FAMILY BRITAIN

FAMILY BRITAIN

1951–1957

David Kynaston

Walker & Co.
New York

Published by Walker Publishing Company, Inc., New York

All papers used by Walker & Company are natural, recyclable products made from wood grown
in well-managed forests. The manufacturing processes conform to the environmental regulations
of the country of origin.

LIBRARY OF CONGRESS CATALOGING-IN-PUBLICATION DATA HAS BEEN APPLIED FOR.

ISBN: 978-0-8027-1797-9

Visit Walker & Company's Web site at www.walkerbooks.com

First U.S. edition 2010

10 9 8 7 6 5 4 3 2 1

Typeset by Hewer Text UK Ltd, Edinburgh
Printed in the United States of America by Quebecor World Fairfield

Contents

A THICKER CUT

Author's Note

Tales of a New Jerusalem is a projected history of Britain between 1945 and 1979. The first volume, *Austerity Britain*, comprises two books, *A World to Build* and *Smoke in the Valley*. The third and fourth books, *The Certainties of Place* and *A Thicker Cut*, form this second volume, *Family Britain*.

THE CERTAINTIES OF PLACE

To my mother, Gisela Hunt

PART ONE

I

All Madly Educative

On Tuesday, 1 May 1951, three days after presenting the FA Cup at Wembley, King George VI was at Earl's Court for the British Industries Fair. 'On one Stand there was a large collection of printed rayon cloth with ultra-modern design,' noted the Cotton Board's Sir Raymond Streat, guiding the royal party round the textile section. 'The King glanced at them and said, "What are those for?" I replied that they were fabrics for ladies' afternoon or evening dresses. He gave another glance at them and muttered, "Thank God we don't have to wear those things." ' At the end of their statutory two hours, the King and Queen announced that they had been 'impressed by the great variety of British products and by the resilience of British industry'.

Two days later an ill-looking George was on public display again. 'Rushed off after breakfast to see the procession,' Gladys Langford wrote in her diary: 'Took my stand at Ludgate Hill where I saw the Royal Family very well. Just before they came along a fox terrier raced along the middle of the road. People yelled & cheered & the poor beast was frantic. About 20 yds behind came another terrier also with its tongue lolling out. After the procession had gone by, I saw the two poor beasts in Farringdon St. The first was lying as tho' dead on the pavement, the other stood over him . . .' The procession was on its way to St Paul's, where after a service the King stood on the steps and declared the Festival of Britain to be officially open. 'Let us pray,' he said, 'that by God's good grace the vast range of modern knowledge which is here shown may be turned from destructive to peaceful ends, so that all people, as the century goes on, may be lifted to greater happiness.' That Thursday evening the King was on the newly created South Bank to open the Royal Festival Hall – an occasion marked by an all-British concert, with Handel an honorary Englishman. It was a proud moment, the Festival Hall being Britain's first new public building since the war (though involving the demolition of the magnificent Lion Brewery). But on that mild evening an observant reporter found something just as stirring in Friday Street at the back of St Paul's: 'A bombed site had been cleared and on it nearly 5,000 young people gathered to sing around a big camp fire. Nearly three tons of wood had been gathered from the East End and the flames lit up a wide area.'[1]

Next morning the King and the rest of the world (including Princess Margaret, her foot accidentally trodden on by an over-keen young reporter, Keith Waterhouse, just down from Leeds) were back on a now rainy South Bank. Over the next five months the Festival of Britain would take many forms – including pleasure gardens in Battersea Park, a science exhibition in South Kensington, a travelling exhibition in the Midlands and the north, a festival ship, an 'Exhibition of Industrial Power' in Glasgow, and a multitude of local events and celebrations. But the incontrovertible centrepiece was the South Bank. There, amidst twenty-two pavilions and much sculpture, three constructs took the eye: the Royal Festival Hall itself, the Dome of Discovery and the Skylon. Ralph Tubbs's impressively monumental Dome (briefly the largest in the world) featured an escalator, enabling the royal party and other VIPs to reach a gallery illustrating the solar system – a means of ascent that so captivated Winston Churchill, a taxi rather than a Tube man, that he kept going down and coming up again. As for the Skylon, designed by Philip Powell and Hidalgo Moya, it made the most instant of impacts: an elegant, 300-foot steel and aluminium 'toothpick' of a tower, especially spectacular at night. Yet transcending everything, in terms of first impressions, was the sheer unabashed pervasiveness of primary colours. 'Whole walls of decoration are made of squares of coloured canvas pulled taut in geometric shapes and triangles, to be lit with a variety of colours,' noted a largely benevolent Cecil Beaton. 'A screen is made by hanging Miró-like coloured balls against the distant chimney pots of the city. Arches underneath the railways are painted strawberry pink or bright blue . . .'[2] It was a style that, after a decade of almost unremitting black, brown and grey, could hardly have struck a brighter, more optimistic note.

'The King has done his stuff at the opening ceremonies,' the rather curmudgeonly Anthony Heap (a local government officer living in St Pancras) recorded on the Friday evening, 'and the crowds are beginning to pour in, despite the damp, dismal and damnably unfestive prevailing weather, to gaze upon its wonders.' Among the 60,000 or so visitors on Sunday the 6th was Kenneth Williams, still a struggling young actor. 'It's all madly educative and very tiring,' was his characteristic reaction. 'Beautifully cooked!!' Ten days later it was the turn of another diarist, Vere Hodgson, to sample the pavilions:

> I wandered into the Schools, but I did not like them much – awful steel chairs, all modern, no grace and no beauty and no elegance. I avoided the Health and the Sport. But I searched for the 1851 Pavilion and found it. We climbed some stairs and there was a model of the Crystal Palace and Queen Victoria opening it ... Then I found the Lion and the Unicorn. This is a MUST for everyone. It is the British character. Obstinacy and imagination or whatever you like to call the two best characteristics of the British race. There was Magna Carta and Habeas Corpus. I was very pleased about this.
>
> By this time it was dark and the lights were on. Now it is all lovely. The Skylon looks fine inside the Exhibition and also the beam of light from the Shot tower moving round ...

'I did enjoy myself,' she concluded. 'I came away at 10.15. I got a cup of tea and roll and butter for 6½d. Good.'³

Whatever individual visitors felt about it, no one could deny that the Festival of Britain was a major national event, the most important yet since the war. For some, looking backwards, it marked the reward for six attritional years of gradually edging towards some sort of peacetime normality; for others, looking forward, it was the welcome harbinger not only of Britain's long-awaited revival as a major force after her early post-war difficulties but of a whole way of more contemporary living. Most people took from the Festival what they wanted to find, and to its creators' credit it was rich and various enough for that to be possible.

It was in a way a minor miracle that there was a festival for anyone to see. For years it had been dogged by a mixture of poor publicity (much of it whipped up by the Beaverbrook press, led by the *Daily Express*) and the pervasive sense that it was going to be not only an unaffordable expense at a time of national belt-tightening but also worthy, bureaucratic and dull. 'He's got a lonely, miserable look, like the Festival of Britain on a Sunday,' was how Jimmy Edwards described a lovelorn Dick Bentley in the radio comedy *Take It From Here* in December 1950. There were also protracted on-site labour troubles – none from a seventeen-year-old electrician from Durham, Bobby Robson, who at his father's insistence was carrying on his daytime trade as a 'spark' while training three evenings a week at Fulham FC, but plenty from Brian Behan, Brendan's Communist brother, who had only recently arrived from Dublin as a labourer. The Labour government, above all Herbert Morrison, expended considerable political capital ensuring that, even after the Korean War had begun, the Festival went ahead; and it was fortunate that the Director of Architecture, Hugh Casson, responsible for a team of more than 40 architects and designers, was a well-connected figure who combined to a high degree the qualities of charm, ambition and determination.[4] Even so, it was still nip and tuck whether the Festival opened on time, and in the event the Battersea Pleasure Gardens were delayed until after Whitsun.

'Don't run away with the idea that the Festival of Britain is going to be solemn,' Gerald Barry had declared in *Picture Post* at the start of 1951:

> Not a bit of it. It will afford us all the opportunity, as occasion allows, for some harmless jollification. After more than a decade of voluntarily-imposed austerity we deserve it, and it will do us good. But the main purpose of the Festival is, all the same, strictly serious. It is intended as an act of national reassessment. The whole of Britain will be 'on show' – to herself, and to the world ...
>
> It will put on record the fact that we are a nation not only with a great past, but also a great future ... It will help to put us on our toes, to raise our morale at home and our prestige among other nations ...

Barry himself, editor of the *News Chronicle* but also the Festival's originator and now its director-general, was one of the progressive, public-spirited, high-minded 'herbivores' (as opposed to 'carnivores', in Michael Frayn's classic coinage) running the show. The emphasis on the future, above all on the Festival's modernity, was at the very heart of what he and the others were trying to achieve. But crucially, it was a restrained, Scandinavian-style, 'soft' Modernism – startlingly novel to most British eyes, but in fact familiar to the cognoscenti since the 1930s – and far removed from the 'hard' Modernist precepts of Le Corbusier and his followers. It was a future, in other words, that came with a warm, unthreatening, scientific yet somehow companionable aura – a future imbued with benevolent, rational and deeply paternalistic assumptions.[5]

Inevitably the Festival got a mixed reception. 'Don't Let's Make Fun of the Fair' was the title of Noël Coward's seemingly supportive but in fact condescending song, while the increasingly anti-Modernist John Betjeman was only relieved that he had not found 'gambolling functionalists trying to be funny'. The conductor John Barbirolli bit his lip so effectively that it was not until four years later, on a visit to Australia, that he unguardedly described the Royal Festival Hall as 'a black spot on the landscape if ever there was one'. The writer and broadcaster Marghanita Laski would for one have disagreed, hailing it as 'the most exciting conception and achievement in the whole exhibition'. So too Dylan Thomas, who in a broadcast in June on the Welsh Home Service extolled 'the shining Skylon, the skygoing nylon, the cylindrical leg-of-the-future jetting', discovered in the Telecinema 'a St Vitus's gala of abstract shapes and shades in a St Swithin's day of torrential dazzling darning needles', and evoked at night-time 'the lit pavilions, white, black, and silver in sweeps of stone and feathery steel'. Among architects, 'hard' Modernists like Ernö Goldfinger were of course underwhelmed, but the overall professional consensus was very positive, certainly among the 'softs'. 'The great thing is that in a single stride, though working under every possible handicap, our designers have unmistakeably taken the lead,' declared the young, idealistic Lionel Brett in the *Observer*. 'And they have put on a show so impossible not to enjoy that there is a real hope that it will mark the beginning of a modern style which will be generally accepted.' John Summerson, perhaps the most distinguished architectural critic of the day, was almost equally enthusiastic. The Skylon was admittedly 'a silly toy, a pretty toy and a dangerous one, whose merciless descending point is luckily just out of reach', but otherwise, the buildings were 'so good, so witty, so full of invention, so oddly and amusingly grouped' that he was able to reassure his *New Statesman* readers that the South Bank was 'an out-and-out winner'. For him, as for others, it was the optimistic start of a distinctive British Modernism.[6]

As for the public at large, the conventional wisdom is that the Festival was a resounding hit. The exhibits on the South Bank attracted almost eight and a half million visitors; a Gallup poll during the summer found that 58 per cent of people had a favourable impression of what they had seen and/or heard of the Festival; and 'Skylon' became an instant nickname for the long-limbed. Yet there are some debits to be entered. The American-style funfair rides at Battersea (such as the Skywheel, the Bubble-Bounce and the Flyo Plane) pulled in just as many daily visitors as the more worthy attractions on the South Bank; among those attractions, the less than educational 'Home of the Future' pavilion was the most popular exhibition; the overall figures for the South Bank would have been markedly less impressive without a 50-per-cent cut in evening ticket prices after early targets were not reached; those evening figures were further distorted by the South Bank's increasing reputation as an easy pick-up place; and, in the country as a whole, there seems to have been apathy at least as much as enthusiasm – an apathy typified by the Festival's lack of impact in Reading (notwithstanding the inevitable historical pageant), the flop of J. B. Priestley's carefully timed novel *Festival at Farbridge*, and the unremarkable listening figures for BBC Radio's almost saturation coverage (a trend that started when a repeat of *Mrs Dale's Diary* on the Light Programme topped the audience for the Home Service coverage of the opening ceremony on the South Bank). Three schoolboys had perhaps representative experiences. John Simpson (seven) 'saw the Skylon, and put on red and green plastic spectacles to watch a film in 3-D, and listened to a recording of the accents of England and someone saying in a Cockney accent, "Come on kettle, boil up" '; Robert Hewison (eight) was 'disappointed to discover that the soaring narrow pod of the Skylon was held up by wires'; and George MacBeth, about to go up to Oxford, won third prize in the North-East Regional Festival of Britain Competition with an unashamedly mocking poem in which the 'rather depressed look of the dome', the 'finicky skylon confessing its failure on legs' and the Festival Hall 'on its very best behaviour' induced between them no more than an adolescent 'yawn'.[7]

A headache for the organisers in the early weeks was litter, but the situation improved once the public-address system began to say loudly and frequently, 'This is *your* exhibition; please help to keep it tidy.' The problem had been ironed out by the second Monday in June, when Henry St John, a misanthropic civil servant living on his own in Acton, paid 5s to take his father to 'the South Bank exhibition' on what seems to have been a particularly busy morning:

> We explored part of the Dome of Discovery, but a broadcast voice asked people to keep on the move, as others outside were waiting to get in. The Dome contained exhibits on synthetic dyes, electrical instruments, mutation of species, physiology of sex, a megatherium or ground sloth, a developing embryo, and many other things which require, but did not get, unhurried study . . .
>
> After a long wait in another queue, we had a fair lunch at 3/3 each in a cafeteria. D showed some desire to go in the shot tower into which however a long queue was winding, so we had a superficial look round the health pavilion, which dealt with blood, the nervous system, vaccination, training of nurses, surgical instruments, burns etc. The only noticeable foreigners I saw at the exhibition were 2 Asiatics, 2 American servicemen, 1 negro, and 1 woman talking French.

Another diarist, Anthony Heap, waited until a Tuesday evening in mid-July:

> From what I'd read and heard about the Exhibition, I'd surmised that there was very little in it likely to appeal to anyone of my unscientific, unmechanical and generally unprogressive turn of mind. And how right my surmise proved to be! 99 per cent of the exhibits on view in the various pavilions are devoted to different aspects of the 'Land' and the 'People' of Britain and the entire contents of the dimly-lit Dome of Discovery were of no interest to me whatsoever.
>
> Admittedly the whole thing is handsomely designed, laid out and, at nightfall, illuminated. And, unlike the Pleasure Gardens at Battersea Park, there are hundreds of comfortable chairs all over the place where one can rest one's weary limbs free of charge – as well as a continuous supply of good tuneful music relayed through amplifiers so that it can be heard where e'r one wanders – or sits.
>
> Even so, the evening scarcely seemed worth the 6/6 it cost me . . .

Next evening his wife Marjorie went. 'M thinks the South Bank Exhibition an absolutely wonderful show,' noted a fair-minded Heap, 'and, after dark, a really enchanting spot.'[8]

It was not just on the South Bank that a clear drift towards the modern was under way. July 1951 saw not only the publication of the first (*Cornwall*) of the *Buildings of England* series by the broadly pro-Modernist, anti-Victorian architectural critic Nikolaus Pevsner but also the gathering at High Leigh, a rather rundown Victorian mansion near Hoddesdon in Hertfordshire, of the delegates from CIAM 8 – the eighth meeting of the Congrès Internationaux d'Architecture Moderne, a body which since the 1930s had in large part been devoted to the ideals of Le Corbusier, who was himself president. As usual, the application of the very latest technology to the problems of mass housing was CIAM's particular preoccupation; the Congress looked ahead in its familiar utopian way to 'an unlimited, inexhaustible, universal and completely flexible flow of atomic and molecular materials and energy ... the age-old dream, hope or demand for unlimited, universal, automatic, and almost magical abundance and leisure'. Nevertheless, there was on this occasion some criticism of the Modernist dream, to judge by the account of a dissenting home delegate, Frederic Osborn: 'I was amazed, and momentarily encouraged, by support from all the French housing planning people present, whose spokesman not only brilliantly exploded Le Corbusier's mad 14-storey glass-house at Marseilles [the renowned Unité d'Habitation, nearing completion], but expressed astonishment that England, the envied country of the family home with garden, should be increasingly piling houses on top of each other,' he reported soon afterwards to Lewis Mumford in America. 'The high officials of our own housing and planning ministry were undoubtedly impressed by these attacks, which were really unanswerable.'

Osborn, in charge of the Town and Country Planning Association, had for years been waging a doughty campaign in favour of dispersal from the unhealthy, overcrowded inner city to new towns and, if necessary, elsewhere, and against what he saw as the multi-storey, high-rise fallacy. His letter went on about 'high officials':

But the drift of things is simply too much for them. I am more and more convinced that we must lose unless somehow we can bring the force of

popular opinion to bear – and I just don't see how to do it. I can't get the
money, and I can't get together even a dozen passionate enthusiasts to splutter
along with me. I feel spent and futile, and can take no pleasure in dialectical
triumphs that are just throwing the sand against the wind. Your way is the
only way: to write books that build new foundations of thought. But that is a
twenty-five year process, and therefore not for me at my age [66].

'I shudder at what will happen in the meantime,' he ended bleakly. 'And
so I pursue the short cut route which isn't open.'[9]

A month later, on 15 August, the winner was announced of the
competition to design a new cathedral for Coventry, to be built next to
the ruins of the blitzed old one. Three assessors – all of them architects,
selected by the Royal Institute of British Architects – chose an up-and-
coming Scottish architect, Basil Spence, who had been responsible for the
Sea and Ships pavilion on the South Bank and whose design for Coventry
was very much in approved 'Festival' style. 'It is the one I should have
chosen myself,' declared the Bishop of Coventry. 'It is imaginative,
modern and magnificently sensitive to the site.' One of his clergymen,
however, begged to differ. 'So far I have only seen the reproduction of
the original rough sketch,' the Rev. H.N.M. Artus of Arley Rectory
wrote immediately to the local paper. 'It appeared to be yet one more
super-cinema, mammoth insurance company's offices, or even a block
of flats. I was just wondering why there was a bit of a church attached to
it when I saw, to my amazement, that this was the prize-winning design
for Coventry Cathedral.' In short, 'I think this thing is a horror'. N. B.
Waddell of 384 Radford Road, Coventry, agreed: 'A lot of people, with
great affectation, will make much of it because it is the winning design,
but for me it is no more satisfying than the paintings in a modern style
which deface some of our art exhibitions.'

Over the next few weeks – as the architectural journals sang an almost
unanimous chorus of praise, interrupted only by some Modernists
wondering whether Spence had gone far enough – a flurry of other
letters appeared in the *Coventry Evening Telegraph*. Not all were
negative, but D. Kaye, chairman of the Coventry Society of Architects,
was clearly on the defensive when he insisted that the new cathedral
would 'aesthetically be a jewel in the heart of Coventry'. His assertion
earned a memorable riposte from F. Bliss Burbidge of Belvedere Road,

Coventry: 'I should like to repudiate the idea that only architects can estimate the beauty of a cathedral; it may be flattering to their own conceit but it will not hold water.' The controversy rumbled on through the autumn, with Spence at one point reassuring a sceptical Coventry Diocesan Conference that 'modern science can produce as beautiful work in cement as our predecessors did with stone'. But by early 1952, once he had amended his design so that the large glass screen dividing the porch from the nave no longer needed to be lowered below the level of the floor (a feature that had prompted the phrase 'push-button Cathedral'), it was clear that the people of Coventry were eventually going to get a new, signature place of worship. 'What I feel absolutely certain of is that it is honest and that it is original,' Pevsner pronounced on radio's Third Programme. 'What it may lack in monumentality, it will gain in life.'[10]

The battle in 1951 between the old and the new was played out perhaps most piquantly on two summer evenings at the Royal Festival Hall. On the first, 14 July, Princess Elizabeth was present at an explicitly 'traditional' concert put on by the National Federation of Jazz Organizations. Humphrey Lyttelton, Monty Sunshine and Wally Fawkes (the cartoonist 'Trog') were among the musicians, with Deryck Guyler as compère. A performance of 'Rock Island Line' by Mick Mulligan and his Magnolia Jazz Band introduced the night's first vocalist, George Melly. 'He began the song cleverly but failed to hold on to his advantage,' noted *Melody Maker*'s rather sniffy reviewer, Max Jones. 'I began to fidget before it was through.' Indeed, Jones's verdict on the concert as a whole was pretty disparaging: 'For the experienced listener I believe it became something of a bore before the evening was out. Certainly there were moments when I wished I was on the North Bank.' Two evenings later there was no royal presence at an equally explicitly 'modernist' concert, this time with Steve Race the compère, the Johnny Dankworth Seven (Cleo Laine on vocals) the undoubted star turn, and the American critic Leonard Feather as *MM*'s reviewer. 'British jazz came of age last Monday night,' began his piece, and he declared that the concert had gone far to 'helping to prove that modern music in Britain need not consider itself a mere Cinderella sister of the American family'. Perhaps, though, the Princess did not unduly mind missing 'the very cool groove of "Seven Not Out" '.[11]

There were a few last diarist-visitors to the Festival. 'I arrived early and joined a queue, a vast, orderly line of people,' recorded the 25-year-old John Fowles on 29 August. 'The Festival I saw in a morning, skimming through it. All the cleverness and the practicality and the didacticism I found rather repellent.' About the same time, on a rainy evening, the slightly older Lawrence Daly, increasingly prominent as a Communist activist on the Fife coalfield, 'splashed around for two hours, visiting the Dome of Discovery, the People of Britain, Land of Britain, Power & Production, & souvenir stalls' – all of which he found 'a magnificent show, of great educational value'. The final diarist was perhaps the best qualified to offer an insightful view:

12 September. At last to S. Bank Festival. Arrive 12 – go straight in – first impression good – smaller exhibits – schools, sports, '1951' – seaside – enjoyable while not too tired. Larger – engines – boats – begins to crowd – Dome of Discovery – gloom – unorganized wandering – symbolic of muddled mind – addled with too much knowledge . . . Did not see all – too tired & hot – Polar Expedition exhibit informative. 'Lion & Unicorn' quite charming – quite obvious. Designs in pottery & silks delightful. Stayed 2½ hrs – enough for one day.

16 September. To Festival 12.45 – fine day, stayed till nearly 5 . . . Homes & Gardens delightful – especially bedsitter for elderly lady – obviously having seen better days. All well designed & colour – avoidance of 'suites' – chairs in different colours but same pattern . . . 'The Country' good large picture mounted on central rod for each month – amusing material (padded) picture of Womans Institutes. Certainly humour + invention allowed. Sad to see livestock there, especially Dartmoor pony . . .

The writer was Grace Golden, a talented but in many ways frustrated commercial artist. She returned on Friday the 28th for a concert at the Royal Festival Hall, whose interior she examined with an acerbic eye. The setting for the orchestra was 'like the crude models of cardboard I make for my own use – different colours stuck together with sticky paper & drawing pins which must surely be at the back of three walls which don't join the ceiling!' The sounding board was 'like parts of a model not yet stuck together'. And the boxes 'only remind one of the balconies outside the flats in Camden Town – needed only washing hanging to be complete'. All of which made her ask herself whether the human race had 'developed sufficiently for it to be exposed against such nakedness as modern architecture'.[12]

'It will be remembered as a moderately successful venture,' reckoned the *Manchester Guardian* next day at the start of the Festival's final weekend – exactly a week after a record 158,365 had flocked to the South Bank, many of them lured by the spectacle of Charles Elleano crossing the Thames on a tightrope. The mood to the last was determinedly cheerful. Saturday the 29th was Gala Night (with Gracie Fields, at her insistence paid in dollars, topping the bill in the open-air cabaret), while on Sunday there was a Thanksgiving service at the Festival Hall. That evening the Archbishop of Canterbury, in lieu of the ailing King, addressed the nation on the radio, declaring that the Festival had been 'a good thing for all of us' and had 'brought encouragement just when it was needed' – that in fact it had been 'a real family party'. On the South Bank itself, there were almost 65,000 visitors during this final day, with well-nigh half still there by 10.00 p.m., when there began on the Fairway (the open space between the Dome of Discovery and the Transport pavilion) community singing to the accompaniment of the massed bands of the Brigade of Guards. The favourites followed one after another: 'Land of Hope and Glory', 'John Peel', 'Danny Boy', 'Loch Lomond', 'Rule Britannia', 'Jerusalem', 'The Old Hundredth'. Then at about 10.17 came the announcement over the loudspeakers, 'Stand by for general black-out', and all the lights duly went out as the three Festival flags were lowered. Then at 10.20 the lights were on again, as the still unsated crowd lustily sang 'God Save the King', 'Abide With Me' and, with hands linked, 'Auld Lang Syne'.

Now it really was over. 'Good night, for the last time, good night,' said the voice over the loudspeakers, efficient and brisk as ever. According to the report in the by now reconciled *Daily Express*, it was not only the paying visitors who left in good order and good humour. As the site emptied, 'the Men in Grey – the attendants – smiled as they dispersed with, they said, only one in ten having a job to go to'.[13] A generation earlier, the Festival's somewhat smug herbivores might have legitimately reflected, there would have been no such relaxed confidence about what their future held.

2

A Narrow Thing

Mercifully for listeners, radio programmes during the second summer of the 1950s were not entirely about the Festival of Britain. 'We read till 8.15 and Twenty Questions,' noted Nella Last on a Monday in Barrow-in-Furness. 'Whatever it "lacks", it's not happy "friendliness".' Another housewife on another Monday had a more chequered time. 'Woman's Hour started today,' recorded Marian Raynham in Surbiton. 'A nuisance but I must listen, it is interesting. Also Mrs Dale & Bob Dale actress & actor were changed today & I like neither as well as last ones. This Mrs D. has a bit of a scrape in her voice, & the Bob is quite different.' In the last three weeks of August, a BBC survey found that 59 per cent of housewives always or often listened to *Mrs Dale's Diary*, 57 per cent to *Housewives' Choice* (musical requests) and 30 per cent to *Woman's Hour*. *The Archers* was not included, but it was during this time that a third diarist-housewife, Mary King in Birmingham, wrote of 'feeling very angry with Phil Archer for not telling Grace Fairbrother what his real thoughts towards her were'.[1]

That summer there was one new programme – in time iconic – that none of the diarists mentioned. 'This series is based upon a crazy type of fun evolved by four of our younger laughter-makers,' promised the *Radio Times*: 'The members of this entertainingly eccentric quartet are old friends. They met during the wartime perambulations of the "Stars in Battledress". Since then Secombe and Sellers have joined the successful company who can top-the-bill. Ex-Etonian Michael Bentine has won his spurs in the West End and Spike Milligan is making a reputation both as a comedian and writer (it is he who has compiled the "Goon Show" material). Now it remains to be seen what will happen when their differing brands of comedy are fused in one show.'

Thus a somewhat nervous BBC launched *Crazy People* – 'featuring Radio's Own Crazy Gang "The Goons" ' – on Monday, 28 May on the London Home Service, before gradually extending to other regions. The format was initially the traditional variety one of sketches interspersed with music; few of the subsequently famous characters had yet been created; and by the end of the series in September, with the shows being repeated on the Light Programme, listening figures were respectable (at around 16 per cent of the radio audience) rather than remarkable. 'This series has drawn divided opinions,' noted the BBC report summarising the reactions of its listeners' panel, 'and the Appreciation Indices [going up to 100] have been low in the 50s. One section of the audience found this an amusing and original show, but there are apparently many still listening to it for whom the "crazy" type of humour and accompanying "noisiness" have no attraction.'[2] Still, the consolation for the quartet – whose humour was arguably a subversive take on the *ITMA* radio shows of the 1940s – was that the BBC did commission a second series for early 1952. This time it would, as they had always wanted, be called *The Goon Show*.

One of radio's biggest stars, the already notoriously irascible Gilbert Harding, spent the summer in enforced rustication from his trademark quiz programme, *Twenty Questions*, after an unfortunate outburst in April. 'I hope that pompous "superior" Gilbert Harding never gets back on to this programme,' reflected Last. 'He seemed to delight in snubbing poor Jack Train!' But by September and its 200th show, he was back in the chair. 'I think Gilbert Harding must have had a "lesson",' noted a relieved Last. 'He has thrown off that over-bearing "superiority".' He had also found a new game-show vehicle, this time on television – a development unrecorded by Last, who like at least nine in ten adults did not have a set. The programme was *What's My Line?*, requiring a celebrity panel to work out, through replies and miming, the occupations of contestants. It made a Harding-free debut on Monday, 16 July, sandwiched between *Men O' Brass* (with the Fairey Aviation Works Band) and *The Lights of London* ('A visit to the South Bank to watch the scene as its buildings are floodlit. Commentator, Richard Dimbleby.'). 'What made last night a pale imitation of the transatlantic original was the sogginess of the experts,' was the stern verdict next morning of Leonard Mosley in the *Daily Express*. 'Barbara Kelly spent much of the time scratching her pretty head. Miss [Marghanita] Laski looked as if she were only there because of the money. And the two male experts [Jerry Desmonde and Ted Kavanagh] just seemed puzzled.' The following week they tried out Harding in the chair, but because of a mix-up over his cards it proved a fiasco, as he confused a male nurse with a motor mechanic. 'It was a simple mistake,' he told a reporter afterwards. 'They put the wrong chap in the wrong place, but there was no trouble nor unpleasantness.' Soon, though, he was a regular on the panel, with Eamonn Andrews equally a regular in the chair, and by the end of August as many as 86 per cent of sets were turned on for it, with of course no competing channels in existence.

The show's almost instant popularity no doubt reflected a winning formula – fascination with the variety of jobs on display (most famously the saggar maker's bottom-knocker in the pottery industry) and the almost novel attraction of seeing ordinary people on television – but there was also fascination with Harding himself. Partly it was his sheer rudeness ('I am tired of looking at you,' he famously snapped at one particularly sphinx-like contestant), partly because the former schoolmaster's manifest intelligence seemed so out of place, and partly because it was impossible not to speculate what lay behind that moustachioed, sometimes self-pitying face almost invariably wreathed in cigarette smoke. Indisputably he was the dominant television star of the first half of the 1950s, with an off-air persona just as crusty and dogmatic, not least through a regular crusading column in the *People* that tackled bureaucrats who were giving individuals a hard time. 'All who remember him know he bristled with prejudice,' noted John Betjeman in a subsequent appreciation: 'They knew his feelings about American civilisation, the Irish Roman Catholic hierarchy, about so-called progress, about plastics, and his deep mistrust of majority opinions, civil servants and everything that goes with officialdom and the suppression of the individual. In his way Gilbert Harding, by being his irascible, generous self, did more to encourage the individual against domination by the State and heartless theorists than any television personality of his time.'[3] That such a set of attitudes could, so soon after the '1945' welfare-state revolution, strike such a chord was suggestive indeed.

The film of the summer, premiered about a fortnight before the launch of *What's My Line?*, was undoubtedly *The Lavender Hill Mob*, an Ealing comedy starring Alec Guinness in which the police were treated somewhat less deferentially than in the previous year's *The Blue Lamp*, but not radically so. Gore Vidal would claim that Guinness modelled his part on the young actor-turned-critic Kenneth Tynan, especially 'the way that Tynan stagily held a cigarette between ring and little fingers'. Tynan himself, signed up by the *Evening Standard*, was now making his mark. Danny Kaye at the Palladium was first in his sights ('trades on sex-appeal too openly ever to be a recruit to the small troupe of great clowns'), then the 'periwinkle charm' of Vivien Leigh, starring that summer with her husband Laurence Olivier in *Antony and Cleopatra*: 'Hers is the magnificent effrontery of an attractive child, endlessly indulged at its first party.' Letters of disgust immediately followed, but Tynan was unconcerned; Noël Coward soon afterwards found him to be 'charming, very intelligent and with a certain integrity'. Neither was at the Coventry Hippodrome in early September for the first night of *Zip Goes a Million*, an American-style musical about a man who has to spend a million dollars in order to inherit a fortune of seven million. 'George Formby is the undisputed star of the show, an eminence he gains by being determinedly and more than ever George Formby,' declared the local paper. 'He displays his old genius for provoking laughter by the least of his broad-vowelled asides. Once again he is the one-man pantomime that never palls.' Admittedly the ukulele-playing Lancashire comedian told 'a clamant audience' at the end of the performance that there had been 'a bit of a muck-up at times', but there was justifiable confidence that the under-rehearsed production would be in good order by the time it got to London the following month.[4]

The summer's big sporting drama, attended by massive publicity, was also an Anglo-American affair. No one gave Randolph Turpin, a black boxer from Leamington Spa who had been a cook in the navy, a chance in his fight on 10 July at Earl's Court against the legendary Sugar Ray Robinson for the world middleweight title. In the event he won quite comfortably on points – even though the radio summariser, the fruity W. Barrington Dalby, badly misled almost twenty-five million listeners by pronouncing that 'only a whirlwind grandstand finish can possibly snatch it for Turpin', an assessment with which Raymond Glendenning ('portly, pertly-voiced commentator with handlebar moustache', in Frank Keating's words) concurred. Dalby afterwards claimed that he had meant 'clinch' not 'snatch', but that did not save the patrician pair from an avalanche of criticism. Just over a fortnight later, the far from proletarian Dorian Williams was the television commentator for the *Horse of the Year Show* at White City stadium. 'My cup of happiness was full,' recorded Vere Hodgson (there in person), 'for we saw Foxhunter jump with Colonel [Harry] Llewellyn riding and we saw Rusty with Miss Kellett and we saw Miss Pat Smythe. We all held our breath while Foxhunter jumped, and then he was cheered to the echo . . .' Later, Hodgson went round to the stables and fed the mighty Foxhunter with sugar. It was exactly a week later, on the Saturday at the start of the August Bank Holiday weekend, that Wally Hammond, the great Gloucestershire and England batsman of the inter-war era, was persuaded to come out of retirement to play against Somerset at Bristol. A crowd of 10,000 saw him survive a first-ball lbw appeal from Horace Hazell and then scratch around for 50 minutes, making only seven, before being clean bowled by Hazell. The future actor Milton Johns, then a Bristol schoolboy, was taken to the match by his father, complete with 'a flask of tea and enough tomato sandwiches to feed half the crowd'. Owing to three changes of bus they arrived too late, 'Oh dear' being his father's restrained comment on seeing the scoreboard. 'He had slipped through my fingers and was lost forever, leaving me with a lifelong conviction that one should never go back, but always forward,' reflected Johns over half a century later. 'Did Wally Hammond feel the same, as he mounted those long pavilion steps that day? Maybe, or should I say probably?'[5]

There were no twilight shadows for Margaret Rose, 21 later that month. Whole packs of reporters pursued the glamorous, vivacious, fairy-tale princess to Balmoral, where their lack of access did not prevent torrents of gushing, breathless prose about the latest developments. 'Yes, HE WAS on the 9.46,' started the despatch from Mamie Baird in the *Daily Express* on the actual morning of her birthday. 'He' was 24-year-old Billy Wallace, who had arrived to join the royal party having 'at the last minute changed his plan to drive all the way from

London to Balmoral in a dashing red sports car'. Next day the paper's Eve Perrick gave the lowdown:

> The Princess's birthday party was such a cosy affair.
>
> After dinner – grouse again – at Balmoral Castle, the green carpets were rolled back, the radiogram moved in, and Princess Margaret's grand birthday ball began.
>
> After all the scarcely suppressed excitement there was no shiny dance floor swept by the trains and trailing skirts of romantic gowns, no famous bands, no floodlit gardens, no coronets, and no fuss.
>
> Just high spirits and friendly fun, with the two Princesses, their best friends, and some of the Duke of Edinburgh's cousins participating . . .

But *The Times*, in its leader to mark the occasion, warned against a new intrusiveness – 'having wished her many happy returns of the day and been told how in general she spent it, her fellow-citizens would be glad if the family party were left undisturbed' – before concluding that 'her future will be followed with kindly good wishes by all, in every corner of the Commonwealth, who know the priceless value of a happy home background'.[6]

A month earlier, on 17 July, illness had prevented the King from opening the Steel Company of Wales's huge new continuous-strip mill at Port Talbot, though he did send a message heralding its contribution to 'our ability to maintain our historic position in a free world'. Instead, Hugh Gaitskell, as Chancellor of the Exchequer, did the honours – appropriately enough, given that the steel industry had recently been taken into public ownership. The site had previously been some 500 acres of marshland and sand dunes, and it was claimed that the conversion into steelworks was the biggest single project in Britain since the railway age. 'Today the 200-ton ladle was seen to pour metal from one of the eight new open-hearth steel furnaces into moulds,' reported the man from *The Times* at the opening ceremony. 'The 20-ton ingots, still brilliantly red, were run one by one down to the slabbing mill to be rolled into slabs. The process was controlled by a flick of the finger and a movement of the foot.' It was a great day for the locals, not only in terms of future employment prospects, as Gaitskell led a party of some 1,200 luminaries, including (in the words of the *Port Talbot Guardian*) 'the most fabulous names in British industry'. But steel was not quite everything, and that Tuesday evening, at a meeting of the Port Talbot Borough Council, there was a disquieting moment as Councillor Idwal Hopkins alleged that burial forms were being issued incompletely. He cited a recent case: 'The husband of the family had died, and the funeral had been all-male. The only son had gone away for six weeks following the funeral, and he had left it to the undertaker to point out the grave to the widow and daughter-in-law. This the undertaker had done, and during the six weeks he was away – every Sunday – the women had placed flowers on the grave. When the son returned he, too, went to the grave, and found that they had been placing the flowers on the wrong grave.' It was an episode that had, in Hopkins's words, 'caused considerable distress'. However, the fact of an all-male funeral was, in this part of south Wales at least, taken for granted.

Clive Jenkins, the son of a railway worker, had grown up in Port Talbot. 'He was a precocious child,' noted an obituary, 'and seemed set for a good schooling when his father died and he was obliged to go to work at 14. This disappointment had much to do with his future attitudes.' Now, in the summer of 1951, at the age of 25, he was a member of the Communist Party and a full-time official for the Association of Supervisory Staffs, Executives and Technicians (ASSET), with particular responsibility for organising workers at London (Heathrow) Airport, where he was rapidly increasing union membership. Shortly after his hometown's hour in the sun, he was at the centre of the civil aviation industry's first significant dispute, causing the state-owned British European Airways (BEA) to cancel more than 800 fully booked services. 'Angry passengers "squatted" at Kensington Air Station this morning, waiting to be flown to Nice,' reported the *Daily Mail* at the height of the dispute. 'They had been told that the Argonaut plane chartered for last night's flight in the B.E.A. cheap-rate service was not available . . . Passengers cried "Iniquitous!" and "What about our bookings?".' Soon afterwards, a ministerial intervention by another self-confident operator, Alfred Robens, settled the matter, very much in favour of the white-collar supervisors and technicians whom the already deeply ambitious Jenkins represented. 'This was my first major national dispute and gave me my first sense of real satisfaction as a collective bargainer,' Jenkins recalled. 'Deeply influenced by this set of events, I learned that it was possible to have disputes which were immensely interesting to the public as well as being attractive to potential members as long as they were in high-technology industries.'[7]

The major industrial strike of the summer, though, was at the Austin Motor Company's works at Longbridge, Birmingham. Eventually involving more than 10,000 workers, it was called on Wednesday, 20 June by shop stewards after management had dismissed (and, despite an existing agreement, refused to redeploy) seven men, including Sid Pegg, who was not only an Amalgamated Engineering Union (AEU) shop steward but also Secretary of the Communist Party's Longbridge branch. Pegg's close colleague, Dick Etheridge, works convener and himself an active CP member, insisted to the *Birmingham Post* that he 'had proof' of 'blacklisting', adding: 'We are not silly over redundancies. Shop stewards have not said that they will not accept redundancy in any circumstances.' It was, in other words, a case of victimisation – which it undoubtedly was. Nevertheless, another prominent shop steward, John McHugh, was adamant that it was not a political dispute, asserting that of the 350 stewards at the meeting that had decided on strike action, only 50 had 'Communist sympathies'. The crunch came with a mass meeting at Cofton Hackett Park (next to the works) on Monday the 25th. It was, reported the not entirely objective *Post*, a 'stormy' affair:

Part of the uproar was due to a denunciation by Mr [Dick] Nester, chairman of No 5 Machine Shop stewards, of Communist activity in the factory, which, he said, he had watched for 18 months. Communist propaganda went on daily, he added.

As he went on to describe the events which led up to the stoppage there were shouts of 'Take him off!' and the microphone was taken from him by Mr George Varnon, chairman of the shop stewards committee. This seemed to incense many in the crowd who demanded a hearing from Mr Nester.

When Mr Varnon said he abided by the decision of the workpeople, somebody in the crowd said 'You've got to!'

Mr Varnon was shouted down when he tried to tell the workers again of the need for continued support of the strike. There were cries of 'We've heard all he's got to say', 'We want to get back to work', 'Put the resolution and let's vote on it'.

As the shop stewards convener, Mr R. Etheridge, was putting the motion to continue to strike before the meeting there were cries of: 'You are trying to mislead us'.

Eventually, those in the crowd of more than 6,000 who were in favour of returning to work were asked to move to the right, those against to move to the left. A 'big majority' moved rightwards. There were two almost immediate outcomes to this humiliating defeat for the more militant shop stewards: the ultra-astute Etheridge privately decided never to call another mass meeting, and the sacked Pegg was soon replaced as CP branch secretary by a young toolroom worker, Derek Robinson, the future 'Red Robbo' of tabloid demonisation.[8]

Elsewhere in Birmingham, at about the time of the Longbridge dispute, a young researcher called Michael Banton took a walk along Sparkbrook Road, looking at the cards in newspaper-shop windows. He counted more cards from people advertising rooms that stipulated 'No Irish' than 'No Coloured'. But his main research was in Stepney, where during the summer he sent out questionnaires to 40 employers in the clothing and building industries in order to gauge their attitude to the employment of black immigrants. He found that whereas the largely Jewish-run clothing industry saw 'the coloured man at little disadvantage', it was different among builders and contractors, where 'there was a considerably greater resistance to the idea of engaging coloured workers', particularly on the part of small firms. 'You have to consider how other people would feel, especially the other employees,' replied one. 'There's not enough work for English people and many of the coloured people only got here by smuggling themselves away.' Overall, Banton reckoned that 'from the small numbers employed there is probably a fair amount of discrimination in employment in this trade', and that 'in a time of unemployment it would increase'.

Housing was even more susceptible to prejudice. 'I have been carrying out a small experiment with the help of my friend O.,' the left-wing writer Mervyn Jones related in August: 'We copied down the addresses of ten rooms advertised as "a let" outside a Notting Hill Gate newsagent's shop. O. went round and asked for rooms; I went to the same addresses twenty minutes later. His score: rooms available at two places, all rooms gone at eight. My score: rooms available at seven, a share offered at another, all rooms gone at two. An odd result; but whereas I belong to what E.M. Forster called the pink-grey race, O. comes from Nigeria.' In most parts of the country, of course, a black person was still a considerable rarity. The experience of Ian Jack, growing up near Bolton and six in 1951, was probably typical. 'The first black person I ever saw was on the Piccadilly line, somewhere near Hammersmith,' he remembered. 'We'd come to stay with my granny and to see the Festival of Britain. A black man, who wore a smart suit, sat across the train's aisle and smiled at me. I think my father encouraged me to smile back. Perhaps I had been staring.'[9]

The kindness of strangers was probably more common between whites. In June, barely a month after he had started at RADA ('O bliss!'), a young aspiring actor from Leicester, Joe Orton, was taken to the bosom of another new, more prosperous student, Kenneth Halliwell. 'Move into Ken's flat,' recorded Orton on 16 June, before four expressive entries:

17 June. Well!
18 June. Well!!
19 June. Well!!!
20 June. The rest is silence.

It was also in June that an almost equally young Jeffery Bernard, four months after he had gone AWOL from National Service in Catterick, gave himself up, ringing the police from the Gargoyle Club in Soho at two in the morning. There ensued two brutal days and nights at a military detention centre near Scotland Yard, with Bernard being kicked every few hours by a Scots Guards sergeant, before he was sent back to Yorkshire. His biographer records how 'when he was being hauled across the concourse at King's Cross, handcuffed to a Military Policeman, strangers came up and gave him cigarettes, money, sandwiches and a magazine and shouted "good luck, mate" and "don't let the bastards get you down".'[10]

Summertime, naturally, was also holiday time. 'It's been a perfect summer's day,' noted Nella Last in Barrow on the last Monday in July, after she and her husband had gone in the afternoon to a nearby beach:

I watched with real concern at chalk white bodies & limbs in bathing suits – both sex & every age – lying and playing in the strong sea air, many already looking 'burned', knowing the *agony* many would be in tonight. I was sorry for the hapless children, some already beginning to squirm & scratch their sunburned flesh, and I didn't see *one* tube of 'cream' or oil being used. Long queues constantly stood at a big ice cream stall, fresh supplies were brought twice, but till after 8 o'clock they sold as quickly as they could make sandwiches.

Over and above day trips, or the traditional lodging house at a popular resort, there was also the recent, increasingly popular phenomenon of the holiday camp. At about the same time as Last was tut-tutting, the writer C. H. Rolph visited one on Canvey Island, run by the local landowner, councillor and magistrate Colonel Horace Fielder. Rolph asked why he charged £5 (double the usual rate) for a chalet in August. 'Keep out the rough stuff,' replied the Colonel. 'I don't need the money – this place makes thousands. But it'd be a nightmare here at £2 in August.'

The research organisation Mass-Observation was also intrigued, and in September sent two investigators to Butlin's at Clacton. There, like previous M-O investigators at Butlin's in Filey, they found a world all of its own. In the dining hall, where Kent House and Gloucester House had separate sittings, the House Captain (a Redcoat called Len) addressed the company through a microphone: 'He invariably started off with: "Good morning, you smashing campers of Gloucester House, and good morning, staff – HI-DE-HI!" to which we answered: "HO-DE-HO".' Len himself was born to his role: 'Tall, swarthy and spivvy, he appeared to be tireless. He was always cracking jokes, pretending to chase the girls and generally clowning. He was enormously popular.' Most evenings there were Redcoat-compèred 'sing-songs' in the Jolly Roger bar, with 'its olde worlde oak-beam decor'. 'As well as community singing, individual campers were invited to perform. There was one young man who performed regularly and excruciatingly. He was regarded by the audience as a great "card" and received a tumultuous welcome.' There was also the already time-honoured 'Personality Girl' contest, won by Greta: 'She was chosen by outside judges and the choice was unpopular with the campers. Her forwardness and general brashness were disliked – disapproved of by the elderly and resented by the young. Contestants were judged not only on their appearance, but also on their talent. (Greta's talent consisted of singing "Too Young".) When asked her ambition, one girl said she had already achieved it in marriage, and we were interested to note the loud applause.' The week ended, as usual, with the Campers' Concert. 'For an amateur show the standard was quite high,' the M-O team found. 'Greta, who was accorded a tepid reception, exhibited an unexpected versatility and sang "Nevertheless". The most popular turn was given by a boy of fifteen, who did farm-yard imitations.' And, they added in a reference to the radio programme on the BBC in the 1940s, moving to Radio Luxembourg in the 1950s, *Opportunity Knocks*, 'his performance was better than that of most of Hughie Green's discoveries'.[11]

Everywhere, this sixth summer after Labour's landslide victory, the welfare state was in daily, ubiquitous action. 'There were medicine bottles of orange juice and jars of Virol to pick up from the baby clinic for my sister,' Carolyn Steedman recalled about moving in June as a four-year-old from Hammersmith to Streatham Hill. Or take the experience of a nine-year-old living with her mother and stepfather in a converted railway carriage at Wraysbury in Berkshire. 'The school health inspector said that I was too skinny, and that I was suffering from malnutrition,' Christine Keeler remembered. 'He arranged for me to be sent to a holiday home in Littlehampton to be fattened up for a month. When I arrived there were sixteen boys staying, but no girls. We were all skinny as rakes. We bathed and played ping-pong and one of the older boys taught me how to play chess.' 'It was,' she added, 'the first time I felt myself aware of a boy.'

For most adults, it was still quite hard just getting by. 'What is the main problem facing you and your family at the present time?' asked Gallup in July. Fifty-six per cent replied that it was the cost of living. Nevertheless, as the very worst of the immediate post-war austerity became a memory, things were continuing to ease somewhat – but only somewhat – in the shops. 'We went for the meat,' noted Nella Last in mid-August. 'I got best frying steak for 1½ rations, & stewing steak for 1½ books, and was lucky enough to get a kidney too.' Later that month, Judy Haines in Chingford was similarly grateful: 'Meat ration much increased [to 1s 10d worth, the highest for ten years] and

I have steak as well as a joint this week.' Soon afterwards, on Saturday, 1 September, there was an important symbolic event, with the opening in bombed-out Plymouth of the new Dingle's, the old one having been destroyed in an air raid. It was the first big department store to have been completed in the country since 1939, and some 40,000 eager shoppers visited on the first day. 'Nylons were the main object of the early arrivals,' reported the *Western Morning News* as a queue quickly formed at the hosiery counter 'and at one time snaked through several departments on the ground floor'. In the crowded food hall, 'the grocery counters were besieged'. Tellingly, 'women who had secured the goods they required then stopped to admire a refrigerated window full of meat'.

That same day, in the Dorset parish of Loders and Dottery, there took place the annual gymkhana, held in the park of Loders Court. 'The Gymkhana was good for our souls,' the Rev. Oliver Willmott wrote in due course in his Parish Notes:

In previous years the weather had always smiled on us, and we sometimes wondered how we would face up to it if the weather frowned. Now we know. Rain fell mercilessly most of the morning and afternoon, but the competitors turned up, some of them from a distance, and 'the show must go on' became the order of the day. The entries reached the surprising number of 87, and this encourages the supposition that fine weather would have made the day eminently successful. The cosiest spot on that boggy field was Mrs Harry Legg's tea emporium under the cedar tree. There the sweetest smiles of herself and her bevy of lady helpers atoned for the rain. The eyes of many customers turned to her warm stove, but it could not be come at for the ice-cream man, who seemed glued to it . . .[12]

'We listened to Mr Attlee's political party broadcast,' noted Marian Raynham in Surbiton on 19 September. 'It turned out to be an announcement of an Election on Oct 25th. Dear, I hope this crew doesn't get in again. That would be awful. I can't vote Tory, but I would prefer the Tories in.' For several months Attlee had been coming under sustained pressure from King George – to the effect that if there was going to be an election, it had better be sooner rather than later, so that it was out of the way before he began a lengthy Commonwealth tour in early 1952. Attlee, who felt an intense personal allegiance to the King, had eventually given in, informing the monarch on 5 September of the election timetable. By the time of the election announcement a fortnight later, however, there was a new, unforeseen twist. 'The King seems very ill,' Raynham added in her entry. 'Has nine doctors.' Four days later he was under the knife, as another diarist, Gladys Hague (in her mid-fifties, living with her sister in Keighley), recorded: 'King George VI has had a serious lung operation so everyone is anxious.' But by now it was too late to reverse the decision, and an election on 25 October it was going to be.

'It certainly seems very strange that the P.M. shd have launched the Election at this moment,' reflected Harold Macmillan the day after the three-hour operation for the removal of a lung. 'What will happen if the King dies?' The larger question was whether Attlee needed to call an election at all. It is true that his parliamentary majority of only six had become increasingly frayed at the edges over the summer, with the Tories using every device to keep the Commons sitting for unconscionable hours – so much so that half a century later Roy Jenkins recalled 1951 as 'the most burdensome summer of all my thirty-four years in the House'.[13] Even so, the Labour government probably could have carried on into 1952, waiting for the adverse economic effects of the Korean War to lessen; but Attlee was weary, his ministers were weary, and to someone like Attlee the appeal of a clear-cut resolution to a difficult, unsatisfactory situation would have been considerable.

The Prime Minister himself exuded reassurance and steady-as-she-goes during the three weeks of the campaign. 'He is sincere, straightforward, clear, concise, sometimes witty, and on rare occasions angry in a dignified kind of way,' observed one reporter, Ian Mackay, in the course of following him around the country (as usual driven by his wife Vi). 'His great strength is his sincerity and simplicity.' In policy terms, though, there was on the part of both Attlee and his party a palpable sense of exhaustion, with little being offered for the future that was either new or exciting – and certainly no specific promise of any further extension of public ownership, with instead only a vague reference in the manifesto to how 'we shall take over concerns which fail the nation'. Instead, there was a twofold emphasis: domestically, on the welfare and employment gains since the war, invariably compared to the 'hungry' 1930s; and internationally, partly in the context of difficult current situations in the Middle East, on depicting the Tories, above all Churchill, as warmongers. The latter theme was especially highlighted by the strongly Labour-supporting *Daily Mirror*, whose insistent question, 'Whose Finger on the Trigger?', passed into electoral folklore.

'You have to make up your minds,' William Warbey, Labour's candidate in Luton, told his listeners as he toured the Farley Hill Estate just over a fortnight before polling day. 'Which sort of government is more likely to safeguard peace, maintain full employment and preserve fair shares for the ordinary working man and woman of this country? Would you trust a Tory Government to keep this country out of war? I wouldn't.' And later that afternoon, addressing a crowd of women, he added: 'We don't want a great man of war like Churchill, we want a man of peace like Attlee.' Later that Wednesday, Aneurin Bevan was in the nearby, equally marginal Watford constituency, where he spoke at the town hall 'filled to capacity, with people standing even at the back of the gallery' and, at one point, a scuffle breaking out after someone shouted 'Vermin'. Inevitably the NHS was a focal part of his speech: 'The Service introduced a conception of ethical priorities, said Mr Bevan. "Rubbish," shouted a heckler. "It's no good shouting 'Rubbish'," rapped out Mr Bevan. "We have now converted the Tory Party to it!" '[14] The sitting MP was John Freeman, who in the spring had, with Harold Wilson, followed Bevan by resigning over the question of charges for dentures and spectacles. But even though the Labour conference at Scarborough at the start of October had seen a clear upsurge of party members' support for what were becoming known as 'the Bevanites', a firm lid was successfully kept on internal differences during the campaign.

Crucial to the Labour case was the contrast between past immiserisation and present amelioration. 'The Last of the Sandwich-Men' was the title of a Kenneth Allsop piece in *Picture Post* some six months before the election. 'It's a depth that some men still plumb, but bit by bit that depth is being levelled up,' he wrote. 'The process that in the past turned human beings into sandwich-men is no longer regarded as inexorable.

Already the sandwich-man has the stamp of a relic, a sad survivor of an age we've grown out of.' Such an assumption was fortified during the election by the publication on 15 October of *Poverty and the Welfare State*, the fruits of a recent (October 1950) survey undertaken in York of more than 2,000 families. The authors, B. Seebohm Rowntree and G. R. Lavers, found that whereas in a comparable survey in 1936 nearly one-third of that city's working-class population had been in poverty, now it was just one-fortieth. 'By far the greatest part of the improvement since 1936 has been due to the welfare legislation introduced since 1945,' Lavers declared in an accompanying newspaper article, which ended with a bold, unambiguous claim: 'To a great extent poverty has been overcome by the Welfare State.' Unsurprisingly, the report was, in the words of David Butler (in the first of his magisterial series of election surveys), 'eagerly seized on by the Labour Party as impartial and irrefutable evidence of their general thesis about the benefits of their rule, and it was often quoted by their speakers, particularly in answer to hecklers'. But perhaps it was not really such good news. Not only has a recent detailed study of the Rowntree/Lavers findings significantly downgraded the sharpness of poverty reduction between 1936 and 1950 (suggesting that nearly 12 per cent of working-class households were still in poverty), but the very fact of a widespread perception that poverty was a thing of the past implied that a central part of Labour's historic mission had been completed.[15]

The exact nature of the Tory mission for the 1950s and beyond was still unclear. The day after the election was announced, Churchill's physician Lord Moran brought him some notes on the Health Service. 'He put them in his pocket without reading them,' Moran recorded. ' "We don't want detail," he protested impatiently. "We propose to give the people a lighthouse, not a shop window." ' In practice, moderation and circumspection were the keynotes for Churchill and his colleagues. One rising young Tory politician, David Eccles, may have told Harold Nicolson at a *Spectator* lunch in early October that, in the face of the difficult economic situation, 'the only cure is to "release the pound" and remove all exchange controls', but no such ultra-free-market nostrums appeared in *Britain Strong and Free*, in effect the Tory manifesto. Instead, stress was laid on improving but not replacing the NHS; keeping intact most of the nationalised industries; promising to 'consult the leaders of the Trade Union movement on economic matters and discuss with them fully, and sympathetically, any proposals we or they may have for action on labour problems'; and holding fast to the previously announced target of building 300,000 houses a year. It was telling that in her Dartford election address, Margaret Roberts (about to marry Denis Thatcher) significantly toned down the right-wing fundamentalism that had characterised much of her previous election campaign, while in Barnet the instinctively more consensual – and Keynesian – Reggie Maudling declared without a qualm: 'I do not think we shall have any serious argument with our opponents over the question of employment,' that indeed 'the difficulty today is not to find jobs for people, but people for jobs.'[16]

Even so, there was still a far from minuscule difference between the pitches of the two main parties. *Britain Strong and Free* included a key passage about the safeguarding of 'our traditional way of life' as integral to 'the Conservative purpose': 'A worthwhile society cannot be established by Acts of Parliament and Government planning. Adequate rewards for skill and enterprise and for the creation of wealth, belief that saving and investment are worthwhile, diffusion of property, home ownership, the rule of law, the independence of the professions, the strength of the family, personal responsibility and the rights of the individual – these are the true foundations of a free society.' The implications were clear enough: a smaller state, fewer controls, lower taxes. 'Queuetopia' remained Churchill's central metaphor for socialism in action – a term designed specifically to appeal to housewives. 'We are for the ladder,' he declared in his election broadcast. 'Let all try their best to climb. They are for the queue. Let each wait in his place till his turn comes.'

Perhaps most symbolic of the divide was the question of identity cards. These had been introduced during the war, and the peacetime Labour government had shown no inclination to abolish them. Earlier in the year there had been a cause célèbre after Harry Willcock, a businessman who had twice stood as a Liberal parliamentary candidate, had refused to produce his after being stopped by the police for driving too fast along Ballards Lane in Finchley. Willcock eventually lost his appeal in the High Court, but the British Housewives' League held a well-publicised protest outside Parliament, with ID cards being ceremoniously destroyed. The issue did not specifically feature in the Tory manifesto, but everyone knew that a change of government would see the unmourned end of what Sir Ernest Benn (publisher, libertarian and uncle of Tony) liked to call 'the Englishman's badge of servitude'.[17]

As usual there was a round of election broadcasts, which overall were listened to by 36 per cent of the adult population – down two points on the previous year. 'The "higher" the class the greater the listening,' noted the BBC, while even among working-class listeners there was a significantly higher take-up for Conservative than Labour speakers. Churchill this time round, six years after his 'Gestapo' fiasco, gave a masterly broadcast, presenting himself as a national figure above the squalid political fray. 'We shall endanger our very existence if we go on consuming our strength in bitter party or class conflicts,' he declared. 'We need a period of several years of solid stable administration by a government not seeking to rub party dogma into everybody else.' As in 1950, the 'Radio Doctor', Charles Hill, was a star performer for the Tories. 'He is very clever,' commented Vere Hodgson. 'I like his – "will Mr Attlee take the ermine and leave Bevan to deal with the vermin?" ' But in Brixton the morning after there was frustration, with a neighbour telling Florence Speed that she really should have listened to Dr Hill. 'But as I told him,' she noted with some bitterness, 'T.V. has cut radio out in our house.'

On the small screen itself, the only election coverage was a live broadcast by each party, with the Tory turn falling on the same evening (the 16th) as Hill. Leslie Mitchell, one of television's most reassuring presences, interviewed the would-be foreign secretary, Anthony Eden, in a live, seemingly spontaneous dialogue that had in fact been meticulously rehearsed. A passage towards the end gives the fearless, take-no-prisoners flavour of the interrogation:

> *Mitchell:* I wonder whether I may introduce a question which I'm sure
> will infuriate you, but since I'm here, presumably, for that reason . . .
> It has often been said in recent times that the Conservative Party is a
> war-mongering party. Is there a shred of truth in that, or isn't there?
> *Eden:* I must say, I do resent that question. I could resent it very much.
> But I can't believe that, you know, the ordinary socialist leaders
> really believe it themselves. Anyhow, anybody who makes such an
> insinuation is making a very unworthy one, in my view. Because

there's nobody in this country who doesn't want peace: may I add,
especially those who've seen war at first-hand.

Mitchell: No, indeed.

Eden: The last thing we want is any more of it. But of course you can
argue about how to keep the peace, can't you?

Mitchell: Yes, one can . . .

'Certainly you've made the policy very clear, sir,' concluded Mitchell.
'May I say thank you very much indeed for letting me question you?'
Soon afterwards the comedian Eric Barker did a send-up on television
of this ultra-deferential approach. 'We were all anxious about how it
would be received,' recalled his young sidekick Nicholas Parsons, 'and
while it was quite gentle, and viewers enjoyed it, messages were sent to
Eric from above advising him to be careful and not to satirise too many
of his employers' serious programmes.'[18]

After the election, Gallup found that whereas 82 per cent of people had
listened at some point to radio broadcasts (and 12 per cent to television),
only 24 per cent had been to indoor meetings and 10 per cent to outdoor
ones. The electorate's interest in the proceedings was, in other words,
essentially passive rather than active. Even so, from a candidate's point
of view, the primacy of the public, ticketless meeting was still absolute.
'I seldom spoke at fewer than three a night,' recalled Labour's Willie
Hamilton about his campaign in West Fife, where the challenge came
from left as well as right. 'The Communists' most eloquent advocate was
not Mr Lauchlan [their candidate] but Lawrence Daly [Lauchlan's agent],
a young coalminer. He was a fluent public speaker and was well versed in
Scottish culture, especially in the songs and poetry of Robbie Burns. He
was a good singer, too, and loved his drink.'

Heckling at meetings was still frequent, as when the broadcaster and
journalist W. J. Brown (himself standing as a Conservative-supported
Independent in West Fulham) spoke at Luton Winter Assembly Hall in
support of Charles Hill:

Brown: There is only one thing to do at this election –

Heckler: Vote Labour.

Brown: You know how different things would be if you did a bit of
labour.

One of Labour's keenest candidates, the young Peter Parker at Bedford ('It is going to be a tremendously fierce fight, but it is going to be fought cleanly'), even addressed the 6,347-strong crowd as they left the town's football ground on a Saturday afternoon, though he might have thought better of it if the visitors, Aynesbury Rovers, had not lost 3–0. Tellingly, the equally youthful, equally keen Anthony Wedgwood Benn, defending Bristol South-East, encountered disquieting signs. 'People are apathetic and there aren't the young ones at meetings that there ought to be,' he reflected with a fortnight to go. And the following week a local alderman took him to 'my first dinner-hour meeting, outside the Co-op furnishing factory' – but 'not a single soul came out of the factory to listen'. Meanwhile, the journalist Edward Hodgkin was taking the pulse in the capital. 'Any visitor who landed in London last week-end would have found it hard to discover from external evidence which of the two forthcoming attractions – the General Election and Christmas – was due first,' he wrote in the *Spectator*'s final issue before polling day. 'There was no sign of urgency, no passion, indeed no interest discernible . . .'[19]

One constituency, Bristol North-East, was the subject of a detailed academic study. 'In many ways the findings substantiate the rule-of-thumb practices of the professional politician,' noted Mark Abrams, a close observer of social and political trends, in his foreword: 'Each of the two major parties enjoys the support of a substantial core of voters who are undisturbed by issues, candidates, meetings and literature. The Labour Party core is mainly male, working-class and young; the Conservatives draw their solid support from women, the middle class and older people. The typical voter is loyal to an "image" which his party has built up by annexing a limited range of sloganized issues.' Three specific findings were especially striking. About one-third of voters receiving election literature failed to read or even glance at it; under 10 per cent (way below Gallup's estimate) attended even one political meeting; and, perhaps most piquantly, whereas only 7 per cent of Conservative voters agreed with 'certain statements or propositions selected as being typically "Labour" ', as many as 27 per cent of Labour voters agreed with typically 'Conservative' maxims. Perhaps not so much had changed in the 70 years since an aged Disraeli had told a British Marxist that 'it is a very difficult country to move, Mr Hyndman, a very difficult country indeed'.[20]

John Fowles, barely a month after gazing on the unnaturally well-ordered queue lining up to visit the South Bank, might have agreed. 'Election,' he noted at the start of October. 'But now it is a choice between Tory romance and Socialist practicality. The Tories offer nationalism, the Empire, freedom of enterprise and so on; the Socialists increasing uniformity, the death of the *ancien régime* individual. As a social unit, I shall vote for the Welfare State. I vote for what I think best for society.' For another young but already published novelist, Sid Chaplin, the assumption seems to have been that the Labour Party was swinging left – an assumption for which the recent Scarborough conference had given considerable evidence – and that a Labour victory would soon be followed by Attlee's exit. 'Bevan is a brilliant man, but rigid in his old-fashioned socialist prejudices,' he wrote to a friend on the 10th from Ferryhill in County Durham. 'As a Prime Minister he would either be a complete failure or the greatest we've had.' For Jean Rhys, a published novelist since the 1920s but in temporary eclipse, this was a rare moment when politics impinged. 'There is an election going on,' she reported from Maidstone to her daughter in the Far East three days before polling, 'but nobody seems to care much, not in this town anyway.' For which she offered a characteristic explanation: 'Perhaps they are too *exhausted*.'

Who was going to prevail? 'Jim thinks we may win the election; Tony doesn't,' the veteran Labour politician Hugh Dalton noted after lunching with his two protégés Callaghan and Crosland the day after Attlee's election announcement. The general expectation, not least on the part of Churchill himself, was that the Tories would win. 'He told me how Liverpool had cheered him, and as he spoke of the "love and affection of the people" his eyes filled with tears,' recorded Moran after seeing him during the campaign. ' "There was rapture in their eyes. They brought their children. I'm not conceited," he said, "but they wanted to touch me." ' Even so, the Tory lead in the weekly Gallup poll steadily narrowed – from eleven points at the end of September to four and a half points by 19 October. 'But on the figures we should be home,' Macmillan sought to comfort himself on that last Friday, while acknowledging that 'it is all on the knees of the Gods'. And of course, 'a small thing might influence the vital 2% or 3% one way or the other . . .'[21]

The final week coincided with the Motor Show at Earl's Court – including, on the Monday, an appearance by Princess Margaret, 'wearing a salmon-pink off-the-face, feathered hat and veil', with the hat matching 'a waisted salmon-pink coat trimmed with a collar of grey lamb's wool'. Headlines had already been made by the prominent display of a gold-fitted, gold-plated Daimler inscribed with the initials of Lady Docker, the famously free-spending wife of the prominent industrialist Sir Bernard Docker, but more significant was the stylish, streamlined Porsche that marked the German car industry's return to the international market. Reviews were also starting to appear of *Zip Goes a Million*, running from the 20th at the Palace Theatre. Cecil Wilson in the *Daily Mail* was reasonably kind about the Formby performance ('he cracks flat-capped jokes, sings in a thin but oddly tuneful voice, and shuffles at his own gentle tempo through a glittering succession of scenes'), but *The Times* declared that he was 'extraordinary only in his ordinariness'. A few days later, Tynan in the *Evening Standard* was unamused: 'I cannot laugh as he fidgets and gapes and fusses flat-footed across the stage . . . And I am unable to accept the theory that a banality or a catchphrase acquires wit or "philosophy" when delivered in a North-country accent. Simplicity and unaffectedness can be carried to extremes; Mr Formby works with what Henry James called "great economy of means, and – ah – effect".'

'I wish I'd have stayed in bloody Manchester,' Formby told Gracie Fields on the phone. 'At least up there folk know what I'm all about!' His consolation, though, was that the punters did not agree with the critics, and *Zip* was soon settling down for a long run with full houses. In Manchester itself, 'Who's going to win the election?' one misfit young Welshman, Frank Lewis, asked himself on Tuesday the 23rd. 'I couldn't care less. At least, that's almost my feeling. I'm almost indifferent.' Next evening his sole concern was his date with Winifred: 'This time we went to the Grapes, just off Oxford Rd near the Roxy. At 10 p.m. went back to our dark spot, up against the garage wall near Dunlop's. Made physical contact, hand contact all over the body. She called me "Professor Delver" because not only did she invite me "to delve" to use her own word but because I always take note most logically and

humorously of what is going on and comment on the proceedings.'
'She had corset on,' he added rather regretfully. 'She doesn't like me
calling her fat.'[22]

Back in the political arena, there was a significant moment on the
Tuesday when the *Manchester Guardian* followed the example of *Picture
Post* and came out against the desirability of another Labour victory.
Although acknowledging that the party had been 'the instrument of
a mainly beneficent social revolution', the paper could not ignore the
disturbing fact that 'behind their façade of unity there is Mr Bevan
and the hate-gospellers of his entourage'. Meanwhile, the politicians
themselves continued to bang away. John Profumo, Tory candidate for
Stratford-upon-Avon, treated a mass meeting in Coventry on Monday
to some timeless humour ('If we have another five years of Socialist
government in this country, somebody in the Ministry of Education
will have to start re-writing our nursery rhymes – such as "There was
an old woman who lived in a queue", and "Sing a song of sixpence the
value of a pound"'), Churchill was in Plymouth on Tuesday stoutly
denying the characterisation of him as a warmonger ('the opposite of
the truth'), and, that same evening, Hill in Luton gave some female
hecklers short shrift ('All right, girls, shout as much as you like, but
you won't pick the Government').

There was also, played out at schools all over the country, the ritual
of the mock election. One such was at the County High School in
Carlisle, where the candidates were all sixth-formers. 'It was obvious
from the beginning,' recalled Margaret Forster (13 at the time), 'that
the appearance and popularity of these candidates were going to count
more with us schoolgirl-voters than anything they said':

> The Conservative candidate was the most attractive but she wasn't a
> good speaker. She was very pretty, with long, blonde hair, beautifully
> brushed, but her voice was rather squeaky and her manner solemn.
> She went on about Winston Churchill and how he'd saved us from the
> Nazis and how ungrateful we'd been not to vote him in after the war.
> The Liberal candidate wasn't much better as far as the content of her
> speech was concerned, but she had a much louder and more forceful
> voice. She was very sporty too, in all the school teams, and made her
> party seem very healthy, the party for fit people who were not 'stuffy'

like the Conservatives. The Labour candidate was just too emotional. She actually wept when she read out some newspaper report on how the poor were living in our big cities. This was, it seemed, the fault of the Conservatives even though they were not at the moment in government – Labour had done what it could but had only made a start and needed many more years in power to carry on the good work. Then there was the Communist candidate – small, ugly, bespectacled, scruffy, but what a brilliant speaker. Our entire system of government, she bellowed, was a farce. The rich got richer, the poor got poorer and nothing would change until outdated democracy was swept aside and replaced by the people as the state and the state as the people, one for all and no more class divisions, no more inequality . . . I went straight home and announced I had no doubts, I was a Communist.

Forster's parents were deeply shocked, her father even walloping her for cheek, and in the end she gave her vote to the Labour candidate. It hardly mattered: 'The Conservative won with the Liberal a close second and Labour a poor third. The outstanding Communist candidate got only three votes and I was ashamed not to have voted for her.'²³

'Polling Day & a fateful one for the Country,' recorded Florence Speed in Brixton on the long-awaited Thursday. 'If the Socialists are returned for a third time, it is goodbye to the Empire & to everything it has stood for.' Three front pages that morning particularly caught the eye. The final Gallup poll in the *News Chronicle* had the Tory lead down to three and a half points; the *Daily Mirror*'s was a 'Trigger' special, complete with large drawing of a menacing gun and hand; and the *Daily Mail* featured a masterly cartoon by Illingworth, showing a middle-class couple at breakfast with a polling station visible through the window, the wife reading a paper with headlines like 'Inflation' and 'Cost of Living Soaring', and the husband getting up determinedly from the table and saying, 'We Are The Masters Now.' Among the diarists, Haines in Chingford voted Labour and then did her shopping ('how they do keep you waiting'), while Lewis delayed until after work and also voted Labour, before going to the Odeon to see *Valley of Eagles* starring Jack Warner. Speed's brother Fred was a polling clerk. ' "All I want is to see England on her feet again," one old woman said dropping her ballot paper into the box,' summarised Florence. 'She was so poor looking, that Fred thought she would be voting for Labour. And a man said, "Third time lucky. But I suppose there are too many b— LCC [London County Council] flats round here." ' Naturally, though, most voters kept their thoughts and intentions to themselves during a generally dry if rather chilly day. One among millions was the composer Ralph Vaughan Williams. 'I voted Labour in the last election though in my heart of hearts I wanted the Tories to get in,' he told a friend some months later. 'But the old spirit of opposition crept up and with all the country shouting for the Tories I determined to be on the other side.'[24]

The polls closed at nine and the early results started to come through not long after ten – by when, according to Gallup, half the electorate had gone to bed, presumably either calm or indifferent about the outcome. But in Trafalgar Square a crowd of some 15,000 gathered to watch the posting of the results on a large screen, while at the Savoy there were 3,000 guests for the traditional election beano given by Lord Camrose, owner of the *Daily Telegraph*. There the restaurant had been converted into a results room, with cheers every time the Tories won a seat, boos if Labour held on. Cecil Beaton took the visiting Greta Garbo with him. 'So great were her spirits as the Conservative victories came through,' he recorded, 'that she did not seem to mind even the attentions of the photographers.' Macmillan, though, skipped the crush: 'I felt I cd not stand it. I do not like the Noel Cowards etc. It is equally bad whether we win or lose.' Nor was the triumphalism necessarily justified. 'By 3 am,' he noted, 'it was clear that there had really been no swing at all for us' and that 'it will be a stalemate, or a small Tory majority'. Everything would turn, all sober observers agreed, on the results declared on the Friday.

Next morning the writer Ronald Duncan was at Charing Cross:

The voracious station disgorged its crowds of office workers as the 8.15 steamed in. The same anxious poker faces looking a little tired from their debauch of statistics on three cups of coffee. As usual they hurried toward the ticket collector, straining the digestion of the gate.

I walked up the platform, watching a ferret-like porter going up the train, slamming the doors of the empty carriages. From one he retrieved a newspaper which had been left on the seat.

As the train shunted out he paused, to study the Stop Press results, and thoughtfully lit a fag-end. I glanced over his shoulder.

'Good. It looks as if the old man will just get in after all.'

'Which old man?'

'Winston, of course.'

'Did you vote for him in spite of your union?'

'Of course not. Being a working man I voted Labour, but all the same I 'oped old Winston would get in this time.'

'You mean to say you voted Labour although you wanted the Conservatives to get in?'

'It's like this mate. I 'ad to vote for me own side out of loyalty like, but what I say is this' (and here he whispered lest his mate should overhear), 'the proper bloke to have on a footplate is an engine driver, and that's why I'd like to see old Winnie back at No 10, 'cause he knows his way around, having been brought up to it like.'

'It looks as if it will be a narrow thing,' I said.

'So it was at Dunkirk. The old b— likes it narrow.'

At which point 'the noisy arrival of the 8.35' ended their conversation.[25]

In the event it did prove a close-run thing, though in terms of seats not as close as the previous election. 'At 1.0 the two parties were neck and neck,' recorded Anthony Heap in his flat off Judd Street, St Pancras, 'and by 5.0 when the Conservative score reached 313 against Labour's 292 and the Liberals' 5, it was all over bar shouting.' By about six Churchill was Prime Minister, having driven to the Palace in a car flying the flag of the Warden of the Cinque Ports. The eventual Tory overall majority was 17 – a majority achieved despite the somewhat startling fact that, on an impressively civic 82.5 per cent turnout, they had received almost a quarter of a million fewer votes than Labour. Among the youthful losers were Margaret Roberts in Dartford and Peter Parker in Bedford; Willie Hamilton won comfortably in West Fife; Charles Hill in Luton and John Freeman in Watford were re-elected, the latter narrowly; and W. J. Brown lost in Fulham West. If for some Tory supporters there was a sense of disappointment, even anti-climax – 'Conservatives are "in", but alas! only just,' reflected Florence Speed at 6.30 that evening – for others there was an irresistible feeling that the natural order of things had been restored. 'I can date my political awakening,' the theatre critic Michael Billington would recall, 'from the moment a peculiarly detested fellow pupil burst into my public school classroom the day after the 1951 general election shouting: "We're in" – meaning, of course, the Tories. His arrogant assumption that we were all of the same persuasion meant I became a lifelong Labourite on the spot.' Or as Vere Hodgson put it less rebarbatively next day in her West London diary: 'At last I can write it. MR CHURCHILL IS AGAIN PRIME MINISTER. How wonderful!'[26]

During the Cabinet-making that ensued over the weekend, two appointments particularly reflected the less than commanding mandate that Churchill had received. One was for No. 11, where almost everyone had expected Churchill to put in the strongly free-market Oliver Lyttelton, a prominent City figure. Instead, he gave the job to the younger Rab Butler – 'the architect', in his biographer's just words, 'behind the rebuilding of the Tory Party's entire post-war fortunes'. The other crucial appointment, especially in terms of seeking to create the right climate for the new government, was the Minister of Labour. Again, everyone expected a hardliner, Sir David Maxwell Fyfe, but instead Churchill turned to the more emollient Sir Walter Monckton, rather cruelly nicknamed 'the oil-can' and now given express orders not to upset the unions. Churchill also offered a position (Minister of Education) to Clement Davies, the Liberal leader whose party had won only six seats. Davies, at the age of 67, was sorely tempted, but, after referring the question to his executive, he regretfully turned it down. 'Had Davies surrendered to Churchill's blandishments,' Anthony Howard plausibly claims, 'the Liberal Party as an independent entity would have ceased to exist.'[27]

In fact, the Tories would almost certainly not have won the election if the Liberals had not fielded such a puny number (109) of candidates. It was a shortfall largely caused by financial constraints, and the majority of disenfranchised Liberal supporters plumped for the Tories as second-best. Even so, it had needed a makeover for Churchill and his party to return to power. 'I have not given my vote to Die Hard Tories, but to Progressive Conservatives,' Hodgson reflected after her jubilant declaration. 'I don't like profiteers and huge dividends.' Her sentiments perhaps accurately reflected the sentiments of much middle-ground opinion – people who may or may not have actually voted Labour in 1945, but who in that unique context had not been too unhappy about a Labour victory. More generally, it seems that whereas the working class stayed broadly loyal to Labour – though no more than broadly, given that 44 per cent of it voted Conservative – the middle class continued, following on from the February 1950 election, its rightwards drift, especially in suburban seats. As for gender, the Conservatives had a 4 per cent lead among women, in part reflecting the party's sustained emphasis on the whole area of consumption.[28]

Ultimately, of course, men and women alike had for more than six years since the war been feeling the squeeze. 'The electorate was generally fed up with its wartime regime,' reflected Peter Parker in later life on his Bedford experience, 'and Labour was seen to be the party of boring rationing and planning regulations. Their continued existence infuriated a people who had fought nobly, had come through the siege of the immediate post-war reconstruction, and as I heard regularly on the doorsteps, were now buggered if they knew who had won the war.' In the face of such grumbling, it was in vain that Parker and his colleagues claimed that the Tory pledge to 'set the people free from controls' – a pledge that involved ending bulk-buying of foodstuffs by the government, abolishing price controls, reducing subsidies and scrapping the wartime utility scheme – would lead to an explosion in the cost of living. No doubt there was widespread scepticism as to whether a change of government would really lead to a more bountiful, less restrictive future, but enough voters were willing to take the chance.

For much of the middle class, the outcome was a sweet moment. 'What do you think the Labour party stands for?' Gallup had asked during the campaign:

More money for less work. (*Headmaster's wife*)
   Giving the working classes power they are not fitted to use.
   (*Commercial traveller*)
   They say social security but I think class warfare. (*Solicitor's wife*)
   Pampering the working man. (*Dentist*)
   Class hatred, revenge, and grab. (*Engineering technician*)
   To keep down the people with money. (*Butcher's wife*)
   Fair shares for all – if they are working people. (*Managing director*)

During the weeks afterwards there lingered in many middle-class breasts a visceral satisfaction that Britain had at last expelled its socialist rulers. On Guy Fawkes Night at one prep school in Shropshire, the headmaster Paul Denman Fee-Smith (nicknamed 'Boss') solemnly threw effigies of Mr and Mrs Attlee on to the bonfire – a spectacle, especially Mrs Attlee's blazing pumpkin hat, that (according to his biographer) 'deeply distressed' the 11-year-old Bruce Chatwin. 'Mummy, how could he do-o-o this?' he would later say in tears to his mother. But at the time, not wanting to rock the boat, he wrote home circumspectly: 'I enjoyed the fireworks last night. They made a very good display indeed.'[29]

3

You Can't Know Our Relief

In 1951 the Prescotts – father Bert (a Liverpudlian railwayman), mother Phyllis, 13-year-old John and three other children – took their summer holiday at Brighton. There they qualified as finalists for a competition to find the 'Typical British Family', with all the finalists having to return to Brighton for the judging on the first Saturday in November. With a mouth-watering prize of £1,000 at stake, the Prescotts naturally did not hesitate to travel down from their home near Chester. That morning the Corporation gave the nine families a guided tour of Brighton and the Downs, in the course of which Bert spoke freely. 'I won a £206 Tote double at Ascot this year,' he told a local reporter. 'I backed Fleeting Moment in the Cambridgeshire and won £14 having seen it win at Brighton – and now we're hoping to pull this off.' Within hours the interview had appeared in the *Evening Argus* – certainly by the time the judges (mainly local councillors but also including the two impeccably middle-class radio stars Anona Winn and Jack Train) got down to business that afternoon at the Dome in front of an audience of about a thousand people. All nine families were interrogated. 'They were quizzed on such thorny family subjects as washing-up, shopping, making the morning tea, and for the younger members there were questions of school, home life and did Dad use the slipper?' another local paper subsequently related. 'Most of the girls said they wanted to be nurses; nearly all the boys disliked school.'

That evening, as part of a variety show that included Tony Hancock on the bill as well as Winn and Train, the judges gave their verdict. Unanimously they chose the Newcombs, comprising Chief Inspector Frederick Newcomb, his wife and their 12-year-old son Raymond, living in Hemel Hempstead. The tenor of their replies can be gauged from the *Argus* report on what 'Brighton considers the typical British family':

> They must enjoy the simple pleasures. (Mrs Newcomb likes best a quiet evening at home with her husband 'relaxing and making a mess with his pipe and the family watching television' or walking in the country with their dog Rover.)
>
> A husband who doesn't drink, except for a sherry at Christmas, and who doesn't grumble.
>
> A wife who, although told by her employer that she was a career girl who would never enjoy married life, makes a success of it, and who loves making such dainties as lemon meringue pie and fruit flan for a most appreciative husband.
>
> A husband who doesn't mind doing the washing-up on his Sundays off . . .

Phyllis Prescott, years later still bitter about the sheer atypicality of the Newcombs (not least their claim that they never had rows), remembered Hancock as one of the judges.[1] That seems unlikely from the accounts in the press, but even if he had been, the family that so openly and cheerfully enjoyed a punt was probably never going to win. Only a week after the election, it was another sign that the middle class was back in the box-seat.

Another railwayman's son was also destined for disappointment, in his case permanently so. This was the writer Jack Common, whose most ambitious novel, *Kiddar's Luck*, was published in November to considerable critical acclaim. 'This is a rich, tolerant, considered and indeed really brilliant picture of working-class life and a profoundly human one,' declared V. S. Pritchett in the *New Statesman* about Common's largely autobiographical account of a working-class childhood in Newcastle during the early part of the century. 'This book makes most of the novels of working-class life look faked and overstrained.' The *Daily Express* even speculated that 'it may collect the jackpot, as Walter Greenwood did 20 years ago with *Love on the Dole*'. It did not happen. 'Having been,' to quote the historian Robert Colls, 'too late (and perhaps unwilling) for the Proletcult of the 1930s,' Common now found himself 'too early (and perhaps too old) for the Angry Young Man marketing of the 1950s.' Still, one authentic working-class voice from the region was by this time starting to be heard – albeit not south of the Trent. This was the stand-up comedian Bobby Thompson, 'The Little Waster', who since October had been featured about one week in three on the variety programme *Wot Cheor Geordie!* This went out on Tuesday evenings at seven on the North of England Home Service, recruited all its acts from the Newcastle area and was invariably recorded in front of an enthusiastic audience in local theatres or miners' welfare halls. By the time the current series ended in April 1952, Thompson was top of the bill, with *Radio Times* calling him 'a Durham lad who has made quite a hit'. He was in fact 40 and, after years performing mainly in pubs and working men's clubs for little or no money, had just given up his full-time job as a labourer at the Royal Ordinance Factory in Birtley, County Durham.[2]

It was also on a Tuesday evening this winter, 11 December, that the Royal Albert Hall featured, at the bottom of the bill, three six-round contests (one welterweight and two lightweight) of a peculiarly family nature. 'Lew Lazar, Aldgate, displayed a varied selection of punches before knocking out Charlie Kray, Bethnal Green, in the third round,' reported *Boxing News*. 'The Kray twins from Bethnal Green had mixed fortunes. Reg turned in the most memorable performance of the pair to outpoint Bobby Manito, Clapham, but Ron never found an answer to the speedier leading of Bill Sliney, King's Cross, and was well outpointed.' Charlie was 25, Reg and Ron were 18, and (in the words of one of Ron's obituarists) 'the twins' street reputations were the result of successful unlicensed bouts with various local rivals'. Three weeks later there was also violence in the air in Glasgow, at the annual New Year's Day 'Old Firm' match between Celtic and Rangers. Far from unprecedented in the fixture, and invariably fuelled by sectarian chanting and flag-waving, the trouble started this time when the visiting Rangers went 4–1 ahead some 20 minutes from time. 'It was stated by the police,' reported the *Glasgow Herald*, 'that a bottle was thrown from high up on the terracing, and landed in the middle of the crowd, who scattered. There was more trouble and a man was arrested. Bottles were thrown at the policemen, who took the man away.' The trouble then spread as several hundred in the covered enclosure scrambled on to the track surrounding the pitch, some even getting on to the pitch itself, before mounted policemen managed to clear them. Eleven people were arrested, with two of them jailed. 'Something must be done,' declared the *Herald* with feeling rather than originality. 'This hooliganism on the sports field cannot be allowed to go on. The sport of football must be cleaned up.' In fact hooliganism at football matches was still pretty rare – in England in 1951, only 21 incidents of spectator misconduct and disorderliness were reported to the FA – but, contrary to subsequent mythology about a 'golden age', it was not non-existent.[3]

Away from the terraces, this first post-war winter under a Tory government remained for most people a daily struggle. There were reductions in imports of unrationed foods; rationing itself remained firmly in force for the time being; and Churchill even had to announce a cut in the weekly meat ration. It was presumably around this time that, confused by figures and weights, he asked his Minister of Food to show him an individual's rations. 'Not a bad meal, not a bad meal,' said Churchill when the exhibit was produced. 'But these,' responded the Minister, 'are not rations for a meal or for a day. They are for a week.' Inevitably housewives were as much as ever at the sharp end, including of price rises. Nella Last in Barrow, noting 'rail fares up 2/- in the £' and 'coal 3^d or 6^d more a cwt', reflected just after Christmas that 'it seems startling to have to face such "jumps", after the feeling that a change of Govt would make for early betterment'; and in Chingford on New Year's Eve, Judy Haines was told by the 'girl in Dyson's' that 'I have lost my last week's fats, cheese and bacon rations for four as I didn't get them before they stock-took', which got Haines properly 'worked up' before she 'took it up with Manager, who gave no trouble!' Equally inevitably, continuing shortages meant a continuing role for the spiv – a role commemorated in February by the rhyme chanted by an 11-year-old girl living in Hackney:

> We are three spivs of Trafalgar Square
> Flogging nylons tuppence a pair,
> All fully fashioned, all off the ration
> Sold in Trafalgar Square.

'Victoria tells me her brother, aged ten, made it up,' her teacher informed Peter and Iona Opie. 'Victoria and her friends skip to the rhyme very fast with a "bump" on the last word.'[4]

For non-skipping pedestrians, these were fraught times. 'Lots of pedestrian crossings have been swept away in Notting Hill Gate,' complained Vere Hodgson in the same entry that acclaimed the Churchillian restoration. 'I am foaming with rage.' Four days later, on 31 October, new regulations came into effect about the use and markings of pedestrian crossings, against a background of government having asked local authorities to do away with uncontrolled crossings, which had neither traffic lights nor policemen and were being widely ignored. Instead, the emphasis was going to be on the recently introduced zebra crossings, with a £5 fine for pedestrians who lingered unnecessarily. Over the ensuing weeks and months, controversy rumbled on: parents protesting against the removal of crossings outside schools formed human barriers in order to hold up traffic while children crossed safely – protests that stimulated the arrival by the mid-1950s of school-crossing patrols and, in due course, the circular 'children crossing' sign (aka 'lollipop'). Test cases led to judges giving various rulings about the respective rights of motorists and pedestrians at zebra crossings, with the more right-wing press (typified by the *Daily Express*'s anti-pedestrian motoring correspondent Basil Cardew) tending to support those behind the wheel.

Cardew also had a word of sympathy for the unfortunate George Samson, a 57-year-old bus driver who on the evening of 5 December, the day before he was due to receive a medal for 25 years of safe driving, came down a badly lit hill in Chatham and accidentally ploughed into 52 Marine cadets (aged between ten and thirteen) who were marching to the naval barracks for a boxing match. Twenty-four died – Britain's worst road disaster yet. At the trial in January, Samson was fined £20 for dangerous driving and disqualified for three years, after the jury had found him guilty but entered a plea for leniency. Relatives as well as some newspaper columnists were sharply critical of the mild punishment, but the great majority of the 1,500 letters that Samson had received from all over the country since the tragedy had been of a sympathetic nature. 'I am very grateful for the letters appreciating my position,' Samson in tweed overcoat and cloth cap told a reporter over a cup of tea near the Old Bailey. 'I know they are only words, but I want to say again how very deeply sorry I am for the parents of the boys.' And he added, almost in tears: 'Don't forget, I knew many of them. Many of those little cadets used to come to my home. They called me "Sammy".'

It had been shortly before this dreadful accident that the merger had been announced between Morris Motors (largely based at Cowley, Oxford) and the Austin Motor Co. (largely based at Longbridge, Birmingham). Its motives were mainly defensive – in a context of increasing market share for Ford and Vauxhall (both of them American-owned), as well as German, French and Italian car outputs starting to reach almost pre-war levels – and the press gave the decision a generally easy ride. Citing economies of scale and increasing standardisation of parts as future boons, the *Economist* reckoned that 'its promoters may well be justified in claiming that the amalgamation will not only be of advantage to their shareholders, but will be also "in the national interest" '. The merger duly took effect in 1952, with the new combine called the British Motor Corporation – the largest motor company in the world outside the US. Chairman and managing director was the 55-year-old Leonard Lord, who in the 1930s had had an unhappy relationship with Lord Nuffield at Cowley before moving to Austin. No one ever denied his qualities as a relentless, even bullying production man, but whether he would have the requisite vision and skills to oversee Britain's flagship car maker, responsible for almost two-fifths of the country's output, was altogether another question. 'You know what BMC stands for?' Lord himself enjoyed boasting. 'Bugger My Competitors!'[5]

Neither motoring nor television-watching were yet majority pursuits, but it was a major development when the BBC's Holme Moss station opened in October, shortly before the election, at a stroke creating 11 million potential viewers in the north of England. One TV critic, Leonard Mosley, went on an immediate recce, an experience that convinced him that in the north the TV set 'will not (as it often is in the south) be a fill-up for the corner of the lounge, a stand-by when there is nothing on at the local flicks or theatre, or something to keep the children quiet', but instead something much more vital and central to everyday life. A letter in *Woman's Own* at the start of 1952 suggested he may have been right. 'Up to a few months ago I was hardly ever at home in the evenings, but now I find it's much more fun to stay in,' Jane Collins wrote from Manchester. 'The reason for this sudden change is that my father has recently bought a television set. And it's surprising what a difference it has made to our family. Now, instead of going out for entertainment, we stay in our own front room where our friends and relations are welcome to pop in and join us if there's something they particularly want to see.' It was symptomatic that already in November *Radio Fun* had become *T.V. Comic* – though two days later, on Remembrance Sunday, Mary King in Birmingham defiantly noted, after listening to Richard Dimbleby's commentary on the ceremony at the Cenotaph, that 'the picture he drew was quite equal to seeing it on a "Television Set" '. Soon afterwards, a BBC survey of listening habits found that 'those over 50 listened to the Home Service in the evening twice as much as those under 20', whereas on the Light Programme there was no such split. Even so, in terms of individual programmes, 'youngsters listened more than older people to such Light Programme evening series as *Variety Bandbox, Life with the Lyons, Variety Fanfare, Fine Goings On, Family Favourites,* Sport, Dance Music and, of course, *Jazz Club,* whose listeners are almost confined to 16–19 year olds.'[6]

There were presumably some jazz-lovers among the students at Aberdeen University who in November elected a new Rector to succeed Sir Stafford Cripps. The university's liveliest campaign for many years produced a striking outcome: 104 votes for the black singer and campaigner Paul Robeson; 104 votes also for the Deeside laird Captain A.A.C. Farquharson; 370 votes for the celebrated war hero Lord Lovat; and 430 votes for the *Take It From Here* star Jimmy Edwards, only 31 but already known as 'Professor'. 'The students did not put me in as a comedian but as someone to help their interests,' the winner told an Aberdeen paper from his country home in Sussex. 'If there's anything the students want me to do I will do it.' Soon afterwards, *Picture Post* attributed the outcome to how 'a gathering undercurrent of hostility had been swirling to and fro between the students and the "senators", or governing body, with the students complaining of an immoderate and Grundyish interference with their out-of-hours activities'. But if there was just a whiff of the sixties and student rebellion about the choice of Edwards, the fate this same winter of the brilliant mathematician Alan Turing – mastermind behind the cracking of the German Enigma code and arguably the father of the modern computer – was testimony to darker, wholly unreconstructed forces. On the evening of 7 February, just weeks after he had appeared on a Third Programme discussion about whether machines could be said to think, the police came knocking on his door at Wilmslow. His crime, following a brief liaison with a fair, blue-eyed Manchester youth called Arnold Murray, was 'Gross Indecency contrary to Section 11 of the Criminal Law Amendment Act 1885'. At one point Turing gave the detectives a lengthy, handwritten statement, which particularly struck them because of his lack of shame. 'He was a real convert,' one recalled, 'he really believed he was doing the right thing.'[7] The case would be heard at the next Quarter Sessions.

'Message from Churchill to come out to Chartwell,' Harold Macmillan recorded in his diary for the day after the Tories had returned to power. 'Found him in a most pleasant and rather tearful mood. He asked me to "build the houses for the people". What an assignment! . . . Churchill says it is a gamble – make or mar my political career. But every humble home will bless my name, if I succeed.' Macmillan, having hoped for greater things, was initially reluctant to accept the job, but, once he became Minister of Housing, rapidly got stuck in. It proved, in terms of fulfilling the much-vaunted Tory pledge to build 300,000 houses a year, a remarkable success story. Churchill overrode all Treasury objections to the concentration of scarce resources on housing; Ernest Marples, 'a cocky and talkative accountant who had built up a fortune with a construction company' (to quote Anthony Sampson), was a relentlessly hard-working junior minister; Sir Percy Mills, a Birmingham industrialist, was brought in as an adviser and quickly established ten Regional Housing Production Boards; and Macmillan himself combined determination (however deceptively languid), pragmatism and a flair for helpful publicity. Typical of the pragmatism was his decision to rely heavily for the time being on housebuilding by local authorities, with their subsidies even being raised, while starting to encourage more private building than Labour had permitted. The flair for PR was epitomised in a widely publicised speech at Nottingham in January, less than three months into the job. 'I will see that the order book is kept full,' he promised the building industry. 'There will be no arbitrary limitation by an arbitrary programme of 175,000 or 200,000 or any other figure of houses a year. There is no restriction; no rigid ceiling; no artificial limit. And the quicker you build, the more there will be to build. The more you finish, the more you get.' A gratified

Macmillan recorded afterwards how 'a very large audience in the Albert Hall accepted the speech with much enthusiasm', while next morning was even better: 'A wonderful press! We have really hit the headlines. On the whole, a very friendly reception. The *Manchester Guardian* a bit sniffy . . .'

The push for 300,000 came, however, at a price. 'The people need more homes,' Macmillan declared in a booklet, *Houses 1952*, published by his ministry during his first few months. 'They need them quickly. This is the most urgent of all social services. For the home is the basis of the family, just as the family is the basis of the nation. We have to try to meet their needs at a time of great economic difficulty. For we have to expand in a period of general restriction. This surely means that we must try to build the greatest possible number of houses out of the available labour and materials.' In practice, this meant smaller houses, with the ministry setting out revised guidelines for local authorities that involved reductions of up to 100 square feet on minimum floor areas. The litany by one housing historian – 'the omission of cupboards in bedrooms, smaller kitchens, and entrance halls reduced to a lobby in which there was space for neither coats nor prams' – gives a good idea of the consequences for what was now officially dubbed 'The People's House'. It is true that standards had been becoming less generous towards the end of the Labour government, but it was under Macmillan that they seriously tightened. 'If we can reduce the size of houses to rabbit hutches of course we can build more houses,' grumbled Bevan, who during his five years as minister had refused to compromise on space standards, and clearly he had a point. But for Macmillan it was not a difficult choice. 'Drove through Leicester to a little village called Desford,' he noted the day after his Nottingham speech. 'Here had descended (like locusts) a host of photographers, BBC men, television, news-reel reporters and the like – all to see me open 2 houses – the first built to the new simplified design.'[8]

Macmillan's politically ambitious, top-down, numbers-driven approach would have profound implications in the context of a continuing acute housing shortage, but what really mattered for many thousands of people was getting into a new house or flat and starting to enjoy appreciably better amenities (indoor lavatory, a bathroom, hot and cold running water, more privacy, often a garden) than they had had before. 'As one of the 15–16,000 on West Ham's waiting list, I say give us somewhere to live, house, flat or prefab, anything, so long as it has four walls and a roof, and we can call it our own,' was how W. R. England of Plaistow put it to the local paper in April 1952. 'But we want these places now – not in 25–50 years!' A huge migration was by this time already well under way – away from the often slum-ridden or blitzed inner cities and out to existing suburbs, newly developed suburbs or even beyond. 'The largest part of this migration was voluntary,' declares its historian, Mark Clapson, according to whom 'the majority of people who moved were working-class couples with children, or couples who were just about to have them'. He adds that 'within the working classes this voluntarism was most strongly located within the younger and relatively wealthier'.

The most symbolically resonant part of the migration was to the twelve New Towns designated since 1946, though in fact by the end of 1951 only 3,126 dwellings had actually been completed. The first New Town was Stevenage, whose youthful pioneers would in time look back with some wonder on the dusty, muddy experience:

> We had no floor coverings except in the bathroom, and a hearth rug before the open fire in the living room, and every evening I polished the Marley tiles in the living room, hall and kitchen. This may lead you to suppose that I was a houseproud housewife. No way! While I was grateful to have a home of our own after five years of living in other peoples', and proud of our achievements in home-making, it was sheer necessity that caused me to do housework in the evening ... We had no gardens, no roads, no pavements or footpaths, no telephones, no shop nearer than the Old Town, and no car and we were surrounded by construction. It doesn't take much imagination to picture the outlandish conditions in which we lived. Fortunately that first summer was dry ... *(Thelma Sultzbach, a GI bride with a two-year-old daughter, arrived May 1951)*
>
> Well we gradually got a bit straight, and I got into some sort of routine. We got to know our neighbours who were all quite friendly. There were still a lot of unfinished houses all around us, but they gradually became occupied. Footpaths were laid. A pillar box was installed in Rockingham Way. The first time I went to post a letter I had to clamber over a pile of bricks to get to the pillar box. *(Marjorie MacLeod, two small children*

and expecting a third, previously living with in-laws in New Southgate,
November 1951)

The day we moved in, the footpath at the front of the house wasn't complete, there was a gap, and the furniture removers walked down two planks; there was mud everywhere. I got down on my knees, and I scrubbed the place from top to bottom. I was finishing the last bit around the corner of the brown tiles, Anne stood there at the bottom of the stairs – looking up (she did not know I was there as she could not hear me) and she said: 'What a beautiful house but how in the name of God am I ever going to clean it!' *(Mick Cotter, previously living in Hornsey with pregnant wife and two small children, February 1952)*

I was thrilled with the home, it was really lovely – to think I had my own sink, my own bathroom, two toilets, one up and one down. I felt I was on holiday for months and months; the children thought it was great. There was a green dell at the side of us, and they just ran round and round. They felt free. *(Anne Luhman, moving from a Tottenham flat without running water, June 1952)*

'To us it was an exciting time,' recalled Huw and Connie Rees, who with their new baby had left a requisitioned flat in Hackney for a new house in Stevenage in September 1952. It was a time that included 'a vision of the future, a prospect of being able to live in ideal surroundings, a healthy environment for children and full employment locally'. Or, as they also put it more prosaically, and perhaps realistically, the people who moved to Stevenage New Town 'wanted no more than the basic right of a home of their own, somewhere to live and to bring up their children in a decent environment'.[9]

Economic self-sufficiency was crucial to the thinking behind the New Towns – in Stevenage, for example, one usually could not get a house without the nomination of a local employer – and in October 1951 there was a revealing case study, scrutinised by the writer Roy Lewis, when an entire firm, Sunvic Controls, moved from 'a warren of workshops' in Covent Garden to a spanking-new factory in the industrial estate of Harlow New Town. The firm's employees were given the option of coming too, and, after an exploratory coach trip to Harlow, more than two-thirds decided to take it and in the process uproot their lives. From some there was positive enthusiasm for the move, especially at the prospect of significantly improved housing conditions, but from others there was more reluctant acquiescence, mainly motivated by not wanting to let go of a good, paternalistic employer. 'It's what you'd expect,' one told Lewis after the coach trip:

> The sort of thing the planning boys dream up, but which doesn't work out. Social classes all mixed up, for example: nobody likes that, you know, people like to keep to their own class, in practice. Then, there's no privacy – think of it, *front gardens in common*. And the back gardens divided only by wire, so your neighbour knows all about you. And to think of it on washing-day. *And* there's going to be a community centre. Yes, it's not a joke, there really is. A community centre! Planners are nuts on palliness. Go? Oh, *of course* I shall go!

Lewis visited Harlow in January 1952 to see how the newcomers in their three-bedroom houses were getting on: ' "I wouldn't go back for anything," was the comment of all those who remembered the single room, the in-laws, the days of inadequate accommodation. "I've not been back to London since we moved," added one housewife, "and I don't want to go." "It would seem a backward step," said another.' As for the inevitable complaints he heard, some were likely to be addressed earlier than others:

> The mud – that will be stabilised. The lack of street lighting – that will be remedied in time. Some wives who don't go to the factory find, even with children, that a labour-saving house leaves them with more time than they know what to do with. These ladies do feel the need of the cinema already. More than that, however, they feel the need of shops. Old Harlow supplies the rations – but life, they find, without acres of suburban shop frontage, lacks a vital quality: they must window-shop, and they want the shops they know. C & A was mentioned wistfully. Epping and Stortford do not satisfy them: they want a strip of Oxford Street; this must remain a dream till Harlow has its planned civic centre . . .

Even so, Lewis noted with satisfaction that many of the women had already started to develop a social life – 'Friendships are springing up with next-door neighbours; TV parties are arranged' – and concluded optimistically that whereas 'to give people a new suburb is to give them nothing but "housing", to give them a new town is to give them and their children a chance to be free and independent men and women learning and teaching the central lessons of civic life'. Not that Lewis himself proposed to share in the adventure, living as he did in a 'genuine early Victorian' house in Notting Hill – albeit (as his author's note cheerfully if insincerely added) 'with every inconvenience which makes you wish you lived in a Harlow house!'

Of course, despite Lewis's passing put-down, it was for the new suburbs that most of the outward migration was destined. These included the extensive and (at this stage) predominantly mixed-development, low-rise Bell Green and Tile Hill council estates starting to take shape in the early 1950s on the outskirts of Coventry, where the Labour-run local authority openly defied Macmillan by announcing in December 1951 that it would be sticking to its ratio of only one licence in five for private building, whereas the minister wanted that sector to receive up to 50 per cent of licence allocations. Bell Green never enjoyed a particularly good press – not least on account of its bleak, windswept, almost treeless appearance – but the Tile Hill Neighbourhood Unit was for several years something of a showpiece. The direct brainchild of the visionary City Architect Donald Gibson, it would, declared an admiring *Coventry Standard* in August 1951, 'ultimately comprise a self-contained township on the outskirts of the old city', with the paper adding that 'great care has been taken to enclose in this town within a city a cross-section of the whole community'. In order to speed up the rate of completions, Gibson and his deputy, Fred Pooley (who actually lived on the Tile Hill estate), reached an agreement with the building firm George Wimpey by which most of the new houses and flats, in Bell Green as well as Tile Hill, were built along the 'no fines' system, involving a coarse cement mixture poured into moulds. This in practice meant a somewhat monotonous surfeit of 'colour-washed' concrete (with a tendency to dampness) and grey, pebble-dashed frontages, though whether this mattered to the first generation of residents is doubtful.[10]

Or take, near the south coast, the enormous Paulsgrove estate, with more than 10,000 people living there by 1951. Situated on Portsdown Hill, this estate had been developed by the City Architect's Department

in Portsmouth to house some of that blitzed city's working class. 'Ask
a Paulsgrove resident if he likes it there, in the post-war "paradise" on
the hill, and more often than not the answer will come back: "Yes, but
. . .," ' began a graphic front-page story in the *Hampshire Telegraph* in
February of that year on 'Paulsgrove: A Paradise Lost?':

> Sometimes the 'but' means that he thinks it is too isolated, that he misses
> the cinema, or his favourite bar; that it is a long ride home, or 'too far from
> Mum'. Very much more often though, it means that he is about to launch
> into a dissertation on the community's No. 1 problem – children . . .
>
> One of the qualifications for securing a house under the 'points' system
> is children. It was the big families who went to Paulsgrove. The result is
> that of the entire population of the estate, at least half are under 15. It is
> nobody's fault, but it is having an unfortunate effect. Very few grown-
> ups think of any of their neighbours' children as anything but scamps.
>
> Everywhere it is the tale of a broken window, of a bell that rings too
> often at dusk, or of footprints in unfenced gardens.

There followed the usual litany of a new estate's failings – no boys' clubs,
no cinema, no pub, one church, only about ten shops (all temporary),
the long bus journey to either Portsmouth or Cosham. But the report
also emphasised that, despite the estate's 'as yet impersonal tangle of
modernity' and its 'strange 20th Century motley of brick, steel and
curiously Continental-looking structures', mainly a mixture of two-
or three-bedroom houses and three-storey blocks of flats, 'the average
tenant is not unduly bothered', for 'after all, his new home is intensely
practical'. Certainly, the gratitude was unmistakeable:

> Hitler did a good job when he blew up my parents' house in Portsea. I
> wouldn't change this for anything.
>
> You can't know our relief when we moved in.
>
> At last, something I can take a pride in.
>
> I have a garden now and we catch the sun all day in the front room –
> no need for candles in the daylight now.

Just over a year later, the paper returned to the estate and focused
on how the work of 'the magnificent new schools' had resulted in a

significant improvement in youthful behaviour, in spite of class sizes averaging around 40. 'How can they talk of us as the hooligan schools!' declared one head teacher. 'We have children here of all types and I say they are a perfectly wonderful lot. The parents are splendid, helping us in every way they can to do the most for their children.' The report itself optimistically identified 'a growing community spirit' on the estate generally; and it predicted that 'the association of the words "Paulsgrove" and "hooligan" ' would soon become 'totally obsolete'.

The outwards migration could also be from villages as well as cities and towns. Such was the case for the family of Lorna Stockton (the future literary critic Lorna Sage), whose remarkable autobiography, *Bad Blood* (2000), relates how her parents in about 1951 moved into a brand-new council semi half a mile 'up the lane' from Hanmer, a Flintshire village just inside the Welsh border. It was a house, complete with open-plan living room, 'designed for the model family of the 1950s ads: man at work, wife home-making, children (two, one of each) sporty and clean and extrovert'. For her grandmother from south Wales, after years of living a proud but discontented life in the local vicarage, 'the raw council estate, where cows wandered over the unfenced garden plots on their way to the fields and *the neighbours could see in*, was Hanmer squared, essence of Hanmer, and she scorned it with a passion'. It was an unprepossessing estate of about a dozen houses – 'built on a flattened field at the top of a windy rise' – and the nine-year-old Lorna, who had also lived at the much more spacious vicarage, 'refused to feel at home there' and spent as much time as possible 'wandering the fields and footpaths in squelching wellies'. Indeed, the whole experience seems to have been a mismatch – 'unlike the other houses, ours didn't have net curtains, an act of impropriety which showed from the start that we didn't know how to behave in our new life' – and not even the arrival of a new three-piece suite could compensate for what Sage unsentimentally records as a (probably far from unique) 'case of emotional claustrophobia'.[11]

One new, much-publicised council estate had no country fields anywhere near.[12] This was the Lansbury estate in the bombed-out East End, named after the legendary inter-war Labour politician George Lansbury and serving during 1951, in its incomplete early development, as the 'Live Architecture Exhibition' for the Festival of Britain. 'Here at Poplar you may catch a glimpse of that future London which is to arise from blitzed ruins and from the slums and chaotic planning of the past,' declared a Festival brochure with typical confidence and forward-lookingness. John Summerson, visiting the estate in June, identified some key elements:

> The general idea is the redevelopment of a 'neighbourhood' as envisaged in the Abercrombie-Forshaw plan of 1943. The old street-pattern is wiped out and a new pattern, with fewer streets, imposed; houses and flats are loosely and agreeably mixed, there is fluent adequacy of open space, and churches and schools are well sited . . . The completed dwellings include three-storey blocks of flats and a longish row of small houses . . . The market place or shopping centre, designed by Mr Frederick Gibberd, is a challenging departure. No traffic enters it and the shops are recessed under the buildings, arcade-wise . . .

Chrisp Street market (London's first pedestrianised shopping centre), complete with clock tower, was indeed designed as Lansbury's heartbeat – though revealingly, when Gibberd offered to design new stalls for the traders, they told him they preferred to carry on with their untidy, shabby old ones.

The verdict of most critics was at best lukewarm ('not overwhelmingly impressive', reckoned Summerson overall, 'worthy, dull and somewhat skimpy', thought J. M. Richards), while only 87,000 people visited the site during the Festival's five months. But as usual, most of those (mainly drawn from Poplar itself) who moved in to the new houses and flats were pleased to be doing so. 'Our new place is just a housewife's dream,' Mrs Alice Snoddy told the press in February 1951 after her family (husband Albert a welder, she a part-time paper-sorter, two young children, one mother-in-law) had been the first to be given keys, in this case to a ground-floor flat. 'There are fitted cupboards and one to air clothes in, a stainless-steel sink, hot water tanks. It's the sort of home to be proud of.' During 1952 two well-disposed sociologists, John Westergaard and Ruth Glass, interviewed several hundred of those who had moved in. 'I never thought I'd see such luxury,' was the heartfelt assertion of a lorry driver's wife; 'I can't stop laughing to myself – I'm so happy,' confessed a housewife who with her husband and two children had been living in one room in a condemned house in Stepney. Equally predictably there were complaints – the new market's layout was too congested ('you can't take a pram round') as well as discouraging to those wanting to have an initial recce before buying anything, there were too few facilities for mothers with small children, the kitchens were too small for eating in, the rents were on the high side. But overall, 'the view that Lansbury offers a fundamentally satisfactory environment is shared by most of the people within and around the new neighbourhood'. Mrs Snoddy herself was settling in for the long haul. Three decades on, in the mid-1980s, she told the BBC that when she first saw her flat, 'I can't say I was all that keen on it, I would have preferred to have gone and lived in a house.' But by 2001 she was happy to concede to the *Guardian* that 'once other people from Poplar began to move on to the estate, I soon began to adjust', adding, 'I must have adjusted rather well as I'm still here 50 years later.'[13]

On almost all the new council estates, severe financial constraints – sometimes allied to a lack of imagination and drive – resulted in a damaging absence of those accompanying facilities that might have made the ideal of a complete neighbourhood unit closer to reality. In March 1952, for example, when Glasgow Corporation's Sub-Committee on Sites and Buildings heard an application from Pollok Estate Tenants' Association 'requesting the erection of a hut or hall for the use of the tenants of the flats for aged persons at Kempsthorn Crescent as a recreational centre', it was compelled to refuse it; at the same meeting there was a similar response to an application 'for an area of ground at Drumchapel for the purpose of erecting a cinema in the new Drumchapel township'. The sociologist Charles Madge published that year a striking audit of community facilities on 100 post-war housing estates:

Facility	Number planned	Number built
Day nursery	13	0
Nursery school	46	1
Infant welfare clinic	24	6
Infant play space	22	2
Open playground	52	14
Health centre	33	0
Community centre	50	4
Branch library	46	11

On all estates, whether built before or since the war, there was also the problem of maintaining facilities. 'What we really want is a supervisor on the lines of a park ranger, whose full-time job it would be to patrol the flats and find the culprits,' declared a tenant in October 1951 after it emerged that children at the huge, showpiece Quarry Hill estate in Leeds were in danger of losing their three playgrounds unless vandals methodically destroying sets of swings were detected. 'The police can't be here all the time.'

The following June the subject arose on *Any Questions?* of the social status of public housing. 'Of course I don't think for a moment it's degrading to live in a council house, obviously that goes without saying,' declared the young, ambitious Labour MP Anthony Crosland. 'But there certainly was a time obviously, twenty years ago, when it was considered degrading to live in a council house, to some extent.' This was, he insisted with undisguised egalitarian passion, an issue of central importance:

Today the situation is much better, partly because council houses obviously are so improved in quality that it's nonsense to say that they're worse than other houses. They're extremely good on the whole now; and partly also because council house estates are manned by a much wider social group than they used to be, I mean they're much more widely drawn. Now I feel very strongly about this because I'm a Socialist and my definition of Socialism quite simply is a classless society – it's a society in which people don't think of themselves as belonging to the working class, or the middle class, or the upper class, or whatever class you like, they haven't got that feeling. Now at the moment I think very strongly what still allows this sense of class to persist, isn't so much income differences that people have, it's differences in education and housing and general social and family background like that. And the most important thing that one could do to eliminate the sense of class in Britain today, isn't now so much to tackle income differences – although that's still important – as to tackle these sort of things like housing and education and to make certain – and this is the crux – that you can't tell that a person belongs to this class, that class or the other class, by looking at the sort of house he lives in or by asking him what school he went to. And when we've got to that state of affairs we shall have a jolly good society . . . HEAR. HEAR. APPLAUSE.

The implacable fact remained, though, that type of housing and social class were inextricably linked. It was mainly the working class (though at this stage often the respectable, improving working class) that occupied council houses and flats, while owner-occupation was almost entirely a middle-class preserve. Also in 1952, a Gallup poll revealingly found that 65 per cent of the people interviewed, of whom 56 per cent were Labour voters, approved of the sale of council houses to tenants – a controversial policy being applied rather nervously and ineffectually by the new Tory government. 'Socialist voters were not so wholeheartedly against the sale of council houses as Socialist councils were,' a Ministry of Housing official reflected on the findings. Telling also, on that *Any Questions?* programme, was the contribution of the next panellist, the bluff, right-wing Wiltshire countryman Ralph Wightman, who deployed a sarcasm that, however unattractively, did its job in undercutting the indignant upper-middle-class product of Highgate and Oxford:

> On that point of Tony Crosland's I would suggest that they have made a completely new class, a superior class, living in council houses, they're the only class in the community – the only class of tenants whose rents can be raised by their landlords. They're the only class of tenant who can be turned out if they take a sub-tenant, if they don't cut their front lawn in conformity with the Council's instructions. LAUGHTER. They are a completely privileged class . . . LAUGHTER . . .[14]

'Had party in the evening,' recorded John McGarry, a 15-year-old schoolboy living in Bournemouth, on 8 January 1952. 'Dorothy came, had super time. Dots really got me. Finished at 11 took Dot home. Mum said something very offending about her when I got back. Feel very rotten about it. Why can't she leave me alone?' Three days later, a Friday, he saw Dot in the evening: 'Had super time, better than talking at scouts. Decide to stay in Mon, Tue, Wed to do some swotting. Dad and Mum do not want me to enjoy myself, surely that's what the life is for. Bed at 10.45 feeling very happy as well as discontented.' The downs and ups of adolescence continued unabated over the next few weeks:

13 January. Decide to join the Navy.

17 January. Dull day at school ... All they talk about is exams, exams, exams what rotten fun.

22 January. Dot came round in the evening, spent quite a good evening together, but she seems very cold hearted tonight.

24 January. History exam in the morning, did terribly about 15% or less.

25 January. Had a super evening. Get a long way with Dorothy. She's lovely, the best girl I've ever had.

4 February. Go round to Dorothies at 7.45 and spend the last evening of my life, so far, there. Had super time ... Got real warmed up at some spots ...

6 February. Find my history book at school ... Dull morning. THE KING DIES AT 10.45 all very strange, everybody seems quiet over the strange news.

Strange but true – at 7.15 that Wednesday morning, King George had been found dead in his bed at Sandringham by an under-valet. He was 56, and it was less than a fortnight since the *Daily Mirror* had published a brief but to-the-point letter from Mrs Florence Price of Dunvant near Swansea: 'Surely we had a great example of the value of prayer during our beloved King's recovery from his severe illness.'[15]

At about 11.00, less than two hours after Churchill had been informed, a Mass-Observation investigator was on a number 6 bus going to Marble Arch via Edgware Road in London:

There was an undercurrent of talk in the bus – and now and again Inv. caught the words 'Princess Elizabeth' and 'the King' and 'It's a pity – she'll have to come back [i.e. from Kenya] I expect'. Everybody seemed to be talking softly, and the expressions on their faces looked solemn. Inv. had a feeling something had gone wrong, so turning to the bus conductress who was standing nearby she asked 'Is there anything wrong?'

Bus conductress – 'Haven't you heard? – it's just come thro' on the wireless – the King died in his sleep.'

Other people on the bus on hearing this remark added – 'Shame isn't it?' – 'Oh well, it's a mercy the way it ended – he had it coming.' 'I'm sorry for the old Queen – Queen Mary – it'll be the death of her.'

An hour or so later, another M-O investigator was in Hammersmith, where he asked people how they felt about the news:

> Pretty rough. If anybody's patriotic they're bound to feel something. I think most people feel something about it. *(M 40. Engineer)*
>
> I'm sorry for the King and I love him very much. *(M 20. Apprentice to watch repairer)*
>
> *(Didn't know.)* I think I feel shocked. Sort of bewilders me I guess. The King died? Oh gee. *(F 20. Typist)*
>
> *(Didn't know.)* Oh I think it's dreadful – I'm terribly sorry. How sudden. I feel most terribly sorry. I feel as shocked as if it was someone belonging to me. *(F 40. Dept Store Buyer)*
>
> Bit of rough that's all. Can't say very much about it at all. Sorry to hear he's gone that's all. *(M 40. Pipe Fitter)*
>
> Well not at all pleased – it's a funny question. *(M 40+. Fitter)*
>
> Very sad and can't help being very sad. Very sad indeed. *(F 40+. Housewife)*

Among the diarists, Nella Last in Barrow heard the news from a neighbour and 'wasn't very surprised', with her 'pity and concern' going 'in a rush of sympathy to Princess Elizabeth, whose youth dies at 26'; Judy Haines in Chingford was also told by a neighbour, with the two of them settling down for 'a cup of tea' and 'a pleasant chat'; 'hope he didn't take a wrong pill', was the rather sardonic reflection of Marian Raynham in Surbiton, adding that 'it will be picturesque to have such a young Queen & Consort, a real Queen'; and Henry St John, working in the Ministry of Food in central London, mainly concentrated in his entry on how the cold in his head had 'reached a stage of sore throat' and 'more nasal discharge', though noting that 'I never saw King George VI.' As for the left-leaning political class, Richard Crossman, a prominent Labour backbencher who also wrote prolifically for the *New Statesman* and *Sunday Pictorial*, noted how 'no one I have met [in the Commons that afternoon] genuinely feels anything about this, except Clem Attlee'.[16]

For many people, the most striking aspect of the day was the absence of normal radio programmes, apart from weather forecasts and news bulletins. There was close-down for most of the afternoon and then again after the six o'clock news (listened to by 54 per cent of the adult population), apart from four further bulletins, one of which was followed by a short memorial service listened to by 46 per cent. 'The evening seemed so strange without the wireless,' reflected Last. 'We joined in silently to the really lovely little service after the nine o'clock news.' For Frank Lewis in Manchester, it was a mixed evening. 'DATE WITH WINN,' he noted. 'SHE DIDN'T TURN UP, probably due to the "King" business.' So instead, with all cinemas and theatres closed for the day (though not pubs), he went to the Chinese restaurant in Mosley Street: 'I found I couldn't eat it all – I'd been eating too many sweets earlier on. 4/5d it came to, I left 6d tip; I don't intend leaving more. I like those meals though, I must go more often to these places.' But for John McGarry in Bournemouth, the death of a monarch was not something to be shrugged off so easily: 'Dull afternoon, get home at 3.15 do homework . . . Mum's do is off she's heard. Says she's going to have a party instead. Fancy on such a sad day. Go out at 7.30, meet Dorothy. Go out for stroll on cliffs and have lovely time, stroll back through the chine stopping at every seat. Get back at 9.45 to find every body having a good time. What disgusting manners.' The young, burdened diarist went to bed at 10.30 'feeling very tired and sad'.

The new Queen returned home on Thursday the 7th. 'The most prosperous-looking among the waiting women wore black furs and hats, and the men wore black ties, but the most touching things were the bows of painstakingly tied cheap black ribbon and the homemade crêpe-paper armbands pinned on many shabby coats,' observed Mollie Panter-Downes (in her regular London letter in the *New Yorker*) about the silent crowd in the Mall watching Elizabeth drive by. Elsewhere the sartorial code seems to have been reasonably relaxed – 'surprised to see so few black ties being worn,' noted Anthony Heap in St Pancras, adding that 'when George V died [in 1936], practically every man in London donned one immediately' – and cinemas and theatres reopened. That evening (the same evening that detectives called on Alan Turing), Churchill paid an eloquent radio tribute to the late King. 'It was the best piece of prose I have heard or read from him,' reflected an appreciative Macmillan. The next day Kenneth Preston, an English teacher in Keighley, recorded how 'many people have spoken of the fine funeral oration that Churchill pronounced on the wireless last night.'[17]

By this time the radio was also proving a source of considerable discontent. 'The BBC proposes to continue scrapping its normal advertised programmes and substituting dreary "modified" ones – mostly made up of what one of my office colleagues expressively describes as "gut-aching" music,' complained Heap on the 8th, with a week still left until the State Funeral and a return to radio normality. 'I can see no justification whatever for this.' Marian Raynham agreed: 'Mrs Dale's Diary on radio again, but am missing my funny men.' Still, these were bumper days for the popular press, with Crossman noting the following week how the *Daily Mirror* had 'put on half a million' and the *Star* (a London evening paper) 'more than doubled its circulation', while the *Sunday Pictorial* (effectively the Sunday version of the *Daily Mirror*) 'put on 150,000 circulation, although this was the fourth day after the King's death and there was no news'. His unimpeachable conclusion was that royalty was 'the one inexhaustible subject'.

Crossman was present on Monday the 11th when the lying-in-state began at an 'extremely cold, dark and dank' Westminster Hall. 'There was a bang,' he recorded, 'the doors opened and the coffin was carried in by eight Grenadiers and heaved on to the catafalque, with only the crown on top. After the coffin came the most extraordinary sight, the Queens and Princesses, looking more like eight [in fact seven] Muslim women, clothed in dead black, swathed and double-swathed with veils so thick that they couldn't read the order of service through them.' Next morning the *Daily Express* carried an instantly famous (or infamous) photograph of the grieving 'three Queens', ie Mary and the two Elizabeths – a decision in 'execrable taste' according to Nella Last, who found that 'everyone else I met when out shopping had the same "disgust" ' at 'such "*shocking* bad taste" '.

Over the next few chilly nights and days, some 300,000 mourners passed solemnly through Westminster Hall to pay their last respects. 'Never safer, better guarded lay a sleeping King than this, with a golden light to warm his resting place and the muffled tread of his devoted people to keep him company,' ran Richard Dimbleby's suitably hushed radio commentary on the Tuesday evening. 'They come from a mile away in the night, moving pace by pace in hours of waiting, come into the silent majesty of the scene and as silently leave again.' Among those next day inspecting the tomb of 'George the Faithful' (in Dimbleby's characteristic coinage) was the novelist Barbara Pym, struck by 'the still figures guarding the catafalque – the nose and chin of a very young officer of the Household cavalry – so pink and smooth – eyes hidden'. Virginia Potter, an American living in England, was there on the final evening. 'It was,' she reported to her mother, 'a very awe-inspiring sight – hundreds of people slowly filing through that enormous and dimly-lit hall, and *no sound* except a quiet shuffling of feet.' Afterwards, 'we walked out into the street where the thousands of people were standing, completely silent, in the cold night air'. Yet for millions of others that week, the frustration mounted. 'My husband was so "fidgety" – couldn't settle to read, wouldn't have a game of card patience,' noted the long-suffering Last on Tuesday evening. 'He counted up the days till he could expect the wireless programmes he likes. They are certainly dreary. Without being "gay", I'm sure a "lighter" style of broadcast would not have been "disrespectful" to a man who loved "Itma".' She added that 'a few plays could have easily been included' in the schedule, whereas 'they left in the mawkish "Mrs Dale's Diary", a real sick maker if there was one!'[18]

On Friday morning the coffin was put on a gun carriage and marched in slow time to Paddington Station by men of the Household Cavalry. All along the route there were crowds who, in Panter-Downes's words, 'had slept through the icy night beside their thermos flasks'. The 'Bloomsbury' diarist Frances Partridge was in north London that morning, but hoping to get across town to have lunch with her son in Kensington. 'My bus decanted me at Selfridges,' she wrote, 'and all at once – like a bucket emptying its contents on me – I saw a horde of human beings advancing towards me. The procession must just have passed as their faces distinctly showed traces of a cathartic experience, like blackboards after a teacher had wiped them.' From Paddington two trains took the world's leaders and royal families as well as the coffin to Windsor, where the service and burial were in St George's Chapel. 'Had hours of King George VI's funeral on television,' noted Judy Haines in Chingford. 'Pamela suddenly said, "Mummy, I *am* having an unhappy time" . . . I wondered aloud who would be looking after all the V.I.P.s over here for the funeral, and Abbé [her husband] said they'd be hurrying home to do their "pools". I did laugh.'

But if private irreverence about foreign dignitaries was one thing, public irreverence about the only royal family that properly counted was quite another. 'In Fleet Street two young men who refused to keep the 2 minute silence, & clumped down the street, were nearly lynched,' noted Florence Speed next day, '& had to take refuge in a block of offices, & then have police protection, the crowd was so furious. One woman hit one of them with an umbrella . . .' Similarly, Panter-Downes recorded in her next letter the widely expressed view that 'the week's events had proved beyond doubt the impossibility of Britain's ever entering into any European federation, since Britons are already federated into a family that has loyalties and traditions bred in its bones and planted in its blood stream'; for her own part, she added that 'this has certainly been brought home with new and moving force'. Even so, looking back in the same letter on the ten days of mourning since the fateful news, she did observe that 'there are few English who do not say frankly that the time has dragged like a year and who are not relieved that it is over'.

Soon afterwards, a BBC survey found that 59 per cent of people had disapproved of the way programmes had been altered during this period, with only 29 per cent approving. Younger people disapproved much more than older people and men more than women, while in terms of class, the further down the social ladder, the greater the weight of disapproval. The findings were arguably a sign of an age of deference, if it had ever existed, starting to fray at the edges – though the accompanying BBC report emphasised that those who disapproved did so 'not on the grounds of abstract principles but because they were deprived of the programmes they liked and offered a service which in general they considered to be "highbrow", with the result that they felt left out in the cold'. The sense of relief at one house in Surbiton was probably typical. 'Radio goes back to normal, Korea, Suez, etc & no King business,' noted Marian Raynham the day after the funeral: 'Some think B.B.C. overdid the mourning. We certainly had a lot of lovely, if solemn music. Daddy [i.e. her husband] simply hated all the Royalty part. He got so tired of it & gave up listening to the news. I enjoy it all, though sorry the King had to go, though these young normal ones seem more cheerful.'[19]

4

Hardly Practicable

Kenneth Barrett ran the John Hilton Bureau, in effect a citizen's advice bureau subsidised by the *News of the World*, which each week printed a selection of the problems sent to the Bureau and its responses; Dr W. Hartston was Senior Medical Officer of the London County Council. The two men started to correspond in February 1951, and before long Hartston was looking forward to meeting Barrett and 'discussing the health aspect of public alarm, public ignorance, public anxiety and public opinion that are our mutual interest'. In late June the meeting of the well-meaning paternalists duly took place in Cambridge (where the Bureau was based). Soon they were in action together, seeking to inch the New Jerusalem just a little closer to reality:

> *3 August, Barrett to Hartston.* By the way, would you like to do something for me? I am enclosing herewith a file which tells its own story. I think I mentioned the case to you when we were together. Somebody ought to kick somebody else's bottom in the L.C.C. Housing Department. If you read through the file from the beginning, it's just possible you may feel like exercising your own muscles.
>
> *11 August, Hartston to Barrett.* I propose to investigate as far as I dare (you will appreciate the difficulty of poking my nose into a Housing Department matter, but difficulty does not mean no poking!) why this long delay and what can be done for Sage both medically and architecturally.
>
> *28 August, Barrett to Hartston.* These housing tragedies sometimes send me home nearly in tears, because there's so little one can do and I realise that Local Authorities are by and large doing their best. What I cannot stand is the holier-than-thou complacency of the London County

Council and some other Authorities. What I cannot stand also is their bloody laziness. Obviously no real investigation has ever been made.

30 October, Hartston to Barrett. Now concerning the matter of our pore [*sic*] friend Sage. I failed to impress the Professor of Medicine at the London Hospital but *have* succeeded in getting Dr Richardson, one of the kinder consultants at St Thomas's Hospital, to see Sage & advise (& arrange) any treatment that might help him. At the least it will show Sagey that he's not altogether abandoned. I've spoken to Sage's family doctor who, while not terribly enthusiastic, acquiesces. So honour, peace and warmth flow all around – I hope.[1]

For Barrett, Hartston and Sage alike, there was by now a Tory government in office, barely six years after the momentous Labour landslide of 1945. How committed would it be to upholding the broadly socialist – certainly collectivist – settlement that the Attlee government had put in place? Would it seek a return, no doubt with a twist of paternalism-cum-modernity, to the verities of social individualism and economic liberalism? One particularly intelligent observer did not see turning back the clock as a realistic option. Britain, argued Albert Camus on the Third Programme shortly after the election, was doing better than Continental countries at social justice, and as a consequence this meant it was winning the Cold War, even if at the price of austerity. Camus went on confidently: 'The Conservative Government, if it wishes both to maintain peace and discourage aggression, will have to leave intact the main social reforms of which Britain is enjoying the benefit.'

He was proved right, in the sense that, broadly speaking, the settlement held in the months and years after October 1951. There was no meaningful attempt to reform, let alone dismantle, the NHS or the welfare state more generally; the only industries to be denationalised were steel and road haulage; the goal of full employment remained sacrosanct; rent controls stayed in place, at least for the time being; and the position and privileges of the trade unions were positively enhanced. Even so, all the evidence is that what was involved was a lukewarm acceptance of the settlement motivated by essentially pragmatic considerations, in the context of an uncomfortably narrow parliamentary majority.

'I have no doubt about the wisdom of making severe cuts in Government expenditure,' one of the Tory elders, Lord Woolton, wrote to Churchill not long after the election. But he went on: 'We shall find ourselves in politically difficult waters if we begin by making serious cuts in the social services ... and leave ourselves open to the charge that what we have saved by this means we have later spent in the reduction of taxation.' Or, as Conservative Central Office revealingly informed party workers in January 1952, 'there is every sign that after six years of the Welfare State elaborate education is necessary to introduce each unpopular measure'. Significantly, as opinion polls consistently showed, the welfare state was almost as popular with the middle as with the working class. As for the lack of extensive denationalisation, which would have carried much less political risk given the public's relative indifference to the subject, the key constraint seems to have been economic, with the new Chancellor, Rab Butler, telling Churchill that a mixture of balance-of-payments problems and insufficient liquidity in the economy made such a policy impracticable. There was also perhaps an element of loss of nerve. 'Houses and meat and not being scuppered,' Churchill famously if privately summed up his less than heroic aims after his first five months back in harness. The electoral catastrophe at the end of the war had cut deep, and the parliamentary party – including its many stolid, gentlemanly, landowning backbenchers, as well as its near-octogenarian leader – had little appetite for needless hostages to fortune.

The conflict between political and economic constraints on the one hand and non-socialist instincts on the other was embodied in the person of Butler – architect of the 1944 Education Act, creator of a more emollient brand of post-war Conservatism and surprise choice as Chancellor. What is striking about his early record at No. 11 is the extent to which he *did* seek to adopt distinctively Tory policies. The infusion of anti-inflation monetary policy (tainted by association with the inter-war Bank of England under Montagu Norman and thus in cold storage throughout the 1940s) as a counterpoint to the ruling Keynesian orthodoxy, moves towards a significant loosening of controls (including over prices and direct investment), old-fashioned Treasury parsimony towards the departments of health, education and even housing – all were significant pointers that culminated in March 1952 with Butler's first Budget. In it he raised Bank Rate from 2½ to 4 per cent, cut a swingeing £160 million from food subsidies (provoking angry cries of 'class war' in the Commons) and made tax changes in such a way as to appeal specifically to the skilled, better-off worker, clearly seen as politically detachable from the working class as a whole. For the first time since the war, declared an appreciative *Financial Times*, people had been given 'a Budget which genuinely provides incentives'. An aged Tory diarist was even more enthusiastic. 'There is a new festival spirit about,' exulted 'Chips' Channon. 'A young Queen; an old Prime Minister and a brave buoyant Butler budget. Has he put us in for a generation?'[2]

All bets would have been off if Butler had had his way just a fortnight or so earlier. 'Operation ROBOT' was a top-secret plan that took its memorable name from the three officials – Sir Leslie **RO**wan (Treasury), Sir George **B**olton (Bank of England), '**OT**to' Clarke (Treasury) – most closely associated with its formulation during the winter of 1951–2.[3] In essence, ROBOT involved simultaneously making sterling readily convertible into other currencies and floating the pound so that it found its own level. The plan was in part a panic reaction to a widening balance-of-payments deficit and rapidly shrinking reserves; in part an attempt to restore the City of London as a leading international financial centre, with sterling as its authentic international currency; and in part a deliberate strategy to trigger a supply-side revolution through unleashing the market forces of convertibility and floating – shock treatment that would make the economy more competitive. The immediate domestic implications were undeniably deflationary, and from the first there were doubters at both the Bank and the Treasury. 'The move would be violently controversial and contrary to the trend of economic thought since Keynes,' warned one of Clarke's colleagues, E. R. Copleston. 'There would be severe industrial unrest, and it would be political suicide for the Government – the discipline of the gold standard, the rule of the Bankers etc . . .'

Briefly it seemed that ROBOT had political legs. 'C of E sold, PM interested and great hopes favourable decision,' Bolton buoyantly noted on 20 February. Two days later, Churchill received a Bank deputation, headed by 'Kim' Cobbold, the Governor, formally advocating the plan. They were, he reported afterwards, 'a fine, patriotic body of men, anxious to do what was right for the country'. But by the end of the month, following two lengthy Cabinet discussions, opposition to the plan had both spread and hardened. Butler, although seemingly a believer, made a weak, unconvincing case; Sir Anthony Eden, the Foreign Secretary, was convinced that its implementation would jeopardise the recently established European Payments Union; and Churchill himself, though instinctively in favour of liberating the pound, was not only alarmed by Eden's hostility but swayed by two of his closest advisers, Lord Cherwell and Sir Arthur Salter – who seldom agreed on anything, but who were, this time, in unison, as Churchill observed. At one of the discussions, there was a particularly telling contribution by the Lord Privy Seal. 'Under democratic government with universal suffrage such violent reversals of policy were hardly practicable,' insisted the Tory grandee Lord ('Bobbety') Salisbury. 'Even if the case for this change were abundantly clear on the merits, there would be very great difficulty in persuading the public to accept it. Moreover, the adoption of this policy would create an unbridgeable gap between the Government and the Opposition . . .' Eden, walking away from that meeting with Macmillan, agreed. 'The country are not ready,' he told his colleague, 'to cast away the whole effort of years and return to "Montagu Normanism" without a struggle.' Put another way, the shadow of the inter-war slump was still as psychically oppressive in 1952 as it had been seven years earlier.

Did the burial of ROBOT matter? Almost certainly, yes. 'At the very least,' Nigel Lawson has claimed from the Thatcherite side of the fence, 'it is hard to believe that the conduct of British economic policy, and our national economic performance, would have been as lamentable as they were during the 1960s and 70s had the liberating economic logic of ROBOT been allowed to prevail' – that in fact the decision represented 'the fork in the road'. But if for Lawson the tantalising might-have-been was 'the progressive post-war adoption of the market economy rather than the stultifying interventionist consensus which was to reach its nemesis in the late 1970s', there was also a might-have-been on the other side of the fence – the '1945', post-war-settlement side. Specifically, one can argue that although the failure of ROBOT undeniably reflected the political impossibility of attempting to turn the clock back to a pre-Keynesian paradise, at the same time the lack of significant opposition to the *goal* of achieving full sterling convertibility – a goal to which the government was fully signed up by the end of summer 1952 – revealed, through its concomitant underpinning of sterling as a reserve currency, the limits of Keynesianism. The rejection of ROBOT may have suggested that domestic priorities had a higher status than international ones, but the convertibility target distinctly implied otherwise. 'Our economic survival in the next year or two will largely depend upon world confidence in sterling,' Macmillan privately reflected. But even that instinctively Keynesian prestidigitator must have wondered whether the competing priorities were truly compatible.[4]

The post-war settlement was also under apparent threat on another front. *The Social Services: Needs and Means* was the title of a January 1952 pamphlet by two rising youngish Tory politicians, Iain Macleod and Enoch Powell. The general tone was sober and far from hostile to the welfare state, but one early passage attracted considerable attention. 'The general presumption,' the authors insisted about the social services, 'must be that they will be rendered only on evidence of need, i.e. of financial inability to provide each particular service out of one's own or one's family's resources.' And: 'The question therefore which poses itself is not, "should a means test be applied to a social service?" but "why should any social service be provided *without* test of need?"' Whatever the financial pressures on funding the services, such a concept of selectivity was of course wholly antithetical to those committed to the principle of universalism – a principle owing much to the deeply resonant stigma attached to means testing between the wars.

Few were more committed to universalism than Richard Titmuss, who on the Third Programme the following month repudiated as 'too simple a view' the Macleod/Powell line that the social services existed only for a portion of the population, with the other portion putting in more than they took out. Rather:

> Redistribution now takes place at some time or other over the life span of nearly everyone. Children put nothing in and take out in the form of education, subsidised milk, family allowances, income-tax rebates (if their parents are better off), medical care by doctors largely trained at the community's expense, and so forth. As adults, people are constantly moving in and out of the territory of socially provided or subsidised

services according to varying need and circumstances. In old age, as in childhood, most people take out more than they put in . . .

Without universalism, Titmuss stirringly concluded, 'the social services would lose their citizenship quality which we found imperative in time of war'. Powell, who had written most of the pamphlet, took to the microphone in April:

> The contention, in fact, is that participating in the benefits of the social services has come in the twentieth century to be a mark of membership of the community. Here we see the significance of the term 'the social service state', the conception that the very nature of the state is determined by the social services which it assures to its members.
>
> This is, in the fullest and, if I may risk a paradox, the non-party, sense of the word, the *socialist* conception.

The logical fulfilment of such a conception would lead, declared Powell, to 'the equalisation and elimination of private property'. The underlying question for the future was 'whether we shall have "the social services" or "the social service state" '.

It is easy in retrospect to underestimate Titmuss, the intellectual most closely associated with the post-war welfare state (the term itself in common usage by the early 1950s). For example, half a century before Vernon Bogdanor made the entirely persuasive retrospective point that 'the success of the welfare state depended on a belief in the beneficence of those in power', Titmuss (in his May 1951 inaugural lecture at the LSE, marking his appointment to London University's new chair in Social Administration) warned emphatically about the dangers of professional interests within the social services – interests 'resistant to social change, and sometimes resistant, therefore, to needed changes in the social services'. Or, as he strikingly put it right at the end of the lecture, 'We shall not achieve a better balance between the needs of today and the resources of today by living out the destinies of tradition; by simply attending to the business of the State.'

Take indeed his address almost exactly a year later at the Jubilee Conference of the Institute of Hospital Administrators. There, to the probable discomfort of his audience, Titmuss's approach was tough-minded, critical and, above all, looking at things from the patient's point of view. Recent improvements (better food for patients and arrangements for parents to see their sick children) had come about not through 'any ferment of self-examination in the hospitals themselves or from the professional ranks of nurses and doctors', but instead through 'pressures from without the hospital'; the increasing complexity of hospital administration was liable to lead to 'excessive preoccupation with means' and accordingly 'the danger that the hospital may tend increasingly to be run in the interests of those working in and for the hospital rather than in the interests of the patients'; 'advances in scientific medicine', and ensuing division of labour, were making it 'harder to treat the patient as a person'; and complaints like 'No one told me anything,' 'Nobody asked me' and 'I don't know' exemplified the recurring theme of 'the discourtesies of silence'. Almost his most damning observation was that 'the practice of talking between doctors and nurses over their patients still goes on although it is now known that hearing is the last conscious function to disappear with anaesthesia'. Although cheering up his audience by applauding their motives – such things were 'done unthinkingly by people who are devoted to their calling, working unselfishly and for long hours in the interests of the sick' – Titmuss's was altogether a coruscating analysis. A Liberal in his youth, he would never lose his deep attachment to the values of individual freedom and individual dignity, even as he inexorably moved into a more collectivist intellectual orbit.[5] It would have been a happier story for Labour, and collectivism generally, if during the third quarter of the century it had been truer to liberal values and less trusting of the state and its appointed experts.

The debate about the post-war settlement briefly threatened to explode on 27 March 1952. That evening, as the Commons debated the relatively modest health charges now being added to those so controversially introduced by Hugh Gaitskell almost a year earlier, Gaitskell's old foe, Aneurin Bevan, was in particularly vigorous form. Calling the NHS, still closely identified as his creation, 'a very great experiment, one of the greatest experiments in human behaviour that the world has ever seen', he condemned the Tories for their 'mean-spirited attitude towards the social services' and claimed that 'the arms programme of Great Britain is now being made by the Conservative Government into an excuse to dismantle the Welfare State'. As it happened, the next speaker was Powell's co-author, Macleod, who at once caught the chamber's (including Churchill's) attention by calling Bevan's speech 'vulgar, crude and intemperate'; he followed up with a highly personal, somewhat unfair, but nevertheless very effective attack on Bevan's tortuous relationship with the whole question of prescription charges when he had been Minister of Health.

Yet although a great parliamentary performance, and one that was almost instantly mythologised, Macleod's speech did not itself seek to stake out any new intellectual ground. There was, in the economist John Vaizey's subsequent regretful words, 'no critique of the basic concepts of Health Service finances, free treatment at point of service, a state monopoly of medical supplies, state employment of almost all doctors and nurses, and owning all the hospitals'. Not that anyone else was staking out such ground; for, as Vaizey added, surely correctly, the already 'striking contrast' with the health systems in America and Continental Europe was 'not commented upon because nobody thought to do so', and 'nobody thought to do so, because in essence the National Health Service was a bipartisan invention, agreed upon and accepted by both parties' – an invention that, whatever the rumbling disquiet over its costs, was 'obviously immensely popular'. Less than six weeks after his joust with Bevan, Macleod was appointed Minister of Health. 'He is shrewd, has a rapier-like brain, is ambitious and clear-minded,' 'Chips' Channon had recently noted about the GP's son from Yorkshire; this seasoned observer reckoned that the 38-year-old would 'go far', even though 'he is bald and limps, and is unattractive, except for his old man's smile'.[6]

––––––––

Bevan himself by the spring of 1952 was more in the public eye than at any time since his high-profile resignation from the Attlee government a year earlier – a year during which there had emerged in the Parliamentary Labour Party a recognisable group of some three dozen 'Bevanites'. The 26-year-old Anthony Wedgwood Benn was not among them – 'particularly obnoxious do I find the complacent assumptions by the Bevanites that the ark of the socialist covenant resides with them', he reflected in November 1951 – but they did include Barbara Castle and Harold Wilson as well as Richard Crossman. 'The fact is,' Crossman justifiably observed in

December, 'that Bevanism and the Bevanites seem much more important, well-organised and machiavellian to the rest of the Labour Party, and indeed to the U.S.A., than they do to us who are in the Group and who know that we are not organized, that Aneurin can never be persuaded to have any consistent or coherent strategy and that we have not even got to the beginning of a coherent, constructive policy.' Even so, he rightly claimed that 'what we have, and it is very important, is a group of M.P.s who meet regularly, who know and like each other and who have come to represent "real Socialism" to a large number of constituency members'. He added that this had produced 'an extraordinary bitterness among those who support the Gaitskell line', having 'convinced themselves that we are demagogues who are deliberately exploiting the simple-mindedness of the rank and file for our own ends'.

By March the bitterness had if anything increased, as Bevan and 56 other Labour MPs refused to support the Attlee leadership's broad endorsement of the government's armaments programme, in the continuing context of the Korean War. The by now far from left-wing *Picture Post* soon afterwards dubbed them 'the Bevanly Host' and sought to assess the implications: 'Among Labour supporters in the country, Bevan and his brigade are popular. They're lively, personable, forceful. And many are B.B.C. stars [including Michael Foot on television] – in short, they are a draw. But the Party and the trade unions set more store by loyalty than by brilliance and invective.' Or as Labour's newest MP, Denis Healey, had already pointed out, 'whereas Bevan's proletarian virility has always hypnotised many middle-class intellectuals, the trade unionists tend to see in him the familiar figure of the self-seeking agitator'.[7]

Yet whatever one thought of him, there was no doubting the hold that Bevan exercised over many people's imagination during the 1950s. They included Sue Townsend, growing up in Leicester:

I was wearing my school uniform, eating Golden Syrup sandwiches and reading a book. The lumbering black and white television in the corner was turned on, but I paid it no attention. Then on to the screen came the image of Mr Bevan who was making a speech in a large hall. I was immediately mesmerised – first by his lovely voice, then by his looks. I put my book down and watched as he spoke. His body dipped and swooped as he started to make a point and then jerked upright to ram the point home. His voice wheedled seductively, dropped until it was only a whisper and whooshed back up the register, ending in a shouted joke. Because there was much audience laughter I thought at first that he was a comedian and I half expected him to break into a song and dance routine as comedians did in those days.

There ensued 'a pre-pubertal crush' – and 'when I found out that he was married to Jennie Lee I was tormented with jealousy'. But if Bevan's oratory was legendary, it came perhaps at the expense of other qualities. Shirley Williams has identified 'a certain waywardness and caprice, an unwillingness to harness his energy, eloquence and charm to the single-minded pursuit of political power', and she is surely right. Or, in the equally acute retrospective testimony of one of his main lieutenants, Crossman:

> Nye was flawed, because at that critical moment he just wasn't there. Bevan would have a bad cold on a critical problem. He hated fighting, quite honestly, he hated it. He kept saying 'Why should I submit myself to this kind of ignominy of fighting people like Gaitskell? Gaitskell will fight; I don't want to fight. I would like to lead this party; I don't want to fight it in this ignominious way.' He hated the in-fighting which you have to do in politics. He wanted victory given to him on a plate . . . Nye was constantly giving up, constantly depressed, lying down in his tent like Achilles. He was that kind of a moody creature; he was brilliant and deeply moody . . . Nye wasn't cut out to be a leader, he was cut out to be a prophet.

Was Bevan, though, really cut out to be a prophet? One youngish, notably intelligent Labour MP, Wilfred Fienburgh, apparently thought so, declaring in the *New Statesman* in April 1952 that 'he has the capacity to be both the philosopher and the architect of the social revolution in the second half of the twentieth century'. Fienburgh was writing just days after the publication of Bevan's *In Place of Fear*, his only book-length testament of political beliefs. The reviews, according to Mollie Panter-Downes, 'mostly ranged from irritable to hopping mad'; half a century on, it is difficult to disagree with the *TLS*'s verdict that the book was 'a dithyramb with meanderings into the many side-tracks of Mr Bevan's private and public experience' and that 'except in mood, its many compelling passages do not cohere'. Crucially, just at the point when Labour in opposition was considering its future direction, Bevan's treatise failed to provide an authoritative statement of Bevanite doctrine for the rest of the 1950s and beyond. Whether in the case of the assumed superiority of public over private ownership, or in that of central planning over Keynesian demand management, there was little in the way of detailed, hard-headed analysis and prescription. In theory looking ahead, in practice much of *In Place of Fear* was addressing the problems of the 1930s, a deficiency at least in part explained by the fact that sizeable chunks had been drafted long before 1952. One particularly striking pre-1945 passage – attacking suburbia as 'an aesthetic monstrosity, an ethical crime, an economic nightmare, and a physical treadmill' – was in the event dropped from the book. In similar vein, however, he moralised about the difference between good and bad consumption, declaring that 'the attempt of Democratic Socialism to universalize the consumption of the best that society can afford meets with resistance from those whose sense of values is deformed by the daily parade of functionless wealth'. Bevan himself was far from an ascetic puritan in his private life, yet it is somehow typical that the final page includes the disapproving anecdote of visiting war-ravaged Italy in 1948 and seeing imported steel being used on the non-essential, profligate task of building cinemas.[8] Perhaps one of them was Cinema Paradiso.

Only a few weeks later, there appeared another work of Labour political thought – this time the Crossman-edited *New Fabian Essays*, a collection of variable quality by mainly youngish MPs (including Healey and Roy Jenkins), with perhaps the highlight being Anthony Crosland's lucid, crisply written 'The Transition from Capitalism'. At the heart of Crosland's analysis was the claim that 'by 1951 Britain had, in all the essentials, ceased to be a capitalist country', that indeed it had become after six years of Labour government a post-capitalist society. Realistically, he accepted that the character of this new society was 'a mixed one so far as the traditional categories are concerned':

It is capitalist to the extent that private ownership of industry predominates, that most production is for the market, and that many of the old class divisions persist. It is non-capitalist to the extent that market influences are subordinated to central planning, not over the whole detailed field of labour and production, but in certain strategically decisive sectors; that the power of the state is much greater than that of any one particular class; and that the distribution of the national income is consciously a matter of political decision and not the automatic consequence of market forces. It is managerial to the extent that the control of industry has largely passed (subject to state controls) into the hands of the managerial class, which has usurped the position of the old capitalist class. It is socialist in that the distribution of income is far more egalitarian, that much economic power and parts of industry are socialised, that a national minimum and a welfare cushion exist, and that planning is largely directed to traditional socialist ends.

Welcoming 'the higher employment, generous social services, less flagrant inequalities of wealth and opportunity', Crosland saw the shift from capitalism to post-capitalism as an unequivocal good, claiming that 'the new society is infinitely more humane and decent than the old'.

The final section of his essay was devoted to the question of how to get from this new society (which he rather awkwardly called 'Statism') to socialism. He began by defining 'socialism' as the pursuit of greater equality – not just greater economic equality and greater equality of opportunity (though in both cases he applauded how these two types of equality had increased since 1945) but also greater *social* equality. 'Class feeling, and general social *malaise*, still persist in England to a deplorable extent,' he declared. 'Britain still is, and feels itself to be, a class society.' He then identified various possible ways of trying to achieve a classless society – the expansion of free social services, more extensive nationalisation of industries, more widespread controls, more redistributive taxation of income – but ruled each out. Instead, he identified three other areas as potentially far more fertile: first, fiscally attacking the skewed ownership of wealth (with Crosland pointing out that 'the still gross maldistribution of property enables the upper classes, by spending out of capital, to live at a standard of luxury which their post-tax income would never alone permit'); second, reforming the structure of the educational system, so that there was no longer 'a social hierarchy of schools'; and third, seeking to transform 'the psychology of industrial relations, and the general tone and atmosphere in industry', so that the worker was given 'a new social status' and no longer felt 'the basic class hostility which stems from his total exclusion from either rights or participation'.

But was the creation of a classless society a realistic aspiration? 'No one should think that this will be a short or an easy task,' began the only moderately uplifting peroration:

> The pace will be limited, not only by the need to preserve the necessary minimum of social peace and cohesion, but also by the difficulty of engendering enthusiasm for further change in a population largely employed and enjoying rising standards every year. There will be no revival of the angry dynamic of revolt against the obvious miseries and injustices of capitalism. The temper of the people will be more contented and therefore more conservative, and public opinion will take time to acclimatise itself to the prospect of each further radical advance.

Accordingly, 'these difficulties make it the more urgent that we should have a clear vision of where we want, as socialists, to go'.

Crosland's essay marked the authentic start of the revisionist project – in essence, an attempt to wean the Labour Party away from fundamentalist allegiance to the cause of public ownership and instead, against a background of successful demand management ('Keynesian techniques are now well understood,' he noted), shift the emphasis at least as much to social as to economic issues. Yet in terms of the project's chances of success, it did not help that Crosland himself, for all his undeniable power of intellect and personal charisma, possessed serious flaws. An incorrigibly arrogant streak not only put off potential allies but was also reflected in a thoroughly top-down approach to policy-making; a disordered personal life was complemented in the early to mid-1950s by a deep unwillingness to play the tedious, time-consuming parliamentary game; and his repeated, immoderate denunciations of what he saw as inexcusably outdated social mores appealed as little to respectable trade unionists (the backbone of the Labour Party) as they did to most middle-class floating voters. 'It's quite obvious that the general result of the unwritten laws is to make people a great deal more miserable than they would otherwise be,' he told an *Any Questions?* audience in Bristol (on the evening, as it happened, that Attlee surrendered power to Churchill). 'We are a nation of very unsmiling and depressed people and we ought to be far more gay and far more cheerful, and far more hilarious, than we are. We're not nearly hilarious enough as a nation, and the reason why we're not hilarious enough is because of these miserable unwritten laws, and so I'm wholly against them.' All of which was said in an 'attractive, drawling, affected donnish tone of voice', as an admiring if ultimately critical friend would describe it.[9]

In December 1951 the veteran Labour politician Hugh Dalton might well have wished it was his handsome protégé Crosland who was helping him make a party political broadcast. Instead, his two colleagues were Tony Benn ('very useful, moves through life like a cat, attractive, has reserves and sense of humour, but not quite to be trusted') and Michael Young ('better at this than at policy making'). Young, principal author of Labour's historic 1945 manifesto, was still working in the party's research department, though not for much longer. There exists the first draft of an undated essay by him, 'Is This The Classless Society?', probably written during the second half of 1951 and almost certainly rejected for *New Fabian Essays*. A fascinating piece, it anticipates not only Young's own *The Rise of the Meritocracy* of seven years later but also the concern felt by Crosland (with whom he was friendly) about the inadequacy of equality of opportunity as a goal.

'If we base our hopes on equal opportunity alone we may find our destination is not Utopia but America,' Young roundly declared at the outset, before detailing some of the ways in which there had emerged greater equality of opportunity over the past decade. These included a better standard of education for working-class children, the rise in real wages, full employment, the rise of service industries, mass production (bringing an increasing range of goods, such as standardised clothes, within everybody's reach) and greater geographical mobility. Significantly, these were all examples of levelling up rather than down; he gave the example of public schools, noting that 'if the last decade is any guide, these schools will take a very long time to die'. In an obvious sense, of course, Young welcomed enhanced equality of opportunity – but not if it came at the expense of enhanced equality of status, nor if its American-style pursuit was psychologically destabilising. 'In a genuinely classless society, people would not be foes but brothers,' he insisted.

'But by stressing competition as the partner of equal opportunity, men are being turned into foes of each other. The stress is on success. The effort is to excel. The aim is to do better than your fellows. The result is a strain on ordinary people which ordinary people are not built to bear.' Near the end came the direct political message: 'We want neither rule of the elite or dictatorship of the proletariat, but rule by all of the people.' And Young called on Labour to develop 'a practical programme for diffusing power on the grand scale' – a programme which, 'particularly by enabling housewives to share power, would sweep the polls'.

Young himself by the end of 1951 had almost certainly come to the conclusion that both he and Labour would find fulfilment through a greater, more subtle understanding of how British society worked and how it was changing. In short, sociology called. It would not, though, be sociology as conventionally practised. In a specially striking passage in his essay, as part of his analysis of the plight of the losers in an increasingly competitive society, he turned to what he saw as the emotionally unnourishing position of the nuclear, non-extended family:

> The couple with the young children – are they so well off? They have established themselves in a city suburb, living neatly and comfortably in their little house, going to the pictures when they can find a watcher for their one or two children. But they seldom have any sense of belonging, and would as soon move on as stay. One suburb is much like another in an atomised society. Rarely does community flourish. How can it when people do not live long enough in one place to know more about their neighbours than their names and jobs and the colour of their irises?[10]

The instincts of the two main parties remained, whatever the internal debates, fundamentally different in the early 1950s. 'There is an intense distaste for the type of fiscal policy which the Welfare State demands,' declared Crosland in his Fabian essay of his Tory opponents – an understandable distaste on the part of the better off, given that by the end of the Labour government marginal tax rates were at times reaching 98 per cent, death duties 80 per cent, and there was also in existence a new differential profits tax at a high rate. The desire to regain some fiscal ground was particularly strong on the part of the Tory rank and file, as shown by the overwhelming majority at the party conference in 1952 for the motion that 'public expenditure has increased, is increasing and ought to be diminished'. As for Labour, the overriding instinct – on right as well as left of the party – was towards greater social and economic equality. The question of means provoked lively comment, even bitter controversy, but that was the shared aim. Moreover, the distinction between the two parties was just as sharp when it came to the very basic, day-to-day issue of private consumption. The Tories before and after the 1951 election did not disguise their desire to dismantle, as soon as economic dictates allowed, the elaborate wartime apparatus of rationing and ensuing austerity, but Labour took comfort from the belief that its electoral defeat had really been a moral victory (in terms of the popular vote) and that Tory promises aimed at grumbling housewives in the butcher's or baker's queue were already being revealed as, in the April 1952 words of the chairman of the National Conference of Labour Women, 'empty and dishonest'. One party, in short, wanted to 'free the people', according of course to a particular definition of freedom; the other did not, or at least not with any great urgency.

Yet in policy-making practice there was considerable compromise and overlap – as opposed to consensus – between the two parties. Full employment, Keynesianism, a mixed economy (including a significant nationalised sector), a welfare state: such proved the inescapable policy framework of the new Tory administration. The underlying psychological realities behind what was essentially a pragmatic response, by a party in which pragmatism was bred in the bone, were arguably threefold. First, the sheer pervasive, emotional power of folk memories of the 1930s as capitalism's never-to-be-repeated human catastrophe; second, the powerful collectivist legacy of the wartime experience; and third, the deep post-war desire on the part of the middle class, just as much as the working class, for a secure, not overly cut-and-thrust life. 'The pressures making for statism are far too strong to be held back,' accurately predicted Crosland, 'and the Tories are too intuitive a party indefinitely to play Canute.' One young Canadian political scientist, closely observing the British state of play in September 1952, was so convinced about the narrowness of the gap that he quoted with approval the Edwardian statesman Arthur Balfour about how the two great parties of the country were 'so sure of their own moderation that they are not dangerously disturbed by the never-ending din of political conflict'.[11] The Canadian was Robert McKenzie, for whom no swing between parties was too small to be of interest.

This is not to deny some wider resonance to the very fact of the Tory restoration – a restoration whose most obviously symbolic early action was the systematic, undeniably vengeful demolition of the entire Festival of Britain infrastructure on the South Bank, with the unavoidable exception of the Royal Festival Hall. For John Vaizey, recalling his Cambridge days, the restoration was mirrored by a generally less congenial local scene: 'The ex-soldiers went; and there came the little sports cars, the ex-National Service officers in cavalry twill, flapped sports jackets and flat caps, the debs and near-debs, the braying voices.' Nevertheless, the fact was that, at an intelligentsia, 'activator' level anyway, the political colouration of the 1950s remained obstinately 'left' rather than 'right' – irrespective of the change of government, and epitomised by the *New Statesman*'s dominance (in both circulation and, largely, reputation) over the *Spectator*. David Marquand would recall how, as an Oxford undergraduate in the mid-1950s, the conventional wisdom he encountered that 'the Tories were the stupid party' and 'the cleverer you were, the more likely it was that you voted Labour', had almost 'the status of a law'.

What were the implications of that prevailing, unquestioned colouration? In April 1979 – a pregnant moment – the chairman of the Supplementary Benefits Commission, David Donnison, valuably summarised the key assumptions over the previous quarter of a century or so of 'liberal, progressive, social democrats, men and women of the centre-left':

(1) The growth of the economy and the population would continue.

(2) Although inequalities in earnings thought to be required to keep the economy moving would persist, they would be gradually modified by a social wage provided by social services distributed with greater concern for human needs, and by the growing burden of progressive taxes required to finance those services.

(3) Despite fierce conflicts about recurring but essentially marginal issues, the people who constitute the broad middle ground of the electorate – the people with middling skills and incomes: 'middle England'

you might call them – could gradually be induced to give general support to these ideas and the programmes which follow from them.

(4) Therefore government and its social services, accountable to this central consensus, were the natural vehicles of progress. Equalizing policies would be carried forward by the public services, propelled by engines of economic growth which would produce the resources to create a juster society without anyone suffering on the way.

(5) Therefore, too, among the generally trusted instruments of progressive social change were doctors, teachers, town planners, nurses, social workers, and all the professions which man the public services.

(6) 'Social' policies were regarded as dealing with the redistribution of the fruits of economic growth, the management of its human effects, and the compensation of those who suffered from them. Thus social programmes were the concern of 'social' departments of government responsible for health, welfare, social security, housing, education and social control. The economy could be left to the economists and the departments of government concerned with economic management.

Not all these rather comfortable assumptions were fully in place by the early 1950s, but already they were unmistakably in the air. Even so, a 1952 Gallup poll surveying what qualities people thought contributed most to a successful marriage – with agreement on politics (6 per cent) bottom of the list – was perhaps a salutary reminder that activator assumptions were not necessarily everyone's assumptions.[12]

'I've yet to meet a Communist who wasn't interested in money,' the hero of *Biggles Follows On* tells Algy, Ginger and the rest. 'It's not having any that makes him a Communist. He wants some, and the only way he can think of is to get his hands into the pockets of those that have.' This latest W. E. Johns yarn (subtitled *A Story of the Cold War in Europe and Asia*, pitting Britain's most popular aviator against his old wartime foe Von Stalheim, now employed by the Russians) was published in 1952 – by which time the Cold War was, with the Korean War continuing, still at permafrost intensity. 'I had a political argument with my father in which he called me a communist and I called him a warmonger,' Kingsley Amis reported in July to Philip Larkin. 'All quite as usual, you see.'

Earlier that month there was a revealing episode concerning the Red Dean of Canterbury, the notoriously pro-Soviet Hewlett Johnson. Returning from a visit to China, where local Christian leaders had presented him with an appeal protesting against what they claimed to be American bacteriological warfare in North Korea and north-east China, he found himself at the centre of a storm. To *The Times* he was 'irresponsible', to the *Economist* 'malignant'; even the *Manchester Guardian* condemned 'his credulity, his capacity to believe nonsense, his ecclesiastical pomp'. The Chinese Christian protest was, in one historian's words, 'buried beneath a welter of personal abuse that suggested to the public that it was Johnson who was responsible for the germ warfare allegations'. Predictably, he received zero support from his archbishop, the establishment-minded Geoffrey Fisher, and in the ensuing House of Lords debate, Johnson was accused – virtually without demur – of being a traitor, a Communist Party lackey, an 'enemy of Western civilisation', and an agent of Moscow doing 'the greatest mischief he can to the Anglo-American amity'.

Positions were just as entrenched in intellectual life generally, typified by how difficult the innovative new historical journal *Past & Present* – set up by the Historians' Group (including Eric Hobsbawm and Christopher Hill) of the Communist Party of Great Britain and characteristically subtitled 'a journal of scientific history' – found it to get contributions from non-Marxist historians. Later in 1952 the prevailing climate was encapsulated in a hostile review of Jack Lindsay's *Byzantium into Europe*. 'Marxian historiography is fundamentally opposed to the canons of western scholarship,' declared the prestigious *TLS*, calling this a fact that 'raises the question, which will have seriously to be faced, sooner rather than later, by those concerned with academic appointments, whether, in fairness to his pupils, any individual who adheres to the Communist doctrine can be allowed responsibility for the teaching of history'. As for Lindsay himself, he had presented 'a picture of Byzantine civilisation which will be wholly unrecognisable by anyone on this side of the Iron Curtain who is neither a Communist nor a fellow-traveller'. The following week a letter from Christopher Hill deplored the use of a *TLS* review 'to advocate a witch-hunt in the historical profession', but soon afterwards an editorial broadly supported the paper's reviewer. At the same time, in a shameful episode, the long-standing editor of the *New Statesman*, Kingsley Martin, sacked Basil Davidson – who had recently written a series of superb articles on the rise of Black Nationalism in Africa – because the word was out, in fact misleadingly, that he was a fellow-traveller. He soon became, in the words of Martin's generally favourable biographer, 'a skeleton in Kingsley's cupboard'.[13]

Increasingly by this time there was focus on the shop floor – in part reflecting a shift in Communist Party thinking after its electoral disaster in 1951 (100 seats contested, none won, deposits lost 98). *The Communist Technique in Britain* was the title of a 1952 Penguin by Bob Darke, a Hackney-based bus conductor who had recently left the CP after 18 years. It was, Mark Abrams wrote in his review, a powerful, compelling piece of testimony:

> He never rose to the top ranks, and he never had much use for the Party's intellectuals and theoreticians. From beginning to end he was merely a tireless N.C.O. fighting and leading his platoons in the trenches of the class war. He was never without a role in one or more sectors of the working-class movement – branch chairman of the National Unemployed Workers' Movement, official of the Fire Brigades Union, of the Hackney Trades Council, the London Trades Council, Hackney Borough Councillor, convener of Peace Campaign meetings, organiser of Tenants' Committees, patron of youth cycling clubs. At every one of these and a dozen similar tasks, the author worked single-mindedly, not for his constituents, but for the Communist Party. He describes calmly and factually how a handful of Party members, always prepared to use chicanery, barely disguised embezzlement, bullying, lying, forgery, conspiracy, steadily exploited for the advancement of the cause, the poverty, political laziness and altruism of their neighbours and workmates. Almost every trade union branch and most large factories in the borough came under their influence.

Darke's revelations made quite an impact, helped by a four-part series of extracts in *Picture Post*. 'If Your Wife Objects, Leave Her!' and 'Some Of The People – Some Of The Time' were typical headlines, as was the caption to a photograph of the scene outside Austin's at Longbridge, Birmingham: 'The man: R.A. Etheridge, former Communist

Parliamentary Candidate, Convener of 350 Shop Stewards. The Audience: some of 20,000 workers engaged upon export work. General Thesis: The Party Line. The Message: Strike!' Almost certainly, though, the Communist threat in the workplace was much exaggerated. The party generally was in numerical decline (fewer than 40,000 members by the early 1950s); barely half were also members of trade unions; and as a CP member somewhat wryly commented at a meeting of industrial cadres in early 1953: 'Once many Lab workers come up against our policy cannot argue against us. But have reserve about are we agent foreign power.'[14]

Inevitably, Labour attitudes towards Communism, and in turn Soviet Russia, varied considerably. 'The Communist Party hates social democracy even more than it hates Toryism,' declared the formidable Bessie Braddock, herself a former Communist but now on Labour's Gaitskellite rather than Bevanite wing, in the TUC-backed *Daily Herald* in August 1952. 'It is astonishing,' she added, 'how many supporters of Labour still fail to grasp this fundamental fact.' A few weeks earlier, Gaitskell himself had privately pondered on the increasingly prevalent anti-Americanism since the start of the Korean War in 1950:

> The truth is that we have a dilemma. We do not like to admit our relative weakness, because we should then look much too like a satellite. But if we try and live up to a military standard we cannot afford, that means economic trouble. A poor relation who is driven to live beyond his means by his rich cousins will not feel well disposed to them. Faced with this dilemma people search for an escape. In England there is not much serious neutralism but there is a great deal of wishful thinking – chiefly about the Commonwealth. It is easy to see how powerful anti-American prejudice can be when to this already difficult relationship is added the genuine fear felt by many people that America will land us all in war. Moreover the war if it comes will engulf and destroy Britain and Europe while very probably leaving the territory of America physically untouched.

Naturally, he went on, anti-Americanism was especially widespread on the left: 'The left is more open to communist propaganda. It is still somewhat sentimental about the Russian regime: it is even more sentimental about the Chinese communists: the mere fact that America is large and powerful stimulates some opposition among those who instinctively favour the poor and the weak . . .'

Where did Bevan, Gaitskell's great rival, fit into that typology? On the one hand his unambiguous belief in parliamentary democracy led him to castigate the CP as 'the sworn inveterate enemy of the socialist and democratic parties'; on the other hand, his whole-hearted belief in scientific planning ('society must be brought under control in exactly the same way as man has tried to bring natural forces under control') inevitably meant that he tended to adopt an indulgent, uncritical stance towards Russia's command-style economic achievements. He also, of course, remained adamant that the Russian military threat was exaggerated and that the best way to combat the spread of Communism was to devote resources not to military hardware but to (as he put it in *In Place of Fear*) 'the provision of the industrial equipment which the under-developed areas of the world must have if they are not to go on bubbling and exploding for the rest of the century'. It was a logical enough position: yet as long as the Cold War lasted, Bevan and the Labour left more generally would be acutely vulnerable to the charge of being soft on Communism, even of being labelled as fellow-travellers.[15]

None of which much concerned Doris Lessing, who in 1949 had come to London from Rhodesia as a young, as yet unpublished novelist. Three years later, in the summer of 1952, she performed what she would famously describe as 'probably the most neurotic act of my life'. In time it inspired some of the most eloquent passages of her remarkable autobiography, *Walking in the Shade* (1997):

I decided to join the Communist Party. And this at a time when my 'doubts' had become something like a steady, private torment. Separate manifestations of the horror that the Soviet Union had become were discussed, briefly, in lowered voices – the equivalent of looking over one's shoulder to see if anyone could hear. I do not remember one serious, sit-down, in-depth discussion about the implications of what we were hearing. Rather, sudden burstings into tears: 'Oh, it's so horrible.' Sudden storms of accusation: 'It's just anti-Soviet propaganda anyway.' Marital quarrels, even divorces . . .

The first and main fact, the 'mind-set' of those times, was that it was taken for granted capitalism was doomed, was on its way out. Capitalism was responsible for every social ill, war included. Communism was the future for all mankind. I used to hear earnest proselytizers say, 'Let me have anyone for a couple of hours, and I can persuade him that communism is the only answer. Because it is obvious that it is.' Communism's hands were not exactly clean? Or, to put it as the comrades did, 'There have been mistakes'? That was because the first communist country had been backward Russia; but if the first country had been Germany, that would have been a very different matter! Soon, when the industrially developed countries became communist, we would all see a very different type of communism . . .

Arthur Koestler said that every communist who stayed in the Communist Party in the face of all the evidence had a secret explanation for what was happening, and this could not be discussed with friends and comrades. Some of the communists I knew had decided that yes, the reported crimes were true – though *of course* not as bad as the capitalist press said – but that Comrade Stalin could not possibly know about what was going on. The truth was being kept from Uncle Joe. My rationalization, my 'secret belief' was that the leadership of the Soviet Union had become corrupt but that waiting everywhere in the communist world were the good communists, keeping their counsel, and they would at the right time take power, and then communism would resume its march to the just society, the perfect society. There was just one little thing: I didn't realize Uncle Joe had murdered them all.

About the same time that Lessing joined up, the uncompromising, hardline, immensely gifted folk singer Ewan MacColl wrote his 'Ballad of Joe Stalin'. Sung to a banjo accompaniment, it was a favourite of the future historian – and, at this stage, ardent Communist – Raphael Samuel, who three decades later would quote with honesty but palpable discomfort the final verse:

> Joe Stalin was a mighty man and he made a mighty plan;
> He harnessed nature to the plough to work for the good of man;
> He's hammered out the future, the forgeman he has been
> And he's made the worker's state the best the world has ever seen.[16]

5

What Will Teacher Say?

March 1952 was the month of Barbara Pym's most popular novel ('*Excellent Women* is England, and, thank goodness, it is full of them,' declared John Betjeman), of Richard Gordon's shrewdly amiable *Doctor in the House* (eighth impression by July), of Terence Rattigan's masterpiece of repressed emotion *The Deep Blue Sea* ('Kenneth More is our best answer to Marlon Brando so far,' Kenneth Tynan) – and of a cri de coeur from a young jobbing actor and would-be playwright. 'The general policy is reactionary to say the very least of it,' John Osborne complained in the *New Statesman* about the state of repertory theatre and its managers. 'Even the plays they present (under admittedly difficult conditions, which, however, they resolutely do nothing to overcome by decent endeavour) have changed little in twenty years. Indeed, so often they are the very same plays, only too familiar to any actor who has had the experience of working for these play factories which turn out their perennial and vulgar farce-drama-thriller cycle twice nightly to audiences who would be as well served by a nude revue.' The letter ended with an already characteristic mixture of irony and anger: 'If planned economy ever takes a complete hold upon the resources of this country, it seems almost certain that the Theatre, at least, will remain the jolly playground of free enterprise, the burial ground of art and integrity, and, incidentally, of the artist.'

The revolution that Osborne implicitly called for might have actually happened only three months later. Rodney Ackland's *The Pink Room* 'gave a glimpse', Richard Eyre has argued, 'of what theatre might have been had audiences, critics and the censor been ready to face the uncomfortable truths that he put on the stage.' A state-of-the-nation play set in a Soho drinking club in 1945, *The Pink Room* dealt among other things with escapism, political apathy and the Holocaust, as well as taking a notably sardonic view of the war as a time of unimpeachable heroism. The London opening was at the Lyric, Hammersmith on 18 June, with a cast including Hermione Baddeley and Betty Marsden, and the critical reaction was merciless. 'Loneliness whiskey momentary euphoria another whiskey deeper layers of loneliness oblivion loneliness whiskey momentary euphoria more whiskey,' was T. C. Worsley's *New Statesman* encapsulation of Ackland's 'appallingly relentless eye and ear'; to Eric Keown it was 'as dreary a collection of human beings as any stage can have carried for a very long time'; Harold Hobson in the *Sunday Times* called it 'an evening of jaw-aching soul-obliterating boredom'; even Tynan in the *Evening Standard*, instinctively sympathetic to any attempt to break out of the drawing room, asserted that it took a 'heart' larger than the playwright's 'to write about the small sins of small people without sentimentalism or shallow moralising'. The run lasted less than a month, and a devastated Ackland had to wait until 1988 for a new, uncensored production (the play renamed as *Absolute Hell*) and belated critical acclaim.[1]

Perhaps back in 1952 it was the homely touch that was missing. 'They are my friends,' one housewife told the BBC that spring. 'I find myself thinking of them at all times.' Another housewife agreed: 'I feel as if the family were relations of mine or very close neighbours. I know how they will react to any given situation. Each of them is such a definite character.' The Listening Panel had been asked why they went on listening to *Mrs Dale's Diary*, by now in its fifth year. ' "Everyday" events, rather than sensational stories, are probably most welcome to Panel members,' the report concluded. 'For instance, one group mentioned the episode in which Gwen discovered a missing pearl necklace and won a reward. This, they felt, struck completely the wrong note.' Tellingly, the only disliked character was the unpleasant Mrs Mountford. It was much the same with *The Archers*: 'Again the appeal of "real" people and ordinary, homely credible incidents was very much in evidence, so also were the objections to unusual happenings and excursions outside the stereotype formed of the Archer family circle. In addition, however, there was much appreciation of the country atmosphere and the "little lectures" on farming: this gave many towndwellers a pleasurable feeling of contact with rural life . . .' *The Archers* was only in its second year, but in a recent poll conducted by the *Daily Graphic*, asking its readers to choose between the two radio soaps, some 78 per cent had plumped for it. William Smethurst, in his demythologising history of the programme, is at pains to demonstrate how in fact there was a strongly melodramatic element to the storyline in these early years, but that was not why the 19 per cent of the adult population who listened to it on any one day liked to think they tuned in.

Although the travails of the mentally ill featured in neither soap, in March the BBC did broadcast a groundbreaking talk on the Third Programme by the Scottish poet and critic G. S. Fraser. After sensitively, non-emotively describing his recent experience in a mental hospital, he finished by asking listeners to 'remember the mentally sick sometimes in your prayers'. It was a timely plea. Another Scot, Ronald Laing, fresh from studying medicine at Glasgow University, was spending part of his National Service working at the British Army Psychiatric Unit at Netley, near Southampton. There he encountered a grim world of insulin shock therapy being applied to patients in deliberately induced comas, of indiscriminate ECT treatment, of routine lobotomies, of padded cells, of a huge, unbridgeable gap between staff and patients. By the time he left in the summer, Laing was deeply perturbed. These seemed to be 'ways of destroying people and driving people crazy', he recalled. 'How could the whole of psychiatry be doing the opposite of what I assumed psychiatry was about – treating, curing if possible, arresting the course of mental illness?'[2]

At least the mentally ill were not actively targeted as criminals – unlike homosexuals in 1952. The much-publicised flight to Russia the previous year of the two spies Guy Burgess and Donald Maclean, both homosexual, had badly rattled the establishment, and the new Tory Home Secretary, Sir David Maxwell Fyfe, was now making the active prosecution of homosexuals almost his highest priority, allied to the introduction of 'positive vetting' in the Civil Service in order to unroot 'serious character weaknesses'. Police activity hit a new, startling intensity, reflected in the comparative England and Wales figures for 1938 and 1952: cases of sodomy and bestiality up from 134 to 670; attempts to commit 'unnatural offences', including indecent assaults, up from 822 to 3,087; offences of gross indecency between males up from 320 to 1,686. Behind these and similar figures lay many, many human tragedies, typified by a trio in 1952. Alan Turing, tried at the Quarter Sessions in Knutsford, Cheshire, some seven weeks after his arrest on the evening of the King's death, was humiliatingly sentenced to a course of organo-therapy treatment at Manchester Royal Infirmary, rendering him impotent and making him grow breasts; the camp, highly popular Lancashire comedian George Williams ('I'm not well . . . I'm not well at all . . . In fact I'm . . . proper poorly!') was charged with a homosexual offence and sentenced to two years' imprisonment, effectively ending his career as a top-of-the-bill performer; and the much-decorated war hero Michael ('Mad Mike') Calvert was court-martialled for 'gross indecency with male persons' and dismissed from the army, quite possibly on trumped-up charges. Progressive opinion, moreover, was not always as progressive as it might have been. About this time the liberal-minded man of letters Stephen Spender asked the leader of the British Communist Party about its attitude to legalising homosexuality. ''Ec!' replied Harry Pollitt. 'We'll have noon o' that filth and roobish, when we coom to power.'

Nor was it generally a subject for bold, uninhibited treatment. 'He isn't married then?' one of the characters in *Excellent Women* asks of the vicar. 'One of *those* . . . I mean,' she adds apologetically, 'one of the kind who don't marry?' Or take *The Deep Blue Sea*, written by Rattigan after his male lover had begun an affair with another man and eventually gassed himself to death. Rattigan knew, though, that neither the Lord Chamberlain nor the theatre-going public would accept such an explicitly homosexual drama, and the result was a heterosexual adjustment. By contrast, there were few punches pulled in either Angus Wilson's first novel, *Hemlock and After*, published in July, or the *Sunday Pictorial*'s 'Evil Men' series appearing a few weeks earlier. 'His picture of homosexual relations – and it is a very large and striking picture – is one of utter desolation, a life without love or satisfaction,' reassuringly argued J. D. Scott in his *New Statesman* review of the Wilson – true only up to a point. As for 'Evil Men', a three-part investigation by Douglas Warth, it began as uncompromisingly as it intended to go on:

The natural British tendency to pass over anything unpleasant in scornful silence is providing cover for an unnatural sex vice which is getting a dangerous grip on this country.

I have watched it growing – as it grew in Germany before the war, producing the horrors of Hitlerite corruption, and as it grew in classical Greece to the point where civilisation was destroyed. I thought, at first, that this menace could best be fought by silence – a silence which Society has almost always maintained in the face of a problem which has been growing in our midst for years. But this vice can no longer be ignored. The silence, I find, is a factor which has enabled the evil to spread.

Homosexuality is an unpleasant subject, but it must be faced if ever it is to be controlled . . .

Most people know that there are such things as 'pansies' – mincing, effeminate young men who call themselves 'queers'. But simple, decent folk regard them as freaks and rarities. They have become, regrettably, a variety hall joke.

There will be no joking about this subject when people realise the true situation.

Public schools and Oxbridge were identified as particularly virulent breeding grounds, while garrison towns, resorts like Bournemouth and particular quarters of big cities (though 'Chelsea, once notorious, has been cleaned up') were apparently where male prostitutes especially flourished. Prisons were also hotbeds of homosexuality, and in the final article Warth argued that homosexuals should instead be sent to special clinics where 'they may be kept in treatment and custody until they threaten society no more'. In short, he declared, 'society must demand that the doctors and police work together to find a final cure'.[3]

For Anthony Heap in St Pancras, writing his diary in May, there were other candidates for the 'evil men' tag:

Apparently it is not enough that black stowaways should be allowed to flock into England in their thousands, remain here to live on public assistance funds or the proceeds of dope peddling, occupying housing accommodation sorely needed by our own population and cause still further overcrowding through having half-breed children by the filthy white sluts who live with them, but we must needs have – according to this morning's papers – a nigger preaching in St Paul's Cathedral to a mixed congregation of blacks and whites . . .

It is impossible to know how representative Heap's views were, but it is clear that by 1952 the question of West Indian workers migrating to Britain was starting to be seen as a 'problem', even though the actual numbers were still only about 2,000 a year. In June an American academic, Ruth Landes, argued at the Anthropological Institute that the British were fundamentally 'inhospitable' to 'everyone who did not speak English and who were not born on the isles', adding that 'the Negro's incomprehensible and perhaps theatrical zest and spontaneity challenged the English at some vulnerable level'; the same month, Bishop Barnes of Birmingham referred to 'semi-foreign areas' and to how 'in districts where there is a considerable foreign element in the population, neither moral standards nor social behaviour are satisfactory'; in July *The Times* insisted that the key to racial harmony lay 'less with Governments than with ordinary people' and emphasised 'the supreme importance of spontaneous social contacts'; and in September a piece in *Picture Post*, 'Breeding a Colour Bar?', focused on 'Brixton's Little Harlem' and was reasonably optimistic, though it did show a wall daubed with the initials 'K.B.W.', short for 'Keep Britain White'. It is even possible that the Rev. W. Awdry's *Toby the Tram Engine*, published in 1952 and featuring 'a funny little engine with a queer shape', drawn as brown by the illustrator C. Reginald Dalby, was intended as a story of racial marginalisation and assimilation. Police attitudes seem to have been mixed. Officers in the Met, to judge by their reports, were generally hostile towards West Indian immigrants, described as 'loathsome creatures' and as 'cunning unprincipled crooks living on women and their wits'. The Chief Constable of Sheffield described to the Home Office how the Jamaicans in his city 'use face cream, perfume etc. to make themselves attractive to the females they meet at dances, cafés etc.' but his counterpart in Middlesbrough, also reporting in October 1952, was adamant that 'on the whole the coloured population are as well behaved as many local citizens', with no evidence of unduly high rates of criminal activity.

There was, in terms of race relations as a whole, one undeniably positive development in 1952. This was the opening of the Shah restaurant in

Drummond Street, near Euston Station, by Sheikh Mohammad, some ten years after he had arrived almost penniless from Mysore in south India. The Shah was a hit from the start, discovered first by junior doctors from University College Hospital, and soon there were queues outside, with an average wait of 25 minutes for a table. It was not quite Britain's first Indian restaurant, but it was the unmistakable start of a revolution in eating out, combining affordability with a sense of luxury – a revolution especially embraced by the indigenous white working class.[4]

It was an all-white line-up when in April, two months into the new reign, *Picture Post* picked 'The New Elizabethans'. Forty-two men and five women were chosen, mainly predictable enough: 'Rab' Butler and Nye Bevan as politicians, Benjamin Britten and Sir William Walton as composers, Graham Greene as novelist, Henry Moore as sculptor, Graham Sutherland as painter, A. J. Ayer as philosopher, Fred Hoyle as mathematician and so on. The main surprises were thespian, with Alec Clunes as one of the two actors (Alec Guinness the other), Celia Johnson as actress and Glynis Johns ('still recognisable as the girl-round-the-corner') as film star. The other three women were the economist Barbara Ward, the barrister Rose Heilbron (Britain's only female QC) and Margot Fonteyn ('almond-eyed and mystically beautiful, she is quiet, modest, still a little shy, only occasionally obstinate') – with no place for the recently married Margaret Thatcher, not yet an MP though author of a recent *Sunday Graphic* article on the position of women 'At the Dawn of the New Elizabethan Era'.

In fact Thatcher was about to experience a great sorrow, for in May her beloved father, Alfred Roberts, was voted out as a Grantham alderman following Labour gains in the council elections. Still wearing his aldermanic robes, and speaking 'with evident emotion' in front of a crowded gallery, Roberts observed that he was the first alderman in a quarter of a century to be displaced by an opposing political party. There then took place, as reported by the local paper, a dramatic farewell:

'It is now almost nine years since I took up these robes in honour, and now I trust in honour they are laid down.'

He recalled that he bought the robes himself and voiced pleasure at being able to present them to the Corporation.

As he was taking his leave, he declared: 'No medals, no honours, but an inward sense of satisfaction. May God bless Grantham for ever!'

And with this he turned abruptly to leave the Council chamber.

Presumably there was less lip-trembling emotion in Oxford about the same time, after a thrusting Australian undergraduate had stood for secretary of the University Labour Club and, in defiance of the rule against open canvassing, had campaigned on the slogan, 'Rooting for Rupert'. Complaints were made to the club's chairman, Gerald Kaufman, who initiated a tribunal. The outcome was that young Murdoch was not allowed to stand for office.[5]

For most people, talk of a new Elizabethan Age – essentially got up by the press – was at most a momentarily pleasing irrelevance. Instead, in the context of a general relaxation of price controls, what was far more preoccupying was the question of the cost of living. 'Have had a notice from the electricity board today that they will put the charges of electricity up without notice to individual customers, in future,' recorded Kenneth Preston in Keighley barely a fortnight after the King's death. 'That is the sort of thing that is so infuriating nowadays. We have absolutely no power to protest or complain. Monopolies – monopolies all over and prices always up and up and again up.' So too with Gladys Langford in north London. 'Laundry price controls are to be removed next Monday,' she noted in June. And two days later: 'Chatted with a plain but pleasant woman in the 'bus who said she had given up her car as she could no longer afford to run it. She said 'phone charges are to be raised.' When the previous month Gallup had asked people about their standard of living, 40 per cent had said it was going down and only 29 per cent going up; while in June one in five told the pollsters that they were trying to cut down on 'everything', compared with just one in twenty-five the previous summer. Moreover, there was still widespread rationing – meat, fats (including butter, margarine and cooking fats), cheese, tea, sugar and sweets – together with periodic shortages. 'Ione has half holiday and I was glad of excuse to go out to lunch,' recorded Judy Haines in Chingford on a Thursday in June. 'Went to Silverthorn Café. Only "mixed grill" at 12 o'c! This "damned Government!" (our joke since we heard it so often of Labour Government and never at all now.)'⁶

Inevitably, so much depended on vantage point and comparison. 'The Rhondda: 1952' was the title of Geoffrey Goodman's upbeat reportage for the *New Statesman* in April. 'The four Labour Exchanges are rather like museum pieces from a wicked age,' he declared, noting that whereas between 1931 and 1935 an average of more than 16,000 had been out of work in the Rhondda, together with many more thousands only partly employed, now just some 2,500 were jobless. 'New clothing shops, food stores, electrical and radio shops have all elbowed their way into the cramped hub, and shop-space is now virtually unobtainable,' was his description of Pontypridd. 'Glass and chrome have come to the valleys' market town and over rough, cobbled streets run high-heeled shoes, nylons and West End drapes ...' Soon afterwards, in nearby Merthyr Tydfil, 'grateful people packed High Street Chapel to give thanks for returned prosperity', while the local paper also reported the almost euphoric speech by the President of Merthyr Chamber of Trade at the new Mayor's installation luncheon:

> Mr Evans claimed that the Chamber, in co-operation with the Council, had done magnificent work in terms of trying to bring new industries to the borough. They felt very proud of what they had done and that Merthyr was now 'on the map'. There was also a happy relationship between management and workers since the advent of new industries and there had been very little labour trouble. Business people had beautified their premises and the town looked more prosperous than it had been for many years. He maintained that the future of the borough was rosy.

Less reliance on coal, iron and steel was undoubtedly a sensible strategy, but there was a shock in June when Hoover, whose factory was situated just outside the town, dismissed some 300 employees, almost a quarter of its workforce. 'Cessation of shipments of washing machines to Australia' was the company's explanation – a sharp reminder of the precariousness of the new prosperity.

'England: the most civilized country on earth, but also the most boring!' the German political theorist Hannah Arendt wrote from Manchester to her husband in New York a week or so later:

A dull blanket of fear lies over the country, which is softened, though, by the fact that they've been eating too little for such a long time that they barely notice the difference anymore. And yet it's almost unbelievable. Not just what the shops look like – groceries and so on, everything scarce, everything of bad quality (which is quite new for this country), but also their genius to make life uncomfortable. Everything set up as if expressively to make life difficult, or at least to challenge you to muster so much cheerfulness that everything can be overcome.

And yet I admire no other people as I admire the English, as a people I mean. Everything we like so much about America, the decency, the lack of hypocrisy, no to-do, fairness, etc is Anglo-Saxon. But all of this without the slightest zest and also without vitality.

Soon afterwards Arendt was in Durham. 'A small English suburban town near Newcastle in the middle of a mining district,' she reported. 'But all of England looks like it's mainly made of coal. Everything black from 150 years of coal dust. The people here are doing well, and the rise of the working class is much more palpable than in London.'

For two less occasional observers of the English scene, these were difficult times. 'All through this last year I have been in trouble – it's the result, I think, of switching my career, leaving politics and preparing to start in at the bottom again in a new field,' Michael Young wrote in early July to Dorothy and Leonard Elmhirst in Dartington. He was just back from a 'most stimulating' trip to Lancashire (in the middle of a textile recession) and Yorkshire:

I interviewed dozens of families, and have I think done as much as possible until I can begin on a more systematic research programme. The slum district I stayed in in Manchester was full of warm and friendly people. It was repeatedly amazing to see the intelligent eyes, the humour and the self-assurance of mothers in dark, crowded rooms cluttered up with broken-down furniture. Even the thousands of women in the dole queue at Blackburn were smiling and joking, and in their smart Marks & Spencer coats they presented a sharp contrast to the mill-girls of the 'thirties with their shawls & clogs. M&S may have done as much to create the social revolution as the Labour Party . . .

So many good things were said. One of the best was Gwen's char-lady who said 'I don't know where any of my babies came from. I've never been a willing partner. I've always turned my back on him.' I went to see this lady, who had 114 close relatives, extending over 5 generations . . .

Later that month, a less enthused, patronless Sid Chaplin, staying in a Nottingham hotel, described to a friend his 'pilgrimage to the castle (where D. H. Lawrence took *his* Marion) just to try to recapture the Lawrencian spirit':

> I'd have spent my time better reading 'Sons & Lovers'. They have now installed a restaurant after the pattern of British Railways, administered by three pleasant sluts. People were sunbathing on the lawn. The sun beat down like a Pittsburg blast-furnace being tapped. And there it was, below the dowdy blackened old spinster of a castle, belching power-station stacks, factories, high, hard roads, as remorseless as the roads to hell, sidings, the foul & filthy Trent, and smog (not honest smoke).

Working full-time for the National Coal Board's magazine *Coal*, involving a monthly feature and much travel, Chaplin was acutely conscious of his lack of progress with his creative writing. 'This last 2½ yrs,' he added, 'have been hard to bear.'[7]

Irrespective of such glooms, it was never realistic that a new reign meant the turning of a moral corner. In late April the *Brighton & Hove Herald* reported 'a wave of wanton destruction by teenage hooligans' striking the seafront, with 'juvenile gangsters' vandalising property and assaulting passers-by; soon afterwards, 'Disgusted' of south Wales complained to the local paper about vandalism in Aberfan's cinema and attributed it to 'lack of parental control'. Increasingly, the focus was on the pernicious consequences of the widespread importation of American 'crime' and 'horror comics', with *Picture Post* in mid-May publishing an investigation which found that they were extensively read by schoolboys, adolescents generally and National Service men. 'Unknown before the war, the first copies arrived with the American troops, who had grown up with them. Now you can buy them all over the country, especially in big towns.' The comics themselves all used the picture-strip technique, were 'concerned almost exclusively with crime and violence', and 'depend for their appeal on violence, sex and racial hatred'. The article (by a Communist teacher called Peter Mauger) demanded that children be protected. The connection between these comics and rising juvenile delinquency was seemingly obvious, and not long afterwards Gallup found two in three adults approving of a blanket import ban. Nor was it just American comics that appalled the moral majority. 'I saw rows of "Life in the Future", "Tales of Thrills & Horror", "True Love Stories", etc, etc,' recorded Nella Last in June after spending part of a Saturday looking at a big magazine stall in Barrow's market. 'I've often said lightly "my breath nearly stopped" – but felt it true this morning. I never imagined such sexy – pornographic – pictures & captions, such sadistic, grim "torture", such "might is right" type of trash. How they got past the censors who ban books is a mystery.'[8]

Fears of unhealthy American influence were also in play when it came to the question of commercial broadcasting. A fortnight after the King's death, and four months ahead of the renewal of the BBC's Charter, Crossman was told that at a recent meeting of Conservative MPs there had been a heavy vote in favour of ending the Corporation's monopoly. 'No doubt the increased agitation is due to the high-handed B.B.C. performance during the King's funeral,' he reflected. 'If there had been a rival, the B.B.C. couldn't have closed the service down in the way it did.' There ensued in late March and early April, ahead of an expected White Paper, a bout of agitated correspondence in *The Times*. 'This is the age of the common man, whose influences towards the deterioration of standards of culture are formidable in all spheres,' warned Lord Brand. 'It is discouraging to find that it is in the Conservative Party which one would have thought would be by tradition the party pledged to maintain such standards, that many members in their desire to end anything like a monopoly, seem ready to support measures which will inevitably degrade them.' Violet Bonham Carter agreed: 'We are often told the B.B.C. should "give the people what they want". But who are "the people"? The people are all the people – including minorities. Broadcasting by the B.B.C. has no aim but good broadcasting. Broadcasting by sponsoring has no other motive but to sell goods.'

It was not just Tory and Liberal grandees who were alarmed, but also the bulk of Labour MPs, including one of the youngest. 'It is a great pity,' observed Anthony Wedgwood Benn, 'that those who are understandably suspicious of monopoly should automatically extend their suspicions to public service broadcasting itself. That is quite a different matter.' On the sparsely represented other side, the most striking contribution was by Hughie Green, a child star of the 1930s who after the war had remade his name presenting *Opportunity Knocks* on the radio. Writing from 169 Chiltern Court, NW1, he extolled the drama available to watch on commercial TV in the States: 'Great plays, star names, excellent direction, and a variety of sets in a fleeting hour can be compared with – in this country – one dreary set and a torrent of words that seem to go on to eternity.' About television in general he added: 'Its main aim in a democratic country should be the same as that of any advertiser – to please the public. Why this great outcry against the advertiser? The British free Press seem to get along with him very well.' In the same issue, however, *The Times* called for the BBC's monopoly to be upheld, largely on the basis that it was now 'a proven British institution'.

The White Paper on 15 May did confirm the monopoly in sound broadcasting, but left the way open for a commercial television competitor. In the House of Lords later that month, Lord Reith – in the public mind still the figure overwhelmingly identified with the BBC – claimed that the introduction of commercial television would be a national disaster comparable to 'dog-racing, smallpox and bubonic plague'. It was an intervention that infuriated Churchill. 'I am against the monopoly enjoyed by the BBC,' he told his physician Lord Moran soon afterwards. 'For eleven years they kept me off the air. They prevented me from expressing views which proved to be right. Their behaviour has been tyrannical. They are honeycombed with Socialists – probably with Communists.' In a fairly humdrum Commons debate in June, Herbert Morrison claimed that there would be 'a competitive drive in a downward direction', while John Profumo spoke for the vanguard of Tory MPs in favour of such competition: 'We are not a nation of intellectuals. The average men and women who form the vast majority of the public deserve the best possible entertainment. We are not a nation of old-fashioned die-hards, and the Government should foster a spirit of experiment ... If there is any doubt about what the people really desire, surely the answer is to try it out and allow the people to find out for themselves.' Going somewhat over the top, he also pronounced himself 'horrified by the philosophy which recognises a State-run organisation as the sole arbiter of our taste and even our entertainment'. His reward was a decisive majority, on a whipped vote, in favour of the White Paper. It was not yet a done deal, but for the three hard-headed men – the former BBC executive Norman Collins, the free-market stockbroker and electrical magnate Sir Robert Renwick and C. O. Stanley of Pye Radio – at the heart of the campaign to break the monopoly, this was a sweet moment.

What did the people want? 'The Parties have got sponsoring all wrong,' Hugh Cudlipp, soon to become the dynamic Editorial Director of the *Daily Mirror* and *Sunday Pictorial*, told Crossman shortly after the Commons vote. 'The staunchest Tory supporters are all against it but a large number of people who vote Labour would really like sponsored variety programmes.' Crossman himself reflected: 'I'm sure that this is true in Coventry [his constituency], where most of my supporters would love sponsored programmes.' Although Gallup found opinion evenly divided – roughly one-third in favour of a new television channel sponsored by advertisers, one-third against, one-third undecided – the instincts of Cudlipp and Crossman were surely correct. Morrison may have worried that television was something 'we can have too much of', claiming that 'when listening and looking it is impossible for anyone to work or read, although women can knit', but almost invariably once people started watching they were hooked – and wanted more. 'I am very interested in television as a viewer,' an engine-driver member of the BBC's Viewing Panel wrote in during the spring. 'It must have altered the habits of thousands of working people, as it has mine. It has opened a vista of sights scenes and educational items to which we could never have aspired. I no longer listen to radio, I rarely go out in the evenings, I have visited the cinema once in 18 months.' He added a postscript: 'I have also resigned my seat on the Town Council, and politics.'[9]

One of the new medium's great attractions, of course, was its coverage (though still somewhat patchy) of major sporting events. In a memorable Derby, the 16-year-old Lester Piggott was ruthlessly outmanoeuvred by the veteran Charlie Smirke on Tulyar, the triumphant winning jockey taunting Piggott by saying, 'What did I Tulyar?' as he dismounted; in the First Test at Headingley against India, England took the field under its first-ever professional captain, Len Hutton, who had a formidable weapon in his fiery fast bowler Fred Trueman – rugged, quick-tongued, no lover of the old guard; and in the Olympics at Helsinki, just as it seemed that Britain was going to go home without a gold medal, Colonel Harry Llewellyn jumped a clear round on Foxhunter, best-loved British horse of the era. There were other entertainments available in August. Churchill one evening went to see *The Yeomen of the Guard* at Streatham and, according to 'Jock' Colville, who accompanied him, 'was received with immense acclamation by the audience'; the American singer Frankie Laine was an instant sell-out at the London Palladium, though an unimpressed Tynan noted in his review how 'he spreads his arms out like a wrestler, and then hits a mad, toneless head-note, holding it so long that you expect him to drop like a stone at the end of it'; and the northern comedian Frank Randle continued to break all records at the Central Pier, Blackpool, with his twice-nightly *Randle's Summer Scandals*. It was not, though, a trouble-free summer for Randle, long the target of Blackpool's Chief Constable Harry Barnes, a strong Methodist. Eventually, Barnes got him summonsed on four charges of obscenity, with the police identifying the part of the show they objected to:

> A silent Chinaman shuffled across the stage. Randle asked the audience, 'Is that King Farouk?'
> CINDERELLA, to Buttons (Randle): 'I'd like to do you a favour.'
> BUTTONS: 'A'd rather have a boiled egg.'
> And CINDERELLA again: 'I'd like to talk to you.'
> BUTTONS: 'It's nowt to do with me. It'll be me father agin.'
> And finally, 'There's a flea loose in the harem and the favourite will have to be scratched.'

Found guilty on all counts, Randle was fined £10 on each summons, with fines also for the rest of the cast and the theatre manager.[10]

There was one dreadful natural disaster during the summer. 'Deaths about 30 [in the end 34] in Lynmouth, the holiday makers and the villagers equally in flood,' recorded Harold Macmillan on Sunday, 17 August, after a deluge had broken over Exmoor. 'Apparently this happened on Friday night, but was not in Saturday's newspapers. As we never listen to the wireless, I had not heard the BBC account on Saturday night.' Over the next few days the BBC, the press and the newsreels all gave blanket coverage to the tragedy, though Churchill was not deterred from going to his Gilbert and Sullivan on Monday evening. By then Macmillan, as Housing Minister, was in north Devon, where he spent Tuesday morning surveying the spectacular damage and persuading the locals 'to concentrate on getting immediate work done before arguing as to exactly who is to pay'. Although criticised in some quarters for his extravagant language ('like the road to Ypres') and dress (cloth cap and walking stick), Macmillan himself believed that his visit had been 'very well received'.[11]

Soon afterwards, in early September, Raymond Chandler arrived in London for a month's stay. There were some pleasingly Chandleresque touches in his letters back home. 'Today is an English Sunday and by God it's gloomy enough for a crossing of the Styx,' he told his publisher. 'I thought England was broke but the whole damn city is crawling with Rolls Royces, Bentleys, Daimlers and expensive blondes.' And, no doubt reflecting the cuisine at the Connaught, he added: 'Never thought I'd get sick of the sight of a grouse on toast or a partridge, but by God I am.' Even so, by the time he got back to California and sent his report to his old Dulwich College contemporary Bill Townend, his overall verdict was favourable: 'The present generation of English people impressed me very well. There is a touch of aggressiveness about the working classes and the non-Public School types which I think is something new and which I personally do not find at all unpleasant ... And the real Public School types, or many of them, with their bird-like chirpings are becoming a little ridiculous.'

There was nothing sanguine about 'Love is Dead', the opening essay of John Betjeman's *First and Last Loves*, a mainly architectural collection published in September. 'We are told that we live in the age of the common man,' he declared:

He would be better described as the suburban man. There is a refinement about him which pervades everything he touches and sees. His books are chosen for him by the librarian, his arguing is done for him by Brains Trusts, his dreams are realised for him in the cinema, his records are played for him by the B.B.C. . . . He collects facts as some collect stamps, and he abhors excess in colour, speech or decoration. He is not vulgar. He is not the common man, but the average man, which is far worse.

He is our ruler and he rules by committees. He gives us what most people want, and he believes that what is popular is what is best. He is the explanation of such phenomena as plastic tea-cups, Tizer, light ale, quizzes, mystery tours, cafeterias, discussion groups, Chapels of Unity, station announcers . . .

As for what the future held under this rule of the mediocre, Betjeman offered a startlingly uncuddly, dystopian vision:

I see the woman with a scarf twisted round her hair and a cigarette in her mouth. She has put the tea tray down upon the file on which my future depends. I see the man on the chain-belt feeling tired, not screwing the final nuts. In a few months I see the engine falling out of the motor car. I see eight porters, two postmen and an inspector standing dazed for forty minutes on a provincial station, staring into space and waiting for what was once the Great Western which is now forty minutes late. I see those sharp-faced girls behind the buffet and the counter insulting the crowds who come to buy. Too bored to think, too proud to pray, too timid to leave what they're used to doing . . . We know how many tons of coal are produced per week, how many man-hours there are in a pair of nylons, the exact date and the name of the architect and the style of a building. The Herr-Professor-Doktors [ie Pevsner] are writing everything down for us, sometimes throwing in a little hurried pontificating too, so we need never bother to feel or think or see again. We can eat our Weetabix, catch the 8.48, read the sports column and die; for love is dead.

'One of the most savage Jeremiads on English life today that I have ever read,' thought the architectural writer (and semi-Modernist) John Summerson. 'It is a little embarrassing.' But to the young, aggressive, left-wing art critic John Berger it was worse than that. 'Why bother to consider the book at all?' he asked in *Tribune*. 'Because it shows, I think, how silly an imaginative and knowledgeable writer can become, if he loses touch with the real issues of the time.'

All too late, in any case, for Mahmood Hussein Mattan – a 28-year-old Somali seaman (and father of three) hanged in Cardiff Prison on 8 September for the murder in March of Lily Volpert, a shopkeeper in the Cardiff docks area. The key prosecution witness was a carpenter called Harold Cover, subsequently convicted in 1969 of attempting to murder his own daughter. That failed to persuade the Home Secretary of the day, James Callaghan, to reopen Mattan's case, but in 1998 the Court of Appeal did reconsider it and found that Mattan's conviction could no longer be regarded as safe. 'The court can only hope that its decision today will provide some crumb of comfort for his surviving relatives,' said Lord Justice Rose. Mattan's widow, Laura, though, was unappeased by the quashing of the conviction. 'I'll probably be angry until my dying day,' she told reporters outside the court. 'He has been cleared, but it should never have happened in the first place. He should have been cleared way back then.'[12]

'Crikey', 'Yarooh', 'I say, you fellows', 'Leggo, you beasts' – the soon familiar cries of the 'Fat Owl of the Remove' were first heard on television on the Tuesday after the King's funeral. Initially, each episode of *Billy Bunter of Greyfriars School* was screened twice, at 5.40 for children and then at 8.00 for adults, both times performed live. Significantly, the opening episode got an excellent Reaction Index (from the BBC's Television Panel) of 79 for the earlier performance, but only 61 for the later. 'There was some feeling among adults that the programme lacked some of the pace and rumbustiousness they associated with the original Billy Bunter stories, and there was a minority of viewers who do not share the view that the stories were worthy of television portrayal.' The *Daily Sketch*, a right-wing tabloid, was more succinct, calling the programme 'dull, dated, boring'. But for many children it was an irresistible draw, above all when the gimlet-eyed form-master Mr Quelch (initially played by Kynaston Reeves) uttered the irresistible words, 'Bend over, you wretched boy,' or when Bunter's sadistic, snooty chums (Harry Wharton, Bob Cherry, Hurree Jamset Ram Singh) tormented their fat, nouveau-riche schoolfellow. Did it worry them that Bunter was played by a padded-out 29-year-old actor (Gerald Campion, in his forties by the time of the last series in 1961)? Or that the world of Greyfriars School – first created in 1910 in the boys' weekly *Magnet* by the prolific, indefatigable

Frank Richards, who now wrote the television scripts – was so infinitely removed from the experience of most children? Probably not. Back in 1940, George Orwell had famously accused Richards of snobbishness, diehard Toryism and being stuck in an Edwardian time warp. 'Human nature, Mr Orwell, is dateless,' Richards had replied. 'A character that lives is always up to date.'[13]

These japes at a minor public school hit the screen just as the sheep-and-goats selection system for state secondary education came for the first time under serious, dispassionate scrutiny. Philip Vernon, professor of Educational Psychology at London University's Institute of Education, published in the *Times Educational Supplement* in early 1952 a two-part investigation of 'Intelligence Testing', based on experiments carried out under his direction. His key finding was that 'systematic coaching' made a significant difference to a child's chances in the eleven-plus exam, and for several weeks the *TES* was flooded with letters, one of which – from James Hemming in Isleworth – castigated the prevailing system as 'unscientific, uneducational, wasteful, unjust, and brutal'. The *TES* itself, in a measured editorial, noted how intelligence tests, as set in the eleven-plus, had 'seemed a heaven-sent technique for approximating to that "equality of opportunity" which the nation is pledged to offer its children', in that 'the tests, it was declared, measured potentialities that were proof against the accidents of birth and early fortune'. The paper did not call, though, for their abolition as such, but rather for more emphasis in selection to be placed on 'attainment tests' (in English and maths) and what it called 'scaled teachers' estimates'. The controversy eventually reached *Picture Post*, though its reporter, Fyfe Robertson, embodiment of Scottish common sense, somewhat evasively concluded that 'when we can manage to give every child the best schooling we can devise, life will do the selecting better than any mathematically-minded educational psychologist'.[14]

In the early 1950s it was not just Labour Party policy that was hostile to tripartism (grammars, secondary moderns and thin-on-the-ground technical schools), but a gathering mood on the left as a whole. Typical was Wilfred Fienburgh, who argued in the *New Statesman* in March 1953 that there had been no advance in equal opportunity since Butler's 1944 Act – largely because the system was too 'chancy', though he also emphasised the continuing existence of private education. Added to the chanciness, he declared, was an inherent cruelty: 'We grade our material at the age of eleven when it is acutely conscious of itself as a person, is aware that parents are anxious, and is, above all, very alive to the chances of success or failure.' Accordingly, 'what we need are schools catering for all the children in a neighbourhood regardless of wealth *or* ability'. In similar vein, he called for public schools to be turned into 'national residential sixth forms' available to all.

An editorial in the same issue, describing the British school system as 'the outstanding example in the Western world of educational privilege', supported only the first half of Fienburgh's prescription and demanded the end of the eleven-plus: 'It is socially pernicious. Taking the Grammar school cap is a more potent emblem of privilege than the old school tie. Public school snobbery affects a few children. The snobbery of the local Grammar school sets the tone in every city and country.' Accordingly, the comprehensive school – of which there were precious few yet in existence – was the answer. Many Labour-controlled local education authorities (LEAs) were in fact still doubtful, even in some cases hostile, but not so the Labour majority on the education committee of the London County Council. 'It aims neither at levelling up nor levelling down, but at giving every child full opportunity to develop according to its own ability,' declared (in April 1952) Helen Bentwich, until recently chairman of the committee, about the LCC's ambitious plan for comprehensives. 'The understanding between workers by hand and brain which must exist when they are educated in the same schools is the best of all preparations for the socialist society. The comprehensive schools, as planned by the L.C.C., will be schools of which any community may rightly be proud.'

The defence of grammars came partly from the left – 'it's part of the folklore of the old Labour Party that the great thing was to give our boys a chance to go to grammar schools,' the sociologist A. H. Halsey would recall with some exasperation – but inevitably mainly from the right. A key figure was the new Education Minister, Florence Horsbrugh. Generally ineffective at resisting Treasury pressure to squeeze education spending (a particularly ill-timed squeeze given that the 'bulge' babies were just starting to enter the school system), she was not helped by her exclusion from the Cabinet for almost two years. Even so, for all her lack of clout and charisma, she was recognised as a conscientious minister, and in October 1952 she unambiguously told the Conservative Party Conference that she saw 'no educational advantage in the comprehensive schools that could possibly outweigh the disadvantages in connection with their enormous size'. A motion deploring any attempt to replace tripartism with comprehensive schools was duly passed, with only one dissenter.[15]

The spring-term edition of *Spur*, the magazine of Raynes Park County Grammar School in Surrey, offers a nice glimpse of a grammar in 1952. 'House Notes', written by the respective house captains, had all the usual phrases – 'most encouraging . . . to be congratulated . . . untiring work . . . steady effort . . . cups not won by one boy alone, however brilliant he may be . . .' – but it is the Chess Club notes, written by a teacher, that take the eye:

> There is a regrettable tendency among juniors towards playing too much chess. The problems of playing in form rooms were partially solved by including two lunch-time meetings during the week, besides the normal Friday evening meeting. But this for some was not enough, for I have found people playing chess at any odd moment during the day in any odd corner. I welcome their enthusiasm but it must yield not only to School discipline, but also to the discipline of good chess playing. If the standard of chess in the School is to improve, players must learn from previous errors or miscalculations, and the only way to do this is to employ the discipline of thinking before you move, and that means both thinking before you make your move and thinking of what your opponent is planning. And the atmosphere of the 'odd moment' is not conducive to this sort of planning.

The same teacher also regretted 'a continued lack of original verse' being volunteered at meetings of the Poetry Society. 'The Society may show outward forms of prosperity,' he reflected, 'but the lack of original verse is a sign of serious decay.'

Irrespective of a certain narrowness and joylessness in their pursuit of excellence, as well as making their own sheep-and-goats division at an early stage, the grammar schools were still the generally favoured destination – if only for negative reasons. 'Teachers themselves, and particularly middle-class parents, would do almost anything to stop their children from having to go to secondary modern schools,' D. S. Morris of the National Foundation for Education Research starkly told a meeting of the Notts Federation of Parent-Teacher Associations in April 1953. 'As things are arranged at the moment, and speaking as a parent, I don't blame them.' Rosalind Delmar was one of many children for whom the pressure was truly on. In 1952 in her final year at a junior school near Redcar, mainly for the children of steelworkers, she had a mother not only soured by the experience of not having been allowed to go to secondary school herself, but also clinging to 'her hope for a schoolteacher daughter who would look after her in her old age'. Moreover, in the school itself, 'work was geared towards the eleven-plus with weekly tests in spelling, maths, grammar'. In the event, only four (including Delmar) passed. So too at a London primary, where in the early 1950s a young, progressively minded black teacher, Beryl Gilroy, encountered a martinet of the old school. 'Mrs Burleigh thought I was endangering the children's eleven-plus potential and wanted the five-year-olds streamed into good, bad and indifferent,' she recalled in her remarkable memoir, *Black Teacher* (1976). 'Her mind was hermetically sealed.'

The chances are that most primaries had a Mrs Burleigh or two – someone who 'disliked most children' and in remembrance stood out 'like some figure in a stern, admonitory religious painting'. Gilroy 'often saw the Devil in Mrs Burleigh's face and frequently heard him in her voice':

> She never once treated me as a colleague and credited me with any kind of teaching know-how. This didn't worry me a bit. As far as her teaching ideas were concerned, they reminded me of a donkey-christening back home [British Guiana].
>
> The poor donkey was tethered to a post by three or four feet of stout rope. Each time its name was shouted it was whacked with a stick. After a dozen or so blows, the donkey reacted to the sound, and it was assumed that it understood its name. In like manner these children were verbally tethered to their seats and punished by smacks, jibes and sneers for breaking Mrs Burleigh's rules. No parent, as far as I knew, ever protested. Like their children they accepted the punishment as an act of God. Some parents even praised her strictness but to me she was simply a bullying adult.

Moreover, with or without a Mrs Burleigh, most schools tended to be authoritarian places that seldom encouraged parental involvement, let alone interference or criticism. There is a strikingly nervous, even apprehensive tone to a May 1952 diary entry by Judy Haines in Chingford. 'Ione [aged five] forgot her skipping rope and was tearful,' she recorded one hot Thursday:

> I promised to bring it at playtime and since Pamela [her younger daughter, not yet at school] had a fruit pop and it is a scorching day, took Ione one. I felt very guilty being in playground and worse when I caught echo of a grown-up's remark, 'You've just had your milk. What will teacher say?' I hung around and felt better when I saw from the park Ione go back into school quite confidently. Pamela and I went to meet her though, as if there had been any bother I wanted to apologise and clear the air. But Ione had just dumped the fruit pop before returning from play (she said she knew I wouldn't want her to eat before dinner and couldn't find a cool place) and all was well. I bought them another one each and was so relieved.[16]

'A dirty red street of huddled little houses jammed together in the bricky wastes of Oldham,' was how Blanche Street struck the *Daily Mirror*'s William Connor (aka 'Cassandra') in June 1952. Living at no. 7 with his wife and two sons was the 39-year-old Frank Benson, a cotton spinner in the Royton Mill, but working only three days a fortnight. 'All my points for last month's sweet ration were unused,' explained Mrs Benson about the sharp drop in their standard of living as a result of the slump in the Lancashire cotton industry. 'The kids ask for them, but I simply cannot afford sweets. Eggs we will soon have to do without, although I managed to get six last week. We have had to cut out biscuits and cakes or things like jellies and fruit which the children are especially fond of.' Connor then asked her husband what he did with his time:

> He was sitting there looking strangely tired and the question seemed at first to puzzle him.
>   'What did you do *yesterday* morning, for instance?'
>   'Well, I read the paper.'

'Did you help with the washing up?'

His wife laughed a little and said: 'I haven't let him do that yet!'

'Well, what DID you do?'

'I helped her with washing the clothes – the heavier stuff, you know.'

'Anything else?'

Benson looked around gloomily and then said brightly: 'Oh, yes. I mended the step-ladders.'

Their plight was not unusual, for that summer 33 per cent of spinning operatives in Lancashire, and 22 per cent of weaving operatives, were either unemployed or on short time. 'Widespread unemployment, but amazing cheerfulness,' another visiting journalist remarked to a union leader, Archie Robertson of the Oldham Cardroom Association. 'Cheerfulness?' Robertson replied. 'And what were you expecting then? When did you hear of Lancashire folk not being cheerful?'

A young researcher, Peter Townsend, paid a more protracted visit – probably in September, not long before the situation started to ease – and found that 'relatively few of the unemployed in Lancashire have applied for national assistance'. This was partly due to 'ignorance or misunderstanding about the regulations', but also reflected 'a strong reluctance on the part of many people to apply for "charity", as they still tend to regard it'. He attached some revealing case-study notes:

> Parent-family in no position to help her, and her savings were sufficient only to help her in the first month of unemployment. Obviously a little ashamed to go to public authorities for help because of her two illegitimate children. *(Unemployed woman, late twenties)*
>
> She now receives national assistance, about 40s a week but delayed seeking it and feels ashamed that she has to have it. 'As soon as I start work fully I'm going to start paying insurance contributions. You have to tell the public assistance people so much of your affairs. It's like charity too.' She has reduced spending on the meat ration, on clothes, coal and household incidentals. She has stopped her former practice of going to the cinema three or four times a week but refuses to stop going to local football matches (costing her 1s 9d a visit plus fares). *(Woman on short time, two daughters)*

All expenditure stopped on sweets, 'luxuries' such as ham and fresh fruit. The man changed from cigarettes to smoking a pipe. An effort to maintain spending on necessary clothing for the girl at school was made and also on an occasional visit to the cinema. A small amount is spent on a budgerigar and a dog. (*Unemployed couple with daughter and dependent mother*)

The sense of self-respect ran deep. In the words of a 37-year-old widow, who went without proper food to ensure that her 11-year-old daughter had as much as possible, but who was determined to delay getting what she called 'public assistance' as long as she could: 'I'd have to be on my beam-ends before doing that.'[17]

Inevitably this recession, coming after seven surprisingly prosperous years, provoked much internal conflict and recrimination among the leaders of the different sections of the Lancashire cotton industry. The man with the unenviable job of banging heads together was Sir Raymond Streat, chairman of the Cotton Board since 1940. Perceiving overproduction as the curse of the world industry as a whole, he was largely responsible for initiating and organising the International Cotton Textile Industry Conference, held at Buxton in September and specifically intended to try to avoid a repeat of 1930s-style Japanese competition. Streat's attitude towards the Japanese was moderate, unemotional and constructive – quite unlike that of one increasingly prominent figure in the industry. This was the short, aggressive, ambitious, bull-like Cyril Lord, who by this time was in his early forties and, in addition to a notable business in Northern Ireland, owned three spinning and three weaving mills in Lancashire. 'The leaders of the trade here seem to be just flotsam and jetsam,' Lord told a press conference in July, prompting Streat to arrange a face-to-face meeting. 'I went to see the little man at his astonishing headquarters at No. 1 Harley Street,' he recorded afterwards. 'The conversation was completely devoid of any rationality. He was constitutionally unable to listen to me and there was nothing to do but listen to him until the time came to go.' Lord was especially scornful, in public as well as private, of Streat's decision to extend an invitation to the Japanese, and he found a powerful ally in the *Daily Express*. 'My Friends the Japs by – Sir Raymond,' was a typical headline in Beaverbrook's finest. Lord was also critical of Streat for not making a better fist of his representations to government, but here there was an immovable block in the form of Peter Thorneycroft, President of the Board of Trade. 'No government can in fact sustain your industry unless you yourselves put yourselves into the best competitive situation,' he almost brutally told Cotton Board members in October. 'The Government has no feather-bed to offer you and very little shelter in the harsh winds of competition which are blowing through the world today.'[18]

Streat, unlike Lord, had a sense of perspective, and knew that the slump had a variety of immediate causes – including not just increasing Japanese competition, but also Korean War stockpiling, import controls in Australia and untimely price-fixing arrangements by the Yarn Spinners' Association. But what no one, including Streat, knew was whether it was just a deeply unpleasant blip or the herald of long-term, irreversible decline. 'Cotton is far from finished and it may well be a power in the export field again,' stoutly declared the *Oldham Chronicle* in July. 'We have had slumps and booms many times before. Cotton will be the staple industry in this area for years to come ...' Clearly, though, there was work to be done if Thorneycroft's bracing yardsticks were to be met. The modernisation of machinery and buildings still had a long way to go; productivity had increased only marginally since the war; and the sociologist Ferdynand Zweig depicted a workforce 'eager to keep to their traditional ways of doing a job and their traditional standards of performance, such as the "four looms to a weaver system"'. Nor, according to a US productivity team that toured the industry in 1952, was conservatism confined to the workers. Not only were 'large elements of both management and labour dominated by an inertia which prevents them from seeing the future clearly', but 'their main effort at the moment seems to be directed towards the protection of the least efficient producers and the preservation of antiquated arrangements'.

The obvious solution was economies of scale involving the integration of spinning, weaving and dyeing. But for many small, specialist firms in Lancashire, in small, tight-knit towns like Nelson or Rochdale, the prospect of becoming part of a large group was still unthinkable. Yet arguably the Lancashire cotton industry was doomed whatever it (or even the government) did or did not do. Such anyway is the fatalistic view of its most authoritative historian, John Singleton, who in his overview of the post-war years contends that 'the industry's failure to modernise its fixed capital stock and to reform its working practices could be seen as the product, not of managerial slackness, but of a judicious assessment of the long-term state of demand'. He adds that 'Lancashire's self-confidence had been shattered by the experiences of the 1920s and 1930s, and the events of the 1940s and 1950s failed to persuade its businessmen that there was any alternative to the further contraction of the industry'.[19] Pessimism, in short, was an entirely rational response, and ultimately the question was how best to manage decline. Of course, for those depending on the mills for their livelihoods, it was rather harder to take the Olympian view.

From an even more Olympian perspective, transcending Lancashire's parochial concerns, the 1952 textiles crisis was a clear signal that it was time to stop privileging the great nineteenth-century export staples – coal, cotton, steel – and instead start prioritising the new, scientific, high-tech industries that could realistically be seen as having a future in the twenty-first century. Indeed, the historian David Edgerton has forcefully argued that the British economy was *already* by the 1950s far more technological in character than has generally been assumed, especially with defence production (including for export) running at unprecedentedly high peacetime levels. These Cold War years were, he claims, dominated by 'the search for what might be called technological security' – a search that involved massive expenditure by central government on military research laboratories. For those brought up on the familiar trope – Victorian heyday, inter-war trauma, post-war inexorable decline – it is a reading that offers a salutary counter-perspective, even though Edgerton perhaps exaggerates when he dubs the Britain of these years as a 'warfare state' rather than a welfare state.

'Science was big in the 1950s,' the poet Hugo Williams has recalled about his boyhood. 'First there were mottled celluloid fish, magnets, Chinese water-flowers, the drinking bird, the diving man, Meccano, metal puzzles, balsa wood, the smell of "dope". Glitterwax was so modern after austerity Plasticine. Then there was Silly Putty (in a mottled egg), Slime, Mud and that stuff in tubes for making your own balloons ...' Son of a distinguished actor-playwright, young Hugo probably did not have Formica in his kitchen at home. Millions, though, did experience the wonders of the brightly coloured, labour-saving, recently developed plastic laminate in the course of the decade. 'Lucky the mother whose table is Formica-topped,' extolled an advertisement in the September 1951 edition of *My Home*. 'No need to scrub – one wipe with a cloth and it's clean.' Five months later, on 23 February 1952, came another sign of the popular lure of things scientific when the first issue of the boys' comic *Lion* featured on its front page 'Outlaw of Space', an errant rival to *Eagle*'s Dan Dare. Or take motor racing. The 22-year-old Stirling Moss was one of *Picture Post*'s 'New Elizabethans'; Raymond Baxter was becoming the usual commentator on both radio and television; and the animated John Bolster, with handlebar moustache and deerstalker hat, gave the latest news from the pits. For Baxter, a suave figure who had been a Spitfire pilot in the war and never lost his schoolboyish enthusiasm for the latest gadgetry, the task of spreading the word about technological prowess, preferably British, would always be more than just a job.[20]

Another of Baxter's regular assignments was the Farnborough Air Show, which in September 1952 had everyone, in Mollie Panter-Downes's words, 'caught up in a wave of excitement and optimism about what was going on over their heads'. It was a dramatic enough week. 'All-day wait – then came THE BANG,' headlined the *Mirror*'s report for Tuesday the 2nd:

> Late this evening, when many spectators had gone off home, Neville Duke, flying Britain's new Hawker Hunter 'super-priority' fighter, provided THE BANG – the noise made when an aircraft breaks through the sound barrier.
>
> We had waited for it since the ban on faster-than-sound flying at the show was lifted.
>
> And the bang that Neville Duke gave us was a MAGNIFICENT BANG, one of the experts here said.

Four days later, a Saturday crowd of 120,000 watched aghast as a prototype de Havilland 110 jet fighter broke up after going through the sound barrier, with an engine ploughing through spectator stands and a car park. The test pilot John Derry, his observer and 26 spectators were killed, including 14-year-old Ray Lord from Wallington. 'Raymond was a grand kid,' a family friend told the press. 'He wanted to be an aircraft designer.' Next day was the last scheduled day, and, despite the tragedy and heavy rain, the show went on, with 150,000 attending. 'I shall press on as usual,' Duke said before he took off in the supersonic Hawker Hunter and again went through the sound barrier. On Monday he received a short, heartfelt note from Churchill: 'Accept my salute.'

The glamour of aviation – typified by the ambition of many adolescent girls to become air hostesses – was seemingly matched by a vibrant, successful British aircraft industry. 'As the weird and wonderful prototypes flashed across the sky above the placidly earthbound cows munching in the quiet Hampshire pastures,' reflected Panter-Downes of her inspiriting Farnborough experience, 'the ordinary English were enormously heartened by the feeling that the peculiar national inventive genius for machines, which created so much wealth in the steam age, is as good as ever in this uncomfortable atomic one.'[21] In fact, certainly as far as the civil-aviation side was concerned, some serious negatives were already apparent.[22] Several immediate post-war projects had ground to a sticky, embarrassing halt, typified by the prestigious but fatally lumbering Bristol Brabazon; the industry was badly fragmented, with some 20 different aircraft companies; overly close government involvement, partly in the context of the main airlines (BOAC and BEA) being nationalised, meant an overemphasis on 'prestige' considerations as well as a tendency to featherbed; and, above all, in terms of matching the American aircraft industry, there was nothing like the huge, competitive domestic market that US manufacturers enjoyed. In practice, much rested on the fate of one particular pioneering British plane – a plane rushed through by de Havilland from drawing board to commercial operation in record-breaking time.

The Comet, the world's first passenger jet aircraft, entered service on 2 May 1952 with a flight from London to Johannesburg, though with several stop-offs on the way. An event that generated huge media attention and popular enthusiasm, it was the subject of the television documentary *Comet Over Africa* (1952), described by one member of the Viewing Panel as 'a memorable record of an historic occasion, that gave us all a great thrill'. It seemed that Britain had a world-beater – 'We may have ordered the market for a generation,' Lord Swinton, Minister of Materials, claimed in July after Pan Am had ordered ten Comets – and Panter-Downes soon afterwards at Farnborough unsurprisingly noted how every morning there were queues 'to clamber aboard the Comet'. Most pundits reckoned that the Comet had a lead of about three to four years, ie before the production of rival American jet planes, and a flurry of articles examined whether production difficulties would be sufficiently overcome for this window of opportunity, in terms of capturing world markets, to be exploited to the maximum. The question, however, that no one in the press raised was whether the Comet itself, for all its elegance and smoothness, was technically sound. The fact that there were fundamental doubts on the part of the Royal Aircraft Establishment (RAE) about the plane's ability to withstand metal fatigue – and that de Havilland, BOAC and the Ministry of Supply had between them connived to postpone exhaustive tests until after the plane's keenly awaited commercial launch – was known to few indeed.[23]

For a boy in the 1950s, if being an airline pilot seemed too nerve-racking, there was now the dream of becoming an atomic-energy engineer. 'Andrew is intelligent and go-ahead,' started a typically improving strip cartoon in the *Eagle*. 'He thinks there is a great future for Engineers in this Atomic Age.' Mary King in Birmingham, approaching the end of her life, found moral comfort in the new age. 'The first Atomic Power Heating apparatus was opened today at Harwell [the nuclear research station near Oxford],' she noted in November 1951. 'I cannot carry the details in my mind, but it is so good to hear of these wonderful researches by man being put to use for the good of man, and not fiendish War bombs.' She was only half right. Certainly there was a civil nuclear energy dimension to the unfolding technology – reflecting not so much a fanciful mirage of some golden age of cheap, limitless power as a pragmatic concern about the future of coal supplies in the context of significantly increasing electricity consumption – yet military considerations were paramount. 'The first small and impure billet was produced at Windscale,' Sir Christopher Hinton recorded in his diary in March 1952. The gifted, demanding Hinton had been charged soon after the war with the task of producing fissile material for bombs; the billet was of plutonium, with the first consignment travelling south the following month under police escort to Aldermaston.

On 3 October, more than three years after Russia had exploded its first atomic bomb, Britain belatedly exploded its own. Hinton in his unpublished memoirs blamed many people and factors for the lag – including the Ministry of Supply and the Treasury for recruitment problems, the Ministry of Works generally ('completely unsatisfactory at first'), and the general uselessness of Lord Portal as Controller of Atomic Energy for five and a half years from March 1946 – but in October 1952 the press reaction to the spectacular explosion off the Monte Bello Islands, complete with smoke plume topping out at 15,000 feet in the clear western Australian air, was one of elation. 'Today Britain is GREAT BRITAIN again – in the eyes of the world,' began the *Daily Mirror*'s front-page report: 'The orange-coloured flash of the explosion of Britain's first atomic bomb did more than signal the unleashing of a new and terrifying weapon of war. It changed a world still ruled by power politics. It signalled the undisputed return of Britain to her historic position as one of the great world powers. Today she stands alongside America and Russia in possessing not only the secret of the atomic weapon, but also the power to produce it.' Or, as the *Daily Mail* proudly put it, 'Those both at home and abroad who have written off Britain as a second-rate Power will have to revise their views.'[24]

This particular autumn, though, the application of science had a more immediate, domestic relevance. 'There's a war between manufacturers of soap powders now going on,' noted Gladys Langford towards the end of September. 'Lever Bros have launched a new powder "Surf" and send thro the post coupons to those on the voting list, which entitle the recipients to buy 1/11 size for 7d which only goes to show how much profit is made normally. Meanwhile Crossfield's – Persil manufacturers – advertise extensively and hold housewives' meetings & what not to popularise *their* production.' There was indeed a war. Tide, originally developed in the US by Procter & Gamble, had built up a strong share of the market in detergent powders since its British launch in 1950, and rival manufacturers were determined to pull it back – not least through the impending noisy launch (in November) of Daz, reputedly 'the most efficient washing product in the world'.

Tide, however, knew this was its time. 'Until Tide came in, it would have been absurd to talk of doing the weekly wash without rinsing,' ran part of a full-page advertisement in the *Mirror* three days after the news from Monte Bello. 'But you never had anything like Tide! It's something new in this world. It's not just a little better than other products. It's miraculously better!' The ad also featured a drawing of two young housewives looking at the washing. 'Look – It's *True*! Dazzling Clean! Without Rinsing!' says one. 'I'd *Never* Have Believed It!' responds the other. Meanwhile, an older woman looks on enviously and remarks: 'If Only We'd Had Tide In *My* Young Days!' But perhaps most expressive of all was the chorus at the foot of the ad, seemingly oblivious to the dangers of false consciousness, let alone reification:

Week after week millions of women see it – say it – sing it!
CLEAN! CLEAN! CLEANEST WASH OF ALL![25]

PART TWO

6

Not Much Here

'My father hadn't minded Lancashire,' Ian Jack recalled in the 1980s:

> The terraced streets shut my mother in, but my father, making the best
> of it, found them full of 'character'; men in clogs with Biblical names –
> Abram, Eli – and shops that sold tripe and herbal drinks, sarsaparilla,
> Dandelion and Burdock. He bought the *Manchester Guardian* and talked
> of Lancashire people as more 'go-ahead' than the wry, cautious Scotsmen
> of his childhood. Lancastrians were sunnier people in a damper climate.
> They had an obvious folksiness, a completely realised industrial culture
> evolved in the dense streets and tall factories of large towns and cities.
> Lancashire meant Cottonopolis, the Hallé Orchestra playing Beethoven
> in the Free Trade Hall, knockers-up, comedians, thronged seaside
> resorts with ornamental piers. In Fife, pit waste encroached on fishing
> villages and mills grew up in old market towns, but industry had never
> completely conquered an older way of life based on the sea and the land.

After twenty-two years in England, Harry Jack, a maintenance
engineer, took his family (including seven-year-old Ian) back to
Scotland in October 1952. They travelled by train. 'Red-brick
terraces with advertisements for brown bread and pale ale on their
windowless ends gave way to austere villas made of stone. The
wistfulness of homecoming overcame my parents as we crossed the
border; Lancashire and Fife then seemed a subcontinent distance
apart and not a few hours' drive and a cup of coffee on the motorway.'
After speeding across the Forth Bridge at dusk, they were met on the
platform by Harry's father-in-law:

Nobody kissed and nobody touched (we never did; did anybody there, then?), but my grandfather was pleased to see us. 'Come in, come in, you'll be hungry.' A refugee from the pits and now retired from his later work as a riveter's labourer, he lived as a widower at the top of an old house with crowstep gables and a pantile roof. Plates of chips and mutton-pies arrived at the table. The gas mantle was lit – plop! – while my mother took a torch and led me downstairs to the outside lavatory. Then I dozed on a makeshift bed as my parents talked about their journey, idly and endlessly as adults always did.

'Thon was a queer-like chap who got on at Preston. Him and his fancy socks and his meat-paste sandwiches.'

'Och but there was no harm in him. He was a cheery soul.'

'The English are great ones for their meat-paste, right enough.'

Next morning Ian woke to the noise of riveters drilling in the nearby shipyard and express trains whistling along the embankment by the sea. 'The smells of damp steam and salt, sweet and sharp, blew round the corner and met the scent of morning rolls from the bakery. Urban Lancashire could not compare with this and, like my mother, I never missed it.'[1]

It was different again at the Red Lion at Blaina, a south Wales town of about 8,000 with an ironworks and nearby collieries as its main sources of employment. In 1947, while the Jacks were still in Bolton, a Mass-Observation investigator embedded himself there and got to know the all-male regulars. Owen Williams, secretary of Blaina's rugby club, worked for the County Council at Abertillery, voted Liberal (the family tradition), and usually wore a sports jacket and grey flannel trousers: 'Call him sane or level-headed or anything you like but his general attitude towards life is reflected in his drinking habits. He drinks half pints when everybody else is drinking pints.' Jimmy Jones, a former miner and factory worker, was now on the dole, supposedly too ill to work, but did enough odd jobs to keep himself in plentiful beer. 'There is not much here except going to have a drink and a smoke,' he reflected. 'You can't go racing because there is not a track around here. I usually spend my time having a few drinks and meeting the boys.' Tom Wathan, an undertaker's assistant, was 'a strange-looking individual' never seen to smile, who sat for hours with his fat old spaniel in the corner beside the fireplace in the public bar and broke his taciturn silence only to tell lewd stories about his corpses. His reward was to be 'one of the privileged few who are allowed to stay after hours for a few bolters in the corridor'. Eli Curtis, a collier who doubled as a notably inefficient, unhygienic part-time barman, was handicapped as a drinker by his busy, purposeful wife being in charge of his pay packet: 'Inv [Investigator] has watched him sitting in the public bar with an empty half-pint glass in front of him for the whole of the afternoon. He just sits still gazing ahead with a cow-like expression on his face. He prides himself that he can sit the whole afternoon and think of absolutely nothing . . .' Bert Lawrence, a boilerman in the pits, was king of the darts board: 'As soon as he comes into the pub he looks around for prospective players. Bert drinks pints, but when playing darts tips his half-pint winnings into his pint glass.' Evan Davis, surface foreman at the colliery, had a boxer's face, permanently played the tough guy and as a special treat would bring his quiet, much more intelligent wife to the Lion on a Saturday night to drink a glass of bottled beer. Gwn, the milkman, had a pint every afternoon at the end of his round, still wearing his tie and full-length brown overalls: 'He seems to be a chain smoker and Inv has always seen him with a Woodbine sticking out of the corner of his mouth.' And Dai Minton, the dentist, had a red face, a glass eye, always kept his overcoat on, and drank heavily, sometimes becoming bad-tempered and vindictive. 'However much people dislike going to him as a dentist because of his drinking habits it would be difficult for them to go anywhere else and probably more costly.'[2] Were they lives of quiet desperation? The Inv did not say. But they were real lives lived in real time in a real, intensely circumscribed world.

Women also had lives, and in their 1951 survey, *English Life and Leisure*, B. Seebohm Rowntree and G. R. Lavers included a decent sprinkling among their adult case histories (some of them supplied by Ferdynand Zweig):

Miss R. is a copy-typist in a large office. She is 21 or so, and lives in a bed-sitting room. She finds it difficult to make both ends meet but is happy because she is free, because she has plenty of boyfriends and plenty of entertainment. She is quite promiscuous and sees no harm in it. Indeed, she doesn't see why people make so much fuss about it; it just seems natural.

She is most of all interested in 'boys,' then in clothes, then in dancing and cinemas. She hopes to marry one day and settle down, but not for a long time.

She reads a daily paper and an evening paper, and always the *News of the World*. She doesn't bother about radio except sometimes the Light Programme.

She doesn't gamble usually, but sometimes in the office they put up 1s each and back a horse just for fun.

Not a churchgoer. She thought the very idea funny. 'Me – like all the stuffy people in their best clothes? That's a good one. Fat lot of difference it seems to make to them anyway. No, not me.'

Miss Z. was formerly Mrs X. But she divorced her husband and resumed her maiden name. She is a rather dull and disillusioned woman of about 35. She divorced her husband for cruelty after he had beaten her with a dog whip in a drunken fit, and had been found by the neighbours with both hands around her throat shaking her.

Miss Z. works in a factory and is happy enough there, but is lonely in the evenings in her bed-sitting room. She is fed up with men and has enough of women all day.

She does a football pool coupon, and most days has a shilling or two on a horse.

Not interested in religion. 'Went to church once too bloody often I did,' she says, referring to her wedding.

Drinks two or three glasses of Guinness each night on her way home from work. Is a chain smoker.

Her world really has just come to pieces with the failure of her marriage. She mopes because there is nothing she really wants, or that really interests her except a home and a husband, and she knows she is too dull and unattractive to have a chance of a second marriage.

Mrs N. is a working-class housewife of about 45. She has three sons. Her husband always gives her his wage packet intact. She allows him £1 for beer and tobacco, another 10s for five dinners in his works canteen, and 5s for fares. She is left with 'less than £4 10s' for all household expenses, and that includes 10s family allowances. They live in a council house and Mrs N. says that her whole life is 'scraping and pinching to make do'. She can afford no recreations for herself – no smoking or drinking, although Mr N. sometimes brings her a bottle of beer from the public house.

She cannot afford to go to the cinema except as a very rare treat, and as for going to church she says she spends 'enough time on my knees scrubbing floors without kneeling on Sundays'. She adds, 'Anyway, what good does it do?'

She likes listening to the radio and her greatest joy is sometimes during the daytime, when everyone is out, to make a cup of tea and sit down and listen to *Woman's Hour*.

Mrs B. is a widow of about 55–60. She is in full-time employment as caterer-cook at a small industrial canteen. She earns a good living and is able to save the whole of a small pension as well as part of her wages towards the time when she cannot work. She is a simple woman with no enemies, no close friends and few relatives. She is not unhappy, having a small comfortable flat and enjoying her work.

She does not drink or gamble but smokes occasionally.

She listens a good deal to the radio and goes occasionally to the cinema. She reads novels from the 2d library and reads the *News of the World*.

She says she is better fed now than she has ever been in her life and her wages are bigger than her husband ever earned. He died some years ago and she speaks of him quite impersonally.

Went to chapel as a girl but has not been for years. When asked why not replied, 'Well, people used to go years ago. It's different now. I don't see I'm any worse for it.'

Rowntree and Lavers also included the case histories of some teenage girls. 'Miss F. has a great desire to "make the best of" herself and to marry someone who can give her a "nice" home,' they noted of a 17-year-old who was the oldest of five daughters and worked the telephone switchboard in a solicitor's office. 'She is fond of children and hopes to have two of her own. She thinks it is unfair on the children to have more than two as it reduces their material prospects.'[3]

So many individual lives, so many individual fates – inevitably it makes one wonder about the validity of terms like 'class', 'culture' and 'community'. Yet at the level of generalisation, one can plausibly argue that in some sense British society was 'frozen' during the ten or so years after the war, that there was for most people, following the shake-up of the war, an instinctive retreat to familiar ways, familiar rituals, familiar relations, all in the context of only very slowly lifting austerity and uncomfortably limited material resources. The continuing bombsites in city centres could hardly have been a more visually eloquent symbol of this protracted hiatus pending a barely imagined onslaught from the – far from unwelcome – forces of change. This was the final authentic phase of what before long would come to seem a distant, irrecoverable epoch of urban civilisation, stretching back to the late nineteenth century and rent asunder from the mid-1950s.

7

A Different Class of People

'And then there was this business of Britain's class system,' recalled Doris Lessing about leaving Rhodesia in 1949 and coming to London. 'It shocked me – as it does all colonials . . .' One day she and an ex-RAF friend from Rhodesia went into a pub in Bayswater: 'It was the public bar. We stood at the counter, ordered drinks. All around the walls, men sat watching us. They were communing without words. One got up, slowly, deliberately, came to us, and said, "You don't want to be 'ere. That's your place," pointing at the private bar. We meekly took ourselves there, joining our peers, the middle class.' The following year another young writer, Dan Jacobson, arrived from South Africa and was struck by 'the appetite the English had for "placing" not only a stranger to the country like myself, but perhaps even more pressingly those who were not strangers, who were native to the islands, and whose hands, faces, accents, clothes and bearing would, if studied with sufficient attention, reveal valuable items of information about them: the most important of these, inevitably, being the social class to which they belonged'. He added that it was a 'kind of detective work' that reminded him of 'an insect stroking an object ahead of it with its feelers, or of a cat sniffing a person's shoes' – and that the process reflected a society 'deeply, obsessively divided by a host of invidious, criss-crossing "social indicators" that would go a long way towards determining relations between its members'.

It was indeed a society of class consciousness – 90 per cent of the 11,000 respondents to a 1950–51 questionnaire printed in the *People* unhesitatingly assigned themselves to a social class – and class separation. Janet Madge in 1948 investigated 'Some Aspects of Social Mixing in

Worcester' and, as a result of fieldwork in the city's social clubs, sports clubs and societies generally, concluded that there was 'little evidence of inter-class association'. It was also a society that functioned along deeply entrenched hierarchical lines: when Tom Bottomore in the early 1950s immersed himself in the voluntary organisations of 'a small English country town' unhelpfully called 'Squirebridge', he found a significant degree of correlation between occupational status and status in those organisations. The first flowering was now appearing of what would become the golden age of British empirical sociology, and a particularly rich study was that made by Margaret Stacey of Banbury. 'The techniques of acceptance or rejection are subtle,' she wrote about the frontiers between the classes in a town pervaded by class. 'You must possess appropriate characteristics: occupation, home, residence area, income (suitably spent), manners, and attitudes. You must know or learn the language and the current private "passwords" of the group. You must be introduced. If you fail in these particulars you will simply be "not known". Nothing is said or done. The barrier is one of silence.' Moreover, she went on: 'This is also true for those who are dropped for some offence against the code of their class; they may never discover what their alleged offence is and certainly have no chance of defence. They simply find that invitations cease and backs are turned at the bar.'[1]

Even a list can only hint at the ubiquity of class. 'A working man speaks a language of his own, while the middle-class man generally speaks the King's English,' asserted Ferdynand Zweig in his 1952 survey *The British Worker*. 'As soon as a man opens his mouth everybody knows to which class he belongs.' At home, towels were a reliable status indicator (Alan Bennett ruefully compared his childhood towels – 'thin, ribbed, the nap long since gone' – with the almost unimaginably luxurious 'thick fleecy' variety), while the middle class only reluctantly abandoned its pre-war habit of having the breakfast marmalade spooned in and out of special pots each morning in order to conceal its shop-bought origins. 'Dinner in the evening is probably still the mark of the upper-middle and upper class,' T. H. Pear remarked in his sound but disappointingly bland 1955 survey *English Social Differences*. 'For the working class, the substantial evening meal is "tea," whether "high" (including meat) or not.' The middle class went to bed appreciably later than the working class, with widespread complaints in Birmingham in 1949, when BBC television began its Midland service, that 8.00 p.m. was too late for the start of evening programmes, that indeed the first main one would not have finished before normal bedtime. Audience research revealed in 1950 that only 25 per cent of viewers with incomes of £1,000 or more approved of music-hall programmes, against 65 per cent of viewers with incomes of less than £350; as for listening habits, BBC figures in 1947 showed that on a typical evening, the Third Programme was heard at some point by 24 per cent of the upper middle class, 12 per cent of the lower middle and only 3 per cent of the working class. At the cinema, according to a detailed study done in Wales, the working class almost invariably stuck to the stalls, the middle class to the more expensive balcony. So too with other leisure pursuits. Long-established climbing clubs had vigilant gatekeepers to exclude the proles; tennis clubs were notorious for the face having to fit; athletics was dominated by the cult of the well-bred, well-behaved amateur; the social chasm between rugby union and rugby league was absolute; and in the still Victorian, two-class (amateurs and professionals) world of cricket, there was a deathless announcement over the tannoy at Lord's one Saturday in May 1950 when a young Middlesex pro was walking out to bat against Surrey: 'Ladies and Gentlemen, a correction to your scorecards. For "F.J. Titmus", please read "Titmus, F.J.".'[2]

Of course, nothing stood entirely still. 'The differences between the working class and middle class are becoming less pronounced,' was the optimistic view of Zweig in 1952:

> The workers' security of employment and earning capacity are constantly improving; education is rapidly reducing the differences between the standards of the classes, and standard English is becoming more widespread, especially on account of the wireless ... The classes now dress more alike than they used to, and it is becoming difficult to distinguish a workman from a black-coated worker on Sundays. The income differences between classes are also growing smaller, and many craftsmen earn more than clerks and officials. The differences in the sizes of families are diminishing as well; birth control is more and more being practised in poor homes. Council houses too are getting rid of the class barriers which formerly existed between districts.

There was also a generational dimension. 'Compare the young couple in a prefab or a post-war Council house with their working-class parents,' Michael Young wrote in his 1951 essay 'Is This The Classless Society?':

> Observe the disappearance of the parlour as a room, seldom used, where precious photographs, old children's encyclopaedias and horsehair shoes were placed on show. Look at the furniture obtained on hire purchase, almost indistinguishable from that in the larger privately-owned houses. See the gadgets in the kitchen and the use made of the opener for the tins, of mass-produced foods which flow endlessly into bigger as well as smaller houses. Notice the collection of crockery and cutlery, and the similar ways in which the table is now laid for meals. See the radios in the kitchen waiting for *Woman's Hour* and the television sets sprouting out of the roofs in all quarters of the town. Note the occasional Penguin or library book in the corner of the shelf. Watch the son in his pin-stripe drinking his light ale in the Saloon Bar, and his girl-friend sipping a gin and orange, while down the road in the Public Bar father takes his pint of wallop and mother takes her Guinness.

One factor that neither Zweig nor Young mentioned was the war. Some historians have seen it as the supreme agent of social change in modern Britain – thereby ignoring the overwhelming extent to which social and cultural life reverted after 1945 to familiar patterns. Just as the war was ending, a young Donald James (the future writer Donald James Wheal) had a chat with his father:

> 'We're working class,' I remember him saying. 'For the moment anyway. It might not look it but we're on the move. I think this war has got a lot of people on the move.'
> 'Because they've been bombed out?'
> 'I'm talking about the way people are beginning to think now. The different classes have all rubbed shoulders in this war, because of the bombs and evacuation, much more than they did in the last one. We'll all come out of this a bit different to what we were when we went in. The working classes have seen that upper-class people can be scared or brave, bright or dim, same as anybody else. And the upper classes are beginning to see that if the working classes *are* sometimes found keeping coal in the

bath, they don't do it by choice. They do it because the way they live, there's nowhere else to keep it.'

'Does that mean all these different classes are coming together?'

'It's a nice thought, but it's a lot to hope for.'

'Do you have to have a lot of money to be upper-class?' I asked him.

He shrugged. 'Not necessarily. Some people at Whitelands [a block of private flats in Chelsea where he was head porter] can hardly find enough for a Christmas tip for the porters. It's more than just money. It's a generation or two of education that kicks it off, Dee. Then it's the way the upper classes live. The way they dress, they way they talk. And then there's masses of customs, ways of saying things, for instance, that people like us don't know anything about. If you don't say the right thing, or don't say it in the right way, then you're not one of them. They laugh up their sleeves at you. I've seen it at Whitelands.'

'Is that how you know about all these things?'

'I don't.'

This shocked me. 'You mean, *you* make mistakes?'

'Dozens, I expect,' he said. 'But I don't know when I'm doing it. And if I tried too hard not to, I'd just make a fool of myself. That's the other catch – you mustn't try too hard.'

'I think it'd be better if we were all just one class.'

'It's never happened anywhere in the world yet, Dee. And it's not likely to. Class differences are here to stay. In themselves they're not important. It's the senseless part of class discrimination that hurts people.'

Judy Haines would surely have agreed. 'She would worry about what other people thought of her at times,' her daughter Pamela recalled in somewhat (if not totally) different 2007. 'She was self-conscious, I think, about coming from a rather poor background in Leyton, and moving to the slightly more "up market" Chingford she found people snooty and unfriendly. People tended to jostle for social position there after the war. North Chingford looked down on South Chingford, and South Chingford looked down on Walthamstow, which in turn looked down on Leyton!'

It was the same – but even more so – by the Cam. Ted Hughes (son of a small shopkeeper, Mexborough Grammar School) went up to Pembroke College in October 1951. 'Well aware of the class divisions that permeated the university,' according to his biographer, 'he held on all the more obstinately to the Yorkshire accent that would have been used to place him instantly.' Hughes himself subsequently attributed the destructive effect of university on him to 'social rancour'. Joan Rowlands (daughter of an engineering draughtsman, Stockport High School for Girls, later Joan Bakewell) went up to Newnham College the same month. 'It wasn't only my clothes that weren't right,' she recalled about the jumpers and cardigans lovingly knitted by her Manchester aunties:

> Neither was my accent – at elocution tests I had always scored badly. Living in Stockport, I hadn't got the hang of what supposedly correct speech sounded like. At Cambridge I could hear at once that some of the grander girls spoke in braying, honking tones that indicated class and money. Perhaps I should copy them, I thought. I made the switch instantly – and disastrously – affecting a sound locked somewhere at the back of my throat that emerged through tightened lips in a parody of speech that was in itself an affectation. I hadn't the confidence to be myself.

Two months later Alan Bennett (son of a Co-op butcher, Leeds Modern School) arrived at Sidney Sussex College for his entrance examination. 'That weekend was the first time I had ever come across public schoolboys in the mass, and I was appalled,' he remembered in his preface to *The History Boys*. 'They were loud, self-confident and all seemed to know one another, shouting down the table to prove it while also being shockingly greedy . . . Seated at long refectory tables, the walls hung with armorial escutcheons and the mellow portraits of Tudor and Stuart grandees, neat, timorous and genteel, we grammar schoolboys were the interlopers; these snobs, as they seemed to me, the party in possession.' Bennett added a coda on the radio in 2008: 'I also realised they had been better taught than I had and more individually taught. They were coming to this examination very much better prepared than I was and I thought that was unfair when I was 17. And that view has never changed.'[3]

In a world of limited social mobility and generally sharp inequalities of opportunity as well as wealth, it was a truism among many activators that access to grammar schools (which the 1944 Education Act had made free), followed by access to higher education, was the crux if significantly more of the working class – especially the semi-skilled and unskilled working class – were ever to have the chance fully to exercise their talents.

The figures were not altogether encouraging. A 10 per cent sample of those entering English grammar schools in 1946 revealed that the numbers of children of skilled and semi-skilled manual workers were broadly in line with the national occupational breakdown, but that the number of children of unskilled manual workers was less than half of what it 'should' have been; five years later, Hilde Himmelweit's sample of four grammars in Greater London showed the working class taking only 52 per cent of the places – some 20 per cent fewer than they 'should' have taken. Indeed, Ross McKibbin in his survey *Classes and Cultures: England 1918–1951* has concluded that 'in most parts of the country the proportion of free places won by working-class children was no higher in 1950 than in 1914, and in some places lower', adding that 'at no point did it equal the proportion won by working-class children in the 1920s'. Moreover, an authoritative 1954 report, *Early Leaving*, found that, once at grammar school, more than half of the children of unskilled or semi-skilled parents obtained fewer than three O-level passes and that a third did not stay on to the sixth form. As for the universities, their full-time student intake was gradually increasing – 70,405 in England and Wales in 1955, compared to 39,438 in 1937 – but the composition of that intake was obstinately out of line with a society that was about 70 per cent manual working class. Only 26 per cent of the men admitted to English universities in 1955 were sons of manual-working fathers, while of that year's male intake who had attended grammar schools, 64 per cent were sons of non-manual-working fathers (ie middle or upper class), 30 per cent were sons of skilled manual-working fathers, 5 per cent of semi-skilled, and just over 1 per cent of unskilled manual workers.

Predictably, the Oxbridge figures in 1955 were even further out of line: just 9 per cent of sons of manual workers in the Cambridge male intake and 13 per cent at Oxford. Both universities had, of course, a traditionally high public-school intake: in the academic year 1953–4, for instance, 36 out of the 74 blues awarded for football (association and rugby) and cricket went to public schoolboys. The public schools themselves were now clear for the time being of any political threat. 'Though the 1944 Education Act will no doubt greatly increase the amount of social mobility in Britain,' the sociologist David Glass remarked in 1954 in the generally downbeat introduction to his pioneering survey *Social Mobility in Britain*, 'there is an upper limit to that increase which the Act itself imposes by leaving the independent public school system substantially intact.' This was, he added, a fundamental inequality of educational opportunity 'likely to cut across the line of social mobility, blocking ascent to, and limiting descent from, the upper reaches of social status'. Still, as the Tory politician Angus Maude had put it the previous year, there had been since 1944 blessedly no longer any case to answer: 'So long as the clever child of poor parents is given a free place in a school which will develop his aptitudes to the full, the parent who is prepared to make sacrifices to provide his child with better-than-average schooling has as much right to spend his money on that as on a better television set.'[4]

'Another day of silence, listening to other people's trivialities – a dreadful hour at night when all the completely banal information gained from a visit of relatives is repeated and reviewed,' John Fowles wrote in his journal on 24 September 1949. The family tobacco firm was struggling, Fowles's parents were leading lives of genteel poverty, and vacations at 63 Fillebrook Avenue, Leigh-on-Sea, far from suited the intolerant Oxford undergraduate:

> Another appalling half-hour of talk. When screaming was close. Talk of the utmost banality, on prices of mattresses, on Mrs Ramsey's daughter who married a doctor in Montreal. A few comments are made on poetry. So hopeless to try and explain. They would never understand. No mention of art can ever be developed in case we are 'highbrow' – God, how I hate that word! . . . Then there is 'niceness' as a standard of judgement – God, how I hate that word, too! – 'a nice girl', 'a nice road'. Nice = colourless, efficient, with nose glued to the middle path, with middle interests, dizzy with ordinariness. Ugh! (*30 September 1949*)

Spasm of hate. Trying to listen to Mozart 465 Quartet when M [Fowles's incorrigibly talkative mother] seems, almost deliberately, to spoil it ... Finally (in the middle of the third movement) the decision that the decorations should be put up: 'Everyone else has put them up. The Farmers have put them up.' We're out of line, horror! Father, up till now a passive spectator, infuriates because he remains passive, i.e. instead of saying, 'Whenever! It can wait,' he mumbles, 'Better get it done,' and starts fiddling about with the streams of coloured paper. Partly I feel this is to annoy the highbrow in me. I switch off the wireless, and help in a savage, couldn't-care-less way. *(16 December 1949)*

Quai des brumes. Beautifully made film. Simple tragedy of sordidity, Kafkaesque despair ... I hate the damned condescension of Basil G [Basil Glover, a stockbroker neighbour, slightly older than Fowles], who says of the film 'one of them things about life in the raw' – in an amiable, tolerant, amused sort of way, as if life in the raw is something of a joke, and not real compared to the silly, conventional routine of a suburban semi-man-about-town. *(6 April 1950)*

In August 1951 – Oxford behind him, a writer's life still a distant dream – Fowles saw *The Cherry Orchard*. 'The characters seem mysterious, unreal, but their mood I recognise at once,' he reflected. 'It is the mood of this town – the ubiquity of futility; the genteel descent into oblivion, where no one is capable of saying what their heart says.'[5]

Fowles while at New College had presumably never encountered Madge Martin. The middle-aged wife of an Oxford clergyman, she enjoyed without any self-loathing – but not qualmlessly – a very middle middle-class way of life and culture. Take 1952. In January there was a car outing, including lunch at the department store Heelas ('always nice') in Reading; in February she and her husband took their annual holiday in Brighton, staying at the Old Ship Hotel; later that month there was a rather guilty coffee morning with Mrs Pegler on Ash Wednesday ('it was *not* a proper Ash Wednesday thing to do, and I ought to have called it off'); in March, another annual routine: the Ideal Home Exhibition at Olympia ('better than ever, with a beautiful décor, and lots of nice things to look at'); in August the annual holiday in Scarborough ('the food is *vastly* better, this year'); and in December a 53rd birthday that featured a visit to the Royal Opera House for *Swan Lake* ('a perfect birthday treat') and presents that included nylon stockings, blue table napkins, a blue scarf, yellow wool gloves, a silk cami-knicker, a Helena Rubinstein lipstick and a kitten cake tin. At year-end she looked back on her cultural highlights. *The African Queen, Singin' in the Rain, The Quiet Man* and *Limelight* were among the most enjoyable films, *Waters of the Moon* (seen at the Oxford Playhouse) and *Paint Your Wagon* (at the New Theatre) among 'the best plays'; while in terms of novels (probably mainly borrowed from circulating libraries), she gave four stars to Paul Gallico's *The Small Miracle* and three to Barbara Pym's *Excellent Women* and Stella Morton's *Turn by Days*, but only two to *Young Shoulders* by Ruby M. Ayres. The following February it was back to Brighton – ' "We've arrived – and to prove it, we're here," as Max Byfield [ie Bygraves], the radio comedian, always says' – and on a Tuesday in March 'another lovely, carefree day': 'Sometimes I think I lead too easy a life these days, but am certainly enjoying them, and feel relaxed. The mornings are always fully occupied, with house-work, shopping, and cooking, but I almost feel guilty and sluttish when I have my adored hour's rest, with my favourite radio programme, "Woman's Hour," and feel I should be doing more constructive work of some sort.' Still, a glimpse of a different life came in April with a trip to Essex for a wedding: 'Southend – though rather awful – wasn't half as common and noisy as we had imagined, but of course this is not "the season." '[6]

The 1951 census put the middle class at around 28 per cent of the population, compared with 22 per cent twenty years earlier. The middle class – in some ways best defined as 'not working class' in terms of attitudes, assumptions and self-image – included the professional class and the self-employed petite bourgeoisie (typified by small shopkeepers) that had emerged strongly in the nineteenth century, as well as the managerial class that had begun to flourish during the inter-war rise of the large corporation, not to mention the ever-expanding lower middle-class legions of clerks, salesmen, insurance agents and shop assistants. There were also, in terms of specific occupational trends, two rapidly growing sectors within the middle class: first, in the science/ technology/engineering fields, in part driven by the increasing number of non-arts university students (doubling between the 1930s and late 1940s), and second, in the public sector, especially social services and the nationalised industries. Overall, it was a far more salaried middle class than it had been, say, half a century earlier – and also appreciably more meritocratic in terms of both intake and subsequent performance evaluation.[7] But not entirely. 'Like many doctors' children, I had from my earliest schooldays come to look upon a medical qualification like a hereditary title,' the young hero notes at the outset of Richard Gordon's *Doctor in the House* (1952). The rest of the first chapter sees him going up to St Swithin's, the teaching hospital where his father had been, and undergoing interviews in which the crucial considerations are a) public-school background, b) ability to pay the fees and c) ability on the rugby field. He satisfies the first two criteria and fortunately, in a hospital already stuffed with forwards, is a wing threequarter and gets the nod.[8]

Perhaps inevitably, significantly more than 28 per cent of people perceived themselves as middle-class. In Geoffrey Gorer's extensive 1950–51 survey of what social class people saw themselves as belonging to, 2 per cent identified themselves as 'upper middle', 28 per cent as 'middle', and 7 per cent as 'lower middle', totalling 37 per cent. Within the sample, a realistic 31 per cent of men claimed to belong to one of those three non-working-class groups – compared to 41 per cent of women, with women (especially those over 45 who were unmarried or widowed) having a particular preference for 'middle'. Gorer's findings were not wholly out of line with a British Institute of Public Opinion survey shortly before. Here, 6 per cent claimed to be 'upper middle', 27 per cent 'middle', and 15 per cent 'lower middle', totalling 48 per cent, but this time, men were almost as likely as women to allow themselves a questionable self-ascription. Still, as most respondents would probably have replied if confronted by the occupationally classified census figures, if you felt you were middle-class, then you were middle-class.

So, no doubt, it was in 1948 when Mass-Observation asked the largely middle-class members of its panel to say something about their class identity:

I feel that anyone who has to consider prices and be economical at every turn cannot claim to belong to the 'Middle Classes'. This term seems in my mind to be synonymous with prosperity, not yet wealth, but with carefree liberality in all things costing money. On the other hand perhaps people who, like myself, had a secondary education or, like my husband, a University education, can be promoted to the ranks of the

Middle Classes, whatever the bank balance! *(Housewife, married to a civil servant)*

I am something of a hybrid. I was brought up middle-class and am financially in that position but my husband [a printer on a London newspaper] retains his working-class breeding which causes most (not all) middle-class people to drop us. *(Housewife)*

The professional upper middle class. There has never been much money in the family, and often very little indeed. But we consider we have obligations to fulfil rather than demands to make, which I think is a characteristic of this solid upper middle class. *(Retired schoolmistress)*

I consider that I belong to the middle class of society. It is so because I have had a Grammar School education, my home is in Pinner (semi-suburban), and amongst other people whose houses are furnished, and are kept in a good condition, as mine is ... Hammersmith is a typical working-class district, and it is from here that I make my comparisons. I see houses with torn, dirty (I know that this is almost unavoidable in London) curtains, broken windows mended with cardboard, for months not days, and generally slovenly appearance. Children are admitted into hospitals (mine in particular) with filthy clothes, skin, hair, etc. *(Student nurse)*

'I am not prejudiced,' Ms Pinner added, 'but cleanliness should come naturally.'

Predictably, a palpable pride, even smugness, shone at times through the replies:

Middle-class. Because I have a civic conscience, am internationally minded, have a feeling of responsibility towards people I don't know and time for enough leisure to be able to use my education (school, social and cultural) to a culturally satisfying end. *(Housewife)*

Middle-class. Because I am not an aristocrat, nor am I a plebeian. My parents were of excellent breeding, and we have as a family the attributes of what is known as the middle-class type – independence, hatred of charity, sans patronage and sans servility, delight in doing one's job thoroughly but with a soul that can rise above it occasionally without fanaticism. *(Housewife)*

The following year pride was redoubled when the panel was asked what value it attached to 'the continued existence of the middle classes':

> Today, when the 'workers' and their families have unprecedented power in this country, the 'middle class,' I think, have one special role: to try to maintain a high level of culture and social responsibility in the country at a time when the trend is in a downward direction. (*Journalist*)
>
> It would be almost impossible for any Government to carry on if the middle classes went out on strike on every possible pretext in the way the – so called – working classes do. (*Chartered accountant*)

'The chief value of the middle classes,' succinctly summarised a housewife, 'is that their way of life represents a standard which the working class can emulate.'[9]

Constantly bubbling up below these moral certainties, there was no doubting the anxiety, even the bitterness, of the newly servantless, highly taxed middle class during the immediate post-war period. 'How grievously,' wrote Roy Lewis and Angus Maude in their 1949 paean to threatened virtues, *The English Middle Classes*, did this group's 'cherished ambitions conflict both with the egalitarian philosophy and with recent political tendencies!' Crucially, this bitterness was not decisively assuaged by Churchill's return to power in 1951. 'The New Poor' was the title of a *Daily Express* series two years later, depicting an oppressively taxed middle class struggling 'to keep up appearances' and reliant on its unique qualities of 'standards, ambitions, self-discipline, education, and immense adaptability'. In truth, though, the middle class as a whole was not doing too badly during, say, the ten years after the war. Its numbers were expanding; the widespread introduction for more senior employees of tax-free 'perks' (such as subsidised mortgages, company cars, and insurance and pension contributions) significantly cushioned things; and in actual practice as opposed to theory, it was the children of professionals and businessmen who disproportionately won the free grammar-school places created by the 1944 Act, with those children about six times more likely to pass the eleven-plus than working-class children.[10]

Instead, if the middle class had any real cause to complain, it was the specifically *lower* middle class.[11] Their children were being squeezed out of free grammar-school places by more prosperous members of the middle class who had previously paid for those places; their salaries were increasing by appreciably less than the wages of manual workers in a full-employment economy; and, as Lewis and Maude pointed out, they were in equal measure despised by the working class for their social pretensions and subservience, looked down on by the upper middle class and cruelly mocked by the intelligentsia. 'Clerks had to live at an address approved by the bank, they had to ask permission from the bank manager to get married, they had to have "appropriate hobbies", and they were evaluated once a year for such qualities as their appearance, their demeanour, and their loyalty,' the sociologist Mike Savage has written on the basis of a close study of bank clerks. 'To be a salaried worker did indeed involve selling yourself: in this respect the perception of male manual workers was entirely accurate.'

A clutch of authentic lower middle-class – or anyway, self-ascribed lower middle-class – voices comes through among M-O's 1948 panel:

Lower-middle class. My income suggests nothing higher. Living in a working-class neighbourhood I find I am rejected, presumably because I don't call my neighbours 'mate'. I try to maintain certain standards of manners and morals and have received a university education which I have endeavoured to extend by selected experiences such as travel, music etc. Upper middle class life as I have once experienced it seems expensive, artificial and insincere. Working class would reject me (some of the worst snobs I've ever met are of this class) mainly because I think I have the audacity to think for myself and not accept ready-made 'headline' opinions. (Schoolteacher)

Lower middle-class. By birth, upbringing and wish I feel I belong to this class. I am not working-class and not true middle-class, which I consider needs the qualification of private means of some sort for a generation or two and a public-school education. Yet I am of the professional class and therefore some sort of middle. (Dental surgeon)

Lower Middle Class. Wages now about £460 a year. Feel that wages are the first consideration together with standard of living adopted. There are probably a considerable number of men earning more than I do whom I consider to be 'working class' because of their standard of living. (Bank clerk)

'E.G.,' he added to cheer himself up, 'earning £11 a week, perhaps living in some slum property and spending £6 or £7 a week on beer, tobacco and pools.'[12]

The whole question of how the working class was generally perceived is a difficult one, not least because – just as much as sex, politics and religion – class was traditionally not a fit subject for polite conversation. Back in the 1930s it had taken protracted agonising by the BBC before allowing a series of radio talks (wholly innocuous in the event) on the topic. Things were changing by the early 1950s, but not very fast, with honest, realistic, non-caricaturing/non-sentimental portraits and assessments of working-class life still largely off limits. 'Beautiful, safe and middle-class is what you had to be, like Virginia McKenna,' was how Sheila Hancock, brought up in King's Cross, ruefully recalled her 'difficulty getting launched' as a young actress. It was different up to a point in the cinema – for instance, *It Always Rains on Sunday* (1947) was a convincing depiction of East End life – but only up to a point, while it was essentially the same in fiction. 'Novels of working-class life are extremely rare, both in general and among the writers who succeed in being taken up by the arbiters of taste in the literary reviews, on the BBC, etc,' the American sociologist Edward Shils observed as late as 1955. Moreover, to write about the working class was to risk the unmistakeable sniffiness of the brief *TLS* review two years earlier of Catherine Cookson's Tyneside-set *Colour Blind*: 'The general effect is noisy in the extreme, as though she were writing at the top of her voice; but presumably life in a crowded slum is in fact very noisy.' Much, as Shils implied, turned on assumptions about the BBC as chief cultural arbiter. Pending the arrival of competition, it was still largely cast in an unrepentantly hierarchical Reithian mould. 'A broadly based cultural pyramid slowly aspiring upwards,' was how the director-general, Sir William Haley, conceived of the radio audience in 1948. 'This pyramid is served by three main Programmes [ie Third, Home and Light], differentiated but broadly over-lapping in levels and interests, each Programme leading on to the other, the listener being induced through the years increasingly to discriminate in favour of the things that are more worth-while.'[13] It was not a vision that willingly embraced the demotic.

Unsurprisingly, the dominant sense is of the working class as living in a world apart from most other people – a world looked upon (inasmuch as it was not just simply ignored) with a mix of emotions, most of them negative or at best condescending. 'The working man's needs are simple,' asserted Mr Buckle of Leicester in a 1946 letter to *The Times* explaining why incentives for increased production were unlikely to do the trick. 'He wants a house to live in, a wife to cook his meals and look after his children; he wants a little to spare for a trip to the pictures with his wife, a pint or so of beer and a few smokes; and he wants money to keep up to this standard.' Six years later another letter-writer was Phyllis Willmott, on the subject of the day care of young children. This contribution to an ongoing correspondence led to an invitation to a meeting held in a large, elegant room overlooking a Bloomsbury square. 'There,' she recalled, 'I found myself facing a bevy of women seated around a long table. "Oh, Mrs Willmott," exclaimed one of them who had rushed over to greet me, "we have all been so curious to meet you – for we couldn't help wondering who could be writing to *The Times* from *Hackney*." ' Schools of course had their moments of collision between different worlds. The poet Tony Harrison (born 1937) grew up in a working-class part of Leeds and was brusquely told off by his English master at Leeds Grammar School for mispronouncing the word 'us' – an episode caught in his celebrated early poem 'Them & [uz]'. Or take the case of the teacher Donald Lindsay, who after leaving Portsmouth Grammar School in 1953 to become headmaster of Malvern College was told on arrival, 'We don't want any of your state school ideas here.'[14]

There persisted an undeniably pervasive fear of the 'common'. 'If there was one consideration that determined my parents' conduct and defined their position in the world it was not to be (or to be thought) common,' Alan Bennett has memorably written; elsewhere in Leeds, Sheila Rowbotham, daughter of a salesman, had a childhood defined by her mother's aversion to 'common' children who 'scream and play rough games and get dirty'; while in Liverpool, John Lennon's Aunt Mimi (whose husband ran a dairy business) was, in Hunter Davies's words, 'very protective, looking after him all the time, trying not to let him mix with what she called common boys'. There was perhaps no one more snobbish than the seaside landlady. 'The older ones lament the difference today from pre-war times, when Newquay was filled up by professional people and middle-class families generally,' reported *Picture Post* from Cornwall in 1952. 'Higher wages and holidays with pay and the poverty of the middle classes have changed all that. Now "it's a different class of people we get. They're nice enough. But there's just no comparison with the people we used to have." ' That same year, the *News Chronicle* reported an agitated debate in Littlehampton about the 'disorderly parking of coaches on the sea-front' and the resulting 'tripper menace':

> For 1¾ hours the chairman banged for order while 176 ratepayers voiced protests at the 'gradual decline of the town'.
>
> Women in evening dresses cat-called and jeered across the ballroom where the meeting was held, and one said: 'I have lived here a long time and seen this very nice town become horrid'.
>
> A man in tweeds said: 'Let us consider how we may exercise a gentle control of the trippers' activities'.
>
> Another said: 'Let us park the cars and coaches away from the seafront and increase charges to dissuade certain types'.

The future lay with the fun-seeking south London working class, and in due course a coach park was built. 'Is it necessary to so encourage day trippers?' a local woman forlornly asked at another meeting. 'This is a free country,' replied the chairman, 'and we are powerless to stop them.'[15]

Was there an element of sexual envy? Probably – though when Mass-Observation in 1949 asked its panel about the ideal size of a family, with particular reference to working-class families, mention of the act of procreation was noticeable by its absence. No occupations were given, but the addresses confirm one's impression of an overwhelmingly middle-class set of respondents:

> There is still a need to increase the knowledge of birth control amongst working-class families. (*'Stonycroft', Rockland Road, Grange-over-Sands, Lancs*)
>
> Working-class families seem to have more children, either through laziness or ignorance. (*Gresham Road, Staines*)

They [ie working-class families] could perhaps have more children as they wouldn't want to educate them privately. (*Castle View Road, Weybridge, Surrey*)

No children, unless they could afford to keep them properly. (*Somerset Road, Farnborough, Hants*)

Lack of education allows them too much money & freedom, & lack of self control. ('*Kemp House*', *The Avenue, Birtley, Co Durham*)

Owing to greater crowding of homes, the children can get companionship from neighbours. A smaller family will suffice. (*Greenbank Drive, Edinburgh 10*)

If the working class do not get a better knowledge of what a civilised human being should develop like, I would suggest NO CHILDREN. (*Combe Park, Bath*)

Two only [compared to an ideal of five for the middle class] if income low. (*Belgrave Crescent, Sunbury-on-Thames*)

It would be desirable to reduce the number of children to two [four for the middle class], as working-class families breed a poor stock too rapidly, resulting in too many of this class in proportion to the others. (*Harcourt Road, Redland, Bristol*)

One of the replies came from Dr Alex Comfort (Honor Oak Road, SE23), future bestselling author of *The Joy of Sex* (1972) in a somewhat less censorious age. Comfort declared that working-class families, 'when living in a genuinely social community, display better maternal physique and morale, and can contemplate larger families provided they have a genuine option'.

There is little doubt what one Islington teacher thought about the working class. 'Notice in so many windows of Council flats the model of an Alsatian dog in plaster where once the aspidistra stood,' observed Gladys Langford in 1949. 'These highly coloured figures are even less beautiful than the plants.' Three years later, by this time retired, she went one Friday afternoon in June to Chapel Street market:

It was very crowded. Nearly every woman of child-bearing age was pregnant and many were pushing prams as well and these often had more than one infant in them already. It was shocking to see how many of these women were very dirty. They practically all had a smear of lipstick and most of them had had their hair 'permed' at some time but their eyes were gummy, their necks & ears were dirty and their bare legs grimy. These are the people who are multiplying so fast and whereas once a number of their children would have died now, thanks to pre-natal and post-natal clinics, most of their children will live – and will choose those who are to govern us. Anyhow I shall be safely dead by that time.

Her distaste extended to the people's friend, a Yorkshireman who as never before on British radio gave a platform to working-class voices. 'For the first – and last – time I listened to Wilfred Pickles who was speaking about his visit to Hoxton,' she noted in 1953. 'How people can endure his programme [*Have a Go!*] week after week, I do not know. He is nauseatingly cheerful, telling people how wonderful they are, exhorting bed-ridden people to "keep smiling" and asking sodden beer-drinkers for their "philosophy".'

So too, at least on the surface, for another middle-class diarist, Nella Last. 'Trippers poured in – some of the "lowest" type I've ever seen,' she recorded in 1947 while on holiday in Scarborough: 'Dirty old women who have come on charabancs as if on a works or street outing, the worse for drink just after lunch & bawling & singing & sitting helplessly round. I thought we had seen some queer ones at Blackpool but Yorkshire mill workers seem more uncouth & "rough" both in speech & behaviour – the children I've heard threatened with a "real good battering"!' Even so, three days later in her hotel, she had something of an epiphany. Almost certainly she was referring to middle-class as well as working-class people, and it is perhaps a salutary reminder of not only the limits of class analysis, but also the abiding importance of the fundamental, essentially Victorian, supra-class divide between the respectable and everybody else: 'Somehow looking round the dining room, hearing little snatches of conversation between children & parents, seeing the love & "ordinariness" of the little families, makes me feel more convinced of "things all coming right". Over sexed, neurotic, & down right *silly* people get into the news, but we have a solid layer of "ordinary" folk, decent in their ways, loving home & children & doing each day's tasks well, neither looking back or too far forward . . .'[16]

To the despair of Marxists, respectability also mattered intensely on the working-class side of the fence. 'The main social distinction was probably between unskilled labourers and those working-men who prided themselves on traditional artisan values,' Peter Stead has written in an illuminating essay on post-war Barry in south Wales. 'The tone of the town was determined by the way in which railwaymen, coal-trimmers and other workmen came together with clerks, teachers, shopkeepers and shopworkers to maintain older standards of respectability.' It was, he adds, a 'social alliance which had been forged in churches and chapels'. In Fife – where he had the misfortune to live above a 'naturally noisy' family that 'smashed firewood and coal on the kitchen floor with an elderly axe-head', roared at their pet mongrel Rover, and 'spat great streaks of phlegm' on the 'shared concrete path' – it was not so different in the case of the once religious, now atheist Harry Jack, a fitter by trade. 'For all his socialist convictions I don't think my father ever saw social divisions in purely political or economic terms,' wrote his son Ian:

> He would make ritual attacks on the big local landlords, the Earl of Elgin and the Marquis of Linlithgow, and on people who showed how they 'fancied themselves' by sending their children to piano and elocution lessons ('Aye, but do they have books in the house?'), but it was an older moral force which generated the most genuine heat in him, and the class conflict as I most often heard it expressed was not so much between classes as internal to each of them; it was 'decent folk' versus the rest. This may be a simple social analysis; it was certainly a relevant one. A strict application of socialist theory would mean that our natural allies were the Davidsons (crash, thump; 'Where's ma fuckin' tea?') and that we would be bound to them for life . . .

It was, according to Ian, 'the embers of Calvinism' that freed his father from 'class-bound loyalty' – a freedom encapsulated in one of the elder Jack's 'favourite concluding statements' at the end of a conversation: 'There's good and bad everywhere.'

In general, though, it seems to have been mainly for women that the question of respectability trumped that of class. 'Working-class women divide themselves not so much by the jobs their husbands do

– and still less by the jobs they themselves do – but rather by ways of life,' concluded Ferdynand Zweig on the basis of extensive empirical investigations:

> They would more often say: 'This is a *superior* woman,' meaning in education and way of life, living in a good house, well serviced, with lots of leisure time or 'this is a *respectable* woman,' who keeps herself right and knows how to cope with her family and her husband, while all the others are of a lazy irresponsible type who fall below these standards. The main line of division is respectability, and the sense of respectability, i.e. conformity to accepted standards, is much stronger among women than men. A labourer's wife, if she is respectable and leads a clean reasonable life, doing her bit and coping sensibly with adversities, is much more respected and classed higher in the social hierarchy than a craftsman's wife who leads the irresponsible life of a waster.

Zweig did not deny that 'women who go out to work regularly' had 'a greater class consciousness, in the male sense of the term, than those who stay at home' – but overall still insisted that 'the idea of class solidarity', central to the class consciousness of the male working class, had relatively limited appeal or even meaning to working women.[17]

Yet for all this, there remains a certain irreducible sense in which the working class of the late 1940s and early 1950s did indeed see itself as 'working-class'. Whatever the internal divisions (including of skill and pay as well as of gender and lifestyle), it was still generally the case that the *larger* divide was between the working class and the much less numerous everyone else – a divide accentuated by the fact of an overwhelmingly white society as yet uncomplicated by major ethnic divisions. 'I have always had to earn my living by working with my hands,' explained a member of M-O's panel in 1948 about calling himself working-class:

> Despite forty years of hard work I have never been able to lift myself out of this class. I am paid a weekly wage and not a salary . . . Until recently I could be sacked at an hour's notice, or sent home in the middle of the week because there was no work in hand . . . I have never had an account at the bank. The small amount I have been able to save from time to time

being in the Post Office Savings Bank. I have not been able to buy my own house. The above reasons are sufficient, I think, to give me the right to be called working class.

'We are working-class – the sort that call the mid-day meal "dinner",' declared a 32-year-old married woman from Bournemouth not long afterwards in Geoffrey Gorer's respondent-rich survey of how the English mostly recognised and accepted their class position. Others were similar: 'One of the people, an ordinary everyday worker'; 'Usually known as working-class or manual workers'; 'Average lower paid worker, who you would see at any football match or at the local'; 'I am a typical working-class man, I go to work in the morning and come home at night and I take my £5 10s a week, and that's how it goes on week after week, just like everyone else.'

Still, these and similar voices get one only so far, for as Zweig shrewdly explained in his pioneering study of the British male worker, 'class subconsciousness is much more common, and more marked, than class consciousness' – a subconsciousness 'expressed more by people's behaviour and reactions than by what they say' and 'produced by common experiences, common attitudes, behaviour and common environment'. Obvious examples of this subconsciousness-moulding behaviour included shopping habits (a residual suspicion of department stores and a strong preference for chain stores, corner shops and the Co-op), sporting preferences (above all football and rugby league) and choice of daily paper. 'I read the *Herald*,' a 60-year-old unskilled worker told an M-O inquiry in 1949. 'I like to read about the working man.' A 25-year-old labourer plumped for the *Mirror*: 'You get good articles in it. And also it's a paper for the working-class man.' Nevertheless, ultimately it was something rather more intangible that defined working-class identity. In 1953 a survey of 631 people (of roughly equal sexes) in Derby who claimed to be working-class asked which of certain given factors was the most important in deciding whether another person belonged to the same class as themselves. A lowly fourth, with only 7 per cent, was 'job'; 'education' came third with 12 per cent; and 'family' was second with 19 per cent. Easily top, on 44 per cent, was a factor called 'beliefs and feelings' – with the authors of the survey glossing that 'one of the more fundamental reasons for identifying yourself with a particular social class is a feeling that your outlook on life is similar to that of people belonging to the class in question'.[18]

Was there an underlying working-class resentment towards the rest of society? 'The worker's attitude towards the middle classes is different from his attitude towards the upper class,' reckoned Zweig:

> He rather dislikes the middle class, especially its lower stratum with which he often comes into contact. People of the lower middle class often snub him, regard themselves as superior to him, take away his money in the shops, or order him about in the offices. These are the people who have cushy jobs, while he has to sweat. These are the climbers, while he stays put. They look at everything in terms of money, while for him money is merely a medium of exchange, not something to accumulate for its own sake.
>
> For the upper classes, on the other hand, he has no dislike at all; often, in fact, he has admiration for them. They are, he thinks, genuine, as he is; and have not a foot in both camps, as the middle classes have. They do not climb in the world, or make their money; their position and wealth are inherited. The worker admires a man with money he has made by gambling or money he has inherited, but he does not like a man who is out to make money. The upper-class man is primarily a sportsman, like himself; he breeds horses and bets on them, the workman breeds dogs and bets on them. They both like gambling . . .

The rigidly enforced apartheid between rugby union and rugby league provided a telling example of prevailing attitudes. In particular, there seem to have been two reasons for rugby league's refusal until as late as the 1990s to challenge rugby union's almost McCarthyite policing of this sporting segregation. 'First, the leadership of rugby league for all its northern self-confidence was fundamentally deferential to those of a higher social class,' reflects Tony Collins, the historian of rugby league. 'To challenge rugby union in the courts would bring accusations of undermining traditional social structures. Second, and apparently paradoxically, this deference sat alongside a deep-going sense of moral superiority towards union; a conviction that not only was theirs a better sport to play and watch, but also that it was democratic and meritocratic in comparison to union's exclusivity. Every union ban and restriction simply added weight to that belief.'

In general, 'deference' and 'moral superiority' also had to be weighed alongside what one might term fantasy interest vis-à-vis stolid indifference. For instance, in 1950 almost a third of the adult population in London and the Midlands listened to the Boat Race, but less than 20 per cent in Wales and the north – and only 4 per cent in Scotland. Or take the unwaveringly middle-class world of *Mrs Dale's Diary*. Margaret Forster's mother, married to a Carlisle factory worker, 'loved Mrs Dale's life because it was the life she felt she should have had – the life of a doctor's wife, perfect'; and 1951 figures showed that whereas 25 per cent of the upper middle class listened to it every day, and 43 per cent of the lower middle class, no fewer than 52 per cent of the working class did so. Yet away from the lure of soap operas, the fundamental applicability remained until well into the 1950s – and arguably beyond – of George Orwell's wartime 'nightly experience in any pub to see broadcast speeches and news bulletins make no impression on the average listener, because they are uttered in stilted bookish language, and, incidentally, in an upper-class accent'. The overwhelming sense is of a deep linguistic-cum-cultural apartness – allied to a stubborn dislike of being patronised. 'They make me sick,' declared 'Rose', Doris Lessing's fellow-lodger in a rundown Notting Hill boarding house in about 1950, after returning from the cinema and smoking several cigarettes to get over her crossness:

It was a British film, see. I don't know why I ever go to them sometimes. If it's an American film, well, they make us up all wrong, but it's what you'd expect from them. You don't take it serious. But the British films make me mad. Take the one tonight. It had what they call a cockney in it. I hate seeing cockneys in films. Anyway, what is a cockney? There aren't any, except around Bow Bells, so they say, and I've never been there. And then the barrow-boys, or down in Petticoat Lane. They just put it on to be clever, and sell things if they see an American or a foreigner coming. 'Wotcher, cock,' and all that talk all over the place. They never say Wotcher, cock! unless there's someone stupid around to laugh. Them people just put it in to be clever, like the barrow-boys, it makes the upper-class people laugh. They think of the working-class as dragged up. Dragged up and ignorant and talking vulgar-ugly. I've never met anyone who spoke cockney. I don't and no one I know does, not even Flo [the landlady], and God knows she's stupid enough and on the make to say anything.

'Well,' she added, 'that's what I think and I'll stick to it.'[19]

Working-class attitudes were at their most cohesive in somewhere like Featherstone in Yorkshire: a virtually single-class town, dominated by one industry, coal mining. 'The working man,' wrote Norman Dennis, Fernando Henriques and Clifford Slaughter in their classic study (*Coal Is Our Life*, 1956) of that mining community based on early-to-mid-1950s fieldwork, 'thinks not in the abstract terms of social and economic relations, but in a more concrete way. For example, his pride in being a worker and his solidarity with other workers is a pride in the fact that they are real men who work hard for their living, and without whom nothing in society could function ... Nothing provokes more anger among working-men than to hear from non-manual workers exaltations to increased effort.' Two other significant findings, both negative, also emerged from this study: first, that a deep, historically shaped awareness of 'them' and 'us' far from automatically translated into political action, with most miners instead offsetting their dangerous, insecure work with as vigorous a pursuit of secular pleasures as possible; and second, that this pursuit ran along entirely conventional working-class lines (pub, club, rugby league, etc), with no apparent wish to imitate middle-class lifestyles. It was seemingly much the same in Ebbw Vale when Kenneth Allsop visited 'Steel Town' and found a new prosperity, but with memories of the 1930s still acting as 'a brake of caution' in 1952. 'A joint family weekly income of £40 net isn't out of the way, but there is no aspiration to middle-class standards: the house remains uncompromisingly working-class. There is no sign of a car-and-TV splurge.' That particular splurge was, of course, only a matter of time; but between them, Dennis et al and Allsop offered a useful pre-emptive warning against the imminent pseudo-sociological assumption that acquisitiveness was inevitably accompanied by embourgeoisiement. Or, as a latter-day sociologist, Mike Savage, has put it, the concept of 'rugged individualism' is one that avoids either/or and helpfully reconciles two diverse strands that most working-class men from traditional working-class cultures had within themselves.[20]

So much turns on the question of social mobility and aspirations to social mobility. But here there is a real problem, given the inevitable dominance in our historical imagination of the apparently many upwardly mobile winners. Joe Orton, growing up on a Leicester council estate, was driven by an ambitious mother and, in his biographer's words, 'would not accept the fatalism of working-class life', a non-acceptance that included elocution lessons; Tom Courtenay's mother, frustrated by her lack of education, was determined that her son should do better; as in Hull, so in Holmfirth near Huddersfield, where 'I don't want my lad to wear overalls' was the watchword, said in a broad Yorkshire accent, of the mother of the future Labour MP Rowland Boyes, son of a lorry driver; and the mother of the future literary critic John Sutherland was the daughter of a Colchester labourer, craved to move up in the world as a result of what she had seen during the war, and put so much pressure on her son to perform academically that he ruefully called a chapter in his autobiography 'The Family Racehorse'.

The defining life-event was usually the eleven-plus, both the exam itself and the preparation leading up to it. Sometimes the successful working-class child was self-motivating – 'I didn't want to become one of the hapless ones who went off to work at Ford's in Dagenham or drove a lorry at Tate & Lyle's in Silvertown,' is how Terence Stamp has explained what got him to Plaistow Grammar School – but more often the push was external, either a teacher or a parent, usually the mother. Lynda Lee-Potter, daughter of a Lancashire miner-turned-painter/decorator married to a former shoe-shop assistant, wrote half a century later the classic account:

> For a year before the exam we talked of little else. I practised writing what we called 'stories' and we did extra sums after school. My mother had an agile mathematical brain and she could reckon up a column of figures like a computer. For months before the scholarship examination [as the eleven-plus was for a long time also called], we did mental arithmetic together. The dress I was to wear on scholarship day was washed and immaculately pressed weeks in advance. On the Friday evening before the exam, she filled the tin bath with hot water and put it in front of the fire so that I didn't have to use the tiny, freezing downstairs bathroom. On the Saturday morning, neither of us could eat but we had a cup of

hot, sweet tea. 'Give it all you've got, love,' she said and there were tears in her eyes.

The scholarship exam was held in a school in the centre of Leigh and I walked there with two other girls. I was desperate to do my best and make my mother happy. She did so much for me and passing the scholarship was the one thing I could do for her. I sat down and looked at the title of the composition, which was where my greatest hopes of success rested. To this day I can remember my feelings of hopelessness when I saw the dreary, uninspiring title. 'Write a composition,' it said, 'on the difference between an apple and an orange.'

I was heartbroken and I walked home convinced I'd failed. My mother put her arms round me and we cried in despair together. 'Never mind, love,' she said, 'I'll put the kettle on and we'll have a cup of tea,' which was her antidote to failure, heartache and desolation. Three months later we got the letter telling me that I'd passed and I think it was the happiest day of my mother's life.

Lee-Potter hardly needed to add that she 'couldn't wait to take me to Danby's, the drapery shop in the centre of Leigh, to buy my uniform'.[21]

Unfortunately, for every real-life Billy Elliot – this was Terry Gilbert, a miner's son who won a scholarship to Chesterfield Grammar School and at 16 entered the Ballet Rambert School, becoming in due course a celebrated dancer and choreographer – there were many, many mute inglorious Miltons. And fundamentally, for the great majority of working-class people in the immediate post-war period, that does not seem to have been a cause for regret or even concern. The crux was attitudes to the value of formal education, with Elizabeth Roberts concluding, on the basis of her extensive interviews in north-west England, that 'a few parents were overtly hostile to the whole system, many were indifferent, and a growing minority very enthusiastic'. These findings were entirely consistent with F. M. Martin's 1952 Hertfordshire survey, revealing that the further down the social scale one went, the less serious parental thought was given to a child's secondary education. Moreover, even if a working-class child did make it to grammar school, there was an all-too-familiar syndrome. 'It was like a portcullis coming down,' the writer Alan Garner recalled. 'A friend's mother told me I wouldn't want to speak to them any more. And while my family was initially pleased, they didn't realise that getting an education is not like getting a car. The child expands and the family cannot cope.'

The value of education tended to be particularly dimly perceived in the case of daughters; but either way, whether a son or a daughter, at a grammar or a secondary modern, the pressure was almost always there to leave as early as possible and get a job. The 1951 census showed that around 80 per cent of young people (aged 15–19) were in full-time employment, and the basic fact was that their contributions were often vital to working-class households, especially (Zweig found) those with two or more children under 14, or lacking an adult male wage-earner. The imperatives of the family budget and the deep socio-cultural divide separating the working class from the rest of society were a formidable combination indeed. The still huge British merchant navy did provide an important, historically underestimated escape valve for many troubled male adolescents; but, like National Service, it seldom shook up predetermined life-chances. That needed the educational route – a route that simply was not on the typical working-class road map, inasmuch as such a map even existed.

'Theoretical', with 'little practical bearing on everyday life', was how Eliot Slater and Moya Woodside summarised the far-from-impressed view of education on the part of 200 working-class soldiers and their wives whom they interviewed just before and just after the end of the war. 'Beyond what was immediately useful, the ability to read, write and reckon, it was nearly all forgotten. It formed no cultural background for reading and study in later life; and most of them felt that all they had learned that was worth learning had been from their experience of life itself. Their schooldays had been irksome and irrelevant to the real business of living.' Or as one mother eloquently put it in relation to her son: 'I am not going to let him learn anything; I want him, if need be, to be able to put his hand to everything.'[22]

———

Still, it all depended. Brian Thompson's father, Bert, was working-class in origin, but as a youngish adult had been transformed by the war into a ruthlessly upwardly mobile figure. 'The former telephone linesman wore a RAF Association scarf, a heavy grey overcoat and the first of a long series of brown trilbies,' is how his son memorably depicts him in peacetime:

> He gave the civilian world his burly truculence, signed off papers with a beautifully assertive signature, blanked the weak and venal. In shops, buying his cigarettes, he would proffer his money and at the same time specify the change he was to receive ... In politics he was a working-class Tory, with a fine disdain of lefties, commies, poofs, conchies, spivs, scroungers, tarts and of course, above all, Yanks. The French were gutless, the Italians pitiable, the Spanish more akin to gypsies than anything else. The Jocks could be tolerated for their qualities of courage and nippiness but there was never a kind word to be had from him about the Taffs. Paddies were treated with indulgence, the way simple-minded people are ...

In the spring of 1951 he took Brian in hand and coached him hard for the new exams called 'O levels'. Brian, who was at a grammar school, duly passed all ten – one of only three in his county to do so – but had already been told by his father to leave school and get a proper, money-earning job. A timely visit from the headmaster persuaded Bert otherwise. 'You go into the sixth form when the new term starts,' an unabashed Bert announced to his son after the head had left. 'And you work. No more pissing around, you understand? Now wipe that look off your face and get out there and mow the lawn.' Cambridge and ultimately a writer's life beckoned for the boy. It had been a close-run thing, for as his still unmistakably working-class, cruelly put-upon mother, Peggy, innocently asked after Bert's pronouncement: 'What the bloody hell's the sixth form?'[23]

8

It Makes a Break

'It is rare for anyone to "go out" straight from work although the men may call in at a public house on the way home,' Doris Rich explained in her account (based on 1948–9 fieldwork) of a typical weekday evening in working-class Coseley, near West Bromwich:

> The evening starts when the men get home from work and all the family sit down to a cooked 'tea'. After tea the workers wash in the kitchen, rather than the bathroom, if there is one, or, if they live in a back-to-back house, in a basin on the living-room table. Any youngsters (15 to 20s) in the house wash, change their clothes and go straight off to visit friends or to the cinema. The man of the house changes his clothes if he is going to the club, or on a special outing with his wife, but he may not change if he is staying at home or only going to his usual public house nearby. At home the evening passes with the wife knitting or sewing and her husband playing with the children, resting (sometimes sleeping) and reading the newspapers. The wireless may be on in the background: some people had the wireless on while being interviewed and appeared to be oblivious to it. At about 9 pm the husband may go to his usual public house ('it makes a break'), leaving his wife to put the children to bed or continue with her knitting. When he comes in they have 'supper', generally a cold snack, and then go to bed.

'In some households,' added Rich, 'while the men are at the public house, the women (particularly the older Black Country women) may go out to get a bottle of stout from the "outdoor" and some fish and chips for supper.'

Neville Holder (born 1945, son of a self-employed window cleaner, nicknamed 'Noddy' at school) was brought up in the Black Country, in his case Walsall. 'Our council house was at the end of a long terrace,' he recalled about an entirely characteristic working-class domestic backdrop to his childhood:

The front door opened directly on to the pavement and you walked straight into the front room, which was only used on special occasions. My mum said it was 'to be kept for best'. You then passed into the living room, where there was a dining table and chairs and a couple of armchairs around a big black coal-fire stove. A huge black kettle, full of hot water, would always be resting there. The living room was also the setting for my Friday night scrub-down in an old tin bath . . . A door opening on to the stairs took you up to two bedrooms. There was no bathroom or indoor toilet. If you were caught short during the night, you used a chamber pot under the bed . . . Downstairs, the room at the back of the house had a gas stove and a large sink where clothes were scrubbed clean by hand. The back yard was shared with three other families and the only toilet was at the end of the yard, with a bolt on the inside of a rickety wooden door . . .

There were cultural compensations. Listening with his parents to light-hearted entertainment shows on the radio; accompanying them on a Friday or Saturday night to the local working men's club (Walsall Labour Club) and collecting the balls from the snooker-table pockets in order to put them back on their spots, as well as (in 1953) making his performing debut singing Frankie Laine's 'I Believe'; and, during the week, waiting for his generally good-natured father (betting and watching sport his other favourite pastimes) to return drunk from the pub after boozing with his mates. The premium placed on habit and conformity was undeniably heavy. 'We always sat at the same table, in the same seats, as did everyone else in the room,' he remembered about the working men's club. 'It was part of the reason that you rarely met anyone you didn't already know.' And: 'No one we knew ever went abroad.' Altogether, Holder concluded, 'it really was an incredibly insular way of life' – but, as he also insisted, 'everyone we knew was happy with their lot', in that 'as long as you had work, your sport and you could go for a drink, you considered yourself lucky'.[1]

Holder lived at 31½ Newhall Street, but there was no more emblematic working-class street in the country than Newcastle's Scotswood Road – emblematic of a way of life that flourished for the best part of a century before 'the great disruption' of the late 1950s and early 1960s.[2] Celebrated in folk anthem ('Gannin along the Scotswood Road to see the Blaydon Races'), it was by the 1950s still a vibrant, populous thoroughfare running for 3 miles near the banks of the Tyne. Pubs (of which at one time there had been forty-four) included the Ordnance Arms, the Hydraulic Crane, the Mechanics Arms and the Moulders Arms, all names that reflected the area's main source of employment, the vast Vickers-Armstrong works; while among a plethora of small shops on the north side that dealt in food there were as many as eighteen (five grocers, two general dealers, two bakers, two fishmongers, two fish-and-chip shops, two fruiterers, two butchers and one confectioner) on the quite short stretch between the Crooked Billet pub and Atkinson Road. On the south side, a series of streets ran sharply down to the Tyne, with, across the river, the six tall, belching chimneys of Dunston power station. It was at the top of one of those streets (Clara Street) that Bert Hardy in 1950 took his evocative, touching rear-view photograph of a mother hand-in-hand with her small son.

Liverpool's Scotland Road, heartbeat of that city's working-class life and close to both the centre and the docks, was almost as emblematic. 'A city within a city', with distinct Irish, Welsh, Scottish and Italian migrant communities as well as the native Scousers and pockets of Germans and Poles, it was still imbued in the early 1950s with strong sectarian divisions. Two young Catholics, both attending St Antony's School, were James Melia (born 1937, one of eleven children of a cobbler) and Priscilla Maria Veronica White (born 1943, daughter of a docker): the former became a scheming, prematurely balding midfielder for Liverpool; the latter, Cilla Black. 'Home was our flat at 380 Scottie Road, above George Murray's barber's shop, behind a branch of Midland Bank and next door to Mrs Lee's Chinese laundry,' she recalled. 'Our home was full of music when I was a kid. We listened to records, and always had the radio on ... Me mam was always singing, especially on Monday mornings, which was washday in our home; and me dad was forever playing his mouth organ when he wasn't tending his budgerigars.' He was also 'a very dapper man who loved his waistcoats' and 'a very quiet, shy man until he was in the company of men', especially in the pub. For his wife, though, there was just one all-consuming ambition. 'We didn't have one of the highly prized two-up, two-down terraced houses. Me mam would have killed to have one of those, because living in the flat meant we didn't have our own front door. We either had to come in through the barber's shop, which me mam hated doing, or when the shop was closed we came in through the back entry on William Moult Street.' And one day, after it transpired that the flat was to be 'upgraded' (including a new bathroom), young Priscilla returned from school to find her mother 'crouched on the stairs crying with frustration' – because this meant that the family would slip down the queue for a council house with its own front door.

The mother is a figure writ large in most memoirs of a working-class childhood. *An Immaculate Mistake* is a marvellous evocation by Paul Bailey (born 1937) of growing up in Battersea during and after the war – a two-storey terrace, with poky rooms, by the railway; the application of Lifebuoy soap each Friday evening on the visit to the public baths; Maggy Brown's pie-and-eel shop; magazines as 'books', with hardly any real books in the houses in Bailey's street; cold rice pudding left out in case he got back late – but it is his mother who is the emotional centre. She was a domestic help, her husband was a roadsweeper; 'if people ask you what your father does for a living', she would instruct the young Paul, 'tell them he works for the council.' The gods she worshipped were tidiness and cleanliness; books were 'dust traps'; Churchill she disparaged as a warmonger; her views on the aristocracy were mixed, but ultimately she was a 'feudalist'; an obsession with money and not being in debt involved methodical saving for her funeral ('the day of your funeral is the most important day in your life'); and her reaction to the subject of sex was profoundly negative. 'If your poor father hadn't gone and died [in 1948], you would be dancing to a different tune, make no mistake,' she would say to the book-reading, classical-music-listening, actor-aspiring and generally moony, moody adolescent Paul. 'Why is that?' 'The back of his hand is why. You'd soon keep a civil tongue in your head if you knew he was there to clip your ears.' Paul was also realising in his teens that he was homosexual – a realisation provoking, unsurprisingly in that milieu, 'feelings of confusion and shame' that lasted until his early 20s.

There seem to be, sad to record, conspicuously few authentic working-class diaries for these years. One that does exist is by William Hayhurst, who lived at 8 Parcel Street, Beswick, Manchester 11, and appears to have been employed by Manchester Corporation as a coach driver, usually for day excursions. The entries tend to be bald, with little in the way of either description or reflection, but cumulatively they yield an impression of a hard-working, self-respecting working man of the period. They also, more disconcertingly, remind us through their very baldness of how little we really know about these distant lives and almost still voices:

> *16 August 1945, Wednesday.* Garage 7.30 am. V.J. party for all the street. Fine weather. Had a real good time. Beer. Fireworks. Dancing round bonfire. 12 midnight.
>
> *3 June 1946, Monday.* Kendall St. Private to Blackpool. Dead end kids.
>
> *24 July 1950, Monday.* Day off. Sunny. Hannah [his wife] & I go to town. Bought chip pan. Go to New Royal at night. Bill [probably their son] booked railway tickets for holidays.
>
> *24 November 1950, Friday.* Stayed with Dad afternoon . . . Said goodnight Bill, God bless. These were his last words.
>
> *4 November 1952, Tuesday.* Day off. Raining all day. 11.00 am City Hall exhibition. Women & Home. No good. Go to Hippodrome. Charlie Chester etc. Very good.
>
> *8 January 1953, Thursday.* Foggy. Up at 5.00 am. Garage 6.30 am. No 3 Duty. Called for haircut on way home. Mother called at night with firewood. All at home. Made football coupon out.
>
> *14 January 1953, Wednesday.* Up at 5.00 am. Garage 6.20 am. Number 4 Duty. Hannah went to Lewis's for cotton 5½d. I dressed aunty's foot again. Little better. Mother brought a bag of coke. On our own, Bill out.
>
> *28 January 1953, Wednesday.* Day off. Hannah & I go to circus at Belle Vue matinee. On our own at night.
>
> *28 March 1953, Saturday.* Backed winner of Grand National 'Early Mist' 20 to 1.
>
> *15 June 1953, Monday.* Rainy. 11 coaches for old age pensioners. Manley Park [Manchester] & Albert Park [Salford]. Police escort through B/pool. Raining. No meals. They had meals at Woolworths. Left 7.00 pm. Home 10.00 pm.
>
> *16 June 1953, Tuesday.* 8.15 am. 5 coaches to Rhyl. Brooke St old age

pensioners. Dinner & tea at Ira's Café. Raining slightly all day. Left at
7.00 pm. Home 11.00 pm. OK.
22 April 1954, Thursday. Up at 5.15 am. Made fire. Garage 6.25 am. No 5
duty. On our own at night watching T.V. Mother called with coupons.
8 May 1954, Saturday. T.V. poor.[3]

Papers, cigarettes, drink: those were the three staples of the working-
class, especially male working-class, way of life – call it 'culture'.

Despite up to a fifth of the adult population being illiterate or semi-
illiterate, the reading of newspapers was a boom activity in post-war
Britain: by 1952 the average total weekday circulation was 29 million,
comprising 16.1 million for national morning papers (almost double
the 1930 average), 2.5 million for provincial morning papers, 3.4 million
for London evening papers and 7 million for provincial evening papers.
On Sundays, when most people read more than one paper, the average
total circulation was an extraordinary 31.7 million, more than double
the 1930 average. UNESCO figures around the same time revealed that
daily newspaper circulation in Britain, about 610 per 1,000 inhabitants,
was decisively ahead of all other countries, with Sweden next on 490
and France on only 240.[4]

Which papers did the working class favour? The following, according
to the authoritative Hulton Survey of 1949 (based on a national sample
of more than 7,000 people), were the most popular six titles:

News of the World: 55.0 per cent (ie read by 55 per cent of the working
   class)
People: 35.9 per cent
Sunday Pictorial: 33.8 per cent
Daily Mirror: 28.6 per cent
Daily Express: 25.7 per cent
Sunday Express: 15.1 per cent

By contrast, only 3.4 per cent of the working class read the *Daily
Telegraph* and only 1.2 per cent the *Observer*, while men read more
than women, with 59.3 per cent compared to 51.3 per cent in terms of
the *News of the World*.

The Press and Its Readers was the title of Mass-Observation's illuminating 1949 survey. 'You know it is all reading, sort of thing, something to read,' an unskilled working-class woman explained about her *Daily Mirror* habit. 'To see how things are going on in the world. I like to hear about murders, I hear about all the murders going on, how it all happened. Proper blood curdler for that sort of thing I am.' The survey included a rich array of other testimony:

I read the *Mirror*. Not anything particular I like about it at all, except the cartoons. I don't read any particular page, just if anyone says anything interesting I pick it up and read it, but I don't bother with it much. *(Unskilled working-class man, 45)*

I've had the *News of the World* for years. I like to read all the crimes and sensational things, and the medical part too. *(Unskilled working-class woman, 35)*

I read the *News of the World*. It seems to me to have all straightforward news in it, and we've been having it for years. *(Artisan-class woman, 50)*

I read the *People*. I like the fashions and all that. *(Unskilled working-class woman, 36)*

I read the *Express* . . . All the sport, see? *(Unskilled working man, 19)*

I read the *Mirror*. I open it at the Live Letters – I read that when I'm feeding the baby. *(Unskilled working-class woman, 30)*

I read the *Sunday Express* . . . I always read the letters – that's the first thing I always read – they have columns about tittle tats from all over the world. *(Woman, artisan-class, 19)*

I read the *Pictorial*. I buy it for the baby to look at the pictures. *(Housewife, unskilled working-class, 30)*

When I've the time, I look at the *Mirror* – Live Letters – they seem to learn you a bit, they give you the answers, you know. And Jane! I've not much time to read really, but when I do I prefer the *Mirror*. *(Unskilled working man, 35)*

The last word went to a middle-aged charwoman. 'Lord love a duck!' she replied to being asked why she read her local paper. 'What a lot of silly questions. Just for curiosity of course. Not for anything in particular.'

The undaunted investigators also watched readers in action in public libraries. A couple of examples were reasonably typical:

> Picks up the *Daily Graphic* [forerunner of the *Daily Sketch*] and looks at front-page headlines. Reads 'Woman Recluse 89 Dead in Trunk'. Reads length of column, turns to back page and continues to read further column (as continued from front page) about the murder (time 4 minutes). Reads column 'Anne's Wedding etc.' (1 minute), back again to front page – reads column on extreme right 'The Dyke', etc. Turns to centre pages, looks at pictures (another minute). Turns to page 2 and reads 'Money is no object'. Puts elbows on table. Also reads article on lower page 2 – '20 years on your age' (5 minutes). Turns over to page 3 – reads cartoon 'Blondie'. Looks up and sees that another woman has finished with magazine *Britannia and Eve* – leans over and takes it. (*Skilled working-class woman, 45*)
>
> Picks up *Daily Mirror*, glances at front page news items (headlines only). Opens *Daily Mirror* to page 3 and reads cartoon – glances at remaining reading matter but doesn't settle down to read anything special. Turns to page 4 – reads 'Jane' – looks at pictures. Leaves *Daily Mirror* open centre page – walks away. (*Unskilled working-class man, 30*)

'On the whole, although the majority of people look at the political news, it is only to glance at it,' was M-O's key, unambiguous conclusion. 'Relatively few ignore it completely, but on the other hand equally few show signs of any real interest in it. And although most of people's reading time, insofar as dailies are concerned, is devoted to news, it is largely the sort of home news that is partly gossip, and that has an easy personal appeal.'[5]

By far the two most popular dailies in the country as a whole were the *Daily Mirror* and the *Daily Express*, each selling around four million copies by the early 1950s. But whereas the *Mirror*'s readership was overwhelmingly working-class, the super-patriotic, drum-beating, right-wing *Express* enjoyed a strong following across the classes – helped by its three leading adult cartoons (Osbert Lancaster, the Gambols and Giles), each having a different class subject matter and, presumably, appeal. The paper's editor was the legendary Arthur Christiansen, for whom the test of a story was reputedly whether it would appeal to someone living in the backstreets of Derby. As for the *Mirror*, two of its most distinctive features were its American-style strip cartoons – usually about seven on any one day, including 'Buck Ryan', 'Belinda' and 'Garth' as well as 'Jane' – and its 'Live Letters', answered since 1936 by the Old Codgers, definitely not American. 'I am informed by my comrades that I could be fined £2 for taking my place in a fish and chip queue out of turn. Is this true?' asked 'Fishy' from RAF Hednesford in July 1951. 'If we had a queue jumper to deal with we'd tell him the same,' was the reply. 'No, laddie, we're not spoiling it for your comrades.' Celebrity featured strongly – in this same issue Judy Garland and Noël Coward on the French Riviera, Vera Lynn's summer season at Blackpool and 'freckled' Glynis Johns's make-up for her latest film role – while editorial space devoted to hard news (excluding crime and sensation) was significantly less than in the worthier, TUC-backed, commercially struggling *Daily Herald*. 'We've taken the *Mirror* since 1940,' a 30-year-old gas fitter explained to M-O. 'I forget what particular reason it was now, I believe it was something to do with some women's patterns that my wife liked ... Well, myself I like it because the sports page is quite enterprising, and we all clamour for Jane, and the comic strips.'[6]

Kingpin of the Sunday papers was the *News of the World*, with a circulation of around seven million, a readership of around eighteen million, and a relentless diet of crime-based stories. 'He Felt a Darkness – And Found Death' jostled on 23 November 1952 alongside 'Scandal Exposed by Writing on the Wall' and ' "I Let Him Have It With The Hairpin" ', not to mention 'Attack in Cubicle Number 38' and 'He Trailed Wife's Car and Got a Black Eye'. There was also in this issue a leader advocating the return of flogging, an article by the high-profile Tory MP Robert Boothby on how 'Empire Can Show The World The Light', Brian Vesey-Fitzgerald's 'Care of Your Cat' column ('How Clever Are Cats?'), a lengthy investigative article ('Vice in the Heart of the Capital: A Stain on Britain's Good Name') about the Paddington district, and a fashion competition (1½d entry fee for two coupons, £500 prize) requiring contestants to arrange in order of merit 'photographs of a distinguished West End model wearing nine different jumpers or cardigans taken from Selfridge's stock'.

Tellingly, though, the paper's dominance did not extend to Scotland, where instead the obligatory Sunday reading for a staggering 77.3 per cent of adults in 1949 was the altogether homelier, more down-to-earth, Glasgow-published *Sunday Post*. Typical items on this particular Sunday included 'Our Food Reporter' on the latest prices and supplies, 'Magic Tricks for the Xmas Party: Priscilla Tells You the Secrets', a story called 'The Silken Web', and the 'Pass It On' column of domestic tips from readers, including Mrs M. Dunnett of 4 Main Street, Clackmannan: 'A half-burnt coal on the last fire at night can be saved by making an air hole with the poker in the centre of the fire. The flames die out quickly, leaving the charred coal for easy lighting in the morning.' There were also, as ever, the latest adventures of the long-running cartoon characters, notably 'The Broons' and 'Oor Wullie', with the latter's strapline entirely characteristic:

> Oor Wullie's job of paper lad
> Aye makes him late for school. Too bad!
> He's bolted twice, and more to come,
> But third time's lucky for our chum!

Oor Wullie was a tenement boy with dungarees and boots, his spiky hair invariably uncombed and ungelled; his creator was Dudley D. Watkins, a devout member of the Church of Christ in Dundee; and the world he evoked was, in the subsequent words of the Scottish publisher Bill Campbell, 'a Scotland of quaintness, kindness, and community intimacy, where political thoughts or aspirations are taboo'.[7]

In the Sunday press as elsewhere there was abundant, wholly shameless advertising of the joys of smoking. ' "The cigarettes for me" says football genius Stanley Matthews,' ran an ad for Craven 'A' in the *News of the World* in December 1952, while earlier in the year, in *Autosport*, the up-and-coming 'speed merchant' Stirling Moss was positively eloquent: 'I'm a light smoker, and that makes the taste of the cigarette an important consideration. Craven "A" gives me all I want of a smoke – and nothing I don't!' It is impossible to exaggerate the ubiquity of smoking. 'People smoked at work, at home, in the cinema, down the pub, on public transport,' remembers Anton Rippon (born 1944) about his Derby childhood:

One of my earliest memories of floodlit football at the Baseball Ground is of thousands of cigarettes glowing in the darkened stands. Abstainers just had to lump it. I grew up in a house full of tobacco fumes. My father [a linotype operator] smoked cigarettes and a pipe – St Bruno tobacco for his briar and either John Player's Navy Cut or Gold Flake cigarettes. He was never without one or the other and could smoke a cigarette down to the tiniest nub. Still alight, it stuck to his bottom lip and wobbled up and down when he spoke ...

Phil Vidofsky lit one cigarette from another as he cut hair at his barber's shop ... Ted Barker, a butcher whose shop was at the top of Gerard Street, smoked as he prepared Sunday joints, his fingers stained brown by nicotine, ash falling on the meat. Nobody seemed to mind ...

It was much the same for John Sutherland (born 1938). 'I was brought up in a household as thick with fumes as a kippering shack in Arbroath,' he recalls of his more or less working-class childhood in Colchester. 'I was routinely woken up by a morning chorus of hacking, or phlegmy or dry coughs, as distinctively identifiable as the voices of the coughers. I could, from my earliest years, distinguish "Willy Woodbines" from Senior Service or Three Castles Virginia by their smell alone.'

In fact, almost half the adult population were only passive smokers. The Hulton Survey for the first quarter of 1949 revealed that whereas 79.1 per cent of men were smokers (mainly of cigarettes only), only 37.7 per cent of women were. Moreover, women who did smoke averaged just 6.5 cigarettes a day, compared to 14.9 for the average male cigarette smoker. Importantly, smoking was a thoroughly cross-class activity: not only were members of the working class just as likely (or unlikely) to smoke as members of other classes, but if anything their men on average smoked slightly fewer cigarettes daily than better-off men. If beyond that there was a specific working-class twist to smoking, it was perhaps threefold: a marked disinclination to smoke pipes; on the part of the poorer working man an economically enforced penchant for roll-ups, with the French-owned Rizla by this time already a brand leader; and an almost tribal loyalty to untipped Woodbines, often sold in corner shops in ones and twos out of an opened packet kept by the till.[8]

'Should We Smoke Less?' asked *Picture Post* in September 1948, exactly two years before the publication of the first British research – only slowly disseminated – on the link between smoking and lung cancer. The context was a serious tobacco shortage, brought on by balance-of-payments difficulties, and graphic photographs of anxious queuers outside London tobacconists were accompanied by some eloquent captions about the smoking motivation:

Mrs Mary Whittle, of St George's Buildings, London E., goes into a queue twice a day to collect five a time for her two sons. They get cigarettes on the way to work, but rely on her to make it up to 20 a day each. 'They don't drink, they work hard, and Charlie would rather go without his dinner money than be without a smoke. They've smoked since they were men, and I don't see why they should stop. It's their only bit of consolation.'

The old age pensioner in the trilby is a regular. He is Alfred Harris of Ashmore Road, Paddington, who rations himself to ten a day because of the price. He has his coupon allowance and works as an assistant stoker because it helps with his tobacco money. He couldn't afford it otherwise, and he can't give up smoking. He has tried but his resolution lasted only a couple of days. He became irritable and went back to ten Woodbines. Tobacco, he says, soothes him and helps him at work.

John Equilant, plumber, once gave up cigarettes altogether because of the cost. Smokes twenty a day now because it is 'comforting'. His assistant, Gerald Tubbs, smokes fifteen a day. Won't give it up or cut it down.

Mr R Meatyard is a GPO linesman. He gets through a packet of twenty a day – sometimes more. He tried to stop smoking when the price was raised in the last Budget, but after three days ended the struggle. 'Why should I give it up, anyway?'

Perhaps most typical of all, though, was the 20-a-day, 35-year-old factory worker highlighted soon afterwards by Rowntree and Lavers in their study *English Life and Leisure*. 'Cannot afford so many because he is married with two children, but cannot do without,' noted his mini case history. 'Has tried several times to give up smoking, but becomes so irritable that home life is impossible and his wife begs him to start smoking again.'[9]

So too with the demon drink. 'Drinking is *definitely* [double-underlined] a form of escapism from the pits – from the steel works

– from the surroundings – from the depressing atmosphere of a small mining town,' declared Mass-Observation's investigator in his 1947 report on drinking in Blaina, south Wales. In fact, consumption of alcohol was on a long-term downward trend: annual per-head intake of beer (overwhelmingly the most popular drink) had been some 27.5 gallons before the Great War, 14.2 gallons by 1938, and by 1951–2 was down to 12.5 – though even that last figure worked out at well over three-quarters of a pint a day for every beer-drinking adult, with relatively little difference across the classes. Of course, there were those (including in the late 1940s about 22 per cent of the male working class and 61 per cent of the female working class) who never drank beer; while for women who were not teetotallers, there was by the early 1950s a new, sparkling drink available in the form of the affordable (1s 3d), brilliantly marketed 'champagne' perry with the appealing Bambi deer symbol. Babycham's creator was Francis Showering (of the Somerset cider-making family firm), who thereby at last freed women from the dismal inexpensive alternatives of, in an obituarist's words, 'milk stout, sweet cider or the sickly VP wines'.[10]

How much drunkenness was there? When Mass-Observation undertook in 1947–8 a comprehensive survey of drinking habits, involving some 5,000 hours being spent in pubs and clubs by its team of investigators, the striking result was 'less than a dozen cases reported at first hand of people being violently drunk'. Three years later the findings were much the same in an M-O survey (involving Bristol, Cardiff, Leicester, Nottingham and Salford) that focused specifically on the question. 'Pretty free from drunkenness,' a Bristol policeman avowed. 'It all depends what you mean by drunk. Somebody out cold or just merry. I mean unable to look after themselves. There's not very much in this particular town. For myself I expect to see one drunken person per day when I'm on duty.' He added that the 'really drunk' tended to be 'the very lowest class person'. Also in Bristol, a middle-aged, working-class woman (and ex-licencee) living near a pub agreed that times had changed. 'Nothing like it used to be,' she declared. 'People know more how to conduct themselves now-a-days. People used to be more free and easy. Now the police have got more control. They didn't used to mind.' Amid much continuing 'activator' whittering about the drink problem – typified by the disapproving, deeply condescending chapter in the Rowntree/Lavers survey – this relative new sobriety was a deep disappointment to the defiantly non-puritanical Raymond Postgate, pioneer of the *Good Food Guide*. 'When I was small, in a provincial town in the reign of Edward VII, there was real drinking, heavy continuous drinking by great masses of people,' he fondly recalled in 1949. And once, when he had pointed out to his mother a swaying, tottering, shouting man on the pavement in broad daylight and asked why he was behaving like that, she had answered casually: 'He is a working man, my dear; he is drunk.'

Even so, there was still a significant amount of drinking being done in post-war Britain – not only in pubs, but also in a dense urban network of workplace clubs (typified by the Finch Lane social centre for Liverpool Corporation conductors and drivers, with George Harrison's bus-driver father, Harold, as Saturday night MC), a rich, diverse array of sports and social clubs, and the 3,000 or so working-men's clubs attached to the Working Men's Club and Institute Union. These clubs had, for their predominantly male members, several distinct advantages over pubs: more liberal opening hours; greater selectivity, ie keeping out women (except at weekend concerts) and rowdies; often better games facilities, for instance snooker, as well as less constrained gambling; and what M-O identified as 'an atmosphere of trust that does not often appear in pubs', exemplified by the men on entering the Grafton Club in York leaving their hats and coats on pegs by the door. In Coseley, Doris Rich asked some members (of working-men's clubs and other social or sports clubs) what they liked about them and why they attended:

> Sooner come to this club than others . . . all your own folks from round about home.
> No women.
> Satisfaction of knowing profits.
> Much the same as a public house but more free and easy.
> Handy.
> Somewhere to go.
> Nothing else to do in Coseley.
> Pass an hour away watching people play.
> It's a break after being at work all day.

I pass an hour ... play dominos and talk different things ... as regards
   politics I'm not interested.
There's never no falling out.
Never no bad language.
Force of habit.

Ultimately, though, as Dennis et al made clear in their study of
Featherstone, a smallish mining town with six working-men's clubs,
it all came down to the liquid amber: cheaper than in the pubs, and
free to each member – up to eight pints anyway – during each of the
Christmas, Easter, Whitsun and August bank holidays. 'In essence,'
they concluded, 'the Working Men's Club is a co-operative society for
the purchase and sale of beer.'[11]

Pubs by contrast were already on a long, slow retreat. In 1904 there
had been 99,500 in England and Wales; in 1919, 83,400; by 1950 it was
73,500 (compared with 19,200 licensed clubs, almost triple the 1904
total). 'There is a general awareness that there is less drinking going on,'
an M-O investigator reported from Cardiff in 1951. 'People talk about
the pubs being empty and some publicans complain about a drop in
trade.' In particular, pubs during the early post-war era seem to have
had a problem attracting young people. The sociologist John Mogey in
his composite portrait of the Jolly Waterman at St Ebbe's, a traditional
working-class district in Oxford, emphasised that virtually all the
regular clientele were over 55; while Donald James Wheal, growing up
in White City, recalled 'most London pubs' as 'unappealing places for
the young', with 'spilt beer, ancient Scotch eggs and a bar dominated by
the middle-aged'.

One should not exaggerate the retreat. After all, M-O's 1947–8
survey of drinking habits found that 79 per cent of men and 49 per cent
of women said that they went to the pub. Within these overall figures
there was little in the way of occupational differences, but some regional
variations, with overall (ie men and women) pub-going percentages of
69 in London, 67 in Middlesbrough (men 81, women 53), 64 in Bolton,
63 in Birmingham and 49 in Blaina (reflecting the Welsh temperance
tradition, with men 73 and women 24). As for *frequency* of pub-going,
'the most regular drinkers are working-class people earning £4–6 a
week, nearly all are over 25, and most of them married with children'.

One of those regulars was a Dagenham milkman. 'I get home fairly early on my job,' he told M-O, 'but soon after six my wife turns to me and she says, "It's time for me to get the kids to bed, come on, get out of my way," so out I come, round here to the pub.'[12]

Pubs varied hugely in character, facilities and opening hours as well as size, but almost certainly the majority, certainly in those many working-class districts where pubs were still thick on the ground, were physically not all that different from the Cannon in Cannon Street, Middlesbrough, where at nine on a typical Monday evening in September 1947 there were 27 people in the public bar, all of them male, all of them working-class:

> The Cannon is situated in a lower working-class area and surrounded by rows of small brick cottages rapidly assuming the condition of a slum district. Both inside and out this pub is an enlarged version of any of the dilapidated dwellings which it serves. Crumbling exterior brickwork, grimy windows, and blistered paint introduce one to the conglomeration of small dirty rooms inside with bare rough floorboards, stained tables and walls, and a general atmosphere of poverty and depression.

It was only a little smarter in the Jolly Waterman, where there was a serving hatch, not a bar counter, and the only room for general use had 'plain wooden benches around the wall, a chair or two, one dark much-painted table screwed to the floor, a dart-board, a notice-board, and an open cast-iron Victorian fireplace'. Even so, there had been since the 1930s a clear trend under way towards a mixture of modernisation and what one might call cosification, with George Orwell in 1946 praising his mythical pub, The Moon Under Water, not least because it had neither 'glass-topped tables or other modern miseries' nor 'sham roof-beams, ingle-nooks or plastic panels masquerading as oak'. Five years later a letter in the *Daily Mirror* saw it all as a sinister plot:

> Publicans whining because their takings are down deserve all the desertions they're getting. They've paid so much attention to making their places fit for women – pretty lampshades, rows of bottles with lights behind 'em – that they're not fit for men.

> There are too many women in pubs anyway. There was a time when the pub was Everyman's Club. That was in those happy days when no decent woman dared be seen in licensed premises.

The writer was 'Nobby' from Birmingham, and he signed off with a single, expressive word: 'Heigho!'

In practice, it was only a part-time threat to male well-being. 'Though women are not prohibited from entering the public houses during the week,' Dennis et al noted in their Featherstone study, 'in fact it is only at week-ends in most cases that they are to be found there.' And they added pointedly that 'only *old women* go to the public house during the week unaccompanied'. Moreover, even if a woman did go to a pub, it was likely to be on certain strict territorial conditions. 'I walked across to the Royal Oak, plucked up courage and walked into the public bar,' related a female M-O investigator in Middlesbrough. 'All the men looked up and there was a dead silence. I tried to head for the bar but a man of 40 stopped me and said, "You're in the wrong place, you want the other door." He walked to the door and pointed to where I should have gone. I went without a murmur.' She did not tell exactly where she had been directed to, but evidence from other pubs is suggestive. In the Red Lion at Blaina, women were usually relegated to the back kitchen; in the Marquis of Granby in Derby, there was a tiny 'snug', invariably occupied by three old ladies nursing bottles of milk stout; in the Ring of Bells in Coventry, there was a long passage, again the preserve of old women; and in Coseley, as in Blaina, it was the back kitchen again or, if they were lucky, 'with the young couples in the smoke room'. At the Jolly Waterman in St Ebbe's there was only one room – but there, the women sat 'around the walls' acted 'as a fringe to the men', still sitting separately even on 'convivial Saturday nights'. Nevertheless, some sort of progress *had* been made. 'You never saw women in pubs here before the war, at least, very few indeed,' asserted Mr Evans in Blaina in 1947. 'The war has brought it on, believe me. A woman who came into a pub before the war was looked upon as a "bad un". Sometimes they used to go into the smoke room but never outside. The changes that do come!'[13]

Women also came in from the cold through the newly booming pub sport of darts, with ladies' darts teams being among the several thousand teams across the country playing in leagues sponsored by the major breweries. M-O reckoned darts to be 'the commonest and by far the most organised' of games played in pubs, with 'the straight 301' as the most popular type of darts. There were plenty of other pub games, including 'dominos and shove ha'penny' as 'fairly universally popular', as well as 'crib and whist', but M-O's belief was that music and singing were no longer all that frequent in pubs and that 'on the whole those who want concerts now go to the club instead'. Most pub games could generate significant betting. 'The amount of gambling that went on, especially on dominos, was shocking,' one customer at the Lion & Lamb in Newgate Street, Newcastle in the 1950s recalled. 'There were the regular, expert domino sharps who sat with their backs to the windows and invited mugs to join in the game. Disinterested men at the bar would appear to be discussing the fate of friends in court or in prison. What they were doing, of course, was using jailbird slang – like two half stretches – to tell their mates in the game exactly what the mugs had in their hands . . .' M-O in its report pointed out that gambling in pubs was illegal and 'frowned upon by the police', but added that 'few regular pubgoers see anything reprehensible in it at all'.

Pubs were also often the centre for a range of other activities. 'One in each district of Coseley houses a lodge of the Royal Antediluvian Order of Buffaloes [a friendly society], two house Pigeon Clubs and one a Fishing Club,' itemised Rich in the Black Country. ' "Death and Dividend" and "Sick and Draw" "clubs" are based on some and members gather together weekly or fortnightly to pay their subscriptions and have a drink and a chat. Such "clubs" are still very popular in Coseley . . .' But of course, in any one pub a huge amount depended on the individual landlord in terms of both activities and atmosphere. The West Midlands brewers Mitchell & Butlers may in 1950 have been providing bowling greens to more than 150 pubs in the Birmingham area alone, but for a few more years yet it was the publicans who, relatively speaking, called at least some of the shots; and for whatever motives, many of them did so in such a way as undeniably to enhance working-class associational life.[14]

The beer-drinking itself, though, was not a peripheral matter. Reputation counted, certainly in early 1950s Byker (Newcastle), where the Grace Inn was reckoned to have the best ESP on Shields Road and the Addison's popular landlord, Tommy Shaw, was highly rated for his Bass, McEwan's Special and the Guinness which he bottled himself. As to type of beer generally drunk, M-O's 1947–8 survey found that the most frequent mentions were given to bitter, mild, stout, mild and bitter, Guinness, brown ale and light ale; that overall 'nearly half of all beer drinkers drink mild and/or bitter'; and that within that there were big regional differences, with for instance 34 per cent of Middlesbrough beer drinkers favouring bitter, only 5 per cent mild, and those proportions being more or less reversed in Bolton. An investigator got talking to a couple of drinkers one August evening in the Wilton Arms, Fulham:

> Working man, aged 55–60. Drinking pints of mild. Accepted one. Said mild was most popular drink, 'What we call "wallop".' Said most working men drink mild – cannot afford bitter, and *anyhow prefer mild.* Said 'ladies' like stout or pale ale (no spirits in this pub). Two to three pints usual evening consumption for him – quite enough – home to bed etc.
>
> Woman, aged 50 – cook – drinking *mild.* Agreed with above remarks regarding popularity of mild, stout etc. – comes in about three times weekly. Two to three pints mild or else sometimes stout for a change.

Almost certainly most beer drinkers were deeply conservative in their habits – a conservatism epitomised by the failed introduction, as a result of a beer shortage, at Blaina's Red Lion of a dark Mitchell & Butlers beer, with most left unsold and going sour. 'The Welshman likes a light beer so that he can see through it and tell whether it is clear or not,' explained M-O's man on the spot. 'They are very sceptical about anything new and the fact that they could not tell whether the beer was cloudy etc. was enough to put them off it.'[15]

What did the working class talk about in pubs? 'Conversation in public-houses is confined almost entirely to the men,' reckoned Mogey on the basis of his St Ebbe's research. 'Topics which are preferred are largely escapist, about horse racing and football bets, about seaside holidays and coach trips.' Tellingly, he added that 'the world of personal references is harsh and full of jokes' – a way, he thought, of preventing 'close inquiry into individual lives'. Certainly the escapism comes through in M-O's survey. 'There is solid evidence in pubs that football is the main topic when in season,' was the Birmingham finding, while in nearby Aston a drinker bluntly asserted: 'Football and beer, that's the only two things you'll find up here.' Or take the Golden Lion in Fulham High Street during the August 1947 convertibility crisis, when 'although Parliament was in the public eye when Inv. was visiting the pub, he did not hear any particular discussion about the crisis'. During a December evening at the Red Lion, Blaina, there were three main topics: the cold weather ('If it freezes then Griffins [the local bus company?] will go off the road'); the discovery of a baby's body in a nearby lake ('It might not have been anybody local, see'); and the imminent outing from the pub to Newport Pavilion to see a show ('Is Bill going, Mrs Jones?' someone asked the landlord's wife).

The fullest rendition we have comes from Room Three of the Cannon in Middlesbrough, where one Monday evening the patient investigator listened to Gerry, Bob and Mrs Richards, all three of them regulars. The topics discussed were, in toto:

The Boys' chances against Derby County at football
The landlord of the Cannon's ban on singing
A forthcoming 'do' in the select room of the Cannon
The service at the pub called the Turf
The beer being weak – 'the rain's got in' says Bob
The weather (train of thought from the last topic)
Deadness of the pub at the moment
The Boys' chances against Derby
The forthcoming 'do' at the Cannon
The quality of the beer
A street outing to Borsbeck
The local looney bin
Gerry's woman friend
Deadness of the pub
The cost of the pub chairs
Gerry's pipe
The Boys' chances against Derby
People's ages
The current pantomime and the week's films
The quality of the beer

The forthcoming 'do' at the Cannon
The outing to Borsbeck
Pubs and landlords in general
Leeds as the best town in the county
Beer pumps with glass tubes
Lack of 'everything' in Middlesbrough

Repetitive, reassuring and deeply familiar, this was a conversational world that, as Dennis et al reflected about comparable conversations in Featherstone's working-men's clubs, privileged 'concrete details' and not only mistrusted but rarely ventured upon 'the level of general principles'.[16]

Why did people go to pubs? M-O's survey found the favourite reasons were 'for the company' (42 per cent), 'to get a drink' (23 per cent), 'for a change' (13 per cent) and 'to pass the time' (10 per cent). This predominantly *social* motivation was confirmed by John Barron Mays in his study of inner-city Liverpool in the early 1950s – describing pubs as 'popular rallying points in the neighbourhood where one can be sure of finding warmth and fellowship' – and almost movingly evoked by the M-O investigator's description of a cold December night at Blaina's Red Lion: 'The mere fact that people congregate closely together around the fires seems to make them open their hearts as it were and talk personally. Groups seem to be closer together and everybody one large family.' Yet in practice, the pub as a social centre operated in a very specific, carefully defined way, with a huge premium on familiarity. 'People generally have one or two favourite "publics" to which they are faithful,' Rich discovered in Coseley. 'At weekends they arrive at their public house early, take up their usual seats and stay until closing time ... Everyone knows everyone in the public houses, for few strangers come to them unless they are situated on a main road.' The M-O survey concurred, finding that the 'average' pub-goer was a working-class person going 'steadily' to his 'favourite pub', often a 'little back-street pub' like the Cannon in Middlesbrough. Moreover, not only did 46 per cent of pubgoers have a favourite pub, but the survey also produced a remarkable study of 529 groups (ie two or more people) drinking together. Of these, 397 were of the same sex, 426 were of the same class, 363 were of the same age group – and only three 'contained a mixture of different sexes, age and classes'.[17] Put another way, pubs acted as central reinforcements of working-class certainties in an era when those certainties – above all of place (in both senses) and gender – still unquestioningly applied. But, for all their psychological importance in underpinning a strong, cohesive sense of identity, they were certainties of exclusion as well as inclusion.

———

'Hobbies give a man something to love and something in which to find freedom,' reckoned Ferdynand Zweig. 'A working man has very little freedom and must often do what he dislikes. Work is often simply something which gives him a living, something he dislikes and would not do unless he is forced to it. But in his hobbies he regains his freedom ...' The extensive 1953 Derby sample (predominantly working-class) revealed gardening as easily the most popular male hobby, followed by (in no particular order) woodwork, decorating, cars and motorcycles, music and art, photography and animals – a list that broadly endorsed Zweig's generalisation that for the British worker 'handicrafts, like carpentry, toy-making, aero-modelling, leather-work, pewter-work, and so on, are much more popular than purely artistic and cultural pursuits'. As for women, the Derby sample showed knitting and needlework to be easily the most popular hobbies, followed a long way behind by gardening, music and art, reading, and rug-making. Not that everyone had a hobby: 46 per cent of the working-class element of the Derby sample had no hobby at all – 54 per cent in the case of the semi- and unskilled working class – while 38 per cent had just one hobby, and only 16 per cent had two or more hobbies. By contrast, only 31 per cent of the middle-class element of the Derby sample were – or anyway, admitted they were – hobbyless.[18]

Even in the case of gardening, moreover, it was only a minority who did so on a regular basis: around seven million men and four million women. Nevertheless, it was a minority that – especially in the case of men – tended to garden on a very keen, sometimes competitive basis. 'Growing would take every spare minute you had and you couldn't go on holidays,' recalled a bodymaker at Standard Motors who was also a leading member of the Coventry Chrysanthemum Society. 'I've said to the wife, "Well, I'm frightened tonight, I'm going to have to fetch them in," ' he added about those tense, foggy times in the autumn as the 9-inch blooms matured. 'So we've rolled the carpet up in the house here and I've had a hundred pots and I've had the flowers touching the ceiling. And kept ready for doing the show.' Some working men – but in Coseley only 11 out of Rich's sample of 112 – rented allotments, with Dennis et al in Featherstone finding holders who 'spent so much time there as to separate themselves from their families for considerable periods'. The electrician father of Janet Bull (later Street-Porter) certainly found solace in his vegetables. 'Like his father he liked nothing better than spending a Sunday afternoon smoking continuously while digging his allotment in Bishop's Park,' she remembered about her childhood in working-class Fulham. 'He would spend hours there, tending an immaculate plot of potatoes, leeks, onions and carrots, and we were most definitely not welcome. But these home-grown vegetables helped the family budget go further . . .'

Mr Bull's other main leisure activities were watching speedway and football, in the latter case standing on the terraces at Craven Cottage. Again, one should not exaggerate how common a type of pursuit this was. 'Three men and one woman in ten visit sports grounds,' Geoffrey Gorer discovered from his massive 1950–51 *People* survey, 'but for most people this is only an occasional outing.' He also found that young men were the most regular spectators at sporting events; that 'people in the North-East and North are far the keenest on sports, with over a quarter of the population going to sports grounds'; and that 'members of the upper working and working classes are much the most assiduous visitors', but that those with a weekly income below £8 'apparently can't afford to spend money on sports'. Watching was one thing, playing another: according to the 1953 Derby sample, only 18 per cent of that city's working class (with a strong bias towards the skilled worker) played sports at all, compared to 51 per cent who watched sports at all. Predictably (taking working and middle classes together), men were over twice as likely as women to play a sport and almost twice as likely to watch one.[19]

Overwhelmingly the most popular spectator sport was football, watched by huge crowds in the late 1940s and early 1950s. After the all-time peak of 41.3 million people at Football League matches during the 1948–9 season, there was a gradual decline – a decline probably caused by a mixture of widening leisure as well as consumption choices and higher admission prices – but in the 1953–4 season the aggregate was still a healthy 36.2 million. Even in the League's least-watched division, Third Division North (spiritual home of Accrington Stanley), there was an average attendance of 7,339 in the 1954–5 season. Who were the spectators? The stereotype of the cloth-capped, working-class man faithfully supporting his home-town club is not wholly off the mark, but nor is it quite the complete picture. The 1953 Derby sample revealed that 28 per cent of football-watchers were middle-class, while research by Gavin Mellor into the composition of football crowds in the north-west between 1946 and 1962 likewise suggests a significant middle-class, often car-owning element, as well as pointing to a sizeable sprinkling of out-of-towners (helped by Lancashire's excellent, pre-Beeching rail network) and the existence of loyalties to city or region that, to an extent that would soon be inconceivable, transcended a narrowly partisan allegiance to a particular club. 'Then [in the 1950s] it didn't make any difference if you were a football supporter and you came from Manchester,' recalled Dave McCormack in the 1990s. 'If you were United you wanted United to win first and foremost, whoever they were playing, and you wanted City to be somewhere near, just below you. If you were a City supporter, you wanted City to win and United just to be perhaps two or three places below.'[20]

The essence of the experience was still pretty unreconstructed: packed, often uncovered terraces, dominated by working men and their sons; primitive facilities; frequent outbursts of a great, collective roar; and, throughout the match, what Subrata Dasgupta, recalling his first childhood visit to Derby's Baseball Ground in 1953, describes as 'the perpetual, raucous, nerve-grinding, encouraging clamour of furiously whirling rattles'. Yet for all the noise and the endemic bad language – B. S. Johnson's lower middle-class father, 'normally restrained to the point of near-inarticulateness', swore 'with a vigour and comprehensibility which surprised and delighted me', the novelist remembered about their trips to Stamford Bridge – these were usually sober, orderly crowds carrying little or no threat of physical violence. 'On leaving the field at the end the referee was vociferously booed and pelted with orange peel and cigarette cartons,' the *Barnsley Chronicle* unusually reported in January 1952 after a disappointing home draw with West Ham United.

'The angry Oakwell partisans can be pardoned for their verbal action for they were placed under extreme provocation but to hurl missiles was carrying things a little too far . . .' The actual football these crowds watched was also for the most part orderly. Intensely physical, yes – one obituary of the iron-hard Welsh centre forward Trevor Ford evoked 'a weekly miscellany of shuddering physical confrontations frequently played on appalling pitches with a leaden ball by men wearing heavyweight footwear' – but with an underlying honesty and lack of gamesmanship. 'Whilst open charging and crunching tackles were seen as integral to the game, particularly in the North,' the historian Richard Holt has noted, 'shirt pulling, elbowing, spitting at opponents, kicking and punching off the ball and behind the referee's back were not acceptable to most fans.'[21]

It was not invariably a benign relationship between supporters and players. 'England were now very often better in midfield play but had lost the art of shooting, particularly spontaneous shooting in the penalty area,' asserted the FA's Technical Sub-Committee (set up after the 1950 World Cup humiliation) in 1952. 'This was thought to be due to the player's reaction to the crowds, in that he feared blame if an opportunity was taken and he missed scoring.' Or take Middlesbrough's England defender, the handsome, well-dressed George Hardwick. 'Ooh, Gorgeous George,' at least one lifelong Boro fan would coo sarcastically, batting his eyelids up and down. Generally, though, this was an era of close, mutual identification. Not only did maximum-wage regulation ensure that players' earnings were not grossly out of line with those of skilled workers, but the players themselves were a visible – sometimes too visible – part of the local scene. England's captain, Billy Wright, paid his tuppenny fare every morning to get the bus to the Wolves ground, while after a match the young Liverpool defender Ronnie Moran would join the fans on the tram home, 'so if I'd played a stinker I'd slouch down in the front seat with a cloth cap pulled down over my face'.[22]

A notable quartet suggests the strength of the relationship. Tom Finney, the gifted but also modest and loyal Preston and England winger, was approached in 1952 by the Italian club Palermo and offered financial rewards way beyond what he was getting at Deepdale. 'Listen to me,' the Preston chairman, a wealthy retired housebuilder called Nat

Buck, told him, 'if tha' doesn't play for Preston then tha' doesn't play for anybody.' Finney stayed – a victim of the archaic retain-and-transfer system that in effect made slaves out of professional footballers – and the story leaked out. 'For some,' recalled Finney years later, 'I was the target of abuse, labelled a "traitor" for even considering leaving my hometown club. However, there were others, and the overwhelming majority at that, who believed I had not been given a fair crack of the whip.' Bert Trautmann was a former German POW who signed for Manchester City in 1949 amid a torrent of abuse in the local press, not least from Jewish and Ex-Servicemen's organisations, but gave such masterly as well as courageous displays in goal that he quickly established himself as a firm Maine Road favourite. Jackie Milburn – 'Wor Jackie' – was perhaps the ultimate local hero. It was not just his prowess as Newcastle's centre forward that made him so cherished; it was also the fact of his personal background as a young miner, having been brought up in the large mining village of Ashington some 15 miles north of Newcastle, and his sheer unassuming one-of-us-ness. A history of Ashington includes a touching photo of him flanked by two boys. It was soon after he had scored the two goals to win the 1951 Cup Final that, one Sunday morning, the boys simply knocked on his door at Ellington Terrace and asked to have their picture taken with him. Stanley Matthews, perhaps inevitably, completes the quartet. The outside right's fame by the early 1950s extended far beyond Blackpool, and he was *the* national footballer, guaranteeing large gates at away matches. One historian, Tony Mason, persuasively suggests three main reasons for the hold he exercised on the popular imagination during these years: his apparently unimpressive physique ('thin body, slightly hunched shoulders, receding hair and bony knees') made him easy for the average football-watcher to identify with; his dedication to fitness and his seeming agelessness were sources of profound admiration; and his matchless craftsmanship on the field, allied to modesty and restraint off it, made him the very epitome of the skilled, respectable working man.[23] Finney, Trautmann, Milburn, Matthews: together they represented the reassuring best of what was still the people's game.

The other great winter sport, for much of the northern working class, was rugby league. Mount Pleasant, Batley; Wheldon Road, Castleford; Crown Flatt, Dewsbury; The Boulevard, Hull (the fishermen's team);

Craven Park, Hull Kingston Rovers (the dockers' team); Parkside, Hunslet; Lawkholme Lane, Keighley; Hilton Park, Leigh; The Watersheddings, Oldham; Knowsley Road, St Helens; Naughton Park, Widnes; Central Park, Wigan – the very names of ground and club were a litany of a deeply entrenched, unashamedly insular sporting culture. Part of that culture was an intense, narrowly focused partisanship. When St Helens in 1948 took on the touring Australians, the response to a half-time loudspeaker request to home supporters to stop cheering every time an Australian got injured was, according to the journalist (but not yet commentator) Eddie Waring, 'groans and derisive laughter'. So too at Post Office Road, home of Featherstone Rovers and, like most rugby-league grounds, an intimate affair, including terraced houses and their washing lines along one side. 'Two thousand teas are thrown at t' back o' t' fire' was the semi-serious local joke about what happened on Saturday afternoon if Rovers lost, causing a near-universal loss of male appetite.

Win or lose, every supporter worth his salt had a view. 'I would like to pass my opinion about the state of affairs at Odsal,' wrote 'Northernite' in September 1951 to his local paper about what was going wrong at Bradford Northern:

> First, if instead of going to New Zealand they had brought players of the calibre of Legard (Dewsbury to Leigh), White (Wigan to Halifax), Poole (Hull to Leeds), and Ike Owens (Castleford to Huddersfield) they would have done better.
>
> Secondly, every team Northern meets seems to be five yards faster in the first ten yards.
>
> Thirdly, everybody's half-backs put ours in the shade.
>
> Fourthly, forwards seem to play without plan. Very seldom do they pass the ball – just head down and trust to providence.
>
> And finally, it's no use Joe Phillips kicking goals if he concedes points in his defensive play.
>
> Obviously what is needed is some sound coaching and really hard training.

The game's uncompromising, uncomplaining physical hardness was taken for granted. 'I had my head to Mellor's backside, waiting for the ball to come between his legs,' begins David Storey's novel *This Sporting Life* (1960), based on his experience of playing for Leeds in the early 1950s. 'He was too slow. I was moving away when the leather shot back into my hands and, before I could pass, a shoulder came up to my jaw. It rammed my teeth together with a force that stunned me to blackness.' Hard, yes, but also a game that was, in Colin Welland's admiring words, 'scrupulously honest, demanding total discipline and absolute commitment' – qualities, he argues, that sprang directly from 'the priorities and values of northern working-class life'.[24]

Two of the most working-class sports were animal-based. Greyhound racing was an inter-war phenomenon that, like speedway, enjoyed a briefish golden age after the war, peaking as early as 1946, when total attendances of 30 million were not far short of football and the night of the Greyhound Derby at White City stadium coincided with no fewer than 44 race meetings on other British tracks. Floodlit, it gave the urban male working class easy access to a night out with a bit of a flutter – other London courses included Harringay, Catford, Wandsworth, Park Royal and New Cross – though even among that target group only a small, hard-core minority regularly attended, caught for ever by the marvellous closing sequence of *The Blue Lamp*, filmed at White City. The other, more participative animal sport was pigeon racing. Its roots lay in the nineteenth century, but it was still thriving in the 1950s with some half-a-million fanciers, especially in the form of long-distance races such as the Great Yorkshire Amalgamation's Caen Race, the London North Combine's Berwick Race and the West Yorkshire Federation's Rennes Race. It was a highly competitive sport – 'it is safe to state that the present team represent the combination of all that was the very best of the Lulhams, Jurions, Delmottes and Wegges, fully trained for the intended onslaught upon the prizes offered within the confines of the London North Road Competition,' ran an advertisement in February 1952 for the auction of the birds, baskets, clocks and lofts of the late Charlie Fleming – but also sociable, including (in Richard Holt's words) 'the trip down to the club, usually a back room of a local pub, for the synchronising of clocks, the ringing, and the filling in of forms'. Yet, as Orwell had already warned in the 1930s in *The Road to Wigan Pier*, there was a looming threat. 'There seems to be a lot of trouble in places about keeping pigeons on council estates,' Frank Sant wrote in 1952 to *Racing Pigeon*'s 'North-West Jottings' column. 'We in Middlewich always invite the chairman, officials and a few councillors to our club dinners. There has never been any trouble here. Perhaps you would pass on the tip.'[25]

In general, Zweig had no doubts on the matter. 'Sporting events form an incessant topic of conversation with men not only in pubs and clubs, but also at home and at their works,' he asserted in *The British Worker*. Moreover, he pointedly added, 'a man who can forecast the result of an event is held in high esteem, as a win or a loss depends on his opinion'. Or as the *Economist* put it in 1947 with characteristic humanity: 'The great support for organised gambling once came from the bored and ill-educated aristocracy; it comes today from the bored and ill-educated proletariat.'

Betting in Britain was the title of a 1951 report by The Social Survey based on a socially representative nationwide sample. It found that 'betting in Britain today is an almost universal habit'; that 'more than three-quarters of the adult population go in for some form of betting'; and that, in terms of the most popular form of betting – namely horse-racing – the most regular punters were middle-aged, working-class men earning between £5 and £10 a week. Altogether, 44 per cent of the inquiry's sample bet on major horse races, 39 per cent did the football pools, and 4 per cent bet on dog races, with in each case a bias towards men. But there were of course other popular forms of gambling. Rowntree and Lavers in their survey included pin-tables and other illegal gambling machines in amusement arcades, sweepstakes and raffles, and newspaper competitions, while an example of the way that gambling could pervade working-class culture was the working-men's club in Middlesbrough officially called the North Eastern Club but locally always known as the Tote. 'Its whole activity centres on gambling,' reported M-O. 'In it there are the bar, piano, billiard tables, and the like which typify most clubs, but as well there is a tape machine and one end of the main room is especially built with eight small hatches in the wall for placing bets, and a large blackboard near the hatches for price-marking. The bookmaker is also the club manager.' And M-O quoted a member: 'It's packed here during the day, when the betting is going on. There won't be many people in today, there's no betting, but tomorrow and Saturday the place will be packed out, you won't be able to move.'[26]

Betting shops as such had been illegal since 1853, which meant that for most working-class people, unable to spare the time and money to get to horse-race meetings and lacking the necessary phone and credit to bet via credit accounts with well-established bookmakers like William Hill, there was no alternative but to use the 'street bookie' and his many 'runners'. Fred Done was 15 when in the late 1950s he began working with his father in the family bookmaking business and discovered a well-established machinery for circumventing the increasingly anachronistic, deeply paternalistic Victorian legislation:

He traded in Knott Mill, one of the rougher areas of Manchester, under a tarpaulin in a back yard. He would open the shop from 11 to 3 and from 5 to 7 for the evening dogs. Bets were written on any scrap of paper, with a nom de plume on the back. We had runners in all of the factories in Trafford Park, one of the biggest industrial complexes in Europe. We would send a taxi round every day, and the bets would be handed over in clock bags [ie ensuring that bets had not been placed after a race had started]. There were no books, there was no income tax, no betting duty. What you had at the end of your day was profit. The only payment you had to make was bribe money to the police, two or three quid a week to keep them off your back. If they were going to raid you, they'd let you know. Of course, punters were not as well-informed then. I once said I felt sorry for them and my father said, 'If I ever hear you say that again . . . Always remember, skin 'em and stamp on 'em'. You had to be tough to stay in the industry. We had runners in all the pubs as well, and there was a lot of competition. The pubs were probably worse than the factories to control.

Everywhere the urban working class lived, the street bookies and their runners (usually on 10 per cent commission) were there too. At Blaina's Red Lion a runner was invariably in the public bar on Friday afternoons taking bets, usually 2s each-way; in inner-city Liverpool, noted Mays, 'in the early afternoon clusters of men, mostly unemployed, gathered together in Wessex Street to await the pay-out from the bookies after the results become known', playing 'pitch and toss or dice in small clusters' while they waited, 'with look-outs posted at strategic points to warn of the approach of the police'; at every working-men's club in

Featherstone there was a runner, 'often disabled workmen who make a "bit on the side", as they say, by being available at the club to take bets'; and in Derby, at a bookie's in Wilson Street based in a house entered via the back garden, the young Anton Rippon, taking an adult bet that had been scribbled in pencil on an old sugar bag, found a smoke-filled room occupied by 'dozens of men, many of them Irish labourers who lodged in the area, listening intently to a race commentary coming over a wire service'. It was an early, unsentimental education. 'Mary, aged 11, was absorbed in her Rorschach,' Madeline Kerr related in her vivid account of the people of Ship Street, another rundown part of central Liverpool, in about 1952–3:

> Suddenly she stopped, looked at the clock and said with urgency, 'I must run an errand for me dad. I'll be back in two minutes.' It was 2.20 pm and she had instructions to put 2s on a horse for her father with a bookmaker round the corner. She had been given the money. The bet had to be on by 2.30. She had her little sister Mildred, not yet five, with her. She tried to leave Mildred with me. Mildred howled. Mary picked Mildred up and ran from the house. She returned out of breath but beaming, still carrying Mildred. The bet had been made in time.

'When asked,' Kerr added, 'what would happen if she had forgotten, she said, "He'd shout." '[27]

Liverpool – in the form of Littlewoods and Vernons – was also home to the flourishing football-pools industry, an industry which during the 1949–50 season involved some 10 million people filling in their weekly coupons. Poolites came from all social backgrounds, but the Hulton Survey of early 1949 conclusively showed the working class to be the most assiduous coupon-fillers, running at about 55 per cent of the working class in the case of men and 20 per cent in that of women – the latter figure perhaps an underestimate, given Zweig's assertion that 'about one in three women workers go in for pools'. How much did the working class stake each week? Exact estimates varied, but the average stake – around 2s 6d for a reasonably well-off working man – represented an affordable loss. Overwhelmingly the favourite punt, introduced soon after the war, was the treble chance: in effect the challenge of predicting eight draws (each worth three points) from fifty-five fixtures. The rewards of pulling it off were huge – up to £75,000, a ceiling voluntarily agreed upon by the pools companies after a recommendation in 1951 by the Royal Commission on Lotteries and Betting – but the chances were slim indeed.

Sociologically, the overriding impression is of doing the pools as an absolutely normal part of the urban working-class routine. 'Most of the dockside dwellers accept the filling up of the weekly coupon as casually and uncritically as a trip to Goodison or the evening in the corner pub,' remarked Mays in Liverpool. 'It is a part of life as they have always known it . . .' All over the country, the ritual of checking the scores was sacrosanct. 'The women in the family were always friendly, it was a happy atmosphere,' recalled a close friend of the future fashion designer Ossie Clark (born 1942), brought up in Liverpool and, later, Warrington. 'But everyone had to be quiet as his father [a P&O chief steward] listened to the results as he religiously did the football pools. There was John, Carol, Ossie and myself and sometimes we would be squabbling together – his eyebrow would twitch with annoyance, he'd tell us all to shut up and then disappear behind his copy of the *Liverpool Echo*.'[28]

Why did working men gamble? A trio of industrial workers spoke in the late 1940s to a TUC inquiry:

> I gamble every week because there is nothing to do at home, and it is amusing to work out the selection.
>
> I gamble because I want to. The Churches are such hypocrites to say that I am sinning.
>
> When we do the football pools every week it is the only time that the family is really together, and it gives us so much pleasure working something out together. We spend very little really, only about 2s 6d each.

Such responses would not have surprised Ferdynand Zweig. ' "It's fun and you give yourself a chance," was the most frequent opinion, and it is difficult not to regard this sort of gambling as an innocent and inexpensive pastime,' he wrote about the working-class addiction to the pools. ' "You can't get anything worthwhile for a shilling nowadays," they say, "but there you have something to look forward and hope for." And a man complains bitterly: "I am so hard up that I can't do even the bloody pools." '

Yet there was a darker side to Zweig's analysis of working-class gambling more generally. Not just those unhappy types, 'men who go short of the essentials of life so that they continue to gamble', to be found 'mostly at dog races', but also, more broadly, the sense in which gambling acted as a substitute for a satisfying way of life, above all in the workplace:

> 'Anyway,' a good observer among workmen told me, 'I have found that the more a man stays put and the more fed up he is with his life, the more he will set his hopes on gambling. A man with the initiative to do something in life, to look for another job and change the way of his life, will be less likely to go in for gambling.' And another man confirmed him with: 'I'm sick of hearing: "If I win on the pools." People keep on and on saying it . . .'[29]

Unlike most of the anti-gambling lobby, still a significant force, Zweig knew far too much about the crooked timber of working-class humanity to be a puritan. His critique carries a charge, even if only at an existential level, that transcends progressive pipe dreams about the active, informed, rational citizen.

⸻

'Such excitement, and such cheering on those late nights in August in the Forties as we welcomed the heroes at the Cross back from the victories at the Eisteddfod,' recalled the television journalist John Morgan about his childhood in Morriston, whose all-male Orpheus Choir won first place for four successive years. 'They were the most powerful and made the loveliest of tenor sounds. Ivor Simms [the conductor] would always insist the choir was ahead of the note, and would permit no self-indulgence.' But in many Welsh colliery towns and villages, it was the Miners' Eisteddfod, from 1948 held each year in the seaside resort of Porthcawl, that mattered at least as much. 'All of you come – you're welcome – men and women, young men and youths, boys and girls – yes; cats and dogs, too, and the sheep from the valley – all are welcome!' was how in 1950 one of the event's prime movers sought to encourage local musical talent. And, having quoted him, Sid Chaplin, writing his monthly piece for the National Coal

Board's house magazine, commented warmly: 'That's the spirit of the singing valleys. A culture that can be shared, a welcome in song and speech, and a place always ready by the fire, with the kettle hospitably on the boil.'

Elsewhere, musical talent could be expressed through the long-established, still vigorous brass-band movement. 'Fodens Motor Works Band [from Sandbach] defends its national title against 16 contenders in the most open championship since the war,' the *Daily Herald* announced on the last Saturday of October 1951 (two days after the general election) about its National Brass Band Championship, following exhaustive area contests earlier in the year. Among the bands competing that day at the Royal Albert Hall, in front of an audience of 7,000, were Brighouse and Rastrick, Fairey Aviation Works, Hanwell Silver, St Dennis Silver (from Cornwall, founded 1837), Morris Motors – and, from Queensbury near Bradford, the Black Dyke Mills Band, returning after a rule-enforced absence following its 1947–8–9 triple win. Altogether, the bands included more than 400 men, but only one girl cornetist, Hazel Joll of Falmouth Town Band. Almost inevitably, Black Dyke Mills came through to win, with their acclaimed performance of Percy Fletcher's *An Epic Symphony*. After their great day out, wrote the *Herald* consolingly, 'the players go home to re-enter their workaday world as miners, motor craftsmen, china-clay workers, shipwrights and masons'. But for the triumphant Yorkshiremen, mainly textile workers, there was both a victory march back home on the Monday evening – 'all the village is expected to turn out to cheer', anticipated the Bradford paper – and, 17 years later, a starring role in the first batch of Apple singles.[30]

Choral singing and brass bands, though, were not the urban working-class norm. Something else was, as the 15-year-old Robert Douglas discovered in Maryhill, Glasgow:

'Are you no away tae the dancing, yet?' Uncle Jack looked at me as though considering reporting me to the police. Every time we had visitors during the summer of 1954 somebody would ask that question. You leave school, get a job and start going to the dancing. It was written down somewhere. Tribal. Another rite of passage . . . 'Everybody starts going tae the jigging when they leave the school. Best puckin' night oot

in the world.' He drew on his Capstan Full Strength. 'Aye, a night doon
the Locarno or the Barrowland. Ye cannae beat it. Time ye were away.'

The *Economist* reckoned in 1953 that ballroom dancing was the second-
largest entertainment industry, with annual admissions at dance halls
running at about 200 million, while that same year the mainly working-
class Derby survey found that whereas 34 per cent of the 16–24 age
group went dancing regularly, only 6 per cent of the 25–34 age group
did, and even fewer as they got older still. Kerr in her study of inner-
city Liverpool put it bluntly: 'Dancing is extremely popular with the
girls until marriage, when it is dropped at once.'

What were those dance floors like? Dennis et al in their Featherstone
study have a nice description of the large Saturday-evening dances
at the Miners' Welfare Institute – several hundred people, almost all
in their late teens, 'dance floor crowded, conversation not urgently
necessary, often limited to a narrow range of remarks on the size of
the crowd and the quality of the band' – but the most vivid evocation
is by Steven Berkoff (born 1937), who by his early teens was going
to the vast Tottenham Royal, a Mecca in almost every sense. It was a
milieu where 'you were who you wished to be – warrior, lover, Jimmy
Cagney, Tony Curtis, villain, spiv, leader, loner, heavy, Beau Brummel';
where 'in your drapes and rollaway Johnny Ray collar you sprounced
into with the expectation of a dream'; where as you entered 'the smell
of the hall had a particular aroma of velvet and hairspray, Brylcreem
and Silvikrin lacquer, cigs, floor polish'; where 'the band, usually Ray
Ellington, would be up the far end'; where 'the Stamford Hill crowd
would stand on the left-hand side and the crowd from Tottenham
would stand on the right', with 'no mixing unless you felt cocky and
wanted to fraternize'; where the underlying behavioural assumption
was that 'this was the mating game and the locking of horns'; where
'you wore your costume and walked the hall beneath the glittering ball
and when you saw someone that you felt was about your stamp you
asked her for a dance'; and where 'as the clock ticked away until the
terrible hour of 11 pm when the band would stop, you became more
and more desperate to find someone you could take home and crush for
half an hour of fierce kissing and squeezing and creating sparks as your
gabardine rubbed against her taffeta'.

Nevertheless, for all the sexual subtext, most dance halls were essentially respectable: managements imposed minimum sartorial standards, including collar and tie for men; they were not licensed for alcohol; and, until the more gymnastic jive gradually took over in the course of the 1950s, they tended to be places where the patrons followed the strict, graceful codes of ballroom dancing ('slow, slow, quick quick slow') as ordained in print and broadcasting by Victor Silvester. Anyway, a glance at one of the best-known bandleaders of the day – the shrewd, dapper, smiling, indefatigable Joe Loss – was enough to demonstrate the underlying conservatism of the milieu.[31]

Nothing yet, though, rivalled the appeal of the flickering screen:

> Every day of the week [noted PEP (Political and Economic Planning) in 1952, several years after the medium's all-time peak] there are, on average, about 3¾ million admissions to the 4,600 cinemas in Great Britain, which is roughly equivalent to every person in the country going to the cinema twenty-seven times a year [easily more than anywhere else in the world]. Not everyone, of course, goes to the 'flicks', but four out of ten adults and five out of ten children do so at least once a week. In all, the British public spend over £100 million annually on cinema-going, which is twice as much as the total amount they spend on going to theatres, concert-halls, music-halls, dance-halls, skating-rinks, sporting events and all other places of public amusement.

Within that huge overall audience, there were certain clear patterns and trends by the early to mid-1950s. The preponderance of women had almost disappeared; the lower middle-class component was declining, the working-class component rising (to 82 per cent of the adult audience by 1954); and there were signs that the cinema would increasingly be a place for the young, among whom pupils from secondary moderns were three times more likely than grammar-school swots to go more than once a week. There were also telling regional variations: annual admissions per person ran at around 36 in Scotland and the north of England, around 26 in London and the Midlands, and only about 18 in the altogether less urban south-west and East Anglia. What about the refuseniks? 'No, I've gone right off it,' a 30-year-old working-class London woman told Mass-Observation in 1950. 'They just don't convince you. Look at the maids in Hollywood films. Do they look as if they've ever done a hard day's work?' A 40-year-old working-class woman was similarly disenchanted: 'If you've seen one, you've seen the lot, and too many of the same type just gets on my nerves. They're all the same, either murder, or mystery, or something to do with shooting and killing. Well, we've lived through enough of that.' And a 25-year-old working-class woman had the best of reasons: 'It's baby – since I've had baby, and she's seven months, I don't think I've been once . . . Well frankly, it doesn't worry me whether I go or not . . . I'd rather sit by the fire and listen to the wireless.'[32]

What were the 4,600 cinemas (of which the majority seated over a thousand) like? A handful of memories give the distinctive flavour:

In the 1940s within a mile or so of where we lived in Armley in Leeds there were at least half a dozen cinemas. Nearest was the Picturedrome on Wortley Road but others were just a walk or a tram-ride away – the Lyric down Tong Road, the Clifton at Bramley, the Palace off Stanningley Road and the Western a bit further on . . . Suburban cinemas were often pretty comfortless places. While the entrance could be quite imposing with the box office generally at the top of a flight of white marble steps, presumably to accommodate the rake, the auditorium itself was often not much more than a hangar, the aisle carpeted but the seats on lino or even bare concrete . . . We always called it 'the pictures', seldom 'the cinema' and never 'the movies'. To this day I don't find it easy to say 'movies' . . . *(Alan Bennett)*

Colchester boasted five cinemas. They ranked hierarchically, from the Regal (a custom-built picture palace, with restaurant, portraits of stars, pile carpet), the Playhouse, the Hippodrome (the last two converted music halls, the latter with some fine interior décor), the Headgate (a converted chapel) to the Empire, the town fleapit – still gaslit in the 1950s. And I seem to recall the usherettes going up and down in the intervals with Flit guns. Perhaps there really were fleas. *(John Sutherland)*

The only downside, so far as I was concerned, was the continuous performance where the main film and the 'B' movie (usually a black and white British cop drama), together with the newsreel, just kept rolling from 2 pm until the stampede to beat the National Anthem at about 10 pm. My father was a man who wouldn't be hurried, so instead of dashing to make the start of the main feature, we'd always arrive in the middle of the film. The whole programme would continue until the point I always dreaded, when my father would nudge me and say, 'I think this is where we came in.' Up we'd get and stumble out in the dark . . . *(Anton Rippon, Derby)*

There was always a queue if the film was at all popular, which invariably resulted in fights as people tried to push in front of others, and even inside no one was safe. Every cinema had its share of gropers prowling the dark looking for young women sitting on their own, and these encounters would erupt like mortar-bomb explosions all through the film. Suddenly there would be a screech and the sound of a face being slapped followed by a lady shouting: 'You dirty fucking bastard!' Ushers would arrive and the shame-faced dirty fucking bastard would be thrown out. *(Michael Caine, Elephant and Castle)*

'I always went the same way to every cinema, and I could traverse those same streets now,' is how the film director Terence Davies recalls his picture-going Liverpool childhood. 'I can still remember where I saw certain films, where I sat, who I went with. It's *still* that vivid.'[33]

Cinema-goers fell into different types. Two film historians, Sue Harper and Vincent Porter, have usefully distinguished between the indiscriminate, the regular and the occasional, while Peter Miskell in his study of the cinema in Wales (where the habit was broadly in line with the British average) has emphasised the intensity as well as the breadth of the medium's appeal, with at least half of a typical audience comprising those who went at least twice a week. How important was the actual film? Kathleen Box's 1946 inquiry into cinema-going, based on adult samples, found that more than two-thirds either went to the same cinema 'whatever the film being shown' or chose a film from a limited range of local cinemas, with fewer than one-third making the film itself the sole criterion of choice. 'Broadly speaking,' commented Rachael Low in 1948 in *The Penguin Film Review* on the implications of Box's findings, 'the lower economic and education groups show the greatest rigidity in their cinema-going, tending to go very often and without exercising much choice.' She went regretfully on:

To them the all-important thing is that films should be available in sufficient quantity to provide one or two full evenings a week at the pictures, with all that this implies of escape from home and job, outings with friends and, for the young, a comfortable and socially accepted place for wooing. The unimportance of artistic nuances is nowhere so marked as in the Sunday-evening houses in such an area, where bad reissues and worse second features are received with indifferent tolerance by a skylarking audience, whose sole expression of emotion, whether of amusement, embarrassment or even surprise or tension, seems to be an uncontrolled guffaw.

Low drew a contrast with those from 'a financial and educational background' encouraging 'more diffused cultural interests'. They, happily, were 'inclined to exercise more rigorous selection, only going to the pictures when there is a particular film they wish to see'.[34]

Examined close-up, the whole business could have an undeniably haphazard feel to it. *London Town*, starring the comedian Sid Field, was Britain's first major Technicolor musical; in the autumn of 1946, at the time of its much-publicised release, Mass-Observation elicited a range of working-class responses, mainly from the King's Cross, Battersea and Waterloo districts, as it asked how people had heard about the film, what they knew about it and whether they wanted to see it:

Well Missie you see, I don't know much about them things, but if you say it's Sid Field, I might take the missus of a Saturday afternoon – she'd enjoy it you know – she likes something cheery over the weekend. *(M50)*

No, I don't know nothing about that sort of thing. *(F50)*

No! – I can't talk ducks – look! I've got no teeth. *(F55)*

I don't get much time to find out about these things really – being at work all day. *(F55)*

I'd be very keen on seeing it – especially the wife – frankly between you and I it's the cheapest form of entertainment for the working man. I go with the wife and kid once a week – usually on a Saturday, and we go out to tea, and that's about as far as the pocket will allow. *(M30)*

Well, I expect we shall go and see it because of my wife. Yes, it's a pity she isn't here really – she'd tell you all you want to know – she's a great film fan. But being a *dutiful* husband as I said – I expect I shall have to go. *(M35)*

I don't really care one way or the other. *(M35)*

Well as a matter of fact, the daughter came round on Sunday and suggested we should go, but the missus was feeling a bit off colour and didn't want to go so far – you know as how it is. *(M65)*

The generally downbeat tone accurately presaged *London Town*'s fate: despite the best efforts of Field himself, Kay Kendall, 'Two Ton' Tessie O'Shea and a 14-year-old Petula Clark, as well as a clutch of supposedly favourite 'Cockney' songs, it proved a resounding flop.

Four years later, expectations were more modest for the altogether lower-budget *Chance of a Lifetime.* This was an 'issue' film, in which the actor-director and writer Bernard Miles depicted industrial relations in a small tractor-manufacturing firm; against its wishes, Rank was compelled by the Labour government to release the well-meaning drama on its Odeon circuit. When M-O asked people as they came out of London Odeons in June 1950 what they had made of the movie, the working-class response was mixed:

It was too dull. It didn't have any life in it. It was all talking all the time. *(F20)*

I think it was trying to say that the Bolshies are not so bad as some people make out. *(M40)*

It was trying to say that the workers and managers should work together harmoniously all the time and not always be going on strike. *(F30)*

It was very true to life and it wasn't far-fetched like some films are today. *(F40)*

I liked the other film [*Arson Inc*, an American picture] that was on with it best. *(M35)*

I haven't thought about it, I just sat back and looked at it, that's all. *(M40)*

I usually go anyway once a week and that seemed about the best to go to that week. *(M35)*

We generally come each week – we didn't know what was on – when we saw Basil Rathbone [in fact Radford] we thought it was a funny. *(F40)*

I'm not much of a judge myself. I don't go in for being a critic exactly. But I think that it shows that you just can't sit back and let things go on, because they just won't. *(M55)*

> To tell you the truth, I thought it was a bit drawn-out. I don't know
> how to put it – it sort of hung fire somehow. *(M65)*

A 50-year-old middle-class woman did not mince her words. 'It tried to show some of the lower classes,' she pronounced outside the Wimbledon Odeon, 'that their conduct today is outrageous – and that that "I'm as good as you" policy is simply outrageous if you haven't got the sense or education to back it up.' In the event, Rank's commercial fears were amply realised. 'The biggest flop we have ever touched,' claimed one Scottish exhibitor, thereby endorsing the initial scepticism of the novelist Elizabeth Bowen (an independent member of the Board of Trade committee) that for all its meritorious qualities it 'lacked the more obvious kind of drawing power'.[35]

A little realism went a long way, as Sydney Box found. During and immediately after the war, Gainsborough Pictures had produced a series of critically ravaged but highly successful historical costume films – bodice-ripping melodramas aimed unerringly at the working-class female audience. Box took over as Head of Production in 1946 and demanded a greater degree of realism, exemplified by his artistically much more ambitious (and expensive) *The Bad Lord Byron* two years later. But he had fatally misread his market and the film flopped, marking the end of Gainsborough's glory days. So too at Featherstone in the early to mid-1950s, where Dennis et al discovered that the key ingredients for box-office appeal were action and escapism: 'The most popular types of film are the coloured "western", the spectacular adventure story, and the slapstick comedy. Pictures about the 1939–45 war are also popular. Musical romances appeal to the women. All these films resemble one another in their irrelevance to the problems of the day . . .' It was similar in Liverpool, where years later two working-class women evoked the pull in the 1950s of the American Dream as played out in Hollywood film musicals. 'They were a life-saver, the musicals,' recalled one, while the other made an unanswerable defence of their sustaining emotional power: 'You should have seen the house where we lived in Cunningham Street. This is a palace compared to it. The worst slum I have ever seen in my life. To live like that and then to enter that magical world. Who can despise it? Only them that's got a lot more can despise it.'

The gulf between 'good' taste (which on the part of the established middle class, ie not the lower middle class, often included a strong element of anti-Americanism) and working-class taste was epitomised by what one might call the Shiner paradigm. Ronald Shiner (born 1903) was an actor who, in the words of one obituary, 'seemed to embody and realise everybody's notion of the archetypal cockney – inquisitive (a long, apparently probing nose assisted him in this), quick-witted, brilliant improvisation when trouble threatened, and ready to face difficulties with an aggression that was always obviously compounded of equal quantities of bluff, self-reliance, and desperation'. His big breakthrough came on the stage towards the end of the war with *Worm's Eye View*. This comedy by R. F. Delderfield about the sufferings of aircraftmen billeted in a Lancashire seaside boarding house ran in London for 1,700 performances, and Shiner not only played the lead-swinging Private Sam Porter but was also director. A film version appeared in 1951 and for the most part was either ignored or patronised by the more upmarket critics. 'In the film,' thought *The Times*, 'the simple farce is perhaps even broader, heartier, and more obvious, but it is a fine distinction.' Commercially, however, it came up trumps, 'a real money-spinner' and 'the turn-up of the century', according to *Kinematograph Weekly*, which in its review of the year declared that 'it made many a more costly British film look sickly at the box-office'. Soon afterwards, Shiner starred as Sergeant Bell in the similarly farcical *Reluctant Heroes*, which according to *KW*'s review of 1952 was 'frightened out of the West End by the critics' before again proving 'record-breaking' and one of the 'big money-takers' of the year. That was the peak of Shiner's career, but later in the fifties there were parts as Alf Tubbe in *Dry Rot*, Marine Ogg in *Girls at Sea* and Gunner Slocum in *Operation Bullshine*.[36]

It was not just cinema that was poised for a great fall, but also live Variety. Yet at the time, like cinema, it still seemed a sure-fire formula, nicely evoked by a local paper's favourable review in September 1953 of the 'Celebration Rag' show twice nightly at the Coventry Hippodrome. Top of the bill was Donald Peers 'singing the songs the radio audiences enjoy and managing to carry off the most banal rhyme with a kind of infectious enthusiasm'; other acts included the Tanner Sisters ('zip through their numbers'), Georges and Lennette ('perform nonchalantly on a high wire'), and Sonny Burke and Jimmy Clitheroe ('an original conjuring act that throws fresh light on the ever-ready volunteer from the audience'), the midget not yet radio's 'The Clitheroe Kid'. Best of all, there was Jimmy James, with his 'sly way with comedy', for instance 'as the drunk with wife trouble, the chap-who-knows-his-way-about, the man who can tell you esoteric things about the fish and chip business', so that 'towards the end of the evening' he had 'only to lift a massive eyebrow and we laughed'.

Variety sometimes took place in the fewish surviving Victorian music halls, such as the Queen's in Poplar High Street or the Metropolitan in Edgware Road (where the young, not-yet-screaming David Sutch watched two-hour, twelve-act shows 'ranging from singers and comics to fire-eaters, magicians and trick cyclists') or the Queen's behind Glasgow Cross, 'small and profoundly proletarian', in one observer's words. More often, though, it took its turn in theatres such as the Bristol Empire, the Brighton Hippodrome or the dreaded – by southern comedians – Glasgow Empire. The joy, perhaps as much in memory as at the time, was in the variousness: the magician Ali Bongo ('The Shriek of Araby'), the illusionist Cingallee, the pigeon act Hamilton Conrad, the animal and bird impersonator Percy ('I Travel the Road') Edwards, the drag act Ford and Sheen, the mind-reader The Amazing Fogel, the lady whistler Eva Kane, the male impersonator Hetty King, the foot juggler Levanda, the comedy acrobats Manley and Austin, the rope-spinner and raconteur Tex McLeod, the yodelling accordionist Billy Moore, the human spider Valantyne Napier, the mental telepathists The Piddingtons, the novelty xylophonist Reggie Redcliffe, the speciality dancer Bunty St Clare, the pianist Semprini, the aereliste Olga Varona, and many, many others – inhabitants of a lost world.[37]

What conclusively destroyed that world was of course television, but it was not just television. It was also the coming to the halls – for good short-term commercial reasons in terms of male bums on seats, but with ultimately disastrous consequences in terms of family entertainment – of nudity, something inconceivable as yet on television. It was admittedly nudity of a very specific, controlled sort: the Lord Chamberlain's rules insisted on the girl or girls staying completely motionless, prompting the well-known revue number, 'It's all right to be nude, but if it moves, it's rude'. Variety's early nudes included Phyllis Dixey (the 'Peek-a-Boo Girl'), 'Jane' (based on the *Daily Mirror*

cartoon and usually accompanied by her little dachshund, Fritzi) and
Blondie ('Godiva') Haigh. A key figure in the rise of the touring revue
with a Nude Show at its heart was Paul Raymond, the future 'King of
Soho'. Topless girls posing in saucy tableaux were his speciality, and by
the early 1950s his show had, an obituary recounted, 'evolved into the
Festival of Nudes (a cheeky wink at the Festival of Britain) and then
Moving Nudes, where naked lovelies were perched high in the air on
precarious wooden platforms'. The poor man's Raymond was Terry
Cantor, whose touring revue (*All Shapes and Surprises*, playing at the
Palace Theatre, Preston) was profiled by Trevor Philpott in early 1954.
'Is it what the customers want?' he asked rhetorically after describing
how the chorus girls took off their dressing gowns to present what had
been announced as 'a tableau in stark reality entitled "The Kill"'. 'The
box office says so,' was his answer. 'The show was losing steadily until
the nudes were brought in, three years ago. Pantomimes and "family-
shows" are having leaner times, year by year; but "Jane," doing a strip-
tease, filled this same theatre in November.' Philpott reflected that it
was 'a sad thing to think on', but the last word went to Cantor: 'My
show's got to suit my audiences. We give the public what they ask for.'[38]

The rapid decline of Variety later in the 1950s would be no laughing
matter for its front-rank comedians, not necessarily equipped to
make the transition to the small screen. Each had his (occasionally
her) own following and distinctive style. Max Miller, no longer quite
the dominant force he had been before and during the war, was still
the original cheeky chappie, the 'eternal commercial traveller', in
Roy Hudd's words, whose art was that of 'suggestion, innuendo,
the unspoken' and who seldom ventured north of Birmingham; the
double act of Jimmy Jewel and Ben Warriss (the latter as the snappily
dressed, brilliantined know-all mercilessly tormenting his gormless
partner) was the bridge between Flanagan and Allen before the war
and Morecambe and Wise from the 1960s; Tommy Trinder specialised
in the brash, abrasive, cockney putdown; Nat Jackley's greatest asset
was his rubberneck; Dave Morris played long seasons in Blackpool
depicting in drag a domineering local landlady; Freddie Frinton's
calling card was his 'Dinner For One, Please, James' sketch, with
Frinton as the bumbling manservant to an autocratic old lady; Doris
Droy, famous for her impersonation of a drunken office cleaner, was

the loud-voiced doyenne of the Queen's in Glasgow; Eddie Gray ('Monsewer'), one of the Crazy Gang, had on his own a line in the burlesque that anticipated Tommy Cooper. Some generalisations are possible. Variety humour combined identity-reinforcing macro-conservatism with a streak of anti-puritanical micro-subversiveness; was strongly working-class in both manner and appeal; and ultimately, for good or ill, was profoundly escapist. M-O in 1950 found that music-hall humour was not only little different in subject matter from ten years earlier – with most jokes still being about sex, ill-health (often accidents) and domestic affairs (including mothers-in-law), and very few topical and/or political ones – but that the jokes themselves were almost word-for-word and largely unchanged.[39] It was, in short, a humour that still spoke to its audience.

The wireless version, more or less following strict BBC guidelines, was a somewhat tamer affair, but presumably not wholly different. Catchphrases proliferated in radio comedy, including 'I thought, "Right monkey!" ' for Salford's Al Read, less escapist than most and hailed by the *Daily Mirror* in 1951 (the year of his first series) as 'the pieman who has become the white hope of Northern comedy'. It was a justified hope, as Read over the years rolled out in his show a succession of recognisable characters from everyday working-class life, such as (to quote Hudd) 'the wife in the kitchen, the "know-all" decorator/football fan/car park attendant, and the embarrassing small son'. Or, in the apt words of Alan Bennett, an early fan: 'Radio was at the kitchen sink long before Arnold Wesker.' Read's counterpart from the north-east was Bobby Thompson, who following his successful stints in *Wot Cheor Geordie!*, had from 1953 his own series, *Bob's Your Uncle!*, transmitted on the North of England Home Service and subtitled 'A running commentary on the wife and hard times of a plain working man, with music and songs for the silver lining'. A sketch from an early show, called 'Buying a New Suit', began with Thompson's recreation of a husband-and-wife meeting of minds:

> I gets me cap on for the club – then it starts!
> 'Just look at the mess ye are! That suit's an absolute disgrace! All the money ye keep out of your pay ye'd think ye'd get yourself a new 'un.'
> 'Why,' I says, 'don't take on pet. It's all right to go to the club in.'

'The club? That's where ye got all them stains, spillin' that muck ye drink.'

'Thaa's wrong there, Phyllis,' I says. 'Beer's awer dear to spill.' I says, 'Lend's a quid to go to the club, an' when I come back thaa can guess how much change I has!' Why, she blows up then . . .

'Lend ye a quid to go to that club? Over my dead body . . . an' get that look out of your eye. You're not going to the club again until ye've been for a new suit! If my mother was to drop dead the day ye haven't a decent suit for the funeral! An' she can't live for ever poor soul.'

'No,' I says. 'But she's having a good try!'

'What was that ye said?'

'I said I'd have a good cry.'

'Ye'll do nothing of the kind. Ye've that much beer inside ye, they could bottle your tears an' sell them for best bitter. I've warned ye though . . . ! That suit's going on the fire, so ye'd better get out of it unless you're thick-skinned. I don't want my man lookin' like a rag bag. Ye drink like a lord, so ye might as well look like one!'

Wives generally fared poorly in Thompson's humour. 'We got off the train at Blackpool,' ran a favourite gag. 'The porter says: "Carry your bag?" Aa said: "Let her walk." ' As for homosexuals, they seldom featured in his patter, but in real life he loathed them and once, according to his biographer, 'finished with a theatrical agency because the partners were thought to be gay'.[40]

No comedian in the late 1940s and early 1950s, though, could match Halifax's Wilfred Pickles for week-in, week-out radio popularity. His prime vehicle was the untesting, good-natured quiz *Have a Go!*, with its invariable, much-loved features: Pickles's opening catchphrase, ' 'Ow do, 'ow are yer?'; the amiable chat with the mainly working-class contestants about their lives; a large round of applause if a contestant turned out to be over 60; a few questions, including one about the contestant's most embarrassing moment; the banging of the gong by Pickles's wife-cum-manager Mabel if the answer was wrong; Pickles's call to the producer, 'Give 'im the money, Barney,' for a winning contestant; and, at the end, the buoyant, singalong theme song ('That's the show, Joe/You've been and had a go'), with piano accompaniment from Violet Carson (the future Ena Sharples of *Coronation Street*). 'A small, slight, spruce man with slickly brushed sandy hair,' was how the *Sunday Pictorial* in January 1947, four months after the quiz show had gone national on the Light Programme, profiled the 42-year-old son of a builder, adding that he had 'no stomach for fussy foreign cooking' and, of course, was 'not interested in politics'. As for his humour, 'there's certainly nothing sophisticated or "smart-alec" about it', being instead 'of the people' and 'healthy, "pub" humour, the type of gag that has no basis in unkindness'.

It was not long before more than half the adult population was regularly tuning in. 'To my mind, the most human Radio personality,' the middle-aged wife of a waiter told M-O in 1949. 'As a listener, I feel straight away, what a wide sense of homeliness has been created. I admire his tolerance, thoughtfulness and humble approach to one and all. His voice sounds very sincere and he has a kindly manner.' Pickles's sincerity does not seem to have been in question, but it was an image that he guarded carefully. 'I had no choice,' he explained in September 1951 about his last-minute refusal – having seen the script – to appear at the London Palladium in Tallulah Bankhead's distinctly American *Big Show*. 'British listeners wouldn't have recognised me. I didn't recognise myself. I'm just an ordinary bloke at home and enjoy myself talking to and mixing with ordinary folk. I don't use scripts and I'm not a slick wise-cracker.' Two months later he introduced in *Radio Times* the sixth series of *Have a Go!*. The first quiz was due to come from 'that snug little Lancashire town Rawtenstall, where they make slippers and speak their minds', and he declared that the programme was 'made of people, with all their qualities and failings, their hopes, fears, ideals'. Charges of sentimentality, even of pandering to certain comfortable, mainly northern self-images, are difficult to deny. But as one of his helpers on stage, the young June Whitfield, would justifiably emphasise half a century later, the endemic stuffiness of so much of the BBC's output meant that 'Wilfred's voice and unaffected ordinariness were like a breath of fresh air.'[41]

'I fancy that the BP [ie the British public] *en masse* is not likely to take to walking over the hills,' was how one Tory backbencher consoled himself in 1949 about that year's National Parks and Access to the

Countryside Act, adding that 'charabancs, main roads and pubs are what the majority of holiday-makers like'. He was right. Two years later the Peak District became Britain's first national park, but at least until the widespread coming of the family car most people stuck to the tried and tested when it came to day outings. Rich had already noted in Coseley how organised outings run by working-men's clubs and suchlike 'usually go to the seaside, especially to Rhyl, Llandudno, Blackpool (especially during the "illuminations") or Weston-super-Mare', while in 'Ashton' (ie Featherstone), Dennis et al observed that 'the people who go on the trips from Ashton clubs in fact seek out those activities in the places they visit which most closely resemble those provided in Ashton', including a high proportion of visits to other working-men's clubs within a 25-mile radius. Even for unorganised daytrippers, there was a high premium placed on the familiar and the popular, as on the first Sunday of June 1950, Newcastle's hottest day of the year so far:

This is what happened.

GETTING THERE: A Newcastle Central Station ticket-collector called it 'pandemonium'. It was, but it was good-humoured pandemonium. From noon until late afternoon, four-deep queues snaked from the platform barriers through the station and out into Neville Street. It was a non-stop queue for the coast resorts.

Buses were stampeded, too. Mothers, fathers and children swarmed into bus after bus. Always, people were left behind. But the queue philosophy says, 'There will always be another bus – or train.' And there was – and everybody got there in the end.

THERE: Tynemouth's sands are golden. But yesterday they were a vivid moving mosaic of blues and reds and yellows and greens. All Tyneside was there – or so it seemed.

And Tyneside queued to enjoy itself. It queued for jugs of hot water for countless picnic teas; it queued for lemonade and candy floss; it queued for the privilege of bathing in the overcrowded swimming pool; it queued for 'funny' paper hats; it queued to get on the beach; it even queued to get off the beach.

'And most of all,' ended the report, 'it queued for ice cream. It must have queued for hundreds of thousands of ice creams.'[42]

Day trips mattered, given that the nationwide Social Survey found in 1949 not only that almost half the adult population had not had a holiday away from home that year but also that for those who had not holidayed, just over half had had day trips instead – thereby leaving some 23 per cent of adults who had had neither a holiday nor a day trip during the whole year, notwithstanding the Holidays with Pay Act in 1948, which gave every employed adult a paid fortnight off. Other findings were that holiday-making was more frequent among the better-off and those in urban occupations with a tradition of paid holidays; that the 26 per cent who had not taken a holiday 'for many years' mainly comprised older people; that less than 2 per cent of holidays were taken abroad; that almost two-thirds of holidays were by the sea; that about two-fifths of holidays involved staying with friends or relatives; and, startlingly, that 32 per cent of holiday-makers went away entirely on their own.

Locally speaking, especially in industrial towns and cities, the annual holiday period was a momentous event, with the nineteenth-century 'Wakes Week' custom still strong and factories shutting down in unison. 'Holiday-Bound Multitude Leaves City', reported the *Coventry Evening Telegraph* on the last Saturday of July 1953:

> Coventry people have been streaming away from the city in their tens of thousands during the past 24 hours.
>
> Fortunately the clouds cleared as the factories closed down yesterday for the fortnight's break, and perfect weather gave the holidaymakers a propitious start for their journeys. At Coventry Station, many of those who departed throughout the night were in a jolly mood, and singing, accompanied by the music of accordions, took the tedium out of the waiting period.
>
> About 25,000 – the same number as last year – travelled by train during the rush period. There was a smooth system of queuing outside the station entrances. As each new train came into the station, its queue was admitted in an orderly crocodile on to the platform.

'Traffic was very heavy this morning,' added the report, 'particularly for Llandudno and Blackpool between 6 am and 7 am,' while 'coaches, solidly booked up this year, were leaving Pool Meadow for all the popular seaside resorts.' Rail had traditionally been far and away the most popular form of travel to and from holiday destinations, but by the mid-1950s visiting figures for Skegness were showing a roughly even divide between rail, coach and car, with coaches able to provide convenient pick-up and drop-off points as well as being cheaper.[43]

An increasingly popular seaside destination was the holiday camp, by now entering its heyday. In addition to the two main, highly successful 'industrial' chains – Butlin's and Pontin's, each providing almost military-style round-the-clock service and entertainment – there were the rather smaller-scale Warner's camps and a host of family-run individual holiday camps tending to the rudimentary but homely, typified by Potter's at Hopton-on-Sea in Norfolk. Most accounts of holiday camps (including M-O's) have a whiff of middle-class condescension about them, playing up the 'Hi-de-Hi' vulgarity, but Valerie Tedder's recollection of a respectable, tight-knit working-class family from Leicester enjoying in 1950 its first proper holiday offers a salutary corrective. Warner's in Hayling Island was the carefully chosen venue for her parents, her little sister and her 16-year-old self, a venue that provided order, fun and a sense of camaraderie in roughly equal proportions:

We made use of the baby listening service a couple of times, but always checked on Julie every half an hour. All one had to do to alert the staff that there was a baby sleeping in the chalet, was to tie a large white handkerchief on the door knob. Any child heard crying was reported by the night staff on patrol and the message was given out over the tannoy system in the ballroom. The compère would stop the evening proceedings the minute he received a message to say, 'Baby crying in chalet number . . .' It was expected that a parent would return to their chalet immediately and they usually did. It was noticeable that many fathers did the honours, leaving the mothers to enjoy the evening undisturbed.

At the end of the evening the entertainment came to a close with the singing of 'Goodnight Campers' to the refrain of 'Goodnight Sweetheart', followed by the National Anthem. Quietly we left the ballroom and bars to stroll back to the chalets. Some youngsters went for midnight swims in the floodlit pool, but if there was any noise whatsoever they were reprimanded by the security patrols who kept a sharp watch on proceedings. Loud noise and shouting was banned and anyone misbehaving in this manner was warned only once. If they persisted, next morning they were asked to leave and were escorted off the premises. Rarely was there any trouble of this nature because the organisers were strict and kept their word. In addition there was always the backing of the family campers . . .

The organisers of the sporting events appeared to have thought of everything and we were encouraged to participate in the heats, playing against one another in our own time until the finals were reached on the Friday morning. Some enthusiasts, we noticed, took part in so many of the sports that they seemed to be doing nothing else all week. We restricted ourselves to the fun sports like the obstacle, sack, three-legged and egg and spoon races. Julie was encouraged to enter the children's events. Dad and I entered the swimming gala, struggling and roaring with laughter at the antics the compère got up to while we were trying to take the races seriously . . .

Dad and I won third prizes for dressing up on Topsy Turvy night. This was for adults only, but it was all clean fun and the children were as much involved as their parents. They enjoyed watching the adults making fools of themselves in their outrageous outfits. We borrowed clothes from one another and there was a great sense of fun and friendliness. Offers to lend items of apparel were readily forthcoming . . .

Other activities they participated in included the plate-collecting competition (from the deep end of the pool), the Donkey Derby, and the fancy-hat and fancy-dress competitions – as well as happy hours by themselves on the beach. 'The week went by very quickly and before we knew it we were saying farewell to many friends. Our first venture with holiday camps was declared a great success . . .'[44]

Whether for holiday camps or for British seaside resorts more generally, there was by the early 1950s an inexorably growing demand, against a background of full employment and enhanced collective bargaining power. 'Early in 1951 the majority of workers still had a basic holiday entitlement of one week, while a minority could expect a fortnight,' notes the historian of occupational welfare, Alice Russell. 'The following year the proportions had been reversed.' The result was keen competition between the resorts, and typical magazine ads in early 1954 included Blackpool ('All the Best and Best for All'), Bournemouth

('For Sea, Sands and Sunshine'), Ramsgate ('Where Jolly Holidays in Bracing Air Suit Health and Pocket'), Walton-on-the-Naze ('England's friendliest resort'), Penzance ('Bathed in the Western Sun') and Fleetwood ('For a Tonic Holiday'). Resorts were especially competitive in the area of illuminations. At Blackpool, the acknowledged market leader, the hugely elaborate display of illuminated tableaux ran each year (after their return in 1949) from early September to late October, attracting some three million visitors; at Morecambe, noted *The Times* in 1953, 'skilful floodlighting has enhanced the natural beauty of Happy Mount Park, and there is floodlighting for three miles and a half along the promenade'; Southport and Southend each had spectacular pier illuminations; Bournemouth specialised in candlelight displays, with some 30,000 candles lit by tapers distributed among holiday-makers; and Paignton's renowned speciality was swinging lanterns.[45]

Most seaside resorts were predominantly for the working class, but predictably there were some social gradations. 'All over Britain,' Ian Jack has recalled, 'smaller resorts drew the kind of people who were offended by too much vulgarity and alcohol, and therefore preferred Millport over Rothesay [both of them favourite destinations, 'doon the watter', during Glasgow's holiday fortnight, Glasgow Fair, in the second half of July], Southport over Blackpool, Teignmouth over Whitley Bay, Mablethorpe over Skegness. I think of their preferences as towns marked by an improving hush, with dads bending over rock pools and mums knitting on the promenade.' There were certainly distinctions when it came to the bestselling postcards of Donald McGill, for whom Blackpool, Scarborough and Brighton were his surefire resorts. 'Ultra-respectable towns, like Eastbourne and Frinton, won't display them,' he remarked in 1954. 'They say they are vulgar – I suppose you might say that of Shakespeare? People who think joke cards are vulgar are worthy people who have forgotten how to laugh – they can only snigger.'[46]

Each resort, respectable or less so, had its own characteristics. Newquay was identified by Arnold Russell on his 1951 *Reynolds News* tour of seaside resorts as a 'bright, breezy, clean resort', no longer reliant for its living on pilchard fishing, and where 'on every side one hears the accents of Scotland, the Midlands and London'. Great Yarmouth, holiday destination for 'a huge, essentially decent, working-class population', he praised as ahead of the post-war curve with its 'clinics and crèches where children can safely be left in the care of professional nurses, paddling pools and toddlers' centres'. Bracing Skegness had a similar clientele. 'We went there every year for as long as I can remember, local people like us tended not to go too far away from home,' remembered the shotputter Geoff Capes, one of a ganger's nine children, about his childhood in the Lincolnshire fens. 'I used to fish off the pier, caught shrimps, went cockling, went back to the caravan and boiled them up.' Up the coast in Scarborough, where some three-quarters of each summer's two million or so visitors were from Yorkshire, attractions included Corrigan's Fair, the Spa's dance halls, cafés and bandstand, Tom Perry's Aquatomics in the huge swimming pool at the far end of the South Bay, and the twice-weekly packed terraces of the Open Air Theatre, with some 8,000 watching shows like *The Desert Song*. In Morecambe, or 'Bradford-on-Sea', the theatrical highlight each summer was the return of the local-born Thora Hird to star in the comedy *Ma's Bit of Brass*. 'A bit mawkish, sometimes, but a brilliant comedienne,' recalled Robert Stephens about acting with her, adding that 'people were hanging from the rafters, you couldn't get a seat'. These were booming times for Morecambe – typified by how 13 'specials', including one train bringing 3,600 holiday-makers from Yorkshire, came even during the 'mackintosh Whit' of 1952 – as they were also for the somewhat more upmarket Douglas on the Isle of Man, each summer a home from home for thousands of Mancunians and Liverpudlians. Its ballrooms, including the Villa Marina, the Palace and the Derby Castle, were among the largest in Europe. 'I like the Palace dance hall best,' noted one appreciative observer, John Betjeman. 'It has a parquet floor of sixteen thousand square feet and room for five thousand people. It is in a gay baroque style, cream and pink inside, and from the graceful roof hang Japanese lanterns out of a dangling forest of flags. A small and perfect dance band strikes up – ah, the dance bands of the Isle of Man! Soon a thousand couples are moving beautifully, the cotton dresses of the girls like vivid tulips in all this pale cream and pink, the sports coats and dark suits of the men a background to so much airy colour . . .'[47]

Nowhere quite beat Blackpool. The Golden Mile, the Tower (including its ballroom with Reginald Dixon at the Mighty Wurlitzer, its circus with the multi-instrumental, much-loved Clown Prince Charlie Cairoli), the Big Wheel, the Pleasure Beach (including the legendary Big Dipper), the three piers, top live shows seemingly everywhere (to take just one week in July 1951, Vera Lynn at the Opera House, Elsie and Doris Waters at the Palace Variety, Wilfred Pickles in *Hobson's Choice* at the Grand, Ted Heath and his Music at the Empress Ballroom, Al Read at the Central Pier, Dave Morris at the South Pier), the Ice Show, the Tussaud waxworks, boxing, wrestling and greyhound racing – all this, and Stanley Matthews too, made Blackpool a secular heaven for millions. The Blackpool landlady, traditionally 'all bosom and bark', in reality not quite so fearsome, did her bit in the town's countless guest houses; but even her mainly sympathetic historian, John Walton, concedes that in the 1950s 'price-cutting and the resultant corner-cutting remained permanent features of the less prosperous end of the industry, and complaints of "full board" which only amounted to two frugal meals a day, or of surcharges for basic services, still flowed freely every season'.[48]

Overall, it was not a place that much commended itself to a political class bent on ever-wider social and cultural improvement. 'Blackpool, with its ugliness and high prices, is the supreme example of the commercial exploitation of working-class limitations,' declared the *New Statesman*'s 'Critic' after the Labour Party's 1949 conference there:

All the pleasures of a big industrial city have been concentrated on a stretch of Lancashire coast where sea-bathing is almost impossible, trees find it difficult to survive, and beauty is excluded by every device of man's contriving. The only noble feature of the place is the trams, which are handsome and very fast. Walking on the sea-front in the evening you can see the mountains of Cumberland a few miles to the north, and reflect on what Cyril Joad [the well-known radio philosopher] has called the 'drainage system' which preserves the quiet of our countryside by canalising working-class holiday-makers into places like Blackpool and Southend, where their year's savings are painlessly removed from their pockets in a few days.

Still, at least it was not Blackpool's rival further up the coast. 'I have just got back from Morecambe,' Clement Attlee told his brother after the party's conference there three years later. 'Architecturally it ranks a good second to Blackpool, the former beats it in the atrocious ugliness of its buildings, but Morecambe pulls up on complete absence of planning. Our hotel wing was, however, very comfortable.'

Broadly speaking – with going abroad effectively not an option in terms of either affordability or available foreign currency – the British holiday-maker took what he got. Some July 1951 vox pop, 'picked at random' by the local Blackpool paper from 'the crowds on central promenade', suggested a fairly high degree of satisfaction:

This is the fourth year we have come. We like your ballrooms and swimming pools, they are so lovely. We can't think of anything we don't like. Blackpool to us is just wonderful. *(Audrey Milburn and Jean Stanley, 20-year-old unmarried girls from Shepherd's Bush)*

The big thing about Blackpool is that when it rains there are plenty of places to go. There are lovely entertainments without going to the sideshows on Central Beach. *(Mrs P. Anderson of Grangemouth, Stirlingshire, on her second visit in two years)*

Blackpool has some lovely walks, that's what I like about it. I don't like drinking but I do like to pop in and have a pot and continue my walk. *(Mr J. J. Murray, 64, of Bishop Auckland, Co Durham, who had started coming to Blackpool with his father before the Great War)*

There is only one Blackpool, but I do feel that the prices of things for the children – toy windmills, buckets and spades, and other things for the sands – are sometimes high. A charge of 1s 9d for a toy windmill is, to my mind, too big. *(Mr I. Blackwood, of New Cumnock, Ayrshire, with his wife on their first holiday since their wedding two years earlier)*

You can have a quiet holiday or a gay one. It caters for everyone – and the air is so wonderful. *(Mr and Mrs W. Hallas, of Eastmoor, Wakefield)*

More generally, not just in Blackpool, it seems that two criteria mattered most to holiday-makers. The first, articulated in September 1951 by a *Reynolds News* reader ('J. F.' of Carlton Vale, London NW6), was value for money:

My wife, two children and I went to Ramsgate.
BOUQUETS:
To a landlady for perfect digs, spotless rooms, good food, moderate charges within anybody's reach (I am a postman). To kind, courteous townspeople and shop assistants. To reduced prices for children at cinemas.

BRICKBATS:

A large one to the corporation for charging 2d for the lifts from beach to promenade, with additional charges for prams and bathchairs.

A second big one for the number of slot machines out of order (children lose shillings a week), three charges a day for deck chairs, and the prices for so-called children's amusements.

The other criterion was wet-weather facilities, with Blackpool clearly an exception rather than the rule. 'On a wet day what has Morecambe to offer?' a disgruntled Mr W. Dixon of Halifax rhetorically asked a local reporter in August 1951. 'I went for a walk on Sunday morning and saw visitors crowding into every available inch of shelter. They all looked miserable, and cast anxious looks towards the sky . . .' Soon afterwards Arnold Russell, having completed his tour of seaside resorts, echoed the complaint: 'In Scarborough and Margate, South Wales and Hastings, I saw families soaked to the skin, staring hopelessly at emptying grey skies, fervently wishing they were home again. Disappointed youngsters had become fractious, mother was near a nervous breakdown, and Dad was ready to emigrate – on his own.' For these unhappy families, he added, there was 'no option but to trail back to an already overcrowded boarding house, to a landlady who didn't want them while she did her cleaning and cooking'.[49]

'There are queues for everything,' Russell at the start of the August Bank Holiday weekend had reported from Margate, widely acknowledged as the Blackpool of the south and a particular magnet for holiday-making Midlanders. 'For cinemas and theatres, for milk bars and pubs, at ice-cream kiosks and at whelk stalls . . .' Nowhere was more crowded than Dreamland, 'jammed with hilarious holiday-makers finding out if the Butler really did see what he wasn't supposed to, pouring thousands of pennies into every kind of amusement machine, shrieking themselves into hysteria on giant dippers and whirling cars, and capping every thrill with an endless succession of plates of cockles'. What exactly was Dreamland? An advertisement in June 1953 extolled its Amusement Park ('open all day and every day', featuring 'Europe's newest thrill – the giant Sky Wheel'), its illuminated Magic Garden and fully licensed Swiss Beer Garden ('A Five-Acre Enchanted Fairyland'), and its cinema, ballroom and Sunshine Theatre (mainly for Variety).

It was probably later that summer in Margate that Lindsay Anderson shot his 11-minute *O Dreamland*, eventually shown in 1956 as one of the pioneering Free Cinema films. Against a soundtrack alternating between the canned laughter of a mechanical dummy policeman and a jukebox playing two of 1953's big hits – Frankie Laine's 'I Believe' and Muriel Smith's 'Hold Me, Thrill Me, Kiss Me' – he produced a social document of, in Gavin Lambert's fine analysis, 'a deep, already troubled ambivalence':

> The candid camerawork, mainly in close shot, shows faces reacting to everything with the same almost catatonic lack of expression. A child blinks at Rosenberg strapped in the electric chair [a macabre recreation of the execution of the atom spy], a tired elderly woman slurps tea as she stares at an 'artistic' nude statue, Bingo players intone the numbers after the caller, like churchgoers mechanically repeating the Lord's Prayer after the minister. The camera also explores other body parts, feet shuffling across ground fouled with litter, tremendous buttocks spilling over counter stools. There is no spoken commentary, only an implied unanswered question: If this is Dreamland, what kind of nightmare is everyday life?
>
> Sometimes the crowd seems as ugly and mindless as the lunatic cackling dummy, sometime as pathetically trapped as the lion in its cage . . .[50]

Was this deal – for people's precious spare time – enough? Were they happy? Or just resigned? For better or worse, *O Dreamland* marked the start of a new, increasingly high-profile phase in the long, difficult, love–hate relationship of the left-leaning cultural elite with the poor old working class, just going about its business and thinking its own private, inscrutable thoughts.

9

I've Never Asked Her In

Before slum clearances and high-rise, before affluence, before mass immigration, before social mobility, before the spread of car ownership and the ubiquitous coming of the box in the corner – was there that most precious, most elusive thing we call 'community'? Ricky Tomlinson, recalling in 2003 his working-class Liverpool childhood in the 1940s and early to mid-1950s, seemingly had no doubt that, notwithstanding the city's Protestant/Catholic sectarianism, such a thing truly existed on the most local, intimate scale:

No one was rich and no one was poor in Lance Street. We were all in the same leaky boat – struggling to make ends meet . . .

Everyone knew everyone in Lance Street. No doors were ever locked. You just knocked and walked in. The street was just wide enough for two cars to pass although I can't remember ever seeing two cars in the street at the same time.

There were around sixty houses and most had children. I can name virtually every family. The Flemmings had seven boys and the Muskers seven girls. Then there were the Taggarts, Moores, Bains and Jennings . . .

In the long twilights we played catch and chase games on the street like 'Tic' and 'Alalio'. Most of the boys had wooden tommy guns or sometimes the real thing, with the firing pin removed. These had been bought for a couple of coppers after the war when fellas would come round the streets with handcarts selling old rifles.

Every 5 November the pride of Lance Street was at stake. A huge bonfire blocked the road, built from wood that had been stockpiled for weeks. Floorboards were ripped out of bombdies [ie bombed-out houses] and packing crates were broken down. Anything we couldn't scrounge we stole, organising raids on neighbouring streets . . .

'Lance Street no longer exists,' he added. 'Nor do the short cuts, hiding places and most of the landmarks from my childhood. Heyworth Primary is now a recreational park full of drug addicts on the dark nights and there is no Garrick pub or Everton Picture Palace. All the houses and shops were bulldozed in the sixties when Liverpool City Council decided that the two-up-two-downs were slum housing . . .'

Over the years there have been many accounts like Tomlinson's, prompting one exasperated historian, Joanna Bourke, to argue in 1994 that the very term 'working-class community' needs to be approached with the greatest suspicion, given the cumulative weight of largely romantic 'working-class autobiographies and oral histories, where social relations are often recalled through a golden haze: conflict is forgotten in favour of doors that were always open; the neighbour who was never seen is neglected in favour of the neighbour who always shared; tiring workdays are ignored in favour of nearly forgotten games which diverted children even during difficult times'. Equally culpable in her eyes have been generations of socialists, for whom the concept of 'community' has 'represented the innate socialism of the workers' – in essence, she asserts, 'a rhetorical device' rather than objective, empirical description.

Another historian, Robert Colls, strongly takes issue with Bourke's overall claim that communities are retrospective constructs. In his superbly crafted 2004 essay 'When We Lived in Communities', he evokes the sense of community he experienced himself, especially through the forceful street presence of strong-minded women, as a boy (born 1949) in working-class South Shields. Colls also repudiates Bourke's argument that the working-class neighbourhood was (in his paraphrasing words) 'essentially a *contracting society*, bidding for scarce commodities and resources', a view he sees as part of the Thatcher-era turn against traditional class-and-community collective history in favour of the concerns of 'a post-industrial, post-colonial, post-masculine, post-Christian world of fluid identities, ethnic diversities and global markets'. And he places much long-term emphasis on how, going back to the nineteenth century, the working class had built and then maintained 'an entirely new civil society based on free association', including involvement in a whole range of voluntary institutions.

Clearly there is no alternative but to go back to contemporary sources to try to resolve the matter. What, though, does 'community' – that 'warmly persuasive word', as Raymond Williams would call it in 1976 – actually mean? As early as 1955 a sociologist listed 94 major ways of defining a 'community'. But here, on commonsensical rather than theoretical grounds, three criteria will suffice for consideration: the extent to which people living in the same locality did indeed engage in associational activity; the extent to which they positively identified with the place where they lived; and the extent to which relations between them were conducted on a basis of friendliness, trust and mutuality.[1]

Beyond the pub, the working-men's club and, arguably, the football or rugby-league terrace and perhaps the bowling green, it is difficult – to judge by the sociological fieldwork of the day – to discern outside the workplace a particularly rich or thriving associational life in working-class Britain of the late 1940s and early 1950s, a Britain in which the coming of the welfare state had sharply reduced the need for collective forms of self-help such as the friendly societies.

'The leisure time of Coseley people is predominantly spent in informal social activity within the family group,' Doris Rich found in the Black Country, adding that apart from the pub and the club there was 'no strongly felt need for more public facilities'. Mark W. Hodges and Cyril S. Smith, two social scientists studying a Sheffield housing estate built between the wars, reckoned that 'for the most part more passive forms of entertainment preponderate' and that 'on the whole spare time is spent at the cinema, the public house, and the "dogs" '; furthermore, 'except for visits to the public house, there appears to be little evidence that the housewives take part regularly in social activities outside the home'. They also told the sad story of the estate's community centre, defunct – like the garden guild and the tenants' association – from lack of interest. Similarly, in the rundown St Ebbe's district of Oxford, John Mogey found that only 10 per cent of his sample 'actually said they had joined a voluntary society, or had become members of an informal group', despite apparently ample opportunities – with Mogey ascribing 'the loyalty of the normal person to the family hearth' to 'social insecurity' in what most people believed to be 'a hostile and dangerous world'. It was even starker in Liverpool's 'Ship Street', where Madeline Kerr bluntly titled one of her sections 'Lack of Associations', noting that 'the men have work associations but the women have nothing'.

Easily the fullest survey of associational life is the Derby one of 1953. Defining associational activity in terms of membership of clubs or societies, a full range of such activity was undeniably available in this medium-sized city: social clubs (including working-men's clubs), fraternal orders (eg the Royal Ancient Order of Buffaloes), women's clubs and institutes, youth clubs, old people's clubs, Service and ex-Service associations, nationality clubs (eg the Welsh Society), sports clubs, recreational clubs, horticultural associations, hobbies clubs, film societies, dramatic societies, music and choral societies, art clubs, literary clubs, photographic societies, archaeological, historical and geographical associations, scientific societies, educational associations, religious and church clubs, business and professional clubs, political clubs, international associations (eg the United Nations Association) and welfare associations. 'Subscriptions – where they exist at all – are generally so low as to present an obstacle to few people,' noted the authors. 'It is fair to say that most of this wide range of club activities is open to all who might wish to take part.' The sample comprised 1,200 men and women aged between 16 and 69, and these were the key findings about the number of clubs or societies joined:

	None	1	2	3 or more
	%	%	%	%
Men	38	38	15	9
Women	67	22	6	5
Middle-class	42	30	14	14
Working-class	58	29	9	4

Neither age nor marital status made much difference – certainly by comparison with both gender and class. Predictably, the survey also found that 'the most popular type of club is the social club', usually 'for drinking purposes', but there was no doubt about what were the two most striking revelations: namely, that 67 per cent of women (predominantly working-class women, given that the sample broadly reflected Derby's strongly working-class character) belonged to no clubs or associations; and that 58 per cent of working-class people (men and women) likewise belonged to none.[2] In short, the evidence is overwhelming that working-class associational life in Derby (a not atypical place) was at best patchy – and certainly not rich.

What about identity with place? 'Coseley isn't bad, I'm used to it,' 'Coseley is all right for them's bred and born there,' and (from a man who never went away on holiday) 'Coseley is as healthy as anywhere else' were some representative sentiments quoted by Rich, who reckoned that Coseley natives 'had a very strong local patriotism' – even though 'those who had come to Coseley from elsewhere more often expressed the opinion that "it's the last place on God's earth" or "it needs an atom bomb" '. It was much the same in Bethnal Green, or at least among the elderly who in about 1955 filled 11 coaches and went to Brighton for the day. 'We're from good old Bethnal Green,' bystanders were told, as (in an observer's words) 'the 400 made their way, in slow-moving groups, to the end of the central pier'. Richard Hoggart, in his part-reminiscence, part-reportage of Hunslet in *The Uses of Literacy* (1957), asserted that the focus of loyalty was a much smaller 'tribal area', recalling how by the age of ten he and his Hunslet contemporaries knew 'both the relative status of all the streets around us and where one part shaded into another', so that 'our gang fights were tribal fights, between streets or groups of streets' – an experience very similar to Tomlinson's in Liverpool. But loyalty could also be to a whole city, or even a region, according to Bill Lancaster's powerful if debatable reading of Newcastle, where (for him) 'Geordie' identity has historically trumped class identity.

Could there be loyalty to a newly or recently built council estate? Almost certainly yes, or at least after a passage of time, with the Hodges/ Smith Sheffield study arguing that 'the feeling of "belongingness" which now exists' on a particular (unnamed) estate had to a significant degree been fostered by hostile outsiders, in that 'unfavourable opinions about the estate are widely held and expressed strongly enough for the residents to have no illusions about their reputation, whether they regard it as justified or not'. Even so, there is surely much truth in the point made by Alison Ravetz, partly on the basis of her study of the Quarry Hill 'Model Estate' in Leeds. 'It is very important,' she notes, 'for people living respectably not to be identified either with the estate as an entity or with undesirable social elements within it.' All the more important, she adds feelingly, when this attempt to live a decent life, 'according to the norms of society', is seemingly 'knocked by exposés, or even by investigations that are moderate in tone but nevertheless treat the estate as a homogeneous entity'.[3]

One cannot avoid the role of sport. 'It is a strange commentary on our modern way of life,' grumbled the *Bolton Journal* in 1949, 'that a football team like the Wanderers may do more to foster the sense of community in Bolton than does a governing body like the Town Council. We may regret this, but we scarcely deny it.' Or take Newcastle United's Cup triumph three years later, when it was not just that city's people who got behind the Magpies but also (in accordance with Lancaster's regional-identity thesis) the people of Sunderland, Hartlepool and, in the *Newcastle Journal*'s proud words, 'the Northumberland farms and the Easington pits'. Crucially, most people still supported their local team, not a club several hundred miles away, a state of affairs that owed much to the equalising effect of almost non-existent television coverage and the continuing maximum wage for players. One should not exaggerate – small clubs like Aldershot continued to potter along in Third Division South – but at the start of a season it was mercifully impossible to forecast with near-certainty who would occupy the leading places of the First Division.

Whether at top or bottom, whether football or rugby, local pride was at stake, inevitably quickening and reinforcing attachment to the local. 'Each game is an occasion on which a high proportion of Ashton's males come together and participate in the efforts of Ashton to assert its superiority (through its representatives) over some other town (through their representatives),' Dennis et al somewhat primly observed of Featherstone's rugby-league team, while the Workington team's homecoming after winning the Rugby League Challenge Cup at Wembley in 1952 epitomised an annual exultant northern ritual. 'We travelled North by train and then went across country by coach from Scotch Corner,' recalled one player. 'And every village in Cumberland turned out to cheer us home. When we reached Workington you could hardly get near the Town Hall.' Adrian Smith's bittersweet 1994 essay, 'An Oval Ball and a Broken City', on the rise and fall of Coventry's rugby-union club tells a larger truth (though perhaps not the only truth), informed by deep personal knowledge. 'Individual areas acquired their own identities, but work and play still focused strongly on the city centre,' he wrote about the Coventry that still existed in the 1950s. 'Coventry people cultivated the belief that everyone still knew everybody else's business. The city's sportsmen, its eccentric personalities, and above all the evening paper, all acted as common points of reference. Individual families were known either for their sporting prowess, or for their notoriety. All families were proud of their city, and of their own particular localities.'[4]

On a Sunday morning in March 1953, just after winning his third Welsh cap, the rugby-union player Terry Davies was still in bed in his council-house home in Pen-y-graig, Llwynhendy, when (in his biographer's words) 'his mother roused him with the news that two strangers with a large briefcase wanted to talk to him':

> They were Wigan [ie rugby league] representatives intent on persuading him to 'go North'. It got to the point where sums ranging between £5,000 and £9,000 were being discussed, and £5,000 in notes were actually piled up on the kitchen table. Terry heard his mother's gasp as she glimpsed the fortune through the dividing curtain: *Arglwydd mowr, drycha ar yr arian 'na, Ted!* (Lord God, look at that money, Ted!). Such a sum in 1953 would have bought sixteen houses in Llanelli or three local farms! He rejected his would-be Wigan captors as he would later reject Leeds and Bradford. Like his father before him his roots went deep, and more to the point his newly acquired status as a Welsh international had even conferred a certain distinction on his mother as a faithful member of Soar Baptist Chapel! With so much to savour at home it was no time to 'go North'. As for the fortune he spurned he would, as he said phlegmatically, most probably have misspent it.

The desire not to move away from one's familiar environment was undoubtedly a widespread one. 'Although today with the beginnings of new housing estates and movement of people from the slum houses these neighbourhoods are becoming less well defined, they are still characteristic of the region,' Rich found about the different 'villages' (each originally growing up around a coal mine or iron works) that made up Coseley. 'On the whole, people, particularly the women, are still attached to their own neighbourhood and like to remain in or near to it. Most of them have been to the same schools, and many go to the same workplace.' So too in inner-city Liverpool in the early 1950s, where John Barron Mays was adamant that 'contrary to the belief of those who advocate a semi-rural, suburban housing scheme there are very many people who prefer to live in the city and more particularly in the central and most heavily built-up areas', adding that 'the city way of life seems to suit their requirements and many have formed strong attachments to the dockside neighbourhoods in particular'. Or, as an elderly Bethnal Green woman told an investigator not long afterwards: 'I want to stop here in Bethnal Green and die. My roots are here. I want to be carried out of here.' Kerr in her study of Liverpool's 'Ship Street' offered the most interesting explanation of why long-established residents, especially the 'Mums', of slum or semi-slum property told her 'with surprising uniformity' that they did not want to leave the neighbourhood. 'It is not because of friends or human relations in general that the family wishes to remain,' she argued. 'The reason seems to be a vague undifferentiated feeling of belonging and the security of moving around in a well-known territory.'[5]

It is hard to be certain, though, that in terms of the larger national picture this was the predominant working-class sentiment. 'People wanted to get out of New Cross,' the historian Roy Porter insisted about his childhood. 'We were on the London County Council housing list, but that was regarded as an unfunny joke ("You'll be dead before they'll offer you a place").' Often it depended on what stage one had reached in life. 'Among those who were parents, moving tended to be justified by its presumed benefits for children, although the latter might well be ignorant of these,' reflects Ravetz. 'People living in older districts of terraced housing thought it particularly desirable to remove their children from the streets where they played, and to give them gardens instead. In satisfying the children's interests, grandparents and other relatives were left behind in the old neighbourhood, and this was a sacrifice that was noticed but felt to be justified.'

The historian who has argued most strongly that very many working-class people – although, on the face of it paradoxically, less so in the case of those living in the very *worst* conditions – had a decisive desire to move out and thereby improve their and their children's material lot is Mark Clapson. In particular, he cites two studies of Birmingham conducted during the 1950s which, in his words, 'found that a majority of slum dwellers wanted to move to improved homes in the suburban rings around Birmingham, although a sizeable minority liked their old house and district'. In his pioneering study *Invincible Green Suburbs, Brave New Towns* (1998), he draws a largely convincing picture of a great, mainly *voluntary* dispersal from the inner cities during these post-war years, especially on the part of younger couples. And he also shows how, whatever their original misgivings, most people in practice were pleased to have made the move. Or, as one of the 90 per cent of Mogey's Barton sample without a good word to say about their former accommodation told him about life on a new estate by Oxford's ring road: 'It's like heaven after what we've been used to. People today don't know of the times when we had to live in old broken-down houses because we could afford nothing better. But today we are given nice little houses to live in . . .'⁶

That leaves mutuality – the truly central question in any discussion of 'community'. Hoggart in *The Uses of Literacy* cited emblematic exchanges from *Have a Go!*: ' "Ay, and what do you dislike most, then?" asks Wilfred Pickles. "Stuck-up fowk." Roars of applause. "Jolly good! And will you just tell me what you like most?" "Good neighbourly fowk." Increased applause. ". . . and very right too. Give her the money." '

Context is everything here, and the key contextual point is to reiterate the extent of status divisions *within* the working class. Robert Roberts, in his justly celebrated evocation *The Classic Slum* (1971) (about Salford either side of the Great War), identified an 'English proletarian caste system' that divided working-class people living or working in the same place; it is clear that this system was still alive and well after the Second World War. 'The East Enders could be incredibly snobbish and class-conscious in their social gradings,' Jennifer Lee (later Worth) found as a Poplar-based midwife in the early 1950s, while at about the same time Jimmy Boyle, growing up in Sandyfaulds Street in Glasgow's Gorbals, saw two cultures thriving in one place:

All the buildings were identical, but of the fifty or so close-mouths, three were different because the people in them were 'toffs', and in a way there was a resentment even amongst the kids from our closes against those who stayed in them, to such an extent that we wouldn't even rake their midgies [ie search their bins] for 'lucks'. The exterior of their part of the building was no different from that of ours. The difference lay in the interior as their windows were always beautiful with a fresh appearance about them, nice curtains, coloured glass, bright paint making the houses look very warm and cosy, like palaces. The close-mouth was always clean, with white chalk running up the sides and it smelled of fancy disinfectant when washed. It was really a sharp contrast from the houses in the rest of the street, though they weren't rich enough to have doors on their closes to prevent strangers getting into their back courts. The kids in these three closes kept together when playing and none of them ever played with us in the poorer closes. However, this didn't bother us as our parents called them 'half-boiled toffs', and when clustered around the closes at night our mothers used to gossip about them, mimic their proper accents and laugh at them . . . Their kids were always clean as new pennies with their hair combed neatly and their nice clothes, with stockings pulled up to the knees, a clear sign of a toff. Most of them were in the Boy Scouts or the Cubs and wore the uniforms . . .

Elsewhere in Glasgow, on the housing estates, there was also a deep internal division. 'The dirty tenants are usually found to be irregular at paying rent and the children are the most destructive,' reported the Corporation's Medical Officer of Health in 1951. 'Most of them are below par mentally and often they have large families. It has been found that the chief reasons for dirty tenants are domestic worries, money worries, wives not getting a fair share of the husband's wages, low mental standard, gambling, drink, criminal history, and just laziness.' The respectable working class had to put up with such unsatisfactory, 'problem' families even in Norwich. 'Dear Sir,' began an anonymous letter in 1948 to the council's households committee:

This [Mrs Carlisle], who you had at your office this morning about her house and two children which are dirty. People have helped her and given her clothes which she has sold again. She is a disgrace to other women who are clean to what she is. I hear the children have no bed to lay on. She has been working at Pearl Laundry now and don't care. Pictures and a smoke is all she care. Her legs are awful and smell too. So I trust this letter of advice help you. Woman at laundry have helped her but it's no good.

'From one who has given her things,' the less-than-forgiving, neighbourly letter signed off.[7]

Inevitably the picture was not uniform. James Robb, studying relatively homogeneous Bethnal Green in the late 1940s, discovered even there 'certain areas which are normally regarded as better or worse than the greater part of the borough', with 'better' areas such as most of Old Ford Road having inhabitants who 'occupationally are not easily distinguishable from the rest of Bethnal Green, but are conscious of their greater respectability'. By contrast, Hodges and Smith in their Sheffield study found that only about a quarter of the residents were conscious of the social difference between the 'top' and 'bottom' ends of their estate ('It's better at the top – always Sunday up there' and 'They say the top part is better, and you get the scruffs down here'), whereas 'the answers of the vast majority indicated either that they recognise no such distinction between the two ends of the estate, or else that they had no experience which enabled them to form a judgement'. Or take Liverpool's 'Ship Street', where, according to Kerr, 'in general the competitive attitude of keeping up with other people is lacking', so that 'conduct such as cruelty to children or stealing from your mother may be heartily disapproved of but the people of Ship Street do not feel called upon to dictate to others what furniture they should have or what conduct they should pursue'.

It was very different in Braydon Road in the Houghton district of Coventry. 'It would be misleading to assume that, because the residents are predominantly "working class", they are homogeneous with reference to anything other than occupation,' was Leo Kuper's conclusion, backed up by some acutely status-conscious vox pop (from around 1950) about neighbours, including their children:

Mr Williams is always saying, 'I can grow bigger flowers than anybody else', or 'I've got bigger plants than anybody else', and he's always talking about how much money he has in the bank – the things they've got, and that he gets paid 9s 6d an hour. Perhaps he hasn't been used to anything before.

She gets up to see her husband off at 6 am, then right away she cleans her doorstep, and when the milkman and the postman come she's talking to them loudly, so that everybody knows she's been up and working. Then she'll appear at her front door early in the morning, all dressed up, even to a necklace, and come right out for everybody to look at. Then at night, she'll parade in front of her window in pyjamas, all got up neatly for everybody to see. She strikes me as the type who's not used to much.

She once saw our two younger girls walking past, dressed up, and she said to Mrs Rice: 'Look at that; they had nothing when they came up there. They're getting on very nicely, I must say.' Well, that was nasty; of course, everybody wants to get on if they can.

I hate to see her [ie the speaker's daughter] playing with the children round here, but she'll play with anybody.

The other day Tony (aged three) came in and said a certain word. I was astounded! There was only Arthur (aged fourteen) and me in. And I looked at Arthur: he blushed and looked down at the table, so that I knew he knew what the word meant ... My husband said: 'My God, if he says that when he's at my mother's, she'll have a fit.'[8]

Braydon Road would never inspire a madeleine moment, but perhaps was not so different in its infinite snobberies from Proust's Combray.

Crucial to the economic as well as the social ecology in all working-class neighbourhoods was the small shopkeeper. 'The local corner shops helped many people to survive during the 1930s depression,' unambiguously declares one historian, Avram Taylor, of working-class credit about a time when the pawnbroker was in decline (though far from vanishing), but the small local retailer still flourished – as he continued to do for a generation or so after the war. Moreover, though the 1950s were not the 1930s, many families would have found it difficult to survive without these small shops. 'Virtually the whole of a wife's "wage" in Ashton is spent on food, on the immediate needs of the week,' noted Dennis et al in Featherstone, 'so that by Wednesday and Thursday the pennies are being counted, and most things bought in the shops are "on tick".' So too in Birmingham's Ladywood district. 'Gerry Marshall was a jolly fat man with horn-rimmed glasses and short white jacket,' recalled Carole Anne Stafford (born 1945) about the grocer on the corner of Melson Street and Summer Hill:

> He was always very friendly to his many women customers, too friendly some husbands thought. But the shop was extremely popular, not just because of the man himself but because of the strap. If money ran out during the week, which it often did, Mom could send me down to Gerry's with a note asking that it be put on the bill. Gerry would note it down in his little black book for payment on the following Friday.
>
> To anybody who did not pay on the due day, Gerry Marshall's friendly manner would vanish instantly and you would be likely to find your name and address and the amount owed on a post card on his front window. This usually did the trick, and there were few cards that stayed up for long.
>
> There was another advantage to Mom shopping at Gerry's. Sometimes when she had paid off a strap bill on a Friday, and all the other bills, she would find herself short of cash to last through the coming week. Gerry Marshall would lend Mom £3 or even £4 in cash until the next pay day. Dad did not know about this and would have gone up the wall if he had; I was under threat of death never to mention it in front of him. As you can appreciate, it was near impossible for Mom and lots of the other women ever to clear their bills with Gerry, and of course, this is what he wanted. He never added anything to the strap bill or charged interest on the loans, but when I brought Mom a sheet of notepaper with the list of items she had bought over the week, she would sit down and check carefully through it.
>
> 'That Gerry Marshall's a crafty bugger,' she would say running her finger down the list for the third time. 'I never 'ad two lots of bacon did I? An' I never 'ad no biscuits this week, I know that fer a fuckin' fact.'
>
> But she always paid up despite her misgivings about the bill, for to fall out with Gerry would mean no more strap and no more cash loans . . .

If there was an element of trust, of mutual interdependence between shopkeeper and customer, in Gerry Marshall's approach, that seems to have been less the case with Lorna Sage's elderly relatives who ran a small general shop, Hereford Stores, in Tonypandy. 'It was the sort of shop that had almost as many customers when it was closed as when it was open,' she remembered. 'Feckless, improvident types rattled at the door at all hours wanting a few fags or half a loaf. And, of course, in search of that increasingly rare commodity that was turning out to be Katie and Stan's special stock-in-trade: tick.' One day Stan took young Lorna on a tour of his booty. Piled up high in his loft were handlebars, wheels and seats from dismembered bicycles, wheels from prams, sometimes even whole prams, and sacks full of ivory piano keys. 'His plan had been to confiscate people's most vital possessions – their mobility and their music – as pledges against bad debts. They were never redeemed. Yet Stan didn't mind, didn't mind at all. In fact, he was as excited and pleased as if he'd invented his own currency and was a secret millionaire in it . . .'[9]

Shops were not only for shopping. 'Every day the husband meets his workmates in the factory and the canteen, and there has his social contact and his conversation,' noted the authors of a 1953 report on Southampton's housing estates, arguing that the New Towns had got it wrong by being unduly restrictive about shops in residential neighbourhoods. 'For the woman whose workplace is the home, the counterpart is often the shop; and one has only to "listen in" at a "dispersed" shop to realise the intimate personal knowledge of family affairs which is shown, and the range of topics, from dress materials to local happenings, which are discussed. This adds to life something of the zest of a small community . . .' Zest perhaps, but in shops and elsewhere the all-consuming staple of female conversation was almost invariably gossip. 'The balconies for the tenement women were equivalent to the streets of the terraced house dwellers,' recalled Jennifer Worth about her Poplar days. 'So close was the living space, that I doubt if anyone could get away with anything without all the neighbours knowing. The outside world held very little interest for the East Enders, and so other people's business was the primary topic of conversation – for most it was the only interest, the only amusement or diversion.' Or take this reminiscence of 1940s street life in working-class Bristol:

Monday was a real old gossip day. With so many women wielding a brush or going great guns with a polishing duster, they could pass the time of day to the neighbour over the way, or with the metal polish tins still in their hands, they would linger in little knots to discuss any recent happening in the street. Net curtains twitched as their owners peeped to see who was talking to who, and the whole street became like an Indian settlement, with gossip like smoke signals drifting in all directions.

Some of these older working-class women could be formidable figures. 'No-one came or went without Ma's observation and no-one got by Ma until she had her gossip,' began Evelyn Haythorne's description of 'Old Ma Barrowcliffe', living in a fictional but true-to-life Yorkshire pit village in the early 1950s:

> Most were ready to talk, the walls were paper-thin, so they'd be daft not to, but a lot genuinely wished to share their troubles and worries. Others just passed the time of day but few willingly crossed her, for she had a great knowledge of what went off in the backs. Usually, though, she didn't spread and one could trust Ma. If you were genuine you were all right, but she 'adn't time for petty illnesses or for nit picking, though she had a great sympathy for real heartaches.[10]

In short, gossip was ubiquitous in well-established working-class neighbourhoods – and, put simply, Al Read would not have won such renown for his monologue of the nosy, talkative housewife if it had not been rooted in reality.

How benign were the effects of all this gossip? 'An activity that in spite of its general disparagement was the channel for neighbourhood lore and wisdom, and a mechanism for enforcing mores,' is Ravetz's largely positive view, while Colls has no doubts:

> Women were streetwise. They kept clear the channels of communication. They knew who was who and where they lived, and they drew on all this as common knowledge ... To the men, women's street talk was just gossip. But to those who needed information about a job, a useful contact, or local resource, or a house swap ('key money'), women's gossip was a standing committee on public safety. David Reeder and Richard Rodger [two urban historians] once famously referred to cities as the 'information superhighway' of their age. At street level, where

the flow of information was heaviest, no one knew this better than the mothers. What came to be called community was simply another way of referring to their world.

In reality it was surely a more mixed picture. 'It is not surprising that savage fighting frequently broke out in the tenements,' notes Worth at the end of her passage about the all-consuming nature of gossip for East Enders; Geoffrey Gorer in his 1950–51 *People* survey of English habits found a significant level of complaints about the gossip of neighbours and reflected that 'the proverbial "village pump" attitude seems to bedevil the life of many', while in his detailed Braydon Road study, Kuper tended to emphasise the negative aspects of gossip or, as it was sometimes called, canting:

> The essential triviality of the content of the local gossip is a striking feature. There are very occasional references to extreme cases of immorality. Many comments relate to standards of housekeeping, 'scruffy homes'; of child-care, 'dragging up children'; of bearing to neighbours, 'she thinks she's the great I am'; and to such social problems as 'scrounging'. Gossip acts as a restraining influence on behaviour, both directly and indirectly. The direct channel is the repetition of what was said to the person discussed. But indirectly, pressure to conform arises from fear of what neighbours will say. The Hutton family relaxes in the back garden on fine days; the daughters dress lightly, and Mrs Hutton feels sure that the 'neighbours talk about the "nudity" of the girls'. Visibility is, in fact, so high that it is difficult to get away with only token conformity, such as a highly polished front step and a neglected interior; no one will be taken in by it.
>
> A further function of gossip is to regulate status reputation. General mode of life, care of the children, are assessed, and families evaluated by these criteria. Possessions, the goods neighbours buy and the prices they pay, are of interest. A group of friends quarrelled on precisely this score. One circulated the story that her friend had paid only seven shillings for some garment, but gave out the price as one pound. Women may be suspected of calling in for the sole purpose of examining their neighbours' purchases. Residents deflate the pretensions of neighbours, or assert, in a variety of ways, their own superior social position. Discussions of status are an essential part of gossip.

The residents themselves stress the hazardous aspects. There is the danger of conflict: 'A tale's never lost; they add a bit to it, and it goes round the neighbourhood.' 'It gets round what you've said, and that's how the trouble starts.'

Above all, Kuper went on, 'they emphasise the threat to privacy' – a threat posed by even apparently harmless gossip. 'Does it matter if her neighbours know what she bought at a shop, or whether she goes out with her husband's brother? Yet discussion of these quite neutral topics is resented. Each person maintains a certain sphere of privacy, a private domain, wide or narrow, which is an extension of the personality and an expression of individuality. It is into this private domain that gossip intrudes.'

Again and again, not least in this context of a deep, if often vain, desire for privacy, one is struck by the limits of neighbourliness – indeed of mutuality – in even long-established working-class neighbourhoods. Jimmy Boyle recalled how in his street in the Gorbals 'if someone died the neighbours would go round the houses collecting money in a bedsheet to help the family meet the costs of the burial', and how 'from the extreme circumstance of a death to the simple need of borrowing a cup of sugar, help was always at hand', but Donald James Wheal remembered the still working-class part of Chelsea (before his family moved to White City) quite differently: 'Sensing a slight, women would not speak to each other for the most trivial reasons. Feuds often developed, sadly between neighbours who needed each other. The World's End was as riddled with them as any medieval Italian city state.'[11]

Contemporary evidence, whether qualitative or quantitative, is more reliable. Take for a start Kerr's broadly positive account of 'Ship Street', where she depicted a world of not much neighbourliness in the sense of social intercourse – compared to constant visiting by relatives – but considerable practical neighbourliness, 'especially in times of adversity', and where 'neighbours who are not on visiting terms hold keys of each other's homes' or even 'accompany each other to hospital'. Yet at the same time she did not deny that in what physically was an intensely close-knit world, 'feuds are fairly common and range from simple quarrels, which are not made up, to the most complicated vendettas which produce a series of lawsuits' or even more primitive forms of vengeance. Mogey seemingly did not encounter feuds in St Ebbe's, but nor did he come across much friendly neighbourliness:

> I don't believe in talking to the neighbours; you have to be careful what you say.
>
> I never have a neighbour inside. I am one of those who keep themselves to themselves. Mind you, I'm sociable, I say 'Good Morning'.
>
> I'm not one for going into people's houses unless for illness.
>
> We don't mix with the people round here. We're not gossips like they are: they're not too bad this end of the street but at the far end the people are always standing on the doorsteps gossiping.
>
> It's just a question of knowing people over walls and through doors.

'Of course if anyone wants help, I help,' one housewife added. 'Like the man over the road when his wife was in hospital. I went over when he came back from work to ask if he had any lunch. He said not to bother.' The evidence was also largely negative in the working-men's clubs in Featherstone, where 'with regard to "mutual helpfulness" the club's achievements in this respect are not at all impressive,' noted Dennis et al, adding that 'there is no suggestion of "mutual helpfulness" on the basis of need'. Almost everywhere, whether in an old or a new neighbourhood, the all-important distinction – crucial in ensuring broadly amicable relations – was between 'neighbourly' and 'friendly'. The former, Hodges and Smith reflected on the basis of their Sheffield study, was 'based on willingness to give, or readiness to ask for and accept, help from others'; the latter implied 'a close reciprocal relationship based on trust, affection and respect'. Inevitably, there were also non-neighbourly relationships between neighbours. But in any case, as Hodges and Smith added, 'the degree of contact between neighbours is regulated by convention, and there is probably rather less permitted or desired nowadays than in the past'.

The most striking qualitative evidence was in Kuper's Braydon Road study – the study of a development specifically built to try to encourage intimacy among its residents. The vox pop speaks cumulatively for itself:

It's terrible, you can hear everything.

When I clean my mirror, it bangs against the wall, and she knocks back. My husband says it's best to ignore people like that.

You can even hear them use the pot; that's how bad it is. It's terrible.

People can keep borrowing and not pay back, till in the end you have to refuse them and that is unpleasant.

I don't believe in borrowing and lending.

I don't believe in going into each other's houses – you can keep friendly without that. Usually, they are getting to know one another's business, and perhaps children are standing there listening: though I like to have a neighbour I can depend on, but one that doesn't take your business out of your house, when they've been in your house.

One woman over the road was getting very friendly – coming over at all times of the day. My husband used to be annoyed when he came home and found that the work hadn't been done; so was I, because I like to get things finished.

A friend you can confide in, a neighbour you can't. What you say to neighbours over the garden wall might be passed on and you might get involved.

You can let a neighbour know too much.

If you get too familiar, you've got them on your doorstep for the rest of your life.

I never thought I'd come to hate anybody like I do her.

I've never asked her in. I could see how it was right from the beginning. She was going in people's houses all day long, and I couldn't stand that.

Mrs Adams always used to be coming round. I had to put a stop to it, I couldn't get on with my work; she used to step over the fence, so we put a higher wire up; and I always kept the gate locked, so that she had to knock at the front door, then I needn't let her in if I was busy. She's only been in once lately.

'Stability exists in the area, but does not arise from any feeling of belonging together,' sensibly concluded the *Coventry Evening Telegraph* in 1952 after Kuper's study had gone to the City Council's Planning and Redevelopment Committee. Book publication the following year earned an equally sensible summary by the *TLS* of the study's important but, on the whole, sadly ignored conclusions: 'One is that intimacy forced on people by the position of houses may lead to hatred and instability instead of friendship and stability. Another is that friendship depends on something more than proximity; it depends on the human beings themselves. Another is that social groups of very different status may be more tolerant to one another than groups nearer in status.' 'The district studied was "working-class",' added the reviewer, 'but the inhabitants showed themselves highly aware of social distinctions.'[12]

Fortunately, the quantitative evidence prevents either side of the 'community' debate from making extravagant claims. The Sheffield study asked 153 housewives on the estate which persons they would ask for help in the event of running out of bread. Almost ten times as many opted for a neighbour as for a relative, though more than 30 per cent replied 'nobody'. But in the case of serious illness, the figures changed to 48 per cent looking to a neighbour, almost 47 per cent to a relative or someone else, and 5 per cent to nobody. As for neighbourly relations, a companion study at about the same time of a recently developed Liverpool estate found these prevailing attitudes from a sample of 36 families:

Mutual assistance with expression of good neighbourly relationships: 11
Little contact with neighbours but an absence of adverse comments about them: 14
No contact with neighbours and general disapproval of them: 4
Unwanted contacts with neighbours involving difficult relationships and strong personal criticisms of them: 7

Positive, neutral, negative – the roughly equal proportions may well have been fairly representative. Mogey, meanwhile, found an interesting contrast in Oxford. Whereas in St Ebbe's there was roughly a 40 per cent acceptance of next-door neighbours and a 60 per cent rejection (ie in terms of general attitudes expressed to the interviewer), on the much newer Barton estate the ratio was 80 per cent acceptance and 20 per cent rejection. 'In Barton everything is strange,' explained Mogey. 'The house, the layout of the estate, the behaviour of the people, and even the way you view your children has altered subtly.' Even so, he observed how, among the pioneer families on the estate, the initial burst of 'great mutual friendliness' – when 'groups of people helped one another in all sorts of ways, by shopping, baby minding, helping with the garden, lending, welcoming newly arrived families with a cup of tea, and so on' – had inexorably given way to 'a retreat to the general ideal of "I keep myself to myself" '.[13]

Finally, two national surveys on this vexed subject were confined to neither one place nor one class. 'How well do you know your next-door neighbours?' Mass-Observation asked its largely but not exclusively middle-class Panel in 1947:

> Just by name. *(Metalworker, 29, near Sandwich)*
>
> It wd be difficult to know less about neighbours than we do. *(Musician and journalist, 56)*
>
> I am only acquainted with my neighbour, think well of her, but leave it at that. *(Housewife, 39, Glasgow)*
>
> Neighbours on one side known fairly well (old air raid shelter companions) but we have no interests in common. Not on speaking terms with neighbours on other side because they have quarrelled with my relatives. *(Teacher, 33, Lancashire)*
>
> On one side enough to say 'Good morning,' other side not forgiven us for not fire-watching. *(Office worker, 49)*
>
> Too well – don't like 'em. *(Physicist, 41, Castle Bromwich)*
>
> I dislike neighbours who 'drop in' often at inconvenient times. On one side is a house badly needing decorating and with two or three children and them I boycott. The other side is a pleasant old lady with whom I have passed the time of day. *(Bank clerk, 38, Bradford)*

M-O also asked, 'How many people living in your immediate vicinity do you know, and how well do you know them?' Again, an underlying apartness prevailed:

> There are one or two people with who I may exchange a few words if I see them in their front gardens, and there is one woman with a baby with whom I would walk to the shops if we were going out at the same time. Otherwise we don't know even the names of any of the people who live near. *(Housewife, 32, Leeds)*
>
> I have very little in common with most of my neighbours & I haven't time to spend in cultivating acquaintance unless it promises to grow into a mutual friendship. *(Civil servant, 41, Oxted)*

I know about 4–5 people – not counting children – in the immediate vicinity well enough to say 'good-morning' to them & pass the time of day. That's all. My children play about with the other children living near – about a dozen – but I don't encourage them more than I must for I don't think much of them. *(Housewife, 37, Birmingham)*

I know the names of all the people on our side of the road for about twenty houses along. I have an idea of their occupations. Some I know personally. I do not go into their homes. The road is wide so I know only a few of those who live opposite. We have a little conversation at the bus shelter. *(Housewife, 56, Burnley)*

I do not know anyone in the immediate vicinity with any degree of intimacy. I am just on speaking terms with perhaps half a dozen, though only with one have I any interest in common, and that is slight, in a joint attendance at a WEA class several years ago. *(Accountant, 46, Sheffield)*

Lots I suppose but only to say 'Good morning etc' to or have 'the daily grumble' with either on the road or perhaps in the bus, wherever we happen to meet. *(Housewife, 47, Sunbury-on-Thames)*

One panellist, a man living in Willesden, briskly answered both questions together: 'I know neither my next door neighbours nor any people in the immediate vicinity, except my landlord's family living in the same house. With them I discuss only formal matters; they are in no sense friends.'

Three years later, in his *People* survey, Geoffrey Gorer discovered that 'the typical relationship of the English to their neighbours can probably best be described as distant cordiality', a memorable phrase justified by the fact that fewer than one in twenty knew them sufficiently well 'to drop in on without an invitation'. Could they, though, despite this deliberate distance-keeping, rely on their neighbours' help in a pinch? 'Only a minority,' he found. 'Eight per cent felt they could rely on their neighbours entirely, and another 27 per cent to a large extent; 10 per cent felt they could not rely on their neighbours at all, and 32 per cent only to a small extent. The remainder – just on a quarter – would not commit themselves, and said that "it depends".' Significantly, the regional and class breakdowns behind these figures upset two of Gorer's understandable presumptions. First, it transpired that 'there is no more reliance on neighbours' help in the Northern regions than there is in

London'; second, 'there is greater reliance among the well-to-do, the members of the middle classes, than there is among the poor', ie people with incomes of under £5 a week. 'The middle class has repeated for generations the cliché that it is the poor who help the poor,' he wryly added. 'The poor themselves seem to doubt it.'

There were two other key prevailing emotions that Gorer found in his survey of 'Friends and Neighbours'. One was the heartfelt desire for quietness and privacy, not least from snooping neighbours. 'Their noses are longer than their arms,' typically complained a middle-aged artisan from Cheshire. 'They cannot live their own lives for watching and meddling in others. Curtain shakes.' The other emotion, either revealed or complained about, was that powerful nexus of envy-cum-snobbishness. 'They speak with an *Oxford* accent but work, perhaps in a better paid job, but have to work to live as I do, but they make you think that they are just that bit above you,' was the bitter complaint of a 31-year-old worker from Crawley about his neighbours. From a Yorkshireman (calling himself 'Hard Working Class') from Barnsley the beef was 'the way they begrudge what we have and the way they spend their money on drink and gambling and sending the children with bets to the bookie'.[14] No neighbour, in short, came without baggage – whether real or imaginary.

Like 'juggling with jelly' is how one historian describes the whole question of 'community', and not the least of the difficulties is identifying a 'typical' working-class district. Was it, for instance, Jennifer Worth's Stepney or Roy Porter's New Cross? 'I took many walks around parts of Stepney to see what it was like,' the former midwife recalled:

It was simply appalling. The slums were worse than I could ever have imagined. I walked south of Cable Street, down Graces Alley, Dock Street, Sanders Street, Backhouse Lane and Leman Street, and the atmosphere was menacing. Girls hung around in doorways, and men walked up and down the streets, often in groups, or hung around the doors of cafés smoking or chewing tobacco and spitting. The condemned buildings were still standing, nearly 20 years after they had been scheduled for demolition, and were still being lived in. A few families and old people who could not get away remained, but mostly the occupants were prostitutes, homeless immigrants, drunks or meths drinkers, and drug addicts. There were no general shops selling food and household necessities as the shops had been turned into all-night cafés, which in fact meant they were brothels. The only shops I saw were tobacconists.

It was certainly different – and probably *more* typical – in New Cross:

All the men were in work, many with big local employers such as the council, Surrey Commercial Docks, the railways, London Transport, Borough market or Peek Frean's biscuit factory; women kept house and raised children. Husbands had wives, housewives had breadwinners, and children had parents (and aunts-in-laws and grandparents round the corner). Families stuck together. Menfolk slipped down to the Royal Archer, but there were no notorious drunks or wife-beaters. Nor was there violence or crime. Girls skipped, and we boys kicked a tennis ball in the street, and mothers didn't worry too much: there was little backstreet traffic – no one we knew owned a car – and no fear of child-molesters.

'Nobody liked living in New Cross Gate,' Porter wholly concedes, 'yet there was much to be said for that kind of respectable working-class inner-city neighbourhood that is now [1994] pretty much a thing of the past.'[15]

New Cross was home to Millwall FC, playing at the take-no-prisoners Den in Cold Blow Lane, and arguably 'community' flourished most – assuming it did exist – in the context of an embattled (or anyway entrenched) *contra mundum* group of people sharing the same physical location and a similar set of attitudes towards the dissident, the outsider, the other. Take the oral memories of Danny Brandon, who worked at the Royal Group of Docks, south of West Ham:

In those days you didn't just work on the docks, you lived by dockers, you were a community, the man next door was a docker, the man over the road, you were a very closely knit community. And that's the reason why a scab in those days he certainly took, not his life, in that sense, but he was a man that would be ostracised, not just at work but where he lived, because they cut one and we all bled, it was as simple as that, which was one of the reasons for the militancy in the docks.

In the East End more generally, the immediate post-war years were characterised by an ugly rash of anti-Semitism, with Robb's Bethnal Green survey finding that more than 26 per cent of his sample were 'extreme anti-Semites', regarding Jews as (in the paraphrased words of one of his interviewees) people who were 'mean, operate a black market, drive hard bargains, are unscrupulous businessmen, full of low cunning, unpatriotic, dirty in their habits, have foreign accents and gesticulate'. Or take Coventry, where Kuper's Braydon Road study detailed the deep resentment felt by Coventrians towards the many incomers since the 1930s. 'Friendliness seems to have disappeared these days', 'All out for themselves', and 'Always trying to get on in the world – rush, rush, rush' were typical attitudes towards non-Coventrians, one of whom told Kuper: 'Coventry people always class us as foreigners. They say: "Go back to your own place." There's a lot of jealousy here.' The overall picture is perhaps of an infinite cluster of small, cut-off worlds in which one was either in or out. 'A different code of ethics is held towards people outside the group,' Kerr explained in 1953 about 'Ship Street' to the British Association, meeting that year in Liverpool. 'It is not stealing to shoplift in the big stores, but a dreadful crime to pinch anything from "Mum".' And she added that in that particular small world, 'fear and superstition are predominant'.

So, 'community' or not? Alison Ravetz is surely on the right lines when she argues that 'perhaps a more fruitful concept to apply to traditional working-class life than the ambiguous one of "community" would be "localism",' adding that 'it was the immediate locality that supplied the economy, the shared culture and the frameworks of personal development'. The contemporary evidence, moreover, is clear that most people had a strong – if not necessarily overwhelming – attachment to their own particular locality. Yet if 'localism' is a more accurate term, it undeniably lacks the emotional resonance of 'community'. Moreover, the truth surely is that although the British were indeed a more individualistic people in the 1940s and 1950s than has often been assumed, they were not yet quite as solipsistic as they were to become. In October 1948 the young Enid Palmer, training as a nurse and presumably in uniform, rode out on her bike from her lodgings in Colchester. 'This morning,' she wrote to her parents in Kenya, 'everybody had red cheeks – & they were breathing clouds of vapour into the frosty air. Everybody seemed lively and cheerful – & hundreds of people must have wished me a "good morning" – everybody from the policeman at the corner, the bricklayers, the chimney sweep black under his layer of soot, the baker, postman, etc . . .'[16]

PART THREE

10

Hit It Somebody

Mollie Panter-Downes on 5 October 1952 sent her regular letter to the *New Yorker* not from London but from Morecambe. There, amid 'some of Britain's nippiest blasts', she described the setting for Labour's just-finished party conference, which had provided 'a striking contradiction of the theory that the British are a stolid, unemotional race':

> Shivering delegates, hanging on to their sheaves of agenda for dear life, were blown along the waterfront, together with the more normal visitors – jolly parties of mill girls on the spree, who were having a fine time eating saucerfuls of orange and pink cockles and mussels, buying souvenirs of pottery Alsatian dogs and shaving mugs decorated with the Queen's picture, and not giving a whoop for the drama going on in the Winter Garden Theatre. Inside this ungardenlike spot, a remarkably melancholy Victorian structure with a total absence of ventilation, the conference set to for four and a half days in an atmosphere so thick with cigarette smoke and rancorous passions that the world's press, skied up in the gallery, with the fumes of both rising toward them, were practically kippered where they sat.

What was the drama's import? 'The air at Morecambe buzzed with the sound of explaining voices playing the Bevan successes down, playing them jubilantly up, predicting that they would finish Attlee, predicting that Bevan had bitten off more than he could chew, and so on.'

The defining event of an uninhibitedly fractious, ill-tempered conference – 'Shut your gob,' shouted the right-wing miners' leader Will Lawther at one heckler, while at least two bouts of fisticuffs were reported, one of them involving the heavyweight Bessie Braddock – was the election for constituency representatives on the National Executive Committee (NEC). Six out of the seven places went to avowed Bevanites (including Wilson and Crossman), at the expense of such senior figures as Morrison and Dalton. The union block vote remained firmly attached to the right of the party, but this was still a stunning coup on the part of the Bevanites, increasingly a party within the party.

Then, almost as soon as the delegates had left squally Morecambe, Gaitskell intensified the mood of internecine strife by making a highly provocative speech at Stalybridge. He accused a significant minority of the (increasingly middle-class) constituency delegates of being 'Communists or Communist controlled'; made a derogatory reference to 'mob rule by a group of frustrated journalists' (with the left-wing, Bevan-supporting *Tribune* explicitly mentioned); and called for a restoration of 'the authority and leadership of the solid and sensible majority of the Movement'. Gaitskell was on the panel for the next *Any Questions?*, from Calne, and unsurprisingly the question came up, 'Does the team consider that the split in the Socialist Party will widen in the future?' The farmer-writer A. G. Street believed it would, and earned laughter and applause for his sally that 'the ultra-Left-Wing are those people who wish to be generous to others with other people's money', but the Shadow Chancellor played a pretty dead bat: 'This is the Light Programme, Mr Chairman, and you won't expect a serious pronouncement from me on this matter.' He did promise, however, that by the next election 'we shall have settled that argument one way or the other'.[1]

Attlee as usual proved a resourceful, unflappable fire-fighter. Approaching his 70th birthday, he was determined to stay as leader for as long as it took to ensure that neither Bevan nor Morrison succeeded him; and on 23 October, at a meeting of the Parliamentary Labour Party (PLP), he successfully moved a resolution not only banning all unofficial groups within the party but also forbidding all personal attacks. The result was a semi-ceasefire for the next 18 months or so, but the pro-Bevan *New Statesman* was certain that Bevanism would not die, given that it was 'the expression of a deep fissure between the official Party machine and the mass of everyday Socialists'. To one somewhat disenchanted party worker, writing in the *Political Quarterly* just as he departed the political scene, the puzzle was that Labour had so entirely failed to be a vigorous, coherent opposition to the Tories. 'Why have the Bevanites been allowed to hold the field?' he asked. 'One reason is the extraordinary freak of yet another hair's-breadth election. It can be argued that a government which came so near to winning a third term cannot have been so far wrong.' And he went on: 'The middle-of-the-road voters apparently approved of the moderate (practically non-existent) programme of 1951, without any specific proposals for further nationalisation. Why then adopt more radical policies? All the more reason for avoiding extremism when its chief advocate is Mr Bevan, who is thought of as being as violently disliked by the body of voters as he is violently admired by his followers.'

The party worker was Michael Young, who in November 1952 bequeathed to Labour's Policy Committee a sociologically flavoured report called 'For Richer For Poorer' – a plea, 'in its policy-making for the future', to 'give some prominence to the needs of the family', especially young parents suffering from 'less money, less leisure, and less companionship'. The answer to these shortfalls lay neither in 'the worship of consumption' (a worship, according to Young, fuelled by advertising, radio, films and women's magazines) nor in the welfare state ('the first cold word recalling the smell of carbolic acid and the tough brown paper of ration books ... the second cold word suggesting the Law Court, the Sanitary Inspector and the Recruiting Office'). Instead, he now placed his faith unequivocally in the C-word: 'Revival of the community would relieve the burden of loneliness and overwork.' One way of achieving this revival was 'rehousing people in the central areas of our cities and towns, as part of a great plan of urban reconstruction, instead of forcing them to move to housing estates on the outskirts', but he also wanted to 'lower the barriers of class which divide people from one another by speeding on with comprehensive schools and by distributing power (and prestige) more widely through an extension of industrial democracy'. Predictably, Young's report met the fate of most reports. 'The Policy Committee never had, I think, a 250-page report before – no one read it!' he recalled many years later. 'It was just a sort of embarrassment when they got it. Except for Edith Summerskill [an MP who was also a doctor], who did read a bit of it, about women, and thought it was rather good and said, "How on earth did you think up all this?" That was really the only comment on it at all. But it certainly confirmed my view that politics wasn't for me.'

One immediate bonus was no longer having to fret about the question of nationalisation. 'It is no longer any use discussing in principle whether public ownership would be desirable,' Young declared in his parting pronouncement on the subject. 'We have to get down to cases . . .' He cited shipbuilding, chemicals and insurance (an old favourite) as three potentially fruitful sectors. Another left-wing intellectual, G.D.H. Cole, advocated in January 1953 twofold criteria in terms of Labour's future nationalisation commitments: 'Any further nationalisation will be a success only if the workers like it, and only if it is undertaken, not simply for the sake of smashing capitalism, but also with a positive view to its contribution towards getting Great Britain out of the economic difficulties under which it is labouring.' In fact, to a surprising extent, Labour at this point was relatively unruffled about the whole issue, with instead the major internal fault lines concerning foreign policy, above all attitudes to America. Importantly, there was no Tory threat to the bulk of the nationalisation carried out by the Attlee government, with road haulage and steel as the only two sectors receiving the privatisation treatment. Neither proved hugely contentious, with the latter much facilitated by the support from the steelworkers' leader, Lincoln Evans. Knighted at the start of 1953, and soon afterwards made vice-chairman of the Iron and Steel Board (at a handsome annual salary of £5,000), which had the power to fix maximum prices, he was the epitome of the right-wing trade unionist who placed harmonious industrial relations with management well above socialist ideology.[2]

Privatisation of nationalised health care – aka the NHS – was never on the agenda. But by autumn 1952 there was considerable pressure on the new Minister of Health, Iain Macleod, to get a tighter grip on costs. This pressure came partly from the Treasury, dismayed by the way in which a generous award to doctors earlier in the year had led to a chain reaction of wage claims across the NHS; partly from hard-line elements in the Cabinet, keen on major tax cuts as soon as possible; and partly from the City, which, according to the *Financial Times* in October, was looking for a 're-think' of 'the principles of Government expenditure from the beginning'. The upshot was a decision to appoint an independent committee to examine NHS expenditure – a decision that involved a considerable tussle over both the committee's terms of reference and its composition. The hardliners lost both: they wanted the committee's explicit goal to be a reduction in costs, but instead it was merely asked how to avoid 'a rising charge' on the Exchequer; while the chairman was to be a leftish economist (and Macleod's old tutor) from Cambridge, Claude Guillebaud, abetted by four figures of impeccable political balance. Macleod himself had no desire to dismantle the NHS or significantly reduce the service it provided, and indeed for an ambitious young politician in 1952 it would have been folly to have harboured such aspirations. That autumn Charlie Chaplin paid a much-publicised visit to the London slums where he had grown up and told reporters about the contrast between the 'rotten teeth' he had once known and the 'rosy-cheeked children, vigorous, smiling with confidence' that he saw now. 'They are the future of England,' he added in words that carried a powerful emotional charge, 'and, if for nothing else, socialised medicine, if I may say so, is a grand thing for that reason.' The following spring, a Gallup poll found that seven out of ten were satisfied with the treatment they received under the NHS.

The more consensual Tories were encouraged anyway by the improving political climate. By November 1952 – against a background of the government winning three by-elections in a row, the economic situation (including the balance of payments) looking better, Butler succeeding 'in making the pound suddenly look more bobbish', houses 'going up at a faster clip', food 'all at once far more plentiful in the shops', the 'first cold snap and foretaste of winter unaccompanied, for once, by warnings of a coal crisis', and above all the failure to come to pass of Labour's dire warnings of 'large-scale unemployment, possibly war, and anyhow the pulling down of the welfare state brick by brick' – it was clear to Panter-Downes that the Tories were firmly in the box seat: 'This seems like a really serious moment for the Socialist Party, badgered as it is by Bevan from the rear and faced with the necessity of thinking up a new policy to take the place of the old, outdated emotional appeals to the voters to save their hard-won rights from the wicked Tories.' Nothing mattered more than the increasingly benign economic picture, in large part a reflection of the falling price of raw materials and the start of the long peacetime boom for the industrial West, and in his budget the following April, Butler took full political advantage by taking sixpence off income tax, as well as reducing purchase tax on some household articles. 'Personally I shall not profit very much as my income is so small,' lamented Gladys Langford, still living in a hotel in north London and about to turn 63. 'If only I could give up smoking!' The general reaction, though, was predictably positive – so much so that Gallup soon afterwards found that the government's satisfaction rating was at a well-nigh unprecedented 60 per cent, up some 14 points from January. 'The Socialists have a theme,' Churchill somewhat smugly reflected the day after Butler's budget. 'We have no theme – we just have a way of life.'

Even so, rationing remained widespread. Tea did come off in October 1952 and sweets (this time conclusively) in February 1953, but sugar, butter, cooking fats, cheese, meat and eggs were all still on the ration. So too was margarine, but more generously than butter. 'The Food Ministry should give us more butter,' implored 'Wanderer' in the Dumbarton-based *Lennox Herald*. 'The youth of the nation cannot build up a physique on "marge".' The middle-aged and elderly Chiswick housewives interviewed in November 1952 for Mass-Observation's 'Margarine Survey' would have wholeheartedly agreed:

I 'ates the stuff and I always did. Wouldn't eat bread and marge if you paid me. Often I don't get our ration. I'll tell you what I do – I mix the cooking fat with the little bit of dripping out of the Sunday joint, and if there's a drip of bacon fat I put that in too, and we haves that on our bread with pepper and salt, and it's a lot better than any margarine.

Frankly I don't like the stuff, though it's all right in cakes. I know in a minute if they give me margarine on bread, if I'm out to tea. And as for butter, well, there's butter *and* butter . . . The National butter is several degrees better than margarine, but there's a lot of room for improvement in it. The only good butter is at Sainsbury's. They *call* it National but it's not, it comes from Denmark or Holland and it's lovely.

When you think the war's been over for seven years, it's terrible to think of that miserable two ounces [ie of butter]. Margarine is a lot better than it was years ago, but it's not nice on bread.

I think margarine's horrible stuff, really. I'd give a lot for more butter.[3]

'Can't tell Stork from butter' was for years the optimistic slogan of one of the leading brands of margarine. Or, as my father would provokingly say when I was in one of my sulks as a small boy, 'Can't tell talk from mutter.'

———

Just before 8.20 a.m. on Thursday, 8 October 1952 – barely a month after the Farnborough Air Show disaster – there was carnage at Harrow and Wealdstone station. The night train from Perth, running at least an hour late, crashed into the stationary back of a semi-fast train from Tring to Euston, and then moments later the Euston–Manchester express went headlong into the wreckage on an adjoining track. Amid appalling scenes, as the footbridge came down and those waiting on the platform were swept away like leaves, 112 people were killed and more than 200 injured – England's worst-ever railway disaster. 'To sympathy for the victims and praise for the rescue workers, including many volunteers who rallied to help in the spirit of the air raids, can be added confidence that, after a most detailed enquiry, the facts will be made available,' *The Times* reassured the nation. 'Pride in the record of the British railways is strong and well founded.' And the *Daily Mirror* quoted an American first-aid man at the scene, praising the stoicism of the injured: 'The British don't cry.'

Less than two months later, on Friday, 5 December, a young actress called Mary Sutherland was travelling from Aldershot to London. The journey should have taken about three-quarters of an hour, but 'the train kept stopping and got slower', she recalled half a century later. 'Nobody knew what was going on and then we realised there was very thick fog. The journey took hours. When we eventually got to Waterloo we didn't know we were there. A guard came along hammering on the doors, "Get out. Get out. You've come to the station, get out." You couldn't see the platform, you had to take it on trust.' By late afternoon a greeny-yellow vapour had enveloped the capital, bringing it to a virtual standstill – and that evening it was so all-pervasive that a performance of *La Traviata* at Sadler's Wells had to be stopped because the audience could no longer see the stage. Over the next three nights and days the smog retained its grip:

6 December. The town being enveloped in a thick and filthy fog the whole day through, ventured out only to go over to the TH [St Pancras Town Hall] and back in morning, and with M & F [his wife Marjorie and their son Anthony, nicknamed Frainy] round to Euston & back in afternoon for the opening of the St Pancras Church bazaar by Richard Hearne (now known to televiewers as 'Mr Pastry') in his customary comic old dodderer get up. *(Anthony Heap)*

7 December. Fog. It was simply dreadful. Visibility about six feet. And it got down the throat & nose & stung like pepper. The Automobile Ass. says it is the worst they have known. All buses etc are suspended. I tripped on a curb & fell on my poor old bosom, left side. *(Marian Raynham)*

8 December. Oh! The fog! At 10 am it was so thick I was afraid to cross Holloway Rd. At 4 pm, I had to hold the side of a passing perambulator to guide my steps. There was practically no traffic on the streets ... Kendall [a fellow-lodger] said people were 'panicking' at King's Cross Tube as hordes of passengers who usually use buses sought to board trains. *(Gladys Langford)*

Raynham's experience in Surbiton was particularly telling, given her proximity to the power station opened at Kingston four years earlier and since then belching black smoke into the air as remorselessly as its earlier counterparts in Southwark and Battersea.

The coming of the smog coincided with preparations for the annual Smithfield Show at Earl's Court, starting on the Monday. 'The last of the stock arrived at 2 a.m. on Sunday morning,' related *Farmers Weekly*:

At noon on Sunday the hall seemed almost as full of fog as the street outside and a number of cattle were heavily distressed and were removed to the show's hospital.

Finally, exhibitors of no fewer than ten beasts were compelled to send their animals for slaughter; three other animals died and at least two others were sent home. A very heavy and unprecedented blow.

Probably the most unfortunate of the exhibitors who suffered these losses was Frank Parkinson Farms Ltd, whose lovely Aberdeen-Angus heifer Portia 5th of Stisted was among those which died.

'There is no doubt,' added the report, 'that she would have stood high in the prize list.'

Government response to the overall choking, eye-watering problem was undistinguished. Not only was there an attempt to conceal the true extent of the lethalness of the four-day smog – in reality killing some 12,000 people, mainly elderly, not the official estimate of 4,000 – but the Housing Minister, Harold Macmillan, barely saw it as a government matter and resisted pressure to reduce the burning of coal on open fires and do more to persuade local authorities to exercise their smoke-abatement powers. 'We do what we can,' he wearily replied to one parliamentary critic, 'but, of course, the hon Gentleman must realise the enormous number of broad economic considerations which have to be taken into account and which it would be foolish altogether to disregard.'[4]

The sequence of disasters was completed during the appalling weekend of 31 January/1 February 1953, as a huge storm first sank the *Princess Victoria* car ferry crossing from Stranraer to Larne, with the loss of 133 lives, and then swept down the east coast of England from Lincolnshire to Kent, leading not only to severe flooding but to terrifying, life-threatening walls of water breaking through inadequate sea defences. Crucially, there was no system in place warning people to evacuate as the storm neared them, and surprisingly little use seems to have been made of the radio. Worst affected was Canvey Island in the Thames Estuary – 'all bungalows and jerry-built', as John Fowles had noted mordantly a few years earlier, and entirely below sea level. The storm reached it in the early hours of Sunday morning. 'My mother woke me by bursting into the bedroom I shared with my brother,' Barrie de Lara recalled:

> She stood me up on my bed and dressed me, rapidly pulling trousers, jumper and school raincoat over my pyjamas. I sat down to reach for the *Teddy Tail* annual I had dropped when I fell asleep and found it soggy and swollen. Water was cascading, roaring, four or five feet high, through the front door. My brother, older than me by ten years, earned my lifelong respect by standing up to his knees in water in front of a mirror and putting on a white shirt and his Essex County Cricket Club tie. 'If I'm going to drown, then I'm going to drown decently dressed,' he announced to us all.

There was a scramble for the roof space. Father hauled himself up through the trap door. Then Mother climbed onto my brother's shoulders and was manhandled aloft. I was passed up like a package. Last came my brother . . .

My father had grabbed two cylindrical tins of Player's cigarettes, a bottle of rum, a pack of cards and matches: you could tell he was an ex-Navy man. My mother had collected candles, money, her fur coat and jewel box. My brother had taken his best shoes and his cricket bat.

The de Lara family survived the night, but 58 Canvey Islanders did not, many of them drowned in their beds. Altogether, 307 people on the east coast died in the storm and 32,000 had to evacuate their flooded homes. It was, by any yardstick, a huge, calamitous tragedy. Yet perhaps because it did not chime in with the much-desired early to mid-1950s narrative of material progress and increasing optimism, perhaps also because most of its victims were poor people living on low-lying, marginal land, it failed to achieve a central place in the national memory.

Canvey itself had largely been developed between the wars as a favoured retirement spot for working-class Londoners with enough savings to buy a plot of cheap land and put up an inexpensive bungalow. Now, in their hour of adversity, most of Canvey's flooded-out inhabitants returned to London to find temporary accommodation with their extended families. 'The relatives in Bethnal Green, or Hoxton, or Hackney, were waiting with open doors,' noted one admiring observer, Michael Young, adding that the whole process was a 'remarkable testament to the strength of kinship ties'. Young's fieldwork in March left a marked impression on him, but perhaps he should have been on the bus with Mollie Panter-Downes crossing the causeway from the railway station at South Benfleet some ten days after the storm. She found herself sitting amid many returning evacuees:

A typical greeting shouted across the bus is 'What happened to your place?', and if the answer is 'Well, we've still got three foot of water everywhere, but we can't complain. Lucky to be alive,' the other Canvey Islanders nod and say, 'That's right.' All the same, everyone's raging preoccupation is to get back into his own three feet of water as soon as possible, for the general feeling seems to be that that is far preferable to being high and dry among married daughters, squalling grandchildren, or well-meaning friends. 'Where did you go?' someone on the bus asked a sharp-faced little woman in an oilskin pixie hood sitting beside her grey-faced husband. 'We never went,' the woman replied tartly. 'We just came in a couple of hours ago to buy a few things. We was evacuated in the war and we don't intend to have none of that again.'

Indeed, of the island's population of some 11,000, about 750 people were 'still sticking it out on Canvey'. There, amid the general cold, wet misery and flooded-out houses with names like 'Mon Tresor' or 'Kosy Kot', there was at least one note of defiance: 'Outside a food store stands a moth-eaten stuffed mountain bear holding in its paws a chalked notice that advises passersby to "Bear Up – Canvey Will Rise Again".'⁵

The smog and the storm were two of the few things this winter not blamed on cosh boys. The previous summer the unremittingly hard-line Lord Chief Justice, Rayner Goddard, had used the Lord Mayor's annual banquet at the Mansion House to make a powerful plea for the restoration of corporal punishment, while Gladys Langford was noting by late October how newspapers were 'full of accounts of further "coshings" and letters to the press advocating the return of flogging as punishment for crimes of violence'. The controversy continued unabated in November, with the Magistrates' Association balloting its members on the question. The government, though, remained unmoved, with the Home Secretary, Sir David Maxwell Fyfe, pointing out to the Cabinet Committee that as well as Labour being solidly against it, 'only about 3 or 4 to 1' among Tories favoured restoration. But the issue continued to resonate, prompting Kenneth Allsop to report in December on 'Fear in the Suburbs' for *Picture Post*. 'Acacia Avenue's respectability is being ravaged by thuggery and coshery,' he found. 'A state of nerves certainly exists. I talked to men and women of all classes and callings, and in almost every one the attitude was emotional rather than rational . . . A revival of flogging was in loud demand.' The magazine's readers concurred. 'No good will be done until the whip is brought back,' declared Mrs Marjorie T. Brentnall of Congleton. 'I feel very strongly about this, and so do all decent citizens.' Mrs L. A. Kershaw of South Croydon spoke for the nation's mothers: 'I am a peace-loving housewife and have a grown-up son and feel for the parents of these young boys who take to violence. I am sure most of them would feel as I do – give them a thrashing and, then help them to live decently and become useful citizens.' Soon afterwards the smog provoked a heavily publicised rash of what Langford called ' "cosh" attacks and hold-ups', and in February it transpired that the magistrates' ballot had produced a majority of more than two to one in favour of restoring corporal punishment. Next day, however, a private member's Bill to that effect was defeated in the Commons by 159–63. The politicians had, in the words of Goddard's biographer, 'closed ranks'.[6]

It was in this jumpy, agitated climate that there unfolded during the winter of 1952/3 the case of Derek Bentley, a 19-year-old epileptic with a mental age of 11. On 2 November he and the 16-year-old Christopher Craig, both wearing drape jackets and crepe-soled shoes, attempted to rob the West Croydon warehouse of Barlow & Parkers, confectionery wholesalers. In the process, Craig shot dead Sidney Miles, a middle-aged police constable. The trial, with Goddard presiding, began at the Old Bailey on 9 December and lasted four days. 'I think both little fuckers ought to swing,' was reputedly the private view of Bentley's counsel, while much turned on the police claim that Bentley had shouted out to Craig just before he shot, 'Let him have it, Chris' – words, if uttered, susceptible to more than one interpretation. 'People waited 8 hours to get in to Craig's trial,' Langford in her north London hotel noted after the first day. 'I don't think he or Bentley who is being tried with him will hang. Craig is only 16 and even the police admit the other fellow is mentally sub-normal.' Next day she went on: 'Breakfast time talk among residents and staff centred on Craig's trial. Most people think the verdict will be manslaughter and that Bentley will not hang as he did not actually handle a weapon. Both young men have lied again and again in their evidence. Craig says he "cried for his mother when he was injured" – no tears for the hapless constable shot dead and for his widow.' In the event, after Goddard's strongly pro-conviction summing-up (in the course of which he produced Bentley's spiked knuckleduster), the jury returned guilty verdicts, though with a recommendation of mercy for Bentley. Craig was too young to be executed, but for Bentley the Lord Chief Justice saw no alternative but to put on his black cap.

An appeal on Bentley's behalf was lodged, but dismissed on 13 January. On Friday the 23rd, only five days before he was due to hang, Bentley's family handed in a petition (with 12,000 signatures) at the Home Office. That weekend, with Maxwell Fyfe considering whether to commute the death sentence, the Sunday papers were full of the case. 'If two men go upon some criminal adventure, the one armed and the other knowing him to be armed, the other no less than the one intends the consequences, and if they include a killing the unarmed intends it and is a murderer,' was the unrelenting view of the *Sunday Times*. 'That is not only the law, it is just law, and good plain sense.' Britain's highest-circulation paper, the *News of the World*, did not commit itself to a formal opinion, but devoted much of its front page to the story. 'Bentley's Pets Join Family Circle as The 11th Hour Approaches,' ran the headline, accompanied by a photo of Bentley's sister Iris holding Flossie, a lurcher puppy, and Judy, a Manchester terrier, while Bentley's favourite dog Bob and Banjo the cat looked on. 'The main reason for his reprieve was that, since his arrest, these dogs had been off their food,' an otherwise sympathetic Rayner Heppenstall sourly recalled press calls for commutation.[7]

The following day, Monday the 26th, Derek's father, William, received a letter from the Home Office informing him that the Home Secretary was unable to advise a reprieve, while on Tuesday morning the two most popular daily papers pronounced. The *Daily Express* was unambiguous, accusing Bentley's defenders of 'wallowing in sentiment', but the *Daily Mirror* more cautious, though in the end tacitly endorsing the 'humane' Maxwell Fyfe: 'The fate of Bentley must be read as a warning that there will not be leniency towards anyone who goes along with a man who carries a gun.' That Tuesday evening, with only hours to go, there were not only large crowds of protesters outside Parliament and elsewhere but also angry speeches by Labour MPs, including R. T. Paget. 'A three-quarter witted boy of 19 is to be hanged for a murder which he did not commit, and which was committed 15 minutes after he was arrested,' was how he memorably put it. Crucially, even though some 200 MPs had signed a petition demanding mercy, the Speaker refused to allow a debate on the Home Secretary's decision as such. 'So a human life must go,' reflected the young actor Kenneth Williams in disgust, 'because discussion of his death is "out of order"!'

Bentley was duly hanged at Wandsworth Prison at nine on Wednesday morning, with a crowd of 5,000 outside. 'Just follow me, lad,' the hangman Albert Pierrepoint gently whispered as he put the pinioning-loop upon Bentley's wrists and suddenly made it tight. 'It's all right Derek, just follow me.' A few hours later, shortly before lunch, Maxwell Fyfe entered the Tory club, the Carlton, 'looking white and exhausted' according to the watching, liberal-minded Humphrey Berkeley. 'Suddenly a group of Club members appeared carrying their whiskeys and dry martinis in their hands and clapped Sir David on the back with shouts of "Well done, David." ' Maxwell Fyfe, 'one of the kindest men I have ever met, obviously was repelled by the demonstration'.

Elsewhere, the horror was palpable. 'THIS THING SHOULD NOT HAVE BEEN DONE,' thundered 'Cassandra' in his *Daily Mirror* column that morning, describing Bentley as 'a weak, vicious youth whose parents attempted to keep him away from Craig'; at a junior school in Dormanstown, Teesside, the 11-year-old Rosalind Delmar was asked at morning assembly 'to pray for his soul, with the sense that in London a great injustice was being done' – a moment that for Delmar gave 'a whiff of a wider view of justice as a yardstick with which those in power could be measured'; and in London itself, the visiting Jean Genet was, according to his biographer Edmund White, 'so appalled by the execution that he never emerged from the Regent Palace Hotel'. The chances are, though, that the female diarists more accurately reflected majority opinion. After referring on the 28th to 'the Bentley-Craig gang' and to Maxwell Fyfe's 'terrible position to be in', Nella Last in Barrow was adamant: ' "Emotional" people cannot be let rule – or over-ride wise if terrible decisions.' Judy Haines in Chingford almost certainly agreed. 'I must say,' she wrote that same day after briefly summarising what had happened, 'these young thugs scare the life out of me and it needs some drastic measure to make them think twice.' And Langford three days later was shocked by how the police sergeant who made the initial arrest had apparently been threatened with murder by several people: 'I find it hard to understand the sympathy lavished on that young thug Bentley.' What none of the three could have known was that almost half a century later, following a lifelong campaign by his sister Iris and almost systematic evasion and suppression of evidence by the Home Office, Bentley would have his name cleared by a latter-day Lord Chief Justice, highly critical of his predecessor's direction to the jury. Bentley, declared Lord Bingham of Cornhill in 1998, had been denied 'that fair trial which is the birthright of every British citizen'.[8]

In 1953 itself, there was soon another murder story. 'Three Women Walled Up in House of Two Murders', was the *Daily Express* headline on 25 March, with the paper noting that the bodies had been discovered in the same house – 10 Rillington Place, near Ladbroke Grove – where Timothy Evans had killed his wife and daughter before being hanged at Pentonville in 1950. But the story was not yet front-page news, for on the same day as these grisly discoveries, Queen Mary died. 'What has been her reward for duty bravely done?' asked the *Express*. 'Her reward is the greatest of all honours. Her reward is the tears which are shed today in humble homes throughout the land.' At the *Mirror* it fell to the young Keith Waterhouse to compile a three-part series, 'The Human Stories of Queen Mary', including such characteristic *bon mots* as 'Illness is so tiresome' and 'I have never been bored in my life, and I have no patience with people who are bored.' 'We sometimes smiled at her old-fashionedness and chuckled at her idiosyncrasies,' Waterhouse himself reflected. 'But it was a kind smile and a happy chuckle for Grandmother England.' Soon, though, the two stories were vying on front pages, as the Rillington Place body count rose to six and the house's long-time inhabitant, John Christie, was apprehended near Putney Bridge. That was on the last day of March, by which time in Rillington Place itself Mrs McFadden at no. 5 had organised a petition asking for the name of the cul-de-sac to be changed. 'Every householder signed it,' observed one journalist, 'for somehow a violent death in their midst, brought a sense of social, communal shame to the more decent folk.' Rillington Place in due course became Rushton Close, subsequently demolished.

Christie's trial was still to come, but Bill Field had already had his encounter with British justice. He was a 43-year-old Labour MP, and widely regarded as a rising figure, when in January he was found guilty at Bow Street Court of 'persistently importuning men for an immoral purpose in Piccadilly Circus and Leicester Square'. On the Tuesday evening in question, earlier that month, he had, according to the police, gone to several pubs as well as paying four visits to public lavatories in the course of 90 minutes. 'At any time did you smile at anyone, first of all deliberately . . . what I would call filthily?' asked at one point his QC, a Tory MP called John Maude who gave his services for free. 'No, but I may have smiled at someone subconsciously,' replied Field. Maude also led Field's defence at the appeal in February at the London Sessions, but again to no avail. During it, one of the two policemen who had been keeping watch on the MP 'agreed that entries in his notebook were not made at the time in question and that he had lied about the notebook at the magistrate's court'. To which Maude 'said it was frightening if a man could be convicted on the evidence of a police officer, who had been caught perjuring himself'. On the appeal being dismissed, Field 'sat as though stunned, appeared to wipe away a tear, then hurried out'. Kenneth Williams, on tour that week in Norwich in a production of *Peter Pan*, might have sympathised. 'Everyone at the Copper Kettle stayed up late and talked,' he noted next day after the Saturday-evening performance: 'The awfully boring & hearty commercial traveller became suddenly confidential. He took me aside in the kitchen, in a burst of confession, and explained that he was homosexual. I had to act deliberately nonchalant to cover my dumbfoundedness, confusion and embarrassment. I practically fell over myself in the effort to be casual and burnt my fingers on the gas ring. Life holds so many surprises for us.' Field himself immediately resigned his seat, disappearing not only from politics but also from all his friends. 'He felt the disaster keenly,' recorded his 2002 obituary, 'and to the end he maintained he had been trapped and martyred because he was an MP.'[9]

There were other faces that did not fit. 'Today there is a residential coloured community of about 50,000 here, and that very articulate body of opinion which uses the words "colour prejudice" upon its oriflame insists we take them into our hearts and into our homes,' declared David Divine in a long article in the right-wing *Sunday Graphic* in October 1952. 'Should we?' he asked, arguing that black workers were poor at keeping their jobs and that 'because they live with a perpetual chip on their shoulder they claim that dismissal is always due to colour prejudice'. Divine also asserted that white dislike of blacks was based less on prejudice than a reaction to the 'lawlessness' and 'arrogance' of 'the coloured colony'. Half the letters the following Sunday defended black immigrants, but half did not. 'There should be a colour bar, and I am not ashamed to say so,' wrote in Ralph H. Taylor of Edgware, while Sydney G. Gibbs reckoned that 'the unrestricted invasion of England by the coloured races is a scandal'.

Evidence that a de facto colour bar already existed was given by Henry Gunter, the Jamaican co-founder of the Birmingham branch of the Caribbean Labour Congress, in an article the following February about the situation in that city. Gunter detailed grossly overcrowded living conditions for many black workers there, extortionate rents, a mixture of discrimination and exploitation at work, and a widespread colour bar at hotels, dance halls and social clubs. Traditionally, black migration had been to dockland areas, but by now it was increasingly going inland to the great manufacturing centres. 'The coloured people are concentrated in overcrowded areas where the housing facilities are worst,' the academic Michael Banton noted sombrely in March. 'The absence of friction may be largely attributed to the full employment of the post-war period. And economic recession could easily open the old wounds and cause new ones.' Soon afterwards Catherine Cookson published her third novel, *Colour Blind*, showing the power of love to triumph over Tyneside intolerance to mixed-race relationships, but that basic economic truth was unlikely to go away.[10]

It was all distinctly white and middle-class in Agatha Christie's *The Mousetrap*, which opened in London in November 1952 to no great expectations on the author's part. The play was set in a country guest house, with a cast of eight including Richard Attenborough as Detective Sergeant Trotter, and got a fairly tepid response from the critics. 'The plot is altogether incredible, and there is a bit of cheating into the bargain,' claimed Iain Hamilton in the *Spectator*, though he did concede that it was still 'an entertaining evening for simple souls like myself who don't really care overmuch who killed X'. T. C. Worsley was especially down on the second half. 'It won't do,' he asserted in the *New Statesman*. 'We are thoroughly dissatisfied, for the clearing up has been most perfunctorily done. The stage is left strewn with uneaten red herrings, unexplained presences, unanswered questions.

We find that for once Mrs Christie has been swindling and on a very large scale too. This is unforgivable in detective fiction.' Setting less exacting – and more representative – standards was the strictly amateur reviewer Anthony Heap, present on the first night and enjoying 'a nice entertaining evening of guessing, suspecting, trailing red herrings and coming to false conclusions, to our simple heart's content'. In short: 'Agatha Christie has, in fact, whodunit again. Signifying that the Ambassadors shouldn't be looking for another distraction until well after the Coronation.' Heap was slightly out – the play continued at the Ambassadors until 1974, when it transferred next door to St Martin's – but it was still a creditable estimate. What was the secret of *The Mousetrap*'s phenomenal success? 'There cannot be just one answer,' mused its producer, Peter Saunders, in 1958. 'But it has all the ingredients of the best quiz games, it is dramatic, it has comedy, suspense, and it can be understood by people of every age.'[11]

Ian Fleming's *Casino Royale*, published in April 1953 and marking the fictional debut of James Bond, offered a different kind of thrill. 'An extremely engaging affair,' thought the *TLS*, 'dealing with espionage in the Sapper manner but with a hero who, although taking a great many cold showers and never letting sex interfere with work, is somewhat more sophisticated,' while Simon Raven in the *Listener* acclaimed Fleming as 'a kind of supersonic John Buchan'. The most glowing review was in the *Sunday Times* – for which, admittedly, Fleming worked as foreign manager. Finding it an adult thriller that was a welcome relief from 'the side street and back bedrooms of Graham Greeneland', Christopher Pym, pseudonym for Cyril Ray, went on: 'Here is a new writer who takes us back to the casinos of le Queux and Oppenheim, the world of caviare and fat Macedonian cigarettes. But with how much more pace in the writing, how much less sentimentality in the tone of voice, how much more knowing a look!' Altogether, the reviewer was 'pretty certain' that Fleming was 'the best new English thriller-writer since Ambler'.

He had a case. 'Fleming wanted to inject something of Chandler's gritty realism into the British spy novel,' his biographer Andrew Lycett has observed, and 'to write about an emerging culture of intelligence where spies were no longer amateur adventurers like Bulldog Drummond but professional hard men.' Nothing more gritty and unsentimental than the brutal ending, with the lovely Vesper Lynd revealed as a double agent working for SMERSH. 'He saw her now only as a spy. Their love and his grief were relegated to the boxroom of his mind.' The new hard-faced professionalism came, though, with some distinctly unreconstructed baggage. 'These blithering women', Bond believed, should 'stay at home and mind their pots and pans and stick to their frocks and gossip and leave men's work to the men', while the baccarat players he was pitted against included an Italian who would 'probably play a dashing and foolish game' and the Maharajah of a small Indian state unlikely to alter Bond's maxim that 'few of the Asiatic races were courageous gamblers'. In fact, *Casino Royale* did not sell particularly well – probably because the time was not quite ripe for what the historian David Cannadine has characterised as Fleming's 'fictional brand of great-power nostalgia, imperial escapism and national reassurance'.[12] Put another way, Britain in 1953 was not yet a country in perceived – let alone self-perceived – decline.

Anyway, the undisputed literary event of 1952/3 had already happened: the publication in November of Dylan Thomas's *Collected Poems*. Philip Toynbee in the *Observer* hailed him as 'the greatest living poet', while Stephen Spender in the *Spectator* asserted that Thomas represented 'a revolt' not only 'against the Oxford, Cambridge and Harvard intellectualism of much modern poetry' but also 'against the King's English of London and the South', incapable of 'harsh effects, coarse nature and violent colours'. The initial print run of 5,000 soon proved inadequate. One young writer and emerging literary impresario, however, professed himself impatient with Thomas's 'disastrously limited subject matter'. This was John Wain, who on the last Sunday of April 1953 introduced on the Third Programme *First Reading: A Monthly Magazine of New Poetry and Prose*. On the Home Service at the same time there was a programme about the British Red Cross, including a recorded interview by Wilfred Pickles at a children's hospital in Warwickshire, while on the Light a variety show called *The Pleasure Boat* starred Julie Andrews and Jon Pertwee, but presumably some people listened. First up was an extract (read by the actor Alan Wheatley) from Kingsley Amis's still unpublished novel *Lucky Jim*, with Wain announcing that 'the particular episode we are going to hear opens with the hero, Dixon, suffering from a hangover and a bad conscience'. In fact the typescript of the novel was still with the publishers Gollancz, whose Hilary Rubinstein next day wrote to Amis to say that his firm did indeed want to publish it. Victor Gollancz himself disliked it, but was persuaded (including by his daughter Livia) to sanction the not exactly princely advance of £100.[13]

If the literary scene in the early 1950s was due for new voices and new faces, so too was popular music, still dominated by ballroom dancing, big-band swing and romantic crooners. 'Incredibly bland and lacking inspiration,' was the succinct retrospective verdict of Bill Wyman, especially scornful of moon-in-June ballads 'without any balls'. Even the commercial station Radio Luxembourg, on 208 medium wave, had relatively little to offer restless youth, to judge by its line-up on the evening of Friday, 14 November 1952:

    7.30 – Nat Cole
    7.45 – Hutch
    8 – Vera Lynn sings
    8.30 – George Elrick's Cavalcade of Music
    9.45 – Vic Damone
    10 – Ray Ellington Quartet
    10.15 – Highlights
    10.30 – Tunes of the Times

That same day, though, marked the generally acknowledged start of the modern British record industry. 'For the first time in the history of the British popular music business,' declared *New Musical Express*, 'an authentic weekly survey of the best-selling "pop" records [still mainly 78-rpm shellac] has been devised and instituted.' Even so, the chart's top five (Al Martino, Jo Stafford, the not yet crowned Nat Cole, Bing Crosby and Guy Mitchell) hardly represented seismic change, while the following spring the band leader Ted Heath, accompanied by his vocalists Dickie Valentine and Lita Roza, was top of the bill for the *NME*'s 1953 Poll Winners' Concert at the Royal Albert Hall.

Still, something was undeniably in the air when 'The Nabob of Sob', aka 'The Prince of Wails', aka Johnnie Ray, flew into London Airport in March for his first visit to England. Centrepiece of his tour was a fortnight at the London Palladium, watched by the *News of the World*'s 'Old Trouper': 'When Johnnie walked on, the audience swooned in an ecstasy of hysteria; when he shouted his song down a hand-mic as he threw himself all over the stage, I didn't think they could bear any more. "Cry, Johnnie, cry!" they shouted . . .' Noël Coward attended the opening night – 'He was really remarkable and had the whole place in an uproar' – but even more appreciative was the prominent Labour MP and socialite Tom Driberg. He went to see Ray's act (only about 25 minutes long), spoke 'tenderly' about him, showed him round the House of Commons, had his advances repudiated and wrote a lengthy article ('For Crying Out Loud . . .') in the *New Statesman*. 'His impulses are generous and not anti-social,' noted Driberg, before concluding even more pompously: 'His best service to himself, and to society, would be resolutely to complete his adjustment to adult life. Some of his fans might then start growing up with him, too.'[14]

In the City of London, another new, rather more brutal face was also the subject of condescension, albeit tinged with fear. An entirely self-made man (the son of Russian Jewish immigrants), Charles Clore was in his late forties and had made most of his money in property. A biographer's phrases are striking about this pragmatic, hard-bitten outsider. He possessed an 'utterly ruthless honesty'; his will had 'the force of granite'; a pair of 'cobalt eyes made people cringe'; and 'he expected the worst of people and was rarely surprised'. Another biographer describes Clore as 'virile, sexually gluttonous, often crude and impatient'. Early in 1953 he made a contested bid – an almost unheard-of phenomenon – for the Northampton-based shoe manufacturers J. Sears & Co, parent company of Freeman, Hardy & Willis. In the end, amid palpable City shock, his offer proved too good to refuse. 'We never thought anything like this would happen to us,' were the valedictory words of the departing Sears chairman, while the *Northampton Independent* quoted Clore himself: 'I am, of course, delighted. Now we must take our coats off and get down to business.'

Hard-headed commentators like the *Economist* shed no tears, arguing that 'it is those who make the bids for shares who are paying the greatest regard to economic principles' and warning that 'Government interference with such bids would be a shelter for inefficient directors, inefficient utilisation of assets and inefficient distribution of risk capital'; but Tory backbenchers as well as City grandees expressed disquiet, especially as Clore did not deny that he had further takeover plans. 'Lord Bicester [of the merchant bank Morgan Grenfell] came in to say that he was very agitated about further manoeuvres by Mr Clore,' the Governor of the Bank of England, Kim Cobbold, recorded in June, and a little later he noted that the even more senior Sir Edward Peacock of Barings was 'unhappy about Mr Clore and similar activities which seem to be spreading but he agrees with me in not seeing what on earth can be done about it'.[15] The wider import was unmistakable: the cosy, paternalistic world of family capitalism, deeply embedded in the British economic system even after the rise of the large corporation during the first half of the century, was now under threat as never before.

Leonard Lord, in charge of Austin at Longbridge, was temperamentally in the same domineering, unyielding mould as Clore. In September 1952 he presided over the dismissal of seven hundred workers, seven of whom were shop stewards, including John McHugh, an Austin employee since 1928. Over the next five months, as the economic climate improved, McHugh remained out in the cold. There is conflicting evidence as to whether he himself was a Communist, but it is clear enough from contemporary documents that his dismissal was, in one historian's words, 'a deliberate management attempt to weaken the NUVB [National Union of Vehicle Builders], the Austin Shop Stewards Committee [headed by Dick Etheridge, an avowed Communist] and the left-wing in the factory'. The strike began on 17 February, involving 2,278 of Austin's NUVB members, and Lord that day issued a notice denying that McHugh had been victimised and refusing to give him 'preferential treatment' because he was a shop steward. As usual, the strikers received little sympathy from the press, with *The Times* predictably emphasising the Communist influence in the dispute, and even the *Mirror* expressing its opposition to preferential treatment for shop stewards. Towards the end of March, Lord dismissed 1,800 strikers. 'The N.U.V.B. have asked for a fight and they have got it,' commented the *Birmingham Post*. 'It is in the general interest that they should be thoroughly beaten ... Partnership between managers and workers is essential for our national survival.' A government-appointed Court of Inquiry broadly came down on management's side, and the strike finally ended in early May very much on Lord's terms, with no reinstatement for McHugh or indeed the other six shop stewards. It had not only been the biggest strike in Birmingham since the war but also set a record as the motor industry's largest single-firm stoppage. 'In my opinion,' retrospectively commented Les Gurl (emerging as Etheridge's counterpart at the Morris plant at Cowley), 'this dispute soured the relationship between the Unions and Austin Management for many years.'[16]

The strike coincided with the passing of the world's most famous Communist. 'We touched on the Stalin situation and we agreed it was just as well Eden [the Foreign Secretary, Sir Anthony Eden] was over there as he might be a stabilising influence,' the chairman of the London Discount Market Association complacently reflected after a conversation with the Governor of the Bank of England, as the Russian leader lay on his deathbed. Next morning, 6 March, Stalin's death was duly announced. 'The Radio news-reader did not use the sepulchral tones and make the reverential pause customarily used in the broadcasting of obituary notices,' noted Gladys Langford, probably with some pleasure, but the writer Sylvia Townsend Warner was outraged by 'an account of such gross & vulgar malice' that 'I could hardly believe my ears.' Later that morning, at Yates's wine bar in Manchester, Michael Wharton (the future *Daily Telegraph* satirist 'Peter Simple') joined colleagues from the BBC features department. 'What's the matter? What has happened?' he asked after noticing that they seemed stunned and unhappy. 'Haven't you heard the news? Stalin is dead,' one of them replied. 'Pity he was ever born,' was Wharton's instant response – a response that 'to these people was simply blasphemous', he recalled, with the result that 'they did not speak to me again for a fortnight'.

Public reactions to the death of Uncle Joe inevitably varied widely. 'Never', declared the British Communist leader Harry Pollitt in the *Daily Worker*, 'have I met anyone so kindly and considerate,' but the *Daily Mirror*'s 'Cassandra' offered an unyielding judgement: 'His purpose was evil and his methods unspeakable. Few men by their death can have given such deep satisfaction to so many.' It was a death that offered the possibility of a thaw in the Cold War, especially with the Korean War winding down towards an eventual ceasefire in July. Even so, the experience of the left-wing Reverend Stanley Evans suggested it was a thaw that would take some time to permeate the British establishment. In April, after 17 years in Orders but still without a proper job in the Church of England, he appealed directly to the Bishop of London, explaining that '. . . the cause which I have most espoused, that of friendship between East and West, is of fundamental importance not only for our national future but also for the future of Christianity as a whole.'[17] But despite the Church's manpower problems, he remained out in the cold.

There were two rather more auspicious moments this April, starting at 4.00 on Tuesday the 21st with the first broadcast of *Watch With Mother*. Initially it was shown only two or three times a week, with the well-established *Andy Pandy* more or less alternating with *The Flowerpot Men*, the latter first seen climbing out the previous December. Their creator was Hilda Brabban, whose younger brothers, William and Benjamin, were so mischievous that their mother would shout, 'Was it Bill or was it Ben?' So a catchphrase was born, though the Flowerpot Men's language (officially known as Oddle Poddle) was so incomprehensible that the programme was quite sharply criticised for encouraging immaturity. The other moment was of a different order: Francis Crick and James Watson, British biophysicist and American viro-chemist, publishing in *Nature* on the 25th a description of the double helix – in effect, revealing the structure of DNA, widely acknowledged as the scientific discovery of the century. In fact, much of their data derived from the work of Rosalind Franklin, a brilliant young physical chemist based at King's College, London. To Crick and Watson fell the glory of the Nobel Prize, along with the molecular biologist Maurice Wilkins; to Franklin, an early death from cancer and years of obscurity before her contribution was properly acknowledged.

The last day of the month was a Thursday. For Nella Last in Barrow, domestic life that evening revolved as usual round her fussy, valetudinarian husband: 'He decided he would like to hear the play from 7 to 8 o'clock. Luckily it was an effortless "happy" play. How "fashions" in entertaining are changing, a kind of little "story" in place of the joyous idiocy of *ITMA* & oh dear they *don't* seem very entertaining. Plays, & *Twenty Questions*, *Palm Court*, & the schools broadcast are the best of "light" entertainment. I often feel sorry that *Woman's Hour* & my husband's rest after lunch, should coincide.'[18]

In October 1952, more than eleven years after the worst of the German bombing, Gladys Langford walked tearfully around Homerton, where she had grown up:

> Everywhere seemed so small, the streets so narrow, the devastation so great. The whole place almost unrecognisable ... Many tombstones in Hackney Churchyard have been blitzed – a keeper told me it is planned to clear away the tombs. The lovely old Eagle House (once a doss house) is badly blitzed & derelict. St Barnabas Church is a shell. Brooksby's Walk has lost almost all the houses near the church & 'prefabs' with nice little gardens cover the spot where the pock-marked cobbler wielded his knife & nails ...

In London as in most of Britain's badly blitzed cities, the pace of physical reconstruction continued to be painfully slow. A series in the *Architects' Journal* in 1952/3 was generally dismayed by the lack of vim and vigour on the part of local authorities, typified by 'extraordinarily dilatory' Bristol and the 'niggardly' fulfilment of promises in Portsmouth. Or, as a Southampton MP explained to the Commons in March 1953 about his city, 'very few of the shops, offices and business premises have been reconstructed', while 'one sees a large number of bare and desolate patches of ground which are covered by willow herb and other wild flowers'. A partial exception was Plymouth – where by 1953 work was well under way on Armada Way, the great north–south avenue (pedestrian in character, with sunken gardens) running from the railway station to the Hoe – but even there, Macmillan during a visit the previous autumn noted how he 'cd give out no news about reconstruction', adding that 'this "Capital Investment Programme" is really intolerable'. Given that, when it came to physical reconstruction, all the local authorities were operating under severe financial constraints imposed by the Treasury, this was undoubtedly true not just in Plymouth.

There was, though, another general influence at work: the sheer lack by the early 1950s of any popular appetite for planning and reconstruction. 'Why don't they build some dwellings on that bombsite?' was the recurrent refrain, according to a 1951 report on London. 'The town planning says it's to be open space. What's the use of open space? Isn't there the doorstep and the street? What we want is homes.' Two years later the Labour MP for Coatbridge, near Glasgow, noted that whereas her constituents viewed housing as 'an acute election issue', they saw town planning as 'a fanatic's dream'. There was, moreover, a deep-rooted element of cultural conservatism. In Canterbury the *Architects' Journal* regretfully recorded 'a strong blend of emotionalism present which is reflected in two fears – vandalism and modernity', a blend perhaps even more powerful in Exeter, with its 'general feeling on the part of the public that redeveloped portions of the city should literally resemble the best in the old'.[19]

How different was it in Coventry, national flagship of reconstruction? Certainly there was plenty to be done: in February 1952 a well-disposed observer, Basil Davidson, characterised the city as an 'ugly and half-painted backcloth to huge and clamorous factories, and, for the moment little more'. Four months later, marking the start of work on the Woolworths building in what would become the Upper Precinct, the *Coventry Evening Telegraph* paid tribute to the perseverance shown by the planners of the emerging city centre: 'They have kept Coventry in the lead among blitzed cities in the work of reconstruction, and the public are becoming increasingly pleased with what is being done.' The contemporary evidence for that cosy assumption was, however, only patchy – and the unsentimental historian of Coventry's reconstruction, Nick Tiratsoo, makes it unambiguously clear that by this time, even more than in the late 1940s, private consumption engendered far more enthusiasm than public reconstruction, with zeal for the latter declining to 'little more than a flicker'. This essentially passive acceptance – mixed with some grumbling – was well shown during the public inquiry that began in February 1953 into the city's Development Plan, which among many other things proposed a ground-level Inner Ring Road. More than 540 individual objections were raised, but the Inspector's overall conclusion was that 'considering the positive nature of the Plan, the objections of weight were not many'.

By this time the more immediate focus was on the imminent completion of the six-storey block of shops and offices at the top of the proposed shopping precinct: Broadgate House, designed in the City Architect's department under Donald Gibson. 'Such a monstrosity, darkening half Broadgate, and obstructing the view and traffic from

Broadgate down Hertford Street, could never have been conceived by a Coventrian who loved Coventry,' declared 'Old Boy' in the local evening paper, while the paper itself tactfully sat on the fence, noting that 'to many people its massive proportions are a symbol of Coventry's recovery, to others they are looked upon as municipal intrusion into a sphere of business activity which might well have been left to other agencies'. A relieved council was able to announce that the building was 85 per cent let, and a former Labour Planning Minister, Lord Silkin, was invited to perform the official opening on the first Saturday in May.[20]

No city was in greater need of a physical upgrade than Glasgow, especially with its desperately overcrowded housing conditions. 'This is a very sordid town,' Joyce Grenfell on tour wrote to a friend in 1952, 'and one sees so many spivs, toughs and undersized cripples, tarts, pansies and flotsam and jetsam that it tends to get a girl down.' In the early 1950s the main housing initiative was directed towards huge peripheral estates, just inside the city's boundaries and mainly comprising three- or four-storey tenements. 'Pollok has suffered from growing pains,' the *Glasgow Herald* noted shortly before Grenfell's lament about the scheme to the south-west that was nearing completion, with a projected population of about 45,000. 'The building of houses has outpaced the provision of community services, particularly schools.' By this time plans had been approved for the Drumchapel scheme to the north-west, projected as a self-contained township of ultimately almost 30,000 residents. 'Conforming in its lay-out to the modern conceptions of community planning,' the *Glasgow Herald*'s municipal correspondent wrote hopefully, 'it is intended to be, not a "suburban sprawl", but a place with recognised boundaries, in which a sense of community may be fostered . . .' Soon afterwards, in November 1952, plans went through for Castlemilk, on a hilly site to the south-east and again for about 30,000 people, with work beginning in 1953. 'The architecture and street layouts were monotonous in the extreme,' notes the estate's historian, 'and the large backland areas between houses were like a wilderness enclosed by brick boxes.' He adds that there was 'certainly no consultation with potential tenants over the planning of Castlemilk' and quotes Glasgow Corporation's unashamed – and politically wholly understandable – mission statement: 'To build the maximum number of houses in the shortest possible time'.

The creation of large peripheral estates, for good or ill, was in itself no solution to the age-old problem of inner-city slums. 'Keep it up and drive it home,' was a stockbroker's enthusiastic response to a hard-hitting documentary, *Slums*, broadcast on the Scottish Home Service in April 1953. 'This is the most important subject in Scotland.' A Glasgow housewife agreed: 'We also have had rats; we have no wash-house, no drying green, not even a proper place for the rubbish bins. We know how true this programme is.'[21] The emerging consensus, certainly on the part of activators, was that the solution lay – once financial resources permitted – in major slum-clearance programmes followed by comprehensive redevelopment.

Some cities (like Liverpool, where the City Architect, Ronald Bradbury, was a vigorous proponent of slum clearance) were ahead of the curve, others still somewhat behind it. In Tory-run Newcastle, for instance, the council was petitioned in November 1952 by 458 'residents of dilapidated and insanitary property' who protested 'in the strongest of terms at the complete failure of the Housing Committee to deal adequately with the city's housing needs, and at their entirely negative attitude with regard to slum clearance'. During the ensuing council debate, a newish Labour councillor, T. Dan Smith, objected to the way in which a previous speaker, a Tory councillor, had apparently blamed the condition of Newcastle's slums on the people who lived in them, people who would turn 'the best house' into another slum:

> In my view slum property is more likely to keep people in a state of mind that is not conducive to helping them to develop a sense of pride in their homes, rather than the fact that, if given better houses, they would wreck those houses. Whether we like it or not, there are thousands of houses in this city without baths and water. When they were built a hundred years ago they were built in the belief that that was all the ordinary people were worth. With rat-ridden houses, houses without water, people living four and five in a room and conditions in which people suffer from tuberculosis, we, as public representatives, cannot be complacent. We say we want a plan and must get on speedily.

In short: 'There is not a single problem facing us today, whether in Newcastle or the country, that is not linked up with the social problems of the slums.'[22] On the question of what exactly would replace these slums, though, Smith for the moment was silent.

Architecturally speaking, the force in the early 1950s apparently lay with the 'soft' Modernists, also called the 'New Humanists'. While their most acclaimed work was the Royal Festival Hall, they were also responsible for an increasing number of new school buildings (typified by the bright, airy and generally Scandinavian-style St Crispin's Secondary Modern at Wokingham), Geoffrey Powell's winning entry (admired for its village-like qualities) in the 1952 competition for the Golden Lane housing scheme on the edge of the City of London, and the Alton East (originally called Portsmouth Road) Estate in Roehampton. The Roehampton development was a showcase for the LCC's Architect's Department and attracted much attention when the Alton East plans and models were revealed in November 1951. Across 28 acres there were to be 744 dwellings, 60 per cent of which were in the form of nine 11-storey point blocks, all with central heating; the other 40 per cent were to be, along increasingly fashionable mixed-development lines, a combination of maisonettes and houses. 'An interesting and architecturally exciting scheme,' was the verdict of the *Architects' Journal*, and over the years Alton East, built between 1952 and 1955, would win much praise, not least for its overall composition. Back in 1951, though, not everyone was so delighted by the picturesque possibilities. That December the *Wandsworth Borough News* reported the views of the Labour chairman of the LCC's Housing Committee, which two months earlier had approved the plans. He could offer 'no reprieve' to existing Roehampton residents; accepted that 'we shall be cursed for this in future, for families should live in intimate houses'; but added that 'we have no alternative if we are to solve the housing problem'.[23]

For the mainly youthful British followers of Le Corbusier, the problem with the generally acceptable, soft Modernism of Alton East – and before it the South Bank – was that it did not go nearly far enough. 'The style of the Festival of Britain seemed at best sentimental, at worst effete,' recalled the architect Robert Maxwell. 'It lacked seriousness. It was bland, and it was parochial. Modern architecture had been sold short in Britain.' The great showpiece building by Le Corbusier himself, the Unité d'Habitation near Marseilles, was completed in 1952 – an aggressively modern 20-storey block on free-standing columns, housing 1,600 shipyard workers and their families. It was a building that exercised an almost mesmeric fascination over the up-and-coming generation of architects. By 1951 work was under way on an LCC site on Bentham Road, Hackney to build a large maisonette block along Unité-style 'slab block' lines. One of its architects was Colin St John Wilson (future architect of the British Library), who in an *Observer* article in July 1952 laid into the recently acclaimed Lansbury Estate in Poplar, with its 'pitched roofs, peephole windows and "folksy" details of the current Swedish revival', all of which were in lamentable, hidebound contrast to the Unité's exemplar of 'the grand scale of city life'. Unsurprisingly, Frederic Osborn, doyen of the town-planning movement, had noted shortly before how the fashion for Le Corbusier was 'raging in the Architectural Association School in London now', with 'the young men under his influence completely impervious to economic or human considerations'.

In June 1952 the LCC's Housing Committee accepted in principle the development plans for what would become the 'hard' Modernism of the explicitly Le Corbusierite Alton West Estate in Roehampton, and the following month the nod was given for the similarly influenced Loughborough Road development near Brixton. Le Corbusier himself visited London in March 1953 to be presented with the Royal Gold Medal at the Royal Institute of British Architects. After speeches by the architectural great and good, Colin Glennie, a student at the AA, spoke for the younger generation:

> It is no use climbing our ivory towers and talking about humanising the modern movement. In those terms modern architecture means nothing. It is the very humanness of the movement which Le Corbusier played so great a part in initiating and the impetus of which he has done so much to sustain, which makes it so wonderfully worth while, and to attempt to stylise and play tricks with it so futile. His life has been devoted to the creation of beauty and essential rightness, which is the true work of the artist and the highest form of human endeavour. Indeed, it is vital if life is to mean anything more than a full belly and a reserve in the bank.

'Le Corbusier is a dreamer,' declared Glennie. 'He is also one of the only truly practical men of our age. He understands the spirit of the 20th century.'[24]

Two of Le Corbusier's most articulate admirers were the charismatic young architects Peter and Alison Smithson, who set up in private practice in 1950 a year after their marriage. Peter 'tempered considerable intellectual arrogance with a streak of dry humour', in the words of the architectural historian Mark Girouard, while Alison 'was opinionated, outrageous, convinced of her own and her husband's importance'. During the early 1950s they were regular visitors to the Bethnal Green home of the photographer and artist Nigel Henderson and his social-anthropologist wife Judith, between them closely observing the day-to-day life of the area and soon leading the Smithsons to realise the importance of the street and the community to their architectural projects. Specifically, their unsuccessful entry for the Golden Lane competition pioneered what would become the hugely influential concept of 'streets in the sky', to be implemented essentially through a system of pedestrian decks.

Soon afterwards, in a lengthy essay on 'Urban Reidentification', the Smithsons elaborated their idea:

> Each part of each deck should have sufficient people accessed from it to become a social entity and be within reach of a much larger number at the same level.
>
> Decks would be places, not corridors or balconies: thoroughfares where there are 'shops', post boxes, telephone kiosks.
>
> Where a deck is purely residential the individual house and yard-garden will provide an equivalent life pattern to a true street or square; nothing is lost and elevation is gained.
>
> The flat block disappears and vertical living becomes a reality.
>
> The refuse chute takes the place of the village pump.

In a piece of writing full of sharply turned phrases – 'New Town development – query, find the new; query, find the town' – the Smithsons robustly confronted the Englishman's traditional castle-on-the-ground dream:

> You might argue that the back garden and front pocket handkerchief are necessary to look out on. But what fills the windows of your day rooms is the houses opposite and the backs behind. Do you really think this is a sustaining prospect? . . .

How many gardens in your street are gardened for other reasons than that of keeping up 'appearances', and for how many is the possession of a garden at all not a personal solution but the only known answer for a civilised existence?

Is your home just what you'd build?

The argument that suburbs are what everyone wants is invalid.

We are not a medieval community that actually directs its individual houses to its taste. Folk-build is dead in England.

The modern, the urban, the vertical (albeit with horizontal decks), the communal: there, unambiguously and without compunction, lay the Smithsonian future. 'If the life lived high-up is worth living then it should be suitable for everyone who wants it,' they insisted. 'No taboo should be put on those with children, to live the lopsided existence of the suburbs; ostracised from town and country, forced into this antiquated way of life. We cannot afford to leave people scattered indiscriminately across the ground.'[25]

Not many were as fanatical about the joys of the vertical, but during 1952/3 the activator mood was continuing to shift in that direction. This included the activators in the Ministry of Housing. Although its manual *Living in Flats*, dated December 1951, had been distinctly cautious – recommending that 'families with several children should as far as possible be accommodated in houses or maisonettes rather than in flats' and adding that 'large estates of flats are apt to be impersonal, and are better developed as a combination of small areas, each a distinct unit' – the mood there seems to have decisively hardened in 1952. In February the ministry warned the LCC against following the example of 'many provincial cities', where an 'unreasoning prejudice against flats' meant that they 'go on eating up the countryside with cottage estates [ie of houses] while their decaying centres cry out for redevelopment at high density'; two months later one of the ministry's mandarins, the formidable Dame Evelyn Sharp, informed a suitably dismayed, dispersion-minded Town and Country Planning Association (still run by Osborn) that in the ministry's forthcoming manual, *The Density of Residential Areas*, 'the standards of density were immensely influenced by the need to conserve land', adding that higher density would also produce 'positively better living conditions'; in his foreword to the

Churchill (*sitting*) and Attlee (*standing*) survey the opening of the Festival of Britain,
4 May 1951

St Bride's, London, June 1951: over ten years after the Blitz

Redgrave Road Residents' Association, Basildon: day trip to Clacton-on-Sea, 1952

Dick Etheridge, leading shop steward at Longbridge, addresses Austin carworkers, 1952

Camden High Street, 1952

Rush for Scotland vs. England tickets, Hampden Park, Glasgow, March 1952

Outside an Ebbw Vale chapel, a summer Sunday, 1952

Petticoat Lane, 1952

Lady Cranbrook recreates the Coronation experience for members of Preston and Langley's W.I., Hertfordshire

Commercial travellers in Maude's Commercial Hotel, Halifax, 1953

City Surveyor and Engineer (Sir Herbert Manzoni) and City Architect
(A.G. Sheppard Fidler) study Birmingham's Inner Ring Road Scheme, January 1954

manual, Macmillan was adamant that 'it is important to save every acre that can be saved'; and in February 1953 his Parliamentary Secretary, the super-energetic Ernest Marples, expressed the wish, in the context of a Commons debate on the loss of agricultural land, that 'the nation as a whole will become a little more flat-minded'. Altogether, it was a hardening of line that reflected not only the failure to question the axiomatic assumption that flats saved land whereas houses gobbled it but also a remarkably effective campaign by the agricultural lobby, headed by the National Farmers' Union. In March 1953 the *Any Questions?* panel was asked in Tavistock whether the nation could support itself in terms of food production. 'The boot is now, ladies and gentlemen, on the other foot – you've got to face it,' solemnly replied the nation's best-known farmer, A. G. Street. 'The thing that will save you from starvation is your home farming, and the make-weight is the little bit that you can buy from abroad, and it'll get less and less and less unless you can work harder and harder and harder.'[26]

There were other high-density, pro-flats opinions expressed, including by architects – increasingly prestigious figures, unlike planners. In Glasgow the fervently pro-flats Sam Bunton put forward plans in January 1952 for the high-rise redevelopment of the bombed area of Clydebank, employing what the *Builder* called 'the cross-wall, multi-flat system' that 'aimed to prove that by a new planning and constructional technique, building into the air is the cheapest and soundest form of providing homes'. Soon afterwards, St John Wilson in the *Observer* declared that the choice in city planning lay between the 'cottage-and-a-cow man', wanting to scale down cities, and 'the supporter of Corbusier's "human" vertical garden city', with Wilson clearly in the latter camp. That autumn the *Glasgow Herald*'s municipal correspondent insisted that 'the new types of flats' going up in the city's peripheral estates were 'in appearance and in practical living conditions far removed from the old conception of the Glasgow tenement', while in December an article in the *Architects' Journal* on the future redevelopment of blitzed, badly rundown inner-city Liverpool called on it to be 'the first city in these isles to undertake some multi-storey building', with 'multi' meaning 15 or 20 storeys. And in February 1953 the *Daily Mirror* declared that 'there is no doubt that this country must save space by building upward and that many more people will have to live in flats', adding that 'if they were all satisfactorily sound-proofed half the dislike of them would disappear'.[27]

A particularly interesting take came from Michael Young's valedictory 'For Richer For Poorer' report in November 1952. There, as part of his overarching theme of revival of the community, he advocated 'rehousing people in the central areas of our cities and towns, as part of a great plan of urban reconstruction, instead of forcing them to move to housing estates on the outskirts'. What did that mean in terms of practicalities? Young conceded that 'it would clearly be quite wrong, and unacceptable to the public, to put everyone into flats', and that 'families with young children need houses with gardens, not flats without'. But in the case of 'old people', he argued, 'most of these can quite well be housed in flats (with lifts) of varying heights'. Quite as much as the Smithsons, Young equated high density with community and low density with social anomie:

> The Garden City type of open development, as represented in many housing estates and suburbs, is unfavourable to community spirit: for one thing, the distances which the mother has to walk, at a time when she is tied by her children, to get to shops, clinics and centres may be so great that she just doesn't go and, if she doesn't go, she doesn't meet anyone. To many of the slum-dwellers and others who are taken from their crowded tenements to new estates, the vast open spaces are not a virtue but a vice, making for dreariness and isolation.

'The higher the density,' in short, 'the fewer will have to move, and the more people will be able to remain near their relatives and friends in the community which they know.' Given that dispersal from the unhealthy, overcrowded inner city had been at the very heart of the progressive '1945' project, and that Young himself had written Labour's 1945 manifesto, this was a striking shift.

The final decision over flats rested with the local authorities, and here too the trend was almost entirely one way, influenced in part by increasingly favourable central-government subsidies for their construction. West Ham in July 1952 broke its own four-storey limit and gave the go-ahead to a ten-storey block of flats, notwithstanding the finding of a recent report that 'the dislike of flats is particularly strong in West Ham'; Liverpool two months later, even before the *Architects' Journal*'s advice, approved 'a number of multi-storey flats up to ten storeys in height' in order 'to make the most of the land in the central areas'; Salford in January 1953 went for a series of seven-storey flats, largely to reduce dependence on overspill housing and in marked contrast to anti-high-rise Manchester; while Coventry's decision in April to have 11-storey flats in its forthcoming housing programme was sold in terms of 'flats with unique heating systems and electric washers included among the fittings'. During the Newcastle debate on slum clearance, Councillor Huddart did note that 'flats are only justifiable for families if the residents have some compensation for the disadvantage of living in flats', but argued that 'in this case [ie in inner-city Newcastle] they can have the compensation of being near their work and entertainment and shops'.[28]

So too in Birmingham, especially with the appointment in 1952 of the flats-minded (though preferably in the context of mixed development) A. G. Sheppard Fidler as City Architect. Early that year, moreover, the council unveiled its development plan, largely the work of the City Surveyor, the arch-engineer Herbert Manzoni. 'The Birmingham of 1972' was the *Birmingham Post*'s front-page headline: 'In 20 years much of the physical aspect of the centre of Birmingham will be changed. It will be a city of tall blocks of offices and flats, traffic congestion will be no longer a problem and underground subways will enable pedestrians to cross the roads without reference to the traffic.' These new roads would include three concentric ring roads, thirteen radial roads and various link roads, while large blocks of flats were also envisaged for the outer suburbs in order to preserve existing agricultural land within the city's boundaries. A public exhibition was held, and the *Post* (generally supportive of the proposals) described the reaction of 'the most incongruous visitor to this apotheosis of modern architecture and town-planning', namely 'a man who shed a metaphoric tear for the back-to-back houses'. Or in his own words: 'They're nice and warm, and cosy and companionable.'

There were other dissenters. Shortly before, the architectural writer John Summerson, in his 1930s youth a convinced Modernist, had offered a thoroughly gloomy appraisal of the LCC's new 20-year development plan. The picture it evoked was, he told the *New Statesman*'s for the most part impeccably progressive readers, 'one of indescribable melancholy, consisting of ranges of near-corbusier "working-class" flats standing on sooty lawns, with concrete kerbs; of schools which might equally be massed lavatories or unemployment exchanges; and of private enterprise office blocks bulging upwards into a silhouette hacked out of space in a battle with rights of light and zoning limitations'. He argued, moreover, that there remained 'a serious psychological barrier between the modern architect and his public, a public which persists in believing that buildings, like people, have their feet on the ground and their heads in the air'. Another erstwhile architectural Modernist, John Betjeman, probably felt the same, for in the autumn of 1952 he came out strongly against Sergei Cadleigh's ambitious 'High Paddington' scheme for a vertical township of 8,000 people above Paddington Station's goods yard area – a scheme blessed by Marples but abhorrent to Betjeman, who pointed out that gardening was a national hobby and asked indignantly whether we were to be turned into a nation made up largely of flat-dwellers. Even Thomas Sharp, in the 1940s a dominant, deeply urbanist architect-planner, now had his reservations. 'We should not advocate the building of high flats merely because we like the look of them aesthetically,' he warned the architectural profession in February 1953. 'We have to measure the sociological, economic and aesthetic problems all together. It's that which makes housing such a tough problem.'[29]

What of society at large? There seems to have been at this crucial time, just as the economic constraints were starting to loosen, remarkably little consultation, but the strong probability is that the great majority of people preferred houses to flats just as much as they had during the wartime surveys. In Crawley New Town, for instance, the development corporation responded to popular feeling in the early 1950s by downgrading the proportion of flats from 15 per cent of the town's total accommodation to 2½ per cent. In Liverpool, John Barron Mays found in his study of an inner-city police division that 'a great many of the police disliked tenements for aesthetic or other reasons not connected with crime', with almost half of them believing that flats 'were breeding grounds for juvenile gangs'. Two of Coventry's councillors did tell the press in May 1953 that flats were 'at long last' becoming popular among Coventrians, but offered no supporting evidence. They would not have convinced Gladys Langford, who the previous November had spent an afternoon walking around Hackney, where she 'grieved to find Woodberry Down so altered':

> It was a most attractive spot – a residential district with the New River & the Reservoirs and their tree-d surroundings to give pleasing views. Now huge blocks of flats, ugly little shops and ludicrous maisonettes scar the mangled roads. Two of the blocks with grey stone look like replicas of Pentonville Prison. Trees have been cut down, the stumps look like rotten teeth in a neglected mouth. There is nothing attractive left. A 'new comprehensive school' is being built. I am sure the character of the residents of London must ultimately be affected – and adversely at that – by such hideous communal life.

'Poor old London!' she plangently concluded.[30]

It is tempting to leave it at that, but ultimately the reality was more complicated. There was indeed much modernity – certainly much Modernist architecture – that was widely disliked by an instinctively conservative society. Yet that same society wanted not only as rapid a solution as possible to the housing crisis but also an easier, more convenient, less laborious everyday life, above all in the home, whether in houses or, if need be, flats. 'Went to the "Press" Pre-view of the Ideal Home Exhibition at Olympia,' Macmillan noted in his diary on 2 March 1953: 'We have an *extremely* good Ministry of Housing exhibit – better than last year. We showed 2 "People's Houses" (one 3 bedroom, one 2 bedroom). One of these is the new "open" design, which will (I think) be popular in the South and with young people. It gives them a large sitting room and dining room and "lounge" all in one room, from wh the stairs go up. (This in place of the old "front parlour" where no one ever sat and which was reserved for the "corpse") . . .' Macmillan's populist instincts were, as was becoming increasingly the case, spot-on. A certain type of light, bright and functional modernity was indeed very acceptable, even positively attractive, especially to the young and especially in a 'service' rather than an 'industrial' broader context. If it had shown rather more humility, not to mention some of that despised 'humanism', the Modern movement, from Le Corbusier downwards, might be remembered a little more fondly than it is.

Furthermore, it is at least arguable that the great drive towards flats and high-rises in the provision of public housing *could* have been less disastrous than turned out to be the case. 'Libra', living in a corporation flat in Glasgow, explained to the local paper in March 1953 that the problem was essentially twofold: first, 'a serious lack of effective insulation against sound', which imposed, especially when children were involved, 'a severe strain upon neighbourly relationships', and second, 'official laxity in enforcing regulations for the common good', with examples including no enforcement of the rule against the keeping of dogs; no sanctions against the use of balconies for 'the beating out of rugs or for hanging out the family washing' even though 'probably most tenants deplore practices that suggest Tin Pan Alley rather than a decent residential area'; no ensuring of privacy for ground-floor tenants in their small, often assiduously cultivated front gardens; and 'no official encouragement' for tenants wanting to tidy up 'the common paths and rear areas'. In short, 'the activities of an anti-social minority appear to be officially condoned'.[31] Zero tolerance worked at Warner's holiday camp on Hayling Island; perhaps it should have been tried elsewhere.

———

'Britain in the Skies' was the title of a triumphalist account on BBC television on 22 April 1953 of the British achievement in aviation – an achievement that now included the Vickers Viscount airliner, which had just entered commercial service. In 1996, after more than 40 years of staunch flying, it was justly recalled as 'the greatest British commercial airliner, blazing a trail with its four Rolls-Royce Dart turbo-prop engines and opening European air routes to millions of tourists and business travellers'. In the early 1950s, though, almost all the popular focus was on the more glamorous, longer-range Comet. Ten days after the broadcast, on Saturday, 2 May – exactly a year after the Comet's hugely publicised inaugural scheduled flight from London to Johannesburg – a BOAC Comet on the Singapore–London service took off from Calcutta at 11.00 a.m. GMT bound for Delhi, with thirty-seven passengers (half of them coming to Britain for the Coronation) and a crew of six. After only six minutes there was complete radio silence amid reports of a severe thunderstorm.

In Coventry, at noon that Saturday, Lord Silkin formally declared Broadgate House open. A particular design feature of the clock on the building's bridge were two models, of Lady Godiva and Peeping Tom, which would come out when the clock struck the hour. A few minutes after noon, they were pushed out manually for the large crowd below to see; but at 1.00, when the clock struck for the first time, the figures stuck – an embarrassing moment. It did not, though, upset the local and visiting dignitaries enjoying a splendid lunch and sonorous speeches in the building's restaurant. None more sonorous than that of Councillor E. M. Rogers, chairman of the Planning and Redevelopment Committee. 'Here in Coventry there is going to be probably a unique example of town planning and civic design, as carried out in this century,' was his bold promise. And, after claiming that it was the first time since the Georgian era that a new town centre, designed as a unified whole, was to be produced, he reached for the architectural stars: 'What Princes Street gives to Edinburgh, the Parade to Leamington, the Royal Crescent to Bath, Broadgate and the precinct will give to Coventry.' The local evening paper agreed. Not only was Broadgate House itself 'a massive symbol of Coventry's triumph over adversity' – which was why when 'ordinary people look at it . . . they rejoice to see it' – but it was also the start of something special: 'Let us make no mistake about it. When this great work is finished the centre of Coventry will be a show place.'[32]

It was also Cup Final day. In the 'Gambols' strip-cartoon in that morning's *Daily Express*, George was asked to settle an argument between his wife Gaye and her friend Polly about who had won the Cup the previous year. This led to Gaye sitting up in bed in tears. 'Besides it doesn't matter *who* won the Cup,' she tells the back of George's head (on the pillow, trying to get some sleep). 'It's the fact that you sided with that woman against your own wife . . . Sniff . . .' Elsewhere in the paper, Desmond Hackett's preview began: 'Stanley Matthews, incredible indelible, 38-year-old master footballer, was in such a tough, fighting mood last night that he convinced me it must be Blackpool to beat Bolton.' This was Matthews's third and (everyone once again assumed) final chance to win a cup-winner's medal, and, as Geoffrey Green put it in *The Times*, his 'presence in a victorious side at Wembley is as eagerly awaited by a man in the street as Gordon Richards' first win in the Derby'. That morning Paul Gardner, a middle-class neutral with a ticket in his pocket, listened in a 'sleazy little café' near Euston Station to one confident Blackpool fan surrounded by his mates. 'It's Stan's year, lads, it's Stan's year, I bloody know it,' he declared. 'I bloody told you so when we beat 'uddersfield, I bloody knew it then, and I'll tell you now, bloody Bolton aren't gonna stop him. Who've they bloody got? Banks [Ralph Banks, the Bolton left-back]? He's a big ox, Stan'll make 'im look bloody daft, he'll wish he'd stayed home with the missus . . . How about anoother coop here, lass?'

A few hours later, just before 'The Coronation Cup Final' got under way, the Queen came on to the pitch to meet the teams. 'As if she bloody cares, one lot's the same as t'other to her,' said a fan near Gardner. For those not at the ground, there was television coverage of the whole match, watched by 7.7 million adults (almost half of them looking at the sets of friends or relatives) and innumerable children. The commentator was Kenneth Wolstenholme, a Bolton fan who manfully managed to stay neutral. Raymond Glendenning was his counterpart on the radio, where a further 7.7 million adults had to wait until the second half for coverage. Among them were Nella Last, very far from a sports aficionado. She and her husband had driven out from Barrow to a local beauty spot, but while he went for a short walk she stayed listening to the car wireless. 'He was back soon after 4 o'clock. I said "I'm wrong, poor Stanley Matthews isn't going to win a Cup Final after all – one of the broadcaster men said 'Bolton is the winner' – and they have 3 goals to Blackpool's 1".' It was indeed 3–1 to Bolton, but in the Royal Box Princess Margaret saw the Blackpool chairman Harry Evans with his head buried in his hands and sought to console him: 'Don't worry, you will win.'

The fightback duly began. 'Soon,' related Nella, 'we were gripped by the intense excitement as the teams equalised. My husband said "there's still a *chance*" but we agreed it was that of a snowball in a hot stove! – right to the very last minute.' In that very last minute, she and her husband listened to Glendenning at his most magisterially impartial. 'Matthews on the edge of the Bolton penalty area,' he almost screamed, 'dribbling right in, past his man, two yards out, squares it, hit it somebody, yes, it's there, it's there, Perry has scored, Perry has scored number 4, laid on by Stanley Matthews, Blackpool have scored

number 4 ...' Near Barrow, as all over the country except in one
Lancashire cotton town, it was a wonderful, unforgettable moment. 'I
found myself clapping heartily – & I laughed aloud at sober working
men who had been listening in, & near parked cars, doing a kind of little
jig!' It only remained for the referee to blow the final whistle, Matthews
to be hoisted aloft by his teammates, and the Blackpool captain Harry
Johnston to collect the Cup. 'Congratulations on a jolly good show,'
the Queen told him as she handed it over.

   That evening, the word from BOAC was that officials were still
clinging to the hope that the missing Comet had come down on an
emergency landing ground. Next morning, though, the wreckage was
found 30 miles from Calcutta. The general assumption was that the
accident had been caused by an extraordinary tropical storm, and Sir
Miles Thomas, chairman of BOAC, announced that the Comet services
would continue without interruption. It was a no-panic approach
praised by the press, with Monday's *Express* calling for 'determination
to go on proving to all men that these new British planes are not only
the fastest and most comfortable, but the safest too'.[33] Barely four
weeks before the Coronation was no time for the nerve of the new
Elizabethans to falter.

11

A Kind of Farewell Party

'I found myself alongside the Duke,' noted Raymond Streat as four days after the Matthews Final he once again accompanied the Queen and Prince Philip to the British Industries Fair, this time including the ICI stand. 'A Terylene man stood beside him on his other side ready to offer any information. The Duke said, "Ah, Terylene. Yes, I remember, this is the new invention. Somebody showed it to me and gave me a shirt." The man beamed and said, "Yes, sir, when you came down to our factory." The Duke said, "Yes, I remember now, and you wanted me to wear it, and I did wear it. Very interesting – clammy, isn't it?" ' By now Philip and his wife, like millions of others, were counting the days. The rest of May 1953 had its share of interest – sudden death for Leading Aircraftsman Ronald Maddison, a volunteer in one of Porton Down's secret nerve-gas experiments; equally sudden death for Accrington Stanley's left-back, Bill Robinson, shot by a jealous husband; a notable Tory win in a by-election at Sunderland South; sharp controversy in Coventry about the new Godiva clock, generally viewed as a needless modern gimmick – but the all-consuming date ahead was Tuesday, 2 June.[1]

As in the case of the royal wedding six years earlier, it had taken a while for public opinion to warm up. 'I think the Coronation is a good thing,' a 15-year-old girl at a West London grammar school had told Mass-Observation in March. 'It revives all the pageantry and colour of the past centuries. It gives us something to think of and be proud of.' Most of her classmates, though, were more critical:

Although I am looking forward to the Coronation very much, I do think that too much money is being spent on it.

Some people are getting too excited and will make it a regrettable day if they don't cool down.

There are too many silly songs and jokes on the wireless about this Coronation year.

I think that the distribution of seats is unfair, and that the 'spivs' are wrangling the seats as they do at the Cup Final.

In my opinion too much fuss, and much too much money is being spent on the Coronation.

A month later, the temperature slowly rising, M-O had asked some Bexley residents about their plans for the big day:

Well, now, if you want my opinion I think that anybody what's getting up at six in the morning to sit in a £5 seat wants their brains testing, do you agree? I should have thought there was better things to do, and better ways of spending what little we have, myself. Of course a lot of people are paid to go, in case enough don't turn up to make a show – I don't know I'm sure. (*59-year-old widow, working as an office caretaker*)

I shall spend Coronation day quite quietly. I can see myself going to bed and there won't be all that noise going on with the bulldozer outside, so I shall be able to sleep peacefully. I'm so tired of the noise of men hammering, it will be so peaceful. I'm very thankful for the holiday for that reason. (*74-year-old woman*)

If I'm not working I think the best thing to do will be to make friends with someone with a television set a week or so before and then drop in casually like, and most likely they'll let you have a look. (*32-year-old baker's roundsman*)

Well, I'd very much like to go, but my husband won't hear of it; he says I'd be a fool to go pushing in all those crowds. He says, what's the point of having television if I go up to town? So I expect we'll just look in, but I must say I yearn to go and see it in the live flesh. (*42-year-old wife of builder's foreman*)

The 55-year-old wife of a clerical officer struck a rare religious note: 'I shall spend a good bit of the day on my knees, praying for that poor soul. She's so young. I don't think she knows what she's let herself in for. But she's got that beautiful husband beside her – hasn't he the loveliest face?'

May was a month of mounting anticipation. 'Everyone is hoping that either this glorious weather will hold for the Coronation, or that it will rain soon, and get it over,' recorded Madge Martin in Oxford on the 12th. Across the country plans for Coronation street parties and celebrations were well under way, though in New Malden, Surrey, it emerged that some organisers had been told by parents that they did not want their offspring to mix with common children, prompting a *People* headline on the 17th, 'They're much too posh for street party'. Class was also not forgotten in Brixton. 'First Coronation decorations up in Vassall Road,' noted Florence Speed two days later. 'Paper strips with portraits of the Queen plastered on every window except one ... All pure Woolworths.' That same day in Manchester a middle-aged man in the textile trade told M-O that everyone he spoke to agreed there was a 'Coronation fever about', and a young working-class woman described how 'it's like the Christmassy feeling in the factory where I work', with pictures of the royal couple 'all over the factory walls'.[2]

Two sometimes grumpy diarists agreed on the 21st that things were astir. 'The Coronation fever is now growing daily and Keighley puts more and more decorations up each day,' noted Kenneth Preston, while Anthony Heap in the capital described how 'the main streets – especially those on the route of the Coronation Procession and subsequent royal drives round London – are rapidly being transformed into newly cleaned, freshly painted, gaily decorated avenues of festive colour', adding that 'the preparations for this Coronation seem to be on a much bigger and extensive scale than were those for the last one sixteen years ago'. All this was not to everyone's liking. 'London is becoming increasingly hellish, swarms of people and a perpetual misery of traffic congestion,' complained Noël Coward on the 24th. 'The streets are chaos owing to the Coronation decorations. It will be a comfort when it is all over.' Madge Martin, though, was closer to the norm on Saturday the 30th: 'The enormous feeling of tension and excitement increases daily. How we shall miss it, when Tuesday is over.' However, as she noted ominously on the Sunday: 'Very cool, unsettled weather.'[3]

One should not exaggerate the euphoria. 'Would you mind telling me how you feel about the Coronation?' an M-O investigator asked during May in working-class Fulham:

They overdo it, it's been going on so long. The press overdoes it till people get sick and tired. *(M70)*

Neither one thing nor the other, I don't mind it, but it doesn't mean a lot to me personally. *(F27)*

Oh rather thrilled, I'm excited to see the children enjoying themselves, we've had our turn. *(F41)*

Well, er, it's rather nice to have the day off. *(M54)*

I feel alright. *(M45)*

I feel it's a good thing if everybody does their little bit to make it a success. *(M71)*

Oh just ordinary. *(F73)*

Well I feel very pleased about it myself, I feel quite worked up about it – you see it everywhere now really, don't you? *(F65)*

I think it's a waste of money. *(M42)*

Well, I'd say it cheers the country up. It's been a bit depressing since the war. Haven't you noticed it? People don't seem the same, do they? A thing like this seems to work up the co-operation a bit. *(M40)*

Definitely I'm all for it, all in favour! *(M58)*

A final reply *(M61)* reminds that the personal always transcends the public. 'I'd get up there if I could but there is not much chance, it means starting off so early, and my wife died last week so I shan't be feeling all that much like it.'

Even so, it seems that it was precisely in traditional working-class areas like Fulham that the Coronation was celebrated most enthusiastically. 'In the poorer areas, the streets are thick with bunting and there is much enthusiasm for street parties,' an M-O panel member suggestively reported in late May about the decorations in Burnley. 'Out of town,' by contrast, 'there are rows of undecorated Semis.' In Fulham itself, Lillie Walk was a narrow alleyway with 42 houses, mostly lived in by labourers and on the local council's 'condemned' list:

Down the entire length of the Walk [noted the M-O investigator on the 30th] there are rows and rows of bunting, while paper garlands and lines of small Union Jacks are strung across from top windows one side of the road to the windows opposite. Every house has pictures of the Queen, Duke of Edinburgh, Prince Charles, and Princess Anne pasted in the parlour window and the two small top bedroom windows. Over the doorways are fixed crowns, gold and silver, large and small, posters with the wording 'God Save Our Queen' or 'Long Live Our Queen' with the initials E.R.II. The outer walls of the front parlours are completely hidden with Union Jacks, more gold and silver crowns or coats-of-arms.

'It'll be the last coronation we'll have down here,' a 60-year-old woman explained, 'because they're pulling the houses down and we're all going to shift, so we're making it a kind of farewell party too.' Money for the street party for the Walk's children had been collected on a regular basis since the previous June. 'Usually lots of people go out on Saturday nights to the pubs, but last week-end and the one before that they were sitting on stools near their front-doors chatting away,' related a middle-aged man about the sacrifices that had been made to pay for the decorations. 'The same goes for the pictures. They put their picture-money away specially to make the Walk look nice and bright. We're all in it. We're all excited and want to make a show.' Or, in the words of a middle-aged woman who had gone without her drink: 'We're all neighbours and we're all happy-go-lucky and it's got to be a day all of us will remember – the kids and all of us.'[4]

By this time the airwaves were pervaded by the impending event, typified by *Coronation Music Hall* on the 30th attracting 91 per cent of the TV public and getting a 'Reaction Index' of 90, the latter figure acclaimed by BBC audience research as the 'highest ever recorded for a Light Entertainment and the highest for any TV broadcast of any kind'. Accordingly, *Woman's Hour* on Monday the 1st, introduced as usual by Marjorie Anderson, included not only the voices of some of the Coronation visitors in London and the latest instalment of Lytton Strachey's *Queen Victoria* but also a talk by a housewife expressing her thoughts on Coronation Eve. She called it 'Dedication':

Last Christmas the Queen asked us all to pray for her on her Coronation Day. She called us, surely, not to lip service, but to share in her personal dedication in the daily round of our own lives.

What can this dedication mean to an ordinary housewife like me? Selfless living so often seems to be something of the mountain top, something difficult to work out in terms of pots and pans, ration books and children fast growing out of their clothes.

Well, first of all, I'm sure it means that the things we long to see in our nation we must first find for ourselves in our own hearts and homes.

My husband tells me that he believes that what happens in the home makes a tremendous difference to a man in his work, whether he is dealing with men or materials. I believe this is just as true of our children. To send out our husbands and children happily in the morning is a way that we women can link ourselves with the great world outside our homes, and feel that we are helping to contribute to the peace we long for so much . . .

The Queen will live to make our nation great, and so must I. While hers may often be in spectacular ways my own dedication may just be in the caring I put into the tiny details of my everyday life. Yes even in the washing up, in things like seeing that I wash most carefully round the handles of cups and saucepans – in the thought and preparation that goes into the cooking – every tiny eye out of the potatoes and spotless hands to cook with . . .

In these small ways, I need to accept fully the responsibility for what my nation is, and for what the world is. The fear, the greed, the hate, which so distress me in the world at large ought to distress me just as much when I see them, in smaller ways, in myself. At least there I can fight it, and in my heart and home I need to build a citadel against these things. During her Coronation service the Queen dedicates herself to serve the cause of righteousness. Let us do the same.[5]

The name of the 42-year-old speaker – living in Wolverhampton, married to a sheet-metal worker, bringing up three sons – was Mary Whitehouse, set to return to obscurity but now having savoured (thanks to the BBC) the buzz of moral exhortation.

There were few more dedicated housewives than Judy Haines in Chingford. 'I don't know how, but I've worked solidly from 7am

to 9pm for days it seems,' she sighed that Monday. 'Sylvia's mother
and Valerie's mother came round to announce the Avenue is to hold
a Coronation Party on June the 13th. Had booked for British Legion
Party, but decided in favour of former one. What a late hour! We gave
10/-.' Another, altogether less domestic diarist, Frank Lewis, was rather
irritably fending for himself at home in Barry, his mother and sister
having gone up to London in the hope of finding a place to watch the
procession. 'I've never had a great deal of interest in Royalty, though
this *IS* a big occasion,' he reflected that day. 'I just can't be bothered
. . .' A sense of adventure, meanwhile, also only partially flickered in
Hampstead:

> I wouldn't go myself, but my boy friend wants me to come, all the time
> from ten o'clock tonight. I'm dreading it. I'm only hoping this rain'll put
> him off. *(F25)*
>
> Yes, we'll be going, a friend of mine and my daughter, we'll be starting
> out about ten o'clock. I'm going to borrow an old tweed coat – this one
> I've got is quite warm, I don't mean that, but I don't want to use it for
> sitting around in the rain, lying out in all night. We'll take some coffee,
> and a packet of Quickies for my face in the morning. My husband's
> furious, he thinks it's barmy. *(F50)*

Poor Gladys Langford went – 'trying to dispel my gloom' – to Marble
Arch to see the decorations:

> It was well nigh impossible to look at the decorations, as the pavements
> were wedged tightly with people. Some sat on the edge of the kerb having
> taken up already their positions for viewing tomorrow's procession . . .
> Outside Selfridge's the throng was at its thickest. People dragged small
> children along . . . Many aged and lame women were milling about. I
> edged out of the crowd into Bond St and thence to Piccadilly. Many
> people with stools, bed, blankets and bags of fodder were on the kerb
> under the portico at the Ritz. Later came a heavy downpour. The doctors
> will be busy after all this for it is quite cold. Here in the hotel [ie the
> one in Islington where she lived] there is to be a bonfire, fireworks and
> punch-drinking – but not for me!

'Everybody – everything – tense and poised,' wrote Madge Martin in Oxford. 'The weather simply horrible – freezingly cold, stormy and unkind.'[6]

It proved a pretty wet night for those camping out in central London, with women outnumbering men by about seven to one. 'People were very scrupulous about saving the places of those absent – for strangers just as much as friends,' noted an M-O investigator. 'There was an empty space near the group with whom Inv was sitting, alleged to belong to "a chap" who was unknown to any of them, yet they had been defending it loyally from all comers for a couple of hours.' Cold and mostly wet continued the weather in the morning, though according to Lady Violet Bonham Carter, in her seat in a stand in the Mall by 7.00, 'the crowds were *most* touching – wrapped in soaked newspapers & plastic mackintoshes but burning with loyalty & full of good humour, tho' many had been there all night'. It was a good humour increased (across the country as well as in central London) by the triumphant news about a British-led expedition – in the *Daily Express*'s immortal headline, 'All This – And Everest Too!' At least one couple, though, was smugly dry in the covered stand in Parliament Square. 'The tickets were an even wiser investment than Denis knew when he bought them,' recalled Margaret Thatcher, 'for it poured all day and most people in the audience were drenched – not to speak of those in the open carriages of the great procession. The Queen of Tonga never wore *that* dress again. Mine lived to see another day.'

For the damp, huddled masses, watching the carriage procession after the three-hour service in Westminster Abbey, there was no doubt who were the two stars of the show. 'It is pouring with rain,' noted another M-O investigator, 'but the Queen of Tonga sits in an open carriage beaming on everyone and waving to the crowds who laugh and point and cheer loudly.' Finally, in a gold state coach drawn by eight greys, came the newly crowned Queen Elizabeth:

The crowd is cheering in a tremendous roar, pushing this way and that to get the best view, standing on tip-toe, jumping up, pressing forward and forward. The cheers are at least six times as loud as they have ever been before . . . But the most anyone gets is a brief view of a pale figure in a shining white dress smiling and waving her hand . . . It is all over so quickly that people seem taken aback. They look at each other and smile almost in a confidential sort of way, there is a kind of sigh, and one or two women are wiping their eyes . . .

'A vast, brown, smiling bundle with a tall red knitting needle in her hat,' was how James Lees-Milne described the intrepid Queen Salote, refusing to have the hood of her carriage drawn. 'The people were delighted. They roared applause . . . Beside her squatted a little man in black and a top hat – her husband. Noël Coward, when asked who he was, said, "Her dinner." '[7]

For the overwhelming majority, of course, the Coronation was experienced through radio or television. Some 32 per cent (11.7 million people) of the adult population listened to at least half an hour of the Service, 29 per cent to the procession to the Abbey and 25 per cent to the procession from the Abbey. The commentators inside the Abbey were two trusty warhorses, Howard Marshall and John Snagge, permitted to describe everything except the Prayer of Consecration just before the Queen took Communion. Other commentators included Wynford Vaughan Thomas at the Victoria Memorial, Jean Metcalfe at Buckingham Palace, Raymond Baxter at Trafalgar Square, Rex Alston at Victoria Embankment and, in an advantageous, well-supplied perch in the Criterion Restaurant, John Arlott at Piccadilly Circus. 'Slowly this Procession makes its stately way round the great sweep of the Circus with a quality that somehow twists the heart in the chest,' he burred, 'and you can feel this coming up down there from the people who have waited so anxiously and are now, by their faces, more than satisfied.' Equally satisfied listeners included Madge Martin in Oxford – 'NO Television for us, but nothing could have been more beautiful than the broadcasting of the Service – with the heart-stirring music, the descriptions of every moment of it, and the picture of colourful splendour' – and Mary King in Birmingham: 'It was such a wonderful ceremony. At the end I was too dazed, too emotionally disturbed physically & spiritually to write any details.' Marian Raynham, at home in Surbiton with her husband, son and daughter, 'listened to it all from 10.30 to 5.30': 'I took advantage of the religious part to put the lunch on the table. They loved the lunch – tom soup, a big salad with nut meat brawn & strawberry blanc mange & jam & top of milk . . . I didn't waste my time. At first part I pulled couch out & spring cleaned behind it & brushed couch well. Did room, later crocheted, later rested. They do do this well. I liked the bit about Justice in the ceremony, & the voice of the Queen & Philip. She never seems nervous ...' The solipsistic civil servant Henry St John went to relatives in Southall to listen. 'One log of an electric fire was switched on, but it was still cold,' was his considered verdict.[8]

Yet it was, undeniably, television's day. No less than 56 per cent (some 20.4 million people) of the adult population watched at least half an hour of the Service – not far short of double the radio audience – with 53 and 51 per cent also watching the processions to and from the Abbey. In fact it had been quite a struggle to persuade the authorities to allow the BBC to cover the Service, with an aggressive campaign led by the Beaverbrook press probably tilting the balance, and even when permission was given it came with certain conditions: four cameras only; no close-ups; no pictures of either the anointing ceremony or the Queen receiving Communion. 'There will be no TV close-up of the Queen at the moment of bum,' Kingsley Amis accurately predicted to Philip Larkin a week before. But even if there had been, it would not have disturbed the hushed, reverential tone of the commentator, Richard Dimbleby, an increasingly integral part of the British constitution. After the Service, after the return procession, there was still plenty for viewers to enjoy: at 5.40 almost sixteen million watched the Queen's appearance on the balcony and accompanying RAF flypast; then, after an early-evening closedown and an edited version of the Service, some ten million watched Churchill's address followed by the Queen's, before a broadcast from *Outside Buckingham Palace*. An unexpected TV turn that night, giving millions their first taste of calypso, was a young Trinidadian performer billed as Young Tiger, real name George Browne, instantly memorialising the day:

> Her Majesty looked really divine
> In her crimson robe furred with ermine
> The Duke of Edinburgh, dignified and neat
> Sat beside her as Admiral of the Fleet.

The song, called 'I Was There (at the Coronation)', was to be given its final outing by Browne at the Roundhouse in 2006, introduced by Damon Albarn.[9]

People watched where they could. 'Nearly all the listeners were in their own homes,' summarised BBC audience research, 'but more than half the viewers of the Coronation Service were in the homes of friends and about 1,500,000 were viewing in public places like cinemas, shops, etc. The average number of people around each domestic television set was about seven, excluding children.' 'We had fully twenty in our workshop viewing it on our set [an Ekco],' noted Barbara Algie, living in Helensburgh, Scotland. 'The Marshalls brought me a coronation cake, and others gave me cakes and sweets.' Improvisation was often the order of the day. 'I sat down on my plastic commemorative cushion in pouring rain outside the DER showroom to watch the Coronation,' recalled David Sutch. 'The whole village clubbed together to rent one, which they put in my father's barn,' remembered Ned Sherrin about a pioneering television experience in rural Somerset. 'I came down from Oxford. It was a sensation. The local squire even came down to watch, with binoculars and a shooting-stick.' Up and down the country, the recipe of the day, a Constance Spry concoction heavily publicised by women's magazines, was Coronation Chicken – cooked, cold chicken in a mild curry mayonnaise sauce with apricots – all ready to be eaten off a tray in front of 'ermine-draped ectoplasm floating about at a rather bizarre séance', as Ann Leslie has nicely described the TV pictures that day when reception was at its fuzziest.[10]

Some children may have been bored, but not on the whole adults, certainly not the diarists. 'Very glad able to see it as happening,' scribbled the commercial artist Grace Golden. 'The Queen, robed and crowned, looked like something from the Arabian Nights – quite unbelievably organised, train bearers all moving with such grace. The Duke of E's lovely voice as he spoke his homage – & the Arch of Cant very fine. Prince Charles in white shirt and ruffles sudden appearance with Queen Mother.' So too Judy Haines: 'Television was perfect and most enjoyable. I liked Prince Charles noticing his mother's new bracelet. I thought the Queen was wonderful, standing up so well to such an ordeal as it must have been.' It is unlikely, though, that the Service was watched in reverential silence, to judge by an account sent to M-O about half a dozen or more people watching it on a TV at a farm (no location given). Comments included:

It's hard on the Queen making her walk as slowly as that. It's a dirty shame I call it.

It's a tiring day for her. 2½ hours in the Abbey. It's the whole day really.

I expect she packs herself up a couple of sandwiches.

I wish some of the ladies-in-waiting would trip over [ie when walking backwards] – give us a bit of fun.

It's the women I want to see. Their dresses.

They put a canopy over her when she's anointed, that's nice for her.

'Their only interest,' the account suggestively noted, 'was to see the Queen – close-ups of her in the coach, getting out of the coach, walking up the Abbey. They didn't stay to watch all the other parts.' Yet perhaps at least as representative was the experience of a youngish, working-class Irish woman living in London who watched it at a friend's home. 'We all thought before it started,' she related to M-O, 'that we could never sit solidly throughout the whole procession and ceremony, and felt we would have to have several "breaks", but once it started we couldn't tear ourselves away from the set, and considered even eating an unnecessary interruption.'[11]

Overall, there is little disputing the conventional wisdom that the Coronation 'made' television in Britain. Not only did anticipation of the event help stimulate licence holders to rise from 1.45 million in March 1952 to 2.32 million by the end of May 1953, but the coverage of the day itself prompted a further rise, up to 3.25 million by March 1954. 'Everyone in the TH [Finsbury Town Hall] today raving over the Television transmission of yesterday's historic events,' ruefully reflected Anthony Heap on the Wednesday. 'Which I must admit, makes me rather enviously wish I had a set myself.' Admittedly Heap added that he was 'not prepared to lay out sixty or seventy quid – half my scanty capital – just to enjoy the special programme I might occasionally want to see', but for him as for many others the seed had been sown. Tellingly, the BBC's own feedback revealed that 'viewers were immensely pleased and grateful that they were shown so much of the actual Service – "far, far more than we ever expected, and obviously more than most of those present could see".' The coverage also, in no small part due to Dimbleby, gave the medium an irreproachable respectability, a sense of it moving for the first time to the centre of national life. 'The BBC has magnificently vindicated the noble idea of a public service,' declared the *Sunday Times*'s television and radio critic, Maurice Wiggin. 'It has behaved with impeccable tact and dignity and has undoubtedly made innumerable new friends . . . After last Tuesday there can be no looking back.'[12]

Away from the box, people marked the day in their different ways. Frank Lewis in Barry played a round of miniature golf 'with 3 rowdy loutish lads'; Kenneth Williams ignored the celebrations and went 'home to bed early'; another troubled soul, the Somerset batsman Harold Gimblett, was playing against Warwickshire at Coventry and, in the only hour of play possible because of rain, deliberately hit a six at about the moment the Queen was being crowned. In the Welsh-border village of Hanmer, ten-year-old Lorna Stockton (later Sage) was dressed for the children's fancy-dress parade as 'a very passable shepherdess complete with black laced bodice, floral panniers, a straw hat and a crook tied with ribbons', giving her second place in the girls' section. Another parade, in rain-sodden Keighley, had a notably unimpressed spectator:

> I had taken the ciné camera [wrote Kenneth Preston] but photography was out of the question. The tableaux when they did come were travelling too fast for one to be able to make much of them. The youngsters standing upon them looked starved to the marrow and the lads who marched in front, carrying a small notice announcing what the tableaux represented, were so cold that their words and notices were almost slipping from their nerveless hands and it was quite impossible, in some cases, to read what was on the notices. The whole procession was a miserable business and in the circumstances represented hundreds of pounds of money wasted.

Lavinia Mynors, married to a distinguished classicist and doing the West End that evening, was altogether more upbeat. Walking back to Chelsea, all the formal celebrations apparently over and the trains and buses full up, she and her niece were in Buckingham Palace Road when at about eleven they heard cheering. 'We turned aside to the front of the Palace,' she recorded afterwards, 'where there were comparatively few people shouting raggedly. There was nothing in our favour except that the balcony was still lit – and we hesitated there for not above four minutes – and then by Jove they came out, the Queen and the Duke, and they didn't hurry back either. We were transported with delight and cheered madly. Then we marched home marvelling at our luck . . .'¹³

Whether on that Tuesday itself or the somewhat drier days after, Coronation celebrations took many forms – concerts, processions, pageants, bonfires, fireworks, etc – but the most emblematic celebration, the one closest to most people's sense of what was fit and proper, was the street party, predominantly but not exclusively for children. This was particularly so in working-class areas. 'In nearly every road there was a party,' was how a Cheshire schoolgirl, in her account of going to her granny's in Lancashire to watch the events on TV, described the gaily decorated side streets off Liverpool's Scotland Road. Sadly, the rain on Coronation Day meant that many parties (including in Lillie Walk) had to be held in nearby halls or schools – 'amid general cries of "Isn't it a shame?" ' as V. S. Pritchett observed in Islington – but many were scheduled for the following weekend or even the one after. 'We had four and a half hours going round street parties, a marvellous show of decorations,' Clement Attlee was thus able to note with satisfaction, adding that 'Walthamstow knows how to do it'; Judy Haines and her two daughters, in nearby, somewhat less working-class Chingford, were among those at Priory Avenue's party:

> Girls looked sweet in Fancy Dresses – Ione as a Chinese lady and Pamela as a Ballet Dancer. Both had flowers in their hair. I contributed 85 cakes to party. I enjoyed some items of local talent. The dancing troupe was 'all tap'. Ione declared the lorries' wheels were oval. How they banged on the impromptu stage – for two hours! At about 10 pm! the children's presents were given out. Girls so very late to bed. Pamela had brooch; Ione propelling pencil and scrapbook. Both had orange and bag of sweets.

The parties were not invariably as decorous as they were decorated. Elaine James, a sheet-metal-worker's daughter growing up in Shoreham, recalled how, as a result of getting it into her head that the Poles had been on the side of the Germans, she lobbed a jelly at the son of a local Polish family and a fight broke out. Moreover, 'once we had finished eating [sandwiches and sweets, washed down by orange squash and Corona cherryade], the grown-ups tried to set games but it all drifted away from organization and we kids were just allowed to run riot'. It was better organised in Soho Street, Glasgow, where 'every lamp-post, doorway and windowsill was decorated with bunting and streamers' and 'trestle tables were set up in the middle of the road, laden with food and drink':

> The celebrations carried on past my bedtime, but I stayed at the window in the twilight, with my chin resting on my hands. People started to sing and dance. My father, who was more than a little drunk, spied me at the window. 'Gi'us a song, Marie, hen', he called out.
>
> I started singing 'In a Golden Coach', a song that had been written for the Coronation [and a current Dickie Valentine hit].
>
> *In a golden coach*
> *There's a heart of gold*
> *That belongs to you and me . . .*

'That,' added Lulu, 'was my first public appearance.'[14]

How was it all done? An M-O investigator drew five broad conclusions on the basis of reports in the *Willesden Chronicle* of 94 children's street parties in that largely rundown, working-class district:

1. The approximate average amount collected for each street party seems to be in the region of £90. Money raised by means of weekly house-to-house collections, raffles, etc. Collections well organised and no shortage of voluntary helpers.
2. Parties generally catering for approximately 100 children.
3. Parties well organised. No expense spared. Bunting, flags and lavish street decorations, a huge swanky tea provided with all the works: sandwiches, jellies, blancmanges, ice-cream; presents; nearly always Coronation cup, saucer and plate, some money (generally a 2/6d or 5/- piece freshly minted), packages of fruit, sweets, etc. Lavish entertainment: Punch and Judy Show, Conjurer or local talent competitions with prizes in abundance.
4. Many reports conclude with thanking local tradesmen for generously providing cakes, toys, etc, etc, for the kiddies.
5. Many small streets pooled their efforts to make a really successful street party . . . much goodwill and co-operation behind efforts judging from reports and pictures.

The reality may not have been quite so cohesively harmonious. Maurice Broady, a young sociologist, uncovered the organisation behind the parties in the working-class Mersey ward of Birkenhead. He found that individual streets or even sections of streets kept themselves very much to themselves – 'We don't interfere with the other parts of the street,' remarked one informant, 'we don't inquire into other people's business'; that volunteers to do the organising (usually middle-aged women with children still at school) were often slow coming forward – 'It was a lot of worry,' said one afterwards, 'wondering if you were doing right, and with nobody coming to help you, you feel you're always in the wrong'; that it was particularly delicate choosing which child would be the street's Coronation Queen – 'It's a question of pleasing one and vexing another'; and that the organisers who had collected the money often avoided patronising the Co-op in case they should be suspected of trying to get the dividend on the street's large order added to their own accounts – 'You can't be too careful with other people's money . . . You've got to do it properly. If you're working among your neighbours, you want everything just so, so there's nothing [ie no complaints or insinuations] afterwards.' Still, whatever the potential pitfalls, parties *were* held, and the great majority of children for whose benefit they were ('the kiddies ought to have something to make up for what they missed during the war') undoubtedly enjoyed them.[15]

Generally, these were not comfortable days for the British left, or indeed the progressive intelligentsia as a whole. 'I am in trouble for a reply at last weekend's brains trust at Lowestoft,' privately noted the rising Labour politician Barbara Castle on the Tuesday evening:

> I said I didn't see what all the fuss was about as the Queen had been exercising her powers perfectly satisfactorily for the last 18 months. I said I hoped this would be the last Coronation of its kind we should see, it was so unrepresentative of ordinary people . . . I think there is no doubt this is a minority view, even among the working class . . . As I write this the Queen's correct & piping girlish voice is enunciating the formulae of dedication; Winston has just introduced her on the radio, exploiting the romantic mood of the moment to its fruitiest uttermost.

Frances Partridge, embodiment of Bloomsbury values, felt much the same. 'The Coronation has come roaring towards us like a lorry heard approaching up a steep incline, and now, thank God, has roared away again,' she reflected two days later. 'I suppose it has meant fun for a great many people, though I allowed myself to be momentarily overcome by dislike for the mumbo-jumbo of the service, with its "holy oil" and the rest, as well as the noisy way the English always pat themselves on the back and say how well the monarchy "works".' Satire was of course a possible outlet, and a precocious ten-year-old at boarding school developed a comic mini-cabaret. 'I would tell this running story about the Coronation and it was about the Duke of Edinburgh being taken short,' recalled Michael Palin in 2008 about arguably the first Python moment.

Not that readers of the *Manchester Guardian* reacted kindly when the paper on Wednesday the 3rd published a cartoon by David Low called 'Morning After', picturing a dazed, bloated family after watching the Coronation on television. Of the well over 500 letters sent during the ensuing controversy, almost three-quarters were hostile:

To say the least it is a joke in bad taste and I feel certain that the 'gentlemen' behind the Iron Curtain are rubbing their hands with glee. Therefore I suggest Mr Low leave your paper and apply there for a job! *(M.B. Sketchley, Heaton Moor, West Stockport)*

The cartoon in today's issue besmirches the reputation of the Manchester Guardian for ever. *(George W. Smith, Blackpool)*

I found Low's cartoon 'Morning After' almost incredibly tasteless and offensive. I am astonished that you should have seen fit to publish it. *(Rodney M. Galey, Woodford, E18)*

I shall cut this cartoon out before I take my 'M.G.' home tonight as I should be ashamed to produce it to my wife & two small daughters. *(J. E. Haygarth, Baildon, Yorks)*

To those many of your readers who were uplifted and inspired on Coronation Day to an extent perhaps never before reached in life, this vulgar buffoonery in our treasured paper is just devastating and unforgiveable. *(Frank Hopkinson, Shipley, Yorks)*

Reaction was much the same to the *New Statesman*'s carping, condescending coverage of the event. 'I listened to the whole service on

T.V. with a very mixed company, including a road man, cook, gardener, etc,' wrote a reader, Mrs C. Anson from a village near Blandford in Dorset, '& I heard no criticism nor were they restless during your "boring" Communion Service. Every house & cottage was decorated & the Queen's speech listened to in silence at the social in the evening. I feel your republic is not very near.'

This profound social conservatism was not lost on Michael Young. 'The heart has its reasons which the mind does not suspect,' began his take on 'The Meaning of the Coronation', a typically engaging piece co-written with the American sociologist Edward Shils. They argued that the occasion had been 'an act of national communion', the Service itself 'a series of ritual affirmations of the moral values necessary to a well-governed and good society', and that throughout the country 'one family was knit together with another in one great national family through identification with the monarchy'. It was not, in other words, just escapism, the desire to break briefly free from the prevailing drabness, that had animated people, but something more profound – ultimately, they asserted, the expression of a post-1945 'moral consensus' behind 'the combination of constitutional monarchy and political democracy'. Altogether it was an analysis unlikely to win many academic friends – one LSE sociologist, Norman Birnbaum, complained scathingly that 'it is a considerable disservice to sociology to present our discipline as a useful handmaiden of the current effort to make a conservative ideology once more orthodox and unquestioned' – but even so, for all the obvious charge of a certain over-cosiness, its intensely helpful starting-point was that the Coronation had been a remarkable episode revealing much about the values and assumptions of British society. And one footnote, backing up their point about how 'parents and wives and children are thought of more highly because they receive some of the backwash of emotion from their Royal counterparts', had a very Youngian touch: 'One of the authors, during an interview in a London slum district, asked a mother the age of her small son. "Just the same age as Prince Charles," she replied, looking at him with a smile of pride and love.'[16]

Four days after the Coronation was a particularly sporting Saturday. At Epsom the just-knighted Gordon Richards, for many years

Britain's greatest jockey, at last managed to win the Derby. 'Beaten – By Dear Old Gordon', declared one headline, after the Queen's horse came second. 'The Queen smiled. "Congratulations," she said. "I am delighted." ' There was less graciousness in the Coronation football final at Glynceiriog, where after a week's competition (also involving Glynceiriog 'B', Llanrhaiadr, Pioneer Corps and Chirk) the local 'A' team met Treflach from Shropshire. Halfway through the second half, with the home side leading 3–2, the referee sent off Treflach's goalkeeper for striking a Glynceiriog forward and also awarded a penalty. Already cross because earlier in the week four of the opposition had played against them in Glynceiriog's 'B' team, and amid chaotic scenes with spectators on the pitch, the Treflach team walked off and refused to come back. Mr H. Roberts, secretary of the competition, called it a 'shameful' finish to an otherwise good, celebratory week. Still, it was all relative to Bertie Buse's calamity that day. The Somerset all-rounder had chosen the fixture against Lancashire at Bath (his home town) for his benefit match, crucial nest egg for any long-serving professional cricketer approaching retirement. A newly laid pitch meant that the contest, instead of lasting the usual three days, was all over before six on the Saturday – a financial disaster. Buse, the faithful pro, sped things along by taking six wickets himself.

Culturally, the post-Coronation weeks had their bruising moments. *Genevieve*, starring the ever-dependable Kenneth More and trumpet-miming Kay Kendall, may have been the immediately acclaimed film hit of the summer – 'achieves that rarest of qualities in an English film – spontaneity,' conceded the often hard-to-please William Whitebait in the *New Statesman* – but the *Evening Standard*'s young, iconoclastic theatre critic, Kenneth Tynan, was finding his position increasingly untenable as readers continued to complain long and hard about his savage attacks on such untouchables as Anna Neagle and Donald Wolfit. Eventually by August he was gone, to be replaced by Milton Shulman, not exactly a soft touch either. But the real cause célèbre was Benjamin Britten's opera *Gloriana*, performed in honour of the Queen at the Royal Opera House two days after the Derby. It did not go well. The performance, noted Mollie Panter-Downes, 'was received with fairly muted enthusiasm by the majority of critics and with frank bewilderment by the distinguished audience', which included the

Queen herself; the intelligence soon reaching Noël Coward was that it was 'apparently a bugger', being 'dull, without melody as usual with Mr B., and not happily chosen'. After the gala performance, at the official party, there were audible sneers about 'Boriana' and 'Yawniana', and the librettist, William Plomer, was perhaps relieved to leave London in July and, to the astonishment of his friends, move to the deep anonymity of Rustington, a Sussex dormitory town near Littlehampton. 'Well, here we are – we have been a week today in this extremely bijou bungalette,' he duly informed Britten, and soon afterwards he wrote some verses in praise of his new surroundings that included the cherishable lines 'The commonplace needs no defence,/Dullness is in the critic's eyes,/ Without a licence life evolves/From some dim phase its own surprise.'[17]

Fear of the commonplace – certainly of the commercial – was now gripping much of the British cultural elite. BBC television's Coronation triumph was thrown into sharp relief by reports from the US that coverage there on commercial channels had included, right in the middle of the ceremony, advertisements featuring the undignified chimp 'J. Fred Muggs', and as early as 4 June a letter from four ex-Governors of the BBC (Lady Violet Bonham Carter and Lords Brand, Halifax and Waverley) appeared in *The Times* warning that 'commercialisation – now imminently threatened – is fraught with dangers to those spiritual and intellectual values which the BBC has nobly striven to maintain', calling on the government to 'yield no further to the intense pressure to which they have been subjected by a comparatively small number of interested parties', and announcing their intention to form a National Television Council to campaign for the BBC's continuing monopoly. The driving force of the NTC was the Labour MP and BBC documentary-maker Christopher Mayhew, who soon produced a stirring pamphlet titled *Dear Viewer* . . . arguing that if indeed TV was 'going to be a dominant force in our national life', then it was crucial to 'make sure it has ideals and integrity or it will ruin us'. Among those meeting at Lady Violet's home later in June to get the NTC rolling were such unimpeachable figures as William Beveridge, E. M. Forster, Harold Nicolson and Bertrand Russell. Soon there was support too from the unusual alliance of the Workers' Educational Association and the Archbishop of Canterbury. Unsurprisingly, the Conservative government now faltered in its support for ending the monopoly.

'Nearly all the best people in the country are opposed to commercial television,' Churchill himself (an old friend of Lady Violet) remarked at Cabinet on the 17th, and soon afterwards Macmillan privately reflected that the antis made 'a formidable combination', adding that 'the real cause of the feeling' was 'a desire to remain different from the Americans'.

Later in June a Gallup poll found that if the BBC were to provide alternative television programmes to the existing ones, then only 19 per cent still wanted commercial stations to be set up – a significant decline in support for commercial television from the previous year, explicable partly by the 'alternative' proviso, partly by the huge boost in prestige that its Coronation coverage had given the BBC. That boost may have been fading by early July, when a *Daily Express* poll showed that 45 per cent favoured 'sponsored TV programmes', 36 per cent objected to them, and 19 per cent were don't knows. There was also by July a rival to the NTC, with the emergence of the cross-party but Tory-backed Popular Television Association, essentially the creation of the powerful triumvirate of the ex-BBC man Norman Collins, the Old Etonian businessman Sir Robert Renwick and Charles Stanley of television manufacturers Pye Radio. The PTA proceeded to lobby at least as hard and as ruthlessly as the NTC, probably more so, and its high-profile supporters included the historian A.J.P. Taylor and the cricketer Alec Bedser. There was little doubt, moreover, which way the popular press was leaning. 'What About The Viewers?' was the *Daily Mirror*'s disloyal headline after Attlee in June had stated that a future Labour government would reverse any attempt 'to allow television to pass into the hands of private profiteers', with the paper asserting that 'the politicians wrangle, but the viewing public stands by, unconsulted, ignored'. Ian Coster, television critic of the *News of the World*, showed himself less than in thrall to the BBC's timeless spiritual values when in July he offered a simple remedy for the small audiences and lack of appeal of the Sunday-night plays on television: 'The solution, which I keep on proposing, is to cut out intellectual drama and put on thrillers and comedies.'[18]

One soap opera, though, had everything. 'The Queen Mother looked very happy and radiant,' a Cheshire schoolgirl wrote in her essay about going to London and attending the Coronation procession, 'but Princess Margaret looked rather sad.' If not sad, certainly preoccupied, for the divorce of the 38-year-old Group Captain Peter Townsend (now serving as Comptroller of the Queen Mother's Household) had gone through the previous December, while the bond between the 22-year-old Margaret and the war hero had grown ever closer. On Coronation Day itself, while the two were standing near each other in an anteroom to the Abbey, an observant foreign reporter noticed how she brushed away 'with a tender hand' a piece of fluff on his RAF uniform. Assumptions of intimacy were made, and next morning the story broke in the New York press. Eleven days later, on Sunday the 14th, the *People* ended the British silence. Under the headline 'They must deny it *now*' and next to photographs of the two, a front-page editorial began: 'It is high time for the British public to be made aware of the fact that scandalous rumours about Princess Margaret are racing around the world.' After identifying Townsend and filling in his background, there followed a passage of 'sheer cant', in Nick Clarke's subsequent apt phrase: 'The story is, of course, utterly untrue. It is quite unthinkable that a Royal princess, third in line of succession to the Throne, should even contemplate a marriage to a man who has been through the divorce courts.' The story then went quiet for the rest of the month, but the decision was taken – by a mixture of court, government and Townsend himself – that he would be posted abroad for two years, as air attaché at the Brussels Embassy, and that the romance would be put on hold until after Margaret's 25th birthday in August 1955. Margaret herself at the end of June accompanied her mother on an official visit to Rhodesia, with the *Daily Mirror* applauding their choice of aircraft: 'The Comets fly triumphantly on. Their designers know them to be world-beaters – and so does our Royal Family.'[19]

In her absence during much of July, public controversy at last flared up. 'If They Want To Marry, Why Shouldn't They?' was the provocative title of Charles Wintour's piece in the *Sunday Express* on the 5th. After a glowing tribute to Townsend – war record, character, not the guilty party in his divorce – Wintour roundly declared that 'the Church should not harm the life of a Princess whose welfare the people hold so close to their hearts'. Other papers also entered the fray, to the consternation of Nella Last in Barrow. 'I'm puzzled about the articles about Princess Margaret & the aide-de-camp Townsend,' she reflected on the 9th. 'Wondering how they could ever think the match would be approved after the Duke of Windsor's affair. There's so much church disapproval.' However, it was not, she mused later in her customary lengthy entry, any longer quite so simple: 'Times have changed – I often feel a bit surprised at the number of divorces in our own town & district. Women don't stand what they used to take for granted – desertion & cruelty, as well as "unfaithfulness", & others claim the same "freedom" as men. *No* one thinks as they used to do – and "thought" is the thing that causes "conduct" – and everything seems so fluid, so chaotic, & people have to solve their own problems, as best they may.' 'My heart bleeds for her I must say,' was Joyce Grenfell's private view next day, but on the 12th the *Sunday Express* revealed that letters from readers had been three to one against Wintour's liberal perspective. 'The stigma of divorce has NOT gone completely,' declared Kenneth Gange of Rainhill, Lancashire. 'There are, I think, a few millions of us who know it is wrong.' Mrs M. Rossiter of Whixley, York, flatly stated that 'I am not one of those who consider a married man with two children suitable for any young girl of about 20.' That same day the *People* ran a front-page story ('Exiled: Why Have They Done This To Her Hero?') about Townsend's imminent posting to Brussels. 'IT MEANS THAT THEY WILL BE GIVEN NO CHANCE TO MEET AND SAY GOODBYE,' screamed the paper, though adding in normal type that their marriage remained 'out of the question because the Queen's sister cannot marry a man who has been through the divorce court'. And it quoted the Archdeacon of Birmingham, the Venerable Michael Parker, who the day before had responded to recent critical remarks about the Church of England's overly prim attitude to the whole question: 'There are many people who are caught up with the secular approach to life, and they have little concept or understanding of the basis of Christian marriage.'

Next morning Britain's best-selling daily paper (having a few years earlier overtaken the *Daily Express*) typically upped the ante. 'The *Daily Mirror* believes,' pronounced a front-page leader, 'that the time has come for the voice of the British people to be heard in the problem of Princess Margaret and her friend, Group-Captain Peter Townsend.' Accordingly, a voting form appeared further down the page, with readers invited to mark the 'yes' or 'no' box as to whether she should be allowed to marry him. All over the country it was now the great talking point. 'My husband was in a dim mood – & Mrs Salisbury [the cleaner] was in one of her most trying,' lamented Nella Last on the Wednesday:

Her *disgust* & indignation about Princess Margaret being 'such a silly little fool' held her up at times ... 'It's *not nice* Mrs Last. I'd belt our Phyllis for acting like that. And a lot of silly girls who copy Princess Margaret's clothes will think they can just do *owt*! ... And fancy her being a *stepmother* ... And I bet she would miss all the fuss she gets. I wonder if she has any money of her own. If she has any, she will find a change from being a Fairy Princess – having every one make a fuss over her.' I felt the ache in my head grow to a real pain.

Noël Coward for one was appalled by the 'journalistic orgy', not least the *Mirror*'s poll. 'It is all so incredibly vulgar and, to me, it is inconceivable that nothing could be done to stop these tasteless, illiterate minds from smearing our Royal Family with their sanctimonious rubbish.'[20]

On Friday the 17th, with Townsend banished and Margaret about to return, the *Mirror* announced the result. More than 70,000 readers had voted, of whom almost 97 per cent thought that she *should* be allowed to marry him. The *Sunday Express* reaction offers a valuable corrective in terms of public opinion as a whole, but this was still a very striking expression of sentiment. There was no doubt, to judge by letters printed by the *Mirror* three days later, about which institution was public enemy number one:

The Church should remember that, had it not been for Group-Captain Townsend and his kind, there would be neither Church nor Throne in England today. (*P. G. Higginson, Stanmore, Middlesex*)

Let us get back to Christian principles, and to hell with the dogmatic attitude of the Church. (*J. Hart, Little Thurlow, Suffolk*)

Don't let the Church spoil the wonderful smile that belongs to our beloved Princess. God gave her a heart. Let her use it as she chooses. (*E. Weller, Stroud, Glos*)

Even Gilbert Harding agreed. 'It seems to me to be silly and pompous for the Church of England, which has fewer than four million active communicants, to put itself forward as "The Church" and to produce rules that we are all expected to follow,' he wrote that weekend in his regular column for the *People*. 'I still wish that people would leave the Princess alone – to marry whom and how she wishes.'

Inevitably the controversy faded, to be put on hold for two years, but before it did so *The Times* offered its troubled thoughts on 'Royal Affairs'. Intensely critical of the recent 'bandying about' of Princess Margaret's name 'in public gossip', it offered only two sentences on the crux of the matter: 'That she shall be happy in all that she does is everybody's wish. That she will choose her path according to duty and conscience as well as inclination, and always in harmonious concert with her beloved sister, is doubted by nobody.' Margaret herself was back on the royal treadmill, including on Tuesday the 22nd. 'I lived in Queen Elizabeth's Close,' recalled Alan Fox about growing up in a prefab next to Clissold Park in north London:

> It was the custom of the Queen Mother, a keen gardener, to visit ordinary people's outstanding gardens. My mum and dad were chosen. Alas, the Queen Mother was unable to attend on the day and Princess Margaret stood in. Her mother's love of gardens and flowers had not rubbed off. At the start of the visit, the court flunky advised my mum 'to keep the conversation going'. What a mistake! Mum could talk nonstop if you let her, and she did, until Princess Margaret, shell-shocked from a botanical barrage, was escorted back to her Rolls.

'Her trip,' he added, 'was immortalised by her very high-heeled shoes which impressed into the tarmac – newly laid just for the occasion.'[21]

By contrast, the Prime Minister was making no public appearances during July – and no one told the public why. In fact he had had a serious stroke barely three weeks after the Coronation, leading to a hastily convened meeting of three press barons (Camrose, Beaverbrook and Bracken) and in effect a gag on the fourth estate. 'The Prime Minister has had no respite for a long time from his arduous duties and is in need of a complete rest,' ran the innocuous bulletin they cobbled together for No. 10, duly released on 27 June. 'Churchill Is Ill: To Rest A Month', was the *People*'s obliging headline next day, with the story stating that 'his trouble is simply tiredness from overwork'. The *Daily Mirror*, anti-Churchill and not part of the magic circle, had its suspicions – to

the extent that its headline on the 29th was 'Should Churchill Retire?'
– but even so the story started with the unambiguous statement that
'Churchill is fagged out,' with no reference to anything more sinister.
'No word of all this has appeared yet in the Press,' noted with relief
the well-connected Tory diarist 'Chips' Channon at the start of July –
more than a week after the stroke – nor did it until the third Monday
of August, by when there had still been no public sighting of the great
man. 'What Is The Truth About Churchill's Illness?' demanded the
Mirror's banner headline, with the story describing how rumours had
continued to mount, including an American paper reporting that he
had had a stroke in late June. 'Is there any reason,' the paper asked,
why the British people 'should always be the last to learn what is
going on in their country? Must they always be driven to pick up their
information at second hand from tittle-tattle abroad?' Churchill's
physician, Lord Moran, had been hoping that morning to go to the
Test at the Oval, but instead was summoned to Chartwell, where he
found Churchill furious about the sheer gall of such a worthless rag.
' "Five million people read that," the P.M. said grimly. "It's rubbish,
of course . . ." '22

The Churchill stroke story was not the only cover-up going on
this summer. On 14 July, the day before John Christie was due to be
hanged for multiple murders at 10 Rillington Place, a government-
appointed inquiry by J. Scott Henderson QC reported – in apparent
defiance of the evidence he had heard – that Christie had lied in
his confession about murdering Timothy Evans's wife and child.
Accordingly, though Christie himself took the drop next morning, it
continued to be denied that there had been a miscarriage of justice in
the case of Evans, hanged in 1950. Subsequently, in Ludovic Kennedy's
bitter words, 'it took thirteen years for officialdom grudgingly to
admit what was obvious in 1953 to all but the wilfully blind; that
there were not two stranglers of women living in 10 Rillington Place,
but one.' In July 1953, it may have been a factor that at the start of
the month a motion to suspend capital punishment for five years had
been defeated in Parliament – a context unlikely to encourage any
immediate official admission of guilt. Still, public opinion was almost
certainly on the side of the parliamentarians. 'Nice young man at
table tonight,' noted Gladys Langford shortly after the vote. 'He says

his uncle is a Detective Sergeant in Liverpool & that he (the uncle) favours the retention of the death sentence and would like the power to administer a birching to be restored.' It was also just after the vote that on 2 July a murder took place on Clapham Common. Two groups of teenagers clashed, words were said ('Walk round the other side, you flash bastard!'), knives were pulled out, a 17-year-old was left bleeding to death on a pavement. Six male youths were arrested, charged and, in the autumn, put on trial at the Old Bailey, with one of them, a 20-year-old labourer called Michael Davies, convicted of murder though in the fullness of time reprieved because it was impossible to know for certain which of the six had actually done the deed. Reports during the trial emphasised how Davies and the others were flashy dressers, liking to get themselves up as Edwardians. It was the start of a new phenomenon: the 'teddy boy'.

There was also fear in the air on the evening of Saturday, 18 July, when at 8.15 – after 'Interlude: The Picnic, by Tissot' and before 'A film of wild life in Africa' – there appeared on the nation's screens one of the earliest dramas specifically written for television. Nigel Kneale's six-part science-fiction series *The Quatermass Experiment*, involving an idealistic government rocket scientist battling the spread of a mind-bending alien vegetable brought home on a spaceship, from the first made a huge impact. 'We were still living in a bomb-blasted Britain and there was the Cold War,' he explained many years later. 'On a day trip to Brighton, I remember seeing promenaders flinch when they heard the buzz of a light aircraft. Was it a Russian rocket?' 'Last night's Terrorvision' was the *News of the World* headline after the fifth episode, with one reader having phoned in: 'I have seen nothing so frightening in my life ... I won't look in next Saturday unless I have someone with me, but I must know what happens.' Viewers' log sheets sent to the BBC confirmed the fearful addiction: 'Wouldn't have missed this for anything. Even missed a day's holiday to see it.' And: 'Everything stopped at our home when serial time came round.'

There was nothing (despite events on Clapham Common) unsettling or futuristic about the programme that made its debut only two days after Professor Bernard Quatermass. *The Good Old Days* came live from the City Varieties Music-Hall at Leeds, reconstructed for the purpose as an Edwardian music hall, with the audience dressing in Edwardian clothes.

The 'chairman' was Don Gemmell, succeeded from the third show by Leonard Sachs, whose speciality – before he finally got to 'Your own, your very own . . .' – was long words in alliterative combinations, provoking 'oohs' and 'aahs' from the almost invariably obliging audience. 'Deeply dejecting' was Peter Black's verdict in the *Daily Mail* on the programme's first outing, because 'the attempt to recreate the atmosphere of 1912 was so pathetically artificial,' but Barney Colehan, the show's producer (who was also responsible for radio's *Have A Go!*), almost certainly knew he had a nostalgia-driven hit on his hands.[23]

Increasingly, though, the present day had its own appeal, with 1953 at last the breakthrough year in terms of moving away from austerity and towards improved living standards and even a measure of affluence. 'We're Buying More Now' was a *News Chronicle* headline in August, on the basis of Treasury figures for the first quarter revealing sharply increased expenditure on food, clothes, shoes, household goods and new cars (nearly 60,000 registrations, compared with about 40,000 in the first quarter of 1952), but relatively less expenditure on drinking, smoking and entertainment – the three staples of the austerity years. The trend continued, with food-consumption figures for the first seven months of 1953 showing meat up by 50 per cent on two years earlier, and bacon up by 24 per cent. Certainly, despite the continued existence of rationing, there was more meat in the shops. It was reported in late June that butchers were able to sell freely once they had provided their registered customers with their 2s 4d weekly ration, while Panter-Downes noted in July that butchers were now finding it difficult to sell their lowest-grade stuff, a development that 'sharply marks the end of the time when housewives meekly queued up and paid for anything the butchers liked to give them'.

There were a couple of particularly emblematic, post-austerity moments in 1953: the opening by Gina Lollobrigida of the Moka coffee bar in Soho's Frith Street, virtually the first café in London to have a gleaming, spluttering Gaggia coffee machine; and the British debut of the Wimpy beefburger, 'the square meal in the round bun', served for the first time at Wimbledon. For most people, material easement had a predominantly domestic focus. 'Explored De Beauvoir Town and the side streets jammed in between Kingsland & Southgate Rds,' recorded Gladys Langford after a long walk in July. 'I may not share the tastes of the masses in window curtaining but I rejoice in that no longer is brown paper stuck over broken panes, there are no scrubby bits of net held in place by bent forks as there were when I started teaching in Hoxton in the 1930s.'[24]

August was holiday time. For day trippers there was a sunny Bank Holiday weekend – on the Sunday almost 10,000 Geordies had arrived by train at Whitley Bay before 2.00 p.m., with every beach hut and deck chair long taken – while on the Kent coast there was the newly opened attraction of Ramsgate Model Village, part of that vogue for the miniature typified by Meccano sets and Airfix models. For the second year running, Anthony Heap took his wife and small son to a boarding house in nearby Broadstairs, where on the third day of their week he reflected that there were only two blots on the landscape:

> One is the deck-chair-hiring system whereby, to save the chair attendants the trouble, one has not only to collect the chair one hires at 6d a time from a certain part of the beach and carry it to wherever one wants to sit but lug it all the way back again afterwards or lose the 6d deposit one also has to pay. The other is the primitive changing room accommodation for bathers – just a yard-square cell with a stone floor and nothing to sit on. Otherwise I remain completely captivated by the sedate elegance and old world charm of this ideal seaside resort for both adults and children – for whom it caters so diligently that even the pubs have special children's rooms.[25]

That same week poor Gladys Langford, some three years after retiring as a teacher, was forced by economic necessity to start a clerical job at Educational Supplies Ltd near Drury Lane:

> *11 August.* Office work wears me down badly. It is so hot in the low ceilinged room and the work is so monotonous. The other clerks I have no doubt find me formidable while I find them foolish. The young ones giggle & chew, the older ones drone about their home affairs.
> *12 August.* My fellow workers most uninspiring – silly little girls tittering and chattering of their boys and older women talking of their children and their ailments. I get not only tired but inexpressibly bored.

> *13 August.* The young girls talk incessantly of films, 'boys' and the Royal Family while the older women chew over illnesses, the doings of husbands & children – and the Royal Family.

Unable to bear it, she left the job a few weeks later.

Among less exclusively female workforces, there was also the topic of sport this remarkable summer. Picking up the Matthews/Richards baton, Tony Rolt and Duncan Hamilton triumphed in June at the gruelling Le Mans 24-hour race, reputedly after a night on the town; over the following weeks, the 22-year-old athlete Gordon Pirie, a bank clerk from Coulsdon invariably known as 'Puff-puff' Pirie, attracted huge publicity with stirring performances over several different distances. Unlike the Oxford-educated Roger Bannister, the other young rising star in British athletics, Pirie made no pretence of being the gifted, effortless amateur. 'No one committed themselves to the grind of training quite like Pirie did,' wrote his biographer. 'He ran, at first, four or five times a week, then daily, then, to the astonishment of his contemporaries, twice a day.' There was also, most compelling of all, the cricket, as England sought to regain the Ashes lost to Australia in 1934. 'A servant showed us into an end room where Colonel Luttrell was sitting watching the Test Match on television,' recorded James Lees-Milne in June after a visit on National Trust business to Dunster Castle in Somerset. 'He did not get up or shake hands but said quite politely, "I must see the end of the match. Sit down where you can." So we did, and when it was over he took us round the castle with much affability.' So too Madge Martin, no cricket-lover. 'I find myself quite interested in Test Match now,' she noted later in June, 'and like listening to the commentaries.'[26] The first four Tests all ended in draws, so everything rested on the fifth, starting at the Oval on Saturday, 15 August.

A full house on the first day included Denis Thatcher, uncontactable for several hours after his wife had given birth to twins in Queen Charlotte's Hospital. Tuesday, the third day, saw the pivotal phase of the match, with Australia batting, recalled soon afterwards by A. A. Thomson, a cricket-loving civil servant:

> Word came to me from a colleague at the far end of my building who, in turn, was receiving signals from some honest workmen who had a

television set in a factory on the opposite side of the road. The progress of the battle was conveyed to me by telephone – an instrument I had not previously admired – and though it started sedately, the tempo of the match perceptibly quickened. There is nothing to affect the blood pressure in a score of 59 for one, but . . . the telephone rang.

'Hello?'

'Fifty-nine for two. It's Hole.'

Pause and ping.

'Hello? Who is it?'

'Sixty for three. It's Harvey.'

'Hello. Who is it?'

'Sixty-one for four. It's Miller.'

Short pause and ping-ping.

'Hello? Who is it now?'

'Sixty-one for five. Now it's Morris. They're on the run.'

The feeling was incredible, outside and beyond human possibility. Sixty-one for five. Hassett, Hole, Harvey, Miller and Morris had travelled the broad road. *We have them.* These wickets had fallen so unbelievably quickly that I could no longer exercise normal patience. Five minutes passed. Nothing happened. Ten minutes. The telephone bell rang shrilly and I snatched the receiver with shaking hand.

'Who is it now?'

'The Foreign Office,' replied a slightly outraged voice, 'if you have no objection.'

That same afternoon Judy Haines and her family were on holiday in Boscombe. 'Several wireless sets on beach and people very friendly passing round the score,' she noted. 'Abbé [her husband] was suddenly missing from his deck-chair. He had gone to toilet and then, fascinated by somebody's wireless, stayed.'

On the Wednesday morning, with England needing only 94 to win, the fast bowler Fred Trueman arrived at the ground with his captain Len Hutton. 'Outside the gates there was already a huge, excited throng, cheering and milling all around, and I remember seeing across the road a cockney chap frantically waving at us a newspaper placard bearing a huge drawing of the Ashes urn, surrounded in massive type by just three words: THEY ARE OURS!' So they were, amid stirring scenes after Denis Compton in due course hit the winning stroke down to the gasometers. But for Judy Haines it proved the most bittersweet of days:

I decided to go to Wimborne Rd Bournemouth, to buy Mum the corsets she had seen advertised. I suggested Abbé stay at home for the Test Match but he wanted to come. The particular shop was miles up the road and a long way out of Bournemouth Town. Abbé *was* fed up. I was annoyed as I had not wanted him to come. He had wanted to be back for the cricket commentary at 11.30. When we regained Boscombe I suggested he go ahead. He and Ione chased off while Pamela and I relaxed. We bought some embroidery (Radio Times Cover) for Ione, and purple knitting for Pamela, and I felt better. We are booked for coach ride to Salisbury. I suggested putting it off as Test Match is coming to a thrilling end. Abbé says 'no'. Despite Kwells, girls were all but sick, and while we were at Salisbury it rained. *Test Match and Ashes won by England*. We wanted to hear John Arlott's summing up at 10.15. I reminded Abbé at 10.10 but he let it go, not wishing to disturb the other guests. In mentioning my disappointment they all expressed theirs. I was *so* miserable in bed I couldn't help sobbing and then had a good cry. Felt better after that.[27]

12

Moral Courage

Ashes to ashes – the day after England had regained the urn, and less than a fortnight after the Russian leader Georgy Malenkov had told the Supreme Soviet that 'the United States no longer has a monopoly of the hydrogen bomb', *Pravda* reported that the Soviet Union had indeed tested a hydrogen bomb, with an explosion showing that the H-bomb's power was 'many times greater than the power of atomic bombs'. Humour was one response to this alarming development – 'the atom bomb with its familiar rococo mushroom plumage will still be useful in minor engagements', reflected the cricket-loving Bernard Hollowood in *Punch* – while most people simply got on with their lives and, more or less successfully, tried not to think about it.

Certainly the Cold War remained, despite the recent end of the Korean War, an obstinate reality, taking a new cultural form in October with the first issue of the monthly magazine *Encounter*. Edited by Stephen Spender and Irving Kristol, it was an explicitly anti-Communist organ (secretly funded by the CIA) of wide intellectual range and high literary quality. At a less rarefied level, Mass-Observation found during the autumn that although twice as many people in Britain were anti- as were pro-Russian, there persisted 'the identification of the Russian people with the "we" group . . . the innocent victims of the machinations of the mysterious "they" '. There were, moreover, mixed feelings towards Americans: admiration for their 'generosity', yes, but also resentment about their 'big-headedness' and for being, most damning of faults, 'all talk'. But predictably, whether towards Russians or Americans, the most common attitude expressed to M-O was that old, deeply insular favourite, 'no opinion'.

Sport for its part did not suddenly stop distracting attention from the momentous issues. 'As usual of course,' warned the *Shetland Times* eight days after *Pravda*'s announcement, 'there are the critics who predict dire results at the hands of an Orkney team,' as the footballers of the two islands prepared to contest that afternoon the Milne Cup. Shetland had not won on Orkney soil since 1929, but on a wet Friday afternoon at Bignold Park, with all places of business in Kirkwall closed, 3,540 spectators saw, in the regretful words of the *Orkney Herald*, 'the Orcadians humbled 3–1 by a much faster and cleverer Shetland side'. Kirkwall City Pipe Band did the musical honours; Shetland's captain, the stopper centre-half Tommy ('Blondie') Newman, received the Cup from the local Liberal MP, Jo Grimond; and on Saturday, still recovering from the Friday evening reception and dance, 'several hundred Orcadians were at the pier' to give the Shetland party (just over a hundred) 'a good-humoured send-off and to have a farewell glimpse of the Milne Cup'. Three weeks later there was another, higher-profile annual ritual with the Last Night of the Proms, as usual conducted by Sir Malcolm Sargent and as usual in front of, according to *The Times*, 'an outsize audience keyed up as if for a Cup Final'. The BBC's head of music had controversially omitted Sir Henry Wood's *Fantasia on British Sea Songs*, an old favourite, from the printed programme – but such was the public outcry that a shortened version was included as an encore. 'As clappers in the horn-pipe, the audience showed a disregard for the conductor's beat that would have won any orchestral player the sack.'[1]

The material world was continuing to improve. 'I began my expedition among the bulging shops of Notting Hill Gate and Paddington,' reported the *News Chronicle*'s David Malbert in early September about a shopping trip round London that revealed the extent to which food rationing was informally if not yet officially ending:

> In a big provision store I bought 1 lb of best grilling steak for 4s; ½ lb of margarine; 2 lb of sugar and 1 lb of back of bacon for 4s 10d. *The subject of ration books did not crop up* . . .
> I went out to the Old Kent Road. 'Will 4 lb do?' the grocer asked when I mentioned sugar. 'I've no ration book,' I explained. He laughed. 'That doesn't matter. Never use 'em now.' In three other shops in the district I bought more margarine, sugar, butter and best bacon. At two others my

umbrella was regarded with slight mistrust and I was reminded: 'Sorry, it's rationed.'

Mollie Panter-Downes confirmed the trend. 'Butchers for some time now,' she observed later that month, 'have been sticking up signs saying, "Anyone served with anything on sale" in their windows,' adding that 'that strange, prized symbol of pre-war good living – pure-white bread – has, for the first time since the war, turned up in the shops for those who can afford to pay more for it than for the subsidised semi-white national loaf'. There was also a signal moment on the 28th. '*Sugar rationing is over*,' recorded Marian Raynham. 'That is wonderful. Now I will have more brown, dem, & some lump. I mostly had granulated because it goes farther.' It was, in Panter-Downes's words, 'one more move toward making a nice little bonfire of ration books'.

The cultural standard of living stayed, from a Reithian perspective, disappointingly poor. 'It appealed strongly to a minority only and was consequently given the low Reaction Index of 54,' noted BBC audience research after the second act of T. S. Eliot's new play, *The Confidential Clerk*, had gone out live in late August. 'The most frequent complaints were that the play seemed difficult, wordy and "highbrow".' A viewer was quoted as saying: 'Couldn't for the life of me pick the story up.' By contrast, the return soon afterwards of the comedy *How Do You View?* ('How do you view? Are you frightfully well? You are? Oh, good show!') won an RI of 76. 'One has only to *look* at Terry-Thomas and one feels a laugh coming,' declared one enthusiastic viewer, another that 'this was grand stuff; interesting, very amusing and *clean*'. Squeaky clean also were *Rag, Tag and Bobtail*, the latest addition to the *Watch with Mother* portfolio, but Nella Last in Barrow was not so sure about the whole phenomenon after listening to her next-door neighbour Mrs Atkinson complain about how her little granddaughter was now always wanting to rush home to watch *Children's Hour*. 'As she talked,' reflected Last, 'I saw plainly how T.V. must be changing a lot of people's habits.' J. B. Priestley had no doubts about the perniciousness. 'Because people spend their evenings watching idiotic parlour games on TV or *Chu Chin Chow* on ice,' he declared in the first of his 'Thoughts in the Wilderness' columns in the *New Statesman*, 'this does not mean that the last glimmer of intuitive perception has been dowsed, though after a few more years of mass communication on this level the crowd may be permanently half-witted.' His next column, later in September, was a lengthy, fiercely anti-American diatribe against the mass media and how it was creating a new world – 'a world I dislike intensely'.[2]

Almost everyone on the left agreed that an improved educational system was pivotal to the country's future health, whether moral and/or socio-economic. 'The child who lives in Merioneth has eight times more chance of going to a grammar school than has a child in Gateshead,' asserted Alice Bacon at Labour's conference at Margate this autumn, calling for an end to 'the grammar school gamble', while Jennie Lee wanted the party to 'put all its enthusiasm and skill into comprehensive schools'. Moreover, although the party had for some time been theoretically committed to the comprehensive principle, there was also considerable – if far from unanimous – rank-and-file enthusiasm for the cause expressed at the conference. Not that it was a cause likely to proceed smoothly so long as Florence Horsbrugh was Minister of Education. Over the winter she largely resisted attempts by Labour-controlled local authorities in London, Coventry and elsewhere to go comprehensive and in particular ensured that, in London at least (where at this point eight comprehensives were being built and four more were on the drawing board), no existing grammar school was lost. One of the planned four was Holland Park Comprehensive, notwithstanding strenuous objections (publicly supported by John Betjeman) from the wealthy residents of Campden Hill, Kensington. 'An educational abortion, a vast factory, mass-producing units for the prefabrication of the classless dictatorship of the proletariat,' ran a typical super-Nimby cry of despair to the local paper.[3]

Increasingly, a central plank of the pro-comprehensive case was that the eleven-plus method of selection for grammar schools was not just cruel and divisive but also inefficient in terms of measuring intelligence. A key figure was Brian Simon, a Communist who as a youngish teacher at Salford Grammar School in the late 1940s had been much struck by how the handful of boys each year who passed a 'transfer' examination from the secondary modern to the grammar *then* flourished more than some of the original eleven-plus passers. 'Did this mean, given the opportunity, that there were potentially hundreds of 11-plus failures perfectly capable of doing well at grammar school?' was how he recalled his thinking. During the early 1950s, by now based at Leicester University's School of Education, he started to conduct research leading in late 1953 to a short but highly focused study *Intelligence Testing and the Comprehensive School*. Even the pro-selection *Times Educational Supplement* conceded that it was 'a formidable indictment of the theory and practice of intelligence testing', while John Garrett, headmaster of Bristol Grammar School and a virtuoso publicist for the grammar-school system, wrote in the *New Statesman* that the case 'deserves respect and demands an answer'. Simon's ultimate conclusion was that intelligence testing essentially tested the differences of social class and that it was time to concentrate, without selection, on the educability of the ordinary child.

Quite apart from the generally high prestige of grammar schools ('Your school and other schools like it, represent what may be called the cream, and it is the object of schools such as yours to direct students to walks of life that call for leadership, ability, character and high standards – in a word, endeavour,' declared Air-Marshal Sir Francis J. Fogarty in July 1953 before handing out the prizes at Purley County Grammar School for Boys), it was not quite so cut-and-dried even in Labour ranks as Simon might have wished. 'Nearly all the delegates either were at grammar school or had their children at grammar schools,' Richard Crossman astutely noted at Margate, while the following month the veteran local Manchester politician Wright Robinson privately confessed himself a 'heretic':

> My own points are first a strong exception to any one type of education being regarded as It, the complete super type justifying the exclusion of all others. The argument is that all other valid types are comprehended within this perfect common school. It is further contended that it cannot be successful unless the competition of its most powerful rival is removed from its catchment area. The grammar school must go. Given free choice the parents will prefer to send their children to a grammar school. Parents are not the best judges of what is best for their children, it is said ... London which has wholeheartedly gone in for the C.S. is building one seven storey and one nine storey school, vast education factories with most of the features of the mass production workshop, in order to produce, or mass produce, ready made democrats. We jeer at the

totalitarian methods of the Soviet, and ape them ourselves by trying to impose in a compulsory system of education, one common pattern, one type of school.

Crossman may also have had further reservations after dining at about the same time with the headmaster of Maidstone Grammar School. 'Claydon made an extremely good impression on me,' recorded the Wykehamist diarist:

> What he really believes in is building up the maintained grammar schools on the one side, and making the Modern schools really good on the other. His central argument is that the comprehensive school really does neglect the differences in intelligence. 'When you talk of Eton being a comprehensive school, it's sheer nonsense,' he said. 'Every boy at Eton, however stupid, is far above the average intelligence. You don't understand the average intelligence, and you will flood the grammar school and kill it if you try to mix the average Modern school child with the grammar school child.'[4]

With the political temperature over selection starting to rise, it was a potentially acrimonious debate set to run and run.

Lorna Stockton (later Sage) – fresh from her semi-triumph on Coronation Day – began that autumn at Whitchurch Girls' High School in Shropshire. 'The high school cultivated the air of being somehow still fee-paying, it was designed to produce solid, disciplined, well-groomed girls who'd marry local traders and solicitors like their fathers,' she recalled. 'The eleven-plus had let in a leavening of out-of-towners and outsiders, but that had only made it more vital to insist on sub-public-school mores – uniforms, "houses", and an elaborate hierarchy of prefects and deputy prefects whose job it was to remind their juniors to stand up straight, and send them out to run up and down the playing field at break in wet weather instead of huddling in the cloakrooms.' Social distinctions were naturally acute on the bus from and to the village where she lived:

> The back seats were reserved for big girls of fourteen and fifteen who went to the secondary modern, but only just. They had perms, boyfriends

and jobs lined up, and they wore their school uniforms in a sketchy, customised way, with extra bits and bits missing, and nylons whose ladders they fixed surely with nail varnish. They had a lot to talk about and laugh over in private. They painted their nails on the way home and picked off the varnish the next morning . . .

The secondary modern boys were younger for their age and scuffled about in the middle seats, playing at being wild, priding themselves on the filthiness of their ties and wearing spare cigarettes behind their ears. Although they sometimes looked up girls' skirts and told dirty jokes, they were second-class passengers, the bus was girl territory, the real tearaways among the boys didn't stoop to catch the bus, but biked to school on the days when they weren't truanting.

And the grammar school boys and high school girls, a conspicuous and shifty minority, distributed themselves around the front seats as they boarded. Grammar school boys stood out sacrificially in bright purple blazers and caps. At least the high school's navy blue matched the majority – although only at a distance, there was no getting around the stigma . . .

'In theory,' Sage added, 'we who'd passed the eleven-plus were supposed to despise the secondary modern kids for being common and thick. In practice we envied them for knowing how to be outsiders and as we grew older we aped their style: caps and berets balled up in pockets, greased and lacquered quiffs of hair, secret lockets and chains with rings on them under their shirts.'

The real fee-paying schools inhabited in every sense a separate world. 'If they believed in equality of opportunity,' Crossman's fellow-Wykehamist Hugh Gaitskell was reported as telling the party conference, 'they could not continue with a system of education under which wealthy parents were able to buy what they and most people believed to be a better education for their children.' At the same time, Gaitskell insisted that he was 'not attacking public schools, or the parents who sent their children to them, but the system was wrong and must be changed'. Alice Bacon, for all her left-wing credentials, disagreed, declaring to conference that the far more important priority was to focus on 'privilege within the State system' and that any attempt to outlaw private education 'would lead to a black market in private tutors and the privileged classes would send their children abroad to be educated'. At which point the whole issue, virtually moribund since 1945, returned to its slumbers. One brave soul, John Wilkes, personally sought to cross the chasm between the worlds by deciding at the end of 1953 to give up the headmastership of Radley in favour of becoming a poorly paid vicar in the heavily working-class Hunslet district of Leeds. His reward was to be treated by his mother-in-law (wife of a former headmaster of Eton) 'as if he had forged a cheque'.[5]

———————

'This will be the first time a British actress has appeared as leading lady at Drury Lane, home of the American musical, since before the war,' noted the *Daily Mirror*'s Eve Chapman on 1 October (the same day as Labour's education debate). The musical was *The King and I* by Rodgers and Hammerstein, and the somewhat surprise choice for the role of the governess was Valerie Hobson, the subject of Chapman's profile, with her 'pale, ladylike looks, her well-bred clothes, and her quiet hobbies – she likes embroidery and painting'. Opening night was exactly a week later. 'Valerie Hobson was most charming and made a triumphant success,' applauded Noël Coward; 'more divinely fair and gracefully dignified than ever', agreed another diarist, Anthony Heap. The weeklies were somewhat less obliging. The *Spectator*'s Derek Monsey found the whole thing only 'adequate', especially given that 'the brilliant glow of *Oklahoma!* [the Rodgers and Hammerstein musical that had hit London six years earlier] still warms and lights our memories', though he did praise Hobson for her 'grace and sincerity'; while according to the reliably acerbic T. C. Worsley in the *New Statesman*, she was 'deficient in voice but works the charm hard'. Later in the year, during the Christmas holidays, the Eton schoolboy Hugo Williams, whose theatrical parents knew Hobson, saw the show. 'I went to meet her in the star dressing room, said to be the most beautiful in the world,' he recalled. 'It had been freshly painted pink and white for her, and was like entering a risqué French apartment. There were three adjoining rooms: vestibule (for casual visitors), softly lit drawing room and brightly lit dressing area, the holy of holies, where Miss Hobson was taking off wide padded hips. I still have her autograph, but not that of her husband, who wasn't famous yet.'

He was John Profumo, who two days after the first night was, like other Tory backbenchers, at Margate for his leader's much-awaited speech to the party conference. This was Churchill's first major public appearance since his stroke, and he spoke for 50 minutes, standing throughout. To the faithful's obvious relief, it was a passable version of vintage:

> All the old mannerisms were there [reported the *Observer*] – the pretended search for the exact word, the delighted childlike glow that comes over his features as he nears a joke. When, as is his way, he got rather confused in some statistics about food, he put it all right by happily reflecting: 'How lucky it was I wasn't complicating it by percentages.' . . . Later on when he drank a glass of water he confided – again with that cherubic smile – 'I don't often do that.' And then as the hall roared its appreciation: 'I mean when I'm making a speech.'

Not everyone shared the enthusiasm for the 78-year-old's evident determination to stay in office. 'London is very miserable at the moment,' Kenneth Williams wrote soon afterwards to a friend, 'the leaves falling in the parks, the evenings becoming colder and foggy and everywhere, the depression wrought by a Conservative government – O to be out of England, now that Winston's in.'[6]

By-election of the autumn was at Holborn and St Pancras South, whose Labour MP, Dr Santo Jeger, had died in September – 'a rank red, and one of the ugliest little yids you ever did see', generously noted a constituent, Anthony Heap. The party's candidate was Jeger's widow, Lena, who during the campaign was canvassing in a block of flats when she met a woman in the lift and addressed her on the issue of German rearmament. 'People have been pissing in this lift,' replied the woman. 'What are you going to do about it?' To which Jeger said that, if elected, she could not promise to be able to stop this. 'Well,' riposted the woman, 'if you can't stop people pissing in lifts, how are you going to stop Germans rearming?' Jeger got home with a narrow majority on 19 November, just a few days after Crossman had spent 'a disturbing weekend' at meetings in the West Midlands. 'Both at Coventry and at Leamington, Nye [Bevan] got an audience but he had to do all the lifting of it,' he reflected. 'I would say that there was absolutely no swing so far towards Labour and that, on the whole, the vast majority of the electorate are plain uninterested in party politics of any kind. This matters far less to a Tory Government than it does to a Labour Opposition.'

Crossman's gloom about the passivity of the electorate would have deepened if, on the day of Jeger's return, he had read Catherine Heath's article in the *Manchester Guardian* about her recent experience dispensing citizen's advice from the John Hilton Bureau, recipient of over 3,000 letters a week:

> I sometimes felt that all politicians should work for a few months in such a bureau. It was to us the homeless wrote, and the old age pensioners, and the disabled soldiers. What startled me was the utter helplessness of these people in the face of the complexity of modern society; the failure of deserving cases to make use of welfare agencies existing for their benefit because they are ignorant of them. We often told a starving old age pension couple about National Assistance, or a lame man about the disabled persons register, and received a grateful letter back. Often, too, people would put themselves out of benefit, lose the right of pension appeal, &c, simply because they were quite incapable of reading a form right through and thus failed to realise there was a time-limit until it was too late.

There were also the victims of 'swindles' – 'it was pitiful to realise what easy game for the unscrupulous many were, and how easily terrified by threats of legal proceedings' – and altogether, she concluded, 'a vast mass of our population live their days in a perpetual state of terror and confusion, and life is a fast game of which they do not understand the rules'.[7]

One life-rule that almost every gay person in 1953 Britain did understand was the advisability of keeping secret their sexual orientation. The febrile atmosphere surrounding the whole subject was epitomised by the furore in September after Benny Hill made a televised gag about New Scotland Yard's phone number as 'WHItehall Home-Away-Home-Away'. It was, complained the War Office, 'in deplorable taste' that there should be this 'reference to homosexuality' on a BBC programme being broadcast live from the Nuffield Centre for service personnel. Historians have differed as to whether there was a systematic, McCarthy-style witch-hunt in operation at this time against homosexuals, but certainly 1953–4 did mark a peak of prosecutions, with key men at the top – Sir David Maxwell Fyfe as Home Secretary, Sir Theobald Mathew as Director of Public Prosecutions, Sir John Nott-Bower as Metropolitan Police Commissioner, Sir Lawrence Dunn as Chief Metropolitan Magistrate – all actively hostile towards what Dunn called 'male harpies' or 'the lowest of the low'. Or, as Maxwell Fyfe put it in December 1953 to the House of Commons: 'Homosexuals, in general, are exhibitionists and proselytizers and a danger to others, especially the young. So long as I hold the office of Home Secretary I shall give no countenance to the view that they should not be prevented from being such a danger.'

There were several causes célèbres around this time, among them the case of the writer Rupert Croft-Cooke, found guilty in October of committing acts of gross indecency with two naval ratings – even though the corroborative evidence had been secured by the police in the most dubious way – and sentenced to nine months' imprisonment. There was also the case of Lord Montagu of Beaulieu, his cousin Michael Pitt-Rivers and the *Daily Mail*'s diplomatic correspondent Peter Wildeblood, all three of whom were arrested in January 1954 for homosexual offences and conspiracy to incite acts of gross indecency (the latter charge being wheeled out for the first time since the trials of Oscar Wilde). Kenneth Tynan stood bail for Wildeblood, a move that – the editor of the *Evening Standard* enjoyed informing his proprietor, Lord Beaverbrook – provoked 'a great roar of laughter of Fleet Street'. Later that month, the Admiralty issued new Fleet Orders highlighting 'the horrible character of unnatural vice' and insisting that naval officers 'stamp out the evil'. Recommended methods included inspection of jars of Vaseline or hair gel for tell-tale pubic hairs, while officers were also encouraged to secure 'the help of the steadier and more reliable men on the lower deck' in order to counter the regrettable tendency 'to treat these matters with levity'.[8]

One case, in October 1953, had a special piquancy. 'Sir John Gielgud in the news – fined £10 for "persistent importuning" in Chelsea,' noted Gladys Langford on Wednesday the 21st. 'He pleaded that he was the worse for drink. There must be a crusade against homosexuality just now.' The theatrical community mainly closed ranks – 'Who's been a naughty boy, then?' was how Dame Sybil Thorndike, wagging her finger, broke the ice as Gielgud sheepishly returned to the Theatre Royal, Haymarket, for rehearsals of N. C. Hunter's *A Day by the Sea*, while on its first out-of-town performance in Liverpool the following Monday there was a standing ovation when the fearful actor came on the stage – but reaction elsewhere was less tolerant. Not only were posters outside the Haymarket smeared for at least a week with 'Dirty queer' graffiti, but the *Sunday Express*'s ultra-right-wing columnist (and former editor) John Gordon penned a fiercely anti-homosexual piece, though without actually using the word. Calling Gielgud's offence one that was 'repulsive to all normal people', he declared that this 'widespread disease' had 'penetrated every phase of life' and 'infects politics, literature, the stage, the Church, and the youth movements, as the criminal courts regularly reveal to us'. He went on:

> The suggestion that peculiar people should be allowed peculiar privileges is arrant nonsense. The equally familiar plea that these pests are purely pathological cases and should be pampered instead of punished is almost as rubbishy.
>
> It is time the community decided to sanitise itself. For if we do not root out this moral rot, it will bring us down as inevitably as it has brought down every nation in history that became affected by it.
>
> There must be sharp and severe punishment. But more important than that, we must get the social conscience of the nation so roused that such people are made social lepers.

Gordon finished by suggesting that 'the nation might suitably mark its abhorrence of this type of depravity by stripping from men involved in such cases any honours that have been bestowed upon them'. Gielgud himself had been knighted only that summer, and it was perhaps no wonder that in the immediate aftermath of the case Noël Coward privately lamented, 'How could he, how could he, have been stupid and so selfish?', perhaps guessing that his own knighthood would now be long delayed – in the event, another 17 years.

'Concern has been expressed recently at the standard of morality in this country,' observed a member of the *Any Questions?* audience at

Parkstone the Friday after Gordon's outburst. 'What are the team's views?' Whereupon the unreconstructed Tory politician Julian Amery called for 'a moral revival in England', but John Arlott was adamant that such calls were irrelevant: 'If a person is not sexually normal, that is not cured by punishment or the law, or by home influence, it's solely a question of the way the person is, and I don't believe that by detection, punishment, religion, or spiritual guidance, you will change a person's basic fabric ...' Tellingly, during the whole discussion, there was no mention of 'homosexuality' as such. It is impossible to be certain whether Amery or Arlott was closer to the centre of public opinion, but the chances are that it was Amery. Two days later, the letters page of the *Sunday Express* noted that, in 'an exceptional response' to Gordon's column, 'most expressed strong approval'; while a few years earlier, Mass-Observation's survey of sexual attitudes had found 'a more genuine feeling of disgust towards homosexuality ... than towards any other subject tackled'. This was hardly surprising, given the lurid, wholly unsympathetic approach of the popular press. 'For many people crime reporters were the only source of information about homosexuality,' the historian Richard Davenport-Hines has commented, 'and they concluded that all homosexuals were chorister-molesting vicars or men who groped other men in subterranean lavatories in a fetid atmosphere of urine.'

Even at the quality end of journalism there was great reluctance to cover the subject in a sober, detached way, not least at the BBC. 'It would be a waste of time to do any serious work on the subject,' asserted Donald Boyd, a senior figure in the Talks Department, in an internal memo in November 1953, having already in another memo called homosexuality 'a distortion of the natural appetite which is incurable and unpredictable'. Moreover, his ultimate boss, the director-general Sir Ian Jacob, was adamant that the time was not right for such a programme, rumours about which were causing consternation to the Church of England's Council for Sex, Marriage and the Family. At least one Christian, though, saw things differently. Chad Varah moved in the autumn of 1953 from a parish in Clapham to St Stephen's Walbrook in the City of London, where within weeks he started the Samaritans. 'In the early days,' he recalled, 'a frequent cause of a suicidal intent or attempt was that a male homosexual had been discovered to be such by some ill-disposed person who was blackmailing him.'[9]

The topic was briefly alluded to when *Take It From Here* returned on 12 November for its seventh series. It was in its way a historic transmission. 'Our family, the Glums, are very *ordinary* people,' declared the announcer David Dunhill about halfway through, heralding the birth of a new radio family. 'They might be *you* or *you* or *you* ... all five of them are shifty, obstinate, argumentative and dim.' They were in short, as the writers Frank Muir and Denis Norden fully intended, very different from cosy, upstanding families like the Dales, the Archers and the Huggetts (which several years after the films still had their own very popular radio comedy series). Jimmy Edwards played the rascally Mr Glum, Dick Bentley his mentally challenged son Ron, and June Whitfield (a newcomer to the show, just pipping Prunella Scales for the role) Ron's loyal, long-suffering fiancée Eth. It took a while for the characterisation to emerge fully, but an exchange from the first episode already gave a flavour:

> MR GLUM: Well, now, you two, what can I say? You're embarking on the Great Adventure in very unsettled times. There's trouble on the borders of Treest, uprisings in British Guinea – they're clamping down on vice in the West End – I tell you the future looks black.
> RON: Dad, what you don't seem to realise is, we *are* the future. Me and Eth. The torch has been handed on. We're trying to build a world that's strong and splendid and fearless and – and – what you scratching for, beloved?
> ETH: I think it was that dog. I'll sit on the sofa if you don't mind.

Long afterwards, Whitfield explained that she had based the way she played Eth on her mother's daily, who not only 'had a high-pitched voice and a terribly earnest way of speaking', but 'kept a very tight grip on her grammar, as though terrified that it might let her down, revealing her to be impolite'. The other female newcomer was the singer Alma Cogan – 'a large, happy girl', in Muir's words, with a 'swinging, chuckly style of singing' – and *TIFH* was soon more popular than ever, with the Glums an immediate hit, occupying the whole second half of the show. 'I never thought I'd miss Joy Nichols so little,' noted Nella Last after the fourth episode. 'One of the girls [presumably Whitfield] seems to have picked up her "vital" style.'

Other popular newcomers this autumn were the new Anglia and the new Prefect – essentially Ford's answer, in the small-car range, to the Morris Minor, Austin Seven and Standard Eight. The Anglia, applauded *Autocar*, was 'austerely furnished', but with a 'very modern and pleasing appearance', while the Prefect was 'a clean-looking car devoid of unsightly frills'. Altogether, 'the comfort standards of today's small cars are a far cry from the time when almost anything was good enough for the man with a slender pocket'. Even so, the magazine did note that whereas Britain 'continues to scale down her larger familiar models', French designers (for instance of the 750cc Renault or 385cc Citroën) had 'sat down in front of a clean sheet of paper and banished, with considerable success, all thoughts of the previous products of their companies'. As usual, Dagenham's finest were unveiled at October's annual Motor Show, an event opened by Prince Philip in characteristically robust, go-ahead form. 'I am not always convinced,' he declared, 'that the driver's comfort is given enough thought. Why is it that there always seems to be a handle or a knob just opposite one's right knee?' Later in his speech he called on the motor industry to produce 'a Comet of the car world', in other words 'something really revolutionary in price and overall performance'. And after noting the increasing amount of freight on the roads and the ever-greater congestion, he concluded: 'However much some people may regret it, you cannot put the clock back. An efficient road system is essential to the industry and commerce of this country both in peace and war.'

The royal hold on the popular imagination continued unabated. 'Girls dressed up as Queen and Duke of Edinburgh in my bridal head-dress and Abbé's battle-dress respectively,' recorded Judy Haines in Chingford on the third Monday of November. 'I was the crowd waving and cheering.' Exactly a week later, on the 23rd, at least 6,000 were at London Airport to see the couple leave for a six-month tour of the Commonwealth – an event to which the *Mirror*, calling the tour 'a rendezvous with the future', devoted the best part of six out of sixteen pages. 'It was immensely moving,' reflected Noël Coward after watching the television coverage. 'The Queen looked so young and vulnerable and valiant, and Prince Philip so handsome and cheerful. A truly romantic couple, star quality *in excelsis*. True glamour without any of the Windsors' vulgarity.' Their departure meant an adjustment to one rather different rendezvous. In early December the *Mirror* announced the result of its Teen Queen contest in which young female readers voted for their escort of choice. Max Bygraves, Tony Curtis and Gregory Peck all came close, but number one was Prince Philip, sadly unavailable. Instead, the Teen Queen – Olwen Evans, a shorthand typist from Ashford, Kent – was awarded a date with the number two, Dirk Bogarde. 'Goodness knows what agonies he went through,' speculates his biographer, 'but he was usually stoic.'[10]

Philip also missed, by just two days, 'The Match of the Century' as it was tagged even before kick-off. 'I defy all logic,' proclaimed the *Mirror*'s Bob Ferrier on the fateful Wednesday the 25th. 'I defy all reason. I refute all argument . . . I have a hunch. The hunch is that England will beat Hungary at Wembley today . . .' England had never lost at home, while Hungary were unbeaten in 25 matches, so that afternoon something probably had to give – and Ferrier was adamant that 'moral courage' would see the English through. It did not. Hungary won 6–3, a triumph epitomised by their marvellous third goal, a silky dragback by Ferenc Puskás (leaving the England captain, Billy Wright, flat on his bottom) before a rasping shot into the roof of the net. It was a stunning reversal near the end of a year of almost unbroken British sporting glory. Even during the first half, wrote the journalist Peter Wilson, 'the grey ranks huddled round the rims of the great stone bowl fell silent, as mourners at a national funeral rather than spectators at a national sporting festival'. Even so, A. Brook Hirst, chairman of the FA, took a cheerful line at the post-match dinner for the two teams: 'We are not downhearted and not disturbed by the defeat we have sustained.' Replying, the Hungarian vice-minister of sport was graciousness itself: 'We are looking forward to the coming visit of England to Hungary and hope you have better luck in Budapest next May.' As for the press, few differed from Alan Ross's verdict in the *Observer* that the difference between the two teams (England's including a 'sluggish' Alf Ramsey at right-back) had been 'the difference between artists and artisans, strategists with a flair for improvisation and stumbling recruits bound by an obsolete book of words'.

It was a match that kept its lustre over the years – Jean-Luc Godard in his 2005 film *Notre Musique* claimed that it was the last great triumph for socialism because the English played individually and the Hungarians collectively – while in its more immediate aftermath the *Orkney Herald*'s regular diarist 'Islandman', pseudonym for the poet George Mackay Brown, remarked that listening to the radio commentary had made him quote Kipling to himself about Nineveh and Tyre. England's 'defeat on this particular occasion was refreshing', he added, 'just as Orkney's defeat on the Bignold Park last August was refreshing'. Would the humiliation make English football alter its parochial ways? It was certainly a deeply insular society in which the weekly ritual was played out, as instanced about this time by the distinctly tepid response to Philip Harben's new television series *Continental Cookery*. The first programme, giving his recipe for 'Onion Soup from France', earned a Reaction Index of only 62; the second, with his recipe for 'Pasta, from Italy', got 60; and there were calls from the BBC's Viewing Panel for 'more everyday dishes', as well as 'remarks to show that the "foreign introduction" was not always popular'.[11]

'Cratered and pocked with bomb-sites,' was how Liverpool struck Lorna Sage as she regularly went there during the winter of 1953–4 for dental treatment. She 'saw in reality the cityscape of the newsreels – the remains of blitzed tenements, wallpaper, fire grates and private plumbing exposed, clinging to walls which were buttressed with wooden props while they waited for demolition', while around the Anglican cathedral lay 'a great emptiness where swathes of streets had been razed to the ground'. All that, in other cities as well as Liverpool, lay ripe for development even before, in early November, Macmillan opened a new front. After telling the Commons that there were at least half a million 'slum houses' that needed to be demolished as soon as possible, he went on:

> We can no longer afford to put off, to put aside, the question of the slums. We can no longer leave people living in cramped, dark, rotten houses with no water, sometimes no lavatories, no proper ventilation and no hope of rescue . . . I shall ask each local authority to set before me a definite programme setting out the size of their slum problem and the methods by which they propose to deal with it . . . In some great cities it will take perhaps 10, 15 or 20 years for us to clear away the whole thing.

There had already been a certain amount of slum clearance since the war, but these words signalled an imminent step-change.

What about those actually living in the slums? Shortly before Macmillan's announcement, all five families residing in damp, rundown, now condemned houses in Battersea Church Road declared unambiguously that they did not want to be rehoused in flats. 'This place is small and dirty, but it is a little home of my own,' explained Mrs Essex at no. 7 (where she had been for 44 years). 'You don't get any privacy in flats.' Her next-door neighbour Mrs Bonard did not want to go at all. 'I have lived here since 1915, and I should hate to move. With a little repair these could be quite nice homes.' She was not alone. 'Strangely enough,' Liverpool's City Architect, Ronald Bradbury, explained to the Housing Centre in London in February 1954, 'there is no desperate anxiety among many slum dwellers, specially older folks, to get out of the slums':

> Some of them have lived their whole lives in the same slum house which holds for them those memories which somehow turn a dwelling, no matter how poor it may be, into 'home'. Many wish to stay and die where they are. One tenacious old lady has refused no less than ten offers of suitable accommodation. Her refusal to move meant that the building of many new dwellings was delayed, and, kindness and persuasion having failed, the Housing Committee was obliged to have her evicted. This is an extreme case, but a great deal of persuasion and salesmanship has to be exercised to secure the rehousing of many slum families.

But 'eventually', he added, 'there comes the glorious day when the demolition contractor's men reduce the old dwellings to rubble and cart it away'. During discussion after his talk, he noted that 60 per cent was a realistic target in terms of the proportion of the existing population that could be rehoused in the central areas, and that 'at present mainly flats were being built in central areas, so that as many people could be rehoused as quickly as possible'. He 'agreed that flats were not ideal, but he thought that if a man had to live near to his work, then he must make do with a second best'. Someone raised the question of provision at these blocks of flats for children's play. 'Mr Bradbury said areas were being set aside for this purpose, and apparatus provided, some of which lasted while some did not. At present they were investigating the possibility of designing a concrete tree, but did not know whether it would last any longer than a real one!'[12]

The prospect of slum clearance gave a new urgency to architectural and planning debates generally, not least the long-running clash between the 'urbanists', who saw the future as predominantly lying in the big cities, and the 'dispersionists', who did not. Michael Young, the new sociologist on the block, was moving ever more towards the former camp. By late 1953 he was starting to write up his LSE thesis, 'A Study of the Extended Family in East London', based on 96 interviews conducted between April and October that were almost equally divided between the traditional working-class district of Bethnal Green and the just-completed LCC out-county estate of Debden in Essex to which many Bethnal Greeners had moved since the war.

In the East End he found an intensely attractive world of its own, a world quite different from the London he had known hitherto:

> When dusk is falling, the homing pigeons glide down over the Mansion House, the Stock Exchange and the Bank of England before fluttering into the backyards of Bethnal Green. As the country-bound business men hurry away from their offices in Lloyd's or Mincing Lane a few hundred yards away, Mr Smith gets back from the docks, waters the flowers in the window-box and settles down to his tea. Mrs Smith pulls the curtains aside to see if she can spot her children playing under the railway arches. All she can see is the rush-hour trains to Ilford and Colchester steaming out of Liverpool Street Station and gathering speed past her windows . . .

It was, Young discovered, a deeply intimate world, with the mother/daughter relationship at its functional as well as emotional heart. 'I don't think,' Mrs Silverman told him, 'I'd like to move out of Bethnal Green. You see my family's always lived here. Mum's always lived in Bethnal Green. I was bred and born here.' Mrs Arding agreed: 'I was bred and born in Bethnal Green and my parents and their parents before them: no, I wouldn't leave Bethnal Green, I wouldn't take a threepenny bus ride outside Bethnal Green.' In two key sentences, Young tried to sum up what had 'struck one observer from outside': 'Bethnal Green has a sense of community; it has a sense of history; it has a kinship system.

These are all independent variables, and yet in this district they are closely connected in such a way that each reinforces the other.'

It was utterly different 12 miles away:

> Debden is separated from Bethnal Green by half an hour in the train and an age in behaviour. Instead of the bustle and shouting of the street markets, there are the hygienic halls of a few multiple stores. Instead of the fierce loyalties of the turnings, there are the strung-out streets in which everyone is a stranger. In Debden the bevy of groups which surround the household has disappeared. Instead of the compact group of kin there is the geographically isolated household. Not that geography makes a gulf. Many families at Debden do preserve some contact with their relatives. But compared to the people of Bethnal Green, the families of Debden are on their own.

'In Bethnal Green you always used to have a little laugh on the doorstep but there is none of that in Debden,' a reluctant Debdenite told him. 'You're English, but you feel like a foreigner here, I don't know why. It's like being in a box to die here.' Above all Young was struck by the malign consequences of Debden's dearth of a public domain:

> In Bethnal Green the lack of space inside the home is compensated for by a rich variety of community provision, from pubs to cinemas, from clubs to markets. People are driven out of the home by its very inadequacy – the wife with no copper or bath to the wash-house or the public bath where she has dozens of other wives to gossip with, the husband with no space in the evenings to the fireside at the pub where he talks football with his cronies. In Debden things are the other way round. The homes have spaces, they have baths, hot water and gardens, and the community has virtually nothing. And so life is lived behind the garden gate and the front windows are shrouded by curtains.

Most symbolic of this privatised lifestyle was the television set – at this point in almost twice as many of Debden's households as Bethnal Green's. 'Instead of going out to the cinema or the pub, the family sits night by night around the magic screen in its place of honour,' Young wrote somewhat bitterly. 'Television is something which complements, and reinforces, the isolation of the immediate family and the lack of opportunities for community life. Its influence will not diminish.'

Young was also during 1953 laying plans for a new organisation. 'The Welfare State recognises that it is the common responsibility of all to relieve the material distress of anyone,' was how he began his proposal for what would become the Institute of Community Studies. 'What is much less widely recognised is the need, not only to relieve distress, but to prevent it.' And after defining the surest way of prevention as being to find out the best conditions for family and community life to flourish, he went on:

> Perhaps the outstanding need is for studies of family and community life in the working classes. Britain is still in significant respects two nations composed of the working classes on the one side and the expanding middle classes on the other, and there is consequently a very real danger that the one class will not understand the other. Failure of communication is particularly serious in so far as it affects the social services. If the middle-class people who draw up policy for the social services do not understand the needs of working-class people, these services will fail to achieve their purpose. Studies of working-class families and communities should therefore be particularly valuable as guides to social policy. This is the main reason why it is proposed that the new Institute should be set up in the working-class district of Bethnal Green.

'The Institute,' he added, 'will have another primary object: to make social science intelligible to the interested layman. Every effort will be made to keep reports free from the deplorable jargon which afflicts so much of sociology.' Young managed to secure adequate funding (soon coming primarily from the Ford Foundation), and the ICS was duly launched in January 1954.[13] From the start, Young's principal day-to-day colleague there was Peter Willmott, who like him had worked in Labour's research department and was an impressive, clear-eyed figure, with little of Young's increasingly emotional attachment to the virtues of the traditional working class.

The architectural zeitgeist was becoming ever more urbanist and Modernist, typified by the experience in 1953 of Ian Davis on his first day at a school of architecture:

I handed my tutor the usual form indicating name, age and home address: Hillside Drive, Edgware, Middlesex. He read my form and gave me a probing stare, followed by: 'I take it that you live in one of Edgware's semi-detached houses?' My affirmative prompted the observation that I should make early plans to move to a more civilised address, such as Camden Town. Later the same morning the First Year were gathered together for an initial briefing on the course and Modern Architecture in general. We were strongly recommended to find out about a Swiss architect called Le Corbusier, 'the greatest living architect in the world'. We were advised to read his books and visit his buildings as soon as possible. Thus, before our first coffee break, the process of indoctrination was well under way. Architecture in 1953 was to do with great events that happened in Marseilles (or for that matter Camden Town), but very definitely not in Edgware, Middlesex.

Or take the recollections of William Howell, one of the idealistic team in the LCC's Architect's Department that was designing the 11-storey Corbusierian slabs for the Alton West Estate. 'We went to Roehampton thinking we had a certain mission,' he explained in a radio interview in 1972. 'We felt this would turn the tide back from the suburban dream . . . A return to the excitement of the city . . . This is what we must do; we don't want to rush out and live in horrid little suburbs and semi-detached houses.' Why had they hated the suburban dream so much? 'Because,' he replied, 'we felt that it discarded the positive things from the city and got very little in exchange. We saw this in terms of the fact that we wouldn't want to go and live there because everything from the bright lights to the art galleries, the continental restaurants, in short "life", the thing one goes to the city for – it didn't seem to be happening out in the suburbs.'

Peter and Alison Smithson fully shared these sentiments, but with of course the 'streets-in-the-sky' twist that made them an unlikely, ultimately unwelcome ally of Michael Young in the cause of urban 'community'. 'It is the idea of the street that is important – the creation of effective group-spaces for filling the vital function of identification and enclosure making the socially vital life-of-the-street possible,' they declared in 1953's *Architectural Year Book*. It would take a while for streets in the sky to become a reality, which eventually they most famously did in Sheffield's Park Hill development. The City Architect there from early 1953 was J. Lewis Womersley, who in September addressed the Town and Country Planning Summer School in Bristol. After asserting that planners of new housing schemes should try to foster 'the friendliness of the slums', he continued:

> In it lies the essence of the community spirit which we planners talk about so glibly. These people like to talk to one another without dressing up and making special calls. The women like to sit on their doorsteps and chat on warm summer afternoons and their small children like to play together in a common garden outside their houses where they are safe from traffic.
>
> The terrace, the small house group round the square or garden, are ideal for these fundamental requirements. To fence each family in and to separate it from its neighbours is to completely misunderstand the problem by seeking to impose upper-class snob-idealism on the less inhibited members of the population.
>
> The policy for housing which should be pursued has to lie somewhere between that of the advocates of high flats for all city dwellers and the 12-to-the-acre adherents who claim that an area only the size of Devon would be used up if every family had a house and garden.

In Park Hill itself, there was little such compromise. The original idea had been to develop the whole, slum-ridden Park area in such a way that, in the words of Park Hill's historian, Christopher Bacon, 'the community and many of its existing buildings [including pubs, corner shops, small businesses, pigeon lofts and places to keep hens and pigs] and roads could be preserved', but, in a fateful decision, that plan was 'scrapped' in late 1953, and 'the idea now was to clear the whole area completely'. Jack Lynn – a young architect who, in tandem with another young architect, Ivor Smith, was most directly responsible for the ensuing Park Hill design, but always answerable to Womersley – would later rather wistfully recall: 'There were some misgivings among us that the community structure would be irrevocably upset, as indeed it was.' By 1954 the design had been completed for four huge blocks overlooking the city centre – blocks which long pedestrian bridges connected into one continuous building, with decks on every third floor.[14]

A further indication of the ascendancy of this bracing urbanism was the increasingly tarnished reputation of the new towns, hitherto almost sacrosanct flagships for the dispersionists. So linked were they with the 'New Jerusalem' aspirations of the Attlee government that the Tories throughout the 1950s were at best lukewarm towards them, authorising only one new one (Cumbernauld in Scotland) and on the whole denying the existing new towns proper financial resources, let alone much in the way of encouragement. 'What a mad venture,' Macmillan reflected privately after a visit to Basildon in May 1952. 'No water; no sewerage; no river to pollute; no industry – and jolly few houses.' Just over a year later, the leading architectural journalist J. M. Richards launched a devastating attack. 'It is a sad moment to have reached,' he declared in the *Architectural Review*, 'when we have to acknowledge the failure of the new towns. But someone must candidly do so ...' Richards's general tone was regretful rather than vindictive – and his attack was particularly telling given that he was far from an out-and-out 'hard' Modernist – but there was a distinct edge as he accused the architects of the new towns of 'eating up valuable acres of agricultural land', of 'scattering houses along either side of draughty expanses of roadway' and of 'marooning the unhappy housewife on the distant rim of their sentimental green landscapes so that she has to tramp for miles with her shopping basket and is altogether cut off from the neighbourliness of closely built-up streets'. The usual champions of the new towns, headed by the indefatigable Frederic Osborn, predictably sprang to their defence. But even Osborn's great American friend, Lewis Mumford, was disobliging enough to observe in the *New Yorker* in October 1953, after a summer visit to Britain, that 'monotony and suburbanism' were the result of their rather unimaginative design, adding that 'where the open spaces gape too widely, and dispersal is too constant, the people lack a stage for their activities and the drama of their daily life lacks sharp focus'. In short: 'Because the new planners were mainly in revolt against congestion and squalor, rather than in love with urban order and co-operation, the New Towns do not yet adequately reveal what the modern city should be.'[15]

The actual experience of living in the new towns was inevitably mixed. Oral histories of the early settlers at Harlow have evoked a distinct sense of isolation (in particular, young wives missing

Mum), of taking a long time to get used to the open-plan design of the houses, and of dismay at the smallness of the kitchens in terms of fitting cookers, fridges and washing machines. Moreover, in new towns like Hemel Hempstead where there was already an established old town, there tended to be very little integration between the two populations. 'A town within a town without adequate mixing', was how a *Daily Telegraph* report in 1952 put it, while one early Stevenage resident recalled how 'we used to get some terrible looks from the Old Towners when they saw our shoes covered in mud'. As for the original ideal of integration between the social classes, that was proving by the mid-1950s to be increasingly unattainable, not least because of the distinctly sniffy attitude of the middle class. 'Senior management tended to look for a house outside the new town,' recalled a member of Stevenage Development Corporation about these early, formative years. 'If they didn't want to live in a village, then by and large their wives did.' The managers, he added, 'tended not to want to live in what they regarded as council estates', but 'preferred to pay a lot more for inferior housing, sometimes outside the town'. And even when a new town like Crawley did, under pressure from central government, allow a higher proportion of private housing, it still proved a hard sell to attract middle-class settlers.

Yet there was a positive side, albeit largely under-publicised. Above all, there continued to be, for the great majority of newcomers, the sheer satisfaction of moving somewhere that had, broadly speaking, adequate domestic facilities and a sense of space outside the home – space that was especially valued in terms of what it offered children. 'Moving from Lewisham in 1953 was wonderful,' recalled John Brian about Crawley. 'I was only nine and we had the River Mole with rainbow trout, horses, rabbits, all manner of wildlife and forests to play in with hectic construction going on all around. It was just amazing . . .' For young wives, moreover, the sense of isolation could lessen once they had their first baby. 'Pram Town' soon became the nickname for Harlow, and one of its historians notes how young women came 'into contact with each other as they tramped over the mud fields pushing their large prams to the shops and the baby clinics before the roads were made up'. There was also quite strong social cohesion when it came to trying to attain specific, practical, communal objectives. This was particularly the case in Stevenage, including a sustained, widely supported campaign after it seemed that the original plans for an up-to-date pedestrianised town centre were, under pressure from sceptical large traders like Woolworths, being abandoned – without any consultation with the recently established Town Forum, intended to encourage dialogue between the planners and the planned-for. Following appeals to the press and the ministry, a crowded public meeting was held at Stevenage Town Hall in January 1954, resulting in a unanimous, enthusiastic vote for a pedestrian centre, which eventually came to pass.[16]

What about the LCC's out-county estates? Was the prevailing atmosphere really as melancholic and lifeless as Young suggested it was at Debden? The largest of these overspill estates – in all of which flats formed only a smallish proportion of the housing stock – was Harold Hill in Essex; among its 25,000 or so inhabitants by late 1953 was the writer Sid Chaplin, still working for the National Coal Board's *Coal* magazine. 'Fully centrally heated and controlled by a thermostat which works with uncanny silent efficiency,' he reported to a friend, while his wife and children enjoyed the large garden. Maureen Kent's family was also in Harold Hill, having moved from the East End in 1952. Her mother, she recalled, had been 'convinced that the climate would be healthier for my brother and I, rather than the London street and traffic'. In Harold Hill, where the Coronation celebrations did much to help new neighbours get to know each other, 'they were, by and large, friendly people whose main concern was their own family and home with a great deal of pride in the appearance of house and garden'; but with 'only one parade of small shops within walking distance', her mother 'missed the street markets so a visit to Romford market once a month was a must', involving 'a half-hourly bus some 20 minutes walk away'. Overall, 'we were very content with life at Harold Hill for the next few years, despite the lack of amenities' – notwithstanding that Maureen and her brother never quite attained the rosy cheeks that her mother had admired on some children during her first visit there.

Another of the out-county estates was Borehamwood in Hertfordshire, like all the others predominantly single-class, ie skilled working-class. 'Notes on Life in a London Satellite' was the title of the journal that an inquisitive, rather puritanical *Observer* journalist, Cyril Dunn, kept while he and his family lived there in 1953–4. A couple of more or less exasperated early entries emphasised the difficulties of an estate still undergoing teething problems:

> What we want are the ordinary facilities that make urban life tolerable. This imprecisely identified creation – neither a suburb nor a New Town – has an urban population, administered & serviced as if it were a village. It is governed by a rural district council. Bus service of infuriating inadequacy. No telephones. Assumption that Estate people don't use telephones. Qs at the kiosk. Stretches of rural blackness, morning & night. Police. Schools. Children left at bus stop. If this is overspill, why not pour some metropolitan resources out with it?
>
> The kiddies have no playgrounds. Odd that in a place where half the population is well under school-leaving age there should be no special provision for children. Every evening at least a dozen children play in the road outside this house. They sound like a hundred. Within a few yards are two vast school playing fields, but from these the Authorities exclude the kiddies. The main playground is the houses in course of construction. A favourite game – to proceed from A to B in follow-my-leader style without touching the ground. As the house-walls grow, the kiddies are frequently well above ground-level and it speaks well for their chamois-like agility that they rarely suffer any really serious injury. But as houses are finished and occupied, the kiddies are squeezed into the streets. They are not allowed to play much in their own gardens: the flowers are not for them to kick. More might be done for them if they had the vote. But they show few signs of minding.

In the course of the winter, Dunn became almost obsessed by the intractable problems of building a community from scratch. 'Community?' he asked rhetorically. 'Building just *houses* and a few shops – like building the auditorium of a theatre & no stage – and then making a lot of speeches about "the new theatre", "the problems of the new theatre" and occasionally getting irritated with the audience for not showing a spirited appreciation of the play.'

Yet it was not just the absence of facilities that vexed Dunn, a theoretically strong supporter of the working class who in practice found it left something to be desired. 'Parson deeply moved by hearing children sing "Maybe it's because I'm a Londoner," ' he recorded. 'Yet it's *this* parochial chauvinistic ill-founded conceit that works *against* new community. Won't build a new community until *forget* they're Londoners & try to be proud of being B Woodsmen.' And by early 1954, after noting that all the various 'community' organisations, including the Community Centre itself, were 'failures', he had reached a conclusion that combined pessimism and pique:

> I am not at all convinced that the Estate people *want* an organised community life. They are inclined to 'keep themselves to themselves' and almost everything in their lives has encouraged them to do so, however gregarious they may have been in the communities from which they came here. There is only one small cinema; in the absence of an Odeon, many of our neighbours have rented a TV set. For this they pay 16/- a week. If they spend up to 5/- a week on the pools, that's a pound a week out of an average wage of £8. They can scarcely afford any other, communal entertainment; and all the time they are acquiring the settled habit of staying in. Having come from years of living in one room, most families can have only a limited amount of furniture. We suspect that we have not been invited back by the neighbours we have entertained because they are insufficiently proud of their homes. Besides, the rooms are too tiny for big parties. And then there are the kiddies. They are usually too small to be left alone at night; they certainly never are by our neighbours. If M. [his wife] invites a young Mum for afternoon tea, it's a safe bet that she'll bring the kiddies as well. And as party manners are not a common attribute of the Estate children, inviting Mum for afternoon tea involves a special effort of the will.

'It may be,' Dunn added, 'that only time can make a community. To create a community out of thousands of adult strangers must need a very special creative effort . . .'[17]

———

The Magyar magicians were destroying England on 25 November 1953 just as Lord Hailsham opened a two-day House of Lords debate. This followed the recent White Paper that had recommitted the Tory government to commercial television, though now to be supervised by a BBC-style 'Second Authority'. No one doubted Hailsham's political loyalty, but he was adamant that 'you destroy the principle of public service, without securing the advantages of private enterprise, by trying to create competition between a public service and something else which is not a public service'. His eventual peroration could not have been bettered by Lord Reith himself:

> We are fighting for our lives in the present generation, no less than in the period of the war. During the period of the war, when in Europe men had to suffer the peril of death to hear the truth, there was a voice of freedom to which attention was universally paid. It was the voice of Britain and it was the voice of Britain's public service broadcasts. Are we now to condemn this as a dangerous monopoly, as a weapon which we tremble to use in peace as in war? Are objective truth, objective justice, objective standards of duty and of conduct so utterly unworthy of advertisement that we must hand over to purely commercial interests the greatest instrument for good that has been devised since the printing press?

'They are very high-minded, very sincere – but so were Cromwell and his Puritans,' countered the Postmaster General, Earl de la Warr, about the government's critics. 'These people probably feel that they could run our lives extremely well. But I do not think the British people have the slightest intention of living like that . . .' Later that afternoon, the Wembley humiliation over, the Archbishop of Canterbury proclaimed his hostility to the very notion of more programmes on the nation's screens: 'I ask: Is it wise to multiply opportunities of spending time in this way at the expense of other possible occupations for reasonable and intelligent persons? So I ask: Do we really need more television? And my answer is, so far: No, we do not.'

Next day, at the end of a debate that had seen the biggest turnout of peers since the American loan debate in 1946, the government comfortably won the vote by 157 to 87. The *Manchester Guardian* – hostile to the breach of the BBC's monopoly – dubbed the Tory peers as the government's 'herd of dumb, driven cattle'. Soon afterwards, the Commons had their own two-day debate. It ran along predictable enough lines, with perhaps Anthony Wedgwood Benn's the most memorable contribution. 'The burden of our argument,' he declared, was that 'under commercial television there is no room for those who are in television because they believe in its capacity for improving itself in that medium and making a programme for its own sake.' And after asserting that 'any programme on commercial television of any country is like a wounded man who has to be carried on a stretcher by his sponsors one at each end' – on which principle 'we are bound to get more and more programmes appealing to mass audiences' – he went on to warn that 'Ted Ray and Terry-Thomas are going to have to look to their laurels against the canned entertainment programme of Bob Hope and Jack Benny.'[18] Again, the government won the vote, and the Reithian nightmare moved one stage closer.

If the herbivorian establishment shuddered, there was reassurance in December for the carnivores. Over the autumn it had emerged that two of the financial world's outsiders, Charles Clore and the property developer Harold Samuel, were between them seeking to engineer the takeover of the Savoy group of hotels, including Claridges and the Berkeley as well as the Savoy itself. This was a source of considerable consternation to many leading City figures. Not only did they (like Churchill) greatly value the hospitality of these places, but the Clore/Samuel move was an ominous sign that the aggressive takeover bid was becoming a regular part of financial life, an assault in fact on the accepted norm of keeping things in the club. However, through some complicated manoeuvres masterminded by the Savoy's Hugh Wontner and much abetted by the stockbroking firm Cazenove, the bid was thwarted. The dominant mood in the City was one of relief – a mood encouraged by the Bank of England, whose Governor, Kim Cobbold, had been strongly urging the banks 'to use special caution in respect of any invitations coming before them which appear to be connected with these take-over operations', on the grounds that 'in some at least there would seem to be a considerable speculative element'. Accordingly, with the bankers compliant, the nasty, unpredictable threat of hostile takeovers was for the moment stayed.

An altogether less resistible rise under way by 1953 was, against the helpful background of full employment, that of what would eventually become known as the fifth estate. 'The most warm-hearted movement in the whole of this country,' was how Wedgwood Benn on 11 December described the trade-union movement to an *Any Questions?* audience in Waterlooville, a statement greeted with repeated laughter. Three days later the warm-hearted National Union of Railwaymen called, in the outraged words of the journalist and television personality W. J. Brown, 'a strike on the railways to start next Sunday – 4 days before Xmas day!' He added that 'the Railwaymen have, as a matter of fact, a good case on wages', but that 'the choice of this date will put the whole country up against them'. 'Back to 1926' was the *Financial Times*'s dramatic headline, with the paper declaring on Tuesday the 15th that 'there can be no pretence that the railwaymen's conduct is anything but extremely irresponsible'.

Wednesday evening, however, saw a dramatic intervention. From the outset of his return to power, Churchill had been determined to keep on cordial terms with organised labour, a determination reinforced in recent months by increasing signs of industrial militancy, and this dispute was no exception. 'We cannot have a railway strike, it would be so disturbing to all of us,' he flatly informed his Chancellor, Rab Butler. 'You will never get home, nobody will be able to see their wives.' Churchill knew he could rely on his Minister of Labour, the emollient Sir Walter Monckton, and shortly before midnight Monckton compelled General Sir Brian Robertson, the retired army administrator recently appointed to take charge of the British Transport Commission, to yield to the union demands. 'Walter and I have settled the railway strike so you won't be troubled any more,' Churchill over the phone informed the absent Butler. 'On what terms have you settled it?' asked Butler. 'Theirs, old cock!' was the insouciant reply. 'We did not like to keep you up.' Monckton would subsequently claim that it had been Churchill and Butler who had been 'weak', wanting 'peace at any price'. But either way, there was no doubt about the Churchillian dictat.

'Monckton has done wonderfully well,' was Macmillan's immediate reaction. 'There will be quite a price to pay – but we all had the impression that public opinion favoured the railwaymen.' Most of the press did not disagree. 'Peace With Honour' was the Conservative-supporting *Sheffield Telegraph*'s headline; the *FT*, though conceding that the settlement was undeniably inflationary and liable to open the floodgates to other unions, insisted that 'managements as a whole must redouble their efforts to increase productivity' and that 'in the last resort, theirs is the responsibility'; while *The Times*, in a bland editorial on 'Better Railways', refrained from outright criticism of the government and hoped that 'this time the promises of higher productivity are not illusory'. Only the *Economist* really put the boot in, using terms like 'funk', 'retreat from reality' and, most pejorative of all, 'Munich'.[19] Over the years it would become one of the mainstays of Thatcherite contemporary history that the government's craven climbdown in December 1953 had set the tone for the next quarter-century of industrial relations – a version given added teeth by Andrew Roberts's coruscating 1994 essay on Monckton in his *Eminent Churchillains*. But as Churchill himself had observed, most people just wanted to get home, not least five days before Christmas.

For this year's Christmas film, there was a runaway winner. On that busy last Wednesday in November, Rank held a sneak preview of *Trouble in Store* – Norman Wisdom's screen debut – at the Gaumont, Camden Town. The first big laugh (in a screenplay originally written by Michael Foot's wife Jill Craigie) came at the sight of Jerry Desmonde in his limousine and little Norman being left behind on his bike, and at the end the audience cheered and clapped. 'If you don't laugh at Norman's antics as the downtrodden worker in a big store, trying to get promotion to a window dresser, there is something wrong with your sense of fun,' insisted the *Daily Mirror*'s reviewer some three weeks later. Not all the critics were completely bowled over. Although acknowledging that 'he is a funny, endearing little man with a big future', Virginia Graham in the *Spectator* thought Wisdom's style overly 'knockabout' and wanted him to learn from the performance in the film of Margaret Rutherford, her humour 'a blend of tones and half-tones graded with infinite cunning'. *The Times* too, though praising 'an unsophisticated British farce with few inhibitions and, mercifully, no ideas above its station', thought it 'a mistaken kindness' to compare Wisdom, as the *Evening Standard* had done, to the early Charlie Chaplin: 'His ill-fitting suit, his losing battles against authority, his air of battered chivalry outwardly support the comparison, but as yet Mr Wisdom relies more on grotesque appearance and manufactured situation than inner inspiration.'

Such reservations mattered not a jot as the film (featuring Wisdom's hit song 'Don't Laugh At Me') was given a blanket release on the vast Odeon circuit and over the next month broke almost all box-office records, including at 51 out of the 67 London cinemas where it played. 'The most astonishing phenomenon in British post-war entertainment,' was how *Picture Post* at the end of January called 'the little man' with 'the wondering face and the battered destiny'. Wisdom at this time was also starring every night at the huge Empress Hall, London, in the panto *Sinbad the Sailor on Ice*. 'He hardly does anything at all, except run about on the enormous stage and in the aisles, shaking an impotent fist at the audience,' noted the magazine. 'He skates a little, sings a little, drives about in an old yellow car. Yet whatever he does, or fails to do, the public responds ecstatically.'[20]

The balance between two rival media was shifting irrevocably. 'It was a T.V. Christmas, which isn't my idea of Christmas,' recorded Judy Haines on Christmas Day, but not long afterwards she was enjoying 'a very fine performance' by Googie Withers in *The Deep Blue Sea*. 'I don't understand unfaithfulness in marriage though & feel it is unnecessary.' The New Year saw the first weather forecasters on television, the Yorkshireman George Cowling and the Londoner T. H. Clifton. 'Both have a nice sense of humour, though Mr Clifton sometimes forgets to relax,' was one viewer's response. 'But he and his colleague are so understanding, and have made up to me for all the affronts I suffered in the old days when I listened to the evening forecasts for *farmers* and *shipping* and we poor housewives were forgotten.' About the same time, BBC's audience research reflected how the new series of *Have a Go!* had had 'an audience of 30%', which was 'as relatively good in these days of television competition as the previous series in 1951/2' – adding not only that 'the reaction of listeners was more mixed than in the past' but that 'there were complaints of staleness in the material and of some uneasiness of manner in Wilfred Pickles himself'.

One should not exaggerate the shift – 'the most relaxed and comforting time of my day', was how Madge Martin in January referred to 'my precious "Woman's Hour" ' – but at the end of that month there was just a whiff of the last hurrah about *The National Radio Awards of 1953–4*, sponsored by the *Daily Mail* and going out live on the Light Programme from the Scala Theatre. Franklin Engelmann was the MC, Sidney Torch and his Orchestra supplied the music, and Gilbert Harding almost inevitably won the award (voted for by listeners) as Personality of the Year. 'The Most Entertaining Programme' was a tied vote between *The Archers* and *Take It From Here*, with the latter's stars doing a special Glums sketch for the ceremony. One exchange had a particular resonance:

DICK: Dad, Eth doesn't like wireless. We're not having one in our home.

JIM: (AGHAST) You're not having a wireless? Oh, son, a home's not a home without a wireless. Think of the long winter evenings . . . ! What are you going to listen to while Eth's talking?

JUNE: I think wireless is just a drug, Mr Glum.

JIM: Oh, that's nice, isn't it? So me and my family are just drug-haddocks! You listen to me, Eth – wireless is a – is a – a modern *miracle*, it is.

JUNE: But there's other forms of entertainment, Mr Glum.

JIM: Who's talking about entertainment? I'm talking about the BBC! The BBC is part of the English heritage. Like suet pudding and catarrh.

The future lay elsewhere, and *Picture Post* had already predicted its 'bright stars of Television in 1954'. They included Morecambe and Wise ('streamlined patter and natural, apparently oblivious, craziness', but no Christian names given), Benny Hill ('combines personal charm with a gift for mimicry and self-effacing comedy') and Billie Whitelaw ('made an immediate impact on viewers when Caryl Doncaster cast her last year as the young wife in the series, *The Pattern of Marriage*'). 'She takes direction well,' Doncaster told the magazine, 'and she has a quality of sincerity which is essential for television. You can't use tricks on TV – and get away with it.'[21]

By early 1954 two national champions were in trouble. 'Awful about that Comet crash in Mediterranean,' noted Marian Raynham on 12 January, two days after all 35 on board had perished off the island of Elba. BOAC had no alternative but to suspend all Comet services while technical examinations took place. 'There could be no doubt of the shock it gave everybody,' reflected a melancholic Raymond Streat a week after the crash:

It was not merely that some people had been killed, though that always shocks everybody's feelings. It was the awful thought that the Comet aeroplane might not be the successful achievement of British scientists and engineers which we have all believed it to be in the past few years. In a very special way it has comforted us as a country and a people during a period in which so many emblems and tokens of our former power and glory had been stripped away from us.

The other troubled champion was Churchill. The *Daily Mirror* had seldom been friendly, but its headline on the 26th, 'Should Churchill Retire?', took its attacks to a new level. Worse, because less predictable, occurred a week later, on 3 February, with the appearance of the latest *Punch*. On one page was a large, striking drawing (unsigned, but by Leslie Illingworth) of an aged, weary Churchill, with the caption, 'Man goeth forth to his work and to his labours until the evening'; opposite was a signed piece by the editor, Malcolm Muggeridge, about 'Bellarius', reputedly an emperor in ninth-century Byzantium. 'The spectacle of him clutching wearily at all the appurtenances and responsibilities of an authority he could no longer fully exercise,' he wrote in Gibbonian style, 'was to his admirers infinitely sorrowful, and to his enemies infinitely derisory.' The magazine in the past year had sharpened up under Muggeridge, but this was something else. '*Punch* goes everywhere,' an infinitely hurt Churchill next day told his doctor Lord Moran. 'I shall have to retire if this sort of thing goes on. I must make a speech in a fortnight's time; it is necessary when things like this happen.'[22]

13

Can You Afford It, Boy?

Things were moving on the literary front. ' "Can't you tell me, Mr Lumley, just what it is that you don't like about the rooms?" ' was the opening sentence, set in the dingy Midland town of 'Stotwell', of John Wain's first novel *Hurry on Down*, published in October 1953. 'There was no mistaking the injured truculence in the landlady's voice, nor her expression of superhuman patience about to snap at last. Charles very nearly groaned aloud. Must he explain, point by point, why he hated living there? Her husband's cough in the morning, the way the dog barked every time he went in or out, the greasy mats in the hall? Obviously it was impossible.' Wain's own background was solidly middle-class – son of a Potteries dentist, Oxford, lecturer in English at Reading University – but his hero Charles Lumley was, in the words of the *TLS*, 'in flight from his parents, from academic culture and gentility, from a manner of speech and a way of living'. The review quoted his resolution as a window cleaner – one of several defiantly non-middle-class jobs during a series of picaresque, unmetropolitan adventures – to 'form no roots in his new stratum of society, but remain independent of class, forming roots only with impersonal things such as places and seasons'. The novel's reception was broadly positive – 'Mr Wain, in his grim and gritty and tough-minded way, can be very funny indeed,' reckoned Walter Allen in the *New Statesman* – but some reviewers could not refrain from moralising. 'Mr Wain endows his hero with an obscure desire to get outside society, or to live in it without belonging to it, or something of the sort,' observed Graham Hough in the *Listener*. 'He has not thought very hard about this, and I don't think you need either.' For Geoffrey Bullough in the *Birmingham Post*, the 'weakness' of a 'very amusing' book lay in the hero's 'drifting negativeness'. Still, *The Times* was able to offer reassurance. The hero 'gets mixed up in some very queer adventures indeed', it noted, before adding that 'this is not a sordid book'.[1]

The following month another grammar-school product, Dylan Thomas, died in New York. Barely two months later, on Monday, 25 January 1954, his 'play for voices', *Under Milk Wood*, had its British premiere on the Third Programme, starring the young Richard Burton in the part Thomas himself would have played. It proved, despite or perhaps because of its plotlessness, a great moment in radio history. 'I was spellbound from start to finish,' declared the *Listener*'s Martin Armstrong, by 'the gradually unfolding impression of a living community' (a small fishing town in south Wales called Llareggub, spelled forwards) and a 'dazzling command of language which kept the listener in a state of delighted surprise'. William Salter in the *New Statesman* found it 'lyrical, impassioned and funny, an *Our Town* given universality', asserting that 'by comparison with anything broadcast for a very long time, it exploded on the air like a bomb – but a life-giving bomb'. Listeners mainly agreed, with the broadcast getting 'the exceptionally high Appreciation Index of 81' and being 'received with a rare enthusiasm'. 'True,' the audience research report added, 'there was a small minority to whom it seemed unedifying, verbose or confusing. But for most of the audience, the wit, vigour and beauty of the writing combined with a flawless production to make a memorable broadcast.' Sadly, Thomas's home town of Laugharne was unable to receive the broadcast, and the Welsh Home Service declined to repeat it, on the grounds that it was not 'for family or home listening'. 'The chapel influence,' plausibly reckons one of Thomas's biographers, 'balked at suggestions of Welsh hypocrisy and saw only malicious satire.'[2]

Thomas's admirers did not include Kingsley Amis, then a 31-year-old lecturer in English at the University College of Swansea. 'So that crazy Welch fellow has paid the supreme penalty,' he wrote to Philip Larkin soon after the news of Thomas's death. 'Many were the long faces here, and much anger there was with the English department for keeping their faces short.' He amplified in a further letter: 'I think him a bad poet and a bad influence . . . I cannot mourn his passing. A Bloomsburyite to his *dirty* fingernails, that was him, and only sentimentalising, ignorant horsepiss about his Welchness can conceal the fact.' Two months later, on the same day as the *Under Milk Wood* broadcast, Amis's first novel, *Lucky Jim*, was published by Gollancz. That evening he and his wife Hilly went out for a celebratory dinner, presumably missing the Third's finest. 'Can you afford it, boy?' the Welsh waiter asked after he ordered a bottle of Veuve Clicquot.

As it happened, a hostile review had already appeared the day before in the *Sunday Times*. An 'ignorant buffoon' was how the novelist Julian Maclaren-Ross dismissed the central character Jim Dixon, with Amis found guilty of confusing 'farce with comedy, schoolboy grubbiness with wit'. Thereafter, Amis was able to relax. John Metcalf in the *Spectator* on 29 January called the novel 'that rarest of rare good things: a funny book'; Allen in the *New Statesman* acclaimed Amis as 'a novelist of formidable and uncomfortable talent'; Anthony Powell in *Punch* (the Churchill issue) reckoned him 'the first promising young novelist who has turned up for a long time'; and John Betjeman in the *Daily Telegraph* on 5 February thought *Lucky Jim* the funniest novel he had read since Evelyn Waugh's *Decline and Fall*. A certain staidness might have been expected from the *TLS*, but its reviewer found the book 'often richly comic' and 'extremely enjoyable', while detecting in Dixon part of an emerging pattern: 'He is the anti- or rather sub-hero who is beginning to figure increasingly as the protagonist of the most promising novels written by young men since the war – in, for example, the work of Mr Ernest Frost, Mr William Cooper, and Mr John Wain – an intelligent provincial, who, after getting a scholarship and an Oxford or Cambridge degree, finds his social position both precarious and at odds with his training.' Arguably the most pregnant response came, late in the day, from a rare female reviewer. Amis, reflected the historical novelist-cum-biographer Hester W. Chapman in the *Listener* in March, 'knows so much already about the vagaries of the human heart that one feels a little anxious that his eye should one day become dulled, his resilience slacken'.[3]

At the risk of reductionism, where exactly was Jim Dixon to be 'placed' in the political, social and cultural landscape of 1954? The *TLS* reviewer made an attempt, but it was Amis himself some four years later – in a surprisingly full response to an inquisitive American academic – who offered the definitive analysis:

Dixon is supposed to be the son of a clerk, an office worker (like myself). He is a Labour Party socialist and probably took part in student politics when younger (like myself). One is meant to feel that he did well enough in his student academic career to make it natural for him to become a history lecturer, which he did without much thought. Though he finds the academic world decreasingly to his taste, he sticks at it because he does think university teaching an important job, and also because he is afraid of venturing out on his own. I think he is a plausible figure in his world: there are certainly many like him in that they are the first generation in their families to have received a university education, they have won their way up by scholarships all through, they are not the conventional Oxford–Cambridge academic type, they don't embrace the manners, customs and pastimes of that type (sherry, learned discussion, tea-parties with the Principal's wife, chamber concerts) but stick to their own, to the ones their non-academic contemporaries share (beer, arguments in pubs, amorous behaviour at – and outside – dances, jazz). Dixon has seen, throughout his life, power and position going to people who (he suspects) are less notable for their ability than their smooth manners, their accents, the influence they or their fathers can wield. The money thing is less important; Dixon is hard-up himself, and is a bit suspicious of the rich, but is far more so of Oxford-accented 'culture'.

That was surely the crux. 'If he were closely questioned about this,' the Oxford-educated ingrate concluded with a typically light touch, 'he would probably admit in the end that culture is real and important and ought not to be made the property of a sort of exclusive club which you can only enter if you come from the right school – culture ought to be available to everyone who can use it; but such an avowal would be very untypical of him and you would probably have to get him very drunk first.'

Lucky Jim was a commercial success from the first (though Amis long afterwards pointed out that 'it did not start to reach the public substantially for a year or so'), and such a perspective did much to explain its appeal, especially to younger readers, quite apart from the humour and sheer enjoyability. 'I read *Lucky Jim* under the best possible circumstances, which is to say, surreptitiously,' Brian Aldiss recalled:

At that time I was working in Parker's bookshop in Oxford. Literacy was not encouraged on the staff, who were instructed to dust but not to read the store of volumes. So my illicit copy had to be carried inside my jacket and snatched at at intervals, while I pretended new-found interest in the Logic section or the Nicaean Fathers. I literally could not put the book down, or it would have been lost behind rows of eighteenth-century sermons.

To say the novel made me laugh is to claim too little. I laughed all right, and still do [in 1990]. I also identified strongly with Dixon. Like Dixon, I was in an undesirable situation (from which I hoped my writing would enable me to escape), like him I felt under-educated; and, like him, I had some interest in women and drink. I can't think of any novel which ever spoke to me so directly. Many of my friends, in those ghastly postwar years, felt the same.

From the start, though, it stirred a strong counter-reaction – arguably already signalled by Victor Gollancz's initial reluctance to publish on the grounds that it was 'vulgar and anti-cultural'. Anthony Powell remembered how, after publication, it 'seemed to some an unforgivable attack on civilised cultural values', how indeed 'in certain quarters *Lucky Jim* was looked on quite simply as a shower of brickbats hurled by a half-educated hooligan at the holiest and most fragile shrines of art and letters, not to mention music'. One phrase, in particular, stuck. 'He heard the clinking of a plug-chain, then the swishing of tap-water. Welch, or his son, or Johns was about to take a bath. Which one it was was soon settled by the upsurge of a deep, untrained voice into song. The piece was recognizable to Dixon as some skein of untiring facetiousness by filthy Mozart.' Given that Amis himself had become in recent years a huge admirer of Mozart, the mandarin assumption of philistinism was unfortunate.[4]

For Larkin, so long Amis's literary mentor, but still himself little known as a poet and now working as a librarian in the 'frightful hole' of the Queen's University, Belfast, this was a difficult time. He had been invaluable to his friend during the novel's prolonged gestation, carefully going through at least one draft and sharpening its focus, and just before publication read a finished copy. 'Of course *Lucky Jim* sends me into prolonged fits of howling laughter,' he wrote on 23 January to his friend Patsy Strang. 'It is miraculously and intensely funny, with a kind of spontaneity that doesn't tire the reader at all. *Apart* from being funny, I think it is somewhat over-simple.' On 3 February, having just read Powell's encomium in *Punch*, Larkin wrote again to Strang. 'I suppose I'd better mention *Lucky Jim*,' was how he reluctantly, itch-scratchingly returned to the subject. 'Well, well. Success, success. I must say, he is doing all he can to sound nice about it. And of course the Kingsley humour I think quite unrivalled, quite wonderful. It's in the general thinness of imagination that he falls down . . .'

What Larkin did not mention in either letter was that he, following the birth of Amis's daughter Sally on 17 January, had almost at once written a touching poem for her, 'Born Yesterday', dated the 20th – the last thirteen lines telling a rarely told truth:

> May you be ordinary;
> Have, like other women,
> An average of talents:
> Not ugly, not good-looking,
> Nothing uncustomary
> To pull you off your balance,
> That, unworkable itself,
> Stops all the rest from working.
> In fact, may you be dull –
> If that is what a skilled,
> Vigilant, flexible,
> Unemphasised, enthralled
> Catching of happiness is called.[5]

Ultimately, as neither man could yet know, it was the work of Larkin – unassuming laureate of the quotidian – that would last. *Ars longa, vita brevis*, as both assuredly did know.

A THICKER CUT

To my stepfather, Bill Hunt

PART ONE

Tolerably Pleasing

'Problems which will arise if many coloured people settle here,' was how Winston Churchill introduced (in the paraphrasing words of the Cabinet minutes) the Conservative government's discussion of 'Coloured Workers' on Wednesday, 3 February 1954. 'Are we to saddle ourselves with colour problems in UK?' he asked. 'Attracted by the Welfare State. Public opinion in UK won't tolerate it once it gets beyond certain limits.' The decisive contribution came from Sir David Maxwell Fyfe, the Home Secretary. After explaining that the non-white population (predominantly from the West Indies) now stood at some 40,000 – sharply up from 7,000 before the war, but still only a few thousand newcomers each year – he weighed up controls: 'We have to admit in Parliament the *purpose* of legislation was to control admission of coloureds. There is a case on merit for excluding riff-raff. But politically it would be represented and discussed on basis of a colour limitation. We should be reversing age-long tradition that British subjects have right of entry to mother-country of Empire. We should offend liberals, also sentimentalists.' Accordingly, 'on balance, scale of the problem is such that we shouldn't take these risks today'. He finished with a shrewd, cynical thrust: 'The coloured populations are resented in Liverpool, Paddington and other areas – by those who come into contact with them. But those who don't are apt to take liberal view.'

Next day it was an entirely monocultural tragedy on which the Wigan Coroner conducted an inquest. Four brothers from Platt Bridge, aged between nine and thirteen, had the previous Saturday got three-quarters of the way across the frozen Perch Pond when the ice cracked – and all four boys drowned. Twelve-year-old Peter Gorton, also from Platt Bridge, had gone out sliding with them, initially on frozen puddles, but not on the ice. 'I told Frank [the oldest brother] I was not going on as my dad had told me not to,' he related. 'They all told me I was soft.' The Coroner, after sombrely recording verdicts of accidental death, observed: 'It is a great pity these four boys did not follow the example of the more cautious child who had been warned by his parents not to go on the ice.' Tellingly, though, he added: 'It is impossible to remove all danger from our lives and it might not be a good thing if all danger could be removed.'

Friday saw the Minister of Housing in a favourite position, the spotlight. Queen's Tower was the predictable name given to Birmingham's first 12-storey block of flats, in Duddeston; performing the opening ceremony, Harold Macmillan took the opportunity to announce the gratifying housing figures for 1953 – a record 318,779 completions. 'It is a good job, half done,' he continued. 'For can we honestly claim to be more than half-way when we haven't been able to tackle slum clearance for 14 years?' He then inspected the flats themselves, took tea with one of the tenants and was on his way. He left behind an optimistic mood, summed up by the Vicar of Duddeston in his parish magazine: 'I have already visited many of the newcomers, and I am pleased to say that they are happy in their new homes and are finding the surroundings tolerably pleasing.'

They were also newcomers, but not quite such new newcomers, at Adeyfield, part of Hemel Hempstead New Town. 'We must do something to wake the people up,' an exasperated Mr S. Douglas declared on Monday the 8th at a poorly attended meeting of the Adeyfield Neighbourhood Council in the Adeyfield Hall. 'There are people in this organisation and in others, about whom you get the nasty feeling that they are only in it for what they can get out of it. When they first join they are keen and helpful, but after a while they seem to become quite satisfied to sit at home, accept the decisions, and benefit from them.' What, he asked, was the reason for this distressing state of affairs? 'We are getting down to almost the only answer,' he went on. 'Television. People get home at night and just don't seem to have any desire to join in with the social activities.' Mr G. Brook Taylor, Public Relations Officer of the Development Corporation that ran the new town, then warned against becoming 'too gloomy' – 'When people come into a new town, they have a strong spirit of adventure and are very lively,' but 'once they have made a few contacts and friends, it is only natural that they should withdraw into their family life' – before a final, forthright contribution came from Mr D. Ritchie: 'An artificially stimulated organisation sheerly for the sake of getting together is a complete waste of time.'[1]

The following week, Tuesday the 16th, was honours time at Buckingham Palace. Among those knighted by the Queen Mother, with her daughter still away on a lengthy tour of the Commonwealth, were Jacob Epstein, the Football Association's A. Brook Hirst (so unshaken and unstirred about the recent humbling by the Hungarians), and 'the Prime Minister of Mirth' – aka George Robey, octogenarian veteran of the Edwardian music hall, but now wheelchair-bound and clutching his trademark small brown cane. Elsewhere in London that day, at the West Kensington headquarters of the catering firm J. Lyons and Co, there was unveiled what the *Evening News* called 'Britain's new electronic brain'. This was an early computer (though the report did not actually use that word) called LEO which 'works out a complicated wages statement involving numerous details for nearly 2,000 people employed at a bakery'. J.R.M. Simmons, largely responsible for its development, claimed that LEO was 'the only one of his kind on commercial work in the world' and would 'revolutionise the keeping of industrial accounts and records', being able to do the work of nearly 400 clerks. What did LEO look like? Disappointingly, the report merely noted that there was 'nothing at all to satisfy the romantic conception of a robot as a "mechanical man" ', and generally the emphasis was on reassurance: 'It cannot do anything except in response to instructions fed into it on punched cards. And the human hand and eye are needed to guide the controlling "nerve centre".' In short, LEO was 'not one of those machines which imaginative writers like to think may one day get out of hand and dominate the world'.

Instead, the more potentially disturbing news that Tuesday came from Birmingham. This was the announcement by Harry Watton, chairman of Birmingham Corporation's transport committee, that a ballot would be held of the city's bus workers (many of them Irish), asking the question, 'Have you any objection to the department employing coloured workers?' Watton himself, as controversy mounted over the next few days, was unapologetic. 'Our first task is to keep buses running,' he insisted. 'Although it is regrettable there should be objections among some bus crews to employing coloured workers it is a fact.' So too the workers' representative. 'The union has no objection to coloured people, a number of whom are already working in garages [about 28 of them, as mechanics or cleaners],' stated Harry Green, the Transport and General Workers' Union's district secretary. 'But we have been told that many of the 1,400 clippies would walk out if non-Europeans were introduced on platform staffs.' Eventually, on the 24th, the ballot was called off, though Green continued to get up to 300 letters a day, mainly anonymous and about evenly divided about the prospect of black conductors. As it turned out, Birmingham had already had a black bus driver, let alone conductor, for almost 20 years – Edward Irons, currently working the number 8 Inner Circle route. 'He is kindness itself, always has a smile for everyone, and is respected by everyone,' vouched a regular passenger, but the T&G's Green was still sceptical: 'How the 1,400 conductresses will react to working with coloured folk remains to be seen.'[2]

It also remained to be seen what was going to be done about the increasingly hot potato of homosexuality. On Friday the 19th, the maverick Tory backbencher Sir Robert Boothby made a widely reported speech in which he gave publicly the reasons he had given privately to Maxwell Fyfe for a royal commission to review the relevant laws. Describing homosexuality as 'a biological and pathological condition for which the victim is only to a small degree responsible', Boothby claimed that 'the existing laws dealing with homosexuality are medieval' and that 'what consenting adults do in privacy may be an issue between them and their Maker, but it is certainly not an issue between them and their Government'. Five days later, when the Cabinet discussed the twin subjects of homosexuality and prostitution, Maxwell Fyfe suggested that in both cases the time had perhaps indeed come for an inquiry, though without yet committing himself. 'Remember that we can't expect to put the whole world right with a majority of 18,' warned Churchill, and Maxwell Fyfe himself was no natural reformer. 'I am not going down in history,' he bluntly told Boothby, 'as the man who made sodomy legal.'[3]

The same day as Boothby's speech, there was domestic drama in Chingford. 'Reported leakage of gas in kitchen to North Thames Gas Board,' noted Judy Haines:

They came along almost at once. Leakage behind tiles! At tea-time, another representative called and estimated that cost of yanking up floor boards between hall and kitchen and replacing pipe would be approximately £5.10.0! I gasped. He asked that we telephone instructions tomorrow. Girls lost no time in informing Daddy Gas Man had been. His immediate reaction was, 'We'll have an electric cooker.' I knew he'd have an answer. I'm quite willing.

Next day, Saturday the 20th, was even more satisfactory: 'Abbé [her husband] and I went out to the Electric Showrooms & chose an Eastern Electric White Cooker. It looks lovely! Brought girls home a choc-ice each.'

The good times were coming, for earlier in the week the government had announced that meat and bacon rationing would at last end during the first half of July, in effect the final major step in the dismantling of the wartime rationing system. Arguably those good times had already started to arrive; yet when Nella Last in Barrow went shopping about the same time as the Haines girls were enjoying their choc-ices, the experience proved curiously deflating for a diarist (by now in her mid-sixties) who had recorded more faithfully than anyone the long years of austerity:

There was very little doing in the market. I reflected how 'blasé' we get & so quickly – though rising prices would account for 'indifference' to the piles of 'top grade Lakeland eggs' 3/3 a dozen? 'Best' bananas at 1/2, & two grades of 'seconds', one of brown skinned ones, were actually marked 6d a pound. Pork, rabbits, boiling fowls were plentiful. Meat too was apparently off ration with it getting towards the market closing. *Such* good woollen & rayon remnants left me utterly indifferent. I wish I could feel a bit more interest generally, things don't seem 'worth worrying over' & I so *quickly* tire.[4]

2

Butter is Off the Ration

'Every night the Harringay arena is packed; every night throngs of converts – mostly young people – crowd up at the end of the service to the bare space below the rostrum, thence to be conducted by "counsellors" to a room where they are interviewed and given tracts.' John Betjeman, writing soon after the start on 1 March of Billy Graham's Greater London Crusade, was as an Anglo-Catholic personally unsympathetic to the Evangelical, revivalist approach – 'the technique of microphones, massed choirs, trumpets and advertising campaigns' – but found in Graham himself 'a humble likeable young man who regards himself merely as an instrument of the Holy Ghost'. Another observer, Trevor Philpott, was there on the first night and noted how all 12,000 seats were filled, how the 2,000-strong choir comprised mainly young women and how several hundred converts came forward. Over the next 11 weeks or so, the arena continued night after night to be full to overflowing, with from late March landline relays to packed churches, halls and cinemas. There was also the nightly ritual on the way back from Harringay. 'The trains are packed with these singing multitudes,' a letter explained to the *Daily Telegraph*'s largely non-revivalist readership. 'One cannot fail to observe the effect it has on the passengers who board the trains at subsequent stations. After the first surprise many smile sympathetically and often enter into conversations; others begin with disapproving looks but soften considerably during the journey.' What accounted for the whole phenomenon? 'Many people', remarked Mollie Panter-Downes in her invariably shrewd 'Letter from London' in the *New Yorker*, linked it to anxiety about the hyrodgen bomb – tested by the Americans at Bikini Atoll on the very day that Graham began his crusade – and given that that explosion was some six hundred times as powerful as the bomb that had destroyed Hiroshima nine years earlier, it was a plausible connection.

Graham during his visit was careful not to be drawn on the vexed issue of homosexuality. 'I canNOT see what homosexuality has to do with the State,' Gladys Langford in north London had privately reflected in January, while in early March an interim report by the Church of England Moral Welfare Society, consisting of Anglican clergymen and doctors, had explicitly recognised that though homosexual acts were a sin in the eyes of the church, this did not mean that they should be treated as crimes punishable by the state. Soon afterwards, on 15 March, the eight-day trial began in Winchester of Lord Montagu of Beaulieu, his cousin Michael Pitt-Rivers and the *Daily Mail*'s Oxford-educated diplomatic correspondent Peter Wildeblood. 'Poor Wildeblood is sensitive, nervous, emotional and intelligent,' recorded the 'Bloomsbury' diarist Frances Partridge after a day at the Assizes. 'He clasped the edge of the dock with long thin fingers and listened intently to every question before quietly and thoughtfully replying.' The key prosecution witnesses were two airmen, John Reynolds and Edward McNally, who in reward for turning Queen's evidence were granted immunity despite having been involved in 24 other homosexual affairs. The proceedings were shot through with class, as when the prosecuting counsel, G. D. 'Khaki' Roberts, fruity-voiced and with a bottle of bright pink cough mixture always at hand, cross-examined Wildeblood:

It is a feature, is it not, that inverts or perverts seek their love associates in a different walk of life than their own?

I cannot accept that as a deduction. I have never heard any suggestion that that is the ordinary rule.

I mean, for instance, McNally was infinitely – he is none the worse for it – but infinitely your social inferior?

That is absolute nonsense.

Well, perhaps that is not a very polite way of answering my question.

I am sorry, I apologize.

Please do not apologize. I know very well you are under a great strain.

Nobody ever flung it at me during the War that I was associating with people who were infinitely my social inferiors.

At the end, after a summing-up in which Mr Justice Ormerod all but directed the jury to reach verdicts of guilty, there were prison sentences of between 12 and 18 months for all three. 'The case for the reform of the law as to acts committed in private between adults is very strong,' commented the *Sunday Times*, far from renowned at this time for its social liberalism. 'The case for an authoritative enquiry into it is overwhelming.'[1]

Another controversial topic had mercifully gone past the inquiry stage, for the time being at least. The Television Bill published by the government on 4 March contained, in Asa Briggs's words, 'far more don'ts than do's' and was aimed foursquare at defusing the opposition towards commercial television on the part of some Tory MPs. 'The ITA [Independent Television Authority] is to have greater supervisory powers than anybody had expected,' the *Economist* somewhat regretfully noted, while the proposed legislation made it unambiguously clear that there would not be US-style programme sponsorship, but instead 'spot ads' judiciously inserted in programmes at 'natural breaks'. None of this stopped some predictably bitter Parliamentary debates, but Richard Crossman's observation in May – two months before the bill became law – that 'there are far more Conservative voters who object to commercial television than Labour voters and there is no sign that the Labour Movement as such feels strongly about the fight against the Bill' was merely an acceptance of reality, by this time very much in line with opinion-polling evidence.

Increasingly, as sets mushroomed around the country and the prospect of a commercial rival to the BBC hove into view, there was a tendency, in both progressive and establishment circles, to disparage the medium itself. 'People are glued to their television sets and are more interested in the latest rude remark of Mr Gilbert Harding than in what is being said and done around them,' complained one of Labour's rising stars, Barbara Castle, in a March speech at Newtown in Wales, while in April a poignant picture by the diarist James Lees-Milne of the attritional struggles of an impoverished country gentleman called Major Edmeades – 'The place [Nurstead Court, near Gravesend] terribly down at heel, messy, smelly . . . I went on the roof. It is perished, tiles off, lead rotten, water pouring through in wet weather. No servants. Poor major! How are the gentry fallen . . .' – included the detail that 'he showed me some of his trim labourers' cottages, all with television'. That summer, after the art historian and unimpeachable upholder of high-cultural values Sir Kenneth Clark had been announced as the ITA's first chairman, he entered the dining room of the Athenaeum, as a guest, and was roundly booed. He may or may not have taken comfort from a letter published not long afterwards in *Picture Post* from Harry Ward of Evesham, Worcs: 'Sponsored TV, if not strangled at birth by the dead hand of the State, will give people what they want, and not what the "long hairs" think they jolly well ought to have. Heigho, then, for sponsored television. Bring on Les Girls – and the BBC can keep Science Review.'[2]

It was perhaps with the threat of commercial television in mind that the BBC on the second Thursday in April had already launched the Groves on the viewing public. 'Everything that happens *could* happen, but we shall show the highlights rather than the humdrum,' explained their creator, Michael Pertwee, in advance. The family, living in Hendon, comprised Dad (a middle-aged jobbing builder, played by Edward Evans, with steak and onions as his favourite food), warm, plain-speaking Mum, irascible Greatgrandma Fagg, Jack (24), his sister Pat (21), and the two youngsters, Daphne (13) and Lennie (12, played by Christopher Beeny, the future Edward in *Upstairs Downstairs*) – and for ten minutes Pertwee introduced them in brief, character-establishing scenes. 'Tell him to keep his passes for the football field,' grumbled the normally good-natured Bob Grove on hearing that his elder daughter had been asked to dinner by a local centre forward.

Next evening, at 7.50 on the 9th, *The Grove Family*, British television's pioneer adult soap, had its first episode proper. Called 'A House of Your Own', it centred on Mr Grove in upbeat mood, having just paid off the mortgage after 20 years, and his wife starting to get ideas about washing machines and new curtains. Early reaction was mixed – 'A catchy signature tune, an admirable cast, sensible settings, efficient production, and a twenty-minute parade of the accepted suburban lower middle-class virtues, chores, domestic economics and humour,' was Bernard Hollowood's rather non-committal, not unfriendly verdict in *Punch* – but from about the fourth episode the members of the BBC's Viewing Panel started to become positively enthusiastic. 'Look forward to meeting this family and feel we know them now,' wrote one, another that 'it is very natural and human', with the only flaw being that 'some of the aged people looking in may wonder if they appeared quite as selfish and trying as "Grandma" to their families'. The series had initially been commissioned for only 13 episodes, but by the 12th the panel's Reaction Index was up to 70 (out of a possible 100), a typical response was that 'the Groves are very real and homely', and they and their fans were apparently settling in for the duration. One humane but demanding critic, Philip Hope-Wallace, was perhaps less ecstatic about the prospect. 'What will happen next week?' he rhetorically asked in the *Listener*. 'Will Gran have caught a chill? Will Pat come back from Paris using too much lipstick? And whatever will those two little mischiefs get up to next? The suspense is almost intolerable.' Still, far more important was the fact that one of the soap's many regular viewers (up to a quarter of those with a television) was the Queen Mother. Few would have demurred from her reputed verdict: 'So English! So real!'

There was no royal imprimatur yet for Eric Morecambe and Ernie Wise. 'A real lusty-laughing audience – that's what we want,' rather nervously declared their producer, Bryan Sears, in the *Radio Times* ahead of the launch of their first television series, *Running Wild*, on 21 April. The series – six fortnightly shows, with Alma Cogan as 'resident songstress' – flopped resoundingly, as the critics from the start put their knives in: 'Their gags were weak, their sketches corny' (*Daily Sketch*); 'TV's worst effort for months' (*Daily Herald*); 'TV should try to hammer out its successes in the rehearsal rooms – NOT drawing rooms' (*Reynolds News*). The Viewing Panel agreed. 'Poor in the extreme – even the few novelties were ruined by "amateur" treatment and poor comedy,' asserted one member. 'This was a third-rate seaside concert party show!' The Reaction Index level did pick up a little (having started at a dismal 43), but by the time that one newspaper critic in late May reckoned that 'it looks as though Morecambe and Wise might have a good show just as it's due to be brought off', it was too late. For the two comedians personally, both still in their twenties, it was a demoralising time, not helped by Eric's mother, Sadie. 'What the devil are you two playing at?' she screamed down the phone from Morecambe after the first show. 'I daren't show my face outside the house. We'll have to move. We'll have to change our name.' In the ensuing post-mortems, some attributed the flop to Morecambe and Wise being too 'Northern'; but their biographer, Graham McCann, as plausibly pins the blame on Sears's lack of faith and scriptwriters who did not understand them.[3]

There was more to April 1954, though, than small-screen ups and downs. In fact, three events had significant implications.

There were, Churchill told the Commons on 5 April during a debate on the H-bomb, 'two main aims' of British policy: 'One is to lose no opportunity of convincing the Soviet leaders and, if we can reach them, the Russian people, that the democracies of the West have no aggressive design on them. The other is to ensure that until that purpose has been achieved we have the strength necessary to deter any aggression by them and to ward it off if it should come.' This statement of the latter aim clearly presaged the Cabinet's decision, taken that summer, in favour of Britain manufacturing its own H-bomb – the rationale being, as Churchill put it, that 'we could not expect to maintain our influence as a world power unless we possessed the most up-to-date nuclear weapons'. More immediately, two main consequences flowed from Churchill's unusually plodding, unnecessarily partisan Commons performance, a display that led to shouts of 'Guttersnipe!' and 'Swine!' 'Things didn't go as well as I expected,' Churchill said next morning as he looked at the highly critical press, failing to comprehend the widespread acceptance that his days at No. 10 were numbered. The other consequence was the politicisation of the whole question of the bomb – already under way since Bikini Atoll, but now accelerating. Later in April, over the issue of establishing an Atomic Energy Authority, some 60 Labour MPs sought to prevent it from being able to manufacture hydrogen bombs; and in Coventry, the Labour-controlled city council decided to abandon civil-defence preparations, on the grounds that they were futile in the H-bomb era, leading to instant accusations in the local press of 'throwing in the sponge'. The emerging progressive orthodoxy was well caught by the bitterly sarcastic lines of 'Sagittarius' (Olga Katzin), the *New Statesman*'s resident versifier:

> Strong is the sense of moral indignation
> But Britain the realities must face,
> Defence remains the first consideration,
> With competition in the atom race.

> Our weapons of complete annihilation
>   With greater Atom-Powers keeping pace,
> To yet more strenuous exertions spurred,
> Since in atomic strength we rank but third.

Which way would popular opinion jump? There were as yet few signs, but it did not help the cause of a mature democracy that the BBC refused to air the issue from anything other than an entrenched Cold War position. In particular, Bertrand Russell tried his hardest to get a hearing, but it was not until December that the Corporation reluctantly broadcast his talk 'Man's Peril from the H-Bomb'.[4]

The second April event, three days after Churchill's parliamentary debacle and an hour or two before the first sighting of the Groves, was the third Comet crash in less than a year. A South African Airways plane came down near Naples, killing all 21 passengers and crew, and almost instantly all other Comets were grounded. Later that year, experts at the Royal Aircraft Establishment in Farnborough concluded that metal fatigue had caused the disasters – in effect, sending the whole Comet project back to the drawing board and thereby forfeiting the technological lead that the British aircraft industry had enjoyed in the early 1950s. 'It is not the case that there are better American aircraft either available now, or available in two years' time, or available in five years' time,' blustered Anthony Crosland (whose South Gloucestershire constituency included the company manufacturing Britannias) on *Any Questions?* in January 1955, but 16 months later Tim Raison's question in *Picture Post*, 'Is there any likelihood of Britain building a jet airliner capable of competing with the Boeing 707 and the Douglas DC8?', was all too pertinent. By this time the first generation of American jets was expected to fly commercially in 1958, and in October 1956 the British government reluctantly gave permission to BOAC to buy 15 Boeing 707s – provided, of course, they used British Rolls-Royce engines. Meanwhile, there were a couple of other pregnant developments. In 1955 the young, entrepreneurial Freddie Laker began his first scheduled service, using converted Bristol freights to shuttle cars and their passengers between Southend and Calais; while the following year, the creation within the Ministry of Supply of the Supersonic Transport Aircraft Committee marked the start of the Concorde story, fuelled by the dream of once again taking the transatlantic lead.[5]

Back in April 1954, the third event was on the 14th, six days after the Comet crash, when the increasingly restless, disenchanted Aneurin Bevan resigned from the shadow Cabinet primarily over the issue of Labour's support for the NATO policy of rearming West Germany – support that he and his followers portrayed as subservience to, in the words of his biographer John Campbell, 'the American view of international politics as a holy war against world Communism, controlled from Moscow'. The resignation did not play well even with the usually pro-Bevan *New Statesman*, which accused him of a 'streak of wilfulness', while according to Panter-Downes after this 'second public walkout' (ie following his resignation from the Attlee government almost exactly three years earlier), 'there are those who predict that it will prove fatal to the Party's chances of getting back at the next election, and those who predict (often without displeasure, needless to say) that it will merely prove disastrous to the man'. Next in line to replace him in the shadow Cabinet was Harold Wilson, who had resigned with Bevan in 1951 and been mercilessly tagged as 'Nye's dog'. Now he decided to bark and, to Bevan's disgust, took the place. Wilson's public letter justifying this action, largely on the grounds of party unity, 'reeked of humbug', and that verdict by his biographer Ben Pimlott was shared at the time on both the left and the right of the party, leaving him an isolated, mistrusted figure, though still grudgingly respected for his manifest ability. ' "Wilsonism" we read of now in *The Economist*,' noted the former Labour minister Hugh Dalton. 'But who is a Wilsonite? He's a clever little chap, with a sure political touch, but not magnetic.'[6]

There was also by April the rise of the teddy boys, or the 'Edwardians' as they were still usually termed. The widely publicised 'Battle of St Mary Cray' late on Saturday the 24th marked their indisputable coming. The *Orpington & Kentish Times*'s horrified headline – ' "Gang Battle" At Railway Station: Edwardian Youths In Half-Hour Fight: Wooden Stakes, Sand-Filled Socks As Weapons' – prefaced an account of a pretty unpleasant half-hour encounter between 'rival gangs of youths from Downham and St Paul's Cray', the gangs 'sporting "Edwardian" suits with stovepipe trousers and velvet-coloured jackets'. Trouble had started earlier in the evening when 'a rowdy party of youths and a few girls from Downham Estate, Bromley, arrived at St Paul's Cray Community Centre, where St Paul's Cray Sports and Social Club were holding a dance'. At the Centre, 'a knife was drawn when a member of the band objected to being jostled', while 'one man had a glass of orange juice thrown in his face during an exchange of words'. The MC, George Couchman, found himself in an unenviable spot: 'I warned the crowd police were standing by and also took the precaution of having the band play only calming music – no quicksteps. Several older people felt there might be trouble and left. I felt the few of us responsible for keeping order were in a precarious position, and I breathed a sigh of relief when 11 o'clock came.' The crowd dispersed quite peacefully – but then came the fight at the nearby station, until broken up by the police, with some 40 youths held overnight. And when the police returned to inspect the damage in daylight, they found a message scrawled on a fire-bucket: 'It is time St Mary Cray was woken-up'.

The appearance of the Edwardians was undeniably distinctive. 'Round the fire stood a few youths dressed in the Edwardian style and with fabulous hair-dos, of the American fashion known as D.A. [short for "duck's arse", reputedly pioneered in Britain by the Hounslow hairdresser Len Pountney],' recorded the somewhat misanthropic Cyril Dunn in his Borehamwood diary the previous winter about 'Saturday Night in the Elstree Way':

> This hair-do is unbelievable, a huge *helmet* of hair. It grows thick down the back of the head and is brushed in from each side towards a centre-line. Over the crown of the head it is swept back, but allowed to grow long and high, and to fall forward in front like the brush-plume of an ancient Greek helmet. The effect is of infinite and mannered attention. In fact, the result is wholly feminine, but without making the youths look effeminate. The clothes are black. The jacket is long, coming down well below the buttocks; the trousers are narrow and taper to the ankles. Here the whole elegant ensemble is suddenly and wildly contradicted. Where one expects something slender and pointed, there are bright socks and cumbersome crepe-soled shoes. The effect of the whole décor is thin, mean and sinister, and is obviously meant to be.

Dunn also watched them in action. 'They never for a moment stopped acting,' he observed. 'The model is patently a screen villain; with a little repellent research one might even identify the actor, though it could be a composite of several actors. The role evidently has several simple conventions. When "the men" are talking to each other, they never smile; the face muscles are held rigid, as if the mood is one of controlled and watchful hate.'

Unsurprisingly, they were not the flavour of the month after the St Mary Cray episode. 'It is about time drastic action was taken to put a stop to these scenes of violence caused by irresponsible youths called "Edwardians",' wrote Robert Hadden of 3 The Avenue, Bickley to the local paper. 'The only remedy now is imprisonment and the birch. Fines are useless.' Elsewhere in suburbia, the Mayor of Kingston upon Thames agreed. 'Directly these silly young idiots get out of hand,' he publicly declared, 'then I'm coming on them with a bang. I don't agree with this rot about spoon feeding.' In late May an investigative article by *Picture Post*'s Hilde Marchant – 'The Truth about the "Teddy Boys" ', based on several visits to the Mecca Dance Hall in Tottenham – sought to allay fears. There she had found 'little to criticise – a touch of vanity, perhaps, a gesture of exhibitionism', but 'harm and violence did not seem to be among them', while she quoted how the manager kept saying to her, 'No trouble at all, these boys.' She did not deny the existence of *gangs* of teddy boys, sometimes leading to criminal actions, but they, she insisted, were the minority. In short: 'Of course, there are "Teddy Boys" with evil ways; but there is a vast majority of young men who merely wish to wear Edwardian clothes as a change from boiler suits and factory overalls.'[7]

The younger generation was – up to a point – better behaved at St Swithin's. *Doctor in the House*, based on the novel by Richard Gordon, was released this spring and proved *the* box-office smash of 1954. On a Wednesday evening in late April, the civil servant Henry St John intended to see it at the Gaumont in Acton, 'but there were queues outside, no seats under 3s 1d, and apparently few of those'. He then tried Ealing, but the queue 'stretched from the Broadway Palladium to Bentalls'. A trio of diarists did manage to watch it, starting with Gladys Langford at the Highbury cinema on the evening of St John's frustrations. 'I did not care for it,' she recorded. 'The technicolor effects were not pleasing to me,' while 'the girls all looked like advertisements for sun-tan cream'. Three days later, the local government officer Anthony Heap was at King's Cross Gaumont and found it 'gay, bright, witty, cheery and joyously irresponsible' – in fact, 'the best and funniest British screen comedy since "Genevieve" ', with Kenneth More and Kay Kendall in both. A youngish writer in Hampstead, earning his crust teaching foreign students, disagreed. 'How banal British films are, how overpraised,' complained John Fowles on 12 May. 'A futile chain of stock situations, played out by stock characters.'

Notwithstanding which, if there was one of the four trainee doctors who made the film, it was undoubtedly diffident Simon Sparrow, played by Dirk Bogarde in an overdue break from his gangster and/ or neurotic roles. 'Sparrow has no family money to support him and has arrived at St Swithin's on merit,' astutely notes the film historian Christine Geraghty. 'He is training to be a GP rather than the more traditionally powerful surgeon and his major success is in helping with a home birth.' Bogarde himself during the filming (at Pinewood and University College London) had tended to keep himself apart, retreating to his Rolls-Royce. 'Oh, he's Ginger, inne?' the camera crew sometimes called out – as in 'Ginger beer', cockney rhyming slang for 'queer' – but Bogarde was always a cat who walked alone.[8]

It was about the time that his Simon Sparrow was starting to woo audiences – as the very model of the idealistic young doctor in the new, inclusive NHS – that the acclaimed, also youngish writer Angus Wilson considered on the Third Programme the future of the English novel in the context of the Welfare State. He was broadly positive, arguing that that future lay with 'a new generation' of novelists coming from 'the new ruling class – that strange mixture of business experts, bureaucrats, social scientists, and the rest of the Welfare set-up'. There ensued an unusually lively correspondence in the *Listener*. 'For novelists who will have perforce to embrace the values and outlook of the Welfare State,' asserted 'a young critic' called R. C. Burlingham, 'there offers in all probability a prospect of arid, conforming Byzantinism.' Kingsley Amis, fresh from his *Lucky Jim* triumph, took issue. 'Does Mr Burlingham believe all that stuff about the thought police and the Ministries of Culture and *1984*?' he asked, before concluding that 'Mr Burlingham should stick to complaining that he does not want to pay for other people's wigs and false teeth.' In his riposte, Burlingham accused Amis of being 'insufficiently aroused' to the fact that 'the Robin Hood State – whichever party governs – is the clear heir to the future', and he declared that in an ever-more egalitarian society, 'the middle-class phenomenon of a liberal, lively, curious, disinterested, travelled, cultivated novel-writing intelligentsia and novel-reading *literati*' was 'unlikely to be among the amenities provided by this secular heaven'. At which point in the controversy, Amis let it rest.

Something was stirring on the right flank, albeit heavily camouflaged by the ruling orthodoxy that there existed between the main parties a broad Keynesian-cum-welfare consensus on domestic issues – a somewhat misleading orthodoxy recently embodied in the *Economist*'s February coinage of the celebrated 'Mr Butskell', a play on the Conservative Party's leading moderate, Rab Butler, and Labour's leading moderate, Hugh Gaitskell. But in his riposte, Burlingham noted how 'an attack on the Welfare State' had 'been recently undertaken with devastating point and with no concessions to fashion by an able economist, Mr Colin Clark, who has presumably taken his life in his hands by doing so'. Clark's attack was in the form of a well-publicised pamphlet, 'Welfare and Taxation', in which as a conservative Catholic (in his case Australian) he argued that there was a moral as well as economic imperative to reduce taxation, and that social services should as much as possible be provided by a mixture of local authorities and voluntary associations rather than by the centralised, dictatorial state. Not long afterwards, in May, the One Nation Group in the Conservative Party published a collection of essays, *Change Is Our Ally*, whose contributors included Enoch Powell and which placed much stress on the virtues of free-market competition. Even so, an explicit distinction was made between those virtues and red-in-tooth-and-claw capitalism. 'To the Tory the nation is not primarily an economic entity,' asserted Powell with deliberate emphasis. 'It may place political and social ends above economic ones, and for their sake may justifiably on occasion seek to prevent change or divert it.'[9]

There would be few stronger defenders of the welfare state – and fiercer critics of its inadequate scope – than the sociologist Peter Townsend, who in February 1954 joined Michael Young and Peter Willmott at the Institute of Community Studies in Bethnal Green. He was soon under way with what ultimately became *The Family Life of Old People* (1957), beginning in late April with pilot interviews in Hampstead. His interviewees included a 65-year-old 'spinster' living in 'a tiny attic room with sloping roof' in Parliament Hill, working 'part-time as a cook 10–2 nearby for a large family in Downshire Hill', and paying 30s a week for furnished accommodation: 'I don't think it's right [she told Townsend]. But there you are. Hampstead rents always were high. She's [ie the landlady] doing pretty well out of it, I don't suppose. She's very particular though. But the house is always very clean. But you can't tell me these landladies don't make much out of it all. They do. I'm sure they do.' Townsend also asked her about entertainment. 'I don't go out much,' she replied. 'Not to these pictures. I don't like them. I go to a Presbyterian nearby every Sunday. I meet my friend from Muswell Hill there sometimes . . . I don't see anyone living nearby. I don't like prying neighbours.' Townsend enquired about family. 'Well, they're all dead now. I wouldn't mind seeing a bit more of my nephew at Ipswich but I don't want to move there. I don't like Ipswich.'

He also interviewed a more prosperous seventy-three-year-old widow, who as a result of having run a small laundry in Fitzrovia now owned a two-floor Edwardian house in Worsley Road, where she lived on the first floor with a nonagenarian friend, while eight relatives (aged between seventy-four and three) shared the ground-floor flat. Townsend described her as looking 'rather like a female version of Charles Laughton in one his seedier roles', but she sounded benign enough: 'We're a happy family. What I like best is when they're all up here for the television. We sit and watch it after our Sunday dinner. Fred [her 47-year-old adopted son] usually falls asleep. Every day the baby [ie the three-year-old] comes up here at 4 o'clock. He has to look at the television. He comes running rag, tag and bobtail every day at 4 . . .'[10]

———

'There is almost as much speculation about the size of tonight's crowd as about the result of the match,' noted the *Yorkshire Post* on Wednesday, 5 May. 'If the ground record of 70,198 is approached, which seems doubtful in view of travelling difficulties, the fact that most of the spectators will be arriving at much the same time will test Bradford Northern's big-match organisation to the full.' Bradford Northern's ground was Odsal, neutral venue for the replay of the Rugby League Cup Final between Halifax and Warrington, after a draw at Wembley. In the event – in a cavernous ground with, in Geoffrey Moorhouse's words, 'terracing made of nothing more substantial than railway sleepers, and the players reaching the field through the crowds, down a long cascade of steps from their dressing-rooms on the amphitheatre's rim' – the *Post*'s prediction was seriously out. Amid chaotic scenes, during which 'some, unable to see the game, climbed to the roof of the old stand, and despite loud-speaker appeals refused to budge until the end', 102,575 spectators packed the ground, a world record for a rugby league match, as Warrington won 8–4. 'Many could not see all the game,' reported the *Bradford Telegraph & Argus*, and the paper's 'obvious conclusion' was that 'much has to be done at the stadium before it can be considered as the "Wembley of the North" '. But soon afterwards, a stirring article ('The will of the north') in *Rugby League Review* argued that the match had 'demonstrated to the rulers of the Rugby Football League in a clear and unmistakeable manner' that people 'desired the final of the game's major trophy to be played in their midst'. The debate would rumble on – though, given the BBC's continuing indifference to the game, not as a debate of much resonance south of the Trent.

The morning after the Odsal crush, it was a distinctly southern, public-school-educated Oxford University cricket team that took the field at the Parks against Yorkshire. On a bitterly cold, windy day, with first a marquee and then a sight-screen being blown down, the visitors made 293 for 4 before declaring at teatime, leaving the students a tricky final session to bat. A fiery young fast bowler, no lover of the amateurs and their fancy caps, took the new ball. 'The second ball of Trueman's first over bowled Marsland, the fourth bowled Williams and from the sixth,' reported J. M. Kilburn in the *Yorkshire Post*, 'the ball jumped from Cowdrey's glove to be caught at short leg by Appleyard, fielding substitute . . .' That left the university 0 for 3 at the end of the first over; by 5.45, after two interruptions for showers, they were 19 for 6, with Trueman on 5 for 5; and eventually, at close, they were all out for 58. By then, however, the odd enterprising spectator might have decided to cross Oxford in search of other sporting fare.

In any case, there were only some 2,000 spectators, each paying 2s 6d, at the Iffley Road track to see Roger Bannister, Oxford graduate and now medical student at St Mary's Hospital, Paddington, make a long-planned attempt to run the mile in under four minutes. The race was due to start at 6.00, and it was only a last-minute improvement in the weather that decided Bannister and his Austrian coach Franz Stampfl not to postpone the attempt. Helped by his pacemakers Chris Brasher and Chris Chataway, Bannister ran a fast race and finished first. Had he done it? 'The result of event No 9, the One Mile, was as follows,' announced a deadpan Norris McWhirter through the loudspeakers, before a lengthy, agonising, deliberate pause. 'First, No 41, R.G. Bannister – in a time which, subject to ratification, is a new track – English native – British national – British all-comers – British Empire – WORLD record. The time is 3 . . .' The rest of the announcement was drowned by the crowd's noise, including repeated chants of 'He's done it, he's done it,' while an exhausted Bannister was surrounded by admirers. For several minutes the rest of the programme was delayed, until at last McWhirter declared: 'Life must go on.'

Bannister himself, once he had been allowed to change, left the stadium with a patriotic sentiment – 'It is a great thing to think that an Englishman has been the first to do a four-minute mile' – and then stopped off briefly at the Oxford sporting club, Vincent's, before heading for London in a BBC television van. *Sportsview*, fronted by Peter Dimmock, had just started as a weekly sports magazine, and later that evening Bannister was at Lime Grove ready to be interviewed after the programme had shown a recording of his epochal run. Next day, the press chorus was triumphantly patriotic. 'So Britain has been the first to conquer Everest and to achieve the four-minute mile,' crowed the *Halifax Daily Courier*, speedily making up for the town's Odsal disappointment. 'Both feats may be equalled, but they will never be erased, for first is always the first. Britain has pioneered the way. So let us have no more talk of an effete and worn-out nation.'[11] Bannister's run may not in reality have been quite the carefree, gloriously amateur effort that it was almost immediately portrayed as, but it was still the apogee of the determinedly hopeful, optimistic 'New Elizabethan' moment.

'I listened to Queen's return on wireless sometimes,' noted Marian Raynham in Surbiton just over a week later, on Saturday the 15th. 'Had our last coal fire. It's still cold.' Amid saturation BBC coverage – from the moment the Royal yacht *Britannia* sighted land off Plymouth Sound – the Queen was returning from her epic six-month Commonwealth tour. Richard Dimbleby was as usual the main man, including at the point of disembarkation at Westminster Pier, where it looked as if the three-year-old Princess Anne might get into the royal carriage ahead of her mother. 'On royal occasions these days,' he reassured viewers, 'you can never be sure what's going to happen next.' The crowds were huge, among them Madge Martin and her clergyman husband, who lived in Oxford but happened to be in London that day and on the spur of the moment decided to watch (at the Horse Guards gate) the Queen on her route to Buckingham Palace. 'What a thrill!' she wrote. 'Worth all the hours [11.00 to 3.45] of waiting – and somehow *being* there in a crowd of good-tempered enthusiasts – on a typical London day – rather grey – but fine – such a really *English* day for her to come back to.' That evening, some 28 per cent of the adult population tuned into radio's Gala Performance – introduced by Jack Buchanan and Margaret Lockwood, with stars including Peggy Ashcroft, Max Bygraves, Eddie Calvert, Tony Hancock, Edmund Hockridge, Al Read, Michael Redgrave, Beryl Reid and Terry-Thomas – while later there was *Dancing by the River*, featuring Ted Heath and His Music playing on the promenade of the Royal Festival Hall. For the police on the ground in central London, many drafted in from the suburbs, it had been a relatively unstressful but long day. 'There were four in Inv's carriage, all looking hot, rather grimy and tired,' recorded a Mass-Observation investigator about her train journey back to Sutton that evening:

> They loosened their collars and belts, settled down to look at the evening papers or leant back and closed their eyes. One remarked: 'There'll just be time for two pints. I was afraid we shouldn't make it!'
>
> An American woman in the same carriage offered sweets all round and tried to get them to talk, but mostly they didn't seem anxious to respond. Inv overheard one policeman say 'they'll be having their bread and jam by now' and another 'I'll be seeing them again soon. I'm going to the garden party.'

'The American woman thought this was serious,' added the investigator, 'and the other policemen laughed when he went on, "Oh, yes. We're always there. Outside the gates!"'

Next Saturday it was the turn of Billy Graham, for the last time on his crusade, to attract the crowds. Some 65,000 came that afternoon to White City Stadium, followed in the evening by 100,000 at Wembley Stadium, as well as another 22,000 on the playing area itself. 'Some 2,000 people waded through the mud to respond to the Invitation,' Graham himself recalled about that Wembley meeting, and, according to a newspaper report, 'they were of all ages, of all classes of society'. Altogether, over the twelve weeks, Graham and his team had attracted more than two million people to meetings and won thirty-eight thousand 'decisions for Christ' – a remarkable achievement. That same rainy Saturday evening, Henry St John was at the Chiswick Empire. 'I saw a variety show which included an American singer named Diana Decker, and a comedian called Peter Sellers,' he dutifully noted. 'The show could not be rated higher than fair; the songs were rubbish, and, as usual, jokes about excretion earned some of the biggest laughs.' But for the evangelist, there was one final meeting before he headed home to North Carolina. 'Tell me, Reverend Graham, what is it that filled Harringay night after night?' asked a gloomy Churchill at No. 10 on Monday. 'I think it's the Gospel of Christ. People are hungry to hear the word straight from the Bible. Almost all the clergy of this country used to preach it fruitfully, but I believe they have gotten away from it.' A sigh accompanied Churchill's response: 'Yes. Things have changed tremendously. Look at these newspapers [early editions of the three London evening papers] – filled with nothing but murder and war and what the Communists are up to.'[12]

Between Wembley and Downing Street there was Budapest. 'Have we any chance of victory?' the *Daily Mail*'s Roy Peskett asked ahead of England's return match against Hungary on Sunday the 23rd, almost exactly six months after the previous autumn's humiliation. 'No England team is beaten until the final hand-shake, but I have viewed other matches with greater confidence . . .' Even so, 'if the ball can be wrested from Puskas and Co their defence will be in trouble'. The outcome was even worse than before: this time, 7–1 to the Magyar masters. 'Until we can win or at least hold our own in such contests,' argued the British minister in Budapest in the continuing Cold War context, 'it will be better to avoid arranging them with countries such as the Satellites whose propaganda made largely at the expense of our own prestige it cannot be our policy to further.' The Foreign Office bluntly replied that 'it would be *much worse* propaganda if it got around that the West would not make fixtures with the Iron Curtain because they were afraid of losing', and thus 'the only remedy for this admittedly sorry state of affairs is for us to concentrate on getting good enough to win'. There were still a few weeks to regroup before the World Cup – during which Birmingham's Diane Leather became the first woman in the world to run a mile in under five minutes but received barely a tithe of Bannister's instant fame, and the eighteen-year-old Lester Piggott won his first Derby on Never Say Die at 33–1, coolly telling reporters that 'it was just another race' – but by Saturday, 26 June it was quarter-finals time at Basle, with England up against a Uruguay team that the previous Saturday had thrashed Scotland 7–0. 'I seem to be the only person in Switzerland who gives England a chance,' wrote the incorrigibly optimistic Peskett. 'I feel they can win if they attack from the start . . .' Uruguay duly won 4–2, leaving Peskett to praise 'a gallant performance' in 'a heart-breaking match' – and to make the glancing but obligatory flick at 'the prima-donna attitude of certain of the Uruguayan players'.[13]

There was no footballing subtext in Iris Murdoch's first novel, *Under the Net*, published three days before the Budapest mauling. Its themes were existential – befitting an Oxford philosophy don who had recently written a study of Jean-Paul Sartre – and at one point the solipsistic narrator Jake, for whom life was 'a private conversation with myself which to turn into a dialogue would be equivalent to self-destruction', offers a brief political critique: 'English socialism is perfectly worthy, but it's not socialism. It's welfare capitalism. It doesn't touch the real curse of capitalism, which is that work is deadly.' Reviews were mixed. 'A brilliant talent', acclaimed the *TLS*, while Amis in the *Spectator* acquitted Murdoch of 'philosophical gallimaufry' and called her 'a distinguished novelist of a rare kind'. But Betjeman in the *Telegraph* disliked the book's 'intellectuals, washouts, and seedy characters in general', the *Guardian* thought it 'sentimental . . . strictly for those who can take their fantasy neat', and for John Raymond in the *New*

Statesman it was 'a bluestocking fantasy, a brilliant but long-winded piece of café writing'.

None of which stopped the novel from being a considerable commercial success (including a 215,000 print run for the Reprint Society book club), and J. B. Priestley may well have had Murdoch in mind, along with Wilson, Amis and probably John Wain and perhaps William Cooper as well, when in June his 'Thoughts in the Wilderness' column in the *New Statesman* considered new English novelists and found them sadly wanting. Not only were their settings insufficiently realistic ('rather like stage scenery out of drawing and queerly coloured'), but their central characters were 'too deliberately unheroic, and often seem such bumbling nitwits that it is hard to sympathise with them in their misfortunes'. In their attitude to society, moreover, these characters were 'artful dodgers rather than open rebels', and, he went on, 'It is impossible to imagine any buying a house, bringing up children, paying taxes, organising a business, serving on a committee, standing for Parliament. They are simply not with us. They no more live in our political and economic world than children of six do.' It was an escapism that Priestley found profoundly disturbing, given that 'not since the Wars of the Roses has literature been held in such low esteem', so that 'any television mountebank is now more important than any poet, novelist, dramatist'.[14] That was no doubt to exaggerate, but his critique as a whole was more than just an older writer's jealous gripe.

June was also notable for the varying fortunes of three young performers. 'The tension of this dramatic play was maintained by excellent team work,' reported the *Whitby Gazette* on the Spa Theatre Company's presentation of Agatha Christie's *Murder at the Vicarage*, running at the local theatre for a week from the 10th. Five actors were singled out for praise, including David Baron – 'assured as the sophisticated artist, mixing charm and ruthlessness to bring the character always in focus'. The actor's real name was Harold Pinter, not yet a playwright; but soon afterwards he left Whitby under a cloud, having resigned from the company when the young assistant stage manager, with whom he had been having an affair, was sacked by the company's manager after being reported by her landlady for staying out into the early hours. 'You'll never work in the theatre again,' were the parting words of the manager (a local butcher) to Pinter. But it was onwards and upwards for Benny Hill, who on television's *Showcase* on the 21st set the nation talking by performing virtuoso live parodies – involving, in his biographer's words, 'super-fast changes of costumes and props' – of Barbara Kelly, David Nixon, Lady Isobel Barnett and of course Gilbert Harding, the four regular panellists on *What's My Line?*. 'Benny Hill is the most original and refreshing comedian that British TV has discovered,' declared the *Sunday Dispatch*, and many agreed. The third performer was Gerard Hoffnung, who on the 29th appeared with Petula Clark and Julie Andrews on television's latest panel game, *Music, Music, Music!*, 'a musical battle of wits' chaired by David Jacobs. 'This infectiously happy character blew his tuba to such effect,' noted an appreciative critic, 'that he nearly saved newest entrant in the Panel Games Stakes from the fate of an "also ran".'[15] Cartoonist and raconteur as well as gifted musician, the 29-year-old Hoffnung, who had left his native Germany just before the war, slipped comfortably into the role of an ageing, pipe-smoking music master and was well on the way to becoming one of the great British humorous eccentrics.

June also saw tragedy. Back in April the Cabinet had reluctantly agreed to allow the Home Office a departmental committee on the legal aspects of homosexuality and prostitution, while in May all four members of the *Any Questions?* team (the prominent Liberal figure Lady Violet Bonham Carter, the farmer-writer A. G. Street, the BOAC chairman Sir Miles Thomas and the already famed foreign correspondent James Cameron) had answered in the affirmative to the question, 'Should the law relating to homosexuality be altered?' That was on the 21st at a secondary modern in Yeovil – not so far from Wells, where five days later at the Somerset Assizes seventeen men were found guilty of 'unnatural acts and acts of gross indecency'. Nine of them aged between 23 and 46 received prison sentences of between one and four years; six aged between 18 and 21 were bound over for up to two years, three of them on condition that they received 'treatment'; and two others were put on probation. 'Once this vice gets established in any community,' gravely stated Mr Justice Oliver, 'it spreads like pestilence, and unless held in check it threatens to spread indefinitely.' Gilbert Nixon, 37-year-old holder of the Military Cross and director of a firm of manufacturing chemists in Liverpool, was given only a 12-month sentence, but within a few minutes he had fatally taken poison. That was tragic enough, but something even more resonant

occurred exactly a fortnight later, when the great mathematician Alan
Turing, pioneer of Artificial Intelligence, dipped an apple in a cyanide
solution and took several bites. After his arrest in February 1952 for
homosexual offences, he had undergone, in a biographer's words, 'a slow,
sad descent into grief and madness'. During the rest of the summer, with
the committee due to start work in the autumn under the chairmanship
of John Wolfenden, university administrator and former public-school
headmaster, the persecution of homosexuals perceptibly eased. But the
huge human damage had already been done.[16]

For most people, though, the summer's dominant discourse was
quite different and altogether more benign. '*Butter is off the ration,*'
gleefully recorded Marian Raynham in May. 'And *margarine* which
I never want to see again, & cooking fat, & Trex is back. The price is
supposed to be high, I *think* it is sure to be cheaper soon.' No one
benefited more from growing consumer confidence and possibilities
than Marks & Spencer, which had just opened a huge new store in
Coventry that was 25 per cent bigger than the one destroyed during
the war and, according to the admiring local paper, incorporated
'all modern department store features, with fluorescent lighting,
illuminated wall panels, furniture (other than counters) of steel, air
conditioning, and terrazzo flooring'. At M&S's annual meeting in
June, the visionary Simon Marks reported record turnover and an
increasingly encouraging environment:

> The general conditions in which the business operates have changed
> markedly in the last two years. The most notable factors have been the
> removal of Government controls and the increasing availability of raw
> materials. With more abundant supplies at our disposal, and the lifting
> of restrictions which for so many years hampered our freedom of action,
> we have been able to take steps systematically to improve our values over
> a wide range of goods . . . There is no doubt that our goods are making
> a considerable appeal to the widening section of the community we now
> count as customers.

'The miracle has happened,' claimed even more euphorically the usually
cautious *Economist* at about the same time, 'full employment without
inflation.'

Not that austerity habits were set to disappear overnight – and certainly not in the pages of women's magazines. 'All action, no waste!' declared the advertisement in *Woman's Own* at the start of July for Gibbs toothpaste, sold by the tin. 'A little Gibbs equals a lot of toothpaste, with *concentrated* Gibbs you can clean your teeth twice a day for as little as 1d a week.' Elsewhere, the 'Handy hints' part of the letters page saw readers like Miss W. of Southsea still obeying the god of thrift. 'I save the rubber rings from bottled fruit and use them in place of string on pudding basins,' she confided. 'They can be washed and used many times.' Or take the ad in *Woman* for a surprisingly popular coffee and chicory essence: ' "Camp" is concentrated to save you money. Every drop is used. Not a drop is wasted.' And in the more upmarket *Lady*, an article by Alison Settle on 'Wardrobe for a Careerist' pointed out that 'terylene suits such as Harrods sell (at £15) will last (in my experience) for years, keeping their pleats, and allowing the worker to wear pale shades', while an ad from Express Handbag Repairs of Stamford Hill, N16, positively reeked of make-do-and-mend, or at least make-do-and-mend-by-somebody-else: 'Don't discard that damaged handbag when it can be relined & renovated . . . Crocodile handbags renovated as new from 60s. Every type of repair by experts . . . Thousands of delighted customers.'[17]

For the thrifty and less thrifty alike, this first weekend of July 1954 was memorable enough. It began on Friday afternoon, the 2nd, when the bespectacled, slightly portly Czech exile Jaroslav Drobny won the Wimbledon men's singles title at his 11th attempt, beating the 19-year-old Australian prodigy Ken Rosewall. 'Good tennis and good sportsmanship,' noted an appreciative Judy Haines in Chingford, adding that 'Wimbledon has kept me going this week', while according to the *Daily Telegraph*'s Lance Tingay, 'the warmth of Drobny's reception as champion could not have been greater had he been a genial Englishman'. For several years it had been a joke in a long-running West End comedy – 'Anyone for tennis? I fancy old Drob's got a real chance at Wimbers this year' – and now at last this modest accountant had done it. That evening, while Marian Raynham 'listened on radio to the Piltdown man skull & why it is a fraud, or hoax', the Minister of Housing and his wife were at Petworth House, stately home of his friend John Wyndham. 'We stayed till 3am,' recorded Harold Macmillan. 'The ball was a tremendous success and seemed like a return (for a few hours) almost to the pre-1914 world. Many old friends – from all over England; all the jewels out of the banks (or out of pawn), champagne; two bands (dancing indoors and out) and the glorious pictures, statues, furniture – all looking superb.'

There was more Wimbers on Saturday afternoon. 'Very sorry Louise Brough didn't beat that cockey little Maureen Connolly in the Women's Singles,' commented Haines after the 19-year-old 'Little Mo' took her third successive title. It was not a contest that registered with Iris Murdoch, torn between two (or possibly three) men. She met one of them, the young literary critic and academic John Bayley, at Victoria station, and that afternoon, after a feverish conversation beside the lions in Trafalgar Square and a scratch lunch in St Martin's Lane, they retreated to the London Library in St James's Square in search of privacy: 'I followed J. upstairs. It was fantastic. We walked up & down the long dark alleys of books. Always there was here & there a reader, hidden. We kept climbing up more & more iron stairways. At last we found a floor where there was no one. We leaned against the shelves in the half darkness & clung to each other. J. wept. After a long time we went out, & I came with him in the taxi to Paddington . . . What will come of all this?'[18]

Saturday's great event was still ahead – namely, at midnight the end of meat rationing, so that henceforth only mothers with children entitled to free milk had to keep their ration books. Generally, this end of rationing after 14 long years was marked with surprisingly little fanfare. 'All the celebrations we promised ourselves seem to be a bit pointless now,' a Leeds housewife explained to a paper. 'I suppose it is because we expected all rationing would end at the same time. We certainly never thought it would be nine years after the war ended.' Nevertheless, this evening there was a ceremonial tearing up of ration books in Trafalgar Square, and in the Sussex town of Heathfield an even more ritualised procession and bonfire.

The procession, reported the *Sussex Express & County Herald*, was headed by an undertaker 'in official garb' and 'behind him, two by two, came local representatives of those who had been most involved in rationing':

There were housewives (Mrs R. W. Pink and Mrs Behennah), a draper (Mrs Jermyn), grocers (Mr N. Farley and Mr M. Barrow), dairy farmers (Mrs Anne Mortlock and Mr E. Richardson), baker and confectioners (Mr D. Phillips, Mr W. Flower and Mrs Hackett), general store-keepers (Mr F. Godley and Mr J. McKay), millers (Mr W. Ashby and Mr W. Bucking), a poultry farmer (Mrs J. Collins), farmers (Mr E. Seymour and Mr Penfold), and, finally, as being the last to be released, two butchers (Mr E. Haffenden and Mr E. J. Hamper).

And after them, hand in hand, danced a long ring of happy children, who had always accepted rationing as part of the natural order of things, and had gradually seen one control after another removed.

A 14-year-old lad, Colin Saunders, was chosen to light the bonfire . . .

After the procession had circled the flames, but before everyone in the crowd threw their ration books on to the bonfire, there came the dramatic high point. Mr R. D. Sparkes, an official from Eastbourne Food Office, was present, and suddenly he was 'seized, shoulders and feet, and hoisted into the air (still clutching his briefcase and rolled umbrella) and swung heartily towards, but not quite over, the flames, three times, before being set on his feet again'. This was done by pre-arrangement, and Sparkes remained calm throughout, but for the spectators it was a glorious, avenging, Ealing-film-like moment.

The weekend had a last twist. On Sunday afternoon in Berne, West Germany beat the hot favourites Hungary and won the World Cup. 'As usual with Continental teams,' disapprovingly noted an English paper, 'the referee (Mr W. Ling of Cambridge) came in for some criticism from the losers.'[19] The German economic miracle was already under way, and this outcome was richly symbolic, especially after the recent British football humiliations. As yet, however, there was only the barest perception in the old country that we had won the war, but – for all the material easement – were losing the peace.

3

The Right Type of Fellow

'We have attacked these furry salad killers with everything we've got,' declared the *Daily Mirror*'s 'Cassandra' (the fiery columnist William Connor) on 20 July 1954. 'Including that unpronounceable, unspellable, unspeakable disease myxomatosis.' He went on:

> This revolting plague which we have spread all over the land has now been reported in half of the fifty-two counties of England and Wales. Thousands of dead and dying rabbits can now be seen in the infected areas. Brer Rabbit himself has been seen on the side of a barn as he longs to die and escape from this horrible torment . . .
>
>   Brer Rabbit can't write, can't spell and hasn't even written to *The Times*! And no protest meeting has taken place in Trafalgar Square because rabbits are not allowed in Trafalgar Square – by Order of the Westminster City Council.

'So die you damned diseased bunnies,' he concluded bleakly. 'Die. Die. Die.'

The drastic, rabbit-destroying disease had arrived in Kent the previous autumn and then spread, including to the Flintshire village of Hanmer. 'The whole countryside stank for weeks of decomposing rabbit flesh, sweet and foul, and unforgettably disgusting,' recalled Lorna Sage. 'And everywhere on the roads and paths rabbits staggered about dying by inches, blind, their heads swollen and fly-blown, so that it was a kindness to kill them quickly.' Tellingly, she added that 'local people didn't know (or didn't say) that myxomatosis had been introduced deliberately to destroy the rabbit population and save millions and the crops they plundered'. But if the farmers, deliberately propagating the virus, were on one, unsentimental side of the question, Cassandra's deliberately emotive column, following even more widespread infection, made clear that not everyone agreed – notwithstanding that the destruction of rabbits was long-established government policy. Over the next few months, a Labour backbencher, Dr Horace King, compared myxomatosis to 'the Nazi crimes at Auschwitz'; the Dean of Winchester called it a 'diabolical evil'; and polls conducted by local papers found overwhelming majorities hostile to extermination. It was an opposition based on a variable mix of motives – including a distinctly non-ethical concern about the potential loss of a favourite cheap meat, romantic notions about the countryside, an instinctive pity for the suffering of rabbits, and deep distrust for anything that savoured of Nazi-style genocide – but it was not enough to persuade the government to criminalise intentional transmission of the disease. In the event, of course, the indomitable little breeder survived. 'The rabbit has won the day,' wanly noted *The Times* by 1956. 'It will never be completely exterminated.'[1]

Sage in her memoir of Hanmer correctly identified myxomatosis, 'this act of viral warfare', as 'all part of the drive towards efficiency' – a drive typified by the increasingly intensive use of pesticides and fertilisers as well as by the rapid proliferation during the 1950s of tractors (by the end of the decade outnumbering horses on British farms by two to one), combine harvesters (superseding the inter-war reaper-binder) and milking machines (virtually replacing milking by hand). Together with falling real wages and often primitive living conditions in tied cottages, this highly mechanised second agricultural revolution was responsible for a relentless drift away from the land, running at some 60 farm workers in England and Wales every working day between 1947 and 1955. 'A few years ago, you see, they used to have all their enjoyment here, a sing-song, three or four times a week,' the publican in the semi-deserted Oxfordshire village of Sibford Gower told *Panorama* in 1956. 'And of course all that's dying out now you see through their going to these factories in Banbury to work. Of course they get more money than they did on the farm . . .' That same year, in a small north Buckinghamshire village, the rector spoke eloquently at his harvest festival. 'The drift from the land will only be stopped when the whole of society begins to realise that the farm labourer is not a clod-hopper, but a highly skilled craftsman, and the foundation stone of civilisation,' insisted the Rev. J. Franklin Cheyne, against a backdrop of the mill gone, the blacksmith's shop now a bus shelter and the school closed, with the children having to travel to nearby Newport Pagnell. 'To the true countryman,' he went on, 'work is not something you do between pay days; it is his life. There is a satisfaction and contentment which the machine-minder in the factory, mass-producing a part for a part of another machine, can never experience. Perhaps that is why he gets a higher wage – to make up for the lack of satisfaction in his job.'[2] The name of the village was Milton Keynes.

'Although food rationing ended at midnight on the night of July 3rd–4th,' lamented the solipsistic civil servant Henry St John on Monday, 5 July 1954, 'there was no improvement in the canteen menu, on which rissoles were featured, and the only carcase meat was the inevitable beef.' Soon, though, there was more choice at the butcher's, while meat prices after an immediate spike started to return to more normal levels. 'We want in modern Britain to have an understanding between the producer and the housewife,' declared the Chancellor, Rab Butler, in a well-publicised speech on the 10th at a Conservative rally at Kingsholm Rugby Ground, Gloucester. 'We want her to be as "choosey" and independent as she likes and we want the producer to produce more of what the public wants. We want the consumer to decide and not the man in Whitehall.' Some three weeks later, buying meat in Barrow market, Nella Last found herself behind a distinctly choosy consumer:

> She surveyed all the cuts of sirloin, rib & 'round', & pointing to a particularly good piece of the latter, asked for it to be weighed. I wondered if she felt as startled as I did, when the butcher said '18/6'. She said a bit breathlessly 'oh *no*, it's far too much for me,' & the pleasant young fellow serving her said 'I'll cut you a smaller piece' – but it was 9/3 & the woman again shook her head. As cheerful as if it was a pleasure, he said 'I'll cut another piece' & this time it was 7/8 & she took it. I felt I'd not have had the courage! – realising what a lot of 'confidence' housewives *have* lost.

Last herself retained an open-minded thriftiness. '*Such* a dear way to buy cheese, in round boxes of segments in silver paper,' she reflected shortly before about Kraft cheese, 'but cheaper, in that I can keep it longer than "bulk" variety, without it going stale.'

A new shopping era was now dawning, but it was not one that Kenneth Preston, a high-minded English teacher at Keighley Boys' Grammar School, necessarily welcomed. 'Re-emerging from the [cathedral] close we felt to be stepping into a different world – and how much inferior!' he declared in Peterborough towards the end of July in the course of a cycling tour with his wife Kath. 'We wandered round and looked at the shops until 7 pm. Shops now are becoming woefully alike so that when you have gone round one town's shops you have gone round all . . .' By this time, Phyllis Willmott had moved, together with her husband Peter and two small children, into an attic flat in the handsome house in Victoria Park Square, Bethnal Green, that was about to be the permanent base of the Institute of Community Studies. Shrewd and keen-eyed, with a natural flair as a diarist, she began a 'Bethnal Green Journal'. 'Shopping is an occupation to be enjoyed in most of Bethnal Green,' she noted among her early impressions around the end of July:

> The women seem to *like* to shop every day. Yet refrigerators are becoming a sign of status and success. What will the mothers do with them? If families were still as large as they used to be, the 'fridge' would be full, no doubt, with each day's shopping. But with today's smaller families will the fridge stay half-empty, or will the wife stay away from the shops? In Roman Road all the customers seem to know the shop people personally. They stand about and joke and chat. They enjoy shopping and are in no hurry, and it's little use anyone else being!

'East Enders are fussy about their bread,' she added. 'Good bread is hot new bread.' And: 'Bethnal Greeners do not like to seem niggly in their shopping. They like to be buying plenty. In a district that has known poverty this is easily understood. Hospitality means *plenty* of food. Refinement in the cooking is unimportant. It is probably possible to attribute other food habits to this poverty line of the past. A half-penny bun to fill up a hungry tummy. A bag of chips at any hour of the day . . .'

All traditional enough, but an important marker for the consumer-durables future was the Board of Trade's removal on 14 July – barely a week after the end of rationing – of restrictions on hire-purchase agreements for such items as radios, television sets, gramophones, refrigerators, vacuum cleaners, motor cars and motorcycles. 'The export problem now is to sell different goods, not to produce them,' reflected sanguinely enough *The Times*'s City editor. 'Metals and other materials are abundant, while defence claims have eased.' Noting that hire purchase was no longer called 'the never-never', the paper argued soon afterwards that whereas in the 1930s 'hire purchase was a working-class device (house buying apart) for obtaining, not luxuries or even semi-luxuries, but such necessaries as furniture', now the post-war middle class, highly taxed and with little capital, was widely using HP, so that 'the class tincture of being a hire purchaser has vanished altogether'. It was not overnight all free and easy – there was still a £50,000 limit of new capital in any one year for hire-purchase finance firms – but the trend was unmistakable.[3]

There was an undeniable class tincture to the question of who should captain England's coming cricket tour of Australia, with two realistic candidates: the incumbent, Len Hutton, a seasoned Yorkshire professional, and the far from seasoned Sherborne-educated Cambridge graduate David Sheppard, an amateur playing for Sussex. The cricket writer likely to have the most influence over the MCC, who had to make the decision, was the pontifical E. W. Swanton. 'There is no better fellow than the average modern cricketer,' he reassured his *Telegraph* readers on 12 July. 'But he does want looking after, and he will react for better or for worse according to how he is handled.' In short, it was quality of leadership – in fact, of man management – that should be the decisive criterion. There followed some sharp words on Hutton's captaincy: 'It is fair to say, that his own strong accent on defence has apparently repressed the younger English batsman ... As in batting, so in tactics, choosing the bolder of two courses does not come easily to his nature.' Sheppard, by contrast, was 'a young cricketer of strong character and much determination to whom leadership comes naturally'. Swanton did not formally plump for either man, but it was obvious which he wanted.

This was too much for the *Daily Mirror*'s Ross Hall. 'Let's be able to cheer the rout of the hypocrites,' he declared two days later, insisting that Hutton be speedily named captain. 'Only the woollen-headed snobs, who have played havoc with English Test cricket abroad in the past [an entirely justified barb at the selection policy for the previous tour of Australia], turn blind eyes to the fact that golden boy David Sheppard is still a learner compared with Hutton.' And he claimed that 'at Lord's and its surrounds', Sheppard's 'amateur claims' were 'supported by an influential majority'. That same day there started the annual Gentlemen (amateurs) versus Players (professionals) match at Lord's, with Sheppard not helping his cause by scoring 4 and 0 as well as being guilty of, in Hall's perhaps not entirely objective appraisal, 'poor handling of the bowling'. In the event, the MCC stuck with Pudsey's finest – unanimously according to Hutton's biographer, Gerald Howat, by one vote according to Swanton's great rival, John Arlott. 'I'm relieved to know that the MCC selectors have thought I'm the right type of fellow to take the England team to Australia,' was Hutton's characteristically dry response to the announcement on the 19th. Next day in *The Times*, John Woodcock was broadly supportive of Hutton – 'at once the most completely equipped batsman in the world and a shrewd tactician' – but could not forbear from referring a little wistfully to Sheppard's 'infectious enthusiasm'.[4]

Enthusiasm of any kind was thin on the ground on the evening of Saturday the 24th, when Richard Crossman, visiting his Coventry constituency, held an open-air meeting outside the Wyken Pippin pub:

> We've never failed to get a good meeting since we put the loud-speaker at the bus-stop, facing across to the pub, which has a huge garden outside, and they come out with their mugs of beer, sit on a little wall and ask questions. I had all three Councillors, and the *Coventry Evening Telegraph* had had the whole front page announcing that the Home Secretary had appointed three Civil Commissioners to take over Coventry's civil defence, so heaven knows there were enough things to talk about. We talked for an hour and a half, and there were never more than five people listening.

'True,' added Crossman, 'it was the first night of the holiday fortnight and 25,000 people had left Coventry station, but there were probably 180,000 people left in the city . . .'

Next week, for Madge Martin and her clergyman husband, it was a few not wholly satisfactory days in London in late July before the real holiday began. On one day: 'We hadn't time for a leisurely dinner, so I had a revolting sandwich at Fortes . . .' And on another, on a bus along the Finchley Road, fondly remembered from pre-Blitz days: 'All the large, romantic houses were shattered, and now just blank spaces, surrounded by dense foliage. I expect the next step will be blocks of horrid flats.' Still, on Saturday the 31st it was off to Scarborough, as usual staying at the Burghcliffe Hotel. Then came the big disappointment:

> We heard horrid things about the new Spa arrangements, but didn't dream just *how* awful the changes were. There is an Ice Show – entirely covering the old space around the open-air band-stand, and enclosed in huge, disgusting striped awning, cutting off the lovely sea-view . . . The Spa has always been our great joy, and we never asked for anything different – and now, to see it so devastated and made so common . . . We could have screamed . . .

That same Saturday, there were mercifully no flies in the ointment, or clouds in the sky, at Loders Fete. 'To have got a fine day in this wettest of summers for fifty years was luck superlative,' recorded the grateful vicar, Oliver Willmott, in his next Parish Notes:

> To match the occasion the organisers presented the best entertainment they have ever concocted. First, the Mayor of Bridport gave a sample of the town crying that has more than once made him champion town crier of England. Then he adjudicated the efforts of eight miserable locals who had been compelled by Miss Randall to dress up, march to a rostrum and imitate the Mayor. They looked like state prisoners going to the block, but the crowd enjoyed it hugely. Green draperies suggestive of the toga and a little cross-gartering had transformed the ample figure of our worthy village butcher into another Nero; academic cap and gown had changed the Vicar's churchwarden into another Frank Sinatra as he would look in the act of receiving an honorary doctorate of Law at Chicago University; and a greenish bowler hat capping the moustachios of the sporting landlord of The Crown had converted him into Old Bill of the 1914–18 war. Old Bill was an easy winner, and with native

generosity he tossed the fruits of victory into the treasurer's lap for the good of the cause. Then followed a display of dancing typical of various nations by Miss Sally Bryant's school of dancing. Loders Court [home of Sir Edward and Lady Le Breton] made the perfect background for this, and the dancers delighted the crowd by doing much more than they had promised. A tent-pegging race in which the horses were gentlemen, the chariots wheelbarrows, and the charioteers ladies, leavened the decorous proceedings with spills and thrills. For the aesthetically minded there was a ladies' ankles competition won by Mrs Rudd junior (who, we hear, always wins, at any fete). In a competition for the knobbliest male knees the Vicar's churchwarden came into his own . . .

The profit was a record – more than £160 – and 'another such fete next year should complete the amount needed for the overhaul of the organ'.[5]

During these mostly damp summer weeks there was plenty of theatrical interest – a Home Service run-out for Robert Bolt's *A Man for All Seasons* ('some quality in its rather stolid way', according to the critic J. C. Trewin), with Noel Johnson of Dick Barton fame as Henry VIII; the sad demise of the Bristol Empire as a live theatre, with a last Variety hurrah featuring among others the impressionist Wally Athersych, renowned for his air-raid noises; curtain up at the Whitehall, with Brian Rix as actor-manager, for John Chapman's hugely successful *Dry Rot*, a farce about dishonest bookmakers – but no serious competition, among theatre-goers anyway, for the star event. This was the musical *Salad Days*, principally the work of the 24-year-old, Eton-educated Julian Slade and performed at the Vaudeville by the Bristol Old Vic company. As usual, there on the first night, 5 August, was Anthony Heap. 'This quaint little musical fantasy', he called it in his diary, with 'a plentiful supply of gay little lyrics set to nimble little tunes', and altogether 'quite a captivating little frolic'. Even so, the curmudgeon in him added: 'I don't know that it called for such an excessively ecstatic reception as the exceedingly well-disposed first night audience saw fit to accord it.' Just over a fortnight later, passing through London on their way back from Scarborough, the Martins went to it. 'A most unsophisticated, almost amateurish, but fresh, unusual and charming little musical, which seems to have

caught on with sophisticated audiences,' was her verdict, adding that
'this one was rapturously enthusiastic'.

Salad Days was set to run and run – fittingly until 1960, for no show
was, at least on the face of it, more quintessentially of the 1950s. 'It is
winsome, coy, escapist, terminally adolescent, pathetically repressed,
and, in its artfully wide-eyed way, exceptionally camp,' declared a
fiercely hostile critic, Alastair Macaulay, about a 1996 revival of what
for him was clearly something from a distant, pre-enlightenment
world. But Macaulay might also have noted not only that – for all
their refined voices – the central characters Jane and Timothy, just
down from university, marry secretly and look after the magic piano
because she does not want to be married off by her mother to a suitable
husband while he cannot face being fixed up with a safe job by one of
his influential uncles, but also that the piano's infectious ability to make
people dance is a severe affront to the hypocritical Minister of Pleasure
and Pastime. It was, all in all, a thoroughly English piece – though
failing, perhaps inevitably, to break the stranglehold of the American
musical.[6]

A week or so after Jane and Timothy found themselves something
to do, George Allen & Unwin published *The Fellowship of the Ring*,
the first volume of J.R.R. Tolkien's *The Lord of the Rings* trilogy.
Naomi Mitchison, along with Tolkien's friend C. S. Lewis, had already
contributed praise to the dust jacket, and now they wrote appropriately
laudatory reviews. 'Like lightning from a clear sky,' declared Lewis
in *Time & Tide*, while Mitchison in the *New Statesman* called it 'a
story magnificently told, with every kind of colour and movement
and graveness'. Most reviews were positive, though not uncritically
so. 'Whimsical drivel with a message?' asked J. W. Lambert in the
Sunday Times. 'No,' he answered. 'It sweeps along with a narrative and
pictorial force which lifts it above that level.' He did, however, note that
it had 'no religious spirit of any kind, and to all intents and purposes
no women'. The *Daily Telegraph*'s Peter Green claimed that the prose
style 'veers from pre-Raphaelite to Boy's Own Paper', albeit conceding
that the novel had 'an undeniable fascination'. And in *Punch*, where
under Anthony Powell's literary editorship it received the briefest
of reviews, Peter Dickinson frankly stated: 'I can think of nothing in
the book to account for the fact that I find the whole thing absolutely

fascinating, despite some of the most infuriating fine writing.' The most heavyweight critique came from a major literary figure, the Scottish poet and critic Edwin Muir. 'To read it is to be thrown into astonishment,' he gladly conceded in the *Observer*, but insisted that in terms of 'human discrimination and depth' there was a fatal shortfall: 'Mr Tolkien describes a tremendous conflict between good and evil, on which hangs the future of life on earth. But his good people are consistently good, his evil figures immutably evil; and he has no room in his world for a Satan both evil and tragic.' Commercially, the book flourished, being reprinted after six weeks, ahead of the publication in mid-November of *The Two Towers*, second in the sequence. It was not yet a cult, though, nor – away from the public prints – was it everyone's cup of tea. 'Don's whimsy' was the private verdict of Angus Wilson, to whom in his own mind the future belonged.[7]

A different sort of saga rolled on at Ambridge. 'Dan and Doris Archer seem to be universally popular figures, old friends, with familiar but by no means unpleasing idiosyncrasies,' an internal BBC report on *The Archers* noted in August. 'They are a solid, sensible pair, "absolutely real" to listeners.' Other characters, though, were not wholly above criticism from the 756 listeners, the great majority of them regular followers of the series, who had completed questionnaires. Peggy Archer, 'in the throes of marital unrest' with Jack Archer, was seen by a minority as 'an unsympathetic wife, shallow and shrewish', while a minority also criticised Jack himself for 'behaving too queerly and unreasonably for too long'. Even Walter Gabriel, for all his 'hosts of admirers', had his critics, with his 'gravelly tones' being 'the source of irritation (and alarm) in certain quarters'. There was also annoyance about the love angle. 'Phil's protracted romance with Grace has evidently become too much of a good thing,' found the report. 'Listeners do not always want to see the couple married but there is a strong feeling that Grace should return from exile so that the matter can be settled once and for all.' These, however, were all minority grumbles – and the report's conclusion did nothing to dent BBC confidence that *The Archers* had become a permanent fixture of daily life: 'For 90% of the regular listeners this serial continues to be as interesting as ever.'

The summer holidays were drawing to an end when on the last Monday of August (not yet a Bank Holiday), Judy Haines in Chingford,

her two daughters and her friend Phyllis took a trip to the Tower of
London:

> We arrived dead on time – 10.30, having bought a film for camera at
> Liverpool Street, which we reached by trolleybus. After seeing the
> shipping from London Bridge we went to Lyons for coffee and
> orangeade. Then we saw the Tower. Armour very interesting. Picnicked
> in the grounds. It's getting very warm and I'm in a muddle with the
> lunch – hard boiled eggs, cut loaf, butter, tomatoes, jelly and swiss roll.
> I have three little buttons off my green coat, which I am unhappy about.
> Lunch over & I'm just as cluttered up with my one long and two short
> frig. boxes. After buying jumping beans we went aboard Thames boat
> to Westminster Pier. Phyllis suggested Battersea Park from there. We
> waited ages for bus & then it was a dickens of a way. We 'did' the fun fair
> in Park – girls wanted everything. (I'm hard up and hadn't bargained for
> this.) Called a halt after train ride, ride on Muffin [ie the Mule] and horse
> respectively, ride on swan round Fairyland, ice cream and candy floss.
> Came out of F.F. and sat in Park – too long! Mistook time by 1 hour.
> Arrived home par-boiled and exhausted at 6.45 pm!

Most of the holidays had been spent without an increasingly ubiquitous
parental aid. 'Television comes home after being away about 4 weeks!'
she noted a few days later. 'New transformer.'[8]

By now the new football season was under way, including in Scotland.
'Woodburn ran the soles off his boots trying to cover up the mistakes of
everybody around him,' ran the *Sunday Post* report of Rangers losing
3–1 at home to Clyde on 21 August. The praise was typical: the 35-year-
old Willie Woodburn had been at the heart of the usually formidable
Rangers defence (the 'Iron Curtain') for many years. 'Always a fiercely
uncompromising tackler,' in an obituary's words, 'the worst of his fouls
were committed in retaliation' – none worse than at Ibrox a week later,
with Rangers two up against Stirling Albion:

> In the very last minute [reported the *Sunday Post*] Woodburn became
> involved with young Patterson in the game's only nasty incident, and
> was ordered off. Mr Young [the referee, from Aberdeen] seemed to
> hesitate before sending the pivot indoors.

Query, just how biased can a football crowd get? They loudly booed the referee for this decision. The poor fellow had no option.

Woodburn had been suspended for violent conduct several times before, but this was something else – a punch (admittedly in retaliation after a foul) on a 19-year-old debutant who, ironically, had idolised Woodburn. Over the next few days, nursing a burst lip and three dislodged teeth, a disenchanted Alec Patterson needed much persuasion from his manager before he agreed to go on playing senior football.

Then on 14 September came 'The Woodburn Bombshell', as the Referee Committee of the Scottish FA decided – by the chairman's casting vote – to suspend Woodburn *sine die*. The news was instantly a national talking point, and the *Sunday Post* took some vox pop:

> He's a quick-tempered player, not a deliberately dirty one. His punishment is too harsh. (*Alec Sprul, 82 Bellrock St, Cranhill, Glasgow – a Clyde supporter*)
>
> There's only one man to blame and that's Willie Woodburn himself. He's the guilty man and now he should take his punishment . . . I've seen youngsters hero-worship Woodburn. For their sakes, he should accept his punishments for his indiscretions. (*John Fox, Maltbarns St, Glasgow*)
>
> This sentence is far too drastic. I've never seen Woodburn play a dirty game. (*Thomas Henderson, 13 Minto St, Edinburgh – a Hearts supporter*)

Most people seem to have agreed that the punishment was unduly severe, but by the time the SFA revoked the ban, three years later, Woodburn was too old to resume his career. Roy Race, by contrast, would prove ageless. In early September, while Woodburn waited to hear his fate, the boys' comic *Tiger* – billed as 'The Sport and Adventure Picture Story Weekly' – made its bow, featuring Roy of the Rovers on an all-colour, all-action front page. 'Only two minutes to go in the local Cup-Tie . . . And the score 0–0! With all his pals of the Milston Youth Club F.C. played to a standstill, centre-forward Roy Race was the one member of the team still tireless and on his toes. Could he score before the final whistle blew?' The outcome was never in doubt, but, unknown to Roy, watching on the touchline was the pipe-smoking, green-felt-hatted Alf Leeds, talent-spotter for mighty Melchester Rovers. 'He's got talent,' he sagely remarked to a spectator, as Roy and his teammates celebrated in the background, 'but he'll have to work hard and take knocks to become a pro.'

The Last Night of the Proms on the 18th – four days after the Third Programme's live broadcast from Venice of Benjamin Britten's new opera *The Turn of the Screw*, with David Hemmings as Miles – as usual signalled the end of summer. The second half saw two traditions instantly created: live television coverage (introduced by Alvar Lidell) and a running order of 'Land of Hope and Glory', the 'Sea Songs' (in truncated form), 'Rule Britannia!' and 'Jerusalem'. There was nothing contemporary included even in the first half, and Sir Malcolm Sargent in his annual 'farewell speech' asked living composers to bear in mind that the great works of art had always sprung from the heart and the affections, adding that 'if your music be the food of love, play on', but otherwise 'shut up'. 'Flash' Sargent's populism was unabashed – 'if people can get as enthusiastic about music as about football,' he also remarked, 'that is all to the good' – and over the years he would have no problems about the coming of the cameras encouraging the already raucous Promenaders to, in David Cannadine's words, 'wear ever more outlandish clothes, and to bring their union flags and streamers and bunting and umbrellas and funny hats'.[9] But Melchester Rovers, in the end, always had the numbers.

———

On 15 September 1954, having passed his eleven-plus, Mike (as he still was) Jagger had his first day at Dartford Grammar School – and started to drift apart from his old schoolfriend, the much less middle-class Keith Richards, who went to the technical school in ill-favoured north Dartford. Not so far away that same week, between Blackheath and Eltham, there opened London's first purpose-built comprehensive, Kidbrooke School. In a sense it was not yet truly a comprehensive – a mixture of ministerial and parental pressure had prevented it from incorporating Eltham Hill School, a girls' grammar – but both physically and symbolically it made a considerable impact.

Kidbrooke 'is a huge triangle of buildings of brick and glass and cedar-wood, with a low copper-covered hall in the middle of it, big enough to hold all two thousand girls at prayers every morning', wrote Anthony Sampson some years later. 'Inside there are rows of glassy, brightly painted classrooms, including a room of typing girls, a room of dressmakers, a row of model kitchens, a pottery, a model flat, laboratories, libraries and three gymnasia. It certainly has some of the appearance of mass-production ...' At the time, the *News Chronicle* called it 'Britain's new palace of educational varieties, a blaze of colour – crimson, yellow and blue', while there was much focus on the headmistress, the tall, firm, humane Mary Green, who had run a grammar school in Bristol until becoming disenchanted by the arbitrary finality of the eleven-plus selection system. 'Each "stream" will follow the same syllabus,' she told the sceptical but not unfriendly local paper before the gates opened for the first time, reassuringly adding that 'how much of any course each group takes and the way in which it is interpreted will depend on the girls' aptitude and ability'. Moreover, the first year's 15 forms would each be 'of roughly equal ability', based on Green's own assessments and former heads' reports. On Friday the 17th the Bishop of Woolwich held a service in the vast hall to launch Kidbrooke. Not once during his address, according to the local paper's mole, did he mention the school itself, but instead 'he urged the girls to build their lives on sound Christian principles and to pay attention to spiritual matters'.[10]

Even before Kidbrooke (starting at the same time as the first comprehensives in Bristol and Coventry), the debate was gathering momentum. 'The battle for the survival of the grammar school is, in its implications, the most crucial political struggle that modern Britain has known,' declared the historian Max Beloff in June at the end of an *Encounter* article arguing that 'British democracy has been as successful as it has, largely because it has succeeded in being so undemocratic', and stressing the dangers of egalitarianism to the survival of this uniquely effective formula. On the whole, though, the wind was starting by 1954 to blow the other way. In August an article in *Education* highlighted the parental predicament that summer in Nottingham, where 447 grammar places had been available, competed for by 2,716 out of the more than 4,400 children coming up for secondary school. Other telling signs were the Central Advisory Council for Education's *Early Leaving* report, revealing the relatively poor academic performance – and high drop-out rate – among working-class children at grammars;

P. E. Vernon in the *TES* publishing work that threw further doubt on the reliability of intelligence testing; and the academic impact of David Glass's *Social Mobility in Britain* collection, finding a generally low level of mobility, with the young sociologist A. H. Halsey concluding that 'the comprehensive school would provide an educational environment which, while catering for the variety of education needed in a technological society, might contribute also towards a greater social unity'. Most striking of all was a *Picture Post* article ('A Hope for *Every* Child – Comprehensive Schools') in December, in which Trevor Philpott went to inspect the Anglesey experience (going back to 1949) and concluded that it was the way ahead, the only alternative to a system in which children were 'robbed savagely' of their 'opportunities' before their 12th birthday. Earlier in the year, however, there had been an instructive Scottish experience for the Labour politician Richard Crossman. 'His little girl Margaret is at Glasgow High School, where she pays £7 a term plus books and uniform in the Junior and will pay much more in the main school,' he recorded after staying with the 'keen, hard, absolutely materialistic, loyal, nice, dull' Chief Convenor of the Albion motor-car works. 'Blackwood is a Councillor, and I said how did this square with Comprehensive schools? He told me that other Councillors were very angry with him, but his little Margaret was going to have the best.'[11]

The human aspect of the eleven-plus system was undeniably cruel – and perhaps increasingly so, given its controversial nature. The following summer, a *New Statesman* piece by M. Lehmann described the overwrought girls in a junior school listening to their teacher (Lehmann herself?) read out the names of those who had passed. Bettie's was not among them:

> Bettie, of whom everyone had been so sure, whom her parents had called the brainy one of the family (having apparently little faith in the talents of their other three daughters), Bettie who was one of the best in the form. Bettie did not cry; she produced a smile on her white little face. Then Doris, always such a proud girl, began to sob, and Mary, too, disconsolately, because her parents had had her coached for six months and she knew how much it had cost them. And then Rachel began because her elder sister had managed to pass two years ago . . .

Then teacher said something comforting to the effect that what they had learnt was not wasted, that they would always be able to use it when they were grown-up. But they knew it was not true. Why and how should they ever be asked again to work out in exactly 24 seconds (not one more) how far it is round a square field whose side is three furlongs? And anyhow, now they had to go home, what would their parents think and say, or – most dreaded thing of all – the neighbours? That they were failures. Failures, ten years old, some 'already' eleven. And it all happened in the Year of Our Lord 1955.

The social hurt could cut the other way, as Kaye Winterbottom, brought up in Rochdale's working-class Spotland district, found in 1954 after passing her eleven-plus and winning a place at Bury Grammar School for Girls:

I suddenly found that the children I knew and had been friends with all my life refused to play with me and said I was a snob. I was really upset and thought it was an injustice. A woman who lived nearby knocked at our front door and told my mother she'd come to let her know it was a waste of time sending girls to grammar schools . . . When I went to Bury I found it very difficult to adapt. When I started fighting the other girls just turned away as if in disgust. I found it very difficult to understand them. No one admired me for the things I was good at – fighting, rampaging, being wild. I broke a bottle of calamine lotion over a girl's head and was threatened with expulsion. I was forever in trouble for one thing or another. They told me I was a disgrace. Girls from Prestwich and Whitefield were from a different culture from girls from Rochdale, and we were the minority.

'The headmistress called us "gals",' she added, 'and we had to wear a hat at all times. You couldn't speak to boys wearing it; you couldn't eat with it on; you couldn't do anything. Of course, I hated it . . .'

None of which cut much ice with Sir David Eccles, the intelligent, ambitious, arrogant Wykehamist – 'tall, sleek of head, handsome of visage', in the historian Correlli Barnett's words – who in November 1954 replaced the largely ineffectual Florence Horsbrugh as Minister of Education. 'My colleagues and I,' he flatly stated at the start of 1955,

'will never agree to the assassination of the grammar schools.' That
spring, addressing the National Union of Teachers and unveiling the
slogan 'Selection for everybody', he directly attacked the comprehensive
school as an 'untried and very costly experiment', suitable only when
'all the conditions are favourable, and no damage is done to any existing
school', which if strictly adhered to would in practice mean only in
new housing estates and perhaps new towns. Later in the year, he was
true to his word when he blocked attempts by the local authorities
in Manchester and Swansea to open comprehensives. 'A multilateral
school,' the Swansea delegation vainly told him, 'was better suited to
the needs of the pupils, who out of school did not ordinarily divide
themselves into secondary modern and grammar groups. If there was
to be a common culture, a common means of communication, it was
necessary to plan for a system which did not strengthen and deepen such
distinctions.' Eccles responded by saying that the pro-comprehensive
argument was fundamentally made on social, not educational grounds,
and that as Minister of Education he would not countenance destroying
any of Swansea's four existing grammar schools. Admittedly he did
sanction two comprehensives on Swansea's new housing estates, but
this was a concession only at the margins.[12]

What about the secondary moderns (educating seven out of every
ten children in state secondary schools)? It could have been one of a
thousand speech days all over the country when in July 1954 the Mayor
of West Hartlepool, Councillor J. W. Miller, sought to soothe the parents
at the Golden Flats County Primary School over the disappointment of
their children not securing a grammar place:

> Some parents think it is the end of the world. Don't you believe it. I did
> not gain entry to a grammar school, but I claim that I have made a success
> of life. A secondary modern school education is as near as possible to
> that at a grammar school. We cannot all be academically minded or
> professional people and if your children get a good solid grounding
> in secondary modern school education they will benefit as much as a
> grammar school child does.

The following February, the *Economist* offered some hard-headed
perspectives on the secondary moderns. 'At first they had little idea

where they were going,' it reckoned about the immediate post-war years, whereas more recently 'some of them have been rising in the world'. Specifically, in addition to 'about one in four' being 'now housed in glittering new buildings', they had found a sense of purpose: 'For the most part this purpose is frankly vocational. Taking a leaf from the book of the secondary technical schools [of which there were relatively few], a number of modern schools have begun to offer to their older children "biased" courses, in which vocational instruction offers anything up to a third of the teaching time; and traditional subjects, in order to stimulate interest, are linked to vocational study as far as possible.' As for the more strictly academic aspect, in terms of 'provision for the average or above-average child', the paper cautiously endorsed greater exposure of such pupils to public examinations. But whether vocationally or academically, the hard fact remained that 'only about one in three or four of the modern schools' were giving their pupils 'something that they can get their teeth into'.

No one appreciated the need to make up this shortfall more clearly than Eccles, fully aware that, in the context of a growing challenge from the comprehensive model, the Achilles heel of the grammars was the poor reputation of the secondary moderns. 'To allow 4 out of 5 of our children and their parents to feel that the children who go to the secondary school [ie the secondary modern] start life impoverished in education would be to sow the seed of discontent throughout their lives,' he reflected in an April 1955 memo, soon afterwards in another memo observing that 'the disappointment and jealousy felt by parents when their children failed to qualify for a grammar school' had not only not disappeared, contrary to the hopes after the 1944 Education Act for 'parity of esteem' between the different types of school, but that 'the resentment appears to be growing'. The policy implication was stark: 'Selection for everybody means developing in each secondary modern school some special attraction and giving parents the widest possible scope.' Accordingly, as early as July, the Ministry's Circular 289 conceded that 'boys and girls do not fall neatly into distinct types' and that 'the Minister therefore regards it as essential that no modern school pupil should be deprived of the opportunity of entering for the examination for the General Certificate of Education if his Head thinks that he has the necessary ability and persistence'.[13] Could it work? Or,

in terms of perceptions – and self-perceptions – was the sheer fact of
the eleven-plus simply too divisive to allow the subsequent chasm to
be bridged?

————

There was another high-profile first term in September 1954. 'The
controversial school at Hunstanton today opens its doors to 450 children
from all over West Norfolk,' noted the *Lynn News & Advertiser* about
a week before Kidbrooke began. 'This building of unusual design,
which has many critics and as many supporters, is now completed
and equipped to take children in the secondary modern channel of the
educational system.' The architects were the young, iconoclastic Alison
and Peter Smithson, and apparently some county councillors had already
publicly called it – on the resort's outskirts, just off the High Road to
King's Lynn – 'an eyesore'. It was undeniably eye-catching. A steel and
glass creation, inspired directly by Mies van der Rohe's Illinois Institute
of Technology, it was, in the admiring words of Peter Smithson's *Times*
obituary, 'a brilliant planning solution of classrooms and staircases over
two storeys and around a succession of small courtyards that eliminated
all corridors'. Bryan Appleyard has referred to 'the brutally exposed
surfaces and the sheer frankness of the entire fabric', while according to
Dan Cruickshank, 'the clarity and simplicity of its design, the ruthless
logic of its planning, the way materials and methods of construction
are honestly displayed, the elegant integration of the services and the
suave minimalism of the fully glazed elevations make the school, in its
way, a masterpiece'. From the start it was associated with the emerging
term 'New Brutalism', and the Smithsons themselves allowed it to be
photographed only on condition that there were neither children nor
furniture and fittings to spoil the effect.

The *Architectural Review* ran a laudatory piece, but not everyone
admired this flagship of hard modernism. 'In that this building seems
often to ignore the children for which it is built, it is hard to define it
as architecture at all,' grumbled the *Architects' Journal*. 'It is a formalist
structure which will please only the architects, and a small coterie
concerned more with satisfying their personal design sense than with
achieving a humanist functional architecture.' Even the *Architectural
Review*, generally sympathetic to the unyieldingly unsentimental

urbanism of the Smithsons, published dissenting letters. 'I should hate to go to school there,' declared Peter Beresford. 'All the rooms look hard and clattery. The stairs give a grim promise of canings and theoretical physics on the first floor. Even outside the place looks windswept and offers no shelter.' The most resonant critique came from a Greek architect. 'The inhuman brutality with which it strikes one is so violent that there is no doubt that it must have shaken even the most die-hard "pseudo-modernist",' wrote E. D. Vassiliadis. 'I have studied architecture in England and have come to love the warm, human quality of its architecture. I consider the Hunstanton School not only a bad piece of architecture but also utterly un-English.'

Nor did the locals learn to love it. 'Will boys and girls who misbehave themselves in Hunstanton be sent to the glasshouse?' was within weeks overheard in the town's court, while after Peter Smithson's death in 2003 a former teacher at the school, J.T.A. Shorten, stated bluntly that 'his reputation in the Hunstanton area is such that the decision to award him and his wife the prize for the winning design for the secondary school there has for ever been regretted'. Informed by Shorten's 37 years of personal experience, starting in 1955, there followed a detailed, devastating catalogue of how appallingly badly the pioneering building had functioned in day-to-day practice: the leaking concrete roof, cracks in the glass sounding like rifle shots during lessons, dangerous glass panels at both ends of the gymnasium, excessive heat in the summer and cold in the winter, dreadful noise and congestion at lesson change because of the absence of corridors, non-soundproofed classrooms, no available places for displays of pupils' work, unpainted classrooms (specifically decreed by the Smithsons), no way of blacking out the assembly hall in order to show films – altogether, 'it was probably more suited to being a prison than a school'. And, he justly added, 'it illustrates the folly of allowing architects' whims to flourish without consulting the people who will work in the resulting buildings'.[14]

The Hunstanton statement came at a particularly pregnant moment in the complex, interrelated worlds of architecture, planning and housing. Cumulatively, four underlying trends in 1954–5 would do much to destroy the '1945' dream.

'We discussed the problem of the Local Authority programmes,' noted Harold Macmillan in September 1954, shortly before handing over the

housing and local government portfolio to Duncan Sandys, Churchill's
son-in-law. 'As we hope to see some 150,000 private enterprise
(unsubsidised) houses completed in 1956, it becomes necessary to
curtail the allocation for L.A. [local authority] building. This is not
an easy operation, and will lead to political trouble. All the same, it is
certainly right . . .' Building controls were ended in November, enabling
private house-building to go full steam ahead, already encouraged by
Macmillan having reduced mortgage requirements, and Sandys the
following spring introduced legislation intended to end subsidies for
'general needs' building by local authorities, which instead were to
concentrate on the new slum-clearance programmes. The annual figures
for permanent dwellings built in England and Wales reflected the start
of a fundamental shift:

	Local authorities	Private builders
1952	176,897	32,078
1953	218,703	60,528
1954	220,924	88,028
1955	173,392	109,934

New homes increasingly to be built by private enterprise, new
homes increasingly to be lived in by owner-occupiers – the political,
Tory-benefiting implications were obvious enough at the time, as in
retrospect is the fact that this was the beginning of the long, painful
process of 'residualisation', by which those living in local-authority
housing would sink ever further below the average income and status
of the population as a whole.[15] Plenty of new public housing still lay
ahead – not least in the context of slum clearance – but the terms of
trade were changing.

The second trend was also pro-private – namely, the declining
prestige of town planners, mostly employed by local authorities, and
bureaucrats generally. To a degree this reflected the Conservative
government's post-1951 dismantling of the state planning apparatus
of the 1940s, typified by the revoking of the 100-per-cent 'betterment'
tax on property development that had been such an emblematic part
of the 1947 Town and Country Planning Act. The profession of
town planning itself was growing rapidly – its numbers rising tenfold

between 1940 and 1957 – but at the same time becoming markedly introverted: not only were planners increasingly remote in a day-to-day sense from the general public, but they were also bitterly resented by architects, especially when they had the temerity to turn down out-of-the-ordinary designs. 'Many town planners are apt to fashion their schemes in the image of too abstract or incomplete a picture of human society,' reflected in 1954 the not unsympathetic William Ashworth, historian of town planning, and he added that 'the danger is the greater because they remain unaware of the nature of this error'.

The planners' cause was only partially helped by the continuing chequered progress – and reputation – of the best-known 'reconstruction' cities. Profiling Plymouth's new city centre in May 1954, Trevor Philpott conceded that it was 'supremely efficient', with free-flowing traffic and plenty of room on the pavements, but personally found it to have 'as much cosiness and charm as an average stretch of the Great West Road between Hammersmith and Slough'. Or in the words of a local man: 'Before the war it was a picturesque town. Now it's a draughty barracks. We call that place [nodding towards Armada Way] Pneumonia Corner. On a winter's day it's cold as charity.' It was no better in Bristol, with the journalist Cynthia Judah observing later that month that the 'bold and dominating' new Council House, housing the local authority, was 'violently disapproved of by most Bristolians'. There was also the wretched Broadmead shopping-centre development, on which work had begun in 1949 (in defiance of the wishes of most Bristolians, who had wanted their new centre to be on the site of the old, blitzed one) and was at last taking sterile, unimaginative shape. As for Coventry, the local paper in January 1955, not long after the opening of the huge, slab-like Owen Owen department store on the north side of Broadgate, quoted a couple of elderly reactions to the city-centre redevelopment. 'I had not seen the new buildings before,' said one. 'I must admit I was a bit awed by what I saw.' And the other: 'I'd rather remember Coventry as it was.' About the same time, the visionary principally responsible for that redevelopment, Donald Gibson, abruptly resigned as City Architect, apparently on the grounds that he and his staff were being poorly treated by some of the councillors. It was Gibson who in 1940 had seen the Luftwaffe's destruction of the city as a once-in-a-lifetime opportunity, and his departure arguably marked the end of glad, confident morning in the Coventry story.

Two episodes both revealed and consolidated the hardening public mood. In July 1954 the Minister of Agriculture, Sir Thomas Dugdale, resigned in the wake of an official inquiry (by Sir Andrew Clark QC) that had been strongly critical of the refusal of his civil servants to sell back to its original owners some 725 acres of farmland at Crichel Down, Dorset, which had been compulsorily purchased for an airfield before the war. Clark's report, declared *The Times*, was 'almost unbelievable in its catalogue of errors of judgement and misleading advice and in the arrogant temper which it discloses among those who are meant to be public servants', while the *Daily Mirror* agreed that Dugdale had no alternative but to 'carry the can for his arrogant bureaucrats'. That autumn there was almost as great a storm after the tragic suicide of Ted Pilgrim, a middle-aged toolmaker living in Collier Row, Essex. Four years earlier he had taken out a £400 mortgage to buy a half-acre plot of land next to his bungalow – mainly to stop noisy children using it as an unofficial playground – but now it was under a compulsory purchase order, for housing purposes, with Romford Borough Council offering only £65. 'Surely the greatest possible indictment against an age gone mad with a rigmarole of rubber stamps, restrictions, and baffling red-tape,' was the verdict of the *Romford Times*, and the *Daily Express* led a national campaign to vilify the Romford bureaucrats and, behind them, the Ministry of Housing officials. 'Why have you done this man to death – you and your minions?' Churchill angrily asked Macmillan, while a last, poignant word went to the widow: 'Ted and I were so happy in our little bungalow in Marlborough Road. My husband was a quiet sort of man and liked nothing better than to potter about in the garden he loved so much.'[16]

Dispersal – moving people out of the overcrowded, unhealthy, rundown Victorian cities – had been a key strain of 1940s planning, and a third trend clearly visible by the mid-1950s was the reaction against this. 'We Are MURDERING Our Countryside' was the stark title of Trevor Philpott's *Picture Post* article in July 1954. Noting that a farm of 150 acres was vanishing every day, with potentially grave implications for security of food supply, he went on: 'After the war we thought our Planners would save our countryside. But the bulldozers move over the farmland as relentlessly as ever. The new "estates" spread, like a rash, over the meadows . . .' There was a predictable riposte from the Town and Country Planning Association's tireless Frederic Osborn – plenty of land was still available for growing food, and 'the excellent object of countryside preservation must not be turned into a space blockade of our less fortunate fellow citizens now living in slums, narrow streets, and treeless and gardenless surroundings' – but his side of the argument no longer had the momentum. 'OCTOPUS' declared the *Birmingham Gazette* in February 1955. 'Where will it all end – this creeping red rash that is pushing the countryside further and further from our doors? While there's still time – stop it!' The new Housing Minister, Sandys, was sympathetic, announcing two months later that 'for the well-being of our people and for the preservation of the countryside, we have a clear duty to do all we can to prevent the further unrestricted sprawl of the great cities'. There followed in August his 'Green Belt' circular, intended to create 'rural zones' round built-up areas and prevent their further development. Dame Evelyn Sharp, his formidable Deputy Permanent Secretary at the ministry, was careful to emphasise that some dispersal of population was still envisaged *beyond* the green belts, but it was still a fundamental shift of emphasis.

It was a shift that owed something to Nimbyism, something to the instinctive desire of those living in attractive out-of-town environments to keep the proles firmly in those towns – and something also to a visceral, largely intelligentsia-led dislike, even hatred, of suburbia. These haters included, for all his humanity, Ian Nairn. This remarkable, passionate young man, fresh from National Service and still wearing a dyed RAF overcoat, spent much of 1954 hanging around the *Architectural Review*'s offices in Queen Anne's Gate until at last he was given a job. His first signed piece appeared in March 1955 – 'the more the English plan, and the more tenderly they feel towards ancient monuments, the faster they seem to put the wrong thing in the wrong place with the best of intentions' – and then three months later he wrote the magazine's special 'Outrage' issue:

This issue [he began] is less of a warning than a prophecy of doom: the prophecy that if what is called development is allowed to multiply at the present rate, then by the end of the century Great Britain will consist of isolated oases of preserved monuments in a desert of wire, concrete roads, cosy plots and bungalows. There will be no real distinction between town and country. Both will consist of a limbo of shacks, bogus rusticities, wire and aerodromes, set in some fir-poled fields: Graham Greene's England, expanded since he wrote in the 'thirties from the arterial roads over the whole land surface. Upon this new Britain the REVIEW bestows a name in the hope that it will stick – SUBTOPIA.* Its symptom will be (which one can prophesy without even leaving London) that the end of Southampton will look like the beginning of Carlisle; the parts in between will look like the end of Carlisle or the beginning of Southampton.

The asterisk directed the reader to the foot of the page: 'Subtopia: Making an ideal of suburbia. Visually speaking, the universalization and idealization of our town fringes. Philosophically, the idealization of the Little Man who lives there (from suburb + Utopia).' Nairn did concede that suburbia had its place 'in the scheme of things'. But 'what is not to be borne', he insisted, was that its 'ethos' should 'drift like a gaseous pink marshmallow over the whole social scene, over the mind of man, over the land surface, over the philosophy, ideals and objectives of the human race'.

The main body of the special issue was a detailed verbal and photographic examination of the whole ugly subtopian phenomenon – 'the steamrollering of all individuality of place to one uniform and mediocre pattern' – before Nairn ended by addressing the reader directly: 'You *have* eyes to see if you have been exasperated by the lunacies exposed in these pages; if you think they represent a universal levelling down and greying out; if you think that they should be fought, not accepted.' The special issue made a huge, gratifying impact, so much so that within weeks the Duke of Edinburgh was telling the Royal College of Art that 'we have a new word now – subtopia – which is proof of a new awareness' and that therefore 'there seems to be no excuse for unattractive design'.[17] For Nairn it was the start of a notable, roller-coaster career; for the dispersionists, a grievous blow.

The obvious, inescapable implication was urban high density – and that in turn meant high-rise flats, the fourth trend. 'Like it or not, we must design more and more blocks of flats,' declared Philpott in his

Picture Post piece (the paragraph emotively headed 'Do We Have to Starve?'), 'and set limits to our suburban sprawls.' In retrospect, these were the years, 1954–5, when the advocates of the high-rise solution won the day. This victory did not result in immediate dramatic change – in 1955 only 29 per cent of new housing output in England and Wales was in the form of flats and maisonettes – but it did set an unmistakable course for the medium-to-long-term future.

There was of course some lingering scepticism. 'All in the future, nothing in the present,' reflected John Fowles towards the end of 1954 about Le Corbusier's increasingly influential 'cities in the sky' vision. 'He sees the present *mess*, of course; but not the present psychology of the individual and society. He takes no account of the conservatism of the human being, his need to have roots in the past, roots in living soil, not in museum pieces, monuments, skylines.' Soon afterwards, in January 1955 at the annual conference of the Society of Housing Managers, the assertion by the Ministry of Housing's Parliamentary Secretary W. F. ('Bill') Deedes that 'it is, I think, accepted beyond question that in many cases we shall have to build up, and that means multi-storey flats' provoked a measure of dissent. After Mrs I. T. Barclay had bravely declared that in new urban developments 'we need some individual houses, and perhaps the more the better', not least for 'the real dog-lovers', a Liverpool councillor, N. A. Pannell, went truly off-piste about 'slabs of buildings like flat boxes standing on end': 'I have a lurking suspicion that the urge to build these multi-storey flats stems from a desire on the part of municipal architects to give expression to their skill and ability. They are oppressed and depressed by the necessity always of having to build these trim little terraced houses, and they are given no scope at all for their undoubted skill and ability . . .'

The sharp-eyed *Economist* also refused to buy the conventional wisdom, picking up in early March on two damaging revelations at a recent RIBA-organised 'Symposium on High Flats' (at which Dame Evelyn Sharp had declared that 'there is nothing more appalling, more deadening, in the urban landscape than a uniform mass of low buildings covering acres and acres', before quoting a poem about the beauty of high towers). One was an authoritative set of recent statistics showing that 'the cost per square foot rises from 32s for a two-storey house to between 55s and 80s or even more for six to twelve storey buildings', with 'almost the entire extra cost of flat construction' being 'borne by the central government, by means of a special subsidy'. The other revelation had come from the London County Council's sociologist Margaret Willis, according to whom 'two out of three of the tenants on the upper storeys of the tall LCC blocks – despite all the attractions of fresher air, greater quiet, and a fine outlook – would still prefer a house and garden'. The *Economist*'s conclusion warranted banner headlines rather than being tucked away in a short, inconspicuous piece: 'There is certainly a place for a few tall flats in local authority schemes; but the suspicion remains that in some of the present mass development schemes – to the tenants' distaste and with the Minister of Housing's express encouragement – far too many authorities and architects are merely building exciting monuments to their own ingenuity.' Regrettably, the left at this critical moment felt unable to break ranks with public-sector-led modernity, an acceptance typified by Mervyn Jones's ultra-enthusiastic *New Statesman* article in October 1954 about a visit to the newly completed Oatlands Court, an 11-storey point block on the Ackroydon Estate on the eastern fringe of Putney Heath – part of the LCC's monumental Putney/Roehampton development that, in Jones's words, 'beats private enterprise hollow for sheer quality and desirability'.[18]

Outside London it was two northern, Labour-run cities that now particularly took up the high-rise cause. One was Leeds, where the City Architect was a committed modernist, R.A.H. Livett, who had been primarily responsible for the pioneering Quarry Hill estate before the war. In 1954 work began on the ambitious Paxton Gardens development, a slab block modelled on Le Corbusier's celebrated Unité d'Habitation at Marseilles and making liberal use of bare concrete. In the same year, a report by the city's housing managers found a significant minority of the Leeds public refusing to apply for flats and instead holding on until a house became available. But this did nothing to deter Livett, who insisted that the multi-storey block was the only way forward if the city's serious housing problems were to be met, especially given the double context of slum clearance and green belt. 'Big cities have to face up to this problem of land shortage and it is up to them to see that all their land is put to the best possible use, particularly in the central areas,' he told the *Yorkshire Post* in 1955 soon after the Sandys circular.

'I refer in particular to the importance of building high. By building high we are getting all we can out of our land and at the same time increasing rateable values.' Livett had the Corporation fully behind him, and this last argument made a very direct appeal.

The other city was Sheffield, several of whose councillors submitted a report in March 1955 following a tour the previous autumn of more than half a dozen large housing schemes on the Continent. They had been much impressed by what they had seen – especially the way in which 'the multi-storey flat can give exceptional amenities in the form of open space, community buildings, services and equipment' – and their conclusion was unambiguous: 'In the circumstances now obtaining in Sheffield – land shortage, ever increasing distances between homes and workplaces, immobility of heavy industry and the urgency for slum clearance – the deputation is convinced of the need to introduce schemes of multi-storey flats, particularly in the redevelopment areas, as a means of solving the housing problem and reducing overspill.' Accordingly, the report specifically recommended that the existing design for Park Hill be accepted, asserting that this would result in 'a comprehensive multi-storey housing project of high standard'.

The recommendation duly went through, and a few weeks later the *Sheffield Star* was reporting 'streams of people' passing through Sheffield Town Hall to look at the striking deck-access, streets-in-the-sky model. 'This new block of flats, it is expected, will set a standard for the country,' proudly declared the paper, adding that 'the scheme will replace 800 old type premises [mainly back-to-backs] with 2,000 modern flats, in a block which will be self-contained down to the local pub'. For the City Architect, J. Lewis Womersley (who had accompanied the councillors on their Continental swing-through), it was a proud moment. 'I was tremendously excited by the dramatic topography of the city and I felt that the opportunities which the site afforded had been completely lost by covering all these hills with small two-storey houses,' he recalled some eight years later about the exciting possibilities that had originally aroused him, including the prominent site of the badly rundown Park district, lowering over the main railway station. 'I saw the possibility of replacing these with towers of flats on hill-tops with open space as a foreground to them so that in their redevelopment people could see the transformation that had been brought about.'[19]

How would it all work out? Britain, claimed Deedes in his address
to the housing managers, was 'in the throes of what we can only
describe as the Second Industrial Revolution', and he went on: 'In this
Second Industrial Revolution we are setting social conditions not in the
background but in the forefront of our new development. This time
we are not, we hope, creating new slums . . .' Michael Young, from his
Bethnal Green vantage point, was part of the debate, contributing a
trio of articles to *Socialist Commentary* between September 1954 and
June 1955. In them he argued against any expansion of the new-towns
programme and insisted that although most people did indeed want
new (or, at a pinch, reconditioned) houses, they wanted them *inside*
the cities, where – for all their large stretches of decay and disrepair –
community spirit and the extended family still flourished. But if the
moral superiority of the inner city over the suburb or new town was
a given, what about the thorny issue of high density and flats? Young
pinned his hopes on a mixture of renovation of the existing housing
stock, ruthless expulsion of space-consuming railway marshalling
yards and goods depots, building of space-saving flatted factories – and,
for those who positively did not dislike living in them, a modicum of
flats. Could the circle be squared? If it could, the rewards, in his mind,
were very great: 'Families would not be forced to move out against
their wishes, and the generations would be kept together. There would
not be so many places like Harlow which has more grandchildren and
fewer grandparents than almost anywhere else on earth. The new towns
of the future would be in Hulme and Hackney.'[20]

4

Bonny Babies, Well-washed Matrons

Two young Canadians arrived in London in the autumn of 1954. 'The houses in Orsett Terrace are all alike with thousands of chimneys on each roof,' the 15-year-old Lynn Seymour, taking up a scholarship at the Sadler's Wells School in Barons Court, wrote home in September. 'The district is not very pretty. I think we got Kensington mixed up with Paddington.' She was staying with what seems to have been a fairly normal middle-class family (the father a civil servant), but her letters over the next few weeks recorded an alien world:

> I bought some Kleenex and a roll of toilet paper. The kind the Fishers have is rather like paper for dress patterns. In fact the toilets themselves are so odd. You have to pull a little chain or string . . .
>
> I have a little radiator in my room and it goes on after you insert a shilling and light a match. The heat stays on a couple of hours, then you must repeat the process . . .
>
> There are a lot of odd characters in London . . . Eccentricity is tolerated here far more than at home . . .
>
> Don't forget to send vitamins, instant coffee and Breck shampoo . . .
>
> We usually have sausages and piles of potatoes at the Fishers' because meat is so expensive. I dream of having a lean juicy steak . . .

The other Canadian was the seven-year-old Michael Ignatieff, who with his family came ashore at Southampton and, 'in sepulchral gloom at four o'clock on a November evening', travelled up to London on the boat train. 'Fog closing in,' he recalled. 'All the English spaces being different; the railway carriages being narrow, different smells, Woodbines in the air, the pervasive dampness, fog and chill everywhere, characters in cloth caps with white scarves, incredibly gnarled old gents carting your luggage to the train.' London itself was a 'cramped, struggling, grimy, dirty old world' – a world that an 'entranced' Ignatieff found 'very magical, very exciting, very dense . . . a very adult world'. Unlike Seymour, the Ignatieffs did manage to locate Kensington (staying that first winter in an 'absolutely freezing apartment' in Prince's Gate), and although at the local private school he 'hated all these little grey woolly socks, the little grey Marks and Sparks uniform', the sheer excitement of London's 'thundering noise' and 'these huge red buses looming out of the fog with their lights all smeared by the fog' made up for it.

Ignatieff was not so far from Stanhope Court, the South Kensington hotel that inspired Terence Rattigan's *Separate Tables*, opening at the St James's Theatre on 22 September with Eric Portman and Margaret Leighton in the lead roles. Comprising a double bill, *Table by the Window* and *Table Number Seven*, it tackled the themes of class and sex with an unexpected incisiveness and even radicalism, though 'homo' in the second play had to be discreetly disguised as 'hetero', if only to protect against the Lord Chamberlain's red pen. For most theatre-goers, though, the appeal lay elsewhere. Anthony Heap, there on the first night, acclaimed it as an 'acutely observed, deeply poignant study in loneliness', adding that 'our leading contemporary playwright' was 'back on the top of his form again', while for Gladys Langford a few weeks later, 'the awful loneliness of the human flotsam and jetsam in a guesthouse was only too well portrayed'.

Separate Tables was a critical as well as a commercial success, but for the *Observer*'s gifted, impatient new theatre critic, it was not enough. The repressed agonies of majors in Bournemouth private hotels were all very well – 'as good a handling of sexual abnormality as English playgoers will tolerate', he conceded – but something else was needed. 'Look about you,' demanded Kenneth Tynan at the end of October:

> Survey the peculiar nullity of our drama's prevalent *genre*, the Loamshire play. Its setting in a country house in what used to be called Loamshire but is now, as a heroic tribute to realism, sometimes called Berkshire. Except that someone must sneeze, or be murdered, the sun invariably shines. The inhabitants belong to a social class derived partly from

romantic novels and partly from the playwright's vision of the leisured life he will lead after the play is a success – this being the only effort of imagination he is called on to make. Joys and sorrows are giggles and whimpers: the crash of denunciation dwindles into 'Oh, stuff, Mummy!' and 'Oh, really, Daddy!' And so grim is the continuity of these things that the foregoing paragraph might have been written at any time during the last thirty years.

'We need plays about cabmen and demi-gods, plays about warriors, politicians, and grocers – I care not, so Loamshire be invaded and subdued,' he ended his call to arms. 'I counsel aggression because, as a critic, I had rather be a war correspondent than a necrologist.'[1]

The poets and novelists were ahead of the playwrights. 'It is bored by the despair of the Forties, not much interested in suffering, and extremely impatient of poetic sensibility, especially poetic sensibility, about "the writer and society," ' pronounced the *Spectator*'s literary editor J. D. Scott in a bold, term-coining article ('In the Movement') at the start of October. 'The Movement, as well as being anti-phoney, is anti-wet; sceptical, robust, ironic . . .' Several letters to the magazine followed: Evelyn Waugh beseeching that 'the young people of today' be allowed to 'get on with their work alone' and not be 'treated as a "Movement" ', the young poet Alan Brownjohn asserting that there needed to be 'a more original intellectual content to the new movement before it can support a genuine claim to transform the literary scene', the even more youthful Malcolm Bradbury calling for the start of a new magazine in England to represent the Movement, and the critic Denis Donoghue identifying the Movement's five key figures as Donald Davie, Thom Gunn (whose first collection, *Fighting Terms*, had just been published as he left Cambridge), John Wain, Iris Murdoch (a case of mistaken identity) and Kingsley Amis, with no recognition yet for Philip Larkin, though his 'Church Going', completed a few weeks earlier, would later be recognised as *the* Movement poem. Amis himself, writing to Larkin, tactfully called Scott's article 'a load of bullshit'.

If the Movement was indeed a movement, arguably three defining characteristics stood out: a zealous heterosexuality, with little taste for effeminacy, let alone homosexuality; an instinctive dislike of Modernism; and, especially on the part of Amis and Larkin, what Davie would many years later regretfully call an 'aggressive insularity'. There were also similarities in background, immortalised soon afterwards by Philip Oakes's 'Identikit' 1950s writer: 'Born: Coketown 1925. Parents: lower middle-class. Educated: local council school, grammar school and university ... Enthusiasms: Orwell, jazz, Doctor Leavis ...' Jazz – traditional, *not* modern – was important, and this autumn saw, at Raynes Park County Grammar School, the formation of a Jazz Club, though only after the headmaster had 'expressed a wish' that its members 'might later gravitate to the serious side of music'. The notes in the school magazine suggested somewhat hesitant beginnings: 'Programmes this term have included a personal choice, an excellently illustrated history of jazz, and a rather controversial programme of music by [Gerry] Mulligan and [Stan] Kenton. It has only been possible to arrange programmes for alternate weeks, owing to the lack of programme material, which in turn is the result of members either having no records to illustrate their topic or being too shy anyway.'[2]

Not all grammar-school boys were jazz-lovers, and in October one of them, the first of his family to go to university, went up to Oxford, still dominated by public-school boys. The awful truth hit Alan Bennett the moment he entered the college lodge:

> It was piled high with trunks; trunks pasted with ancient labels, trunks that had holidayed in Grand Hotels, travelled first-class on liners, trunks painted with four, nay even *five*, initials. They were the trunks of fathers that were now the trunks of sons, trunks of generations ... I had two shameful Antler suitcases that I had gone with my mother to buy at Schofields in Leeds – an agonizing process, since it had involved her explaining to the shop assistant, a class my mother always assumed were persons of some refinement, that the cases were for going to Oxford with on a scholarship and were these the kind of thing? They weren't. One foot across the threshold of the college lodge and I saw it, and hurried to hide them beneath my cold bed.

The following month, a public-school boy who had come down from Oxford four years earlier returned for a weekend. 'The University seemed young, offensively callous,' noted an unimpressed John Fowles. 'On Sunday morning, little groups of earnest young men in dark suits and college scarves – the scarf seems sadly ubiquitous now, though the uniform can surely never be a symbol of freedom of thought – hymnbooks in hand. An oppressive air of religiosity everywhere, everywhere . . .'

Class was as pervasive as ever. 'He carries rather too much of a chip on his shoulder about the middle classes,' reflected Hugh Gaitskell in early October about one of Labour's rising MPs, George Brown, son of a Southwark van driver. 'But his record in speech and working is excellent. He has unlimited courage and plenty of sense.' Soon afterwards, on Friday the 8th, this class warrior was on *Any Questions?* at the Town Hall, Lydney. 'We stayed at the Feathers Hôtel,' recorded a seasoned fellow-panellist, Lady Violet Bonham Carter. 'Ralph Wightman and Mrs Wightman rolled up later – & at dinner [ie before the programme] a new member of the Team – George Brown – Attlee-ite Labour who was Minister of Works . . . Everyone was agreeable to him – but he was obviously lacking in "touch" – or any kind of "amenity" or intercourse.' Then came the programme itself, as ever going out live: 'George Brown's "form" cld not I thought have been worse. He made 2 really "bad form" howlers – one a quite gratuitous & irrelevant insult to the Liberal Party – the other an allusion to my age!' The transcript reveals that his crack against the Liberals was that 'they hardly have any conference worthy of the name', while he did indeed make a jocose reference to Lady Violet's 'present age of 26 or thereabouts'. Yet more unpardonable was still to come. 'When we returned to the hôtel (our BBC hosts having left us) & we sat up talking he hectored & harangued us & addressed me repeatedly as "my dear Violet". I was frozen – but did not I fear freeze him. I have never before – in the course of an unsheltered life, spent among all sorts & conditions of men – met anyone so completely un-house-trained.'[3]

Brown was on the right of the Labour Party, at a time of continuing discord between Bevanites and Gaitskellites. 'How can you support a public school boy from Winchester against the man born in the back streets of Tredegar?' Bevan in June had furiously asked Sam Watson, leader of the Durham miners, about their decision to support Gaitskell, not himself, for the party's vacant treasurership. Gaitskell duly won it, announced in late September at the party conference in Scarborough, during which Bevan as usual spoke at the *Tribune* rally:

This took place [recorded the pro-Bevan Crossman] in a ghastly hall with dim lights and an audience fanning out all round into the darkness. Typically enough, Peggy Duff [tireless left-wing campaigner] hadn't arranged the chairs on the platform or tested the microphones, which looked like broken chrysanthemum stems. You pulled them up to your level and they had a brilliant habit of slowly sinking down again in sight of the audience.

When Nye started, I don't know what he had intended to say, but he spent forty minutes in a long attack on the press, prefaced by a statement that he never believed in personal attacks. Then there was a wild sloshing at unnamed, terrible, adding-machine leaders and a tremendous attack on trade union leaders. It was all very incoherent until the last fourteen minutes, when he did some excellent stuff on foreign policy. There was some quick applause, people began to file out and then the 'Red Flag' was sung, not very satisfactorily.

The 'adding-machine' passage was when Bevan bitterly declared that he now knew that 'the right kind of leader for the Labour Party is a desiccated calculating machine who must not in any way permit himself to be swayed by indignation', even 'if he sees suffering, privation or injustice', for to do so 'would be evidence of lack of proper education or absence of self-control'. This may well have been in reference to Attlee, but it was widely assumed to be Gaitskell, thereafter indelibly associated with the description. Gaitskell contented himself with the briefest of ripostes in his first post-conference newspaper article – 'by the way we do need arithmetic for social progress' – and Crossman privately reflected that 'the Right wrongly think that Nye has finished himself'.[4]

The increasingly troubled industrial scene was starting to attract at least as much attention as the political. 'No newspapers today,' noted Marian Raynham in Surbiton on 11 October. 'A strike. They strike, the dockers strike, everybody wants to strike.' Two days later, Anthony Heap took up the chorus: 'Strikes, strikes, strikes. First the docks, then the newspapers, now the buses, one sixth of which failed to run today.' And after another two days, Raynham again: 'The strikes go on, the bus & dockers strikes. It is very serious.'

In the event, it was the docks that were the most serious concern, with Merseyside members of the giant Transport and General

Workers' Union unofficially supporting – to the undisguised fury of their fiercely right-wing, anti-Communist national leader, Arthur Deakin – the striking London dockers who belonged to the more left-wing National Amalgamated Stevedores and Dockers. That union was, Deakin publicly declared, 'led by a moronic crowd of irresponsible adventurers'. It was generally a very bitter dispute, turning on the question of whether overtime was compulsory, and on the 29th it emerged that the Lord Mayor of London, Sir Noel Bowater, was cancelling a Mansion House banquet in aid of the Docklands Settlement – essentially a charity for children in the Docklands area – 'in view of the attitude of the dock workers'. In fact, following a government-appointed court of inquiry which recognised the need to require 'reasonable overtime' in the docks, the end was nigh, with the dockers returning to work at the start of November. Just before they did so, Crossman went to speak at a meeting at Huyton, Harold Wilson's Merseyside constituency. 'As I entered the door,' he recorded, 'five enormous dockers stood towering over me, saying, "What have you written in the *Sunday Pic* about £30 a week for dockers?" Apparently, next door to my column there was a news story saying that, by working overtime to make up for the strike the dockers might earn as much as £30.' Crossman added that both there and at Toxteth, where he had spoken earlier in the day, all the party officials, dockers to a man, had spoken about Deakin 'in terms which are almost impossible to reproduce, since they clearly regard him as the greatest single enemy of the people'.

Who had won? 'My dear Walter, hooray – hooray – many congratulations on yet another triumph,' an exultant Attorney-General, Sir Reginald Manningham-Buller, wrote to the Minister of Labour, Sir Walter Monckton, while Harold Macmillan saw the outcome as, with any luck, 'a set-back for the Communists and "fellow-travellers"'. But for an increasingly prominent dockers' leader in London, the fiery Jack Dash, establishing that 'never again could the dock employers threaten compulsory overtime' was 'perhaps the greatest victory won by the united action of the portworkers for fifty years'. The real loser, according to the leading socialist intellectual G.D.H. Cole, was Deakin's 'unmanageably huge and clumsy' T&G, and he drew a wider lesson for the trade-union movement as whole:

The centralisation of collective bargaining has done a good deal to encourage the belief among leaders that they own their members, rather than are owned by them. If trade unions are to be truly democratic bodies, they will need to devise new ways of fostering free activity at branch and workplace levels in order to offset the atrophy of local life which is all too marked a feature of current trade union practice.

In the wake of the dispute, the *News Chronicle*'s industrial correspondent, Geoffrey Goodman, spent three weeks touring all the docks, in the process discovering 'astonishing inefficiencies, poor management bordering on the absurd, corrupt trade union practices and a bewildered workforce'. At his insistence, before the paper printed his three-part series, Goodman put his findings to Deakin: 'He eyed me with great suspicion and demanded to know my sources for what he regarded as "scandalous inventions". Of course he knew I would not, could not, divulge any names, so he simply dismissed the whole business as a "load of malicious anti-T and G lies", and warned me against publishing the material. The paper ignored his threats . . .'

Goodman added, in his recollections of covering the tangled post-war industrial scene, that a major problem was 'the casual, lazy assumption', including on the part of 'the average news desk', that 'all disputes and certainly all unofficial strikes, were the work of the Communist Party and its army of industrial activists' – usually an unjustified assumption. Still, the Communist rhetoric could be ambitious enough. On the day the dockers returned to work, the party's West Ham North branch considered a report stating that the aim for the coming year was 'to organise 15 comrades who must be capable of political leadership and Marxist approach to working-class problems', which if achieved 'could lead to our Branch becoming of the size, character and vigilance necessary to lead the people to political power in West Ham and indeed to be the key to the winning of the Labour Movement for a decisive end to capitalist power in Great Britain'.[5]

Yet Albion in 1954 was no longer – if it ever had been – in a convertible state. 'Well-dressed young mothers air their bonny babies, well-washed matrons and healthy looking men pace the streets,' had been Gladys Langford's experience a few weeks earlier in the East End as she walked 'the length of Commercial Street', which she had known half a century earlier. ' "Itchy Park" is no longer a weed-ridden waste but a well-planned garden and its benches are no longer tenanted by lousy tramps and aged crones. Well-dressed young housewives wheel fat infants along its paths.' That same Saturday, 9 October, Nella Last in Barrow was chatting to the manager of the local 'Co-op Furnishing Shop', and he told her, 'I can sell more washing machines & these new "steam" electric irons than anything else.' White goods mattered, as an unwell Judy Haines reflected on the last Monday, ie wash day, of November: 'Thanked God and Abbé for the washing machine – but I let it over-run! Mopped up half a bucket of water.' Apart from some concerns about inflation, running at around 3.5 per cent, the economic indicators for the year had been undeniably good – industrial production, employment, exports and consumer expenditure all continuing to rise – and in mid-December the finance subcommittee of Labour's National Executive Committee discussed, at Crossman's suggestion, 'the problems of Socialism in a boom':

> Gaitskell was in the chair and immediately suggested that we should ask the opinions of four representative economists on the prospects of the boom's continuing. After some consultation with Harold Wilson, Gaitskell named Richard Kahn, Austin Robinson and Sir Donald MacDougall. I myself was baffled as to what these eminent gentlemen are to do and, as a division bell rang at that moment, I asked Gaitskell in the lobby. He explained to me that, from his strict economic point of view, the sort of questions I was putting were irrelevant: I was talking about a psychological boom, not an economists' boom.

'He seemed to feel,' added Crossman even more tellingly, 'that I should be content with this reply.'[6]

––––––––

Radio still largely meant BBC radio, but one evening this autumn Gladys Langford rather surprisingly went to 'the Lucozade sponsored Quiz programme run by Radio Luxembourg'. The compère was Hughie Green – 'a poor comedian I thought' – and Langford was struck by how he 'in many instances practically put the words for answers into the contestants' mouths'. As for those around her, 'the majority of the audience was of the charwoman and "Teddy boy" type'. On the BBC itself, this was the autumn that the Goons, with their fifth series, were at their hugely popular zenith. Certainly it was the high point of John Lennon's addiction to them, an addiction that involved a mastery over all the voices and catchphrases, not least Bluebottle's 'Dirty rotten swine!' Episodes in the series included 'The Whistling Spy Enigma', 'The Affair of the Lone Banana' and 'Dishonoured, or The Fall of Neddie Seagoon', but probably the most celebrated went out on 12 October, three days after Lennon's fourteenth birthday. 'The Goons (Home) have been talking, rather confusedly, about batter puddings,' was the somewhat starchy reaction of the *Listener*'s drama critic J. C. Trewin to 'The Dreaded Batter-Pudding Hurler (of Bexhill-on-Sea)', written wholly by Spike Milligan. 'There were sharp crackles, "By the light of a passing glue factory I saw that Eccles was wearing only one boot"; and only once or twice I heard a curious hissing noise and knew that my teeth were bared.' A crucial part of *The Goon Show* mix, and presumably appeal, was its jibes against such sacrosanct institutions as the church, the army and the Foreign Office – jibes 'embedded in the madness', in Philip Norman's apt words, 'like hooks in blubber'. But late in the year, in 'Ye Bandit of Sherwood Forest', they went too far by including a banquet scene in which Churchill (impersonated by Peter Sellers) was under the table 'looking for a blasted telegram', prompting the BBC to ban forthwith any further such impressions.

From Tuesday, 2 November, there was a new entrant in the comedy lists. *Hancock's Half Hour*, written by the youthful pair Ray Galton and Alan Simpson, made its debut on the Light Programme at 9.30, immediately after John Gielgud and Ralph Richardson in *The Adventures of Sherlock Holmes*, and was facetiously billed in the *Radio Times* as 'the first of a series of programmes based on the life of the lad 'imself from the files of the Police Gazette'. Those appearing, in addition to the 30-year-old Tony Hancock, were the future stalwarts Sidney James and Bill Kerr, Moira Lister (in the unenviable role of Hancock's girlfriend), Gerald Campion (television's Billy Bunter) – and Kenneth Williams. 'BBC 10 a.m. Camden Theatre,' he noted the previous Saturday. 'Recording of "Hancock Half-Hour" went very well really, and I got through OK.' This opening episode was called 'The First Night Party', with Hancock hosting a reception for BBC chiefs and newspaper critics.

'It is easy to imagine the comic potentialities of this idea,' claimed the *Radio Times* in advance, while afterwards Trewin described how 'the expansively ecstatic 'Ancock presided, with intermittently contagious good spirits, over a new comic medley ("Higgins!" he cried to the Park Lane butler, "Cut another sturgeon!")'.

Inevitably it would take a while for the fully formed Hancock persona to emerge (first on radio, later on television also), but once it did it was unique, perhaps best distilled by Roger Wilmut:

> Anthony Aloysius St John Hancock II, of 23 Railway Cuttings, East Cheam; dressed in a Homburg hat and a heavy overcoat with an astrakhan collar of uncertain age; a failed Shakespearean actor with pretensions to a knighthood and no bookings; age – late 30s but claims to be younger; success with women – nil; financial success – nil; a pretentious, gullible, bombastic, occasionally kindly, superstitious, avaricious, petulant, over-imaginative, semi-educated, gourmandising, incompetent, cunning, obstinate, self-opinionated, impolite, pompous, lecherous, lonely and likeable fall-guy.

Hancock was undoubtedly *the* comedian of the 1950s, acutely mirroring many of the prevailing aspirations and frustrations, above all social and sexual. *Hancock's Half-Hour* was also a pioneering type of radio comedy. 'Non-domestic with no jokes and no funny voices, just relying on caricature and situation humour,' was Galton and Simpson's firm intention from the start, and though they were initially thwarted precisely by (among other things) Kenneth Williams's funny voices, increasingly there was, as Peter Goddard has put it, 'a naturalism of language, characterisation and location allowing for almost-believable story lines and audience identification'.[7]

Radio's nemesis was implacably gaining ground – 163,872 new television licences were issued during October, a monthly record, taking the total up to some 3.8 million – but Gladys Langford continued to resist. 'I still dislike TV,' she reflected after watching the arrival of the Emperor of Abyssinia on a fellow-resident's set at her north London hotel. 'The figures are so tiny. I thought the Queen looked very drab, the Duke of Edinburgh slouches and the Duke of Gloucester was wearing spectacles. Winston Churchill looks a very, very old man.'

There were three especially notable new series. *Fabian of the Yard* was a Scotland Yard drama series filmed in documentary style and based on a real-life detective; *Zoo Quest*, produced and presented by a very fresh-faced David Attenborough, had not only film of an expedition to West Africa but also, in the studio, some of the animals brought back to London Zoo; and *Ask Pickles* was self-explanatory. 'As soon as I saw that lean face, perfectly creased by years of practice into the right, warm smile, leaning into my parlour to say " 'Ow do," ' wrote a relieved James Thomas in the *News Chronicle*, 'I thought: "Doan't thee wurry, lad, tha's picked thisen another winner." ' Thomas did identify a possible problem of intrusiveness, but overall applauded Pickles because he 'risks putting before the biggest audience in Europe an unrehearsed string of ordinary folk who make you wonder what they are going to *say* next'. Bernard Hollowood disagreed, laying into the blessed Wilfred in his regular *Punch* column on television. He accused Pickles of wallowing 'smugly in a nauseating glue-pot of mawkishness' and making 'a public parade of emotion that is essentially private', as he 'unites long-separated lovers, friends and relatives, parades the afflicted, champions the hopeless ambitions of the untalented'. In short, declared Hollowood, he 'persuades millions of viewers to become Peeping Toms, eavesdroppers, keyhole snoopers'.[8]

Far more controversial, though, was Nigel Kneale's powerful television adaptation of George Orwell's *Nineteen Eighty-four*, including a particularly disturbing brainwashing scene. It went out live (including a live orchestra) on the evening of Sunday, 12 December, immediately after *What's My Line?*, and starred Peter Cushing as Winston Smith. Although 'put on with many a caution toward the kiddies and old and susceptible' (in Philip Hope-Wallace's caustic words), the protesting phone calls flooded in almost from the start, followed over the next few days by press outrage and Commons motions accusing the BBC of needlessly frightening its viewers. 'Many said it should not have been broadcast on a Sunday – the evening of "family viewing",' was a common opinion among the BBC's Viewing Panel (giving a Reaction Index of only 39), while ' "it should not have been broadcast at all, because it wasn't entertainment" was a frequent statement'. Among those also watching was the writer Sid Chaplin. 'Bad, I thought, in several ways,' he told a friend. 'Reaction of many shocked people was

I think a true instinct – human beings have proved themselves bigger than the diabolical torturers pictured. The end was just disgusting.' He did add, though, that it was 'good that 1 mill – perhaps more – should see this exposure of social engineering'. On Thursday the 16th a second performance, this time straight after *Sportsview*, won the biggest television audience since the Coronation. It was, predictably, a talking point on next evening's *Any Questions?*. 'I like to see the BBC showing a bit of courage,' declared Anthony Wedgwood Benn from the County Secondary Modern School at Ilminster, 'and if there was public protest about this I think it was quite right in view of the nature of the play for the BBC to go ahead with it. (*A little applause.*) I'm glad anyway one person in the audience agrees with me.'

'Two hours of absorbing horror comic for the delectation of millions,' was Hollowood's verdict on the adaptation, and amid a renewed storm of public outrage about American horror comics the allusion was deliberately topical. 'A bit of Christmas shopping (I am getting on very early with it, this year),' noted Madge Martin in mid-November, 'then to an exhibition, held in the N.U.T. [National Union of Teachers] headquarters near St Pancras, of "comics" for children. It was to show how dreadful the "horror" comics are, and a campaign is being launched, successfully, to ban them. They certainly are revolting.' Soon afterwards, Peter Mauger in *Picture Post* reiterated his call of two years earlier, declaring that 'either we can protect the "freedom" of a few unscrupulous publishers to make money by degrading the minds of our young people – or we can protect our children's freedom to develop normally, free from this dangerous drug'. But given that the sales of such comics were in fact far lower than those of British comics, was legislation to ban them really the answer? 'A sample number of copies were produced and handed round by the Home Secretary,' a flippant Harold Macmillan recorded after a Cabinet discussion in early 1955. 'There were not quite enough copies for us all – so cries were heard "come on, now, David, let's have a look" or "I say: Fred, you might give a chap a chance" and so on . . .' Eventually, bowing to public opinion and resisting Roy Jenkins's stirring parliamentary defence of freedom of expression, the government did go ahead and legislate.[9]

Freedom of artistic expression was probably not Gladys Langford's credo either. 'I shall go to no more modern art shows unless they are free for I get no pleasure out of contemplating modern art,' she reflected in October after inspecting an exhibition of 'British Painting & Sculpture 1954' at the Whitechapel Art Gallery. She had wisely (from her point of view) skipped the solo show by the 26-year-old John Bratby. 'Bratby does his vehement damnedest to extract the last ounce of desperate passion from the spectre-eyed ladies and the higgle-piggle of objects crowded on the kitchen table that are his subject matter,' reckoned the *Spectator*'s M. H. Middleton. 'On goes the paint, trowel-thick, in great linear strips that follow the form like livid weals.' And overall, 'the result too often suggests rather a desperate desire for intensity than a desperate intensity'. Other critics, though, were much more receptive: John Russell in the *Sunday Times* asserted that Bratby's rendition of a cornflakes packet edged Velázquez's *Rokeby Venus*; *Studio Magazine* ranked him with Rembrandt and Goya; and in the *New Statesman* the young, very left-wing John Berger declared that Bratby had created a style entirely his own: 'To enter the Beaux Arts Gallery is to enter Bratby's home. This is partly because his subjects are his wife, his sister-in-law, his kitchen table, his dog, his groceries: but far more profoundly because you are compelled to share his most intense and personal emotions. His personality is a desperate one and you are held by his glittering eye.' Indeed, asserted Berger, he paints 'as though he sensed that he only had one more day to live', and 'a packet of corn-flakes on a littered kitchen table as though it were part of a last supper'.

In fact, Bratby was part of a loose quartet of young, broadly social-realist painters from the Royal College of Art who had all recently exhibited at the Beaux Arts – Derrick Greaves, Edward Middleditch and Jack Smith being the others – and in December probably the most influential art critic of the day, David Sylvester, grouped them together in an *Encounter* article, 'The Kitchen Sink', that gave the name to a movement for which the everyday was paramount. 'If there is life and exultation in Bratby's work,' Sylvester noted in a largely hostile piece, 'there is also the drawback that in expressing the disorder of reality it is itself disordered.' Bratby himself the previous year had married the talented painter Jean Cooke (after first locking her in his room in case she escaped), and over the years, as his own fortunes dwindled, he would treat her appallingly, permitting her to paint for only three hours in the morning, slashing her pictures if he disapproved of them and painting over them if he had run out of canvas. 'A tiny woman,' noted an admiring obituarist in 2008, 'she had an indomitable spirit, and was affectionately celebrated for always having her say at Royal Academy meetings.'[10]

Sylvester's 'Kitchen Sink' article was just about to appear when on 30 November, to mark Churchill's 80th birthday that day, there took place in Westminster Hall a ceremony that Macmillan called 'dignified, restrained and noble'. Apart from speeches by Attlee and Churchill himself, its main elements were Parliament's two presents: an illuminated book signed by almost every MP and a portrait of Churchill painted by Graham Sutherland. 'He is a magnanimous man & a great one,' reflected Marian Raynham after listening to the ceremony on the radio. 'Some did not sign in the book of names presented. To him that meant, I don't know how to put it, freedom & the right of the people to make decisions.' There was less magnanimity about the portrait, which Churchill had first seen a fortnight earlier and immediately loathed, partly because it made him look as if he was straining on the lavatory. 'One painful moment when the curtain concealing Sutherland portrait was drawn back,' recorded Clarissa Eden (wife of Anthony) in her account of the ceremony, 'and Winston turned to look at it with loathing, and he then said, "This is a remarkable example of modern art," whereupon the blimpish Tories let out a yell of laughter & Sutherland blushed.' Attlee privately sympathised. 'I don't like Graham Sutherland's stuff,' he wrote to his brother soon afterwards. 'I tell people that it's lucky that he did not depict the Old Man in plus-fours with loud checks with one foot in a grave. That's his usual style.' The painting was never displayed in public, and after a year or so Clemmie Churchill had it secretly cut up and burned. As for Churchill himself, all the birthday fuss had, despite the disagreeable portrait, a rejuvenating effect. 'He now has a firm reputation – for the first time in his life – as a reliable and far-seeing statesman *in peace*,' Henry Fairlie observed a few days later in his first political commentary for the *Spectator*, arguing there was no reason why Churchill should not lead the Tories into the next election.

English football, after a rocky time, was returning to Churchillian form – and although the national team beat West Germany 3–1 in a Wembley friendly the day after his birthday, the principal flag-bearers were the pacey, muscular, long-passing Wolverhampton Wanderers, under the authoritarian management of Stan Cullis. Floodlit friendlies against prestigious international opposition were a considerable novelty, but in late 1954 there were two at Molineux, in both cases the second half being televised. 'RUSSIANS FEAR WRIGHT' was a confident headline on 16 November before that evening a crowd of 55,184 saw Billy Wright's team thrash Spartak 4–0, making (in Geoffrey Green's euphoric words in *The Times*) 'the sort of history that has been awaited by Englishmen chafing under the yoke of Continental dominance in the whole wide field of football'. On 13 December the visitors were Honved, six of whose team (including Puskas) had played in Hungary's historic 6–3 victory against England just over a year earlier. Honved were two up at half-time, but then the nation cheered as it watched, to words by Kenneth Wolstenholme, Wolves turn it round on a quagmire of a pitch and win 3–2. Hailing 'another decisive blow for British football', Charles Buchan in the *News Chronicle* claimed that Wolves in the second half 'not only got on top, but rubbed the noses of the Honved players in the Molineux mud'. And he explained how they did it: 'By close marking and quick tackling, they cut all the rhythm out of the Honved team and then sledge-hammered a way past their defenders. It was British football at its best.'

Christmas was approaching, the first one since the end of rationing. 'We went out early by car this morning to get the last of the shopping for the holiday,' Phyllis Willmott recorded in Bethnal Green on Christmas Eve, a Friday:

> We went to Roman Road. It was not crowded, but there were people about. The women were out with their big, flat bags. And the husbands were out with packets in their hands, looking as if they were really enjoying this day off work.
>
> At the end of the road we parked for a moment, and I watched the world go by. We were outside a butcher's. A big, well-made woman pushing a pram stopped outside. She was shabbily dressed. Two children were walking with her – a boy of about nine or ten, in long trousers; a girl of about six with thin, white legs, cotton socks, and a coat with the hem let down badly. She had her hands in her pockets and looked cold in the sharp wind. 'You stay outside,' said the mother to her. The girl stayed, holding the pram, while the boy followed his mother into the

shop. At first, I thought there were two children in the pram. Another look showed that there were three: a boy of about four, a girl of three (with a dummy in her mouth and a rosy, bonny face) and a baby under the hood of perhaps a year or fifteen months. The girl standing holding the pram stared in at us; she didn't smile. I felt how unfair life is. More so now, perhaps, than ever. They are becoming such a minority group, the large 'poor' families.

It was, on the whole, an easier life in Chingford. 'Abbé has today off, too,' noted a contented Judy Haines four days later. 'How I do love to have him at home. He took us to see Glynis Johns in "Mad about Men". All about a mermaid. We all thoroughly enjoyed it, and I am resolved to wear lighter colours and step up the glamour a bit. Resolution No 1 for 1955.'[11]

5

A Fair Crack at the Whip

Modernisation was in the air in early 1955. On Monday, 24 January
– hours after 17 had been killed when a diverted York–Bristol
express jumped the points at Sutton Coldfield – the British Transport
Commission's chairman, General Sir Brian Robertson, unveiled
a £1,240 million *Plan for the Modernisation and Re-equipment of
British Railways* that aimed by 1970 to electrify the main lines and
many of the major suburban lines, make increasing use of diesel, and
phase out steam trains. Against a background of rising coal prices,
the strategy made obvious sense, whatever the undoubted widespread
emotional attachment to steam, for all its dirtiness. Press reaction was
generally positive, if somewhat sceptical of the ability of the ossified
BTC to deliver change. Moreover, as the *Economist* fairly pointed
out, 'the measures that are proposed will, after fifteen years, put
this country's railway system no further ahead than, say, the Dutch
railways today'. There was also the continuing here and now of a
badly rundown, poorly performing network. 'In 1962 the train now
standing at Platform 6 will be air-conditioned, radar-equipped and
faster than sound,' announced a station loudspeaker in an Osbert
Lancaster pocket cartoon a few days after the plan, 'but tonight it will
be running a leetle behind time!'

A large part of the problem facing the railways by 1955 was
increasingly intense road competition, especially in freight, and on 2
February the Transport Minister, John Boyd-Carpenter, announced a
major programme of expenditure on roads over the next four years.
This would include the start of construction of London–Yorkshire
and Preston–Birmingham 'motor roads' (ie motorways), a crossing

of the Firth of Forth, the Dartford–Purfleet tunnel and the rebuilding of London's Albert Bridge. 'Throughout its length it will have two carriageways,' helpfully explained *The Times* about the London-to-Yorkshire project. 'The motor road will be carried over or under all existing roads and at important junctions there will be fly-overs or under-passes.' Against a background of the number of motor vehicles having nearly doubled since 1938, Britain's roads were, by common consent, inadequate and dangerous – epitomised by the A1, or Great North Road, condemned by *Picture Post* later in 1955 as 'the bloodiest country lane in Britain' – so, as with the rail plan, there was little opposition. However, the town planner Colin Buchanan offered a word of caution. 'The road improvements will be, in the main, open-country schemes, and they will benefit the motorists, industry, and indeed the country,' he wrote in early 1956. 'But in the towns, where journeys begin and end, the extra motor vehicles may come to be regarded as a very mixed blessing.'[1]

Less than a fortnight after Boyd-Carpenter's announcement, it was the turn of Geoffrey Lloyd, Minister of Fuel and Power, to flourish a ten-year plan. 'This is a historic day for Britain,' he declared. 'It offers the possibility of a continuing increase in the standard of living of our country . . . Here is new scope for our traditional genius – the mixing of a small proportion of imported materials with a large amount of skill and ingenuity.' Lloyd was announcing the building of 12 nuclear power stations, a programme ahead of anywhere else in the world. The new stations (known in time as the Magnox stations, after the special alloy of magnesium in which the uranium fuel rods were clad) were to be built by private enterprise but operated by the Central Electricity Authority, reconstituted in 1957 as the Central Electricity Generating Board. That body's first chairman would be Sir Christopher Hinton, who in 1955 itself was, as a key figure at the Atomic Energy Authority, the public face of nuclear power for peaceful purposes. His arguments were compelling and seldom criticised: not only was the demand for conventional fuels growing rapidly, but the more easily worked coal deposits were becoming depleted, the price of coal was inexorably increasing, and there were continuing recruitment problems in the mines. Moreover, construction work at Calder Hall in Cumberland, intended to be the first station to generate large quantities of electrical power from atomic energy, was progressing satisfactorily, while in the north of Scotland, work was under way at Dounreay to build a 'breeder reactor'. In March, Marian Raynham in Surbiton heard Hinton give a typically authoritative talk on 'Atomic Energy in Industry' on the Home Service. 'I loved to hear it all just roll off his tongue about the Calder reactor & uranium & gases & power & fission material etc,' she recorded. 'All so easy it sounded.'[2]

Inevitably, the question began to be asked, especially in relation to the nationalised sector: would modernisation work without higher productivity and improved industrial relations? The railways were now temporarily replacing the coal mines as the focus of most attention, especially in the wake of a threatened national strike in the second week of 1955 that had, as was becoming a familiar pattern, been averted only by the deft ministerial use of a tame Court of Inquiry. The Cabinet was divided about its recommendations, but most knew that public opinion (74 per cent according to Gallup) was firmly on the side of the low-paid railwaymen. Churchill had no appetite for an industrial fight, and, as Macmillan put it in his diary to justify acceptance of significant pay rises for little or nothing in return, 'we are enjoying the greatest boom in history', so 'how can 700,000 industrial workers be asked to forego their share?' The *Economist* as usual fulminated – 'There is no substitute for competition . . . One of the dreams that finally died last week was the dream that industries could be planned or rationalised or co-ordinated into efficiency' – while Enoch Powell warned in a speech in his Wolverhampton constituency that without greater financial realism 'we shall get into the nightmare situation of everybody subsidising everybody else's wages', but as yet there was zero political traction for the concept of extensive denationalisation. Instead, Tory hopes were pinned on the leaders of organised labour doing their honourable bit as they saw the fruits of the government's capital investment coming through. 'There is really a great opportunity here of doing a big thing,' Macmillan privately reflected shortly before the announcement of the rail plan. 'We *must* – at all costs – get the Unions on our side from the start, if we are to get the benefit of modernisation.'

Among railwaymen themselves, morale was near rock-bottom. Their relative standard of living had deteriorated sharply since the war, skilled men (including drivers and firemen) were leaving in droves, and too many recruits were of questionable quality and being promoted too quickly, compromising safety standards. Brian Thompson's first vacation job as a Cambridge undergraduate was to work as a relief porter at sooty, sulphurous, 'massively overmanned' Liverpool Street station in the run-up to Christmas 1955. The prevailing cynicism, he found, was total:

> You could describe railway portering of the period as money for Old Holborn. It was unskilled labour in all but one regard: there was a knack in dropping a promising-looking box just hauled from the goods van at exactly the right height onto its most vulnerable corner. When it was done properly, the packaging shattered and the contents were revealed. The rest was sleight of hand. The first time I saw this done, I had to blink twice to believe it, the more so because it was effected under the nose of a foreman porter there on purpose to prevent it. The theft that followed was accomplished as smoothly and routinely as a laundress folding sheets.
>
> We took our breaks in an underground mess at the end of one of the platforms, an unheated hell-hole littered with the crusts of sandwiches, newspapers and cigarette packets. Rats ran round the walls the way they do in pantomime sketches, as if drawn by strings; nobody seemed to notice. Some had come to work only to sleep, others to add to an open-ended seminar on horse-racing . . .
>
> A seasoned porter called Chas took me on as his assistant and for half the ten-hour shift we would walk, a couple of buckets of sand in each hand, up some stairs and across a creaking cast-iron gantry before leaving them in a corner while we nipped into Bishopsgate for a wet. Then we would stagger back with them to our underground cave for a smoke. The only time anything like despatch was shown was the day the royal family set off for Sandringham. On that morning half the station staff mobbed the train, hustling for the honour of lifting a suitcase into the compartments assigned to the entourage. The knack here was to avoid the equerries, who had seen a thing or two before joining the Palace, and go for elderly ladies-in-waiting, who responded with bewildered gratuities.
>
> 'I'm afraid I don't have any coin in my purse,' one said.

'Don't you worry about that, ma. Me and my family wish you and yours a very Merry Christmas.'

Blushing, she passed across a green pound note.

Altogether, it was 'the perfect antidote to romantic idealism about the unawakened working class'.[3]

Another industry with inadequate growth in labour productivity was the Lancashire cotton industry. There, dismay had greeted the announcement in early 1954 of the Anglo-Japanese Payments and Trade Agreement, which in effect opened up the whole sterling area to Japanese imports. 'It was not to be expected that this freeing of trade would be popular in Lancashire, but if it cannot be liked it will just have to be lumped,' noted an unsympathetic *Spectator*, adding that there persisted in that county 'bitter memories of Japanese competition between the wars'. Predictably, the man who made most noise at this point was the combative, publicity-seeking mill owner Cyril Lord, who accepted an invitation from *Picture Post* to discuss the matter with Kyoshi Fujise, a Japanese trade representative in Britain. He pitched in from the start:

> *Lord:* The point is that the Japanese have now got unlimited access to our Colonial markets. Why should they send stuff here? I can only speak from the commonsense aspect as far as this country goes. I am vitally interested in textiles, having twelve mills and over 5,000 workers. It is an industry I've been in all my life – and I have seen the economic distress caused solely by our attitude to Japan. I am sorry to bring this up Mr Fujise, but the appreciation of what we have done for Japan pre-1939 was shown by Pearl Harbor on December 7, 1941. What has Japan ever done for us? Why should we do anything for Japan?
>
> *Fujise:* I admit that Japan did a very bad thing in starting war by attacking Pearl Harbor. But she lost the war. It might be God's judgement – that I don't know, and cannot say. But I think that Japan does not have to remain an outcast nation in the world.
>
> *Lord:* That is true. But why should Britain destroy herself economically for Japan? Are you suggesting that *we*, and not America, should help you to attain the standards of conditions that exist in this country? After all, it is America that is building you up as a buffer state against Communism. I am speaking personally. I would not care whether

you were Communistic, Democratic, or what you were, because
whichever way the wind blows, that way you will go. If it suits you to
go Communistic, you will.

Fujise: I am not prepared to discuss that matter.

Lord then went on to accuse Japanese industrialists of being subsidised
by their government, lamented that the stinginess of British banks
prevented the Lancashire cotton industry from modernising and
declared that 'we have been sold down the river by the Government'.
Proceedings concluded on a sour note:

Fujise: I understand your feelings, and I do not expect goodwill from
   you. But I should like to end this meeting in a sincere and honest way.
Lord (shaking hands before leaving): Thanks. Your boys were shaking
   hands in Washington at the time they attacked Pearl Harbor.
Fujise: I am sorry that you've mentioned that. If I may say this frankly:
   Japan has been, and is, looking forward to a lead from this country
   and from the British Commonwealth, and they take what they say,
   and write, very seriously. I myself am very much for the British, not
   against them. But, quite frankly, I am rather disappointed with Mr
   Lord's attitude. I respect his argument. I am not talking about that. But
   I was disappointed at his way of saying farewell to me. I look to you
   British as the gentlemen of gentlemen.

In the event, the Japanese threat to Lancashire's colonial markets
proved to be exaggerated, and by 1955 the focus had moved to the
Commonwealth, with the industry campaigning for import controls on
cheap cloth first from India and then from Pakistan and Hong Kong also.
'The hangman of Lancashire' was Lord's typically judicious term for
Peter Thorneycroft, President of the Board of Trade, but Thorneycroft
was adamant that, in the context of the government's wider policy of
liberalising trade, Lancashire could not be made a special case.[4] The
cotton industry, in short, was on a one-way ride.

———

'Not for the first time in our history we have a Colonial problem on
our hands, but it's a Colonial problem with a difference,' began Robert

Reid's voiceover at the start of the television documentary, *Has Britain a Colour Bar?*, transmitted on the last day of January 1955. 'Instead of being thousands of miles away and worrying other people, it's right here, on the spot, worrying us.' And he asked about the West Indian immigrants: 'How do they fit in to our ways and standards of life, coming, as they do, from places where customs, standards of life, are much different, and, very often, lower than our own?' The main body of the programme saw René Cutforth in investigatory mode in Birmingham, home (in a manner of speaking) to some 10,000 West Indians. 'Well, let's face it,' he said, 'they are different. They look different and they behave differently . . . they sound different and their tastes in matters of food are different.'

The strength of the documentary, which made a considerable stir, was in its interviews, and next day the *Birmingham Post* asserted that through them Cutforth had 'sought to show that while official circles are careful to ensure that there is no colour-bar, prejudice is encountered in the daily life of the newcomer'. Thus an estate agent 'agreed that he hesitated to let houses to coloured persons, who might overcrowd them', a white factory worker 'stated bluntly that the sooner all coloured people were sent home the better he would be pleased'; and Harry Green, district secretary of the Transport and General Workers' Union, emphasised 'different traditions' and warned that 'real trouble was possible in the event of a trade slump'. For William Salter, television critic of the *New Statesman*, 'probably the most depressing thing of all was the spectacle of trade union leaders having to defend and attempt to justify their members' xenophobia', and his overwhelming impression was that legitimate concerns about 'problems of economics [ie employment] and housing' were 'rationalisations of attitudes of mind inadmissible to the public view'. He may well have been right, for although Cutforth had tried to interview the white bus crews at Hockley bus garage, scene of the recent dispute over the Corporation's employment of black workers, they had refused to talk on camera and had prevented their black colleagues from doing so either. Reid for his part would receive an unambiguous postcard from one viewer: 'You and your black friends ought to be put up against a wall and shot.'[5]

There was no doubting the proliferation, not least in London. 'The number of negroes and coloured people about is amazing,' noted

Gladys Langford neutrally in April 1955. 'They seem to be everywhere.' Altogether, in terms of the mid-1950s surge after America had shut its doors to West Indian immigration from 1952, Home Office figures for net immigration are probably the most reliable guide:

	West Indies	India	Pakistan	Total 'Coloured' Commonwealth
1953	2,000	–	–	2,000
1954	11,000	–	–	11,000
1955	27,000	6,000	1,800	42,700
1956	30,000	5,500	2,000	46,850

Traditionally the West Indian newcomers had been almost entirely adult males, but in 1955 virtually one-third were women and children, with the great majority of those newcomers as a whole coming from Jamaica.[6]

Inevitably they encountered a range of reactions. When the eighteen-year-old Morris Gurling arrived in London in 1955 to study engineering, it took him eight hours and endless rejections before he finally got a room in Camden Town, sharing a house with young white men mostly working at the BBC. Another 1955 arrival was Carmel Jones, a future Pentecostal minister:

Biggest shock was, one, the cold, and two, having gone to church for the very first time – so elated, so delighted that I'm coming from an Anglican church back home, I went to join in worship, and so I did – but after the service I was greeted by the vicar, who politely and nicely told me: 'Thank you for coming. But I would be delighted if you didn't come back.' And I said, 'Why?' He said, 'My congregation is uncomfortable in the company of black people.' That was my biggest shock. I was the only black person in that congregation that Sunday morning, and my disappointment, my despair went with me and I didn't say anything to anyone about it for several months after that.

At least one newcomer this year had a somewhat more welcome time of it. 'When you gave a passenger his change and ticket, besides marvelling at the fact that you actually spoke English and that you gave him the correct change, he would also grab hold of your hand and then shout to all the bus that your hands are warm,' remembered a Jamaican migrant (in Donald Hinds's rich 1966 book, *Journey to an Illusion*) about his early experience as a London bus conductor. 'Some, of course, gave your hands a vigorous rub to see whether it was dirt that made you black. So many people put their hands on my hair for good luck in the first year of my working on London buses that I was in fear of going bald prematurely.' It was better yet for 'Melon', a Jamaican who in 1955, after eight years of lodging in rundown parts of Notting Hill, Elephant and Castle, Brixton and Stoke Newington, was able to buy his own house. 'When Melon moved into a short quiet street at the northern end of Brixton,' recorded Hinds, 'his was the only "coloured house" for many a street around. The neighbours showed no hostility. In fact, one helped him to decorate his rooms cheaply, and taught him how to mend electric fuses . . . The children in the street used to gather around Melon and ask him what time it was. They were disappointed when he showed them his gold watch; they laughed happily when he looked up to where the sun ought to be and then guessed the time.'

Nevertheless, for most immigrants, whether new or well established, the question of a colour bar was becoming all too topical. 'Did your reporters visit Moss Side?' asked a reader from Sale after *Picture Post* in early 1954 had claimed there was 'no colour bar' in Manchester, mainly on the grounds that no heads turned when 'a negro bank clerk' went into the cocktail bar of the Grand Hotel. 'Did they interview any Colonial students who had tried to find lodgings, without success?' And about Manchester as a whole: 'There are many ignorant people who fear those with coloured skins. There are people who will not sit next to negroes on buses.' Or take Birmingham, where, quite apart from the television evidence, there was the case in November 1954 of Kenneth Goodman, a black organist due to give a recital in the Town Hall, being refused accommodation at 23 hotels. 'One cannot deny the existence of considerable prejudice against the coloured immigrants,' reflected the *Birmingham Post* a fortnight before Cutforth's programme. 'The difficulties of finding accommodation, the undoubted lack of social amenities, the occasional hurtful taunts they suffer because of their colour, all tend to generate bitterness.' So too elsewhere in the West Midlands: in Coventry, at the General Wolfe pub in Foleshill Road, there was a well-publicised case in February 1955 of two rooms being off limits to 'coloured people', mainly Indians, while soon afterwards there was a furore when the landlord of the Red Cow pub in Smethwick instituted a colour bar in his Men Only smoke-room – a move only half-heartedly opposed by Smethwick's Labour MP, Patrick Gordon Walker.

The general upshot, in terms of day-to-day life, seems to have been a broad acceptance on both sides of separate spheres. 'The West Indians take a passive attitude to any incipient discrimination,' found a *Manchester Guardian* reporter in January 1955 about immigrant life in Brixton. 'In the shopping areas the women keep as much as possible to themselves and make little attempt to mix or chat with their white-skinned neighbours. Most of the immigrants are anxious not to provoke incidents . . .' But sometimes there was a flashpoint, as in a series of tense nights in Camden Town in August 1954, culminating in an attempt by an aggressive group of white men to set fire to a house in Baynes Street occupied by West Indians, after first entering it and smashing up all the furniture. 'Then they come into my shop, they do nothing but complain and ask for a quarter of a pound of this and that,' a white resident of the street told a journalist soon afterwards. 'It's not worth serving them.' And another: 'Those girls with them – up at Clerkenwell [ie magistrates' court] every week, I'll bet.' And a third, using the inevitable, all-purpose adjective: 'They're dirty . . .'[7]

Turning to the workplace, there was a positive aspect, especially in the prevailing full-employment context. 'Faced with a growing list of vacancies, transport concerns somewhat reluctantly recruited coloured conductors and drivers, West Indians especially,' noted Michael Banton later in the 1950s in his eminently judicious survey of *White and Coloured*. 'London and Manchester early led the way with small numbers of coloured transport workers, then in 1954 Birmingham Corporation had to recruit them in larger numbers, and in 1955 Sheffield, Nottingham, Coventry and other towns followed suit.' As for the wider industrial scene, a January 1955 despatch from Coventry in the *Manchester Guardian* quoted the personnel manager of a large car factory: 'Frankly, we would be completely lost without our coloured workers. Our foundry just would not keep going. They don't mind how hard they work . . .' Yet overall it was a far more mixed picture. In Coventry itself, according to Steven Tolliday in his study of that city's engineering workers, recruitment practices at the major firms meant that 'most blacks never got inside the factory gates', while as for Birmingham the *Post*'s analysis of race relations noted that 'several large firms' still operated a colour bar.

Such a policy, there and elsewhere, to a large degree reflected employers' awareness of shop-floor anxieties and prejudices, with the trade unions far from distinguishing themselves in terms of mediating those attitudes. Even where non-white workers were allowed, they tended to be treated by their representatives as second-class members, with *The Times* observing in November 1954 that 'the trade unionists, excepting such undertakings as the Post Office and London Transport, where it is a point of honour that there shall be no colour bar, often have an understanding with managements that the hallowed rule of "last in, first out" shall not apply to whites when coloured immigrants are employed, and that coloured workers shall not be promoted over white'. Soon afterwards, Emrys Thomas, General Secretary of the Ministry of Labour Staff Association, spelled out the facts of life about 'West Indian Workers' for *Socialist Commentary*'s progressive, socially liberal, middle-class readers:

> Practically only about 25 per cent are skilled or semi-skilled in the sense that they can walk straight into a job of work and begin to produce. The rest are just not up to the quality of the white workers. The man who says he is a carpenter turns out to have done only rough work and has no tools. Worse, he is not used to the industrial discipline of this country; the necessity to stick at the job and not spend too much time at the lavatory or smoking and talking. He is unfamiliar with the things in industrial life which are second nature to the white worker. He appears, often, to be unused to the idea of completing his stint each day and every day.

Ultimately, Thomas envisaged a policy of 'limitation', but meanwhile, 'so long as the proportion of coloured people in the white community is low and well-dispersed, then the complicated relationships are minimised and hardly obtrude themselves'.[8]

One local dispute in February/March 1955 suggested that things were already quite 'complicated'. This was at West Bromwich, where busmen took strike action in protest at the hiring of an Indian trainee conductor. C. H. Mullard, a bus driver for 18 years, issued a union-sanctioned statement: 'The platform staff are deeply concerned about this matter because, owing to our low rate of wages, we know that if we accept an influx of coloured labour we shall be brought down to a 44-hour week on which it would be impossible for a family man to exist.' Tellingly, the busmen received little public sympathy, typified by a letter to the local paper that described West Bromwich conductors and conductresses as 'the most ill-mannered, bad-tempered and ignorant lot I have ever met'. Bkika Patel himself, who had previously worked with the Bombay tramway service, understandably opted for caution – 'I have no wish to cause any trouble and I am keeping clear of the dispute' – and ultimately, as in several other similar public-transport disputes in the Midlands this year, it was the white strikers who largely won the day in the form of (to quote Clive Harris, historian of the non-white 'industrial reserve army') 'the imposition of a quota on the number of black workers taken on, their confinement to specific duties and agreements about redundancy'.

There was a piquant footnote to the West Bromwich episode. After the Bishop of Lichfield had condemned the striking busmen as unChristian, the MP for Wolverhampton South-West (in the Black Country, like West Bromwich) wrote to him to argue that it was not racial considerations as such that had motivated the busmen, but rather their dislike of a foreign group muscling in, as with the Durham miners when they had gone on strike over the employment of Italians. The MP, Enoch Powell, suggested that the time had come for an amendment to the 1948 British Nationality Act, in order to 'distinguish' Jamaicans 'from citizens of this country', and he concluded piously: 'In seeking to prevent while it is still possible the creation here of perhaps insoluble and intractable political problems, I hope one is not necessarily in breach of any obligation of humanity or Christianity.'[9]

In general, the question of immigration controls was starting – but only starting – to become a politically high-profile issue. In March 1954, a few weeks after the inconclusive Cabinet discussion on 'Coloured Workers', Lord ('Bobbety') Salisbury, Lord President of the Council and a key figure in the Tory Party, sounded an apocalyptic note to the Colonial Secretary: 'We are faced with a problem which, though at

present it may be only a cloud the size of a man's hand, may easily come
to fill the whole political horizon . . . Indeed, if something is not done
to check it now, I should not be at all surprised if the problem became
quite unmanageable in 20 or 30 years time. We might be faced with very
much the same type of appalling issue that is now causing such great
difficulties for the United States . . .' The decisive argument, however,
had already been made a few days earlier by the Commonwealth
Secretary, Lord Swinton, writing to Salisbury: 'If we legislate on
immigration, though we draft it in non-discriminatory terms, we cannot
conceal the obvious fact that the object is to keep out coloured peoples.
Unless there is really a strong case for this, it would surely be an unwise
moment to raise the issue when we are preaching and trying to practise
partnership in the abolition of the Colour Bar.' There the matter rested
for the moment, though one historian, Kathleen Paul, has argued that
it was from this point that the government initiated what she calls 'a
deliberate campaign to sway public opinion in favour of control'.

By the autumn of 1954 it was obvious that the number of West Indian
immigrants was rising sharply, and on 5 November a Labour backbencher,
John Hynd, secured a half-hour Commons debate on the immigration issue.
'If there is a sudden influx of outsiders, whether they be Jamaicans, Poles,
Welshmen or Irishmen, it upsets the balance,' he declared, before going on
to excuse the proprietors of a dance hall in his Sheffield constituency who
had imposed a colour bar. In response, a Colonial Office minister, Henry
Hopkinson, could only say that the whole question was receiving 'very
careful attention'. Three days later *The Times* warned against the powder-
keg implications of the new wave of immigrants becoming concentrated
in areas of serious housing shortages – 'What are likely to be the feelings
of more than 50,000 would-be white tenants in Birmingham, who have
waited years for a decent house, when they see newcomers, no matter what
their colour, taking over whole streets of properties?' – while on the 12th, in
his Smethwick constituency near Birmingham, Gordon Walker came out
for a policy of control: 'I don't think any country has a moral obligation to
import a racial problem . . . I am a great believer in Commonwealth unity,
but I cannot see that there will be any danger to it if Britain takes powers
over immigration.'[10]

At Cabinet, the issue came to a head in January 1955, shortly before
the BBC documentary and amid considerable press coverage of some

spectacularly big-number disembarkations of Jamaicans at Plymouth. 'More discussion about the West Indian immigrants,' noted Macmillan on the 20th. 'A Bill is being drafted – but it's not an easy problem. P.M. thinks "Keep England White" a good slogan!' In the event the Cabinet shied away from action. The reasons were probably a mixture of disinclination to accept the potential seriousness of the issue, uncertainty about the state of public opinion and concerns about the implications for the 'Old' [ie white] Commonwealth. Irrespective of the question of 'should', *could* Churchill have done more? 'I think it is the most important subject facing this country, but I cannot get any of my ministers to take any notice,' he privately informed the *Spectator*'s editor, Ian Gilmour, though the truth surely was that at this particular point in his political career he was little inclined for major controversy, in the domestic sphere anyway. About the same time, a right-wing Tory MP, Cyril Osborne, tried and failed to introduce a private member's bill in favour of restrictions. He seems to have been sat on by the government, even to the extent of having to pretend to be ill, while it did not help his cause that Princess Margaret was about to visit Jamaica in celebration of the tercentenary of British sovereignty there. But on the ground, the issue was far from going away. 'I believe in international democratic Socialism, and I don't like the idea of controlling the movement of people, but when a city is faced with a problem like Birmingham's, with a shortage of houses, a shortage of house-building land and workers from many countries flocking to it, it seems to me that we Socialists must do some re-thinking,' publicly declared Frank Price, an ambitious Birmingham local politician, in March. 'If the present situation continues without control, conditions in the city, already very difficult, will become chaotic. What the city council can do to meet the problem has yet to be worked out, though my view is that it demands national consideration and action by the Government.'[11]

It is not easy to judge the state of public opinion as a whole by this time, including in the many areas of Britain where the sighting of a non-white person was still a rarity. In November 1954, following a *Picture Post* article on mixed marriages, there was strikingly rosy testimony from 'a young coloured man happily married to an English girl': 'Thank God, I can honestly say not one person I have met has brought up the question of my colour. I think I can speak with some authority, since I have completed a hitch-hike tour of the British Isles. On this tour I was treated with every kindness conceivable, and more than one driver went out of his way to oblige me.' However, there were far more letters to the press of an essentially negative kind. To quote a handful from 1954/5:

> I would have been far happier to stay among my own people. Now I find that there is nowhere I can go without being stared at. Even in church many hesitate to sit next to me just because I am dark. *(Indian student, Bradford)*
>
> The real problem is not the dope pedlars, but the tens of thousands of hard working types who in so many cases find white wives and promptly produce larger families than their white neighbours. *(Les Pritchard, Llandaff)*
>
> One must face facts. There is a Colour Bar growing, as the hundreds of West Indians pour into our isle, seeking 'paradise'. This flow must be greatly restricted. As the American says, 'Don't get me wrong'. I want the West Indians to have a fair crack at the whip, but not at the expense of the strife and turmoil that a Colour Bar brings. *(Anthony Alton, Lancashire)*
>
> At the present influx of coloured people it will be a rarity to hear an English voice on our city streets in a generation, or so. We are known as a hospitable people, but have we not opened the doors of our national hospitality too wide? *(C. Corfield, Birmingham)*
>
> The influx of coloured people into this country continues. Some firms now employ more West Indians than Englishmen. Are British workers blind to the threat to their welfare or can they see no farther than across the road? *(O. Duncan, London SE15)*

Unfortunately, there is no satisfactory (or even semi-satisfactory) statistical survey of attitudes, and what we do have from this time conveys a jumbled message. Gallup in April 1955 asked, 'Do you think it is right or wrong for people to refuse to work with coloured men and women?', to which only 12 per cent thought it was right, whereas 79 per cent thought it wrong. (In the same poll, to the question 'Do you personally know or have you known any coloured people?', 58 per cent replied in the negative.) Also in 1955, the sociologist Anthony

Richmond, in a report entitled *The Colour Problem*, estimated that the majority of Britain's white population was prejudiced against black people, with about one-third believing that they 'should not be allowed in Britain at all'. Finally, there was the *Daily Sketch*, a right-wing tabloid. In January 1955, on the back of a 'special inquiry' by the paper into West Indian immigrants which had found that 'too many of them will be doomed to poverty relieved only by the public purse', it polled its readers: 97.6 per cent were against unrestricted entry and 81.3 per cent were in favour of stopping entry altogether.

For all too many West Indian newcomers, irrespective of these various figures and estimates, there was often huge ignorance to overcome, abetted by an instinctive suspicion or resentment of 'the other', and further compounded by the time-honoured English vice, hypocrisy. One West Indian, A. G. Bennett, offered this wry but heartfelt sketch in his 1954 book *Because They Know Not*:

> What is wrong is with what they style the 'neighbour'. Since I came here I never met a single English person who had any colour prejudice. Once, I walked the whole length of the street looking for a room and everyone told me that he or she had no prejudice against coloured people. It was the neighbour who was stupid. If we could only find the 'neighbour' we could solve the entire problem.[12]

'It's a good programme on Thursday night,' Nella Last in Barrow noted gratefully on 13 January 1955. 'When I look at my husband sometimes, I wonder *whatever* I'd do without the wireless.' The following evening, *Any Questions?* came from Taunton, and among those dealing with the first question, 'Are the measures taken to deal with travel difficulties due to seasonal frost adequate?', was the Labour MP for South Gloucestershire, just back from a lengthy trip to the States. 'I haven't the faintest idea whether the measures are adequate or not – I don't know what measures are taken,' impatiently declared Anthony Crosland. 'As far as I'm concerned, the weather as a subject of conversation after three months away from it, is out.' Last did not yet have a television, but by this time more than four million households did, and the following evening, Saturday the 15th, saw the debut of *The*

Benny Hill Show. 'A career that owes all, or nearly all, to television,'
remarked *Radio Times* about 'the burly, chubby-cheeked young man
who made such a hit as compère of *Showcase*,' and the 29-year-old,
who had left school at 16 and still lived 'quietly and modestly in a
North London boarding house', was indeed the first British comedian
to forge a style specifically tailored for television. 'Even though he was
prone to be "saucy",' his biographer Mark Lewisohn has observed, 'he
traded on a larky, good-natured, boy-next-door image, epitomised by
his cheeky looks and grin,' and at this point his appeal to the television
audience was 'universal – across the classes and generations'. No
doubt this was partly a reflection of the still relative novelty of the
medium, with BBC audience research finding soon afterwards that
'there seems to be far less "class difference" in viewing habits than
in listening habits'. As it happened, Hill's was not the only notable
debut programme this mid-January weekend, for on Sunday afternoon
there featured for the first time *The Sooty Show*. It was almost seven
years since Harry Corbett, a Yorkshire engineer-surveyor who also
tried his hand at amateur magic, had bought a teddy-bear hand puppet
in a Blackpool shop for 8s and called him Sooty. Now, having gone
full-time with his little friend in 1952, he was at the start of what
would become one of the world's longest-running children's television
programmes.[13]

Mid-February also had its moments. 'Although *Picture Book* will
set out to interest its very young viewers and awaken in them a sense
of wonder and discovery, no attempt will be made to *teach*,' solemnly
promised *Radio Times* about the latest addition ('Pages turned by
Patricia Driscoll') to the *Watch with Mother* line-up, going out for the
first time on Monday the 14th between 4.00 and 4.15. Two days later,
at the Strand Theatre, the curtain went up on *Sailor Beware!*, a kitchen
comedy that made an overnight star of the foghorn-voiced, 38-year-old
Peggy Mount. In a performance 'instinct with horrid truth', according
to the *Spectator*'s Anthony Hartley, 'she roars and bullies, snaps and
frets with the immense and hideous gusto of one whose mission it is to
make other people's lives a hell on earth'. He added that, as the raucous
Emma Hornett, she was also 'extremely funny', and 'the audience
rolled in the aisles'. 'Peggy, you will never play glamorous roles,' one
cruel-to-be-kind producer had told her. 'Even if you were slim, you've

got a character face, character arms, a character body, a character voice.'
Next evening, on the 17th, a less endearing – but almost as enduring
– battleaxe appeared on screen. 'John and Phyllis Cradock, the Bon
Viveur husband and wife cookery team, present an unusual style of
cooking to a studio audience at the Television Theatre,' was how *Radio
Times* signalled the first *Kitchen Magic*. John and Phyllis were soon
much better known as Johnnie and Fanny – with little doubt about who
wore the trousers – and that evening their three party dishes comprised
a Swiss roll, éclairs and soufflé *en surprise*, prepared for eight people
at a cost of just over 6s. The *Listener*'s Reginald Pound called it 'one
of those put-up-job programmes in which the characters try hard to
appear as if the inspiration for it has only just come to them', but the
short-tempered, snobbish, attention-seeking Fanny was poised to
become post-war Britain's first celebrity chef.

The difference between her and two longer-established cookery gurus
was considerable. 'Philip Harben and I weren't celebrities,' Marguerite
Patten recalled half a century later. 'We were informers, much less
important than the food. Our role during rationing was to guide people
through interesting meals when what you could buy was so limited.'
But by the mid-1950s rationing was passing into history, and food was
starting to become about display as well as nourishment. In short, the
mood music was just right for some culinary flamboyance, even some
conspicuous consumption. 'ANOTHER BOOM YEAR IS HERE',
pronounced the *News Chronicle* on the first Monday of 1955, on the
basis of a Gallup poll showing that 80 per cent of adults expected to
earn at least as much as in 1954. 'In booming, buoyant Britain,' declared
the paper, 'people are getting ready for a spending spree in which
millions will be poured out on TVs, cars, houses, washing machines and
refrigerators.' Or, as Mollie Panter-Downes not long afterwards told
her American readers, Britain was turning into a land of 'new television
masts sprouting from roofs, new cars in garages, and markets bulging
with every conceivable necessity and luxury'.[14]

One new car was in Chingford. February started well for Judy
Haines – 'England have won Fourth Test in Australia and consequently
retained the Ashes,' she wrote on the 2nd. 'Lovely!' – and then got
better. On the 15th a local car dealer returned, at her husband Abbé's
request, the deposit for a Ford Anglia: 'Can't wait for car indefinitely.

We are all delighted the way is clear to negotiate for a Standard 8.'
The following Saturday was cold and snowy: 'Just sat around fire
and dreamed of a Standard 8 and much better weather.' And then on
Saturday the 26th, after Abbé had bought the car but not been able to
bring it home because of still needing insurance: 'Thrilled! He went off
to see Leyton play Watford. Pity they had to lose on this lovely day.
I can think of nothing but cars, especially 825 CEV.' The great day
came on Saturday, 5 March: 'Excitement runs high. Abbé went off to
Lamb's and brought home the beautiful Standard Eight de Luxe 825
CEV. The girls were watching from window. "It's a black Standard!
It's CEV! It's 825 – it's Daddy!" ' Two days later Abbé was going to
work in central London by car, which soon had the family nickname
'Kevin'. The Standard Eight was a four-door saloon, launched two
years earlier, and from May 1955 even the non-de luxe version of it had
winding windows and trimmed door panels, at the cost of an extra £28
6s 8d. The Standard Motor Company, explained the *Economist* rather
sniffily, 'has now accepted the fact that motorists are prepared to spend
quite substantial sums for details that add nothing to a car's mechanical
efficiency and little to the physical comfort of driving it'. From Judy
Haines herself, there remained gratitude for anything that made day-
to-day life easier. Or as she eloquently wrote in early May, 'My back is
aching. Oh how lovely to have a washing machine.'

It did not yet feel like boom time in Bethnal Green. There for a week
in March, at the request of Peter Townsend, a dozen old people (as they
were categorised then) kept a daily diary. A trio of entries for Monday
the 21st gives the flavour of a family-centred world where the new
affluence was still just a distant rumour:

> *Mrs Tucker, 16 Bantam Street, aged 60, living with infirm husband in*
> *terraced cottage.*
> *7.45 am.* I got up, went down, and put my kettle on the gas – half-way
> – then I raked my fire out and laid it, swept my ashes up, and then
> cleaned my hearth. Then I set light to my fire, then sat down for a
> while, then I made tea and me and Dad had a cup.
> *9.20 am.* I went out for the *Daily Mirror* and fags for Dad. About eight
> people said 'Good morning' with a nice smile, then I replied back.
> Then I went home and prepared oats and bread, butter and tea and me

and Dad sat for breakfast. When we finished I cleared away and swept and mopped my kitchen out.

11.15 am. I started to get dinner on, then Mrs Rice, a neighbour, asked me to get her coals in, and she will take my bag-wash, also get my dog's meat. We had a nice chat about Mothers' Day. I showed her my flowers and card which Alice sent. It was very touching, a box of chocs from John, stockings and card from Rose, card and 5s from Bill, as I know they all think dearly of me.

1 pm. My daughter Alice came with baby. We had dinner together.

2 pm. My daughter Rose and husband came. I made them a cup of tea and cake.

3.15 pm. Dad and I sat to listen to radio.

5 pm. We both had tea, bread and cheese Dad, bread and jam myself. When finished I cleared away again.

7 pm. My son John and his wife called to see if we were all right before they went home from work.

8 pm. I did a little mending.

10 pm. We went to bed.

Mr William James, aged seventy-three, widower, living alone in two-room flat on first floor in Gretland Street. Formerly a market porter.

7.45 am. Got up, made a cup of tea.

8 am. Started to clear the place up. Cleared the fireplace out. I had the sweep coming between 9.30 and 10 and they are very strict on time. And at 9 had some bread and marmalade for quickness and he came at 9.45. He stayed about 20 minutes – another 5s gone. Well, I had to sweep up and clear the place up and got out at 11.15.

11.15 am. Went to the paper shop, got my *News Chronicle* and my ration of twenty Woodbines and went to my daughter's place in Thirsk Street at 11.45. Sat down for a while and had a smoke.

12.15 pm. Washed her breakfast things up, swept the kitchen up and then had another sit down talking to Mr Bird (budgie). Then found some cold meat, so I boiled some potatoes and had some dinner with a nice cup of tea.

1.30 pm. Sat down and read the paper and listened to the wireless and of course dozed off till 3 pm. Got up, washed up and got ready for the girl to come home at 4.20, made a cup of tea, then the grandchildren came home at 4.40 and you know what they are for talking and at 5.30 I went home, buying the paper as I go along. Got home at 5.50.

5.50 pm. First thing light the fire, then lay the table, make the tea, boil an egg and finish up with marmalade. Then sat down and read the paper. Then got up, washed up, had a wash, sat down till 9. Then went to the club and had a chat and a game of cards till 11, then home and so to bed 11.30.

Mrs Harker, 12 Peacock Street. Widowed, aged sixty-two, living alone.

Got up at 8.30, lit the fire 9.0, then had breakfast, tea and toast. 9.20 my grandson brought my dinner in to cook. 9.45 cleaned my budgie out and settled her. 10.0 peeled the potatoes. 10.15 started my clearing up, made the bed and washed up. 11.0 put my dinner on to cook and then did a little washing. 12.30 had my dinner, bacon and potatoes, fed the dog. After sitting a while got up and washed up. 2.10 got myself ready to go and see an old neighbour. 2.30 went over to my neighbour. After sitting talking about the family, made a cup of tea and had a cake, after that we finished our conversation. 4.0 washed up. 4.30 left her to come home to catch my daughter's club man [her daughter was an agent for a clothing club, collecting weekly payments for clothing and shoes] but he didn't turn up, so at 5.0 got my tea and sat resting by the fire. Then I got up. 6.30 a friend came in to pay her club. We sat talking about the family, and in the meantime my grandson and his friend came in to take the dog for his night's run. My friend left at 7.15. After that I cleared the fireplace up and tidied up the room. 7.30 sat down and had a read of the paper. 7.45 started to write a letter to my son in Dorset. 9.0 got my supper, a boiled egg and toast, and cleared away. After that I sat and had another read. 10.20 went to bed.

'Balls to say as administrators do more neighbourliness & more services for elderly,' Townsend himself jotted down not long afterwards. 'Important thing is what is happening to family. Help family to help itself.' Meanwhile, his colleagues Michael Young and Peter Willmott continued to work away at what would become *Family and Kinship in East London* (1957). '800 Bethnal Green families now lie massed on a big office table,' Young noted in May after a big push on the interviews. 'How shall we convert them back again into flesh and blood people? Social research is a strange job. Pouring information from one bottle into another, making people into words and always hoping for the creative leap which will make facts into life.'[15]

Things were also tight at Woburn Abbey. Family seat of the dukes of Bedford, it was in a decrepit state when the 13th Duke inherited it in 1953, along with a crippling bill for death duties not far short of £6 million. After initial dismay, he went to work with a will and in April 1955 opened it to the paying public, complete with children's zoo, playground, boating lake and tearoom. His wife Lydia helped out as a guide, and during the first week a man came up to her and, with the words 'That's for you, ducks', put a sixpenny bit in her hand. More than 180,000 visitors came in the first year, well above expectations, and despite some murmurings of disapproval, a razzmatazz future lay ahead for the ancestral home. The Indian writer Nirad Chaudhuri, visiting England about the same time as the opening, noted 'the growing habit of visiting the country houses' and, on the basis of personal observation, tried to explain why: 'One motivation of a practical order must be ruled out altogether, and that is the wish to get ideas about building, furnishing, and living in such places. Even historical interest in them or the families did not seem to be very strong, because many of the visitors had to be supplied with such information. Those who went to see them appeared to derive some immediate and direct satisfaction from the mere sight of the houses and their contents.' Even so, these were grim times. 'In 1955 alone,' according to the architectural historian J. Mordaunt Crook, 'country houses were coming down at the rate of one every two-and-a-half days. There had been nothing quite like it since the Dissolution of the Monasteries.' And this summer there was particular dismay when Lord Lansdowne demolished a large, Adams-built part of Bowood House in Wiltshire, on the grounds that it had gone beyond any possibility of economic repair and, even if repaired, would be uneconomic to maintain. 'In France and Italy Bowood would be a classified monument,' James Lees-Milne from Brooks's fulminated to *The Times*. 'The fate that now awaits it would not be tolerated in these two countries for a moment.'

Henry St John, the misanthropic civil servant, continued the almost commentless chronicling of his life. 'In Ealing the trolley-bus driver refused to move until some people who he stated to be standing upstairs were removed,' he recorded on Saturday, 16 April. It was a situation that might have appealed to Tony Hancock, whose second radio series – hard on the heels of the first one finishing in February – was due to start the following week. Unfortunately, he had done a runner, booking himself in at a cheap *pensione* on the Neapolitan Riviera. The frantic producer turned to another comedian, who good-naturedly agreed to stand in, and on Tuesday evening it fell to Robin Boyle to announce, 'This is the BBC Light Programme. We present *Hancock's Half Hour*, starring – Harry Secombe . . .' Soon afterwards, Hancock himself (or his agent) gave a quote to the *Sunday Pictorial*: 'I'm the kind that can't relax. It doesn't matter how many times I play a scene, I'm always trying to add something to it. It frays my nerves to a frazzle and suddenly my system won't take it any more.' Since the previous November he had been performing twice-nightly in *The Talk of the Town*, a revue at the Adelphi Theatre. Now, he eventually returned to the fray, but not before Secombe had deputised twice more. The rest of the series, however, proved a triumph, as (in one biographer's words) 'public enthusiasm built quickly' and 1955 turned into the year 'in which the country became truly conscious of the Hancock phenomenon'.

Radio, not television, was still the universal medium, with figures in June showing that whereas some 40 per cent of middle-class households had a TV set (still quite an expensive item), only 26 per cent of working-class households did. Class, though, was not the sole determinant, for whereas 41 per cent of families with a child aged between eight and fifteen had a set, the same was true for only 26 per cent of families without such a child. Or in the nicely understated explanation of Mark Abrams, in his analysis of 'Child Audiences for Television', there existed 'a widening appreciation among parents that television can take from their shoulders the burden of keeping their children silent in the hours between returning from school and going to bed'. Abrams in April 1955 systematically investigated the viewing habits of children (eight to fifteen) and revealed as never before the medium's addictive qualities: 'As far as the majority of children are concerned, the tea-time viewing [ie of programmes specially for children] is at best a mere warming-up, a preliminary flexing of the eye muscles, before the main diet starts at 7.30 pm [ie after the so-called toddler's truce, with no programmes at all while parents got their small children to bed]; over 70 per cent of children in TV homes said they had watched at least part of the adult TV programmes on the evening before the interview.' Moreover, 'middle-class parents who own TV sets are only a little more restrictive than working-class parents with TV sets when it comes to letting their children stay up and watch adult programmes'. All in all, 'the average child in a TV home spent 1½ hours every evening watching adult television', with half of those in the 11-to-13 range still being in front of their sets after 9.00 p.m. And unsurprisingly, when children were asked to name their favourite programmes, only 34 per cent of their votes went to children's programmes, with far more plumping for *Ask Pickles* (a particular favourite of working-class children), *The Grove Family* and *Fabian of the Yard*.[16]

This spring the annual outcomes to the football season had a more than usual resonance, in retrospect at least. Newcastle United won the FA Cup for the third time in five seasons; Chelsea won their first league championship, overcoming an early 5–6 home defeat to Manchester United; Luton Town, watched by increasingly prosperous Vauxhall car workers, gained promotion to the First (ie top) Division; and the supporters of Accrington Stanley went through the emotional mill, faithfully recorded by the *Accrington Observer*. Only one team would be promoted from Third Division North, and Stanley started the Easter programme four points clear of Barnsley at the top (only two points then for a win). After a battling draw at York City on Good Friday ('a grand slam set-to with plenty of good football, thrills and he-man stuff'), humiliation came next day, 9 April, as in bright sunshine and in front of a crowd of 11,250, they crashed 5–2 at home to Hartlepool, with Stanley 'more and more disorganised and ragged, until, by the final whistle, the rout was complete'. By the 23rd, after more indifferent results, it was a case of 'something of a miracle needed', but over the next week things suddenly swung back Stanley's way, so that by the 30th, the last Saturday of the league season, 'hope will, indeed, be very much alive' if Stanley could win at Chesterfield. Sadly, they slumped to a 6–2 defeat – 'Oh dear, oh dear, what an anti-climax!' – and the same afternoon Barnsley wrapped up promotion. Still, a 3–0 win at Bradford City the following Wednesday secured second place. 'At any rate,' optimistically reflected 'Jason' of the local paper, 'Stanley are now "on the map" and a team and club to command respect.'

For almost four weeks this spring, sporting and other deeds went largely unreported in the national press. As the result of a dispute involving the Amalgamated Engineering Union and the Communist-dominated Electrical Trades Union, a national newspaper strike began on 25 March, affecting almost all London-published daily and Sunday titles. Harold Macmillan's diary recorded some early developments:

> *27 March*. There have been no papers obtainable for two days except the *Manchester Guardian* and the *Yorkshire Post*. No Sunday papers – an immense relief! . . .
>
> *31 March*. Today, I am told, the whole London consignment of the *Yorkshire Post* was stolen at Kings X, by some ingenious speculator, for re-sale at an enhanced price . . .
>
> *1 April*. The newspaper proprietors are losing heavily. Those which have a great range of papers, periodicals etc (like Amalgamated Press etc) are sound enough. The *Daily Chronicle* [ie *News Chronicle*] is said to be rocky. And the *Daily Herald* too. So perhaps the only tangible result of the strike may be to silence the Socialist and Radical press! . . .

Eventually, after the inevitable Monckton-appointed Court of Inquiry, there was a settlement, and the papers reappeared on 21 April. 'For all the people who are connected with newspapers the strike has been a difficult period, a time they will long remember as one of anxiety, suspense and frustration,' declared the pink paper that was starting to cover the British economy as a whole and not just the City. 'For many papers, including the *Financial Times*, it was the first time in their history that they altogether failed to appear.' At least one diarist was less fussed. 'It is extraordinary,' reflected Madge Martin in Oxford the same day, 'how everyone got on quite well without them.'

Had they? 'Results show, in general, a picture of frustration (not always unhappy), a good deal of anti-strike feeling, a broad awareness that the strikers want wage increases and a vague knowledge of the pros and cons of the matter,' Mass-Observation found during the strike on the basis of its familiar mix of interviews, observations and overheards. 'People are adjusting themselves to the strike: some with irritation and signs of nervous strain as they search for *anything at all* to read; some with relief as, freed from apparent compulsion to read, they decide that the strike has compensations. For most, however, the loss of newspapers is a big loss . . .' Of 500 carefully watched Londoners travelling to work by Tube on the first Monday in April, 59 per cent were sitting and doing nothing, while the same morning at Surbiton station at about 9.00, the usually very busy bookstall made only three sales in ten minutes. 'A young clergyman bought *Robin*, a children's paper; a young man bought *Automobile*; a middle-aged man bought the *Christian Science Monitor* after picking it up between thumb and finger and enquiring sarcastically "What is *this*?".' M-O also included some vox pop, mainly but not entirely negative:

My husband gets very depressed. The paper's a part of his life. I feel utterly lost. (*Tailor's wife*)

Not reading *The Times* is like not cleaning your teeth. (*Middle-class man, retired*)

You know there's something missing. It's getting a bit tight to light the fires. You have to scrape round the boy's scrapbooks and his comics. (*Working-class housewife*)

I miss my bit of scandal in the Sunday newspapers. (*Young working-class shop assistant*)

It's a nuisance to men, not so much to women, they don't have time to read. (*Wife of Post Office worker*)

Oh, I do miss the newspapers. For one thing I never know the date and then there is nothing to argue about on the bus going to work. (*Wages clerk*)

I think it's rather a nice change not to have newspapers, not to read about Atom bombs all the time. (*Electrician*)

It saves me a bit of money – 2s 6d a week. (*Trade representative*)

I think it's a jolly good thing. It gives people a chance to read stuff that's more valuable. (*Local government official*)

Those – the majority – who said they had been personally affected by the strike were asked to identify what in the papers they had missed in particular. Sport (including the pools) was easily top on 35 per cent, followed by the news (20 per cent), crosswords (7 per cent) and cartoons (4 per cent). Among that last small but dedicated group, feelings seem to have run especially high. 'There is a rumour that they are printing papers for themselves in Fleet Street,' a female reader of the

News Chronicle said. 'Does that mean that when the papers start again we shan't know what has happened to Colonel Pewter for a fortnight?'

One visitor, staying at London's Connaught Hotel, felt only modified rapture at the return of the fourth estate. 'Would you please have someone tell the *Daily Sketch* that not only would I not do a piece of writing for them but that I wouldn't use their rotten rag even to stuff up a rat hole,' Raymond Chandler requested his British publisher on 27 April. 'Our press is no bargain, but your gutter press is fantastically bad.'[17]

6

A Lot of Hooey

People were also asked during the newspaper strike what stories they would like to have read about. 'Oh, bits about accidents and murders and thrilling bits, you know,' replied a 29-year-old cleaner in a cafeteria. 'Any boxing news or football. The Don Cockell fight . . .' answered a 51-year-old mechanic. 'I think only the small news items, nothing special, just the little bits,' said the 24-year-old wife of a transport driver. It was left to a 54-year-old builder's labourer to stake the high ground: 'Well, I missed the splash they would have made about Churchill and now there's the general election, still we won't have to read a lot of hooey, will we?'

The interviews were probably on about 18 April, only three days before the papers in fact returned, but thirteen days after the announcement that Churchill was at last stepping down. 'Tears rolled down my cheeks,' wrote Nella Last after hearing the news on the radio. 'It's been an honour to have had him for a leader, though if I'd been able to have "given him a wish," it would be that tonight he went to bed, happy but sad, & in his sleep started his last journey & never woke as the King he served so well did.' Next day, Wednesday the 6th, Sir Anthony Eden became Prime Minister, an event treated by the still toothless BBC as a pre-ordained coronation virtually above politics. The handsome, charming, highly strung Eden had, like many crown princes, waited a long time – too long – for this moment. 'It is a pretty tough assignment to follow the greatest Englishman of history, but I feel sure Eden will make a good job of it,' Harold Macmillan optimistically reflected that day, but the greatest Englishman himself had on the eve of his departure – after entertaining the Queen to dinner at No. 10 – declared with a sudden vehemence to his principal private secretary: 'I don't believe Anthony can do it.'

The following week, on Friday the 15th, Nella Last heard on the six o'clock news that Eden would be making a radio broadcast at 7.30. But before then, her next-door neighbour, Mrs Atkinson, dropped by:

> She said, 'What *can* Eden have so important to say? Do you think it's about Princess Margaret marrying Townsend?' She is so very interested in every scrap of news of them. I said, 'I shouldn't think it would be a Prime Minister's job to tell us.' My husband said, 'More likely he's got the newspaper strike settled.' I said, 'Well, I don't think he has anything to do with *that* either.' My husband said, 'What *can* it be then?' Without a thought in my head it could be a solution, I said, 'Only thing *I* can think is a sudden decision to have an Election.' They both were doubtful.

Nella was right, with Eden setting the election date for some six weeks hence, 26 May. This was barely three and a half years since the last election, and the Tories still had an eminently workable majority, but quite apart from the natural wish to secure a personal mandate, Eden had another reason for going early. 'Anthony has thought for a year now that we will run into trouble with our trade,' his wife, Clarissa, had noted in her diary in February. 'Anthony wonders if a snap election immediately after taking over may not be the best chance. He feels sure we will lose if we wait till the autumn.'[1]

Four days after the date had been set, Rab Butler presented what could not but be seen as a highly political budget, cutting the standard rate of income tax by 6d and freeing 2.4 million people from paying the tax altogether, while at the same time publicly pinning his faith on 'the resources of a flexible monetary policy' in order to counterbalance this fiscal generosity. The *Financial Times*, once back in action, argued that Butler had been 'right to take his risks on the side of expansion', though did concede not only that the budget had been inflationary, but also that 'the condition of the economy still needs to be watched with great care'. Gaitskell as Shadow Chancellor bitterly accused Butler of placing political popularity above economic prudence, but it was the *Manchester Guardian* that called the larger game correctly: 'Mr Butler may indeed have cause to regret his generosity later in the year . . . And then the laugh would really be with Mr Gaitskell. But the prospect of Mr Butler "eating his words" at some time in the autumn is not going to win this election.'[2]

Almost certainly a third reason for Eden's timing was the desire to exploit the recent, particularly intense bout of rancorous discord within the Labour Party. As usual, Bevan and his arch-foe Gaitskell were in the thick of things, and the issue was the H-bomb, which the government had announced in February that Britain would be making. Bevan did not – unlike some Bevanites – oppose that as such, but in a direct assault on Attlee's cautious, deliberately ambiguous line, he insisted that it was Labour's job to pressurise the government into abandoning its suicidal policy of 'first use' and reorientating its whole foreign policy. 'We have now reached a situation,' he told the Commons in early March, 'where Great Britain can, in a few short years, run the risk of extinction of its civilisation, and we cannot reach the potential enemy [ie Russia] in an attempt to arrive at an accommodation with him because we are now at the mercy of the United States.' More than 60 Labour MPs then rebelled with him against the official party line, and it was not long before Attlee was having to resist a concerted attempt by Gaitskell, who hugely exaggerated the organisational size and coherence of 'Bevanism', to get Bevan expelled from the party. 'There are extraordinary parallels between Nye and Adolf Hitler,' Gaitskell told an incredulous Crossman on the 22nd. 'They are demagogues of exactly the same sort.' A week later, Bevan apologised to Attlee, and once again, as in 1951, an implausible façade of unity was just about created for the widely expected imminent election.

Importantly, 'the Bomb' itself as an issue had only limited traction outside the Westminster village. There was as yet no hint of a meaningful protest movement, and although 51 clergy and ministers did sign a petition urging the British people to 'reject the monstrous and cynical policy which the Government has imposed upon them', the Archbishop of Canterbury, Geoffrey Fisher, still had his bishops firmly in line behind him. Soon after the government's February announcement, Crossman discussed the matter first with the *Daily Mirror*'s political editor Sydney Jacobson, and then with a former Labour minister, Arthur Creech Jones. Jacobson told him that after his paper had devoted two successive front pages to the H-bomb, arguing that Britain had to have one, they had received a grand total of only ten letters on the subject, while Creech Jones frankly observed about the underlying attitude of most people: 'They're not interested because they always assumed we'd got it already and that, even if we hadn't, we were bound to make it in a world as crazy as this.' So too during the general election in May, when the octogenarian Bertrand Russell, speaking on a Labour platform, tried to energise the electorate over the proposition that amid the dangers of chemical, bacteriological and nuclear warfare, 'the only alternative to living together is dying together'. On the day, according to Alistair Cooke's humorously ironic report in the *Manchester Guardian*, Russell got a decent round of applause, but the overall response was a collective shrug of the shoulders.[3]

If not the H-bomb, what were the voters thinking and talking about? During the campaign, *Picture Post* featured some electoral vox pop:

Government? This Government or any other – I haven't got much time for 'em. To tell the truth I never voted last time. Whenever we put in for a rise we get the same answer – whoever's in. My basic rate's £6 11s 6d. With two young kiddies it's not enough, I'm not jokin'. This five and ninepence a week we have to pay the Government – a waste o' money, I call it! The Conservatives put their foot in it there all right. (*Charlie Quentin, roadsweeper, Liverpool, voting Labour*)

The whole of the Socialist programme tends to restrict trade rather than to expand it. Britain is a trading nation. We must stand well financially and economically in the eyes of the rest of the world. (*Charles Purnell, stockbroker, London, voting Conservative*)

I never did vote Conservative and never shall. I'll never forget what happened a few years after the First War. They knocked our money down from forty-eight shillings to thirty-two shillings in one week. I think it was a Conservative Government – Conservatives were in it, anyway. (*Tom Mason, herdsman, Eggington, Beds, voting Labour*)

I dislike intensely the term 'working class'. We are all working people and I think the Tories legislate for all of them. Labour seems to think that if you wear a collar and tie you are the dregs. (*Mrs Jones, doctor's wife, Liverpool, voting Conservative*)

We're worse off than we were under the last lot. The rent's gone up 1s 6d a week, but we're not grumbling about that. No, it's the prices of things. Coal is scandalous – 6s 5d a hundredweight. Labour are more for the working people. If they got in we'd all be better off. (*Mrs Woolfrey, housewife, Liverpool, voting Labour*)

I think this lot have not done badly, not bad at all. The country's certainly a lot more prosperous now. We old age pensioners are 7s 6d better off. Though the rent has gone up threepence, and food costs a bob or two a week more than it did, I still think I'm a bit better off. No, I don't think that Labour will improve things that way. Course, they're all for the trade unions, and they're the people who keep our wages up. (*H. Hogden, newspaper seller, Manchester, voting Labour*)

I used not to be interested in politics, but I became a Conservative. Actually, I'm more anti-Socialist than pro-anything. I'm not all that politically minded – I don't think much about the H-Bomb – but the principle of free enterprise is right up my street. (*Dick Brittain, haulage contractor, South Benfleet, voting Conservative*)

On this job it's all work and a bit of bed. I've got to earn a decent wage as the wife and I are buying our own house, with a nice little greenhouse, too. The basic wage is only £6 16s a week, and I've got to put in about 25 hours' overtime to get a wage worth picking up. The work's rough, dirty and wet, and ruins your clothes. Still, I don't think any of this is the Government's fault. It was no better when Labour were in. If Sir Anthony Eden can't sort things out, I don't think anybody can do it. (*John Wells, haulage worker, Carnforth, voting Conservative*)

The magazine's Kenneth Allsop also spoke to a hundred out of the two million first-time voters (twenty-one still the minimum voting age). 'What emerged very strongly – even amongst those who declared themselves for Conservative or Labour – was a dislike, almost amounting to rebelliousness, against domination by the two major parties,' he reported. 'One after another, they expressed abhorrence at the highly-organised and disciplinarian structure of the House of Commons. "Just two huge voting machines," "a three-line whip system," "they're as different as chalk and chalk" – these were some of the phrases used. It may be out of this discontent with the present two-party game of pitch-and-toss that a Liberal revival is grown.' Allsop concluded that 'Young Britain is in a militant mood for more individuality, for less conformity and political rigidity', but if so one of his interviewees, a barrow-boy called Ron Gibbs, had not heard. ' "Me? I'm voting Conservative, mate," ' ran the caption underneath a photo of him. ' "Should think so, too," said his uncle, owner of the stall. "We don't want them Labour stranglers back." '[4]

It was not an election that ever really caught fire. 'Electioneering seems to be leaving people cold,' noted Gladys Langford on 11 May, with just over a fortnight to go. 'The newspapers report that at a meeting at which Douglas Jay was to speak only 7 people turned up and one of these represented the Press so the meeting was cancelled.' When, right at the death, Attlee went to speak at Sittingbourne football ground, in Britain's most marginal constituency, the attendance was described by the *Faversham Times* as one that would have been poor for a match. The broadcasting figures told a similar story. An average of 15 per cent of the adult population listened to party political broadcasts on the radio, while on television the average was 14 per cent. Even assuming no overlap of audience, the combined total of 29 per cent was significantly below the 36 per cent average for radio broadcasts in 1951 (when there were no television broadcasts). No doubt the shortfall of interest was partly a reflection of the seeming inevitability of the outcome, with the opinion polls for all three weeks of the campaign proper consistently giving the Tories a lead of 3 to 4 per cent. At one point Nella Last's husband did have a flutter of anxiety about a Labour win, but she calmly predicted to him an overall majority for the Tories of around 45 to 50.[5]

Television coverage of the election was confined to party political broadcasts (all done live), so relatively speaking they mattered more than they would in later elections. Labour on the whole fared indifferently. 'A nice, gentle person, the kind of neighbour from whom one can borrow a lawn mower, but a bit tedious,' was how the habitually taciturn Attlee came across to the *Manchester Guardian* reviewer as, in the company of Mrs Attlee and sitting on a cretonne-covered easy chair by a rustic brick fireplace, he was interviewed by a supportive journalist. 'One imagines that he neither won nor lost a single vote.' Soon afterwards it was the turn of Harold Wilson and the formidable Dr Edith Summerskill (the party chairman) to pretend to be a married couple in order to demonstrate the sharp rise in the cost of living under the Tories – a performance significantly impaired by Summerskill sticking the butter price label into the cheese and vice-versa, while the butter and cheese themselves respectively melted and dribbled under the hot studio lights. Wilson just about managed to keep his composure, calling the notion that Labour would bring back rationing 'a deliberate

Tory lie', and was praised by the *New Statesman*'s television critic, William Salter, as 'forthright, unsmiling, the grim efficient executive'. By contrast, in a question-and-answer session a few days later involving a quartet of Labour figures, James Callaghan was condemned by Salter as 'altogether too brash and cock-sure', with the broadcast generally getting 'completely out of hand', including far too much 'bonhomie', for Salter 'only bearable on panel games'.

The Tory broadcasts also had some mixed fortunes – the appearance and style of Macmillan, thought Salter, was 'guaranteed to re-establish in voters' minds the stereotype of the Tories as an upper-class party' – but overall were appreciably more professional in approach. Their last one was a virtuoso solo performance by Eden, speaking direct to camera and making benign references to 'our Socialist friends'. Salter called it 'a superb achievement . . . impressive and persuasive', while according to Panter-Downes, 'though the language was hardly Churchillian, the faithful clichés, plus an easy manner that is apparently a television natural, seemed to have hit the spot – the slow, sensible norm of the British, who detected their sincerity and liked it'. A faux-intimacy perhaps, but the public had never before been so close-up to the Prime Minister of the day.[6]

Outside the studio, Labour's campaign was, by common consent, poorly co-ordinated and uninspiring, with little fresh to say. 'A rehash of an indigestible dish,' was one commentator's retrospective verdict on the manifesto, with Attlee in particular inevitably very much seen as yesterday's man. 'Wake up this election!' he vainly implored one audience. 'The Tories hope to keep it quiet and to sneak back into power before the nation realises what has happened.' For their part, the Tories relentlessly emphasised the domestic economic aspect – rising standard of living, housing records smashed, increasing ownership of televisions, cars, washing machines and suchlike – while at the same time claiming that Labour's return would inexorably lead to an austerity reprise of (as the Tory manifesto put it) 'shortages and queues, ration-books and black markets, snoopers and spivs'. Still mindful of lingering memories of the 1930s, they were also careful not to frighten the horses. Take Enoch Powell in Wolverhampton, where in his election address there was, in a biographer's words, 'not a hint of his misgivings about certain aspects of welfare spending as he emphasised (in bold print) not only that NHS spending had increased and extra school places had been provided, but also that "retirement and other pensions, insurance benefits, family allowances, have been increased by 50 per cent or more" '.

The Tories also had in Eden a genuine electoral asset. 'He said nothing memorable, but said it very well,' observed David Butler, and it was the second half of that verdict that mattered especially. Eden himself, in a tribute to the efficiency of his party machinery, later claimed to have found the whole exercise 'less exacting than rowing number seven in the boat'. Two episodes in his campaign had a particular resonance. 'The car came to a halt in a strange district and we were surrounded by men staring curiously at us,' remembered his wife, Clarissa. 'I asked where we were and was told "the Gorbals." I had a frisson of apprehension – then they recognised the person in the car and, smiling, they banged on the bonnet and the windows. Extraordinary. They were all going to vote Labour, but they supported *Anthony*.' The other episode was at a naval base, where Eden was taunted about endangering the sons of other men. This was too much for him, and he spoke emotionally of his own son, a wartime pilot who had gone missing over Burma. 'Frightfully good stuff, sir, you should do it more often,' said his young personal assistant, Peter Tapsell (a future Tory MP). But Eden, as Tapsell recalled long afterwards, felt only shame at his loss of self-control.[7]

Two of the more interesting candidates were standing for Essex seats. One was John Arlott. 'I was the world's worst canvasser,' he shuddered afterwards about his three weeks in Epping. 'I went to two houses only. The first one, I asked the lady who came to the door if she felt she could support the Liberals in the election. "What election?" she said: and the second one I asked the same question, and she slammed the door in my face.' One evening he went looking for votes at the Royal Auxiliary Air Force officers' mess at North Weald and found himself drawn into a costly game of liar dice at the bar, with a young Norman Tebbit among those playing.

The other candidate was the 24-year-old Shirley Catlin (the future Shirley Williams), standing for Labour at Harwich. 'I enjoy the campaign very much,' she told the local paper, 'but sometimes when I'm in a hostile neighbourhood speaking in the van, and never get a friendly wave, I feel after about ten minutes I could give up politics altogether. But you just have to carry on.' The paper itself praised her as 'a mistress of the apt phrase' and gave an example: ' "Good morning, ladies and gentlemen," she announced on a cold, grey morning in Brightlingsea. "It's a windy day, isn't it? Vote Labour and temper the wind to the shorn lamb." ' The *Harwich & Dovercourt Standard* was, like most local papers, far from Labour-supporting, but after it was all over felt moved to observe that 'there is no doubt that N.E. Essex has a soft spot for "Shirley" '.

At her nomination meeting, Catlin had hard words to say about the Tories: 'Out of the 600 candidates they are putting up, no less than 80 went to Eton and 80 per cent went to public schools. They are still a party of a small class.' She might also have mentioned that ten members of Eden's eighteen-strong cabinet were Old Etonians, with five of those ten, including Eden himself, having then gone on to Christ Church, Oxford. 'Gravy for Etonians: thin gruel and skilly otherwise,' subsequently noted the colourful, proto-Thatcherite Tory MP Gerald Nabarro (educated at a London County Council school), adding that 'the rest of the Eden Cabinet, with the exception of the Mancunian Lord Woolton, were almost as well born'. Nevertheless, if there was an emblematic Tory candidate in this election, it was not one of the silver-spooned, but Barnet's candidate, the solidly upper-middle-class, but far from upper-class, Reginald Maudling. Still in his 30s, he had just been made Minister of Supply, prompting the *Spectator*'s gifted new political commentator, Henry Fairlie, to call him 'the first dimpled child of Butskellism', in tribute to his consciously moderate, progressive brand of Conservatism. During the campaign he spoke widely in other constituencies, but was also conscious of potential danger in Barnet itself, which now included the LCC out-county estate of Borehamwood – politically an unknown quantity. 'We have done the things we have said we would do,' he proclaimed at a meeting in Cockfosters the Saturday before polling day. 'At home, taxes have been cut, controls lifted and more houses than ever built. The charge of being warmongers was made against the Tories, but we have ended the wars we inherited. It was said that there would be a million unemployed under a Conservative administration. In fact, employment is at a record level.'[8] Maudling, one of life's optimists, trusted it would be enough.

'General Election: the futility of politics,' John Fowles bleakly reflected, not so far away in Hampstead, in a diary entry covering both polling day and the next day, Friday the 27th. 'The helplessness of the self before the vast mass of blind public opinion. In this election, too, the apathy is significant and healthy; people are no longer interested in politics . . .' Judy Haines, unusually for her, did not even mention the election. 'I was very keen to see Alistair Sim & Joyce Grenfell in "The Belles of St Trinians" at Highams Park, Regal,' she noted on the Thursday. 'Decided, therefore, to miss Keep Fit and take girls [whose school was being used for voting]. Very disappointed, and I dropped off to sleep here and there.' Three other diarists – unlike her, all Conservative-supporting – were more engaged. 'I *would* have loved to stay up till 12 o'clock, but my husband said the wireless would disturb him, so I'll have to be patient,' recorded Nella Last. Florence Turtle, a 58-year-old buyer for British Home Stores, who lived with her two brothers in Wimbledon Park, had not only no husband to make a fuss but also a television to watch:

> *Thursday night:* At 9.30 pm Richard Dimbleby started to broadcast the Election results. Cheltenham was the first to come through with a 2 per cent swing to Conservatives – the same trend was notable at Salford East & West . . . I retired to bed at 3.0 am as we could keep awake no longer. We got rather excited when first Watford & then Central Wandsworth fell to the Conservative & celebrated accordingly.
>
> *Friday:* Well the Country is saved from bankruptcy for a bit. One thing the Conservatives are more efficient than the others & also for the good of the whole nation . . .

That Friday in Barrow, Last had a chat 'over the fence' with 'the two old women next door' (presumably not the Mrs Atkinson side): 'Poor old dears. "It had made us real poorly last night after watching T.V. We were sure that Labour were going to win, & oh dear if that nasty fat Bevan had got any power, it would have been really dreadful." ' Or, as Anthony Heap in London concisely put it a few hours later, 'Hap-hap-happy day.'[9]

The Tories had won a very comfortable overall majority of 58 (including a majority of seats in Scotland), with Labour having lost sixteen seats, the Liberals staying on six seats, and seventeen unsuccessful Communist candidates managing only 33,000 votes between them. Turnout was down from 82 to 76 per cent, with Labour having lost a million and a half votes, the Tories half a million. Among the individual outcomes, neither Arlott nor Catlin were close to winning; the voters of Borehamwood failed to come out for Labour and thereby ensured an easy win for Maudling; Barbara Castle just squeaked home in Blackburn; Michael Foot lost his seat at Plymouth Devonport; Anthony Crosland also lost (at Southampton Test, having at almost the last minute ditched South Gloucestershire because of redistribution worries); and Willie Whitelaw was the new MP for the safe Tory seat of Penrith and the Border, despite a heated scene at the count when William Brownrigg, a Carlisle farmer standing for Cumbrian Home Rule, accused Whitelaw of filching 'bundles and bundles' of his votes. Particularly telling were the results in prosperous, emblematic Coventry: all three seats stayed Labour, but in each there was a disconcertingly large drop in the majority. 'The factory gate meetings were moderately attended,' one Coventry MP, Richard Crossman, wrote soon afterwards about his campaign, 'but with very small collections and no sign of enthusiasm and for the first time since '45 we had workers returning from the factories turning thumbs down when they saw a socialist car.'[10]

Some 17 months after the youngish Labour MP Roy Jenkins had remarked to Crossman that 'the electorate is extremely Conservative-minded and we can never win except with the kind of attitude represented by the right-wing leadership' – by which he meant Gaitskell and followers like Crosland and himself, all united in opposition to Bevan – Labour's decisive defeat in May 1955 inevitably provoked internal analysis. None of that analysis quite got to grips with the clear evidence of a continuing gender gap (ie with the Conservatives now far better than Labour at tapping into the concerns of women in general and housewives in particular), but three early contributions made important, valid points.

'Since 1951 the Tories have had good luck with the economic climate, people are generally better off and the end of most shortages has enabled rationing to be ended on everything but coal,' privately reflected an even younger Labour MP, Anthony Wedgwood Benn, in June. 'There has been no unemployment. A family in a council house with a TV set and a car or motorcycle-combination on hire purchase had few reasons for a change of government.' Soon afterwards, a leading article on 'Equality with Quality' in *Socialist Commentary*, the magazine of

the right wing of the party that was edited by Rita Hinden, argued
that what was needed in society (and therefore in Labour policy) was a
levelling up, not down:

> Despite the rise in material standards and welfare, this is still a squalid
> country and all too many people are still compelled to lead squalid lives.
> Look at the ugly towns, at the mean streets, the cramped and shoddy
> houses. Look at the crowded classrooms, the scarcity of teachers and the
> wretched playgrounds. Look at the amenities for community life offered
> to most of our people. Then ask how near we have come to building
> Jerusalem 'in England's green and pleasant land'.

Even so, the editorial insisted on limits to any future Labour
revisionism, despite the clear evidence of lack of public enthusiasm
for nationalisation: 'Equality with quality can only be won through
increased public ownership, public enterprise and public expenditure.
This must remain the crux of any socialist programme.'

The July issue also included a piece by Gaitskell himself,
'Understanding the Electorate', in which he noted that during the
campaign he had 'never known so few people seem to feel themselves
really involved'. As to why Labour had lost, the crux – he asserted in
italics – was *'the lack of fear of the Tories derived from the maintenance
of full employment, the end of rationing and the general feeling that
"things were better"'*. He then tried to explain what lay behind all this:

> I fancy that in the last year or two more and more people are beginning to
> turn to their own personal affairs and to concentrate on their own material
> advancement. No doubt it has been stimulated by the end of post-war
> austerity, TV, new gadgets like refrigerators and washing machines, the
> glossy magazines with their special appeal to women, and even the flood of
> new cars on the home markets. Call it if you like a growing Americanization
> of outlook. I believe it's there, and it's no good moaning about it . . .

Gaitskell, his eyes on 1959 or 1960, ended with a prediction that was
also a warning: 'We certainly cannot assume that the next General
Election will be nicely timed to coincide with an economic crisis.'[11]

PART TWO

7

A Fine Day for a Hanging

On May Day 1955, as Stirling Moss was becoming the first Englishman to win the Mille Miglia (a thousand miles of open roads in Italy), the leader of the Transport and General Workers' Union (T&G), Arthur Deakin, collapsed and died while addressing a rally at the Corn Exchange, Leicester. He had been more responsible than anyone for delivering the trade union moderation of the immediate post-war years, and amid an increasingly acrimonious industrial scene it was hard not to see his death as symbolic of the passing of an era. Over the next month, even during an election campaign, the atmosphere continued to deteriorate: in early May an unofficial strike in the Yorkshire coalfield, at one point involving some 115,000 workers at 95 pits, marked the start of a long leftwards journey on the part of the Yorkshire section of the National Union of Mineworkers; on 24 May there began a six-week dock strike, centring on Merseyside, that was essentially another bout of inter-union turf warfare between the T&G and the much smaller National Amalgamated Stevedores and Dockers; and then from midnight on the 28th, two days after the election, there was a national rail strike, as the footplatemen (ie drivers and footplate staff) who belonged to the Associated Society of Locomotive Engineers and Firemen (ASLEF) sought to re-establish their pay differentials over the much more numerous, generally less skilled members of the National Union of Railwaymen (NUR). 'At Ealing Broadway main line station,' noted Henry St John on Whit Sunday (the 29th), 'a chalked-up notice stated: "Owing to labour trouble all advertised services are cancelled."'

A hapless victim of the strike was Marion Crawford, 'Crawfie', the former royal governess who long after she had become persona non grata on account of her revelations in *The Little Princesses* continued to write her *Woman's Own* column based on the fanciful premise that she was still on the inside track. 'The bearing and dignity of the Queen at the Trooping of the Colour ceremony at the Horse Guards' Parade last week,' she wrote authoritatively in the issue dated 16 June, 'caused admiration among the spectators', before going on to describe, with a similar show of intimacy, the scene at Royal Ascot ('an enthusiasm about it never seen there before'). Unfortunately, the issue had already gone to press *before* the rail strike – consequent on which, the Trooping of the Colour was cancelled and Royal Ascot postponed. Unmourned by the unforgiving Palace, it was the end of Crawfie the scribe.[1]

Although declaring a state of emergency on 31 May, the government's approach remained essentially non-confrontational. This was especially so in relation to the economically more damaging dock strike, where Sir Walter Monckton (still the Minister of Labour) relied on a mixture of personal mediation and the good offices of the TUC, with the Cabinet apparently not even considering the possibility of bringing in troops. As for the railway strike, Eden did in a radio broadcast insist – at his wife's urging and against the strong advice of Monckton and senior civil servants – that the railwaymen had to return to work before negotiations could begin, but in the event it ended on 14 June in the familiar manner of Monckton effectively buying it off, on what Macmillan next day privately called 'satisfactory terms'. Eden himself seems to have gone quietly, perhaps conscious of Cabinet unease ('it is very dangerous to take up too firm a position in these affairs', reflected Macmillan on the 13th), but did for a moment look as if he was going to try to do something big about the whole issue of strikes, with compulsory secret ballots the most mooted option. However, when he set up a special ministerial committee, the overwhelming weight of evidence, particularly from Monckton and the British Employers' Confederation, emphasised the intractable practical and political problems involved in enforcing such legislation, and Eden decided to shelve the matter. Monckton instead, conscious that a full employment environment was always likely to give organised labour the whip hand, pinned his hopes on a more gradual, intangible process, telling colleagues in July that it was 'desirable to educate public opinion about the problems of industrial relations in contemporary society, and particularly about the limitations of the strike as an industrial weapon', adding that through discussions on radio and television 'much could be done'. A well-meaning paternalist to his highly intelligent fingertips, he presumably believed this could really happen.

'The public, which to date has had a good deal of sympathy for the seemingly underpaid express-locomotive drivers, is now beginning to feel sick and tired of being caught between the unions' crossfire at increasingly frequent intervals,' recorded Mollie Panter-Downes at the start of June. 'The British are a good-tempered people who lumber toward rage at a majestic rate, but they seem to be on the move.' A degree of rage was probably felt at the Woodstock Hotel in Highbury Park, north London, where at breakfast on the 3rd a resident held forth to Gladys Langford about how he had been 'calling at a firm yesterday which had suffered from 3 strikes in one day', while three days later Langford herself noted, in relation to Eden and the railwaymen: 'I do hope he succeeds in breaking the strike but I doubt his success.' Soon afterwards, on the 8th, Judy Haines in Chingford went to the post office with a present to send: 'Assistant gave me corrugated cardboard & I packed it all up. Too heavy! Parcels over 8 oz cannot be accepted during rail strike! I said, "Oh well, if my troubles are no worse than that . . ."' Assistant appreciative of my bright spirit and said most people moaned frightfully, as if it was *his* fault.' The novelist and playwright Patrick Hamilton was among the moaners. 'A singularly depressing and, *I* think, rather muddled, strike,' was how he described it to his brother on the 10th, adding that it merely confirmed his increasing feeling that the proletariat was 'as moribund a class as the "aristocracy" '. Or, as Florence Turtle in Wimbledon Park put it about the whole phenomenon when a rail settlement was finally announced, 'Am fed up to the back teeth with everlasting strike.'[2]

Yet the underlying reality was that for most people the natural desire to get back to normal life vastly outweighed any larger considerations. 'There is a general handing out of compliments and medals, as if some unpopular war had ended,' rather caustically noted Panter-Downes on the 15th, with cheering in the Commons for the 'brilliant and popular' Monckton – for whom congratulations poured in from all quarters, including Miss Riley of 27 The Drive, Wallington, Surrey, 'and all her friends who travel with her on the 8.30 from Wallington'.

Crucially, there was not yet, despite widespread grumbling about the inconvenience of strikes, a stigma attached to the unions as such. 'Generally speaking, and thinking of Britain as a whole, do you think Trades Unions have been a good thing or a bad thing?' Gallup asked in August. To which 67 per cent said 'good' and only 18 per cent 'bad'. Gallup also revealed who in the public's opinion 'are not paid enough' (railwaymen, schoolteachers, factory workers and engineers), who 'are paid too much' (dock workers, lawyers, miners and civil servants) and who 'take life too easily' (civil servants, schoolteachers, builders and dock workers).[3]

Another area politically off-limits, beyond a very modest extent, was privatisation. On 3 June, in the middle of the railway strike, the *Any Questions?* panel – comprising Lady Violet Bonham Carter, the farmer-writer A. G. Street, Gerald Nabarro and James Callaghan – met at a hotel before that evening's broadcast from a factory in Poole. Nabarro, 'a very a-typical Conservative' in Lady Violet's words, was according to her 'very proud of being of humble origin & told F.G. [Freddy Grisewood, the chairman] to announce him as having started life as a builder's labourer & been a private in the Army'. Then came the pre-programme dinner: 'The conversation was painfully & tediously "class conscious" – one long harp on how many Etonians were in the Cabinet etc., in all of which Nabarro joined "con amore".' And in the broadcast itself, there took place 'a terrific slanging-match between Callaghan & Nabarro on the merits & demerits of nationalization'. It included, in the context of a question about whether workers in nationalised industries should have the freedom to strike, this exchange:

> *Nabarro*: What is wanted, I think, is a very much greater sense of responsibility in the nationalised industries, as well as in other industries, where strikes have taken place or are pending, and I must add there that it is not without significance in our industrial economy, that the majority of recent strikes seem to have taken place in nationalised industries, where labour relations are generally speaking infinitely poorer than in private industry.
>
> *Callaghan*: So what?
>
> *Nabarro*: Denationalise them as much as you possibly can. (*Applause.*)
>
> *Grisewood*: Yes Jim, Jim Callaghan.

Callaghan: Denationalise the coal mines? Come on, let's have a straight
answer.

Soon afterwards, to more applause, Nabarro reiterated his point that
'the answer is to try and denationalise as many industries as possible'.

The programme ended with a question from Sam Holt about why
people in the south of England, compared to those in the north, were
'generally surrounded by a high wall of shy reserve'. This provoked
Callaghan into asserting that the answer was 'quite simply and shortly
because people in the South are more snobs than people in the North',
adding that 'there's still far too much forelock-touching in the South
of England, especially in the County areas, still far too many class
distinctions and rigidities'. To which Lady Violet replied, 'I entirely
disagree. I would say, with all respect to Mr Callaghan, it takes a snob
to see a snob.' This sally earned, she noted with satisfaction afterwards,
'thunderous applause', leaving Callaghan, with no time to come back,
'distinctly annoyed'. But the most resonant event this Friday took
place in a Hammersmith flat, concisely recorded in the pocket diary of
a young actor and budding dramatist: '*Look Back in Anger* finished.'
It had taken John Osborne precisely four weeks and a day, including a
week's sojourn in Morecambe to play a small part in the naval comedy
Seagulls over Sorrento.[4]

This particular Friday was also the final day of the Messina
Conference, a gathering of the six member states of the European Coal
and Steel Community that led directly to the creation of the European
Economic Community in 1958. Britain deigned to send an observer,
but by this time he had already departed for home, reputedly with the
words: 'I leave Messina happy because even if you continue meeting
you will not agree; even if you agree, nothing will result; and even if
something results, it will be a disaster.' Eden, the Foreign Office, the
Treasury and the Ministry of Agriculture were all dead set against
British participation in the new organisation. The Commonwealth
weakened, free trade undermined, further European integration (even
a federation) on the cards, industry exposed to increased competition
– such was the Cabinet's assessment, with only one policy outcome
possible. Moreover, even if it had been accepted by the political elite, the
very concept of a pooling of sovereignty would at this stage have been

almost impossible to sell to the British people. Not long afterwards, English football's new league champions, Chelsea, encountered a pure Little Englander in action when the autocratic secretary of the Football League, Alan Hardaker, bullied the club into agreeing not to take part in the first European Cup (forerunner of the Champions' League). A dyed-in-the-wool northerner, he subsequently confessed, with a little grin, to the football writer Brian Glanville why he preferred not to get involved with football on the Continent: 'Too many wogs and dagos.'⁵

One European now doing business in England was the 32-year-old bouncing Czech Robert Maxwell, who on 15 June endured *un mauvais quart d'heure* in Winchester House, Old Broad Street, as almost two hundred publishers and their advisers listened to the official receiver's report on the collapse of the book-wholesaler Simpkin Marshall, some four years after Maxwell had taken control of it, promising the *Bookseller* as he did so that 'this will prove to be a long and successful chapter' and that 'nothing will be spared to promote the completeness and efficiency of this service in every way'. Also on the 15th, at Lord's, the young England amateur batsman Colin Cowdrey scored 47 on his first appearance of the season, looking, reported the *Evening Standard*, 'assured and immensely powerful, with no hint of any difficulty regarding footwork'. He had recently been discharged from National Service in the RAF on the grounds of 'a long history of foot trouble', thereby provoking a storm of hate mail and public attacks (including from Nabarro, who in the Commons accused him of dodging the column), but by early July he was back in the England team, playing under its new amateur captain, Surrey's Peter May.

This same summer, the 18-year-old Paul Bailey more deliberately evaded National Service through a virtuoso performance at the medical: a confession to bed-wetting did the trick, even before he mentioned possible homosexual tendencies. ' "I'm ashamed of you," said my mother. "Whatever will people think?" "Which people, Mum?" "Everybody. The whole street. They'll think there's something wrong with you." ' Bailey only found out later that the evening before his medical she had paid a rare visit to the local parish church in Battersea in order to pray for his acceptance by the army. Dennis Potter, 20 years old and from the Forest of Dean, was meanwhile reluctantly sticking out his National Service, having been transferred to the War Office in

London on account of his knowledge of Russian. 'God! those long afternoons in summer when you could hear the clock on Horse Guards Parade strike every quarter-hour, and it would be stiflingly hot and all those nerds would have their tightly furled umbrellas and their bowler hats on,' he recalled almost 40 years later. 'And having to go through that ridiculous "permission to speak – Sah!" routine every time you opened your mouth. That little phrase seemed to me to sum up the whole of English life at that time.' He was hoping to go up to Oxford in the autumn, but failed his Latin responsions and had to wait another year.[6]

Five days after Cowdrey's cameo, the trial began at the Old Bailey of the 28-year-old Ruth Ellis, accused of murdering her lover, an unsuccessful racing driver and two-timing socialite called David Blakely, outside the Magdala pub in Hampstead on Easter Sunday – a week or so after he had hit her so hard in the stomach that she had suffered a miscarriage. Ellis herself, daughter of an abusive professional cellist who had made her older sister Muriel pregnant, was a club hostess, sometime prostitute, occasional model and single mother of two. 'Ruth Ellis: I Shot To Kill Him', 'Model Weeps: I Was a Jealous Woman' and 'Model Smiles at Murder Verdict' were three of the *Daily Mail*'s headlines during the two-day trial, and generally there was a censorious tone to much of the press coverage, with great emphasis laid on Ellis's platinum-blonde hair and smart black suit with astrakhan collar and cuffs, as well as her unwomanly lack of emotion on hearing the guilty verdict. As for the trial itself, the judge, Sir Cecil Havers, refused to allow her counsel, Melford Stevenson, to argue provocation as a defence, while the jury reached its unanimous verdict in less than half an hour.

After the trial, Ellis refused to appeal, probably because of not wanting to implicate Desmond Cussen, a sugar-daddy accountant who had driven her to the pub and provided the gun, and who now promised to look after her children. On 23 June the execution date was fixed for 13 July at Holloway Prison. 'I have been tormented for a week at the idea that a highly civilised people should put a rope round the neck of Ruth Ellis and drop her through a trap and break her neck,' the still visiting Raymond Chandler wrote in the *Evening Standard* on the last day of June. 'This was a crime of passion under considerable provocation. No other country in the world would hang this woman.' And he finished with a reference to 'the medieval savagery of the law'. But at least as typical, perhaps more typical, was the reaction in Kingston-upon-Thames of Jacqueline Wilson's mother, Biddy, to a newspaper serialisation of Ellis's story. 'I read over Biddy's shoulder,' recalled Wilson. 'She tutted over Ruth's blonde hair and pencilled eyebrows and dark lips. "She's obviously just a good-time girl. Look at that peroxide hair! Talk about common!" '[7]

Sir Alfred Munnings – past President of the Royal Academy, tormentor of Henry Moore, and scourge of all things modern and Modernist – was probably not an abolitionist. On Monday, 4 July, he performed the annual ceremony, in the Village Hall at Brantham, Suffolk, of 'Dubbing the Knight'. After the ceremony, and the singing of 'When a Knight Won His Spurs' and 'The Maid's Song', it was time for Munnings to speak, as reported by the *Stowmarket Mercury*:

> Showing signs of emotion, he wiped his eyes and blew his nose in a large, gaily-coloured handkerchief. 'These are fine words,' he said, 'and they rhyme too. Not like these modern poems.'
>
> He told the children they were lucky to be living in the countryside where they could daily see the miracles of God in every hedgerow and tree top. 'A thrush can better Sir Malcolm Sargent and all his philharmonic host.' Parts of Britain were still unspoiled by industry, and they should take advantage of that: they were lucky, too, that they did not have to go to school by bus to some big town to be taught in a huge classroom by 'urbanised teachers'.
>
> He told the girls: 'The place of every woman is the home. Learn to cook, and to cook well.' And to the boys: 'Marry a good, useful woman, not one of these silly asses who want to go to the pictures every night.'

'As the meeting ended,' concluded the report, 'the children crowded round Sir Alfred waving autograph books.'

Four days later, on Friday the 8th, the Lord Mayor of Coventry officially opened the city's Upper Precinct, a pedestrianised shopping area with a first-floor level. 'There is certainly nothing like it in Britain,' one of the architects involved proudly told a local paper. 'There may be something as new in Europe, but nothing quite the same.' Even so, for all its importance as a symbol of Coventry's pioneering reconstruction, it did not prove a huge success, partly because of the decision – whether on aesthetic or financial grounds is unclear – not to have access ramps, but instead to rely on stairs. 'The Precinct shops on top floor hardly did any business,' remembered one Coventrian. 'As quick as they opened, they tended to change or close. I don't think Coventry people were too keen on climbing up steps and going to shops at different levels. I think everybody had got so used to being on the ground floor.' There was also for the ruling Labour councillors, viscerally committed to the 1940s concept of the new Coventry, the wider problem of continuing trader-cum-Tory resistance to pedestrian shopping – a resistance sufficiently strong to make it a real possibility that a new motor road was going to drive through the whole pedestrian shopping area. But some three months after the opening of the Upper Precinct (with the Lower one still under construction), the Labour proposal that a new central thoroughfare, Market Street, should become a traffic-free shopping street was carried. 'We are going to keep our heads in front,' declared Alderman George Hodgkinson, for many years the dominant local politician behind Coventry's reconstruction. And he added: 'This resolution is a test of faith in the adventure we have begun.'[8]

'LAST BID TO SAVE RUTH ELLIS' ran the *Daily Mirror*'s front-page headline the day after the Upper Precinct opening, with a story about the mass petitions flooding in to the Home Office. But this Saturday, the 9th, her fate was not on the mind of Frederick Sanderson, a 30-year-old Dalston man travelling on a 73 bus along the Essex Road in London. 'You foreigners come to this country and take away Englishmen's jobs,' his wife said, during a row with the non-white conductor, Irvin Obadiah, who had been living for the previous two years in Hackney. To which, by his own account, Obadiah replied, 'If I was a foreigner I should not be ashamed of being one.' But by Sanderson's account he called her 'an English pig'. In any event, Sanderson bopped him one – leading in due course to a 10s fine (and £2 costs) as well as a rebuke from the Bench at Old Street Magistrates' Court: 'Why you want to make all this trouble on a bus and hit a man much smaller than you, I don't know. He's got his job to do and it's a difficult one.'

It was a pity that PC George Dixon was not around to calm things down. Last seen shot dead in *The Blue Lamp* (1950), he miraculously returned to the screen – but this time the small screen – at 8.45 this Saturday evening for the debut of *Dixon of Dock Green*, subtitled in *Radio Times* 'The stories of a London policeman on his beat'. As before, Jack Warner played Dixon and the writer was Ted Willis, while the part of the sensible daughter, Mary Dixon, went to Billie Whitelaw. Willis would subsequently stress that in the television series he had wanted to convey the reality of a London copper's day-to-day life – 'traffic duty, drunks, night-beats, answering questions, handling minor criminals' – and that 'Dixon couldn't be Dixon in a programme which was full of wailing sirens, screeching brakes, gun fights, murderers and crazy mixed-up kids'. The formula worked. 'So wise, so fatherly, he earns everyone's respect,' noted Philip Hope-Wallace in the *Listener* of Dixon in the opening episode (called 'P.C. Crawford's First Pinch'), while after the third episode the *Spectator*'s John Metcalf wrote of how 'P.C. Dixon saunters amiably about his beat catching bicycle thieves, reuniting fallen daughters with forgiving fathers, worrying about his day off and dodging the sergeant', in all of which 'the true ring of authenticity comes quite often', adding up to 'a vast improvement on the routine mechanics of *Fabian of the Yard*'. So too, on the whole, the members of the BBC Viewing Panel. 'Pleasant, and suitable for family viewing' and 'Setting and action were refreshingly true to life' were two early reactions, with further praise following at the end of the series: 'Very fine series – we always have this programme marked as a "must see".' And: 'Very high class and like Oliver Twist, I ask for more.' More than 360 episodes indeed lay ahead, often starting with Dixon's genial 'Evenin' all', eventually creating – and reinforcing – a cosy, rose-tinted image of the police that would take a long time to shift.[9]

The weather was hotting up. 'Another lovely day,' recorded Florence Turtle on Sunday the 10th:

> Went to Church but Amy was not there. Home & put roast pork in the oven on a very low flame & then went by car with Bernard [her brother] & Dinah to Richmond Park. Bernard brushed out car whilst I threw sticks for Dinah. We then made our way round to the Kings Arms at Roehampton past the Skyscraper Flats which are ruining the whole area & had a drink apiece. Home, cooked vegetables & Roast Pork with sage & onion stuffing, all of which were delicious, plus fresh fruit salad.

Rested & then got tea consisting of Tinned Salmon & Salad. Crocheted a bit, then B [her sister Barbara] came on the phone & suggested my meeting her & Fred on the Towing Path, which I did & repaired to the Star & Garter for a very pleasant Session.

'Brian [her other brother] started to lay linoleum in lavatory at 7 pm,' ended her entry, '& was still at it when I got home at eleven.'

' "I'M CONTENT TO DIE" SAYS RUTH ELLIS' was the *Mirror*'s front-page headline on Monday morning, with only 48 hours to go before her appointment with Albert Pierrepoint. An announcement was expected this day as to whether there was to be a reprieve from the Home Secretary, and it duly came. 'Ruth Ellis is NOT to be reprieved,' recorded Gladys Langford at the end of Monday. 'She is to hang on Wednesday. How grim the intervening hours must be for her and her parents. Poor unfortunate children too. Thank God I had a good mother. Bad thunderstorm tonight & such clammy weather all day.' And next day she wrote: 'There are still agitations to obtain a reprieve for Ruth Ellis. She has been in my mind all day; worthless as she is, it is a grim thought that she is to be hurled into eternity in this golden weather.' Other diarists this Tuesday concentrated on the weather rather than Ellis. 'A sweltering day – hottest of year so far' (Heap in St Pancras). 'A real heat wave now, with terrific sunshine all day, and most places having thunderstorms which don't break up the heat' (Martin in Oxford). 'Hot enough to keep one perspiring tonight' (Raynham in Surbiton).[10]

What to wear during this exceedingly hot spell? 'I have been wearing a straw boater and a bow tie in London,' John Betjeman told the readers of his 'City and Suburban' column in the *Spectator*. 'In Bond Street the glances of the women and men were so contemptuous of this ageing Teddy Boy that I had to take off my hat and expose my bald head to the sun.' This summer there was all too little male sartorial distinction around, at least according to Cecil Beaton. 'Young "teddy boys", with their bright blue or scarlet corduroy pants, seem to show spirit,' he observed, 'but generally men still go about in dirty old mackintoshes, shiny, striped City trousers, and greasy bowlers. The English have not recovered from the war, and it shows itself in the torpor of their vestments.' It was not torpor, though, that bothered E. W. Swanton, a stickler for the maintenance of cricket's traditions. 'One was left wondering,' he grumbled in the *Daily Telegraph* after the Varsity match at Lord's in early July. 'Does the shoddy dress of many of the undergraduate spectators, the shedding by the cricketers of part of their historic uniform [a reference to Cambridge caps and Oxford sweaters], derive from the same basic cause, a weakened sense of personal dignity and good manners? Are the young gentlemen of 1955, outwardly so polite to their seniors, intentionally cocking a snook at the past?'[11]

There was a late twist to the Ruth Ellis story. On the Monday evening she sent for the solicitor Victor Mishcon, who had handled her divorce, and told him about how much Pernod she had been drinking before she fired the gun and of the role played by Cussen. But despite Mishcon's best efforts next day, no reprieve was forthcoming. Wednesday dawned fair, the start of another scorcher. 'It's a fine day for hay-making,' declared 'Cassandra' (William Connor) on the front page of the *Mirror*. 'A fine day for fishing. A fine day for lolling in the sunshine. And if you feel that way – and I mourn to say that millions of you do – it's a fine day for a hanging.' Outside Holloway Prison, where Ellis was due to be hanged at 9.00 a.m., a large crowd, thousands-strong, surged behind a massive police cordon. And in the playground of a boys' school in Middlesex, the headmaster came across four pupils, all under the age of 11, standing still. One had a watch in his hand and was saying, 'Only four more minutes and she is going to swing. One, two, three, four, she has had it boys.' Gladys Langford surely had it right when she asserted in her diary later that day: 'I feel sure that if executions were in public there would be as great crowds today as ever there were. People don't change.' For one young writer, the whole thing made a considerable impression. 'I daresay she was a vulgar little tart with a predilection for wearing crosses round her neck, but to sentence her to die at such and such a time, in *that* way, is to make her into a dying goddess,' reflected Frederic Raphael. 'London shuddered in the heat, and so it should. Executions are unnatural crimes.'

Almost half a century later, in 2003, Ellis's sister Muriel was at last able to ask the Court of Appeal to quash the murder conviction and instead substitute a verdict of manslaughter on the grounds of provocation and/or diminished responsibility. Despite all the eloquence of Michael Mansfield, acting for her, the appeal was rejected, being described as 'without merit'.[12]

8

It's Terribly Sad

'Whew! The Men Are in Revolt' exclaimed the *Daily Mirror* on Saturday, 16 July. It was three days since Ruth Ellis had been hanged – days that had included a sharp controversy in Blackpool over the Chamber of Horrors exhibiting a wax effigy of her, dressed in a low-cut black evening gown with a black tulle stole – and the heat wave was unabated. The male revolt was about not being allowed to wear cooler clothes, and the *Mirror* quoted the hard-line general manager of a big London store: 'Whatever the weather our men must dress in a grey suit, collar and tie. The public expects them to look smart. If we allowed them to dress anyhow, the place would look very tatty indeed.' In the City that week, not far from his Cloth Fair home, John Betjeman's sartorial eyes were opened. 'I was walking down Newgate Street with a girl in the hot weather,' he wrote soon afterwards. 'She remarked on how unattractive men were. Looking at their clothes, I realised she was right – retired tea-planters bursting out of linen suits; youths with rows of pens and pencils in their pockets, and badges and combs and tubular grey-flannel trousers; businessmen in dark suits minus the waistcoat, with the sweat showing through their shirts.' On the other hand, Betjeman had nothing but praise for 'the cheap cotton dresses' bought from chain stores. And he offered a considered compliment: 'I cannot believe that English women have ever looked prettier than they have done in the summer weather of this year.'[1]

It was probably an unhappy weekend for Edward (E. P.) Thompson in Halifax. 'This long, tendentious volume,' the anonymous reviewer (in fact, the writer James Pope-Hennessy) in the latest *TLS* called his first major book, *William Morris: Romantic to Revolutionary*. 'Heavily biased by Marxian thought, his book is also splenetic in tone. It is perhaps a remarkable feat that he manages to sustain a mood of ill-temper through a volume of 900 pages.' After asserting that Thompson's study 'merely serves to emphasise aspects of Morris which are better left forgotten', the review finished: 'Mr Thompson is too shrill to be persuasive – and when he declares that Morris's *A Factory as it Might Be* is not an unpractical poet's dream but has been already "fulfilled" in the Soviet Union, readers of common sense will part company with him for good.' Thompson himself, in a 1976 postscript to a revised edition, subsequently conceded some ground – 'It is true that in 1955 I allowed some hectoring political moralisms, as well as a few Stalinist pieties, to intrude upon the text' – but at the same time emphasised the larger context, namely that 'the book was published at the height of the Cold War' and 'intellectual McCarthyism was not confined to the United States'.

He might also have mentioned the deep rut which history itself was in by the mid-1950s. John Drummond went up to Cambridge in October 1955 to read the subject and was intensely disappointed: not only were the dons remote, but the history they taught was 'both fractured and partial', with 'no sense of a whole society', while 'the very phrase "social history" was disallowed'. That last point was not quite true, but what G. M. Trevelyan, doyen of social history, meant by the term was something essentially Whiggish and patrician, rather than concerned with the lives and struggles of ordinary people. For Drummond, the sterile, top-down approach in Cambridge was epitomised by Geoffrey (G. R.) Elton (whose hugely studied *England under the Tudors* appeared in 1955): excellent on government and pipe rolls, much less so on music, literature and architecture. Thompson himself, a Cambridge graduate, consciously preferred to stay outside the academy, instead teaching adult-education classes in West Yorkshire. The two men were of the same generation – Elton born in 1921, Thompson in 1924 – and over almost four decades would battle it out for Clio's soul.[2]

At Aintree on the 17th, the Sunday of this July weekend, Stirling Moss became the first British driver to win the British Grand Prix, albeit driving a Mercedes and possibly because the world champion, Juan Manuel Fangio, was happy to let Moss triumph on home soil. Next day, Ford unveiled its latest Anglia, a small two-door, four-seater family model. 'From every aspect the Anglia is a good-looking, well-proportioned car,' acclaimed *The Times*, 'yet the comfort and convenience of the passengers have not been sacrificed for the sake of appearance,' adding that 'the close view of the road surface ahead should be of great benefit when driving in fog', a tacit reference to the continuing frequency of smogs. The age of the all-dominant car was dawning fast, not least in Birmingham, where on Friday the 22nd the Minister of Transport, John Boyd-Carpenter, formally opened the road-widening scheme at Digbeth, converting a bottleneck into a dual carriageway, with some stirring words: 'This scheme in this great city, the heart and centre of the industrial Midlands, will contribute directly towards providing an efficient transport system to serve the industry of this country, by which every man, woman and child in this country lives.' One dissenter, viewing the motoring phenomenon as part of a wider, disagreeable pattern, was Philip Larkin. 'The pubs here are nightmares of neo-Falstaffianism, coughing laughter well soused with phlegm,' he grumbled from Cottingham, just outside Hull, to a friend on the 28th. 'The village smells of chips. The town smells of fish. And everywhere creep the new cars with L on the front, Auntie Cis and co. learning to drive i.e. clog up the roads some more & further endanger my life.'

Next day, Madge Martin arrived in Scarborough for her annual holiday there, noting that the Spa 'thank goodness is fully restored to its former dignity and beauty', while Judy Haines took her two girls to the Odeon to see Mr Pastry (aka Richard Hearne) in *The Happiest Days of His Life* and Walt Disney's *The Vanishing Prairie*: 'Both very good. Pamela regretted Mr Pastry's film was not in colour.' Saturday the 30th saw the start of the Bank Holiday weekend, with the forecast good and the holiday rush starting early. Liverpool was typical. From 7.00 in the morning, buses to the city centre were full of 'bucket-and-spade laden families and haversack-carrying teenagers'; city shops were 'crowded by families making last-minute purchases before going on holiday', with a particular rush for cheap seaside shoes, 'sun dresses' and men's socks; packed trains were leaving Lime Street station, with 'many people going to North Wales standing in the corridors or crowded in the guard's van', while from Exchange 'trains to Blackpool and Morecambe were full long before they were due to leave'; motor coaches were also fully booked; and there were long queues for the three steamers going to the Isle of Man, though an official was adamant, 'There is no danger of anyone being left behind.' Sunday morning was spent by an appreciative Martin 'listening to an orchestra on the Spa with the well-dressed audience, which is still, in a minor way, the custom', and then on Bank Holiday Monday the Haines family treated itself to a car outing to Chelmsford (with a picnic stop on the way), where they watched Essex play Worcestershire. 'Instead of lining up for cup of tea, at my insistence we had 2/6d set tea,' wrote Judy. 'It was delicious. Dainty sandwiches, bread and jam, delicious cakes, two pots of tea instead of watering down first lot. Girls charged half. A lovely sunny day and we stayed till end of match – 7 pm. Bought fish and chips at Epping, so no cooking on arrival home. Opened tin of peaches. What a lovely day!'[3]

Two days later, on Wednesday, 3 August, the first English production of Samuel Beckett's *Waiting for Godot* opened at the small Arts Theatre in Great Newport Street. Directed by the 24-year-old Peter Hall, it proved a fraught evening. Hall would recall how 'on the line, "Nothing happens, nobody comes, nobody goes. It's awful", a very English voice said loudly: "Hear! hear!" ', while the line 'I have had better entertainment elsewhere' provoked ironical laughter, and when a character yawned, so too, loudly and pointedly, did someone in the stalls. A sizeable part of the audience left at the interval, and at the end, remembered Peter Bull (who played Pozzo), 'the curtain fell to mild applause, we took a scant three calls and a depression and sense of anti-climax descended on us all'. The reviews over the next day or two did not help. Not all the critics were as outrightly hostile as the *Daily Mail*'s Cecil Wilson – his piece adorned by the headline 'THE LEFT BANK CAN KEEP IT' – but Derek Granger's mildly amused condescension in the *Financial Times* was fairly typical, calling it 'a cast-iron copper-bottomed, rubber-lined, water-proof, high-brow's delight with knobs on' and adding that 'even its "great thoughts" seem just the kind that we ourselves might have fathered given moody enough circumstances and a dull day'.

The turning point came at the weekend, as Harold Hobson in the *Sunday Times* and Kenneth Tynan in the *Observer* both wrote in very positive terms about the play's uniqueness, and from that moment the size of the audiences quickly picked up and its London future was assured, not least as a talking point. In due course it fell to *The Critics* on the Home Service to offer their assessment. 'Tremendously funny, deeply sad,' thought J. W. Lambert. 'Could have gone on listening to it for ever,' declared Colin MacInnes. 'A play of profound religious symbolism,' asserted G. S. Fraser. Upon which the fourth critic, the humorist Stephen Potter, announced that, although he had disliked the play when he had seen it, 'for the first time on record my opinion has been somewhat changed by the opinions of the other critics', and he went on to praise it as 'a masterpiece of production – beautifully acted . . . a very refreshing change from the average West-End play'. Potter slipped up, however, by further remarking that while watching it 'I thought the play had no real centre – it's exactly like Peer Gynt's onion'. To which Lambert scornfully riposted, 'That seems to me practically the whole point of it.'4

Eight days after *Godot*, on a Thursday morning in Soho, there took place the so-called 'Battle of Frith Street'. London's two dominant gangsters of the era were undoubtedly Jack Spot (real name Jack Comer) and Billy Hill, and this was a knife-fight between Spot and one of Hill's sidekicks, Albert Dines. It ended in a greengrocers, where a large fruiterer, Bertha Hyams, finished proceedings by hitting Spot with a brass weighing-pan. Spot duly found himself at the Old Bailey, were he was charged with affray and successfully defended by Rose Heilbron. 'Thank you very much,' the East Ender yelled to the jury. 'I have suffered enough.' Which earned a sharp rebuke from Sir Gerald Dodson, Recorder of London: 'Behave yourself!' It soon transpired that key evidence – including from an octogenarian Anglican clergyman badly in debt to his bookmakers – had been rigged and bought, provoking John Gordon to ask bitterly in the *Sunday Express*: 'Are the JACK SPOTS above the law?' In fact the best days for both Spot and Hill were past them, but the Krays were still just limbering up, with Reg perfecting his celebrated 'cigarette punch', offering a cigarette with one hand and breaking the jaw with the other. For most people, though, the persistent fear was less of criminal godfathers than of teddy boys. One evening that summer, a Ted sat on a bus next to a friend of Gladys Langford and 'pinched her legs & stroked her bosom and she was afraid to complain to the conductor lest she was razor-slashed – so she left the 'bus & got on one following'.5

On Saturday the 13th, two days after the Soho fracas, Philip Larkin made the memorable journey, on a slow, stopping train from Hull to London, that he eventually transmuted into 'The Whitsun Weddings'.[6] The return trip involved different emotions. 'I had a hellish journey back, on a *filthy* train,' he wrote to the friends he had stayed with, 'next to a young couple with a slobbering chocolatey baby – apart from a few splashes of milk nothing happened to me, but the strain of feeling it might was a great one . . .' Soon afterwards, reviews starting appearing of Kingsley Amis's second novel, *That Uncertain Feeling*, which were generally favourable and, as with *Lucky Jim*, viewed him as offering something different from most other contemporary novelists. 'He is brashly, vulgarly, aggressively unsensitive, and the world his characters inhabit is the world that has succeeded the posh,' declared V. S. Pritchett (under the pseudonym Richard Lister) in the *New Statesman*. 'It is the world of the Welfare State in all its crudity, and Mr Amis is a literary Teddy boy.' Pritchett elaborated on this 'new world' – one of 'sitters-in [ie babysitters], and nappies and half-washed tea-cups, and multiple stores and mass-producing tailors' – and reckoned that Amis depicted it 'with a mixture of two parts disgust and three parts farcical comedy'. Amis himself reflected that 'the reviewers have been very decent on the whole, but all this "vulgar" stuff makes me wonder where they live and where they go on their free evenings'. August also saw the publication of the first *Guinness Book of Records*, compiled by Norris and Ross McWhirter after the Irish brewery had turned to the statistically minded twins to compile a reference book that would settle pub arguments. It would become the best-selling work of non-fiction after the Bible.[7]

Larkin's thank-you letter of the 17th included a scribbled addition – '*Am going to buy some 6^d postal orders tomorrow, for Football Pools*' – and three days later the football season began. For the first time, Saturday-evening television was able to show in a programme called *Sports Special* some highlights of the afternoon's action, though up to a total maximum, insisted the Football League, of only 15 minutes each week. On the opening day itself, the most heartwarming scene was at Southend United, who entertained Norwich City in Third Division South for the opening of the new Roots Hall ground, entirely financed by supporters (who apparently never thought of trying to achieve ownership). Before the kick-off, there was music by the band of the United Supporters Club, a service of dedication by the vicar of Prittlewell and everyone standing to sing 'Abide with Me'. On a baking-hard surface on a hot afternoon, Southend ran out 3–1 winners in front of a 17,000 crowd, which after the final whistle swarmed over the pitch. The new season also featured Roy Race and Blackie Gray making their first-team debuts in *Tiger* for Melchester Rovers, at home to Elbury Wanderers. 'The pals struck their best form right from the kick-off. Then the crowd roared as Blackie snapped up the ball, and sent a perfect through pass to Roy. Roy flicked the ball past an Elbury back, followed up and shot first time. "Goal!" "Good old Roy! Up the Rovers!" "By thunder! That new lad Race can certainly shoot!" ' The match finished three apiece, with a brace for the blond-haired Roy of the Rovers, a centre forward with a long, turbulent career ahead of him.[8]

On the same day that Southend was *en fête*, John Fowles and his girlfriend opted for a different coastal destination, going to Littlehampton for a week's holiday and staying 'with a Mrs Sopp in an archetypal seaside lodging-house':

> A great lump of a groaning, creaking, aging, double-bed; to make love on it was like driving a lorry of old iron down a bumpy lane. A religious text lord of the mantelpiece, guarded by two drab China Alsatian dogs. Three faded pictures. 'The Letter', 'The Ride', 'The Important Message'. A faded chromotint of men herding sheep in Australia. The enamel wash stand with basin, jug and soapdish – quite redundant, with a modern bathroom next door, but kept, one felt, for the essential artistic effect.

This summer holidays it was the customary Wales for the Fulham-based Bull family, making the journey in a second-hand van, with no windows in the back. 'We had all the usual rituals, the 6.30 a.m. start, no breakfast till we reached somewhere called Brownhills north of Birmingham, where Mum put on an apron and cooked a fry-up of bacon and eggs on a primus stove in a lay-by,' remembered Janet Street-Porter. 'Oh, how I longed for a meal in a café like other people! The journey up the A5 was as interminable as ever, and my sister was reduced to counting milk churns to pass the hours, while I read till I felt car sick.' For the 12-year-old Mike (not yet Mick) Jagger, this August was the month not of holidays but of work – a summer job on an American base near Dartford. There he played American football and baseball, drank Coke, and met a black cook, José, who introduced him to rhythm and blues. The newly Americanised Jagger would have to go back to school in September – unlike Mary O'Brien, a 16-year-old who decided this summer, having left St Anne's convent school in Ealing, that the time had come for a complete makeover. In the privacy of her bedroom, out went the sensible, librarian look, and instead (in her biographer's words) 'on went the tall blonde beehive wig, the glamorous French pleated dress and grown-up high heels', while 'in a gesture of teenage daring' she 'put around her eyes layers of Indian kohl, false eyelashes and heavy black mascara'.[9] It was the start of Dusty Springfield.

'Educational opportunities here should be as good as in any grammar school,' Mrs H. R. Chetwynd, head of the just opening Woodberry Down comprehensive school in Hackney, told the *Hackney Gazette* on the first Tuesday in September. 'We would like people to know that this will be one complete school. Pupils will not be called grammar, central or modern, but will all belong to one school with the same chances.' The school itself, noted the paper approvingly, was 'one of the latest and best equipped in the country', having taken five years to build, and could accommodate 1,250 pupils. There were three four-storey buildings, 'extensive use of prefabricated construction', and altogether 'the whole lay-out is large and impressive', enabling courses to be 'planned to meet the needs of children of varying ability'. A handful of other new comprehensives were also opening this term, including Woodlands in Coventry. Amid significant local reservations about the change of educational direction, Alderman S. Stringer was careful to insist at the formal ceremony in October that 'it was never the intention of the Education Committee that such schools should be competitive with the grammar school type of education', but rather they should be complementary, giving 'opportunities that probably would never have been there otherwise'. By contrast, the Lord Mayor, Alderman T. H. Dewis, was entirely unabashed, boasting that with this new comprehensive Coventry was in 'the exalted position' of 'giving a lead to the country'. That was not strictly true, but there was no doubt that the comprehensive experiment was by now starting to take real, tangible shape. And soon afterwards, Margaret Cole expressed the hope in *Tribune* that people might at last stop assuming automatically, on the basis of no evidence, that 'a comprehensive school "must be" a perpetual traffic-jam, a universal sausage machine of mediocrity in which the child is a lonely atom and all individuality and all initiative suppressed'.

Meanwhile, the majority of secondary-age children continued to attend secondary moderns. With its '118 airy rooms, including laboratories and lecture halls', a library (with one wall completely made of glass) stocking 3,000 books (half of them non-fiction), laboratories 'with sinks and gas points to permit a maximum number of individual experiments', woodwork and metalwork rooms 'so well equipped that it would be reasonable to describe them as small factories', blackboards 'on the roller principle', floors 'laid with non-slip plastic bricks' and corridors into which 'light streams through transparent plastic domes' – it was no wonder that the *Chorley Guardian* was ecstatic about Southlands School, the Lancashire town's new secondary modern. So too with the new Dick Sheppard School in Tulse Hill, a secondary modern-cum-technical school for 900 pupils. 'The keynote of the whole school is lightness and brightness with glass walls used wherever possible,' noted the *South London Press*, arguing that it 'cuts at the root the deep-seated prejudice of parents and Londoners that unless a child wins a grammar place in the eleven-plus examination its career is crippled'.

It was a quite different, much less optimistic take that John Laird offered. A New Zealander who had taught at five London secondary moderns – none of them in 'bad' or 'slummy' areas – in the previous two years, he delivered in the *News Chronicle* in September a devastating three-part exposé. 'What seems to have happened,' he asserted, 'is that the tradition of respect for the teacher and all that he represents has broken down. Consequently the young teacher has to fight his battle alone, unaided by any accepted background of discipline.' The title of one piece was 'Jungle in the Classroom', and Laird emphasised the futility of hoping for any parental support: 'London parents of secondary modern children apparently do not regard education as very important. They take little interest in school unless they suspect that their children are being maltreated.' Laird reckoned that 'about 30 per cent leave school semi-literate', stated that 'very few pupils read books as distinct from comics', and concluded bleakly that 'we are still turning out from our State schools a very large number of children who in speech and writing recognisably belong to a "lower order" '. Unsurprisingly, many middle-class parents were loath to leave matters to chance when it came to the eleven-plus, and a few days after Laird's articles Judy Haines in Chingford noted that several neighbouring girls were having 'private coaching in sums'.[10]

Just as the autumn term was starting, Wolverhampton was hit by an overtime ban on the buses. The reason was familiar – a protest against the employment of too many (ie more than 5 per cent) non-white workers – and there was the usual disclaimer by the white busmen that they were racially motivated. The local *Express and Star* printed some passenger overheards, including on the Dudley-to-Fighting Cocks trolley route:

> Well, these foreigners can come willy-nilly into the country – and they've got to work somewhere!
>
> I don't see why the black men shouldn't be on the buses. They're nearly always polite to me, and often help me off the platform.
>
> Well, I think the unions have to draw a line somewhere with this coloured problem. The trouble is that the coloured men can just drift into the country, without any special training.

'The Wolverhampton bus dispute has brought to a head a great deal of racial bitterness,' reflected the paper on 10 September. 'Human nature is such that it fears what is strange. A colour problem exists in the Midlands and it is no use to pretend that it does not.' Yet for one West Indian, recently arrived in London, there was unbridled hope and excitement about the future. 'Boy, London is a confusing place, a complication of traffic and geography,' Sylvan Pollard wrote in August to his wife in British Guiana:

> You just have to see London to believe it. Immense, giddy. There's going to be a good life for you and our children here. Opportunities keep knocking all the time and there's no barrier to success if a man works hard and invests in the future.
>
> I've been admitted into the printers' union since last Monday. I do printing like I did at the Chronicle, but what a difference. Work starts

at 8 am, but nothing is done before 8.30 except reading newspapers and some smoking and talking. Stop at 10 for tea and cakes. Lunch hour from 12.30. I go sight-seeing every day and catch a snack outside. I knock off at 5 pm don't work Saturday nor Sunday. On top of all this they pay me £9 10s. Sounds good eh. Well it is way above what the average Englishman earns but it is not enough for this worker. I can save more than half my salary per week.

Thanks for sending a parcel, but don't – save it for yourself and the girls.

An ocean of love and a kiss on every wave . . .'[11]

'I would not care to say categorically that this was the most nauseating programme I have ever seen on TV, for I have been pretty appalled in my time by *Ask Pickles*,' declared the *New Statesman*'s television critic William Salter, who went on to refer to 'endless tins of treacle' and to how 'it is the inflation and debasement of feelings that should be private that one abhors'. The programme in question was *This Is Your Life*, the creation of Ralph Edwards (an American who had popularised it in the States) and launched here by the BBC on 29 July 1955. 'We can assure our readers that the secret of the victim's identity is being well kept,' *Radio Times* had promised, and in the event the first outing, fronted by Edwards himself, had the well-known radio and television personality Eamonn Andrews as its subject. Thereafter, it was he who became the compère, as he also did from 14 September of another new television series, *Crackerjack*. This featured comedians, speciality acts and participatory games such as 'Double or Drop', with a Crackerjack pencil for all who took part, and in an accompanying *Radio Times* article its originator and producer, Johnny Downes, explained that 'all our guests must be over twelve years of age and able to reach the Television Theatre by five o'clock without missing any of their school day'. The same month, there were a couple of other BBC television developments: from the 4th, the faces as well as the voices of newsreaders, with Richard Baker and Kenneth Kendall the first to be seen, though at this stage without the vulgarity of their identities actually being revealed; and from the 19th, the reinvention of *Panorama* (hitherto a rather scrappy affair) as the Corporation's current-affairs flagship, offering a weekly 'Window on the World' presented by the trusted, authoritative figure of Richard Dimbleby.[12]

By this point the BBC was bracing itself for an imminent, potentially dangerous challenge: the coming of commercial television, due to start on Thursday, 22 September. Programmes at first would be available only to viewers in London and its surrounds – from Hitchin in the north to Horsham in the south, from Wallingford in the west to Burnham-on-Crouch in the east – while even in that restricted area only a minority of sets had yet been converted to take ITV. Nevertheless, almost everyone realised that this was the start of a new, more competitive era in British television. 'I am prepared to stick my chin out a yard and make a prophecy here and now,' declared Godfrey Winn in *Picture Post*. 'Independent TV, once its growing pains (which may well last a year) are over, is going to settle down into a wow of a success.' He went on to claim that this could only be good for the BBC, 'cossetted in the cotton wool of a cosy monopolist atmosphere for years', and that at last the viewer would be sovereign: 'The referee of the fight, and the final decider of the contest, will be the public themselves. Always before, "They" have been in a position to give the public what, in their Olympian way, they considered was "good" for it. But, starting with D-Day, the public will have the big guns ...' In the same issue, Kenneth Adam, a former Controller of the BBC Light Programme, expressed caution about the television phenomenon as a whole. He accused the BBC of already moving downmarket ('lowering its sights in order to meet the threat of competition'), argued that the ideal schedule, in terms of quality control, was only three hours of programming each evening, and called on everyone involved, on both sides of the television divide, 'to use this new force of incomparable, even frightening, potency in the best possible way for the enrichment rather than the impoverishment of our family life'.

The BBC did have one card up its sleeve on the fateful Thursday evening. At 6.45, just half an hour before commercial television was due to go on air, some 25 per cent of the adult population tuned in to the usual Light Programme broadcast of *The Archers* – and, to their almost uniform dismay, listened to its most sensational episode yet: a fire breaking out in the stables at Grey Gables Country Club, the newly married, pregnant Grace Archer dashing in to save her horse Midnight, a beam crashing down and Grace dying in Phil Archer's arms ('Phil ... I love you, Phil ...') on the way to hospital. 'I am terribly upset,' one typically devastated listener, Mrs Mary Holmes of Edgbaston, Birmingham, told a journalist. 'It's like losing one of the family.' Nor were the cast best pleased. 'This is the third death,' one complained amid huge publicity over the next few days. 'At this rate we shall all be out of work in no time.' But the scriptwriter, Edward J. Mason, was adamant: 'We must mirror life or *The Archers* will turn into a drawing-room exercise. We shall now see how the Archers react to tragedy.' Only the *Manchester Guardian*, with some verse by Mary Crozier, dared a little humour:

> She was well loved, and millions know
>   That Grace has ceased to be.
> Now she is in her grave, but oh,
>   She's scooped the ITV.

The BBC itself stoutly denied that the timing of Grace's death had been a deliberate spoiler. But as Rooney Pelletier, controller of the Light Programme, had privately reflected in May: 'The more I think about it, the more I believe that a death of a violent kind in *The Archers* timed if possible to diminish interest in the opening of commercial television in London is a good idea.'[13]

Undeterred, ITV's special evening began at Guildhall, London, with the televising of the official inaugural ceremony. After some opening words from Leslie Mitchell (whose voice had launched BBC Television 19 years earlier), John Connell described the guests as they arrived; the Hallé Orchestra under Sir John Barbirolli (recently appointed musical adviser to Associated-Rediffusion, the company responsible for weekday programmes in London and the home counties) played Elgar's *Cockaigne* overture followed by the national anthem; and there were uplifting speeches from the Lord Mayor, the Postmaster-General (Dr Charles Hill) and the chairman of the Independent Television Authority (ITA), Sir Kenneth Clark. Clark's role was in effect to lend cultural respectability to the new channel, but afterwards he confessed privately that the ceremony had left him feeling as if he had constructed a handsome building that was being lived in by barbarians. Then, from 8.00, with Muriel Young as announcer, came the programmes themselves.

They included a variety show compèred by Jack Jackson, a trio of brief drama sequences (including Dame Edith Evans as Lady Bracknell), professional boxing from Shoreditch Town Hall, and the news read fluently by Christopher Chataway. But inevitably, the real novelty lay in the advertisements. 'And now the moment you've all been waiting for,' declared Jackson at 8.12, 'it's time for the commercial break.' The evening's advertisers had drawn lots for which should have the privilege of the first slot, and the winner was – 'It's tingling fresh, it's fresh as ice, it's Gibbs SR toothpaste'. Or, as Bernard Levin put it in his *Manchester Guardian* review of the evening's entertainment, 'a charming young lady brushed her teeth, while a charming young gentleman told us of the benefits of the toothpaste with which she was doing it'. Next up were Cadbury's Drinking Chocolate and Summer County margarine. As for overall viewer reaction, fewer than 200,000 sets tuned in, but among those who did watch, Gallup found that only one in ten was critical, while two in three thought the new venture had got off to a good start.[14]

Over the next few days a handful of future favourites made their bows. *Dragnet* and *I Love Lucy* were both American imports – respectively, a realistic police series (significantly tougher-edged than *Dixon*) and television's pioneer sitcom, starring the zany Lucille Ball, her real-life husband Desi Arnaz and, in due course, 'Little Ricky'. *The Adventures of Robin Hood* was a hit from the start, filmed at Walton-on-Thames and starring Richard Greene as the hero and Bernadette O'Farrell as Maid Marion. Blessed with an infectious theme tune, it employed not only quality directors like the young Lindsay Anderson but also blacklisted American writers using pseudonyms. Arguably most quintessential of the new channel, though, were the two big quiz games, marking a clear break from the BBC's no-prizes policy. *Take Your Pick* was a vehicle for the New Zealander Michael Miles, with the stentorian voice of Bob Danvers-Walker announcing the prizes – ranging from the seriously valuable to the booby, depending which of 13 numbered boxes the contestants picked. 'The green lights of envy,' reckoned an acerbic Bernard Hollowood in *Punch*, 'came up from the audience like traces.' The other well-rewarded game was *Double Your Money*, introduced by the egregious, sincerity-challenged, canny Hughie Green and featuring, for contestants who got past the early stages, the 'Treasure Trail' to an ultimate prize of £1,024.

First contestant on the first programme was Alan Hardy, an Arsenal-supporting clerk from New Southgate with heavy spectacles, jacket and tie. He agreed to be called 'Alan' by Green, who, after each correct answer – to fairly simple questions, such as naming three European capitals – would give the audience a complicit look of mock astonishment followed by the inevitable 'Let's give him a big hand'. At one point a member of the audience shouted out an answer, earning this reproof from Green: 'Please don't try to help any of the contestants ... We do try to play the game.' After the commercial break, the contestants were two married couples. The first, elderly and working-class from Balls Pond Road, mainly answered questions about the music hall and were given a characteristic Green send-off: 'You've been such darned good sports here tonight that we're going to give you £6.' The other couple, newly married and lower middle-class, answered questions on the RAF, with the wife saying, 'If he says so' and Green quickly interjecting, 'Isn't she sweet?' At the end of the half-hour, he finished with words directly to the viewer: 'Thank you for allowing us to come into your homes. Good night.'[15]

There was also *Sunday Night at the London Palladium*, which on the 25th made an inauspicious start. According to the *News Chronicle*'s James Thomas, the bill-topping Gracie Fields gave 'a brief and rather uninspired performance', the US-exported *Beat the Clock* interlude (in which married couples, often honeymooners, played quickfire silly games in order to win prizes) was 'a rather dreary parlour game', and all in all the whole thing 'turned out to be just another TV variety show'. But soon – under the watchful eyes of the impresario Val Parnell and ATV's Lew Grade – it became the new channel's consistently most popular programme, helped each week by the front-man skills of the sardonic comedian Tommy Trinder ('You lucky people') as well as an early appearance from Norman Wisdom. It is impossible to be sure, but the very fact that this glamorous show, live from the heart of London's West End, was transmitted on a *Sunday* evening perhaps gave an extra, irresistible frisson. More improbably, a certain frisson was also attached to commercial television's news coverage. Masterminded by Aidan Crawley, a former Labour MP and now the first editor-in-chief of Independent Television News (ITN), it deliberately sought to be less deferential, and generally have a more personal touch, than the still almost parodically stilted BBC version. In addition to Chataway, already well known for his achievements as an athlete, the other early star was a youngish, bow-tied Robin Day, who soon developed the art of the tough, even aggressive political interview – never before seen on British television. 'He puts his blunt, loaded questions with the air of a prosecuting counsel at a murder trial,' was how by 1956 one television critic was describing Day in action. 'As he swings back to face the cameras, metaphorically blowing on his knuckles, one detects the muffled disturbance as his shaken victim is led away.'[16]

Inevitably the new channel got a mixed critical reception in its early weeks. 'We expected the I.T.A. to borrow ideas, programmes and films from American television,' Hollowood wrote in *Punch*. 'We knew that the advertising agencies would fashion their "spots" on the American plan. What we didn't bargain for was an entire service geared to the American way of life.' By contrast, Isabel Quigly in the *Spectator* praised the ITA for having 'managed to shed a good deal of that frowstiness, that mincing intellectual gentility that was rampant and ruining so much that was good on the BBC', and she gave a particularly high mark to Chataway for his 'refreshing vigour' on the news, so different from the BBC's 'elegant but often baffling understatement'. Moreover, the advertisements had 'turned out to be quite inoffensive', if 'mostly mediocre'. Against that, she identified an unattractive streak of vulgarity, epitomised by *People Are Funny*, 'where unfortunate (though idiotic) members of an audience are called up on the stage and subjected to various indignities and then consoled with a washing machine or a wireless or a bunch of pound notes'. This Saturday-night programme was compèred by Derek Roy – 'a silky, suave operator', according to *Picture Post* – and amid widespread condemnation of it as tasteless and exploitative was eventually dropped by the ITA.

The viewers themselves seem to have been mainly positive about the new channel. When Gallup in early October interviewed those with access to both services, it found that twice as many thought ITV better than BBC as the other way round. An increasing number of sets, moreover, began to be converted, up to almost half a million by early November. Mass-Observation's Panel was predominantly middle-class, and thus not wholly representative, but this autumn a quartet of members gave their views:

I can & do receive ITV on my set & except for Professional Boxing & a more lively news service the programmes seem to be inferior copies of BBC ones or moronic public quizzes or filmed series – mostly American. (Though I admit to being a Robin Hood serial fan!) (*Married man, 36, insurance clerk*)

The advertisements are not nearly as obnoxious as I feared – in fact they don't bother me at all although I hate advertising in general. I just don't want all their sports and fights, nor their games and knockabouts, but have had – oh quantities of programmes I have enjoyed very greatly (not least the Shell/Betjeman adv. features). But SO difficult now to remember which were BBC and which features were Commercial. I switch continually. Some really excellent plays. (*Widow, 50+, secretary*)

On the whole the advertisements are better than the programmes. They are lively and amusing – eg Westclox on the day when clocks had to be put back. All the family chuckle over Murray Mints. (*44, housewife*)

I think it is one of the most awful betrayals of codes of free speech and decent behaviour. (*Single woman, 57, part-time social investigator*)[17]

———

'I have several times suggested that what I call the "Establishment" in this country is today more powerful than ever before,' Henry Fairlie wrote in the *Spectator* on 23 September, the day after commercial television's debut:

By the 'Establishment' I do not mean only the centres of official power – though they are certainly part of it – but rather the whole matrix of official and social relations within which power is exercised. The exercise of power in Britain (more specifically, in England) cannot be understood unless it is recognised that it is exercised socially. Anyone who has at any point been close to the exercise of power will know what I mean when I say that the 'Establishment' can be seen at work in the activities of, not only the Prime Minister, the Archbishop of Canterbury and the Earl Marshal, but of such lesser mortals as the chairman of the Arts Council, the Director-General of the BBC, and even the editor of the *Times Literary Supplement*, not to mention divinities like Lady Violet Bonham Carter.

Reactions were predictable. Bonham Carter herself dismissed the idea of an Establishment as 'a fiction', Randolph Churchill (Winston's son) accused Fairlie of having 'idiotic bees' in his bonnet, and John Sparrow, Warden of All Souls, implausibly asserted, on the basis of having sat on selection boards for the Foreign Service (according to Fairlie, a male bastion where what mattered was knowing the right people), that 'candidates from grammar schools, and from working or middle-class homes, have (to say the least) as good a chance of success as others'. Fairlie's article made a considerable impact and was the first significant post-war attempt to unpick the connections, and penetrate the secrecy, of what was still at the top a very closed elite – or what an exasperated William Cobbett a century and a half earlier had called 'The Thing'. Fairlie might also have mentioned the Treasury, which on the home front was still a top-drawer institution of great prestige as well as mystique. In 1954 an American political scientist, Samuel Beer, submitted to officials the draft of his book about the Treasury, following several years of diligent, ingenious research, and encountered a nervous, even hostile reaction. The matter passed across the desk of the Cabinet Secretary, Sir Norman Brook, who reflected that 'the real problem is whether we can allow the publication of a book which gets so near the knuckle in describing, evidently on the basis of some inside knowledge, how the Treasury works on the inside'. An essentially secretive, mandarin culture ran very deep, and the eventual upshot was that Beer was able to publish in 1956 only after having made extensive, emasculating revisions. One reviewer, the well-connected economist Roy Harrod, took away from Beer's study the 'comforting confidence' that, whatever else ailed Britain, 'this country remains supreme in the world in one field – top-level administration'.

In September 1955, 'Establishment' was not the only term becoming part of the general vocabulary. The current issue of *Encounter* included a typically witty piece by the novelist Nancy Mitford entitled 'The English Aristocracy', with most attention focusing on the passages in which she quoted from the philological work of Alan Ross, a professor at Birmingham University seeking to distinguish between upper-class and non-upper-class English usage, or what he called 'U' and 'non-U':

Cycle is non-U against U *bike*.

Dinner: U-speakers eat *luncheon* in the middle of the day and *dinner* in the evening. Non-U-speakers (also U-children and U-dogs) have their *dinner* in the middle of the day.

Greens is non-U for U *vegetables*.

Home: non-U – 'they have a lovely *home*'; U – 'they've a very nice *house*.'

Ill: 'I was *ill* on the boat' is non-U against U *sick*.

Mental: non-U for U *mad*.

Note paper: non-U for U *writing paper*.

Toilet paper: non-U for U *lavatory paper*.

Wealthy: non-U for U *rich*.

To these I would add:

Sweet: non-U for U *pudding*.

Dentures: non-U for U *false teeth*. This, and *glasses* for *spectacles*, almost amount to non-U indicators.

Wire: non-U for U *telegram*.

Phone: a non-U indicator.

(One must add that the issue is sometimes confused by U-speakers using non-U indicators as a joke. Thus Uncle Matthew in *The Pursuit of Love* speaks of his *dentures*.)

The magazine had printed extra copies in advance, but still sold out in days. Or, as Mitford's friend Evelyn Waugh wrote to her in Paris soon afterwards, 'In England class distinctions have always roused higher feeling than national honour: they have always been the subject of feverish but very private debate. So, when you brought them into the open, of course everyone talked, of course the columnists quoted you and corrected you. Letters poured in to the various editors, many of them, I am told, unprintably violent.'[18]

Alan Dyer was definitely non-U among the miners at Manvers Main Colliery, Yorkshire. There, on the Silkstone seam, an unofficial strike in October proved shockingly divisive. Seven miners refused to come out, eventually leading, after the strike's collapse, to a mock trial at which five of the seven confessed their regret for having worked on, one 'sick' was excused, and the seventh man, the 27-year-old Dyer, failed to turn up and instead went to the pit, where a Sunday shift earned him £4 overtime for filling 13 tons of coal. Accordingly, in a move that provoked national attention and much criticism, doing considerable damage to the trade-union movement as a whole, he was 'sent to Coventry' by his fellow-miners, who refused to work within sight of him. Eventually, the colliery manager weakly agreed to send him away from the pit to dig manholes half a mile from his nearest neighbour. 'Why should I say sorry?' an unrepentant Dyer asked the press. 'I've done nowt wrong.' With no help from the National Union of Mineworkers, but fortified by his mother-in-law's declaration that 'he's a reet good worker is Alan', Dyer indignantly refuted malicious rumours that he had worked through the strike only because he was in debt. 'Look at them, all stamped up,' he said as he showed journalists the hire-purchase cards on which he had bought his furniture. 'I don't owe anybody a penny. The television set's paid for, too, and we've had it over two years. I've not done bad since I've been married, 'ave I? We reckon to put a fair bit by each week. We're having a baby car in the spring. Though I put another idea into t'wife's head last night – fourteen days on the Italian Riviera. £32 all in. Mind you, it'll cost about eighty pounds for the three of us. Must take the kid [his three-year-old daughter]. That's who the holiday's for.' Coming hard on the heels of several other well-publicised victimisation cases – including one in which an ostracised engineering worker in Warrington had gassed himself – it showed 'the great labour movement', in *Picture Post*'s words, 'taking on all the dignity of a lynching mob'.

'A fine semi-documentary film with Michael Redgrave acting splendidly,' noted Madge Martin in Oxford on 18 October after going with her husband to see *The Dam Busters*. It was already five months since the royal premiere (Princess Margaret present), but only six weeks since the film had gone on general release. *The Dam Busters* was not every critic's all-time favourite – the young Alan Brien rated it in the *Evening Standard* as only 'a near miss' – but elsewhere there was almost uniform praise: 'One of the best war pictures yet made' (*Daily Mail*); 'The finest war picture' (*News Chronicle*); 'Excuse me while I rave' (*Daily Mirror*). There was special praise for the film's restraint, with Richard Mallett observing in *Punch* that 'almost the only attempt at an emotional effect comes with the death of a favourite dog', but seeing no need to mention that the dog's name was Nigger. *The Dam Busters* proved an irresistible success – in commercial terms, definitely the British film of the year, arguably of the decade – and much of its appeal was down to a skilful script by R. C. Sheriff and 'The Dam Busters March' by Eric Coates, soon a hit record. Redgrave played Dr Barnes Wallis (creator of the bouncing bombs that breached the Ruhr dams), Richard Todd was Wing Commander Guy Gibson, in charge of 617 Squadron, and there were parts elsewhere in his crack team for Nigel Stock, Robert Shaw and Bill Kerr. It was not a film that even for a nanosecond questioned the existing class structure, with a strong showing in 617 for Oxbridge blues, while to convey the theme of imperial unity there was also a sprinkling of Australasians. 'Hardly a Welsh or a Scottish accent to be heard,' observes John Ramsden in his acute study of the film, 'nor indeed one from the East End, the West Midlands or the North.'

The Dam Busters was of course only one example of the genre. At least 29 war films had already been released earlier in the 1950s, including *The Wooden Horse* (1950) and *The Cruel Sea* (a huge box-office success in 1953, starring Jack Hawkins), while immediately ahead would be at least 17 others in the next two years, including Kenneth More as Douglas Bader in the big 1956 hit, *Reach for the Sky*. For the most part with only minor variations, the formula was tried and trusted: plenty of action and plenty of insouciant, stiff-upper-lipped British heroism in a noble cause. Nor was it just films, given the ubiquity of 'The War', possibly even more in children's lives and imaginations than their parents'. 'As a child all the games I played were war games,' recalled Richard Eyre (born 1943). 'I fired sticks and mimicked the high stutter of machine guns in the woods, and flattened the long grass as I dive-bombed my friends with ear-damaging howls and flung my small body into the arc of heroic death. Or I sat in the cockpit of a large paratroop glider, whose still intact but inert carcass lay in an orchard at my friend's house, wearing a gas mask as a pilot's helmet and taking turns to sit in the pilot's seat and steer the flak-torn fuselage through heavy bombardment towards its target.' Or take Airfix Spitfires: sold by Woolworths for 2s, they proved to be, after their introduction in 1955, the toy firm's most popular model, prompting Robin Blake to remember half a century later how he had 'spent many a short-trousered hour, half stoned on glue, clumsily cementing together the moulded plastic sections'. Among boys' comics, the issue of the *Rover* for 29 October 1955 was pretty typical. '3 FULL PAGES OF WAR PICTURES' promised the front cover, while stories included 'The Battle Against the Flying Bomb' ('Braddock, Ace Pilot of the Last War, is in Action against this Deadly German Weapon'), 'Sergeant Allen of the Fighting 15th' ('The sky over Holland is dark with aircraft as the British Airborne Division drop in on Arnhem to write a glorious page in their history!'), and 'The Eyes that Never Closed' ('How the Allies sought out and destroyed the German Submarines'), beside all of which the football story, 'It's Teamwork that Counts', rather paled into insignificance.[19]

On 19 October, the day after the Martins went to *The Dam Busters*, Anthony Heap made one of his regular trips to the theatre:

> At last catch up with the much discussed 'Waiting for Godot' which was produced at the Arts to a very mixed press early in August, and, on the strength of a surprising last minute rush on the Arts box office, unexpectedly transferred to the Criterion some six weeks later. The more exalted half of the critical fraternity deemed it a subtle, witty, sublime and moving masterpiece; the more low-brow reviewers, a meaningless morass of words, a conglomeration of tripe, a glorification of the gutless. Well, as I suspected, the latter were dead right. This obscure, verbose, unintelligible, and utterly infantile brainchild of James Joyce's secretary Samuel Beckett, concerning the wearisome waiting of a couple of dreary decayed tramps for a never-appearing GODot is, in fact, as pretentious and preposterous a piece of highbrow-poppycock as ever I've had the misfortune to see.

Altogether, concluded Heap, it was 'a crashing, exasperating bore'. Others agreed. John Gielgud 'loathed' it, Somerset Maugham called it 'two dirty old men picking their toenails', and the character actor Robert Morley, after brooding in his bath for an hour, came to the conclusion that 'the success of *Waiting for Godot* means the end of the theatre as we know it'. According to Terence Rattigan, indisputably the leading British dramatist of the day, 'all Mr Beckett has done is to produce one of these things that thirty years ago we used to call Experimental Theatre – a movement which led absolutely nowhere'.

But even amid the catcalls, inside the Criterion as well as outside, the fact was that *Godot* was playing to packed houses every night – so much so that when John Fowles tried to see it nine days after Heap, on the grounds that 'everyone goes, so we must', he found there were 'no seats for three weeks'. In early November there was a stormy meeting of BBC Radio's drama department on the subject of experimental productions. 'Heaven defend us from an outbreak of *Godot*-scripts where the tricks only just hide an almost complete lack of anything to say,' was the uncompromising view of the old guard, headed by Val Gielgud, brother of John. But the argument was won by Barbara Bray, a leading young script editor: 'Third Programme planners will have to be prepared not only to be daring initially, but also to persist in the face of possible audience resistance long enough for public taste to accommodate itself.' Not long afterwards, the *Evening Standard* drama awards were held for the first time, with feelings running high among the judging panel. After the conductor Sir Malcolm Sargent had threatened to resign if *Godot* was given the prize for best play, an ingenious compromise was brokered: best play to go to Jean Giraudoux's *Tiger at the Gates*, while the prize for *Godot* was 'most controversial' play of the year – a one-off award, never given again.[20]

October was not a happy month for Rab Butler. His give-away budget in April – directly leading to the Tory election win in May – had been predicated on the Bank of England exercising monetary control over the banks, but by July a mixture of inflationary and balance-of-payments pressures had made it all too clear that the strategy, for all its immediate political pay-off, had been economically flawed. Butler in late July had announced a round of credit-restricting measures, but during October severe pressure on sterling led to him having to introduce an emergency budget on Wednesday the 26th, involving significant cuts in government spending and an increase in purchase taxes. 'These were steeply raised on everything from a car to a lipstick, and clamped for the first time on lots of hitherto free household goods, which the Tories gloomily fear will hardly induce the housewife to love the Conservative Party,' noted Mollie Panter-Downes next day. 'Labour currently has its best chance in months for an all-out attack on the Government, and will certainly take it.' This particularly applied to Hugh Gaitskell, who delivered in the Commons an uncharacteristically personal, bruising attack on Butler:

He has persistently and wilfully misled the public about the economic situation and he has done it for electoral reasons ... The April Budget – a masterpiece of deception – certainly encouraged instead of damping down additional spending. Now, having bought his votes with a bribe, the Chancellor is forced – as he knew he would be – to dishonour the cheque ... He has behaved in a manner unworthy of his office. He began in folly, he continued in deceit, and he has ended in reaction.

The speech, reflected the *Observer*'s political diarist, marked the 'Demise of Mr Butskell'.

As British economic policy prepared to enter the stop-go cycle that would continue for at least the next quarter of a century, there were other signs, this time from the right, that that cosy, consensual, mythical figure was now past the high tide of his influence. At the Conservative Party Conference at Bournemouth earlier in the month, a chorus of louder-than-usual grumbles was heard from constituency representatives about the impact of rising prices on the lifestyles of the middle classes – some of whom, according to the man from Peckham, were 'rapidly arriving at the position' where they 'can hardly afford even a theatre ticket'. Or take the speech some six weeks earlier by J. Gibson Jarvie, chairman of United Dominions Trust and a well-known City personality, at his company's annual meeting. After a disparaging analysis of the British workforce – 'in many factories the most unpopular man is the hardest worker and the fastest' – he turned to the government and directly blamed it for inflation: 'It is their incredible weakness in dealing with organised labour and their demands for goods and services, their calls on the capital market and the inflated national income resulting from unproductive Government employment, which tear our economy to pieces.' Nor, in terms of government, was it just the politicians: 'Beginning with the war years, there has been a sinister abdication of power and authority to the established civil servants. Whitehall is the bureaucrat's paradise. The creation and perpetuation of employment for civil servants seems to have been a prime objective.' Finally, after a swipe at modern youth – 'ambition sadly lacking ... undisciplined ...' – Jarvie called for lower government spending, for lower taxation, and for 'the strike weapon' to 'give way to a more sensible – I could say a more grown-up – method of settling industrial disputes'.

Delivered in the same year that the newly created, incorrigibly pro-market Institute of Economic Affairs brought out its first publication – on the desirability of the free convertibility of sterling – it was not quite a Thatcherite agenda, but not too far off.[21]

———

Butler's budget, *Waiting for Godot*, even *The Dam Busters* – all mattered infinitely less to the British public this October than the unfolding Princess Margaret drama. The final phase of this act had begun on 19 August, two days before her twenty-fifth birthday. 'COME ON MARGARET!' screamed the front page of the *Daily Mirror*, adding, underneath a large photograph of her, 'please make up your mind!' The matter to resolve was whether, two years having elapsed since their enforced separation, she would now seek to marry Group Captain Peter Townsend – and what the price of such a marriage would be. 'She has *not* absolutely decided,' Harold Macmillan noted a week later after a conversation with Eden, who in turn had been talking with the Queen. 'It will be a thousand pities if she does go on with this marriage to a divorced man and not a very suitable match in any case. It cannot aid and may injure the prestige of the Royal Family.'

There things rested until October, when Townsend was due for some home leave. 'Mrs Atkinson came in,' recorded Nella Last on Thursday the 13th as press coverage increased its intensity:

> She had got me some yeast. She said idly, 'Looks as if you're going to be right, that Princess Margaret *will* marry Townsend – seen the paper yet?' We discussed it. We both felt 'regret' she couldn't have married a younger man. Mrs Atkinson too has 'principles' about divorce that I lack. We just idly chatted, saying any little thing that came into our minds, for or against the match. I wasn't prepared for my husband's wild *condemnation* or his outburst about my far too easy-going way of looking at things! . . . I poached him an egg for tea.

That evening the storm-tossed couple had two hours together at Clarence House. 'TOWNSEND VISITS MARGARET' and 'NOW – THE NATION WAITS' were among next morning's headlines. 'Nothing much else than Princess Margaret's affairs is being talked of in this country,' observed the *Manchester Guardian* on Saturday morning, and that weekend the press besieged Allanbay Park in Binfield, Berkshire, where Margaret and Townsend were guests of the Hon Mrs John Lycett Mills, a first cousin of the princess. 'NO RING YET!' announced a disappointed *Daily Mirror* on Monday, with an accompanying photo of Margaret and the bare third finger of her left hand.[22]

Next day, Tuesday the 18th, the Cabinet discussed the question and took a collective view that if Margaret went ahead and married Townsend, she would lose both her rights of succession and her Civil List allowance. On the Wednesday, Nella Last had a visit from two former neighbours, a mother with her married daughter. 'She is a rather silly "bobby soxer" who never really grew up,' she wrote afterwards about the daughter, '& if there's one thing I detest on the whole of God's green earth it's an "adolescent" of 37 or so! How she yammered about the "fairy tale" romance of Princess Margaret – just like you read about in Fairy Tales.' The *Mirror*'s headline of the day, however, was 'MARGARET DINES TONIGHT WITH PRIMATE WHO WON'T MARRY HER TO TOWNSEND', and that evening (while Anthony Heap waited impatiently for Godot) Margaret did indeed dine with the unrelenting Geoffrey Fisher, Archbishop of Canterbury, who did indeed counsel her against. One increasingly exasperated observer of the whole business was Malcolm Muggeridge. 'The probability is, I suppose, that the monarchy has become a kind of *ersatz* religion,' he wrote in this week's *New Statesman* (in a piece called 'Royal Soap Opera'), which was out on Friday morning. And he concluded:

> The royal family and their advisers have really got to make up their minds – do they want to be part of the mystique of the century of the common man or to be an institutional monarchy; to ride, as it were, in a glass coach or on bicycles; to provide the tabloids with a running serial or to live simply and unaffectedly among their subjects like the Dutch and Scandinavian royal families. What they cannot do is to have it both ways.

Muggeridge's reward was an *Evening Standard* editorial accusing him of treasonable views.

This same Friday, the 21st, with 'MARGARET AND PETER TOGETHER AGAIN' the *Mirror*'s unashamedly soap-opera headline, the Queen, watched by the Cabinet and the rest of the Royal Family, unveiled a statue of George VI in Carlton Gardens. 'Much was asked of my father in personal sacrifice and endeavour,' she said in heavy rain in words equally heavy with resonance. 'He shirked no task, however difficult, and to the end he never faltered in his duty.' Gazing sympathetically at the royals as they returned to the Palace was Madge Martin, down in London for the day with her husband. 'We had a grand view of them in the Royal cars,' she recorded. 'The Queen lovely, and delicate; Princess Margaret, pale and strained, under all the nerve-wracking time she's going through now – regarding her possible marriage with Captain Peter Townsend. Poor young thing.' Joyce Grenfell, albeit in New York, felt much the same. 'Papers here full of Meg and Peter,' she wrote later this day to her friend Virginia Graham in London. 'Wish they'd decide. Sad whatever they do. Poor girl.' Saturday found Margaret in the East End – where she opened a new community centre and heard women shouting, amid cheers, 'Good luck, Maggie! You marry him!' – while next day Florence Turtle in Wimbledon Park reflected: 'A lot of gossip in the papers ... Why can't they leave the girl alone? They abuse the freedom of the press.'[23]

Monday and Tuesday were quiet, but the next two days paid for all. 'Princess Margaret' was the authoritative title of the main leader in *The Times* (hitherto standing aloof) on Wednesday the 26th, the day of Butler's emergency budget. Almost certainly the work of the paper's editor, Sir William Haley, in effect this was the Establishment seeking to deliver a knock-out blow in order to end an unseemly, even dangerous controversy. After describing the 'enormous popular emotion' on the subject as 'sentimental' and 'ill-informed', and referring to the press's 'odious whipping-up of these honest and warm-hearted feelings', it defined the fundamental purpose of the Royal Family as to be 'above all things the symbol and guarantee of the unity of the British peoples'. Accordingly: 'There is no escape from the logic of the situation. The QUEEN's sister married to a divorced man (even though the innocent party) would be irrevocably disqualified from playing her part in the essential royal function.' In practice, went on *The Times*, this would entail 'abandonment of her place in the Royal Family as a group fulfilling innumerable symbolic and representative functions'. The editorial ended on an appropriately sententious note: 'Her fellow-subjects will wish her every possible happiness – not forgetting that happiness in the full sense is a spiritual state, and that its most precious element may be the sense of duty done.' This did the job, for Townsend subsequently recalled that, after reading it, he and Margaret had privately agreed that it would be impossible to go ahead. The following day, she called on Fisher and told him that, on the grounds of conscience, she had reached her decision. 'Was her act of abnegation from a sense of duty, or through an unwillingness to lose her title, status and income?' Nick Clarke would ask almost half a century later, and with the passage of time it is hard not to view the latter motive as having been somewhere near the fore.

For the moment, the public was kept in the dark. 'THIS CRUEL PLAN MUST BE EXPOSED' thundered the *Mirror* on Friday the 28th, accusing the 'starchy' Haley of having 'donned the black cap and passed his savage sentence' in 'an ill-disguised attempt to force Princess Margaret into giving up the man she loves by a bullying ultimatum'. The same day, Graham gave Grenfell the latest well-bred buzz: 'Feelings are quite violent about Townsend, some saying that the moment he fell in love with P.M. he should have disappeared for good; or that at least a grand gesture of renunciation would have been appropriate. Others say he is a cad. In the meantime we wait . . .' That evening, *Any Questions?* carefully avoided the topic – although presumably there were questions submitted – but over the weekend the press continued the debate, with the *Sunday Express*'s fiery columnist John Gordon urging Margaret to choose according to her heart: 'Are we going to permit a minority to dictate to the Princess which man she chooses to be her husband?' Next day, Monday the 31st, the *Daily Express* argued similarly and insisted that 'the people will give her their support'. It was a fair claim, given that a recent Gallup poll had found that 59 per cent approved of Margaret marrying Townsend and only 17 per cent disapproved, with the rest claiming not to be interested.[24]

The announcement came this Monday evening, with the BBC reading out Margaret's carefully drafted explanation: 'Mindful of the church's teaching that Christian marriage is indissoluble, and conscious of my duty to the Commonwealth, I have resolved to put these considerations before others.' Among those hearing this over the 9 o'clock news was Jennie Hill. Middle-aged, unmarried, living in a village near Winchester with her rather despotic mother and working long hours in a bakery (which she cycled to and from each day), she had been keeping a full diary since the start of the year. 'I feel so depressed & sorrowful for them both,' she now wrote – the first time so far she had mentioned an event outside her immediate situation. Other diarists responded in their own way:

So that puts to bed all the newspaper claptrap. (*Florence Turtle*)

It is a heroic decision – & rends one's heart. She is so vital, human, warm & gay – made for happiness. And *what* she must be suffering doesn't bear thinking of. (*Violet Bonham Carter*)

Princess Margaret has decided NOT to marry Group Captain Townsend – after all that bother! I suppose her money & position meant more to her than her affection for this rather scrubby looking youngish man. (*Gladys Langford*)

This is a great act of self-sacrifice, and the country will admire and love her for it. I feel rather moved. It will be awkward meeting the Duke of Windsor at dinner after this. (*Harold Nicolson*)

It is a very noble, unselfish decision, and she has all our sympathy and admiration for putting her own feelings to one side for the sake of the prestige of the throne, and to uphold the sanctity of the Marriage vows. (*Madge Martin*)

This is a fine slap in the chops for the bloody press which has been persecuting her for so long. (*Noël Coward*)

'Thank goodness *that's* over!' (*Nella Last, quoting her husband*)

It was a sorrowful night for Jennie Hill: 'Dreamt about Princess Margaret, but I was outside Clarence House crying my eyes out for her.'[25]

Next morning, Tuesday, 1 November, saw the papers more or less evenly divided, with for instance the *Daily Mail*'s 'Who can doubt the Princess has made the right decision?' being counterbalanced by the *Manchester Guardian*'s more ponderous 'In the long run it will not redound to the credit or influence of those who have been most persistent in denying the Princess the same liberty that is enjoyed by the rest of her fellow citizens.' That afternoon a Mass-Observation investigator mingled with the mainly female, working-class crowd, about 200-strong, waiting outside Clarence House in the vain hope that Margaret would appear. Two women, aged 30 and 26, talked it through:

> I'd no idea this would happen. I thought it was all fixed – they looked so happy. I just couldn't believe it. It's terribly sad.
> I can't understand why they don't leave them alone.
> It's not as if she would come to the Throne.
> *(Laugh)* Not with that lot!
> They say it's because he hasn't much money, but there's heaps of things he *could* do. Anyway she's got money of her own – I've been told she's a very rich girl.

As usual, the diarists had their private say. 'Now there will perhaps be an end of all the noise,' reflected Kenneth Preston in Keighley, and Anthony Heap agreed: 'Now, perhaps we'll hear a little less of that over-publicised little lady.' Judy Haines was more sympathetic, but still relieved: 'I do hope Margaret will fall in love again. I must say divorce is very distasteful to me. Separation yes, but remarry – why? Why ask for trouble twice!' As for Jennie Hill, the news continued to dominate her thoughts. 'Cannot get over the tragedy of it all day,' she noted at the end of the day, and then that Tuesday night: 'Dreamt of them again.'[26]

On Wednesday the 2nd, after rather muted coverage the day before, the *Mirror* hit its stride. 'THIS MUST NOT WRECK TWO LIVES' was the front-page headline, with Keith Waterhouse declaring below that 'it would be outrageous if either of them should be made to suffer in any way because of the genuine love they have shown for one another'. Specifically, he did not want Townsend – 'a man of intelligence and great personal courage' – to be banished, and he went on: 'The stiff-collar classes are already crowing in their clubs that Peter Townsend has been shown the door. These are the people who would have bowed the lowest if he had married Princess Margaret.' Finally, he warned: 'THESE ARE THE PEOPLE who, from now on, will watch Princess Margaret like hawks crossed with vultures.' That evening, Richard Dimbleby went to Lambeth Palace to interview the archbishop live on television. Urbane and relaxed, Fisher was adamant that the decision had been solely Margaret's and that 'there was no pressure from State or Church'. The spectacle revolted Gilbert Harding. In his next *People* column, he described Fisher as having been 'at his most unctuous' and Dimbleby 'at his most pompous'.

It was indeed Fisher and his institution that now bore the brunt of the popular outrage, encapsulated in a quartet of letters appearing in the *Express* on Thursday the 3rd:

> As one who tries to practise Christianity, I am disgusted. I never intend to set foot in church again. (*Mrs P. J. Arick, Isleworth*)
>
> As a divorcee and now married to the man I love, and who loves me, I only hope all the self-righteous people who call themselves Christians will now be able to sleep at night. (*Mrs Elliott, Merstham, Surrey*)
>
> Princess Margaret has made a mistake and those clergy who influenced her decision should have it on their conscience. (*Mrs Jean Hamilton, Hendon*)
>
> I have always been a member of the Church of England, but from now onwards I never again enter that Church. (*Mrs Winifred Barkby, Sheffield*)

That afternoon, M-O secured an 'overheard' in Chelsea by a 30-year-old working-class woman: 'The typing pool at Morgan's Crucible Works [in Battersea] is simply seething. They *all* think she ought to have married him.' And at about this time, Gallup conducted its post-renunciation poll, finding that only 28 per cent agreed – and 59 per cent disagreed – with Fisher's ruling that the Church of England should not remarry a divorced person so long as the other party was still alive. Firmly in the 'disagree' camp were Lindsay Anderson, James Cameron, Humphrey Lyttelton, Wolf Mankowitz, John Minton, Ronald Searle, Kenneth Tynan and Sandy Wilson, who on behalf of 'the younger generation' sent a striking letter to the *Express* that appeared on Friday the 4th. They explained what the episode had shown:

> First, it has revived the old issue of class distinctions in public life.
>
> Second, it has shown us 'The Establishment' in full cry, that pious group of potentates who so loudly applauded the Princess's decision.
>
> Third, it has exposed the true extent of our national hypocrisy.
>
> But, above all, the Townsend affair brings up the general question of 'national dignity', and its encroachments on personal freedom.

Finally, after complaining about 'the alliance of a swollen bureaucracy and an elderly oligarchy', the writers concluded: 'It is not to be wondered at if some young people are seriously considering quitting this country in search of one less restrictive in its patriotism and less stifling in its conventions.' That evening, *Any Questions?* was predictably silent on the dominant question of the day.[27]

Unsurprisingly, in the same directive in which it asked its largely middle-class Panel about commercial television, Mass-Observation also sought to gauge reaction to the no-marriage announcement. The difference between the two sexes could hardly have been greater, starting with the men:

My interest in this matter has not been raised above the 'luke warm' stage and I have no opinions on this very personal subject. (*25, single, local government officer*)

Her action was a crushing blow to the sloppy sentimentality showed by some of our less responsible newspapers over this affair. I am quite sure that she has done the right thing. (*33, single, audit clerk*)

I don't care a tinker's cuss what happens either to P. Margaret or to G. Capt. Townsend. Of course she has done the 'right' thing. (*41, married, schoolmaster*)

I feel that Princess Margaret has made the correct decision. I also feel that had Group Captain Townsend been a Gentleman he would not have put the Princess to the necessity of making such a decision. He would have gone off to Darkest Africa to shoot elephants or something. (*47, married, commercial traveller*)

It is a pity she did not marry Townsend and thereby leave the country. I am no lover of Princess Margaret and the National Press does not help by its continuous publicity of this so called glamour girl. Princess Alexandra beats her hands down. (*36, married, bank cashier*)

Stupid to get herself into such a situation. Townsend should also have known better. (*48, married, warehouseman*)

I just don't care one way or the other. (*32, married, research chemist*)

A very sound decision. (*56, married, Inland Revenue valuation clerk*)

She has put herself in the right, which is always a good thing to do. (*37, married, journalist*)

'Indifferent,' replied a 41-year-old married schoolteacher, 'but my wife showed enough interest for two people. She was firmly pro-Princess and a happy ending. I cannot know enough of the true facts to be able to pass judgement.'

By contrast, the Panel's women were divided in their opinion about the decision, but with few exceptions emotionally engaged by the human dimension:

I think she has done the right thing. The Princess belongs to the royal family & cannot behave as any ordinary girl. She is well paid for any work that she does, & she should not do anything to lower moral standards. She is young, but not too young to set an example. (*58, single, retired teacher*)

I feel that Princess Margaret should not have put state and religious interests before her personal happiness. But I am not convinced he was the right husband for her. According to the newspapers, he loves country life and quietness, and Princess Margaret is known to love a gay city life with parties and theatres. Their only thing in common apart from their love for each other would seem to be horses! (*28, married, housewife*)

I am *very sorry* for Princess Margaret – as I feel, their decision has been a *hard* one. At the same time, she realises that Great Privileges imply Great Responsibilities, which the Duke of Windsor was *too selfish* to do! (*65, single, retired teacher*)

At my age, you know that the world is seldom worth losing for love. (*62, married, housewife*)

If she really wanted to marry him, and presumably she did, she has done the wrong thing. (*27, married, housewife*)

I really do think that a man of his age & experience need not have allowed the equivalent of a schoolgirl crush to develop into a grand passion. The man's a Cad. (*34, single, secretary*)

I felt the disparity of age was rather great, & as a member of the Mothers' Union I ought not to feel any tolerance towards divorcees, 'innocent' or otherwise. As a member of the church I ought to have the same sentiments but am 'confused' & cannot make up my mind about re-marriages. (*45, married, housewife*)

It is said by some, that the reason Prince Philip opposed the marriage was because at one time he had his eye on her, before he chose Elizabeth.

This of course is pure gossip. A friend of mine said people might snub her if she married a commoner. What utter drivel!! I had hoped she would hold out. (*80, widow*)

I'm deeply distressed by her decision. It came as almost a physical shock. It was as if we had suddenly started to move back towards the darkness of some primitive jungle – as if a beautiful young girl had been sacrificed to its gods. (*50, single, technical librarian*)

The 50-plus widow who found the television advertisements 'not nearly as obnoxious as I feared' also had something to say about this matter. 'Is the glow of romance enough?' she asked. 'Of course not – or only in novelettes. Would she have liked being a stepmother, and a déclassée princess? Not Margaret!!!'

Perhaps the last word, some three months after the announcement, should go to Christopher Isherwood's mother. 'M. disapproves of Princess Margaret, thinks her a show-off,' he noted during a rare visit back home. 'This is very important – for M. always seems to me to embody British upper-middle-class opinion.'[28]

9

Family Favourites

Dab-it-off, Windolene, Dura-glit, Brasso, Brillo, Rinso, Lifebuoy, Silvikrin, Amm-i-dent, Delrosa Rose Hip Syrup, Mr Therm, Put-U-Up, Toni Perms, hair-nets, head-scarves, Jaeger, Ladybird T-shirts, rompers, knicker elastic, cycle clips, brogues, Clark's sandals, Start-rite (that haunting rear view of two small children setting out on life's path), Moss Bros, tweed jackets, crests on blazers, ties as ID, saluting AA patrolmen, driving gloves, Austin Cambridge, Morris Oxford, Sunbeam Talbot, starting handles, indicator wings, Triumph, Norton, sidecars, Raleigh, Sturmey-Archer, trolley-buses, Green Line, I-Spy, Hornby Dublo, Tri-ang, Dinky, Meccano, Scalextric, Subbuteo, Sarah Jane dolls, Plasticine, Magic Robot, jumping jacks, cap guns, Capstans, Player's Navy Cut, Senior Service, Passing Clouds, cigarette boxes, Dagenham Girl Pipers, Saturday-morning cinema, Uncle Mac, Nellie the Elephant, The Laughing Policeman, fountain pens, Quink, napkin rings, butter knives, vol-au-vents, Brown Windsor soup, sponge cakes, Welgar Shredded Wheat, Garibaldis (squashed flies), Carnation, Edam, eat up your greens, Sun-Pat, Marmite sandwiches, hard-boiled eggs, semolina, shape, sucking oranges through sugar cubes, Tizer, Quosh, Kia-ora Suncrush, dandelion and burdock, Tom Thumb drops, Sherbet Fountains, Spangles, Trebor Chews, barley twists, blackjacks, fruit salads, aniseed balls, pineapple chunks, Big Chief Dream Pipe, flying saucers, traffic-light lollipops, gobstoppers. The agonising dilemma at the ice-cream van: a big one for 6d or two small ones for 3d each?

None of which quite did it for David Hare, growing up in Bexhill-on-Sea. 'I think anyone who wants to return to Britain in the Fifties is on to an insane project,' the playwright declared in 1999. 'The society was so oppressive and so false, particularly sexually. Neighbours had this prurience and primness and this awful kind of policing of each other's lives.' Next year, in another interview, he came back to his unfavourite decade: 'Nobody could now imagine how dull things were and how respectful people were and how dead they were from the neck up. We knew we were in the trauma of some great event but had missed the event that explained the behaviour; and that was everyone wanted a quiet time.' The 'great event' was of course the war, and in 2004 he reiterated that 'for most of us' a reprise of the 1950s 'would represent a return only to repression, to hypocrisy and to a kind of willed, pervasive dullness which is the negation of life'. It was a very real sentiment that Hare was challenging. 'We have got to try to recover from the permissiveness of the Sixties,' Margaret Thatcher had told the *Daily Mail* back in 1988, towards the end of her premiership. She did not need to spell out that ergo the non-permissive previous decade was a good thing.

The 1950s came particularly to the fore during the national soul-searching in the immediate wake of the Jamie Bulger murder in 1993. 'It was the best of times,' asserted Ian Jack, warmly recalling full employment, steady material progress and a widely shared sense of certainty about life. 'It was the worst of times,' insisted Lynn Barber, 'the most exciting event of the Fifties' being 'the advent of the Birds Eye Roast Beef Frozen Dinner for One'. The debate continued. When in 2007 the BBC's website magazine sought to create a people's history of the decade, some contributors were negative, but it was Jill Morgan of Aldershot who spoke for the majority:

I was a child growing up in the fifties. We walked to school, had open fires and no central heating. Sweets were a treat, not part of lunch. We played in the street with our friends and were safe, we climbed trees, skinned our knees and ripped our clothes, got into fights and nobody sued anybody. We got a clip round the ear when we had been naughty, and Mum gave us a teaspoon of malt and cod liver oil each morning before school. Yum! There was no day-time TV, and we played cards and board games and TALKED to each other and our friends. We were allowed to answer the phone on our birthdays as a special treat. It was an innocent time, gone forever . . .

'Bring back,' she concluded, 'the values of the 1950s!!!'

Was Bexhill itself, anyway, quite so awful? 'I had always rather despised the idea of Bexhill,' recorded the generally tolerant Madge Martin in February 1954, 'but in spite of being modern and with no particular charms, it managed to be rather appealing . . . The shops are very good . . .' Yet Hare had a point, as did the Goons in their choice of staid setting for the terrors of batter-pudding hurling. 'We all hated getting the Bexhill run,' the folk singer Shirley Collins remembered about working in the mid-1950s as a bus conductress:

Bexhill was posh, people there were wealthy and generally arrogant and rarely said 'please' or 'thank you'. Some ladies were too delicate to give you their fares; they would drop their coins from their gloved hands into your palm as if to avoid contamination. 'I beg your pardon?' I asked one lady. 'I didn't say anything,' replied the customer. 'Oh, I'm sorry,' I said. 'I thought you said thank you.' It was petty, but reasonably satisfying.[1]

'Good Friday: contempt for the real meaning of the day,' bitterly reflected John Fowles (far from a signed-up Christian) in April 1955. 'It is no longer remembered for what it is. Now all holidays are the same – relaxation after tension, relief from routine. Strolling crowds, daffodils, spring sunshine . . .' Was Britain already such a secular society? The historian Callum Brown argues forcibly in *The Death of Christian Britain* (2001) that it was the 1960s that marked the great, sudden step-change in the process of secularisation: 'People's lives in the 1950s were very acutely affected by genuflection to religious symbols, authority and activities. Christianity intruded in very personal ways into the manner of people's comportment through their lives, through the rites of passage and through their Sundays. Religion mattered and mattered deeply in British society as a whole in the 1950s.' Is he right?

Widespread outrage at the church's apparently heartless interference during the Princess Margaret affair might suggest otherwise. So do vox-pop findings from earlier in the 1950s, themselves following on from Mass-Observation's *Puzzled People* survey soon after the war, uncovering deep antipathy to what was seen as the hypocrisy of most

Christians. 'You ask whether religion attracts hypocrites,' a London carpenter replied to Ferdynand Zweig. 'I say certainly it does.' Zweig himself noted how, 'whenever the problem of religion is raised' during his interviews with British working men, 'hypocrisy is mentioned as the chief argument against the organized Churches'. He was also struck by two other strands. 'The workers often say that "If the Church leaders had their way the world would be too gloomy for words". Nothing joyful would be allowed.' And: 'How often is it repeated: "It doesn't matter what people believe but what they are and do. The personality is all that counts." ' Rowntree and Lavers in their 1951 study *English Life and Leisure* also encountered plenty of mistrust:

Don't talk to me about parsons! They've got a pretty soft job, if you ask me. Telling decent working folk how to behave! What do they know about it? Never done an honest day's work in their life, most of them. (*Working-class widow in late middle age*)

When I had T.B., mate, and was off work for fourteen months I can tell you who looked after me and the missus. It wasn't all those — — — people from the chapel. It was my mates from the boiler shop. (*Working-class man*)

My boss is a great man for the chapel but he'll give short weight if he can, and he makes plenty of mistakes adding the bills – all on his own side. (*Male shop assistant in early middle age*)

It doesn't encourage you much to go to church, does it, when you see an old skinflint like him? He'd squeeze the last penny out of anybody, and then up he gets on Sundays bold as brass and reads the lessons. I think they're all the same. (*Middle-class housewife speaking about her landlord*)

Richard Hoggart later in the 1950s found much the same in working-class Hunslet, where phrases like 'nice work if y' can get it' and 'wonderful what y' can get paid for nowadays' were typical of what he called the prevailing 'cheerful cynicism towards the clergy'.[2]

Churchgoing figures are also a problem for the Brown thesis. Geoffrey Gorer's extensive *People* survey in 1950–51 revealed that only 15 per cent attended a church or religious service at least weekly, 45 per cent intermittently (less than weekly, but at least once or twice a year) and 40 per cent never, unless for a wedding or a funeral. Just over two years later, a detailed survey of leisure habits in Derby found that 27 per cent of people never went to church, while only 13 per cent went once a week or more. Women accounted for almost two-thirds of church attendances, with a bias towards the elderly, and a middle-class person was at least twice as likely to go to church each Sunday as a working-class person. In December 1954, the BBC commissioned Gallup to undertake a major nationwide investigation. 'If the decline in churchgoing needed confirmation it obtains it from this survey,' declared the ensuing report. 'Six out of ten non-churchgoers say they "used to go", seven out of ten occasional churchgoers say they used to go more often and so do three out of ten frequent churchgoers. Yet the vast majority of all three groups went to Sunday School or Bible Class in their youth – most of them for several years.' As to the headline figure, 63 per cent attended religious services either never or only once or twice a year. Finally, in February 1957, another Gallup survey found that only 14 per cent had been to church the previous Sunday.[3]

The rites of passage, however, tell a rather different, less secular, more nineteenth-century story. Take the proportion of infants baptised in the Church of England. Whereas in 1900 such baptisms had run at 609 out of every 1,000 live births, by 1956 the figure was 602. The decline was more marked – but still relatively mild – in the case of religious (as opposed to civil) marriages: between 1900 and 1957, a fall in England and Wales from 85 per cent to 72 per cent, in Scotland from 94 per cent to 83 per cent. In other words, a church wedding remained the overwhelming custom. As for the third rite, cremations increased notably after 1945 (up from 4 per cent in 1939 to 50 per cent by 1966), but in the 1950s anyway, Hoggart's finding in Hunslet that most people disliked them as 'unnatural' was probably widely shared. And he detailed the elaborate provisions that 'the more careful families' made towards what was called a 'proper' funeral or a 'decent burial' or even 'putting 'im away splendid', usually involving the parish church.[4]

And belief? 'He has doubts about whether the supernatural parts of Christian teaching should be taken literally but "cannot imagine" himself just vanishing when he dies,' reported Rowntree and Lavers about a middle-aged, self-made engineer. 'He thinks there must be some other existence. He attaches great importance to the part of Christian teaching that says one should love one's neighbour, and he claims that he has tried to practise it all his life.' Other interviewees offer a flavour of the faith/non-faith spectrum:

> She is not interested in religion. She says if saying her prayers would get her a house she would say them, but 'everyone knows it's all nonsense'. (*Labourer's wife*)
>
> Mrs O. says she is a Christian. She does not bother to go to church but she was brought up as a Christian, and is sure the Bible is true. (*Bus driver's wife*)
>
> He is not an atheist and he believes in some Supreme Power that he calls fate. He thinks nobody can alter fate and therefore it is no use praying. He hardly knows what to believe. (*Bus conductor*)
>
> Mr H. does not call himself a religious man and he never bothers to go to church, but he thinks it important that people should act decently towards those whom they meet because otherwise the world would be an impossible place. (*Milkman, 45*)
>
> Mrs R. has absolutely no religious beliefs and thinks that going to church or not is just like going to a cinema or not, 'It's a matter of what suits you.' (*Female factory worker, 30*)
>
> She hardly knows why she does, but she thinks that Christianity really corresponds with the good life she would like for herself and her family. But she does not believe in the 'supernatural' parts. (*Professional man's wife*)
>
> 'I don't know what I believe, but I don't believe all this "God is Love" stuff. When I was a kid I had a text in my bedroom, "God is Love". Since then I've been in two wars, been unemployed eighteen months on end, seen the missus die of cancer, and now I'm waiting for the atom bombs to fall. All that stuff about Jesus is no help.' (*Lower middle-class man*)

Overall, it was still, more or less, a believing people. Gorer found not only that two-fifths of adults in England made prayers 'a regular part of their lives', and another one-fifth in times of peril or grief, but also that 47 per cent believed in an afterlife, with another 30 per cent uncertain. That envisaged afterlife tended to be positive, often taking what Gorer called 'a very material nature':

It will be a wonderful place with everything just right and there will be plenty of lovely food without rationing I hope. (*Married woman, 41, West Bromwich*)

More peaceful than the present one, with no cold, wars or washing up. I hope there will be animals, music and no towns; a kind of ideal earth in heaven. (*Married woman, Berkhamsted*)

I believe it will be a very happy place, with no colour bars, no 'class' distinction, no intonation of speech, a place where everyone will have a job to do, no matter whether he was king or peasant in this world, a place where there will be a common language. Jesus Christ and his twelve disciples will be a form of Government, there will be no opposition, for there will be nothing to oppose. (*Young woman, Bishop's Stortford*)

Similar to life here but no sex life. (*Divorced working-class woman, 41, Oldham*)

Gorer's figures were broadly confirmed by Gallup's 1957 survey: 71 per cent believing that Jesus was the Son of God, 54 per cent believing there was life after death, and only 6 per cent denying outright the existence of 'any sort of spirit/god or life force'. For most believers, ethics trumped metaphysics. 'The workers,' noted Zweig, 'are not interested in theology and you cannot make them discuss any of the theological problems which seem so important in religious literature. They believe that the supreme being exists and they think that this is enough.' Hoggart encountered much the same amid the Hunslet working class's understanding of religion: 'doing good', 'common decency', 'helping lame dogs', 'doing unto others as y'would be done unto', 'we're 'ere to 'elp one another', 'learning to know right from wrong'. Crucially, Hoggart emphasised the peripheral nature of these ethical precepts in people's actual daily lives. 'Doing your best, but remembering the "real world" outside, the world of work and debts,' he wrote in an illuminating passage, informed by deep personal knowledge. 'Life is making the best of things in this world, is "rubbing along" as best you may; you may have "Christ's teaching" somewhere at the back of your head; you may, when you think of it, admire it; but still, when it comes to the living of life itself, well "you know . . .".'[5]

If Hoggart is correct – that the ethical basis of most people's Christian beliefs counted for relatively little in practice, by implication perhaps little or no more than the ethical convictions of non-believers – it is hard to see how Britain in the 1950s can, in any meaningful sense, be called a Christian society. Nevertheless, it was still a society in which religion had a greater day-to-day weight – was more deeply embedded – than would subsequently be the case.

Starting with religious affiliation. Here, Gorer revealed that more than three-quarters of the English adult population assigned themselves, however loosely, to some religion or denomination, predominantly the Church of England. The bond between people and churches was kept intact especially through Sunday schools – 'a national custom' (in Gorer's phrase) to which the majority of parents in his survey sent their children, even though most of those parents were themselves not churchgoers on any regular basis. Not long afterwards, the Derby survey revealed that 63 per cent of children aged between four and ten, and 56 per cent between eleven and fifteen, attended a Sunday school. Parental motives were not exactly spiritual: getting the children out of the house, reckoned Hoggart, allied to 'the notion that Sunday school is a civilizing influence, that it helps the children to avoid "getting into bad ways" '. Churches were also involved in all sorts of youth groups, boys' clubs and so on, while explicitly Christian organisations ranged from the Mothers' Union to the Boys' Brigade, whose Glasgow battalion in the 1950s ran the world's largest football league, with some 200 teams competing on Saturday afternoons.

Religious broadcasting was still hugely important to the BBC, whose Gallup survey in 1954 found over two-thirds of the sample listening frequently (37 per cent) or occasionally (31 per cent) to such programmes. Generational tensions surfaced that year when the BBC objected to Don Cornell's chart-topping 'Hold My Hand', on the grounds of the profanity of the line 'This is the kingdom of heaven'. An amended line ('This is the wonder of heaven') was overdubbed for purposes of airplay, but the Archbishop of Canterbury, Geoffrey Fisher, still publicly criticised the song when Cornell came to Britain on tour. The American balladeer expressed his annoyance – breaking some furniture in front of the press – and everywhere the audiences loyally shouted out, 'Sing your banned song, Donny boy!'[6]

Sundays remained special – and, for most younger people anyway, specially awful. The boredom, the sense of nothing happening or ever likely to happen again, seemingly affected everything:

Empress of Britain under construction: Fairfield's Shipyard, Glasgow, January 1955

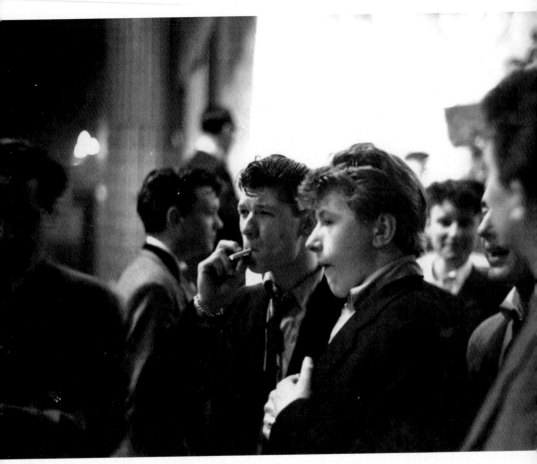

Mecca Dance Hall, Tottenham, May 1954

Coupon-checkers at Littlewoods Pools, Liverpool, 1954

Inverness, 1950s

Woolworths, 1955: the Christmas rush

Mulberry Street Primary School, Manchester, 1956

New Union Street, Coventry: reconstruction, c.1955

British Amateur Ballroom Dancing Championships, Blackpool, 1955

Leeds, 1957

West Indian immigrants wait at Customs, Southampton Docks, May 1956

Elswick, Newcastle upon Tyne, 1957

The streets of Carlisle would be totally empty as if a bomb had gone off – no shops, no pubs, no life, no everything. My father would not even allow me to ride my bike on a Sunday, let alone play football in the street, read the *Dandy* or *Beano* or do anything much that smacked of pleasure and enjoyment. Not that he was religious or went to church . . . (*Hunter Davies*)

Sunday lunch: family favourites, mum scraping veg, he [father] carving the lamb. I always tried to be out before *Billy Cotton's Bandstand* [in fact *Band Show*]. Wakey wahhhkey. (*Ossie Clark, Warrington*)

Cinemas opened, but only briefly, and no God-fearing person would be seen going to the pictures on a Sunday. So after the Light Programme's lunchtime diet of *Two-Way Family Favourites*, *The Billy Cotton Band Show* and *Educating Archie*, it was either a game of Ludo or a good stiff walk. The weather had to be particularly bad for my father not to suggest the latter option. (*Anton Rippon, Derby*)

On fine days, we went out as a family for long walks or rode our bikes past hatted church-goers (which we weren't) in stilled villages. Apart from the occasional newsagent, no shops were open, nor cinemas, nor pubs. Small railway stations closed and the signals on many lines stood all day disappointingly at red. Neighbours chatted over the hedge as they dug their gardens, church bells sometimes tolled. Otherwise, a great external quietness meant to encourage reflection in our internal souls. (*Ian Jack, Fife*)

In 1953 a Labour MP, John Parker, introduced a Sunday Observance Bill seeking to repeal the existing legislation and allow a greater range of Sunday entertainments. This was not only voted down by 281 to 57, with Churchill refusing to allow a royal commission on the subject of Sunday observance, but a Gallup poll found that most people were opposed to professional sport, let alone horse racing, on a Sunday.[7]

Two developments in September 1955 signalled a degree of change in the air. The first concerned the Duke of Edinburgh's penchant for playing polo or cricket on Sundays, behaviour strongly attacked by the Free Church of Scotland in its monthly magazine. The *Daily Mirror*, in a characteristic leader on 'The Duke's Sunday', returned fire:

Who in Britain thinks it is a crime to play cricket on Sundays?

Who in Britain thinks it is a crime to play polo on the Sabbath?

VERY FEW PEOPLE.

People whose ideas are as out of date as the penny-farthing bicycle.

A few days later a reproachful Archbishop Fisher wrote to Prince Philip, in effect accusing him of giving 'great encouragement' to 'all who now are constantly seeking to invade the domesticity of Sunday rest and recreations, and who when the time comes will press very hard for legislation to remove all restrictions upon the full secularisation and commercialisation of Sunday'. Philip's shortish, rather breezy reply – 'I don't think there is any need to be apprehensive about Sunday observance . . .' – yielded nothing. Later that month arrived commercial television and *Sunday Night at the London Palladium*, decisively supplanting radio's more decorous Jean Pougnet and the Palm Court Orchestra, coming from the Grand Hotel. 'The most daring Sunday programme yet,' asserted *Picture Post*'s Denzil Batchelor, who wondered what was going to happen to 'the English Sunday as we know it' if, driven by the very commercial dictates of the new channel, 'the most exciting cricket, the top boxing and athletics, find their way to the TV screens':

> I think the coming of competitive TV will see the end of the British Sunday as a day of rest, church-going and good works – and nothing more. Whether, as a result of this, church-going itself will fall off – whether, in fact, in some cases it *could* fall off – I would not care to prophesy. It is possible that it may increase, when people know that the rest of their holy day is to be regarded as a holiday – as it was in the glorious past when Britain was a Christian Country.[8]

Deference, respectability, conformity, restraint, trust – these were probably all more important than piety in underpinning 'the 1950s'.

Despite the egalitarian effects of the war, deference still ran deep in British society, whether towards traditional institutions, or senior people in hierarchical organisations, or prominent local figures (the teacher, the bank manager, the JP, the GP), or older people generally, or the better educated, or that increasingly influential phenomenon, the somewhat stern but more or less benign expert, for example in childcare. Hard empirical evidence for this deference is surprisingly elusive, but three brief vignettes are evocative. First, in that ultra-hierarchical, status-conscious, age-respecting, largely male preserve, the City of London, where in most offices it was still 'Mr this' and 'Mr that', with no ready assumption of first-name terms. 'You may call me Ernest,' the merchant banker Thalmann (of Warburgs) announced towards the end of the decade to a recent recruit, Peter Spira, and the proverbial pin was heard to drop when the young man eventually mustered the courage to do so. Or take the response in August 1954 after the *Sunday Pictorial* had dared to speculate on what sort of school the almost six-year-old Prince Charles would be going to and had printed an accompanying coupon asking readers to send in their views. '1-in-4 say M.Y.O.B. [ie Mind Your Own Business],' rather ruefully noted the following week's headline, a view typified by G. A. Septon of Glebe Gardens, New Malden: 'If half the parents in the country were as good and conscientious as the Queen and the Duke of Edinburgh there would be little cause for concern anywhere. Trust the Queen and Prince Philip.' A few months later, Richard Crossman (Winchester and Oxford) was at Hearsall, on the outskirts of Coventry, addressing a Parent-Teachers' Association about the city's comprehensive experiment. 'Rather ominously,' he recorded afterwards, 'in the vote of thanks one parent said that it was so nice to have the thing explained by somebody who talked English properly, unlike some Councillors, who had tried to teach parents how education had been organised but obviously were not educated themselves.'[9]

It was hard to avoid – or evade – the culture of respectability. 'I found it quite easy to alter all the Boot's things, and of course I perfectly well understand the reason for it all,' Kingsley Amis wrote in February 1955 to his editor at Gollancz after concern had been voiced about some expressions in *That Uncertain Feeling* that might lead to the novel being banned by Boots Circulating Library and possibly other libraries also. ' "Balls" and "a quick in and out" were very easy, and I found the best treatment for the "buggers" was to alter each one on its merits rather than trying to devise an equivalent for the word.' Few patrolled the boundaries of respectability more assiduously than Winifred 'Biddy' Johnson, all-powerful editor of the mass-circulation *Woman's Weekly*, first port of call for most Mills & Boon serialisations. Doctor–nurse romances were her preferred genre; the doctors themselves had to be unimpeachable, and neither the language nor the drink were permitted to be strong. 'Do Johnson women go to pubs?' an exasperated author asked Alan Boon as his hero Bruce was about to take Trudi out for a drink. 'I always think "country inn" sounds so ingenuous, especially if they go for *supper*, even if it's bread and cheese and a gallon of wallop ... Anyhow I shall write it that way for the book, and we can always make it a milk bar or something when we approach Johnson.'

An intrinsic part of respectability was what the film critic Penelope Houston called 'that celebrated English custom of ignoring a disagreeable fact, on the assumption that if left alone it may quietly go away', and she complained with justifiable bitterness about how this meant that 'many areas of experience are closed off to the British film-maker', or at least a film-maker who wanted any degree of commercial success. The BBC did not help. 'I want you to see yourself as – well – as having become an officer in a rather good regiment' was how the new recruit Robin Day was welcomed to the Radio Talks department in 1954. It was in general a slow-moving, highly bureaucratic organisation with precious little appetite for taking risks or giving offence. News bulletins remained, in David Hendy's words, 'pillars of grammatical rectitude'; for most of the decade there was, to Peter O'Sullevan's considerable irritation, a complete ban on any betting information in horse-racing broadcasts; and, down with flu in December 1954, John Fowles noted how 'everyone on the BBC talks as if they are a little bit older and cleverer than anybody else, but they're doing their damndest to conceal it'.[10]

'We were never encouraged to think that we were better than anybody else,' Alan Titchmarsh reflected in 2006 about his Ilkley childhood, as a plumber's son. 'If anything, we were taught that we were just the same. The most important thing in life seemed to be to blend in and get on with everybody, and I suppose that's what I've spent the rest of my life doing. Blending in.' The conformist ethos in the 1950s was much the same in Stockton-on-Tees. 'It was certainly not a place, in those days, for much deviation from a pretty dour norm, let alone for anything in the nature of artistic affectation,' recalled the novelist Barry Unsworth. 'To carry an umbrella or ask for wine in a pub was to put your virility in question. Suede shoes were for "lounge-lizards". Beards were out of the question.'

Dress, indisputably, was the crucial shibboleth, however uncomfortable it might be to wear. 'There are many branches,' noted the Westminster Bank's house magazine, 'where the putting on of a soft collar instead of a stiff white one will mark a man down as unambitious and unworthy of the higher reaches of his profession,' while on the Stock Exchange the insistence on sartorial uniformity was even more exacting. As well as the regulation bowler hat and rolled umbrella, remembered the stockbroker Dundas Hamilton, 'I came to work in a short black jacket and striped trousers, and we all wore white shirts and stiff white collars. We also had a ban on the soft shirt or the coloured shirt, and if I'd worn a striped shirt and a soft collar people in my office would have said to me, "Why haven't you got out of your pyjamas yet?" ' Dirty looks greeted the young Brian Thompson when he wore a green thornproof suit and Hush Puppies on the Central Line, and another writer, Derek Robinson, recalled how, growing up in Bristol, men's clothing 'boiled down to sports-jacket-and-flannels or single-breasted suit', though 'you could get away with a sweater in the countryside'. Suits tended to be from Burton's, and for much of the decade being measured for a first suit at one of its many shops remained a classic male rite of passage for the 'trainee adults' (in Thompson's resonant phrase) that mainly comprised British youth. Still, by the mid-1950s, there were signs of change, for women as well as men. The image projected by Burton's in its advertising started to have a less regimented feel, while in London a young Mary Quant, just out of art college, was looking with dismay at what most women wore. 'What I loathed was the unsexiness, the lack of gaiety, the formal stuffiness of the look that was said to be fashion,' she recalled. 'I wanted clothes that were much more for life – much more for real people, much more for being young and alive in.'[11]

Not much, apart from the Monday washing, was yet being hung out. 'Life in London, even in the most crowded streets, seemed like a film of pre-talkie days,' recorded the Indian writer Nirad Chaudhuri about his visit to England in 1955. 'I had an uncanny sensation when I saw unending streams of people going along Oxford Street, and heard no sound. As they moved into the Underground stations they looked like long lines of ants going into their hole.' He met 'the same silence' in pubs, restaurants and buses – a silence, a 'dreariness of public behaviour', utterly different from what he was used to in India. The English were no less reserved, he found, when they did speak, with 'their habit of tacitness, which they call understatement'.

Yet it would be wrong to assume that Britain in the 1950s was invariably a land of self-restraint and a carefully calibrated politeness. Philip Larkin's Scottish holiday in July 1953 was significantly spoiled, he grumbled to friends, by first 'the drunk man in the train from Shotts, Lanarkshire, with no teeth & very few fingers, who engaged me in incomprehensible bawdy jesting', and then '*two* drunk men in my sleeping compartment, Glasgow–Birmingham, who smashed a bottle, threatened me with a niblick, sang, & had me swallowing tea & White Horse at 6 the next morning'. Or take the emotive issues of litter and bus queues. 'It took me five minutes to find a litter basket in London's big Victoria Station,' a reader from Herne Bay complained to the *Daily Mirror* in August 1955, the same year as the formation (owing much to Elizabeth Brunner, chairman of the National Federation of Women's Institutes) of the Keep Britain Tidy pressure group. 'Good job I wasn't in a hurry to catch a train,' continued Mrs I. S., 'or I might have been tempted to add my junk to the awful mess on the floor.' As for bus queues, it seems there was a particular problem in the capital. 'There is some order until a bus arrives at a stop, but that little goes then,' a Burnley clergyman informed *The Times* the previous autumn. 'If two arrive together, the situation is worse. It is true there is no violence, but a lot of people sidle on the buses out of their turn with great skill and an appearance of disinterestedness. It would not come off in these parts.' A letter to the *Sunday Express* almost exactly a year later took up the charge. 'What has happened to the shape of the bus queues?' asked Morris Aza of 8J Hyde Park Mansions, N1. 'I recall their neat and orderly double-file formation during the war. Today they straggle and lack not only their former parade-ground precision but also bonhomie.'[12]

Helped by informally policed public spaces – by bus conductors, by park-keepers, by lavatory attendants – and by a police force that was largely admired, this was for the most part an era of trust. 'I liked my half-hour's walk through the quiet suburban streets,' Jacqueline Wilson recalls about being a six-year-old in Kingston-upon-Thames, adding that 'it wasn't that unusual to let young children walk to school by themselves in those days'. Ken Blakemore, who grew up in a large Cheshire village, remembers not only the front door of his home being left unlocked, but bikes generally being left untouched or unchained at the bus stop or the railway station. This even applied to motorbikes, for, according to John Humbach, it was not until about 1957 that British motorcycles were fitted with locks or keys of any kind. Humbach himself had a Triumph 500cc bike. 'It had no locks and I never had a chain and padlock (and never knew anyone who had),' he wrote in 1996. 'Yet this bike remained parked every night outside my house in a street which was then pretty slummy (Stadium Street, London SW10). The bike was never stolen and I was never worried that it might be.'

It would be easy to exaggerate levels of honesty – Rowntree and Lavers in their 1951 survey *English Life and Leisure* reported quite widespread minor dishonesty – but the fundamental fact was that, following the quite sharp upward spike in the immediate post-war years, crime declined markedly during the first half of the 1950s, before starting to move up again from 1955. The figures for 1957, the end of the 'high' fifties, are striking, indeed startling, compared with 40 years later. Notifiable offences recorded by the police: a little over half a million in 1957, almost 4.5 million in 1997. Violent crimes against the person: under 11,000 in 1957, a quarter of a million in 1997. It was, in short, a different world – a world, at its trusting best, evoked by S. Hickson, a Prudential agent ('The Man from the Pru') servicing the market gardeners and bulb growers of Spalding in Lincolnshire during the 1950s:

Although at first, when I used a push-bike, I could not get home to lunch, there was never any need to take sandwiches. There was always a place set for me and I can still see those heaped plates of steamed apple puddings, followed by an equally generous plate of meat, often home-cured bacon, and vegetables. Invariably they served the pudding first. How many cups of tea I swallowed on a cold day rather than refuse the hospitality so generously given! . . . Later, when I acquired a bright yellow Austin Seven of very ancient vintage – which the local folk referred to as 'the flying bedstead' – it sometimes resembled a greengrocer's cart when I arrived home from my day's collecting. Then there were the places I used to get the key: in the spout over the kitchen window; under a piece of brick near the side door; on a nail in the shed; and then I would let myself into the house and find the books and premiums which had been left in some convenient place. All this was to save me a back call when the housewife was working in the fields. Many times I would find also a hastily scribbled note: 'Please take an extra sixpence and post these letters' . . . 'Fill in this form' . . . 'Tell the doctor Johnnie is not so well' . . . 'Tell my mother I cannot get home this week' . . . 'Leave this parcel at Mrs Brown's' and many others of like sort.[13]

1950s Britain was also an authoritarian, illiberal, puritanical society. Not entirely, of course, but the cumulative evidence is overwhelming.

School life set the tone. David Jones (later Bowie) peeing on the classroom floor soon after he had started school in Brixton and being too scared to tell anyone, a tearful Jacqueline Aitken (later Wilson) being forced to eat up the fatty meat at her school dinners before going to throw up in the smelly lavatories, John Major-Ball (later Major) hating the institutionalised bullying at Rutlish in south-west London, Peter Cook at his public school (Radley in Oxfordshire) being tormented and beaten by an imperious, cricket-playing prefect called Ted Dexter – the consolations of fame were still a long way off. Inevitably, memories have loomed large:

> School discipline was strict and the boys were caned and the girls got an occasional rap on the knuckles with a ruler. Things were learnt by rote and the tables test, once a week, was a nightmare. No one questioned authority then, but it didn't mean to say that we weren't resentful at times. (*Pamela Sinclair, junior school, London*)
>
> Being caned was a particular preoccupation. Depending on the teacher, you could be caned for any infringement of school rules – like being inside the school buildings at playtimes. Who used a cane, who used a rubber strap, if you could make it sting less by pulling your hand back at the moment of contact or spitting on your hand before, were all subjects of endless discussion. (*Rosalind Delmar, junior school, Dormanstown*)
>
> Our Latin teacher, Westy, was a grizzled veteran of the Great War who wore woolly combinations and chewed garlic in class. 'Got a cherry

bottom, have you? Well, here's sixpence to let me have a squint.' Sixpence bought two Mars Bars in those days, so Westy did a brisk trade. (*Michael Barber, prep school, Thanet*)

Teachers thumped kids quite frequently. The PT master beat boys on the backside with a large wall-map of the world, rolled around the strip of wood from which it normally hung. He was short and stout, and the map was very long, so he had to stand well back in order to make his swing, a bit like W.C. Fields playing golf. When he got his follow-through right he could knock a boy clean off his feet. (*Derek Robinson, secondary school, Bristol*)

There was no talking, no running, and you had to wear your hat and your gloves in the street or you used to be reported, and then you'd be in for it! I always had trouble with the uniform and I remember once they made me kneel for three hours on the hall floor for not having a white collar: I didn't have one because we couldn't afford one. (*Dorothy Stephenson, girls' convent school, Sheffield*)

The ogre, the teacher everyone feared and loathed, was Mr Garrigan who taught maths. He was small, ugly, bespectacled, very sarcastic. I had only been at the school a few months when he called me out for some reason and made some catty comment about my accent, asking where I had come from. I said Dumfries. He asked which part. I said the outskirts of Dumfries. 'I never knew Dumfries had skirts.' A really stupid, obvious, banal joke, but of course the whole class laughed uproariously, keeping in with Garry, enjoying my discomfort, glad that they were not being picked upon. I used to dread his lessons so much that I often bunked off, sitting in the drying room of the cloakroom in the dark, along with a few other pathetic specimens, in order to miss his lessons, shaking in fear in case we got found out. (*Hunter Davies, secondary school, Carlisle*)

It really wasn't very pleasant. There was far too much pen-pushing and masses of homework. And far too much petty discipline. Incredible petty rules about uniforms and stuff. (*Mick Jagger, grammar school, Dartford*)

Not all memories are negative, but relatively few seem to be positively enthusiastic. 'Little boys wore grey school shorts and long grey socks all year round and little girls wore dresses or pinafore dresses and blouses,' Sheila Ferguson recalls in neutral mode about her junior school at Harringay in north London. 'The school cap and beret were de rigueur. We learned to write with nib pens on wooden holders which we dipped in ink wells and learned from Janet and John books.'[14]

Education in theory was becoming less Victorian – by 1957 the Ministry of Education would be noting that it saw a school 'no longer as a mere machine for giving lessons but as a social unit concerned with the all-round developments of boys and girls' – but on the ground, especially in secondary schools, the main progressive, child-centred push still lay ahead. Take for instance the no-leeway, almost militaristic tone to the timetable for a Birmingham secondary modern's visit to London in 1951. 'Rise, wash and visit lavatories,' it began. 'Make your bed, pack your belongings in haversack and take it with you.' Then, in London itself, there were visits to the Houses of Parliament ('Pay great attention to your hosts and guides'), Westminster Abbey ('Keep with the official guide') and St Paul's ('Keep with your leader'), lunch at Trafalgar Restaurant ('Choose a main course dish at 1/1d, a sweet at 5d, tea 2d or coffee 2½d. Your leader will pay. Choose tables as close together as possible . . .') and two compulsory lavatory stops (by Westminster underground station and near Tower Bridge). Three years later a diarist's six-year-old daughter was being little encouraged to express herself. 'Pamela said she felt simply awful when they weren't allowed to talk – penalty name on paper,' noted Judy Haines after the third day of term in September 1954. 'She said she felt stifled.' About the same time, at Colston's School in Bristol, an independent, these were some of the strictly enforced rules:

No boy may have his hands in his pockets on meeting a master or other senior person. Boys are expected to raise their caps on meeting any masters, masters' wives or ladies of the staff . . . There must be no communication of any kind between boys in the Sick Wing and other boys – e.g. dropping notes onto the Parade, lending books etc. Private wireless sets and gramophones are forbidden. Association football is forbidden. No boy may keep in his possession a sum of money larger than two shillings. Only English comics are permitted. All American publications of this kind are banned. In addition, cheap novelettes and such like reading matter are forbidden, but it is understood that this prohibition does not extend to Penguins and reputable publications of the same kind.

As for the corporal punishment that helped to enforce such rules, a national poll of teachers in 1952 found that 89 per cent wanted such punishment to be retained. Still, the probability is that its frequency was starting to diminish. 'Masters dare not touch little Willie or mistresses cane little Mary,' complained Dr N. S. Sherrard of Beccles in July 1954 in an address to parents at the Alderman Woodrow Secondary School, Lowestoft. 'People would be up in arms today if they did. As they cannot do it, you must do it yourself in the home.' Even an essentially kindly person like the clergyman Oliver Willmott, who took Scripture lessons in the village school at Loders, grumbled in his Parish Notes the following February that the Dorset Education Committee was no longer following the biblical precept 'Spare the rod, spoil the child'. And he wondered whether the Committee's members responsible for their 'precious rules' had 'children of their own, or have ever taught in school'.[15]

Juvenile delinquency, and the moral welfare of youth generally (not least in the context of their disturbingly expanding wage packets), remained a pressing concern – even before the coming of rock 'n' roll. In Gerald Fairlie's *The Return of the Black Gang* (1954), a Sapper-style Bulldog Drummond yarn, Sir Bryan Johnstone, Director of Criminal Investigations at Scotland Yard, offers his analysis of what, in the context of the rise of 'cosh boys', was going wrong: 'A strange lack of parental control in these modern days, caused by mistaken kindness and the fallacies of modern psychiatric education. The hysterical clamouring of youth for any sort of adventure ...' Plenty of other voices also called for a tougher approach. 'There is,' declared Stanley Smith, Brigade Secretary of the Boys' Brigade, in a 1951 talk at the Athenaeum on juvenile delinquency, 'a dangerously soft attitude present which whittles away all personal responsibility for wrong doing, and the child comes to regard himself not as sinful, but just as "a psychological case".' The police agreed, to judge by John Barron Mays's analysis not long afterwards of a police division in inner-city Liverpool. 'Stress was generally placed on punishment [including the birch] and behind many of the criticisms was the old idea of retribution,' he found. 'It was clearly only a minority who appreciated that a juvenile court was not a watered-down adult court, that ascertainment of guilt and consequent dismissal or punishment were not the main issues. They

were either unsympathetic to, or ignorant of, the true purpose of the
juvenile court, which is broadly therapeutic and concerned more with
the rehabilitation of the child than the punishment of transgressors.'[16]

What about youth organisations? The still very popular Boy Scouts
undoubtedly did their bit – *The Scout Song Book*, published in 1952, included
such Ralph Reader favourites as 'Comrades Are We', 'The Day Is What
You Make It', 'It's Great to Be Young' and of course 'Crest of a Wave' – but
Basil Henriques, doyen of the Boys' Club movement and veteran magistrate
in the East London Juvenile Court, worried about what happened when
boys left the Scouts, the 'greatest leakage' being between 13 and 15:

> Of those who leave [he wrote in 1955] many have the potentialities for
> becoming splendid men, while others are boys of a lower calibre who will
> not knuckle down to discipline or accept the demands made on them.
> Can the club 'sink' hold both these types? Does the club movement, like
> the Scouts, concentrate on the better grammar-school boy, and thereby
> neglect the difficult, mediocre boy who is driven out of the 'sink' down
> the 'drain', or is it inclined to concentrate on the sub-standard boy, and
> thereby drive the better type out of the 'sink', not necessarily down the
> 'drain', but into the non-co-operative and unsocial 'stream'?

That October, a report entitled *Citizens of To-morrow*, by four working
parties of educationalists, sociologists and industrialists, identified a
fateful 'gap both in education and in life' opening from 15 to 18. 'The
Youth Service which caters for these crucial years,' noted the *Observer*
in its summary of the report, 'has been condemned to a losing battle
against penury, with too few trained leaders and too many "dingy
surroundings," "outworn techniques and obsolete habits of thinking."
The results are garnered by the Forces [ie for National Service] in
recruits with poor physique and poor education, who lack "religious
knowledge, self-confidence, initiative and sense of responsibility." '

The article was called 'The Trouble with Youth', a trouble that not
even Frankie Vaughan could fix. The crooner was a prominent supporter
of youth clubs, and in November 1955 *Picture Post*'s Robert Muller
described how this 'serious young man from the slums of Liverpool,
with perhaps the greatest juvenile following after Dickie Valentine, and
a passion to do good', had recently spent a week on a tour of them,

judging talent contests and sometimes performing himself. 'Yet to do good,' reflected Muller, 'was not made easy for Vaughan':

> In some mixed clubs, members preferred to roar and yell and scream at the idol in the blue serge suit to putting on a show of their own. And always there were the girls. Thousands of them, swelling the mixed clubs to bursting point, infiltrating the boys' clubs as friends and relatives. They were the girls who had not come to perform, or see the boys perform, but merely to pay their customary homage to a pop singer, to indulge in their weekly bout of exhibitionism. They were not content with adjudication. They wanted performance. They were not content with autographs or pictures. They wanted kisses.
>
> On one such an occasion, as the girls screamed, and the boys hooted, he shouted: 'Do you know what you are? You are a disgrace!'

'The god showed his wrath,' concluded Muller, 'and the congregation was silent.'[17]

Occasionally, the views and voices of the trainee adults themselves come through. Mays in Liverpool in the early 1950s discovered that schoolboys were 'almost unanimously in favour of the retention of corporal punishment', having 'the advantages of swiftness and brevity in its execution reinforced by long tradition', whereas alternative punishments, including 'a withdrawal of such privileges as attendance at the baths or playing fields', would generate far more resentment. About the same time, Pearl Jephcott was investigating youth organisations in various working-class districts of London and Nottingham, to which around a third or just over of adolescents belonged. She was particularly interested in those who had left:

> Not interested in learning knots. (*Girl Guide, 14*)
> Started going out with boy. (*Girls' Life Brigade, 15*)
> Packed it in when I started courting. (*Club boy, 16*)
> Too stuffy in the Crypt. (*Club boy, 14*)
> Don't like it, don't like religion. (*Club girl, 14*)
> Too much of a family clique. (*Club boy, 17*)
> Boring – you just sit there and can't get any games because the boys bag them all. (*Club girl, 15*)

One group safe to be left alone by the sociologists was the Young Conservatives, aka 'the marriage market of the suburbs', which during its 1950s peak had a membership of around 170,000. 'Their dances were famous,' according to Raphael Samuel (probably not on the basis of personal experience), 'incomparably preferable, for the protective parent or the aspiring maiden or youth, to the roughness of the Locano or the dowdiness of the Church Hall; their car rallies – an innovation of the late 1940s – were a field day for show-offs.' There were no doubt some YCs among the students at Bristol University:

> We could not have been picked out as students in a crowd [recalled Helen Reid, 1954–7]: men wore blazers and flannels, or cords if they were arty, girls wore long full skirts with paper taffeta petticoats, jersey tops and ballerina shoes, and in the winter, tweed suits ...
>
> Social life hinged on hops: there were about ten dances and balls a term. Mostly they were cattle markets held at the Vic Rooms, where the 'men' gathered in groups round the bar (orange juice in half pint beer mugs, 3d a glass, was popular) while the girls hugged the walls, waiting to be singled out and kicked to pieces in the quickstep, under the flicking lights of the witchball.
>
> Like Cinderella, every girl wanted to go to THE ball, in this case the annual Union Ball, a most formal affair where officers of other unions were invited, and the top men were expected to wear tails.
>
> When the great day came, your partner, if he was properly trained, would present you with a corsage and hand you into a taxi, with your stole and your evening bag, your long gloves and your agonising high heels ...
>
> We all sat down to an austere institutional dinner, the Sauternes flowed like Tizer, and there were heavily witty undergraduate speeches, loyal toasts and singing of the University song, pinched from Gilbert and Sullivan.
>
> 'Though I myself have said it, and it's greatly to my credit, I am a Bristol man,' sang the girls ...

'In fact, though we didn't know it,' concluded Reid a little wistfully, 'we were elderly before our time.'[18]

Elderly, and perhaps also under-sexed, given that Mass-Observation's 'Little Kinsey' survey back in 1949 had found only 32 per cent (mainly men) denying the possibility of 'sexless' happiness. 'Generally it seems fairly clear that people's approach to sex,' the report had noted, 'tends to be limited not only by their intentness on doing what they regard as socially "correct", but also by anxiety and fears, particularly fears of transgressing the bounds of "normality", and which may be all the stronger for their vagueness.' The British through the 1950s remained ill at ease with the whole subject. 'The kind of sex she suggests is warm, uninhibited, completely natural,' Dirk Bogarde wrote in *Picturegoer* in 1955 about making *Doctor at Sea* with Brigitte Bardot, but at the same time expressed a rather haughty scepticism about her future in the British film industry: 'Even without her French accent, Brigitte would be too much for British studios to handle. You see, Brigitte takes the trouble to put across sex as an art. For most of our girls it's a farce.' Bogarde himself exuded a smouldering, ambiguous sexuality, though that was hardly true of the other three most bankable British male film stars of the fifties – Jack Hawkins, Kenneth More and Norman Wisdom. As for comedians, in addition to Wisdom's asexual gormlessness, one has only to think of the hugely popular Benny Hill, whose 'leering comedy' was, in the apt words of his biographer Mark Lewisohn, 'rooted in the Variety stage, where many seemingly mild-mannered comedians, acting as if they were stags, brashly hinted at sex and ogled at women but when faced with the genuine prospect of intimacy would stammer, not stiffen'.

Perhaps the dominant sentiment was prudishness. 'Saw "Pal Joey" [the American musical] at the Prince's Theatre last night and found it most offensive,' recorded Gladys Langford in April 1954. 'All my natural Puritanism rose in revolt. The chorus girls were near-nudes . . .' Or take the reaction in 1953 (as recorded by Mass-Observation) to the publication of extracts from Alfred Kinsey's new study *Sexual Behaviour in the Human Female*, some three years after the *People's* editor had forbidden Geoffrey Gorer to include in his survey an explicit question about female orgasms:

Kinsey? Stupid rot in the newspapers. They should never print the stuff. (*Travelling artist, 36*)

That dreadful man who wrote that book about women. (*Widow, 66*)

I'm glad to say that I did not stoop low enough to read his articles.
(*Fitter, 45*)

Not very nice reading. Enough said. (*Railway platelayer's wife, 53*)

He's been minding other people's private lives and making money out
of it. (*Miner, 54*)

Almost anything, it seemed at times, was liable to give offence. 'The
fact is that to certain people and their families (and they include quite
intelligent and ordinary people) the male body in tights, especially
white tights, is quite shocking,' asserted the BBC's Cecil McGivern,
Controller of Television Programmes, in a 1954 memo. 'I must insist
that great care is taken. The dressing of male dancers *must* be supervised
and producers of ballet must shoot male dancers so dressed in such a
way that the risk of offence is minimised.'[19]

One way and another, the result was near-unmentionability. 'Sex
was not a matter for general discussion,' Penelope Lively bluntly
recalls about being a young woman then, and most children of the
fifties would nod in agreement. Women's magazines were particularly
circumspect in their treatment, with analysis of the *Woman's Own*
problems page in 1955 showing that 'Mary Grant' went to almost any
length – 'an important part of marriage', 'physical love', even 'intimate
love-making' – to avoid the dreaded word *sex*, a circumspection almost
matched by the letter-writers themselves, for whom a favourite phrase
was 'the intimate side of married life'. The Mills & Boon authorial rules,
not just guidelines, were strict – passion fine, 'sex' or titillation far from
fine – while generally in fiction, films and plays there was an almost
systemic lack of frankness in approach to sexual matters, an inhibition
in part the direct result not only of censorship but also of a major
government-cum-legal campaign in the mid-1950s against anything
even faintly obscene, a campaign that among other cases saw the artist
Donald McGill, king of the seaside postcard, briefly banged up for his
depiction of an outsize, almost vertical stick of rock.

Inevitably, a conspiracy of silence meant in turn deep sexual
ignorance. Lively also recalls how she and her female generation 'found
out by trial and error, and mistakes ended in marriage or abortion'; for
Joan Bakewell, her 'total innocence of birth control' as a Cambridge
undergraduate was shared by her mother (unsurprisingly, given that

only one in six of M-O's 'Little Kinsey' street sample had had any sex education); and a common theme to *Growing Up in the Fifties*, a 1990 collection of female testimony, is embarrassment about sex and secrecy over menstruation. Boys were also stumbling in the dark. 'Sex education did not feature on Quarry Bank's syllabus, and [Aunt] Mimi could not be interrogated on such matters in other than the most general and theoretical terms,' notes John Lennon's biographer Philip Norman. 'Like most of his generation, John had to piece together the facts of life from dirty jokes and diagrams on the walls of public urinals.' As in Liverpool, so in Bristol. 'At my school,' remembered Derek Robinson, 'the two periods of biology scheduled to cover human reproduction left many of us more confused than before. That tangle of plumbing created in chalk on the blackboard: did it really have something to do with our bodies? There was a rumour that sex was supposed to be fun. It didn't look like fun. The way the biology master described it, it sounded slightly less fun than unclogging a drain with a bent plunger.'[20]

Another area long shrouded by secrecy, rumour, guilt and fear was homosexuality. Admittedly there was a comic tradition of the effeminate queen, but it was not a tradition that ever embraced realistic portrayal. During most of the 1950s, moreover, the Lord Chamberlain's Office resolutely refused to allow any discussion of the subject on the licensed stage, while it remained strictly off-limits in British cinema (notwithstanding Frankie Howerd playing Willie Joy in 1955's *Jumping for Joy* and ordering a double ginger beer). In another sense, though, things were probably starting to change by the mid-1950s, amid the widespread prosecution of homosexuals, the establishment of the Wolfenden Committee in 1954 and quite extensive press coverage. 'The subject was taboo and never openly discussed,' Basil Henriques noted in 1955. 'Lately it has become an ordinary topic of conversation, openly talked about by people of all ages and both sexes in each other's company.' Free and frank exchanges of view were perhaps in reality not quite so prevalent round the dinner table, but it was significant that Henriques himself, for all his generally high moral tone, strongly encouraged parents to show 'the utmost sympathy' towards homosexual sons.

Inevitably, evidence to Wolfenden varied hugely, but it was arguably the British Medical Association that carried the most weight. In a lengthy written submission, it sat on the fence about what Wolfenden should recommend in terms of legalisation or otherwise, but did assert that prison was 'not usually the most suitable place' for 'dealing' with the homosexual offender and referred to 'the apparent disproportion of sentences imposed' as 'sometimes greatly disturbing'. Even so, there was no disposition on the BMA's part not to regard homosexuality as a problem requiring treatment. That treatment could take several forms, but subsequently released Home Office papers showed the quite widespread use in the 1950s of electric-shock treatment and oestrogen (a female sex hormone) in order to try to turn homosexual prisoners into heteros. 'The desire for medical treatment is often expressed but much more rarely sincerely felt,' was the typically caustic remark of prison staff in the report presented to the Home Secretary, and indeed in the majority of cases the 'inverts' (as they were called) refused treatment.

Only three professed homosexuals gave evidence to Wolfenden: Peter Wildeblood, Patrick Trevor-Roper (a Harley Street eye surgeon and brother of Hugh) and Carl Winter, director of the Fitzwilliam Museum in Cambridge. All three were well-connected professional men, and Winter described with some satisfaction his extensive circle of very civilised homosexual or homosexual-tolerant friends:

> We are all completely at ease in one another's company and the world in which we live, which is a much more extensive world, I think, than many people would suppose. We visit each other's houses, go abroad, travel, look at the sort of things that interest us, art, exhibitions, ballet, and have a satisfactory life within that sphere. Somebody from outside is every now and then caught up in it. Somebody presents himself at one's door and if he is in character a sympathetic person he is admitted, if not, he is excluded . . .

It was a million miles away from the world of cottaging, smelly urinals and furtive encounters in parks – the world that, perforce, most other homosexuals inhabited. Accordingly, none of the three asked the Committee to recommend decriminalising homosexual activities in general, including in public places; all they wanted was legalisation inside the home, or, in Wildeblood's words, 'neither corrupting others nor publicly flaunting their condition'.[21] Their evidence, in short, was still in its way a milestone, but it was very far from a rallying cry.

Most homosexuals, before and during the Wolfenden Committee's entirely private deliberations, got on with life as best they could. Two leading television personalities, the covertly homosexual Gilbert Harding and the covertly lesbian Nancy Spain, kept up a bantering, somewhat camp relationship for screen and press, even permitting suggestions of marriage; Dirk Bogarde reputedly paid annual visits to University College Hospital for aversion therapy; equally reputedly, Edward Heath was warned by police in 1955, during vetting to become a Privy Councillor, to stop his cottaging activities; the writer and radio producer Hallam Tennyson was staying in his marriage despite becoming aware of his underlying homosexuality, a process movingly described in his 1984 memoir *The Haunted Mind*; the young Peter Maxwell Davies, growing up in working-class Salford, knew enough to stay mum ('keeping it secret became second nature'); and Alan Bennett, uneasily asked by his father if he was 'one of them', quickly replied, 'Oh, Dad, don't be daft.' A gay couple during these long dark years were Daniel McCairns and Harold Smythe, even though they were living in Maryhill, one of the toughest parts of Glasgow. 'I'd like to have asked them how the hell they got away with it,' McCairns's great-nephew reflected in 2005 following their deaths after over half a century together. 'What was it like to spend your entire public life never showing any affection? Did you ever tell anyone else? But to ask would have been inconceivable, which is, perhaps, the answer to how they got away with it. No one dared hint at it.'[22]

The Wolfenden Committee did not just consider the question of 'Huntley's', as Wolfenden termed homosexuals to spare the feelings of his female secretaries. There was also the problem of 'Palmer's', as he called prostitutes. It was a problem partly of numbers: the National Council of Women of Great Britain reckoned in its evidence that about a quarter of a million men visited prostitutes each week in London (perhaps an overestimate), while in 1958 the number of full-time streetwalkers there was gauged at 3,000 (perhaps an underestimate). But above all, in the eyes of the authorities, it was a problem of visibility. In particular, members of the Cabinet and senior Home Office officials were appalled by the sheer affront to decency and thus in 1954 sanctioned the subject as a last-minute add-on to homosexuality; while the following year, from a rather different standpoint, the American sexologist Alfred Kinsey was shown round the West End on a Saturday night and counted a thousand prostitutes at work, saying afterwards that he had never seen so much blatant sexual conduct.

Almost certainly there was little sympathy for the position of these women. 'Disapproval is not only strong but general,' M-O's 'Little Kinsey' found in 1949 about prostitution as such, with 'moral objections' being 'largely directed against the prostitutes themselves', viewed by most people as 'hard, bad and degraded'. Those attitudes probably hardened during the more prosperous 1950s, as the traditional economic justification became less applicable. Yet to read *Women of the Streets* (1955) – undertaken for the British Social Biology Council, edited by the invariably humane C. H. Rolph, and typically for its era subtitled *A Sociological Study of the Common Prostitute* – is to encounter voices that should have reminded Wolfenden and his committee members that each prostitute (here based mainly in Soho or Hyde Park) was a unique individual working in a heartless industry:

You don't know the things they do and the things they want. Be all right walking down the street, talk to you ever so nice, but when they get alone with us women, well, some of them are like rats in holes. A woman doesn't know a man; if a wife knew what her husband was really like she'd never live with him no more. We have to chain them up and beat them and jump on them . . . Sometimes a man sits beside me and I shudder away from him, if only people knew what you were like, you awful slimy toad, I think. (*Bessie*)

Some of the men even want to kiss you! Why, they'd mess all your lipstick up . . . I get so mad when a man says to me, 'But you must get some pleasure out of it, else you wouldn't do it' . . . you know, it's funny, but once I get the money I change. Maybe going to my place in the car we have to talk, and I try to make myself nice and ask what they do, though sometimes I say 'If you were a bank-robber I wouldn't care.' But the moment we get in and I get the money I feel fed up with them and keep on saying to myself, 'Hurry up, hurry up and get out' . . . One thing I can't stand in business is anyone touching my breasts. I can't bear it and nearly scream if they try. (*Edna*)

Ten shillings a time, unless they don't know the value of money, say a foreigner, then we charge them more. Of course, in the Park you don't have the full intercourse; at least, you have to on the grass or on a chair, but you say 'The grass is too wet, dear.' You keep your legs together and the men don't know any different. (*Gwyneth*)

I like to have my eyes open. I'll never take a man who offers me more than I ask. I only want thirty shillings, and if one offers me £3 I know it's fishy. He'll try to get me to take off my clothes and then get his money . . . We get a lot of sadists and men who want beating – they're usually Army captains. (*Kathleen*)

I hate the sort of man who says, 'Of course my wife doesn't understand this sort of thing.' Judging from them I wonder which one it is doesn't understand. They can be so dull! Anyway, I don't think they should discuss their wives with me. Their relation with me is something apart. (*Priscilla*)[23]

'The time in Britain is twelve noon, in Germany it's one o'clock, but home and away it's time for *Two-Way Family Favourites*.' Every Sunday, after the signature tune 'With a Song in My Heart', these words were heard on the Light Programme, spoken by (as Denis Gifford fondly recalled) 'the warm, ladylike, yet subtly sexy tones of Jean Metcalfe, BBC lady *par excellence*'. There followed an hour and a quarter of record requests, linking Armed Forces personnel in West Germany with their families at home, and invariably including the 'Bumper Bundle', the week's most popular choice. Metcalfe herself, a railway clerk's daughter, was married to the avuncular, rock-steady Cliff Michelmore – the two having met over the microphone in the late 1940s, when he was temporarily the presenter in Hamburg – and under her the programme became a household fixture, attracting weekly audiences of around 12 to 13 million. It was unique in its ability 'to stimulate both the digestive juices and the heartfelt emotions of the nation at the same time', remembers Ken Blakemore from his Cheshire childhood. 'The air was laden with that theme tune and with yearning messages, the aromas of roast lamb and gravy, and the sounds of new potatoes being scraped and mint being chopped. *Two-Way Family Favourites* was, in short, the distilled essence of 1950s family bonding.'[24]

Normative assumptions identifying the moral and social health of the nation with the moral and social health of the family were close to the heart of the era's official and semi-official discourse – a discourse predicated on the perhaps exaggerated perception that the great disruption of the war and immediate post-war years had been hugely damaging to the cohesiveness of family life. To an unprecedented, almost cultish extent, children were seen as the future, and it was to them, more than any other section of society, that the new welfare state was devoted. The welfare state alone, though, could not do it all, and almost all activators were agreed that it was the family that provided the indispensable framework for a child's development. A key conduit for the message were women's magazines, by the early 1950s approaching their zenith of circulation and devoting page upon positive, glowing page to family matters, typified by *Good Housekeeping* starting a regular 'Family Centre' feature that dealt with all aspects – parental, marital, practical – of family life. Almost invariably applied to nuclear rather than extended set-ups, the very word, moreover, was ubiquitous. 'To Be One of the Family' was one of the adult stories in the randomly chosen 1 March 1952 issue of the *People's Friend*, while for children there was 'The Snowdrop Family Goes to Town'.

Marriage itself was the unassailable norm. 'Never before,' reflected Richard Titmuss towards the end of the 1950s, 'has there been such a high proportion of married women in the female population under the age of forty and, even more so, under the age of thirty.' Or take 'gross nuptiality' indicators, ie the percentage probability of marrying before the age of 50:

	Men	Women
1900–02	88.0	81.6
1951–55	93.5	94.6
1956–60	94.1	96.0
1995	65.4	68.7

Unsurprisingly, given such figures, Gorer found on the basis of his *People* survey that the English placed 'a very high valuation' on 'the institution of marriage'. Put another way, marriage was the all-pervasive expectation, especially of course among as yet unmarried adolescents,

above all working-class girls. 'From "having a boy" to "going steady",
and from "going steady" to "getting married",' noted Pearl Jephcott on
the basis of her Nottingham study in the early 1950s, 'were the proper
steps for any dutiful daughter to take in her teens and to have completed
by her early twenties.'[25]

It seems that at least a quarter of couples (of all social classes) first
met on the dance floor, while on Sunday evenings – in south Wales
anyway, and probably elsewhere – there was the so-called monkey
parade. 'Gaggles of girls strolled in their finery: hoop skirts, stockings
and a flash of scarlet across the lips; gangs of boys marched by in their
Vaseline-sculpted Tony Curtis hair – big DA at the back and quiff
in the front,' wrote Robin Eggar in his biography of Tom Jones. 'All
evening they criss-crossed, exchanging glances and giggles, sometimes
pairing off for a sneaked coffee, but more often relying on flirting and
safety in numbers.' Jones himself, Tommy Woodward at the time, got
married at Pontypridd register office in March 1957 at 16, the same age
as his heavily pregnant bride, Linda. 'Nobody can touch me now I'm a
man,' he reckoned to himself after first seeing the baby some six weeks
later. In less rushed circumstances, the wedding would probably have
been at a church or chapel, though in any case a proper honeymoon
was far from invariable. 'We went and stayed at my brother's house,'
recalled a mid-1950s bride from the north-west about what followed
the reception at the Co-op. 'Of course, we didn't have a lot of money,
but we had bought a house of our own, so we just went away for a long
weekend and then came back to our home to settle in.'

Divorce was highly unusual through the decade, running at an
annual rate of around two divorces per thousand married people once
the immediate post-war upwards blip had played itself out. In part this
reflected what was still the largely restrictive, judgemental, illiberal
law, requiring guilt – usually in the form of adultery – on the part of
either husband or wife. A Labour MP, Eirene White, did try in 1951
to achieve a measure of reform and in the process inspired a notable
speech by the young Tory politician Reginald Maudling, who declared
that 'broadly speaking, we are dealing not with the misdeeds of men
and women but their follies and misfortunes, which are much harder
to deal with'. The Attlee government took fright, however, and set
up a royal commission – which, lawyer-dominated, took five years to

report, and then inconclusively. Although the Mothers' Union refused to admit the divorced, attitudes in general towards divorce seem to have been conflicted: often an inability or unwillingness to imagine that it might be a possible outcome to one's own marriage, however unhappy or imperfect, as well as a certain censoriousness towards well-known figures (for instance J. B. Priestley or the comedian Max Wall) whose marriages had failed; but at the same time, a certain underlying pragmatic tolerance towards the concept, allied to instinctive dislike of those, like the church, seen as too inclined to go on the high horse. By 1955, moreover, there were significant straws in the wind: not only the widespread sympathy for Princess Margaret in her wish to marry a divorced man but also the arrival as Counselling Officer at the National Marriage Guidance Council (precursor of Relate) of John Wallis, who would oversee a shift away from guidance in order to save marriages and towards counselling aimed at maximising individual fulfilment.

Even so, whatever the precise mix of social attitudes, divorce itself was still so much the exception that the psychological burden on the children of divorce remained considerable. 'I was eight, relieved at a more peaceful homelife but very embarrassed about having divorced parents,' Angela Hogg remembered more than 30 years later about the aftermath of her parents' 'very stormy' marriage ending in 1955:

> I shrivelled in history lessons about Henry VIII when his divorces were mentioned. After the divorce my brother, sister and I [living with their mother in Bristol] were handed over to my father on neutral territory – the White Tree roundabout – every third weekend. My father then lived in Birmingham but rented one room as a base. He cooked us meals on a one-ring stove but took us out to 'places of interest'. Both parents married again. It was very hard to balance loyalties. In those days nobody ever thought of counselling the children or sorting out the huge problems of being adolescents in two households. We kept our agonies to ourselves and hardly dared discuss them with each other.

'Things,' she concluded with heartfelt relief about using the past tense, 'were kept much more under the carpet in those days.'[26]

Outside the statistically insignificant world of the open-marriage leftish intelligentsia – A. J. Ayer, Anthony Crosland, Kingsley Amis – it is all but impossible to know the extent of extramarital affairs. Virtually the only guide we have is M-O's 1949 'Little Kinsey' survey, which asked its unrepresentatively liberal, middle-class National Panel and found that 'one husband in four, compared with one wife in every five, admits to experience of sex relations outside marriage'. The historian of adultery, Claire Langhamer, suggests that 'there was a very real public perception that extra-marital affairs were more common across social categories than had previously been the case', but for most of the 1950s her only contemporary evidence is *The Times* in May 1954 reporting the fear of the prominent, morally upright Judge Denning that 'we have unfortunately reached a position where adultery, or infidelity or misconduct, as soft-spoken folk call it, is considered to be a matter of little moment'.

That, though, is as much about attitudes as practices, and in terms of attitudes we do indeed know more. 'Little Kinsey' revealed that although there was in theory widespread condemnation of sex outside marriage (63 per cent of the street sample), people when it came to particular cases were, in Langhamer's words, 'unwilling to make judgements without an understanding of individual circumstances'. Soon afterwards, in Gorer's survey, the majority of responses to the question of what a husband/wife should do if the other was found to be conducting an affair had 'the implicit or explicit assumption that adultery should not terminate the marriage (if that can possibly be avoided) and does not justify the wronged spouse in adopting violent and aggressive behaviour'. A 30-year-old woman from St Helens advised: 'First of all discuss it calmly with him, then do nothing but wait. Let the affair die a natural death and the man will return. In the meantime, she can buy some new clothes and have her hair permed, make herself as attractive as she can. Spend more on herself than on the house.'

This measure of tolerance seems to have become the norm, to judge by what Marian Raynham heard on *Any Questions?* in December 1954:

My goodness, I nearly exploded. One question was 'whether one act of adultery should be a cause for divorce'. The 'holy' Archbishop Fisher said it shouldn't, there was forgiveness, & the marriage could go on happily as before. This was in the paper the other day. Well, I'll be blowed, not one of those specimens, including Mary Stocks, had the courage to take another view. What a revelation. The other three were Tom Driberg M.P.,

Nigel Balchin, Sir Godfrey [Llewellyn, a prominent Welsh Conservative]. Well, I'm shocked to the marrow. So married people are allowed a ration of one adultery, leaving the marriage as before. The other innocent party not minding a bit presumably . . .

There was less sympathy for the plight of the third party. 'He is talking nonsense about divorcing her,' bluntly replied 'Mary Grant' (running the *Woman's Own* problems page) to a single woman who had been asked by her lover to wait for his divorce. 'Stop seeing him.'[27] The marriage, almost whatever the situation, came first and last.

What about premarital sex? Again, hard evidence is patchy, although we know from Eustace Chesser's extensive cohort-based survey (conducted in 1954 and somewhat skewed towards the middle class) that it was probably becoming more common during the first half of the century, 19 per cent of women born before 1904 reporting having had premarital sex, compared with 43 per cent born between 1924 and 1934, with generally those from wealthier backgrounds more likely to have had it. And again, attitudes are easier to ascertain. Gorer found that 52 per cent were opposed to premarital sexual experience for young men and 63 per cent for young women, adding the telling gloss that 'whether pre-marital experience is advocated or reprobated, the effect on the future marriage is the preponderating consideration'; while when Chesser asked single women under the age of 21, 89 per cent said that for the success of their future marriage it was 'important or fairly important' that they did not have premarital intercourse, with 78 per cent wanting that stricture to apply to their future husbands also. On the reasonable assumption that more than 11 per cent of women and 22 per cent of men were having premarital sex by the 1950s, there was clearly something of a gulf between aspiration and reality, not least in the context of the continuing taboo about the loss of female virginity.

This taboo came through markedly in some of the responses to Gorer from unmarried men:

I, when I marry, want a pure girl, so the least I can do is to be the same myself. (*20, North London*)

I think all women should be married in white and can't do so if she has had sexual exp. with men. (*19, Liverpool*)

Would not like my future wife to have had sexual experience with other persons prior to our marriage. Matter of principle also. (*21, Lincolnshire*)

I think it is wrong for anybody to gain experience at the expense of somebody else. I should hate to think somebody had tried married life out on my wife to be. (*23, Tilbury*)

Women's magazines agreed, with 'Mary Grant' assiduously pushing the idea of the female chaperone for any girl worried about being induced to go too far. Moreover, for any girl who *had* gone too far, the cult of virginity was such that this could effectively mean the end of choice in terms of deciding on a husband. 'When we 'ad rows,' somewhat ruefully recalled a working-class woman from Birmingham some 40 years after marrying in 1957, 'well I used to think "well I can't fall out with 'im because – or break up with 'im – because I've 'ad sex, I'd be used goods for somebody else." '28

For most couples, of course, there was always the question of birth control – at a time when the size of the family was changing significantly. Archbishop Fisher may have told the Mothers' Union in 1952 that 'a family only truly begins with three children', but as a young father in a rundown outer London borough unsentimentally informed an enquiring sociologist at about the same time, 'Our parents had too many children: we want to give ours a good start in life, so we shan't have more than we can afford.' Chesser in 1956 confirmed the trend – 'A family of four or more children is now regarded as large' – and Gallup the following spring, asking about the ideal size of family, found that two children was easily the most popular. It was no coincidence, presumably, that matters of contraception were at last moving into the mainstream: almost every week a new family planning clinic opened, while in November 1955 Iain Macleod's well-publicised visit, as Minister of Health, to the Family Planning Association ended almost overnight the media's reluctance to discuss the whole subject. But there was still a long way to go. Many parts of the country did not have clinics, while new clinics were often viewed with considerable suspicion. Moreover, as Kate Fisher stresses in her study of birth control, widespread ignorance persisted, especially on the part of women. As for method, a subsequent survey of two working-class cohorts who had got married in the 1950s found the following about their early married lives: 37 per cent mainly using condoms (for which there was no British Standard until 1964); 33 per cent mainly relying on withdrawal; 15 per cent mainly using female methods such as diaphragms or IUDs; 12 per cent not worrying about contraception; and 3 per cent other. Quite apart from no single method being wholly reliable, there were other practical concerns. 'Shaped like a doll's bowler hat, with a hard rim of black rubber,' was how Phyllis Willmott unfondly remembered the Dutch cap. 'When I put it in I felt like a stuffed chicken.'[29]

There was one great, oppressive shadow, seldom openly spoken about. 'Abortion was the awful spectre for girls,' recalled Penelope Lively. 'Each of us knew someone to whom the worst had happened, with accompanying whispered horror stories about backstreet addresses and £100 in a brown envelope.' Some 12,000 abortions a year were performed legally, on the grounds that terminating a pregnancy would prevent the woman from 'being a mental and physical wreck', but the great majority were not, leading directly each year to some 70 or more registered deaths from dangerously conducted criminal abortions. There still prevailed, according to Barbara Brookes, historian of abortion, 'an atmosphere of secrecy and shame', though it does seem that public opinion was slowly moving in a more liberal direction. Not only did a newspaper poll in 1956 find majority support for abortions by doctors 'at the request of the mother-to-be', but there was an increasingly low rate of conviction for professional abortionists. Were there any real-life Vera Drakes? Jennifer Worth, an East End midwife during the 1950s, took issue in 2005 with Mike Leigh's depiction of a heroine acting on principle and never taking payment. 'I very much doubt that this was ever the case,' she asserted. 'From everything we heard, abortionists were in it for the money (the going rate was between one and two guineas). I never heard of one who was conducting a philanthropic practice.' Significantly, she added: 'It was not their fault they were medically untrained; the legislation was to blame. Fatalities among women undergoing an abortion were high, but they were far higher among women who tried to do it themselves, unaided.'[30]

Illegitimacy rates were low through the 1950s, running most years at or below 5 per cent, or in the mid-1950s around 33,000 illegitimate babies a year. Of those babies, a little under half (about 13,000 a year) were given up for adoption. Why? A report in 1950 about the Church of England's moral-welfare work in London is suggestive of some of the acute practical difficulties faced by unmarried mothers:

> Few people realise how seldom an affiliation order is made against the father of an illegitimate child. Many girls have insufficient evidence on which to apply for a summons. In other instances they have lost touch with the man and are unable to give an address at which he can be found. Workers find a general unwillingness on the part of the mother to take action, especially in cases where the man concerned is married. She, and very often members of her family too, dread the publicity of a Magistrate's Court. What is due to the child is forgotten or passed over in the confusion caused by other people's interests and emotions . . .
>
> The Worker's chief difficulty lies in finding accommodation for the mother who wishes to keep her baby. Often the girl who beforehand has felt adoption to be the only solution to her problem entirely changes her mind when the baby is born. More Hostel accommodation is needed for mothers who can go out to work, and leave the children safely cared for during the day . . . Sometimes the best type of mother, after a great struggle, turns to adoption in the end as a means of gaining security for her child.

Many young, unmarried mothers lacked the skills for adequately paid employment; landlords seldom welcomed such tenants; and it was not until the late 1970s that council waiting lists were opened up to unmarried mothers. Also, there was often pressure from mother-and-baby homes, mainly run by welfare societies of a religious character and from where some 15 per cent of illegitimate births took place. 'It was presented as in the best interest of the unsupported child to lose the stigma of illegitimacy and to have a stable upbringing with two adopted parents: the homeless child for the childless home,' notes Gillian Clark in her study of mother-and-baby homes. 'It was a telling argument for a girl ill-equipped to support them both.'

Above all, there was the stigma itself – a stigma that unmarried mothers felt not only from their immediate families (especially their fathers), but from society at large. A flavour comes through in the response of *Daily Mirror* readers in October 1953 to another reader's suggestion that it was 'high time' that 'unmarried mothers had some status in this country':

Why should unmarried mothers be given 'status'? It is a pity that they do not think of the status they give to their children when they choose to defy the moral conventions, the backbone of family life, and live with other women's husbands. (*Mother, Stroud*)

My husband knows that, if he left me to set up with some fancy piece, I would do all I could to make her name smell, so that, even if vanity blinded her, her neighbours would see her as a shameless thing. Once she was left unprotected I would swoop down and grab everything I could get, even if it meant that her children were left on the rates. (*Mrs D., Portsmouth*)

Unmarried mothers must always remain without 'status' so that they may serve as a good warning to young girls. (*'Happily Married', Bolton*)[31]

Marriage was an integral part – arguably *the* integral part – of the 1950s deal. It was not a deal open to those who, deliberately or otherwise, appeared to be circumventing the terms and conditions.

In 1955 the readers of *Woman's Own* voted for their favourite radio voice. The winner was a family favourite. 'For me,' Nan Wigham from Durham wrote in, 'Jean Metcalfe's voice depicts all the qualities I think every woman ought to have. Sincerity, humour, understanding, reliability and tact.' So much was now being demanded of what Simone de Beauvoir ironically called *The Second Sex* (English edition in 1953). Woman as embodiment of femininity, woman as dutiful, good-companion wife, woman as ingenious, cost-effective, uncomplaining homemaker, woman as strict yet infinitely loving mother – it was a daunting, home-centred, fourfold role.

'How to Dress to Please Men' was the expressive title of a series in *Everywoman* in the early 1950s, with a special emphasis on personal grooming ('He likes you to be soft and silky'). Other women's magazines relentlessly pushed the ideal – indeed the indispensability – of feminine physical attractiveness. 'She won't get far without polishing up her good points and disguising her bad ones so that he's completely befogged by glamour!' advised *Woman's Own* in 1951. 'It's at this stage that the romantic compliments are paid and the diamond engagement rings get shopped for!' Operating at an elite level above the mass-circulation magazines, there were two particular cynosures of beauty and elegance. Barbara Goalen, *the* British mannequin of the era until her retirement in 1954, was recalled for how 'her haughty demeanour, delicate bone-structure and wasp waist came to represent the height of glamour', while for older women the great exemplar was Margot Smyly, who in the pages of *Vogue* assumed the persona of 'Mrs Exeter', remembered as a 'chic matron' and 'a very feminine social being in her luncheon suits, cocktail dresses and well-wielded fur stole'. One shrewd observer, who had long ago reconciled herself to the cultivation of non-physical charms, found the whole phenomenon altogether too much. 'On T.V.,' reflected Barbara Pym in 1955, 'I thought that women have never been more terrifying than they are now – the curled head ("Italian style"), the paint and jewellery, the exposed bosom – no wonder men turn to other men sometimes.'[32]

For wives, there were competing messages. Officially this was the dawning age of the companionate, shared-interests, no-separate-spheres marriage – as ordained in 1949 by the Royal Commission on Population, with its manifest approval for the by now increased emphasis on 'the wife's role as companion to her husband as well as a producer of children', as given cinematic wifely flesh by the stylish, witty Kay Kendall in three mid-1950s comedies, *Genevieve*, *The Constant Husband* and *Simon and Laura*. Yet equally powerful, arguably more powerful, was the discourse stressing that good companions did not mean equal companions. 'Don't try to be the boss,' warned Monica Dickens in her *Woman's Own* column in 1955 as she attacked 'the slightly abnormal woman who wants to have her cake and eat it'. In other words: 'She wants a man to give her love, companionship, a home, children, and the wherewithal to support life comfortably; but she cannot bring herself to let her man be the head of the household.' It was the same in the marriage bed, at least as laid down by Dr Mary Macaulay's *The Art of Marriage*, first published in 1952 and subsequently as a Penguin. Not only was 'the success of the erotic side of the marriage chiefly the husband's responsibility', but it was 'a shocking thing' to hear of a wife refusing her husband's sexual advances, in that 'such an attitude would be impossible in any woman to whom loving and giving were synonymous'.

Sex was conspicuously – if predictably – off the agenda when

Woman's Own in 1955 asked 'Are You a Perfect Partner?' and put some leading questions:

> Some weeks after you suggest an idea, *he* offers it afresh as his own . . . Would you (a) Let it go and say nothing? (b) Remind him that it was your idea originally? (c) Accuse him of having a terrible memory?
>
> He loves animals and wants to get a dog, you are not so keen . . . Would you (a) Give in because it's what he wants? (b) Argue against it? (c) Forbid it?
>
> He's buying you presents that he can't afford . . . Would you (a) Accept his presents and say nothing? (b) Tell him you love him just as much without his presents? (c) Show anger at his wasteful extravagance?
>
> You earn more money than he does . . . Would you (a) Offer to pay for both of you? (b) Go 'dutch'? (c) Suggest some entertainment you know he'll be able to afford?
>
> He keeps comparing you unfavourably with other girls . . . Would you (a) Fume inwardly and say nothing? (b) Tell him sweetly to take out the girl he obviously prefers? (c) Make uncomplimentary remarks about him?

The correct answers were a, a, b, c and b. Full marks, and 'you will be the perfect wife and deserve a perfect husband'; high marks, and 'you will make some man very happy'; but a low score, and 'you need more tolerance and a greater understanding of the man you love'.

The perfect partner was also the perfect homemaker, not least in the context of the enhanced prestige of the housewife in the eyes of the newly servantless middle class. It was a role played out above all in the kitchen. 'A woman's place?' almost needlessly asked *Woman's Own*. 'Yes, it is! For it is the heart and centre of the meaning of home. The place where, day after day, you make with your hands the gifts of love.' More generally, the vogue for domesticity was nurtured and spread across the land's villages and small towns by Women's Institutes – at the peak of their popularity, flower-arranging a particular speciality – while the strongly perceived need to pass on housewifery skills across the generations was summed up by a Bolton councillor, Mrs Heywood, pronouncing in 1953 on the importance of washday: 'If the laundry goes out of the home, a child will have no training in house management.'[33]

An undeniable judgementalism was involved, typified by television ads for washing powder and the like unashamedly equating the moral worth of the wife with the whiteness of her husband's shirts. Happily, for those afraid of falling short, help was at hand, especially as the range of consumer products rapidly expanded from the mid-1950s. The Good Housekeeping Institute was assiduous in its advice, with its compendious guide to *The Happy Home* (1955) including detailed chapters on 'The Good Steward', 'Easier Housework', 'Home Laundrywork', 'Cooking Craft' and 'The Perfect Hostess', and of course women's magazines were suffused with practical tips and information. Here, the special emphasis was on making good the shopping and culinary skills that had been lost during the long years of austerity and shortages, a tutorial service exemplified by the 'Wooden Spoon Club' in *Woman* and 'Cecile's Cookery Class' in *Woman's Weekly*. 'A very great part of a woman's life is spent choosing, buying and preparing goods for her own and her family's consumption,' reflected Mary Grieve, editor of *Woman* all through the 1950s. 'Success is as cheering and vitalising to her as it is to a man in his chosen career, failure as humiliating.'

A couple of gender stereotypes seem to have remained near-sacrosanct. One was male assumptions about – whatever her apparent intentions – female extravagance. 'Do you like it, dear?' the strip-cartoon character Gaye Gambol asked her husband, George, in the *Sunday Express* in January 1955 as she showed him her new dress. 'Er . . . yes . . . but,' replied George, before she blithely went on, against the background of a black cloud gathering over George's long-suffering head: 'I got it in the sales – it was reduced from £5 to £4 – I saved a pound. And I saved ten shillings on these shoes and nearly two pounds on all this dress material. You're always saying that we must economise so I'm going shopping again tomorrow to save some more money.' Arguably the matching female assumption was how the housewife's control of the day-to-day domestic domain ultimately if covertly gave her the whip hand. 'The woman of the house is the most important person in it,' was how *Woman's Own* put it in 1957. 'Her husband may be stronger and cleverer than she is. He may be a business tycoon, or a genius or a famous personality. His wife may seem inferior to him in the more obvious ways – but there is one subtle way she can outdo him every time, and that is in her influence in the home . . .'[34]

Yet however exalted, a housewife did not exist on the same plane as a mother. Early in 1954, Oliver Willmott's wife explained in his Parish Notes that whereas the members of their WI had 'learnt to do many practical things' and 'seen demonstrations' that had 'helped us to improve our cooking, sewing, handicrafts, and the interior decorations of our houses', the purpose of the Mothers' Union was altogether more spiritual, being 'a society of Christian women pledged to help one another in performing faithfully the duties they owe to their husbands, their children and their God'. She added that 'we come to the monthly meeting of the M.U. to refresh our ideals, and to reaffirm the mother's motto, which is "I serve" '. The key cinematic text was *Mandy* – a 1952 Ealing drama (and Jane Asher's screen debut) in which Phyllis Calvert played the endlessly devoted, endlessly warm mother of a deaf-mute daughter – but one figure above all was identified with the coming centre-stage of the idealised mother, a phenomenon no doubt in large part the inevitable legacy of the involuntary paternal disappearing act during much of the 1940s. This was the psychoanalyst John Bowlby, who in the early 1950s relentlessly and brilliantly propagated his research findings about the crucial influence of mother-love on the formation of a child's character and personality. Typical was his conclusion to a *News Chronicle* article (bluntly headed 'The Mother Who Stays at Home Gives Her Children a Better Chance') in 1952:

> Babies need mothers because a child's emotional development depends on his relationship with his mother in his very early years.
>
> If she neglects him when he is small there will be trouble afterwards.
>
> So the mother who stays at home is giving her children a surer foundation for mental health than costly equipment and an expensive education can provide.
>
> Research shows that the deprived children of today are the delinquents and neurotics of tomorrow.

The following spring there appeared his best-selling Penguin, *Child Care and the Growth of Love*, which comprised two self-explanatory parts, 'Adverse Effects of Maternal Deprivation' and 'Prevention of Maternal Deprivation'. It was a message instantly and widely endorsed.

'That every infant born into the world does need individual affection is not just sentiment, it is a cold scientific fact demonstrated by Dr John Bowlby in a way which leaves no room for argument,' Anne Cuthbert declared in *Housewife* in September 1953, and her article's title was even less ambiguous: 'Nothing Takes the Place of a Mother's Love'.

There is no better place for locating the expected norms of being a woman, certainly a middle-class woman, than *Woman's Hour*, presented for much of the 1950s by either Jean Metcalfe or Marjorie Anderson. Mary Hardie's 'Diary' was transmitted on 9 February 1955 – part-realistic, part-idealistic, and almost sublimely representative:

Oh and yesterday – yesterday was one of those days. It began with Richard all sniffy and sneezy so he had to stay home from school. It went on with shopping that took longer than usual and a friend who called in for a moment and stayed till lunchtime – so lunch was late and the housework was completely out of hand and the dusting still wasn't done – and it ended with an attempt to make a cake with the children's help. It's no good – it's always a mistake. This cake started off with every intention of being a Victoria sandwich. But just as the margarine was in the mixing bowl the 'phone rang. As I went to answer it Richard called out: 'Shall we chop up the margarine with the spoon, Mummy?' and I gaily said, 'Yes, do, that'll be a great help.' When I got back to the kitchen the margarine was certainly chopped into small pieces – but it was on the table instead of in the bowl. The bag of flour had been most helpfully got out – there was flour on the floor, flour on the chairs and flour on the children – and a valiant attempt had been made to cream the margarine into the flour. I stood in the doorway, shocked into silence for once. 'Stevie did it,' said Richard in eager self-defence. And Stevie was certainly pretty well caught in the act. I was *very* cross and shooed them back to their bricks and cars and railway. Then I went back to the kitchen and got out more margarine – the other would just have to be used for pastry – and (let me hope Ann Hardy [the programme's culinary expert] doesn't hear me) I put it in the oven just for a moment, just to soften a little. Then I felt ashamed of myself for being so cross with the children – after all they had been trying to help – so I went to tell them so. We had a very pleasant conversation on the principles of making a cake by the creaming method and in the general orgy of forgiveness, the margarine in the oven softened out and melted and practically sizzled. So the Victoria sandwich ended up as a Yorkshire parkin, because that's the only thing in my repertoire where the recipe begins 'Melt the margarine . . .' It was quite good parkin.[35]

———————

Contrary to subsequent mythology, the 1950s were not entirely bereft of ambitious, independent-minded women. Sheila van Damm was a leading long-distance rally driver before she retired in 1956 to run the Windmill Theatre; Margery Fish was liberated as a gardener after her husband's death in 1947, digging up his concrete paths and giving the thyme and daisies their freedom, a process celebrated in her acclaimed 1956 book *We Made a Garden*; Rose Heilbron became a household name as one of the outstanding defence barristers of the era, specialising in high-profile murder trials; even Bethnal Green's Beverley Sisters (Joy, Babs and Teddie) had a certain pink-and-white chutzpah. One determined woman, though, remained thwarted for most of the decade. In late 1954, having twice fought unwinnable seats in nearby Dartford, Margaret Thatcher sought to secure the Tory nomination for the eminently winnable Orpington. She failed – largely, it seems, because leading local Tories believed her candidacy would be incompatible with having two small children. A bitterly disappointed Thatcher wrote to Central Office in early 1955 that accordingly she would abandon 'further thought of a parliamentary career for many years'.[36]

The normative pressures around women and work were considerable. 'No two women have exactly the same capacities and I would never interfere with the right of the minority to prefer outside work,' conceded Evelyn Home, *Woman*'s trusted counsellor for millions of women, in 1951. She went on: 'But it is safe to say that most women, once they have a family, are more contented and doing better work in the home than they could find outside it.' So too that same year *Woman's Weekly*, with graphic running subtitles to a short story about a mother eventually renouncing her hateful work: 'Home-making is the most useful of all the talents. To make a man feel happy and comfortable and to make a child feel cherished. No Woman's Work is more important than these.' Of course, women's magazines knew that many women *did* work, but the prescribed life-pattern they tended to assume and foster was (in the words of Stephanie Spencer) 'school, job, job and marriage, child care and full-time domesticity followed perhaps by later return to part-time (and, rarely, full-time) employment'.

The status of female paid work remained low – no overall equal-pay legislation, average female wages running at only 59 per cent to those of men – and the prevailing assumption was that women worked for 'pin money', not a living wage in its own right. Neither the Labour Party nor the trade unions (both of them very male-dominated) pushed at all hard to increase the status of female work, while as for men in general, Elizabeth Roberts found in her extensive oral history of north-west England an adamantine twofold conviction: that a husband's wages should be higher than his wife's; and that a man should be able to support his family off his own bat. Mass-Observation in 1957 interviewed 644 married men in a nationwide survey, among whom only 23 per cent, with a bias towards the better-off, expressed unqualified approval of married women going out to work. 'A woman's place is in the home,' was the blunt reason given by 79 per cent of those who were against married women having jobs, and a few expanded:

When a woman goes out to work, the home soon falls apart. (*Tin plate worker, 39*)

If the husband brings home a fairly good wage, then the wife should be made to stay at home. The trouble is some women don't know how to handle money and in that way never have enough. (*Coal miner, 43*)

Working women are one of the main causes of child delinquency. (*Engineer, 47*)

If I wanted just a housekeeper I would have got one without having to marry her. Her place is at home with the kids. She gets plenty [ie money] to keep her at home in any case. (*Miner, 44*)

One married woman who had abruptly stopped working some years earlier was the actress Valerie Hobson, on the instructions of her politician husband, John Profumo.[37]

Separate capacities and potential were entrenched from an early age. 'What a pretty doll,' says Janet in a *Janet and John* learn-to-read book. 'One day I will go in a big ship,' says her brother John. Or take Enid

Blyton's *Five Get Into Trouble*: ' "Dick! *I'll* make your bed," cried Anne, shocked to see it made in such a hurried way.' In *The Education of Girls* (1948), John Newsom, Chief Education Officer for Hertfordshire, had set out his views, declaring that 'the future of women's education lies not in attempting to iron out their differences from men, to reduce them to neuters, but to teach girls how to grow into women and to relearn the graces which so many have forgotten in the last thirty years'. To judge by Mary Evans's memoir about attending a girls' grammar school from 1956, the reality was not so far different:

> The responsibilities of the housewife and the mother were given full credit by the staff and 'making a home' was an ideal which was accorded full status by a staff that was largely unmarried. So having a 'working' mother was regarded as slightly peculiar, and rather eccentric . . . When the school debated the issue that 'A Woman's Place is in the Home' the school decided that this was certainly the case.

As for higher education, growing steadily if not yet spectacularly, by 1958 female students still comprised only 24 per cent of the whole university intake, exactly the same as back in 1920. Moreover, studies of women graduates through the twentieth century have shown that by the 1950s they were rejecting the marriage-and-motherhood model far less than previous generations. 'She must avoid both the rocks of aggressive insistence on her status and also the mud-flats of self-deprecation,' reflected Judith Hubback on 'the educated wife of today' at the end of her 1957 survey *Wives Who Went to College*. 'She must be both feminine and masculine, but not lean too far one way or the other.' So much depended on the husband – but 'with his love, his trust and his help she will do great things'.

A few key figures flesh out the bigger picture. Between 1951 and 1957 the proportion of married women in the total female workforce rose appreciably from 43 to 49 per cent. Most of these new jobs for married women were part-time, particularly in manufacturing industry, which was operating at virtually full capacity. Among married women as a whole, those in paid employment rose from 26 per cent in 1951 to 35 per cent by 1961 – still a minority, but significantly less conspicuously (or pejoratively) so.[38]

Whether full-time or part-time, whether for the married or the unmarried, the sort of work realistically available remained on the whole extraordinarily limited. Lulie Shaw, in her case study of a working-class London suburb in the early 1950s, found that 'the range of occupations for the women was even narrower than for the men', with more married women being 'employed in laundry work than in any other single occupation', followed by 'clerical and office work, then domestic work, then packing or assembly jobs in light engineering, food, cosmetics or patent medicine factories'. At Alfred Herbert's (the well-known machine-tool firm in Coventry), a study by Ken Grainger observes, 'none of those women who were recruited and trained as semi-skilled machinists to substitute for scarce (white) male labour – either during the war or in the early 1950s – ever gained skilled status', with Grainger adding that 'a similar group of men could not have been treated in this way without provoking serious unrest in the factory'. The 1950s was also the apogee of the all-female typing pool, including the one in Holborn unfondly recalled by Anne Henderson:

> It was a bit like being at school: there'd be about twelve girls in the pool, all sitting in rows with their typewriter on a desk in front of them. And the supervisor would be sitting in front of you like a schoolteacher would. It was very strict. You couldn't talk to the girl sitting next to you; you couldn't smoke and you couldn't eat. You would go up and collect your work in a folder, take it back to your desk, type it, take it back to the supervisor and then she would check it. If it was no good you'd have to collect it and do your mistakes. If that happened we'd all sort of moan and groan and pull faces. It was very boring work.

And of course, at any sort of elevated level, whether in most professions or in industry or in politics or even in large parts of the welfare state, the presence of a woman still tended to be a rarity.

Inevitably, the marked rise in the number of married women (often with children) deciding to work caused considerable hand-wringing. Take the telling stance of *Picture Post*, which had once campaigned for more and better day nurseries. Now, in January 1956, it ran an article by Venetia Murray called 'The Children of Women Who Work' that not only prominently quoted the Bowlby-following child expert Doctor Ronald MacKeith ('for a mother of a child under five to have to leave her baby is a tragedy that can have disastrous consequences'), but included several typically striking photographs of sad-looking children, including a toddler sitting forlornly behind the bars of a cot, with the emotive caption, 'The Child Whose Home Life, On Many Days Of The Week, Begins At Five-Thirty In The Evening'. Murray highlighted a nursery situated in a Lancashire cotton mill and paid for by the mill itself in order to attract and keep female labour: 'The sight of those desolate baby faces waiting for their mothers at the end of the day was heartbreaking. The sudden blazing delight when she came in, collected him over the counter, hugged him and took him away – this seemed proof enough that Doctor MacKeith is right.' And Murray asked: 'Could you, would you, should you take the chance with your child's future that he might be wrong?'[39]

The other question, though, was what working women themselves actually thought and felt about the whole issue of paid work outside the home. 'Women preferred to have casual, part-time work because that enabled them to put the needs of their children first,' reckons Elizabeth Roberts on the basis of her 1990s oral history of Barrow, Lancaster and Preston. She goes on:

> Working women's perceptions were that whereas it was acceptable – indeed desirable – to earn money on their own account, it was not 'right' to have a job which demanded long hours of work and the taking of responsibilities which would leave them too tired, both physically and emotionally, to care 'properly' for their families. Besides, who was to look after the children? There was inadequate childcare provision; but even had it been better, it is not certain that many women would have used it. It was assumed that children should be cared for within the family. No respondent complained about her low wages – particularly low when compared to those of her husband. Women's wages were regarded as being for 'extras' while men's wages were for essentials.

Her conclusions are broadly consistent with the contemporary evidence. 'The attitude of the married women to work was that they were glad to have the extra money,' noted Lulie Shaw about her working-class London suburb, 'but that they valued almost as much the "company at work" – they appeared to have no interest in work as such.' John Smith in 1955 conducted fieldwork in the Peek Frean biscuit factory in Bermondsey. There he found that 'what most of the women wanted was an opportunity to earn money to raise the standards of living of the family as a whole', and that as long as there was 'a steady flow of work which would enable them to make the best use of their limited hours in the factory', then they were content, especially if it was piecework in 'a really well-organized department'.

Easily the most systematic, representative survey of attitudes was Mass-Observation's in 1957. In it, 73 per cent of married women workers gave 'financial reasons' as their main motive for going out to work, though with the emphasis far less on dire necessity than on upgrading their standard of living, seen by most as making a direct contribution to the quality of their marriage and family life:

> It has made it possible to keep a good standard. (*Teacher*)
> Well, we'd have been very poor sometimes if I had not taken a job. I feel I've been a real help to my man. (*Factory cleaner*)
> We have been able to afford a nicer home because of my work; we can buy all sorts of extras or a holiday. (*Filing clerk*)

Non-financial reasons given for going out to work included 'need of mental stimulus' (13 per cent), 'enjoy it' (7 per cent) and 'need of social stimulus' (6 per cent), with a cinema cleaner's response possibly typical: 'With all the children at school, there is not so much to do at home: it passes the morning.'

M-O also interviewed full-time housewives, of whom 53 per cent said that they would not like a job, with 'no one to look after the children' easily the main reason given (52 per cent), followed by 'health not good enough' and 'husband disapproves' (10 per cent each). Of the other 47 per cent who did want a job, the overwhelming preference was for part-time work; and though 'financial reasons' were predictably top of the list (again, 73 per cent), some of the working-class respondents also expressed other wishes:

I get fed up and morbid spending nearly all day alone; I feel it would keep me younger having a job. (*48, one child*)

I'd enjoy it, I'd have more company and get taken out of myself. (*30, two children*)

It would break the monotony. I'd see more of life and get to know more people. (*35, three children*)

Oh, it would be smashing to get a break. To get away from this lot for an hour or two – it would be like heaven! (*32, nine children*)

A middle-class woman agreed. 'Getting away from the housework and the children just for a short time each day,' said a 30-year-old with two children wistfully. 'Everything is the same day after day. It would be so refreshing to get away.'[40]

Marriage and its accompanying responsibilities – these were things almost everyone had a view about. 'From twenty-six years' experience of truly perfect marriage,' Mrs H. of Nantwich wrote to the *Sunday Pictorial* in February 1954, 'I say the way to keep a man happy and contented is to satisfy his main needs – his love-life, his meals, his home comforts.' Next week Mrs E. C. of Stepney exploded: 'The letter made me mad. Has she ever thought of those wives who go out to work? Why should the husband always be the one to be kept happy? Isn't a woman who has had a healthy, hard day's work entitled to feel tired and not up to sex-life?' Or take the reaction in September 1955 to a recent letter in *Woman's Own* on the issue of whether wives should work, with readers' opinions 'about equally divided under two headings: "Yes, within reason" and "Not in any circumstances" '. Mrs V. Norman of New Malden represented the 'Yes' camp: 'The most cherished addition to our home is our baby son, now growing up a placid, happy little soul. This is partly because I am not a harassed housewife, thanks to my labour-saving devices – none of which we would have been able to afford had I left my job when we were first married.' Mrs J. Parker of Troon headed the opposition. 'The wife comes home from a day at the office, tired and easily upset – and then there's a house to clean and meals to cook,' she wrote. 'In that state, quarrels easily flare up and small misunderstandings seem more serious than they are.' Miss Y. H. of Birmingham agreed: 'If a man cannot support a wife, he doesn't deserve one. I don't mind cooking, sewing and cleaning for him – so long as the place he asks me to do it in isn't too small – but I will *not* go out and work for him, too.'

Inevitably it was a debate shadowed by the question of guilt. 'A whole generation of (mainly middle-class) British mothers was made to feel guilty about "separation anxiety",' Ann Dally declared unforgivingly in 1990 after Bowlby's death. 'Though educated and trained, they stayed at home for many years, some happily but many basically unhappily.' It was not just a new conventional wisdom that married working women had to contend with, but deeply entrenched cultural assumptions, particularly in somewhere like Wales, with an economy dominated by heavy industry and, before the 1960s, only about a quarter of all women of working age being in paid employment, most of them single women. 'If you went out to work they used to say, "Oh well, they can't be doing for the children," and it did used to make you feel very guilty,' recalled Esme Williams, who in the 1950s had started work in a light manufacturing concern near Merthyr Tydfil. 'If you went out to work you didn't think you were a good mother. A mother's place was in the home, you shouldn't go out to work.'

What would be the attitude of the next generation of married women? Eustace Chesser's 1954 survey asked 160 unmarried under-21s, and 324 unmarried between the ages of 21 and 30, in both cases finding that only 10 per cent would want to work after they had married and had children. The following year, replies to a *Woman's Own* questionnaire revealed that, among unmarried young women, more than four-fifths intended to be a full-time homemaker after the birth of their first child, although the great majority envisaged working after marriage but before children. And in 1956 a survey by Joyce Joseph of 600 adolescent girls, attending a range of schools in the home counties and the West Country, found 61 per cent planning to work after marriage, but 50 per cent not anticipating a return to work even after their children were old enough to be left.

The girls were also asked to write autobiographical essays as if looking back at the end of their lives. The issue of work after marriage featured in most of them, though of course in different ways:

I was thrilled to be married but a little anxious as I wanted to keep on with my career. All the people at work thought that I should stay at home, but I was restless and wanted to be out.

I was married and I carried on another year at the library, but as I wanted a family I left.

During the time my children were at primary and grammar school I stayed at home because I considered I was of more use to them and that a mother's place is at home, especially when children are at the secondary school age, because the strain of school work at A level demands smooth running in the house.

My husband had a good job with good pay so there was no need for me to go out to work. I always believed that a woman's place is in the home, unless it is necessary for her to go out to work.

My daughter now got married, but unlike myself continued with her work for quite some time after marriage.

'From the attitudes to work and marriage which emerged in this inquiry,' concluded Joseph, 'most of these girls are not thinking in terms of carrying on in a vocation throughout their married lives, but rather in terms of home-making as their vocation, and full-time or part-time work outside the home as a secondary interest. These girls see their future role primarily as "Mum" . . .' But it could be Mum quite happily without Dad, to judge by a couple of the girls' scenarios:

I was left Alan's money and the house and settled down to an easy life, no work, and no worries to bother with.

I was forty when my husband was killed in a plane crash. I was broken-hearted but it could not be helped. Now I went to a lot more dances, I was hardly home at night.[41]

'You did a lot of visiting to relations,' John Kerridge recalled about his childhood in Wood Green, north London, in the early 1950s. 'But you didn't have a choice. "Sunday afternoon, you're coming with us to see gran," and that was it.' Even though the conventional wisdom by this time was that industrialisation and urbanisation had already gone a long way towards killing off the extended family, there was evidence that it still had some life left in it. 'They dislike the idea of separation from their old home because mother is there and she is the one they still turn to for comfort and companionship,' noted John Barron Mays about young wives in nuclear families in inner-city Liverpool, while across the Pennines in Featherstone, not only did 'a typical housewife see a good deal of her kinsfolk' but there was also, according to Norman Dennis et al in their *Coal Is Our Life* study, a particularly strong, life-long attachment between miners and their mothers, 'visiting them regularly and helping them when they can' as well as 'in this single case' being 'able to speak of love without embarrassment'. So too in Lulie Shaw's working-class London suburb, where two-thirds of her 101 nuclear families lived within easy walking distance of near relatives. 'The grandmothers, especially the maternal grandmother, played an important part in the lives of many of the families,' she added, and in general she found the kinship network operating an extensive system of mutual help.

No observer or sociologist was more preoccupied with the extended family than Michael Young. 'It is quite clear that in our part of London there are very few immediate [ie nuclear] families standing on their own,' he explained in November 1955 to the National Council of Family Casework Agencies about the research in Bethnal Green that he and his colleagues (principally Peter Willmott and Peter Townsend) were doing at the Institute of Community Studies. As a vivid but typical example, he cited a widow in her sixties, living alone save for dog and budgie:

> She is infirm and rarely goes out. A married daughter lives two minutes' walk away with her five children. One grandson does her shopping, another collects and returns the washing which is done by another married daughter living ten minutes' walk away. A young grandson often stays a night with his grandmother. The widow cooks lunch for one of her daughters and two of her grandchildren, and all four sit down together for the meal. The grandchildren do all kinds of odd jobs; they fetch her papers, chop firewood and take the dog out. The second daughter collects the pension every Friday and her mother spends every Sunday in her home. One son keeps a stall in the market, brings vegetables every morning and gives his mother 10s a week. He lives five minutes' walk

away with his wife and child. A second married son lives in Norwich and that is where the widow spends a fortnight's holiday every summer. Fifteen relatives are seen at least once a week, several of them every day.

Crucially, Young went on, 'the Extended Family Welfare Association', as he only half-jokingly called it, benefited *all* generations:

> The extended family, far from giving help merely to old people, is an agency of mutual aid for the exchange of reciprocal services. The wife, for example, has to go out to work to make up the rent money; after they come back from school the children go round to have their tea at Grannie's. The wife is ill in bed; Grannie comes in to do the cooking and look after the home. The wife has to go to the Out-Patients' Department; she leaves her young children with a sister. She runs out of money on a Thursday – she borrows from a brother and pays it back the following night after she has had her housekeeping allowance. For material help, for advice on all sorts of questions and for emotional comfort, she turns to her relatives.

In sum, the extended family was 'a source of aid and comfort' – a source, Young emphasised, that it was time that the framers of social and housing policy belatedly recognised.

Inevitably, and not wholly ignored by Young in his talk, there was potentially a darker side. Selfish, exploitative motives for helping kin, a sense of obligation breeding a festering resentment, the all-powerful grandmother as an oppressive, even malignant figure – all these, along with more positive elements, come out in Elizabeth Roberts's oral history. Moreover, whether for good or ill, the inexorable trend was *away* from the large extended family. Women were having fewer children, and Gorer's detailed evidence revealed that by the early 1950s the break-up of the extended family was already well advanced in the south of England, hastened by dispersal and the motor car, if not yet in the Midlands or the north. In short, the small, nuclear family represented the future – a future predicated on two core relationships: husbands and wives; parents and children.[42]

———

Realism as well as romance determined most choices of spouse. 'In half an hour, it was over,' wrote *Picture Post*'s Brian Dowling in a 1952 account of an East End white wedding. 'The children, till then under everyone's feet, had been awed into cherub-behaviour. There had been no tears, nor any great jubilation. The register was signed. The wedding was a fact.' Natalie Higgins, in her groundbreaking study of working-class marriage in mid-twentieth-century England (based on interviews in the 1990s with people from Birmingham and Hull who had got married in the 1930s and 1950s), argues that 'the qualities women looked for most in potential husbands were commitment to work and to their role as provider', adding that 'respondents often described the men that were to become their husbands with the words "clean," "decent" and "hard-working" and they valued men that were not "pushy" in sexual terms'. Tellingly, Higgins is struck by 'how many women enjoyed dancing above all else before they married, and yet eventually chose as a lifetime partner a man who could not or would not dance, and this included women who met their future husbands at dances'. Her overall thesis is broadly consistent with Eustace Chesser's 1954 survey, showing that for single women it was physical strength rather than good looks that was important in the choice of a future husband, preferably allied to a similar sense of humour. Harder to be sure about are the spousal criteria for men, although Higgins's view is that during the courting process they more consciously fell in love, a love that often included a strong element of sexual attraction. Nevertheless, when Gorer in 1950/51 asked men to nominate the most important qualities a wife should have, relatively few (even among the single men) mentioned beauty or good looks; instead the winning criterion was the thoroughly unromantic 'good housekeeper'. In short, marriage was a contract, a well-understood lifetime arrangement based on mutual interest.

At the heart of that mutual interest was usually a very traditional division of labour: the husband as breadwinner, the wife as homemaker, even if she was in part-time paid work. 'While he is at work she should complete her day's work – washing, ironing, cleaning or whatever it may be – and she must have ready for him a good meal,' explained Norman Dennis et al about the 'very consciously accepted' compact in the Yorkshire mining town of Featherstone. As a fairly standard display of anger if that compact was broken, they cited the husband who 'when presented with "fish and chips" from the nearby shop on returning from work, threw them into the fire', telling her that it was her job to cook a proper meal, not (in his words) 'a kid's supper on the street corner'.

For husbands generally in the 1950s, their side of the deal involved a particular strain, in the context of full employment and plenty of overtime work being readily available for both skilled and unskilled men. 'Some of the men conveyed in their interviews,' notes Higgins, 'almost a compulsion to work to the point of exhaustion, in the process often neglecting their wives and growing families.' She quotes the poignant recollections of 'Joe Dixon', a textile worker in Hull who had married in 1951:

> Didn't 'ave much sex, you know, because I worked and worked, I grafted an' grafted, I did all the overtime, an' I warn't at 'ome much even when I got, when we got the 'ouse, I worked an' worked an' I din't see much of me two sons, 'cos I was allers at work, 'cos I even got a night job, and you'd be amazed the hours I did, 'cos I thought 'well, I've got to make a life fer them, an' this is it, if it kills me I, I will work'.

Higgins plausibly speculates that an influence on the more driven 1950s male interviewees – compared to her more fatalistic 1930s male cohort – may have been 'a new and positive feeling that the images of family homes portrayed at the cinema, on television and in advertisements was not anywhere near as unattainable as they had been for their parents' generation'.[43]

It was most wives, though, who truly knew what long hours meant. In the spring of 1951, a Mass-Observation survey involved 700 working-class housewives in Islington, Wandsworth, Camberwell, West Ham and Hendon for a week keeping daily diaries, which cumulatively revealed that their average weekday was one of at least fifteen hours, with at least half of those housewives spending between three and four hours daily in and around the kitchen. A typical day is exhausting simply to read:

Forenoon	*Afternoon*
Got up; washed	Started to cook lunch
Cooked and ate breakfast	Cleaned hall while lunch cooked
Dressed baby	Lunch
Cleared breakfast	Washed up lunch
Tidied and swept nursery	Ironing
Made children's beds	Brought in washing
Put baby out in pram	Tidied self and baby
Got dressed herself	Fetched boy from school
Made own bed; tidied bedroom	Tea
Tidied bathroom, cleaned basin, polished floor	Wrote letter
	Went to post
Cleaned out grate; tidied living room	Cleared tea
Tidied kitchen; washed up breakfast	Bathed children and put them to bed
Laundry; hung out washing	Washed up tea
Took out rubbish; brought in coal	Cooked supper
Went out to shop	Supper
More laundry	Sat and knitted
	Read evening paper
	Went to bed

'Much of her day,' observed M-O about the housewife generally, 'may be spent in total isolation from adults.'

Three years later, Dr Irene Green, Medical Officer of Health for St Faith's and Aylsham Rural District Council in Norfolk, contrasted in her annual report the shorter hours of the worker, holidays with pay and regular half-days, which had all 'reduced the strain on large sections of the population', with the conditions in which many housewives and mothers still worked. 'The burden of the housewife with young children has been little affected by these changes,' she went on, 'and her hours of service to the family are still as long as ever they were. Everyone needs a day or even a few hours off occasionally and I am shocked to find some mothers never enjoy this luxury and no one seems to think they should.' There had apparently been little change by the spring of 1956 when, exactly five years after its first survey, M-O again investigated 'The Housewife's Day' and again found it was at least 15 hours long. Nevertheless, it did emerge that working-class housewives were now 'spending rather less time on domestic jobs', especially preparation of meals and housework, 'and more on both part-time work and leisure', including watching TV, than had been the case in 1951. Partly this was down to labour-saving devices, above all automatic washing machines, but their spread was still patchy and most homes were not yet temples of white electrical goods. 'The job with the 100-hour week' was how *Picture Post* in March 1956 profiled Anne Driver, a mother of four living in Hunstanton, married to a council worker, and busy through the day and into the night 'cooking, cleaning, scrubbing, window-cleaning, house decorating, washing, ironing, first-aid, nursing, carrying coal, humping laundry, sewing, mending, patching, darning, cleaning sinks and drains, helping neighbours, caring for pets, and polishing'.[44]

Did these homemakers resent their assigned role? There simply does not exist for these years the weight of contemporary evidence to enable a definitive answer, but the probability is that by and large they did not, or at the least, if they did resent it, then they were broadly resigned to it. 'Restricted to the home as they are,' Dennis et al explicitly stated in their Featherstone study, 'wives do not actively resent it. When pressed they will acknowledge jealousy of their husband's freedom, but many of them say that they find satisfaction in the care of their children.' Oral testimony suggests a degree of positive enthusiasm. 'I was mistress in my kitchen and that is how I liked it,' recalled Pamela Woodland, who as a young teacher in Rotherham had married in 1953. 'I did everything. I knew where everything was. My kitchen was like a very, very efficient workshop ... It was my ambition to run the house to the best of my ability.' Similarly, interviewing a range of women about their post-war experiences, the historian Claire Langhamer has found that they 'rarely fail to express pleasure in at least some aspects of their domestic work'. She quotes the working-class 'Jean', who married in 1955: 'I just enjoyed having it nice and putting your nice tea set out and that sort of thing, you know. It was all part of the pleasure ... This home-making thing to me was nice, you know.' Attitudes are never static, and the very fact of an increasing appetite among married women for part-time work was a harbinger of change on the way, but at this specific time – the early to mid-1950s – not only were traditional gender roles still largely set in stone, but the zeitgeist as a whole overwhelmingly enhanced and fortified the self-worth of the homemaker, a self-worth already fortified by the ingenuity and resourcefulness needed to survive the austerity era.

Of course there must have been many moments of discontent, and lives of outright unhappiness, but they surface surprisingly rarely, even in the diaries. Nella Last, however, allowed herself one such moment in June 1954. 'I *did* so hope to get him to see Danny Kaye [in *Knock on Wood*], but had to be content when he agreed to go on the Coast Rd,' she recorded after a Friday outing with her husband. 'I proposed tea at a very good little café, it would only have been 3/6 or 3/9 for the two, but he pointed out, "very little more, & it would be the price of a cwt of coal, & anyway, nothing could be nicer than our own bread, butter, jam & cake." I thought peevishly "except making them always" . . .'[45]

A rigid division of labour inevitably meant a high probability of husband and wife living most of the time in separate spheres. 'The comedian who defined "home" as "the place where you fill the pools in on a Wednesday night" was something of a sociologist,' noted Dennis et al in relation to Featherstone's miners. 'With the exception of a small minority, the husbands for preference come home for a meal after finishing work and as soon as they can feel clean and rested they look for the company of their mates, i.e. their friends of the same sex.' So too in working-class Liverpool, where according to Mays 'male solidarity is a conspicuous feature of social life' and 'men and women tend to segregate the social activities'. Significantly, when Gorer asked the married readers of the *People* to rank factors making for a happy marriage, 'comradeship' and 'shared interests' came well down, at sixth and eighth respectively, while in terms of factors making for an unhappy marriage, 'each going own way' was a lowly twelfth. The ideal, in other words, of a so-called 'companionate marriage', with an emphasis on teamwork, partnership and shared interests, was clearly not universally practised – and indeed, on the basis of her interviews in Preston, Lancaster and Barrow, Elizabeth Roberts bleakly concluded that it had been 'difficult to find many companionate marriages in this study up to 1970'.

Much turned on male attitudes to housework, and here the contemporary sources largely endorse Roberts's assertion that 'women continued to be chiefly responsible', with 'little evidence of a corresponding increase in the amount of work their menfolk did around the house' to match the increasing amount of paid work that their wives did outside the home. In Gorer's survey, 'selfishness' was easily the main fault that wives found in their husbands, though there were also dishonourable mentions for 'taking wife for granted', 'lazy, sleepy, won't help in house' and 'untidiness'. Soon afterwards, in a survey of married women working in the higher grades of the Civil Service, Margot Jefferys found that '1 in every 4 husbands either did not help at all or did so only inconsistently, and only 1 in 5 put in as much as half the hours spent by their wives on domestic tasks'; in 1954, Dr Green in Norfolk noted how 'many husbands seem particularly selfish' in the sense of 'never offering to be child-minders to allow their wives a little relief from this duty'; while in a letter to *Woman's Own* the following year on the question of whether a man could run a house as efficiently as a woman, Mrs M. Titterington of Enfield waxed sarcastic: 'Men manage the home on their own? Oh Yes! manage to dodge most real work. Methodical? Certainly. Their method is to get someone else to cope with the situation.' Or, as Richard Hoggart observed in Hunslet, '. . . many wives come home from work just as tired as their husbands and "set to" to do all the housework without help from them'.[46]

Nevertheless, things were starting to change, especially in the case of younger couples. 'Some working-class husbands will share the washing up if their wives go out to work, or will take turns with the baby if their job releases them early and not too tired,' noted Hoggart. Shaw similarly in her working-class London suburb recorded how a young wife had 'volunteered the information that she and her husband could talk about everything and anything together, she thought that modern girls were not afraid of their husbands, as the older generation had been, and so they could be companions for each other and do things together'. As for the East End, Young and Willmott were pleasantly surprised by 'the new sight of young fathers wheeling prams up Bethnal Green Road on a Saturday morning, taking their little daughters for a row on the lake or playing with their sons on the putting green'. Moreover, the drift outwards of many of these younger couples during the 1950s further encouraged a more companionate marriage. John Mogey in Oxford discovered that a strictly demarcated division of labour between husband and wife was over three times less common on the new Barton estate (off the ring road) than it was in the rundown St Ebbe's district in the city centre. And in Debden, for all its shortcomings in terms of a wider sense of family and kinship, Young and Willmott observed marriages that were much more a 'partnership' than those in Bethnal Green, with the husbands often having given up beer or going to football matches and generally being much more focused, like the wives, on their shared home. Indeed, Elizabeth Bott in her 1957 study *Family and Social Network* argued that what decisively pushed couples towards a more companionate approach was the absence of extended family networks, in effect throwing husband and wife on themselves and their own resources.[47] Given that the outward migration was set to continue, and similarly the decline of the extended family, the era of the companionate marriage was clearly – if still patchily – under way.

Even if it was a partnership, it was not necessarily a partnership of equals. 'She was a big heavy woman, on the short side, but broad and very strong, with a strength of mind even greater than the strength of her body,' was how Adam Faith (born in 1940 as Terry Nelhams), recalling his Acton childhood, described his mother, whereas his coach-driver father, Alf, was 'the kindest, most passive of men', in charge of his life only when behind the wheel. Or when Frank Girling, an anthropologist, spent 18 months in the mid-1950s investigating life on a Scottish housing estate largely occupied by unskilled workers, he found that the women had 'a dominant position in the social life of the area and also in their own homes', regarding 'all male activities with tolerant amusement', and that the men 'lack the self-confidence and assertiveness of their wives'.

Overall, however, the evidence suggests that more often than not it was the husbands who called the shots, perhaps in part because by this time they tended to be several years older than their wives, which had been much less the case before the war. Mays in inner-city Liverpool, for instance, depicted a world in which girls were anxious to get engaged – and thereby raise their status – as soon as possible after leaving school, followed by marriages in which there was 'an acceptance of a male-dominated home', with 'a great amount of deference paid to the husband as wage-earner and as the traditional head of the family'. Many husbands were tyrants. 'My father would bellow, "GET YOUR ELBOWS OFF THE TABLE" at everyone,

including my mother, whose apron had to be spotless at all times,'
recalls Janet Street-Porter about her father at meal times in working-
class Fulham; another compelling memoir, *Silvertown* by Melanie
McGrath, describes the unblinking brutality and exploitiveness of her
grandfather Len Page, running the Cosy Café in the East End; Billie
Whitelaw's autobiography evokes a loveless marriage to an older actor,
Peter Vaughan, increasingly irate as her star rose; and the bullying,
hectoring Labour politician George Brown used his long-suffering
wife Sophie as little more than a doormat who, in their daughter's
words, 'just put up with hell, basically'. Sophie might have secretly
sympathised with Florence Parsons. 'I only did it to please him,' she
explained on 1 January 2000 (her 100th birthday, and 21 years after
her husband's death) about her long years of voting Labour. 'When
he'd gone, I changed to Tory.' Just occasionally, in a world largely run
by men for men, the worm could turn. In the spring of 1955, a Derby
County club-house went not to Stewart Imlach and his wife, who
had been promised it, but instead to a new signing. The manager, Jack
Barker, showed the Imlachs an inferior house and tried to sweet-talk
Mrs Imlach, whereupon she whacked him with her handbag. 'I can't
believe I did that,' she remarked half a century later – and the result, in
a display of marital unity, was an immediate transfer request.[48]

Two especially key areas in the husband/wife balance of power were
money and birth control. From a range of evidence, it seems clear
enough that most male wage-earners reserved part of their wage for
personal spending purposes and then gave the rest to their wives for the
housekeeping, often without revealing how much they had held back.[49]
'Unlike many of my friends,' recalled the Scottish miner Lawrence
Daly rather ruefully, 'I showed my pay slip to my wife and discussed
with her what was I thought a fair share for pocket money. My friends
thought this proved that I was, as they said, a hen-pecked husband. My
wife, on the other hand, saw no virtue in this whatsoever as it was what
she had been brought up [in middle-class Worcestershire] to expect.'
What is also clear is that the division of the weekly wage packet was
usually inequitable. In 1949 a Mass-Observation survey found that only
14 per cent of husbands spent less than 5s on themselves, compared
to 52 per cent of wives; two years later an assessment of why many
married women wanted paid work argued that a principal – perhaps *the*

principal – reason was in order to avoid having to ask their husbands for the money 'for a new dress or hat'; Michael Young in 1952 argued that housekeeping allowances had failed since 1939 to keep up with rising earnings; and soon afterwards, Dennis et al in Featherstone discovered that wives there had virtually no personal spending power. 'They give out the housekeeping money as if it were a gift,' a 54-year-old middle-class wife from Weston-super-Mare complained to Gorer, and others echoed her bitterness:

> Treat their wives as paid housekeepers. Not let his wife know how much money he has. (*Wife, 30, Wigan*)
>
> Meanness or rather hard over money matters. This refers to my husband. (*Working-class wife, 49, Bury St Edmunds*)
>
> Spending too much on cigarettes, betting and the 'local' when the wife needs it more for the home and the children. (*Lower-middle-class wife, 29, Bromley*)
>
> They do not understand high cost of living. They do not go shopping with their wives to find out where money goes to. (*Wife, 30, Birmingham*)
>
> Many men deliberately keep wives short of money on pretence of saving for old age, but nothing makes a woman age quicker than having to scrape and do without when children are young. (*Middle-class woman, 56, Birmingham*)

As for birth control, the pioneering work of Kate Fisher has decisively overturned long-standing assumptions that it was women who cared more about this aspect of marriage and who determined the arrangements. Instead, on the basis of extensive oral histories in Blackburn, Hertfordshire, Oxford and south Wales, she has concluded that not only was 'men's knowledge of birth control more extensive than women's', but that 'men were frequently given ultimate power to determine whether or not birth control would be used, what method was chosen, and the regularity with which it would be employed'. One of her interviews, with 'Larry' (a builder and foreman bricklayer) and his wife 'Doreen', has a particular piquancy. They had married in Blackburn in 1946 – he twenty-nine, she twenty-four – and they had had two sons:

LARRY: We never discussed it.

DOREEN: What?

LARRY: This business of, er, family breeding.

DOREEN: I asked you 'Please could I have, try for another child?' You know that. You kept saying 'No, I don't want a football team.'

LARRY: I said I didn't want a big family.

DOREEN: Well, I didn't get one. You said 'We're just right, we've a two-bedroomed house and we've two boys, it means moving, no.' That's what you said.

LARRY: Well, I thought you were in the same mind.

DOREEN: No, I wanted to try for a girl and you wouldn't say yes.

LARRY: Well, I thought it might've been a boy.

DOREEN: Well, if it had've been, I'd've tried again for a girl.

LARRY: Well, that's why I'd'a – stop . . . that's why I put a stop to it.

DOREEN: Huh! Yeah, he's the bo – . . . he was the boss.

LARRY: Well, I was the boss then.

Unsurprisingly, Larry had also not permitted Doreen to work: 'I felt as though I could keep her.'[50]

Sex itself was the subject of only one systematic survey during the 1950s – Eustace Chesser's *The Sexual, Marital and Family Relationships of the English Woman* (1956), based on questionnaires completed in 1954 by more than 6,000 female informants, located via GPs and with a middle-class bias. The married women were asked about their degree of 'sexual satisfaction in sexual intercourse', to which 43 per cent replied they had 'a lot', 36 per cent 'a fair amount', 16 per cent 'a little' and 5 per cent 'none'. Three other suggestive findings emerged: the higher up the occupational ladder the husband was, the more sexual satisfaction his wife was likely to get (or at least claim to get); among wives not fully enjoying intercourse, the four most common reasons given were 'husband ejaculates too quickly', 'husband does not pet enough before intercourse', 'too frequent intercourse' and 'husband expresses too little tenderness'; and overwhelmingly it was felt by wives that men wanted sex more frequently than women did. Over the years the methodology behind Chesser's survey would be much criticised – Chesser himself, a doctor, wrote prodigiously on sexual matters – but it remains a key source.

Do his findings suggest a broadly satisfied or dissatisfied female population? Much turns on that ambiguous phrase 'a fair amount', but overall it is hard to be sanguine, given other contemporary evidence and subsequent oral testimony. 'Fifty out of every hundred wives still go through their years of married life without discovering that physical satisfaction can, and should, be as real and vivid for them as it is for their husbands,' claimed Dr Helena Wright, on the basis of 'hundreds of talks' with her patients and much correspondence, in her *More About the Sex Factor in Marriage*, a 1947 follow-up book that was in wide circulation all through the 1950s. Or take a matter-of-fact sentence in Shaw's account of family life in a working-class London suburb: 'The impression gained from the remarks volunteered by many of the women in all age groups was that they did not enjoy intercourse, but rather regarded it as a necessary part of married life.' It was probably even worse in Featherstone, where according to Dennis et al 'very few women stated real satisfaction with their sex lives', with the authors noting that for the men there, sex was essentially 'a matter of conquest and achievement'. Nor did the fundamental misalignment necessarily ease with age. The Bethnal Green sociologists did not greatly concern themselves with sex, but Peter Townsend in his study of old people there did record his impression that 'some women had rarely experienced sexual satisfaction and found it difficult to give a husband "his rights" when they became infirm'. The most vivid evidence – perhaps not altogether representative, but surely far from wholly atypical – comes from the recollections of Renee Lester, a Scunthorpe mother of six:

> I wasn't one of the lucky ones. Every night I'd maybe read for a bit and keep my eye ready on the clock for when he came home from the pub. He'd be home around ten to eleven. When I heard footsteps I'd blow the lamp out and pretend to be asleep. He would come home full of beer and start mauling me. I just wanted to sleep and it used to cause no end of trouble if I refused him. You'd get a swipe if you didn't. And sometimes they'd say, 'Oh bugger you if that's the way you feel.' I didn't care if he said that, but mostly they demanded their rights. There was no affection with it, no love, they just wanted sex. It was a duty, a horrible duty to me, I didn't like it. A woman didn't get satisfaction from sex then, she was just disgusted with it, if she was owt like me. And you'd lie there

and you'd be looking at the cracks in the ceiling thinking, 'Oh that crack could do with filling in, that could do with a bit of whitewashing.'

'It was no fun,' she concluded bleakly, 'it was just nasty, dirty and degrading.'[51]

How much did unsatisfactory sex lives matter to those involved? Probably quite a lot, in that among Natalie Higgins's 1950s cohort (much likelier to complain about the subject than the 1930s cohort had been) 'some women expressed disappointment that sex only lasted "two minutes," that their husbands did not act tenderly toward them during sex, or said that they would have liked "a bit more foreplay" ', while 'some men wished that their wives had instigated sex sometimes, or were simply more active during intercourse'. Particularly for women, notwithstanding their underlying pragmatism about marriage, the ubiquitous messages of the era must have made a significant difference, heightening expectations and, all too often, increasing subsequent disappointment. Those messages, of course, were less to do with sex itself than romance and the ideal of the happy, mutually contented, indissoluble union, but it did not take a huge leap of the imagination to picture that ideal as finding its most perfect expression in the bedroom. The cruel gap between aspiration and reality – arguably the master-theme of the 1950s – comes out in the bitter tone of some of the complaints made to Gorer:

> Treating their wives like servants instead of partners, and being very selfish and demanding in sexual matters. (*Lower middle-class wife, 29, Bromley*)
>
> Expect a woman to submit to love-making because it is 'their duty' whether they like it or not. (*Working-class wife, 28, Castleford*)
>
> Excessive sexual demands. A wife should be entitled to say no if she wants to, and not be forced. (*'A typical housewife of the Working Class', 35, Maidenhead*)
>
> Taking wives for granted. Wanting intimacy without much love-making first. Not troubling if wife is sexually satisfied or not. (*Middle-class wife, 33, Hove*)

A.J.P. Taylor famously described the English between roughly 1880 and 1940 as 'a frustrated people' on account of inadequate methods of contraception. Those methods improved significantly after the war – even before the Pill – but the chances are that the frustration, for men as well as women, largely continued.

Yet there is always the danger of 'presentism'. Just because we live in an age of, relatively speaking, more companionate marriages and more reciprocal sexual relationships, we assume that their absence fatally blighted our parents' or grandparents' lives in the 1950s. This rather condescending assumption does not hold up, if Higgins is right in her core argument about marriage in mid-century Britain that so long as both parties to the contract did what they were supposed to do – husband as breadwinner, wife as homemaker – then the marriage was a viable one. 'Neither romantic love nor sexual passion were given a high priority,' she insists, though she adds that 'there was a general wish for companionship and censure for domestic violence'. Geoffrey Gorer, an almost unfailingly perceptive observer, would have agreed with her. Highlighting in his study of the English character 'the great importance for English men and women of the institution of marriage and the seriousness with which they consider it', he went on: 'It is marriage itself which is important, not, I think, love or sexual gratification: a marriage is living together, making a home together, making a life together, and raising children.'[52] The greatest priority was to keep the family show on the road, even if that show involved untold frustrations and resentments, few of which could yet be openly talked about.

It is undeniable that many 1950s parents – especially fathers – could be harsh or authoritarian or remote figures to their children. 'From as young as I can remember we were all regularly beaten, bullied and victimised by our father,' recalled John Davies about his childhood in Machen, south Wales, soon after his younger brother Ron had resigned as Welsh Secretary in 1998:

We would get picked on for something as trivial as playing out in the garden without permission. I can vividly remember my father lining us up in the garden and interrogating us – hitting out with a leather strap he had specially made. He would use violence until one of us gave in to confess, then punish us even more. We would regularly be black and blue at our father's hands. He would fly into a rage at the slightest thing – dinners would end up all over the walls and we'd all get beaten.

Jacqueline Wilson's father, Harry, was not violent, but still inflicted terrible, unpredictable rages on his family. 'When he was in full rant,' she remembered, 'his face would go an ugly red and the veins would stand out on his forehead.' Or take Christine Keeler's stepfather ('Dad') as she grew up in a converted railway carriage at Wraysbury in Berkshire: 'It was always Dad who gave me orders and told me how to help around the house. Mum just carried on waiting on me hand and foot, cooking and serving food, washing and ironing and making the bed. Dad was the law . . . Once I brought a field mouse home. I held it out in my cupped hands, very pleased to have such a warm, living thing to play with. But he took it away from me, threw it on the floor and crushed it with his foot. I remember it squeaking.' In the case of Rosalind Delmar, growing up in Dormanstown, both her parents insisted on no wavering from moral absolutes: he 'believed that might was right and that children should obey paternal discipline without question', whereas her absolutes ranged from 'the right way to cook a pie or scrub a saucepan – "cleanliness is next to godliness" – to iron precepts which told you what to do, say and think', precepts that usually reflected her strong Catholicism. What was so often missing was physical intimacy. 'Ours had been a typical 1950s relationship,' Angela Phillips wrote in 2005 after her father's death. 'We were affectionate and respectful but – I realised as I held his hand that last night – we had barely touched since I was a baby.' And she went on: 'Mine was the Truby King generation. Reared by the book. We slept in our own beds after a good-night kiss and a story. No snuggling into the parental bed, no curling up on a lap and falling asleep in front of the TV. At adolescence even the good-night kiss had to stop. Distance was maintained. Children need to be tough, resilient, independent (in case of another war?) . . .'[53]

Amid all this and much similar testimony, however, it is easy to forget that 1950s parents were, taken as a whole, significantly less old-school than the previous generation of parents. The oral evidence alone is striking: Margaret Williamson, on the basis of interviews in the ironstone mining district of East Cleveland, found post-war fathers appreciably more involved and willing to play with their children than pre-war parents had been; the same applies to the Higgins interviews from Hull and Birmingham; while in the post-war north-west, Roberts reckoned that 'families became much more child-centred', so that 'parents were on the whole closer to their children, less authoritarian than their own parents and less feared'. Among contemporary observers, a particularly informed reading came from Shaw in her working-class London suburb:

> The families in the younger generation showed the prevailing tendency to put the children first, and fathers as well as mothers seemed to be aware that a high standard of child health and upbringing is required today by the health and social services. Both made sacrifices so that their children might have the vitamins, the clothes, and the toys which the 'good parent' is expected to give them. The idea of the 'good parent' which the younger generation seemed to have was in contrast to that of the older; it was not uncommon for a young mother to speak of her father's strictness in her childhood and to add 'but fathers mustn't be like that today, must they?' . . .
>
> Most of the parents in the under-forty group were markedly indulgent and permissive in their handling of their children. The main burden of care necessarily fell on the mothers during the pre-school years, but fathers played with their children when they came in from work, took them out at week-ends, and made toys for them . . .

The overall sense is of parenthood on the cusp of fundamental change by the early to mid-1950s; tellingly, replies to Gorer near the start of the decade revealed that a continuing attachment to the need for discipline in the home was combined with a marked distaste (apart from a smallish minority) for corporal punishment which went beyond a spank or a slap.

This incipient revolution came at a parental price. 'Five out of the sixteen men who were married in the 1950s expressed frustration with the conflicting pressures of their roles of breadwinner and father,' notes Higgins about this time of 'more work than people to do it', and she quotes a Birmingham grocer who had married in 1954: 'I only saw them [ie his children] a short time at night before we put them to bed, when I got 'ome 'cos I mean I used to work at Stechford, an' I lived at 'Andsworth.' This pressure to do something for the kiddies, which in practice usually meant long hours of overtime, was often complemented on the mother's side by a gnawing anxiety about the best way to bring up her children, an anxiety probably exacerbated rather than relieved by the burgeoning advice (including Dr Spock's *Baby and Child Care* from 1955) on the subject. 'The mother of a first baby wanted to know if we disapproved of thumb sucking,' noted Shaw:

> She had been told by the Health Visitor to stop her baby from doing it, but 'the gentleman on the wireless' (in *Woman's Hour*) said that it might do psychological harm to prevent a baby sucking his thumb. One mother of a pre-school child asked for advice about her son's sleep disturbance and fear of cats. She explained that she felt very guilty because she had, once, failed to hear the child crying when he awoke suddenly.

Even the thoroughly well-balanced and mostly cheerful Judy Haines was prone to moments of doubt. 'Ione asked to go and play with sand and in other gardens,' she recorded in 1951. 'I managed to resist this ... The children are welcome to come in but I don't like our girls running wild. I hope I am right. I believe in an organised life for them while young.' Chingford was a very different world from inner-city Liverpool, where a pessimistic John Barron Mays found that 'the degree of supervision and discipline exercised by parents differs enormously between family and family':

> There are still a number of fathers who when roused to anger employ an excessive amount of physical violence. It seems that 'a good hiding' or 'a battering' is the only method they know. The result is that many children genuinely fear their fathers and some mothers deliberately conceal their children's misdemeanours from their husband because they dread excessive punishment. Children are quick, too, in such cases to exploit their mother's sympathy to secure indulgence. It seems clear that training in parenthood is still at a most primitive level and, in so far as discipline goes, men and women either imitate the treatment that was meted out to them as children or react strongly in the opposite direction.[54]

No more than any other decade did the 1950s, with enough problems of its own, have 'the answers' for the problems of the future.

———

So, happy families or not? It is a very real historical difficulty that, happiness only writing white, some of the very best, most compelling memoirs of the era – for instance by Lorna Sage or Carolyn Steedman – record largely dysfunctional families and essentially miserable childhoods. Things become more mixed if one moves down a literary level or two. To pick just a trio from the biography shelves: Adam Faith remembers from Acton 'a very free and easy-going home' in which 'Mum never minded much what we got up to – as long as it didn't bring trouble to the front door'; John Sergeant, son of a clergyman, depicts 'a happy childhood' in the Oxfordshire village of Great Tew ('the village was heaven for children who wanted to build igloos in the winter, to ride bikes in the summer, to chase bullocks in the field, to shoot catapults and on one glorious occasion to try to escape from home altogether'), though he was largely unaware that his parents were incompatible and wholly ignorant that they had made a ten-year agreement to stay together only while the children grew up; and Kenny Everett (real name Maurice Cole) had, according to his sister, a suburban childhood in Liverpool that was 'perhaps too cloistered, too sheltered', but nevertheless was within 'a very close, very loving family'.

Clearly it is impossible to say that any one childhood or family was 'typical', but Ken Blakemore's memoir *Sunnyside Down*, about growing up in the Cheshire village of Bunbury, has a particular – and attractively unassuming – authenticity about it. He was born in 1948 (the day the NHS began), had three much older siblings and seems to have enjoyed his childhood. But for all the memoir's rich, atmospheric period detail, the keenest interest lies in the portrait of his parents. His father (Wilfrid) ran, undynamically and unprofitably, a small workshop servicing motor cars, and generally was a somewhat distant figure who 'lived for coming home, putting his feet up and retreating into another world behind the paper or a historical novel'; his mother (Beryl) 'was basically cheerful, and had an infectious laugh, but there was no mistaking the fact that, as the 1950s went on, eddies of discontent sometimes swirled into her moods'.

Blakemore includes an evocative setpiece of a typical family teatime, circa 1955:

5.30 pm. Mum is getting the evening meal underway. The contents of three misshapen aluminium saucepans are beginning to bubble on a small, grey electric cooker that has one larger solid heating plate, glowing red, and one smaller one. Mum is wearing a 'pinnie' with a faded flower pattern on it, and frowns as the cooker gives her a painful electric shock when she touches one of the knobs. She inserts some lamb chops under the uncertain grill.

5.40 pm. Enter Dad, through the front door. He is carrying a rolled-up *Daily Telegraph* and is whistling, partly to announce his arrival and partly to show that he is pleased to be home. He talks to Mum, running through his day. Each news item is preceded with the phrase 'I see', as in, 'I see there's been another horrific accident at Fourways.' She responds appropriately, but looks distracted as she checks the chops, pokes the potatoes and washes some sprigs of mint under the tap at the sink.

5.55 pm. As the weather forecast for land areas starts on the radio in the kitchen, Dad, on cue, makes his way upstairs to wash.

6.00 pm. The news headlines follow the Greenwich Time Signal on the Home Service, and the radio is switched off. Mum calls me in from the garden. Dad appears, wearing trousers and a short-sleeved shirt, looking pink and scrubbed.

6.05 pm. Everyone is now sitting at the table except Mum, who is serving up each meal on plates in the kitchen. She brings plates through, starting with Dad's first, apologising as she does so for the way she's cooked the food. Each plate has on it a lamb chop, a number of boiled potatoes, peas (picked from the garden) and carrots. 'I don't know if you'll really like these chops,' admits Mum. 'They weren't very good to start with – that Tony's a real twister – but I've burned them a bit as well.' No one responds to these apologetic remarks; we're used to them, and also know that the chops will be delicious.

6.08 pm. We all start eating, except Mum, who hasn't sat down yet nor brought a plate of food for herself. No one comments on this. We know that, about half-way through the first course, she will bring a much smaller, scrappier portion of food into the living room for herself. I have an uneasy feeling, looking back on this, that, like a lot of women in low-income families, Mum was regularly cutting back on her own food so her children and husband could have enough. She would eventually sit down reluctantly and say things like, 'You don't really fancy the food you've cooked yourself. I'm fed up with looking at it.'

6.20 pm. The first course is over. Dad has left two boiled potatoes on his plate, a small gesture to signal that he had been given more than enough and is satisfied – a pointless gesture that annoys Mum.

6.21 pm. Mum, who has hardly touched her food, brings in the second course, which is rhubarb crumble, made with rhubarb from the garden – and Bird's custard. Mum apologises again for the poor quality and the predictability of this pudding idea, and doesn't have any herself. We all enjoy it.

6.30 pm. The males finish their rhubarb crumble. Mum goes out to the kitchen to put the kettle on for tea. Dad says something about the weather. Mum returns with teacups and saucers, a milk jug and a sugar bowl. She goes back out again, to the pantry this time, returning with a brown loaf, butter in a butter dish and a slab of red Cheshire on a plate, with a small cheese knife. Dad gets up and stretches his arms, then stands surveying the garden, swaying gently at anchor. Mum, who has gone out to the kitchen yet again, comes back in with a large metal teapot.

6.35 pm. The atmosphere is suddenly more relaxed. Dad and Mum share a joke, then Dad picks up his cup of tea and the *Daily Telegraph* and wanders through to the front room to read, chewing a Rennie's digestion tablet. We all chat as Mum butters thin slices of bread and we all help ourselves to slivers of moist, red cheese. This is the food Mum likes best. The tea in my cup is strong and brown and has thick Jersey milk in it, with two teaspoonfuls of sugar.

7.00 pm. Mum washes up.

Blakemore adds that generally, in terms of the domestic economy, there were 'two big flies in the ointment' for his mother. The first was the increasingly inadequate housekeeping money. 'Dad left a certain amount of money on top of the bureau in the kitchen, every week. He seemed to assume that Mum would discover it, with a little cry of pleasure and surprise, as she went about her dusting. The actual amount that was needed to cover the cost of the week's groceries, coal and milk was never discussed. On Planet Dad, it seemed that a full catering and fuel supply service could be obtained by leaving a modest amount of cash like this under an old butter dish.' The other problem was boredom. 'She had been left with all the responsibility of what to make for tea, but basically she had gone off the idea.' And Blakemore quotes her remark to him in the 1970s, after Wilfrid had died: 'At last! No more cooking. I can eat what I really like – *sandwiches*!'[55]

PART THREE

10

Less Donnie Lonegan

The winter of 1955–6 was a chilly affair, especially February. The 1st was the coldest day since 1895, and later that month Richard Ingrams arrived in 'incredibly cold and very primitive' Aldershot to begin his National Service. So too, as ever, in Cambridge. 'I wear about five sweaters and wool pants and knee socks and *still* I can't stop my teeth chattering,' Sylvia Plath (there on a Fulbright scholarship) wrote home on the 24th. 'The gas fire eats up the shillings and scalds one side and the other freezes like the other half of the moon.'

Yet it was also the winter that popular music at last began to generate some real heat. Initially down as 'a foxtrot' in the Decca catalogue, '(We're Gonna) Rock Around the Clock' by Bill Haley and his Comets hit the charts on the back of being featured in *Blackboard Jungle*, recalled by Ray Gosling as 'a cheap film about a high school in America where the teenagers beat up the teachers ... a jolly good boo, clap and foot-stamping film'. It entered the Top 20 on 15 October, supplanted Jimmy Young's 'The Man from Laramie' to go number 1 on 12 November, and stayed there for seven further weeks, fending off Mitch Miller's 'Yellow Rose of Texas', the Four Aces' 'Love Is a Many Splendored Thing' and Dickie Valentine's 'Christmas Alphabet', before finally (on 14 January) giving way to Tennessee Ernie Ford's 'Sixteen Tons'. Selling a million copies in the UK – the first record to do so – this achievement effectively marked the advent in Britain of rock 'n' roll. Moreover, hard on the heels of the all-American Haley was an East Ender of Irish ancestry. He was Lonnie Donegan, whose 'Rock Island Line', a Leadbelly song with a hard-driving narrative (sung by George Melly at the Royal Festival Hall in 1951), peaked at number 6 on 11 February and altogether was in the Top 20 for 19 weeks. For the 16-year-old John Ravenscroft (later Peel), growing up in Cheshire, but going to Shrewsbury School, the performance had 'a sense of space and freedom, a kind of take-it-or-leave-it spirit that made everything that had gone before sound overcooked and claustrophobic' when he heard it on a radio request programme, probably either *Housewives' Choice* or *Two-Way Family Favourites*.

'Rock Island Line' almost overnight started a teenage craze – skiffle. The keynote was do-it-yourself. 'The double-bass, a broomstick implanted in a tea-chest, and the washboard plus a few thimbles to extract the obligatory rasping sound from it, could be acquired by rummaging through grandma's (if not mother's) junk room,' fondly recalled a Donegan obituarist. 'For the rest, a simple acoustic guitar (or banjo) could be acquired for a tenner. And no great mastery of that instrument's potential was required. Three chords played in a few different keys enabled many a canny practitioner to strut the stage without his musicianship being called into question.' Over the next year or so, skiffle groups mushroomed around the land, including in Liverpool the Quarrymen with John Lennon on a cheap little mail-order guitar, at first mainly playing at church halls and suchlike. Ravenscroft, meanwhile, began to perfect the role of embattled believer. 'Lolly Dolligan' was his businessman father's invariable wind-up, while at the end of the Easter term his report urged, with owlish schoolmasterly humour, 'less Donnie Lonegan and more of the constructive effort'.[1]

Another popular new phenomenon was also the object of condescension. 'Watched commercial television for the first time,' noted John Fowles in January 1956. After referring to 'the dreadful obsequiousness of the compères and performers' he went on:

> The drinkers in the pub sat in silence, watching, not drinking. Transfixed by the shimmering screen; like the first cavemen to make fire. Agape. And such rubbish . . . Desecration of most sacred themes – death, birth; American voices and manners; and the viewers all sad, bored, when the publican turned the lights on again; a deprivation of opium that forced them to drink again.

There was no doubt which channel viewers preferred if they had the choice: in December 1955, three months into the new television era, 57 per cent told Gallup that ITV was better than BBC whereas only 16 per cent expressed a positive preference for BBC – a humiliating result for the Corporation.

Instead, the pressing problem facing commercial television was building up sufficient critical mass, especially before the Midlands and the North came on stream, which they did in February and May respectively. Accordingly, the sense of crisis in late 1955 and early 1956 was palpable – and the brutality of the solution all too predictable. 'Although prepared to cater for minorities who appreciate more serious programmes,' announced a spokesman not long before Christmas, 'we have decided to put on such programmes outside peak viewing hours. Programmes like the Hallé Orchestra, documentaries and discussion features just aren't popular with the public. As a commercial organisation we have to give the public what it wants.' Unsurprisingly, there ensued considerable controversy about independent television's 'retreat from culture', but ATV's Richard Meyer frankly informed ITA's director-general, Sir Robert Fraser, in February that 'the lot of the pioneer programme contractor is not a very happy one financially and we do feel that we must use every possible endeavour to obtain maximum audiences in the initial stages of the development of the medium so that we can be certain of getting worthwhile sales of advertising space'. Or, as one of Meyer's colleagues rather more crisply told a Birmingham paper shortly before ATV's opening, 'I think the public want good light entertainment and that is what we shall try to give them.'[2]

As usual this winter, the cultural pageant continued. 'It seems that what listeners like about the series is not its breadth or its occasional excitements, but rather its stable continuity and the absence of any harrowing tragedies,' observed *Radio Times*, marking the 2,000th episode on 14 November of *Mrs Dale's Diary*. Later that month, 'few listeners had a good word to say' about a dramatisation of *Lucky Jim*. 'Many were baffled and to others who were not, the play was ugly and vulgar in tone', their dissatisfaction not allayed by 'the sound effect (dustbin lid) used to herald Jim's soliloquies'. Altogether it earned a Reaction Index of 47, 30 less than a recent radio production of J. B. Priestley's *An Inspector Calls*. In December the arrival of *The Woodentops* (joined in their 'little house in the country' by Sam, Mrs Scrubbit and of course Spotty Dog) completed the *Watch with Mother* portfolio, while *The Ladykillers* was in retrospect the last major Ealing comedy, if criticised at the time by the *New Statesman*'s William Whitebait as 'stylish but just a bit of a bore'. The by now ritualised 'Books of the Year' saw a warm mention in *The Times* for Philip Larkin's hitherto ignored new collection *The Less Deceived*, the first in which he revealed his authentic voice, though the reading public as a whole voted for Nicholas Monsarrat's *The Cruel Sea*, Paul Brickhill's *Reach for the Sky* and Alistair MacLean's *HMS Ulysses* as the best they had read in 1955.

There was a short-lived literary storm after Somerset Maugham on Christmas Day had launched a full-scale attack in the *Sunday Times* on the boorishness of Kingsley Amis's young male characters, calling them 'scum' and much else besides, but for the really young in the early part of 1956 the two words invariably on their lips were 'Davy Crockett', as a hit song and an avalanche of merchandise (Davy Crockett buckskin outfits, Davy Crockett bows and arrows, Davy Crockett 'Whistling Pipes of Peace', above all Davy Crockett raccoon-skin hats (ten million sold at 12s 6d each)) relentlessly sharpened appetites for the Disney film *Davy Crockett, King of the Wild Frontier*, to be released in early April – or, as Iona and Peter Opie put it not long afterwards, 'the most ambitious adult-organised assault on the juvenile imagination since before the war'. Elsewhere, the Great Drawing Room of the Arts Council's headquarters in St James's Square was the scene on 9 January of Britain's most uncompromisingly modern concert yet (featuring Harrison Birtwistle as well as Peter Maxwell Davies, and scornfully attacked by the *Daily Mail*), while exactly a month later, at the National Film Theatre, there were long queues for the first Free Cinema showing of documentary shorts, mainly about working-class life (still an unusual subject) and including Lindsay Anderson's *O Dreamland*. A working-class girl made good by this time was Blackpool's 19-year-old Norma Sykes, better known as Sabrina. 'What Sabrina has "got" is no mystery,' declared *Picture Post*'s Robert Muller. 'With her forty-inch bust and very blonde hair, she has become the Teddy Boy's symbol for opulent sex. Incessant Sabrina propaganda had turned Norma Sykes into a national tonic, a seaside postcard brought to life, sex for the unimaginative, inflated into absurdity.' For another blonde, two days after her *cri de froid*, 26 February was a date with destiny, as Sylvia Plath (dressed in red and black, with thick crimson lipstick) met Ted Hughes for the first time, at a noisy, drunken party at the Cambridge Women's Union – an electrifying encounter that ended with blood running down Hughes's bitten cheek. 'This man is terrific . . . He is the best of the best,' was, however, a BBC viewer's reaction to the end on 3 March of the first series of *The Dave King Show*, showcasing a comedian with a relaxed, engaging, mildly subversive style. 'We shall miss him sadly,' said another. 'A great favourite in this house.'[3]

In the immediate wake of the Ruth Ellis case, a Gallup poll had found that only 50 per cent agreed with the death penalty, compared to 37 per cent wanting abolition and 13 per cent don't knows. By November 1955 a major abolitionist campaign was under way, including a mass rally at Central Hall, Westminster, with speeches from Gilbert Harding, J. B. Priestley and Lord Pakenham (the future Lord Longford), though when Kingsley Amis attended a demonstration in Swansea, he was struck by how it comprised largely 'the professions, the middle-class intelligentsia and the young'. Opinion, moreover, was shifting back, with Gallup in late November finding that the abolitionists were down to 25 per cent and then, in early February, to 21 per cent. Even so, a free vote in the Commons on 16 February produced an unexpected majority of 31 for experimental suspension of the death penalty, with most of the 37 Tories who swung the vote having only been elected the previous May. If this was indeed 'the sign of a genuine liberalisation of public opinion', as Richard Crossman hoped after the vote, no one had told Anthony Heap. 'Emotionalism scored its greatest and most deplorable triumph over reason,' he snorted next day, with the '37 Tory idiots' making him especially indignant: 'They ought to be shot.' He need not have worried, because five months later the Lords, spearheaded by Lord Goddard (still Lord Chief Justice), repeated their 1948 action and rejected any form of abolition by 238 to 95.

A nationwide survey undertaken by Mass-Observation in December 1955 fleshes out the bald narrative. This broke down attitudes to the notion of a five-year trial suspension, finding among other things that 34 per cent approved (well over double the 1948 figure in a similar survey); that 48 per cent of men disapproved, compared to 42 per cent of women; that women had been 'particularly influenced towards disapproval of capital punishment by the emotional influence of the case of Ruth Ellis'; that younger people were more inclined to favour a trial suspension; that members of the Church of England and the Church of Scotland were least likely; and that – perhaps surprisingly – differences in social class were 'insignificant'. The vox pop had their usual pungent, M-O flavour:

Oh no, don't please. They'd murder us all. (*LCC female nursery helper, Kentish Town, 46*)

If they've done a murder they should be punished. They should be *tortured.* (*Engine driver's wife, Crewe, 55*)

There was the case of Craig and Bentley. I think the wrong person got the string, and that's what makes me feel the whole system wants changing. (*Parcel packer, Shoreditch, 25*)

You hear about these Teddy boys – we saw some at Blackpool, and one had a razor in his lapel. These teenagers need a firm hand. I know, I've got a daughter, she's a good girl, but we have to pull the rope tight. The things she comes back from the Youth Club and tells me! (*Housewife, married to grocer's assistant, Sheffield, 39*)

I think it was dreadful to hang Ruth Ellis. I was ill all the time the trial was on. I could not believe they could hang her, especially a woman. She loved him and did not mean to kill him, it was done on the spur of the moment. I would stop this horrible death penalty. (*Housewife, married to fitter, Greenock, 40*)

I think Ruth Ellis deserved to swing. Women can be as vicious as men. More so in some cases. (*Cinema odd-job man, Birmingham, 21*)

It seems a bit medieval to hang people. (*Male teacher, Romney Marsh, 23*)

Death penalty should be kept. I don't think they should have done away with the cat. It might have helped to curb these Teddy boys. I think they're too lenient in schools these days. I'm old-fashioned and I believe in the cane. (*Middle-class widow, Chesterfield, 65*)

There'd be a few wives slaughtered lying about. It would be cheaper than divorce. (*Male taxi proprietor, Hereford, 25*)

I just know that if it was someone belonging to me I'd help put the rope on myself. (*Male film coater, Brentwood, 55*)

I am a Catholic, but God forgive me I do believe in a life for a life. To think of the MPs voting for no hanging is absolutely disgraceful. (*Female lavatory attendant, Tottenham, 44*)

There were also a couple of nice linguistic manglings. 'No, I think it had better stay as a detergent,' stated a 47-year-old cashier's wife, while the other was unattributed: 'It's hanging I don't like. They should have elocution, as in America.'[4]

Race and class, meanwhile, continued to provoke deep fault lines.

On 3 January 1956 – exactly two months after the Cabinet had decided, under threat of resignation from the Colonial Secretary, Alan Lennox-Boyd, not to back the Home Secretary, Gwilym Lloyd George, in his wish to introduce legislation to control immigration from the New Commonwealth – the 12-year-old Mike Phillips arrived in London from British Guyana. Living with his parents in the De Beauvoir Town area between Islington and Dalston, at the top of a crowded three-storey Victorian house with a clothing factory in the basement, he slowly adjusted to school life with working-class London boys: bollock-grabbing before the teacher came in, spitting on the ceiling of the bicycle shed, frequent fights, and always the regular, repetitive use of 'words like fuck, piss, shit, cunt, bastard and bloody', which he had never heard before 'used in such a casual and vacuous manner'. He was not especially victimised, as he and the other 'foreign' boys sat apart in a corner of the classroom and were also taught how to box, but outside, 'I'd bump into a man or a woman in the street, or trip over someone's bag, and if it wasn't the first thing they said, it might be the last thing: the inevitable question, "Why don't you go back where you came from?"' The writer Colin MacInnes, picking up on how London was starting to change rapidly with large-scale black immigration, assembled in March 'A Short Guide for Jumbles (to the Life of their Coloured Brethren in England)', whose Q&As included:

What is *a Jumble?* – You are, and I, if we are white. The word's a corruption of 'John Bull', and is used by West Africans of Englishmen in a spirit of tolerant disdain.

Do Africans not like us, then? – Not very much, because our outstanding characteristics of reliability and calm don't touch them, and we lack the spontaneity and sociability they prize.

Is there a colour bar in England? – I've not yet met an African or West Indian who thinks there isn't. The colour of the English bar, they say, is grey. Few of us love them, few of us hate them, but almost everybody wishes they weren't here and shows it by that correct, aloof indifference of which only the English know the secret.

Is it possible for a white man, and a coloured, to be friends? – One hastens to say 'Yes'; but then, remembering the *distant* look that sometimes comes into the opaque brown eyes – that moment when they suddenly depart irrevocably within themselves far off towards a hidden, alien, secretive, quite untouchable horizon – one must ultimately, however reluctantly, answer, 'No.'

The next month, London Transport started to recruit staff from Barbados (and subsequently Trinidad and Jamaica), lending the money for their sea fares and arranging accommodation on their arrival. It was soon axiomatic that the capital would grind to a halt without this imported labour, doing work that the white working class was unwilling to do.

North Oxford's Cutteslowe Walls – erected in the 1930s, 7 feet tall, with a set of revolving iron spikes running the entire length – were not quite as notorious a symbol of continuing social divisions as the Gentlemen versus Players fixture at Lord's, but in early 1956 a sociologist, Peter Collison, surveyed the pleasant, trim, almost entirely middle-class private estate on one side of the Walls and the almost entirely working-class council estate (the Cutteslowe Estate) on the other side. In answer to the question 'Should the Walls Be Taken Down?', 88 per cent on the council side said they should, in comparison with only 29 per cent on the private side, though 58 per cent there did concede that 'a passage through them for pedestrians should be provided' – not unreasonably, given that on the council side convenience of access to the bus stops on Banbury Road was overwhelmingly the main reason for wanting the Walls down. What motivated the private side? The key considerations, according to what residents told Collison, were (in descending order) traffic, social class and property value. He quoted some respondents:

The Walls should never have been there in the first place, but as they have been up for twenty years, and many people on the estate bought their houses on the assumption that there would never be any through traffic, *I* think that they should stay up.

If the Walls are taken down traffic will be diverted and cause child casualties.

After all we are private owners and pay a lot more money, especially with increased rates. And there is a lot of riff-raff on the other side.

At present children on the other side of the Wall fight those from this side. If the Walls were taken down the fighting would be much worse and as a mother I feel strongly about this.

An undertaking was given that the council estate houses should not be built near the private estate and when the Walls are taken down the value of the property will drop.

A lot of folk have bought their property here and I think it [ie removal of the Walls] might devalue it.

On the council side, quite apart from the significant daily inconvenience, there was clear, understandable resentment. 'People over there are no better than we are,' said one. And another: 'People on the private estate would become less toffee-nosed if the walls were removed.'⁵ But for the moment, they stayed put.

Anthony Eden this winter probably felt he had more working-class than middle-class supporters. Just before Christmas, as Harold Macmillan replaced the economically discredited Rab Butler at the Treasury, Mollie Panter-Downes reckoned that 'this looks like a moment of some gravity for the Conservative Party' and identified 'continuing high prices' as a principal cause of its popularity being 'at a low ebb'. Then on 3 January came the hammer blow of the *Daily Telegraph* – solid, reassuring organ of the middling classes, the paper they could trust – turning savagely on Eden and demanding, in what became a famous phrase, 'the smack of firm government'. Soon the middle-class chorus of complaint was becoming incessant. 'Wanted: An English Poujade?' was the stirring headline given by *Picture Post* in late January to a letter from Miss M. Edwards of Holywell, Cheshire, detailing the latest price and purchase-tax rises; '. . . am very worried at the way prices are soaring', lamented Florence Turtle in Wimbledon Park on 1 February; and later that month, a more occasional diarist, Rose Uttin in Wembley, wrote her first entry since 1949 in order to grumble that 'food is so dear it might as well be rationed', not helped of course by '3 weeks of awful weather below freezing every day'.

The same month, a package of anti-inflationary emergency measures (including higher interest rates, tightened hire purchase and reduced subsidies on bread and milk) predictably brought no early increase in the government's popularity, while on the 27th a strong editorial in *The Times* on the plight of the middle class – over-taxed and struggling, especially if on fixed incomes, against the ravages of inflation – prompted a flurry of unburdening letters. Typical was John Lewis of Cradley Rectory, near Malvern, claiming forlornly that 'we creep through each quarter only with extreme care' and calling for 'credit facilities for educational purposes' in order to avoid middle-class children being 'squeezed out of the public schools by financial considerations'. Eden himself had already been castigated by Malcolm Muggeridge in the *New Statesman* as 'Boring for England', but it was politically much more damaging when the *Spectator* in early April ran a full-length attack on 'The Lost Leader', whose 'irremediable faults appear to be an exceptional lack of vision or originality and an excess of vanity'. Later in April came the formation of The Middle Class Alliance, with Henry Price, Tory MP for Lewisham, as founder-chairman. Claiming more than 25,000 members already, and setting out a litany of grievances about the high cost of living and increased taxation, Price told *The Times* that it was 'not a purely selfish, sectional movement', but instead wanted 'to preserve the middle classes for the service of the nation'.[6] The suburbanites were at last getting restless – having been largely taken for granted ever since Lord Salisbury's tactically brilliant creation of so-called 'Villa Toryism' in the late nineteenth century.

The new leader of the Labour Party was indisputably middle-class, though of the upper variety. Attlee's retirement had long been expected, and when he stepped down in December 1955 there was a three-way choice for Labour MPs, with the 49-year-old Hugh Gaitskell in the event trouncing Aneurin Bevan and Herbert Morrison, in effect a generational step-change. 'It would have been better had they chosen Nye Bevan,' complained Harold Nicolson, but a more typical reaction was Henry Fairlie's in the *Spectator*, assessing Gaitskell as 'emotionally and intellectually equipped for the highest political office'. One of his most loyal followers was Roy Jenkins, who in the 1970s, recalling Gaitskell, accepted that 'he was stubborn, rash and could, in a paradoxical way, become too emotionally committed to an over-rational position which, once he had thought it through, he believed must be the final answer'. Jenkins also conceded that Gaitskell was 'only a moderately good judge of people', before going on:

> Yet when these faults are put in the scales and weighed against his qualities they shrivel away. He had purpose and direction, courage and humanity. He was a man for raising the sights of politics. He clashed on great issues. He avoided the petty bitterness of personal jealousy. He could raise banners which men and women were proud to follow and he never perverted his leadership ability. He was informed by sense and humour and by a desire to change the world, not for his own satisfaction but in order that people might more enjoy living in it. He was rarely obsessed, either by politics or himself. He was that very rare phenomenon – a great politician who was also an unusually agreeable man.

But what about Gaitskell's relationship with the electorate? In an editorial the day after his elevation to the leadership, *The Times* reflected that a major challenge ahead was to 'prove his sympathy with people (with their aspirations and their individuality) as well as he has done, sincerely, with the people's cause'.

His replacement as Shadow Chancellor was Harold Wilson, who during the autumn had produced a substantial report on the weaknesses in Labour's political machine – a machine that meant that 'compared with our opponents', he bluntly stated, 'we are still at the penny-farthing stage in a jet-propelled era'. The report, asserted the *New Statesman* at the time, made Wilson 'for the first time, a figure of real political importance', and the magazine speculated that in him Labour 'may have found the manager it has needed so long – young, vigorous, modern-minded and able to see that a party machine must be an inspiration to party workers and not merely the means of disciplining them'. In January, some three weeks after the change of leadership, Gaitskell recorded George Brown bitterly telling him that 'he found it very hard to stomach Harold Wilson, and much preferred Nye', to which Gaitskell reassuringly countered that 'although he [ie Wilson] was a cold fish I thought he knew the need for loyalty' and 'was not really dangerous because he would not have much support if he made trouble'. Wilson himself at this time was on a visit to the Soviet Union, on his return telling the *Daily Mirror* that rapid scientific and technological advance there, together with effective centralised planning, had now convinced him that 'in the next generation Russia's industrial challenge may well dominate the world economic scene'. It was the start, his biographer Ben Pimlott noted, of 'his "modernization" approach to economic policy, with its emphasis on planning and controls'.[7]

It was likewise with the economic challenge from the Soviet Union specifically in mind that Eden, also in January, gave a speech at Bradford asserting that 'the prizes' would in future go to those countries 'with the best systems of education' and pledging that educational resources would be made available to ensure that the demand for 'many more scientists, engineers and technicians' was met. There followed in February a White Paper entitled *Technical Education* that, under the auspices of Sir David Eccles as Minister of Education, outlined a new structure of Colleges of Advanced Technology (CATs) to exist alongside the universities, with, below them, an extensive tier of regional colleges, as well as detailing Russia's lead over the West in the output of engineers and technicians. Yet even if these ambitious plans were to be implemented, there remained a major shortfall at secondary level because of the 'Cinderella' status of technical schools, of which by the late 1950s there were only 267 in England and Wales, compared to 1,252 grammar schools and 5,493 secondary moderns.

More generally, 'declinism' seems – despite the recent advances in material prosperity – to have been well under way by 1955–6. 'Do you remember the post-war joke about the Germans' new secret weapon – hard work?' asked Fyfe Robertson in August 1955 in a typically spirited letter to *Picture Post* warning about the dangers of inflation. 'We thought it a good crack then. But it's not so funny now. The Germans are steadily taking over our markets. They've rebuilt their cities, re-equipped their industries, and achieved a remarkable degree of prosperity in a remarkably short time – *with scarcely any rise in prices.*' And Robertson wondered whether the difference between the two countries was 'simply that too many British people are not giving a fair day's work for a fair day's wage'. Three months later the magazine published an inquiry into why the British shipbuilding industry – still the biggest in the world – was starting to lose out to German shipyards, while about the same time an ambitious, gifted young football writer, Brian Glanville, brought out a book, *Soccer Nemesis*, about the decline of British football. The following February the financial journalist Harold Wincott visited industrialists in the Midlands, where he found them deeply conscious of 'the Germans and the Japanese breathing down your neck the whole time'. Another concerned observer was Aidan Crawley, who soon after leaving ITN in early 1956 made for BBC television a documentary series called *The Edge of Success* about British industry and whether it was using new methods and competing with its European rivals. He was particularly struck, he recalled, by the arthritic state of the declining industries and their lack of responsiveness to fresh challenges. When for instance he asked General Sir Brian Robertson whether the lack of time-keeping equipment accounted for the notorious unpunctuality of British Railways, Robertson accused Crawley of 'bowling him a fast one'. As for the shipbuilding industry, 'almost all shipbuilders refused to take part in any programme', though they eventually permitted the filming of 'the welding of steel plates on to the deck of a ship', which because of demarcation problems proved an 'interminable' process.

Crawley's series neatly dovetailed with another BBC television series, presented by Christopher Mayhew, about the whole question of Britain's 'decline'. Ahead of it, the BBC in the winter of 1955–6 commissioned a survey of 416 adults, of whom 46 per cent reckoned Britain had declined as a world power over the previous half-century, compared to 17 per cent who thought Britain was now more powerful. In terms specifically of Britain's ranking among the world's economies, 28 per cent saw decline (mainly blaming the trade unions) and only 10 per cent saw improvement, with the rest unwilling to venture an opinion. There was also a 'Way of Life' question: here, 39 per cent perceived decline, 23 per cent improvement, with the declinists citing as evidence:

> day-to-day cases of selfishness; attitude of trade unionists to their leaders; the attitudes of children and teenagers; the size of cinema crowds; monopolies in industry; the retaining of emergency powers by Government; use of troops to break strikes; length of military service; the

fact that 'anything different is frowned on'; the way that people 'expect things to be done for them'; overcrowding; traffic chaos.

As for causes of this deteriorating way of life, the most frequently given were '"too much welfare and state care" (which makes people "do less for themselves"); the quantity of mass entertainment readily available; American films and comics; insufficient discipline and training of youth; growth of state controls and red tape'.

Still, amid all this pessimism, one future worldbeater took to the streets on 8 February. Defying the cold snap, RM 1 – London's first Routemaster bus – left Cricklewood Garage that Wednesday morning to ply route 2 (Golders Green–Crystal Palace). Sadly for the history-making passengers, the heating system obstinately refused to work.[8]

———

On Saturday, 24 March there was the usual huge crowd for the Grand National at Aintree, with Lancashire's Chief Constable, Eric St Johnston, having to make sure that the royal party (including the Queen Mother and Princess Margaret) did not run into the Russian party (including the former Premier Georgy Malenkov and Foreign Minister Andrei Gromyko, guests of the Central Electricity Authority). The Queen Mother, in her usual ice blue, had a particular interest, with her horse Devon Loch, ridden by Dick Francis, being strongly backed at 100/7. The *Manchester Guardian* described the race's sensational denouement:

> Devon Loch was five lengths clear of ESB, with Francis already stretching out a hand for his bay leaves. Then the astonishing happened. Devon Loch's hind legs buckled and he went down on his stomach. In what can have been no more than two seconds but it seemed like an age, Francis threw his weight forward and his mount struggled to his feet. Could he still do it? It looked as though he might. The first royal victory in the National since 1900 – only 40 yards away. But down went the hind legs again as ESB rushed past. Francis dismounted, threw down his whip and wept when he heard the applause for his effort.

Over the years there would be many theories why Devon Loch collapsed – a reaction to the huge, excited, cheering noise around him, trying to jump an imaginary fence, cramp, even a Soviet conspiracy. As to the royal response, Harold Nicolson was given the inside dope a few days later when at luncheon he sat between the Queen's Private Secretary and the young Duke of Devonshire. 'The Queen Mother never turned a hair,' he recorded afterwards. '"I must go down," she said, "and comfort those poor people." So down she went, dried the jockey's tears, patted Peter Cazalet [the trainer] on the shoulder and insisted on seeing the stable-lads who were also in tears. "I hope the Russians saw it," said Devonshire. "It was the most perfect display of dignity that I have ever witnessed."'[9]

'The whole press (all over the world) is full of the accounts of Khrushchev's speech (or speeches) attacking Stalin and his memory,' noted Macmillan on 19 March, five days before the National. 'He seems to have accused him of almost every known crime. This amounts to the biggest "volte-face" since the Stalin-Ribbentrop pact in 1939.' It was indeed a momentous development, with reports being leaked of Nikita Khrushchev's 'secret' speech on 25 February at the Twentieth Congress of the Communist Party of the Soviet Union, acknowledging and exposing something of the reality of Stalinism. Among British Communists, the focus inevitably was on the party's Twenty-fourth Congress, to be held in Battersea Town Hall at the end of March. There, it proved too soon for any revisionism. 'Comrade Stalin,' declared the former Communist MP, Willie Gallacher, 'was the steel sprung mattress around which the best comrades gathered,' while the General Secretary, Harry Pollitt, insisted that 'the Soviet Union is and remains the greatest Socialist power in the world', where 'exploitation of man by man has been abolished'.

Such reactions engendered a profound sense of disenchantment on the part of two gifted, charismatic figures. 'It is the biggest Confidence Trick in our Party's history,' Edward (E. P.) Thompson wrote from Halifax on 4 April to a fellow Communist historian, John Saville, in Hull. 'Not one bloody concession as yet to our feelings and integrity; no apology to the rank-and-file, no self-criticism, no apology to the British people, no indication of the points of Marxist theory which now demand revaluation, no admission that our Party has undervalued intellectual and ideological work, no promise of a loosening of inner party democracy ...' The other figure was the Scottish miner (by now workman's safety inspector)

Lawrence Daly, secretary of the 1,200-strong Glencraig miners' branch of the party and justly described by the *Daily Worker* the previous year as 'a self-educated man of immense talents who speaks with fluency and knowledge'. On 29 April, he wrote to the party's headquarters in King Street, Covent Garden, arguing that the British party had to dissolve itself and start again in order to be free to criticise the Soviet Union – a suggestion that in due course brought a stern response from John Gollan (who had just succeeded Pollitt), informing Daly that his proposal involved 'a negation of everything you have tried to do since you joined us 16 years ago as a lad of 15'.[10] For Thompson, for Daly, for many others, it was the start of a painful, ultimately liberating process, in which the 'New Left' was born.

As it happened, Khrushchev, accompanied by the Russian Prime Minister Marshal Bulganin, was visiting Britain during April. It was a visit that made waves even in advance. 'They've arranged that we should have them to tea,' Prince Philip (visiting Coventry for the laying by the Queen of the new Cathedral's foundation stone) told Richard Crossman on 23 March. 'I don't know what the hell we shall give them. I think it's bloody silly. But they think we should give them too much importance if we had them to lunch.' Three days later, at the Free Trade Hall in Manchester, Malcolm Muggeridge (who a quarter of a century earlier had exposed the huge human cost of Stalin's collectivisation programme) told a protest meeting that 'expecting B. and K. to reform their ways as a result of seeing our free way of life is liking asking two professional ladies from the Moulin Rouge to attend Roedean in the hope that they will marry Archdeacons and settle down to a life of quiet respectability'. During the visit itself, running for ten days from 18 April, 'Bulge and Crush', as they were nicknamed by the press, 'somehow assumed', noted James Cameron early on, 'the character of an experienced double-act in a touring vaudeville', and almost the only time they were embarrassed in a public context was when, attending the Oxford Union, banners like 'Joe for Prof' and 'Big Brother is Watching You' were held aloft by students, with 'Poor Old Joe' being sung ironically. The event was televised, and Florence Turtle recorded with glee how 'the Russians did not know what was being sung & waved & cheered!'

But shortly afterwards, on the 23rd, there was a more serious contretemps at the Commons dinner given to them by the Labour

Party. 'Khrushchev made a speech saying that it was Russia alone who defeated Germany,' related Nicolson two days later, once again on the basis of inside knowledge:

> George Brown exclaimed, 'May God forgive you!' Khrushchev broke off and asked the interpreter what he had said. It was translated. Khrushchev then banged the table and said, 'What I say is true!' George Brown is not the mild type of Socialist. He replied, 'We lost almost half a million men while you were Hitler's allies!' *Silence pénible*. At the Speaker's luncheon yesterday George Brown went up with outstretched hand to apologise, but Khrushchev put his hand behind his back and said sharply, '*Niet!*' My [Labour] friend told me that in a long experience of unsuccessful banquets, that will live in his memory as the most acid failure that he has ever witnessed. Apparently the Russians are furious at the undergraduates ragging them at Oxford . . .

There were two other piquant aspects to Labour's ill-fated dinner. 'I will never forget his contemptuous attitude to us,' Crossman recalled about Khrushchev's aggressive, bullying speech, 'his couldn't-care-less suggestion that we should join the Russians because, if not, they would swat us off the face of the earth like a dirty old black beetle.' The other aspect concerned Harold Wilson, who that evening probably met the 24-year-old Marcia Williams (later Lady Falkender) for the first time. She was taking shorthand notes, on behalf of Labour's general secretary, and afterwards Wilson drove her home. 'Something of significance must have happened that night,' subsequently reckoned Joe Haines (Wilson's future press secretary), because 'discussions recalling that evening always made Marcia jumpy, so much so that it became a standing joke among a few of us that if I wanted to induce a panic in her, I would simply send her a postcard with the numbers 23456 on it.'[11]

Bulge and Crush were gone almost a week when on Thursday, 3 May, the Manchester-based Granada launched commercial television for 400,000 homes in Lancashire and Cheshire, with transmissions across the Pennines to follow in the autumn. 'Good entertainment – with a sense of responsibility', was the self-professed motto of its main man, Sidney Bernstein, determined to combine profitability and quality, in the advertisement breaks as well as the programmes themselves.

'You can use Granada advertisements as a trustworthy guide to wise spending,' viewers were reassured at the end of the first night. 'Wise spending eventually saves money . . .' At this point most Mancunians were probably looking ahead to Saturday afternoon and City's chances in the Cup Final, still an entirely BBC preserve. In a compelling encounter, their German goalkeeper Bert Trautmann broke his neck a quarter of an hour from the end, but played on, as Manchester City overcame Birmingham City 3–1 – widely praised courage that was an important moment of Anglo-German reconciliation. Three days later, Tuesday the 8th, saw John Fowles and his wife-to-be Elizabeth fielding laborious questions from a private detective in order to facilitate her divorce ('the profoundest things in life treated so naïf-mechanically'), Christopher Mayhew winding up his TV series about whether the British were in decline ('about the only Socialist who does not infuriate me', noted Turtle), and – the start of a theatrical revolution.

'First Night of "Look Back In Anger" at the Royal Court,' recorded the inevitable, invaluable Anthony Heap:

> The English Stage Company will surely have to find better new clothes than this excruciating first effort by a young actor named John Osborne if its repertory venture is not going to come a serious cropper. What we had inflicted on us tonight was, in fact, not so much a play as one long mortifyingly monotonous monologue by one of the most insidiously and insufferably boring characters it has ever been my misfortune to encounter as a playgoer – a too awfully bitter and so terribly cynical young neurotic with an outsize chip on his shoulder and a pathological hatred of everything and everybody. He begins ranting, railing and raving in the most pretentiously puerile manner as soon as the curtain goes up and, except to make himself equally objectionable by occasionally playing some hideous 'blues' on a trumpet off-stage, never – or hardly ever – lets up to the bitter end. There are, it is true, one or two other characters – the dreary little long-suffering pregnant wife who leaves him for a few months ere mournfully returning after a miscarriage, her tarty little actress friend who 'fills in' for her in the interim and the oafish numbskull who virtually lives with them in their squalid little one room attic flat. But as their only function is to serve as targets for the tiresome tirades of the futile, nauseating, self-pitying boor in question,

they don't help very much. Neither, for that matter, does the acting of Kenneth Haigh (the 'unhappy mixed up Bid'), Alan Bates (the doltish Dobbin), Mary Ure (the woebegone wife) or Helena Hughes (the stand – or rather lay – in), their best though they doubtless do in the unfortunate circumstances.

'Look Back in Anger, indeed!' he concluded. 'What else can one be expected to do after wasting a dollar and an evening on such wearisome rubbish.'[12]

Some reviewers in the next few days agreed with Heap. 'Its total gesture is altogether inadequate,' reckoned *The Times*; '. . . the most putrid bosh', declared the *Evening News*; '. . . self-pitying snivel', asserted Milton Shulman in the *Evening Standard*. Even so, they were far from universally discouraging. The unashamedly middle-brow Cecil Wilson (*Daily Mail*) predicted that Osborne would write 'a brilliant play' once he had 'let a little sunshine into his soul', John Barber (*Daily Express*) conveyed a sense of excitement – 'It is intense, angry, feverish, undisciplined . . . But it is young, young, young . . .' – and Derek Granger (*FT*) identified it as 'a play of extraordinary importance' whose 'influence should go far, far beyond such an eccentric and isolated one-man turn as the controversial "Waiting for Godot" '.[13] Above all, there was the verdict in the *New Statesman* of Cuthbert Worsley, who on the first night had only with difficulty prevented Terence Rattigan from following the example of the West End impresario Binkie Beaumont and walking out. Worsley found the play 'a remarkable piece of writing', called Jimmy Porter a 'Wolverhampton Hamlet', and declared that in his soliloquies 'you can hear the authentic tone of the Nineteen-Fifties, desperate, savage, resentful, and, at times, very funny'. Still, Osborne and his backers were undeniably grateful when the two Sunday heavyweights entered the lists on his side. 'A writer of outstanding promise,' asserted Harold Hobson in the *Sunday Times*, while for Kenneth Tynan in the *Observer* the play was a wonderfully fresh, accurate, life-enhancing portrait of 'post-war youth as it really is' – 'the drift towards anarchy, the instinctive leftishness, the automatic rejection of "official" attitudes, the surrealist sense of humour (Jimmy describes a pansy friend as "a female Emily Brontë"), the casual promiscuity, the sense of lacking a crusade worth fighting for and, underlying all these, the determination that no one who dies shall go unmourned'. Tynan finished with a characteristic encomium: 'I doubt if I could love anyone who did not wish to see *Look Back in Anger*. It is the best young play of its decade.'

So too for Brian Thompson, a grammar-school boy who was now a Cambridge undergraduate. 'Jimmy Porter spoke for our generation: both the anger in his voice and the self-pitying,' he recalled half a century later about going to the first night with his girlfriend. It was a performance given an extra resonance for him by an incident just before the start:

A burly man and his wife who could easily have been Alison's parents [ie in the play] accused us of sitting in their seats. I showed him the stubs and he rolled his head like a maddened bear. He was drunk and so, to a lesser extent, was his wife.

'Don't make yourself ridiculous,' she said, leaning over me. 'Just hop off.'

'I don't think it's us that looks ridiculous.'

'Educated people might say, "It is we",' she corrected icily.

We had the undivided attention of three rows by now.

'We're not shifting.'

'All right, chum,' the man said. 'Okey-dokey. We'll see, shall we?'

The front of house manager was called and we showed the ticket stubs again.

'Bloody man's in our seats,' the theatre-goer insisted. 'Won't budge, impudent little shit.'

We were in his seats but his tickets were for the following evening's performance. He stumbled away, cooed on by that peculiar English disdain that does not have to raise its voice. Then the curtain went up and little by little I saw what I should have said.[14]

11

No Choice

'A bluebook full of whitewash' was how 'at first glance' the report of the Guillebaud Committee – set up by Iain Macleod three years earlier to examine the cost-effectiveness of the NHS – struck *The Times* on its publication in January 1956. 'It advises no major change in the structure or financing of the service, and sees no opportunity for a substantial saving on any part of it or for funding fresh income outside the Budget. It proposes no new charges on users of the service. Indeed, it suggests the eventual dropping of some charges and increased spending in some services.' But the paper conceded that on closer inspection the committee had 'argued their case with considerable thoroughness', in particular demonstrating incontrovertibly that 'the service's share of national resources has dwindled steadily since 1949'. Such an outcome – effectively shooting the fox of the Treasury and the more right-wing Tories – owed much to the committee having turned for expert advice to a young, brilliant, idealistic Cambridge economist, Brian Abel-Smith, reputedly 27th in line for the throne and a committed Labour supporter ever since his hateful time at Haileybury. He proceeded to work closely with Richard Titmuss, joining him at the LSE in 1955, and together they provided the statistical ammunition that underpinned the report. Bevan's baby, still only seven years old, was safe in its present form for the foreseeable future, though the *Spectator* was justifiably scornful of the committee's decision 'not', in Guillebaud's words, 'to visit formally any hospitals or other establishments concerned with the working of the National Health Service'.

There was no doubting the NHS's broad-based popularity. When Gallup asked patients later in 1956 'how they felt about the service',

90 per cent answered favourably and only 3 per cent unfavourably. Moreover, 87 per cent thought that their doctor was doing a 'good' job (and 9 per cent a 'fair' one), while 86 per cent found their doctor's waiting room 'satisfactory'. As for the prescription charge of 1s, some 64 per cent of patients accepted that as fair.[1] Of course, the popularity of the NHS cut both ways. On the one hand, it made it politically unthinkable that any party would seek fundamentally to dismantle it; on the other, people's sense of gratitude – however undemonstrative – for the relatively austere, no-frills NHS they had been given made it easier for governments to continue to run it on a tight fiscal rein. Put more harshly, the very fact that the NHS in the 1950s and for quite a long time thereafter was not on the political front line inevitably encouraged, on the part of this paternalistic monopoly provider, a certain degree of complacency and even mediocrity.

Gallup's question 'Do you feel your doctor is also a friend in whom you can confide or not?' scored a surprisingly high 79 per cent 'Yes', even though – or perhaps in part because – most GPs did not stray too far from the advice of Stephen Taylor, in his 1954 guide to *Good General Practice*, that 'the better the clinician, the less often does he diagnose neurosis'. As for keeping the patient in the loop, Taylor quoted a GP interviewee: 'I make it an absolute rule never, under any circumstances, to tell a patient what his blood pressure reading is. Instead I say "Not bad for your age", or "Quite reasonably satisfactory". Once a patient knows he or she has hypertension, symptoms multiply enormously, and misery grows . . .' What if a patient was dissatisfied with his or her GP? Hard evidence is elusive, but Titmuss noted in 1957 that 'among patients today', following Ministry of Health restrictions imposed in 1950, 'an impression has gained ground that it is impossible or almost impossible to change one's doctor'.

The patient was even more disempowered in hospitals – many of them grim, sometimes dilapidated, often Victorian buildings, with no new hospitals yet built since the war. Outpatient departments tended to be particularly dismal, time-wasting places, as typified by Richard Gordon's 'St Swithin's': 'The queue shifted up the wooden seat as each patient was called inside by the stern-faced nurse at the door: the movement was slow and spasmodic, like the stirrings of a sleepy snake.' Fyfe Robertson in 1954 highlighted the issue. 'Too many patients feel that to too many outpatient doctors they are not *people* at all, but card numbers and diseases,' he observed in the context of recent patient surveys. 'Probably most criticism today concerns outpatient treatment.' Labour's research department did the previous year consider whether it might be possible to end the cattle-like system of block bookings, but concluded limply that although 'it is desirable wherever possible that hospitals should endeavour to operate an appointment system', the problem was 'very difficult'.

For inpatients, not only were there punishingly long hours (the ludicrously early wake-up still sacrosanct), but for child patients the great majority of hospitals did not allow daily visits, with some not allowing visits at all. David Widgery (a future radical East End GP) was a child in the 1950s and had lengthy stays in hospital:

> Among my memories of the kindness of the nurses and the other patients, the presence of doctors seemed occasional and special, arriving in troupes to discuss the progress of one part of your body while you, rather embarrassed, stared at the ceiling, tried not to cry and pretended not to be getting in the way. After they had safely left the ward, patients would confer about what was decided, most importantly whether there was any chance of discharge. The junior nurses would join in the guesswork. I grew to understand that the patient was usually wrong about everything, that once you got your bedpan you would probably be stranded, perched on it for an hour, that the patients had only the dignity, status and rights they could squeeze from the system, and we all remained in ignorance about our progress because it was nobody's job to explain, except the houseman, who was half-asleep anyway. We were not people, we were a 'tib and fib', a 'Charnley', and 'two fractured necks of femurs'.

The ever-alert Titmuss reflected in 1957 how 'autocratic behaviour among hospital staffs, with behind them a long tradition deriving from military discipline, didactic teaching and Poor Law regimentation, is strengthened by the invasion of scientific techniques, by increasing specialization and by the growth of professional solidarities' – and he warned against what he chillingly called 'a danger of a new authoritarianism in medicine'.

Did the British Medical Association (BMA) have anything to say about the treatment of patients? 'Doctors' pay was *the* subject at BMA House,' recalled Paul Vaughan, who in 1955 got a job there in the public relations department. 'It was generally assumed it was what the BMA were there for . . .' Vaughan added that, when Bevan's name came up, it was 'usually pronounced Bev-Anne . . . usually with a sort of grimace'.[2]

Almost half the NHS's beds in the mid-1950s were occupied by the mentally ill, for the most part in large mental hospitals built on the pattern of jails, with the patients living in huge, often locked wards. In a poignant entry by a far from wholly sympathetic diarist, Anthony Heap in October 1955 describes visiting his wife, Marjorie, who for the past seven months had been at Friern (previously known as Colney Hatch) Mental Hospital:

> Grieved to find M not only transferred to another, grimmer, more remote ward on account of getting out of hand in the other one, but in a much worse condition, dopey and more deluded than ever. The insulin and electric shock treatment she's been having only seem to have had a detrimental rather than a beneficial effect on her, and I can't believe that being confined to the prison-like ward with the cell-like bedrooms that I saw her in this afternoon is going to do her any good either.

A few months later, Philip Larkin visited his mother at Carlton Hayes Hospital, near Narborough in Leicestershire, where she was being treated for some form of mental illness or instability. 'Large and dingy as a London terminus,' he told a friend, 'it was filled with the apathetic or moping inmates and their stolid families and in the very centre stood a tea trolley, at which a small queue endlessly waited.' The only thing he could compare it to was 'a German expressionist film', and he added that 'around the walls and corridors lingered the hospital servants (all harmless certifieds) grinning as you passed'. Mercifully, there were some exceptions. 'A place of calm and lightness, set in beautiful gardens maintained by the patients,' was how Ken Worpole half a century later recalled visiting his father in Runwell Hospital, one of the larger Essex asylums. 'It was designed on a parkland-villa system of low-rise buildings, with patients organized into smaller residential groups, and was run with great dedication by medical staff who supported the ideals of the therapeutic community movement.'

Friern, though, was almost certainly more typical, and as Heap suggested, this was still the era of physical methods of treatment, principally threefold: ECT (electroconvulsive treatment), deep insulin therapy (involving risky, even fatal comas) and pre-frontal leucotomy. However, the last two treatments were being increasingly questioned by the mid-1950s, and from about this point the focus moved more to powerful new psychotropic drugs such as chlorpromazine, marketed from 1954 as Largactil. The dramatic emergence of these tranquillisers undoubtedly helped to shift the balance of psychiatric opinion away from institutional care and towards treatment in the community, but the historian Simon Goodwin has emphasised the role of other important 'new initiatives' by the 1950s, such as 'the "open door" policy, the development and use of new physical treatments, and the "de-designation" of some mental hospital beds', all of which 'reflected the increased emphasis being given to the treatment, rather than simple containment, of mentally ill people'. One young psychiatrist, based in the mid-1950s at Glasgow's Gartnavel Royal Mental Hospital, preferred to go his own way. There, Ronald Laing set up the so-called Rumpus Room, in which a dozen particularly unpopular, seriously disturbed patients were removed from the danger and smell of the wards, placed in pleasant surroundings, allowed to wear ordinary clothes and treated by carefully selected nurses as real human beings with real human feelings. This largely successful experiment became the basis for the book he started writing in 1956 – *The Divided Self*.[3]

Elsewhere on the medical front, two diseases in the news in 1956 were polio and lung cancer. 'After much doubt and hesitation,' recorded Heap in March, 'decide to apply to have Frainy [his young son] inoculated with the new anti-polio vaccine, with which the first so many thousand children between the ages of two and nine are, if the parents agree, to be injected this summer.' This was the first year that the vaccine was available, and as yet, quite apart from parental misgivings, there were not sufficient quantities. Accordingly, some 3,000 people (mostly children) contracted polio during the summer's epidemic, though in the year as a whole only 114 died, one of the lower post-war totals up to this point. As for lung cancer and its causal link with smoking, the new Health Minister, Robin Turton, took much the same stance as his predecessor Macleod: a public acceptance that the two were probably linked, but a disinclination either to stop smoking himself or to wage a public-information campaign. Anyway, there was little political will for such a campaign: 'I only hope it won't stop people smoking!' noted Macmillan (suddenly conscious of the Treasury's fiscal needs) of Turton's May statement, while about the same time Rab Butler reflected that the government should not 'assume too lightly the odium of advising the general public on their personal tastes and habits where the evidence of harm which may result is not conclusive'. The issue was raised on *Any Questions?* following Turton's statement, and after the countryman Ralph Wightman had related how he had begun smoking at the age of 11, his fellow-panellist Ted Leather, a Tory MP, told jokes about Churchill's smoking. And not long afterwards, at its annual conference at Brighton, it was only with considerable reluctance, amid vocal protest, that the BMA agreed on a one-day smoking ban during proceedings. Still, Kingsley Amis in Swansea was taking no chances. 'I have taken to using a filter-holder,' he confessed to Larkin later in the year, 'in dear smear dread of l+ng-c+nc+r, and chose the more modest, less ornate type of the two offered. It is the lady's type, I find.'[4]

Inevitably, for all its understandably alluring promise of universalism, not everyone benefited equally from the NHS. Fyfe Robertson asserted in 1954, on the basis of survey evidence, that it had 'made least difference to poorer employed people, and most to women (especially middle-aged) and the old of both sexes', adding that 'the difference has been greatest among the lower-paid middle class'. Provision undeniably varied. Taylor in the early 1950s, researching *Good General Practice*, found that the less effective, lower-grade GPs tended to be in working-class industrial areas, while in purely quantitative terms, the 'obstructionism of the BMA' (in the words of Charles Webster, historian of the NHS) largely blocked attempts to correct regional imbalances in the supply of GPs – imbalances that heavily favoured 'the metropolitan regions and their neighbours'. As for take-up, an official 1955–6 survey of general practice revealed that patient consulting rates were failing to compensate for the well-known class bias in national patterns of mortality and morbidity. The same applied, noted Abel-Smith and Titmuss in their research for Guillebaud, to working-class use of hospital services, which anyway were available very unevenly around the country, with for instance Sheffield Regional Health Board having only nine beds available per thousand population, compared to the South West Metropolitan RHB's fifteen.[5]

What about the elderly, who along with women generally were, according to Robertson, the great beneficiaries? No doubt they did benefit overall, but another NHS historian, Geoffrey Rivett, has drawn on a 1954 national survey of services for the elderly to paint a less sanguine picture: GPs sometimes no longer referring elderly patients because of long waiting lists; hospital accommodation often 'in long rambling draughty buildings far from other hospital services', with in one case 'an outside cast-iron staircase' serving 'one ward on the first floor over a boiler-house and a paint store'; and physicians who either 'did not believe in geriatrics' or were indifferent. Indeed, it seems to have been axiomatic among hospital administrators and health authorities that geriatric patients, being 'chronic', only merited a lower budget, including for food, than acute patients. Altogether, as Abel-Smith and Titmuss concluded in their study, 'by and large the older age groups' were 'currently receiving a lower standard of service than the main body of consumers' and there were 'substantial areas of unmet need among the elderly'. Put another way, a war had been won, a new world was being constructed, and it was not the old who represented the future.

Poverty was an almost taboo word in 1950s Britain, but that – despite the best efforts of the Welfare State – was what sizeable pockets of elderly people still lived in. A quartet from Bethnal Green spoke to Peter Townsend in around 1955:

When we were both working we had £10 a week coming in. If we wanted to buy something for dinner, we went out and got it. Now anything a bit tasty is out. But it's when you're getting on you need it. I'm telling you this in confidence. People think we're comfortable and I wouldn't have them know otherwise. But we're not . . .

I used to have two pints of milk a day, and I said to the milkman, 'I don't like to owe you money,' so after that I'd only have one pint. We used to have eggs for supper, or a kipper, but not now. We have p'rhaps a bit of toast. But we always have dinner. We always have something hot. We had to cut down on everything, I can tell you. He [her husband] doesn't even smoke now. And he doesn't drink. But I like a drink when I can, I don't mind admitting. And he has to put his shilling on the pools . . .

I don't have any breakfast. I mostly have boiled beef when I get meat, and with it I have carrots or parsnips or brussels sprouts and potatoes. Sometimes I make myself a pease pudding . . .

The money goes like anything. It costs me a £1 for my rations. Last Saturday our joint was 7s 6d and it was only a little one, but we spun it out till Monday . . . We can't afford luxuries. I just have a bit of toast for breakfast and a cup of tea. I can't afford eggs . . .

In many such cases, Townsend asked why they had not applied for the still means-tested National Assistance. 'I've never liked to cadge', replied one, another that 'I don't want to tell people all my affairs', a third that 'I'd starve rather than ask for a penny'.[6]

Would they have agreed with Macmillan when in 1955 he privately described the UN Secretary General, Dag Hammarskjöld, as 'suffering from the endemic disease of Scandinavia (esp Sweden) – gutlessness' and hypothesised: 'I suppose after another generation or two of the Welfare State we shall be the same!'? Or with Gilbert Harding when the following year, in his preface to *The Gilbert Harding Question Book* (devised by W. H. Mason, pipe-smoking Senior English Master of Manchester Grammar School), he complained that 'this is an age of moving pictures, gramophone records, radio, television – all for nothing or for so little as to make them not worth having', adding 'that is what I suppose is meant by living in a welfare State'? Perhaps they would, but the problem of poverty as such, and not only among the elderly, was unlikely to disappear overnight. Much of course turned on definitions, but in a retrospective study of a 1953–4 Ministry of Labour national survey of the expenditure and income of nearly 13,000 households, Townsend found that a total of roughly 5.3 million people – including 1.75 million primarily dependent on wages – were in what could reasonably be described as poverty. Even so, a poll in 1956 showing that 49 per cent of mothers neither recognised nor were able to define the term 'welfare state' must have been somewhat disconcerting to those emotionally committed to the welfare state and its founding values.[7] And they might even have speculated that, should a 'New Right' ever take shape and attain critical mass, the popular opposition to it might turn out to be dangerously flaky.

1956 was notable for so many reasons, including in relation to the urban environment. To take a mere ten: the Clean Air Act came on the statute book (four years after the infamous London smog) and, although dealing only with smoke rather than with industrial pollution generally, would among other benefits double Manchester's quota of winter sunshine; the Ideal Home Exhibition featured a Smithsons-designed 'House of the Future', a rectangular, windowless box that was gadget-filled, but without private space; on his father getting a job at the de Havilland factory, the ten-year-old Donovan Leitch (the future folk singer) moved from inner-city Glasgow to Hatfield New Town in Hertfordshire and discovered *rus in urbe*; an office-building boom was under way, especially in London, with Sir Howard Robertson's design for the Shell building on the South Bank being shown at the Royal Academy Summer Exhibition, a design that – according to one appraisal soon after – 'lies heavily on the human spirit, redolent with undertones of 1984'; the new Housing Subsidies Act made it much more advantageous for local authorities to build high-rise, giving three times as much subsidy for a flat in a fifteen-storey block as for a house; the Irish dramatist Brendan Behan visited Leeds and, he told the *New Statesman*, 'saw, with interest as a former slum dweller and building worker, the beautiful flats at Quarry Hill estate', the 1938 showcase of municipal flat-building; that estate's creator and still City Architect for Leeds, R.A.H. Livett, told the *Yorkshire Post* that he no longer believed in rehousing families in flats and that it was 'the speculative builder' who had the right answer, in that 'he builds semi-detached houses because he knows what the people want' – a recantation that came too late to stop the high-rise juggernaut in his city; in Bristol, a rundown but still viable Georgian area, Kingsdown, that was rumoured to be on the condemned list was visited by a young local journalist, Tom Stoppard, who found himself enchanted by 'a glimpse of a quieter contented world' and concluded that 'the traditionalists are right'; John Betjeman spoke ('Let us not write the Victorians off as no good') in protest at the proposed demolition of the City of London's 'impressive, vast and exquisitely detailed' Coal Exchange for the purpose of road-widening; and in Newcastle, an unemployed, one-eyed Welshman, Jimmy Forsyth, acquired an aged Rolleiflex camera and started making a visual record of the Scotswood Road area just as it began to be razed.[8]

In 1956 there were two cities – both with sectarian divisions, both with apparently solid commercial and industrial bases, both larger-than-life – that were particularly on the cusp of fundamental change.

One was Glasgow, the British city with the worst housing problems. There, in varying degrees, the three not mutually exclusive solutions of dispersal beyond the city boundaries, dispersal to just inside the city boundaries and inner-city redevelopment were all being pursued. The Tory government in the 1950s designated only one New Town, and that was Cumbernauld in late 1955, some 13 miles to the north-east and specifically intended for Glasgow overspill. The choice of site owed much to the agricultural lobby's refusal to yield the best land, which in turn resulted in a far from ideal open, hilly setting, susceptible to frequent rain and strong winds. 'I want to see a compact urban area, with higher overall densities than have been adopted in most of the post-war schemes [ie including the existing New Towns], achieved, not by a lowering of standards, but by the use of higher blocks and the omission of much of the so-called "amenity" open space (expensive to maintain and inimical to urbanity),' Hugh Wilson explained soon after his appointment in 1956 as chief architect and planning officer of Britain's 15th New Town. 'We have,' he added, 'an opportunity to design a "cellular" town, the houses within walking distance of the centre,' which itself would be pedestrianised, and he clung tenaciously to the concept of Cumbernauld Hill as the focus for a tight-knit settlement that would not be too alienating for deeply urbanised Glaswegians.

Dispersal to some 4 or 5 miles out was the fate for the 130,000 or so people destined for the four giant peripheral estates, mainly comprising rows of three- and four-storey flats. Pollok to the south-west of the city was more or less completed by the mid-1950s, Drumchapel to the north-west and Castlemilk to the south-east had tenants moving in by 1955, and Easterhouse to the north-east had its first tenants arriving in October 1956. 'The great challenge to the tenants of many of the new Glasgow housing estates is that of remoteness,' asserted the *Glasgow Herald* two months later. 'The men are aware of remoteness from their work; the women of remoteness from shops ... and perhaps also remoteness from relatives and friends to whom they could formerly turn in times of trouble ...' There were other serious problems in what the historian Seán Damer has called these 'windswept canyons', including lack of facilities (especially shops, schools, entertainment and transport) and lack of open spaces. Castlemilk was typical – described by another historian, Charles Johnstone, as 'a high-density residential area where you could not even get a haircut without travelling into the city centre'.

Yet the probability is that at this point the great majority of Castlemilk's new residents were broadly happy to be there, at least to judge by their recollections over thirty years after arriving:

I moved from Bluevale Street in the east end in October 1955. We got to Castlemilk in the dark and there was no light on the stair. We took the furniture up the stairs by the light of a bicycle lamp. We had no gas connected and no light. We couldn't even light a fire because the coal nest was missing! You had to depend on neighbours that day – being kind and giving you hot water and heating up your dinner. But everybody rallied round. You knew your neighbours because we all came together and moved up the same close or round about – so it didn't feel too bad. (*Nan Tierney*)

I QUALIFIED! I had been on the housing list for twelve years. You had to come up to be at the allocation of the new houses. I wanted top flat, 2 up and I got it! I had lived ground floor before in a room and kitchen. We moved into our 3 apartment in Croftfoot Road in March 1956. My husband and family were all delighted. (*Agnes Dickson*)

We moved into our five apartment in Croftfoot Road [in 1956]. We had both a back and front garden for the very first time. I had four children and soon my back door became the meeting place for all the kids. I would make candy and tablet and my husband would have a ball for them to play with. Sitting at the front you would have a blether to folk as they passed. (*Isa Robertson*)

We moved into a flat in Glenacre Drive in 1957. In the old tenement back-courts, everything was divided by railings and there wasn't much light because of the high tenement buildings. Here everything was so bright, clean and green. (*May Martin*)

Thoroughly unhappy were those living in the nearby private housing estates of Croftfoot and Cathcart. 'A complaint was made that following the occupation of houses in Castlemilk numerous depredations have occurred in Croftfoot gardens,' balefully noted the Cathcart Ward Committee in late 1955. 'Flowers have been destroyed and coal stolen. Young children had been hawking papers on Sundays in the avenues . . .'[9]

As for inner-city redevelopment, the first area chosen was the highly symbolic Gorbals, specifically its Hutchesontown part. By 1954 plans were on display by Corporation architects who envisaged its transformation into a series of tower blocks – to the horror of Frederic Osborn. In *Town and Country Planning* that June he not only offered a detailed analysis of why this approach would cost far more than a predominantly low-density solution, with the unhoused to go to overspill, but pleaded with the Corporation to consider 'family living conditions 25, 50, or 100 years ahead'. It was to no avail. 'This time there will be no rubber-stamp semi-detacheds,' declared a local journalist, Alastair Borthwick, in his 'Scottish Diary' for the *News Chronicle*. 'The ground is too valuable. This time they will have to build upwards, monumentally. Also, the slate will be clean. The man who gets the job will be able to compose an entire town within a city.' The following April, the Corporation finally gave its go-ahead. 'In place of drab four-storey tenements in hollow squares,' reported the *Glasgow Herald*, 'there will be well-spaced housing, a striking feature of which will be towering blocks of flats of 10 storeys or more mingled with flats of the more orthodox type up to four storeys, roughly in the proportion of 50 per cent of the multi-storey type.' Some accompanying figures took the eye: of the 26,860 people living in the area, only 10,179 would be rehoused there; the existing 444 shops would be replaced by four shopping centres containing a total of 57 shops; and 48 pubs would be reduced to nine.

Did the old Gorbals really have to go? 'The broad streets, flanked with their uncompromising cliffs of classical tenements diminishing into the distance, have an air of dilapidated, littered grandeur . . . a sort of stricken elegance,' wrote a visitor while it still stood. But of course, behind that faded grandeur lay many years of landlord neglect-cum-exploitation and some harsh facts: acute overcrowding (87 per cent of Hutchesontown's flats having only one or two rooms), few facilities (only 3 per cent having baths and only 22 per cent internal

WCs) and many utterly squalid back courts, often used by small firms for such occupations as grease-manufacturing and fish-curing. In short, large-scale tenement refurbishment would have taken a long time and cost a lot of money – and the mood of the moment, as faithfully recorded by Borthwick, was for something altogether new and different. That at least was the Corporation's mood, because we simply do not know about the wishes of the residents, who as usual were not properly consulted. What we do know, from a survey conducted later in 1956 by Glasgow University's Tom Brennan, is that some 60 per cent wanted to stay in the immediate area – a wish that, under whatever form of redevelopment, was unlikely to be fulfilled.[10]

The other city on the cusp of change was Liverpool. There, 1956 saw both the closure of the Overhead Railway (known locally as the docker's umbrella) and the official opening in June of the ten-storey Cresswell Mount, dominating the Everton scene and the city's first multi-storey dwelling block. 'We thought deeply about whether it was going to be something that would meet our needs,' explained Alderman David Nickson, chairman of the Housing Committee, about the whole question of going vertical. 'As we can see today, it has proved itself very successful – something of which we can be proud.'

If Cresswell Mount represented the future, Crown Street stood for what was poised to become the past. Abercromby ward lay to its west, Smithdown and Low Hill wards to its east, and together they constituted the inner-city, largely rundown 'Crown Street area' that sociologists from nearby Liverpool University (with John Barron Mays to the fore) sought to investigate earlier in 1956. A mixture of crumbling Georgian mansions and quietly decaying nineteenth-century terraced streets, this predominantly working-class (mainly unskilled) area comprised 'slum' property already destined for clearance and 'twilight' property that might or might not survive. It emerged from the survey that 36 per cent did not want to leave their present dwelling, that 25 per cent did want to change residence, but still stay within the locality, and that 39 per cent, fewer than two-fifths, wanted to move elsewhere. In terms of where they might move to, whether voluntarily or otherwise, there was particularly little desire to move to Kirkby, a huge new council estate on the outskirts of Liverpool that already had a population approaching forty thousand, almost entirely overspill from Liverpool's slums and for whom the City Architect, Ronald Bradbury, had pioneered the ten-storey blocks later used on Everton Hill. Back in 1952, soon after the start of the Kirkby development, Barbara Castle had told the local Labour Party, 'This is your chance to build a new Jerusalem.' But four years on the message was yet to reach Crown Street.[11]

Public housing was now – and would remain for the next decade or more – essentially numbers-driven, but to dip into the original reports of Mays and his colleagues is to be forcibly reminded of the primacy and variousness of individuals, with all their individual wants and circumstances:

> Old woman bed-ridden – very happy – delightful relationship with grand-daughter. Pleasant, clean atmosphere. Has lived in the house since 1917. Doesn't think the neighbourhood is anything like it used to be. The old neighbours have gone. 'We haven't got the same class of people. Don't run away with the idea that I think I'm it – but in the old days the children out on a Sunday were real well put on. Many a time I've kept our kids in because they weren't nice enough for Sunday. (*75-year-old widow, living with two daughters (tailoress and barmaid) and one grand-daughter*)
>
> House is reached by steep and narrow stairs, quite unsuitable for old people. Coal has to be carried up, and rubbish down. As there is no backyard they cannot have a dustbin, so must dispose of rubbish as best they may, mainly on the living room fire. Cooking by coal range, no bathroom or hot water supply. Most courteous and informative. (*65-year old watchman in children's playground, living with wife and niece*)
>
> Very distressed at living next door to pub – which has, in her opinion, got out of hand since a woman licensee took over. 'It's got my nerves to pieces. There was a thing in the *Express* "Why don't they have singing in Liverpool pubs?" – believe me they do!' (*51-year-old cleaner, living with husband (warehouse porter) and two children*)
>
> House old, damp, cramped, unhealthy and inconvenient, would like to move to an outlying estate. Cramped, untidy living room, unpleasant

smell, which respondent voluntarily explained as due to the fact that the outside toilet leaks into the back kitchen. House infected by cockroaches. Corporation have been approached about this, but will charge £1 for disinfectation, and neither landlord nor tenant will pay. (*24-year-old housewife, living with husband (deliverer for wholesale newsagent) and three young relatives*)

A well cared for, clean, tidy & well furnished house; wireless, T.V., thermostatic iron, children well-dressed, clean & tidy. General feeling of comfort & well-being, distressed at having to live in relatively mean surroundings. (*29-year-old housewife, living with husband (plumber) and two small children*)

Horrifying visit. Mrs—— could only be described as a mound of decaying flesh. She was too vast to be able to move about – she was partially blind & partially deaf. Her face was covered with sores. The smell was inconceivable, although her room was reasonably clean & tidy & had recently been redecorated. She said her neighbours were very kind & always called in when passing to see if she wanted anything. (*65-year-old widow*)

'Anywhere to get out of this area.' Poor living conditions. There is no bath; water-supply from a tap in the yard; no back-kitchen – they cook in the bottom room; no sink. As they're at the end of the row of houses, their water supply is poor, and all the dirt in the waste water clogs in their drain, & he has to get it out. Nevertheless, a very cheery young couple, who made me feel at home and were very friendly indeed. Can 'pop in' at any time. (*31-year-old builder's labourer living with wife and four young children*)

One interview was with a 28-year-old husband (a labourer at Threlfall Brewery), his 24-year-old wife (a press hand at Meccano) and her brother, a policeman, who happened to be there. The siblings did most of the talking. 'They were very concerned about the state of England – what had happened to all her power? England had in the past done so much for backward countries & now they wanted nothing to do with her.' And: 'How shameful it is that such uneducated people as B & K were heads of state – they hadn't even troubled to learn English – our royal family always took the trouble to learn some of the language of the people they were visiting.' And finally: 'They thought the survey a very good idea & "very good of us to do it"! They thought it very bad that in a free country when the Corporation wanted to pull down houses they merely gave the tenants notice to quit & gave them no choice for their new home.'[12]

12

The Real Razzle-Dazzle

On 19 May 1956, 11 days after the premiere of *Look Back in Anger*, Elvis Presley entered the British charts for the first time with 'Heartbreak Hotel', followed a fortnight later by 'Blue Suede Shoes'. 'Heartbreak Hotel' stayed in the Top 20 for the rest of the summer, but never quite made it to number 1 – unlike such mushy fare as Ronnie Hilton's 'No Other Love' (four weeks), Pat Boone's 'I'll Be Home' (six weeks) and Doris Day's 'Whatever Will Be Will Be (Que Sera Sera)' (five weeks). John Ravenscroft (later Peel) first heard 'Heartbreak Hotel' on *Two-Way Family Favourites* – where Presley was introduced as 'the new American singing sensation' – and the effect on him was 'of a naked extraterrestrial walking through the door and announcing that he/she was going to live with me for the rest of my life'. There was 'something frightening, something lewd, something seriously out of control about "Heartbreak Hotel", and alarmed though I was by Elvis, I knew I wanted more'. So too with Bill Perks (later Wyman), who on leave from National Service bought the record (shellac 78 rpm) and 'played it with the windows to the street open until it wore out'.

The fascination with the singer himself rapidly grew as film clips of his American television appearances occasionally surfaced. 'It was nothing but Elvis Presley, Elvis Presley, Elvis Presley,' remembered John Lennon's Aunt Mimi. 'In the end I said "Elvis Presley's all very well, John, but I don't want him for breakfast, dinner and tea."' The 14-year-old Roger Daltrey, at Acton Grammar School, boldly asked a 30-year-old teacher what he thought of Elvis and got the one-word answer, 'Disgusting'. There was also huge resistance, to rock 'n' roll generally as well as to Elvis, within the popular music establishment, led by *Melody Maker*: first the jazz-loving Steve Race condemned 'the cheap, nasty lyrics on which the Rock and Roll movement thrives', and then Jack Payne (bandleader turned disc jockey) declared of Presley, 'Personally, I don't like his work and nor will, I feel, the vast majority of our listening public.' But as the summer went on, the rock 'n' roll craze became increasingly irresistible, with rock 'n' roll dancing even at the Durham Miners' Gala in July, under the largely tolerant gaze of more elderly onlookers. It was a craze, rapidly taken up by teddy boys, with a strongly sartorial aspect – 'He turns revolt into a style,' wrote Thom Gunn in 1957 in his poem 'Elvis Presley' – while with airplay very limited from the starchy BBC, the mushrooming coffee bars (complete with large, coin-operated American jukeboxes) played a key role in disseminating the new sound. Not all youth succumbed, however. 'In the study I was in [at Shrewsbury School] when rock 'n' roll entered my life,' recalled Peel, 'the records of choice were a recording of Handel's Zadok the Priest from the Coronation of George VI and a recording of the same king's magnificent wartime speech in which he quoted from the poem "A man stood at the gate of the year".'[1]

After Osborne, after Presley, May 1956 still had two further cultural fireworks up its sleeve. 'One of the most remarkable first books I have read for a long time,' declared Cyril Connolly in the *Sunday Times* on the 27th, 'an exhaustive and luminously intelligent study of a representative theme of our time', portentously agreed Philip Toynbee the same day in the *Observer*, and over the next week or so there followed almost unstinting critical praise, as well as instant best-seller status. The philosophical-cum-literary treatise was Colin Wilson's *The Outsider*, the author was 24, and he was widely (if incorrectly) rumoured to have slept nightly on Hampstead Heath while going each day to the British Museum Reading Room to research and write it. There were a couple of cooler assessments – 'a young man has made a desperate attempt to make sense of the conflicting visions of life that have been thrown at him by an immense variety of books', noted the *TLS* on 8 June, while a week later Kingsley Amis in the *Spectator* argued that the best cure for the adolescent, self-obsessed Outsider was 'ordering up another bottle, attending a jam session, or getting introduced to a young lady' – but nothing could stop the phenomenon, one of whose instant effects was to get Ronald Laing writing *The Divided Self*. It was a phenomenon that by July had become part of a broader 'Angry Young Men' phenomenon, essentially a publicity-driven creation that identified the very disparate figures of Osborne, Wilson and Amis as core members, though in fact they were similar only in their lower middle-class origins and robust heterosexuality. There was no place for the 42-year-old Angus Wilson, for whom 1956 was a difficult year: during the spring his play at the Royal Court, *The Mulberry Bush*, was comprehensively overshadowed by Osborne's, while in the early summer his ambitious, Dickensian new novel, *Anglo-Saxon Attitudes*, was widely praised (except by Amis, who called it 'clearly a failure'), but somehow failed to chime with the zeitgeist.[2] Still, even for an AYM the spirit of the times could shift with alarming rapidity.

May's other firework was the first major triumph on home soil for Theatre Workshop, the company based at the Theatre Royal in Stratford (two stops on from Bethnal Green) and the creation of a remarkable working-class, left-wing visionary director, Joan Littlewood. Brendan Behan's *The Quare Fellow*, a prison-yard drama only previously performed in Dublin, had its London debut on the 24th, with no Irishmen in the cast (which included Richard Harris and Brian Murphy), but plenty in the audience, among them several of Behan's old IRA comrades. Reviewing the first night, Brian Inglis noted 'an extraordinary decision to play the Irish national anthem in the middle', with the result that 'one section of the audience stood, wondering whether it ought to be sitting, and another section sat, wondering whether it ought to be standing'. At the end, when the mandatory 'God Save the Queen' was played and most people stood, the IRA contingent remained firmly seated. Behan's unsentimental, bawdy, moving play had a considerable impact and was widely praised (including by Kenneth Tynan), with its abolitionist message having a particular resonance because of the continuing Parliamentary debate about possible suspension of the death penalty. A few weeks later, Behan himself made a famously drunken appearance on *Panorama*, where he was interviewed by Malcolm Muggeridge and managed little more coherent than 'I want a leak', but the publicity did not damage his play, which transferred to the West End in July. 'Just the sort of thing one might expect from the leftist Theatre Workshop to produce' was Anthony Heap's predictable verdict about this 'propaganda play written by some Irish ruffian', though he conceded that Littlewood's production 'makes the utmost of the very raw material on hand'.

Another Irish playwright was entertaining the sticks. *Waiting for Godot* had ended its run at the Criterion in March – 'Couldn't make head or tail of it,' reported Evelyn Waugh to Nancy Mitford after arriving 'rather tight for the second act only' – before in late May embarking on a provincial run, with original cast, that included weeks at Harrow, Cambridge, Bournemouth, Streatham ('where they threw pennies on the stage on the first night', recorded Pozzo, aka Peter Bull, 'but never into the box-office during the week'), Golders Green and Birmingham. Week three of a testing tour that frayed the nerves of all concerned was at Britain's premier seaside resort. Advertised as 'inimitable' and 'priceless', Beckett's play arrived at the Grand Theatre, Blackpool on Monday, 4 June, to find itself up against stiff competition: *The Dave King Show* at the Winter Gardens Pavilion, Albert Modley (supported by Mike and Bernie Winters) starring in *Summer Showboat* at the Palace Theatre, and, twice nightly at the Central Pier, *Let's Have Fun* with Jimmy James, Ken Dodd and Jimmy Clitheroe. It proved to be, reported the local paper, 'one of the stormiest receptions in the theatrical history of Blackpool', as 'a large body of the audience beat a disorganised retreat from the auditorium, others stayed and displaying appalling manners made interjections which must have been audible to those on the stage, and some remained in their seats to enjoy this remarkable play'. It did not help that the audience included a party of OAPs, paying only a shilling each, but far from convinced by the second act that they were getting value for it, and according to Bull's account fewer than 100 altogether of the audience were left at the end, having started at some 700. 'We took one quick curtain,' he added, 'and there were rumours of the police being called out for "our special safety" as it says on some fire curtains.' Houses for the rest of the week were very poor, and by Saturday evening the cast were so desperate to leave town that they agreed on a pause-free performance in order to catch the last London train from Preston – 'oddly enough', recalled Bull, 'the only performance that seemed to go remotely well in Blackpool and, needless to say, we were on the verge of maniacal laughter throughout'.[3]

In the poetry world there were three signal moments this summer: at the Sheldonian in Oxford, W. H. Auden's inaugural lecture as Professor of Poetry – '1¼ hours straight down the middle of the pitch about what poetry was,' noted Lavinia Mynors, and read out 'inexorably in a harsh northcountry voice'; the secret marriage of Sylvia Plath and Ted Hughes in what she called 'the dim little church' of St George the Martyr in Bloomsbury; and the appearance of *New Lines*, a 'Movement' anthology edited by Robert Conquest, and including poems by Larkin and Amis among others, that sought, declared Conquest in his introduction, to be 'empirical in its attitude to all that comes' and to maintain 'a rational structure and comprehensible language', rejecting 'diffuse and sentimental verbiage, or hollow technical pirouettes'. Film of the summer was undoubtedly *Reach for the Sky*, the life story of the disabled war hero Douglas Bader – 'a very moving and stirring picture', according to Heap, made all the better by Kenneth More's 'brilliant underplaying of the character' – while a movie in prospect was the tantalising coupling of Sir Laurence Olivier and Marilyn Monroe in what became *The Prince and the Showgirl*. She arrived at a wet London Airport on 14 July to start filming at Pinewood, and right from the start there was little Anglo-American chemistry. 'SLO is much too remote,' recorded Colin Clark (son of Kenneth, brother of Alan and employed on the set in a lowly role). 'He's going to be her director and that should be a close relationship, but he is quite clearly not in any way concerned with her personally.' Eight days before Monroe's arrival, *Hancock's Half Hour* made its small-screen debut. It was a medium for which 'his infinitely expressive, melted-down features seemed made', recalls an appreciative Simon Callow, and although one member of the BBC's Viewing Panel found the first episode 'senseless bilge from beginning to end', most 'praised it without reservation'. A sense of discontent, the world never quite matching up to his hopes, ran deep in the Hancock persona, and there was no shortage of Tory malcontents this summer, with mass middle-class abstentions almost losing the party a by-election at Tonbridge. 'Those who have shouldered their "personal responsibility" and asserted the "rights of the individual" find themselves worse positioned than those who have bilked the State at every turn,' declared a letter to the *Sunday Times* in its immediate wake, while another writer stated that as a result of the credit squeeze 'the middle class now perceives quite clearly that it is expected to subscribe to total self-extinction'. Modernisation might or might not save the day. On 12 June, Fred Hackett from Newton-le-Willows drove his bulldozer through a hedge in a Lancashire field, marking the start of construction of the Preston Bypass – the first part of what would become the M6. 'A road designed exclusively for the use of motor traffic' was how, next day, the *Manchester Guardian* explained the still novel concept of 'the motorway'.[4]

Through the summer, the Communist drama continued to unfold. On 20 June – ten days after the *Observer* had devoted most of the paper to printing all 26,000 words of Khrushchev's 'secret' speech – Lawrence Daly wrote a long, heartfelt letter (subsequently published in *Tribune*) in which he explained why 'after the most serious, prolonged and painful consideration' he had resigned from the party. Declaring that its 'unquestioning acceptance of the anti-Stalin criticisms' were just 'as reprehensible as was its previous unquestioning acceptance of every aspect of Soviet Policy while Stalin was in power', he went on: 'This attitude of blind loyalty to the Soviet leaders instead of loyalty to Communist principles is the basic error which has led the Communist Party to support and defend (or deny and ignore) the most colossal mistakes and monstrous crimes.' Socialism remained, he insisted, 'the only ultimate answer to the exploitation of man by man', and he described 'the genuine Communist' as 'immeasurably superior' to those people who tolerated such things as 'dictatorship in Spain and elsewhere' or 'the vile racial discrimination practised in South Africa'. Indeed, 'it is the very sincerity of the Communist's burning desire to uplift all the exploited and oppressed that has led them to approve of a heavy price being paid to achieve that end', and although 'that attitude has led to the most terrifying mistakes . . . the motives which inspired it should never be forgotten'.

By contrast, the historians Edward Thompson and John Saville were still within the party when in early July they brought out the first, cyclostyled issue of the *Reasoner*, subtitled *A Journal of Discussion*. The editorial, 'Why We Are Publishing', had a very Thompsonian ring: 'A crisis demands crisis measures. It is now clear to all that the fullest discussion is a necessity.' And: 'We take our stand as Marxists.' Thompson also contributed a piece in which, after proudly asserting that 'our party contains within its ranks many of the best, most self-sacrificing, intelligent, and courageous representatives of the British people', he made a key admission about the consequences of an inward-looking, sectarian culture: 'I am *not* proud of our failure to root ourselves more deeply in British life . . . I am *not* proud of the way in which we have alienated many thousands of the best of the British people by our rigidity and our folly . . .' Some 650 copies were produced, engendering a high degree of positive response from other disenchanted members, and by the end of the summer the two men were coming under serious party pressure not to bring out another issue.[5]

On Saturday, 28 July, the American writer (and chronicler of the Soviet revolution) Edmund Wilson docked at Liverpool. 'Arriving in England is always relaxing,' he reflected. 'In spite of the developments since the last war, the social system is still largely taken for granted, and it is soothing for an American to arrive in a place where everybody accepts his function, along with his social status, and everything operates smoothly – officers on the boat, officials at the customs, conductor on the train, taxi drivers . . .' Not far from Liverpool, at Old Trafford, England were playing Australia with the series still poised. 'A brighter morning and we chanced a day at Westcliff, taking the portable wireless for the Test Match,' noted Judy Haines on the final day, Tuesday the 31st. 'Thought the weather might make the result a draw, but it stayed bright and we won the match! [John Arlott commentating at the last] and therefore retained the Ashes.' Remarkably, the Surrey and England off-spinner Jim Laker had taken a world-record 19 wickets. 'Much jubilation by the men in this office who can talk about nothing else,' recorded Florence Turtle the same day. 'I said it was as bad as when the General Election was on. They said "Surely you realise a test match is far more important." I am afraid many of the English people do think that way!' That evening, Laker made his non-motorway back to London, stopping off at a pub in Lichfield for a beer and sandwich. Because everyone was watching the television, showing highlights of the day's play, no one recognised him.[6]

––––––

'At Longbridge on the outskirts of Birmingham the bus passed one of the motor factories where a big strike started today,' recorded Henry St John on Monday, 23 July 1956, eight days before Laker's triumph, as he travelled from Great Malvern during a touring holiday. 'A lot of men were hanging about (12.25 pm), and some 9 or 10 police, but lights blazed in the building although I saw no one actually working.' A big strike was indeed starting at the Austin plant (part of the British Motor Corporation), and it came at a time when the trade unions were ever more continuously – and controversially – centre-stage.

This new phase had begun the previous autumn, fuelled by inflation running at an unacceptable 3.5 per cent a year and wage increases at 4.5 per cent. First the British Employers' Confederation, then the Federation of British Industries (precursor of the CBI), called on the government to get the unions to exercise wage restraint. The unions themselves were the subject in early 1956 of a lengthy *Sunday Times* 'exposure' of restrictive practices, while Macmillan's credit squeeze in February reinforced middle-class suspicions that they were paying an unfairly heavy price for the irresponsible behaviour of organised labour. Eventually, in March, the government produced its White Paper entitled *The Economic Implication of Full Employment* – 'an undistinguished document, full of platitudes and generalisations', recalled the leading industrial correspondent Geoffrey Goodman of a paper that steered clear of seeking to interfere with the well-established system of free collective bargaining, but did implicitly accept that, as wage claims continued to spiral, the free-market approach could no longer guarantee full employment. The political temperature continued to rise. 'The proletarian peril is back with us again,' noted Tom Burns in early April in the *New Statesman*, citing a recent *Punch* cartoon about how the working class appeared through middle-class eyes: 'Irrational, hostile, nihilistic, getting more and doing less, making each wage increase the preface to a wage demand, refusing to accept the need for higher production, breaking agreements, flouting the law, rejecting elected leaders, enjoying the benefits of full employment and housing subsidies and health services, and threatening the economic system from which the benefits derive.' The same month, on the other side of the fence, the announcement by Standard Motors in Coventry of large-scale redundancies as a result of automation in its tractor factory not only provoked a lengthy strike, but heightened employee anxieties generally, with 'automation' rapidly becoming a bogey word.

At a lunch hosted by Macmillan on 3 May, Lady Violet Bonham Carter sat next to the Treasury's Sir Leslie Rowan, and they agreed that the 'real seat of power' had passed from Parliament to the trade unions, with Rowan 'full of apprehension about the industrial future'. Eden on the 9th personally urged the union leaders to tone down their wage claims, but that evening Woodrow Wyatt (a Labour MP) exposed on *Panorama* the undue influence being exercised by the Communist minority that dominated the Electrical Trades Union, in turn provoking claims of malicious interference in union affairs. 'Well, I feel that this is not only a trades union matter but it is a matter of common political or national interest,' commented Lady Isobel Barnett (of *What's My Line?* fame) on the next *Any Questions?*. 'Call the House of Commons out and I don't really think we'd notice it for quite a long time,' Leicester's former Mayoress added to laughter, 'call the AEU [Amalgamated Engineering Union] out, in even only one section, and at once redundancy becomes obvious in other industries, people are thrown out of work in an ever-increasing spiral, and the consumer, which is you and I, is affected vitally where it hurts most.' On the 25th, Macmillan made a major speech at Newcastle, in effect blaming the unions for inflation and calling on them to behave more responsibly – a speech altogether more measured in tone than the rhetoric of the People's League for the Defence of Freedom, a spiky pressure group formed in June that had the unions squarely in its sights and for a time seriously worried Tory high command about its potential for splitting the right-wing middle-class vote.[7]

It was on this thoroughly combustible scene that Frank Cousins now made his presence felt. 'His commanding physique added to the power of his forceful argument, augmenting an unusual arrogance of manner and style that sometimes made him appear more angry and formidable than he intended,' wrote Goodman (his largely admiring biographer) about his habitual aggression as a rising trade-union official. 'The belligerence was also a reflection of his boundless conviction that *he* was correct, even where he acknowledged that there were, perhaps, some merits in an opposing view.' The union was the Transport and General Workers' Union, Britain's biggest, and the left-wing, 51-year-old Cousins (from a Yorkshire mining background) became its General Secretary in May 1956, after the early death of Arthur Deakin's successor. 'There must be no dubiety as to where we stand as a union,' Cousins had recently written in the T&G's magazine. 'While prices rise wages must rise with them. In other words, wage increases that result from rising output are the workers' share of the extra wealth they are helping to create.' In short: 'We are not prepared that our members should stand still whilst the Government continually hand out largesse to those who are more favourably placed.' Unsurprisingly, the new General Secretary gave a dusty response to Macmillan's Newcastle démarche. 'We are not very impressed by his telling us that if there are no wage increases for twelve months everything will be all right,' he told a union rally next day in Coventry, while soon afterwards, reporting to his executive on the economic situation, he observed that 'hardly a word is directed towards the employing interests and the higher income groups except the customary half-hearted appeal', so that 'once again, apparently, it is the workers who are to stand still while the cost of living continues to rise'. It was a long time since a major union leader had spoken, publicly and personally, in such uncompromisingly strident tones – a cause of consternation to the TUC hierarchy as much as to Tory ministers (with Iain Macleod by now at the Ministry of Labour) and to the middle class at large.

Then came the BMC strike, as witnessed through a bus window by St John. Its cause was the shock announcement in late June that the company was sacking, with immediate effect, 6,000 out of a total workforce of 55,000, with the rest to switch to a three- or four-day working week. Everyone knew that demand for motor cars was in a temporary slough, but this was still completely out of the blue – without warning, without consultation and almost certainly the direct work of the autocratic, bullying chairman, Leonard Lord. 'Of course, one has great sympathy for the workers,' privately reflected Macmillan at the start of July, while Macleod in the Commons carefully distanced himself from the BMC management. Half the redundancies were at Longbridge, whose leading shop steward, Dick Etheridge, scribbled some speaking notes before a meeting on the 7th of Birmingham shop stewards in the motor-car and ancillary industries:

Short time started early JAN
   Since then have met management several times who state redundancy never being discussed
   TYPICAL LORD CONDUCT
   NUMBER SACKED TOO GREAT
   HUMAN TRAGEDIES ARISING

Eventually, in a decision involving 15 unions, but with Cousins to the fore, strike action was called for the 23rd. Results were mixed. Almost half the workforce went on working – involving some roughhouse scenes at Longbridge – but enough disruption was caused for Macleod to get talks started by the end of the month, in due course leading to a full resumption of work on 13 August.

The press, while critical of Lord, was generally unsympathetic to the unions. 'This strike was not only ill-conceived, it was ill-timed,' wrote Fyfe Robertson in *Picture Post* at the start of August, and he was particularly critical of Cousins, who had taken the T&G 'into the first big official strike since the war, only to find that a showdown designed to tighten trade union solidarity has dealt it a grave blow'. Or, as he put it with apparent glee, 'Is Frank Cousins' face red!' In fact, the unions did wrest two significant, unprecedented concessions out of BMC: compensation (though not very much) for the dismissed workers and, crucially, a commitment to consult the unions prior to any further redundancies. 'The thing was that it got our toe in the door over redundancy,' recalled Les Gurl (the equivalent at Morris Motors in Cowley of Etheridge at Austin in Longbridge) with satisfaction in the 1970s. But at the time, he was so disenchanted by the lack of rank-and-file support for the strike (particularly marked at Cowley) that he turned in his shop steward's card and told his 'shop' that he did not want to represent them any more, before then changing his mind. As for the motor industry more generally, the strike's legacy was one of deep, mutual mistrust between employers and employees – a legacy especially damaging at a time when the competition from foreign car manufacturers was becoming increasingly keen, not least in the lucrative European market.[8] Their way, based largely on co-operation, was not on the whole the British way.

What, the Tory government continued to ponder, was to be done about the unions? 'Legislation to make all strikes illegal unless preceded by a secret ballot would be practically impossible to enforce,' Eden privately conceded shortly after the BMC strike. 'You could not fine or imprison large numbers of workers for coming out on strike without having voted to do so.' Macleod agreed, though addressing the party conference in October he gave a different reason why he ruled this out: 'The idea, of course, is that the workers are less militant than their leaders. All I can tell you, speaking frankly, is that this is not my experience, nor is it the experience of any Minister of Labour.' And he added that this view had been the Churchill/Monckton one, so that 'if I am wrong I am in good company'. Arguably, though, it was no longer such a surefire assumption that the rank-and-file was to the left of the leadership – and that, specifically, the advent of Cousins was changing the equation. When the TUC gathered at Brighton in early September, he made a belligerent speech, pouring scorn on Macmillan's offer to come to Brighton to explain government policy ('What does he think it is – a film festival?') and uttered a sentiment that was not quickly forgotten: 'In a period of freedom for all we are part of the all.' It was a speech that alarmed Crossman – 'Mr Cousins is a pretty rough customer and pretty dangerous' – while Macmillan reflected that in electoral terms 'this outburst will frighten and annoy the "middle of the road" characters'. A few weeks later, at the Labour conference in Blackpool, Cousins made a deliberately more restrained speech, welcomed by the Labour leadership, though with Gaitskell noting privately that 'intellectually, it seemed to me to be pretty poor stuff'.

Significantly, despite all that had been going on, the trade unions were still broadly seen, by the population as a whole, as 'a good thing' – by 61 per cent, according to Gallup in August, though that was 6 per cent down on a year earlier. Soon afterwards, a recently elected left-wing Labour MP, Frank Allaun, described a talk he had just given on trade unionism to the sixth form of a grammar school. Most of the questions, he related, had been hostile, and he gave examples:

Do trade unionists who go on strike realise the implications of their actions?
    Was it fair to 'victimise' a man who would not join the union?
    Was it right for trade unionists to send a man to Coventry?
    Should Communists be allowed to infiltrate into unions?

'I don't criticise the boys,' was Allaun's conclusion. 'I blame the newspaper proprietors who deceive them.'[9]

The spendthrift Dockers – Sir Bernard with his yacht and fleet of Daimlers (one of them gold-plated), Lady Norah with her furs and jewels – were seldom out of the popular press in the mid-1950s. But in May 1956, three years after the couple had been excluded from the Royal Enclosure at Ascot, the board of Birmingham Small Arms Company (usually known as BSA, making motorcycles among other things) decided to sack him as chairman and managing director, no longer willing to continue subsidising their lavish lifestyle. Public opinion was split. Most 'working folk', reckoned Fyfe Robertson, saw the Dockers as 'people who do, without making any bones about it, what so many others would if they could', whereas 'probably a majority amongst the middle classes are pretty severe critics'. One of those middle-class critics was Leslie Brown, chief investment manager at the Prudential, BSA's largest shareholder. At a crowded, stormy meeting on 1 August, held in the ballroom of Grosvenor House, Docker tried to get himself reinstated and received noisy support from some of the individual shareholders; but it was Brown (a grammar-school boy from Croydon who had come through the ranks as a trained actuary) who rose above the hubbub, quietly yet firmly explaining why Docker was unacceptable. Institutional investors like the Pru were the rising force in the City – unglamorous, professional, judicious – and Brown's successful repudiation of Docker marked an important symbolic defeat for the freeloading, buccaneering model of capitalism.

Eight days later came a more '1956' event with the opening of the *This Is Tomorrow* exhibition at the Whitechapel Art Gallery. Indeed, J. G. Ballard in 2008 would recall this 'wonderful exhibition' as *the* defining event of the year, especially Richard Hamilton's painting *Just what is it that makes today's homes so different, so appealing?* and an installation by Peter and Alison Smithson imagining what someone would need in order to survive after a nuclear war. 'I thought: here is a fiction for the present day,' reflected Ballard. 'I wasn't interested in the far future, spaceships and all that. Forget it. I was interested in the evolving world, the world of hidden persuaders, of the communications landscape developing, of mass tourism, of the vast conformist suburbs dominated by television – that was a form of science fiction, and it was already here.' At the time, it was the Hamilton collage – also on the exhibition's poster – that stole the show, a pioneering piece of Pop Art shown as part of an eye-catching installation that among other things included a juke-box, an outsize bottle of Guinness and the 16-foot-long Robbie the Robot, previously seen in the film *Forbidden Planet*. Significantly, Ballard further identified the exhibition as the moment that marked the usurping of the respectable avant-garde, embodied by Henry Moore, Barbara Hepworth and Graham Sutherland, all of them 'artists in favour with the Arts Council and the British Council'. The young architect Jim Stirling was also part of the exhibition, in what was supposed to be a collaboration with sculptors, but the experience was sufficiently unsatisfactory to ensure that henceforth he would work with neither artists nor sculptors – thereby 'confirming', according to the cultural historian Martin Harrison, 'a megalomania in architects that has undermined most collaborations of this kind'.[10]

This Is Tomorrow was still showing at the Whitechapel when, in the last week of August, the *Rock Around the Clock* 'riots' began. Jiving in the gangway, ripping up seats, occasional actual or threatened violence – this was the teenage (especially teddy-boy) reaction, night after night, in West London cinemas like the Prince of Wales in Harrow Road and the Gaumont in Shepherd's Bush to the cheaply made 'U' film starring Bill Haley. 'This rhythm is the real razzle-dazzle,' 15-year-old Alfred Harper of Latimer Road told a reporter. 'It gets you, man. I've been here three times this week. And I'm coming again.' A cinema manager was also quoted: 'It's a great rhythm. I've even danced it with the wife in the kitchen. But that's no reason why it should make people into hooligans.' By early September, as the movie began to be released across the country, it was becoming a major controversy. 'A cinema, sir, is a place where people go to enjoy films and not a centre for tribal dancing or the relief of sexual neuroses or inhibitions,' R. D. Cole of Sidcup Road, SE9 wrote to the *News Chronicle*. Sheila and Jennifer Baxter of Sanderstead, Surrey agreed: 'As normal teenagers we are disgusted at repeated reports of the riots following the showing of the film "Rock Around the Clock". Do the film selectors require even further proof that this film should be banned?'

In fact, during the middle weeks of the month, it was banned in many places, including Bristol, Ipswich, all of Gloucestershire, Blackburn, Birmingham, Brighton, Gateshead and Bradford. 'In London, more than a quarter of a million young people find Beethoven as exciting as roll and rock,' proudly declared the ever-mischievous Sir Malcolm Sargent at the Last Night of the Proms, while in a radio discussion a 27-year-old aspiring Liberal politician, Jeremy Thorpe, observed that 'what worries me is that a fourth-rate film with fifth-rate music can pierce the thin shell of civilisation and turn people into wild dervishes'. Undoubtedly the film – where it was shown – did generate some significant law-and-order problems, including a large-scale riot in Manchester after nearly 2,000 youths had blocked a main street, but the fact was that, according to the relevant Home Office file, there were complaints about behaviour at only 25 of the 400 cinemas that showed it. Some of the 375 were probably in Liverpool. 'I went to see *Rock Around the Clock*,' claimed John Lennon subsequently. 'Nobody was singing and nobody was dancing. I was all set to tear up the seats, too, but nobody joined in.'[11]

Also in September, *Panorama* featured a hard-hitting report by Christopher Chataway (recently lured from ITN by the BBC) on the colour bar at British Railways. 'Well, there is a general reluctance by men to work with these coloured chaps,' the goods agent at the Smithfield depot told him, while there was also a revealing exchange between Chataway and an NUR representative. Question: 'But now, not every coloured man surely is much slower than every Englishman; you *can't* judge a whole race like that?' Answer: 'No, I'm talking now of the majority of the particular type of coloured man that I've contacted ...' About this time, Michael Banton was finishing a survey drawn from six localities (Ipswich, Coventry, Alcester, Leeds, Hawick and Leith). From it, he concluded that 'colour prejudice is not widespread in Great Britain', with for example 52 per cent thinking it was wrong for landladies to show racial discrimination in their letting policies, but that 'the evidence of discrimination is undeniable', with for instance 23 per cent either doubtful or outright negative about the prospect of working with 'a coloured man'. Banton's broadly sanguine findings were markedly at variance with a 1956 survey of a thousand people in Birmingham, many living in 'immigrant areas'. In answer to the question, 'Would you have a coloured person in your house as a lodger?', only 15 – a mere 1.5 per cent – replied 'Yes', while almost two-thirds of the sample expressed the view that coloured people were intrinsically less intelligent than white people. Among the black immigrants themselves, a telling change occurred this summer. Up to this point there had been a tradition of free parties – invitations for which were 'not infrequently', recalled Donald Hinds, 'extended to the unknown coloured man who shared the same compartment on the train, or to those who complained about the weather on the bus', with the parties themselves 'an important social gathering' where 'a man could spread the word around that he was about to take over the vacant possession of a house, or that his employers had vacancies', as well as being 'a place to meet the women'. Now, however, it became obligatory to bring a 'bottle of something', and soon afterwards there came what Hinds (who had himself arrived from Jamaica in 1955) called 'the hideous commercial parties', with 'pounding, toneless music' and no place for those 'shy immigrants anxious to make the right impression on the neighbours'.[12]

The second issue of the *Reasoner*, received at the LSE library on 11 September, was still an all-white affair. It appeared about a fortnight after Thompson and Saville had been summoned to King Street to appear before a specially convened Political Committee. 'Edward and I made separate statements,' recalled Saville, 'and one of the striking things about the general discussion which followed was that no member of the Committee talked about the social and political structures within the Soviet Union and why it was so important for the whole membership to appreciate how the crimes described by Khrushchev could occur in a society that called itself socialist. We were talking into very thin air and nothing we said would have any impact or relevance.' The two historians explained that the second issue was already on its way, and in due course it was made clear to them that a third issue would mean expulsion.

The September issue itself included a long letter from Doris Lessing, who expressed concern that the journal, despite its 'admirable' motive of 'trying to restore intellectual conflict', could 'easily be interpreted as an attack against the party leadership', and she defended the long silence of British party members about the realities of Stalinism:

> The facts are that, up to the 20th Congress, if those of us who knew what was going on – and it was perfectly possible to know if one kept one's mind open and read the plentiful evidence available – if we had said what

we thought, in the only place open to us, the capitalist press, we would have been cast out by the party and branded as traitors, and inevitably isolated by bitterness and recrimination from a world movement in which we believed, and of which we wished to remain a part.

That is why we kept silent. We believed that Communism had a vitality and a moral vigour that would triumph over the brutality and intellectual dishonesty that had undermined it. We were right to think so.

'We have all,' she concluded, 'been part of the terrible, magnificent, bloody, contradictory process, the establishing of the first Communist regime in the world – which has made possible our present freedom to say what we think, and to think again creatively.' If Lessing was emotionally still very much holding on to the party, Lawrence Daly had already made the break. In the same issue, his letter from West Fife had a notable passage:

However inadequate and hypocritical British capitalist democracy may be, the average worker does feel that he has the right, more or less, to express his own opinion freely on political and other affairs, worship freely in his own way, get a fair trial if he is arrested, listen to different points of view and make up his own mind, travel almost where he likes (if he can afford it) and so on.

Workers cherish these rights, however restricted, and have refused to give any substantial political support to the C.P. largely because they feared that many of these rights would disappear if it came to power.

It would now appear that their fears were justified.

'There is room for hope,' he ended, 'but *only if* the C.P. begins to show the workers by *deeds* that a genuine change has been made. Can the leadership respond to the challenge? My opinion is that it cannot, but I hope it will yet prove me wrong.'[13]

Moving some further degrees to the right, British social democrats in early October at last had their bible with the publication of Anthony Crosland's compendious and elegantly, but also robustly, written *The Future of Socialism*. In many ways a fleshing out of the themes he had adumbrated four years earlier in *New Fabian Essays*, it advanced six key concepts: the taming by now of the worst excesses of laissez-faire capitalism, though this time Crosland shied away from the term *statism* to describe the existing state of affairs; the urgent need for revisionism – based on current circumstances – within socialist thinking, notwithstanding that 'many working-class militants, and still more some middle-class people who have espoused the workers' cause, feel their whole status and psychological security to depend on preserving a traditional, proletarian philosophy of class-struggle'; the continuing need for a high level of social expenditure, with Crosland wanting 'a generous, imaginative, long-term programme' that would 'make our state schools and hospitals, and all the services that go with them, the equal in quality of the best which private wealth can buy'; the pursuit of greater equality (of outcome as well as of opportunity), involving (among other things) a significant redistribution of wealth through the fiscal system, the integration of private and grammar schools into a single 'comprehensive' state secondary system, and a version of industrial democracy that severely reduced existing status inequalities at the workplace; further attempts to broaden public ownership to be on a case-by-case, non-dogmatic basis ('we cannot go bull-headed at nationalisation without regard to the economic consequences'); and finally, less puritanism and more social liberalism, with Crosland declaring with some exasperation that 'socialists cannot go on indefinitely professing to be concerned with human happiness and the removal of injustice, and then, when the programmes are decided, committing the National Executive, out of fear of certain vocal pressure-groups, to become more orthodox than the bench of bishops'. The book's last sentence was similarly heartfelt: 'We do not want to enter the age of abundance, only to find that we have lost the values which might teach us how to enjoy it.'[14]

Reaction from the Labour left proved predictably hostile, with Will Camp's review in *Tribune* appearing under the headline, 'Socialism? How Dare He Use the Word!'. Camp himself was uniformly negative, among other things accusing Crosland of a mixture of 'optimism about the achievement of "welfare capitalism" and pessimism about the traditional objectives of Socialism'. He ended:

Heaven help the Labour Party if Crosland's 'realism' ever takes a hold on its leaders. The silent coalition between Right wing Labour and 'progressive' Tory which has ruled the country, with a few off moments, ever since the majority Labour Government fell in 1950 will then continue indefinitely. The voters will cease to bother which of the two parties is nominally in power. And as for the Labour rank-and-file, they will lose their faith in Socialism.

Crosland's treatise had a deservedly long shelf life and in 2006 was republished with a foreword by Gordon Brown. 'His breakthrough fifty years ago was telling the Labour Party how a market economy could be made to work in the public interest,' noted Brown, who implicitly identified in Crosland the seeds of the New Labour project, above all through the way he had spelled out the challenge to be 'both radical and credible'. For Crosland himself in 1956, no longer an MP, it was at the age of 38 a huge ambition fulfilled – to have become, in Roy Hattersley's felicitous phrase, 'the political philosopher of the libertarian left'.[15]

At a less platonic level, plenty else was happening during September and October. Plans to drown the Welsh-speaking Tryweryn Valley in Merionethshire, in order to supply water to Liverpool, provided a popular cause for Welsh nationalists, with Plaid Cymru holding in September a Save Tryweryn rally in Bala. Nationalism had been quiescent in the Principality for a long time, but this marked the start of a new, more powerful sense of grievance. Elsewhere, 'squealing women . . . weeping women . . . screaming women . . . fainting women' greeted the arrival of the flamboyant pianist Liberace at Waterloo station on the 25th, according to the *Daily Mirror*, whose 'Cassandra' next day launched a vicious, implicitly homophobic attack on 'the biggest sentimental vomit of all time' – the attack appearing in the same issue as the first of a three-part series by Keith Waterhouse on 'The Royal Circle', which he accused of being 'as aristocratic, as insular and – there is no more suitable word – as toffee-nosed as it has ever been'. The dons were returning, and in the Forest of Dean the working-class Dennis Potter left home to go up to New College, Oxford. Everyone wished him luck at his 'farewell' drink with his parents at the Berry Hill Working Men's Club, 'but, to my shame, I realized that more than anything I wanted to get away from it all, more than ever before that I was glad to be going, glad to be taking this heaven-sent passport to the world of ... what? I wasn't sure, but I knew it was a world where I should be happier, a world where my books were not muddles, where I wasn't on the defensive when putting forward my opinions and value-judgements'. Cultural divides were not only about class, and in the *New Statesman* dated Saturday, 6 October – the day that Bobby Charlton made his Manchester United debut, scoring twice in a 4–2 home win against Charlton Athletic – there was a first outing for C. P. Snow's 'The Two Cultures', ie literary and scientific, with Snow making a cogent case for their bridging. The following week the Tories were at Llandudno for their conference, where Eden made a strong speech that, according to Henry Fairlie, left him safe at No. 10 until the next election in 1960.[16]

The diarists, meanwhile, had mixed fortunes. 'We had coffee at the "Whimpy" in Lyons Corner House,' noted a discontented Madge Martin after a day wandering round Regent Street and Bond Street. 'London is too full of these crowded, meretricious "stand-up" coffee bars. Where are the old days of sitting quietly to elevenses, in a serene, old-fashioned café?' Poor Gladys Langford, who had had a stroke the previous winter and only quite recently resumed her diary, found herself one rainy Monday unable to cross 'a whirling stream pouring across the path' in Highbury Fields. Happily, 'two passing "Teddy-boys" came to my rescue and lifted me over the torrent'. There was a similar experience for Judy Haines, out shopping with her mother in Highams Park: 'We had a good lunch at the A.B.C. (downstairs) and then made our way home. A teddy boy was very kind assisting mum on the moving stairs.' Frank Lewis, now living in Barry but working in Cardiff, was stood up one Tuesday evening by a girl called Julie. 'I seem to be doomed at the Capitol [cinema],' he glumly recorded. 'That's a second time a girl hasn't turned up there ... And after me bloody well rushing to get there ...' He then went 'looking for talent', but as usual to little avail.[17]

That was on 16 October, the same evening that the BBC showed a 25-minute extract (introduced by Lord Harewood) from *Look Back in Anger*, a huge shot in the arm to the Royal Court box office and attracting there a wholly new type of audience, recalled by the stage manager, Michael Halifax, as 'young people gazing around wondering where to go and what the rules were'. As if to prove that John Osborne had not overnight transformed the London theatre, there was a new play at the Duchess, *Plaintiff in a Pretty Hat* by Hugh and Margaret Williams (parents of poet Hugo, actor Simon), which, described by *The Times* as the 'lightest of light comedies' about 'an urbane Welsh peer' trying to get his son out of a breach of promise action, could not have been more polar opposite. Still, the new kept on coming, and on 27 October, the same day that Presley's 'Hound Dog' reached number 2 in the Top 20, there was a first appearance in the charts for Tommy Steele, performing 'Rock with the Caveman', part-written by Lionel Bart. For a fresh-faced Bermondsey boy, discovered at the already renowned 2 I's coffee bar in Soho, this topical ditty about the discovery of a Piltdown man's skull made him Britain's first rock 'n' roll star.[18]

In the midst of all this, on 17 October, Calder Hall at Windscale in Cumberland was officially opened by the Queen and became the world's first nuclear reactor to feed power into a national grid. 'One thing which no one can doubt,' asserted the *Financial Times* on the morning of the ceremony, 'is that from now on the nuclear power programme will be pressed ahead to the limits of the national resources and of technical possibility.' In the *News Chronicle*, 'The Atom Goes to Work for the Housewife' was the title for a bullish article by the leading science writer Ritchie Calder, who called the opening 'a historic and symbolic act – Britain's entry, in the forefront of all the nations, into the Atomic Age, with the atom tamed for domestic and industrial purposes'. At the ceremony itself, the Queen ringingly pronounced that 'all of us here know that we are present at the making of history', a cue for *The Times*'s correspondent to let himself go a little:

Today, with a boisterous wind to display the flags – and nearly wreck the marquees – the colourful and almost Wellsian-looking installation deeply stirs the imagination. Nothing like it exists elsewhere. Truly it has been described as a 'courageous enterprise'; for Calder Hall represents the inauguration of a comprehensive programme of atomic power stations which, in time, will provide Britain with an ample supply of electricity without the use of coal or oil. Therein lies its magic.

Not just magic but, according to Anthony Wedgwood Benn, socialist magic. 'We're told we should be proud of it and we should,' he declared on *Any Questions?* two days later, 'and it is public enterprise both in the Atomic Energy Authority and in the British Electricity Authority which distributes it, and I'm sure Ted Leather [the Tory MP on the panel] in boasting rightly of the achievement of Calder Hall will remember that when the nation as a nation gets down to the job it's capable of leading the world, and I as a Socialist am very proud of that too.' Nor in global terms was he inclined to minimise the achievement itself: 'We've talked since 1945 of the atomic age presenting alternatives of utter obliteration or great hopes for rising standards and up until now we've had a bit too much of the utter obliteration brought before us and not enough of the hope and the possibility for rising standards, and Calder Hall shows what can be done and we're very delighted to see it.'[19]

An innovation a fortnight later was not quite such a cause of national pride. 'The G.P.O. was *packed* – five queues for Pensions,' recorded Nella Last on Wednesday, 1 November. 'By the time I got to the counter, I felt as if I could just push my book, through the little "grill". I said "I've *never* seen such a crowd" and was told "it's been like this since 9 o'clock – it's these Premium Bonds!".' They had attracted some flak on their announcement by Macmillan in his April Budget – a 'squalid raffle' (Harold Wilson), a 'cold, solitary, mechanical, uncompanionable, inhuman activity' (the Archbishop of Canterbury) – but Gallup soon afterwards had found that 54 per cent approved of a government-sponsored lottery and only 31 per cent disapproved.[20] Now on the first day of purchase, the queues in Barrow told their own story. With a top prize of £1,000, it only remained for Ernie next summer to do the honours.

13

Brisk Buying and Selling

'The bright bricks of new homes, hedged with well-tended gardens, sprouted the dubious joys of a TV age,' wrote Geoffrey Goodman after a visit to a council estate in Barnsley. 'Children, happy and healthy, played around the garden fences. A new pub had been built, with a drive-in, chromium and glass saloon bars and plush leather upholstery; there was a dimpled blonde behind the bar, and even in the "public lounge" there were waitresses.' That was in the *New Statesman* dated 26 May 1956, and the same day Harold Macmillan visited his former constituency of Stockton-on-Tees, which had suffered so much during the slump of the 1930s. 'We drove round some of the parts which we knew very well and have been much altered by slum clearance etc,' he noted. 'The wealth and prosperity of the town is incredible. . .' A week or two later, a special feature in *Encounter* on 'This New England' led with an even more emblematic northern town. 'On Saturday afternoons the market-place, which in Orwell's days was full of angry speakers and hungry listeners, is full of brisk buying and selling,' observed Wayland Young in 'Return to Wigan Pier'. And overall, he reckoned that since the publication of *The Road to Wigan Pier* in 1936, Wigan had 'changed from barefoot malnutrition to nylon and television, from hollow idleness to flush contentment'.[1] Barnsley, Stockton, Wigan: the inescapable conclusion was that there was, relatively speaking, a new affluence afoot, a fundamentally different condition.

Another resonant symbol of this changing state of affairs was the declining demand for allotments. 'For the first time in years there is no queue for allotment sites in East Ham,' reported the *Star* in January 1956, quoting a dismayed official from the local Allotment Association:

'What has happened to them all? A few years ago all available ground in the borough was taken up. Today, with fewer sites, we find a great many of our plots are vacant and still more members are giving up this coming season.' But of course it was not just vegetables that were being bought as a mixture of full employment, rising real wages, generally easier credit facilities – including in the flourishing mail-order sector – and few remaining constraints on supply pushed Britain into becoming by the mid-1950s, if not quite yet a fully fledged consumerist society, at least a proto-consumerist one. Indisputably in the vanguard was 'the teenage consumer', as he or she would soon be called. 'Before the war many young workers handed over their earnings to "Mum" and received back an austere allowance of a few shillings to cover fares, snacks, and pocket money,' whereas 'in the post-war world the roles tend to be reversed', noted Mark Abrams, the closest, most alert observer of the phenomenon, in May 1956. Now, he went on, '"Mum" is given £1 or £2 as a contribution to the family's household expenditure and the young earner holds onto the rest', so that in comparison with the generation earlier 'the working boys or girls of today are magnificently well off, and their spending is one of the mainstays of many flourishing markets'. All this was predicated upon a labour market in which unskilled and semi-skilled youth labour was heavily in demand, resulting in the real earnings of teenagers being 50 per cent higher by 1957 than they had been in 1938. 'There was plenty of work,' a teenager in the Brighton area would recall. 'There was no trouble getting work . . . Once you got to the age of sixteen you could go to any builders or garage or anywhere and get a job . . .'[2]

It is impossible to know to what extent advertising fuelled this proto-consumerism, but certainly advertising itself was on the increase – its total expenditure up from 0.77 per cent of GNP in 1952 to 0.93 per cent by 1956, and this despite continuing newsprint rationing until 1956. Women's magazines benefited particularly, with for instance *Woman's* advertising revenue almost quintupling between 1951 and 1958. Another favourite target for advertising agencies was a fairly upmarket but still nuts-and-bolts magazine like *Homes and Gardens*, whose February 1954 issue, page 1, was typically devoted to the actress and singer Florence Desmond extolling the virtues of the Kenwood Chef – 'saves hours of work, and makes a whole range of new exciting dishes possible'. So too *Picture Post*, which regularly in the mid-1950s included a lengthy 'advertising feature' on 'The Modern Kitchen', with the one in February 1956 insisting that 'first-rate kitchen ware is something you will never regret possessing'. By contrast with the print format, television advertising from September 1955 took a while to find its feet, with many of the early commercials being too long and too clunky, remembered unfondly by Ronnie Kirkwood of the Colman Prentis & Varley agency as 'loud-mouthed salesmen who confused shouting with communicating, and bullying with persuading'. Still, there were some palpable hits during the first 15 months or so, including an animated 'Snap, Crackle and Pop' for Rice Krispies and the introduction of subsequently impermissible 'pester power' as a short-trousered boy implored, 'Don't forget the Fruit Gums, Mum'. Gallup polled viewers throughout the first year of commercial television, and despite high marks for Shell's carefully produced miniature travelogues and for Mackesons with their comic animated stout bottles, easily the favourite was the jingling, catchy cartoon for Murraymints. 'Viewers,' noted the *News Chronicle*, 'are amused by the lazy guardsman who refuses to obey orders until he's finished his too-good-to-hurry-mint.'[3]

***

'We queued up to see the incredible "house of the future" – and decided – *no*,' recorded Madge Martin after visiting the Ideal Home Exhibition in March 1956, and she was almost certainly not alone in giving a shudder when she saw the Smithsons' vision. Even so, in the here and now, most new homes in the 1950s were being built along self-consciously 'modern' lines, with the emphasis on informality, flexibility of purpose, the creation of as much space as possible, and the kitchen as an integral part of family life. This particularly applied to private housing, with the builders Taylor Woodrow in 1956 setting out their stall for a £2,195 bargain that was 'the house every woman has dreamed about':

> Design is based on the open-planning idea – a bold step indeed from the orthodox type of house of the 1930s for the whole ground floor is intercommunicated. Entering the house, with its attractive reeded glass door screen and shelves by the front door, is the lounge hall – a

spacious, elegant room, 18½ feet long and 12 feet wide. Along the whole
facing wall are built-in shelves, to hold, perhaps, a few cherished books,
a choice ornament, treasured knick-knacks, or one of those delicate,
trailing indoor plants. These are centred by an electric fitted log fire. The
lounge sweeps through to the dining area, nearly 11 feet square with its
low, wide picture-frame window. It leads to a dream of a kitchen, which
again follows the wide-open look. A feature of this is the bright stainless
steel, double-sided sink unit with built-in cupboards above and below.
Another wall has more long built-in cupboards, and there are yet others
to ceiling height, while still more are built around the most up-to-date of
refrigerators, which is set at eye-level. Perhaps the most unique of all is
a specially made breakfast-table fitment covered with scarlet Formica at
working-top height with a cascade of drawers – one green baize lined for
cutlery – and a space for the washing machine. Yes – this too is included
in the price, and believe it or not, so is the electric clock on the wall.

Nevertheless, there persisted significant working-class resistance to the
open-plan revolution, or anything even faintly resembling it, especially
if the traditional front-room parlour 'for best' was threatened. 'Come
and take a look at what they've done inside,' the Borough Engineer
for Harlow New Town said to Tosco Fyvel, researching a 'This New
England' piece about a development comprising almost entirely young
working-class families. 'It's worth it if you're interested. In my first
ten houses I put in a kitchen dining-alcove and a big living room. Not
a family liked it. They all want a downstairs front and back, even if the
rooms are poky.'
    It was much the same with furniture, with modern styles such as
Robin Day's (imbued with the Festival of Britain ethos) or Ercol (using
natural materials) tending to be embraced with much more enthusiasm
by the upper middle-class than by either the lower middle or the
working class. Even G-Plan furniture, launched in 1953 by E. Gomme
of High Wycombe and seeking, as one of their advertisements put it, to
'combine the best in contemporary styling with sound construction and
the finest finish – all at a moderate cost', probably failed to penetrate
below a certain point in the socio-economic scale. The commercial
limits of Scandinavian-style 'soft' Modernism were pointed up by
an exhibition, *Register Your Choice*, held at Charing Cross station in

1952 and subsequently analysed by Mass-Observation. The choice in question was between on the one hand a traditionally furnished room with dark woods and a three-piece suite, on the other a much more modern room with a light colour scheme and non-suite furniture. 'It seems evident that as yet many people – probably most – judge furniture in terms of its apparent comfort and solidity, and distrust the capacity of contemporary styles to provide these advantages too,' noted M-O in a tone of clear regret about a misguided preference largely coming from the working-class visitors to the exhibition. 'There is much failure even to appreciate the aesthetic attraction of contemporary styles, much emotional resistance to this unfamiliar manner, much tendency to withdraw into the security of the familiar. . .' Fyvel, inspecting the interiors in Harlow New Town in 1956, would have sympathised with M-O's disappointment. 'The houses seemed filled with bicycles, budgerigars, perambulators, and television sets,' he rather sourly noted. 'The rooms certainly struck one as small, perhaps because they were stuffed with unsuitable furniture. Oversize three-piece suites and clumsy sideboards hit the eye. Cheap mass-produced china ornaments stood on the chimney-piece or in the front window: haphazard coloured reproductions hung on the walls. The effect was uniformly ugly.' In fact, he concluded: 'In all the rooms I did not see one single piece of furniture or decoration of even moderately good taste.'[4]

But whether tastes were acceptable or unacceptable, by the mid-1950s the age of DIY was dawning. Importantly, it was a supply as well as a demand revolution, including the emergence of emulsion paint and the paint roller as well as the selling of wallpaper through retail outlets. ICI was quickly on the case, with Dulux on sale by 1953, and in general optimistic white paint was starting to replace dirt-concealing brown as most amateur decorators' colour of choice. So too Black & Decker, which in 1954 decided to enter the domestic market, developing for its electric drill such accessories as a lathe, saw attachment and bench stands – prelude to a major advertising campaign that autumn which resulted in a spectacular increase in sales. There were other landmarks. Bon Marché in Liverpool had by this time already opened its 'Household Boutique', aimed at women as much as men, and other department stores such as Heelas in Reading followed in 1955. DIY's bespoke magazine, *Practical Householder*, was launched in October 1955, while in September 1956 there was the first of the annual Do-It-Yourself exhibitions at Olympia. A glance at the December 1956 issue of *Practical Householder* gives the prevailing flavour, with articles such as 'Disguising that old Fireplace', 'A Contemporary Table Lamp: Made from a Darning Stool and Knitting Needles', and 'Modernising an Old Type Sewing Machine: To Include Built-in Shelves, Drawers, Cotton Wells and Stool'. Elsewhere, a large ad pictured a middle-aged man showing his son and daughter-in-law how to do it. 'It's quite an easy job to re-surface your kitchen table with FORMICA Laminated Plastic, and surprisingly economical,' ran the text. 'Half an hour's pleasant work, and hey presto! you have a table with a top that will never stain, chip or crack, resists heat up to 310°F – a joy for years to come.' The special delight of the magazine was its covers: invariably in bright colours, they almost always depicted a recently married husband and wife working happily together as a team on some ingenious, challenging, but ultimately do-able DIY project.[5]

'Cannon Raises the Level of Cooking – With the Exclusive Foldaway Eye Level Grill', 'Bendix Automatically Makes Washing a Leisure – You Just Set It and Forget It', 'Swirlux – This Is The Way to Wash Your Clothes' – consumer durables, above all washing machines, were starting in the 1950s to transform the everyday lives of millions of housewives. Market leader for washing machines was, by a long way, Hoover, which had moved into the field in 1948 (with its new factory near Merthyr Tydfil) and by 1955 was selling its Mark III Power Wringer, with its boffins still working on the twin-tub concept, while fridge manufacturers included Prescold, Electrolux, Coldrator (an Ambridge favourite), English Electric and Frigidaire. It is easy, though, to exaggerate at this stage the penetration of these so-called 'white goods'. Vacuum cleaners may by 1955 have been in a majority of households, but washing machines were in only 18 per cent and refrigerators in a mere 8 per cent. In Wales, as late as 1960, there were fridges in just 5 per cent of households. On washday, the typical housewife was not the ecstatic figure of the washing-machine ads, nor indeed the duly grateful Judy Haines in Chingford, but rather David Blunkett's mother in a council house in Sheffield, 'pummelling the clothes in the "dolly tub"'. Among those housewives fortunate enough to have labour-saving appliances, a survey was conducted in 1953 in order to guide manufacturers about female criteria for new appliances. Overwhelmingly the main consideration, found the survey, was durability; but it was soon a message wholly ignored, as built-in obsolescence became a deliberate manufacturing ploy, allied to marketing that increasingly emphasised fashion and novelty.[6]

In the kitchen, the possibilities for innovative cooking steadily broadened – Kenneth Lo's *Cooking the Chinese Way* sold 10,000 copies in hardback on its publication in 1954, while the following year, in her preface to the Penguin edition of her *A Book of Mediterranean Food*, Elizabeth David noted that 'so startlingly different is the food situation now (from two years previously) that I think there is scarcely a single ingredient, however exotic, mentioned in this book which cannot be obtained somewhere in this country' – but more important for most people was the increasing availability of convenience foods. New additions in the mid-1950s included Colman's 'Instant Desserts', Birds Eye frozen chicken pie and, most popular of all, Birds Eye Fish Fingers, introduced a fortnight before the start of commercial television and reputedly only saved by a last-minute name change from being called cod pieces. Even so, for all their time-saving advantage, there was often an innate resistance, essentially a social conservatism, that new foods had to break down. 'I'm too old for these modern ideas,' a 64-year-old labourer told Mass-Observation in 1953 about frozen foods (which anyway depended to a large extent on would-be consumers having refrigerators), while an advertisement in 1956 for Batchelors 'Soup Mixes' made much of how 'if you pride yourself on serving *freshly cooked* food, warming up just isn't good enough', whereas in this case bringing the contents of the packet to the boil and simmering for 20 minutes meant that 'you actually COOK the soup yourself' and 'you serve it *freshly made*'. As for drinks, tea-bags had yet to make their commercial appearance, but by 1954 Nescafé instant coffee had doubled its sales since the war and Maxwell House ('America's favourite coffee') was poised to offer real competition. On the alcoholic front, the sales of canned beer for home drinking started to take off from 1956, and that Christmas off-licences reported a sharp rise, compared to previous Christmases, in the sale of wine. In this whole area of eating and drinking, though, there was one particularly emblematic food. 'Collected 15/- Sainsbury chicken,' noted Judy Haines on the first Friday of August 1956. 'My! It was good!' It may well have been a chicken produced by John Eastwood, Nottinghamshire pioneer of factory farming methods that in time transformed chicken from one of the most expensive to one of the most affordable dishes; and it may also have been about the time that when I was having Sunday lunch at my uncle and aunt's Shropshire farm, my little cousin piped up as the trolley was wheeled in, 'Oh no, not another bloody chicken!' My mother, living in Grove Park in south-east London, where chicken was still a special treat, could not get over it.[7]

In any domestic setting, nothing could stop the irresistible spread of the television set. By 1956 there were sets in some 48 per cent of households, with a majority at this stage having access to BBC programmes only, and generally during the early to mid-1950s there was often keen competition to be the first in a street to have one. In Neasden the father of Lesley Hornby (the future Twiggy) was one such pioneer, and as an inveterate DIY man, 'forever making "improvements"', he quickly knocked up a cabinet for it. Crucially, in terms of the ecology of working-class homes, the set more often than not invaded the hitherto sacrosanct parlour, including in miners' houses in the Forest of Dean. 'The little screen found its place amongst the cumbersome best furniture and the heavily flowered, deep-bordered wallpaper,' recalled Dennis Potter some years later:

> And, of course, when the family began to watch, furniture got moved around, a few superfluous things were slung out, a giant change in domestic habits was being made . . . Instead of a coal fire once a week 'to air the room', to preserve the mausoleum from the damp, fires were lit throughout the winter; some people even began to have a glass of beer or a flagon of cider, to keep on their working clothes and boots, consciously to relax over it all, to create a genuine living space in what had been the lifeless clutter of the old Front Room. When this happened, the former wallpaper was discovered to be irritating and out-of-tune, the best china 'a pity to keep for looking at', the heavily framed picture 'a bit miserable', and a minor revolution was finally consummated when supper was eaten in the room to the pale flicker of the Lime Grove light . . .

Inevitably, attitudes varied. In Michael Palin's intensely respectable, middle-class home in Sheffield, the TV was usually covered with a knitted antimacassar; while from a left perspective, Doris Lessing adamantly refused her son's entreaties for a set, and she recalled that in her circle the typical attitude to the medium was, 'Our children's minds would be rotted by this monstrous new invention,' and 'What could we all do to save ourselves?' There was less agonising in working-class homes. 'In one household,' reported Michael Young and Peter Willmott about an interview in Debden, 'the parents and five children of all ages were paraded around it in a half circle at 9 p.m. when one of us called; the two-month-old baby was stationed in its pram in front of the set. The scene had the air of a strange ritual. The father said proudly: "The tellie keeps the family together. None of us ever have to go out now."' Or as one of the Crown Street sociologists recorded after interviewing a middle-aged press tool setter and his wife: 'Own T.V. – they paid £69 for it – saved up over a long period. Wife admitted that she thought T.V. good because "after you've been married for a long time you run out of conversation."'[8]

Overall, a greater home-centredness was accompanied by changing patterns outside the home. The cinema-going habit was significantly weakening (an average of 22 visits in 1956 for each person over the age of 16, compared with 34 visits ten years earlier); football and cricket attendances were also steadily declining; and in Bethnal Green in the mid-1950s, Young and Willmott noted how 'all the publicans lament the loss of trade', as 'the men stay at home with their wives and children', occasionally fetching a bottle in to drink while watching the TV. By contrast, expenditure on motoring quadrupled between 1945 and 1956, and over the same period roughly trebled on hobbies such as playing sports, gardening, photography and looking after pets. Meanwhile, there was an increasing trend for eating out, with the start of the Berni Inns in 1954 – offering a half-pound Argentine rump steak with chips and peas, roll and butter and pudding or cheese for 7s 6d – particularly emblematic. As for holidays, at least half the population took a vacation away from home in the course of 1955, with some 8 per cent of those going abroad, and an increasing proportion using a caravan. In short, mobility and choice were beginning to define consumer behaviour, although both concepts still had a long, long way to go. Moreover, just because Mary Quant had opened a shop (Bazaar) on the King's Road in late 1955, it did not mean that the rest of the country was even incipiently ready to swing.[9]

———

'Here are just a few of the shops I used, starting with Alfred Street South,' recalled Joan Priestley about being a housewife in the 1950s in the largely working-class St Ann's district of Nottingham:

> Farnsworth's Pork Butchers, Barnes Dales little dairy sold Colwick Cheeses, Barber Len for son's haircut, Coupe's Furnishing and round the corner into the Square was Plunkett's Gents Outfitters, Atkin's Wine Shop, Winfield's the Butcher. If you'd had some coal delivered, it was up to Brown's the Coal Merchant to pay the bill on Union Road, down again to the Square, there was Carnill's Pork Butchers, Briley's Ladies' and Children's Wear, past the imposing Westminster Bank. Crossing over and passing the Cromwell Pub to the Co-op Butchery and Greengrocer's, Morley's Cake Shop, Dean's for Ladies Fashion, past the Cavendish Cinema, then there was Mr Ash, an excellent Fishmonger for many years . . .
>
> Such a variety of shops, there was no need to go into town . . .

Most of these shops (including also 'Meakin's the cobbler, Marsden's, Mr Chettle the dentist, Ridgards for cookers, Mr Clarke the Chemist, Hopewell Furnishers and Wayne's Poodle Parlour and Pet Shop') probably flourished, and would continue to do so for a while yet, but it was already becoming a different story away from the main shopping streets. In the Crown Street survey, 'an irascible old lady who is very acute and capable' was the proprietress of 'a small corner general shop', and her incisive views on the plight of such shops in the area were paraphrased by the interviewer in February 1956:

> Nowadays, there is too much competition in this kind of retail trade. This is one reason why it is necessary for them to stay open from 10 a.m. till 9.00 p.m. and often for a spell on Sunday mornings too. They are tied to the shop, and are just about making a living.
>
> The local people purchase only small quantities of goods at a time as they require them. For teas, they wait until their children come home

from school & ask them what they want, & then send out to the corner shop for it. Although they come in for 'a little tittle-tattle', their custom is not regular, and 'they only make a convenience of these little shops', or ask credit in them.

'When goods were rationed,' she added bitterly, 'people did a constant trade here. Now they come in only for odds & ends.'

Even a reasonably thriving independent shop was coming under increasing competition – but not yet intolerably stiff competition, given continuing resale price maintenance – from the chain stores, whose share (excluding the Co-op) of the total grocery provision market rose from 19.9 per cent in 1950 to 26.9 per cent by 1961, while that of the independents (defined as less than ten stores) declined from 56.8 per cent to 52.3 per cent.

The two most emblematic chain stores (or multiples) were, in their different ways, the Co-op and Marks & Spencer. 'All the Co-ops were laid out the same,' remembered Geoff Phillips, who grew up in Newcastle's Byker area:

On the left when you went in were dry goods. On the right were bacon and cheese and meat. At the back were fruit and veg. The fruit was polished and displayed in doilies and silver paper. One person served you at the dry goods counter, then one person at the bacon counter, and so on. They would then put all your purchases together in a parcel which was tied up with string. Most women had baskets with a cloth cover. If required, a boy on a bike would deliver your groceries to your home. You had to quote your store number and get a ticket so as to claim your divi. The Co-op dividend was sometimes as high as a 1/- in the pound.

Largely stuck in its ways, though, the Co-op was in slow but sure decline, its grocery share going down from 23.2 per cent in 1950 to 20.8 per cent by 1961. The fortunes of M&S were, by contrast, almost vertiginously rising, to the point where it was fast becoming a national institution – an institution whose purpose was, declared Fyfe Robertson in a lengthy 1955 panegyric, 'to serve the new mass-prosperity market by bringing good quality, and good design and finish, within the reach of moderate purses', and he noted that 'sample analysis shows that the proportion of the firm's customers in each economic group is about the same as their proportion in the population'. The same year another, more radical journalist was equally impressed by the democratisation of demand being fostered by this highly acceptable face of capitalism. 'Before the Welfare State there were broadly two classes of consumers, the middle class who had the money, and the working class who hadn't,' wrote Laurence Thompson in the *News Chronicle*. 'Now there is only one class and I am told that many a débutante wears a Marks & Spencer nylon slip beneath her Dior dress as if she were just a Gateshead factory girl.'[10]

As for the traditionally inegalitarian department stores, the 1950s now seem like their heyday. 'Fish paste and cress sandwiches' in the restaurant, served by 'tired, kindly women in little pinafores and frilled caps', the food department in the basement where 'assistants in white cotton coats' stood at the counters 'weighing out tea' and 'cutting cheeses with wire', haberdashery where one could buy 'tape and elastic, bales of bias binding, Sylko in any shade of any colour you needed, dress-making shears, very small scissors, their blades fashioned like a stork's beak', and a shoe department in which 'the children would be bought crepe-soled sandals and peer at their weird black bones in the x-ray machine' – so Penelope Mortimer recalled going, as a young mother, to John Barnes in Finchley Road. Even so, department stores by the mid-1950s were increasingly conscious of both rising competition from the chain stores and an untapped, newly affluent working-class potential clientele that they had previously ignored, prompting the managing director of Selfridges to assert in the *Financial Times* in May 1955 that it was only through 'providing an environment and attractions, which convert shopping from a chore to an interesting relaxation', that they could hope to 'win back trade'.

Later that year, Mass-Observation conducted a survey on behalf of Browns of Chester to try to establish what local people felt about a department store that over the years had been known as dear and exclusive. The resulting all-female vox pop showed social class alive and well in Cheshire, with 'B' denoting upper middle-class, 'C' lower middle-class, 'D' skilled or semi-skilled working-class, and 'E' unskilled working-class:

I never go there now. I think they have lowered their standards. I wouldn't go into a shop that has placards in its windows advertising credits and hire-purchase. I think it's dreadful for a firm of such old standing to sell clothes on credit. *(60B, wife of proprietor of newsagents)*

It's a lovely shop of course. You can walk round and you're under no obligation to buy. One time they used to cater for one class, and now they seem to cater for all. I think that's all their hire purchase and credit schemes have come into being. *(43C, wife of plumber and pipefitter)*

You pay just to breathe the air of that shop. I keep away. *(32C, wife of cattle dealer)*

Well, everything's very expensive. When you go to the shop you never feel comfortable. *(38C, wife of manager of furniture shop)*

I don't go there. They're expensive people. I'm just frightened to go in and ask anything there. *(34C, wife of cash clerk)*

If you've got the money all well and good, but it's definitely not for working classes. *(41D, wife of aircraft labourer)*

Well, I think to go to those stores you've got to be posh. I know it's the same money but I think the assistants seem different. *(37D, wife of wagon repairer)*

I think it's too superior for people like me – I would be scared of the assistants. *(51DE, wife of engine driver)*

Too many women about in it looking down their noses at you. *(48D, wife of farm worker)*

It was a further sign of the need for department stores to broaden their appeal when Beatties of Wolverhampton, wanting to advertise its January sale in 1957, became the first to use television. Still, there was always the danger of alienating the traditionally well-heeled base – and when in 1956 the venerable Whiteley's in Bayswater tried to introduce self-service, there was such a revolt that, in the words of the historian Bill Lancaster, 'the ageing, fixed-income clientele won back their cherished counters', thereby condemning Whiteley's to a further cycle of stagnation and decline.[11]

Self-service itself was steadily on the rise (including at the Co-op), up to about 3,100 stores by 1956: still less than 3 per cent of all food shops, but accounting for over 10 per cent of food sales. M-O that year undertook a survey for the International Tea Company, asking housewives in Liscard – a largely middle-class village near Wallasey – what they thought of the concept. Opinion was about evenly divided:

> Very good. You can walk round and everything's out for you to see, everything's out in front, and you're not waiting in a queue to be served, you can just pick out what you want and get away.
>
> Oh, I don't know. I think you're just as well off with assistants to serve you. You know what you want and you've only to ask for it.
>
> Some do like them, but I don't because I feel you just don't get that personal attention.
>
> I think they're too impersonal. You just go wandering round and out. I'll tell you what I really dislike – seeing the bacon and cooked meats all sliced in the window – dark and dry-looking.
>
> I think it's quite a good idea myself. You see what you want and the price is on everything. You can see what different makes they have.
>
> I rather like it myself – it's more convenient. The only thing is that sometimes a lot of people get at the paying counter and you have to wait.
>
> Well, I *like* to be served – it's so much more personal.
>
> Well, to be quite honest with you, I'm not at all keen on them. I prefer to see the cheese cut before my eyes, and potatoes and vegetables – I like to choose them and see them weighed. I don't like them in these bags.
>
> I think it's very good. You see things you wouldn't normally see if you had to ask for them.

The great majority of self-service shops were on too small a scale properly to be called supermarkets, of which there were only about a thousand at the most by 1956, with for instance Tesco opening its first true supermarket that year, in a disused cinema in Maldon, Essex. The miles of aisles still lay ahead, while out-of-town shopping was barely a gleam in anyone's eye.

Nor was shopping yet a leisure activity, but rather a daily or near-daily drudge, with the prevailing lack of refrigerators meaning that housewives by 1957 were still making an estimated average of 7.6 visits per week to the grocers and 3.3 visits to the butchers – visits that, in the context of early closing on Wednesdays and very limited Sunday trading, often had to be carefully planned. Of course, some housewives enjoyed shopping more than others, but the replies of the Liscard housewives, asked by M-O whether 'shopping for groceries and day to day things like that' was 'something you like, or not', probably give a fair sense of how housewives generally felt about this taken-for-granted (by others) part of their lives:

Oh, I don't mind. It's a change to get out for a bit of fresh air – a change from doing housework.

Well, I don't dislike it. It's a part of housekeeping isn't it? I think it's just a matter of looking after the family.

Well yes, I like shopping all right, but it's simply terrible the prices these days.

Oh yes, I don't mind it. It's just part of everyday life. I've done it for so many years and you get used to it. It's a habit the same as everything else.

Well, I do like shopping if I have plenty of time.

Well, I ask you, the prices put you off.

Well, you get a bit tired of it, don't you? From day to day the same, but it's got to be done.[12]

———

'More than nine out of ten houses visited showed signs of recent redecoration and alterations – usually a new fireplace,' recorded Tom Brennan in June 1956 after visiting tenements in the Gorbals. 'Several scores of families had obviously spent a lot of time and money trying to improve their one or two rooms. The prosperity of recent years showed very clearly. It has not all been misdirected as is often suggested.' There was indeed a reflex middle-class tendency to criticise the frivolous, extravagant expenditure of the newly better-off working class, a tendency embodied by Nella Last in Barrow. 'Mrs Salisbury often makes me *gasp*,' she wrote a few months earlier about her cleaner. 'She was paddling round in a nasty old pair of rubber soled shoes. I said, "Oh Mrs Salisbury, *look*, you are making marks all over the carpets. Haven't you brought your old slippers?" She said a bit mournfully, "No, they have fallen to bits, these booties are all I've got" – & she is paying for a £108 T.V. set, & a "racing" bicycle for her schoolboy, though he owns one good enough to go to school on it!!' There was also a more general sense of unease, typified by the reaction of the Glasgow-based *Evening Citizen*, about the time of Brennan's interviews, to the pronouncement of the Scottish Under Secretary, J. Nixon Browne, that two vital ingredients for a happy home life were a 'kitchen to be proud of' and a 'room for a TV'. 'Fine,' riposted the paper. 'But many people manage very well without a dream kitchen – and a lot of folk were quite happy before TV existed. Material comforts help, but it is a mistake to over-accentuate them. No home will be a happy one – whatever the amenities – without the mutual love, respect and unselfishness of the family.' From the left, as evidenced by the painful saga of commercial television, there was palpable discomfort with the whole area of advertising and consumption, forcefully though Crosland argued that 'the wide and plentiful diffusion of consumer goods' was a perfectly valid 'route towards social equality'. And from the guardians of high culture and high-mindedness generally, the dismay was almost total. 'All that solemnity in the 1950s, it just seems so remote,' the poet and critic Ian Hamilton poignantly reflected in 2001 shortly before his death:

> It's very close too because it determined so much of one's own thought and action; and yet it is a million miles away. They said: look out, people are doing these demoralising things, we are going to enter a society dominated by mass-communications and consumerism, a society that isn't going to care about the things you care about. You do realise that's the way we're going, don't you? That was the Leavisite cry. And we said: Yes and we must prevent that. And we devoted whole lifetimes to trying to prevent it – and look what's happened . . .[13]

The history train was rolling by the mid-1950s in only one direction. And whatever the concerns, whatever the critiques, nothing was going to derail it.

14

A Pretty Mess

'Terrible 24 hours,' noted Clarissa Eden on 27 July 1956. 'Nasser trying to take over the Suez Canal. Anthony and the Cabinet decide to fight, if necessary alone.' It was a concise, accurate summary, and the same day Macmillan observed that the Egyptian President's speech announcing his seizure of the Canal had been 'very truculent – an Asiatic Mussolini', adding that the Cabinet's 'unanimous view' was 'in favour of strong and resolute action'. Most of the press over the next few days agreed, while in the Commons on 2 August, after Eden had stated that Britain could not allow this to pass unchallenged, Gaitskell laid such stress on Nasser as a 1930s-style dictator that he appeared to be giving support to Eden's firm line.

Away from Westminster and Fleet Street, as the Army Reserve was called up and Royal Navy ships sent to the Middle East, a class dimension was rapidly emerging. 'Arthur rang up,' noted Nella Last on the 2nd about her civil servant elder son. 'He seemed very concerned about the Suez problem, – feared the govt were "rushing things".' Three days later, John Fowles muttered darkly to himself about the 'hideous bellicosity of the Tories' in the 'Suez Canal scare' and described Britain as being 'in a hopelessly immoral position'. But it was Billy Butlin who had his finger on the popular pulse, refusing to allow Egypt's brilliant swimmers to participate in the annual Butlin's Cross-Channel swimming race. 'They've got the Suez Canal,' he was quoted as saying, 'I'm not going to let them have the English Channel.' And for a young David Owen, working on a Costain's construction site in Plymouth prior to going up to Cambridge, there was the painful shock of discovering that his fellow-workers 'were adamant from the start that the Egyptians should not be allowed to get away with it' and that 'the "Gippos" had hit us, so we should hit them'.

Between early August and late October – amidst endless rounds of diplomacy, largely a charade from the British government's point of view – Suez positions steadily hardened. 'The blunt fact is that there is now a clear clash of parliamentary opinion between Government and Opposition on how to deal with Colonel Nasser,' reported ITN's Robin Day from the Commons on 12 September, after Gaitskell had made it clear in a stormy emergency debate that Labour would not support any military action unsanctioned by the United Nations. 'The unity which appeared to pervade Parliament on August 2nd has now completely evaporated.' In the press, there was majority support – but not overwhelmingly so – for the Eden line about the folly of a re-run of inter-war appeasement. And in the public at large, polls revealed a deep mistrust and disapproval of Nasser, but a preference at this stage for going down the UN route rather than taking unilateral action.[1] The pace of events quickened during October. Publicly, the Tory conference at Llandudno was unashamedly hawkish; privately, a meeting at Sèvres (a Paris suburb) on the 22nd saw Britain, France and Israel cooking up an astonishingly disreputable, highly secret scheme by which a week later Israel would invade Egypt, thereby enabling an Anglo-French intervention that could be presented as peacemaking while in reality seeking to regain the Canal and in the process overthrow Nasser. If not quite something out of *Blackadder*, it was not much better.

———

On the evening of Monday the 29th, as Israeli tanks and armoured cars duly crossed Egyptian border outposts and headed for the Suez Canal, the Queen was attending the Royal Film Performance (*The Battle of the River Plate*) at the Empire in Leicester Square. There, accompanied by a possibly nose-out-of-joint sister, she was presented to a galaxy of stars, including the three leading sex symbols of the day – Marilyn Monroe, Brigitte Bardot and Anita Ekberg. 'Marilyn Monroe Captures Britain' was one headline next day, but on the set at Pinewood it was an even more difficult time than usual. 'The trouble is that she takes extra pills when she doesn't feel 100%,' noted Colin Clark, 'without really knowing what effect the pills will have.' He added that 'MM looks more and more vulnerable and I am sorry for her', but chatting the same day to one of the exasperated lighting men, 'veterans of countless Rank films', he was told that 'if it wasn't for our loyalty to Sir Laurence, I'd have edged a spanner off the grid and onto her head'. In Westminster at 4.30 this Tuesday afternoon, Eden stunned the Commons by announcing an Anglo-French ultimatum to Nasser, who was given 12 hours to withdraw his troops from the Suez Canal or face the consequences. The Tories, according to Labour's J.P.W. ('Curly') Mallalieu, 'roared their delight'. But that night there was no mention of Suez in Anthony Heap's diary, which instead lamented how 'those horrible yellow tubular street lights that have been gradually introduced along suburban main roads during the last year or two are now beginning to render central London hideous by night as well'.

On Wednesday morning there was unqualified backing from the *Telegraph*, *Express* and *Financial Times*, while the *Daily Sketch* also weighed in, declaring that 'the critics of Eden are the critics of Britain'. This lurid tabloid had put on some 70,000 circulation since the middle of the year, employing what one press critic, Francis Williams, called a 'formula of cheese-cake, sensation and extreme Toryism of the most old-fashioned jingoist kind' – anticipating Murdoch's prime-era *Sun*. Elsewhere in Fleet Street, both the *Mail* and *The Times* sounded cautious notes, while the *Manchester Guardian* began a notable leader unambiguously: 'The Anglo-French ultimatum to Egypt is an act of folly without justification in any terms but brief expediency. It pours petrol on a growing fire. There is no knowing what kind of explosion will follow.' Anthony Wedgwood Benn reflected later on Wednesday how the paper was providing 'the intellectual leadership in the country', adding that 'the churches, leading figures in science, universities and among professional people are coming out solidly on this'. Two experienced observers certainly felt strongly. 'How they can have done such a thing with the whole of world opinion against us passes my comprehension,' Harold Nicolson wrote to his wife Vita Sackville-West, while Violet Bonham Carter was privately 'convinced that we have made the biggest blunder in our history'. So too at Nuffield College, Oxford, where Raymond Streat spent the Wednesday evening with the fellows. 'The talk went on furiously until a late hour,' he recorded. 'The outstanding emotions I think were horror at the prospect of Britain being branded as an aggressor, horror of a long struggle followed by an interminable occupation in the midst of hatred and nationalistic tactics as in Cyprus, and shock at losing friends in Canada and U.S.A.' By this time, with the ultimatum rejected, British bombers were close to having destroyed the Egyptian air force, to the unstinting applause of Virginia Graham's husband for one. 'Tony,' she wrote from London to Joyce Grenfell in the States, 'is being wonderfully blimpish – he is so convinced that neither England nor the Conservative Party can do wrong – & he is all for us occupying the Canal Zone & to hell with UNO [United Nations Organisation].'[2]

'IT'S ON – AND EDEN STICKS TO HIS GUNS!' proclaimed the *Sketch* on Thursday, 1 November, with an editorial declaring that 'Suez for us means survival or ruin' and that 'if Britain were now forced into an ignominious retreat by a frenzied faction at home, then indeed would our nation be eclipsed and our standing in the world lost for many years to come'. But the *Sketch*'s circulation was still only about a quarter of the *Mirror*'s, which now pronounced on 'EDEN'S WAR': 'There is NO treaty, NO international authority, NO moral sanction for this desperate action.' The *News Chronicle* also came in strong – 'This is folly on the grand scale . . . Only a miracle can save the Prime Minister now' – and *The Times* wondered aloud about the wisdom of President Eisenhower only hearing about the Anglo-French ultimatum from press reports. In the Commons, a censure debate descended into what Mollie Panter-Downes called 'a bear garden', with Reggie Maudling subsequently claiming that Denis Healey had got so angry that steam had come out of his ears.

Among the diarists, both Frank Lewis (going to the Royal to see Hitchcock's *The Man Who Knew Too Much*) and Henry St John (focused on his breakfast conversation with his landlady about her unsatisfactory method of frying his bacon) ignored the crisis, as, more surprisingly, did Anthony Heap, who instead took advantage of the first-day Premium Bonds and bought £10 worth. Up in Barrow, back from the post office after her wearisome queuing, Last had a visit from a friend, Mrs Higham. 'She was so full of "admiration" of Eden's policy I felt envious,' noted Last. 'She laughed to scorn my fears & qualms. I wished so *heartily* I could too.' Madge Martin in Oxford kept things in perspective. 'It does seem awful,' she reflected on the news about the bombings, 'but I still get more worried by personal problems.' Streat, back from the dreaming spires, met Sir Frank Lee, Permanent Secretary at the Board of Trade, who said not only had he known 'absolutely nothing of what was going on in the Cabinet', but that 'he was utterly opposed as a private person to what had been done'. If Streat had stayed in Oxford this Thursday, he might have witnessed a clash between anti-Eden student demonstrators and people with placards proclaiming 'Shoot the Wogs', and conceivably also Isaiah Berlin hurrying to catch the post. 'I should like to offer the Prime Minister all my admiration and sympathy,' he assured Clarissa Eden. 'His action seems to me very brave very patriotic and – I shd have thought – absolutely just.' Over in Cambridge, a motion at the Union opposing armed intervention was carried 218–136, amidst memorably rowdy scenes, while the *Manchester Guardian*-reading Sylvia Plath wrote home. 'This attack is a disaster from every angle – moral, military, political,' she told her mother. 'Britain is dead; the literary and critical sterility and amorality which I long to take Ted away from is permeating everything. God Bless America.'[3]

Suez was not the only world event this autumn. 'What has happened in Hungary during these past days has not been a popular uprising against a dictatorial Government,' declared the *Daily Worker*, organ of the British Communist Party, on 26 October. 'It has been an organised and planned effort to overthrow by undemocratic and violent means a Government which was in process of carrying through important constructive measures. . .' Now on 1 November, in a last-minute piece called 'Through the Smoke of Budapest' for the forthcoming issue of the *Reasoner*, an impassioned Edward Thompson asserted that the popular uprising in Hungary was part of the whirlwind being reaped by 'Stalinism'. What of the immediate future, with the Russian troops having apparently backed off? 'No chapter would be more tragic in international socialist history,' declared Thompson, 'if the Hungarian people, who once before lost their revolution to armed reaction, were driven into the arms of the capitalist powers by the crimes of a Communist government and the uncomprehending violence of Soviet armies.' And Thompson went on to attack the *Daily Worker*, which in its editorial columns 'has done nothing to express our thoughts or to assert our honour in the past few weeks'. High emotion in Halifax this Thursday was matched by yet higher emotion in Swansea. 'Even if you wanted Hilly twenty times more than I do, that would not make me any more inclined to let her go,' Kinglsey Amis wrote in a long, stern, entirely unhumorous letter to the priapic Henry Fairlie, in effect telling him to lay off his wife and accusing him of being 'selfish and ruthless by nature' as well as 'excitable to the point of instability'.[4]

Friday morning (2 November) brought predictable Suez reactions – a letter from Bertrand Russell in the *Manchester Guardian* declaring that 'the criminal lunacy of the British and French Governments' action fills me with deep shame for my country', a lengthy article by Michael Foot in *Tribune* claiming that 'not since Neville Chamberlain presented Hitler's terms to the Czechs in 1938 has a powerful Western nation treated a small nation with such brutal contempt', a *New Statesman* editorial condemning the British government 'for a crime not merely against Egypt, but against the whole edifice of international law' – but also less predictable. The *Spectator* had often in its history been a magazine of Tory reaction, but now under the editorship (and proprietorship) of Ian Gilmour it was more liberal and less easy to call. 'Was the action taken appropriate?' it now asked, in a leader that also hinted at collusion with the Israelis. 'And, if so, was it timely? The answer to both questions, it is now clear, is – no.' The other weekly to come out against Eden was the much-respected *Economist*, which accused him of 'a strange union of cynicism and hysteria' that could 'arouse no confident support in the country'. Everywhere there seemed discord and division. 'This Suez business is setting men by the ears,' reflected Kenneth Preston in Keighley, adding that in the staffroom at his grammar school there was 'a sharp cleavage of opinions'. Virginia Graham had lunch with 'a gaggle of ladies', she reported to Joyce Grenfell. 'Of course we thrashed about like puzzled whales. Most people seem to be shocked & depressed, & even the most pro agree it's got to be a success. Whatever "it" is.' Nella Last continued to feel 'sick at heart', not to mention 'baffled & bewildered', though took some comfort from her acquaintance Mrs Preston quoting to her Mr Preston: 'If we had given in, we were *done* for.' In Chingford, Judy Haines knew her mind. 'The Country is split as to the advisability of our action without permission from United Nations,' she recorded. 'I'm all for law.' Perhaps the most disconcerted person this Friday was the undergraduate Brian Thompson. 'I joined an anti-war protest march that was forming up outside the Cambridge Labour Club,' he recalled. 'An old man tottered out of the premises, reversed his walking stick and struck me a nerve-numbing blow on the arm. "Not a soldier among you," he shouted, beside himself with rage.'

Arguably, though, the prize for discombobulation went to poor Freddy Grisewood. As usual he was in the chair for the Light Programme's *Any Questions?* which, this Friday evening, came from the Wilton Carpet Factory in Wiltshire. The panel comprised a couple of MPs, the all-round great-and-the-good Mary Stocks, and Henry Fairlie, presumably still mulling over the Amis missive. 'Now before we have the first question,' announced Grisewood, 'I must point out that the question which very many of our audience have handed in to be discussed cannot be dealt with in this programme because of the 14-day rule.' This rule, imposed by government, stipulated there should be no discussion on radio or television of any question due to be debated by Parliament in the next 14 days, so this was presumably not a surprise to the panel, which nevertheless reacted angrily. 'Monstrous', erupted one of the MPs, 'hear, hear', concurred Stocks, 'absolutely ridiculous', exclaimed the other MP, and it was left to Fairlie, unable to top that, to assert 'it seems to me a most nonsensical rule'. Over the next half-hour or so, the panel, inspired by Fairlie, proceeded to lead an increasingly irate Grisewood a merry dance, going to elaborate lengths to discuss the burning issue of the day. 'We're all under the illusion that Britain has invaded Egypt,' said Fairlie. 'I want to talk about the other invasion which has been ignored, which is that Britain has invaded a country called Ruritania.' That directly led to the plug being pulled on the broadcast for a few minutes, and on its return Grisewood struggled through to the end as best he could.⁵

'RAF ROCK 'N ROLL 'EM ROUND THE CLOCK' was the *Sketch's* front-page headline on Saturday the 3rd, surpassing itself, and the report started: 'The last remnants of Colonel Nasser's air force lay in smouldering ruins in the desert dust last night. . .' Three papers in the other camp – *Manchester Guardian*, *News Chronicle* and *Daily Mirror* – all noted bulging postbags running heavily against Eden's action, though both viewpoints were represented, as in the *Mirror*:

When I heard of the bombing on the news this morning, I said to my husband: 'We don't want war. What can we do about it?' And his reply frightened me. 'There's nothing we can do about it. We voted the Government into power and it's their policy we have to abide by,' he said.

I've never written to a newspaper before, and I have no political affiliations, though I voted Tory last time, but I can remember the horror of the last war. There must be some way of stopping Eden. *(Mrs E.H., Windsor)*

Thank heaven at last this country is going to stop being pushed around by all and sundry. Old Eighth Army 'rats' welcome the news that we are landing to protect the Suez – despite the cowardly bleats of the Socialists. *(J.M., Barnet, Herts)*

Between noon and 3.00 p.m. there was in the Commons what Richard Crossman called 'another bear-garden', including 'boos and catcalls' for the Foreign Secretary, Selwyn Lloyd, before the focus switched to Eden's television and radio broadcast that evening. 'All my life I have been a man of peace,' he almost pleadingly insisted, but he was adamant that 'chaos in the Middle East could permanently lower the standard of life in this country and in Europe, as well as in many poorer countries in the world', and he continued to call the Anglo-French intervention no more than a 'police action'. The diarists privately gave their verdicts:

A dishonest but able performance. *(Nicolson)*

An odious performance to me but effective. *(Benn)*

One of the most plangent appeals I have ever heard to the soapy floating voter and the liberal conscience. *(Crossman)*

Sounded tired, understandably, & I thought it could be better. *(Marian Raynham)*

Sounded a very tired man. *(Preston)*

Not everyone tuned in. 'It was no use planning to stay up till 10 o'clock to listen to Eden's speech,' ruefully noted Last, 'it would have destroyed any chance of sleep for both of us. . .' Fairlie, back from the West Country, also almost certainly missed it. 'Now, of course, things have been diversified by the arrest of Henry for not appearing before the bankruptcy courts,' related a not entirely displeased Amis next day to Larkin, adding that 'he spent last night in Brixton'.[6]

On Sunday morning the most celebrated – and execrated – editorial of the Suez Crisis appeared. The action against Egypt, asserted the *Observer*, 'endangered the American alliance and Nato, split the

Commonwealth, flouted the United Nations, shocked the overwhelming majority of world opinion and dishonoured the name of Britain', while an accompanying piece on the same page accused Eden's government of 'crookedness' as well as 'folly'. This made an appropriate appetiser to the main event of the day: a mass 'Stop the War' rally in Trafalgar Square, attended by at least 10,000, with many holding aloft 'LAW NOT WAR!' banners. The main speaker was Aneurin Bevan, whose beautifully delivered putdown would be a clip deservedly played again and again over the years: 'If Sir Anthony is sincere in what he says – and he may be – then he is too *stupid* to be Prime Minister.' After the demo, in the early evening, several thousand surged down Whitehall and headed for ungated Downing Street (where an apprehensive Cabinet was in session), only to be blocked by mounted police. Gaitskell, meanwhile, was rehearsing his 10.00 p.m. broadcast reply to Eden. 'What he had to say was so compelling,' noted an admiring Benn in the wings, 'that all the technicians stood completely silently and listened to every word. What a contrast to their usual lulling and whispering and hurried glances at the sports news from the evening papers.' In the broadcast itself, Gaitskell stressed the international aspect: 'We are doing all this alone, except for France: opposed by the world, in defiance of the world. It is not a police action; there is no law behind it. We have taken the law into our own hands.' Near the end, ill-advisedly, he called on potential Tory rebels to come out and force Eden's resignation – a call that, with just a few exceptions, served to reinforce Tory tribalism. It also stuck in many people's gullets that he was adopting such a critical tone only hours before British forces were due to go into battle on enemy territory, not least in the gullets of the troops themselves. 'Such expressions of fury and disgust and revulsion as I have rarely seen among grown men' was how Anthony Howard, on one of the troopships steaming towards Port Said, recalled their reaction.[7]

Over the weekend there had been another, heartbreaking international dimension. 'SOVIET TANKS CRUSH RESISTANCE' was the *Manchester Guardian*'s bleak headline on Monday morning, as it became brutally clear that the Russians had taken advantage of the Suez situation to exercise their military might over the Budapest rebels. 'One feels guilty at one's impotence – & our *folly* has distracted the attention of the world from this tragedy,' bitterly reflected Violet Bonham

Carter on the Sunday. 'I cannot forgive it.' Next day, the *Mirror* had no compunction about making the link. 'Once British bombs fell on Egypt the fate of Hungary was sealed,' asserted its leader. 'The last chance of exerting moral pressure on Russia was lost when Eden defied the United Nations over Suez.' Almost certainly Khrushchev would have acted as he did anyway, sooner rather than later, but undeniably Suez provided opportune cover. For Edward Thompson and John Saville, putting the final touches to the new issue of the *Reasoner*, there was just time on the Sunday to write an editorial taking account of 'the tragic news of the attack':

> The intervention of Soviet troops in Hungary must be condemned by all Communists. The working people and students of Budapest were demonstrating against an oppressive regime which gave them no adequate democratic channels for expressing the popular will. The fact that former fascists and those working for the restoration of Capitalism joined the revolutionaries does not alter this central issue. The criminal blunder of unleashing Security Police and Soviet forces against these crowds provoked the mass of the people to take up arms, in the name of independence, liberty and justice, against an oppression that was operated in the name of Communism.

This evening the British Communist Party ran true to form, its executive committee issuing a statement that 'the Soviet Union, in responding to the appeal made to them to help defend Socialism in Hungary, is also helping to defend peace and the interests of the world working class'. And next morning the *Daily Worker*'s main headline, 'NEW HUNGARIAN ANTI-FASCIST GOVT IN ACTION', was matched only by its blithe sub-head: 'Soviet troops called in to stop White Terror'.[8]

Elsewhere in the press, on this Monday the 5th that saw British paratroopers landing on Egyptian soil, there was the now usual daily barrage of correspondence, including from Leslie Meek of Wembley. 'I am firmly convinced,' he declared in the *Daily Mail*, 'that before long the majority of people in this country will be saying "Thank God for Eden" – just as we said "Thank God for Churchill" during the last war.' Eva Faithfull of Reading disagreed. After explaining in the *News Chronicle* how as an Austrian she had 'lived in Vienna during the whole

Nazi regime' and felt a 'sense of acute shame at the actions of my own country', and how she had then moved to England after the war and felt 'happy and secure', Marianne's mother went on: 'Now, as a grown woman, I am experiencing at the present time the same sense of helpless shame at the actions of our Government'. During the day, Raynham spotted Surbiton graffiti ('Gaitskell is a Traitor' scrawled just outside her gate and 'We want Eden' across the road), while Kenneth Williams passed a time of rare harmony with Tony Hancock: 'We talked of Suez – the action of Eden in Egypt – we deplored it.' This afternoon in the Commons featured the by now customary acrimonious scenes. 'Has the Prime Minister exchanged congratulations with Mr Khrushchev?' Healey asked Eden, to loud cheers from Labour MPs, and Bevan, 'red-faced and bursting with fury' according to the *Mirror*, 'banged the despatch box and shouted, "Will the Government stop lying to the House of Commons?"'.[9]

In the West End, the shock news came through at about four o'clock that, in view of the international situation, Buckingham Palace had requested the cancellation of this evening's Royal Command Variety show. 'I just cannot believe it's true,' declared a distraught Sabrina, who had been due to sing 'Temptation', backed by the Nitwits. 'And there was I insisting that they made the neck higher so that no one should protest about my appearance. It's ... oh, I don't know *what* to say.' Still, quite apart from bonfires and fireworks, there were plenty of alternative attractions this evening. Madge Martin in Oxford saw another MM ('certainly an enchanting creature') in *Bus Stop*; Tommy Steele gave his first major live performance, at the Sunderland Empire; on the box there was the debut of Granada's *What The Papers Say*; and in Gravesend, Benn addressed three protest meetings, though the poor turn-out 'rather confirmed what I had suspected: that ordinary people are not yet moved on this issue'. A better-attended protest meeting was at Colchester Town Hall, where the speaker was the pro-Soviet Labour MP Konni Zilliacus. 'He had quivering, fat jowls,' recalled John Sutherland, and 'in his Finnish accent he asked rhetorically: "What must a British soldier feel, as he drives his tanks against Egyptian women and children?" "Make the buggers run!" shouted back a member of the Young Conservative claque, who had taken over several of the front rows. Uproar ensued.'[10]

The main political news on Tuesday morning, offsetting the successful landing at dawn of the main invasion force, was a Gallup poll – conducted late the previous week – showing that only 40 per cent agreed with Eden's Middle East policy, whereas 46 per cent disagreed and 14 per cent were don't knows. Among the letters to the papers, probably the pick was Peter Ustinov's to the *Manchester Guardian*, attacking the 'odious hypocrisy' of the government's claim to have been conducting no more than a 'police action'. Another letter was from C. P. Snow to his brother Philip. 'I don't think a total war is likely,' he cautiously predicted, 'but one can't be sure that it's impossible & perhaps we ought to make emergency plans.'

The crucial information Snow did not have was that during the morning's Cabinet, Macmillan as Chancellor had outlined the severe pressure that Britain's financial reserves were now under and the unwillingness of the Americans to come to the rescue by offering dollar loans, with Macmillan concluding that in economic terms there was no alternative but to end the military action. Accordingly, a consensus emerged that a ceasefire would be announced later in the day. Eden duly did so in the Commons in the late afternoon, to resounding cheers from the Tories behind him. 'One of them said aloud, "What exactly are we cheering?",' recorded Benn on the basis of information emanating from Bob Boothby. 'Gerald Nabarro, who was beside him, exclaimed in a stage whisper, "We are cheering the last chance to save our political bacon, old boy. That's what we're cheering and make no mistake about it."' According to Crossman, 'the general Labour view' as members left the Chamber was that 'this was the greatest climb-down in history and that Eden couldn't survive'. In the short term, they reckoned without the BBC, which had been Eden-friendly almost throughout the crisis and now treated the ceasefire news as, in the words of the historian Tony Shaw, 'a vindication of the government's daring action rather than what it actually was, an enforced and humiliating halt'. Among the diarists there seems to have been a prevailing sense of relief – 'shameful relief' in Nicolson's case (as he told his wife), while for Last, despite this good news, 'the waste, destruction & chaos makes me shudder'.[11]

'"Bloody Yanks," muttered my father, without looking up from his *Daily Mail*,' remembered Anton Rippon about the Suez aspect of his Derby childhood. '"They've always been the bloody same."' A similar reaction around the country meant that during the week or so after Eden had announced the ceasefire, there was a perceptible shift of sentiment towards the government – that, in fact, Nabarro had called it right. The cumulative evidence was striking. A poll of 550 people in ten different London districts 'immediately after the cease-fire' found that 272 broadly approved of the government's intervention, 166 disapproved, and 112 had no firm opinion either way; letters sent to the *Yorkshire Post* were starting by the 8th to run strongly in the government's favour, while across the Pennines the voluminous daily postbags arriving at the *Manchester Guardian* showed a steadily declining majority against the action; a Gallup poll taken on the 10th and 11th revealed 53 per cent approving of the government's action and only 32 per cent disapproving; the composer William Walton, who at the start of the month had been equating Eden to Mussolini, was by the 13th fearing that if the Russians 'get Suez they've fairly got us by the balls (or testicles if you will) & they can cut (or bite) them off at any time they please'; and at a by-election at Chester on the 15th, the Tory vote held up sufficiently well to make it clear that, at a time of national crisis, the middle-class revolt against the party had run out of steam. John Fowles saw things differently. 'The Tory Party are fundamentally wrong in their action over Egypt,' began his letter to the *New Statesman* that appeared on the 10th, 'and it seems pretty certain that they have handicapped themselves out of the race in the next election.'[12]

The reverberations of Budapest, meanwhile, were only just starting. The *Daily Worker* on the 9th published a letter from Eric Hobsbawm, who as his alter ego of *New Statesman* jazz critic Francis Newton had recently described Elvis Presley as 'a peculiarly unappealing Texan lad . . . with a line in suggestive belly-dancing'. Here, he called 'the suppression of a popular movement, however wrong-headed, by a foreign army' as 'at best a tragic necessity', though at the same time stated that he was 'approving, with a heavy heart, of what is now happening in Hungary'. Then in the paper exactly a week later, in the same issue in which a group of docker-members of the party (including Jack Dash) stated that 'we regard as fully justified the calling in, at a late hour, of the Red Army to safeguard the working class of Hungary', there was an important piece by Peter Fryer, who in October had gone to Budapest as the paper's correspondent and had now resigned after his reports had not been used. In it he insisted that the Soviet troops who had entered the city on 4 November were not fighting fascists, but instead 'they fought workers, soldiers and students', and 'could find no Hungarians to fight alongside them'. The following week he elaborated in the *New Statesman*. 'From start to finish the *Daily Worker* – or rather the Stalinists who control it – has lied, lied, lied about Hungary,' Fryer wrote. 'Shame on a newspaper which can spit on a nation's anguish and grief. Shame on party leaders who can justify with smooth clichés and lies the massacre and martyrdom of a proud and indomitable people.'

Other *Daily Worker* journalists also left the paper and the party – including Llew Gardner (future television reporter) and Leon Griffiths (future creator of *Minder*) – during these often difficult, even agonising times for many Communists, not just journalists. 'We are both in an awful dilemma,' wrote one Nottinghamshire couple on the 13th to a friend in Leeds who was also a CP member, in his case in the process of leaving. 'When one has devoted a number of years, and sacrificed one's family life, for something we firmly believed would benefit mankind, then one doesn't give up easily . . .' But the fact was that 'we are both terribly disgusted with events in Hungary as we feel sure many comrades are'. Altogether, over the coming days and months, some 7,000 individual Communists did leave the party, representing around one-fifth of the membership. Those who stayed loyal included Hobsbawm, Arthur Scargill and many trade unionists, though not Les Cannon of the Electrical Trades Union; those who went included Thompson, Saville, Doris Lessing and the youthful historian Raphael Samuel, as well as the *Daily Worker* journalists. 'It wasn't easy psychologically for me to leave the Party, even with the events of 1956 as my solid reason,' recalled Jean McCrindle over half a century later. 'I had heard my father [a CP member who stayed] say often that people who left the Party were weak and neurotic bourgeois individualists who usually "ended up" needing Freudian psycho-analysis – another *bête noire* to communists of that generation. I seem to remember Doris Lessing being put in this category after she left. Everything was political. Personal private life was of no consequence compared to the collective comradeship of the fight for the future world revolution.'[13]

Back on the Suez front, there were mixed post-ceasefire fortunes for those parts of the fourth estate that had spoken out against Eden. The

Manchester Guardian lost readers in the north, but gained many more in the south; the *Mirror* and *News Chronicle* took significant circulation hits, of 80,000 and 25,000 respectively; and the *Observer*'s circulation – contrary to subsequent mythology – did not fall (despite Margaret and Denis Thatcher cancelling their subscription), but there was a serious loss of advertising, the start of a long commercial decline for the paper. For the *Spectator*'s Ian Gilmour, these were personally fraught times. 'Eden is indeed unspeakable,' he wrote on 19 November to Hugh Trevor-Roper in Oxford. 'In the present semi-fascist atmosphere up here it is considered treacherous to whisper a word of criticism. When I go into my club [White's], I feel as if I had been cheating at cards or something vile like that! Still we go plugging on even though our readers leave us in shoals.'[14]

Nor were these easy times for many other people. On the 20th – three days before Eden left for three weeks' much-criticised recuperation in Jamaica – it was announced that petrol rationing (a weekly maximum of 200 miles for private motorists) would start in mid-December, a development that led directly to BMC's Leonard Lord inviting back Alec Issigonis, designer of the Morris Minor, to create a new, fuel-efficient car: the Mini. Then on 3 December there were two further announcements: that the British forces would be withdrawing from Egypt and the tax on petrol would rise by 40 per cent. 'Newswise it's altogether a wretched Wednesday morn – petrol up to 6/- a gallon, bread going up, dollar reserves down a wump, a promise of increased income tax,' gloomily reported Virginia Graham on the 5th to Joyce Grenfell. 'It really does seem to have been a disastrous enterprise, & even Tony, who has been staunchly pro-Eden, is beginning to feel it wasn't *quite* the most brilliant idea he ever had.' Eden himself returned to the Commons on the 17th and was greeted, according to Panter-Downes, by 'a decent amount of friendly cheering by some, but noticeably not all, of the Tories, and decibels of ringing silence from the Labour and Liberal benches'. Three days later in the Chamber, he explicitly denied collusion: 'I want to say this on the question of foreknowledge and to say it quite bluntly to the House, that there was not foreknowledge that Israel would attack Egypt – there was not.'[15] The politics of Suez were not yet played out.

It was a crisis that had shown many things: Britain's inability to act independently of her American ally; the futility of clinging on to illusions of Empire; the ability of those in power to practise deceit, with the extent of the collusion not definitively emerging until well into the 1960s; and an undeniable waning of deference, symbolised by the Trafalgar Square demonstration. How much impact did it really have on people at the time? Certainly it is possible to construct a 'high' narrative that sees the Suez Crisis as a turning-point in British geopolitical-cum-economic policy, with for instance the *FT*'s gifted, left-leaning leader writer Andrew Shonfield blasting out a series of editorials calling for a fundamental rethink as well as a longer piece in the January 1957 issue of *Encounter* that strongly urged a downgrading of 'considerations of prestige' and a new realism about Britain's overseas responsibilities. Yet for ordinary people? Florence Turtle, too preoccupied by the pre-Christmas rush at work, made no mention of Suez in her diary, while Panter-Downes at the very height of the crisis noted that 'through all the shaking events and bewilderment of the past week, London has seemed a city of preternaturally calm people, who pause on the street corners to buy their papers and stand there a minute to stare at the headlines with a total lack of expression before tucking the things under their arms and marching on'. A mere three months later, at the start of February 1957, Crossman was much struck when he attended a by-election meeting in Lewisham in support of Labour's young, middle-class candidate. 'He talked far too much about Suez, whereas this election should be decided on rents and the cost of living, as nobody, at least in that audience, wanted to look back and discuss the merits of Suez,' reflected Crossman afterwards. 'We've settled down again in the most amazing way. Though the whole foundations of the country have been shifted by the earthquake, we are inclined to deny it ever occurred.'[16]

Nothing after all had let up in the distracting national pageant. A week after the ceasefire, Gerard Hoffnung and friends gave at the Royal Festival Hall London's first 'crazy concert', a sell-out affair aimed at making concert-going less solemn, though *The Times* reviewer found little amusing in 'Mr Hoffnung's private Tuba joke' or 'a septet of stone hot-water bottles and a quartet of household electrical cleaning devices'. Another week later, filming complete, Marilyn Monroe flew out of London Airport, telling reporters that 'meeting your Queen' had been her biggest thrill, 'I didn't manage to get any of your fish and chips' her biggest disappointment. Granada TV on the 28th gave

Look Back in Anger a full run-out, to complaints only from the *Daily Express*, while Amis on 6 December provided Larkin with a buoyant domestic update: 'I have more or less got my wife back (no Henry for 6 months; resumption of marital relations; much increased cordiality between the partners to the matrimonial arrangement in question) for the time being, and that is sodding good-oh, believe me, sport.' Henry St John remained impenetrable, inscrutable Henry St John. 'Despite the vile weather,' he noted on Sunday the 9th, 'of 13 passengers of both sexes, mostly young, on the upper deck of the trolleybus on which I returned [from Southall to Acton], all but one were hatless, and the one exception had a scarf on her head.' Two days later Fanny and Johnnie Cradock had their hour in the sun, presenting at the Royal Albert Hall, in front of an audience of 6,500 and the television cameras, the Bon Viveur International Christmas Cookery show, sponsored by the North Thames Gas Board. It turned out to be, more than ever before, a TV Christmas. 'Now at least there is the television to fill in the boring hours,' reflected Fowles, back home at Leigh-on-Sea; in St Pancras, the Heaps had only just acquired a set, which on Christmas Day itself was on 'almost continuously' between 3.00 and 9.00; and that day saw the first PG Tips 'chimps' ad, shot in a stately home with Peter Sellers doing the voices. On New Year's Eve there was a hint of satirical times ahead, when at the very small New Lindsay Theatre Club in Notting Hill Gate, Michael Flanders and Donald Swann gave the first performance of *At the Drop of a Hat*, opening with a wry song, 'A Transport of Delight', about the peculiar ways of London buses and their drivers and conductors. The first controversy of the New Year concerned the Honours List, specifically the CBE for Stanley Matthews. Now that 'our leading cricketer [Len Hutton], Association Footballer [Stanley Matthews] and jockey [Gordon Richards] have all received high recognition', grumbled a Hampshire colonel to the *Daily Telegraph*, 'is it too much to hope that the nation will recover a proper sense of values and reserve such honours for those whose services to it have been of greater moment than skill at games and horse-racing?'[17]

———

On the genuine grounds of ill-health, Eden resigned on Wednesday, 9 January. It is a moot point whether he really had a political future, but the striking fact was that, at the point of resignation, 56 per cent of the public were, according to Gallup, still satisfied with him. 'Here's a pretty mess, the Prime Minister resigning like that,' a taxi-driver said to Nicolson, while it was 'no shock' to Nella Last, given how 'his photos have shown him as a very sick man'. She expected Rab Butler to succeed Eden, but it turned out to be Harold Macmillan who had the greater confidence of his party, having generally displayed greater vigour – in both offensive and defensive mode – during the Suez affair. He also had, observed Panter-Downes soon afterwards, 'an extremely original mind, a bitingly witty tongue, and a touch of the showman', though Last's husband refused to believe the news, saying 'now what qualifications has *he* got?' 'THE QUEEN SENDS FOR MACMILLAN' announced the *Evening Standard* in its 'Final Night Extra' for the 10th, as the political wheel took another spin, but tucked away on an inside page its 'Newsbriefs' column was a pleasing reminder of the permanence of the local and particular:

> **Bus fares** at Lowestoft are to be raised to offset petrol rises.
> **Final cost** of a health centre on the Harold Hill estate at Romford is fixed at £35,270.
> **15 budgerigars** offered to Friern Barnet Council have been refused. Reason: no aviary.
> **The Queen** has sent a donation towards a new church on a housing estate at King's Lynn.
> **Police** have been asked by Harlow Council to watch for hooligans smashing street lamps.
> **Minimum charge** fixed by Bexley Council for circuses in parks there is £10 a day.
> **Complaints** of increased noise due to shunting at North Chingford are being investigated.

Elsewhere in Chingford, it was just another Thursday for Judy Haines, who made no mention of Macmillan in her diary. 'Still pegging away at Pamela's frock,' she noted instead. 'As my kitchen curtains are in ribbons, spared time to cut out material from new bought yesterday. I feel more confident with measuring since Dressmaking lessons.'[18]

Afterword

'Good food and plenty of it, full employment, well furnished homes – today's generation knows what Good Living really means!' began an advertisement for New Zealand butter ('the perfect butter with the natural golden colour') in *Woman* in the first week of 1957.[1] Food, jobs, homes: such was the holy trinity of the 1950s, a formula for Tory votes and a widespread, almost wholly welcome sense of security after the tumultuous upheavals and painful privations of the 1940s. 'Kitchencraft is the art of making your kitchen light, livable and labour-saving,' declared the current issue of *Woman and Shopping*, before itemising 'some good buys' – including 'a fluorescent light fitting designed specially for efficient, shadowless light at the cooker and sink', 'a spin dryer which will dry six shirts to ironing stage in six minutes', 'a chair in tubular steel with a foam rubber seat', and 'a "Mixidiser" that operates from a main tap and does your egg whisking, fruit pulping and creaming'.[2] For most people the future, not just in the kitchen, was indisputably modern – yet modern, they hoped, within a familiar, reassuring setting. Modernists, by contrast, had little patience with the recalcitrant forces of social conservatism. The tensions between these two perspectives – one glancing anxiously over the shoulder at a disappearing past, the other forging ever onwards and upwards – would be played out in modernity Britain.

Notes

Abbreviations

Abrams   Mark Abrams Papers (Churchill Archives Centre, Churchill College, Cambridge)
Amis   Zachary Leader (ed), *The Letters of Kingsley Amis* (2000)
BBC WA   BBC Written Archives Centre (Caversham)
Benn   Ruth Winstone (ed), Tony Benn, *Years of Hope: Diaries, Letters and Papers, 1940–1962* (1994)
Chaplin   Sid Chaplin Papers (Special Collections, University of Newcastle upon Tyne)
Crossman   Janet Morgan (ed), *The Backbench Diaries of Richard Crossman* (1981)
Crossman   Diary of Richard Crossman (Modern Records Centre, University of Warwick)
Dalton   Ben Pimlott (ed), *The Political Diary of Hugh Dalton 1918–40, 1945–60* (1986)
Daly   Lawrence Daly Papers (Modern Records Centre, University of Warwick)
Fowles   Charles Drazin (ed), John Fowles, *The Journals: Volume 1* (2003)
Fowles   John Fowles Papers (Special Collections, University of Exeter)
Gaitskell   Philip M. Williams (ed), *The Diary of Hugh Gaitskell, 1945–56* (1983)
Golden   Diary of Grace Golden (Museum of London)
Hague   Frances and Gladys Hague Papers (Keighley Library)
Haines   Diary of Alice (Judy) Haines (Special Collections, University of Sussex)
Heap   Diary of Anthony Heap (London Metropolitan Archives)
Hill   Diary of Jennie Hill (Hampshire Record Office)
Hilton   The John Hilton Bureau Collection (News Group Newspapers Limited Archive, News International Limited)
Hodgson   Diary of Vere Hodgson (held by Veronica Bowater, literary executor)
King   Diary of Mary King (Birmingham City Archives)
Langford   Diary of Gladys Langford (Islington Local History Centre)
Lewis   Diary of Frank Lewis (Glamorgan Record Office)
M-O A   Mass-Observation Archive (Special Collections, University of Sussex)
Macmillan   Peter Catterall (ed), *The Macmillan Diaries: The Cabinet Years, 1950–1957* (2003)
Martin   Diary of Madge Martin (Oxfordshire Record Office)
MNA   Muir and Norden Archive (Special Collections, University of Sussex)
Osborn   Michael Hughes (ed), *The Letters of Lewis Mumford and Frederic J. Osborn* (Bath, 1971)
Preston   Diary of Kenneth Preston (Bradford Archives)
Raynham   Diary of Marian Raynham (Special Collections, University of Sussex)
St John   Diary of Henry St John (Ealing Local History Centre)
Speed   Diary of Florence Speed (Department of Documents, Imperial War Museum)
Streat   Marguerite Dupree (ed), *Lancashire and Whitehall: The Diary of Sir Raymond Streat: Volume Two, 1939–57* (Manchester, 1987)
Townsend   Townsend, P., *Family Life of Old People, 1865–1955* [computer file], Colchester Essex: UK Data Archive [distributor], September 2004. SN: 4723.
Turtle   Diary of Florence Turtle (Wandsworth Heritage Service)

All books are published in London unless otherwise stated.

The Certainties of Place

1 All Madly Educative

1. Streat, pp 581–2; *The Times*, 2 May 1951; Langford, 3 May 1951; *The Times*, 4 May 1951; Gavin Stamp, *Britain's Lost Cities* (2007), p 133; *Daily Express*, 4 May 1951.

2. Keith Waterhouse, *Streets Ahead* (1995), p 14; Richard Weight, *Patriots* (2002), pp 200–201; 'Ralph Tubbs', *Daily Telegraph*, 27 Nov 1996; *The Times*, 'Hidalgo Moya', 4 Aug 1994; *Vogue*, July 1951, p 59.

3. Heap, 4 May 1951; Russell Davies (ed), *The Kenneth Williams Diaries* (1993), p 63; Hodgson, 20 May 1951.

4. MNA, Box 7, *Take It from Here*, 3 Dec 1950; Bobby Robson, *Farewell but Not Goodbye* (2005), p 20; Bernard Adams, 'Brian Behan', *Independent*, 6 Nov 2002; Casson obituaries in *The Times/Daily Telegraph/Guardian*, 17 Aug 1999.

5. *Picture Post*, 6 Jan 1951; Michael Frayn, 'Festival', in Michael Sissons and Philip French (eds), *Age of Austerity* (Oxford, 1986), pp 307–8; Becky Conekin, '"Here Is the Modern World Itself": The Festival of Britain's Representations of the Future', in Becky Conekin et al (eds), *Moments of Modernity* (1999), pp 228–46.

6. David Cannadine, *In Churchill's Shadow* (2002), p 265; Candida Lycett Green (ed), John Betjeman, *Coming Home* (1997), pp 279–80; Charles Reid, *John Barbirolli* (1971), p 295; *Vogue*, June 1951, p 74; Dylan Thomas, *The Broadcasts* (1991), pp 246–51; Nigel Warburton, *Ernö Goldfinger* (2004), p 131; Lionel Esher, *A Broken Wave* (1981), p 304; *New Statesman*, 12 May 1951; Peter Mandler, 'John Summerson 1904–1992', in Susan Pedersen and Peter Mandler (eds), *After the Victorians* (1994), pp 236–7.

7. Frayn, 'Festival', pp 324–5; Iona and Peter Opie, *The Lore and Language of Schoolchildren* (1959), p 105; Becky E. Conekin, *The Autobiography of a Nation* (Manchester, 2003), p 209; Christina Hardyment, *Slice of Life* (1995), p 37; Winston Fletcher, '1951: The Truth', *Guardian*, 9 Apr 1998; Mary Banham and Bevis Hillier, *A Tonic to the Nation* (1976), p 180; Stuart Hylton, *Reading: The 1950s* (Stroud, 1997), pp 12–15; Chris Waters, 'J.B. Priestley 1894–1984', in *After the Victorians*, p 222; BBC WA, R9/74/1, June 1951; John Simpson, *Strange Places, Questionable People* (1998), p 33; Robert Hewison, *In Anger* (1988), p 64; Banham and Hillier, *Tonic*, p 176.

8. St John, 11 Jun 1951; Heap, 17 Jul 1951, 19 Jul 1951.

9. Alison Ravetz, *Remaking Cities* (1980), pp 214–15; Osborn, pp 194–5.

10. *Coventry Evening Telegraph*, 15 Aug 1951, 17 Aug 1951; Nicholas Bullock, *Building the Post-War World* (2002), pp 80–82; *Coventry Evening Telegraph*, 30–31 Aug 1951; *The Times*, 12 Nov 1951; *Coventry Evening Telegraph*, 16 Jan 1952; *Listener*, 17 Jan 1952.

11. *Melody Maker*, 21 Jul 1951.

12. *Fowles*, p 131; Daly, Ms 302/5/3, 31 Aug 1951; Golden, 12 Sep 1951, 28 Sep 1951.

13. *Manchester Guardian*, 29 Sep 1951; Juliet Gardiner, *From the Bomb to the Beatles* (1999), p 57; *Listener*, 4 Oct 1951; *The Times*, 1 Oct 1951; *Daily Express*, 1 Oct 1951.

2 A Narrow Thing

1. M-O A, D5353, 21 May 1951; Raynham, 17 Sep 1951; BBC WA, R9/9/15 – LR/51/2313; King, 29 Aug 1951.

2. *Radio Times*, 25 May 1951; Roger Wilmut and Jimmy Grafton, *The Goon Show Companion* (1976), pp 44–5; BBC WA, R9/74/1, Oct 1951.

3. M-O A, D5353, 14 May 1951, 27 Sep 1951; *Radio Times*, 13 Jul 1951; *Daily Express*, 17 Jul 1951; *Western Daily Press*, 26 Jul 1951; BBC WA, R9/4, 4 Oct 1951; Hilary Kingsley and Geoff Tibballs, *Box of Delights* (1989), p 10; Andy Medhurst, 'Every Wart and Postule: Gilbert Harding and Television Stardom', in John Corner (ed), *Popular Television in Britain* (1991), pp 60–74; Candida Lycett Green (ed), John Betjeman, *Coming Home* (1997), p 381.

4. Gore Vidal, *Palimpsest* (1995), p 148; *Evening Standard*, 29 May 1951, 9 Jul 1951; Graham Payn and Sheridan Morley (eds), *The Noël Coward Diaries* (1982), p 177; *Coventry Evening Telegraph*, 5 Sep 1951.

5. *Guardian*, 10 Jun 2005 (Frank Keating); Hodgson, 5 Aug 1951; *Western Daily Press*, 6 Aug 1951; Milton Johns, 'Wally Hammond', *Journal of the Cricket Society* (Autumn 2006), pp 4–5.

6. Nick Clarke, *The Shadow of a Nation* (2002), pp 59–60; *Daily Express*, 21–22 Aug 1951; *The Times*, 21 Aug 1951.

7. *The Times*, 18 Jul 1951; *Port Talbot Guardian*, 20 Jul 1951; *The Times*, 23 Sep 1999; Clive Jenkins, *All Against the Collar* (1990), pp 30–37; *Daily Mail*, 23 Jul 1951; Jenkins, *All Against*, p 37.

8. Steve Jefferys, 'The Changing Face of Conflict: Shopfloor Organization at Longbridge, 1939–1980', in Michael Terry and P. K. Edwards (eds), *Shopfloor Politics and Job Controls* (Oxford, 1988), pp 66–8; *Birmingham Post*, 21–6 Jun 1951; Alistair Tough, 'Richard (Dick) Albert Etheridge', in Joyce M. Bellamy and John Saville (eds), *Dictionary of Labour Biography, Volume IX* (Basingstoke, 1993), p 76; John McIlroy, '"Every Factory Our Fortress": Communist Party Workplace Branches in a Time of Militancy, 1956–79, Part 2: Testimonies and Judgements', *Historical Studies in Industrial Relations* (Autumn 2001), p 82.

9. Email from Michael Banton, 12 May 2006; Michael Banton, 'The Economic and Social Position of Negro Immigrants in Britain', *Sociological Review* (Dec 1953), pp 49–52; *New Statesman*, 11 Aug 1951; *Guardian*, 30 Oct 2004.

10. John Lahr, *Prick Up Your Ears* (2000 edn.), pp 76, 79; Graham Lord, *Just the One* (1997), p 79.

11. M-O A, D5353, 30 Jul 1951; *New Statesman*, 4 Aug 1951; M-O A, TC58/2/H.

12. Carolyn Steedman, 'Landscape for a Good Woman', in Liz Heron (ed), *Truth, Dare or Promise* (1985), p 118; Christine Keeler, *The Truth at Last* (2001), p 114; George H. Gallup (ed), *The Gallup International Public Opinion Polls: Great Britain 1937–1975, Volume One* (New York, 1976), p 252; M-O A, D5353, 16 Aug 1951; Haines, 25 Aug 1951; *Western Morning News*, 1 Sep 1951, 3 Sep 1951; Michael Willmott (ed), Rev. Oliver Leonard Willmott, *The Parish Notes of Loders, Dottery & Askerswell, Dorset: Volume I*, (Shrewsbury, 1996), Oct 1951.

13. Raynham, 19 Sep 1951; Kenneth Harris, *Attlee* (1982), p 486; Raynham, 19 Sep 1951; Hague, Box 3, 24 Sep 1951; Macmillan, pp 101–2; Roy Jenkins, *Churchill* (2001), p 838.

14. *News Chronicle*, 12 Oct 1951; D. E. Butler, *The British General Election of 1951* (1952), p 50; *Luton News*, 11 Oct 1951; *West Herts and Watford Observer*, 12 Oct 1951.

15. *Picture Post*, 31 Mar 1951; *Daily Herald*, 12 Oct 1951; Butler, *British General Election*, p 108; Timothy J. Hatton and Roy E. Bailey, 'Seebohm Rowntree and the Postwar Poverty Puzzle', *Economic History Review* (Aug 2000), p 536.

16. Lord Moran, *Winston Churchill* (1966), p 342; Nigel Nicolson (ed) Harold Nicolson, *The Later Years, 1945–1962: Diaries and Letters, Volume III* (1968), p 210; Conservative and Unionist Central Office, *Britain Strong and Free* (1951), pp 17–18; John Campbell, *Margaret Thatcher, Volume One* (2000), p 92; Lewis Baston, *Reggie* (Stroud, 2004), p 83.

17. *Britain Strong*, pp 5–6; Joe Moran, 'Queuing Up in Post-War Britain', *Twentieth Century British History* 16/3 (2005), p 287; Michael Caines, 'Identity Crisis', *Times Literary Supplement*, 14 Apr 2006; Deryck Abel, *Ernest Benn* (1960), p 146.

18. BBC WA, R9/9/15 – LR/51/2435; Jenkins, *Churchill*, p 841; Hodgson, 21 Oct 1951; Speed, 17 Oct 1951; Michael Cockerell, *Live from Number 10* (1988), pp 11–13; *Listener*, 25 Oct 1951; Nicholas Parsons, *The Straight Man* (1994), p 114.

19. The British Institute of Public Opinion, *Behind the Gallup Poll* (1951), p 25; Steven Fielding et al, *'England Arise!'* (Manchester, 1995), p 199; Willie Hamilton, *Blood on the Walls* (1992), p 72; *Luton News*, 18 Oct 1951; *Bedford Record*, 2 Oct 1951, 16 Oct 1951; Benn, pp 155–6; *Spectator*, 19 Oct 1951.

20. R. S. Milne and H. C. Mackenzie, *Straight Fight* (1954), pp 5, 87–8, 108–10; Henry Mayers Hyndman, *The Record of an Adventurous Life* (1911), pp 244–5.

21. *Fowles*, pp 135–6; Chaplin, 7/3/1, 10 Oct 1951; Francis Wyndham and Diana Melly (eds), Jean Rhys, *Letters, 1931–1966* (1984), p 90; Dalton, p 556; Moran, *Churchill*, p 345; Macmillan, pp 108–9.

22. *Evening Standard*, 22 Oct 1951; Andrew Barrow, *Gossip* (1978), p 163; *Daily Mail*, 22 Oct 1951; *The Times*, 22 Oct 1951; *Evening Standard*, 26 Oct 1951; David Bret, *George Formby* (1999), pp 190–1; Lewis, 23–4 Oct 1951.

23. *Manchester Guardian*, 22 Oct 1951; *Coventry Evening Telegraph*, 23 Oct 1951; *Western Morning News*, 24 Oct 1951; *Luton News*, 25 Oct 1951; Margaret Forster, *Hidden Lives* (1995), pp 204–5.

24. Speed, 25 Oct 1951; *News Chronicle*, 25 Oct 1951; *Daily Mirror*, 25 Oct 1951; *Daily Mail*, 25 Oct 1951; Haines, 25 Oct 1951; Lewis, 25 Oct 1951; Speed, 25 Oct 1951; Ursula Vaughan Williams, *R.V.W.* (1964), p 323.

25. British Institute, *Behind the Gallup Poll*, p 25; *Listener*, 1 Nov 1951; *Times Literary Supplement*, 2 Feb 1996 (Hugo Williams); Cecil Beaton, *The Strenuous Years* (1973), p 105; Macmillan, p 110; *Evening Standard*, 26 Oct 1951.

26. Heap, 26 Oct 1951; Speed, 26 Oct 1951; *Guardian*, 29 May 2004; Hodgson, 27 Oct 1951.

27. Anthony Howard, *RAB* (1987), p 176; Andrew Roberts, *Eminent Churchillians* (1994), p 252; *The Times*, 23 Sep 2003.

28. Hodgson, 27 Oct 1951; Ina Zweiniger-Bargielowska, *Austerity in Britain* (Oxford, 2000), p 251; James Hinton, 'Essay in Labour Statistics', *Labour History Review* (Winter 1992), p 63; Zweiniger-Bargielowska, *Austerity*, pp 228–9.

29. Peter Parker, *For Starters* (1989), pp 84–5; Zweiniger-Bargielowska, *Austerity*, p 228; John Bonham, *The Middle Class Vote* (1954), pp 76–7; Nicholas Shakespeare, *Bruce Chatwin* (1999), p 64.

3 You Can't Know Our Relief

1. *Evening Argus* (Brighton), 3 Nov 1951; *Brighton & Hove Gazette*, 10 Nov 1951; *Evening Argus*, 5 Nov 1951; Colin Brown, *Fighting Talk* (1997), p 30; Decca Aitkenhead, 'Prezza on the Couch', *Guardian*, 26 May 2008.

2. *New Statesman*, 5 Jan 1952; *Daily Express*, 24 Nov 1951; Robert Colls, 'Cookson, Chaplin and Common: Three Northern Writers in 1951', in K.D.M. Snell (ed), *The Regional Novel in Britain and Ireland, 1800–1990* (Cambridge, 1998), p 175; *Radio Times* (Northern edn), 18 Apr 1952; Dave Nicolson, *Bobby Thompson* (Newcastle, 1994), p 19.

3. *Boxing News*, 19 Dec 1951; Dick Hobbs, 'Ron Kray', *Independent*, 18 Mar 1995; *Glasgow Herald*, 2 Jan 1952, 9 Jan 1952; H. F. Moorhouse, 'Professional Football and Working Class Culture: English Theories and Scottish Evidence', *Sociological Review* (May 1984), pp 301–2; Stephen Wagg, *The Football World* (1984), p 195; Eric Dunning et al, *The Roots of Football Hooliganism* (1988), p 136.

4. Harold Macmillan, *Tides of Fortune* (1969), p 491; M-O A, D5353, 27 Dec 1951; Haines, 31 Dec 1951; Iona and Peter Opie, *The Lore and Language of Schoolchildren* (1959), p 105.

5. Hodgson, 27 Oct 1951; Joe Moran, 'Crossing the Road in Britain, 1931–1976', *Historical Journal* (Jun 2006), p 486; *Daily Express*, 5–6 Dec 1951, 23 Jan 1952; *Economist*, 1 Dec 1951; Richard Overy, 'Sir Leonard Percy Lord', *Dictionary of Business Biography, Volume 3* (1985), pp 856–9; *Guardian*, 16 Apr 2005.

6. *Daily Express*, 30 Oct 1951; David Oswell, *Television, Childhood and the Home* (Oxford, 2002), p 101; King, 11 Nov 1951; BBC WA, R9/74/1, Feb 1952.

7. *Press and Journal* (Aberdeen), 12 Nov 1951; *Picture Post*, 9 Feb 1952; Andrew Hodges, *Alan Turing* (1983), pp 449–63.

8. Macmillan, pp 113–14; Anthony Sampson, *Macmillan* (Penguin edn, 1968), p 97; Anthony Seldon, *Churchill's Indian Summer* (1981), p 251; Harriet Jones, '"This Is Magnificent!": 300,000 Houses a Year and the Tory Revival after 1945', *Contemporary British History* (Spring 2000), p 111; Macmillan, p 134; A.G.V. Simmonds, 'Conservative Governments and the Housing Question, 1951–59', University of Leeds PhD, 1995, pp 92–3; Macmillan, p 134.

9. *Boro' of West Ham, East Ham, Barking and Stratford Express*, 18 Apr 1952; Mark Clapson, *Invincible Green Suburbs, Brave New Towns* (Manchester, 1992), p 49; Simmonds, 'Conservative Governments', p 345; Huw and Connie Rees (eds), *The History Makers* (Stevenage, 1991), pp 71, 79, 42–3; Steve Humphries and John Taylor, *The Making of Modern London, 1945–1985* (1986), p 87; Rees and Rees (eds), *History Makers*, p 3.

10. Roy Lewis, *Moving to Harlow* (Harlow, 1952), unpag; *Coventry Evening Telegraph*, 7 Dec 1951; Grant Lewison and Rosalind Billingham, *Coventry New Architecture* (Warwick, 1969), p 129; *Coventry Standard*, 31 Aug 1951; Andrew Saint, 'Fred Pooley', *Guardian*, 24 Mar 1998; *Municipal Journal*, 22 May 1953; *Coventry Evening Telegraph*, 4 Jun 1952; Bill Lancaster and Tony Mason, 'Society and Politics in 20th Century Coventry', in Lancaster and Mason (eds), *Life and Labour in a 20th Century City* (Coventry, c. 1986, pp 351–2. For a notably positive assessment of Tile Hill, see Nicholas Bullock, *Building the Post-War World* (2002), p 238.

11. *Hampshire Telegraph*, 9 Feb 1951, 14 Mar 1952; Lorna Sage, *Bad Blood* (2000), pp 89–102.

12. Nick Tiratsoo et al, *Urban Reconstruction in Britain and Japan 1945–1955* (Luton, 2002), chap 4.

13. Becky E. Conekin, *The Autobiography of a Nation* (Manchester, 2003), p 72; *New Statesman*, 16 Jun 1951; Percy Johnson-Marshall, *Rebuilding Cities* (Edinburgh, 1966), p 231; *New Statesman*, 16 Jun 1951; *Architectural Review* (Dec 1951), p 363; Tiratsoo et al, *Urban Reconstruction*, p 32; John Westergaard and Ruth Glass, 'A Profile of Lansbury', *Town Planning Review* (Apr 1954), pp 39–41; Tiratsoo et al, *Urban Reconstruction*, p 34; *Guardian*, 11 Jul 2001.

14. *Minutes of the Corporation of Glasgow*, Nov 1951–May 1952, p 1801; Nick Tiratsoo, 'The Reconstruction of Blitzed British Cities: Myths and Reality', *Contemporary British History* (Spring 2000), p 36; Peter Mitchell, *Memento Mori* (Otley, 1990), p 94; BBC WA, *Any Questions?*, 27 Jun 1952; Simmonds, 'Conservative Governments', p 428; BBC WA, *Any Questions?*, 27 Jun 1952.

15. Diary of John McGarry (Special Collections, University of Sussex), 8 Jan 1952–6 Feb 1952; Andrew Barrow, *Gossip* (Pan edn, 1980), p 166; *Daily Mirror*, 26 Jan 1952.

16. M-O A, TC14/1/L, 6 Feb 1952, D5353, 6 Feb 1952; Haines, 6 Feb 1952; Raynham, 6 Feb 1952; St John, 6 Feb 1952; *Crossman*, p 71.

17. BBC WA, R9/13/77; M-O A, D5353, 6 Feb 1952; Lewis, 6 Feb 1952; McGarry, 6 Feb 1952; *New Yorker*, 16 Feb 1952; Heap, 7 Feb 1952; Macmillan, p 141; Preston, 8 Feb 1952.

18. Heap, 8 Feb 1952; Raynham, 8 Feb 1952; Crossman, 15 Feb 1952; *Crossman*, p 73; M-O A, D5353, 13 Feb 1952; *Crossman*, p 74; Leonard Miall (ed), *Richard Dimbleby, Broadcaster* (1966), p 76; Barbara Pym Papers (Bodleian Library, Oxford), Ms 42, fol 11, 13 Feb 1952; Angela Potter (ed), *Shared Histories* (Athens, GA, 2006), pp 275–6; M-O A, D5353, 12 Feb 1952.

19. *New Yorker*, 23 Feb 1952; Frances Partridge, *Everything to Lose* (Phoenix edn, 1999), p 151; Haines, 15 Feb 1952; Speed, 16 Feb 1952; *New Yorker*, 23 Feb 1952; BBC WA, R9/9/16–LR/52/670; Raynham, 16 Feb 1952.

4 Hardly Practicable

1. Hilton, Box 17, London County Council file.

2. *Listener*, 22 Nov 1951; Michael Kandiah, 'Conservative Leaders, Strategy – and "Consensus"? 1945–1964', in Harriet Jones and Michael Kandiah (eds), *The Myth of Consensus* (Basingstoke, 1996), pp 71–2; A.G.V. Simmonds, 'Conservative Governments and the Housing Question, 1951–1959', University of Leeds PhD, 1995, p 8; Harriet Jones, 'The Cold War and the Santa Claus Syndrome: Dilemmas in Conservative Social Policy-Making, 1945–1957, in Martin Francis and Ina Zweiniger-Bargielowska (eds), *The Conservatives and British Society, 1880–1990* (Cardiff, 1996), p 248. Kandiah, 'Conservative Leaders', p 70; John Colville, *The Fringes of Power: Volume Two* (Sceptre edn, 1987), p 298; Alan Booth, 'New Revisionists and the Keynesian Era in British Economic Policy', *Economic History Review* (May 2001), pp 355–6; Neil Rollings, '"Poor Mr Butskell: A Short life, Wrecked by Schizophrenia"?', *Twentieth Century British History* 5/2 (1994), pp 197–8; Lord Butler, *The Art of the Possible* (1971), p 163; R. C. Whiting, 'Income Tax, the Working Class and Party Politics, 1948–52', *Twentieth*

Century British History 8/2 (1997), pp 208–12; *Financial Times*, 12 Mar 1952; Robert Rhodes James (ed), *Chips: The Diaries of Sir Henry Channon* (1967), p 568.

3. Helpful accounts of ROBOT include: Correlli Barnett, *The Verdict of Peace* (2001), pp 152–76; Jim Bulpitt and Peter Burnham, 'Operation Robot and the British Political Economy in the Early-1950s: The Politics of Market Strategies', *Contemporary British History* (Spring 1999), pp 1–31; Butler, *Art*, pp 160–62; Alec Cairncross, *Years of Recovery* (1985), chap 9; John Fforde, *The Bank of England and Public Policy, 1941–1958* (Cambridge, 1992), pp 426–51; Peter Hennessy, *Having It So Good* (2006), pp 199–217; Anthony Howard, *RAB* (1987), pp 185–9; Scott Kelly, 'Ministers Matter: Gaitskell and Butler at Odds over Convertibility, 1950–52', *Contemporary British History* (Winter 2000), pp 40–49; Nigel Lawson, 'Robot and the Fork in the Road', *Times Literary Supplement*, 21 Jan 2005; Donald MacDougall, *Don and Mandarin* (1987), pp 85–108; Keith Middlemas, *Power, Competition and the State, Volume 1* (1986), pp 199–204; Stephen J. Procter, 'Floating Convertibility: The Emergence of the Robot Plan, 1951–1952', *Contemporary Record* (Summer 1993), pp 24–43.

4. Barnett, *Verdict*, p 157; David Kynaston, *The City of London, Volume IV* (2001), p 48; MacDougall, *Don*, p 88; Kelly, p 47; Macmillan, p 149; Lawson, 'Robot'; Kynaston, *City of London*, p 51.

5. Alan Deacon and Jonathan Bradshaw, *Reserved for the Poor* (Oxford, 1983), p 53; *Listener*, 14 Feb 1952, 17 Apr 1952; *Financial Times*, 7 Mar 2001; Richard M. Titmuss, 'Social Administration in a Changing Society', *British Journal of Sociology* (Sep 1951), pp 193, 197; R. M. Titmuss, 'The Hospital and Its Patients', in James Farndale (ed), *Trends in the National Health Service* (Oxford, 1964), pp 273–82; Jim Kincaid, 'Richard Titmuss', in Paul Barker (ed), *Founders of the Welfare State* (1984), p 119.

6. *Hansard*, 27 Mar 1952, cols 883–6; Robert Shepherd, *Iain Macleod* (1994), pp 73–7; John Vaizey, *In Breach of Promise* (1983), p 40; Rhodes James (ed), *Chips*, p 568.

7. Benn, p 160; Crossman, pp 47–8; *Picture Post*, 22 Mar 1952; Denis Healey, *The Time of My Life* (Penguin edn, 1990), p 150.

8. *Observer*, 24 Apr 2005; *Times Literary Supplement*, 26 Dec 1997; Alan Thompson, *The Day Before Yesterday* (1971), p 147; *New Statesman*, 12 Apr 1952; *Times Literary Supplement*, 4 Apr 1952; Michael Foot, *Aneurin Bevan: Volume 2* (Granada edn, 1975), p 365; Aneurin Bevan, *In Place of Fear* (Quartet edn, 1978), pp 200, 203.

9. C.A.R. Crosland, 'The Transition from Capitalism', in R.H.S. Crossman (ed), *New Fabian Essays* (1952), pp 33–68; BBC WA, *Any Questions?*, 26 Oct 1951; Vaizey, *In Breach*, pp 95–6. In addition to two biographies – Susan Crosland, *Tony Crosland* (1982), and Kevin Jefferys, *Anthony Crosland* (1999) – see also Jeremy Nuttall's work on Crosland, including 'Tony Crosland and the Many Falls and Rises of British Social Democracy', *Contemporary British History* (Winter 2004), pp 52–79.

10. Dalton, p 575; Abrams, Box 67, 'The Future of the Labour Party, 1952–1959'.

11. Crosland, 'Transition', p 59; Martin Daunton, *Just Taxes* (Cambridge, 2002), p 229; E.H.H. Green, *Ideologies of Conservatism* (Oxford, 2002), pp 219–20; Ina Zweiniger-Bargielowska, *Austerity in Britain* (Oxford, 2000), p 236; Crosland, 'Transition', p 59; R. T. McKenzie, 'Laski and the Social Basis of the Constitution', *British Journal of Sociology* (Sep 1952), p 263.

12. Vaizey, *In Breach*, p 87; Jeremy Nuttall, 'Labour Revisionism and Qualities of Mind and Character, 1931–79', *English Historical Review* (Jun 2005), p 679; David

Donnison, 'Social Policy Since Titmuss', *Journal of Social Policy* (Apr 1979), pp 146–7; Robert J. Wybrow, *Britain Speaks Out, 1937–87* (Basingstoke, 1989), p 33.

13. Michael Paris, 'Red Menace! Russian and British Juvenile Fiction', *Contemporary British History* (Jun 2005), pp 127–8; Amis, p 287; Dianne Kirby, 'Ecclesiastical McCarthyism: Cold War Repression in the Church of England', *Contemporary British History* (Jun 2005), pp 196–201; Eric Hobsbawm, *Interesting Times* (2002), pp 191, 230–31; *Times Literary Supplement*, 12 Dec 1952, 19 Dec 1952, 2 Jan 1953; C. H. Rolph, *Kingsley* (1973), pp 311–14.

14. John Callaghan, 'Industrial Militancy, 1945–79: The Failure of the British Road to Socialism?', *Twentieth Century British History* 15/4 (2004), p 390; Abrams, Box 57; *Picture Post*, 20 Sep 1952, 27 Sep 1952, 4 Oct 1952, 11 Oct 1952; Richard Stevens, 'Cold War Politics: Communism and Anti-Communism in the Trade Unions', in Alan Campbell et al (eds), *British Trade Unions and Industrial Politics: Volume One* (Aldershot, 1999), pp 175–6, 183.

15. *Daily Herald*, 29 Aug 1952; Gaitskell, pp 317–18; John Callaghan, 'The Left and the "Unfinished Revolution": Bevanites and Soviet Russia in the 1950s', *Contemporary British History* (Autumn 2001), pp 68–70; Bevan, *In Place*, p 163; A. J. Davies, *To Build a New Jerusalem* (1992), pp 188–9.

16. Doris Lessing, *Walking in the Shade* (1997), pp 52–4; Raphael Samuel, *The Lost World of British Communism* (2006), pp 135–6.

5 What Will Teacher Say?

1. Hazel Holt, *A Lot to Ask* (1990), p 160; Kathleen Tynan (ed), *Kenneth Tynan, Letters*, (New York, 1994), p 185; *New Statesman*, 15 Mar 1952; BBC2, *Changing Stages*, 26 Nov 2000; *New Statesman*, 28 Jun 1952; *Punch*, 2 Jul 1952; Charles Duff, *The Lost Summer* (1995), p 154; Geoffrey Wansell, *Terence Rattigan* (1995), p 226; Sam Walters, 'Rodney Ackland', *Independent*, 7 Dec 1991.

2. BBC WA, R9/9/16–LR/52/941; William Smethurst, *The Archers* (1996), pp 37–8; *Listener*, 27 Mar 1952; John Clay, *R.D. Laing* (1996), pp 43–50.

3. Jeffery Weeks, *Coming Out* (Quartet edn, 1990), p 159; Richard Davenport-Hines, *Sex, Death and Punishment* (1990), p 301; Tony Gould, *Inside Outsider* (Allison & Busby edn, 1993), p 97; Andrew Hodges, *Alan Turing* (Vintage edn, 1992), chap 8; 'George Williams', *The Times*, 28 Apr 1995; *Independent*, 5 May 1999 (Ann Treneman); Alison Macleod, *The Death of Uncle Joe* (Woodbridge, 1997), p 28; Barbara Pym, *Excellent Women* (Pan edn, 1989), p 25; *The Times*, 7 Feb 2001 (Benedict Nightingale); *New Statesman*, 2 Aug 1952; *Sunday Pictorial*, 25 May 1952, 1 Jun 1952, 8 Jun 1952.

4. Heap, 12 May 1952; Michael Banton, *White and Coloured* (1959), p 157; *Manchester Guardian*, 7 Jun 1952; John Barnes, *Ahead of His Age* (1979), pp 427–8; *The Times*, 24 Jul 1952; *Picture Post*, 6 Sep 1952; *Guardian*, 18 Jun 2005 (Ian Jack), 16 Feb 2005 (Hugh Muir); Bob Carter et al, 'The 1951–55 Conservative Government and the Racialization of Black Immigration', *Immigrants & Minorities* (Nov 1987), pp 341–2; *Independent*, 16 Sep 1989 (Patrick Matthews).

5. *Picture Post*, 19 Apr 1952; Margaret Thatcher, *The Path to Power* (1995), p 79; *Grantham Journal*, 23 May 1952; William Shawcross, *Rupert Murdoch* (1992), pp 71–2.

6. Preston, 25 Feb 1952; Langford, 11 Jun 1952, 13 Jun 1952; George H. Gallup (ed), *The Gallup International Public Opinion Polls: Great Britain 1937–1975: Volume One* (New York, 1976), p 272; Robert J. Wybrow, *Britain Speaks Out, 1937–87* (Basingstoke, 1989), p 35; Haines, 26 Jun 1952.

7. *New Statesman*, 26 Apr 1952; *Merthyr Express*, 14 Jun 1952, 24 May 1952, 14 Jun 1952; Lotte Kuhler (ed), *Within Four Walls* (New York, 2000), pp 195–8; Dartington Hall Trust Archives, LKE/G/35, 3 Jul 1952; Chaplin, 7/3/1, 21 Jul 1952.

8. William Osgerby, '"One for the Money, Two for the Show": Youth, Consumption and Hegemony in Britain 1945–70, University of Sussex PhD, 1992, p 96; *Merthyr Express*, 3 May 1952; *Picture Post*, 17 May 1952; John Springhall, 'Horror Comics: The Nasties of the 1950s', *History Today* (Jul 1994), p 11; Wybrow, *Britain Speaks*, p 35; M-O A, D5353, 14 Jun 1952.

9. *Crossman*, pp 76–7; *The Times*, 25 Mar 1952, 27 Mar 1952, 3 Apr 1952, 9 Apr 1952; Michael Cockerill, *Live from Number 10* (1988), pp 25–6; Lord Moran, *Winston Churchill* (1966), p 390; *The Times*, 12 Jun 152; Anthony Sampson, *Anatomy of Britain* (1962), pp 606–7; *Crossman*, p 110; Wybrow, *Britain Speaks*, pp 35–6; *The Times*, 12 Jun 1952; BBC WA, R9/4, 19 May 1952.

10. John Karter, *Lester* (1992), p 24; John Arlott, *Fred* (Coronet edn, 1974), chap 5; 'Sir Harry Llewellyn, Bt', *The Times*, 16 Nov 1999; John Colville, *The Fringes of Power, Volume Two* (Sceptre edn, 1987), p 310; Kathleen Tynan, *The Life of Kenneth Tynan* (Methuen edn, 1988), p 98; *Blackpool Gazette & Herald*, 9 Aug 1952; C. P. Lee, 'The Lancashire Shaman', in Stephen Wagg (ed), *Because I Tell A Joke Or Two* (1998), pp 46–7.

11. Macmillan, pp 181–2; David Sandison, *The Golden Years: 1952* (1996), p 39; Macmillan, p 183.

12. Frank MacShane (ed), *Selected Letters of Raymond Chandler* (1981), pp 320, 327; John Betjeman, *First and Last Loves* (Grey Arrow edn, 1960), pp 11, 14–15; Bevis Hillier, *John Betjeman: New Fame, New Love* (2002), pp 483, 485; 'Law Report', *Independent*, 4 Mar 1998; *Daily Telegraph*, 25 Feb 1998 (Terence Shaw).

13. BBC WA, R9/4, Mar 1952; *Daily Telegraph*, 12 Jul 2002; Sonia Orwell and Ian Angus (eds), *The Collected Essays, Journalism and Letters of George Orwell, Volume I* (1968), p 539. In general on *Billy Bunter of Greyfriars School*, see also the obituaries of Campion in *The Times/Guardian*, 11 Jul 2002, and *Independent*, 13 Jul 2002.

14. *Times Educational Supplement*, 25 Jan 1952, 1 Feb 1952, 8 Feb 1952, 7 Mar 1952; *Picture Post*, 30 Aug 1952.

15. *New Statesman*, 21 Mar 1953; *Political Quarterly* (Apr 1952), p 146; *Guardian*, 18 Jan 1994; Alan C. Kerckhoff et al, *Going Comprehensive* (1996), p 62; Anthony Seldon, *Churchill's Indian Summer* (1981), p 277.

16. *The Spur* (Spring 1952), p 10; *Nottingham Guardian*, 20 Apr 1953; Rosalind Delmar, 'Recording a Landscape: Growing Up in Dormanstown', in Jim Fyrth (ed), *Labour's Promised Land?* (1995), pp 310–12; Beryl Gilroy, *Black Teacher* (1976), pp 50–1; Haines, 22 May 1952.

17. *Daily Mirror*, 1 Jul 1952; John Singleton, 'The Decline of the British Cotton Industry since 1940', in Mary B. Rose (ed), *The Lancashire Cotton Industry* (Preston, 1996), p 307; *New Statesman*, 31 May 1952 (Basil Davidson); *Planning*, 1 Dec 1952, pp 130–35.

18. Marguerite W. Dupree, 'Struggling with Destiny: The Cotton Industry, Overseas Trade Policy and the Cotton Board, 1940–1959', *Business History*, Oct 1990, pp 116–18; John Singleton, *Lancashire on the Scrapheap* (Oxford, 1991), p 130; David Hunt, 'Cyril Lord', in *Oxford Dictionary of National Biography, Volume 34* (Oxford, 2004), p 437; *Oldham Chronicle*, 19 Jul 1952; Streat, p 646; *Daily Express*, 23 Aug 1952; Singleton, *Scrapheap*, p 131.

19. Singleton, *Scrapheap*, pp 128–9; *Oldham Chronicle*, 12 Jul 1952; Ferdynand Zweig, *The British Worker* (1952), p 40; Correlli Barnett, *The Verdict of Peace* (2002), p 303; John Singleton, 'Showing the White Flag: The Lancashire Cotton Industry, 1945–65', *Business History*, Oct 1990, p 129.

20. David Edgerton, *Warfare State* (Cambridge, 2006), p 104; *Economic History Review* (Aug 2006), pp 649–50 (Rodney Lowe review of *Warfare State*); *Times Literary Supplement*, 27 Jan 1995; Juliet Gardiner, *From the Bomb to the Beatles* (1999), pp 62–3; Denis Gifford, *Complete Catalogue of British Comics* (Exeter, 1985), p 59; 'Raymond Baxter', *Daily Telegraph*, 16 Sep 2006, *Guardian*, 19 Sep 2006 (Richard Williams).

21. *New Yorker*, 20 Sep 1952; *Daily Mirror*, 3 Sep 1952; Sandison, *Golden Years*, p 45; *Daily Mirror*, 8 Sep 1952; *Guardian*, 6 Dec 2005 (Stephen Moss); *New Yorker*, 20 Sep 1952.

22. Keith Hayward, *The British Aircraft Industry* (Manchester, 1989), chaps 2, 5; Arthur Reed, *Britain's Aircraft Industry* (1973), pp 1–2; Barnett, *Verdict*, chap 17; Geoffrey Owen, *From Empire to Europe* (1999), pp 304–7.

23. BBC WA, R9/19/1, Jun 1952; David R. Devereux, 'State Versus Private Ownership: The Conservative Governments and British Civil Aviation, 1951–62', *Albion* (Spring 1995), pp 75–6; *New Yorker*, 20 Sep 1952; *Picture Post*, 13 Sep 1952; Channel 4, 'Comet Cover-Up', 13 Jun 2002.

24. *Guardian*, 6 Aug 1990 (John Ezard); King, 18 Nov 1951; Margaret Gowing, *Independence and Deterrence, Volume 1* (1974), pp 443–4; Papers of Lord Hinton of Bankside (Institution of Mechanical Engineers), HIN 1/38, 1/4; 'John Challens', *The Times*, 18 Mar 2002; *Daily Mirror/Daily Mail*, 4 Oct 1952.

25. Langford, 27 Sep 1952; T.A.B. Corley, 'Consumer Marketing in Britain, 1914–60', *Business History* (Oct 1987), p 74; David Jeremiah, *Architecture and Design for the Family in Britain, 1900–70* (Manchester, 2000), p 155; *Daily Mirror*, 6 Oct 1952.

6 Not Much Here

1. Ian Jack, *Before the Oil Ran Out* (1987), pp 20–23.
2. M-O A, TC85/9/B.
3. B. Seebohm Rowntree and G. R. Lavers, *English Life and Leisure* (1951), pp 92, 48–9, 85, 88, 119.

7 A Different Class of People

1. Doris Lessing, *Walking in the Shade* (1997), p 54; Dan Jacobson, '"If England was What England Seems"', *Times Literary Supplement*, 11 Mar 2005; Geoffrey Gorer, *Exploring English Character* (1955), p 34; Janet H. Madge, 'Some Aspects of Social Mixing in Worcester', in Leo Kuper (ed), *Living in Towns* (1953), p 278; Thomas Bottomore, 'Social Stratification in Voluntary Organizations', in D. V. Glass (ed),

Social Mobility in Britain (1954), pp 349–50, 381; Margaret Stacey, *Tradition and Change* (1960), p 148.

2. Ferdynand Zweig, *The British Worker* (1952), p 204; Alan Bennett, *Untold Stories* (2005), p 491; Joe Moran, *Queuing for Beginners* (2007), p 11; T. H. Pear, *English Social Differences* (1955), p 184; Anthony Sutcliffe and Roger Smith, *Birmingham, 1939–1970* (1974), p 249; *Manchester Guardian*, 14 Dec 1950; BBC WA, LR/47/379, 14 Mar 1947; Peter Miskell, *A Social History of the Cinema in Wales, 1918–1951* (Cardiff, 2006), pp 96–7; Gordon T. Stewart, 'Tenzing's Two Wrist-Watches: The Conquest of Everest and Late Imperial Culture in Britain, 1921–1953', *Past & Present*, Nov 1995, p 178; Stacey, *Tradition and Change*, p 88; Martin Polley, '"The Amateur Rules": Amateurism and Professionalism in Post-War British Athletics', in Adrian Smith and Dilwyn Porter (eds), *Amateurs and Professionals in Post-War British Sport* (2000), pp 81–114; Tony Collins, *Rugby League in Twentieth Century Britain* (Abingdon, 2006), chap 9; Fred Titmus, *My Life in Cricket* (2005), p 14.

3. Zweig, *British Worker*, pp 206–7; Abrams, Box 67, 'The Future of the Labour Party, 1952–1959'; Donald James Wheal, *White City* (2007), pp 213–14; Email from Pamela Hendicott, 15 Mar 2007; Elaine Feinstein, *Ted Hughes* (2001), pp 26–7; Joan Bakewell, *The Centre of the Bed* (2003), pp 86–8; Bennett, *Untold Stories*, pp 390–91; *Independent*, 25 Jan 2008 (Ciar Byrne).

4. A. M. Carr-Saunders et al, *A Survey of Social Conditions in England and Wales* (1958), p 64; H. T. Himmelweit, 'Social Status and Secondary Education Since the 1944 Act', in D. V. Glass (ed), *Social Mobility in Britain* (1954), p 142; Ross McKibbin, *Classes and Cultures* (Oxford, 1998), p 260; Correlli Barnett, *The Verdict of Peace* (2001), p 462; Carr-Saunders et al, *Survey*, pp 68, 70; John Eggleston, 'Secondary Schools and Oxbridge Blues', *British Journal of Sociology* (Sep 1965), pp 234–5; D. V. Glass, 'Introduction', in Glass (ed), *Social Mobility in Britain* (1954), pp 22–3; Angus Maude, 'The Conservative Party and the Changing Class Structure', *Political Quarterly* (Apr 1953), p 146.

5. *Fowles*, pp 3–5, 11, 27–8, 132–3.

6. Martin, 4 Jan 1952, 27 Feb 1952, 14 Mar 1952, 5 Aug 1952, 20 Dec 1952, end-1952, 2 Feb 1953, 17 Mar 1953, 10 Apr 1953.

7. This analysis derives from: McKibbin, *Classes and Cultures*, pp 44–9; Mike Savage et al, *Property, Bureaucracy and Culture* (1992), chap 3; Harold Perkin, *The Rise of Professional Society* (1989), pp 436–43; David Edgerton, *Warfare State* (Cambridge, 2006), pp 172–80.

8. Richard Gordon, *Doctor in the House* (1952), chap 1.

9. Gorer, *Exploring*, pp 48–9; M-O A, Directives for Sept 1948 (Men's replies, C–F file, Women's replies, A–H file, L–S file), Directives for Jan 1949 (Men's replies, J–L file, M–O file, Women's replies, R–W file).

10. Simon Gunn and Rachel Bell, *Middle Classes* (2002), p 97; quoted in Bill Williamson, *The Temper of the Times* (1990), p 73; A.C.H. Smith, *Paper Voices* (1975), p 149; McKibbin, *Classes and Cultures*, pp 63, 262.

11. Roy Lewis and Angus Maude, *The English Middle Classes* (1949), pp 283–6; John Bonham, *The Middle Class Vote* (1954), pp 65–70; McKibbin, *Classes and Cultures*, pp 65–6, 261–2.

12. Mike Savage, 'Sociology, Class and Male Manual Work Cultures', in John McIlroy et al (eds), *British Trade Unions and Industrial Politics: Volume Two*

(Aldershot, 1999), p 35; M-O A, Directives for Sept 1948 (Men's replies, G–I file, C–F file).

13. Arthur Marwick, 'Images of the Working Class since 1930', in Jay Winter (ed), *The Working Class in Modern British History* (Cambridge, 1983), p 223; *Daily Telegraph*, 11 Jan 2005; John Gross, *A Double Thread* (2001), p 121; *Encounter*, April 1955, p 14; *Times Literary Supplement*, 19 Jun 1953; Sir William Haley, *The Responsibilities of Broadcasting* (1948), p 11.

14. Williamson, *Temper*, p 75; Phyllis Willmott, *Joys and Sorrows* (1995), p 140; *Independent*, 1 Apr 2007 (Michael Glover); 'Donald Lindsay', *The Times*, 3 Dec 2002.

15. Bennett, *Untold Stories*, p 24; Sheila Rowbotham, 'Revolt in Roundhay', in Liz Heron (ed), *Truth, Dare or Promise* (1985), p 193; Hunter Davies, *The Beatles* (1978), p 25; *Picture Post*, 2 Aug 1952; *News Chronicle*, 25 Aug 1952; *Evening News*, 6 Oct 1952.

16. M-O A, TC3/4/A–B; Langford, 16 Mar 1949, 20 Jun 1952, 7 Jan 1953; M-O A, D5353, 7 Jul 1947, 10 Jul 1947.

17. Peter Stead, 'Barry since 1939', in Donald Moore (ed), *Barry* (Barry Island, 2nd edn, 1985), p 457; Ian Jack, *Before the Oil Ran Out* (1987), pp 33–4; F. Zweig, *Women's Life and Labour* (1952), chap 17.

18. M-O A, Directives for Sept 1948 (Men's replies, C–F file); Gorer, *Exploring*, pp 40–41; Zweig, *British Worker*, p 201; John Benson, *Affluence and Authority* (2005), pp 197–8; Mass-Observation, *The Press and Its Readers* (1949), p 98; T. Cauter and J. S. Downham, *The Communication of Ideas* (1954), pp 246, 256.

19. Zweig, *British Worker*, p 206; Collins, p 138; BBC WA, R9/74/1, May 1950; Margaret Forster, *Hidden Lives* (1995), p 209; BBC WA, R9/9/15–LR/51/2313; David Hendy, 'BBC Radio Four and Conflicts over Spoken English in the 1970s', *Media History* (Dec 2006), p 275; Doris Lessing, *In Pursuit of the English* (Sphere edn, 1968), p 113.

20. Norman Dennis et al, *Coal Is Our Life* (Tavistock edn, 1969), pp 33–4; Mike Savage and Andrew Miles, *The Remaking of the British Working Class, 1840–1940* (1994), p 5; *Picture Post*, 16 Aug 1952; Savage, 'Sociology', pp 23–42.

21. John Lahr, *Prick Up Your Ears* (Bloomsbury edn, 2002), pp 49, 57, 69–70; Tom Courtenay, *Dear Tom* (2000); Tam Dalyell, 'Roland Boyes', *Independent*, 21 Jun 2006; John Sutherland, *The Boy Who Loved Books* (2007), pp 56–9; Terence Stamp, *Stamp Album* (1987), p 65; Lynda Lee-Potter, *Class Act* (2000), pp 9–10.

22. Nadine Meisner, 'Terry Gilbert', *Independent*, 21 Sep 2001; Elizabeth Roberts, *Women and Families* (Oxford, 1995), p 173; F. W. Martin, 'An Inquiry into Parents' Preferences in Secondary Education', in D. V. Glass (ed), *Social Mobility in Britain* (1954), chap 7; *Guardian*, 16 Oct 2004; Selina Todd, 'Breadwinners and Dependants: Working-Class Young People in England, 1918–1955', *International Review of Social History*, April 2007, p 78; Email from Ken Worpole, 17 Jan 2008; Joanna Bourke, *Working-Class Cultures in Britain, 1890–1960* (1994), pp 120–21.

23. Brian Thompson, *Keeping Mum* (2006), pp 90–91, 196–200, 231–2.

8 It Makes a Break

1. Doris Rich, 'Spare Time in the Black Country', in Leo Kuper (ed), *Living in Towns* (1953), p 323; Noddy Holder, *Who's Crazee Now?* (1999), pp 1–10.

2. *Independent*, 9 May 1995 (Nick Donaldson); *Kelly's Directory of The City of Newcastle Upon Tyne and Gosforth, 1953* (1953), pp 217–18; Benwell Community Project, *Final Report Series, No 7* (Newcastle upon Tyne, 1979), pp 16–17. See also Jimmy Forsyth, *Scotswood Road* (Newcastle upon Tyne, 1986).

3. Cilla Black, *What's It All About?* (2003), pp 4–5, 11–12; Paul Bailey, *An Immaculate Mistake* (2004); Diaries of William Hayhurst (Manchester City Archives), Mss 573/9–10, 14, 16–18.

4. B. Seebohm Rowntree and G. R. Lavers, *English Life and Leisure* (1951), p 287; T. Cauter and J. S. Downham, *The Communication of Ideas* (1954), pp 168–9.

5. Geoffrey Browne, *Patterns of British Life* (1950), pp 70–72; Mass-Observation, *The Press and Its Readers* (1949), pp 20–73.

6. *Daily Mirror*, 30 Jul 1951; Mass-Observation, *Press*, pp 39, 104.

7. Rowntree and Lavers, *English Life*, p 289; *News of the World*, 23 Nov 1952; Browne, *Patterns*, p 74; *Sunday Post*, 23 Nov 1952; *Guardian*, 11 Jan 2003 (Ian Jack).

8. *News of the World*, 21 Dec 1952; *Autosport*, 6 Jun 1952; Anton Rippon, *A Derby Boy* (Stroud, 2007), pp 22–3; John Sutherland, *The Boy Who Loved Books* (2007), p 141; Browne, *Patterns*, pp 122–5; David Vincent, *Poor Citizens* (Harlow, 1991), p 148; *Financial Times*, 21 Apr 2001 (Andrew Lycett); Lorna Sage, *Bad Blood* (2000), p 40.

9. *Picture Post*, 4 Sep 1948; Rowntree and Lavers, *English Life*, p 201.

10. M-O A, TC85/9/A, 11 May 1947; A. M. Carr-Saunders et al, *A Survey of Social Conditions in England and Wales* (1958), p 251; T. R. Gourvish and R. G. Wilson, *The British Brewing Industry, 1830–1980* (Cambridge, 1994), p 368; Cauter and Downham, *Communication*, p 90; Browne, *Patterns*, p 126; John Ezard, 'Francis Showering', *Guardian*, 8 Sep 1995.

11. M-O A, FR 3029, p 56, TC 85/14/A, May 1951; Rowntree and Lavers, *English Life*, chap 3; *Picture Post*, 18 Jun 1949; Hunter Davies, *The Beatles* (Mayflower edn, 1969), p 56; Gourvish and Wilson, *British Brewing*, p 415; M-O A, FR 3029, pp 158–66; Rich, 'Spare Time', pp 352–3; Norman Dennis et al, *Coal Is Our Life* (Tavistock edn, 1969), p 153. See also Adrian Smith, 'Cars, Cricket and Alf Smith: The Place of Works-based Sports and Social Clubs in the Life of Mid-Twentieth-Century Coventry', *International Journal of the History of Sport* (Mar 2002), pp 137–50.

12. Cauter and Downham, *Communication*, p 91; M-O A, TC 85/14/B, May 1951; J. M. Mogey, *Family and Neighbourhood* (1956), p 103; Donald James Wheal, *White City* (2007), p 215; M-O A, FR 3029, pp 37–8, 96, 99.

13. Ferdynand Zweig, *The British Worker* (1952), p 137; M-O A, TC 85/4/B, FR 3029, p 72; Mogey, *Family*, p 103; Sonia Orwell and Ian Angus (eds), *The Collected Essays, Journalism and Letters of George Orwell: Volume III* (Penguin edn, 1970), p 63; *Daily Mirror*, 30 Jul 1951; Dennis et al, *Coal*, pp 154–5; M-O A, FR 3029, p 49, TC 85/9/B, 6 Oct 1947; Rippon, *Derby Boy*, p 32; Paul Thompson, 'Imagination and Passivity in Leisure: Coventry Car Workers and Their Families from the 1920s to the 1970s', in David Thoms et al (eds), *The Motor Car and Popular Culture in the 20th Century* (Aldershot, 1998), p 262; Rich, 'Spare Time', p 327; Mogey, *Family*, p 105; M-O A, TC 85/9/A, 8 Apr 1947.

14. Tony Collins and Wray Vamplew, *Mud, Sweat and Beers* (Oxford, 2002), pp 32–3, 58; M-O A, FR 3029, pp 113–14, 116, 119; Brian Bennison, *Heady Days* (Newcastle upon Tyne, 1996), p 14; M-O A, FR 3029, pp 121–2; Rich, 'Spare Time', p 326; Collins and Vamplew, *Mud*, pp 28, 33–4.

15. Brian Bennison, *Heavy Nights* (Newcastle upon Tyne, 1997), pp 34, 36–7; M-O A, FR 3029, pp 231–2, TC 85/8/A, 6 Aug 1947, TC85/9/A, 3 Jan 1947.

16. Mogey, *Family*, p 105; Collins and Vamplew, *Mud*, p 24; M-O A, TC 85/8/A, 7 Aug 1947, TC 85/9/A, 2 Dec 1947, FR 3029, p 110; Dennis et al, *Coal*, p 144.

17. M-O A, FR 3029, p 133; John Barron Mays, *Growing Up in the City* (Liverpool, 1954), p 71; M-O A, TC 85/9/A, 2 Dec 1947; Rich, 'Spare Time', p 327; M-O A, FR 3029, pp 71, 79, 103.

18. Zweig, *British Worker*, p 150; Cauter and Downham, *Communication*, pp 84–5; Zweig, *British Worker*, p 151; Cauter and Downham, *Communication*, pp 84–5.

19. *New Statesman*, 15 Apr 1950; Thompson, 'Imagination', pp 258–9; Rich, 'Spare Time', p 311; Ross McKibbin, *The Ideologies of Class* (Oxford, 1990), p 146; Janet Street-Porter, *Baggage* (2004), p 40; Geoffrey Gorer, *Exploring English Character* (1955), p 70; Cauter and Downham, *Communication*, p 79.

20. Dave Russell, *Football and the English* (Preston, 1997), pp 131–5; Carr-Saunders et al, *Survey*, p 246; Tony Collins, *Rugby League in Twentieth Century Britain* (Abingdon, 2006), p 200; Cauter and Downham, *Communication*, p 81; Gavin Mellor, 'The Social and Geographical Make-Up of Football Crowds in the North-West of England, 1946–1962: "Super-Clubs," Local Loyalty and Regional Identities', *Sports Historian* (Nov 1999), pp 25–42.

21. Jeffrey Hill, *Sport, Leisure and Culture in Twentieth-Century Britain* (Basingstoke, 2002), p 30; *Guardian*, 5 Jan 2008 (David Lacey); Subrata Dasgupta, *Salaam Stanley Matthews* (2006), p 40; Jonathan Coe, *Like a Fiery Elephant* (2004), p 53; Collins and Vamplew, *Mud*, pp 72–3; Russell, *Football*, p 138; *Barnsley Chronicle*, 12 Jan 1952; 'Trevor Ford', *The Times*, 2 Jun 2003; Richard Holt, 'Heroes of the North: Sport and the Shaping of Regional Identity', in Jeff Hill and Jack Williams (eds), *Sport and Identity in the North of England* (Keele, 1996), p 155.

22. *Football Mail* (Portsmouth), 15 Mar 1952; *Guardian*, 11 Jan 2008 (Harry Pearson); Billy Wright, *Captain of England* (1950), p 125; *Daily Telegraph*, 27 Jul 1998.

23. Tom Finney, *My Autobiography* (2003), pp 6–14; *Manchester Evening News*, 6–7 Oct 1949; John Ramsden, *Don't Mention the War* (2006), pp 325–44; Richard Holt, 'Football and Regional Identity in the North of England: The Legend of Jackie Milburn', in S. Gehrmann (ed), *Football and Regional Identity in Europe* (Munster, 1997), pp 54–9; Mike Kirkup, *Ashington Coal Company: The Five Collieries* (Seaham, 2000), p 84; Tony Mason, 'Stanley Matthews', in Richard Holt (ed), *Sport and the Working Class in Modern Britain* (Manchester, 1990), pp 175–6.

24. Trevor Delaney, *The Grounds of Rugby League* (Keighley, 1991); Sam Davies, 'The History of Hull Dockers, c. 1870–1960', in Sam Davies et al (eds), *Dock Workers* (Aldershot, 2000), p 192; Geoffrey Moorhouse, *At the George* (1989), pp 50, 30; Dennis et al, *Coal*, p 157; *Telegraph & Argus* (Bradford), 4 Sep 1951; David Storey, *This Sporting Life* (Penguin edn, 1962), p 7; *Independent*, 1 May 1999. In general on rugby league, see Collins, *Rugby League*.

25. Laura Thompson, *The Gods* (High Stakes edn, 2003), p 29; Browne, *Patterns*, p 140; *Picture Post*, 21 Nov 1953; *Racing Pigeon*, 5 Jul 1952, 9 Feb 1952; Richard Holt, *Sport and the British* (Oxford, 1989), p 188; George Orwell, *The Road to Wigan Pier* (Penguin edn, 1962), p 63; *Racing Pigeon*, 5 Jan 1952. In general on pigeon racing, see Martin Johnes, 'Pigeon Racing and Working-Class Culture in Britain, c. 1870–1950', *Cultural and Social History* (Sep 2007), pp 361–83.

26. Zweig, *British Worker*, p 127; Roger Munting, 'Betting and Business: The Commercialisation of Gambling in Britain', *Business History*, Oct 1989, p 72; W.F.F. Kemsley and David Ginsburg, *Betting in Britain* (The Social Survey, 1951), pp 1–2; Rowntree and Lavers, *English Life*, pp 139–44; M-O A, FR 3029, p 158. In general on gambling, see Carl Chinn, *Better Betting with a Decent Feller* (2004 edn); Mark Clapson, *A Bit of a Flutter* (Manchester, 1992); Keith Laybourn, *Working-Class Gambling in Britain, c. 1906–1960s* (Lampeter, 2007).

27. *Independent*, 27 Apr 2001 (Stan Hey); *Observer*, 29 Apr 2001; M-O A, TC 85/9/A, 19 May 1947; John Barron Mays, *Growing Up in the City* (Liverpool, 1954), p 72; Dennis et al, *Coal*, p 149; Rippon, *Derby Boy*, p 48; Madeline Kerr, *The People of Ship Street* (1958), p 34.

28. Laybourn, *Working-Class Gambling*, p 163; Browne, *Patterns*, p 142; F. Zweig, *Women's Life and Labour* (1952), p 145; Laybourn, *Working-Class Gambling*, pp 161–2; Clapson, *A Bit*, p 173; Mays, *Growing Up*, p 72; Lady Henrietta Rous (ed), *The Ossie Clark Diaries* (1998), pp xiv–xv.

29. Laybourn, *Working-Class Gambling*, pp 270–71; Zweig, *British Worker*, pp 142–3, 148.

30. Peter Stead, 'Popular Culture', in Trevor Herbert and Gareth Elwyn Jones (eds), *Post-War Wales* (Cardiff, 1995), pp 120–22; *Coal* (Sep 1950), p 19; *Daily Herald*, 27 Oct 1951, 29 Oct 1951; *Telegraph & Argus* (Bradford), 29 Oct 1951.

31. Robert Douglas, *Night Song of the Last Tram* (2005), p 297; Cauter and Downham, *Communication*, pp 134–6; Kerr, *People*, p 32; Dennis et al, *Coal*, pp 125–7; Steven Berkoff, *Free Association* (1996), pp 34–41; Phil Moss, *Manchester's Dancing Years* (Manchester, 1996), pp 10–11; Dave Harker, *One For the Money* (1980), pp 66–7; *Guardian*, 6 Oct 2007 (Joe Moran); Chris Ellis, 'Joe Loss', *Independent*, 7 Jun 1990; Moss, *Manchester's Dancing Years*, pp 21–2.

32. *Planning*, 5 May 1952, p 249; Sue Harper and Vincent Porter, 'Cinema Audience Tastes in 1950s Britain', *Journal of Popular British Cinema* (1999), p 67; Ross McKibbin, *Classes and Cultures* (Oxford, 1998), p 421; Barry Doyle, 'The Geography of Cinemagoing in Great Britain, 1934–1994: A Comment', *Historical Journal of Film, Radio and Television* (March 2003), p 62; M-O A, TC 17/15/H.

33. H. E. Browning and A. A. Sorrell, 'Cinemas and Cinema-Going in Great Britain', *Journal of the Royal Statistical Society* (1954), p 137; Alan Bennett, *Untold Stories* (2005), pp 159–60; Sutherland, *The Boy*, p 80; Rippon, *Derby Boy*, p 78; Michael Caine, *What's It All About?* (1992), pp 39–40; Paul Farley, *Distant Voices, Still Lives* (2006), p 80.

34. Harper and Porter, 'Cinema', pp 67–9; Peter Miskell, *A Social History of the Cinema in Wales, 1918–1951* (Cardiff, 2006), p 26; Kathleen Box, *The Cinema and the Public* (The Social Survey, 1948), p 2; Rachael Low, 'The Implications behind the Social Survey', in Roger Manvell (ed), *The Penguin Film Review, 1946–1949, Volume II* (1977), pp 109–10.

35. M-O A, TC 17/15/A–C, F; Vincent Porter, 'Feature Film and the Mediation of Historical Reality: *Chance of a Lifetime* – A Case Study', *Media History* (Dec 1999), pp 181–99.

36. Sue Harper, *Picturing the Past* (1994), esp chap 9; Dennis et al, *Coal*, p 163; Joanne Lacey, 'Seeing through Happiness: Hollywood Musicals and the Construction of the American Dream in Liverpool in the 1950s', *Journal of Popular British*

Cinema, 1999, p 55; Vincent Porter and Sue Harper, 'Throbbing Hearts and Smart Repartee: The Reception of American Films in 1950s Britain', *Media History* (Dec 1998), pp 187–8; 'Ronald Shiner', *The Times*, 1 Jul 1966; Vincent Porter, 'The Hegemonic Turn: Film Comedies in 1950s Britain', *Journal of Popular British Cinema* (2001), pp 83–4; *The Times*, 30 Jul 1951; *Kinematograph Weekly*, 20 Dec 1951, 18 Dec 1952.

37. *Coventry Evening Telegraph*, 8 Sep 1953; Millicent Rose, *The East End of London* (1951), pp 271–2; Lord David Sutch, *Life as Sutch* (1991), p 10; Colm Brogan, *The Glasgow Story* (1952), p 153; Roy Hudd, *Roy Hudd's Cavalcade of Variety Acts* (1997). For an evocation of life in Variety, see Brian O'Gorman, *Laughter in the Roar* (Weybridge, 1998).

38. Nicholas Parsons, *The Straight Man* (1994), p 122; G. J. Mellor, *The Northern Music Hall* (Newcastle upon Tyne, 1970), pp 207–8; Roger Wilmut, *Kindly Leave the Stage!* (1985), p 215; Simon Sheridan, 'Paul Raymond', *Independent*, 5 Mar 2008; *Picture Post*, 9 Jan 1954.

39. Hudd, *Roy Hudd's Cavalcade*, pp 120–21; 'Jimmy Jewel', *The Times/Independent* (Denis Gifford), 5 Dec 1995; John Fisher, *Funny Way to Be a Hero* (1973), pp 178–84; Wilmut, *Kindly*, pp 196–7, 199–200; Geoff J. Mellor, *They Made Us Laugh* (Littleborough, 1982), pp 38–9; Brogan, *Glasgow Story*, p 153; Fisher, *Funny*, pp 64–71; Andy Medhurst, *A National Joke* (Abingdon, 2007), chap 5; *Daily Herald*, 4 Jul 1950.

40. *Daily Mirror*, 30 Jul 1951; Hudd, *Roy Hudd's Cavalcade*, p 151; Bennett, *Untold Stories*, p 419; *Bob's Your Uncle!*, 21 July 1953 (Newcastle City Library, L791.4); Dave Nicolson, *Bobby Thompson* (Newcastle upon Tyne, 1996), pp 98, 61.

41. Denis Gifford, *The Golden Age of Radio* (1985), p 110; June Whitfield, *... And June Whitfield* (2000), pp 44–5; *Sunday Pictorial*, 12 Jan 1947; Gary Whannel, 'The Price Is Right but the Moments Are Sticky: Television, Quiz and Game Shows, and Popular Culture', in Dominic Strinati and Stephen Wagg (eds), *Come On Down?* (1992), p 181; M-O A, Directives for July 1949 (Women's replies, F–P file); *Daily Herald*, 15 Sep 1951; *Radio Times*, 30 Nov 1951; Whitfield, *... And June*, p 45.

42. Stuart Ball (ed), *Parliament and Politics in the Age of Churchill and Attlee: The Headlam Diaries, 1935–1951* (Cambridge, 1999), p 581; Rich, 'Spare Time', p 334; Dennis et al, *Coal*, p 151; *Newcastle Journal*, 5 Jun 1950.

43. W.F.F. Kemsley and David Ginsburg, *Holidays and Holiday Expenditure* (The Social Survey, 1951); *Coventry Evening Telegraph*, 25 Jul 1953; John Hudson, *Wakes Weeks* (Stroud, 1992), p 15.

44. Geof Parsons, *'Only One "f" in Geof'* (Lowestoft, 1998), chap 3; Valerie A. Tedder, *Post-War Blues* (Leicester, 1999), pp 76–83.

45. Alice Russell, *The Growth of Occupational Welfare in Britain* (Aldershot, 1991), p 117; *Picture Post*, 2 Jan 1954; *The Times*, 29 Aug 1953.

46. *Guardian*, 1 Jul 2006; Robert Jeffrey and Ian Watson, *Doon the Watter* (Edinburgh, 1999); Elfreda Buckland, *The World of Donald McGill* (Poole, 1984), p 124.

47. *Reynolds News*, 15 Jul 1951, 12 Aug 1951; *Independent*, 22 May 1993; *Picture Post*, 9 Aug 1952; Keith Parry, *Resorts of the Lancashire Coast* (Newton Abbot, 1983), p 196; Robert Stephens, *Knight Errant* (1995), p 15; Roger K. Bingham, *Lost Resort?* (Milnthorpe, 1990), p 255; Moss, *Manchester's Dancing Years*, p 41; Candida Lycett Green (ed), *John Betjeman, Coming Home* (1997), p 300.

48. Moss, *Manchester's Dancing Years*, pp 47–8; *Blackpool Gazette & Herald*, 21 Jul 1951; Parry, *Resorts*, p 190; John K. Walton, *The Blackpool Landlady* (Manchester, 1978), p 196.

49. *New Statesman*, 18 Jun 1949; Kenneth Harris, *Attlee* (1982), p 504; *Blackpool Gazette & Times*, 21 Jul 1951; *Reynolds News*, 23 Sep 1951; *Morecambe Guardian*, 18 Aug 1951; *Reynolds News*, 9 Sep 1951.

50. *Reynolds News*, 5 Aug 1951; Mark Lewisohn, *Funny, Peculiar* (2002), p 143; Julian Demetriadi, 'The Golden Years: English Seaside Resorts, 1950–1974', in Gareth Shaw and Allan Williams (eds), *The Rise and Fall of British Coastal Resorts* (1997), p 51; *Reynolds News*, 5 Aug 1951; *Isle of Thanet Gazette*, 12 Jun 1953; Gavin Lambert, *Mainly About Lindsay Anderson* (2000), p 61.

9 I've Never Asked Her In

1. Ricky Tomlinson, *Ricky* (2003), pp 16–37; Joanna Bourke, *Working-Class Cultures in Britain, 1890–1960* (1994), pp 137–8; Robert Colls, 'When We Lived in Communities: Working-class Culture and Its Critics', in Robert Colls and Richard Rodger (eds), *Cities of Ideas* (Aldershot, 2004), pp 283–307; Raymond Williams, *Keywords* (1976), p 66; Bourke, *Working-Class Cultures*, p 137.

2. Doris Rich, 'Spare Time in the Black Country', in Leo Kuper (ed), *Living in Towns* (1953), pp 358, 361; Mark W. Hodges and Cyril S. Smith, 'The Sheffield Estate', in University of Liverpool, *Neighbourhood and Community* (Liverpool, 1954), pp 92–3, 96, 98–9; J. M. Mogey, *Family and Neighbourhood* (1956), pp 112–13; Madeline Kerr, *The People of Ship Street* (1958), p 101; T. Cauter and J. S. Downham, *The Communication of Ideas* (1954), pp 62–7.

3. Rich, 'Spare Time', p 361; Peter Townsend, *The Family Life of Old People* (Pelican edn, 1963), pp 146–7; Richard Hoggart, *The Uses of Literacy* (Pelican edn, 1958), p 60; Bill Lancaster, 'Newcastle – Capital of What?', in Robert Colls and Bill Lancaster (eds), *Geordies* (Edinburgh, 1992), pp 65–7; Hodges and Smith, 'Sheffield Estate', p 89; Alison Ravetz, *Model Estate* (1974), pp 137–8.

4. *Bolton Journal*, 21 Jan 1949; Jeff Hill, 'Rite of Spring: Cup Finals and Community in the North of England', in Hill and Jack Williams (eds), *Sport and Identity in the North of England* (Keele, 1996), p 103; Norman Dennis et al, *Coal Is Our Life* (Tavistock edn, 1969), p 156; Hill, 'Rite', p 100; Adrian Smith, 'An Oval Ball and a Broken City: Coventry, Its People and Its Rugby Team', *International Journal of the History of Sport* (Dec 1994), pp 507–8. For two case studies of football and identity, see Gavin Mellor, 'Post-war Lancastrian Football Heroes: Finney, Lofthouse and Douglas', *North West Labour History* (1999–2000), pp 44–54; N. A. Phelps, 'Professional Football and Local Identity in the "Golden Age": Portsmouth in the Mid-twentieth Century', *Urban History* (Dec 2005), pp 459–80. For a particularly rich evocation of a football club and its community, see also Andrew Ward and Ian Alister, *Barnsley: A Study in Football, 1953–59* (Barton-under-Needwood, 1981).

5. Huw Richards, 'Terry Davies', in Richards et al (eds), *More Heart and Soul* (Cardiff, 1999), p 62; Rich, 'Spare Time', p 360; John Barron Mays, *Growing Up in the City* (Liverpool, 1954), p 49; Townsend, *Family Life*, p 145; Kerr, *People*, pp 23–4.

6. Roy Porter, *London* (Penguin edn, 2000), p xiv; Alison Ravetz, *The Place of Home* (1995), p 205; Mark Clapson, *Invincible Green Suburbs, Brave New Towns* (Manchester, 1998), chap 3; Mogey, *Family*, p 74.
7. Hoggart, *Uses*, p 86; Robert Roberts, *The Classic Slum* (Pelican edn, 1973), p 13; Jennifer Worth, *Call the Midwife* (2007), p 246; Jimmy Boyle, *A Sense of Freedom* (Pan edn, 1977), pp 8–9; Charles Johnstone, 'The Tenants' Movement and Housing Struggles in Glasgow, 1945–1990', University of Glasgow PhD, 1991, p 91; Becky Taylor and Ben Rogaly, '"Mrs Fairly is a Dirty, Lazy Type": Unsatisfactory Households and the Problem of Problem Families in Norwich 1942–1963', *Twentieth Century British History* 18/4 (2007), p 451.
8. James H. Robb, *Working-Class Anti-Semite* (1954), p 49; Hodges and Smith, 'Sheffield Estate', pp 10–13; Kerr, *People*, p 116; Leo Kuper, 'Blueprint for Living Together', in Kuper (ed), *Living in Towns* (1953), chap 5.
9. Avram Taylor, *Working Class Credit and the Community since 1918* (Basingstoke, 2002), pp 72–3; Dennis et al, *Coal*, p 197; Carole Anne Stafford and Alan Crowe, *Us Kids* (Birmingham, 1998), pp 26–7; Lorna Sage, *Bad Blood* (2000), pp 40–41.
10. P. Ford and C. J. Thomas, *Shops and Planning* (Oxford, 1953), p 44; Worth, *Call*, p 30; Melanie Tebbutt, *Women's Talk?* (Aldershot, 1995), pp 60, 50, 174.
11. Alison Ravetz, *Council Housing and Culture* (2001), p 165; Colls, 'When We Lived', p 298; Worth, *Call*, p 30; Geoffrey Gorer, *Exploring English Character* (1955), pp 60–61; Kuper, 'Blueprint', pp 45–7; Boyle, *Sense*, p 8; Donald James Wheal, *White City* (2007), p 265.
12. Kerr, *People*, pp 102–9, 138–41; Mogey, *Family*, pp 84, 94; Dennis et al, *Coal*, pp 152–3; Hodges and Smith, 'Sheffield Estate', pp 109–10; Kuper, 'Blueprint', pp 14–15, 50–3, 59, 99–101; *Coventry Evening Telegraph*, 28 Apr 1952; *Times Literary Supplement*, 8 Jan 1954.
13. Hodges and Smith, 'Sheffield Estate', p 108; G. Duncan Mitchell and Thomas Lupton, 'The Liverpool Estate', in University of Liverpool, *Neighbourhood and Community* (Liverpool, 1954), p 58; Mogey, *Family*, pp 85–8.
14. M-O A, Directives for Sept 1947; Gorer, *Exploring*, chap 4.
15. John Davis ('New Jerusalem' seminar, Kingston University), 3 June 2008; Worth, *Call*, p 180; Porter, *London*, pp xiv–xv.
16. Fred Lindop, 'Unofficial Militancy in the Royal Group of Docks, 1945–67', *Oral History* (Autumn 1983), p 27; Robb, *Working-Class*, p 115; Kuper, 'Blueprint', pp 37–9; *Manchester Guardian*, 5 Sep 1953; Ravetz, *Council Housing*, p 166; Enid Palmer Letters (Department of Documents, Imperial War Museum), Oct 1948.

10 Hit It Somebody

1. *New Yorker*, 11 Oct 1952; Brian Brivati, *Hugh Gaitskell* (1996), p 172; *Crossman*, p 151; Brivati, *Hugh Gaitskell*, p 176; BBC WA, *Any Questions?*, 10 Oct 1952.
2. Kenneth Harris, *Attlee* (1982), p 506; *New Statesman*, 25 Oct 1952; Michael Young, 'The Leadership, the Rank and File, and Mr Bevan', *Political Quarterly* (Jan–Mar 1953), p 104; Michael Young Papers (Churchill Archives Centre, Churchill College, Cambridge), 2/1/1, 10/3; Young, 'Leadership', p 106; *New Statesman*, 31

Jan 1953; Brivati, *Hugh Gaitskell*, p 181; John Saville, 'Sir Lincoln Evans', in Joyce M. Bellamy and John Saville (eds), *Dictionary of Labour Biography, Volume IX* (Basingstoke, 1993), pp 80–83.

3. *Financial Times*, 8 Oct 1952; Nicholas Timmins, *The Five Giants* (2001), pp 205–6; Robert Shepherd, *Iain Macleod* (1994), pp 84–5; Channel 4, *Pennies from Bevan*, 14 June 1998; Robert J. Wybrow, *Britain Speaks Out, 1937–87* (Basingstoke, 1989), p 38; *New Yorker*, 29 Nov 1952; Langford, 14 Apr 1953; George H. Gallup (ed), *The Gallup International Public Opinion Polls: Great Britain 1937–1975: Volume 1* (New York, 1976), p 294; Mark Pottle (ed), *Daring to Hope: The Diaries and Letters of Violet Bonham Carter, 1946–1969* (2000), p 121; *Lennox Herald*, 2 May 1953; M-O A, TC 67/9/D.

4. *The Times*, 9 Oct 1952; *Independent*, 11 Oct 1999 (Natasha Walter); *BBC History Magazine*, Dec 2002, p 48; Heap, 6 Dec 1952; Raynham, 7 Dec 1952; Langford, 8 Dec 1952; *Farmers Weekly*, 12 Dec 1952; *BBC History Magazine* (Dec 2002), p 49 (Devra Davis); *Hansard*, 27 Jan 1953, col 829.

5. BBC2, *Timewatch: The Greatest Storm*, 31 Oct 2003; *Fowles*, p 14; *Oldie* (July 2007), pp 42–3; *Independent*, 23 Jan 2003 (Michael McCarthy); *Timewatch* (Martin Francis); Michael Young, 'The Role of the Extended Family in a Disaster', *Human Relations* (1954), pp 387–8; *New Yorker*, 21 Feb 1953.

6. Fenton Bresler, *Lord Goddard* (1977), pp 225–6; Langford, 27 Oct 1952; National Archives, C.C. 96 (52), 20 Nov 1952; *Picture Post*, 6 Dec 1952; Langford, 7 Dec 1952; Bresler, *Lord Goddard*, p 234.

7. Michael Collins, *The Likes of Us* (2004), p 154; Donald Thomas, *Villains' Paradise* (2005), p 205; Langford, 10–11 Dec 1952; *Sunday Times*, 25 Jan 1953; *News of the World*, 25 Jan 1953; Rayner Heppenstall, *The Intellectual Part* (1963), pp 136–7.

8. *Daily Express*, 27 Jan 1953; *Daily Mirror*, 27 Jan 1953; *Spectator*, 30 Jan 1953; Russell Davies (ed), *The Kenneth Williams Diaries* (1993), p 87; *Evening Standard*, 31 Jul 1998; Humphrey Berkeley, *Crossing the Floor* (1972), p 127; *Daily Mirror*, 28 Jan 1953; Rosalind Delmar, 'Recalling a Landscape: Growing Up in Dormanstown', in Jim Fyrth (ed), *Labour's Promised Land?* (1995), p 313; Edmund White, *Genet* (1993), p 536; M-O A, D5353, 28 Jan 1953; Haines, 28 Jan 1953; Langford, 31 Jan 1953; *Independent*, 31 Jul 1998.

9. *Daily Express*, 25 Mar 1953; *Daily Mirror*, 25 Mar 1953; *Picture Post*, 18 Apr 1953; *The Times*, 26 Jan 1953; *News of the World*, 25 Jan 1953, 22 Feb 1953; *Daily Mirror*, 21 Feb 1953; *Kenneth Williams Diaries*, p 89; *The Times*, 15 Oct 2002.

10. *Sunday Graphic*, 26 Oct 1952, 2 Nov 1952; Ian Grosvenor et al (eds), *Making Connections* (Birmingham, 2002), p 63; Michael Banton, 'The Changing Position of the Negro in Britain', *Phylon* (March 1953), pp 82–3; Kathleen Jones, *Catherine Cookson* (1999), pp 214–15.

11. *Spectator*, 5 Dec 1952; *New Statesman*, 13 Dec 1952; Heap, 25 Nov 1952; 'Sir Peter Saunders', *Daily Telegraph*, 8 Feb 2003.

12. *Times Literary Supplement*, 17 Apr 1953; *Listener*, 23 Apr 1953; *Sunday Times*, 12 Apr 1953, 5 Nov 2006; Ian Fleming, *Casino Royale* (Pan edn, 1958), pp 157, 89, 61–2; David Cannadine, *In Churchill's Shadow* (2002), p 281.

13. Andrew Lycett, *Dylan Thomas* (2003), p 340; *Spectator*, 5 Dec 1952; Lycett, *Dylan Thomas*, p 340; *Radio Times*, 24 Apr 1953; Humphrey Carpenter, *The Angry Young Men* (2002), pp 54–5.

14. Bill Wyman, *Stone Alone* (1990), p 52; *New Musical Express*, 7 Nov 1952, 14 Nov

1952, 20 Mar 1953; *News of the World*, 29 Mar 1953; Graham Payn and Sheridan Morley (eds), *The Noël Coward Diaries* (1982), p 209; Pottle (ed), *Daring to Hope*, p 119; *New Statesman*, 11 Apr 1953.

15. Charles Gordon, *The Two Tycoons* (1984), p 42; Richard Davenport-Hines, 'Sir Charles Clore', in *Oxford Dictionary of National Biography, Volume 12* (Oxford, 2004), pp 183–4; David Clutterbuck and Marion Devine, *Clore* (1987), p 69; *Northampton Independent*, 13 Feb 1953; *Economist*, 14 Feb 1953; David Kynaston, *The City of London, Volume IV* (2001), p 64.

16. Steve Jefferys, 'The Changing Face of Conflict: Shopfloor Organization at Longbridge, 1939–1980', in Michael Terry and P. K. Edwards (eds), *Shopfloor Politics and Job Controls* (Oxford, 1988), p 68; Etheridge Papers (Modern Records Centre, University of Warwick), 202/S/J/3/3/2, 17 Feb 1953; Tim Claydon, 'Tales of Disorder: The Press and the Narrative Construction of Industrial Relations in the British Motor Industry, 1950–79', *Historical Studies in Industrial Relations* (Spring 2000), pp 12–13; *Birmingham Post*, 28 Mar 1953; John Salmon, 'Wage Strategy, Redundancy and Shop Stewards in the Coventry Motor Industry', in Terry and Edwards (eds), *Shopfloor*, p 198; Anthony Sutcliffe and Roger Smith, *Birmingham 1939–1970* (1974), p 173; Les Gurl Papers (Archives, Ruskin College, Oxford), 57/1.

17. Bank of England Archives, LDMA 1/7, 6 Mar 1953; Langford, 6 Mar 1953; Claire Harman (ed), *The Diaries of Sylvia Townsend Warner* (1994), p 194; Michael Wharton, *The Missing Will* (1984), p 198; Alison Macleod, *The Death of Uncle Joe* (Woodbridge, 1997), p 38; Paul Boyle (ed), *Cassandra at His Finest and Funniest* (1967), p 148; Dianne Kirby, 'Ecclesiastic McCarthyism: Cold War Repression in the Church of England', *Contemporary British History* (June 2005), pp 192–6.

18. *Radio Times*, 17 Apr 1953; 'Hilda Brabban', *Daily Telegraph*, 21 Sep 2002; Brenda Maddox, *Rosalind Franklin* (2002); M-O A, D5353, 30 Apr 1953.

19. Langford, 8 Oct 1952; *Architects' Journal*, 2 Oct 1952, 30 Oct 1952; Nick Tiratsoo et al, *Urban Reconstruction in Britain and Japan, 1945–1955* (Luton, 2002), p 13; Macmillan, p 185; Tiratsoo, *Urban Reconstruction*, p 12; *Architects' Journal*, 24 Apr 1952, 21 Aug 1952.

20. N. Tiratsoo, *Reconstruction, Affluence and Labour Politics* (1990), p 52; *Coventry Evening Telegraph*, 4 Jun 1952; Tiratsoo, *Urban Reconstruction*, p 24; Tiratsoo, *Reconstruction*, p 75; *Coventry Evening Telegraph*, 7 Feb 1953, 11 Feb 1953.

21. Janie Hampton (ed), *Joyce & Ginnie* (1997), p 175; *Glasgow Herald*, 15–16 Oct 1952; Charles Johnstone, 'The Tenants' Movement and Housing Struggles in Glasgow, 1945–1990', University of Glasgow PhD, 1991, pp 315–18; BBC WA, R9/74/1, May 1953.

22. Benwell Community Project, Final Report Series, no 4, *Slums on the Drawing Board* (Newcastle upon Tyne, 1978), p 8; *Proceedings of the Council of the City and County of Newcastle upon Tyne for 1952–1953* (Newcastle upon Tyne, 1953), pp 585–7.

23. Nicholas Bullock, *Building the Post-War World* (2002), p 117; *Architects' Journal*, 8 Nov 1951; Patricia Garside, 'Town Planning in London, 1930–1961', University of London PhD, 1979, p 497.

24. Bryan Appleyard, *The Pleasures of Peace* (1989), p 119; Thom Gorst, *The Buildings Around Us* (1995), p 113; Bullock, *Building*, pp 103, 105; *Osborn*, p 205; *Journal of the Royal Institute of British Architects* (April 1953), p 217.

25. Mark Girouard, *Big Jim* (1998), p 54; Victoria Walsh, *Nigel Henderson* (2001), pp 54–5; Bullock, *Building*, pp 118–19; Alison and Peter Smithson, *Ordinariness and Light* (1970), pp 52, 25, 20–21, 31.
26. Ministry of Housing and Local Government, *Living in Flats* (1952), p 31; J. A. Yelling, 'Expensive Land, Subsidies and Mixed Development in London, 1943–56', *Planning Perspectives* (Apr 1994), p 150; *Town and Country Planning* (Jun 1952), p 292; E. W. Cooney, 'High Flats in Local Authority Housing in England and Wales since 1945', in Anthony Sutcliffe (ed), *Multi-Storey Living* (1974), p 164; *Hansard*, 20 Feb 1953, col 1679; BBC WA, *Any Questions?*, 27 Mar 1953.
27. Miles Glendinning, 'Sam Bunton and the Cult of Mass Housing', in Glendinning (ed), *Rebuilding Scotland* (East Linton, 1997), p 105; *Builder*, 18 Jan 1952; *Architects' Journal*, 28 Feb 1952; *Glasgow Herald*, 14 Oct 1952; *Architects' Journal*, 25 Dec 1952; *Daily Mirror*, 23 Feb 1953.
28. Michael Young Papers, 2/1/1; Patrick Dunleavy, *The Politics of Mass Housing in Britain, 1945–1975* (Oxford, 1981), p 215; *Boro' of West Ham, East Ham, Barking and Stratford Express*, 4 Apr 1952; *Liverpool Daily Post*, 5 Sep 1952; Peter Shapely et al, 'Civic Culture and Housing Policy in Manchester, 1945–79', *Twentieth Century British History* 15/4 (2004), pp 420–21; *Coventry Evening Telegraph*, 4 Apr 1953; *Proceedings*, p 584.
29. Sutcliffe and Smith, *Birmingham*, pp 430–31; *Birmingham Post*, 3 Jan 1952, 10 Jan 1952; *New Statesman*, 29 Dec 1951; *Architect and Building News*, 6 Nov 1952; *Architects' Journal*, 26 Feb 1953.
30. A.G.V. Simmonds, 'Conservative Governments and the Housing Question', University of Leeds PhD, 1995, p 343; John Barron Mays, 'A Study of a Police Division', *British Journal of Delinquency* (Jan 1953), p 193; *Municipal Journal*, 22 May 1953; Langford, 12 Nov 1952.
31. Macmillan, p 215; *Glasgow Herald*, 9 Mar 1953.
32. *The Times*, 9 Apr 1996 (Harvey Elliott); *People*, 3 May 1953; *Coventry Evening Telegraph*, 2 May 1953, 4 May 1953.
33. Martin Johnes and Gavin Mellor, 'The 1953 FA Cup Final: Modernity and Tradition in British Culture', *Contemporary British History* (Jun 2006), pp 263–80; *Daily Express*, 2 May 1953; *The Times*, 2 May 1953; Paul Gardner, 'Blackpool v Bolton Wanderers: The Cup Final, 1953', in Ian Hamilton (ed), *The Faber Book of Soccer* (1992), pp 43–4, 46; M-O A, D5353, 2 May 1953; Radio 4, *The Archive Hour: Back to Square One*, 20 Jan 2007; *People*, 3 May 1953; *Daily Express*, 4 May 1953.

11 A Kind of Farewell Party

1. Streat, p 676; *Independent*, 16 Nov 2004; Mike Jackman and Garth Dykes, *Accrington Stanley: A Complete Record, 1894–1962* (Derby, 1991), p 191; Phil Hubbard et al, 'Memorials to Modernity: Public Art in the "City of the Future"', *Landscape Research* (Apr 2003), p 160.
2. M-O A, TC 69/3/B, TC 69/5/G; Martin, 12 May 1953; *People*, 17 May 1953; Speed, 19 May 1953; M-O A, TC 69/5/F.
3. Preston, 21 May 1953; Heap, 21 May 1953; Graham Payn and Sheridan Morley (eds), *The Noël Coward Diaries* (1982), p 213; Martin, 30–31 May 1953.

4. M-O A, TC 69/9/G, TC 69/5/E, TC 69/9/C.

5. BBC WA, R9/4, 17 Jun 1953, *Woman's Hour*, 1 Jun 1953.

6. Haines, 1 Jun 1953; Lewis, 1 Jun 1953; M-O A, TC 69/5/G; Langford, 1 Jun 1953; Martin, 1 Jun 1953.

7. M-O A, TC 69/5/I; Mark Pottle (ed), *Daring to Hope: The Diaries and Letters of Violet Bonham Carter, 1946–1969* (2000), p 123; *Daily Express*, 2 Jun 1953; Margaret Thatcher, *The Path to Power* (1995), p 78; M-O A, TC 69/6/B; James Lees-Milne, *A Mingled Measure* (1994), p 30.

8. BBC WA, R9/74/1, Jul 1953, R9/9/17–LR/53/1021; M-O A, TC 69/1/C; David Rayvern Allen (ed), *A Word from Arlott* (1983), pp 139–42; Martin, 2 Jun 1953; King, 2 Jun 1953; Raynham, 2 Jun 1953; St John, 2 Jun 1953.

9. BBC WA, R9/9/17–LR/53/1021; Ben Pimlott, *The Queen* (1996), pp 205–6; *Guardian*, 2 Jun 2003 (Stephen Bates); Amis, p 323; BBC WA, R9/9/17–LR/53/1021; Jon Lusk, 'George Browne', *Independent*, 10 Apr 2007.

10. BBC WA, R9/74/1; Diary of Barbara Algie (Glasgow City Archives), 2 Jun 1953; Lord David Sutch, *Life as Sutch* (1991), p 13; *Independent*, 29 Oct 2001; Miriam Akhtar and Steve Humphries, *The Fifties and Sixties* (2001), p 99; *The Times*, 13 Sep 2004 (Stephanie Theobald); *Spectator*, 15 Dec 2001.

11. Golden, 2 Jun 1953; Haines, 2 Jun 1953; M-O A, T69/6/D.

12. Asa Briggs, *Sound and Vision* (Oxford, 1995), p 221; Heap, 3 Jun 1953; BBC WA, R9/13/96; Jonathan Dimbleby, *Richard Dimbleby* (1975), pp 249–50.

13. Lewis, 2 Jun 1953; Russell Davies (ed), *The Kenneth Williams Diaries* (1993), p 91; David Foot, *Harold Gimblett* (Fairfield edn, Bath, 2003), pp 27–8; Lorna Sage, *Bad Blood* (2000), p 125; *Oswestry and Border Counties Advertizer*, 10 Jun 1953; Preston, 2 Jun 1953; Alethea Hayter (ed), *A Wise Woman: A Memoir of Lavinia Mynors from Her Diaries and Letters* (Banham, Norfolk, 1996), p 90.

14. M-O A, TC 69/3/A; *New Statesman*, 6 Jun 1953; Kenneth Harris, *Attlee* (1982), p 510; Haines, 13 Jun 1953; 'Elaine', in Terry Jordan (ed), *Growing Up in the Fifties* (1990), p 85; Lulu, *I Don't Want to Fight* (2002), p 22.

15. M-O A, TC 69/8/A; Maurice Broady, 'The Organisation of Coronation Street Parties', *Sociological Review* (Dec 1956), pp 229–38.

16. Anne Perkins, *Red Queen* (2003), p 119; Frances Partridge, *Everything to Lose* (Phoenix edn, 1999), pp 180–81; *Financial Times*, 28 Jun 2008; *Manchester Guardian* Archive (John Rylands Library, University of Manchester), 223/1; *New Statesman* Archive (University of Sussex, Special Collections), 17/7; Edward Shils and Michael Young, 'The Meaning of the Coronation', *Sociological Review* (Dec 1953), pp 63, 67, 73, 76–7; N. Birnbuam, 'Monarchs and Sociologists: A Reply to Professor Shils and Mr Young', *Sociological Review* (Jul 1955), p 23; Shils and Young, 'The Meaning', pp 78, 81.

17. *People*, 7 Jun 1953; Ronald Frankenberg, *Village on the Border* (1957), pp 120–22; *Oswestry and Border Counties Advertizer*, 10 Jun 1953; Foot, p 36; *Wisden Cricketers' Almanack 1954* (1954), pp 525–6; *New Statesman*, 6 Jun 1953; Kathleen Tynan, *The Life of Kenneth Tynan* (Methuen edn, 1988), pp 103–5; *New Yorker*, 27 Jun 1953; Payn and Morley (eds), *Coward Diaries*, p 214; Peter F. Alexander, *William Plomer* (Oxford, 1989), pp 279–82.

18. Lawrence Black, *The Political Culture of the Left in Affluent Britain, 1951–64* (Basingstoke, 2003), p 94; *The Times*, 4 Jun 1953; Black, *Political Culture*, pp 94–5;

Richard Weight, *Patriots* (2002), p 242; National Archives, CAB 195/11/1, 17 Jun 1953; Macmillan, p 238; BBC WA, R9/4, 13 Jul 1953; Anthony Sampson, *Anatomy of Britain* (1962), pp 606–8; *Daily Mirror*, 15 Jun 1953; *Manchester Guardian*, 15 Jun 1953; Des Freedman, 'How Her Majesty's Opposition Grew to Like Commercial Television: The Labour Party and the Origins of ITV', *Media History* (Jun 1999), p 26; *News of the World*, 26 Jul 1953.

19. M-O A, TC 69/3/A; Pimlott, *Queen*, p 218; *People*, 14 Jun 1953; Nick Clarke, *The Shadow of a Nation* (2003), p 62; Tim Heald, *Princess Margaret* (2007), pp 98–101; *Daily Mirror*, 26 Jun 1953.

20. *Sunday Express*, 5 Jul 1953; M-O A, D5353, 9 Jul 1953; Janie Hampton (ed), *Joyce & Ginnie* (1997), p 188; *Sunday Express*, 12 Jul 1953; *People*, 12 Jul 1953; *Daily Mirror*, 13 Jul 1953; M-O A, D5353, 15 Jul 1953; Payn and Morley (eds), *Coward Diaries*, p 215.

21. *Daily Mirror*, 17 Jul 1953, 20 Jul 1953; *People*, 19 Jul 1953; *The Times*, 24 Jul 1953; *Guardian*, 3 Dec 2005.

22. Roy Jenkins, *Churchill* (2001), p 863; Roy Greenslade, *Press Gang* (2003), p 64; *People*, 28 Jun 1953; *Daily Mirror*, 29 Jun 1953; Robert Rhodes James (ed), *Chips: The Diaries of Sir Henry Channon* (1967), p 580; *Daily Mirror*, 17 Aug 1953; Lord Moran, *Winston Churchill* (1966), p 455.

23. Ludovic Kennedy, *Ten Rillington Place* (Panther edn, 1971), pp 7–11; Langford, 1 Jul 1953; Donald Thomas, *Villains' Paradise* (2005), pp 215–16; Paul Rock and Stanley Cohen, 'The Teddy Boy', in Vernon Bogdanor and Robert Skidelsky (eds), *The Age of Affluence, 1951–1964* (1970), p 291; John Ezard, 'Nigel Kneale', *Guardian*, 3 Nov 2006; Hilary Kingsley and Geoff Tibballs, *Box of Delights* (1989), p 13; *The Times*, 28 Mar 2005; *News of the World*, 16 Aug 1953; BBC WA, R9/19/1, Sep 1953; Kingsley and Tibballs, *Box*, p 12; *Daily Mail*, 21 Jul 1953.

24. *News Chronicle*, 11 Aug 1953; Macmillan, p 264; *Daily Mirror*, 27 Jun 1953; *New Yorker*, 18 Jul 1953; Edwin Heathcote, *London Caffs* (Chichester, 2004), p 18; *Daily Telegraph*, 1 Jun 2002 (Max Davidson); Langford, 3 Jul 1953.

25. Douglas Bond, *1953 Scrapbook* (Newcastle upon Tyne, 1993), p 22; *Independent*, 1 Aug 1998 (Nicole Veash); Heap, 10 Aug 1953; Langford, 11–13 Aug 1953.

26. Alan Henry, 'Duncan Hamilton', *Guardian*, 19 May 1994; *Independent*, 21 Dec 1999, quoting Dick Booth; Lees-Milne, *Mingled Measure*, p 32; Martin, 27 Jun 1953.

27. John Campbell, *Margaret Thatcher, Volume One* (2000), pp 98–9; A. A. Thomson, *Cricket My Happiness* (1954), pp 16–17; Haines, 18 Aug 1953; *Spectator*, 10 Sep 2005 (Frank Keating); Haines, 19 Aug 1953.

12 Moral Courage

1. *The Times*, 20–21 Aug 1953; *Punch*, 19 Aug 1953; Lawrence Black, '"The Bitterest Enemies of Communism": Labour Revisionists, Atlanticism and the Cold War', *Contemporary British History* (Autumn 2001), p 53; *Shetland Times*, 28 Aug 1953, 4 Sep 1953; *Orkney Herald*, 1 Sep 1953; *The Times*, 21 Sep 1953; David Cannadine, 'The "Last Night of the Proms" in Historical Perspective', *Historical Research* (May 2008), p 334.

2. *News Chronicle*, 7 Sep 1953; *New Yorker*, 10 Oct 1953; Raynham, 28 Sep 1953; *New Yorker*, 10 Oct 1953; BBC WA, R9/19/1, Oct 1953; *Guardian*, 20 Sep 2008

(Michael Coveney reviewing Graham McCann, *Bounder!*); M-O A, D5353, 3 Oct 1953; *New Statesman*, 5 Sep 1953, 26 Sep 1953.

3. *The Times*, 2 Oct 1953; *Daily Mirror*, 2 Oct 1953; Brian Simon, 'The Tory Government and Education, 1951–60: Background to Breakout', *History of Education* (Dec 1985), pp 289–90; Brian Simon, *Education and the Social Order, 1940–1990* (1991), pp 171–2; *Times Educational Supplement*, 6 Nov 1953; Bevis Hillier, *John Betjeman: New Fame, New Love* (2002), pp 562–3.

4. Brian Simon, *A Life in Education* (1998), p 58; *Times Educational Supplement*, 15 Jan 1954; *New Statesman*, 27 Mar 1954; Simon, *Education and the Social Order*, p 176; Deborah Thom, 'Politics and the People: Brian Simon and the Campaign against Intelligence Tests in British Schools', *History of Education* (Sep 2004), pp 515–29; *Coulsdon & Purley Times*, 24 Jul 1953; *Crossman*, p 270; Papers of Wright Robinson (Manchester City Archives), Box 11, 18 Nov 1953; Crossman, Ms 154/8/14, 19 Nov 1953.

5. Lorna Sage, *Bad Blood* (2000), pp 143–7; *The Times*, 2 Oct 1953; Alethea Hayter (ed), *A Wise Woman: A Memoir of Lavinia Mynors from Her Diaries and Letters* (Banham, Norfolk, 1996), p 97.

6. *Daily Mirror*, 1 Oct 1953; Graham Payn and Sheridan Morley (eds), *The Noël Coward Diaries* (1982), p 221; Heap, 8 Oct 1953; *Spectator*, 16 Oct 1953; *New Statesman*, 17 Oct 1953; *Times Literary Supplement*, 18 Jul 2008; Martin Gilbert, '*Never Despair*' (1988), p 895; *Observer*, 11 Oct 1953; Russell Davies (ed), *The Kenneth Williams Letters* (1994), pp 30–31.

7. Heap, 25 Sep 1953; Tam Dalyell, 'Baroness Jeger', *Independent*, 3 Mar 2007; *Crossman*, p 276; *Manchester Guardian*, 19 Nov 1953.

8. Mark Lewisohn, *Funny, Peculiar* (2002), pp 201–2; Jeffrey Weeks, *Coming Out* (Quartet edn, 1990), p 159; Richard Davenport-Hines, *Sex, Death and Punishment* (1990), pp 304–5; Weeks, *Coming*, p 159; Cate Haste, *Rules of Desire* (1992), p 169; Davenport-Hines, *Sex*, p 310; Philip Hoare, 'Peter Wildeblood', *Independent*, 25 Nov 1999; Kathleen Tynan, *The Life of Kenneth Tynan* (Methuen edn, 1988), pp 109–10; Davenport-Hines, *Sex*, pp 301–2.

9. Langford, 21 Oct 1953; Nigel Hawthorne, *Straight Face* (2002), p 120; Sheridan Morley, *John G* (2001), p 249; Hawthorne, *Straight Face*, p 120; *Sunday Express*, 25 Oct 1953; Morley, *John G*, p 252; BBC WA, *Any Questions?*, 30 Oct 1953; *Sunday Express*, 1 Nov 1953; Jeffrey Weeks, *Sex, Politics and Society* (1989 edn, Harlow), p 241; Davenport-Hines, *Sex*, p 299; Radio 4, *The BBC and the Closet*, 29 Jan 2008; Chad Varah, *Before I Die Again* (1992), p 170.

10. MNA, Box 13, *Take It From Here*, 12 Nov 1953; June Whitfield, *... And June Whitfield* (2000), p 94; Frank Muir, *A Kentish Lad* (1997), p 151; M-O A, D5353, 6 Dec 1953; *Autocar*, 2 Oct 1953, 9 Oct 1953, 30 Oct 1953; Haines, 16 Nov 1953; *Daily Mirror*, 24 Nov 1953; Payn and Morley (eds), *Coward Diaries*, p 223; John Coldstream, *Dirk Bogarde* (2004), p 198. In general on TIFH, see John Fisher, *Funny Way to Be a Hero* (1973), pp 225–7; Derek Parker, *Radio* (Newton Abbot, 1977), pp 121–2.

11. *Daily Mirror*, 25 Nov 1953; Ivan Ponting, 'Ferenc Puskas', *Independent*, 18 Nov 2006; *Daily Mirror*, 26 Nov 1953; *Birmingham Post*, 26 Nov 1953; *Observer*, 29 Nov 1953; *Guardian*, 20 May 2005 (Peter Bradshaw); *Orkney Herald*, 8 Dec 1953; BBC WA, R9/19/1, Dec 1953. In general on the England–Hungary match and its

context, see the special issue of *Sport in History* (Winter 2003–4), including articles by Peter J. Beck, Ronald Kowalski and Dilwyn Porter, and Jeffrey Hill.

12. Sage, *Bad Blood*, pp 155–6; *Hansard*, 4 Nov 1953, cols 187–8; *South Western Star*, 9 Oct 1953; *Housing Centre Review* (Mar–Apr 1954), pp 20–24.

13. Michael Young, 'A Study of the Extended Family in East London', University of London PhD, 1955, pp 24, 34, 170, 174, 176–7; Dartington Hall Trust Archives, LKE/G/35; Nick Tiratsoo and Mark Clapson, 'The Ford Foundation and Social Planning in Britain: The Case of the Institute of Community Studies and *Family and Kinship in East London*', in Giuliana Gemelli (ed), *American Foundations and Large-Scale Research* (Bologna, 2001), pp 201–17. See also Asa Briggs, *Michael Young* (Basingstoke, 2001), pp 128–37.

14. Paul Oliver et al, *Dunroamin* (1981), pp 27, 19, 21; Nicholas Bullock, *Building the Post-War World* (2002), p 139; *Coventry Evening Telegraph*, 8 Sep 1953; Christopher W. Bacon, 'Streets-in-the-Sky: The Rise and Fall of the Modern Architectural Urban Utopia', University of Sheffield PhD, 1982, pp 115–19.

15. Alan G. V. Simmonds, 'Conservative Governments and the New Town Housing Question in the 1950s', *Urban History* (May 2001), pp 65–83; Macmillan, p 160; *Architectural Review* (July 1953), pp 29–33; *New Yorker*, 17 Oct 1953.

16. Judy Attfield, 'Inside Pram Town: A Case Study of Harlow House Interiors, 1951–61', in Attfield and Pat Kirkham (eds), *A View from the Interior* (1989), pp 215–16, 218; Mark Llewellyn, 'Producing and Experiencing Harlow: Neighbourhood Units and Narratives of New Town Life 1947–53', *Planning Perspectives* (Apr 2004), pp 155–74; Andrew Homer, 'Administrative and Social Change in the Post-War British New Towns: A Case Study of Stevenage and Hemel Hempstead 1946–70', University of Luton PhD, 1999, p 149; Simmonds, 'Conservative Governments', pp 75–6; http://www.francisfrith.com/search/england/crawley/memories; Attfield and Kirkham (eds), *A View*, p 215; Susan Morris, Untitled section in Huw and Connie Rees (eds), *The History Makers* (Stevenage, 1981), pp 83–7; Jack Balchin, *First New Town* (Stevenage, 1980), pp 271–5; Homer, 'Administrative and Social Change', pp 157–63.

17. Chaplin, 7/3/1, 7 Dec 1953, Interview with Rene Chaplin, 18 May 1999; Maureen Kent, 'Harold Hill in the "Fifties"', in Shirley Durgan (ed), *Our Scattered Lives* (Billericay, c. 1980), pp 31–2; Cyril Dunn, 'Notes on Life in a London Satellite' (1953–4), in possession of Peter Dunn.

18. Asa Briggs, *Sound and Vision* (Oxford, 1995), pp 835–6; *Hansard*, 25 Nov 1953, cols 517, 524–5, 531, 555; *New Yorker*, 12 Dec 1953; *Hansard*, 15 Dec 1953, cols 298–300.

19. David Kynaston, *The City of London, Volume IV* (2001), pp 64–5; BBC WA, *Any Questions?*, 11 Dec 1953; Papers of W. J. Brown (Department of Documents, Imperial War Museum), 02/59/3, 1/18, 14 Dec 1953; *Financial Times*, 14–15 Dec 1953; Andrew Roberts, *Eminent Churchillians* (1994), pp 267–8; Macmillan, pp 279–80; *Sheffield Telegraph*, 17 Dec 1953; *Financial Times*, 18 Dec 1953; *The Times*, 19 Dec 1953; Roberts, *Eminent Churchillians*, pp 267, 269; Anthony Howard, *RAB* (1987), p 203.

20. Norman Wisdom, *Don't Laugh At Me* (1992), p 151; Norman Wisdom, *In My Turn* (2002), p 190; *Daily Mirror*, 18 Dec 1953; *Spectator*, 25 Dec 1953; *The Times*, 21 Dec 1953; Wisdom, *Don't*, p 152; *Picture Post*, 30 Jan 1954.

21. Haines, 25 Dec 1953, 16 Jan 1954; Anthony Hayward, 'Bert Foord', *Independent*, 11 Aug 2001; BBC WA, R9/10/1–VR/54/81, 19 Feb 1954, R9/74/1, Jan 1954; Martin, 19 Jan 1954; MNA, Box 38; *Picture Post*, 2 Jan 1954.
22. Raynham, 12 Jan 1954; Streat, pp 705–6; *Daily Mirror*, 26 Jan 1954; *Punch*, 3 Feb 1954; Gilbert, p 950.

13 Can You Afford It, Boy?

1. John Wain, *Hurry on Down* (Penguin edn, 1960), p 7; *Times Literary Supplement*, 9 Oct 1953; *New Statesman*, 24 Oct 1953; *Listener*, 29 Oct 1953; *Birmingham Post*, 27 Oct 1953; *The Times*, 7 Oct 1953.
2. Melvyn Bragg, *Rich* (1988), p 142; *Listener*, 4 Feb 1954; *New Statesman*, 6 Feb 1954; BBC WA, R9/74/1, Mar 1954; Andrew Lycett, *Dylan Thomas* (2003), p 377.
3. Amis, pp 344–5; Zachary Leader, *The Life of Kingsley Amis* (2006), p 300; *Sunday Times*, 24 Jan 1954; *Spectator*, 29 Jan 1954; *New Statesman*, 30 Jan 1954; *Punch*, 3 Feb 1954; *Daily Telegraph*, 5 Feb 1954; *Times Literary Supplement*, 12 Feb 1954; *Listener*, 18 Mar 1954.
4. Amis, pp 522–3, 746; Brian Aldiss, ''im', in Dale Sarwak (ed), *Kingsley Amis* (Basingstoke, 1990), p 40; Humphrey Carpenter, *The Angry Young Men* (2002), p 55; Anthony Powell, *To Keep The Ball Rolling, Volume IV* (1982), pp 158–9; Kingsley Amis, *Lucky Jim* (Penguin edn, 1961), p 63; Neil Powell, *Amis & Son* (2008), p 84.
5. Anthony Thwaite (ed), *Selected Letters of Philip Larkin* (1992), pp 221–3; Philip Larkin, *Collected Poems* (1988), p 84.

A Thicker Cut

1 Tolerably Pleasing

1. National Archives, CAB 195/11/1, 3 Feb 1954; *Evening News*, 4 Feb 1954, *Coventry Evening Telegraph*, 4 Feb 1954; *Birmingham Mail*, 5 Feb 1954; *Hertfordshire Hemel Hempstead Gazette & West Herts Advertiser*, 12 Feb 1954.
2. *Evening News*, 16 Feb 1954; *Birmingham Mail*, 16 Feb 1954, 24 Feb 1954, 25 Feb 1954, *News Chronicle*, 23 Feb 1954, 1 Mar 1954, 2 Mar 1954.
3. Robert Rhodes James, *Bob Boothby* (1991), pp 369–70; *Observer*, 21 Feb 1954; National Archives, CAB 195/11/1, 24 Feb 1954.
4. Haines, 19–20 Feb 1954; *Birmingham Mail*, 17 Feb 1954; M-O A, D5353, 20 Feb 1954.

2 Butter is Off the Ration

1. *Spectator*, 12 Mar 1954; *Picture Post*, 20 Mar 1954; John Pollock, *Billy Graham* (1966), p 165; *New Yorker*, 15 May 1954; Langford, 10 Jan 1954; *Economist*, 6 Mar 1954; Frances Partridge, *Everything To Lose* (Phoenix edn, 1999), pp 198–9; Cate Haste, *Rules of Desire* (1992), p 170; Peter Wildeblood, *Against the Law* (1955), pp 62–3, 80; *Sunday Telegraph*, 10 Sep 2000 (Lord Montagu interview); Sheridan Morley, *John G* (2001), pp 259–60.

2. Asa Briggs, *Sound and Vision* (Oxford, 1995), p 845; *Economist*, 13 Mar 1954; John Corner, 'General Introduction: Television and British Society in the 1950s', in Corner (ed), *Popular Television in Britain* (1991), p 5; *Crossman*, p 331; *Montgomeryshire Express and Radnor Times*, 13 Mar 1954; James Lees-Milne, *A Mingled Measure* (1994), p 60; Kenneth Clark, *The Other Half* (Hamish Hamilton edn, 1986), p 138; *Picture Post*, 23 Oct 1954.

3. *Radio Times*, 2 Apr 1954; Briggs, *Sound*, p 901; Anthony Hayward, 'Edward Evans', *Independent*, 4 Jan 2002; *Reynolds News*, 11 Apr 1954; *Daily Mail*, 9 Apr 1954; www.televisionheaven.co.uk/grove.htm; *Listener*, 15 Apr 1954; *Punch*, 21 Apr 1954; BBC WA, R9/19/1, Jun 1954, R9/19/2, Jun 1954 (2); *Listener*, 22 Apr 1954; Wikipedia, 'The Grove Family'; *Radio Times*, 16 Apr 1954; Graham McCann, *Morecambe & Wise* (1998), p 108; *Reynolds News*, 25 Apr 1954; BBC WA, R9/19/2, Jun 1954 (2); *Reynolds News*, 23 May 1954; McCann, *Morecambe*, pp 109, 115.

4. Martin Gilbert, *'Never Despair'* (1988), pp 968–9; Mark Pythian, 'CND's Cold War', *Contemporary British History* (Autumn 2001), p 134; *Crossman*, p 305; Roy Jenkins, *Churchill* (2001), pp 875–7; Henry Pelling, *Churchill's Peacetime Ministry, 1951–55* (Basingstoke, 1997), p 123; *Coventry Evening Telegraph*, 6 Apr 1954; *New Statesman*, 10 Apr 1954; Anthony Adamthwaite, '"Nation Shall Speak Peace Unto Nation": The BBC's Response to Peace and Defence Issues, 1945–58', *Contemporary Record* (Winter 1993), pp 567–8.

5. BBC WA, *Any Questions?*, 14 Jan 1955; *Picture Post*, 16 Jun 1956; David R. Devereux, 'State Versus Private Ownership: The Conservative Governments and British Civil Aviation, 1951–62', *Albion* (Spring 1995), p 78; Berry Ritchie, 'Sir Freddie Laker', *Independent*, 11 Feb 2006; Thayer Watkins, 'The Concorde Supersonic Transport' (London Conference on Concorde, c. 2000).

6. John Campbell, *Nye Bevan* (1997), p 284; Dalton, p 624; *New Yorker*, 15 May 1954; Ben Pimlott, *Harold Wilson* (1992), pp 184–7; Dalton, p 625.

7. *Orpington & Kentish Times*, 30 Apr 1954; *Daily Mail*, 26 Apr 1954; David Butler, 'Len Pountney', *Independent*, 18 Jun 1997; Cyril Dunn, 'Notes on a London Satellite, 1953–54'; *Orpington & Kentish Times*, 7 May 1954; Paul Rock and Stanley Cohen, 'The Teddy Boy', in Vernon Bogdanor and Robert Skidelsky (eds), *The Age of Affluence, 1951–64* (1970), p 297; *Picture Post*, 29 May 1954.

8. St John, 28 Apr 1954; Langford, 28 Apr 1954; Heap, 1 May 1954; Fowles, EUL MS 102/1/8, fol 123, 12 May 1954; Christine Geraghty, *British Cinema in the Fifties* (2000), p 67; John Coldstream, *Dirk Bogarde* (2004), p 204.

9. *Listener*, 29 Apr 1954, 6 May 1954, 13 May 1954, 20 May 1954; *Economist*, 13 Feb 1954; *Listener*, 20 May 1954; Joan Keating, 'Faith and Community Threatened? Roman Catholic Responses to the Welfare State, Materialism and Social Mobility, 1945–62', *Twentieth Century British History* 9/1 (1998), pp 92–4; Robert Walsha, 'The One Nation Group: A Tory Approach to Backbench Politics and Organization, 1950–55', *Twentieth Century British History* 11/2 (2000), pp 208–12.

10. Townsend, 'Pilot Interviews, 1954', 27 Apr 1954, 29 Apr 1954.

11. *Yorkshire Post*, 5 May 1954; Geoffrey Moorhouse, *At the George* (1989), p 35; *Yorkshire Post*, 6 May 1954; *Bradford Telegraph & Argus*, 6 May 1954; Jeff Hill, 'Rite of Spring: Cup Finals and Community in the North of England', in Hill and Jack Williams (eds), *Sport and Identity in the North of England* (Keele, 1996), p 91; *Yorkshire Post*, 7 May 1954; *Oxford Mail*, 7 May 1954; *Spectator*, 14 May 1954; *The*

Times, 5 May 2004; *Oxford Mail*, 7 May 1954; Briggs, *Sound*, p 775; *Halifax Daily Courier*, 7 May 1954; John Bale, 'How Much of a Hero? The Fractured Image of Roger Bannister', *Sport in History*, Aug 2006, pp 235–47.

12. Raynham, 15 May 1954; *Reynolds News*, 16 May 1954; Martin, 15 May 1954; BBC WA, R9/74/1, Jun 1954; *Radio Times*, 7 May 1954; M-O A, TC 69/8/K; Billy Graham, *Just As I Am* (1997), pp 233–4; Pollock, *Billy Graham*, p 175; David J. Jeremy, *Capitalists and Christians* (Oxford, 1990), p 397; St John, 22 May 1954; Graham, *Just*, p 236.

13. *Daily Mail*, 22 May 1954; Peter Beck, 'Britain in the Cold War's "Cultural Olympics": Responding to the Political Drive of Soviet Sport, 1945–58', *Contemporary British History* (June 2005), p 177; *Independent*, 20 Apr 2004 (Julia Stuart); John Karter, *Lester* (1992), p 27; *Daily Mail*, 26 Jun 1954, 28 Jun 1954.

14. Iris Murdoch, *Under the Net* (Penguin edn, 1960), pp 31, 99; *Times Literary Supplement*, 9 May 1954; *Spectator*, 11 Jun 1954; Peter J. Conradi, *Iris Murdoch* (2001), p 385; *New Statesman*, 5 Jun 1954; Conradi, *Iris*, p 386; *New Statesman*, 26 Jun 1954.

15. *Whitby Gazette*, 18 Jun 1954; David T. Thompson, *Pinter* (Basingstoke, 1985), p 27; Mark Lewisohn, *Funny, Peculiar* (2002), pp 206–7; *Radio Times*, 25 Jun 1954; *Reynolds News*, 4 Jul 1954.

16. BBC WA, *Any Questions?*, 21 Jan 1954; *Somerset County Gazette*, 29 May 1954; David Leavitt, *The Man Who Knew Too Much* (2006), pp 268, 275–6; Richard Davenport-Hines, *Sex, Death and Punishment* (1990), p 315.

17. Raynham, 10 May 1954; Paul Bookbinder, *Simon Marks* (1993), p 136; *Coventry Evening Telegraph*, 22 Dec 1953; *Observer*, 13 Jun 1954; Lord Briggs, 'TV Advertising and the Social Revolution', in Brian Henry (ed), *British Television Advertising* (1986), p 347; *Woman's Own*, 1 Jul 1954; *Woman*, 3 Jul 1954; *Lady*, 1 Jul 1954.

18. Haines, 2 Jul 1954; 'Jaroslav Drobny', *Daily Telegraph*, 15 Sep 2001; *Spectator*, 3 Jul 2004 (Frank Keating); Raynham, 2 Jul 1954; Macmillan, p 322; Haines, 3 Jul 1954; Conradi, *Iris*, p 387.

19. *Yorkshire Post*, 3 Jul 1954; *Sussex Express & County Herald* (Hailsham & Heathfield edn), 9 Jul 1954; *Yorkshire Post*, 5 Jul 1954.

3 The Right Type of Fellow

1. *Daily Mirror*, 20 Jun 1954; Lorna Sage, *Bad Blood* (2000), pp 136–7; P.W.J. Bartrip, 'Myxomatosis in 1950s Britain', *Twentieth Century British History* 19/1 (2008), pp 83–105.

2. Sage, *Bad Blood*, p 137; Alun Howkins, *The Death of Rural England* (2003), p 152; Howard Newby, *Country Life* (1987), p 206; *Financial Times*, 27 Jun 1955; BBC Four, 'The Lie of the Land', 5 Nov 2003; Thomson Collection (University of Northumbria), 'Milton Keynes' file.

3. St John, 5 Jul 1954; *Birmingham Post*, 12 Jul 1954; M-O A, D5353, 14 Jul 1954; Preston, 22 Jul 1954; Phyllis Willmott, *Bethnal Green Journal, 1954–55* (2001), pp 4–5; *The Times*, 14 Jul 1954, 23 Sep 1954.

4. *Daily Telegraph*, 12 Jul 1954; *Daily Mirror*, 14 Jul 1954, 16 Jul 1954; Gerald Howat,

Len Hutton (1988), p 148; John Arlott, *Fred* (1971), p 84; *Daily Mirror*, 20 Jul 1954; *The Times*, 20 Jul 1954.

5. Crossman, MS 154/8/15, fol. 531, 30 Jul 1954; Martin, 28 Jul 1954, 30–31 Jul 1954; O. L. Willmott, *The Parish Notes of Loders, Dottery & Askerswell, Dorset: Volume I, 1948–1965* (Shrewsbury, 1996), Sep 1954.

6. *Listener*, 5 Aug 1954; *Radio Times*, 23 Jul 1954; Terry Hallett, *Bristol's Forgotten Empire* (Wesbury, 2000), p 192; 'John Chapman', *Daily Telegraph*, 7 Sep 2001; Heap, 5 Aug 1954; Martin, 21 Aug 1954; *Financial Times*, 20 Apr 1996; Richard North, 'A Jolly Start to the Revolution', *Independent*, 6 Aug 1994; Dennis Barker, 'Julian Slade', *Guardian*, 20 Jun 2006.

7. Humphrey Carpenter, *J.R.R. Tolkien* (1977), pp 218–19; *New Statesman*, 18 Sep 1954; Carpenter, *Tolkien*, p 220; *Punch*, 8 Sep 1954; *Spectator*, 1 Oct 1954; Carpenter, *Tolkien*, pp 219–21; Colin Wilson, *Dreaming to Some Purpose* (2004), p 131.

8. BBC WA, R9/9/18, LR/54/1303; Haines, 30 Aug 1954, 4 Sep 1954.

9. *Sunday Post*, 22 Aug 1954; Phil Gordon, 'Willie Woodburn', *Independent*, 6 Dec 2001; Brian Glanville, 'Willie Woodburn', *Guardian*, 11 Dec 2001; *Sunday Post*, 29 Aug 1954, 5 Sep 1954; Hugh McIlvanney, 'The Fall of Willie Woodburn', in Ian Hamilton (ed), *The Faber Book of Soccer* (1992), pp 56–65; *Sunday Post*, 19 Sep 1954; Gordon, 'Woodburn'; Peter Acton and Colin M. Jarman (eds), *Roy of the Rovers* (Harpenden, 1994), p 11; *Radio Times*, 10 Sep 1954; David Cannadine, 'The "Last Night of the Proms" in Historical Perspective', *Historical Research* (May 2008), p 334; *The Times*, 20 Sep 1954; Cannadine, '"Last Night"', p 334.

10. Christopher Sandford, *Mick Jagger* (Cooper Square Press edn, New York, 1999), p 23; Stuart Maclure, *A History of Education in London, 1870–1990* (1990), p 174; Alan Kerckhoff et al, *Going Comprehensive in England and Wales* (1996), p 63; Anthony Sampson, *Anatomy of Britain* (1962), p 187; Brian Simon, *Education and Social Order, 1940–1990* (1991), p 173; 'Dame Mary Green', *The Times*, 26 Apr 2004; *Eltham & Kentish Times*, 10 Sep 1954, 24 Sep 1954. In general on Kidbrooke, see Kidbrooke School, *Memories of Kidbrooke School, 1954–2005* (2005); Rebecca Smithers, 'Gold Standard', *Guardian*, 12 Jul 2005.

11. Max Beloff, 'Democracy and Its Discontents', *Encounter*, Jun 1954, p 54; Simon, *Education*, pp 150–51; L. S. Hearnshaw, *Cyril Burt* (1979), p 119; *Times Educational Supplement*, 17 Dec 1954; A. H. Halsey, 'Social Mobility in Britain – A Review', *Sociological Review* (Dec 1954), pp 169–77; *Picture Post*, 4 Dec 1954; Crossman, MS 154/8/14, 6 Apr 1954.

12. *New Statesman*, 4 Jun 1955; Steve Humphries et al, *A Century of Childhood* (1988), pp 135–6; Correlli Barnett, *The Verdict of Peace* (2001), p 480; Simon, *Education*, pp 183–7; Gareth Elwyn Jones, '1944 and All That', *History of Education* (Sep 1990), pp 246–7; Simon, *Education*, p 187.

13. *Economist*, 12 Feb 1955; *Northern Daily Mail*, 2 Jul 1954; *Economist*, 12 Feb 1955; Dennis Dean, 'Preservation or Renovation? The Dilemmas of Conservative Educational Policy 1955–1960', *Twentieth Century British History* 3/1 (1992), pp 14–15; Simon, *Education*, pp 185–6; Rene Saran, *Policy-Making in Secondary Education* (Oxford, 1973), p 54.

14. *Lynn News & Advertiser*, 7 Sep 1954; Lionel Esher, *A Broken Wave* (1981), p 59; 'Peter Smithson', *The Times*, 10 Mar 2003; Bryan Appleyard, *Richard Rodgers* (1986), p 77; Dan Cruickshank, 'Hunstanton School', *RIBA Journal* (Jan 1997),

p 51; Anthony Jackson, *The Politics of Architecture* (1970), p 184; *Architectural Review* (Nov 1954), p 282, Feb 1955, p 82; *Lynn News & Advertiser*, 17 Sep 1954; *The Times*, 19 Mar 2003.

15. Macmillan, p 356; Harriet Jones, 'New Tricks for an Old Dog? The Conservatives and Social Policy', in Anthony Gorst et al (eds), *Contemporary British History, 1931–1961* (1991), p 41; Christopher W. Bacon, 'Streets-in-the-Sky: The Rise and Fall of the Modern Architectural Urban Utopia', Univeristy of Sheffield PhD, 1982, pp 234–5; A.G.V. Simmonds, 'Conservative Governments and the Housing Question, 1951–59', University of Leeds PhD, 1995, pp 41, 110–11, 424–5.

16. Alison Ravetz, *Remaking Cities* (1980), pp 67–8; Gordon E. Cherry, *Town Planning in Britain since 1900* (Oxford, 1996), p 136; Ravetz, *Remaking*, p 200; Simmonds, 'Conservative', pp 160–61; Ravetz, *Remaking*, p 200; William Ashworth, *The Genesis of Modern Town Planning* (1954), p 237; *Picture Post*, 15 May 1954, 29 May 1954; Gavin Stamp, *Britain's Lost Cities* (2007), pp 35–6; Grant Lewisohn and Rosalind Billingham, *Coventry New Architecture* (Warwick, 1969), pp 30–31; *Coventry Evening Telegraph*, 13 Jan 1955; Andrew Saint, *Towards a Social Architecture* (1987), p 163; John Griffith, 'Crichel Down: The Most Famous Farm in British Constitutional History', *Contemporary Record* (Spring 1987), pp 35–40; *The Times*, 20 Jul 1954; *Daily Mirror*, 20 Jul 1954; John Davis, 'Macmillan's Martyr: The Pilgrim Case, the "Land Grab" and the Tory Housing Drive, 1951–9', *Planning Perspectives* (Apr 2008), pp 125–46; *Romford Times*, 6 Oct 1954; Harold Macmillan, *Tides of Fortune* (1969), p 48; *Romford Times*, 13 Oct 1954.

17. *Picture Post*, 3 Jul 1954, 17 Jul 1954; Patrick Dunleavy, *The Politics of Mass Housing in Britain, 1945–1975* (Oxford, 1981), p 268; Simmonds, 'Conservative', p 134; Dame Evelyn Sharpe, 'The Next Million Houses – Where Are They to Be?', *Housing Centre Review* (Jul–Aug 1955), p 4; Colin Boyne, 'Ian Nairn: 1930–83', *Architectural Review* (Sept 1983), p 4; *Architectural Review* (Mar 1955), p 204, (Jun 1955), pp 365–6, 371, 451; Joe Moran, '"Subtopias of Good Intentions": Everyday Landscapes in Postwar Britain', *Cultural and Social History* (Sep 2007), p 406.

18. *Picture Post*, 3 Jul 1954; Miles Glendinning and Stefan Muthesius, *Tower Block* (1994), p 172; Fowles, EUL MS 102/1/8, fol 182, 13 Nov 1954; The Society of Housing Managers, *Report of Conference* (1955), pp 6, 22, 65; 'Symposium on High Flats: Part I', *Journal of the Royal Institute of British Architects* (Mar 1955), p 195; Dunleavy, *Politics*, p 165; *Economist*, 5 Mar 1955; *New Statesman*, 2 Oct 1954.

19. Simmonds, 'Conservative', pp 214–33; City of Sheffield Housing, *Multi-Storey Housing in Some European Countries* (Sheffield, 1955), pp 36–7; *Sheffield Star*, 13 Apr 1955; John R. Gold, *The Practice of Modernism* (Abingdon, 2007), p 215.

20. Society of Housing Managers, *Report*, p 8; Michael Young, 'Must We Abandon Our Cities?', *Socialist Commentary* (Sept 1954), pp 251–3, 'Whose Houses First?', *Socialist Commentary* (Nov 1954), pp 310–14, 'The Two Nations of 1955', *Socialist Commentary* (Jun 1955), pp 168–70.

4 Bonny Babies, Well-washed Matrons

1. Lynn Seymour, *Lynn* (1984), pp 22–30; Jonathon Green, *Them* (1990), pp 90–91; Geoffrey Wansell, *Terence Rattigan* (1995), pp 250–52; Michael Billington, *State of the Nation* (2007), pp 68–72; Heap, 22 Sep 1954; Langford, 16 Oct 1954; Dominic Shellard (ed), Kenneth Tynan, *Theatre Writings* (2007), pp 35–7.

2. *Spectator*, 1 Oct 1954, 8 Oct 1954, 15 Oct 1954; Clive Wilmer, 'Thom Gunn', *Independent*, 29 Apr 2004; Bryan Appleyard, *The Pleasures of Peace* (1989), p 103; Amis, p 405; Alan Sinfield, *Literature, Politics and Culture in Postwar Britain* (Oxford, 1989), pp 79–81, 158–60; Kevin Jackson, 'Exorcising Coleridge', *Independent*, 10 Sep 1990; D. J. Taylor, 'D.J. Enright 1920–2002', *Times Literary Supplement*, 10 Jan 2003; *The Spur* (Autumn Term 1954), p 15. The authoritative account of the Movement remains Blake Morrison, *The Movement* (Oxford, 1980).

3. Alan Bennett, *Writing Home* (1994), pp 32–3; *Fowles*, p 343; Gaitskell, p 334; Mark Pottle (ed), *Daring To Hope: The Diaries and Letters of Violet Bonham Carter, 1946–1969* (2002), pp 139–40; BBC WA, *Any Questions?*, 8 Oct 1954; Pottle (ed), *Daring*, p 140.

4. Philip M. Williams, *Hugh Gaitskell* (1979), p 329; *Crossman*, pp 350–51; John Campbell, *Nye Bevan* (Richard Cohen edn, 1997), p 293; Brian Brivati, *Hugh Gaitskell* (1996), p 198; *Crossman*, pp 352–3.

5. Raynham, 11 Oct 1954; Heap, 13 Oct 1954; Raynham, 15 Oct 1954; Jim Phillips, 'Inter-Union Conflict in the Docks, 1954–1955', *Historical Studies in Industrial Relations* (Mar 1996), pp 107–30; *New Yorker*, 27 Nov 1954 (Panter-Downes); *News Chronicle*, 1 Nov 1954; Henry Pelling, *Churchill's Peacetime Ministry, 1951–55* (Basingstoke, 1997), p 158; *Crossman*, pp 360–61; Andrew Roberts, *Eminent Churchillians* (1994), p 270; Macmillan, p 363; Jack Dash, *Good Morning, Brothers!* (1969), pp 84–5; *New Statesman*, 6 Nov 1954; Geoffrey Goodman, 'The Role of Industrial Correspondents', in Alan Campbell et al (eds), *British Trade Unions and Industrial Politics: Volume One* (Aldershot, 1999), p 29; Raphael Samuel, *The Lost World of British Communism* (2006), pp 123–54.

6. Langford, 9 Oct 1954; M-O A, D5353, 9 Oct 1954; Haines, 29 Nov 1954; *Crossman*, pp 375–6.

7. Langford, 22 Oct 1954; Philip Norman, *John Lennon* (2008), pp 65–6; Roger Wilmut and Jimmy Grafton, *The Goon Show Companion* (1976), p 140; *Listener*, 21 Oct 1954; Norman, *John Lennon*, p 65; Wilmut and Grafton, *Goon Show*, pp 59–60; *Radio Times*, 29 Oct 1954; Russell Davies (ed), *The Kenneth Williams Diaries* (1993), p 105; *Radio Times*, 29 Oct 1954; *Listener*, 11 Nov 1954; Roger Wilmut, *Tony Hancock 'Artiste'* (1978), p 174; Peter Goddard, '"Hancock's Half-Hour": A Watershed in British Television Comedy', in John Corner (ed), *Popular Television in Britain* (1991), p 78.

8. *Radio Times*, 10 Dec 1954; Langford, 13 Oct 1954; Susan Sydney-Smith, *Beyond Dixon of Dock Green* (2002), pp 100–101; *Radio Times*, 17 Dec 1954; *News Chronicle*, 15 Nov 1954; *Punch*, 15 Dec 1954.

9. *Radio Times*, 10 Dec 1954; *Listener*, 16 Dec 1954; Francis Wheen, *Television* (1985), p 111; BBC WA, R9/19/2, Feb 1955; Chaplin, 7/3/1, 14 Dec 1954; *Any Questions?*, 17 Dec 1954; *Punch*, 21 Dec 1954; Martin, 12 Nov 1954; *Picture Post*, 20 Nov 1954; Macmillan, p 388; John Springhall, 'Horror Comics: The Nasties of the 1950s', *History Today* (Jul 1994), pp 10–13.

10. Langford, 9 Oct 1954; *Spectator*, 1 Oct 1954; Andrew Lambirth, 'John Bratby', *Independent*, 23 Jul 1992; *New Statesman*, 25 Sep 1954; David Sylvester, 'The Kitchen Sink', *Encounter* (Dec 1954), pp 61–4; Philip Vann, 'Jean Cooke', *Guardian*, 29 Aug 2008; Andrew Lambirth, 'Jean Cooke', *Indpendent*, 11 Aug 2008.

11. Macmillan, p 368; Raynham, 30 Nov 1954; Daniel Farson, *Sacred Monsters* (1988), p 167; Clarissa Eden, *A Memoir* (2007), p 180; Kenneth Harris, *Attlee* (1982), p 525; Roy Jenkins, *Churchill* (2001), p 890; *Spectator*, 3 Dec 1954; Brian Glanville, 'Stan Culllis', *Guardian*, 1 Mar 2001; Percy M. Young, *Football Year* (1956), p 49; *The Times*, 17 Nov 1954; Subrata Dasgupta, *Salaam Stanley Matthews* (2006), pp 92–3; *News Chronicle*, 14 Dec 1954; Phyllis Willmott, *Bethnal Green Journal, 1954–1955* (2001), p 37; Haines, 28 Dec 1954.

5   A Fair Crack at the Whip

1. Charles Loft, 'Reappraisal and Reshaping: Government and the Railway Problem, 1951–64', *Contemporary British History* (Winter 2001), p 75; *News Chronicle*, 25 Jan 1955; BBC Four, 'The Last Days of Steam', 16 Oct 2008; *Economist*, 29 Jan 1955; Osbert Lancaster, *Signs of the Times* (1961), p 89; *New Statesman*, 24 Nov 2003 (Gerald Crompton); *The Times*, 3 Feb 1955; *Picture Post*, 5 Nov 1955; *Town Planning Review* (Jan 1956), p 237.

2. *News Chronicle*, 16 Feb 1955; Fred Roberts, *Sixty Years of Nuclear History* (Charlbury, 1999), pp 72–3; Sir Christopher Hinton, 'The Atom for You', *Picture Post*, 13 Aug 1955; Raynham, 31 Mar 1955.

3. Andrew Roberts, *Eminent Churchillians* (1994), pp 270–74; George H. Gallup (ed), *The Gallup International Public Opinion Polls: Great Britain, 1937–1975, Volume One* (New York, 1976), p 343; Macmillan, p 378; *Economist*, 15 Jan 1955; Simon Heffer, *Like the Roman* (1988), p 195; Macmillan, p 382; John Stobbs, 'Is Morale High Enough?', *Picture Post*, 14 Jan 1956; Brian Thompson, *Clever Girl* (2007), pp 151–4.

4. John Singleton, 'Showing the White Flag: The Lancashire Cotton Industry, 1945–65', *Business History* (Oct 1990), pp 132–3; Marguerite Dupree, 'Struggling with Destiny: The Cotton Industry Overseas Trade Policy and the Cotton Board, 1940–1959', *Business History* (Oct 1990), p 119; *Spectator*, 5 Feb 1954; *Picture Post*, 20 Feb 1954; Dupree, 'Struggling', pp 120–21.

5. Wendy Webster, *Englishness and Empire, 1939–1965* (Oxford, 2005), pp 159–61; *Birmingham Post*, 1 Feb 1955; *New Statesman*, 12 Feb 1955; *Picture Post*, 22 Jan 1955; John Corner, 'Documentary Voices', in John Corner (ed), *Popular Television in Britain* (1991), p 47.

6. Langford, 3 Apr 1955; *Independent*, 8 Jun 1998 (Mary Chamberlain); Paul Foot, *Immigration and Race in British Politics* (1965), p 126; Michael Banton, *White and Coloured* (1959), pp 157–8.

7. *Independent*, 19 Apr 2000; Mike Phillips and Trevor Phillips, *Windrush* (1998), p 149; Donald Hinds, *Journey to an Illusion* (1966), pp 73, 85–6; *Picture Post*, 16 Jan 1954, 30 Jan 1954; *Birmingham Post*, 15 Nov 1954, 17 Jan 1955; *News Chronicle*, 7 Feb 1955; Foot, *Immigration*, p 57; *Manchester Guardian*, 20 Jan 1955; *New Statesman*, 9 Oct 1954.

8. Banton, *White*, p 163; *Manchester Guardian*, 31 Jan 1955; Stephen Tolliday, 'High Times and After: Coventry Engineering Workers and Shopfloor Bargaining, 1945–80', in Bill Lancaster and Tony Mason (eds), *Life and Labour in a Twentieth Century City* (Coventry, c. 1986), p 207; *Birmingham Post*, 17 Jan 1955; *The Times*, 9 Nov 1954; *Socialist Commentary* (Dec 1954), pp 356, 358.

9. *Birmingham Post*, 28 Feb 1955; *West Bromwich, Oldbury and Smethwick Midland Chronicle & Free Press*, 18 Feb 1955; Clive Harris, 'Post-war Migration and the Industrial Reserve Army', in Winston James and Clive Harris (eds), *Inside Babylon* (1993), p 43; Heffer, *Like*, pp 196–7.

10. Randall Hanson, *Citizenship and Immigration in Post-war Britain* (Oxford, 2000), p 70; D. W. Dean, 'Conservative Governments and the Restriction of Commonwealth Immigration in the 1950s: The Problems of Constraint', *Historical Journal* (Mar 1992), pp 174–5; Kathleen Paul, *Whitewashing Britain* (Ithaca, 1997), p 138; Roberts, *Eminent Churchillians*, p 233; Foot, *Immigration*, p 165; Roberts, *Eminent Churchillians*, p 233; *The Times*, 8 Nov 1954; Foot, *Immigration*, p 56.

11. Macmillan, p 382; Ian Gilmour and Mark Garnett, *Whatever Happened to the Tories* (1997), p 78; Roberts, *Eminent Churchillians*, pp 235–6; *Birmingham Post*, 14 Mar 1955.

12. *Picture Post*, 30 Nov 1954, 17 Apr 1954; *Western Mail*, 14 Jan 1955; *Picture Post*, 12 Feb 1955; *South London Press*, 16 Sep 1955; Gallup (ed), *Gallup*, p 343; *Independent*, 15 Jun 1998 (Randeep Ramesh); *New Statesman*, 17 Sep 1955 (Norman MacKenzie); A. G. Bennett, *Because They Know Not* (1954), p 22.

13. M-O A, D5353, 13 Jan 1955; BBC WA, *Any Questions?*, 14 Jan 1955; *Radio Times*, 7 Jan 1955; *Independent*, 27 Jun 2002 (Martin Kelner); Mark Lewisohn, *Funny, Peculiar* (2002), p 242; BBC WA, R9/9/19–LR/55/1325; James Green, 'Harry Corbett', *Independent*, 21 Aug 1989.

14. *Radio Times*, 11 Feb 1955; *Spectator*, 25 Feb 1955; Anthony Hayward, 'Peggy Mount', *Independent*, 14 Nov 2001; *Radio Times*, 11 Feb 2005; Clive Ellis, *Fabulous Fanny Cradock* (Stroud, 2007), pp 82–4; *Listener*, 24 Feb 1955; Marguerite Patten, 'A Life in the Day', *Sunday Times*, 17 Jun 2007; *News Chronicle*, 3 Jan 1955; *New Yorker*, 5 Mar 1955.

15. Haines, 2 Feb 1955, 15 Feb 1955, 19 Feb 1955, 26 Feb 1955, 5 Mar 1955, 7 Mar 1955, 19 Mar 1955; *Economist*, 28 May 1955; Haines, 2 May 1955; Peter Townsend, *The Family Life of Old People* (1957), pp 296–7, 300, 309–10; Townsend, 20 May 1955; Dartington Hall Trust Archives, DWE/G/11/C, 27 May 1955.

16. 'The Duke of Bedford', *Guardian* (Dennis Barker)/*The Times*, 29 Oct 2002; John, Duke of Bedford, *A Silver-Plated Spoon* (1959), p 214; David Cannadine, *The Decline and Fall of the British Aristocracy* (1990), pp 646–7; Nirad C. Chaudhuri, *A Passage to England* (Hogarth Press edn, 1989), pp 147–8; J. Mordaunt Crook, 'Raffles in the Ruins', *Times Literary Supplement*, 8 May 1998; *The Times*, 24 Jun 1955, 29 Jun 1955; St John, 16 Apr 1955; John Fisher, *Tony Hancock* (2008), p 175; Jack Adrian, 'Robin Boyle', *Independent*, 1 Oct 2003; *Sunday Pictorial*, 24 Apr 1955; Fisher, *Tony Hancock*, p 163; Mark Abrams, 'Child Audiences for Television in Great Britain', *Journalism Quarterly* (Winter 1956), pp 35–41.

17. *Accrington Observer*, 12 Apr 1955, 23 Apr 1955, 30 Apr 1955, 3 May 1955, 7 May 1955; Macmillan, pp 408–10; Lord Birkenhead, *Walter Monckton* (1969), p 299;

Financial Times, 21 Apr 1955; Martin, 21 Apr 1955; M-O A, TC 61/14/A; Frank MacShane (ed), *Selected Letters of Raymond Chandler* (1981), p 388.

6 A Lot of Hooey

1. M-O A, TC 61/14/A, D5353, 5 Apr 1955; Michael Cockerell, *Live from Number 10* (1988), p 27; Macmillan, p 413; Roy Jenkins, *Churchill* (2001), p 896; M-O A, D5353, 15 Apr 1955; Clarissa Eden, *A Memoir* (2007), p 184.
2. David Kynaston, *The City of London, Volume IV* (2001), p 68; *Financial Times*, 21 Apr 1955, 23 Apr 1955; Philip M. Williams, *Hugh Gaitskell* (1979), p 352.
3. John Campbell, *Nye Bevan* (Richard Cohen edn, 1997), p 296; Anne Perkins, *Red Queen* (2003), p 131; *Crossman*, p 410; Dianne Kirby, 'The Church of England and the Cold War Nuclear Debate', *Twentieth Century British History* 4/3 (1993), pp 278–9; *Crossman*, p 389; E. P. Thompson, *The Poverty of Theory* (1978), pp 1–2.
4. *Picture Post*, 21 May 1955.
5. Langford, 11 May 1955; Lawrence Black, *The Political Culture of the Left in Affluent Britain, 1951–64* (Basingstoke, 2003), p 23; *The Times*, 6 Jul 1955; Robert M. Worcester, *British Public Opinion* (Oxford, 1991), p 14; M-O A, D5353, 13 May 1955.
6. *Manchester Guardian*, 12 May 1955; *Independent*, 14 Mar 1992 (Michael Cockerell); Philip Ziegler, *Wilson* (1993), pp 106–7; *New Statesman*, 21 May 1955, 28 May 1955, 14 May 1955, 28 May 1955; *New Yorker*, 11 Jun 1955; Cockerell, *Live*, p 36.
7. Brian Brivati, *Hugh Gaitskell* (1996), pp 216–17; Kenneth Harris, *Attlee* (1982), p 533; Ina Zweiniger-Bargielowska, *Austerity in Britain* (Oxford, 2000), pp 239–40; Robert Shepherd, *Enoch Powell* (1996), p 135; David Dutton, *Anthony Eden* (1997), p 270; Sir Anthony Eden, *Full Circle* (1960), p 279; Eden, *Memoir*, p 207; *Guardian*, 15 Sep 2006 (Michael White).
8. David Rayvern Allen, *Arlott* (1994), p 233; Norman Tebbit, *Upwardly Mobile* (1988), p 47; *Harwich & Dovercourt Standard*, 20 May 1955, 3 Jun 1955, 6 May 1955; Sir Gerald Nabarro, *NAB 1* (Oxford, 1969), pp 126–7; Lewis Baston, *Reggie* (Stroud, 2004), pp 97, 104–17.
9. Fowles, EUL MS 102/1/8, fol 223, 26/27 May 1955; Haines, 26 May 1955; M-O A, D5353, 26 May 1955; Turtle, 26–7 May 1955; M-O A, D5353, 27 May 1955; Heap, 27 May 1955.
10. *Crossman*, p 421; John McIlroy, 'Reds at Work: Communist Factory Organisation in the Cold War, 1947–56', *Labour History Review* (Summer 2000), p 197; Baston, *Reggie*, p 108; Kevin Jefferys, *Anthony Crosland* (Politico's edn, 2000), p 54; Mark Garnett and Ian Aitken, *Splendid! Splendid!* (2002), p 44; Crossman, MS 154/8/17, fol 672, 31 May 1955.
11. *Crossman*, pp 280–81; *Times Literary Supplement*, 17 Nov 2000 (Martin Pugh); Benn, p 182; *Socialist Commentary* (Jul 1955), pp 198–200, 203–6.

7 A Fine Day for a Hanging

1. David E. Martin and Bryan Sadler, 'Arthur Deakin', in Joyce M. Bellamy and John Saville (eds), *Dictionary of Labour Biography, Volume II* (1974), pp 112–17;

C. Slaughter, 'The Strike of Yorkshire Mineworkers in May 1955', *Sociological Review* (Dec 1958), pp 241, 258; Jim Phillips, 'Inter-Union Conflict in the Docks, 1954–1955', *Historical Studies in Industrial Relations* (Mar 1996), pp 107–30; St John, 29 May 1955; Robert Lacey, *Majesty* (Sphere edn, 1978), pp 280–81.

2. Jim Phillips, 'The Postwar Political Consensus and Industrial Unrest in the Docks, 1945–55', *Twentieth Century British History* 6/3 (1995), pp 313–14; Benn, p 221; Andrew Roberts, *Eminent Churchillians* (1994), p 276; Macmillan, pp 437, 435; Correlli Barnett, *The Verdict of Peace* (2001), pp 424–5, 427; *New Yorker*, 11 Jun 1955; Langford, 3 Jun 1955, 6 Jun 1955; Haines, 8 Jun 1955; Sean French, *Patrick Hamilton* (1993), p 245; Turtle, 14 Jun 1955.

3. *New Yorker*, 25 Jun 1955; Roberts, *Eminent Churchillians*, p 276; George H. Gallup (ed), *The Gallup International Public Opinion Polls: Great Britain, 1937–1975, Volume One* (New York, 1976), p 351; *News Chronicle*, 6 Sep 1955.

4. Mark Pottle (ed), *Daring to Hope: The Diaries and Letters of Violet Bonham Carter, 1946–1969* (2000), pp 149–50; BBC WA, *Any Questions?*, 3 Jun 1955; Pottle (ed), *Daring*, p 150; John Osborne, *A Better Class of Person* (1981), pp 264–6.

5. http://www.europarl.europa.eu/summits, speech by Klaus Hansch, 29 Mar 1996; Keith Middlemas, *Power, Competition and the State, Volume I* (Basingstoke, 1986), p 253; Andy Mullin and Brian Burkitt, 'Spinning Europe: Pro-European Union Propaganda Campaigns in Britain, 1962–1975', *Political Quarterly* (Jan–Mar 1995), p 102; Rogan Taylor and Andrew Ward, *Kicking and Screaming* (1995), p 129.

6. Tom Bower, *Maxwell* (1988), pp 54, 73; *Evening Standard*, 15 Jun 1955; *Daily Mail*, 6 Dec 2000 (Ian Wooldridge); Paul Bailey, *An Immaculate Mistake* (Penguin edn, 2004), pp 144–7, 162; Humphrey Carpenter, *Dennis Potter* (1998), pp 52–3.

7. *Daily Mail*, 21–2 Jun 1955; *Evening Standard*, 30 Jun 1955; Jacqueline Wilson, *Jacky Daydream* (Corgi Yearling edn, 2008), p 175. In general on the Ellis case, see Robert Hancock, *Ruth Ellis* (Weidenfeld & Nicolson edn, 1985); *The Times*, 15 Mar 2002 (Carol Midgley); *Guardian*, 12 Sep 2003 (Clare Dyer).

8. *Stowmarket Mercury*, 8 Jul 1955; *Coventry Standard*, 15 Jul 1955; Phil Hubbard et al, 'Contesting the Modern City: Reconstruction and Everyday Life in Post-war Coventry', *Planning Perspectives* (Oct 2003), pp 391–2, 397; *Manchester Guardian*, 14 Oct 1955; *Coventry Evening Telegraph*, 5 Oct 1955.

9. *Daily Mirror*, 9 Jul 1955; *Hackney Gazette*, 9 Sep 1955; *Radio Times*, 1 Jul 1955, 4 Jan 1957; *Listener*, 14 Jul 1955; *Spectator*, 29 Jul 1955; BBC WA, R9/19/2, Aug–Sep 1955; Peter Cotes, 'Lord Willis', *Independent*, 24 Dec 1992. In general, see Susan Sydney-Smith, *Beyond Dixon of Dock Green*, pp 103–17.

10. Turtle, 10 Jul 1955; *Daily Mirror*, 11 Jul 1955; Langford, 11–12 Jul 1955; Heap, 12 Jul 1955; Martin, 12 Jul 1955; Raynham, 12 Jul 1955.

8 It's Terribly Sad

1. *Daily Mirror*, 16 Jul 1955; *News Chronicle*, 15 Jul 1955; *Daily Mirror*, 16 July 1955; *Spectator*, 22 Jul 1955.

2. *Times Literary Supplement*, 15 Jul 1955; E. P. Thompson, *William Morris* (Merlin Press edn, 1977), p 769; John Drummond, *Tainted by Experience* (2000), p 71; David Cannadine, 'The Way We Lived Then', *Times Literary Supplement*, 7

Sep 1990; Drummond, *Tainted*, pp 71–2. For insightful obituaries of Elton and Thompson, see *Independent*, 9 Dec 1994 (Patrick Collinson), 30 Aug 1993 (E. J. Hobsbawm), *Guardian*, 30 Aug 1993 (W. L. Webb). For nuanced historiographical readings, see also Miles Taylor, 'The Beginnings of Modern British Social History', *History Workshop* (Spring 1997), pp 155–76; Jim Obelkevich, 'New Developments in History in the 1950s and 1960s', *Contemporary British History* (Winter 2000), pp 125–42.

3. *Independent*, 6 Jul 2007 (Brian Viner); *The Times*, 19 Jul 1955, 23 Jul 1955; Anthony Sutcliffe and Roger Smith, *Birmingham, 1939–1970* (1974), pp 403–4; Anthony Thwaite (ed), *Selected Letters of Philip Larkin, 1940–1985* (1992), p 248; Martin, 29 Jul 1955; Haines, 29 Jul 1955; *Liverpool Echo*, 30 Jul 1955; Martin, 31 Jul 1955; Haines, 1 Aug 1955.

4. Peter Hall, 'Godotmania', *Guardian*, 4 Jan 2003; *Sunday Times*, 7 Aug 1955 (Harold Hobson); James Knowlson, *Damned to Fame* (1996), p 415; *Financial Times*, 4 Aug 1955; Knowlson, *Damned*, p 415; Alan Jenkins, *Stephen Potter* (1980), pp 188–9.

5. James Morton and Gerry Parker, *Gangland Bosses* (2004), p 211; *News Chronicle*, 24 Sep 1955; John Gross, *A Double Threat* (2001), p 122; *Sunday Express*, 16 Oct 1955; Dick Hobbs, 'Reg Kray', *Independent*, 2 Oct 2000; Langford, 16 Jul 1955.

6. For evidence of the date of Larkin's journey, see Thwaite (ed), *Selected Letters*, p 301, where Larkin specifically recalls in 1959 that it was in August 1955. What we know about his movements that month strongly suggests that it was Saturday the 13th. As for Whit Saturday that year, it was on the eve of a national railway strike, and it is temperamentally unlikely that Larkin would have taken the risk, not knowing how he was going to get back.

7. Thwaite (ed), *Selected Letters*, p 249; *New Statesman*, 20 Aug 1955; Amis, p 452; 'Norris McWhirter', *The Times*, 21 Apr 2004.

8. Thwaite (ed), *Selected Letters*, p 250; Garry Whannel, '"Grandstand", the Sports Fan and the Family Audience', in John Corner (ed), *Popular Television in Britain* (1991), pp 186–7; *Independent*, 5 Oct 2000 (David Conn); *Southend Standard*, 18 Aug 1955, 25 Aug 1955; Peter Acton and Colin M. Jarman (eds), *Roy of the Rovers* (Harpenden, 1994), pp 13–15.

9. Fowles, EUL MS 102/1/8, fol 234, 20–27 Aug 1955; Janet Street-Porter, *Baggage* (2004), p 79; Christopher Sandford, *Mick Jagger* (Cooper Square Press edn, 1999), p 24; Lucy O'Brien, *Dusty* (1989), p xi.

10. *Hackney Gazette*, 7 Sep 1955, 5 Sep 1955; *Coventry Evening Telegraph*, 13 Oct 1955; Douglas Hill (ed), *Tribune 40* (1977), p 106; *Chorley Guardian and Leyland Advertiser*, 3 Jun 1955; *South London Press*, 7 Oct 1955; *News Chronicle*, 14–16 Sep 1955; Haines, 21 Sep 1955.

11. *Express and Star* (Wolverhampton), 1 Sep 1955, 6 Sep 1955, 10 Sep 1955; *Guardian*, 22 Jul 2006.

12. *New Statesman*, 6 Aug 1955; Spencer Leigh, 'Ralph Edwards', *Independent*, 21 Nov 2005; *Radio Times*, 22 Jul 1955; Dennis Barker, 'Johnny Downes', *Guardian*, 25 Jan 2005; *Radio Times*, 9 Sep 1955; Hilary Kingsley and Geoff Tibballs, *Box of Delights* (1989), p 50; Asa Briggs, *Sound and Vision* (Oxford, 1995), p 904.

13. *Picture Post*, 24 Sep 1955; BBC WA, R9/35/4, 22 Sep 1955; William Smethurst, *The Archers* (1996), pp 56–61; *News Chronicle*, 23 Sep 1955; *Manchester Guardian*, 26 Sep 1955; Briggs, *Sound*, p 923.

14. *TV Times*, 20 Sep 1955; Meryle Secrest, *Kenneth Clark* (1984), p 201; Philip Purser, 'Muriel Young', *Guardian*, 29 Mar 2001; *TV Times*, 20 Sep 1955; *Punch*, 27 Sep 1955; Mark Robinson, *100 Greatest TV Ads* (2000), p 16; *Manchester Guardian*, 23 Sep 1955; *News Chronicle*, 23 Sep 1955.

15. Jeff Evans, *The Penguin TV Companion* (2006), pp 254, 423; Tom Vallance, 'Bernadette O'Farrell', *Independent*, 26 Oct 1999; Evans, *Penguin TV*, p 804; Bernard Sendall, *Independent Television in Britain: Volume I* (1982), pp 320–21; *Punch*, 5 Oct 1955; Denis Gifford, 'Hughie Green', *Independent*, 5 May 1997; BBC Four, 'Double Your Money', 27 Mar 2005.

16. *News Chronicle*, 26 Sep 1955; Francis Wheen, *Television* (1985), pp 71–2; Leonard Miall, 'Sir Robin Day', *Independent*, 8 Aug 2000; Robin Day, *Grand Inquisitor* (1989), p 79. In general on *Sunday Night at the London Palladium*, see *Picture Post*, 26 Nov 1955; Sendall, *Independent Television*, p 322; http://www.televisionheaven. co.uk/londonpalladium.htm.

17. *Punch*, 5 Oct 1955; *Spectator*, 30 Sep 1955; *Picture Post*, 10 Dec 1955; Sendall, *Independent Television*, p 321; *News Chronicle*, 6 Oct 1955; ITC records (BFI), 3995707 (barcode number), 3001/4 (file number); M-O A, Directive Replies, Nov 1955, Men, A–G file, Women, G–L, A–F files.

18. *Spectator*, 23 Sep 1955, 7 Oct 1955, 30 Sep 1955; James E. Cronin, 'Power, Secrecy and the British Constitution: Vetting Samuel Beer's *Treasury Control*', *Twentieth Century British History* 3/1 (1992), pp 59–75; Nancy Mitford, 'The English Aristocracy', in E. Hamilton (ed), *The Penguin Book of Twentieth Century Essays* (1999), pp 322–3; *New Yorker*, 8 Oct 1955 (Panter-Downes); Evelyn Waugh, 'An Open Letter to the Honble Mrs. Peter Rodd (Nancy Mitford) on a Very Serious Subject', in Alan S. C. Ross et al, *Noblesse Oblige* (1956), p 65.

19. *Picture Post*, 19 Nov 1955; Martin, 18 Oct 1955; *Evening Standard*, 19 May 1955; *Daily Mail*, 17 May 1955; *News Chronicle*, 17 May 1955; *Daily Mirror*, 20 May 1955; *Punch*, 1 Jun 1955; John Ramsden, *The Dam Busters* (2003), p 67; John Ramsden, 'Refocusing "The People's War": British War Films of the 1950s', *Journal of Contemporary History* (Jan 1998), pp 62–3; Peter Hennessy, 'Modern History in the Making', *Director* (Sep 1992), p 27; Richard Eyre, 'My Voilà Moment', *Guardian*, 12 Apr 2003; Robin Blake, 'Aeronautical but Nice', *Financial Times*, 4 Nov 2006; *Rover*, 29 Oct 1955.

20. Heap, 19 Oct 1955; Geoffrey Wansell, *Terence Rattigan* (1995), p 265; Hall, 'Godotmania'; *New Statesman*, 15 Oct 1955; Fowles, p 365; Joan Bakewell, *The Centre of the Bed* (2003), p 119; Hall, 'Godotmania'.

21. David Kynaston, *The City of London, Volume IV* (2001), pp 68–71; *New Yorker*, 5 Nov 1955; Philip M. Williams, *Hugh Gaitskell* (1979), p 360; Brian Brivati, *Hugh Gaitskell* (1996), p 222; E.H.H. Green, *Ideologies of Conservatism* (Oxford, 2002), p 193; *Birmingham Mail*, 23 Aug 1955; Gerald Frost, *Antony Fisher* (2002), p 62.

22. *Daily Mirror*, 19 Aug 1955; Macmillan, p 464; M-O A, D5353, 13 Oct 1955; *Daily Mirror*, 14 Oct 1955; *News Chronicle*, 14 Oct 1955; *Manchester Guardian*, 15 Oct 1955; Elizabeth Longford, *Elizabeth R* (1983), p 176; *Daily Mirror*, 17 Oct 1955.

23. D. R. Thorpe, *Eden* (2003), p 448; M-O A, D5353, 19 Oct 1955; *Daily Mirror*, 19 Oct 1955; Ben Pimlott, *The Queen* (1996), p 236; *New Statesman*, 22 Oct 1955; Richard Ingrams, *Muggeridge* (1995), p 182; *Daily Mirror*, 21 Oct 1955; Pimlott, *Queen*, p 236; Helen Cathcart, *Princess Margaret* (1974), p 124; Martin, 21 Oct

1955; Janie Hampton (ed), *Joyce & Ginnie* (1997), p 203; Willi Frischauer, *Margaret* (1977), p 107; Turtle, 23 Oct 1955.

24. *The Times*, 26 Oct 1955; Pimlott, *Queen*, pp 238, 596; Cathcart, *Princess Margaret*, pp 124–5; Nick Clarke, *The Shadow of a Nation* (2003), p 65; *Daily Mirror*, 28 Oct 1955; Hampton (ed), *Joyce & Ginnie*, p 204; BBC WA, *Any Questions?*, 28 Oct 1955; *Sunday Express*, 30 Oct 1955; *Daily Express*, 31 Oct 1955; George H. Gallup (ed), *The Gallup International Public Opinion Polls: Great Britain, 1937–1975, Volume One* (New York, 1976), p 357.

25. Tim Heald, *Princess Margaret* (2007), p 104; Hill, 31 Oct 1955; Turtle, 31 Oct 1955; Mark Pottle (ed), *Daring to Hope: The Diaries and Letters of Violet Bonham Carter, 1946–1969* (2000), p 158; Langford, 31 Oct 1955; Nigel Nicolson (ed), Harold Nicolson, *Diaries and Letters, Volume III*, (1968), p 290; Martin, 31 Oct 1955; Clarke, *Shadow*, p 65; M-O A, D5353, 31 Oct 1955; Hill, 1 Nov 1955.

26. *Daily Mail*, 1 Nov 1955; *Manchester Guardian*, 1 Nov 1955; M-O A, TC 69/11/B, 1 Nov 1955; Preston, 1 Nov 1955; Heap, 1 Nov 1955; Haines, 1 Nov 1955; Hill, 1–2 Nov 1955.

27. *Daily Mirror*, 2 Nov 1955; *Daily Express*, 3 Nov 1955; *People*, 6 Nov 1955; *Daily Express*, 3 Nov 1955; M-O A, TC 69/11/B, 3 Nov 1955; Gallup (ed), *Gallup*, p 359; *Daily Express*, 4 Nov 1955; BBC WA, *Any Questions?*, 4 Nov 1955.

28. M-O A, Directive Replies, Nov 1955, Men, A–G file, Women, A–F, G–L, M–Z files; Katherine Bucknell (ed), Christopher Isherwood, *Diaries: Volume One, 1939–1960* (1996), p 575.

9 Family Favourites

1. *Guardian*, 13 Nov 1999; *The Times*, 9 Sep 2000; *Guardian*, 30 Oct 2004; *Daily Mail*, 29 Apr 1988; *Independent on Sunday*, 28 Feb 1993; *BBC News Magazine* (online), May 2007, 'Was Britain Better in the 50s?'; Martin, 22 Feb 1954; Shirley Collins, *America Over the Water* (2005), p 176.

2. *Fowles*, EUL MS 102/1/8, fol 212, 8 Apr 1955; Callum Brown, *The Death of Christian Britain* (2001), p 7; Ferdynand Zweig, *The British Worker* (1952), pp 235–9; B. Seebohm Rowntree and G. R. Lavers, *English Life and Leisure* (1951), pp 326–7; Richard Hoggart, *The Uses of Literacy* (Pelican edn, 1958), p 279.

3. Geoffrey Gorer, *Exploring English Character* (1955), pp 241–2; T. Cauter and J. S. Downham, *The Communication of Ideas* (1954), p 52; BBC WA, R9/9/19–LR/55/192, Feb 1955, 'Religious Broadcasts and the Public'; A. M. Carr-Saunders et al, *A Survey of Social Conditions in England and Wales* (Oxford, 1958), p 260; George H. Gallup (ed), *The Gallup International Public Opinion Polls: Great Britain 1937–1975, Volume One* (New York, 1976), pp 403–4.

4. Brown, *Death*, p 6; Grace Davie, *Religion in Britain since 1945* (Oxford, 1994), p 82; Hoggart, *Uses*, pp 114–15.

5. Rowntree and Lavers, *English Life*, pp 14, 33, 38, 50–51, 55, 67, 355; Gorer, *Exploring*, pp 243–4, 253, 257; *Tablet*, 18 Dec 1999; Gallup (ed), *Gallup*, p 405; Zweig, *British Worker*, pp 236–7; Hoggart, *Uses*, pp 117–19.

6. Gorer, *Exploring*, pp 237–8, 246–7; Cater and Downham, *Communication*, pp 54–5; Hoggart, *Uses*, p 118; *Times Literary Supplement*, 8 Aug 2008 (Bill Knox);

Carr-Saunders, *Survey*, p 261; Spencer Leigh, 'Don Cornell', *Independent*, 1 Mar 2004.

7. Hunter Davies, 'The Church Has Scored an Own Goal', *Independent*, 6 Jul 1998; Lady Henrietta Rous (ed), *The Ossie Clark Diaries* (1998), p xlviii; Anton Rippon, *A Derby Boy* (Stroud, 2007), p 76; Ian Jack, 'Things That Have Interested Me', *Guardian*, 11 Mar 2006; John Parker, *Father of the House* (1982), pp 119–20; Clive D. Field, '"The Secularized Sabbath" Revisited: Opinion Polls as Sources for Sunday Observance in Contemporary Britain', *Contemporary British History* (Spring 2001), p 6.

8. *Daily Mirror*, 5 Sep 1955; Andrew Holden, *Makers and Manners* (2004), p 64; *Picture Post*, 3 Dec 1955.

9. David Kynaston, *The City of London, Volume IV* (2001), p 140; *Sunday Pictorial*, 29 Aug 1954; Crossman, MS 154/8/16, 1 Nov 1954.

10. Amis, p 422; Joseph McAleer, *Passion's Fortune* (Oxford, 1999), pp 241–3; Robert Hewison, *In Anger* (Methuen edn, 1988), p 177; Robin Day, *Grand Inquisitor* (1989), p 64; David Hendy, 'BBC Radio Four and Conflicts over Spoken English in the 1970s', *Media History* (Dec 2006), p 275; Peter O'Sullevan, *Calling the Horses* (1989), p 144; *Fowles*, p 369.

11. Alan Titchmarsh, *Nobbut a Lad* (2006), p 4; Barry Unsworth, 'Stockton and Naples', *Northern Review* (Autumn 1999), p 113; David Lascelles, *Other People's Money* (2005), p 9; Kynaston, *City*, p 140; Derek Robinson, 'It Was Different Then!', in James Belsey et al, *Muddling Through* (Bristol, 1988), p 13; Frank Mort, *Cultures of Consumption* (1996), p 138; Brian Thompson, *Clever Girl* (2007), p 30; Mort, *Cultures*, p 140; Steve Humphries and John Taylor, *The Making of Modern London, 1945–1985* (1986), pp 32–3.

12. Nirad C. Chaudhuri, *A Passage to England* (Hogarth Press edn, 1989), pp 82–6; Anthony Thwaite (ed), *Selected Letters of Philip Larkin, 1940–1955* (1992), p 207; *Daily Mirror*, 20 Aug 1955; Helen Carey, 'Elizabeth Brunner', *Independent*, 15 Jan 2003; *The Times*, 3 Sep 1954; *Sunday Express*, 18 Sep 1955.

13. Jacqueline Wilson, *Jacky Daydream* (Corgi Yearling edn, 2008), p 120; Ken Blakemore, *Sunnyside Down* (Stroud, 2005), pp 159–60; *Independent*, 29 Oct 1996; Rowntree and Lavers, *English Life*, chap 6; Christie Davies, *The Strange Death of Moral Britain* (New Brunswick, NJ, 2004), pp 27–8; Laurie Dennett, *A Sense of Security* (Cambridge, 1988), pp 322–3.

14. George Tremlett, *The David Bowie Story* (1974), pp 15–16; Wilson, *Jacky*, p 95; Anthony Seldon, *Major* (1997), pp 12–13; Harry Thompson, *Peter Cook* (1997), pp 18–19; *BBC News Magazine* (online), May 2007, 'Your 1950s: School life'; Rosalind Delmar, 'Recording a Landscape: Growing Up in Dormanstown', in Jim Fyrth (ed), *Labour's Promised Land?* (1995), pp 311–12; *Oldie* (May 2000), pp 32–3 (Barber); Robinson, 'Different', p 9; Steve Humphries et al, *A Century of Childhood* (1988), p 113; Hunter Davies, *Strong Lad Wanted for Strong Lass* (Carlisle, 2004), p 34; *The Times*, 28 Mar 2000; *BBC News Magazine*, 'Your 1950s' (Ferguson).

15. Donald Simpson, 'Progressivism and the Development of Primary Education: An Historical Review', *History of Education Society Bulletin* (Autumn 1996), p 58; Ian Grosvenor and Martin Lawn, 'Days out of School: Secondary Education, Citizenship and Public Space in 1950s England', *History of Education* (July 2004), pp 385–8; Haines, 9 Sep 1954; John Wroughton, *Mr Colston's Hospital* (Bristol,

2002), p 298; *Guardian*, 23 Jan 2003 (Libby Brooks); *Eastern Daily Press*, 25 Sep 1954; Rev. Oliver Willmott, *The Parish Notes of Loders, Dottery & Askerswell, Dorset: Volume I* (Shrewsbury, 1996), Feb 1955.

16. Elizabeth Nelson, *The British Counter-Culture, 1966–73* (Basingstoke, 1989), pp 14–15; Gerald Fairlie, *The Return of the Black Gang* (1954), p 21; John Springhall et al, *Sure & Stedfast* (1983), p 185; John Barron Mays, *Growing Up in the City* (Liverpool, 1954), p 183.

17. The Boy Scouts Association, *The Scout Song Book* (1952); Basil Henriques, *The Home-Menders* (1955), pp 147–8; *Observer*, 23 Oct 1955; *Picture Post*, 19 Nov 1955.

18. Mays, *Growing Up*, p 69; Pearl Jephcott, *Some Young People* (1954), pp 69–71; Raphael Samuel, *The Lost World of British Communism* (2006), p 12; Helen Reid, 'Salad Days', in James Belsey et al, *Muddling Through* (Bristol, 1988), pp 35–42.

19. Liz Stanley, *Sex Surveyed, 1949–1994* (1995), pp 155, 164; Sheridan Morley, *Dirk Bogarde* (1996), pp 65–6; Sue Harper and Vincent Porter, 'Cinema Audience Tastes in 1950s Britain', *Journal of Popular British Cinema* (1999), p 72; Mark Lewisohn, *Funny, Peculiar* (2002), p 236; Langford, 4 Apr 1954; Martin P. M. Richards and B. Jane Elliott, 'Sex and Marriage in the 1960s and 1970s' in David Clark (ed), *Marriage, Domestic Life and Social Change* (1991), pp 37–8; M-O A, Mass-Observation Bulletin, no 50: March 1954, pp 2–6; Paul Ferris, *Sir Huge* (1990), p 97.

20. Penelope Lively, 'Sex Was a Dangerous Game in the Swinging Fifties', *Sunday Times*, 3 Dec 2000; Richards and Elliott, 'Sex and Marriage', p 38; McAleer, *Passion's Fortune*, p 209; Cate Haste, *Rules of Desire* (1992), pp 175–7; *Guardian*, 22 May 2004; Lively, 'Sex'; Joan Bakewell, *The Centre of the Bed* (2003), p 109; Liz Hodgkinson, 'The Decade of Discontent', *The Times*, 12 Sep 1990; Philip Norman, *John Lennon* (2008), p 72; Robinson, 'Different', p 10.

21. Andy Medhurst, *A National Joke* (Abingdon, 2007), pp 87–9; Holden, *Makers*, pp 60–62; Medhurst, *National*, p 96; Henriques, *Home-Makers*, pp 128, 130; British Medical Association, *Homosexuality and Prostitution* (1955), p 31; *The Times*, 28 Nov 1997 (Valerie Elliott); Patrick Higgins, *Heterosexual Dictatorship* (1996), pp 40–45; Matt Houlbrook, *Queer London* (2005), pp 255–61. See also Frank Mort, 'Mapping Sexual London: The Wolfenden Committee on Homosexual Offences and Prostitution, 1954–57', *New Formations* (Spring 1999), pp 108–11.

22. Andy Medhurst, 'Every Wart and Pustule: Gilbert Harding and Television Stardom', in John Corner (ed), *Popular Television in Britain* (1991), pp 67–8; *Times Literary Supplement*, 19 Nov 2004 (Frederic Raphael); *Evening Standard*, 24 Apr 2007; Angela Pleasence, 'Hallam Tennyson', *Guardian*, 6 Jan 2006; Stephen Moss, 'Sounds and Silence', *Guardian*, 19 Jun 2004 (Maxwell Davies); Alan Bennett, *Untold Stories* (2005), p 143; *The Times*, 12 Dec 2005 (Paul McCann).

23. Paula Bartley and Barbara Gwinnett, 'Prostitution', in Ina Zweiniger-Bargielowska (ed), *Women in Twentieth-Century Britain* (Harlow, 2001), p 219; Jerry White, *London in the Twentieth Century* (Vintage edn, 2008), p 322; Holden, *Makers*, p 66; Paul Ferris, *Sex and the British* (1993), p 157; Stanley, *Sex*, pp 148, 150; C. H. Rolph (ed), *Women of the Streets* (1955), pp 87–91.

24. http://www.whirligig-tv.co.uk/radio/twff.htm; Denis Gifford, 'Jean Metcalfe', *Independent*, 31 Jan 2000; Blakemore, *Sunnyside*, p 133.

25. Cynthia L. White, *Women's Magazines, 1693–1968* (1970), pp 139–40; *People's Friend*, 1 Mar 1952; Richard M. Titmuss, *Essays on 'The Welfare State'* (1958), p 99; David Coleman, 'Population and Family', in A. H. Halsey with Josephine Webb (eds), *Twentieth-Century British Social Trends* (Basingstoke, 2000), pp 58–9; Gorer, *Exploring*, p 155; Jephcott, *Some Young People*, p 66.

26. Rachel M. Pierce, 'Marriage in the Fifties', *Sociological Review* (July 1963), p 219; Robin Eggar, *Tom Jones* (2000), pp 34–6; Elizabeth Roberts, *Women and Families* (Oxford, 1995), p 74; Penny Somerfield, 'Women in Britain since 1945: Companionate Marriage and the Double Burden', in James Obelkevich and Peter Catterall (eds), *Understanding Post-war British Society* (1994), p 66; Claire Langhamer, 'Adultery in Post-War England', *History Workshop Journal* (Autumn 2006), p 94; Lewis Baston, *Reggie* (Stroud, 2004), pp 80–81; Noel Annan, *Our Age* (1990), p 175; Gorer, *Exploring*, p 147; Mary Abbott, *Family Affairs* (2003), p 111; Max Wall, *The Fool on the Hill* (1975), pp 168–9, 173; David Clark, 'Guidance Counselling, Therapy: Responses to "Marital Problems", 1950–90', *Sociological Review* (Nov 1991), pp 772–3; Humphries, *Century*, p 58.

27. Stanley, *Sex*, p 134; Langhamer, 'Adultery', p 99; Stanley, *Sex*, p 132; Langhamer, 'Adultery', p 102; Gorer, *Exploring*, pp 154, 149; Raynham, 10 Dec 1954; Langhamer, 'Adultery', p 104.

28. Eustace Chesser, *The Sexual, Marital and Family Relationships of the English Woman* (1956), pp 311–16; Gorer, *Exploring*, pp 96–7; Chesser, *Sexual*, p 377; Gorer, *Exploring*, pp 98–9; Richards and Elliott, 'Sex and Marriage', p 40; Natalie Higgins, 'The Changing Expectations and Realities of Marriage in the English Working Class, 1920–1960', University of Cambridge PhD, 2002, p 110.

29. Holden, *Makers*, p 43; Lulie A. Shaw, 'Impressions of Family Life in a London Suburb', *Sociological Review* (Dec 1954), p 181; Chesser, *Sexual*, p 455; Gallup (ed.), *Gallup*, p 409; Elizabeth Wilson, *Only Halfway to Paradise* (1980), p 96; Holden, *Makers*, p 44; Kate Fisher, *Birth Control, Sex and Marriage in Britain, 1918–1960* (Oxford, 2006), chap 1; Higgins, 'Changing', p 223; Phyllis Willmott, *Joys and Sorrows* (1995), p 138.

30. Lively, 'Sex'; Joanna Bourke, *Working-Class Cultures in Britain, 1890–1960* (1994), p 57; Barbara Brookes, *Abortion in England, 1900–1967* (Beckenham, 1988), pp 133, 148, 144; Jennifer Worth, 'A Deadly Trade', *Guardian*, 6 Jan 2005.

31. Bourke, *Working-Class Cultures*, p 31; *Picture Post*, 25 Sep 1954; Gillian Clark, 'The Role of Mother and Baby Homes in the Adoption of Children Born Outside Marriage in Twentieth-Century England and Wales', *Family & Community History* (May 2008), p 55; *Quarterly Review of the Church of England Moral Welfare Council* (Oct 1950), p 27; Clark, 'Role', pp 46–7; Tanya Evans, 'The Other Woman and Her Child: Extra-marital Affairs and Illegitimacy in 20th Century England', Institute of Historical Research, 20 Feb 2008; Clark, 'Role', pp 57, 45; *Daily Mirror*, 26 Oct 1953, 29–31 Oct 1953.

32. *Woman's Own*, 20 Oct 1955; White, *Women's Magazines*, p 147; Marjorie Ferguson, *Forever Feminine* (1983), p 60; 'Barbara Goalen', *Daily Telegraph*, 19 Jun 2002; Veronica Horwell, 'Margot Smyly', *Guardian*, 11 Jun 2005; Barbara Pym Papers (Bodleian Library, Oxford), MS Pym 47, fol 10, c. Dec 1955.

33. Summerfield, 'Women', pp 58–9; Christine Geraghty, *British Cinema in the Fifties* (2000), pp 160–67; *Woman's Own*, 6 Oct 1955; Wilson, *Only Halfway*, p 93;

Woman's Own, 1 Sep 1955; Christina Hardyment, *Slice of Life* (1995), p 37; Maggie Andrews, *The Acceptable Face of Feminism* (1997), chap 8; *Bolton Evening News*, 30 Apr 1953.

34. Maggie Andrews, 'Butterflies and Caustic Asides', in Stephen Wagg (ed), *Because I Tell a Joke or Two* (1998), p 54; Good Housekeeping Institute, *The Happy Home* (1955), chaps 2–3, 5, 7, 9; White, *Women's Magazines*, pp 146–7; *Sunday Express*, 16 Jan 1955; Ferguson, *Forever*, p 50.

35. Willmott, *Parish Notes*, Mar 1954; Sue Aspinall, 'Women, Realism and Reality in British Films, 1943–53', in James Curran and Vincent Porter (eds), *British Cinema History* (1953), p 290; Alan Sinfield, *Literature, Politics and Culture in Postwar Britain* (Oxford, 1989), pp 207–8; *News Chronicle*, 23 Apr 1952; *Housewife*, Sep 1953, p 30; BBC WA, *Woman's Hour*, 9 Feb 1955.

36. Rivers Fletcher, 'Sheila van Damm', *Independent*, 26 Aug 1987; Jenny Uglow, *A Little History of British Gardening* (2004), p 286; James Morton, 'Dame Rose Heilbron', *Guardian*, 13 Dec 2005; Deborah Ross, 'Three's Company', *Independent*, 15 Jul 2002; *Daily Telegraph/Guardian*, 15 Nov 2003.

37. White, *Women's Magazines*, p 142; Stephanie Spencer, *Gender, Work and Education in Britain in the 1950s* (Basingstoke, 2005), p 150; Roberts, *Women*, pp 119, 129–31; Viola Klein, *Britain's Married Women Workers* (1965), pp 65–9; John Boyd Carpenter, *Way of Life* (1980), p 108.

38. *Independent on Sunday*, 31 Dec 2000 (Louise Jury); *Independent*, 3 Dec 2003 (Brian Viner); Wilson, *Only Halfway*, p 33; Mary Evans, *A Good School* (1991), p 29; Carol Dyhouse, 'Education', in Ina Zweiniger-Bargielowska (ed), *Women in Twentieth-Century Britain* (Harlow, 2001), p 124; Sarah Aiston, 'A Maternal Identity? The Family Lives of British Women Graduates Pre- and Post-1945', *History of Education* (Jul 2005), p 411; Judith Hubback, *Wives Who Went to College* (1957), p 159; Klein, *Britain's Married*, p 26; Chris Wrigley, 'Women in the Labour Market and in the Unions', in John McIlroy et al (eds), *British Trade Unions and Industrial Policies: Volume Two* (Aldershot, 1999), p 45; Jane Lewis, *Women in Britain since 1945* (Oxford, 1992), p 74.

39. Shaw, 'Impressions', pp 182–3; Ken Grainger, 'Money Control and Labour Quiescence: Shopfloor Politics at Alfred Herbert's, 1945–1980', in Michael Terry and P. K. Edwards (eds), *Shopfloor Politics and Job Controls* (Oxford, 1988), p 98; Humphries and Taylor, *Making*, p 66; Denise Riley, '"The Free Mothers": Pronatalism and Working Women in Industry at the End of the Last War in Britain', *History Workshop* (Spring 1981), p 78; *Picture Post*, 7 Jan 1956.

40. Roberts, *Women*, p 235; Shaw, 'Impressions', p 183; J. H. Smith, 'Managers and Married Women Workers', *British Journal of Sociology* (Mar 1961), pp 20–21; Klein, *Britain's Married*, pp 36–48.

41. *Sunday Pictorial*, 21 Feb 1954, 28 Feb 1954; *Woman's Own*, 1 Sep 1955; Ann Dally, 'John Bowlby', *Independent*, 13 Sep 1990; Victoria Winckler, 'Women in Post World War Wales', *Llafor* (1987), p 70; Simon Phillips, 'The Changing Social & Economic Role of Women within the Valley Community of Merthyr Tydfil during the Twentieth Century', Keele University thesis, June 1992; Chesser, *Sexual*, p 375; April Carter, *The Politics of Women's Rights* (Harlow, 1988), p 19; Joyce Joseph, 'A Research Note on Attitudes to Work and Marriage of Six Hundred Adolescent Girls', *British Journal of Sociology* (Jun 1961), pp 176–83.

42. Humphries and Taylor, *Making*, p 29; Chris Harris, 'The Family in Post-war Britain', in James Obelkevich and Peter Catterall (eds), *Understanding Post-war British Society* (1994), p 50; Mays, *Growing Up*, p 89; Norman Dennis et al, *Coal is Our Life* (Tavistock Publications edn, 1969), pp 204, 242; Shaw, 'Impressions', pp 184–6; Dartington Hall Trust Archive, DWE/G/11/D, Michael Young, 'The Extended Family Welfare Association' (Nov 1955); Roberts, *Women*, pp 180–98, 176; Gorer, *Exploring*, p 46.

43. *Picture Post*, 15 Mar 1952; Higgins, 'Changing', pp 91–100; Chesser, *Sexual*, pp 363–7; Higgins, 'Changing', p 102; Gorer, *Exploring*, pp 125–6; Dennis, *Coal*, pp 181–2; Higgins, 'Changing', pp 180–5.

44. M-O A, Mass-Observation Bulletin, no 42, May/June 1951: 'The Housewife's Day'; *Eastern Daily Press*, 25 Sep 1954; M-O A, Mass-Observation Bulletin, no 54, June 1957: 'The Housewife's Day (2)'; Claire Langhamer, 'The Meanings of Home in Postwar Britain', *Journal of Contemporary History* (Apr 2005), p 358; *Picture Post*, 10 Mar 1956.

45. Dennis, *Coal*, p 203; Miriam Akhtar and Steve Humphries, *The Fifties and Sixties* (2001), pp 91, 93; Langhamer, 'Meanings', p 358; M-O A, D5353, 18 Jun 1954.

46. Dennis, *Coal*, pp 180–81; Mays, *Growing Up*, p 93; Gorer, *Exploring*, p 138; Roberts, *Women*, pp 105, 234; Gorer, *Exploring*, p 129; Margot Jefferys, 'Married Women in the Higher Grades of the Civil Service and Government Sponsored Research Organizations', *British Journal of Sociology* (Dec 1952), p 363; *Eastern Daily Press*, 25 Sep 1954; *Woman's Own*, 14 Jul 1955; Hoggart, *Uses*, p 57.

47. Hoggart, *Uses*, p 57; Shaw, 'Impressions', p 187; Michael Young and Peter Willmott, *Family and Kinship in East London* (Pelican edn, 1962), p 24; Bourke, *Working-Class Cultures*, p 85; Young and Willmott, p 145; Janet Finch and Penny Summerfield, 'Social Reconstruction and the Emergence of Companionate Marriage, 1945–59', in David Clark (ed), *Marriage, Domestic Life and Social Change* (1991), p 22.

48. Adam Faith, *Acts of Faith* (1996), pp 37–8, 31; *News Chronicle*, 11 Oct 1955; Roberts, *Women*, p 88; Mays, *Growing Up*, p 89; Janet Street-Porter, *Baggage* (2004), p 43; Melanie McGrath, *Silvertown* (2002); Billie Whitelaw, . . . *Who He?* (1995), pp 64–9; Peter Paterson, *Tired and Emotional* (1993), pp 31–7; *Independent*, 1 Jan 2000 (Hunter Davies); Gary Imlach, *My Father and Other Working-Class Football Heroes* (2005), pp 63–4.

49. Michael Young, 'Distribution of Income within the Family', *British Journal of Sociology* (Dec 1952), pp 314–15; Shaw, 'Impressions', p 181; C. Slaughter, 'Modern Marriage and the Roles of the Sexes', *Sociological Review* (Dec 1956), p 214; Higgins, 'Changing', p 194.

50. Daly, Ms 302/5/8, p 7; Claire Langhamer, *Women's Leisure in England, 1920–60* (Manchester, 2000), p 164; Wilson, *Only Halfway*, p 32; Young, 'Distribution', p 313; Dennis, *Coal*, pp 210–12; Gorer, *Exploring*, p 132; Fisher, *Birth Control*, pp 188, 194–5.

51. Chesser, *Sexual*, pp 423, 432, 448, 451; Stanley, *Sex*, pp 40–44; Lesley A. Hall, *Sex, Gender and Social Change in Britain since 1880* (Basingstoke, 2000), pp 154–5; Shaw, 'Impressions', p 187; Dennis, *Coal*, p 231; Peter Townsend, *The Family Life of Old People* (Pelican edn, 1963), p 90; Akhtar and Humphries, *Fifties*, pp 175–6.

52. Higgins, 'Changing', p 211; Gorer, *Exploring*, p 133; A.J.P. Taylor, *English History, 1914–45* (Pelican edn, 1970), p 219; Higgins, 'Changing', p 219; Gorer, *Exploring*, p 161.

53. *Guardian*, 3 Nov 1998; Wilson, *Jacky*, pp 181–2; Christine Keeler, *The Truth at Last* (2001), pp 14–15; Delmar, 'Recording', pp 307–8; Angela Phillips, 'A Small Space around a Bed', *Guardian*, 24 Sep 2005.

54. Margaret Williamson, '"He Was Good with the Bairns": Fatherhood in an Ironstone Mining Community, 1918–1960', *Northern History* (1998), p 95; Higgins, 'Changing', pp 260–61; Roberts, *Women*, p 236; Shaw, 'Impressions', pp 188–9; Gorer, *Exploring*, p 191; Higgins, 'Changing', pp 261–2; Shaw, 'Impressions', p 189; Haines, 30 May 1951; Mays, *Growing Up*, pp 83–4.

55. Faith, *Acts*, p 29; John Sergeant, *Give Me Ten Seconds* (2001), p 32; David Lister, *In the Best Possible Taste* (1996), p 5; Blakemore, *Sunnyside*, pp 51–2, 77–80 (edited extracts).

10 Less Donnie Lonegan

1. *Independent*, 26 Mar 1990; Aurelia Schober Plath (ed), Sylvia Plath, *Letters Home*, (1976), p 217; Martin Roach, *Top Hundred Singles* (2002), p 108; Christine Geraghty, *British Cinema in the Fifties* (2000), p 9; Tony Jasper, *The Top Twenty Book* (1994 edn), pp 11–12, 16–19; John Peel and Sheila Ravenscroft, *Margrave of the Marshes* (Corgi edn, 2006), pp 67, 65; 'Lonnie Donegan', *The Times*, 5 Nov 2002; Philip Norman, *John Lennon* (2008), p 93; *Guardian*, 11 Dec 2002 (John Peel); Peel and Ravenscroft, *Margrave*, p 126. For a full account of skiffle, see Mike Dewe, *The Skiffle Craze* (Aberystwyth, 1998).

2. Fowles, EUL MS 102/1/8, fol 262, 10 Jan 1956; *News Chronicle*, 20 Dec 1955; Charles Reid, *John Barbirolli* (1971), p 342; Bernard Sendall, *Independent Television in Britain: Volume 1* (1982), pp 328, 348; *Sunday Mercury*, 12 Feb 1956.

3. *Radio Times*, 11 Nov 1955; BBC WA, R9/2/5, 16 Dec 1955; David Oswell, *Television, Childhood and the Home* (Oxford, 2002), p 66; *New Statesman*, 24 Dec 1955; *The Times*, 22 Dec 1955; *News Chronicle*, 30 Dec 1955; *Sunday Times*, 25 Dec 1955; Steve Humphries et al, *A Century of Childhood* (1988), p 81; Iona and Peter Opie, *The Lore and Language of Schoolchildren* (1959), p 118; Mike Seabrook, *Max* (1994), pp 41–2; *Guardian*, 27 Jan 2006 (Will Hodgkinson), 13 Jun 2008 (Simon Hoggart); *Picture Post*, 25 Feb 1956; Elaine Feinstein, *Ted Hughes* (2001), pp 52–5; BBC WA, R9/19/2, Mar 1956.

4. Robert J. Wybrow, *Britain Speaks Out, 1937–87* (Basingstoke, 1989), p 44; David Cesarani, *Arthur Koestler* (1998), p 437; *Spectator*, 2 Dec 1955; Wybrow, *Britain*, p 44; *News Chronicle*, 17 Feb 1956; Crossman, MS 154/8/19, fol 804, 22 Feb 1956; Heap, 17 Feb 1956; *Picture Post*, 21 Jul 1956; M-O A, TC 72/2/A–B.

5. Randall Hansen, *Citizenship and Immigration in Post-war Britain* (Oxford, 2000), pp 70–71; D. W. Dean, 'Conservative Governments and the Restriction of Commonwealth Immigration in the 1950s: The Problems of Constraint', *Historical Journal* (Mar 1992), pp 180–81; Mike Phillips, *London Crossings* (2001), pp 10–15; Mike Phillips and Trevor Phillips, *Windrush* (1998), pp 145–6; Colin MacInnes, *England, Half English* (Hogarth Press edn, 1986), pp 19–20, 29; Steve Humphries and John Taylor, *The Making of Modern London, 1945–1985* (1986), p 117; *New Society*, 25 Apr 1963; Peter Collison, *The Cutteslowe Walls* (1963), pp 136–41.

6. *New Yorker*, 31 Dec 1955; *Daily Telegraph*, 3 Jan 1956; *Picture Post*, 28 Jan 1956; Turtle, 1 Feb 1956; Rose Uttin Diary (Imperial War Museum), 88/50/1, Feb 1956; Anthony Sampson, *Macmillan* (Pelican edn, 1968), p 113; *The Times*, 27 Feb 1956, 2 Mar 1956; *New Statesman*, 11 Feb 1956; *Spectator*, 6 Apr 1956; *The Times*, 25 Apr 1956.

7. Nigel Nicolson (ed), Harold Nicholson, *The Later Years, 1945–1962: Diaries and Letters, Volume III*, (1968), p 292; *Spectator*, 16 Dec 1955; Lord Jenkins of Hillhead, 'Hugh *Gaitskell* (1906–63)', *Contemporary Record* (Autumn 1993), pp 306–11; *The Times*, 15 Dec 1955; Ben Pimlott, *Harold Wilson* (1992), p 194; *New Statesman*, 1 Oct 1955; Gaitskell, p 410; Pimlott, *Wilson*, p 198.

8. Brian Simon, *Education and the Social Order, 1940–1990* (1991), pp 198–9; P. J. Kemeny, 'Dualism in Secondary Technical Education', *British Journal of Sociology* (Mar 1970), p 86; *Picture Post*, 20 Aug 1955, 26 Nov 1955; *Times Literary Supplement*, 16 Dec 1955; *Financial Times*, 21 Feb 1956; Aidan Crawley, *Leap Before You Look* (1988), pp 316–17; BBC WA, R9/10/3-VR/56/1, 9 Jan 1956; J. S. Wagstaff, *The London 'Routemaster' Bus* (1975), p 7; Travis Elborough, *The Bus We Loved* (2005), p 64.

9. Sir Eric St Johnston, *One Policeman's Story* (Chichester, 1978), p 217; Reg Green, *National Heroes* (Edinburgh, 1997), p 159; *Manchester Guardian*, 26 Mar 1956; *The Times*, 5 Apr 2006 (Lydia Hislop); *Guardian*, 8 Apr 2006 (Stuart Jeffries); Nicolson, *Later Years*, p 299.

10. *Macmillan*, p 544; Glyn Powell, 'Turning off the Power: The Electrical Trades Union and the Anti-communist Crusade, 1957–61', *Contemporary British History* (Summer 2004), pp 3–4; John Saville, *Memoirs from the Left* (2003), p 105; Terry Pattinson, 'Lawrence Daly', *Independent*, 30 May 2009; *Daily Worker*, 26 Apr 1955; Daly, MS 302/3/2, Gollan to Daly, 16 May 1956.

11. *Crossman*, p 483; Richard Ingrams, *Muggeridge* (1995), p 178; John Sutherland, *Stephen Spender* (2004), p 307; *News Chronicle*, 19 Apr 1956; *Evening Citizen*, 23 Apr 1956; Turtle, 23 Apr 1956; Nicolson, *Later Years*, p 300; *Crossman*, p 624; Joe Haines, *Glimmers of Twilight* (Politico's edn, 2004), pp 13–14.

12. *News Chronicle*, 3 May 1956; *Independent*, 29 Mar 1993 (Michael Leapman); *Guardian*, 2 Nov 2004 (Luke Harding); *Fowles*, pp 373–4; Turtle, 8 May 1956; Heap, 8 May 1956.

13. *The Times*, 9 May 1956; John Heilpern, *John Osborne* (2006), p 169; Geoffrey Wheatcroft, 'Milton Shulman', *Independent*, 24 May 2004; 'Cecil Wilson', *Daily Telegraph*, 19 Mar 1997; Michael Billington, 'John Barber', *Guardian*, 10 Dec 2005; *Financial Times*, 10 May 1956.

14. 'John Osborne', *The Times*, 27 Dec 1994; *Guardian*, 21 May 2003 (Samantha Ellis); *New Statesman*, 12 May 1956; *Sunday Times*, 13 May 1956; *Observer*, 13 May 1956; Brian Thompson, *Clever Girl* (2007), pp 191–2.

11 No Choice

1. *The Times*, 26 Jan 1956; Howard Glennerster, *British Social Policy Since 1945* (Oxford, 1995), p 87; 'Professor Brian Abel-Smith', *The Times*, 9 Apr 1996; Peter Townsend, 'Professor Brian Abel-Smith', *Independent*, 9 Apr 1006; *Spectator*, 3 Feb 1956; *News Chronicle*, 6 Jul 1956.

2. Marshall Marinker, '"What is Wrong" and "How We Know It": Changing Concepts of Illness in General Practice', in Irvine Loudon et al (eds), *General Practice and the National Health Service, 1948–1997* (Oxford, 1998), pp 69–70; Richard Titmuss, *Essays on 'The Welfare State'* (1958), p 139; Charles Webster, *The National Health Service,* (Oxford, 2002 edn.), pp 39–40; Richard Gordon, *Doctor in the House* (1952), p 134; *Picture Post,* 9 Oct 1954; Labour Party Archives (People's History Museum, Manchester), Research Department Correspondence, 2.3.1, vol 3, 'Hospitals, 1953' file, Memo on 'Hospital Services'; John Prince, 'A Consumer's View of the National Health Service', in James Farndale (ed), *Trends in the National Health Service* (Oxford, 1964), p 35; Rudolf Klein, *The New Politics of the NHS,* (Harlow, 1995 edn.), pp 46–7; David Widgery, *The National Health* (1988), pp 56–7; Titmuss, *Essays,* pp 201–2; Paul Vaughan, *Exciting Times in the Accounts Department* (1995), pp 71, 61–2.

3. *Spectator,* 3 Feb 1956; Nicholas Timmins, *The Five Giants* (2001 edn.), p 210; Heap, 2 Oct 1955; Richard Bradford, *First Boredom, Then Fear* (2005), p 151; *Times Literary Supplement,* 14 Oct 2005 (Ken Worpole); Geoffrey Rivett, *From Cradle to Grave* (1997), p 77; Simon Goodwin, 'Community Care for the Mentally Ill in England and Wales: Myths, Assumptions and Reality', *Journal of Social Policy* (Jan 1989), pp 30, 33; John Clay, *R.D. Laing* (1996), pp 55–60.

4. Heap, 23 Mar 1956; Channel Four, 'Children of the Iron Lung', 21 Sep 2000; Rivett, *Cradle,* p 59; Virginia Berridge, 'The Policy Response to the Smoking and Lung Cancer Connection in the 1950s and 1960s', *Historical Journal* (Dec 2006), p 1197; *Macmillan,* p 556; Berridge, 'Policy', p 1200; Matthew Hilton, *Smoking in British Popular Culture, 1800–2000* (Manchester, 2000), p 214; *News Chronicle,* 6 Jul 1956; Amis, p 496.

5. *Picture Post,* 9 Oct 1954; Vivienne Walters, *Class Inequality and Health Care* (1980), p 138; Webster, *National,* pp 57–8, 129–30; Charles Webster, 'Investigating Inequalities in Health before Black', *Contemporary British History* (Autumn 2002), p 91; Klein, *New Politics,* p 47.

6. Rivett, *Cradle,* p 76; Zaida Hall, 'Doctor John Agate', *Independent,* 20 Nov 1998; Pat Thane, *Old Age in Modern England* (Oxford, 2000), p 449; Peter Townsend, *The Family Life of Old People* (Pelican edn, 1963), pp 177–9, 183.

7. Macmillan, p 486; Gilbert Harding, 'Preface', in W. H. Mason, *The Gilbert Harding Question Book* (1956), p 6; Peter Townsend, 'The Meaning of Poverty', *British Journal of Sociology* (Sep 1962), pp 211–15; Rodney Lowe, *The Welfare State,* (Basingstoke, 1999 edn.), p 97.

8. Berridge, 'Policy', p 1199; Alan Kidd, *Manchester,* (Edinburgh, 2002 edn.), p 196; David Jeremiah, *Architecture and Design for the Family* (Manchester, 2000), p 173; *The Times,* 30 Jan 2004 (Bob Stanley); *Architectural Design* (Dec 1956), pp 377–8; Peter Hall, *Cities of Tomorrow,* (Oxford, 2002 edn.), p 241; *New Statesman,* 8 Dec 1956; A.G.V. Simmonds, 'Conservative Governments and the Housing Question, 1951–59', University of Leeds PhD, 1995, pp 253–4; John Winstone, *Britain As It Was, 1963–1975* (Bristol, 1990), p 35; Candida Lycett Green (ed), John Betjeman, *Letters, Volume Two,* (1995), p 99; Pennie Denton (ed), *Betjeman's London* (1988), p 53; Anthony Flowers and Derek Smith, *Out of the One Eye* (Newcastle, 2002), pp 9–16.

9. John R. Gold, *The Practice of Modernism* (Abingdon, 2007), p 148; John R. Gold, 'The Making of a Megastructure: Architectural Modernism, Town Planning and

Cumbernauld's Central Area, 1955–75', *Planning Perspectives* (Apr 2006), p 116; *Architects' Journal*, 17 Jan 1957; Gold, *Practice*, p 150; Frank Worsdall, *The Tenement* (Edinburgh, 1979), pp 141–2; *Glasgow Herald*, 26 Dec 1956; Seán Damer, *Glasgow* (1990), p 191; Charles Johnstone, 'The Tenants' Movement and Housing Struggles in Glasgow, 1945–1990', University of Glasgow PhD, 1992, pp 315, 318; Castlemilk People's History Group, *The Big Flit* (Glasgow, 1990), pp 5–7, 20; Johnstone, 'Tenants' Movement', p 324.

10. Ronald Smith, *The Gorbals* (Glasgow, 1999), pp 16–17; *Town and Country Planning* (Jun 1954), pp 277–80; *News Chronicle*, 23 Nov 1955; *Glasgow Herald*, 13 Apr 1956; Smith, *Gorbals*, pp 19–21; *Glasgow Herald*, 25 Jun 1956.

11. *Liverpool Daily Post*, 30 Jun 1956; Selina Todd, 'Affluence, Class and Crown Street: Reinvestigating the Post-War Working Class', *Contemporary British History* (Dec 2008), pp 501–3; John Barron Mays, 'Cultural Conformity in Urban Area: An Introduction to the Crown Street Study in Liverpool', *Sociological Review* (Jul 1958), p 98; J. A. Yelling, 'Residents' Reactions to Post-War Slum Clearance in England', *Planning History* 214/3 (1999), p 7; C. H. Vereker and J. B. Mays, *Urban Development and Social Change* (Liverpool, 1961), p 94; Todd, 'Affluence', p 508; *Liverpool Daily Post*, 30 Jun 1956; Arthur Marwick, *Britain in Our Century* (1984), p 184.

12. Crown Street Survey, University of Liverpool, Special Collections, D416/1/23.

12 The Real Razzle-Dazzle

1. Tony Jasper, *The Top Twenty Book*, fifth edn (1991), pp 18–21; John Peel and Sheila Ravenscroft, *Margrave of the Marshes* (2005), pp 69–70; Bill Wyman, *Stone Alone* (1990), p 63; Philip Norman, *John Lennon* (2008), p 82; *Daily Telegraph*, 7 Jul 2003 (Michael Shelden); Pete Frame, *The Restless Generation* (2007), pp 175, 177; Michael Richardson, *The Durham Miners' Gala* (Derby, 2001), pp 176–7; Thom Gunn, *The Sense of Movement* (1954), p 31; Dave McAleer, *Hit Parade Heroes* (1993), p 43; Peel and Ravenscroft, *Margrave*, p 71.

2. Humphrey Carpenter, *The Angry Young Men* (2002), pp 108–10, 135; *Times Literary Supplement*, 8 Jun 1956; *Spectator*, 15 Jun 1956; John Clay, *R. D. Laing* (1996), p 59; Carpenter, *Angry*, pp 134–44; Peter Bailey, 'White Collars, Gray Lives? The Lower Middle Class Revisited', *Journal of British Studies* (Jul 1999), p 289; *Guardian*, 8 Nov 1999 (Flachra Gibbons); Margaret Drabble, *Angus Wilson* (1995), pp 209–12; *Spectator*, 1 Jun 1956. The fullest account of the Angry Young Men remains Harry Ritchie, *Success Stories* (1988).

3. Alan Strachan, 'Joan Littlewood', *Independent*, 23 Sep 2002; Michael O'Sullivan, *Brendan Behan* (Dublin, 1997), p 207; *Spectator*, 1 Jun 1956; O'Sullivan, *Behan*, p 207; Richard Ingrams, *Muggeridge* (1995), p 177; Heap, 24 Jul 1956; Charlotte Mosley (ed), *The Letters of Nancy Mitford and Evelyn Waugh* (1996), p 386; Peter Bull, *I Know the Face, but . . .* (1959), p 189; *Blackpool Gazette & Herald*, 2 Jun 1956; *West Lancashire Evening Gazette*, 5 Jun 1956; Bull, *I Know*, pp 186–7; *West Lancashire Evening Gazette*, 9 Jun 1956; Bull, *I Know*, p 188.

4. Alethea Hayter (ed), *A Wise Woman: A Memoir of Lavinia Mynors from her Diaries and Letters* (Banham, 1996), p 114; *The Times*, 19 Jan 1998 (Erica Wagner); Robert

Conquest (ed), *New Lines* (1956), pp xii–xv; Heap, 29 Aug 1956; Colin Clark, *The Prince, The Showgirl and Me* (1995), p 68; *Guardian*, 27 Dec 2008 (Simon Callow); BBC WA, R9/19/2, Aug 1956; John Ramsden, *The Age of Churchill and Eden, 1940–1957* (Harlow, 1995), pp 296–7; *New Yorker*, 7 Jul 1956; Joe Moran, *On Roads* (2009), pp 19–20; David Hunt, *A History of Preston* (Preston, 1992), p 263.

5. Roy Greenslade, *Press Gang* (2004), pp 125–6; Daly, Ms 302/3/2, 20 Jun 1956; *Reasoner*, Jul 1956, pp 2–3, 14–15; John Saville, *Memoirs from the Left* (2003), pp 107–8.

6. Leon Edel (ed), Edmund Wilson, *The Fifties* (New York, 1986), pp 369–70; Haines, 31 Jul 1956; David Rayvern Allen (ed), *Another Word from Arlott* (1985), p 212; Turtle, 31 Jul 1956; Alan Hill, *Jim Laker* (1998), p 135.

7. St John, 23 Jul 1956; Robert Shepherd, *Iain Macleod* (1994), p 108; Geoffrey Goodman, *The Awkward Warrior* (1979), p 123; *Sunday Times*, 29 Jan–4 Mar 1956; Goodman, *Awkward*, p 123; *New Statesman*, 7 Apr 1956; Shepherd, *Macleod*, p 110; Mark Pottle (ed), *Daring to Hope: The Diaries and Letters of Violet Bonham Carter, 1946–1969* (2002), p 166; Eric Silver, *Victor Feather, TUC* (1973), p 103; BBC WA, *Any Questions?*, 13 May 1956; Harold Macmillan, *Riding the Storm* (1971), pp 55–7; Ramsden, *Age*, pp 298–300.

8. Goodman, *Awkward*, pp 68, 110, 125–6, 129–30; Macmillan, p 571; Shepherd, *Macleod*, p 111; Richard Etheridge Papers at Modern Records Centre (University of Warwick), Mss 202/S/J/3/3/5; Goodman, *Awkward*, p 130; R. A. Leeson, *Strike* (1973), p 1997; John Salmon, 'Wage Strategy, Redundancy and Shop Stewards in the Coventry Motor Industry', in Michael Terry and P. K. Edwards (eds), *Shopfloor Politics and Job Controls* (Oxford, 1988), p 205; Tim Claydon, 'Tales of Disorder: The Press and the Narrative Construction of Industrial Relations in the British Motor Industry, 1950–79', *Historical Studies in Industrial Relations* (Spring 2000), pp 13–16; *Picture Post*, 4 Aug 1956; Goodman, *Awkward*, p 131; Leeson, *Strike*, p 198; Timothy R. Whisler, 'The Outstanding Potential Market: The British Motor Industry and Europe, 1945–75', *Journal of Transport History* (Mar 1994), pp 5–9.

9. David Dutton, *Anthony Eden* (1997), p 271; Shepherd, *Macleod*, p 113; Goodman, *Awkward*, p 134; *Crossman*, p 510; Macmillan, p 594; Gaitskell, p 615; George H. Gallup (ed), *The Gallup International Public Opinion Polls: Great Britain, 1937–1975, Volume One* (New York, 1976), pp 385, 351; *The Voice of Fords Workers*, Oct 1956, pp 4–5.

10. Laurie Dennett, *A Sense of Security* (Cambridge, 1988), pp 316–17; *Picture Post*, 23 Jun 1956; Anthony Sampson, *Anatomy of Britain* (1962), pp 218–19; *Guardian*, 14 Jun 2008 (James Campbell); Mark Girouard, *Big Jim* (1998), p 85; *Guardian*, 14 Jun 2008 (James Campbell); Girouard, *Big Jim*, pp 85–6; Martin Harrison, *Transition* (2002), p 127.

11. *News Chronicle*, 31 Aug 1956, 6 Sep 1956, 12 Sep 1956; Frame, *Restless*, pp 187, 190, 192; *Picture Post*, 22 Sep 1956; Alan Travis, *Bound and Gagged* (2000), p 109; *Guardian*, 22 Jun 2001.

12. Jonathan Dimbleby, *Richard Dimbleby* (1975), pp 278–9; Michael Banton, 'The Influence of Colonial Status upon Black–White Relations in England, 1948–58, *Sociology* (Nov 1983), p 551; Michael Banton, *White and Coloured* (1959), p 210; Banton, 'Influence', p 552; Banton, *White*, p 210; Banton, 'Influence', p 553; Paul

Foot, *Immigration and Race in British Politics* (Harmondsworth, 1965), p 128; Donald Hinds, *Journey to an Illusion* (1966), pp 118–20.

13. Saville, *Memoirs*, pp 108–9; *Reasoner* (Sep 1956), pp 12–13, 27–8.

14. C.A.R. Crosland, *The Future of Socialism* (1956), pp 67, 98, 148, 295–332, 258–77, 333–50, 487, 522–3, 529. For fuller discussions, see Edmund Dell, *A Strange Eventful History* (1999), chap 10; Radhika Desai, *Intellectuals and Socialism* (1994), chaps 4–5; Martin Francis, 'Mr Gaitskell's Ganymede? Re-assessing Crosland's *The Future of Socialism*', *Contemporary British History* (Summer 1997), pp 50–64; Jeremy Nuttall, *Psychological Socialism* (Manchester, 2006), pp 69–80.

15. *Tribune*, 5 Oct 1956; Gordon Brown, 'Foreword', in Dick Leonard (ed), Anthony Crosland, *The Future of Socialism* (2006), pp ix–x; *Guardian*, 27 Feb 1997.

16. Kenneth O. Morgan, 'Royals since 1945: Political Society', in Trevor Herbert and Gareth Elwyn Jones (eds), *Post-War Wales* (Cardiff, 1995), pp 14, 29–30; *Daily Mirror*, 26 Sep 1956; Dennis Potter, *The Glittering Coffin* (1960), p 76; Leo McKinstry, *Jack & Bobby* (2002), pp 62–3; *New Statesman*, 6 Oct 1956; *Picture Post*, 22 Oct 1956.

17. Martin, 21 Sep 1956; Langford, 1 Oct 1956; Haines, 4 Oct 1956; Lewis, 16 Oct 1956.

18. *Guardian*, 31 Mar 2006 (Mark Lawson); Irving Wardle, *The Theatres of George Devine* (1978), p 185; *The Times*, 13 Oct 1956; Jasper, *Top Twenty*, p 22; *Record Collector*, Aug 2006, p 67.

19. *Financial Times*, 17 Oct 1956; *News Chronicle*, 17 Oct 1956; *The Times*, 18 Oct 1956; BBC WA, *Any Questions?*, 19 Oct 1956.

20. M-O A, D5353, 1 Nov 1956; *Independent*, 30 Oct 2006 (David Prosser); Gallup (ed), *Gallup*, p 376; *Guardian*, 28 Oct 2006 (Jim Griffin).

13 Brisk Buying and Selling

1. *New Statesman*, 26 May 1956; Macmillan, p 561; *Encounter*, Jun 1956, p 5.

2. *Star*, 26 Jan 1956; Richard Coopey et al, *Mail Order Retailing in Britain* (Oxford, 2005), pp 64–5; Nick Tiratsoo, 'Popular politics, affluence and the Labour party in the 1950s' in Anthony Gorst et al (eds), *Contemporary British History, 1931–1961* (1991), p 49; Elizabeth Nelson, *The British Counter-Culture, 1966–73* (Basingstoke, 1989), p 14; Bill Osgerby, '"Well, It's Saturday Night an' I Just Got Paid": Youth, Consumerism and Hegemony in Post-War Britain', *Contemporary Record*, Autumn 1992, p 292.

3. Winston Fletcher, *Powers of Persuasion* (Oxford, 2008), p 31; Christina Hardyment, *Slice of Life* (1995), p 53; *Homes and Gardens*, Feb 1954, p 1; *Picture Post*, 25 Feb 1956; Fletcher, *Powers*, p 35; Mark Robinson, *100 Greatest TV Ads* (2000), pp 48, 27; *News Chronicle*, 22 Oct 1956.

4. Martin, 6 Mar 1956; Miriam Akhtar and Steve Humphries, *The Fifties and Sixties* (2001), pp 119–20; John Burnett, *A Social History of Housing, 1815–1970* (Newton Abbott, 1978), p 300; *Encounter*, Jun 1956, p 12; *Financial Times*, 10 Feb 2001 (Alice Rawsthorn); *The Times*, 16 Jul 2004 (Lucia van der Post); *Picture Post*, 8 Oct 1956; Sally MacDonald and Julia Porter, *Putting on the Style* (1990), 'Traditional Values' section; M-O A, Bulletin No 49, Mar/Jun 1953, 'Furnishing'; *Encounter*, Jun 1956, p 12.

5. Paul Atkinson, 'Do It Yourself: Democracy and Design', *Journal of Design History*, 2006 (19/1), p 6; Carol Kennedy, *ICI* (1986), p 118; James Obelkevich, 'Consumption', in James Obelkevich and Peter Catterall (eds), *Understanding British Society* (1994), p 147; Ralph Harris and Arthur Seldon, *Advertising in Action* (1962), pp 203–4; David Jeremiah, *Architecture and Design for the Family, 1900–70* (Manchester, 2000), p 165; Andrew Jackson, 'Labour as Leisure – the Mirror Dinghy and DIY Sailors', *Journal of Design History*, 2006 (19/1), p 59; Jeremiah, *Architecture*, p 165; *Practical Householder*, Dec 1956, pp 32, 38, 43, 49; Robert Opie, *The 1950s Scrapbook* (1998), pp 12–13.

6. *Picture Post*, 27 Feb 1954; David E. Roberts, 'Sir Charles Colston', in David Jeremy (ed), *Dictionary of Business Biography, Vol 1* (1984), p 756; David L. Wakefield, *The Hoover Story in Merthyr Tydfil* (Merthyr Tydfil, c. 1977), pp 6–7; Opie, *Scrapbook*, p 16; Obelkevich, 'Consumption', p 145; John Davies, 'Wales in the Nineteen-sixties', *Llafour*, 1987 (4/4), p 83; David Blunkett, *On a Clear Day* (1995), p 40; Hardyment, *Slice*, pp 41–2.

7. Nick Smurthwaite, 'Kenneth Lo', *Independent*, 16 Aug 1995; *Times Literary Supplement*, 26 Nov 1999 (Arabella Boxer); Jeremiah, *Architecture*, p 172; Joe Moran, *Queuing for Beginners* (2007), p 152; M-O A, Bulletin No 50, Mar 1954, p 15; *Illustrated*, 21 Jan 1956; *Independent*, 19 Mar 1997 (P. T. Meard); Harris and Seldon, *Advertising*, pp 169–70; *Financial Times*, 12 Oct 1959; *Reynolds News*, 24 Feb 1957; Haines, 3 Aug 1956; 'Sir John Eastwood', *The Times*, 15 Aug 1995; Information from Gisela Hunt.

8. Tim O'Sullivan, 'Television Memories and Cultures of Viewing, 1950–65', in John Corner (ed), *Popular Television in Britain* (1991), p 161; Twiggy Lawson, *Twiggy* (1997), p 15; O'Sullivan, 'Television', p 167; Dennis Potter, *The Changing Forest* (Minerva edn, 1996), p 9; *The Times*, 4 Nov 2004 (Clive Davis); Carole Klein, *Doris Lessing* (2000), p 147; Doris Lessing, *Walking in the Shade* (1997), p 92; Michael Young and Peter Willmott, *Family and Kinship in East London* (Pelican edn, 1962), p 143; Crown Street Survey (University of Liverpool, Special Collections), D416/1/23.

9. A. M. Carr-Saunders et al, *A Survey of Social Conditions in England and Wales* (1958), pp 245–6; Young and Willmott, *Family*, p 24; Carr-Saunders, pp 247–8, 242; 'Frank Berni', *Daily Telegraph*, 12 Jul 2000; Paul Levy, 'Aldo Berni', *Independent*, 20 Oct 1997; Peter Frost, 'Sam Alper', *Independent*, 11 Oct 2002; Geraldine Wilson, 'Alexander Plunket Greene', *Guardian*, 10 May 1990.

10. Ruth I. Johns, *St Ann's, Nottingham* (Warwick, 2002), p 54; Crown Street Survey, D416/1/23; Carlo Morelli, 'Constructing a Balance between Price and Non-Price Competion in British Multiple Food Retailing, 1954–64', *Business History*, Apr 1998, p 47; Geoff Phillips, *When We Were Kids* (Durham City, 2001), p 43; Morelli, 'Constructing', p 47; *Picture Post*, 10 Sep 1955; Marcus Sieff, *Don't ask the price* (1986), pp 169–70.

11. Penelope Mortimer, *About Time Too* (1993), pp 43–4; Sonia Ashmore, 'Extinction and Evolution: Department Stores in London's West End, 1945–1982', *London Journal*, Jun 2006, pp 48–9; M-O A, TC24/9/D; Bill Lancaster, *The Department Store* (1995), pp 196–7.

12. Jeremiah, *Architecture*, p 172; Morelli, 'Constructing', p 49; M-O A, TC78/3/B; Oliver Marriott, *The Property Boom* (1967), p 237; Kathryn A. Morrison,

English Shops and Shopping (New Haven, 2003), p 284; W. G. McClelland, 'The Supermarket and Society', *Sociological Review*, Jul 1962, p 134; M-O A, TC78/3/B.

13. *Glasgow Herald*, 25 Jun 1956; M-O A, D5353, 29 Feb 1956; *Evening Citizen*, 18 Jun 1956; C.A.R. Crosland, *The Future of Socialism* (1956), p 518; *London Review of Books*, 24 Jan 2002.

14 A Pretty Mess

1. Clarissa Eden, *A Memoir* (2007), p 235; Macmillan, pp 578–9; Roy Greenslade, *Press Gang* (2003), pp 131–3; Brian Brivati, *Hugh Gaitskell* (1996), p 260; M-O A, D5353, 2 Aug 1956; *Fowles*, p 378; Sir Billy Butlin, *The Billy Butlin Story* (1982), p 223; David Owen, *Time to Declare* (1991), pp 39–40; Robin Day, *Grand Inquisitor* (1989), p 91; Greenslade, *Press Gang*, p 133; Corelli Barnett, *The Verdict of Peace* (2001), pp 493–4.

2. *Daily Mirror*, 30 Oct 1956; Colin Clark, *The Prince, the Showgirl and Me* (1995), pp 188–9; *New Statesman*, 3 Nov 1956; Heap, 30 Oct 1956; *Daily Sketch*, 31 Oct 1956; *New Statesman*, 3 Nov 1956; *Manchester Guardian*, 31 Oct 1956; Benn, pp 194–5; Nigel Nicolson (ed), *Harold Nicolson: The Later Years, 1945–1962: Diaries and Letters, Volume III* (1968), p 312; Mark Pottle (ed), *Daring to Hope: The Diaries and Letters of Violet Bonham Carter, 1946–1969* (2000), p 173; Streat, p 847; Janie Hampton (ed), *Joyce & Ginnie* (1997), p 216.

3. *Daily Sketch*, 1 Nov 1956; *Daily Mirror*, 1 Nov 1956; *News Chronicle*, 1 Nov 1956; *The Times*, 1 Nov 1956; *New Yorker*, 10 Nov 1956; Lewis Baston, *Reggie* (Stroud, 2004), p 114; Lewis, 1 Nov 1956; St John, 1 Nov 1956; Heap, 1 Nov 1956; M-O A, D5353, 1 Nov 1956; Martin, 1 Nov 1956; Streat, p 848; *Manchester Guardian*, 5 Nov 1956 (Nicolas Walter et al); Henry Hardy and Jennifer Holmes (eds), Isaiah Berlin, *Enlightening: Letters 1946–1960* (2009), p 547; *Manchester Guardian*, 2 Nov 1956; Aurelia Schober Plath (ed), Sylvia Plath, *Letters Home* (1976), p 282.

4. *Daily Worker*, 26 Oct 1956; *Reasoner*, Nov 1956, Supplement, pp 1–2; Amis, pp 489–91.

5. *Manchester Guardian*, 2 Nov 1956; *Tribune*, 2 Nov 1956; *New Statesman*, 3 Nov 1956; *Spectator*, 2 Nov 1956; *Economist*, 2 Nov 1956; Preston, 2 Nov 1956; Hampton (ed), *Joyce & Ginnie*, p 218; M-O A, D5353, 2 Nov 1956; Haines, 2 Nov 1956; Brian Thompson, *Clever Girl* (2007), p 184; BBC WA, *Any Questions?*, 2 Nov 1956.

6. *Daily Sketch*, 3 Nov 1956; *Daily Mirror*, 3 Nov 1956; Crossman, p 538; *Listener*, 8 Nov 1956; Nicolson, p 314; Benn, p 200; Crossman, pp 538–9; Raynham, 3 Nov 1956; Preston, 3 Nov 1956; M-O A, D5353, 3 Nov 1956; Amis, p 491.

7. *Observer*, 4 Nov 1956; *Daily Mirror*, 5 Nov 1956; *Manchester Guardian*, 5 Nov 1956; D. R. Thorpe, *Eden* (2003), p 527; *The Times*, 18 Feb 2003 (Anthony Howard); Benn, pp 201–2; *Listener*, 8 Nov 1956; Tony Shaw, 'Cadogan's Last Fling: Sir Alexander Cadogan, Chairman of the Board of Governors of the BBC', *Contemporary British History*, Summer 1999, p 140; Barnett, *Verdict*, p 496.

8. *Manchester Guardian*, 5 Nov 1956; Bonham Carter, p 174; *Daily Mirror*, 5 Nov 1956; *Reasoner*, Nov 1956, pp 1–2; *Daily Worker*, 5 Nov 1956.

9. *Daily Mail*, 5 Nov 1956; *News Chronicle*, 5 Nov 1956; Raynham, 5 Nov 1956; Russell Davies (ed), *The Kenneth Williams Diaries* (1993), p 127; *Daily Mirror*, 6 Nov 1956.

10. *Daily Mail*, 6 Nov 1956; Martin, 5 Nov 1956; Pete Frame, *The Restless Generation* (2007), p 150; Caroline Moorehead, *Sidney Bernstein* (1984), pp 252–3; Benn, p 205; John Sutherland, *The Boy Who Loved Books* (2007), pp 161–2.

11. *News Chronicle*, 6 Nov 1956; *Manchester Guardian*, 6 Nov 1956; Philip Snow, *Stranger and Brother* (1982), p 112; Robert Cooper, 'A Weak Sister? Macmillan, Suez and the British Economy, July to November 1956', *Contemporary British History*, Sep 2008, p 309; Benn, p 208; *Crossman*, p 541; Tony Shaw, 'Eden and the BBC During the 1956 Suez Crisis: A Myth Re-examined', *Twentieth Century British History*, 1995 (6/3), p 340; Haines, 6 Nov 1956; Nicolson (ed), *Diaries*, p 317; M-O A, D5353, 6 Nov 1956.

12. Anton Rippon, *A Derby Boy* (Stroud, 2007), p 60; Harvey Cole, 'Public Opinion and the Suez Crisis', *Fabian Journal*, Mar 1957, pp 10–11; *Yorkshire Post*, 8 Nov 1956; *Manchester Guardian*, 7 Nov 1956, 12 Nov 1956; Barnett, *Verdict*, p 652; Malcolm Hayes (ed), *The Selected Letters of William Walton* (2002), pp 286–7; John Ramsden, *The Age of Churchill and Eden, 1940–1957* (Harlow, 1995), pp 313–14; *New Statesman*, 10 Nov 1956.

13. *New Statesman*, 22 Sep 1956; *Daily Worker*, 9 Nov 1956, 16 Nov 1956; *New Statesman*, 24 Nov 1956; Tom Steel, 'Llew Gardner', *Independent*, 26 Nov 1990; Jim Roche Papers (Ruskin College, Oxford), Mss 51/20; A. J. Avis, *To Build a New Jerusalem* (1992), p 196; Jean McCrindle, 'The Hungarian Uprising and a Young British Communist', *History Workshop Journal*, Autumn 2008, p 198.

14. Greenslade, *Press Gang*, pp 136–7; Brenda Maddox, *Maggie* (2003), p 64; Richard Cockett, 'The *Observer* and the Suez Crisis', *Contemporary Record*, Summer 1991, pp 27–30; Richard Davenport-Hines (ed), *Letters from Oxford: Hugh Trevor-Roper to Bernard Berenson* (2006), p 210.

15. *Independent*, 9 Sep 1997 (Kate Watson-Smyth); Hampton (ed), *Joyce & Ginnie*, p 222; *New Yorker*, 12 Jan 1957; *Independent*, 15 Jan 2003 (Robert Fisk).

16. David Kynaston, *The Financial Times* (1988), pp 248–51; *Encounter*, Jan 1957, pp 38–44; Turtle, Nov–Dec 1956; *New Yorker*, 10 Nov 1956; *Crossman*, p 572.

17. John Amis, *Amiscellany* (1985), p 114; *The Times*, 14 Nov 1956; *Daily Mirror*, 21 Nov 1956; Moorehead, *Bernstein*, p 266; Amis, p 486; St John, 9 Dec 1956; Clive Ellis, *Fabulous Fanny Cradock* (Stroud, 2007), pp 73–6; *Fowles*, p 385; Heap, 25 Dec 1956; Mark Robinson, *100 Greatest TV Ads* (2000), p 84; Travis Elborough, *The Bus We Loved* (2005), pp 69–71; Tony Mason, 'Stanley Matthews', in Richard Holt (ed), *Sport and the Working Class in Modern Britain* (Manchester, 1990), p 159.

18. Robert J. Wybrow, *Britain Speaks Out, 1937–87* (Basingstoke, 1989), p 48; Nicolson (ed), *Diaries*, p 328; M-O A, D5353, 9 Jan 1957; John Campbell, *Pistols at Dawn* (2009), pp 266–8; *New Yorker*, 26 Jan 1957; M-O A, D5353, 10 Jan 1957; *Evening Standard*, 10 Jan 1957; Haines, 10 Jan 1957.

Afterword

1. *Woman*, 5 Jan 1957.
2. *Woman and Shopping*, Jan/Feb 1957, pp 42–45.

Acknowledgements

I am grateful to the following for kindly allowing me to reproduce copyright material: Evelyn Abrams (Mark Abrams); Ouida V. Ascroft (Florence Speed); Lady Diana Baer (Mollie Panter-Downes); Joan Bakewell; BBC Written Archives Centre; Birmingham Libraries and Archives (extract from the diaries of Mary King, collection reference MS1547); Ken Blakemore (*Sunnyside Down*); Michael Bloch (James Lees-Milne); Bloomsbury Publishing Ltd (extract from *An Immaculate Mistake* © 1991 Paul Bailey); Veronica Bowater (Vere Hodgson); Alan Brodie Representation (*The Diaries of Noël Coward*, on behalf of NC Aventales AG, successor in the title to the Estate of Noël Coward); Rene and Michael Chaplin (Sid Chaplin); Jonathan Clowes Ltd (*Letters* copyright © 2001 Kingsley Amis, *Lucky Jim* copyright © 1953 Kingsley Amis, on behalf of the Literary Estate of Kingsley Amis; extract from *The Reasoner* copyright © Doris Lessing 1956, on behalf of Doris Lessing, extract from *In Pursuit of the English* copyright © Doris Lessing 1960, on behalf of Doris Lessing, extract from *Walking in the Shade* copyright © Doris Lessing 1998); Susan Crosland (*New Fabian Essays* and *The Future of Socialism*); Virginia Crossman (Richard Crossman); Alan Crowe (Carole Anne Stafford); Curtis Brown Group Ltd, London (on behalf of the Trustees of the Mass-Observation Archive, copyright © Trustees of the Mass-Observation Archive; extract from *England, Half English* copyright © Colin MacInnes 1961, on behalf of the Estate of Colin MacInnes); Renée Daly (Lawrence Daly); The Dartington Hall Trust Archive; Hunter Davies; Norman Dennis; Peter Dunn (Cyril Dunn); Faber & Faber Ltd (extract from *Untold Stories* by Alan Bennett; extract from *Free Association* by

Stephen Berkoff; *Selected Letters of Philip Larkin* copyright © The Estate of Philip Larkin; *Letters Home* copyright © The Estate of Aurelia Plath); Margaret Fenton (Sir Frederic Osborn); Margaret Forster; Enid Grant (Enid Palmer); Rachel Gross (Geoffrey Gorer); HarperCollins Publishers Ltd (*Bad Blood* © Lorna Sage 2001; *The Kenneth Williams Diaries* © Kenneth Williams 1993, 1994); Pamela Hendicott (Judy Haines); Hazel Holt (Barbara Pym); Steve Humphries (*The Making of Modern London, 1945–85*; *A Century of Childhood*; *The Fifties and Sixties*); Institution of Mechanical Engineers (Lord Hinton of Bankside); Islington Local History Centre (Gladys Langford); Ian Jack (*Before the Oil Ran Out: Britain 1977–87*, 1987; *The Country Formerly Known as Great Britain: Writings 1989–2009*, 2009); Dan Jacobson; Ruth I. Johns (*St Ann's Nottingham: Inner-city Voices*, Plowright Press 2002, 2006); Little, Brown Book Group Ltd (*Ricky* by Ricky Tomlinson); Ione Lee (Judy Haines); The Marvell Press (extract from 'Born Yesterday' by Philip Larkin from *The Less Deceived*); John McGarry; Jamie Muir and Denis Norden (Frank Muir and Denis Norden Archive); John Murray Ltd (*The Boy Who Loved Books* by John Sutherland); News Group Newspapers Limited Archive (Papers of the John Hilton Bureau); The Harold Nicolson Estate; Ingrid Pollard (Sylvan Pollard Estate); Allan Preston (Kenneth Preston); The Random House Group Ltd (extract from *White City* by Donald James Wheal, published by Century; extract from *Years of Hope* by Tony Benn, published by Hutchinson; extract from *What's It All About?* by Cilla Black, published by Ebury Press; extract from *Who's Crazee Now?* by Noddy Holder, published by Ebury Press; extract from *The Changing Forest* by Dennis Potter, published by Secker & Warburg; extract from *Jacky Daydream* by Jacqueline Wilson, published by Doubleday; extract from *Coming Home* by John Betjeman published by Vintage); Marian Ray and Robin Raynham (Marian Raynham); Rogers, Coleridge & White Ltd (*Diaries 1939–1972* by Frances Partridge copyright © 1999 Frances Partridge) Anton Rippon (*A Derby Boy*); Basil Streat (Sir Raymond Streat); Valerie Tedder; Brian Thompson (*Clever Girl*); Peter Townsend; Sylvia Turtle (Florence Turtle); Roxana and Matthew Tynan (*The Life of Kenneth Tynan* by Kathleen Tynan, theatre writings, letters); Phyllis Willmott; Jennifer Worth; Toby Young (Michael Young).

I am indebted, in many different ways, to archivists, librarians, fellow-historians, friends and acquaintances. They include: Mark Aston; Michael Banton; Paul Barker; Peter Bevington; Piers Brendon; Sophie Bridges; John Campbell; Judith Downey; Elisabeth and Peter Dunn; Eamon Dyas; Helen Ford; Laura Gardner; Kate Gavron; Geoffrey Goodman; John Gross; Janie Hampton; Lynsey Hanley; Sue Harper; Pam Hendicott; Dick Holt; Felix Lancashire; Roy Lumb; Nicholas May; Joe Moran; Blake Morrison; Andrew Motion; Juliet Nicolson; Jonathan Oates; Erin O'Neill; Robert Opie; Jack Ozanne; Stanley Page; Michael Passmore; Alison Ravetz; Andrew Riley; John Roberts; John Southall; Todd Swift; David Taylor; John Wakefield; Andy Ward; Yvonne Widger; Melanie Wood; Ken Worpole. At the Special Collections (including the Mass-Observation Archive) at the University of Sussex, I am grateful for their help to Fiona Courage, Dorothy Sheridan and the staff, including Catrina Hey, Jessica Scantlebury and Karen Watson. The London Library remains London's most congenial, inspiriting library, and I am grateful to the staff for all their constructive kindness over the years. This book could not have been written without ready access to the hard-copy local newspaper collection at the British Newspaper Library in Colindale. I am not the only historian who hopes and trusts that this access will continue, whether at Colindale or elsewhere.

Since 2001 I have been a visiting professor at Kingston University, where over the last few years there have been, under the welcoming auspices of Gail Cunningham and Philip Spencer, a series of (for me) enjoyable and stimulating 'New Jerusalem' seminars run from the Faculty of Arts and Social Sciences. Those attending have included Joe Bailey, Peter Beck, Brian Cathcart, Norma Clarke, Sylvia Collins-Mayo, John Davis, Paul Dixon, Ilaria Favretto, Jeremy Nuttall, John Stuart and Frank Whately.

The following people not only kindly read and commented on all or part of the various drafts, but were also much-appreciated sources of help and encouragement: Joe Bailey; Mike Burns; Gail Cunningham; Juliet Gardiner; Sara Marsh; Dil Porter; Harry Ricketts; David Warren; Phyllis Willmott. I owe a particular debt to Phyllis Willmott, who since we first met in 2002 has been an unfailingly generous as well as shrewd supporter-cum-critic of what I am trying to do.

Getting this book over the line has involved what my father would have called 'a Harry Wragg finish'. I am deeply grateful to the following people: Annalisa Zisman (Back to Balance) for keeping me loose; Amanda Howard (Superscript Editorial Services) for transcribing my tapes with remarkable accuracy against very tight deadlines; Andrea Belloli for her sensitive copy-editing; Catherine Best and Patric Dickinson for reading the proofs; Douglas Matthews for compiling the index; my agent Deborah Rogers and her colleagues Hannah Westland and Mohsen Shah; and at Bloomsbury, the very hard-working trio of Bill Swainson, Nick Humphrey and Anna Simpson, whose good humour as well as good judgement have done much to make this a broadly enjoyable experience.

My largest debt is, as usual, to my family: Laurie, George, Michael and above all my wife Lucy, a pillar throughout of practical, intellectual and emotional support.

New Malden,
Summer 2009

Picture Credits

Churchill and Attlee survey the opening of the Festival of Britain, 4 May 1951 (*Copyright Museum of London*)

St Bride's, London, June 1951: over ten years after the Blitz (*The Times*)

Redgrave Road Residents' Association, Basildon: day trip to Clacton-on-Sea, 1952 (*Courtesy of Anita Woollard*)

Dick Etheridge, leading shop steward at Longbridge, addresses Austin carworkers, 1952 (*Getty Images*)

Camden High Street, 1952 (*Copyright Museum of London*)

Rush for Scotland vs. England tickets, Hampden Park, Glasgow, March 1952 (*NI Syndication*)

Outside an Ebbw Vale chapel, a summer Sunday, 1952 (*Getty Images*)

Petticoat Lane, 1952 (*Copyright Museum of London*)

Lady Cranbrook recreates the Coronation experience for members of Preston and Langley's W.I., Hertfordshire (*Getty Images*)

Commercial travellers in Maude's Commercial Hotel, Halifax, 1953 (*Getty Images*)

City Surveyor and Engineer (Sir Herbert Manzoni) and City Architect (A. G. Sheppard Fidler) study Birmingham's Inner Ring Road Scheme, January 1954 (*Getty Images*)

Empress of Britain under construction: Fairfield's Shipyard, Glasgow, January 1955 (*Herald & Times, Glasgow*)

Mecca Dance Hall, Tottenham, May 1954 (*Getty Images*)

Coupon-checkers at Littlewoods Pools, Liverpool, 1954 (*Getty Images*)

Inverness, 1950s (*Mary Evans Picture Library*)

Woolworths, 1955: the Christmas rush (*Getty Images*)

Mulberry Street Primary School, Manchester, 1956 (*Getty Images*)

New Union Street, Coventry: reconstruction, c. 1955 (*Photographer unknown*)

British Amateur Ballroom Dancing Championships, Blackpool, 1955 (Getty Images)

Leeds, 1957 (Mary Evans Picture Library)

West Indian immigrants wait at Customs, Southampton Docks, May 1956 (Getty Images)

Elswick, Newcastle upon Tyne, 1957 (NCJ Media Ltd)

Index

772 INDEX

OTHER BOOKS BY C. W. CERAM

Yestermorrow (1961)
The March of Archaeology (1958)
The Secret of the Hittites (1956)
Gods, Graves, and Scholars (1951)

These are Borzoi Books
published in New York by
Alfred A. Knopf

HANDS

ON THE

PAST

HANDS
ON THE PAST

*Pioneer Archaeologists Tell
Their Own Story*

Edited by
C. W. CERAM

ALFRED·A·KNOPF   NEW YORK
1966

Library of Congress Catalog Card Number: 66-19372

———◆———

THIS IS A BORZOI BOOK
PUBLISHED BY ALFRED A. KNOPF, INC.

———◆———

First American Edition published September 19, 1966
Second Printing, December 1966
Manufactured in the United States of America

FOREWORD

'Archaeology is at the same time
a science and an art'.

Encyclopaedia Britannica 1950

LIKE EVERY OTHER ENCYCLOPAEDIA DEFINITION, this one is incomplete. Archaeology is, as well as being a science and an art, moreover an adventure, an adventure of spirit and deed. Not only in the nineteenth century, the 'classical' period of great archaeological discovery, but also today, in the mid-twentieth century, the archaeologist has to combat physical forces – in the form of jungle and desert, or of visionless officials, or other obstructions of every sort. Therefore Part One of our book is concerned mainly with modern tomb-robberies and with the struggle of the archaeologists to protect these monuments.

Although the archaeologists' accounts of these kind of adventures, the accompaniment to their serious scientific researches, are very exciting, more exciting by far are the spiritual adventures which the scholar can experience in the quiet of his study – as did Champollion, when he deciphered hieroglyphic script.

We shall find both kinds of adventure in this anthology. The book is not put together like a novel, to be read from cover to cover in one session. The purpose of every anthology is to give as complete as possible a survey of a spiritual landscape; but only a geometrician measures out a landscape systematically, whereas the inquisitive viewer picks out the places amenable to him for a short stay.

The choice of extracts is purely subjective; how could it be otherwise, the material on this subject being as extensive as it is? The primary principle involved was to choose what was *interesting*, but to give it in doses which eventually combined to bring into view the whole picture of archaeological discovery. It would be out of place here to take into account literary merit. Many scholars were very poor narrators of their discoveries, but one or two of these badly written accounts have been included because of the importance of the material. Much had to be omitted because it was available only in a strictly scientific form and quite unreadable for the layman. But a few things have also been 'excavated' which had been lost to the scholar himself for many years.

This book is confined almost entirely to the authentic writings of the archaeologists themselves. In preparing it a basic rule of archaeology was rigorously adhered to – that nothing was to be altered. Every omission is indicated. The very variable spelling of names created quite a problem; but in this case too the original spelling of the names was preserved as far as possible and all the variants in spelling of each name have been entered in the index, where the one in common usage today has been indicated.

My purpose is not to provide a comprehensive anthology, since Jacquetta Hawkes has already done this in her two-volume work, *The World of the Past*, New York 1963 and London 1964. To show the whole scope of archaeological research, also where it has erred, a few of the completely abstruse, nonsensical statements have been included (such as the fantastic analysis of the meaning of the pyramids by Smyth, or the no less fantastic interpretation of hieroglyphic script by Kircher) which illuminate more fully than any description, the amount of wrong directions and by-ways scientific research has had to travel before an acceptable solution was found.

In the introductory chapters, therefore, a few articles have also been included to illuminate the subsidiary problems of archaeology – for example, the exemplary excavations-agreement of Olympia, as well as the archaeologists' experiences with reconstruction, forgers and antique dealers.

Our book covers the period of the first systematic excavations up to the present day, when the excavator with a spade has suddenly had his work made easier and more effective by complicated technical advances. We have restricted ourselves regionally to Europe, North Africa, the Near East and both the Americas. Prehistoric discoveries have not been included because they do not come within the scope of the book.

In conclusion I should like to thank Dr Anne G. Ward, who wrote the biographical notes and who takes the credit for these; she performed a very hard task in an exemplary manner.

C. W. Ceram

CONTENTS

6 CONTENTS

ILLUSTRATIONS

Part One

IN PLACE OF AN INTRODUCTION

The ideal archaeologist

CHARLES LEONARD WOOLLEY

The prime duty of the field archaeologist is to collect and set in order material with not all of which he can himself deal at first hand. In no case will the last word be with him; and just because that is so his publication of the material must be minutely detailed, so that from it others may draw not only corroboration of his views but fresh conclusions and more light. Should he not then stop at this? It might be urged that the man who is admirably equipped to observe and record does not necessarily possess the powers of synthesis and interpretation, the creative spirit and the literary gift which will make of him a historian. But no record can ever be exhaustive. As his work in the field goes on, the excavator is constantly subject to impressions too subjective and too intangible to be communicated, and out of these, by no exact logical process, there arise theories which he can state, can perhaps support, but cannot prove: their truth will depend ultimately on his own calibre, but, in any case, they have their value as summing up experiences which no student of his objects and his notes can ever share. Granted that the excavator is adequate to his task, the conclusions which he draws from his own work ought to carry weight, and he is bound to put them forward; if they are palpably wrong then his observations also may justly be held suspect. Between archaeology and history there is no fenced frontier, and the digger who will best observe and record his discoveries is precisely he who sees them as historical material and rightly appraises them; if he has not the power of synthesis and interpretation he has mistaken his calling. It is true that he may not possess any literary gifts, and that, therefore, the formal presentation of results to the public may be better made by others; but it is the field archaeologist who, directly or indirectly, has opened up for the general reader new chapters in the history of civilized man; and by recovering from the earth such documented relics of the past as strike the imagination through the eye, he makes real and modern what otherwise might seem a far-off tale.

Digging up the Past, 1954

How to buy antiquities

CHARLES LEONARD WOOLLEY

Before the modern archaeologist puts his spade to the earth, all his possible findings are carefully allotted by treaty, and piracy of antiquities has been reduced to a minimum by careful legislation. But however far-sighted the legislators, human nature and the value of ancient artifacts have made even the most painstaking laws liable to abuse.

Rascality where antiquities were concerned was not always confined to the dealers.

I was in Naples, staying with a friend of mine, an Englishman who had lived all his life in Naples, and one day there came along a plumber who had a little house and a small business at a place called Pozzuoli, which is on the outskirts of Naples to the north, and he said he had heard I was there and that he had something of interest to report. He had been enlarging his house, and in digging the foundations he had come upon a number of blocks of marble, some of which were covered with inscriptions and one was carved. He had shown this to his local priest who thought the things were interesting and important, and he wanted to know whether I would come and look, and buy anything that I wanted.

I went along, and there was, among a number of inscriptions, a very large marble slab, about 6 feet high or rather more, and about 5 feet across, with a group of life-size figures carved, one in high relief and two in lower relief. The one in high relief was obviously a member of the Imperial Family of the Emperor Augustus, and the other two were soldiers, and I realised that it was a fragment of an extraordinarily important and beautiful monument.

I said to the man, 'This is absolutely first-class! It's worth a great deal of money, but I can't buy it.' He said, 'Why not?' So I explained, 'In the first place, I could never get it out of the country, and in the second place I haven't got the money to pay for a thing of that sort.'

He said, 'Well, what am I to do?' and I told him, 'There is only one thing you can do. Nobody can smuggle a thing of that size out of

Italy, and if you try you will get into frightfully serious trouble. Go to the Naples National Museum and report what you have found. They will send a proper man along, and they will then take the things and value them, and pay you three-quarters of the sum. They keep one-quarter for the Government, but you will get quite a large sum of money, and that is the best thing you can do.'

He didn't like it – he didn't want to get the Government in at all; but in the end he thought perhaps he had better do what I had told him, and he went and reported it. And the second man in the Museum, who was an Inspector of Antiquities, came to the house. He saw these things and said, 'What a lot of fuss you are making about nothing. Those inscriptions are of interest to us, but they have no commercial value, so I'll take them away and there is no payment for them.'

The plumber asked, 'What about this carving?'

'That!' he said, 'Good heavens! It's absolute rubbish, not worth anything at all – you would be very lucky if anybody gave you £5 for a thing like that. I don't want it, I will leave it in your hands. The Museum is not interested in a thing of that sort!' And he went off with the inscriptions.

The plumber came to me a few days later and told me the story. 'It is very disappointing,' he complained, 'I thought I was going to get quite a large sum of money, and I am getting nothing at all.'

'Well,' I said, 'I can't understand it. That is a very valuable object.'

He said, 'Well, I don't know about that, but yesterday a man did come along' (and he gave me a description of the man and his name). 'He offered me £10 for it – shall I take it?'

I said 'No', and made certain enquiries. The man was an antiquity dealer, and was the brother-in-law of the Inspector, and the whole thing was a put-up job. So I saw the plumber again and explained to him what the law was. I said:

'If they don't want it, they ought to give you a permit for export. I have told you I can't afford to pay the value of the object, and you have got to remember that if you sell it abroad a third of the sum goes to the Government in tax. I can only afford to pay you £60, but you can tell them it has been sold for £100, and I will pay them the £33. That is all the money I can lay my hands on, and it is nothing like the value of the object, but if you would like to sell it to me on those terms and if you get the permit to export, I'll take it.'

He said that was very nice of me, and he would be delighted to do it. So he went round to the Museum, saw the Inspector of Antiquities and said, 'About this stone you don't want, will you give me permission to export?'

The Inspector said, 'You ignorant peasants: You are such fools! You think because a man comes along and offers you a pound or two more than another, and says he wants to export it you are going to profit; but actually you're not, because you have to pay a third to the Government. Now I suppose someone has offered you £15 – well, the most you'll get is £10.'

'Oh no,' said the plumber, 'I am going to pay you £33.'

The Inspector said, 'What?'

He repeated, 'I am going to pay you £33, a third of the price of the thing.'

The Inspector said, 'Look here, you are not going to have authority to export at all. The Museum is not going to take over your sculpture; it is going to remain in your hands, and it is valued at £4,000. I shall put it on the list of National Monuments. You are going to be responsible to the Government for the safeguarding of a £4,000 object. It is at your risk if anythings happens to it.'

The poor man came round to me in tears. He said, 'You have ruined me', and he told me the whole story.

This was in front of my friend, who listened carefully and then said, 'Well, I think, you know, we have got to take a strong line.'

I said, 'Right, I would do anything. The Inspector is an absolute scoundrel, I would do anything to down him.'

He said, 'That's all right if you will give me a free hand – will you?' To which I agreed.

Now at that moment in Italy, the Government party had in Parliament a majority of one. Suddenly the Prime Minister received a letter sent from Naples and signed by a well-known citizen of Naples, saying that it was requested that the Government would appoint a Royal Commission to remove a certain Roman sculpture from the list of National Monuments on which it had been placed by the local Inspector of Antiquities, which made it a thing immovable. The Commission were to remove it from the list and give authority to the peasant owner to export it; failing which, as the result of the sudden and unexpected demise of the three sitting members of Parliament for Naples (who all supported the Government), opposition members would be elected and the Government would fall. The fact was that we had got that secret society called the Camorra to back us, and the Camorra could do anything.

Within three days a Royal Commission came down and hurriedly altered the list of the National Monuments of the South of Italy, and gave permission to export the Pozzuoli stone. And it went off, and is now in Philadelphia – (I was working for Philadelphia at the time). Nobody looking at it in the Museum now would ever imagine that there had been that drama behind the scenes. Actually the Italians themselves did not know what had happened.

About a month later I went into the office of the Inspector of Antiquities, and on the table was a copy of the most recent issue of the Government publication reporting discoveries of antiquities in the country, and there was a large photograph of this particular Augustan monument. When the Inspector came into the room – he was out when I first went in – I said, 'Oh, Doctor Gabrici, what a lovely thing this is! I'll go and have a look at it – is it down in the Gallery yet?'

He said, 'No.'

'Is it in one of your stores still?' He said, 'No.'

'Where is it?' He said, 'It has been exported.'

I exclaimed, 'Why, Doctor Gabrici, you couldn't allow a thing like that to go – it's a National Monument! It's a treasure! Whatever induced you to allow anyone to take it out of the country?'

And he looked at me, and I looked at him, and he didn't know what to say. He didn't know whether I was responsible, and I wasn't going to tell him; but he never gave an explanation of why it had gone, which was his own fault entirely.

As I Seem to Remember, 1962

How to steal antiquities

CARLO MAURILIO LERICI

In 1958 at a meeting of the Rotary Club of Rome the speaker drew attention to the work recently undertaken by the Milan Polytechnic which involved the application of geophysical methods in archaeological research. After speaking of the results achieved by thus exploring a necropolis in the Cerveteri area, he was unable to hold back his own views on the facts which the technicians of the Polytechnic had noted – facts which shed light on the illegal and destructive excavational activities taking place in that same area side by side with the lawful work carried on by the State or by authorized bodies. Then an eminent university personality took advantage of this opportunity to give a spirited defence of the work of the tomb-robbers. He used seemingly paradoxical arguments that were not without a basis of truth, claiming that these people actually forward the cause of culture because it is thanks to them alone that thousands of collectors and scholars have been able to assemble these testimonies to our ancient civilizations under their own roofs. Indeed everyone knows that were it otherwise these pieces would still be unknown because they would have remained buried or been kept in the archives of Italian museums which are overloaded with material that is condemned either to remain for ever unseen or to be squandered or disposed of in other ways.

To this argument which is intended to justify clandestine excavation somewhat from a moral point of view we can add another based on material considerations.

For the most part tomb-robbers come from among the unemployed or under-employed and it is only the need to earn that makes them attempt the undertaking. This is moreover confirmed by the fact that during periods of seasonal agricultural work which require the maximum utilization of auxiliary manual labour, clandestine archaeological research is reduced to a minimum, whereas it is at its height at periods of greater unemployment. There can therefore be no doubt that in many cases there exist motives of necessity among people without means of support – motives which can explain if not justify the phenomenon.

It is true that the law gives the representatives of the Department of Antiquities powers to compensate discoverers of archaeological material with a reward. It is equally true that this reward, however modest, is higher than that which the tomb-robbers can get from the receivers, but they do at least pay straight away, whereas the State's practice is better left unsaid. This is known well enough to the few who have abided by the law, declaring and handing over valuable objects such as collections of coins, bronzes or ceramics, and who, years later, are still waiting to be compensated.

A first attempt to estimate the damage caused

Let us now consider some specific events that have taken place recently.

The reference to examples drawn from the Lazio territories should not lead one to suppose that illegal research is exceptionally prolific in those areas. One should remember that so far the Milan Polytechnic have only been able to carry out their surveys with freedom in the territories subject to the Department of Antiquities of Southern Etruria, which, from the start, has facilitated and encouraged the application of geophysical methods. The numerous bits of information which have reached us from every part of Italy have shown how in many archaeological zones the team of the Milan Polytechnic could have come up with discoveries of a far more important nature than those which it has so far been able to document. But it must unfortunately be stated that local representatives of the Department of Antiquities have not in every case received the Polytechnic's intervention favourably.

In 1957 a team of surveyors from the Milan Polytechnic whose purpose was to give to Southern Etruria's representative of the Department of Antiquities a practical demonstration of new methods of archaeological research based on the use of geophysical apparatus, undertook a campaign in the area of Monte Abbatone. This area was alloted to them by the representative and within it as we all know lies one of the large Etruscan necropolises of Cerveteri.

It was on this campaign which took place during the first term of 1957 that some hundreds of chamber tombs were identified, the greater part of which, although they had been broken into at a much earlier period, still contained material for excavation disregarded by the previous excavators who had only taken away precious objects such as jewels or bronzes. When it came to preparing a topographical measured plan that would show the groups that had been identified and explored it was considered advisable, for the first part which had been explored so far, and which took up about 20 per cent of the total area of the necropolis, to include also the groups that had been opened in the last few years by clandestine excavators. These were easily recognizable because the entrances to the chambers were still open and the numerous fragments of pottery left on the spot pointed without a shadow of doubt to the recent date of many of the fractures. It was thus possible for the first time to prepare a document of exceptional interest in that it allowed one to measure the precise extent of an illegal excavational activity that had taken place during the period since the last war – that is a period of between ten and fifteen years. . . .

Obviously the groups in question were those most easily recognizable even to the superficial observer, who would either examine the vegetation and the typical outcrop that grows on the topsoil of the very contours of the original tombs, or who would concentrate on groups so close to the surface as to be easily 'felt' by tests on the soil made with a long iron point shaped like a kitchen-spit which, as it can pierce down into the soil, enables one to search for the entrance passages or for the surrounding ditches along which the point will penetrate with ease.

The development of the campaign that followed during the years 1957, 58 and 59 led to the identification of over 550 chamber tombs and at the same time it was easy to establish the fact that the proportion of pillaged tombs in the last few years, as illustrated in figure 1, remains constant throughout the area of this important necropolis. It is therefore reasonable to suppose that the tombs which have been 'worked over' since the war by tomb-robbers number in this area alone between 350 and 400 and that the booty acquired can at least be equalled to the amount salvaged by the Department of Antiquities among the tombs discovered by the team of the Milan Polytechnic. Since the latter includes over 5,500 pieces salved by the Department itself at the accepted total of 12 million (lire) one can presume that the material illegally taken has a considerably higher value. Now this hypothesis drawn up from concrete facts such as those we have given here can give some idea not only of the damage caused in this particular case – that is in an archaeological area that is notoriously poor – but also of that caused in the remaining areas of Italy where the phenomenon repeats itself with the same causes and the same results. The example of the necropolis at Monte Abbatone is notedly repeated in thousands of spots all over Italy where there are ancient necropolises – an inexhaustible repository of material for excavation which led Ceram, the well-known author of *Gods, Graves and Scholars*, to claim that Italy still possesses below ground her own and vaster Louvre.

In the successive campaigns that were carried out in other archaeological zones by the Milan Polytechnic the same observations were in fact repeatedly made and to such an extent that it was practically possible to claim that for the preliminary work of fixing the boundaries of necropolises to be explored by geophysical methods, the testimony of external traces of violation still visible on the site is even more helpful than the examination of aerial surveys of individual zones. Tomb-robbers of all time have thus already taken steps to signal out these zones and in some cases, such as the large necropolis of Monterozzi at Tarquinia, they have gone so far as to scratch in the date of their visits.

In this last zone all the groups have been violated indiscriminately over the centuries and traces of violation repeated in different periods are not infrequent. If the Polytechnic team carried on their research here none the less it is because, as is well known, there are painted groups in this necropolis which in part, at least, are still preserved. We shall see, however, how the work of the pillagers has contributed to their deterioration and often to their destruction.

Figure 2 shows the measured plan of another site in the Cerveteri zone to which the Milan Polytechnic team of surveyors had proposed to extend its activities after having determined the extent of the recent devastation already caused by the tomb-robbers. In the course of just two weeks the team thus singled out about forty groups among which there was one whose original wealth was still intact and of exceptional interest. Unfortunately, for want of a formal authorization from the proprietor, the team was obliged to interrupt its work and naturally enough this interruption was very gratifying to the tomb-robbers, who by now have in all probability completed the raid on the other existing groups.

It is not a matter of one isolated case: in some zones in the province of Grosseto which are notoriously plagued by clandestine treasure-seekers the Polytechnic team did not even receive the authorization of the local representative of the Department of Antiquities to carry out a survey – let alone excavation: incredible but true.

Similarly in the neighbourhood of Viterbo, the little cemetery zone, which is illustrated in figure 3, represents another of the very frequent examples that all the Italian archaeological zones offer and that an entire atlas would not suffice to document. Here again it is a question of recent operations, probably carried out in the years 1959-60, and the innumerable fragments that are still visible testify without any doubt to the kind and variety of the goods that were removed.

But we can now add further evidence which reflects what is perhaps the most serious and alarming aspect of the phenomenon of clandestine research.

These 'freelance excavators', for whose benefit we have been so scrupulously objective and have not failed to bring forward the extenuating circumstances which can be considered a partial justification of their activities, these people demonstrate that they have no notion of the value of the material they excavate or of the precautions that should be taken to avoid its damage and destruction. Archaeologists and specialists in excavation know from their own experience what all this means and they are even more aware that almost the entire collection of archaeological groups, particularly those in burial zones or in temples or sanctuaries – these being the richest in marketable material – show clear traces of repeated violations and of the consequences of the clumsy and hurried work of the pillagers. But without going back to far-off times, let us confine ourselves to recounting what happens today or happened yesterday, that is in the case of the very groups shown in the measured plans illustrated in the figures. From a systematic collection of fragments with recent fractures that was put at the disposal of the Department of Antiquities, some have been reassembled, as is illustrated in figures 4-7 which prove how pieces of great value have been overlooked and dispersed owing to haste. Although some of these pieces when assembled have not allowed for more than a quarter or a fifth of the original to be reconstructed, the expense of restoring them has nevertheless been considered justified. But one can well imagine how much more valuable would be pieces for example such as those illustrated in figures 6-7 which were partially reconstructed from the few fragments discovered in the respective groups that had been violated.

But one of the even more alarming bases for indictment is given us by some painted tombs that had already been discovered in the years 1959-60 in the necropolis of Monterozzi illustrated in figures 8, 9 and 10.

These tombs, which are entirely frescoed, and which have, like all the others in the zone, been stripped of their movable furniture, quite clearly betray from the sound of the walls the immediate proximity of a further sepulchral chamber. Now the excavators have not hesitated to demolish entire frescoed walls with their picks, as those traces that are still visible reveal. Only a few traces remain, but these are sufficient to allow one to estimate the original state of preservation of the painted plaster. This is an example which should make one stop and think, the more because it is not an offence of centuries ago but one that has taken place in the last few years and therefore it is unfortunately particularly current.

It is well known that in the cases of almost all ancient sepulchral groups containing household goods and clothing it is very unusual to discover pieces intact even in the very rare cases of tombs that have not been violated. The movements of the earth as it shifts about, such as those caused by earthquakes which have followed one after another in considerable numbers over the centuries in all Mediterranean areas of historical importance, have caused the breakage of collections of pottery or impasto work, leaving in most instances only the small-sized pieces intact. Now illegal excavators steal everything, even the fragments, but they rarely manage to distinguish the value of the different objects, and the very conditions in which their work takes place, often during the night hours, make selection difficult. They moreover neglect, through ignorance, the precautions for preserving pieces that are most likely to suffer from change of temperature or humidity in the atmosphere. So it can happen that even a portion of the goods they take consequently suffers destruction. If, on the basis of the facts established during the campaigns carried out by the Milan Polytechnic, we were to assess the damage caused by the tomb-robbers by reason of the clumsy methods of excavation and collection alone, we think we would not be far off the mark in claiming that a good half of the excavation material that passes through their hands gets irrevocably ruined.

Then over and above the damage that the national heritage suffers on account of the material that is illegally excavated, sold or exported, there is the no less severe damage caused by these ignorant vandals of archaeology.

If in fact the material that is illegally sold or exported cannot be considered lost to the cultural legacy of civilized men, that which is destroyed out of neglect or ignorance can of itself give us the measure of the immense damage that is caused repeatedly and extensively throughout the archaeological areas of the ancient world. And in the face of this, the damage caused by barbarian raids, by the sackings of

history that took place during the great invasions, at the decline of the
Empire, in the Middle Ages and up to those that occurred during
revolutionary and wartime episodes in the nineteenth and twentieth
centuries seems insignificant. Because the vandalism that destroys the
buried archaeological heritage of the nation is an everyday problem in
the thousands and thousands of places that preserve these testimonies of
thirty centuries of history.

How can this be remedied?

The law lays down that anything found in the subsoil is the property
of the state and gives the representatives of the Department of Antiquities the authority to reward the owner of the land and the discoverer
with a recompense which, in the aggregate, must not exceed half the
value of the material discovered. The work of the tomb-robbers and
likewise that carried out by the owners of the sites is therefore illegal
and for this reason it is, as we know, investigated by the officers of the
law. But we know equally well that, given the widespread nature of the
phenomenon and the material impossibility of carrying out inspection
in all the archaeological zones, the law more or less leaves things as it
finds them so that illegal excavations proceed everywhere, the only
fluctuations being due either to the seasonal phenomena of greater
agricultural employment or to the lesser demands of the market. For
obviously even on the open market of antiquities there are fluctuations
due to the differing trends of cultural interest; so for example for some
ten or twenty years Etruscan objects have been 'doing well' owing to
the keen interest of scholars. This interest is clearly indicated by the
blossoming of publications, the success of superb newspaper editorials
which elucidate the more typical aspects of Etruscan civilization and
art, by the art exhibitions shown in the large capitals of Europe, the
increasing interest of foreign cultural tourism and finally by the sensational discoveries due to the introduction of the new scientific research
methods of the Milan Polytechnic. All this goes to emphasize the
gravity of the phenomenon that the law is powerless to suppress.

What is the remedy? Are we to increase the supervision? We should
need an army of police and guardians. And then *qui custodet custodes?*

Contact with these relics of ancient civilizations, which often include
precious objects and coins that can easily be concealed, little by little
exercise a strange charm even over those most in control, and not all are
able to resist it. It is as if a mysterious virus found its way into their
veins, a virus that succeeds in giving life to a fragment, that brings out a
mysterious written document or image, that recalls a moment in the

life of an epoch tens of centuries ago – or perhaps a little ornament or ritualistic object which can summon up a human feeling. One has to live for some time in this strange world to understand all this and to come to appreciate the heroic strength of character of the civil servants in the Department of Antiquities who are able to overcome these temptations.

Given the obvious impossibility of seeing that the law is respected, let us put the question again: What remedy is there? Should the law be altered? And in what way?

The facts we have laid out and those that have been the subject of extremely serious and important journalistic enquiries in recent years, lead us to foresee quite clearly, alongside the gravity of the phenomenon, its possible solutions.

There is obviously something that is not quite right in the law concerning excavations and in the ways in which it is interpreted and applied, but that is not all. Even a perfect law leaves things as it finds them when those responsible for seeing that it is respected lack the powers and the goodwill.

Thus we see the State, the legal possessor of as much as exists under the ground, being plundered every day by illegal excavators and by the proprietors themselves because the Department of Antiquities does not have the means for excavations and the authorities are not in a position to prevent this pillage. And the situation, let us bear this in mind, shows every indication of getting increasingly worse because in a great part of the archaeological zones in Italy large-scale programmes of agrarian redevelopment or reform are under way which bring with them the new deep-ploughing machinery that disturbs and often exposes new groups of tombs. Indeed this is already happening and has been happening for over twenty years in all areas along the Tyrrhenian coastline. The primitive ploughshare of the Virgilian peasant who discovered the relics of the ancient warrior buried in his field (*Georg.* I. 493) is today replaced by the work of bulldozers capable of reaching the most deeply buried archaeological stratifications. The world is marching on rapidly in this day and the unprecedented rate of increase in its population forces men to utilize every strip of ground. The necropolises and the archaeological zones that are productive of material for excavation in a country like Italy take up thousands of square miles and are to a large extent doomed to disappear, swept up by the growing exigencies of modern civilization. The large urban centres set the example, spreading themselves over archaeological areas the importance of which tends to be either concealed or played down in the interests of the constructors. We cannot hold on to any illusions here: the task of looking after buried material of historical or artistic value will simply have to be relegated to the Museums or to well-defined zones that allow for adequate supervision and maintenance.

Lecture to the Rotary Club of Rome, 1958

Translated from the Italian by L. A. Tufnell

A strange bargain

CHARLES LEONARD WOOLLEY

Another curious experience occurred to the late Lord Caernarvon, the man who discovered the famous Tomb of Tutankhamen. He was a very keen collector of Egyptian antiquities, and one day he was in his hotel in Cairo and a man came in and asked to see him, and then said, 'You collect antiquities?'

'Yes,' said Caernarvon.

'Well, I've got something wonderful. Wonderful!'

Caernarvon said, 'What is it; show me.'

'Oh,' he said, 'I can't show you here. It's in my house.'

'Well,' said Caernarvon, 'If it is as good as all that I'd like to see it.'

The man said, 'Yes, you can come and see it, but on my terms!'

'Oh, what are those?'

'You have got to come at night, and you have got to submit to being blindfolded and I shall take you to my house, because I don't want you to know where it is. And,' he said, 'you have got to bring with you £300 in gold.'

Now that sounded an impossible condition. To go with an unknown man, blindfolded and with three hundred gold pounds in your pocket, is not a thing that an ordinary man would do. But Lord Caernarvon was completely reckless and fearless. He said, 'Oh certainly, I will do that,' and he added, 'Is that the price you're asking?'

'Yes,' said the man, 'it's £300, and I'm not taking a penny less, but for £300 you can have the thing if you like.'

So that night after dinner three men came in and said to Caernarvon, 'Come along', and they took him outside the hotel, and on the pathway of the street they carefully blindfolded him and they put him into a carriage and drove for a time and then they took him out and took him inside a house and undid his eyes. He said, 'Where are the antiquities?' and they showed him two objects. One was a small vase of polished stone with a gold cover to it and on the cover was engraved a cartouche of one of the earliest known Pharaohs, a Pharaoh of the First Dynasty. It was a marvellous thing. And the other was even more remarkable.

It was a beautifully made flint knife about 8 inches long, beautifully worked and it had a handle of gold embossed with animal figures. It was clearly earlier than the first Pharaohs, of prehistoric antiquity, and Caernarvon simply opened his eyes and said, 'All right, I'll buy it.' He knew that at the price the things were dirt cheap, so he paid out the £300 and they faithfully gave him the things, bandaged his eyes and took him back to his hotel.

He looked at those things when he was back and it struck him that they were familiar; and he thought they must be duplicates of something he'd seen before. So the next day he went round to the National Museum of Cairo and he went to the case where some of the earliest and greatest treasures were kept, a large desk case with red velvet lining, and various objects on it; and he saw a round spot of dark colour on the velvet: the rest had faded where the sun had hit it. There was another long spot which exactly corresponded to his flint dagger; and he realised that the things he had bought were stolen from the Museum.

So he asked to see the Director, old Professor Maspero, a Frenchman, and he said, 'Professor Maspero, I want to ask you, have you had any valuable things stolen from the Museum of late?'

And Professor Maspero said, 'Good heavens, what makes you say that?'

'Well,' he said, 'I've got a suspicion about it. Is it really true?'

And Maspero heaved a heavy sigh and said, 'Yes, it is. We have lost two great treasures.'

'Have you taken any steps to recover them?'

'No,' said Maspero, 'I daren't.'

And Caernarvon knew what that meant; it meant that the things had been stolen by the Sub-Director, who was a German, and to have accused him would have caused an international incident that they couldn't possibly afford.

Caernarvon said, 'I've got these objects. I got them from a man whom I couldn't possibly trace – he was careful about that; I paid £300 for them. Would you like to buy them back? If so, pay me the £300 and you shall have them, because they are not mine.'

And the Professor said, 'Do you really mean that?'

'Yes,' said Caernarvon, 'certainly, I'm prepared to let you have them.'

The Professor said, 'That is more than generous of you: please bring them along.'

So Caernarvon took the two objects to Maspero's office and handed them over and said, 'Now I want a cheque for £300.'

Maspero said, 'Certainly,' and he wrote a cheque, handed it across and said, 'Now of course you will give me an official receipt.'

Caernarvon said, 'Give you a receipt? Not on your life. I'm not going to give you a receipt for stolen goods.'

Maspero objected, 'Without a receipt I cannot give the cheque.'

And Caernarvon said, 'Without the money I'm not going to hand over the objects. Either you give me a cheque without a receipt or I walk away with the two things.'

Maspero said, 'I must have them back, but I must have a receipt.'

Maspero sat for a while and thought. Then he rang his bell and one of the attendants, a sort of sweeper, came in and Maspero said to him, 'Here is a form. I want a signature to it. Go out into the Bazaar and get hold of the first man you like, give him sixpence and get him to sign his name to this.'

And so that was duly done and in twenty minutes the man came back with a signed receipt for £300 and Caernarvon took his cheque and then handed over the objects, which are still in the Cairo National Museum.

As I Seem to Remember, 1962

Legalized art robbery

All too often in the past the masterpieces of classical art have been subject to the depredations of rich collectors who coveted them only for their unique beauty and not at all for their archaeological value. Every attempt has been made to prevent this by suitable legislation, and now it is almost impossible for an archaeologist to lay claim as an individual to any part of the findings of his 'dig' or to any treasure-trove he may find, but when a really determined collector has the power to create his own laws there can be no defence against his appropriations. A startling example of this occurred when Napoleon's victorious army overpowered Italy in 1796; it was followed by a group of commissioners who were ordered by Bonaparte to annexe for France any major work of art which seemed worthy of their attention, and among the terms of the peace treaty offered to the Pope was an article rendering these transactions legal and binding.

Article 8

The Pope shall cede to the French Republic one hundred paintings, busts, vases or statues, to be selected by commissioners who will be sent to Rome, these objects specifically to include the bronze bust of Junius Brutus and that of Marcus Brutus in marble, both on the Capitol, and in addition 500 manuscripts selected by the above-mentioned commissioners.

Correspondance de Napoléon, vol. I, 1858

Translated from the French by V. M. Conrad

The complete forger

CHARLES LEONARD WOOLLEY

Increasing public interest in the artifacts of the ancient world has created a demand which ingenious forgers have been only too ready to supply. Even the greatest archaeologists have had their moments of unfortunate credulity, such as the time when Sir Arthur Evans enthusiastically acquired the so-called Ring of Nestor, which was later minutely analysed by the Swedish scholar Nilsson and proved to be of modern origin. The methods used by the forgers are well documented as they have several times been caught in the act, as Sir Leonard Woolley relates.

Actually, at one time I was completely taken in. I was really shocked. In Crete in the early years of this century I was stopping with Arthur Evans when he was excavating at Knossos, and one day he got a message from the police at Candia asking him to come to the police station, so we went together – he, Duncan Mackenzie, who was his assistant, and myself. And the most surprising thing had happened.

Evans for years had employed two Greeks to restore the antiquities which he had found. They were extraordinarily clever men – an old man and a young one – and he had trained them, and they had worked under the artist whom he employed there, and they had done wonderful restorations for him. Then the old man got ill and at last the doctor told him he was going to die.

He said, 'Are you sure?' The doctor said, 'Yes, I'm afraid there's no hope for you at all.'

'Right', he said. 'Send for the police.' The doctor said, 'You mean the priest.' 'No I don't', he said, 'I mean the police.' He insisted, and they sent for the police, and the police came and asked him, 'What on earth do you want?'

'Now I can tell you,' said the sick man. 'I'm going to die, so I'm all right, but for years I've been in partnership with George Antoniou, the young fellow who works with me for Evans, and we have been forging antiquities.'

'Well', said the policeman, 'I don't know that that concerns me.' 'Yes,' he said, 'it does. Because we've sold a statuette of gold and ivory which was supposed to be a Cretan one to the Candia Government Museum, and that's a criminal offence. George is a scoundrel, and I hate the fellow, and I've been waiting for this moment to give him away. Go straight to his house and you'll find all the forgeries and all our manufacturing plant there.'

The police went, they raided, and they found exactly what he said, and they asked Evans to come and look, and I never saw so magnificent a collection of forgeries as those fellows had put together.

There were things in every stage of manufacture. For instance, people had been recently astonished at getting what they call chryselephantine statuettes from Crete; statuettes of ivory decked out with gold – there is one in the Boston Museum and one at Cambridge, and one in the Cretan Museum at Candia. These men were determined to do that sort of thing, and they had got there everything, from the plain ivory tusk and then the figure rudely carved out, then beautifully finished, then picked out with gold. And then the whole thing was put into acid, which ate away the soft parts of the ivory, giving it the effect of having been buried for centuries. And I didn't see that anyone could tell the difference!

Then they had got Greek coins. These are sometimes very rare and of immense value; recently one Greek coin at a London sale fetched £3,100; another fetched £2,300 – both unique coins. Of course, such coins are generally the treasured possessions of different museums. The two Greeks wrote round to the museums where there were unique coins and asked to be supplied with plaster casts of them. That is a very common request and it is always granted.

They got the plaster casts, and they had discovered how to make a steel mould from the plaster, so they cast steel moulds from the two sides of the coin, making one as an anvil and the other as a hammerhead. They looked up the catalogues of the coin collection from which the cast came, and they found there the exact weight of the coin in milligrams. It would also give the exact character of the alloy, the silver alloy of which the coin was made. So they imitated the alloy, cut off a lump of the right weight exactly, heated it almost to melting point and put it on the anvil and struck it with the hammer in the fashion of the ancient coiner, and produced something so like the original that nobody could have told the difference. They had got about 100 of these forgeries in stock, and how many of such may have found their way on to the market I don't know, but it really was bewildering.

I said to Evans, 'I shall never buy a Greek antiquity!'

He said, 'Well, even I feel rather doubtful now,' and he was a marvellous judge.

As I Seem to Remember, 1962

The Olympia Convention

This is the agreement between the German and the Greek Imperial Government which was concluded and signed on 25 April 1874. This is a significant document, because it was the first modern, legally clear excavation agreement between two governments and became the prototype for the countless other international agreements which became necessary during the course of the history of excavation.

As well as this the excavation of Olympia became an example in another respect. Under the direction of Ernst Curtius and Friedrich Adler (who were joined by a whole team including the friend and assistant of Schliemann at Troy, the architect, Wilhelm Dörpfeld) here the scientific methods of modern excavation were developed; the results reached their highest peak in our time with the excavation of the great stadium of the Olympic games (where today the torch for the modern Olympic games is lit) and the discovery of the workshop of the most famous of ancient sculptors, Pheidias, under the direction of Emil Kuntze.

THE AGREEMENT

The Imperial German and the Royal Greek Governments have, guided by the wish to carry out excavations together in the area of the ancient Olympia in Greece, decided to conclude a convention and have agreed upon the following points:

ARTICLE I

Each government will appoint a commissar who will check according to his proportion that the following agreements are kept during the excavations.

ARTICLE II

The site of the old temple of the Olympian Jupiter shall serve as starting point of the excavations, which will be carried out on the site of old Olympia.

A later agreement between both governments will decide whether the excavations are to be extended to other regions of the Kingdom of Greece.

ARTICLE III

Whilst the Greek Government gives permission for the excavations on the site of Olympia, it promises to give the commissars every aid in the carrying out of the work, in the obtaining of workmen and in the fixing of the wages of the latter; also the above-named government will put police on the site of the excavation who will see that the orders of the commissars are carried out, and who can supply, should the need arise, for this purpose, armed force, without in any case deviating from the laws of the land. The Greek Government furthermore undertakes to pay compensation to those persons, proprietors or owners of empty land (whether this be fallow or cultivated) who have any kind of right to it.

Article IV

Germany undertakes to pay all the costs of the project, that is to say:

The wages of the officials, the wages of the workmen, the erection of store-houses and barracks, should these be needed. Germany furthermore promises to pay damages for plantations and buildings of every kind, as set out in the laws of the land or in the agreements between the Greek Government and the farmers, which are situated on national pieces of ground, in so far as such damages have a really strong ground or the personal rights of private persons can be justifiably claimed. On no account, however, can the compensation exceed the sum of 300 Drachmas (1 Drachma = 7 Sgr. 2 Pf.) per Stremma (1 Stremma = 1000 sq. metres), even if the Greek Government has ceded part of that piece of land to private persons.

Greece, on its part, promises with the aid of all the means in its power, to carry out the eviction or expropriation of those persons who are at this time in possession of pieces of land in which it seems necessary to undertake excavations.

It goes without saying that the work on the excavations can in no case be stopped or delayed on account of eventual objections or protests of private persons or persons at the moment engaged in building on those pieces of land.

Article V

Germany reserves the right to mark out which pieces of land on the plain before Olympia are suitable for excavating, to employ and to dismiss the workers, and to direct and apportion the work.

Article VI

Greece holds the rights of possession of all works of ancient art and any other objects which the excavations will bring to light. It will make its own decisions whether or not it will give to Germany, as a souvenir of the mutually undertaken work and in reward for the sacrifices Germany has made to this enterprise, the duplicates or repetitions of the objects found during the course of the excavations.

ARTICLE VII

Germany holds the exclusive rights to make copies and casts of the objects which are discovered during the excavations.

These exclusive rights are valid for five years from the time of discovery of each object. The Greek Government also gives the Imperial German Government the right – though not the exclusive right – to make copies and casts of all the antiques in the possession of the Greek Government or which it will find in the future without the co-operation of the German Government on Greek soil. Excluded from this are only those antiquities which in the view of the competent ministerial advisers could be damaged or might deteriorate during the process of casting.

Greece and Germany reserve the exclusive right to publish the scientific and artistic discoveries of the excavations carried out at the expense of the Germans. All these publications will be published periodically in Athens in Greek and at the expense of the Greeks. The same publications are to be published simultaneously in Germany with figures, plates and pictures which are only to be engraved and made in Germany. This last task is to be taken over by Germany and at the same time she promises to send to Greece fifteen of every hundred copies of the first edition of figures, plates and pictures, and thirty-five of each hundred of the following editions.

ARTICLE VIII

Should the Greek commissar entrusted with the guarding of the excavations unexpectedly object to the work ordered by the German scholars, the Royal Greek Foreign Ministry and the Imperial German Embassy in Athens will together, as a last resort, settle such differences.

ARTICLE IX

The present convention stays valid for ten years from the day of its ratification by the representation of the people.

ARTICLE X

Each of the two contracting Governments pledges to put this contract in front of the appropriate representation of the people as soon as possible; yet neither of the two parties is obliged to bring it into action before it has been ratified by the representation of the people.

ARTICLE XI

This convention should, on the proviso that it has had the permission of the representation of the people, be ratified in two months' time, or sooner, and the ratifications be exchanged in Athens.

As witnesses to this document: Mr von Wagner, Ambassador Extraordinary and authorized minister of the German Emperor in Athens, Professor E. Curtius, specially authorized agent on the one hand, and Mr J. Delyanny, Foreign Minister of His Majesty, the King of Greece, Mr P. Eustratiades, Keeper of Antiquities, on the other hand, all authorized by their respective governments and provided with their seals.

Done in Athens, in duplicate, on the 13/25 April 1874.

E. v. Wagner (L.S.)
Ernst Curtius (L.S.)
Delyanny (L.S.)
Eustratiades (L.S.)

Olympia, vol. I, 1870

Translated from the German by C. M. Kaine

Part Two

————◆————

THE BOOK OF THE STATUES

The foundation of the British Museum

Sir Hans Sloane (1660–1753) *was born in County Down, Ireland. He studied medicine in London for four years and then completed his M.D. degree at the University of Orange in 1683. On his return to England he brought with him a considerable collection of plants, and continued to gather curios for the rest of his life; he spent fifteen months in Jamaica as physician to the Duke of Albemarle, and during this short time he added 800 unknown plants to his collection. His professional and scholastic honours were many. He was elected Secretary to the Royal Society, and in 1716 he became the first physician to receive a hereditary title when he was created a baronet. He was appointed successively Physician General to the army, First Physician to George II, and President of the Royal Society. At his death he offered his books, manuscripts and curios to the nation for the sum of £20,000, and the acceptance of the collection formed the nucleus of the British Museum.*

I Sir Hans Sloane of Chelsea, in the county of Middlesex, Baronet, do make this codicil to be annexed to my last will and testament as follows. Whereas I have in and by my said Will given some directions about the sale and disposition of my musaeum, or collection of rarities herein more particularly mentioned. Now I do hereby revoke my said Will as far as relates thereto, and I do direct and appoint concerning the same in the following Manner. Having had from my youth a strong inclination to the study of plants, and all other productions of nature; and having through the course of many years with great labour and expence, gathered together whatever could be procured either in our own or foreign countries that was rare and curious; and being fully convinced that nothing tends more to raise our ideas of the power, wisdom, goodness, providence, and other perfections of the Deity, or more to the comfort and well being of his creatures than the enlargement of our knowledge in the works of nature, I do Will and desire that for the promoting of these noble ends, the glory of God, and the good of man, my collection in all its branches may be, if possible, kept and preserved together whole and intire in my manor house, in the parish of Chelsea, situate near the physic garden, given by me to the company of apothecaries for the same purposes; and having great reliance and confidence that the Right Hon. and other persons hereafter named will be influenced by the same principles, and faithfully and conscientiously discharge the trust hereby reposed in them, I do give, devise and bequeath unto the Right Hon. Charles Sloane Cadogan, Esq:

(Here follows a list of 51 names)

all that my collection or musaeum, at, in, or about my manor house at Chelsea aforesaid, which consists of too great a variety to be particularly described. But I mean all my library of books, drawings, manuscripts, prints, medals and coins, antient and modern, antiquities, seals, &c. cameos and intaglios, &c., precious stones, agates, jaspers, &c. vessels, &c. of agate jasper, &c. chrystals, mathematical instruments, drawings and pictures, and all other things in my said collection or musaeum, which are more particularly described, mentioned and numbered, with short histories or accounts of them, with proper references in certain catalogues by me made, containing thirty-eight volumes in folio, and eight volumes in quarto, except such framed pictures as are not marked with the word (collection) to have and to hold to them and their successors or assigns for ever; to the intent only that the same and every part and parcel of my said collection or musaeum may be vested in the said Right Honourable and Honourable, and other persons upon the trusts, and for the uses and purposes, and subject to the several limitations and directions hereafter particularly specified concerning the same; and for rendering this my intention more effectual, that the said collection may be preserved and continued intire in its utmost perfection and regularity; and being assured that nothing will conduce more to this purpose, than placing the same under the direction and care of the learned, experienced and judicious persons who are above all low and mean views, I do earnestly desire than the king, his royal highness the prince of Wales, his royal highness William duke of Cumberland, the archbishop of Canterbury for the time being, the right honourable Philip lord Hardwick, and the lord high chancellor for the time being, the lord president of the council for the time being, the lord privy seal for the time being, the lord steward of his majesty's houshold for the time being, the lord chamberland of his majesty's houshold for the time being, his grace Charles, duke of Richmond, his grace John duke of Montague, his grace Holles duke of Newcastle, his grace John duke of Bedford, and the two principal secretaries of state for the time being; the right honourable John earl of Sandwich, and the lord high admiral, or the first lord commissioner of the admiralty for the time being; the right honourable Henry Pelham, Esq; and the lord high treasurer, or the first lord commissioner of the treasury for the time being, and the chancellor of the exchequer for the time being, the lord chief justice of the king's bench for the time being, the lord chief justice of the common pleas for the time being, the lord chief baron of the exchequer for the time being, the lord bishop of London for the time being, the lord bishop of Winchester for the time being, the right honourable Archibald duke of Argyle, the right honourable Henry earl of Pembroke, the right honourable Philip earl of Chester-field, the right honourable Richard earl of Burlington, the right honourable Henry lord Montford, the right honourable Arthur Onslow, esq; and the speaker of the House of Commons for the time being, the honourable lord Charles Cavendish, the right honourable Charles lord Cadogan, the right honourable John earl of Verney, the right honourable George lord Anson, will condescend so far as to act and be visitors of my said musaeum and collection. And I do hereby, with their leave, nominate and appoint them visitors thereof, with full power and authority for any five or more of them to enter my said collection or musaeum at any time or times, to peruse, supervise and examine the same and the management thereof; and to visit, correct and reform from time to time as there may be occasion, either jointly with the said trustees, or separately, upon application to them for that purpose; or otherwise all abuses, defaults, neglects, or mismanagaments that may happen to arise therein, or touching or concerning the person or persons, officer or officers that are or shall be appointed to attend the same. And my will is, and I do hereby request and desire, that the said trustees, or any seven or more of them do make their humble application to his majesty or to parliament, at the next sessions after my decease as shall be thought most proper, in order to pay the full and clear sum of twenty thousand pounds of lawful money of Great-Britain, unto my executors or the survivors of them, within twelve months after my decease, in consideration of the said collection or musaeum: It not being, as I apprehend or believe, a fourth of their real and intrinsic value; and also to obtain such sufficient and effectual powers and authorities, for vesting in the said trustees all and every part of my said collection or musaeum before mentioned in all its branches; and also my said capital manor house, with such gardens and out-houses as shall thereunto belong, and be used by me at the time of my decease, in which it is my desire the same shall be kept and preserved; and also the water of, or belonging to my manor of Chelsea coming from Kensington, subject to furnishing or supplying the lord Bishop of Winchester's house as is now used; and also all that the advowson or presentation or right of patronage of the church of Chelsea: To the end, the same premises may be absolutely vested in the said trustees, for preserving and continuing my said collection or musaeum in such manner as they shall think most likely to answer the public benefit by me intended; and also obtain as aforesaid, a sufficient fund or provision, maintaining and taking care of my said collection and premises, and for repairing and supporting my said manor house, water-work and premises, to be vested in the said trustees for ever: And I do hereby further direct and appoint, that my executors do and shall, upon payment of the said sum of twenty thousand pounds, deliver or cause to be delivered unto the said trustees, or any seven or more of them, for, and in the name of all of them, in the presence of the visitors, or any five or more of them, as well the possession of my said manor house and gardens at Chelsea aforesaid, as also all my collection or musaeum before mentioned and described, and every part thereof in all its branches, whole and intire, as the same shall be bound in my said manor house, according to the said catalogues, and together with the several volumes of catalogues thereunto belonging. And further, my will is, and I do hereby also direct and appoint, that in case his majesty or the parliament do accept the said offer, and do pay the sum of twenty thousand pounds unto my executors or the survivor of them, that then my said executors do, within six months after such payment as aforementioned, and obtaining proper powers for effectually vesting in the said trustees all my said collection, and my said capital house and gardens, with their appurtenances, water and advowson, presentation or right of patronage of the church of Chelsea as aforesaid; together with my heir or heirs at law, and all other proper parties, do and shall join in and execute such acts, deed, or conveyances, as shall be thought requisite and necessary for the more perfect and absolute vesting, conveying, and assuring the said premises in, and to the said trustees and their assigns or successors for ever, for the uses, intents and purposes herein mentioned and intended.

Printed Will and Codicils of Sir Hans Sloane, Bart, 1753

A troublesome legacy

HORACE WALPOLE TO HORACE MANN

One of Sir Hans Sloane's legatees, Horace Walpole, took a somewhat rueful view of the charge laid upon him by the will, as can be seen from his letter to a friend.

Arlington Street, 14 February 1753

I have been going to write to you every post for these three weeks, and could not bring myself to begin a letter with, 'I have nothing to tell you.' But it grows past a joke; we will not drop our correspondence because there is no war, no politics, no parties, no madness, and no scandal. In the memory of England there never was so inanimate an age: it is more fashionable to go to church than to either House of Parliament. Even the era of the Gunnings is over: both sisters have laid in, and have scarce made one paragraph in the newspapers, though their names were grown so renowned, that in Ireland the beggar-women bless you with, 'The luck of the Gunnings attend you!'

You will scarce guess how I employ my time; chiefly at present in the guardianship of embryos and cockleshells. Sir Hans Sloane is dead, and has made me one of the trustees to his museum, which is to be offered for twenty thousand pounds to the King, the Parliament, the Royal Academies of Petersburgh, Berlin, Paris, and Madrid. He valued it at fourscore thousand; and so would anybody who loves hippopotamuses, sharks with one ear, and spiders as big as geese! It is a rent-charge, to keep the foetuses in spirits! You may believe that *those* who think money the most valuable of all curiosities, will not be purchasers. The King has excused himself, saying he did not believe that there are twenty thousand pounds in the Treasury. We are a charming wise set, all philosophers, botanists, antiquarians, and mathematicians; and adjourned our first meeting, because Lord Macclesfield, our chairman, was engaged to a party for finding out the longitude. One of our number is a Moravian, who signs himself Henry XXVIII, Count de Reus. The Moravians have settled a colony at Chelsea, in Sir Hans's neighbourhood, and I believe he intended to beg Count Henry XXVIIIth's skeleton for his museum.

I am almost ashamed to be thanking you but now for a most entertaining letter of two sheets, dated December 22, but I seriously had nothing to form an answer. It is but three mornings ago that your brother was at breakfast with me, and scolded me, 'Why, you tell me nothing!' – 'No', says I; 'if I had anything to say, I should write to your brother.' I give you my word, the first new book that takes, the first murder, the first revolution, you shall have, with all the circumstances. In the mean time, do be assured that there never was so dull a place as London, or so insipid an inhabitant of it as

Yours, &c.

The Letters, vol. III, 1903

The controversial bequest of Lord Elgin

THOMAS BRUCE, 7TH EARL OF ELGIN (1766-1841), *succeeded to his title at the age of five. In 1785 he entered the army, where he ultimately rose to the rank of Major-General. In 1790 he began his diplomatic career and was shortly appointed envoy to Brussels and then to Berlin. From 1799 to 1802 he held the post of Envoy Extraordinary in Constantinople, and during this time he secured Turkish permission to record and later to remove many works of classical art from Athens. The sculptures were brought to England in small consignments between 1803 and 1812, and when Lord Elgin himself arrived, he found that he was being violently attacked both for the legality of his appropriations and for the artistic value of the sculptures. He published a memorandum in his own defence, and in 1816 a Parliamentary Committee vindicated his conduct and confirmed the value of his acquisitions by recommending the purchase of the marbles for the British Museum for £35,000 – a sum much lower than their original cost to Lord Elgin.*

In the year 1799, when Lord Elgin was appointed his Majesty's Ambassador Extraordinary to the Ottoman Porte, he happened to be in habits of frequent intercourse with Mr Harrison, an architect of great eminence in the west of England, who had there given various very splendid proofs of his professional talents, especially in a public building of Grecian architecture at Chester. Mr Harrison had besides studied many years, and to great purpose, at Rome. Lord Elgin consulted him, therefore, on the benefits that might possibly be derived to the arts in this country, in case an opportunity could be found for studying minutely the architecture and sculpture of ancient Greece; and his opinion very decidedly was, that although we might possess exact measurements of the buildings at Athens, yet a young artist could never form to himself an adequate conception of their minute details, combinations, and general effect, without having before him some such sensible representation of them as might be conveyed by *casts*. This advice, which laid the groundwork of Lord Elgin's pursuits in Greece, led to the further consideration, that, since any knowledge which was possessed of these buildings had been obtained under the peculiar disadvantages which the prejudices and jealousies of the Turks had ever thrown in the way of such attempts, any favourable circumstances which Lord Elgin's embassy might offer should be improved fundamentally; and not only modellers, but architects and draftsmen, might be employed, to rescue from oblivion, with the most accurate detail, whatever specimens of architecture and sculpture in Greece had still escaped the ravages of time, and the barbarism of the conquerers.

On this suggestion, Lord Elgin proposed to his Majesty's Government, that they should send out English artists of known eminence, capable of collecting this information in the most perfect manner; but the prospect appeared of too doubtful an issue for ministers to engage in the expense attending it. . . .

After much difficulty, Lord Elgin obtained permission from the Turkish Government to establish these six artists at Athens; where they prosecuted the business of their several departments during three years acting on one general system, with the advantage of mutual control, and under the general superintendance of M. Lusieri. They at length completed Lord Elgin's plan in all its parts.

Accordingly, every monument, of which there are any remains in Athens, has been thus most carefully and minutely measured; and, from the rough drafts of the architects (all of which are preserved), finished drawings have been made of the plans, elevations, and details of the most remarkable objects; in which the Calmouk has restored and inserted all the sculpture, with exquisite taste and ability. He has besides drawn, with astonishing accuracy, all the bas-reliefs on the several temples, in the precise state of decay and mutilation in which they at present exist.

Most of the bas-reliefs, and nearly all the characteristic features of architecture, in the various monuments at Athens, have been moulded, and the moulds of them have been brought to London.

Besides the architecture and sculpture at Athens, all remains of them which could be traced through several other parts of Greece, have been measured and delineated, with the most scrupulous exactness, by the second architect, Ittar. . . .

In the prosecution of this undertaking, the artists had the mortification of witnessing the very wilful devastation, to which all the sculpture, and even the architecture, were daily exposed, on the part of the Turks and travellers. . . . The Temple of Minerva had been converted into a powder magazine, and been completely destroyed, from a shell falling upon it, during the bombardment of Athens by the Venetians towards the end of the seventeenth century; and even this accident had not deterred the Turks from applying the beautiful Temple of Neptune and Erectheus to the same use, whereby it is constantly exposed to a similar fate. Many of the statues on the *posticum* of the Temple of Minerva (Parthenon,) which had been thrown down by the explosion, had been absolutely pounded for mortar, because they furnished the whitest marble within reach; and the parts of the modern fortification, and the miserable houses where this mortar was so applied, were discovered. Besides, it is well known that the Turks will frequently climb up the ruined walls, and amuse themselves in defacing any sculpture they can reach; or in breaking columns, statues or other remains of antiquity, in the fond expectation of finding within them some hidden treasures.

Under these circumstances, Lord Elgin felt himself impelled, by a stronger motive than personal gratification, to endeavour to preserve any specimens of sculpture, he could, without injury, rescue from such impending ruin. . . . Actuated by these inducements, Lord Elgin made use of all his means, and ultimately with such success, that he has brought to England, from the ruined temples at Athens, from the modern walls and fortification, in which many fragments had been used as so many blocks of stone, and from excavations made on purpose, a greater quantity of original Athenian sculpture, in statues, alti and bassi relievi, capitals, cornices, frizes, and columns, than exists in any other part of Europe. . . .

The Parthenon itself, independently of its decorative sculpture, is so chaste and perfect a model of Doric architecture, that Lord Elgin conceived it to be of the highest importance to the arts, to secure original specimens of each member of that edifice. These consist of a capital; assizes of the columns themselves, to show the exact form of the curve used in channelling; a Triglyph, and mutules from the cornice, and even some of the marble tiles with which the ambulatory was roofed: so that, not only the sculptor may be gratified by studying every specimen of his art, from the colossal statue to the basso-relievo, executed in the golden age of Pericles, by Phidias himself, or under his immediate direction; but the practical architect may examine into every detail of the building, even to the mode of uniting the tambours of the columns, without the aid of mortar, so as to give to the shafts the appearance of single blocks. . . .

More difficulty occurred in forming a plan, for deriving the utmost advantage from the marbles and casts. Lord Elgin's first attempt was to have the statues and bas-reliefs restored; and in that view he went to Rome, to consult and to employ Canova. The decision of that most eminent artist was conclusive. On examining the specimens produced to him, and making himself acquainted with the whole collection, and particularly with what came from the Parthenon, by means of the persons who had been carrying on Lord Elgin's operation at Athens, and who had returned with him to Rome, Canova declared, that however greatly it was to be lamented that these statues should have suffered so much from time and barbarism, yet it was undeniable, that they had never been retouched; that they were the work of the ablest artists the world had ever seen; executed under the most enlightened patron of the arts, and at a period when genius enjoyed the most liberal encouragement, and had attained the highest degree of perfection; and that they had been found worthy of forming the decoration of the most admired edifice ever erected in Greece; That he should have had the greatest delight, and derived the greatest benefit, from the opportunity Lord Elgin offered him of having in his possession, and contemplating, these inestimable marbles: But, (his expression was,) it would be sacrilege in him, or any man, to presume to touch them with a chisel. Since their arrival in this country, they have been thrown open to the inspection of the public; and the opinions and impressions, not only of artists, but of men of taste in general, have thus been formed and collected. From these, the judgement pronounced by Canova has been universally sanctioned: and all idea of restoring the marbles has been deprecated. . . . From trials which Lord Elgin was induced to make, at the request of professional gentlemen, a strong impression has been created, that the science of sculptors, and the taste and judgement by which it is to be carried forward and appreciated, cannot so effectually be promoted, as by athletic exercises practised in the presence of similar works; the distinguishing merit of which, is an able, scientific, ingenious, but exact imitation of Nature. By no other way could the variety of attitude, the articulation of the muscles, the description of the passions; in short, every thing a sculptor has to represent, be so accurately or so beneficially understood . . .

Under similar advantages, and with an enlightened and encouraging protection bestowed on genius and the arts, it may not be too sanguine to indulge a hope, that, prodigal as Nature is in the perfections of the human figure in this country, animating as are the instances of patriotism, heroic actions, and private virtues, deserving commemoration, sculpture may soon be raised in England to rival the ablest productions of the best times of Greece.

Memorandum on the Subject of the Earl of Elgin's Pursuits in Greece, 1811

The Treasure of Priam

HEINRICH SCHLIEMANN

DR HEINRICH SCHLIEMANN (*1822-1890*) *was born in Neu Buckow in Germany. He was a man of great and varied natural ability, both for scholarship and for business; starting as an assistant in a small shop he amassed a large fortune in trade and was then able to retire and follow out his lifelong ambition to search for the site of Troy. Unlike other scholars of his day, he placed complete faith in the accuracy of the Homeric poems, and by following the topographical descriptions in the* Iliad *he was able to identify the hill of Hissarlik as the site of Troy. His faith in ancient authorities was justified more than once, as it later led him to excavate the citadel of Mycenae, where he discovered an entire pre-Hellenic civilization including a group of royal graves containing an immense burial hoard of gold. He was often misled by his enthusiasm for Homer, and his unscientific methods of excavating would have appalled modern archaeologists, but his discoveries were of the first importance and magnitude. Among his many talents was an outstanding facility for languages; he learned a great many by a plan he devised for himself, which strongly resembles the most recent teaching methods.*

In the new large excavation on the north-west side, which is connected with the one I have just been describing, I have convinced myself that the splendid wall of large hewn stones, which I uncovered in April 1870, belongs to a tower, the lower projecting part of which must have been built during the first period of the Greek colony, whereas its upper portion seems to belong to the time of Lysimachus. To this tower also belongs the wall that I mentioned in my last report as 9 feet high and 6 feet broad and as continuous with the surrounding wall of Lysimachus; and so does the wall of the same dimensions, situated 49 feet from it, which I have likewise broken through. Behind the latter, at a depth of from 26 to 30 feet, I uncovered the Trojan city wall which runs out from the Scaean Gate.

In excavating this wall further and directly by the side of the palace of King Priam, I came upon a large copper article of the most remarkable form, which attracted my attention all the more as I thought I saw gold behind it. On the top of this copper article lay a stratum of red and calcined ruins, from $4\frac{3}{4}$ to $5\frac{1}{4}$ feet thick, as hard as stone, and above this again lay the above-mentioned wall of fortification (6 feet broad and 20 feet high) which was built of large stones and earth, and must have belonged to an early date after the destruction of Troy. In order to withdraw the Treasure from the greed of my workmen, and to save it for archaeology, I had to be most expeditious, and although it was not yet time for breakfast, I immediately had 'paidos' called. This is a word of uncertain derivation, which had passed over into Turkish, and is here employed in place of ἀνάπαυσις, or time for rest. While the men were eating and resting, I cut out the Treasure with a large knife, which it was impossible to do without the very greatest exertion and the most fearful risk of my life, for the great fortification-wall, beneath which I had to dig, threatened every moment to fall down upon me. But the sight of so many objects, every one of which is of inestimable value to archaeology, made me foolhardy, and I never thought of any danger. It would, however, have been impossible for me to have removed the Treasure without the help of my dear wife, who stood by me ready to pack the things which I cut out in her shawl and to carry them away.

The first thing I found was a large copper shield (the ἀσπὶς ὀμφαλόεσσα of Homer) in the form of an oval salver, in the middle of which is a knob or boss encircled by a small furrow (αὖλαξ). This shield is a little less than 20 inches in length; it is quite flat and, surrounded by a rim (ἄντυξ) $1\frac{1}{2}$ inches high; the boss (ὀμφαλός) is $2\frac{1}{3}$ inches high and $4\frac{1}{3}$ inches in diameter; the furrow encircling it is 7 inches in diameter and $2\frac{2}{5}$ of an inch deep. . . .

Next came another cup of the purest gold, weighing exactly 600 grammes (about 1 lb. 6 oz. troy); it is $3\frac{1}{2}$ inches high, $7\frac{1}{4}$ inches long, and $7\frac{1}{5}$ inches broad; it is in the form of a ship with two large handles; on one side there is a mouth, $1\frac{1}{5}$ inches broad, for drinking out of, and another at the other side, which is $2\frac{3}{4}$ inches broad, and, as my esteemed friend Professor Stephanos Kumanudes, of Athens, remarks, the person who presented the filled cup may have first drunk from the small mouth, as a mark of respect, to let the guest drink from the large mouth. This vessel has a foot which projects about $\frac{1}{12}$ of an inch, and is $1\frac{1}{3}$ inches long, and $\frac{4}{5}$ of an inch broad. It is assuredly the Homeric, δέπας ἀμφικύπελλον. But I adhere to my supposition that all of those tall and brilliant red goblets of terra-cotta, in the form of champagne glasses with two enormous handles, are also δέπα ἀμφικύπελλα, and that this form probably existed in gold also. I must further make an observation which is very important for the history of art, that the above-mentioned gold δέπας ἀμφικύπελλον is of *cast gold*, and that the large handles, which are not solid, have been fused on to it. On the other hand the gold bottle and the gold cup mentioned above have been *wrought with the hammer*.

The Treasure further contained a small cup of gold alloyed with 20 per cent of silver, this is the mixed metal called *electrum*. It weighs 70 grammes (2¼ oz. troy), and is above 3 inches high, and above 2½ inches broad. Its foot is only ⅘ of an inch high and nearly an inch broad, and is moreover not quite straight, so that the cup appears to be meant only to stand upon its mouth. . . .

As I found all these articles together, forming a rectangular mass, or packed into one another, it seems to be certain that they were placed on the city wall in a wooden chest (φωριαμός), such as those mentioned by Homer as being in the palace of King Priam. This appears to be the more certain, as close by the side of these articles I found a copper key above 4 inches long, the head of which (about 2 inches long and broad) greatly resembles a large safe-key of a bank. Curiously enough this key has had a wooden handle; there can be no doubt of this from the fact that the end of the stalk of the key is bent round at a right angle, as in the case of the daggers.

It is probable that some member of the family of King Priam hurriedly packed the Treasure into the chest and carried it off without having time to pull out the key; that when he reached the wall, however, the hand of an enemy or the fire overtook him, and he was obliged to abandon the chest, which was immediately covered to a height of from 5 to 6 feet with the red ashes and the stones of the adjoining royal palace.

Perhaps the articles found a few days previously in a room of the royal palace close to the place where the Treasure was discovered, belonged to this unfortunate person. These articles were a helmet, and a silver vase 7 inches high and 5½ inches broad, containing an elegant cup of electrum 4⅓ inches high and 3½ inches broad. The helmet was broken in being taken out, but I can have it mended, as I have all the pieces of it. The two upper portions, composing the crest (φάλος), are uninjured. Beside the helmet, as before, I found a curved copper pin, nearly 6 inches in length, which must have been in some way attached to it, and have served some purpose.

At 5 or 6 feet above the Treasure, the successors of the Trojans erected a fortification wall 20 feet high and 6 feet broad, composed of large hewn and unhewn stones and earth; this wall extends to within $3\frac{1}{4}$ feet of the surface of the hill.

That the Treasure was packed together at terrible risk of life, and in the greatest anxiety, is proved among other things also by the contents of the largest silver vase, at the bottom of which I found two splendid gold diadems ($\kappa\rho\acute{\eta}\delta\epsilon\mu\nu\alpha$); a fillet, and four beautiful gold ear-rings of most exquisite workmanship; upon these lay 56 gold ear-rings of exceedingly curious form and 8,750 small gold rings, perforated prisms and dice, gold buttons, and similar jewels, which obviously belonged to other ornaments; then followed six gold bracelets, and on the top of all the two small goblets.

The one diadem consists of a gold fillet, $21\frac{2}{3}$ inches long and nearly $\frac{1}{2}$ an inch broad, from which there hang on either side seven little chains to cover the temples, each of which has eleven square leaves with a groove; these chains are joined to one another by four little cross chains, at the end of which hangs a glittering golden idol of the tutelar goddess of Troy, nearly an inch long. The entire length of each of these chains, with the idols, amounts to $10\frac{1}{4}$ inches. Almost all these idols have something of the human form, but the owl's head with the two large eyes cannot be mistaken; their breadth at the lower end is about $\frac{9}{10}$ of an inch. Between these ornaments for the temples there are 47 little pendant chains adorned with square leaves; at the end of each little chain is an idol of the tutelary goddess of Ilium, about $\frac{3}{4}$ of an inch long; the length of these little chains with the idols is not quite 4 inches.

The other diadem is 20 inches long, and consists of a gold chain, from which are suspended on each side eight chains completely covered with small gold leaves, to hang down over the temples, and at the end of every one of the sixteen chains there hangs a golden idol $1\frac{1}{4}$ inches long, with the owl's head of the Ilian tutelary goddess. Between these ornaments for the temples there are likewise 74 little chains, about 4 inches long, covered with gold leaves, to hang down over the forehead; at the end of these chains there hangs a double leaf about $\frac{3}{4}$ of an inch long.

The fillet $\H{\alpha}\mu\pi\upsilon\xi$ is above 18 inches long and $\frac{1}{2}$ of an inch broad, and has three perforations at each end. Eight quadruple rows of dots divide it into nine compartments, in each of which there are two large dots; and an uninterrupted row of dots adorns the whole edge. Of the four ear-rings only two are exactly alike. From the upper part, which is almost in the shape of a basket, and is ornamented with two rows of decorations in the form of beads, there hang six small chains on which are three little cylinders; attached to the end of the chains are small idols of the tutelar goddess of Troy. The length of each ear-ring is $3\frac{1}{2}$ inches. The upper part of the other two ear-rings is larger and thicker, but likewise almost in the shape of a basket, from it are suspended five little chains entirely covered with small round leaves, on which are likewise fastened small but more imposing idols of the Ilian tutelar divinity; the length of one of these pendants is $3\frac{1}{2}$ inches, that of the other a little over 3 inches.

Of the six gold bracelets, two are quite simple and closed, and are about $\frac{1}{5}$ of an inch thick; a third is likewise closed, but consists of an ornamented band $\frac{1}{25}$ of an inch thick, and $\frac{1}{4}$ of an inch broad. The other three are double, and the ends are turned round and furnished with a head. The princesses who wore these bracelets must have had unusually small hands, for they are so small that a girl of ten would have difficulty in putting them on.

The 56 other gold ear-rings are of various sizes, and three of them appear to have also been used by the princesses of the royal family as finger-rings. Not one of the ear-rings has any resemblance in form to the Hellenic, Roman, Egyptian, or Assyrian ear-rings; 20 of them end in four leaves, ten in three leaves, lying beside one another and soldered together, and they are thus extremely like those ear-rings of gold and electrum which I found last year at a depth of 9 and 13 metres ($29\frac{1}{2}$ and $42\frac{1}{2}$ feet). Eighteen other ear-rings end in six leaves; at the commencement of these there are two small studs, in the centre two rows of five small studs each, and at the end three small studs. Two of the largest rings, which, owing to the thickness of the one end, certainly cannot have been used as ear-rings, and appear to have been finger-rings only, terminate in four leaves, and at the commencement of these there are two, in the middle three, and at the end again two small studs. Of the remaining ear-rings two have the form of three, and four the form of two, beautifully ornamented serpents lying beside one another.

Besides the ear-rings, a great number of other ornaments strung on threads, or fastened on leather, had been put into the same large silver vase; for above, and below them, as already said, I found 8,750 small objects; such as gold rings, only $\frac{1}{8}$ of an inch in diameter; perforated dice, either smooth or in the form of little indented stars, about $\frac{1}{6}$ of an inch in diameter; gold perforated prisms, $\frac{1}{10}$ of an inch high and $\frac{1}{8}$ of an inch broad, decorated longitudinally with eight or sixteen incisions; small leaves about $\frac{1}{5}$ of an inch long, and $\frac{1}{8}$ of an inch broad, and pierced longitudinally with a hole for threading them; small gold pegs $\frac{1}{5}$ of an inch long, with a button on one side, and a perforated hole on the other; perforated prisms about $\frac{1}{5}$ of an inch long, and $\frac{1}{10}$ of an inch broad; double or triple gold rings soldered together and only $\frac{1}{4}$ of an inch in diameter, with holes on both sides for threading them; gold buttons or studs $\frac{1}{5}$ of an inch high, in the cavity of which is a ring above $\frac{1}{10}$ of an inch broad for sewing them on; gold double buttons, exactly like our shirt studs, $\frac{3}{10}$ of an inch long, which, however, are not soldered, but simply stuck together, for from the cavity of the one button there projects a tube ($a\dot{v}\lambda\acute{\iota}\sigma\kappa o\varsigma$) nearly $\frac{1}{4}$ of an inch long, and from the other a pin ($\ddot{\epsilon}\mu\beta o\lambda o\nu$) of the same length, and the pin is merely stuck into the tube to form the double stud. These double buttons or studs can only have been used, probably, as ornament upon leather articles, for instance upon the handle-straps ($\tau\epsilon\lambda\alpha\mu\hat{\omega}\nu\epsilon\varsigma$) of swords, shields, or knives. I found in the vase also two gold cylinders above $\frac{1}{10}$ of an inch thick and $\frac{3}{4}$ of an inch long; also a small gold peg above $\frac{4}{5}$ of an inch in length, and from $\frac{6}{100}$ to $\frac{8}{100}$ of an inch thick; it has at one end a perforated hole for hanging it up, and on the other side six encircling incisions, which give the article the appearance of a screw; it is only by means of a magnifying glass that it is found not to be really a screw. I also found in the same vase two pieces of gold, one of which is $\frac{1}{7}$ of an inch, the other above 2 inches, long; each of them has 21 perforations.

The person who endeavoured to save the Treasure had fortunately the presence of mind to stand the silver vase, containing the valuable articles described above, upright in the chest, so that not so much as a bead could fall out, and everything has been preserved uninjured.

Troy and Its Remains, 1875

A stolen treasure

HEINRICH SCHLIEMANN

I now come to three smaller treasures, found at the end of March 1873, at a depth of 30 ft on the east side of the royal house and very close to it, by two of my workmen, one of whom lives at Yeni Shehr, the other at Kalifatli. One of them was found in the owl-headed vase No. 232, which was closed by the pointed foot of another vase; the two other little treasures were found, together with the battle-axe No. 828, close by. But as the statements of the labourers differ as to the particular objects contained in each treasure, I can only describe them here conjointly. The two workmen had stolen and divided the three treasures between themselves, and probably I should never have had any knowledge of it, had it not been for the lucky circumstance that the wife of the workman of Yeni Shehr, who had got his share of the plunder, all the articles Nos. 822-833, besides two more pendants like Nos. 832 and 833, had the boldness to parade one Sunday with the ear-rings and pendants Nos. 822 and 823. This excited the envy of her companions; she was denounced to the Turkish authorities of Koum Kaleh, who put her and her husband in prison; and, having been threatened that her husband would be hanged if they did not give up the jewels, she betrayed the hiding-place, and thus this part of the treasure was at once recovered and is now exhibited in the Imperial Museum of Constantinople. The pair also denounced their accomplice at Kalifatli, but here the authorities came too late, because he had already had his part of the spoil melted down by a goldsmith in Ben Kioi, who, at his desire, had made of it a very large, broad, and heavy necklace, with clumsy flowery ornaments in the Turkish fashion. Thus this part of the treasure is for ever lost to science. I can, therefore, represent here only that part which was taken by the Yeni Shehr thief, because it exists, and everybody can see it in the Constantinople Museum. As both thieves declared separately on oath before the authorities of Koum Kaleh that the owl-vase No. 232, with part of the gold, was found by them immediately to the west of the well, and that the two other treasures were found close by, and indicated the exact spot of the discovery, there can be no doubt as to its accuracy.

Ilios, 1880

A Mycenaean ruler

HEINRICH SCHLIEMANN

Mycenae, 6 December 1876

For the first time since its capture by the Argives in 468 BC, and so for the first time during 2,344 years, the Acropolis of Mycenae had a garrison, whose watch-fires seen by night throughout the whole Plain of Argos carry back the mind to the watch kept for Agamemnon's return from Troy, and the signal which warned Clytemnestra and her paramour of his approach. But this time the object of the occupation by soldiery is of a more peaceful character, for it is merely intended to inspire awe among the country-people, and to prevent them from making clandestine excavations in the tombs, or approaching them while we are working in them. . . .

But of the third body, which lay at the north end of the tomb, the round face, with all its flesh, had been wonderfully preserved under its ponderous golden mask; there was no vestige of hair, but both eyes were perfectly visible, also the mouth, which, owing to the enormous weight that had pressed upon it, was wide open, and showed thirty-two beautiful teeth. From these, all the physicians who came to see the body were led to believe that the man must have died at the early age of thirty-five. The nose was entirely gone. The body having been too long for the space between the two inner walls of the tomb, the head had been pressed in such a way on the breast, that the upper part of the shoulders was nearly in a horizontal line with the vertex of the head. Notwithstanding the large golden breast-plate, so little had been preserved of the breast, that the inner side of the spine was visible in many places. In its squeezed and mutilated state, the body measured only 2 ft 4½ in from the top of the head to the beginning of the loins; the breadth of the shoulders did not exceed 1 ft 1¼ in, and the breadth of the chest 1 ft 3 in; but the large thigh bones could leave no doubt regarding the real proportions of the body. Such had been the pressure of the *débris* and stones, that the body had been reduced to a thickness of 1 in to 1½ in. The colour of the body resembled very much that of an Egyptian mummy. The forehead was ornamented with a plain round leaf of gold and a still larger one was lying on the right eye; I further observed a large and a small gold leaf on the breast below the large golden breast-cover, and a large one just above the right thigh.

The news that the tolerably well preserved body of a man of the mythic heroic age had been found, covered with golden ornaments, spread like wildfire through the Argolid, and people came by thousands from Argos, Nauplia, and the villages to see the wonder. But, nobody being able to give advice how to preserve the body, I sent for a painter to get at least an oil-painting made, for I was afraid that the body would crumble to pieces. Thus I am enabled to give a faithful likeness of the body, as it looked after all the golden ornaments had been removed. But to my great joy, it held out for two days, when a druggist from Argos, Spiridon Nicolaou by name, rendered it hard and solid by pouring on it alcohol, in which he had dissolved gum-sandarac. As there appeared to be no pebbles below it it was thought that it would be possible to lift it on an iron plate; but this was a mistake, because it was soon discovered that there was the usual layer of pebbles below the body, and all of these having been more or less pressed into the soft rock by the enormous weight which had been lying for ages upon them, all attempts made to squeeze in the iron plate below the pebble-stones, so as to be able to lift them together with the body, utterly failed. There remained, therefore, no other alternative than to cut a small trench into the rock all round the body, and make thence a horizontal incision, so as to cut out a slab, two inches thick, to lift it with the pebble-stones and the body, to put it upon a strong plank, to make around the latter a strong box, and to send this to the village of Charvati, whence it will be forwarded to Athens as soon as the Archaeological Society shall have got a suitable locality for the Mycenean antiquities. With the miserable instruments alone available here it was no easy task to detach the large slab horizontally from the rock, but it was still much more difficult to bring it in the wooden box from the deep sepulchre to the surface, and to transport it on men's shoulders for more than a mile to Charvati. But the capital interest which this body of the remote heroic age has for science, and the buoyant hope of preserving it, made all the labour appear light.

Mycenae, 1878

To His Majesty King George of the Hellenes, Athens
I am overwhelmed with joy to inform Your Majesty that I have uncovered the tombs which tradition, as set down in Pausanias, knew

as the sepulchres of Agamemnon, Cassandra, Eurymedon and their fellows, all struck down at the banquet by Clytemnestra and her lover Aegisthus. The tombs lay within a double ring of parallel stone slabs, which would only have been erected in honour of the noble persons I have named. Inside the tombs I found a vast mass of treasure consisting of archaic objects made of solid gold. These alone are enough to fill a great museum, which will be the wonder of the world, and which, in centuries to come, will draw to Greece thousands of visitors from every land. Since love of learning alone impels my researches, I naturally make no claim on this treasure, which I am truly happy to hand over intact to Greece. May God grant that this treasure becomes the foundation of a great national prosperity.

Henry Schliemann
Mycenae, 16(28) November 1876

His Majesty's Reply

To Doctor Schliemann, Argos

I have the honour to inform you that His Majesty the King has received your despatch, and has graciously instructed me to thank you for your hard work and devotion to learning and to congratulate you on your valuable discoveries. His Majesty hopes that your future endeavours are always crowned with similar happy success.

Secretary to His Majesty the King of the Hellenes
A. Calinskis
Mycenae, 1878

Telegrams translated from the French by V. M. Conrad

1. The Lion Gate as it must have appeared when Schliemann first came to Mycenae. When, after several years
of work starting in 1874, he succeeded in bringing to
light a whole "Mycenaean culture," he had opened a
new chapter of early European history.

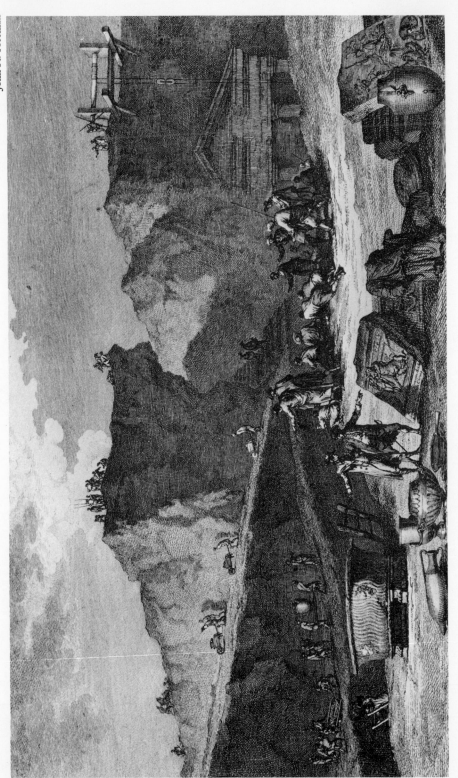

2. Herculaneum in the middle of the 18th century. When the first excavators came, they had to dig through a shield of hardened lava up to 65 feet in depth. The city was buried in 79 A.D., in Pompeii, its twin in disaster, it remains today, more than two hundred years since its discovery, a far from exhausted treasure trove.

Winckelmann in Herculaneum

JOHANN JOACHIM WINCKELMANN

JOHANN JOACHIM WINCKELMANN (1717-1768) *was born in Stendal in Prussian Saxony. His early studies of classical literature gave him a great desire to visit Rome, and in 1754 he was appointed librarian to Cardinal Passionei, adopted the Roman Catholic faith, and settled in Italy. At this time great discoveries were being made at Pompeii and Herculaneum, but the finds were jealously guarded by the excavators, who would not allow observers either on to the site or into the workshops. Winckelmann, with characteristic devious cunning, managed to circumvent this prohibition sufficiently to gather material for several publications.*

In 1768 he went to Vienna, where he was received and honoured by Maria Theresa, but the pecuniary rewards he accepted for his work proved his undoing; on the return journey he was very much too free with his money while staying at an inn at Trieste, and was attacked and murdered by a robber. He was the first archaeologist to study the development of ancient art and to attempt the logical deduction of the history and social background of the ancient world from its surviving artifacts.

A well dug for the prince of Elbeuf, at a small distance from his house, was the first thing that gave occasion to the discovery they are now pursuing. The prince had built this house in order to make his constant residence in it. It lay behind the Franciscan convent, at the extremity of, and upon, a rock of lava near the sea. It afterwards fell into the hands of the house of Falletti of Naples, from whom the present king of Spain purchased it, in order to make a fishing seat of it. The well in question had been sunk near the garden of the barefooted Carmelites. To form it, they were obliged to dig through the lava to the live rock, where the workmen found, under the ashes of mount Vesuvius, three large cloathed female statues. These the Austrian viceroy very justly laid claim to, and, keeping part of them in his hands, ordered them to Rome, where they were repaired. They were then presented to prince

Eugene, who placed them in his gardens at Vienna. On his death, his heiress sold them to the king of Poland for six thousand crowns or florins; which, I cannot positively say. Seven years after my setting out for Italy, they stood in a pavillon of the great royal garden, without the city of Dresden, along with the statues and busts of the palace of Chigi, for which the late Augustus, king of Poland, had given sixty thousand crowns. This collection was added to some ancient monuments, which cardinal Alexander Albani had ceded to the same prince for ten thousand crowns.

On the discovery of these antiquities, orders were given to the prince of Elbeuf, not to dig any further. Thirty years, however, were suffered to elapse, before any more notice was taken of them. At length, the present king of Spain, as soon as by the conquest of Naples he found himself in peaceable possession of it, chose Portico for his spring residence; and, as the well was still in being, ordered the works begun at the bottom of it to be continued, till they reached some buildings. This well still subsists. It runs down perpendicularly through the lava to the middle of the theatre (the first building discovered,) which receives no light but by it. Here an inscription was found containing the name of Herculaneum, which, by giving room to guess what place they had hit upon, determined his majesty to proceed further.

The direction of this work was given to a Spanish engineer, called Roch Joachim Alcunierre, who had followed his majesty to Naples, and is now colonel, and chief of the body of engineers at Naples. This man, who (to use the Italian proverb) knew as much of antiquities as the moon does of lobsters, has been, through this want of capacity, the occasion of many antiquities being lost. A single fact will be sufficient to prove it. The workmen having discovered a large public inscription (to what buildings it belonged, I can't say) in letters of brass two palms high; he ordered these letters to be torn from the wall, without first taking a copy of them, and thrown pell mell into a basket; and then presented them, in that condition, to the king. They were afterwards exposed for many years in the cabinet, where every one was at liberty to put them together as he pleased. Some imagined, they made these two words, IMP. AUG. I shall presently relate how a brazen four-horse chariot was served, by the same engineer's directions.

Don Roche having in time attained a higher rank, the superintendance and conduct of the works in question were committed to a Swiss officer, called Charles Weber, now a major; and it is to his good sense, that we are indebted for all the good steps since taken, to bring to light this treasure of antiquities. The first thing he did was, to make an exact map of all the subterraneous galleries, and the buildings they led to. This map he rendered still more intelligible, by a minute historical account of the whole discovery. The ancient city is to be seen in it as if freed from all the rubbish, with which it is actually incumbered. The inside of the buildings, the most private rooms, and the gardens, as well as the particular spots, where every thing taken out of them was found, appear in this map, just as they would if they were laid quite bare. But nobody is permitted to see those drawings.

The happy issue of the works undertaken at Herculaneum proved a motive for opening the earth in other places; and the doing this soon enabled them to ascertain the situation of the ancient Stabia, and led them, at Pompeii, to the vast remains of an amphitheatre, built on a hill, part of which, however, had been always visible above ground. The diggings in these places proved far less expensive, than the diggings in Herculaneum, as there was no lava to dig through. The subterraneous works at Pompeii are those, which promise most; for there they are not only sure of proceeding step by step in a great city, but have found out the principal street of it, which runs in a strait line. But, notwithstanding all this certainty of their being able to find treasures unknown to our ancestors, the works for that purpose are carried on in a very slow and indolent manner; there being but fifty men, including the Algerine and Tunisian slaves, employed in all these subterraneous places. Great a city as Pompeii is known to have been, I, in my last journey, found but eight men at work on the ruins of it.

To compensate this neglect, the method observed in digging is such, that it is impossible the least spot should escape unnoticed. On both sides of one principal trench, carried on in a right line, the workmen alternately hollow out chambers, fix palms, in length, breadth, and height; removing the rubbish, as they proceed, from every one of these chambers, to the chamber opposite it, that was last hollowed out. This method is taken, not only with a view of lessening the expence, but of supporting the earth over one chamber, with the rubbish taken out of another.

I know, that strangers, particularly travellers, who can take but a cursory view of these works, wish, that all the rubbish was entirely removed, so as to give them an opportunity of seeing, as in the plan of which I have been speaking, the inside of the whole subterraneous city of Herculaneum. They are apt to impeach the taste of the Court, and of those who direct these works. But this is a mere prejudice, which a rational examination of the nature of the spot, and other circumstances, would soon conquer. I must, however, agree with foreigners in regard to the theatre; for it might have been entirely cleared; and it was, certainly, a thing well worth the expence. I am, therefore, very far from being satisfied with their just disencumbering the seats, the form of which could be so easily gathered from the many other ancient theatres still in being; whereas they have left the stage as they found it, though the most essential part of the whole building, and the only one, of which we have no clear and precise ideas. They have, it is true, done something towards giving this satisfaction to the curious and the learned, having cleared the steps leading from the Arena, or Pit, to the stage, so that we may hope to enjoy, one day or another, though under ground, a sight of the whole theatre of Herculaneum.

As to the whole town, I must beseech those who long for a free view of it, to consider, that, the roofs of the houses having given way under the enormous weight of the superincumbent lava, nothing could be seen in that case but the walls. Besides, as those walls which had paintings on them have been cut out, and carried off, that such inestimable pieces might not suffer by the air or rain, no wall, but those of the poorest and meanest houses, would appear entire. Now, I leave any one to judge, how excessively expensive it would be to blow up such a thick and extensive crust of lava, and remove the vast quantity of ashes accumulated under it. And, after all, what would the advantage of it be? That of laying bare a parcel of old ruinous walls, merely to satisfy the ill-judged curiosity of some virtuosi, at the expence of a well built and very populous city. The theatre, indeed, might be entirely laid open at no expence but that of the garden belonging to the barefooted Carmelites, under which it lies.

Those, who have a mind to see the walls of ancient buildings formerly buried in the same manner, may satisfy their curiosity at Pompeii. But few persons, except Englishmen, have resolution enough to go so far on that account. At Pompeii the ground may be dug up, and turned topsy-turvy, without any risk, and at small expence, the land lying over it being of little value. Formerly, indeed, it used to produce the most delicious wine; but that it now produces is so middling, that the country would suffer very little by the entire destruction of its vineyards. I must add, that this country is more subject than any other to those dangerous exhalations called *Musseta* by the inhabitants, which burn up all the productions of the earth. This I had an opportunity of observing on a great number of elms, which, six years before, I had seen in a very thriving way. These exhalations generally precede an eruption, and are first felt in places under ground. Accordingly, a few days before the last eruption, some of the inhabitants dropt down dead on entering their cellars.

It appears by the indolent manner in which these works are conducted, that a fine field of discovery must remain to posterity. As great treasures might perhaps, be discovered at the same expence, by digging at Pozzuoli, Baiae, Cuma, and Misenum, where the Romans had their finest country seats. But the Court is so well satisfied with the discoveries now making, that it has forbid the earth to be dug any where else below a certain depth. Certain it is, that, in the districts I have been mentioning, there are ancient buildings, hitherto little, or not at all, noticed, as appears by what I am going to relate. An English Captain, whose ship lay at anchor two years ago in these parts, discovered under Baiae a spacious and beautiful hall, accessible only by water, in which there still remained very fine ornaments in stucco. It is only since my return from Naples that I heard of this discovery, of which, however, I have seen the drawing. Mr Adams, of Edinburgh in Scotland, gave me a circumstantial account of it. He is a lover of the arts, and intends to visit Greece, and Asia Minor.

A Critical Account of the Situation and Destruction of Herculaneum and Pompeii, 1771

The plaster corpses of Pompeii

AUGUSTUS GOLDSMIDT, ESQ *communicated the following account of the discovery of some skeletons at Pompeii in the spring of the year.*

'Happening to spend last winter in Rome, I made a short excursion during Lent to Naples, being anxious, at the request of several friends, to bring back a particular report of some interesting discoveries of human remains lately made at Pompeii.

'Through the kindness of Signor Vertumni, a Roman artist of some eminence then residing at Naples, I obtained an introduction to the Cavaliere Fiorelli, the government director of the works, who invited me to join a party shortly about to explore the ruins of Pompeii.

'After visiting several of the streets and of the less recently discovered portions of the city, we proceeded to a small museum fitted up under the direction of Signor Fiorelli, and in which he hopes to retain, so far as possible, on the spot the numerous objects of interest daily brought to light in the course of the more extended researches which have been made since the advent of the present government of Italy. In two of the rooms in the museum are deposited the bodies, as nearly as possible in the relative positions in which they were found; and I am much indebted to the kindness and courtesy of the Cavaliere Fiorelli, who afforded me every information on the subject of these discoveries, and also allowed me to inspect the journals which are kept of the progress and result of each day's labour.

'It seems that early in February last the remains of a linen cloth or bag were found in the course of removing the loose soil which now covers the remains of Pompeii, that contained several coins, ornaments, and two iron keys. Close to this a hole was accidentally made by one of the workmen with his pickaxe, and, on investigating this, Signor Fiorelli perceived that there existed a cavity of some extent. He had for some time entertained the idea that there were probably human bodies buried in the ruins of the city, the remains of which might have perished though leaving their impressions in the sandy covering. He therefore caused plaster of Paris in a very liquid state to be poured into the cavity;

this he continued to do, blowing also with considerable force, so as to cause the liquid plaster to permeate the centre cavity.

'As soon as the cavity was filled with plaster, he had the earth round it carefully removed. The ashes in which the bodies were buried must have fallen in a damp state, and hardened gradually by the lapse of time, and as the soft parts of the bodies decayed and shrunk a hollow was formed between the bodies and the crust of soil. This formed the cavity into which the plaster was poured. In the bony parts, the space left void being very small, the coat of plaster is proportionately thin, and many portions of the extremeties and the crania are left exposed.

'So intimately did these ashes penetrate, and so thoroughly has the cast been taken, that the texture of the under garments, drawers, and sort of inner vest with sleeves is distinctly visible. The bodies, it may be noticed, present a tumified appearance in the abdominal region, as if from the action of water.

'In the first room is the figure of a female, apparently about thirty years old, or perhaps more, lying on the right side in a twisted and apparently somewhat contorted position. The left hand is raised, and on the little finger is a ring much corroded, apparently of silver; the head is thrown back, and the hair, which appears to have been very plentiful, is still visible; the folds of the dress are quite distinct; the bones of the feet, which are stretched out, are protruding; the ancles and wrist joints and the extremities of the fingers are most delicately formed, and their slenderness and the great length and better proportions of the thumbs would seem to show that this female was of gentler blood than the two hereafter described.

'In the next room there are two shelves; on the first is the figure of a man lying on his back, with one hand grasping his garment, which he has pulled up to the chest, leaving the whole of the lower portion of the figure exposed, which is of very fine proportions; a curious peculiarity still distinctly traceable is that the hair of the *pubes* is shaved so as to leave it in a semi-circular form, such as may be observed in the statues, and which has, I believe, been generally supposed to be merely a sculptural conventionality. The other hand is extended and strongly clenched, and the limbs in an attitude of rigidity almost amounting to convulsion. These facts, as well as the expression of pain and horror distinctly traceable in the countenance, would seem to show that the unfortunate man died fully conscious of the dreadful fate which awaited him, and against which he vainly struggled. The bones of the feet are exposed.

'On the other slab in the second room lie two female figures, Signor Fiorelli supposes, probably of the family of the man.

'These two are lying with the heads at opposite extremities of the table, so that the lower portion of the one figure is parallel to the other; they are the bodies of a woman apparently from 30 to 40 and a girl of 15 or 16. The woman is lying on the left side, with one arm slightly raised, and the other by her side, apparently in an easier position than the two figures before described, as if she had suffered less.

'The younger is also lying on her left side, the head thus turned in a contrary direction to that of the elder; the face is supported on the left arm, which is placed so as to protect the eyes, and the arm and hand are in an attitude as if holding a cloth or handkerchief over the mouth, apparently protecting herself as much as possible from the falling ashes. The form of this figure is most beautiful, especially the loins and *nates*, which are perfectly modelled; the hand and arm are also very delicate, though both these figures would appear to have been of inferior rank to the first. The tissue of the dress is distinctly visible. I should have mentioned that, in the elder, traces of cloth leglets and the fastenings of a kind of ancle boots are distinctly visible.

'The symmetry of the back and loins of this figure, as well as that of the younger already alluded to, are most remarkable, and, occurring as it does in bodies taken by chance, would seem to go a long way to show that the ancients had actually before them individual specimens of that perfect symmetry which they have handed down to us in those magnificent statues which are still the world's wonder, and that they were not an assemblage of the characteristics of different individuals into one imaginary form.

'These discoveries are in many particulars worthy of the attention of Archaeologists, and reflect much credit on Signor Fiorelli, to whose critical acumen they are due.'

Thanks were returned for these Communications.

Proceedings of the Society of Antiquaries of London, 1863

The discovery of the 'Venus de Milo'

CLAUDE TARRAL

Perhaps the most rewarding age for an archaeologist to live in was the second half of the nineteenth century. Archaeology, regarded as a means of scientific study of the past through its artifacts 'rather than merely a fruitful source of collectors' pieces, was still in its infancy and offered immense scope to scholar and excavator alike. Their findings created the framework upon which the chronology of the classical world has largely been built, but quite apart from the value of these discoveries as historical evidence, statues were excavated which must rank among the greatest treasures of mankind as pure works of art.

It is exactly forty-four years since chance brought to light the enchanting Venus de Milo, the pearl of the Louvre. Unhappily, this short interval has seen the loss of the leading actors in this magnificent triumph over the passage of time. The young ship's ensign, Dumont d'Urville, the first to be struck by the beauty of this precious statue, and who drew and described it with so much understanding, met a tragic death in a railway accident. Fauvel, the last survivor of the Choiseul expedition, the distinguished scholar Quatrèmere de Quincy, the learned Clarac, Forbin Janson, the Marquis de Rivière, Émeric David, are no longer with us. Marcellus, who had the signal honour of receiving the Venus and transporting it to France, died recently while still in his prime. So we are reduced to drawing almost all our information from the records they have left to posterity. M. Brest, France's consular agent at Melos, who displayed such laudable energy in the acquisition of this masterpiece, is still alive; but he is past eighty, and I fear his memory is no longer very accurate; he believes that both his own superiors and the historians have treated him unjustly; to him our ravishing goddess, far from being a joyful recollection, is a source of great bitterness; if, however, his grievances are well founded, we should pity this venerable old man, and in that case there would still be time to soothe the distress of his last years by a speedy restitution. M. Beulé openly declares that France owes the Venus de Milo to M. Brest; this tribute requires a detailed appraisal. I have before me a very full unpublished report, written two years ago by M. Brest, in which he states that he 'purchased the immortal Venus for France, towards the end of 1819, from a Greek peasant, Theodore Kendrotas, for the sum of 600 piastres plus 18 piastres for packing, a total of 618 piastres, at that time equivalent to the same amount of francs'. M. Brest then had the statue transferred to his house, and retained it, in spite of threats from Prince Mourousi; subsequently the torso was stolen and placed on board a disused ship; M. Brest, assisted by lieutenant Berranger and twelve men from the crew of the schooner *Estafette*, recovered it by main force. It was M. Brest, too, who undertook to secure the leading citizens of the island of Melos against Mourousi's vengeance, and had to pay the fine of 6,000 piastres which the despot imposed on them; only ten years later was M. Brest reimbursed for this outlay, but by then the difference in the exchange rate was very unfavourable to him, and he lost 5,000 francs; this loss, with other sums expended, was never repaid him. M. Brest still declares that in the absence of the Marquis de Rivière, M. Beaurepaire, the chargé d'affaires at Constantinople, contrived to trick him into handing over all the documents and receipts which substantiated his claims. These are indeed serious accusations against the dead; we should accept them only with reservations, for it may be that M. Brest's memory is leading him astray unawares. Here are some grounds for doubting the accuracy of his statements. First, M. Brest has never sought public restitution for these numerous injuries he alleges he suffered. He maintains that he bought the Venus towards the end of 1819; as soon as it was detached and lifted from its niche, he had it removed to his house; however, this last statement is contradicted by Dumont d'Urville; at least four months later (19 April 1820) he saw the upper part of the Venus in a Greek peasant's shed, and found the lower part still in its niche. M. Brest also says that no arms were found, and yet d'Urville saw two arms and a hand holding an apple, which were delivered to Marcellus with the Venus and other fragments. M. Brest mentions only two Hermes figures discovered with the Venus; there were three. Here is enough evidence that M. Brest is mistaken in certain factual details; he may be right in others. It is for the Chancellery of France to examine his claims, and if necessary make him honourable restitution, since it would be shameful to France if ingratitude on such a scale were to taint the possession of a monument of unfading glory.

Here is an abridged account of the discovery of the Venus; it is most unfortunate that the circumstances of that discovery are so poorly documented, for a number of important archaeological points are very puzzling. The first description of the jewel of the Louvre is that of the young d'Urville; it is still the best; though not an archaeologist, his instinctive observation is a model for antiquarians. His remarkable report is little known; it deserves serious study, and as it supports my conjecture, I shall quote the most important passages.

'On April 19 1820,' says d'Urville (*Annales maritimes*, Bajot, 1821, p. 150), 'I went to look over some classical fragments found at Melos shortly before our arrival. About three weeks before we reached the island, a Greek peasant was digging in his field, which lay within the bounds of the site of ancient Melos, when he found some pieces of dressed stone; since these blocks are used by the local people for building their houses and have a certain value, he was impelled to dig deeper, and so came to uncover a kind of niche in which he found a marble statue, two Hermes figures, and some other marble fragments.

'The statue was in two pieces, joined by means of two strong iron pins. The peasant, fearful of losing the fruit of his labours, had the upper part of the statue and the two Hermes figures removed to a shed; the lower part remained in its niche. I examined everything carefully, and the various pieces seemed to me to be of fine style, as far as my poor knowledge of the arts permitted me to judge.

'I measured the two parts of the statue separately, and found the whole to be very nearly 6 feet in height. It was the representation cf a nude woman; her left hand was raised, holding an apple, and her right hand supported an intricately folded wrap which fell carelessly from her loins to her feet; but both hands are damaged, and actually detached from the body. The only remaining foot is bare; the ears are pierced, and must have held ear rings. All these attributes would seem sufficiently to fit the Venus of the judgement of Paris; but where, then, are Juno, Minerva and the handsome shepherd? It is true that a foot clad in a buskin and a third hand were found at the same time; however, the name of the island, Melos, is closely akin to the word *melon*, meaning 'apple'. Is it not likely that the chief attribute of the statue indicates this verbal link?

'The two Hermes figures which accompanied it in its niche are undistinguished; one is surmounted by the head of a woman or child and the other has the face of an old man with a long beard. Above the entry to the niche is a marble slab $4\frac{1}{2}$ feet long and 6 to 8 inches broad, carrying an inscription; of this, only the first half has survived weathering; the rest is completely effaced. This loss cannot be evaluated, perhaps we might have gained thereby some light on the history of this island, which by every indication was once most prosperous, but whose fate after the Athenian invasion, that is, for more than twenty-two centuries, is completely unknown to us. We might at least have learnt on what occasion, and by whom, these statues were dedicated. I copied this inscription. The pedestal of one of the Hermes figures must also have carried an inscription, but its letters were too worn for me to decipher. At the time of our journey to Constantinople, the ambassador questioned me about this statue; I gave him my opinion, and I sent M. de Marcellus a copy of the account you have just read. On my return, M. de Rivière informed me that he had purchased the statue for the Museum. I have since learnt that M. de Marcellus reached Melos at the very moment when the statue was awaiting shipment for another destination; but after various difficulties, this friend of the arts finally succeeded in saving this precious relic of antiquity for France.'

In this manner the young naturalist d'Urville personally saw the lower part of the Venus in its niche; he states that the upper part was joined to the lower by two strong iron pins; this would support the belief that the Greek peasant removed them, and that the Venus was entire, and standing upright as M. Brest describes. But other accounts state that the Venus was found in two separate pieces; the clear marks of a spade on the torso bear out this last version. D'Urville is most explicit on the subject of the two hands, the left holding the apple, the right supporting the drapery; he is mistaken in his designation of a Hermes, our little Mercury, which he takes for a woman or child – a fact which shows his lack of classical scholarship; he could not decipher the inscription on its base – which indicates his unfamiliarity with epigrammatic studies. The copy he made of the inscription on the marble slab above the niche has proved very valuable, as I shall show below. It is my belief that Dumont d'Urville played a most important part in acquiring the Venus; M. Brest has no standing in the world of the arts – his opinion could not influence the ambassador at Constantinople; but the enlightened view of d'Urville was a powerful factor in saving this unique monument for France.

Concerning the excavation at Melos, Marcellus has left us some details which seem to be accurate, although they contradict M. Brest.

'Towards the end of February 1820, a Greek named Yorgos was busy digging in his field when he found a kind of oblong niche built in the rock; he managed to clear this little edifice, and also a narrow recess sunk 5 or 6 feet below ground level. Lying there in huddled

confusion he found the top part of the statue, which he at once removed to his shed, three Hermes figures, some statue bases and other
marble debris; a fortnight later, continuing his investigation, he found
the lower part of the same statue and some fragmentary classical
sculptures.' Here now is the description of the Venus made on sight
by Marcellus. 'The statue was made of two blocks, joined together by
an iron pin which has not been recovered; the folds of drapery on the
left hip concealed the line where the two pieces met. The whole mass
of hair (we must understand by this expression only the chignon) was
detached, but quite well preserved and elegant in style. One by one on
the bridge of the schooner *Estafette* I displayed the three Hermes figures
and the classical fragments, which had all been delivered to me.' In
a note Marcellus adds: 'On a marble slab 4½ feet long by 8 inches
broad were some words which seemed to have no connection with the
statue; this inscription was partially effaced, and was left at Melos.'
What extraordinary folly! And yet the intelligent d'Urville had judged
it very important and deplored its debasement! Marcellus makes this
observation: 'Volumes of dissertations in praise of the Venus have
made their appearance; among these works we note the pages of
Quatremère de Quincy, Clarac and Saint-Victor, full of taste and
scholarship. Some sketches of poses conjecturally restored had been
submitted to the King; there had even been an attempt to fit to the
statue's shoulders two arms and a hand holding an apple, which I had
also brought back; but it was easy to see that these roughly shaped
arms could only have belonged to the Venus in a first and crude
attempt at restoration, attributed to the eighth-century Christians.
It was shown (by whom?) that the statue, loaded with robes, gold
necklaces and ear-rings, had represented the Panagia (Holy Virgin) in
the little Greek church whose ruins I saw at Melos.' Here are absurd-
ities if you like; diplomacy does not give a man discretion as an
amateur archaeologist. I have quoted these sentences to show that
Marcellus really did bring to France two fragmentary arms, with a
hand holding an apple, the arms and hand exactly described by
d'Urville. How could Clarac be unaware of this fact, and write the
following: 'It was believed that the left arm was entirely missing; but
on visiting Melos to confirm for himself all that concerned the statue,
the Marquis de Rivière instituted fresh excavations, and the fragments
of an arm and a hand were happily discovered. These, from the quality
of the marble and the workmanship, could be supposed to belong to
our Venus, and we see from the holes of the pin and the marks of

tearing that the arm was fixed to it.' Are this left arm and hand those referred to and brought back by Marcellus? On studying Marcellus and examining the carving of the Venus where the fragment of arm is shaped, one is inclined to tax Clarac with confusion; however, I read in the unpublished report of M. Brest that he was in fact instructed by M. de Rivière to make new excavations at Melos, and that two arms were discovered which M. Brest thought belonged to the Venus. 'The right arm was in three pieces, the fingers of the hand closed on an apple and the left in two pieces, with three fingers closed, and the thumb and the index finger joined, apparently holding something.' M. Brest states that he sent these fragments to Toulon, addressed to M. Bedfort.

In his unpublished report, M. Brest affirms that 'the Venus had no arms; the crumbling of the upper part of the niche could have broken them, and also caused a light grazing on the statue's nose.'

There are a number of divergencies between these historians. M. Brest claims that the Venus had no arms, but d'Urville saw them, and says that the left hand held the apple; Marcellus received the fragment-ary hands from M. Brest and brought them back to France. Clarac speaks of a left hand with the apple, M. Brest of a right hand; but, to be honest, M. Brest could very well be wrong here; otherwise it would mean that two fragments of Venus with the apple were dug up at Melos. Today the Louvre has only one piece of the arm and the left hand; I have taken a mould of these, and there is no doubt that they belong to our statue; I believe these two pieces are the same as those seen and described by d'Urville and brought back to France by Mar-cellus. Clarac only mentions a single arm recovered in the second exca-vation at Melos; M. Brest says he dug up two. M. de Sartiges, ambassador to Rome, visited Melos some years ago, and he assures me that M. Brest told him of the two arms which he sent to France; M. Gobineau, a most distinguished archaeologist although a skilful diplomat, met M. Brest at Constantinople on returning from a mission to Persia; M. Brest reiterated to him the same statements concerning the two arms. What is certain is that several pieces of the Venus, fragments of a right and left arm and a left hand holding an apple, three Hermes figures, a pedestal with a Greek inscription and part of the statue base passed the threshold of the Louvre; here we must admit a deplorable, inexplicable occurrence: today the Museum no longer possesses either the right hand, the fragment of base, or the pedestal of the Hermes-Mercury, adorned with its priceless Greek inscription. M. de Longpérier has made exhaustive investigations to recover them, even excavating the floors of the cellars, but in vain – these fragments are lost for ever. In the arts, as in politics, prejudice, vanity, scholastic pride and ignorance play a large part. The Greeks and Romans had good reason to make the guardians of their art treasures answerable for failure with their lives. In the reign of Louis Philippe, one man with great influence at the Louvre suggested to the King that he could make him magnificent table-tops from the ancient monuments of Egypt; art, said this scholarly architect, would lose nothing thereby, and the furniture of the Crown would gain a good deal. I have heard a fashionable painter and fine speaker declare that if he were director of the Louvre, he would kick all those ugly Egyptians out of the door. How should we explain the mysterious loss of these fragments of the Venus? It was maintained that they could not have belonged to the original statue, that they were restorations, and therefore merely worthless pieces of marble. Clarac, admittedly, thought the inscription important; but it obstructed his theory that the Venus was the work of Praxiteles. All this tended to expose the fragments to destruction; their loss will be a perpetual stigma on the Louvre authorities, since the worst mutilation of the Venus actually took place within the walls of this sanctuary of the arts!

Forty-three years ago in these precincts, your distinguished permanent secretary, Quatremère de Quincy, came to pay a brilliant tribute to the adorable Venus de Milo; his wise and graceful speech moved his audience profoundly, for then as now the Venus was the topic of conversation in every salon, the preoccupation of every artist. Her dreadful mutilation stirred the imagination of antiquarians; men asked what, before the sacrilege, was the pose of this proud goddess. Every man had his own murmured suggestion. And who better than the author of *Jupiter Olympien* could claim to throw light on so knotty a problem? Quatremère explained with his customary lucid scholarship that the noble figure once represented Venus in victory, grouped with or talking to Paris or Mars, that she was the creation of Praxiteles or his school. But even the great authority of Quatremère failed to convince the world; Clarac opposed the idea of a group propounded by Quatremère; he believed the statue stood alone, but related to other figures which could have been Paris and the two goddesses, to whom in proud disdain, she showed the apple, prize of her victory. The conviction of Clarac was short-lived. The scholar Millingen discovered a Corinthian medallion struck under S. Severus: on it, a half-draped female figure holds a shield in her hands, in which she appears to be

admiring her reflection. Using this as a guide, Millingen restored the
Venus of Capua, which is so like our famous statue; but he forgot that
the base of the Capua statue once bore the two little feet of Cupid: all
the same, poor Clarac was seduced by Millingen – the Venus de Milo
must also have been admiring her reflection in a shield; farewell apple,
farewell his pride, farewell the disdain of the victorious goddess!
Emeric David affirmed that the Venus had never formed part of a
group, seeing in her a true statue: 'She does not represent Venus, but
rather the nymph Melos, that is to say, the personification of the island
of Melos.' M. Paillot de Montabert says she is more likely a Muse.
Might she not rather be the courtesan and musician, Glycera of Argos,
a statue executed by that Herodotus of Olynthus who worked with
Praxiteles on the statue of Phryne? Could we not naturally imagine the
lyre which she held in her left hand, while the right prepared to play?
Who will dare to answer these questions? M. de Montabert says only
that our precious Venus 'is no more than a copy which Herodotus of
Olynthus would have disowned'. Finally, other scholars of Montabert's
calibre suppose the Venus in the act of drawing a bow, dressing her
hair, watching her reflection in a mirror, and as a Muse writing history
on a great tablet which would automatically conceal her magnificent
bust. In conclusion, our distinguished national historian, M. Thiers,
believes the Venus to be a Victory blowing a trumpet; he has even
shown me the point where the trumpet was attached to her knee; thus
even this great connoisseur of the arts commits his little peccadillo . . .
(Here the manuscript breaks off)

Revue Archéologique, series IV, vol. VII, 1906
Translated from the French by V. M. Conrad

Max Hirmer

3. The Venus de Milo.

4. The Charioteer of Delphi.

The charioteer of Delphi

Tuesday 28 April 1896 must have been a red-letter day in the annals of the great excavation of Delphi. That was the day on which the team working in the ruins of the house of Kounoupis had just broken down a water conduit, crudely fashioned of baked clay, when there appeared the lower part of a bronze statue (inv. 3484), 1·28 metres in height and wearing a tunic which fell in folds 'with the regularity of Ionic column fluting'. Near by they recovered the life-size back leg of a horse, also bronze (inv. 3485). At the same time they took out of the earth an inscribed block bearing a dedication in verse (inv. 3517). A photograph taken at the actual moment of discovery shows the statue and the inscription still half-buried in soil. Two other bronze fragments completed the find: 'a shaft with reins attached' (inv. 3542) and the bent end of a yoke, also with 'reins' attached (inv. 3543).

On the evening of Friday 1 May, the exploration of the house of Kounoupis brought to light 'the upper part of the statue whose feet had been discovered on Tuesday in the same spot' (inv. 3520). Homolle, at first glance, dated it accurately: 'beginning of the fifth century'. Further bronze pieces were extracted: the right forearm (inv. 3540), with fragmentary reins still in its hand; another back leg (inv. 3538) and a horse's tail (inv. 3541).

Discoveries continued to be made in the same place for a few days longer: on Thursday 7 May, it was a horse's foreleg (inv. 3597) and the other end of the yoke (inv. 3598); finally, on Saturday 9 May, a triangular pad (inv. 3618) concluded the series of finds which might be presumed to belong to the same group.

Such were the circumstances in which the Charioteer came to light. They are related above according to the *Journal of excavations* preserved in the archives of the French School. This record, it should be stressed, contains the only reliable account. Written on the spot, day by day, by one of the members of the School who were supervising the dig, it is the sole source for valuable details. These agree with later reports by the excavators, Homolle, Bourguet and Convert. In the face of these expert testimonies, supported by the text of the *Journal*, which was

contemporaneous with the discoveries, the recollections of an uneducated workman, sought many years later by a foreign scholar who
ignored the authentic records, deserve no credence.

Homolle instantly realised that the find was exceptional. Two telegrams, on 9 and 11 May, alerted the *Académie des Inscriptions*. On
12 May, the Director of the School sent a letter with two photographs
to Paris: he transcribed the inscription, identifying it as a dedication by
Polyzalos the Deinomenid, and briefly touched on the merits of the
statue. On 5 June, he presented an address before the Academy in
which we find for the first time a detailed catalogue of the extant
fragments of the group, a description of the Charioteer, precise notes
on its execution, and an opinion as to its date ('beginning of the second
quarter of the fifth century') and style. Finally, as early as the following
year, he published in *Monuments et Memoires, Fondation E. Piot*, IV,
1897, pp. 169-208, pl. 15-16, an article entitled '*l'Aurige de Delphes*',
which constituted the first scholarly publication on the statue. And so
this work, which satisfied every requirement of scientific study of the
period, offered the evidence to learned scrutiny barely a year after the
discovery.

One does not know which to admire more, the exemplary diligence
of the author or his accuracy of judgement. If certain portions of his
account, on points of minor importance, are now discounted, all the
essential part remains valid. The majority of later commentators have
gone astray in just that degree in which they have diverged from
Homolle. Undoubtedly modern archaeology is more pedantic than
that of a few years ago. It demands minutely detailed descriptions and
a great wealth of measurements and calculations. If these modern
standards give rise now and then to a certain idle ostentation, yet they
are in accord with a very natural feeling, which is the respect for
evidence. So it has become necessary, after fifty years of commentaries
and controversies, to reissue in a more detailed form the masterly
publication of 1897. The work of R. Hampe, in the *Denkmäler* of
Brunn-Bruckmann, work in which valuable observations figure side
by side with glaring errors, made this new publication still more vital.
But the eye which examines is nothing without the spirit which
interprets. Homolle, at first glance, both saw accurately and judged
exactly. This work could not commence without an open tribute to
him. . . .

The Charioteer is an *ephebe* of athletic but slim build: the broad
shoulders denote strength, but the delicate extremities, hands and feet,

have distinction. The general impression of slightness is accentuated by his dress, which is the long charioteer's tunic, the white *xystis* traditionally worn for racing. It comes down almost to his ankles in long, parallel folds from the belt, which is set very high, above the stomach. This positioning of the waistline, distinctly higher than the hips, emphasises the slimness of the outline. Above the belt, the tunic 'blouses' appreciably, especially at the sides. It shapes to a pointed neckline in front and behind, and ends on the shoulders and arms in a seam which holds a mass of gathers. The combined play of this seaming and of a band which passes under the armpits forms elbow-length sleeves.

The Charioteer stands erect, but without rigidity. His bare feet, set close together, are placed squarely, turned a little outwards, toes slightly curled, giving the body adequate purchase on the unyielding floor of the chariot. By a rotation of the body's axis which becomes more and more pronounced, hips, shoulders, head and the direction of the eyes turn progressively to the right: this controlled movement animates the entire figure. The arms were extended to hold the reins, elbow slightly forward, forearm level: the shoulders are supple and rounded, braced for the motion of the chariot. The right arm, alone preserved below the sleeve, is finely modelled, its long muscles indicated with great subtlety. The long, slim fingers, their nails cut round by an engraving-tool, were closed upon a cylindrical object in addition to the reins: here we can restore the goad (κέντρον) The four reins leading to the two right-hand horses must have been held by the thumb against the stock of the goad, then passing between this and the palm of the hand before falling back vertically to waist height. Three of these reins have been recovered still in place. The left hand must have been similarly positioned, holding the four reins from the two left-hand horses of the quadriga.

The head attracts particular notice. Set on a long, powerful neck, it is modelled within a long oval, with the widest point over the temples. The ears, small and prominent, framed by curls of hair in relief, are the only breaks in this rigorous contour. The hair lies plastered on the skull in short strands, engraved rather than moulded, except on the neck and round the ears, where curls spring out. A few wandering locks sketch side-whiskers on the cheeks. A broad band crosses the forehead and confines the hair at the temples; it is summarily fastened on the neck, where the two ends are merely crossed, without a knot. This band was decorated with inlays which have partially worn away:

between two darker bands, a simple meander pattern, each winding being the frame for a Greek cross. The inlays were in copper (horizontal bands) and silver (meander and Greek cross); the lips were perhaps covered with a thin layer of copper.

The features, despite an evident stylization, are extraordinarily lifelike. The heavy, rounded chin flows without a break into the curve of the jaw. The cheeks are full, yet their delicate planes allow the structure of the cheekbones to be seen. The mouth, with its strong lips, is half open and seems to be drawing breath. The lips are outlined by a slight ridge. A little opening is visible at each corner. The rather narrow nose, with its flat, well-marked bridge, would appear pinched, if the nostrils, emphasised by an engraved line, were not dilated as if inhaling. The eyebrows, in low relief, follow the line from the nose, after a sharp change of direction at its root, then lengthen and fade out towards the temples. Finally, the eyes, long and almond-shaped, are unequally opened, the left a little less than than the right. Between the added eyelashes, cut from bronze wire, the eyeballs have retained their poly-chrome inlay. The white of the eye is made of white paste, the iris, of a very light chestnut, is rimmed with a black circle and itself forms a narrow border to the black round of the pupil. The harmony of these hard stones is so perfect that the combination seems a single whole: its polish picks up reflections and imparts to the expression a strange intensity. . . .

Erected to commemorate a victory at the Games, the group dedi-cated by Polyzalos had, above all, to be truthful, but with that higher and more sublime truth which belongs to archaic offerings. It does not represent the winning Charioteer and his chariot: rather, it is identified with the donor, he *is* in a sense the Charioteer, for all time. In addition, he is able, in the dedication, to speak in the first person, within a tradition formula which is not yet emptied of meaning: Πολυζαλὸς μ'ἀνέθηκεν. This vital truth of equivalence, in a testimony intended to defy the centuries, imposed the scrupulous reproduction of charac-teristic features, of functional details, without which the spectator would not have believed in the image. From this springs the careful fidelity both in the anatomical detail of the horses and in the execution of the harness and chariot. From this comes the feeling of presence which the statue creates to this day.

At that period, the consecration of an offering was before everything an act of piety, and the satisfaction of human vanity had as yet intruded only to a minor degree. The Charioteer is the contemporary of

Aeschylus, Pindar and Bacchylides. He belongs to a time of sincere belief; its feeling stamps him. In his slightly stiff bearing, his tinge of lofty reserve, there is something religious, an evocation of the austere nobility of a great chorale. One might say that he was listening to a hymn. He has just bound on the fillet of victory: it is a solemn moment, requiring meditation and devotion. With his skilled, masterful hand – ῥυσίδιφρον χεῖρα πλεξίπποιο φωτός (Pindar, *Isthm.* II, 21) – he has known how to hold back or unleash to good purpose the ardour of his team, and so to gain the favour of Phoebus. He stands there as a good servant both of God and of his prince. The statue is an expression of the man: full of strength and modesty, aware of his achievement, but free from all pride.

More than any other, the severe style in art was fitted to express this attitude. It suited alike the Athenian warriors of Marathon and Salamis and the aristocratic rulers of the Dorian cities, still filled with the greatness of their destiny. In the bronze statue this art finds its supreme expression. The craft of the artist here, by fire and iron, masters an intractable material and bends it to his will. The sculptor, inheriting the swift, continuous advance of generations, still counts it a point of honour to rival nature. But his overriding brain subordinates his creation to an artistic balance. Attracted by subtle indications, the eye may now and then, in the motionless form, catch the trace of a movement. So the work achieves a kind of vibrant stillness, which dazzles.

With admirable conscientiousness, as a craftsman who seeks nothing short of perfection, the sculptor has patiently toiled at his task: he might justly claim to have achieved it. No earthly sensuality is his; no exaltation of the human body as a natural collection of plastic forms. The preoccupation with realism here revealed has no roots in any appreciation of the physical beauty of the world. All is subject to the abstract concept which informs the whole figure, to its very fingertips. It is like a monument where the architect has already calculated every part. Even when it reproduces the model with scrupulous exactitude, one is aware that it has been weighed in the mind and re-ordered.

So abstract a style is hardly conceivable outside Athens. There alone developed, in the archaic period, a new idea of sculpture in which the artist studies the living form as a geometrician, resolving it into form-ulae, a naturalist, observing in order to understand, and a technician, seeing each difficulty as a challenge. So Attic art possesses a quality of purity, of conscious design, of clarity. This lucid and dedicated art stamps its best sculptures with a slightly cold intellectualism which marks them out almost as a signature: so, at Delphi itself, with the metopes of the Athenian Treasury. The Charioteer is of the same spirit. It is because he exists to be understood that he is examined, peered over and turned to once again. He is not for passive contemplation – the cold look of his stone and enamel eyes forbids it.

Fouilles de Delphes, vol. 4, part 5, 1890

Translated from the French by V. M. Conrad

The discovery of the Hermes of Praxiteles

ERNST CURTIUS

ERNST CURTIUS (1814–1896) *was born at Lubeck in Germany. He travelled extensively in Greece and achieved a high reputation as both a historian and an archaeologist, accepting in 1844 the appointment of Extraordinary Professor at the University of Berlin and of Tutor to Prince Frederick William. He is best known, however, for his work at Olympia, where in 1874 he concluded an agreement to excavate the site, which was thereafter entrusted exclusively to German archaeologists. His scholarly and painstaking excavations at Olympia, especially of the Temple of Zeus and the Heraion, brought to light many superb works of Greek sculpture and architecture, but none more deservedly famous than the marble Hermes, thought by many to be an original carving by the fourth-century sculptor Praxiteles.*

A telegram of 8 May eventually brought the most important news. It read: 'Considerable remains of the Heraion 80 metres north of the opisthodom of the temple, 63 feet wide; whereupon one of the oldest and most important buildings within the altis, the length of which Pausanias gives as 63 feet, has been discovered.'

Reports of 8 May give further information on the Temple of Hera. A doric temple with a peristyle and staircase has appeared. A few column drums with twenty grooves, as well as sections of the cella wall 2–3 metres high, still *in situ*; the capitals show ancient forms, the width of the lowest stage is 19·95 metres. How this measurement can be brought into agreement with the incomplete place in Pausanias (V, 16, 1) is still uncertain; the identity of the building has, however, been proved by the finding of a Parian marble statue which Pausanias places in the Temple of Hera. It is a youthful Hermes holding the young Dionysus on his arm, the work of Praxiteles. The statue was discovered in the cella lying on its face where it had fallen, close by the costumed Roman female figure mentioned in Report 17. The arm and the legs beneath the knees of Hermes are missing, as is the upper half of the child; on the other hand, the head of Hermes was found undamaged, and he stands casually supporting himself against a tree trunk which is covered by his discarded cloak; his raised right hand seems once to have held a bunch of grapes. The height of the figure is now 1·80 metres. The composition vividly calls to mind the group of Eirene and Pluto in Munich. A section of the costume which hangs in magnificent folds is formed out of a separate piece of marble; the surface of the whole is superbly preserved. Less important features such as hair and the back are neglected. There are traces of red paint on lips and hair. As a result of this important find everything is being done to excavate as much as possible of the Temple of Hera before the end of this season.

Archaeologische Zeitung, vol. 35, part 1, 1877
Translated from the German by C. M. Kaine

5. The Hermes of Praxiteles.

6. The reconstructed Stoa of Attalus in Athens, with the Acropolis in the background. In 1953 Homer A. Thompson set to work on this most prodigious and expensive (2 million dollars) of reconstructions, faithful to the original in the smallest detail, using the original materials.

The rebuilding of the Stoa

PAUL MACKENDRICK

PAUL MACKENDRICK *is an American, and was educated at Harvard University and Balliol College, Oxford. He was formerly Professor of Classics at the University of Wisconsin, and now holds the post of Professor in charge of classical studies at the American Academy in Rome.*

The Attalids were not content to adorn only their own city. Attalus II (159-138) had been educated in Athens, and in gratitude he built on the east side of the Athenian Agora the stoa that bears his name. Attalus' brother, Eumenes II (197-159), had already set the example by building a stoa on the south slope of the Athenian Acropolis, between the theater of Dionysus and the spot where later the Odeum of Herodes Atticus was to stand. Both served practical purposes: promenade, shopping center, grandstand – the Panathenaic procession passed the Stoa of Attalus on its way to the Parthenon. The Middle Stoa, at right angles to the Stoa of Attalus, half promenade, half market, like the Stoa of Philip V at Delos (to be described later) was probably the gift of Attalus' brother-in-law and fellow-student in Athens, King Ariarthes V of Cappadocia (162-130). What the excavators call South Stoa II belongs to the same period. It served, with the Middle and East Stoas, to separate off a smaller area from the main square. But it was not a commercial agora: the excavators found no shops, booths, stalls, weights, or measures in it.

The Stoa of Attalus has been completely rebuilt, and now houses the Agora Museum, storerooms, and offices. A description of the Agora excavations as a whole is best postponed to the chapter on the Greek world under Roman sway, since the Agora reached its peak of development under Augustus, but this is the place to describe the Stoa and its reconstruction.

Its dimensions (382 feet long, 64 feet broad) and plan (two-storied double colonnade, with twenty-one shops behind on each floor) had been known since Greek excavations of 1859-1862. It was then that the discovery of epistyle fragments bearing King Attalus' name put the identification of the building beyond doubt. Much of the remains had been shielded by the so-called 'Valerian Wall' which was built right through the ruins of the building after its woodwork had been burned in the Herulian sack of AD 267. Under the north end were found several Mycenean chamber tombs, and a room in use in the fifth and fourth centuries was part of a law court, an inference from some jurors' ballots found in it. These are bronze disks with an axle through the middle, pierced for conviction, solid for acquittal. If the juror held the disk by the axle between thumb and forefinger, he could drop his ballot into the urn without anyone's knowing how he had voted. These ballots had apparently fallen by accident at the time the room was abandoned. A gutter-block that had settled out of position proved to conceal a well that yielded sixty-five five-gallon containers of sherds datable 520-480 BC, obviously from a retail potter's shop, since many of the vases were of the same type or even by the same hand. The Hellenistic shops served a variety of purposes; several have been restored for museum exhibits, with shelving modeled on the ancient, whose position was revealed by cuttings in the walls. One shop yielded surgical instruments. At the north end the oldest visible arch in the history of Greek architecture masks the end of a barrel-vault supporting the stairs.

The story of the reconstruction of the Stoa provides one of the most interesting examples in the history of archaeology of scientific inference at work. The guiding spirit was Homer A. Thompson, Director of the Agora Excavations, acutely and ingeniously assisted by John Travlos, the Agora architect. From surviving ancient blocks they knew the materials needed: blue Hymettus marble for the steps, gray Piraeus limestone for the walls, white Pentelic marble for the façade, columns, and interior trim, clay from the claypits of Attica for the roof tiles. Materials from the same places was used when the reconstruction began in 1953. The drums for the columns were delivered from the quarry roughly squared; the corners were then chamfered, and with careful hand work, by sixty marble-workers, using toothed and straight-edged chisels little changed since antiquity, the marble began slowly to assume cylindrical shape. The restorers knew from surviving capitals that the outer columns were Doric on the ground floor, double Ionic above, with a balustrade for safety closing the intercolumniations. Only the outer row of columns was fluted, since fluting depends for its effect on being struck by the sun. The inner row was Ionic on the ground floor, palmleaf above, the latter capital being one much favored by Pergamene architects. The columns of the bottom outer row, since

each consisted of three drums, were best fluted *in situ*, the bottom drum
being unfluted to avoid damage from foot traffic. Teams of four men
worked seventy-six man-days to flute the first column, at a cost of
$300. (The Erechtheum building-accounts show that in 407-406 teams
of five to seven men worked 350 man-days per column, at 350 drachmas per man, but those were taller columns, fully fluted, and of harder
stone.) The original floors had been a rough mosaic of marble chips
(*lithostroton*); the reconstruction uses the same material, which, polished,
is called *terrazzo*. The ancient beams were restored for protection
against fire, in reinforced concrete, revetted with laminated wood
(imported, but so must the wood have been to deforested Attica in
Hellenistic times). The position and size of the beams were determined
from sockets in the ancient stone work. Reinforced concrete piers were
inserted in the heart of the ancient walls, but enough ancient blocks
were bonded with the modern to show the evidence on which the
reconstruction was based.

In September 1956, the finished Stoa was dedicated by the Patriarch
of Athens and All Greece in the presence of King Paul and Queen
Frederica, and 1,500 invited guests, for all of whom the building
successfully discharged its original function of keeping crowds of
people cool on a hot day. Again as in Attalus' time it serves as a screen
between market and city. Since it sits low, it does not compete with
the buildings on the Acropolis or the Hephaistaion, and, as the loving
hand-work weathers, it serves better and better to allow modern visitors
a unique opportunity to appreciate the scale and spatial effect of a
splendid piece of Hellenistic civic architecture. And ten shops thrown
together on the ground floor house the Agora Museum, whose displayed finds, from Neolithic to Turkish, span 5,000 years of Athenian
history. In the lower portico, statues and inscriptions are set up near
where they were found, showing to advantage in a raking light. In the
basement and upper story a large bulk of material (over 68,000 inven-
toried items, plus over 94,000 coins, in June, 1961), unsuitable for
public display, is made accessible to scholars, and a model of the Agora
enables visitors (47,000 the first year, 150,000 the second, the numbers
growing annually) to orient themselves from a point of vantage. Thus a
phil-hellenic gesture of a Hellenistic philanthropist from the east has
been repeated in our time by philanthropists from the west: the new
world redressing the balance of the old.

The Greek Stones Speak, 1962

The London Mithraeum

RUPERT LEO SCOTT BRUCE-MITFORD

RUPERT LEO SCOTT BRUCE-MITFORD (1914-) *was born in London and educated at Christ's Hospital and Hertford College, Oxford. From 1950 to 1954 he held the post of Secretary to the Society of Antiquaries, and since 1954 he has been Keeper of British and Medieval Antiquities at the British Museum.*

The last investigation to be covered by this necessarily brief survey involves a return to the centre of the city.

In topographical terms the site enclosed by the wall consists of twin hills, Cornhill on the east, the hill of St Paul's on the west. These hills are separated by a small shallow valley, that of a stream which since early times has been called Walbrook – a name now preserved by the small street linking the modern Bank area with Cannon Street.

When in 1952 news of impending building developments on the large bombed site on the west side of Walbrook Street made an examination of the area desirable, an east-to-west cutting was undertaken (in broken lengths because of modern obstructions), the purpose of which was to obtain a section across the valley. Since almost the whole site was covered with bomb-rubble to a depth of some feet, the choice of position was, in fact, restricted to a narrow lane through the débris at a point approximately midway along the length of Walbrook Street.

The excavation proved to be one of considerable difficulty because of subterranean water. Most of the trenches were permanently flooded at a depth of about 4 feet below the cellar-floors, and water was present in increasing quantity as the floors of the cuttings were lowered. In spite of this and other handicaps, however, a fairly complete picture of this part of the valley was obtained. The natural profile was established as that of a broad shallow hollow, the western lip of which lay near Sise Lane, while the eastern lip was just to the east of Walbrook Street. The stream in its original 'Roman' form flowed approximately down the middle of this hollow and was thus some distance to the west of the assumed line referred to above. The full width of the channel unfortunately was not seen, but was not more than 12–14 feet; the stream itself was shallow, with a bottom 32–35 feet below modern street level. . . .

This picture is perhaps somewhat different from that which has usually been assumed for the Roman Walbrook, which, as it approaches the Thames, now becomes a squalid brook flowing through an 'undeveloped' area of scattered wooden buildings, more permanent houses and other buildings appearing on the fringes. It was only at a comparatively late date that buildings began to appear in the hollow itself. The first of these to the north, near Bucklersbury, was represented only by a tiny fragment of wall with associated mosaic pavement, presumably (but not necessarily) part of a house the remainder of which had been completely destroyed by later activities on the site. The second was the Walbrook temple of Mithras.

The first indications of this building presented themselves at an early stage in the most easterly cutting. By good fortune they appeared immediately under the cellar floor. As the section was deepened successive floors were uncovered. The latest of these (that is, the first to be encountered), was continuous over the whole surface; at a lower level earlier floors were associated with a sleeper wall aligned with the jamb of the apse and carrying spaced-out concrete 'pads' or 'settings' for columns. On the limited view given by the cutting, therefore, it was possible to decide that the building had originally been of basilican type – that is, a columned hall with at least one apsidal end – which in course of time had been remodelled internally by the removal of the columns and by the raising and re-laying of the floor to convert it into a single compartment. . . .

The Mithraeum was made up of two parts: the rectangular temple proper, about 60 feet by 25 feet, its main axis set east-to-west; and attached to its eastern end a narthex or vestibule, which came to light only at a later stage in the investigation. The body of the building was divided longitudinally by its colonnades into nave and side-aisles. In its original form the interior reflected basic Mithraic practice: the floor of the nave, which was the setting for the ritual, was sunken; those of the aisles, on which the worshippers gathered, were raised; and the number of columns, seven on each side, symbolised the seven grades into which the devotees of the cult were divided. At the western end, the floor of the semicircular sanctuary was raised high above that of the nave; on it would have stood the chief sculpture, Mithras Tauroctonus, the god slaying the sacred bull from whose blood sprang all earthly life. The front of the apse was broken by a slightly raised central portion, probably part of an arrangement involving the use of columns or other supports for a beam to take a curtain, behind which the group would have been concealed, except at the appropriate times in the ritual. Wooden steps provided access from the nave to the sanctuary, and one or more altars would have been set up before it, as well as probably elsewhere in the body of the nave.

At the eastern end the entrance opened from the narthex: the stone door-sill, though badly worn, was well preserved, with the iron collars for the door-pivots still in place in their sockets. Here, too, wooden steps provided for access to the floor of the nave. The narthex floor, which was presumably at Roman street level, was nearly $2\frac{1}{2}$ feet higher; but little is known of the narthex, most of which probably lies under the modern Walbrook: the part that remains has yet to be examined.

A feature of the exterior of the building was the massive external buttresses at the west end. The semicircular buttresses flanking the apse must have given an impression of a triple apse in their complete state: they and a large square buttress on the crest of the apse were added while the building was being erected and clearly reflect the unstable character of the site, with the Roman Walbrook only a few feet away to the west.

The temple in its original form appears to have been built towards the end of the second century AD: a more exact date must depend upon a detailed examination of the evidence now being attempted. In time, however, the building underwent extensive modification. No doubt reflecting the waterlogged condition of the surrounding area, the floor-level of the nave was gradually raised during the third century, and the earlier changes were accompanied by corresponding alterations in the level of the aisles. As an accompaniment to these changes there had been drastic remodelling of the superstructure: the colonnades were removed and finally a uniform floor converted the interior into the single chamber mentioned above.

But before this process was completed trouble, or the threat of it, had overtaken the temple and led to the burial of at any rate some of the most important sacred images. In one hole near the north-east corner of the nave had been placed the heads of Mithras and Minerva; in another near by, with a stone laver, a gigantic marble hand clasping the pommel of a dagger, a small figure of Mercury, and the head of Serapis. All the signs were that here was another instance of the conflict between

Mithraism and Christianity which led the Mithraists to bury their cult-objects and destroy their temples when in the early fourth century Christianity achieved the ascendancy. Yet the Walbrook temple itself does not appear to have suffered a fate parallel to that of the images; at least two floors sealed the pits containing the marbles, to indicate that the building went on in use; and there was no sign of destruction which could be said to be deliberate. . . .

The group of marbles as a whole is without parallel in Britain: all are of foreign workmanship. The Serapis particularly is in almost perfect condition; but Mithras, with the upturned eyes which show that it was derived from a bull-slaying, stands apart from the others in its sensitive rendering. The larger-than-life-size hand presents its own problem; if indeed it was derived from yet another sacrifice-group, the complete work must have been so large than its accommodation in the temple would have been difficult. The many questions raised by these and many other finds, must, however, be left for discussion in another place. Here it must suffice to say that the presence of these and other deities is in accordance with the all-embracing character of the Mithraic cult, which tended to assimilate to itself classical cults with similar or related attributes: such a one was the Graeco-Egyptian god of the underworld, Serapis.

And, secondly, the Walbrook Mithraeum exemplifies the second of the two main aspects of Mithraism. Mithras, god of strength and of the manly virtues, drew his followers largely from the Roman soldiery: his temples are numerous in the military areas of the Empire. But Mithras was also the god of upright dealing and as such a favourite of the merchant community. Mithraea are therefore common in the ports; and the London temple reflects the wealth and the contacts of the city's prosperous commercial class, with its comparatively rare architectural treatment and its wealth of works of art of the highest quality and refinement, contrasting with the often crude but vigorous elements in the military shrines.

Recent Archaeological Excavations in Britain, 1956

Traces of the Etruscans

GEORGE DENNIS

GEORGE DENNIS (*1814-1898*) *made his career in the diplomatic service, holding successive consular posts in Benghazi, Crete, Sicily and Smyrna. During his service in the Mediterranean area, his deep interest in archaeology led to the organization of expeditions to Cyrenaica and Asia Minor, and in 1842 and 1847 to journeys of exploration in Etruria. Largely as a result of his publication on the Etruscans, a model of detail and accuracy for its time, public interest in this civilization revived and a whole new branch of archaeological studies and researches came into being.*

In former chapters I have spoken of the ancient city of Vetulonia, and of various sites that have been assigned to it; and have shown that all of them are far from satisfactory. In the course of my wanderings through the Tuscan Maremma in the spring of 1844, I had the fortune to fall in with a site, which, in my opinion, has stronger claims to be considered that of Vetulonia than any of those to which that city has hitherto been referred.

Vague rumours had reached my ear of Etruscan antiquities having been discovered near Magliano, a village between the Osa and the Albegna, and about eight miles inland; but I imagined it was nothing beyond the excavation of tombs, so commonly made at this season throughout Etruria. I resolved, however, to visit this place on my way from Orbetello to Saturnia. For a few miles I retraced my steps towards Telamone, then, turning to the right, crossed the Albegua some miles higher up, at a ferry called Barca del Grassi; from this spot there was no carriage-road to Magliano, and my vehicle toiled the intervening five miles through tracks sodden with the rain.

Magliano is a squalid, innless village of three hundred souls, at the foot of a mediaeval castle in picturesque ruin. On making enquiries here I was referred to an engineer, Signor Tommaso Pasquinelli, then forming a road from Magliano to the Saline at the mouth of the Albegna. I found this gentleman at a convent in the village, amid a circle of venerable monks, whose beards far outshone the refectory table-cloth in whiteness. I was delighted to learn that it was he who had made the rumoured discovery in this neighbourhood, and that it was not of tombs merely, but of a city of great size. The mode in which this was brought to light was singular enough. Nothing was visible above ground – not a fragment of ruin to indicate prior habitation; so that it was only by extraordinary means he was made aware that here a city had stood. The ground through which his road had to run being for the most part low and swampy, and the higher land being a soft friable tufo, he was at a loss for the materials he wanted, till he chanced to uncover some large blocks, buried beneath the surface, which he recognised as the foundations of an ancient wall. These he found to continue in an unbroken line, which he followed out, breaking up the blocks as he unearthed them, till he had traced out the periphery of a city.

With the genuine politeness of Tuscany, that 'rare land of courtesy', as Coleridge terms it, he proposed at once to accompany me to the site. It was the first opportunity he had had of doing the honours of his city, for though the discovery had been made in May 1842, and he had communicated the fact to his friends, the intelligence had not spread, save in vague distorted rumours, and no antiquary had visited the spot. News always travels on foot in Italy, and generally falls dead lame on the road. I had heard from the antiquaries of Florence that something, no one knew what, had been found hereabouts. One thought it was tombs; another had heard it was gold *roba*; another was in utter ignorance of this site, but had heard of a city having been discovered on Monte Catini, to the west of Volterra.

The city lay between Magliano and the sea, about six and a quarter miles from the shore, on a low table-land, just where the ground begins to rise above the marshy plains of the coast. In length, according to Signor Pasquinelli, it was somewhat less than a mile and a half, and scarcely a mile in breadth; but taking into account its quadrilateral form, it must have had a circuit of at least four miles and a half. On the south-east it was bounded by the streamlet Patrignone, whose banks rise in cliffs of no great height; but on every other side the table-land sinks in a gentle slope to the plain. At the south-western extremity, near a house called La Doganella, the only habitation on the site, was found a smaller and inner circuit of wall; and this, being also the highest part of the table-land, was thus marked out as the site of the Arx.

Though scarcely a vestige remained of the walls, and no ruins rose above the surface, I had not much difficulty in recognising the site as Etruscan. The soil was thickly strewn with broken pottery, that infallible and ineffaceable indicator of bygone habitation; and here it was of that character found on purely Etruscan sites, without any admixture of marbles, or fragments of verd-antique, porphyry, and other valuable stones, which mark the former seats of Roman luxury. Though the walls, or rather their foundations, had been almost entirely destroyed since the first discovery, a few blocks remained yet entire, and established the Etruscan character of the city. From these little or nothing could be ascertained as to the style of masonry; but the blocks themselves were indicative of an Etruscan origin – some being of *macigno*, resembling those of Populonia in their size and rude shaping; others of tufo, or of the soft local rock, like that of Corneto, agreeing in size and form with the usual blocks of this material found on Etruscan sites. Some of the former had been found nine or ten feet in length. But the blocks were not generally of large dimensions, though always without cement. On the spot, where a portion of the walls had been uncovered, at the verge of a hollow, a sewer opening in them was disclosed.

Within the walls a road or street had been traced by the foundations of the houses on either hand. Many things had been dug up, but no statues, or marble columns, as on Roman sites – chiefly articles of bronze or pottery. I myself saw a piece of bronze drawn from the soil, many feet below the surface, which proved to be a packing-needle, ten inches in length, with eye and point uninjured! It must have served some worthy Etruscan, either in preparing for his travels, perhaps to the Fanum Voltumnae, the parliament of Lucumones, perhaps for the *grand tour*, such as Herodotus made, which is pretty nearly the *grand tour* still; or, it may be, in shipping his goods to foreign lands from the neighbouring port of Telamon. This venerable needle is now in my possession.

While it is to be lamented that to future travellers scarcely a trace of this city will be visible, it must be remembered, that but for the peculiar exigencies of the engineer, which led to the destruction of its walls, we should have remained in ignorance of its existence. Other accidents might have led to the uncovering of a portion of the wall; but it is difficult to conceive that any other cause could have brought about the excavation of the entire circuit, and the consequent determination of the precise limits of the city. So that in spite of the wholesale macadamisation, the world is greatly indebted to the gentleman who made the discovery.

Cities and Cemeteries of Etruria, 3rd edition, vol. II, 1883

The Bull of Minos

ARTHUR EVANS

Sir Arthur Evans (*1851-1941*) *was born at Nash Mills, Hertfordshire, educated at Harrow, at Brasenose College of which he became a Fellow, and at Gottingen University. After visiting the Balkans in 1875 he became deeply interested in the archaeology of the region, but his attention was diverted to Crete by a study of engraved gems known to have been found on the island. In 1899 after prolonged negotiation he bought the site of Knossos, and his excavations there revealed a brilliant and sophisticated people antedating even the recently-discovered Mycenaean civilization, to whom he gave the name of Minoans. His large private fortune and all the resources of his extensive scholarship were subsequently devoted to the examination and publication of his findings at Knossos, and to the repair and restoration of the palace. Little is known of the religious practices of the Minoans but their art frequently depicts one of its most spectacular and dangerous rituals.*

The remains of these 'Taureador Frescoes' – as they may be fittingly called – belong to several panels. Although the figures in these are three or four times larger than those of the miniature panels – 32 cm (*c.* 12$\frac{3}{4}$ in) as against 10–8 cm (*c.* 4–3$\frac{1}{8}$ in) – the panels have this in common, that they were comparatively low. The height of that restored in Fig 144 is 72·8 centimetres, including the decorative framing. This height, approximating to 80 cm, corresponds with that conjecturally assigned to the 'Miniature Frescoes'. It also agrees with that already arrived at for the painted friezes of the 'House of the Frescoes'. In these cases the fresco bands seem to have run immediately under beams forming the continuation of those of the lintels and would have been superposed on low dadoes about 1 metre high. In the case of the 'Partridge Frieze' of the Caravanserai Pavilion, however, there is clear evidence that the painted band ran above the level of the lintel beams and, from the artistic point of view, was consequently somewhat 'skied'. In the present case we may suppose that the 'Taureador' panels were set above dadoes

of the full height of somewhat over 2 metres, and this seems best in
keeping with the decorative methods in vogue within the Palace at the
time of the L.M. I restoration, though a lower position, like those of
the 'House of the Frescoes', might have suited the designs better.

It is certainly difficult to place these 'Taureador Frescoes' later than
the First Late Minoan Period. The delicate delineation of some and the
fine enamelled surface, especially in the case of the white paint themselves, point to an age when the art of wall-painting had reached its
highest level. On the other hand certain accessory details, such as the
imitation *intarsia* work on variegated stones that decorates the borders,
betray a certain sympathy with a style of border fashionable in the last
age of the Palace (L.M. II).

The designs were originally distributed in several panels and in the
case of one of these it was possible to restore the whole composition.
Here, besides the male performer of the usual ruddy hue who is turning
a back-somersault above the bull, are two female taureadors, distinguished not only by their white skin but by their more ornamental
attire. Their loin-cloth and girdle is identical with that of the man but
of more variegated hue: his is plain yellow, theirs are decorated with
black stripes and bars. They wear bands round their wrists and double
necklaces – one of them beaded – and, in the case of some of the figures,
blue and red ribbons round their brows. But perhaps their most distinctive feature is the symmetrical arrangement of short curls over their
foreheads and temples, already noticed in the case of the female 'cow-
boy' of the Vapheio cup. . . . Their foot-gear consists of short gaiters
or stockings and pointed mocassin-like shoes.

In the design seen in Fig 144 the girl acrobat seizes the horns of a
coursing bull at full gallop, one of which seems to run under her left
arm-pit. The object of her grip, clearly shown in the enlarged reproduction of this section in Fig 145, seems to be to gain a purchase for a
backward somersault over the animal's back, such as is being performed
by the boy. The second female performer behind stretches out both her
hands as if about to catch the flying figure or at least to steady him
when he comes to earth the right way up. The stationing of this figure
handy for such an art raises some curious questions as to the arrangements within the arena.

Apart from this, certain features in the design have provoked the
scepticism of experts acquainted with modern 'Rodeo' performances.
A veteran in 'Steer-wrestling', consulted by Professor Baldwin Brown,
was of opinion that anyone who had anything to do with that sport

would pronounce the endeavour to seize the bull's horns as a start for a somersault as quite impossible 'for there is no chance of a human person being able to obtain a balance when the bull is charging full against him'. The bull, as he further remarked, has three times the strength of a steer, and when running 'raises his head sideways and gores anyone in front of him'.

'That a somersault was performed over the back of a charging bull seems evident and does not seem to present much difficulty, but surely if the bull were at full gallop the athlete would not alight on its back, but on the ground well behind it?'

All that can be said is that the performance as featured by the Minoan artist seems to be of a kind pronounced impossible by modern champions of the sport. The fresco design shown in Fig 144 does not, as we shall see, stand alone, and the successive acts that it seems to imply find at least partial confirmation in a clay seal-impression and in the bronze group, where the acrobatic feat is illustrated by the diagrammatic figure. . . .

These highly sensational episodes are primarily exhibitions of acrobatic skill. In this respect, as already noted, they differ from the parallel performances of the Minoan cow-boys, the aim of which was rather the catching of wild or half-wild animals. That girls actually took part in this more practical side of the sport, as occasionally in the 'Wild West' of America today, has been shown from a scene on a Vapheio Cup, but the elegance and ornaments of the female acrobats shown in the 'Taureador Frescoes' belong to a different sphere. The ribbons and beaded necklaces are quite out of place in rock-set glens or woodland glades. To the Palace circus they are more appropriate. The animals themselves were no doubt carefully trained. Like the bulls of the Spanish arenas they may often have been of established pedigree and reared in special herds or *ganaderias*. It is clear that in all these scenes the attention of the Minoan artist is largely centred on the animal itself, which is rendered of disproportionate size, as befitting what was to them evidently quite as much as the lion, the King of Beasts. . . .

The idea of the performance as here conceived by the modeller of this bronze group seems to have been essentially the same as that of the fresco painter who executed the original of Fig 44. This design, indeed, fits on to the whole series of gem types such as those illustrated above, and involving three separate actions – the seizure of the horns, the landing over the head, and the final somersault behind, where timely assistance is rendered by an attendant figure.

The first part of this acrobatic cycle, as thus logically conceived, has rightly been shown to transcend the power and skill of mortal man. . . .

That the painted reliefs of bull-grappling scenes such as those that remained in part at least in position above the Northern Entrance Passage at a time when the Greek settlement was already in existence may have left their impress on later traditions of the Minotaur and of the captive boys and girls is itself, as already suggested, by no means improbable. But there is no reason to go farther than this and to suppose that the acrobatic figures of either sex engaged in these dangerous feats actually represent captives, trained like the Roman gladiators to 'make sport' for the Minoan holidays. Still farther are we away from any comparison with the primitive and more ferocious custom, illustrated by the monuments of prehistoric Egypt, in which prisoners of war were exposed to wild bulls.

The youthful participants in these performances – like those of the boxing and wrestling bouts, that can hardly be separated from the same general category – have certainly no servile appearance. They are, as we have seen, elegantly tired, and, specially in the hand-to-hand contests to be described below, often of noble mien. In these champions of either sex we must rather recognise the flower of the Minoan race, executing, in many cases under a direct religious sanction, feats of bravery and skill in which the whole population took a passionate delight.

The lithe sinewy forms of those engaged in the sports of the Minoan arena, with their violent muscular action and conventionally constricted waists, were as much the theme of the contemporary artists as were the more symmetrical shapes of her *ephebi* to those of classical Greece. In both cases it was the glorification of athletic excellence, manifesting itself in feats of which the Gods themselves were witnesses. So, too, the participation of women in the Minoan bull-grappling scenes can by no means be regarded as a symptom of bondage or of a perverse tyrant's whim. It was rather, as we have seen, the natural outcome of the religious organisation in which the female ministers of the Goddess took the foremost place in her service. At Sparta, where the Minoan religious tradition seems to have had a considerable hold, girl athletes continued to take part in the public games.

The Palace of Minos, vol. III, 1930

Reconstruction work at Knossos

ARTHUR EVANS

The preservation of the 'Domestic Quarter' – greatly due to the comparative protection against earthquake shocks afforded by the cutting on three sides into the Neolithic strata of the 'Tell' – had more the aspect of a miracle than anything that excavation might reasonably have been supposed to bring to light. The 'Grand Staircase', especially – of which three flights were unearthed in their entirety and sufficient evidences of two more – now once more restored to such a condition as to fulfil its original functions after an interval of over three and a half millennia – still stands forth as a monument of constructive skill.

In the whole exploration of the Palace site the most surprising development was that which occurred on emerging south from the Corridor of the Bays that flanked the Royal Magazines where the 'Medallion Pithoi' were stored. The pavement that was followed out, resting on the Neolithic clay, seemed to represent the level above and below which it was hopeless to expect further remains in this direction. The hot season had begun and the work of excavation had in fact begun to grow rather weary when, on opening out here a blocked doorway, a landing came to light, beyond which further clearance showed an ascending and descending flight of gypsum steps – afterwards discovered to belong to the second and third flight of a magnificent stone staircase. . . .

Something has been already said of the peculiar difficulties and even dangers encountered in making our way down the lower flights and through the corridors and halls of the ground floor beyond. It was certainly a fortunate circumstance that amongst the workmen then employed were two from the Laurion Mines, and under their guidance we were able, with the constant use of mine props, to tunnel down the lower flights and along the vaults beyond. It was then realised that though the massive wooden framework that played so great a part in the structural features of the last Middle Minoan period, including substantial posts and cross-beams as well as the wooden columns and capitals, was reduced to a carbonised condition – more by chemical action than by fire – the fabric for the most part was still held in position, in places even as far as the level of the second story.

This was the result of the intrusion into the spaces below of fallen materials, mostly, no doubt, sun-dried bricks from the uppermost stories of this part of the building. But the full explanation of the phenomena was not supplied till later, when the 'Caravanserai' on the opposite side of the gorge to the south of the Palace was excavated. It was there found that the springs on that side, which were largely impregnated with gypsum, combining with the native clay and in this case too with crude bricks fallen from above had formed a concretion as hard as cement and which could only be penetrated with sharp steel picks at the cost of considerable time and labour. It is clear that the same result as that naturally produced by the springs from the Gypsàdes hill beyond acting on the clay materials had, in the case of the covered spaces of the lower floors and flights of stairs, been owing to the dissolved effect of rain-water on the debris of the gypsum blocks, pavements, and dado slabs of the uppermost stories. The deleterious effect of rain on the gypsum elements of the Palace is rapid in its action and the progress of disintegration had made itself very perceptible in exposed parts of the building since the first days of the Excavations. The extent to which the gypsum is liable to be thus dissolved depends, it is true, on the individual consistency of the stone. Some of the earlier Palace slabs are of specially fine quality, with waving translucent veins and laminations pale brown and amber tinted, and such seem to have still an almost unlimited power of resisting the elements. But exposed surfaces as a rule are gradually reduced to a rough mass of crystals, and in some cases one is almost tempted to compare the effect of a drop of water on a lump of loaf sugar.

One inevitable conclusion from this disintegrating process was that in order to save any part of such remains it was necessary that they should be covered over. But the excavation of the staircase and the halls it served brought with it still more urgent needs. The hewing away of the clay concretions and the extraction of the various rubble and earthy materials in the intervening spaces left a void between the upper and lower spaces that threatened the collapse of the whole. The carbonised posts and beams and shafts, although their form and measurements could be often observed, splintered up when exposed and of course, could afford no support. The recourse to mine props and miscellaneous timbering to hold up the superincumbent mass was at most temporary and at times so insufficient that some dangerous falls occurred.

New Era in Reconstitution due to Use of Ferro-concrete

To relax our efforts meant that the remains of the upper stories would have crashed down on those below, and the result would have been an indistinguishable heap of ruins. The only alternative was to endeavour to re-support the upper structures in some permanent manner. In the early days of the Excavation the Architect, Mr Christian Doll, who manfully grappled with this Atlantean task, had perforce largely to rely on iron girders brought from England at great expense, and these were partly masked with cement. The shafts of the columns were replaced by stone blocks concealed by a stucco coating and the capitals were actually cut out. Even then wood, which it was hard to obtain properly seasoned, was allowed to play a part in these reconstructions. The cypress trunks and beams that had supported solid masses of masonry in the old work were of course no longer obtainable so we had to learn that even the pinewood of Tyrol, imported through Trieste, which in the chalets of its own country might have resisted the elements for generations – could be reduced to rottenness and powder in a few years by the violent extremes of the Cretan climate.

But with the increasing use of ferro-concrete – the material of which was reinforced by thick iron wires – for constructive work of all kinds, a new era of reconstitution and conservation opened on the Palace site. It has already been shown how in the west wing of the building the new method made it possible much more efficaciously and cheaply to replace upper floors with the old elements at the same time set on their proper level, while columns, capitals, and other features, even those involving elaborate details, had no longer to be hewn and carved from the actual stone, but could be 'cast' wholesale in wooden moulds, which the native carpenters were skilful in turning out. The carbonised beams and posts were at the same time restored by the same methods in the new cement material, while, by flooding it over a temporary boarding, supported by posts below, it was possible to lay out considerable areas of the pavement and at the same time permanently to protect from the weather the gypsum slabs and blocks and other perishable features of the basement rooms and magazines. The whole framework of the building on this side was so well compacted together by this new material that it successfully resisted the severe earthquake of 26 June 1926.

The Palace of Minos, vol. III, 1930

Ventris deciphers the Cretan script

WILLIAM TAYLOUR

MICHAEL GEORGE FRANCIS VENTRIS (*1922-1956*) *was born at Wheat-hampstead and became an architect by profession. From his earliest years he had been deeply interested in languages and in problems of decipherment, and during the war became expert at breaking codes. The method used by the military was largely based on statistical analysis, and it occurred to Ventris that this method could equally effectively be applied to the Linear B tablets, where the problems of translating an unknown language written in an unknown script had hitherto proved insuperable. Finding that he needed the assistance of an expert philologist, he approached Professor J. Chadwick, who was so impressed that he agreed readily to co-operate. When their results were published they were so conclusive that very little opposition was possible, but Ventris did not live to see this triumph of his method, for he was killed in a traffic accident at the age of thirty-four.*

Civilisation by definition in ancient history means a literate society. Indeed the very complexity of civilised society requires a discipline of records to function at all. The Mycenaean civilisation was no exception to this rule, though earlier excavations had provided little evidence of the fact. Some knowledge of writing was inferred from curious signs painted on a certain number of Mycenaean stirrup-jars found at Mycenae, Tiryns, Orchomenos, and Thebes; but not until the excavations, begun at Pylos in 1939, produced hundreds of clay tablets inscribed with a similar script was it realised that the knowledge of writing may have been general and widespread in Mycenaean Greece. These clay tablets were not unique. They had already been found in Crete at Knossos as early as 1900 by Sir Arthur Evans, who from the first recognised their importance. Knossos has produced the largest number of such records, between 3,000 and 4,000, though many of them are fragmentary; but they have also been found elsewhere in that island in the palaces of Phaistos, Hagia Triada, and Mallia. Pylos has the next largest number, just over 1,200, and each year's excavation on that site produces its annual increment. Mycenae so far has accounted for little more than seventy; and the greater number of these come from houses outside the Citadel.

It seems indeed strange that the dynamic centre and inspiration of the civilisation, which we call Mycenaean, should have produced so small a number. The explanation seems to be twofold: the perishability of the substance and perhaps the inability of the earlier excavators to recognise these rather undistinguished lumps of clay for what they were. The latter explanation is a fairly common one given by modern archaeologists, but I do not think that all tablets could have escaped the keen eye of Schliemann who prided himself upon the care with which he collected and preserved what, even to him, were the most insignificant objects. It is true that tablets are not easy to recognise. The so-called Linear B tablets – the only kind found in the Greek mainland – are oblong pieces of clay about three inches in length. Some are much larger and almost square; others are long, narrow, and tapering, like a palm-leaf. In the dust and dirt of excavation tablets could be taken for fragments of coarse pottery, except that one surface to the discerning eye would display incised markings. But unlike pottery they are not baked in a kiln, which would have rendered them indestructible. They were shaped out of ordinary clay, inscribed with a record when the clay was still soft, and then put out in the sun to dry. So long as they were stored in a dry place they were likely to survive, but once subjected to the effects of water they quickly dissolved into a shapeless mass. (This unfortunate fate befell some tablets stored by Sir Arthur Evans in a shed with a leaking roof!) It is largely due to the violent destruction of a site that tablets have survived at all. The fierce fires burnt them to the hardness of pottery; even so, some of them are rather friable.

At Pylos the majority of tablets were concentrated in one area and in the course of excavation it became clear that these represented the palace archives. They were stored near the entrance to the palace in a small room with low benches that supported free-standing shelving, or so it could be inferred from careful observation of the burnt debris filling the room. It could also be deduced that the tablets were kept in wicker baskets, as an impression of the wickerwork was preserved on several pieces of burnt clay found adhering to 'labelling' tablets, that is, tablets stating in an abbreviated form the subject of the contents. Another type of storage seems to have been wooden boxes. Within the Citadel of Mycenae no archives have been found. A few tablets, eight in all, were recovered in 1960 in further excavations of Mycenaean houses within the Citadel and near the Grave Circle, but they were very fragmentary. The circumstances of their findings suggest that they were but a remnant of a large hoard which was all but annihilated by the devastating fire that destroyed the buildings in which they were housed. The surviving tablets were found embedded in conglomerate masses of molten stone, brick, and clay fused to the consistency and hardness of concrete. Spattered about in this rock-like, calcined debris were specks and fragments of a reddish brown substance, which could have been potsherds or bits of disintegrated tablets. If the latter, it would seem that the tablets in this case were stored in stone cupboards or containers. The very evident marks of the fire that destroyed the palace on the crown of the Citadel show that here too the conflagration was of equal intensity and violence to the one farther down the slope of the hill. In this manner any archives that may have existed within the palace would have been obliterated or have left so little trace as to have eluded the vigilance of the excavators.

These records in clay from Greece and Crete, and a few from Cyprus, are practically the only written documents that have survived from the Aegean world of the second millennium. It may well be that other media for writing were used, substances such as wood, leather, parchment, palm leaves, or papyrus, none of which would survive under normal conditions. The conversion of the papyrus plant into a very adequate writing material was a specialised industry of Egypt and there is plenty of evidence of trade relations between the Aegean and that country. Writing in clay was the system adopted in Babylonia and neighbouring kingdoms – there the tablets were oven-baked – and an implement with a wedge-shaped end was used to reproduce the cuneiform script (*cuneus*=a wedge). But the Aegean scribe preferred a stylus or pointed tool and it may be that the more important documents were written on other materials more adapted to such an instrument. The tablets, on the other hand, which could be cheaply and easily produced on the spot, would serve for day-to-day business records, and that is in fact what they are.

How do we know this? So much was deduced by Sir Arthur Evans from pictorial signs on the Knossos tablets recognisable as horses, chariots, weapons, etc., but it was not until recent times, 1952 to be exact, that the many attempts at deciphering the script met with success. This was largely due to the genius, brilliance, and application of a young architect, Michael Ventris, assisted at a critical stage of his work by the Cambridge philologist, John Chadwick. To understand this colossal achievement one must appreciate that Ventris was attempting a far more difficult task than the problem that faced Champollion in solving the riddle of Egyptian hieroglyphics or Grotefend and Rawlinson in the decipherment of cuneiform. These early pioneers had bilingual or trilingual texts to help them and at least they knew the linguistic group to which the language belonged. Ancient Egyptian, though much modified, lived on in the Coptic tongue; Assyrian and Babylonian were related, it became clear, to ancient Hebrew and Semitic languages in general. But Ventris was faced with one script alone and without a clue as to what language it might stand for.

Many of course had preceded Ventris in the unrewarding quest. Sir Arthur Evans himself was a pioneer and laid the foundations for future research. He was able to demonstrate the different stages in the development of the script. First, the hieroglyphic signs that are mainly found on Cretan gems and seal-stones belonging to the first half of the second millennium; a few tablets with hieroglyphs are also known. Secondly, a cursive and simplified version of these signs, which Sir Arthur termed Linear A; this was inscribed on tablets (said to be oven-baked), vases, stone, and on bronze. Finally, a later and more advanced script, closely related to Linear A, which he called Linear B. No exact dates can be given for the periods in which these scripts were in vogue, but it can be said that Linear A overlaps the hieroglyphic script and may have started as early as the eighteenth century. It seems to have gone out of use in the early part of the fifteenth century. Linear B, which is almost exclusively recorded on tablets, begins before or just after 1400 BC. The latest tablets can be dated to around 1200 BC. Linear B is the only form of the script known on the Greek mainland.

In his study of the material, Evans had established certain basic points: that the tablets were lists or accounts, that a numerical system was clearly recognisable, that some of the signs were ideograms (pictures of the objects designated), and that the other signs were most likely syllabic. This list he assumed because he had noted that groups of signs were separated from other groups by vertical strokes; hence each group probably represented a word of so many syllables. Beyond these general conclusions Evans was not prepared to commit himself. Many of his less cautious and immediate followers – and distinguished scholars among them – were to rely too much on guess-work, choosing a language that might be shown to have some affinity with the script and trying to make the two fit. Method was lacking in nearly all these schemes. Without a detailed analysis of the inscriptions there was little chance of success. One of the few who adopted a methodical approach was the American, Dr Alice E. Kober. She was able to demonstrate by her analysis of the Linear B signs that it was an inflected language, that is, one in which words have varying suffixes added to denote gender, plural, etc. (as in Latin). For instance, she noted that the totalling formula for men and a certain class of animals differed from that used for women and another class of animals and this suggested a distinction in gender. But her greatest contribution to the decipherment was her demonstration that certain words made up of two, three or more syllabic signs could have two variants by adding a different sign or by changing their terminal sign into another sign. (An example in English would be: wo-man; woman's; wo-men). Such variations are referred to in linguistic circles as 'Kober's triplets'! Professor Emmett L. Bennett, Jr was also one of the few to use a methodical approach. Apart from elucidating the system of weights and measures used in the script, his most important contribution was the ordering and classification of the whole Linear B signary. The division of the signs into two classes, ideographic and syllabic, was clarified and from a detailed study of variants in the orthography (bad handwriting is nothing new) he was able to narrow down the number of syllabic signs to just short of ninety.

There was one valuable, but deceptive, clue to attacking the problem of decipherment. A related script is found in Cyprus and is referred to as Cypro-Minoan. Only a few tablets have been found there, of which the oldest is said to date from the early fifteenth century and has affinities with Linear A. Two features about these tablets call for special comment. A blunted stylus was used and the tablets were baked in fire. The technique is therefore different from the tablets we have been discussing and is more closely linked to that of the civilisations to the East. This is not surprising in view of the geographical position of Cyprus. Yet another script, the Classical Cypriot script, was in use on the island from the sixth to the third or second century BC and is obviously related to Linear B. In most, if not all, cases Greek was written in it; hence decipherment was possible. Seven of the signs are similar to or can be equated with Linear B and the phonetic values of the Cypriot Syllabary are known. The signs represent either a vowel or a consonant plus vowel. As this is a syllabic and not an alphabetic script, difficulties occur in words where two or more consonants follow one another or where a word ends in a consonant. Using this syllabic script, *'pastor'* would be spelt *pa-so-to-re*.

The final vowel of -*re* would not be pronounced, neither would the *o* of -*so*; such would be regarded as 'dead' vowels. But the choice of the syllabic sign -*so* (from the five syllabic signs beginning with *s*: -*sa*, -*se*, -*si*, -*so*, -*su*) is governed by, and must conform to, the vowel of the syllabic sign following, in this case, the *o* of -*to*. So for '*prison*' the spelling could be *pi-ri-so-ne* (the final 'dead' vowel is always *e*). Yet a further complication in the Cypriot Syllabary is that *n* before a conson-ant is not written. Thus '*contralto*' would appear as *co-ta-ra-lo-to*. It must be clear from these examples that the Syllabary would be a very clumsy method of writing English. It is even more so for Greek. The word *anthropos* 'man' has to be written *a-to-ro-po-se*. Now a very large number of Greek words end in *s* and, as the Cypriot syllabic sign -*se* is identical with one of the Linear B signs, it could easily be demonstrated whether Linear B was a likely candidate for Greek or not. It was found that the -*se* sign very rarely occurred as a terminal sign in the Linear B script. The natural conclusion therefore was that the language was not Greek.

The preliminary, basic, and essential work carried out by Kober and Bennett was invaluable to Ventris who now brought an added dimen-sion to tackle the problem of decipherment, a knowledge of crypto-graphy. In theory any code can be broken provided there is enough coded material to work on. A detailed analysis of the material should reveal certain recurring features and underlying patterns. We have already commented on those that had been noted by Dr Kober. Ventris was able to add to the number of pregnant observations. On the basis of the material available, considerably augmented by the publication in 1951 of Bennett's transcription of the tablets found at Pylos in 1939, he prepared statistical tables showing the over-all fre-quency of each sign. He was able to deduce – and here he had the collaboration of Bennett and the Greek scholar Ktistopoulos – that three of these signs were probably vowels from the fact that they occurred predominantly at the beginning of sign groups. A suffix was provisionally identified as the conjunction 'and', used like -*que* in Latin. Other inflexional variations of words identifiable as nouns were noted and, as some of these occurred with the ideogram of man and woman, it could be seen that in such cases the inflexion was often one of gender rather than case.

The relative accumulated data were arranged by him in tabular form, in what he called the 'grid'. The grid was constantly being revised and rearranged. In one of its latest forms it consisted in the main of fifteen rows of consonants and five columns of vowels; as none of the values of the consonants or vowels was known, these were simply given numbers. Within these seventy-five spaces were arranged the most frequently recurring Linear B syllabic signs (fifty-one out of a possible total of ninety) on the basis of statistical data that had been assembled about them. If the system was sound and the data correctly diagnosed, signs in the same column should share the same vowel and signs in the same row should start with the same consonant. Therefore, if the phonetic values of but a few syllabic signs could be established, the values of the others would automatically follow from the grid.

We have already mentioned that seven of the signs from the Cypriot syllabary can be equated with Linear B signs; it was permissible therefore to experiment with the Cypriot phonetic value of these signs. This Ventris did. Furthermore, he had concluded from the constantly recurring position of certain groups of signs in the tablets that these sign-groups represented the names of places. Working on these two suppositions he made tests with ancient place-names. For the Knossos tablets the choice was naturally made from Cretan names that were known in Classical times or mentioned by Homer – Knossos itself, Amnisos (a harbour town near by), and Tulissos; and they could be recognised in the following syllabic spellings: *ko-no-so*, *a-mi-ni-so*, *tu-ri-so*. These identifications were certainly valid on the Cypriot spelling convention, double consonants (*km*, *mn*) being split into syllables. The *ri* instead of *li* in *tu-ri-so* (Tulissos) was not a difficulty. Ventris had already recognised that *r* and *l* were interchangeable, as they are in several languages, including Ancient Egyptian. One marked difference from the Cypriot is that the final *s* is not written. Similarly *l*, *m*, *n*, *r*, *s* are omitted at the end of a word or when preceding another consonant, and there are other spelling rules imposed by the decipherment that do not correspond with the Cypriot conventions.

If the results of these tests were promising, they still did not provide any clue as to the language concealed in the script. Ventris's own opinion was that the language was Etruscan and to the very last he tried conclusions in that direction. It was only as 'a frivolous digression' (his own words) that in the final stages of the decipherment he experimented with Greek. To his surprise, with Greek many of the tablets made sense. Admittedly as many more remained incomprehensible, but if the language was indeed Greek, it would of necessity be a very archaic form of the tongue that was recorded in the Linear B script a full 500 years before Homer – and Homer's Greek is itself archaic. If the language was Greek, one would expect to find many of these Homeric archaisms foreshadowed in the Linear B texts and the fact that this was so contributed very largely to the favourable reception accorded by the majority of scholars to Ventris's revolutionary pronouncement. One has only to recall the contention and controversy that arose over the success claimed for the decipherment of cuneiform and Egyptian hieroglyphics to marvel at the comparative acquiescence and applause with which this far more spectacular and controversial achievement was received. Opposition to the claim there naturally was, but before it could become articulate a remarkable and dramatic piece of new evidence supervened.

About the same time that Ventris was reaching his solution of the Linear B problem, a tablet was being unearthed at Pylos that went far to confirm the correctness of his system. It was one of about 400 that were discovered during the 1952 excavations. Early in the following year they were being cleaned and studied in Athens by Professor Blegen, their finder. He tried out Ventris's syllabary on several of them, and on this one with striking results. It was a tablet with an inventory of tripods and various kinds of vases, some with four handles, some with three, and one with none; the different ideogram used in every case made this clear. But each ideogram was preceded by a description and, although the meaning of every word in the description was not self-evident, some could be given the following phonetic values – and no other – according to the Ventris syllabary: *ti-ri-po*, *qe-to-ro-we*, *ti-ri-o-we*. The *ti-ri-po* word only appears with the tripod sign. Following the spelling convention previously demonstrated, it is clearly the Greek word *tripos*, a tripod. O-we, which occurs in the three other words given above, means 'eared'; the word 'ear' is regularly used in Greek for the handle of a pot. It is found above in combination with *quetro* (Greek *tetra*, Latin *quattuor*), *tri* (as in *tripos*), and *an*, the Greek negative prefix, i.e. no handles. That the above-given words should only occur with the ideograms to which they refer was beyond the possibility of coincidence. The basic soundness of the decipherment of Linear B as an archaic form of Greek was thereby established and the publication of this tablet in 1953 served to convince many who up till then were only partly converted. But it did not convince all and to this day there is a small minority of scholars who will not accept the decipherment. Nevertheless, their most distinguished protagonist, Professor Beattie, fully appreciates the awkward implications of the tripod tablet and that it must in some manner be explained away. He has therefore been driven to the desperate expedient of suggesting that

Ventris had foreknowledge of this tablet before he arrived at his final solution. Such a suggestion is not only unworthy but completely without foundation.

How is one to explain the opposition, however diminished, to the idea of Linear B being Greek? The objections concern admitted difficulties in translation. Many words still do not make sense and, on account of the great variety of possible alternative readings in certain cases, one cannot always be sure of the Greek form of these doubtful words. . . . It is argued that no scribe could make himself intelligible to another with such an elastic script. For instance, the sign for *ka* may represent as many as seventy different syllables: *ka, ga, kha, kai, kas, kan,* etc. This is so, but it is not true of all the syllabic signs; and signs are not read in isolation but in combination as words. Certain combinations occur again and again. A pictogram is often there to supplement a hesitant memory. But there are many cases in our own language where we have a choice between variant readings. A word like 'invalid' is capable of two meanings and two different pronunciations. . . . Like the Mycenaean scribe we may hesitate for a moment before making a choice; it is familiarity and the context that ultimately decide.

If it is generally accepted today – at least by the greater number of distinguished Greek scholars – that the language of Linear B is Greek, it has to be admitted that the written material so far available is limited in quantity and quality. What is the quality thereof? Inventories for the most part and catalogues: inventories of stores, livestock, and agricultural produce; catalogues of men, women, and children. And of the latter category a great part of the text is taken up with proper names and the occupations of the individuals concerned. At least 65 per cent of the sign groups are proper names. . . . About 200 or so are almost certainly place-names, although quite a number of these cannot be identified geographically. Some 3,500 tablets have been studied and these have yielded a total vocabulary of 630 words, of which about 40 per cent can be read with a fair degree of certainty. The number of texts that contain sentences of any length is limited and consequently our knowledge of grammar and syntax is equally so. These are the 'chariot', 'land tenure', and 'furniture' tablets. It is necessary to emphasise these limitations in order to retain a due sense of proportion. The decipherment of Linear B has enlarged our view of Mycenaean civilisation considerably but we cannot always be certain how much of the picture is in focus.

The Mycenaeans, 1964

Part Three

---◆---

THE BOOK OF THE PYRAMIDS

The tourist and the monuments

AUGUSTE MARIETTE

Auguste Ferdinand Francois Mariette (1821-1881) was born at Boulogne. He first went to Egypt in 1850 entrusted with a mission to seek out and buy for the national collection any suitable manuscripts in the Coptic, Syriac, Arabic, and Ethiopic languages, but he shortly abandoned this intention in favour of active exploration and excavation of the ancient monuments. After discovering the Serapeum where the sacred bulls of Apis were buried, he spent the next four years digging and despatching his finds to the Louvre, of which he was appointed assistant curator on his return. In 1858 he was made conservator of Egyptian monuments, and moved with his family to Cairo. Among the many sites he explored in detail were Memphis and the Saqqara pyramids, Meydum, Abydos and the Thebes necropolis, Karnak, Medinet Habu and Deir el-Bahari, and the temple which had long been hidden by drifts of sand between the paws of the Sphinx. His immeasurable contributions to archaeology were honoured by the Egyptians with the successive titles of Bey and Pasha.

There is no need to enlarge upon the importance of the monuments that cover the banks of the Nile. They are the witnesses of Egypt's former greatness, and, so to speak, the patents of her ancient nobility. They represent in the eyes of strangers the tattered pages of the archives of one of the most glorious nations in the world.

But the higher the esteem in which we hold Egypt's monuments, the more it behoves us to preserve them with care. On their preservation partly depends the progress of those interesting studies which have for their object the history of ancient Egypt. Moreover, they are worthy of being preserved, not only for the sake of all such among us as appreciate them, but also for the sake of future Egyptologists. Five hundred years hence Egypt should still be able to show to the scholars who shall visit her the same monuments that we are now describing. The amount of information already obtained from the deciphering of hieroglyphs, though this science is still in its infancy, is already immense. What will it be when several generations of savants shall have studied those admirable ruins, of which one may truly say that the more they are known, the more they repay the labour bestowed upon them?

We therefore earnestly beg again and again all travellers in Upper Egypt to abstain from the childish practice of writing their names on the monuments. Let anyone, for instance, visit Tih's tomb, at Sakkárah, and he will rest satisfied that this tomb has actually suffered more damage by the hand of tourists during the last ten years than it had during the whole of the previous six thousand years of its existence. Sethi I's beautiful tomb at Bab-el-Molouk is almost entirely disfigured, and it is all we can do to prevent the evil from increasing. M. Ampère, who visited Egypt in 1844 has, perhaps, overstepped the mark in the following lines extracted from his journal; yet we will transcribe them to show to what opprobrium those travellers expose themselves who thoughtlessly engrave their names on the monuments: 'The first thing that strikes one on approaching the monument (Pompey's Pillar) is the number of names traced in gigantic characters by travellers, who have thus impertinently engraved a record of their obscurity on the time-honoured column. Nothing can be more silly than this mania, borrowed from the Greeks, which disfigures the monuments when it does not altogether destroy them. In many places, hours of patient toil have been expended in carving on the granite the large letters which dishonour it. How can anyone give himself so much trouble to let the world know that an individual, perfectly unknown, has visited a monument, and that this unknown individual has mutilated it?' We recommend the perusal of the above lines to the young American traveller who, in 1870, visited all the ruins in Upper Egypt with a pot of *tar* in one hand and a brush in the other, leaving on all the temples the indelible and truly disgraceful record of his passage.

We have no advice to give to those travellers who wish to purchase antiquities and to take them home as souvenirs of their visit to Egypt. They will find more than one excellent factory at Luxor.

But to travellers who wish really to turn their journey to some account, we would recommend the search after papyri. In fact, there is nothing in the way of monuments more precious than a papyrus. One knows fairly well what may be expected from a temple or from a tomb; but with the papyrus one is in the dark. In fact, such a papyrus might be discovered as would prove of more importance than an entire temple; and certain it is that if ever one of those discoveries that bring about a revolution in science should be made in Egyptology, the world will be indebted for it to a papyrus.

As all excavations are interdicted in Egypt and no permissive firman has ever been given, one might imagine that opportunities of purchasing papyri can never present themselves. Such, however, is not the case. All travellers in Upper Egypt must have seen fellahs working in those parts of the ruins where the crude-brick walls are crumbling into powder. What they are seeking is the dust which comes from the crumbling bricks, and which they use for manure. Now and then, however, a piece of good luck awaits them, and it is not an uncommon occurrence for a papyrus to be found in this manure. Nor must it be forgotten that, in spite of all prohibitions, clandestine searches are made, particularly at Thebes, and in this way also, among many other monuments, papyri may be discovered. It is for the traveller to make inquiries and to examine into the matter, not at Thebes only, but at all the stations where the *dahabeah* stops. The fine collection of Mr Harris, at Alexandria, was formed in no other manner; and it was by mere accident that Madame d'Orbiney purchased the papyrus, now in the British Museum, which has rendered her name famous. In the present state of Egyptology, no greater service can be rendered to science than in securing any papyrus which accidentally falls into the hands of the fellahs, and which, sooner or later, must be entirely lost, if not thus preserved from destruction.

Monuments of Upper Egypt, 1877

Excavations in Egypt

JOHANN LUDWIG BURCKHARDT

JOHANN LUDWIG BURCKHARDT (*1784-1817*) *was born in Lausanne and received his education in Germany. He travelled to England with letters of introduction to the President of the Royal Society who was also the founder of the African Association. After three years' study in London and Cambridge he was instructed by the Association to go to Syria to study the Arabic language and customs in preparation for a journey of exploration to the regions south of the Sahara. This he did, and in 1812 he arrived in Cairo but, unable to find a suitable caravan for his intended destination, travelled instead up the Nile, eastward from Shendi to Suakin, thence to Mecca and Modena, through Suez and back to Cairo, arriving in 1815. He remained there for two years, and died without ever carrying out the Sahara expedition.*

You will be pleased to hear that the colossal head from Thebes has at last, after many difficulties, safely arrived at Alexandria. Mr Belzoni, who offered himself to undertake this commission, has executed it with great spirit, intelligence, and perseverance. The head is waiting now at Alexandria for a proper conveyance to Malta. Mr Salt and myself have borne the expenses jointly, and the trouble of the undertaking has devolved upon Mr Belzoni, whose name I wish to be mentioned, if ever ours shall on this occasion, because he was actuated by public spirit fully as much as ourselves. The Committee need not be under any apprehension, that this transaction has caused my name to become of public notoriety in Egypt; which would certainly have been the case, if it had been known that I have had any thing to do with it. The Kahirines ascribe it entirely to Mr Salt and Mr Belzoni, who, they say, send it to England to have it taken to pieces, in order to find the invaluable jewel which it contains. The residence of the French Savans in Egypt has not taught them to form better notions, and the same kind of belief which caused the Shikh of Tedmor to resist my carrying off a small mutilated bust, found near the portico at Palmyra, still operates in every part of Egypt.

The peasants of Gourne reported to me, that the French had in vain endeavoured to carry off this head; and that they had even cut a hole in the lower part of the bust, to blow off part of the stone, and render it thus more transportable. I am ignorant for what reason they relinquished that scheme, but it is somewhat curious to find that in the drawing which they have given of that head, in their great work, they have represented it as it would probably have been, after the lower part should have been destroyed.

The discoveries of Mr Belzoni in Upper Egypt, are too interesting not to deserve notice here. He has half cleared the temple of Ebsambal in Nubia, of the sands that obstructed it. The frontispiece of the temple, which has thus been discovered, is full of hieroglyphics; of the four colossi which stand before it, the face of one only (which I have mentioned in my journal), remains perfect; one of the three others has been reduced by mutilation to a mere lump of rock.

Behind Gourne he has discovered a new tomb of the kings, about one mile distant from the most western 'insulated tomb', as the French laid it down in their map. He says it is beautiful, and larger than any of the others, with a sarcophagus in it. All the paintings are done upon a white stucco, adhering loosely to the wall, and thus easily to be removed.

By digging at Gourne, in the plain between the Memnonium, and Medinet Habou, in a western direction from the two sitting colossi, about half a mile distant from them, he found a mutilated colossal head of granite, of much larger dimensions than the one he carried off, or any other at Thebes, being from ten to twelve feet across the front.

You remember the small pond, within the enclosure of the interior part of the temple of Karnak, towards the side of Luxor, which encircles on three sides an elevated ground. A row of Andro-sphynxes, or whatever they may be called, stand there, which the French had dug up, and of which Mr William Banks carried off last year the two best. In digging farther on in the line in which these statues stood, Mr Belzoni has discovered eighteen others, of similar shape, but of much superior workmanship, all in beautiful preservation; he has brought down six of them to Mr Salt, who had furnished him with money for the express purpose of procuring antiquities; besides the commission to carry off the head. By the side of these figures he has found another statue, of a hard, large grained sand stone: it is a whole length naked figure, sitting upon a chair, with a ram's head upon the knees; the face and body entire; with plaited hair falling down to the shoulders. This is one of the finest, I should say the finest Egyptian statue I have seen; the expression of the face is exquisite, and I believe it to be a portrait. From the beautiful preservation of all these figures, which is so rare in Egypt, Mr Belzoni argues, that the Egyptians used this place to hide their idols, when the Persians came to destroy them, and he hopes, in going up a second time to Thebes, to find at the same place other treasures. He has likewise found at Karnak, the four sided monument, with figures in high relief on three sides of it, of which the French talk so highly in their work, and of which they have given a drawing. But it was in quite a different place from that indicated by them, for Mr Belzoni found it under ground far to the east of the adytum of Karnak. This, with a dozen of Sphynxes, he has been obliged to leave on the shore of the river near Karnark, the boat being already over loaded. The head alone weighs, I believe, from twelve to fifteen tons.

Mr Belzoni, who is as enterprising as he is intelligent, high-minded, and disinterested, further informs us, that he has dug up the colossus, indicated by the French upon their map of Karnak, as laying on the N.W. side of the abovementioned pond, under the name of 'Colosse renversé.' He has turned it up, and finds it to be a torso without head, or feet, about thirty feet in length, of beautiful workmanship; he says that he has seen nothing in Egypt, not even excepting our head, that can be compared to it, as it is a true imitation of nature, not done in the usual hard style, but according to the best rules of art.

If Mr Belzoni had had a flat bottomed boat at his command, he is confident that he should have been able to float down one of the small obelisks of Philæ, about twenty five feet in length. He handles masses of this kind with as much facility as others handle pebbles, and the Egyptians who see him a giant in figure, for he is six feet and a half high, believe him to be a sorcerer. Manual labour is so very cheap in Upper Egypt, that a little money goes a great way: the hire for a Fellah per day, is about four-pence; although upwards of one hundred Fellahs were occupied for many days with our head, and that we paid one hundred pounds for the boat only, and made a present to Mr Belzoni, small indeed, but as much as our circumstances permitted, the total expense incurred by us, as far as Alexandria, does not amount to more than three hundred pounds, and Mr Belzoni's whole expedition, to about four hundred and fifty pounds. The Pasha of Egypt is luckily not yet aware of the value of these statues; if he was, he would probably imitate Wely Pasha of the Morea, and ask for passage money, for he extends his extortions over every article of Egyptian produce, and condescends even to farm out the trade of camel and sheep's dung. Mr Belzoni, who is known in England as a hydraulic engineer, and is married to an English woman, who has accompanied him to Egypt, entered last year the service of the Pasha, as a mechanic, but not being able to contend with the intrigues of a Turkish court, and too honourable to participate in them, he was dismissed as unfit for his business, and five months of pay still remain due to him. So much for the Pasha's encouragement of European artists. They are enticed into his service by his emissaries in the Mediterranean, but are soon left to bewail their credulity.

You will find in the notes accompanying my translation of Macrizi, the account of some other very interesting discoveries, in the Eastern mountains of Upper Egypt; and last month, the old and so often visited pyramid of Djize was so well rummaged, that much curious new matter has come to light. Mr Caviglia, an Italian, and Mr Kabitch, a German, settled here, formed the project of exploring the well in the great pyramid. In the course of the operation they have discovered that a continuation of the descending passage leads to a chamber under the centre of the pyramid, and they find that no other well descends into the passage.

I have been led to believe from various circumstances, that this new discovered continuation of the entrance passage was opened in the time of the Khalif who opened the pyramid, and that it has been choked up ever since. If I am to believe Sherif Edrys, the author of a history of the Pyramids, a book, I believe, unknown in Europe, and which I have lately purchased here, the interior of the pyramid is full of passages and rooms, and several sarcophagi are yet to be discovered. This author wrote in the twelfth century, and himself minutely examined the pyramid.

Travels in Nubia, 1819

A visit to Thebes

DOMINIQUE VIVANT DENON

DOMINIQUE VIVANT, BARON DENON (1745–1825), was born at Châlon-sur-Saone and studied law at Paris. He was a highly versatile man of many talents, and soon turned to arts and letters, writing a successful comedy at the age of twenty-two, after which he took up drawing and painting. He rose to favour in court circles and carried out several commissions, both diplomatic and artistic, for Louis XV. When the Revolution broke out he was on a mission to Naples but he immediately returned to France, where he managed to survive in spite of his aristocratic connection under the protection and patronage of the famous painter David. Napoleon, whose universal mind neglected no possible detail which could lead to the aggrandisement of France, invited Denon to join the group of scholars who followed the army to Egypt to study antiquities, and he made meticulous notes and drawings of all he saw, often conducting his observations with the utmost coolness in the middle of a major battle. He was later appointed Director General of Museums, and followed several other campaigns in the same way.

About noon we arrived at the territory of Thebes; and at the distance of three-quarters of a league from the Nile, we saw the ruins of a large temple, which have never been noticed by travellers, and which may give an idea of the immensity of that city, since, if we suppose that this was the farthest edifice on the eastern side, it is more than two leagues and a half distant from Medinet-Abu, where we observed the most western temple. It was now the third time of my passing Thebes; but, as if fate had willed that I should invariably be in haste, I could take but a hasty view of what so strongly interested me; I therefore confined myself to endeavour to account for what I saw, and to a few notes relating to what I might delineate on my return, provided I should then be more fortunate. I wished to ascertain whether at Thebes the arts had had different epochs and a chronology. If a palace once existed in Egypt, the ruins of it must be sought at Thebes, since this had been the metropolitan city; and if there were in reality epochs in the arts, the result of the first attempts must also be sought for in this capital, because luxury and magnificence have departed progressively from this point of simplicity, since they proceed only in company of opulence and superfluity. At length we arrived at Karnac, a village built on a small part of the site of a single temple, the circumference of which, as has been somewhere said, would require half an hour to perform its circumition. Herodotus, by whom it was not visited, has, notwithstanding, given a correct idea of its grandeur and magnificence. Diodorus and Strabo, who only examined it in its ruinous state, seem to have given the description of its present conditions; and all the travellers by whom they have been copied, have mistaken a great extent of masses for the proportions of beauty, and, having suffered themselves rather to be taken by surprise than to be delighted on an inspection of the largest ruins in the universe, have not dared to prefer the temple of Apollinopolis at Etfu, that of Tintyra, and the simple portico at Esneh, to the ruins in question. The temples of Karnac and Luxor were probably built in the time of Sesostris, when the flourishing state of Egypt gave birth to the arts, and when these arts were perhaps first displayed to an admiring world. The vanity of erecting colossi, was the first consideration of opulence; and it was not then known, that a perfection in the arts bestows on their productions a grandeur independent of their relative proportions: as, at first, it is not ascertained, that the small rotunda of Vicensa is a finer edifice than St Peter's at Rome; and that the school of surgery in Paris is, in point of style, as grand as the pantheon of the French capital; or that a cameo may be preferable to a colossal statue. It is therefore the sumptuousness alone of the Egyptians which must be observed at Karnac, where not only quarries, but mountains are heaped together, and sculptured into massive proportions, the units of which are feebly executed, and the parts aukward in appearance; and these masses are overspread with uncouth bas-reliefs, and tasteless hieroglyphics, as barbarous as the sculpture itself. The only objects there which are sublime, both with regard to their dimensions, and the skill of their workmanship, are the obelisks, and a few remains of the outer gates, the style of which is truly admirable. If in the other parts of this edifice the Egyptians appear to us to be giants, in the last mentioned production they are genii. Hence I am convinced, that these sublime embellishments were posteriorly added to the colossal monuments. It cannot however be denied, that the plan of the temple is noble and grand. But the art of contriving beautiful

plans, has, in architecture, invariably preceded that of the fine execution of the respective parts, and has survived for several centuries the
corruption of the latter, as is proved at once by a comparison of the
monuments of Thebes with those of Esneh and Tintyra, as well as by
the edifices of the reign of Dioclesian, when compared with those of
the golden age of Augustus.

To the descriptions of this great edifice of Karnac, which are already
known, I must observe, that it was but a temple, and could be nothing
else. All that exists at present belongs to a very small sanctuary, and had
been disposed in this way to inspire a due degree of veneration, and to
form a kind of tabernacle. While examining the whole mass of these
ruins, the imagination is fatigued with the mere thought of describing
them. The portico of this temple alone contains an hundred columns;
the smallest are seven feet and an half in diameter, and the largest
eleven. The space occupied by its circumvallation contained lakes and
mountains; while avenues of sphinxes reached even to the very gates.
In short, to form a competent idea of so much magnificence, it is
necessary that the reader should fancy what is before him to be a dream,
for even the spectator cannot believe his eyes. But with respect to the
present state of this edifice, it is necessary at the same time to observe,
that a great part of the effect is lost by its very degraded condition.
The sphinxes have been wantonly thrown down; but barbarism,
wearied with destroying, has spared a few of them; and on examining
these, it is easy to perceive that some of them had a woman's head,
others that of a lion, a ram, or a bull. The avenue which leads from
Karnac to Luxor was of the last mentioned description; and this space,
which is nearly half a league in extent, contains a constant succession
of these figures scattered to the right and left, together with fragments
of stone walls, of small columns, and of statues. The position being in
the centre of the city, the part which was the most advantageously
situated, there is reason to suppose that the palace of the kings or great
people was erected on that site. But though several traces render this
probable, the fact is not proved by any extraordinary magnificence.

Luxor, the finest village in these environs, is also built on the site of
the ruins of a temple, not so large as that of Karnac, but in a better state
of preservation, time not having yet destroyed the masses, nor have they
fallen by their own pressure. The most colossal parts consist of fourteen
columns of ten feet in diameter, and of two statues in granite, at the
outer gate, buried up to the middle of the arms, and having in front
of them the two largest and best preserved obelisks in the whole

country. It is, without doubt, flattering to the pomp of Thebes, that the richest and most powerful republic in the world should not possess means sufficient, not to hew out, or merely to transport these two monuments, which are no more than a fragment of one of the numerous edifices of that astonishing city.

One peculiarity belonging to the temple of Luxor, is, that a quay, provided with a demibastion, secured the eastern part, which was near the river, from the damages which might have been occasioned by the inundations.

This means of defence, which since its origin has been repaired and augmented by brick-work, proves that the river has not changed its bed; and its state of preservation also proves, that the Nile has never been banked by other quays, since no traces of similar constructions are to be met with in other parts of the city.

The entrance of the village of Luxor exhibits a striking mixture of beggary and magnificence, and impresses me with an awful idea of the gradation of ages in Egypt. It appears to me to be the most picturesque group, and the most striking representation of the history of the times: never were my eyes and my imagination so forcibly struck as by the sight of this monument. I often came to meditate on this spot, to enjoy the past and the present, to compare the successive generations of inhabitants by their respective works, which were before my eyes, and to store in mind volumes of materials for future meditations. One day the sheik of the village accosted me whilst sitting down on these ruins, and asked me if it was the French or the English who had erected the monuments; and this question put an end to my reflections.

There are two obelisks of rose-coloured granite, which are still seventy feet above the ground, and to judge by the depth to which the figures seem to be covered, we may suppose about thirty feet more to be concealed from the eye, making in all one hundred feet for the height of these monuments. Their preservation is perfect, the hieroglyphics with which they are covered are cut deep, and in relief at the bottom, and shew the bold hand of a master. What an admirable sharpness must the gravers possess, that could touch such hard materials! what time required for the labour! what machines to drag such enormous blocks out of the quarries, to transport them hither, and to set them erect! There are also two colossi of the same material, but they are worn and decayed; yet the parts that remain shew that they had been completed in the most perfect manner. We may here remark, that the custom of piercing the ears was known to the ancient Egyptians, as these statues still bear the impression of auricular perforations. Two large masses which form the gate are covered with sculpture, representing battles between chariots arranged in lines, drawn by two horses, and containing a single champion.

Nothing can possibly be more grand than the gate just mentioned, nor nothing more simple than the small number of objects of which this entrance is composed. No city whatever makes so proud a display at its approach as this wretched village, the population of which consists of two or three thousand souls, who have taken up their abodes on the roofs and beneath the galleries of the temple, which has nevertheless the semblance of being in a state of desolation.

During the time I was occupied in taking a plan, our cavalry was engaged with a small party of straggling Mamelukes, two of whom were killed, and the others escaped by swimming across the river, leaving behind them their arms, horses, and accoutrements.

Travels in Upper and Lower Egypt, 1802

7. Baron Vivant Denon, shown here preparing to draw the ruins of Hierakonopolis. While Napoleon set out in 1798 to conquer the new Egypt with the sword, an artist in his entourage captured the old Egypt with his sketch pad and pencil.

8. The "second" pyramid of Giza. For a long time nobody knew whether all the pyramids of Egypt were really royal mausoleums. Especially that of King Chefren seemed to be nothing more than a massive hill of stone—until Belzoni, a former circus athlete, discovered the entrance shown here.

The opening of a pyramid

GIOVANNI BATTISTA BELZONI

GIOVANNI BATTISTA BELZONI (*1778-1823*) *was born in Padua and begin his remarkable career as a strong man in a circus. In this capacity he travelled extensively, and in 1815 another aspect of this versatile character became evident when he went to Egypt to offer to the government a hydraulic irrigation machine of his own invention. His offer was not accepted, but his engineering talents were called on when, through the influence of the British consul, he was commissioned to go to Thebes and arrange the transportation for the British Museum of the head of Ramesses II known as the Colossus of Memnon. This he achieved so successfully that he decided to continue his work on Egyptian antiquities, which he did with immense energy and enthusiasm. He explored Edfu, Elephantine and Philae, cleared the sand from the temple at Abu Simbel, excavated extensively at Karnak, discovered the tomb of Seti I which contained a magnificent sarcophagus now to be seen in the Soane Museum, London, and was the first to penetrate the second pyramid at Giza. In 1819 he returned to England to supervise an exhibition of his finds, and in 1823 he was commissioned to undertake a journey to Timbuktoo, but died on the way.*

Before my departure for Thebes I visited the pyramids in company with two other persons from Europe. On our arrival at these monuments they went into the first pyramid, while I took a turn round the second. I seated myself in the shade of one of those stones on the east side, which form the part of the temple that stood before the pyramid in that direction. My eyes were fixed on that enormous mass, which for so many ages has baffled the conjectures of ancient and modern writers. Herodotus himself was deceived by the Egyptian priests, when told there were no chambers in it. The sight of the wonderful work before me astonished me as much as the total obscurity in which we are of its origin, its interior, and its construction. In an intelligent age like the present one of the greatest wonders of the world stood before us, without our knowing even whether it had any cavity in the interior, or if it were only one solid mass. The various attempts which have been made by numerous travellers to find an entrance into this pyramid, and particularly by the great body of French savans, were examples so weighty, that it seemed little short of madness, to think of renewing the enterprise. Indeed, the late researches made by Mr Salt himself, and by Captain Cabilia, during four months, round these pyramids, were apparently sufficient to deter any one. A short time before this period the few Franks who resided in Egypt had some idea of obtaining permission from Mahomed Ali, and by the help of a subscription, which was to be made at the various Courts in Europe to the amount of at least £20,000, were to force their way into the centre of this pyramid by explosions, or any other means that could be suggested. Mr Drouetti was to have had the superintendence of this work. Indeed it had created some difference among themselves who was to have had the direction of the whole concern. Was not this enough to show the difficulties I had to encounter, and to make me laugh at myself, if any thought of such an attempt should cross my mind? Besides, there was another obstacle to overcome. I had to consider, that in consequence of what I had the good fortune to do in Upper Egypt, and under the circumstances above mentioned, it was not likely that I should obtain permission to make such an attempt: for if it could be supposed, that there was any possibility of penetrating into the pyramid, the operation would certainly be given to people of higher influence than myself.

With all these thoughts in my mind I arose, and by a natural impulsion took my walk toward the south side of the pyramid. I examined every part, and almost every stone. I continued to do so on the west – at last I came round to the north. Here the appearance of things became to my eye somewhat different from that at any of the other sides. The constant observations enabled me to see what other travellers did not: indeed, I think this ought to be considered as a standing proof, that in many cases practice goes farther than theory. Other travellers had been also in various places where I had been, and came often to the same spot where I was, but perhaps did not make the observations I did. I certainly must beg leave to say, that I often observed travellers, who, confident of their own knowledge, let slip opportunities of ascertaining whether they were correct in their notions; and if an observation was made to them by any one, who had not the good fortune of having received a classical education, they scorned to listen to it, or replied with a smile, if not a laugh of disapprobation, without investigating whether the observation were just or not. I had often the satisfaction of seeing such travellers mortified by the proof of being wrong in their conjecture. I do not mean to say, that a man, who has had a classical education, should think himself under a disadvantage in regard to knowing such things, compared with him who has not; but, that a man, who thinks himself well informed on a subject, often does not examine it with such precision as another, who is less confident in himself.

I observed on the north side of the pyramid three marks, which encouraged me to attempt searching there for the entrance into it. Still it is to be remarked, that the principal signs I discovered there were not deduced solely from the knowledge I had acquired among the tombs of the Egyptians at Thebes; for any traveller will acknowledge, that the pyramids have little in common with the tombs, either in their exterior appearance, or in any shape whatever: – they are two different things, – one is formed by a vast accumulation of large blocks of stones: – the other is entirely hewed out of the solid rock. My principal guide, I must own, was the calculation I made from the first pyramid, and such was my assurance on this point, that I then almost resolved to make the attempt. I had been at the pyramids various times before, but never with any intention of examining into the practicability of finding the entrance into them, which was deemed almost impossible. The case was now different – I saw then what I had not seen before – I observed, that just under the centre of the face of the pyramid the accumulation of materials, which had fallen from the coating of it, was higher than the entrance could be expected to be, if compared with the height of the entrance into the first pyramid, measuring from the basis. I could not conceive how the discovery of the entrance into the second pyramid could be considered as a matter to be despaired of, when no one had ever seen the spot, where it must naturally be presumed to exist, if there were any entrance at all. I farther observed, that the materials which had fallen exactly in the centre of the front were not so compact as those on the sides; and hence concluded, that the stones on that spot, had been removed after the falling of the coating. Consequently I perceived the probability of there being an entrance into the pyramid at that spot. Encouraged by these observations, I rejoined my companions in the first pyramid. We visited the great sphinx, and returned to Cairo the same evening.

I resolved to make a closer examination the next day, which I did accordingly, without communicating my intention to any one, as it would have excited great enquiry among the Franks at Cairo, and in all probability I should not have obtained permission to proceed in my design. The next day's examination encouraged me in the attempt. I was confident, that, if my purpose had been known to certain persons, who had influence at the court of the Bashaw, I should never succeed in obtaining permission. On the following day therefore I crossed the Nile to Embabe, as the Cacheff who commanded the province which includes the pyramids resided there. I introduced myself to him, and acquainted him with my intention to excavate the pyramids, if it met his approbation. His answer was, as I expected, that I must apply to the Bashaw, or to the Kakia Bey, for a firman, without which it was not in his power to grant me permission to excavate at the harrans, or pyramids. I asked him, whether he had any other objection, provided I obtained the firman from the Bashaw; he replied, 'none whatever'. I then went to the citadel, and as the Bashaw was not in Cairo, I presented myself to the Kakia Bey, who knew me from the time I was at Soubra, and who, on my request for permission to excavate at the pyramids, had no other objection, than that of not being certain, whether round the harrans there were any ploughed grounds, on which he could not grant permission to dig. He sent a message to the above Cacheff at Embabe, who assured him, that round the harrans there was no cultivated land, but that on the contrary it was solid rock.

With such an assurance I obtained a firman to the Cacheff, to furnish me with men to work at the pyramids. My undertaking was of no small importance: it consisted of an attempt to penetrate into one of the great pyramids of Egypt, one of the wonders of the world. I was confident, that a failure in such an attempt would have drawn on me the laughter of all the world for my presumption in undertaking such a task: but at the same time I considered, that I might be excused, since without attempting we should never accomplish any thing. However, I thought it best to keep my expedition as secret as possible; and I communicated it only to Mr Walmas, a worthy Levantine merchant of Cairo, and partner in the house of Briggs. It is not to be understood, that I intended to conceal the attempt I wished to make on the pyramids, for the effects of my work would plainly show themselves; but being near the capital, where many Europeans resided, I could not prevent myself from being interrupted during my operations; and as I knew too well how far the influence and intrigues of my opponents could be carried, I was not certain, that the permission I had procured might not have been countermanded, so as to put an end to all my proceedings.

Accordingly having provided myself with a small tent, and some provision, that I might not be under the necessity of repairing to Cairo, I set off for the pyramids.

My sudden departure from Cairo was supposed to be an expedition to the mountain of Mokatam, for a few days, as I had given out. At the pyramids I found the Arabs willing to work, and immediately set about the operation.

My purse was but light, for very little remained of what I received as a present from Mr Burckhardt, and the consul; and though it had been a little strengthened by the two statues I lately disposed of to the Count de Forbin, who had paid me one-third of the money on account, my whole stock did not amount to two hundred pounds, and if I did not succeed in penetrating the pyramid before this was exhausted, I should have been at a stand, before the accomplishment of my undertaking, and perhaps prepared the way for others stronger than myself in purse.

Two points principally excited my attention: the first was on the north side of the pyramid, and the second on the east. There is on the latter side part of a portico of the temple which stood before the pyramid, and which has a causeway descending straight towards the great sphinx. I thought, that by opening the ground between the portico and the pyramid I should necessarily come to the foundation of the temple, which in fact I did. I set eighty Arabs to work, forty on the above spot, and forty in the centre of the north side of the pyramid where I observed the earth not so solid as on the east and west. The Arabs were paid daily one piastre each, which is sixpence English money. I had also several boys and girls to carry away the earth, to whom I gave only twenty paras, or three pence, a day. I contrived to gain their good will by trifles I gave as presents, and by pointing out to them the advantage they would gain, if we succeeded in penetrating into the pyramid, as many visitors would come to see it, and they would get bakshis from them. Nothing has so much influence on the mind of an Arab as reasoning with him about his own interest, and showing him the right way to benefit himself. Any thing else he seems not to understand. I must confess, at the same time, that I found this mode of proceeding quite as efficacious in Europe.

The works on each side continued for several days without the smallest appearance of any thing. On the north side of the pyramid, the materials which were to be removed, consisting of what had fallen from the coating, notwithstanding the appearance of having been removed at a later period than the first, were so closely cemented together, that the men could scarcely proceed. The only instrument they had to work with was a kind of hatchet or spade, which being rather thin, and only fit to cut the soft ground, could not stand much work among stones and mortar, which latter I suppose, as it fell from the pyramid, had been moistened by the dew, and gradually formed itself almost into one mass with the stones.

On the east side of the pyramid, we found the lower part of a large temple connected with the portico, and reaching within fifty feet of the basis of the pyramid. Its exterior walls were formed of enormous blocks of stone, as may now be seen. Some of the blocks in the porticoes are twenty-four feet high. The interior part of this temple was built with calcareous stones of various sizes, but many finely cut at the angles, and is probably much older than the exterior wall, which bears the appearance of as great antiquity as the pyramids. In order to find the basis of the pyramid on this side, and to ascertain whether there were any communication between it and the temple, I had to cut through all the material, there accumulated, which rose above forty feet from the basis, and consisted of large blocks of stone and mortar, from the coating, as on the north side. At last we reached the basis, and I perceived a flat pavement cut out of the solid rock. I caused all that was before me to be cut in a right line from the basis of the pyramid to the temple, and traced the pavement quite to the back of it, so that there was evidently a spacious pavement from the temple to the pyramid; and I do not hesitate to declare my opinion, that the same pavement goes all round the pyramid. It appeared to me, that the sphinx, the temple, and the pyramid, were all three erected at the same time, as they all appear to be in one line, and of equal antiquity. On the north side the work advanced towards the basis; a great number of large stones had been removed, and a great part of the face of the pyramid was uncovered, but still there was no appearance of any entrance, or the smallest mark to indicate that there ever had been one.

The Arabs had great confidence in the hopes I had excited among them, that if any entrance into the pyramid were found, I would give great bakshis, in addition to the advantage they would derive from other strangers. But after many vain expectations, and much hard labour in removing huge masses of stone, and cutting the mortar, which was so hard that their hatchets were nearly all broken, they began to flag in their prospect of finding any thing, and I was about to become an object of ridicule for making the attempt to penetrate a place, which appeared to them, as well as to more civilised people, a mass of solid stone. However, as long as I paid them they continued their work, though with much less zeal. My hopes did not forsake me, in spite of all the difficulties I saw, and the little appearance of making the discovery of an entrance into the pyramid. Still I observed, as we went on with our work, that the stones on that spot were not so consolidated as those on the sides of them, and this circumstance made me determine to proceed, till I should be persuaded that I was wrong in my conjecture. At last, on the 18th of February, after sixteen days of fruitless labour, one of the Arabian workmen perceived a small chink between two stones of the pyramid. At this he was greatly rejoiced, thinking we had found the entrance so eagerly sought for. I perceived the aperture was small, but I thrust a long palm-stick into it upwards of two yards. Encouraged by this circumstance, the Arabs resumed their vigour on the work, and great hopes were entertained among them. Thus it served my purpose, as the work now went on briskly. I was aware, that the entrance to the pyramid could not be between two stones in this manner; but I was in hopes, that the aperture would furnish some clew by which the right entrance would be discovered. Proceeding farther, I perceived, that one of the stones, apparently fixed in the pyramid, was in fact loose. I had it removed the same day, and found an opening leading to the interior. This sort of rough entrance was not more than three feet wide, and was choked up with smaller stones and sand, which being removed, it proved to be much wider within. A second and third day were employed in clearing this place; but the farther we advanced, the more materials we found. On the fourth day I observed, that sand and stones were falling from the upper part of this cavity, which surprised me not a little. At last I found, that there was a passage from the outside of the pyramid by a higher aperture, which apparently was thought to have had no communication with any cavity. When all the rubbish was taken out, and the place cleared, I continued the work in the lower part beneath our feet; and in two days more we came to an opening inward. Having made it wide enough, I took a candle in my hand, and, looking in, perceived a spacious cavity, of which I could not form any conjecture. Having caused the entrance to be cleared of the sand and stones, I found a tolerably spacious place, bending its course towards the centre. It is evidently a forced passage, executed by some powerful hand, and appears intended to find a way to the centre of the pyramid. Some of the stones, which are of an enormous size, are cut through, some have been taken out, and others are on the point of falling from their old places for want of support. Incredible must have been the labour in making such a cavity, and it is evident, that it was continued farther on towards the centre; but the upper part had fallen in, and filled up the cavity to such a degree, that it was impossible for us to proceed any farther than a hundred feet. Half this distance from the entrance is another cavity, which descends forty feet, in an irregular manner, but still turns towards the centre, which no doubt was the point intended by the persons who made the excavation. To introduce many men to work in this place was dangerous, for several of the stones above our heads were on the point of falling; some were suspended only by their corners, which stuck between other stones, and with the least touch would have fallen, and crushed any one that happened to be under them. I set a few men to work, but was soon convinced of the impossibility of advancing any farther in that excavation. In one of the passages below, one of the men narrowly escaped being crushed to pieces. A large block of stone, no less than six feet long and four wide, fell from the top, while the man was digging under it; but fortunately it rested on two other stones, one on each side of him, higher than himself, as he was sitting at his work. The man was so incarcerated, that we had some difficulty in getting him out; yet, happily, he received no other injury than a slight bruise on his back. The falling of this stone moved many others in this passage: indeed, they were so situated, that I thought it prudent to retreat out of the pyramid, or we might have reason to repent when too late; for the danger was not only from what might fall upon us, but also from what might fall in our way, close up the passage, and thus bury us alive. My expectation in this passage was not great, as I perceived from the beginning it could not be the true entrance into the pyramid, though I had strong hopes that it would lead to some clew for the discovery of the real entrance; but, alas! it gave me none, and I remained as ignorant of it as I was before I began.

Having spent so many days at the pyramids without being discovered by any of the people at Cairo, I did not expect, that my retreat could be concealed much longer, as there were constantly Franks from Cairo making a Sunday's excursion to the pyramids, or travellers, who, of course, made it a point to see these wonders on their first arrival at the metropolis. In fact, the very day I was to have quitted this work, I perceived, in the afternoon, some people on the top of the first pyramid. I had no doubt they were Europeans, as the Arabs or Turks never go up, unless to accompany somebody, to gain money. They saw part of my men at work at the second pyramid, and concluded that none but Europeans could be conducting such an operation. They fired a pistol as a signal, and I returned another. They then descended the angle which led towards us; and on their arrival proved to be Monsieur L'Abbé de Forbin, who had accompanied his cousin, the celebrated Count, into Egypt, but did not proceed higher. With them were the father superior of the convent of Terra Santa. Mr Costa, an engineer, and Mr Gaspard, vice-consul of France, by whom I was introduced to the Abbé. They all entered into the newly discovered passage; but it gave the Abbé less pleasure than a cup of coffee, which he honoured me by accepting in my humble tent. Naturally, after such a visit, all the Franks in Cairo knew what I was doing; and not a day passed without my having some visitors.

I was determined to proceed still farther with my researches, the recent disappointment making me rather more obstinate than I was before. I had given a day's rest to the Arabs, which I dedicated to a closer inspection of the pyramid. It often happens, that a man is so much ingulfed in the pursuit of his views, as to be in danger of losing himself, if he do not quickly find the means either of an honourable retreat, or of attaining the accomplishment of his intended purpose. Such was my case. The success of my discovery of the false passage was considered as a failure. I cared little what was thought of it, but I was provoked at having been deceived by those marks, which led me to the forced passage, with the loss of so much time and labour. However, I did not despair. I strictly noticed the situation of the entrance into the first pyramid, and plainly saw, that it was not in the centre of the pyramid. I observed that the passage ran in a straight line from the outside of the pyramid to the east side of the king's chamber; and this chamber being nearly in the centre of the pyramid, the entrance consequently must be as far from the middle of the face as the distance from the centre of the chamber to the east side of it.

Having made this clear and simple observation, I found, that, if there were any chamber at all in the second pyramid, the entrance or passage could not be on the spot where I had excavated, which was in the centre, but calculating by the passage in the first pyramid, the entrance into the second would be near thirty feet to the east.

Satisfied with this calculation, I repaired to the second pyramid to examine the mass of rubbish. There I was not a little astonished when I perceived the same marks, which I had seen on the other spot in the centre, about thirty feet distant from where I stood. This gave me no little delight, and hope returned to cherish my pyramidical brains. I observed in this spot also, that the stones and mortar were not so compact as on the east side, which mark had given me so much encouragement to proceed in the first attempt; but what increased my hopes was an observation I made on the exterior of the front where the forced passage is. I observed the stones had been removed several feet from the surface of the pyramid, which I ascertained by drawing a line with the coating above to the basis below, and found the concavity was inclined to be deeper towards the spot where I intended to make my new attempt. Any traveller, who shall hereafter visit the pyramids, may plainly perceive this concavity above the true entrance. Such has been the effect of two different hints; first my old guide from Thebes, I mean the spots where the stony matter is not so compact as the surrounding mass; and, secondly, the concavity of the pyramid over the place where the entrance might have been expected to be found, according to the distance of the entrance into the first pyramid from its centre.

I immediately summoned the Arabs to work the next day. They were pleased at my recommencing the task, not in hopes of finding the entrance into the pyramid, but for the continuation of the pay they of course were to receive. As to expectation that the entrance might be found, they had none; and I often heard them utter, in a low voice, the word '*magnoon*', in plain English, madman. I pointed out to the Arabs the spot where they had to dig, and such was my measurement, that I was right within two feet, in a straight direction, as to the entrance into the first passage . . . and I have the pleasure of reckoning this day as fortunate, being that on which I discovered the entrance into the great tomb of Psammethis at Thebes. The Arabs began their work, and the rubbish proved to be as hard as that of the first excavation, with this addition, that we found larger blocks of stone in our way, which had belonged to the pyramid, besides the falling of the coating. The stones increased in size as we went on.

A few days after the visit of the Abbé de Forbin I was surprised by the appearance of another European traveller. It was the Chevalier Frediani, who, on his return from the second cataract of the Nile, came to visit the great pyramids. I had known him at Thebes on his ascending the Nile, and was much pleased to see him, as I thought he might be an impartial spectator of the event of my operations, which in fact he was. He greatly approved of my undertaking, but after being two days with me was ready to take his departure. I suppose he had as much expectation, that I should open the pyramid, as the Arabs who named me the *magnoon*. It happened, that on the very day he was to set off for Cairo, I perceived in the excavation a large block of granite, inclining downward at the same angle as the passage into the first pyramid, and pointing towards the centre. I requested the Chevalier to stay till the morrow, thinking perhaps he might have the pleasure of being one of the first who saw the entrance into the pyramid. He consented, and I was pleased to have a countryman of my own to be a witness of what passed on this important occasion. The discovery of the first granite stone occurred on the 28th of February, and on the 1st of March we uncovered three large blocks of granite, two on each side, and one on the top, all in an inclined direction towards the centre. My expectation and hope increased, as to all appearance, this must prove to be the object of my search. I was not mistaken, for on the next day, the 2nd of March, at noon, we came at last to the right entrance into the pyramid. The Arabs, whose expectation had also increased at the appearance of the three stones, were delighted at having found something new to show to the visitors, and get bakshis from them. Having cleared the front of the three stones, the entrance proved to be a passage four feet high, three feet six inches wide, formed of large blocks of granite, which descended towards the centre for a hundred and four feet five inches at an angle of twenty-six degrees. Nearly all this passage was filled up with large stones, which had fallen from the upper part, and as the passage is inclined downwards, they slid on till some larger than the rest stopped the way.

I had much ado to have all the stones drawn out of the passage, which was filled up to the entrance of the chamber. It took the remainder of this day and part of the next to clear it, and at last we reached a portcullis. At first sight it appeared to be a fixed block of stone, which stared me in the face, and said *ne plus ultra*, putting an end to all my projects as I thought; for it made a close joint with the groove at each side, and on the top it seemed as firm as those which formed the passage itself. On a close inspection however I perceived, that, at the bottom, it was raised about eight inches from the lower part of the groove, which is cut beneath to receive it; and I found, by this circumstance, that the large block before me was no more than a portcullis of granite, one foot three inches thick.

Having observed a small aperture at the upper part of the portcullis, I thrust a long piece of barley straw into it, and it entered upwards of three feet, which convinced me, that there was a vacuum ready to receive the portcullis. The raising of it was a work of no small consideration. The passage is only four feet high, and three feet six inches wide. When two men are in it abreast of each other they cannot move, and it required several men to raise a piece of granite not less than six feet high, five feet wide, and one foot three inches thick. The levers could not be very long, otherwise there was not space in the four feet height to work with them; and if they were short, I could not employ men enough to raise the portcullis. The only method to be taken was, to raise it a little at a time; and by putting some stones in the grooves on each side, to support the portcullis while changing the fulcrum of the levers, it was raised high enough for a man to pass. An Arab then entered with a candle, and returned saying, that the place within was very fine. I continued to raise the portcullis, and at last made the entrance large enough to squeeze myself in; and after thirty days exertion I had the pleasure of finding myself in the way to the central chamber of one of the two great pyramids of Egypt, which have long been the admiration of beholders. The Chevalier Frediani followed me, and after passing under the portcullis we entered a passage not higher or wider than the first. It is twenty-two feet seven inches long, and the works including the portcullis occupy six feet eleven inches in all. Where the granite work finishes at the end of this passage, there is a perpendicular shaft of fifteen feet, and at each side of the passage, an excavation in the solid rock, one of which, on the right as you enter, runs thirty feet in an upward direction, approaching the end of the lower part of the forced passage. . . . Before us we had a long passage running in a horizontal direction towards the centre. We descended the shaft by means of a rope. At the bottom of it I perceived another passage running downward at the same angle of 26° as that above, and toward the north. As my first object was the centre of the pyramid, I advanced that way, and ascended an inclined passage, which brought me to a horizontal one, that led toward the centre. I observed, that after we entered within the portcullis, the passages were all cut out of the solid rock. The passage leading toward the centre is five feet eleven inches high, and three feet six inches wide.

As we advanced farther on we found the sides of this passage covered with arborizations of nitre; some projecting in ropes, some not unlike the skin of a white lamb, and others so long as to resemble an endive-leaf. I reached the door at the centre of a large chamber. I walked slowly two or three paces, and then stood still to contemplate the place where I was. Whatever it might be, I certainly considered myself in the centre of that pyramid, which from time immemorial had been the subject of the obscure conjectures of many hundred travellers, both ancient and modern. My torch, formed of a few wax candles, gave but a faint light; I could, however, clearly distinguish the principal objects. I naturally turned my eyes to the west end of the chamber, looking for the sarcophagus, which I strongly expected to see in the same situation as that in the first pyramid; but I was disappointed when I saw nothing there. The chamber has a painted ceiling; and many of the stones had been removed from their places, evidently by some one in search of treasure. On my advancing toward the west end, I was agreeably surprised to find, that there was a sarcophagus buried on a level with the floor.

By this time the Chevalier Frediani had entered also; and we took a general survey of the chamber, which I found to be forty-six feet three inches long, sixteen feet three inches wide, and twenty-three feet six inches high. It is cut out of the solid rock from the floor to the roof, which is composed of large blocks of calcareous stone, meeting in the centre, and forming a roof of the same slope as the pyramid itself. The sarcophagus is eight feet long, three feet six inches wide, and two feet three inches deep in the inside. It is surrounded by large blocks of granite, apparently to prevent its removal, which could not be effected without great labour. The lid had been broken at the side, so that the sarcophagus was half open. It is of the finest granite; but, like the other in the first pyramid, there is not one hieroglyphic on it.

Looking at the inside, I perceived a great quantity of earth and stones, but did not observe the bones among the rubbish till the next day, as my attention was principally bent in search of some inscription that would throw light on the subject of this pyramid. We examined every part of the walls, and observed many scrawls executed with charcoal, but in unknown characters, and nearly imperceptible. They rubbed off into dust at the slightest touch; and on the wall at the west end of the chamber I perceived an inscription in Arabic . . . and the various interpretations given of it compel me to explain some points, which will perhaps lead to a satisfactory explanation. It appears to me, that all the difficulty lies in the last letters of the inscription, which are supposed to be obscure. This indeed is the fact; but I must say, that these letters were so blotted on the wall, that they were scarcely visible. The transcriber was a Copt, whom I had brought from Cairo for the purpose, as I would not trust to my own pen; and not being satisfied of his protestations of accuracy, though it was copied under my own eyes, I invited many other persons, who were considered as the best skilled in the Arabic language of any in Cairo, and requested them to compare the copy with the original on the wall. They found it perfectly correct, except the concluding word, which indeed appeared obscure; but if it be considered how much that word resembles the right one, we shall find a correct sense, and the whole inscription made out.

Translation of the Inscription by Mr Salame

'The Master Mohammed Ahmed, lapicide, has opened them; and the Master Othman attended this (*opening*); and the King Alij Mohammed at first (*from the beginning*) to the closing up.'

I must add, that the circumstance of the pyramid having been again closed up agrees with what I have said of my finding it so.

On several parts of the wall the nitre had formed many beautiful arborations like those in the passage, but much larger and stronger. Some were six inches long, resembling in shape a large endive leaf, as I mentioned before. Under one of the blocks that had been removed, I found something like the thick part of a hatchet, but so rusty, that it had lost its shape. At the north and south sides are two holes, which run in an horizontal direction, like those that are seen in the first pyramid, but higher up.

Returning out of this chamber we reached the passage below. At the bottom of the perpendicular shaft were so many stones as nearly to choke up its entrance, and after removing these we found the passage running to the north, at the same inclination as above, an angle of 26°.... This passage is forty-eight feet six inches in length, when it joins an horizontal passage of fifty-five feet still running north. Half-way up this passage on the right is a recess eleven feet long and six feet deep. On the left, opposite to it, is another passage, running twenty-two feet with a descent of 26° towards the west. Before we proceeded any farther toward the north, we descended this passage, and entered a chamber thirty-two feet long, nine feet nine inches wide, and eight feet six inches high. This chamber contains many small blocks of stone, some not more than two feet in length. It has a pointed roof like that before mentioned, though it is cut out of the solid rock; for it is to be understood, as I before observed, that, after we entered through the portcullis, all the passages, and the large chamber, as high as the roof, are cut out of the solid rock of calcareous stone. On the walls and roof of this chamber are several unknown inscriptions, as there are in the upper chamber. They are perhaps Coptic. Reascending into the horizontal passage, at the end of it we found grooves for a portcullis like the former; but the stone of granite which served for this purpose had been taken down, and is to be seen under the rubbish and stones near the place. Passing the portcullis we entered into a passage, which ascended in a direction parallel with that above. . . . This passage runs up forty-seven feet six inches. Here we found a large block of stone, placed there from the upper part; and by calculation I found, that this passage ran out of the pyramid at its basis, as, from the upper part of this square block, I could perceive other stones, which filled up the passage to the entrance, so that this pyramid has two entrances to it. Half-way up the horizontal passage, which leads into the large chamber, is some mason's work; but I believe it to be only the filling up of a natural cavity in the rock.

Having made all my observations, we came out of the pyramid with no small degree of satisfaction; and I was highly gratified with the result of my labour, of very little more than a month, the expense of which did not amount in all to £150, though I had accomplished a task, which was supposed would have required several thousands.

The Chevalier Frediani went to Cairo the same day, and the news of the opening of the pyramid soon brought the Franks to visit its interior. As I had no fear that the Arabian women would break the pyramid, I left the entrance open (*pro bono publico*); and in that place where the perpendicular descent, just inside the portcullis, is, I made a stone step for the accommodation of visitors, leaving half of the passage to enter into the lower chamber.

Narrative of Operations and Recent Researches in Egypt and Nubia, 1820

A cache of mummies at Thebes

GIOVANNI BATTISTA BELZONI

A traveller is generally satisfied when he has seen the large hall, the gallery, the staircase, and as far as he can conveniently go: besides, he is taken up with the strange works he observes cut in various places, and painted on each side of the walls; so that when he comes to a narrow and difficult passage, or to have to descend to the bottom of a well or cavity, he declines taking such trouble, naturally supposing that he cannot see in these abysses any thing so magnificent as what he sees above, and consequently deeming it useless to proceed any farther. Of some of these tombs many persons could not withstand the suffocating air, which often causes fainting. A vast quantity of dust rises, so fine that it enters into the throat and nostrils and chokes the nose and mouth to such a degree, that it requires great power of lungs to resist it and the strong effluvia of the mummies. This is not all; the entry or passage where the bodies are is roughly cut in the rocks, and the falling of the sand from the upper part of ceiling of the passage causes it to be nearly filled up. In some places there is not more than a vacancy of a foot left, which you must contrive to pass through in a creeping posture like a snail, on pointed and keen stones, that cut like glass. After getting through these passages, some of them two or three hundred yards long, you generally find a more commodious place, perhaps high enough to sit. But what a place of rest! surrounded by bodies, by heaps of mummies in all directions; which, previous to my being accustomed to the sight, impressed me with horror. The blackness of the wall, the faint light given by the candles or torches for want of air, the different objects that surrounded me, seeming to converse with each other, and the Arabs with the candles or torches in their hands, naked and covered with dust, themselves resembling living mummies, absolutely formed a scene that cannot be described. In such a situation I found myself several times, and often returned exhausted and fainting, till at last I became inured to it, and indifferent to what I suffered, except from the dust, which never failed to choke my throat and nose; and though, fortunately, I am destitute of the sense of smelling, I could taste that the

mummies were rather unpleasant to swallow. After the exertion of
entering into such a place, through a passage of fifty, a hundred, three
hundred, or perhaps six hundred yards, nearly overcome, I sought a
resting-place, found one, and contrived to sit; but when my weight
bore on the body of an Egyptian, it crushed it like a band-box. I
naturally had recourse to my hands to sustain my weight, but they
found no better support; so that I sunk altogether among the broken
mummies, with a crash of bones, rags, and wooden cases, which raised
such a dust as kept me motionless for a quarter of an hour, waiting till
it subsided again. I could not remove from the place, however, without
increasing it, and every step I took I crushed a mummy in some part
or other. Once I was conducted from such a place to another resembling
it, through a passage of about twenty feet in length, and no wider than
that a body could be forced through. It was choked with mummies,
and I could not pass without putting my face in contact with that of
some decayed Egyptian; but as the passage inclined downwards, my
own weight helped me on; however, I could not avoid being covered
with bones, legs, arms, and heads rolling from above. Thus I proceeded from one cave to another, all full of mummies piled up in
various ways, some standing, some lying, and some on their heads.
The purpose of my researches was to rob the Egyptians of their papyri;
of which I found a few hidden in their breasts, under their arms, in the
space above the knees, or on the legs, and covered by the numerous
folds of cloth, that envelop the mummy. The people of Gournou, who
make a trade of antiquities of this sort, are very jealous of strangers,
and keep them as secret as possible, deceiving travellers by pretending,
that they have arrived at the end of the pits, when they are scarcely at
the entrance. I could never prevail on them to conduct me into these
places till this my second voyage, when I succeeded in obtaining
admission into any cave where mummies were to be seen.

My permanent residence in Thebes was the cause of my success. The
Arabs saw that I paid particular attention to the situation of the entrance
into the tombs, and that they could not avoid being seen by me when
they were at work digging in search of a new tomb, though they are
very cautious when any stranger is in Gournou not to let it be known
where they go to open the earth; and as travellers generally remain in
that place a few days only, they used to leave off digging during that
time. If any traveller be curious enough to ask to examine the interior
of a tomb, they are ready to show him one immediately, and conduct
him to some of the old tombs, where he sees nothing but the grottoes

in which mummies formerly had been deposited, or where there are but few, and these already plundered; so that he can form but a poor idea of the real tombs, where the remains were originally placed.

The people of Gournou live in the entrance of such caves as have already been opened, and, by making partitions with earthen walls, they form habitations, for themselves, as well as for their cows, camels, buffaloes, sheep, goats, dogs, and etc.

Narrative of Operations and Recent Researches in Egypt and Nubia, 1820

The Temple of Abu Simbel

JOHANN LUDWIG BURCKHARDT

The rock-cut temple built at Abu Simbel by Ramesses II was drifted over with sand for many centuries, and when Burckhardt made his journey through Nubia only the heads of the Ramesside colossi showed above the surface. It was left to that most energetic of Egyptologists, Belzoni, to clear the sand and explore the temple, which inevitably became a focus of attraction for serious scholars and for adventurous Victorian travellers like Mrs Amelia Edwards, who accompanied a later expedition to Abu Simbel. Its emergence from the sand had endured for only a small part of its long history when it was threatened with a more permanent and more destructive inundation; it was calculated that when the new High Dam at Aswan was finished, the water level would rise to flood the temple and the porous sandstone sculptures would be completely destroyed. An appeal was launched by Unesco in the hope of raising enough money to have the entire structure lifted above water level, but funds for so costly an undertaking were not forthcoming, and, in order to save the temples, it is planned to cut them into 30-ton blocks and remove them for rebuilding beyond the reach of the Nile.

Having, as I supposed, seen all the antiquities of Ebsambal, I was about to ascend the sandy side of the mountain by the same way I had descended; when having luckily turned more to the southward, I fell in with what is yet visible of four immense colossal statues cut out of rock, at a distance of about two hundred yards from the temple; they stand in a deep recess, excavated in the mountain; but it is greatly to be regretted, that they are now almost entirely buried beneath the sands, which are blown down here in torrents. The entire head, and part of the breast and arms of one of the statues are yet above the surface; of the one next to it scarcely any part is visible, the head being broken off, and the body covered with sand to above the shoulders; of the other two, the bonnets only appear. It is difficult to determine whether these statues are in a sitting or standing posture; their backs adhere to a portion of rock, which projects from the main body, and which may represent a part of a chair, or may be merely a column for support. They do not front the river, like those of the temple just described, but are turned with their faces due north, towards the more fertile climes of Egypt, so that the line on which they stand, forms an angle with the course of the stream. The head which is above the surface has a most expressive, youthful, countenance, approaching nearer to the Grecian model of beauty, than that of any ancient Egyptian figure I have seen; indeed, were it not for a thin oblong beard, it might well pass for a head of Pallas. This statue wears the high bonnet usually called the corn-measure, in the front of which is a projection bearing the figure of a nilometer; covered with hieroglyphics, deeply cut in the sandstone, and well executed; the statue measures seven yards across the shoulders, and cannot, therefore, if in an upright posture, be less than from sixty-five to seventy feet in height; the ear is one yard and four inches in length. On the wall of the rock, in the centre of the four statues, is the figure of the hawk-headed Osiris, surmounted by a globe; beneath which, I suspect, could the sand be cleared away, a vast temple would be discovered, to the entrance of which the above colossal figures probably serve as ornaments, in the same manner as the six belonging to the neighbouring temple of Isis. I am also led to conjecture, from the presence of the hawk-headed figure, that this was a temple dedicated to Osiris. The levelled face of the rock behind the colossal figures is covered with hieroglyphic characters; over which is a row of upwards of twenty sitting figures, cut out of the rock like the others, but so much defaced, that I could not make out distinctly, from below, what they were meant for; they are about six feet in height. Judging from the features of the colossal statue visible above the sand, I should pronounce these works to belong to the finest period of Egyptian sculpture; but, on the other hand, the hieroglyphics on the face of the rock are of very indifferent execution, and seem to be of the same age as those in the temple at Derr. A few paces to the south of the four colossal statues, is a recess hewn out of the rock, with steps leading up to it from the river; its walls are covered with hieroglyphic inscriptions, and representations of Isis; and the hawk-headed Osiris.

The temple of Ebsambal serves as a place of refuge to the inhabitants of Ballyane, and the neighbouring Arabs, against a Moggrebyn tribe of Bedouins, who regularly every year, make incursions into these parts. They belong to the tribes which are settled between the Great Oasis and Siout. When they set out, they repair first to Argo, where they commence their predatory course, plundering all the villages on the western bank of the river; they next visit Mahass, Sukkot, Batn el Hadjar, Wady Halfa, the villages opposite Derr, and lastly Dakke; near the latter place, they ascend the mountain, and return through the desert towards Siout. The party usually consists of about one hundred and fifty horsemen, and as many camel-riders; no one dares oppose them in Nubia; on the contrary, the governors pay them a visit, when they arrive opposite to Derr, and make them some presents. The incursions of this tribe are one of the principal reasons why the greater part of the western bank of the Nile is deserted. Whenever they advance towards Ballyane, its inhabitants retreat with their cattle to the temple of Ebsambal. The Moggrebyns, last year attempted to force this place of refuge, but failed, after losing several men.

Travels in Nubia, 1819

Coffee at Abu Simbel

AMELIA EDWARDS

At this juncture, seeing that the men's time hung heavy on their hands, our Painter conceived the idea of setting them to clean the face of the northernmost Colossus, still disfigured by the plaster left on it when the great cast was taken by Mr Hay more than half a century before. This happy thought was promptly carried into effect. A scaffolding of spars and oars was at once improvised, and the men delighted as children at play, were soon swarming all over the huge head, just as the carvers may have swarmed over it in the days when Rameses was king.

All they had to do was to remove any small lumps that might yet adhere to the surface, and then tint the white patches with coffee. This they did with bits of sponge tied to the ends of sticks: but Reis Hassan, as a mark of dignity, had one of the Painter's old brushes, of which he was immensely proud.

It took them three afternoons to complete the job: and we were all sorry when it came to an end. To see Reis Hassan artistically touching up a gigantic nose almost as long as himself: Riskalli and the cook-boy staggering to and fro with relays of coffee, brewed 'thick and slab' for the purpose; Salame perched cross-legged, like some complacent imp, on the towering rim of the great pschent overhead; the rest chattering and skipping about the scaffolding like monkeys, was, I will venture to say, a sight more comic than has ever been seen at Abou Simbel before or since.

Rameses' appetite for coffee was prodigious. He consumed I know not how many gallons a day. Our cook stood aghast at the demand made upon his stores. Never before had he been called upon to provide for a guest whose mouth measured three feet and a half in width.

Still, the result justified the expenditure. The coffee proved a capital match for the sandstone; and though it was not possible wholly to restore the uniformity of the original surface, we at least succeeded in obliterating those ghastly splotches, which for so many years have marred this beautiful face as with the unsightliness of leprosy.

A Thousand Miles up the Nile, 1889

Appeal by Mr Vittorino Veronese

DIRECTOR-GENERAL OF UNESCO

Work has begun on the great Aswan dam. Within five years, the Middle Valley of the Nile will be turned into a vast lake. Wondrous structures, ranking among the most magnificent on earth, are in danger of disappearing beneath the waters. The dam will bring fertility to huge stretches of desert: but the opening up of new fields to the tractors, the provision of new sources of power to future factories, threatens to exact a terrible price.

True, when the welfare of suffering human beings is at stake, then, if need be, images of granite and prophyry must be sacrificed unhesitatingly. But no one forced to make such a choice could contemplate without anguish the necessity for making it.

It is not easy to choose between a heritage of the past and the present well-being of a people, living in need in the shadow of one of history's most splendid legacies: it is not easy to choose between temples and crops. I would be sorry for any man called on to make that choice who could do so without a feeling of despair: I would be sorry for any man who, whatever decision he might reach, could bear the responsibility for that decision without a feeling of remorse.

It is not surprising, therefore, that the governments of the United Arab Republic and Sudan have called on an international body, on Unesco, to try to save the threatened monuments. These monuments, the loss of which may be tragically near, do not belong solely to the countries who hold them in trust. The whole world has the right to see them endure. They are part of a common heritage which comprises Socrates' message and the Ajanta frescoes, the walls of Uxmal and Beethoven's symphonies. Treasures of universal value are entitled to universal protection. When a thing of beauty, whose loveliness increases rather than diminishes by being shared, is lost, then all men alike are the losers.

Moreover, it is not merely a question of preserving something which may otherwise be lost; it is a question of bringing to light as yet undiscovered wealth for the benefit of all. In return for the help the world gives them, the governments of Cairo and Khartoom will open the whole of their countries to archaeological excavation and will allow half of whatever works of art may be unearthed by science or by hazard to go to foreign museums. They will even agree to the transport, stone by stone, of certain monuments of Nubia.

A new era of magnificent enrichment is thus opened in the field of Egyptology. Instead of a world deprived of a part of its wonders, mankind may hope for the revelation of hitherto unknown marvels.

So noble a cause deserves a no less generous response. It is, therefore, with every confidence that I invite governments, institutions, public or private foundations and men of goodwill everywhere to contribute to the success of a task without parallel in history. Services, equipment and money are all needed. There are innumerable ways in which all can help. It is fitting that from a land which throughout the centuries has been the scene – or the stake in – so many covetous disputes should spring a convincing proof of international solidarity.

'Egypt is a gift of the Nile'; for countless students this was the first Greek phrase which they learnt to translate. May the peoples of the world unite to ensure that the Nile in becoming a greater source of fertility and power does not bury beneath its waters marvels which we of today have inherited from generations long since vanished.

Unesco Courier, 1960

Translated from the French

9. The Great Temple of Abu Simbel, some thirty years after its discovery. The structure, with the four enormous seated effigies of Ramses II the Great, is one of the most remarkable monuments of mankind. When it became evident that the erection of the Aswan Dam would lead to the total submergence of the temple under the waters of the Nile, UNESCO succeeded in uniting more than twenty nations in a vast rescue operation.

10. The mummy of Tuthmoses III
as it was found at Deir-el-Bahri.

11. The mummy of Tuthmoses III
after unwrapping.

A hoard of royal mummies

GASTON MASPERO

GASTON CAMILLE CHARLES MASPERO (1846-1916) was born in Paris. In his second year at the École Normale he met the great Egyptologist Mariette, who was in Paris supervising the Egyptian section of the Great Exhibition, and, with his advice and encouragement, concentrated his studies upon archaeology. In due course he became teacher of Egyptian language and archaeology at the École des Hautes Études, and by 1874 he held the Chair of Champollion at the Collège de France. In 1880 he went to Egypt at the head of a team of excavators, and was shortly offered the post of Director General of excavations and antiquities of Egypt, which, apart from three years in Paris from 1886 to 1889, he held until his retirement. He was responsible for extensive work in rehousing and cataloguing the collections, and made many important finds.

For some several years past it had been realised that the Arabs of Gurna had found one or two royal tombs whose whereabouts they refused to divulge. In the spring of 1876 an English general named Campbell had shown me the hieratic ritual papyrus of the high-priest Pinotem, bought in Thebes for £400. In 1877 M. de Saulcy sent me on behalf of one of his friends in Syria, photographs of a long papyrus belonging to Queen Notmit, mother of Herihor, the end of which is now in the Louvre and the beginning in England. M. Mariette had also negotiated at Suez the purchase of two other papyri written in the name of a Queen Tiuhathor Henttaui. About the same time funerary statuettes of King Pinotem appeared on the market, some of fine workmanship and the others coarse. Briefly the fact that a discovery had been made became so certain that as early as 1878 I could definitely state concerning a tablet belonging to Rogers Bey that 'it came from a tomb close to the, as yet, unlocated tombs of the Herihor family'. . . .

To find the site of these royal tombs was therefore, if not the main, at least one of the principal objects of a trip which I made to Upper Egypt during March and April 1881. My intention was not to carry out any sondages or to settle down to excavations in the Theban necropolis; the problem was far more difficult. It was necessary to extract from the fellahin the secret which they had so zealously guarded until now. I had learnt only one thing: the principal dealers in antiquities were a certain Abd-er-Rassoul Ahmed, of Sheik Abd-el-Gurna, and a certain Mustapha Aga Ayad, vice-consul of England and Belgium at Luxor. To harass the latter was not so easy: protected as he was by diplomatic immunity he could escape the proceedings of the Directorate of Excavations. On April 4 I sent an order for the arrest of Abd-er-Rassoul Ahmed to the chief of police at Luxor, and I telegraphed to His Excellency Daud Pasha, Mudir (Governor) of Qena, as well as to the Ministry of Public Works requesting permission to open an immediate enquiry against his person. Questioned on board ship first by M. Emile Brugsch, and then by M. de Rochemonteix who kindly gave me the assistance of his experience, he denied everything that I charged him with, the discovery of the tomb, the sale of papyri and funerary statuettes and breaking up coffins contrary to the almost unanimous assertions of European travellers. I accepted his offer to have his house searched, less in the hope of finding any incriminating objects than to give him the chance of changing his mind and coming to an arrangement with us. Mildness, threats, nothing succeeded, and, on April 6, the warrant arrived to open the official enquiry, so I sent Abd-er-Rassoul Ahmed and his brother Hussein Ahmed to Qena, where the Mudir was demanding their appearance to stand trial.

The investigation was soundly pursued but on the whole gained nothing. The questions and arguments put by the magistrates of the Mudiria (province) in our delegate's presence, the inspector of Dendera, Aly-Effendi Habib, were notable for the number of testimonies evoked favourable to the accused. The foremost citizens and mayors of Gurna swore several times on oath that Abd-er-Rassoul Ahmed was one of the most upright and unselfish men of the district, and that he was incapable of diverting the most insignificant antiquity let alone robbing a royal tomb. The only interesting detail which came to light during the investigation was the insistance with which Abd-er-Rassoul Ahmed asserted that he was the servant of Mustapha Aga, the English vice-consul at Luxor, and that he lived in that person's house. He thought that in making out he was in the vice-consul's service he benefited from diplomatic privileges and came under Belgian or British protection. Mustapha Aga had encouraged both him and his associates in this error; he had persuaded them that in hiding behind him they would be safe henceforth from the local administrative agents, and by this simple trick he had managed to concentrate all the antiquities trade in the Theban plain into his hands.

Abd-er-Rassoul Ahmed was meanwhile provisionally released upon the surety of two of his friends, Ahmed Serour and Ismail Sayid Nagib, and returned home with a spotless certificate of honour conferred upon him by the foremost citizens of Gurna. But his arrest and the two months' imprisonment, together with the severity with which His Excellency Daud Pasha had conducted the enquiry, had clearly shown him that Mustapha Aga was unable to protect even his most faithful agents; it was also known that I intended to reopen the investigation when I returned to Thebes during the winter and that the Mudiria would also make further investigations. Several vague denunciations reached the Museum, and we learnt several new pieces of information from abroad, but the best news of all was of squabbles starting between Abd-er-Rassoul and his four brothers: some thought the danger finally over and the Museum authorities beaten, others thought it might be more prudent to come to terms with the Museum and divulge the secret. After a month of discussions and quarrels, the eldest of the brothers, Mohammed Ahmed Abd-er-Rassoul, suddenly decided to speak. He went secretly to Qena and told the Mudir that he knew the whereabouts of the site which had been vainly sought for several years; the tomb contained not one or two mummies but about forty, and the majority of the coffins had the small serpent on the front, like those seen on the head-dresses of pharaohs. His Excellency Daud Pasha immediately referred this to the Minister of the Interior, who conveyed the despatch to His Excellency the Khedive. His Highness, to whom I had spoken concerning the affair upon my return from Upper Egypt, recognised without any difficulty the importance of this unexpected denunciation and decided to send a member of the museum staff to Thebes. I had just returned to Europe but I had left M. Emile Brugsch, my assistant curator, the necessary powers to act for me in my stead. Having received the order to proceed, he left for Thebes on Saturday, 1st July, accompanied by a trustworthy friend and Ahmed Effendi Kamal, the Museum secretary-interpreter. A surprise awaited him at Qena: Daud Pasha had seized several precious objects at the house of the Abd-er-Rassoul brothers including three papyri of Queen Makere, Queen Isiemkheb and the princess Nesikhonsu. It was a promising beginning. To ensure the happy outcome of this delicate operation that was just beginning, His Excellency had placed his *wekil* at the service of our agents and also several employees of the Mudir. . . .

On Wednesday, the 6th, Messrs Emile Brugsch and Ahmed Effendi Kamal were led by Mohammed Ahmed Abd-er-Rassoul directly to the place where the funeral vault was located. The Egyptian engineer who had excavated it so long ago had laid his plans in a most skilful manner; never was a hiding place more cleverly concealed. The line of hills which separates the Biban-el-Moluk [Valley of the Kings] from the Theban plain here forms a series of natural circular clefts between the Assassif and the Valley of the Queens, of which the best known is that where the temple of Deir el-Bahari was built. In the rock face which separates Deir el-Bahari from the next cleft just behind the hill of Sheikh Abd-el-Gurna, about sixty metres above the level of the cultivated ground, a shaft eleven and a half metres deep and about two metres in diameter had been dug. At the bottom of the shaft, on the west side was the entrance to a passage 1·4 metres wide and 80 cm high. After running for 7·40 metres it turned suddenly northwards and continued for another 60 metres, the measurements never remaining constant: in places the passage was two metres wide and in others not more than 1·30 metres; near the middle five or six roughly cut steps showed a marked change of level, and on the right hand side an unfinished niche indicated that another change in direction of the passage had at one time been considered. Finally it opened out into an irregular, oblong chamber about eight metres long.

The first object which had presented itself to M. Emile Brugsch's gaze when he reached the bottom of the shaft was a white and yellow coffin inscribed with the name Nesikhonsu. It was in the passage about sixty centimetres from the entrance; a little farther on was a coffin of XVII dynasty style, then the Queen Tiuhathor Henttaui, then Seti I. Beside the coffins and scattered on the ground were wooden funerary statuettes, canopic jars, bronze libation vases, and, at the back in the corner angle made by the passage as it turned northward was the funeral tent of Queen Isiemkheb bent and crumpled like a valueless object, which a priest in a hurry to get out had thrown carelessly into a corner. The entire length of the main passage was similarly obstructed and disordered: it was necessary to advance on all fours not knowing where one was putting hands and feet. The coffins and the mummies rapidly glimpsed by the light of the candle bore historic names, Amenhetep I, Tuthmoses II, in the niche near the steps, Ahmose I and his son Siamun, Sequenre, Queen Ahotpe, Ahmose, Nefertari and others. The chamber at the end was the height of confusion but it was possible to see at first glance that the style of the XXth dynasty predominated. Mohammed Ahmed Abd-er-Rassoul's report which had at first seemed exaggerated hardly expressed the truth: where I had expected to find one or two minor kings, the Arabs had dug up a vault full of Pharaohs. And what Pharaohs! Probably the most famous in the history of Egypt, Tuthmoses III and Seti I, Ahmose the Liberator and Ramesses II the Conqueror. M. Emile Brugsch thought that he must be dreaming coming upon such an assemblage so suddenly. Like him I still ask myself if it is true and if I am dreaming when I see and touch the bodies of all these people when we never thought to know more than their names.

Two hours were sufficient for the preliminary examination, then the work of getting the coffins out began. Three hundred Arabs were quickly assembled by the Mudir's officials and put to work. The Museum's boat, hastily summoned, had not yet arrived; but one of its pilots, Reis Mohammed, who was perfectly trustworthy, was present. He descended to the bottom of the shaft and supervised the removal of its contents. Messrs Emile Brugsch and Ahmed Effendi Kamal received the objects and sorted them out as best they could on the ground without relaxing their vigilance for a moment, then the objects were carried to the bottom of the hill and laid side by side. Forty-eight hours of hard work got everything out of the cache; but the task was by no means finished. It was still necessary for the convoy to cross the Theban plain to the river's edge near Luxor. Several of the coffins, lifted only with the greatest difficulty by a dozen or sixteen men, took seven to eight hours to make the journey to the river, and it can easily be imagined what such a journey was like in the dust and heat of July.

At last, on the evening of the eleventh, all the mummies and coffins were at Luxor, carefully wrapped in matting and canvas. Three days later the Museum's steamer arrived and no sooner was it loaded than it set sail back to Bulaq with its cargo of kings. A strange thing happened! From Luxor to Quft on both banks of the Nile the wailing fellahin women with dishevelled hair followed the boat and the men fired off their guns, just as they do at funerals. Mohammed Abd-er-Rassoul was rewarded with five hundred pounds sterling, and I thought it best to appoint him reis of excavations at Thebes: if he serves the Museum with the same skill which he had used for so many years against it, we may hope for some magnificent discoveries.

Institut Égyptien Bulletin, series 2, no. 2, 1881

Translated from the French by P. A. Clayton

A false interpretation of the hieroglyphs

ATHANASIUS KIRCHER

ATHANASIUS KIRCHER (*1601–1680*) *was born at Geisa near Fulda. He entered the Jesuit college of Fulda and in 1618 became a novice of that order. He rose to the position of professor of philosophy, mathematics, and oriental languages at Wurzburg, but in 1631 the upheavals of the Thirty Years War drove him to remove himself to Avignon. In 1635 Cardinal Barberini secured him a position in Rome teaching mathematics at the Collegio Romano, and after eight years in this post he resigned in order to devote himself entirely to the study of antiquities. He was not a scholar of great original genius, and his work, which includes an entirely incorrect solution to the Egyptian hieroglyphics, is valuable only for its historical interest as a demonstration of the errors of earlier archaeologists. The following passage is from his explanatory introduction; there would be no point in including his entirely imaginary hieroglyphic grammar and vocabulary.*

PREFATORY LETTER

To the judicious and benevolent reader

If ever I realised the truth of that Hebrew saying, 'He who increases knowledge increases sorrow', it was surely in the revival of the study of this language hitherto unknown in Europe, in which there are as many pictures as letters, as many riddles as sounds, in short as many mazes to be escaped from as mountains to be climbed. The story clearly illustrates the difficulties which one encounters in undertaking arduous and unfamiliar tasks and opening up untrodden paths without a guide, and the dangers inherent in the investigation of the mysteries of a language which no one has previously studied. However, perseverance has triumphed over the difficulties of this abstruse subject, a consuming interest in the problem has lightened the endless work involved, and the burning desire implanted in me by nature to promote and restore studies neglected by reason of their difficulty has overcome all tribulations. Toil soon issued in rest, dislike was transformed into delight, and the fears which I had entertained as to the difficulties of getting to the root of the problem and solving it were turned into joy.

Knowing that I am to be judged by you, I ought not to fear the criticism of others, nor seek to defend my work. I am conscious, however, of having fallen upon times in which the noblest things are those most exposed to censure, the most serious topics are the most ridiculed and the most honourable enterprises are viewed with the deepest suspicion. Moreover, the minds of many people are such that they are not disposed to believe anything new and strange and outside their experience unless it is proved by convincing evidence and the testimony of reliable men, and unless its practical value is apparent. So, in order to increase confidence in my work and gain greater authority for it, I have thought it worth while briefly and clearly to explain how it came to be written and how the Autograph first came into my hands, adding at the same time an example showing how useful the work will be. In this way I trust I may the more easily escape the absurd but shameful charge of forgery, which the fertile imagination of certain ill-disposed persons might devise.

It happened like this. Urged on by his love of philosophy and antiquity, the honourable D. Petrus à Valle, knight and patrician of Rome, travelled like a second Apollonius through Greece, Palestine, Persia, India, Arabia and almost the whole eastern world, and came finally to Egypt, the fruitful source of all learning, intending to explore for himself the wonders of which he had read. Among the memorable things which he diligently investigated, he came upon this Copto-Arabic vocabulary or word-list, hidden away among men whose ignorant minds were incapable of appreciating it. He examined it carefully, and found that it would be invaluable for reviving the ancient language of Egypt, which had almost perished with age. He therefore purchased it for a considerable sum, and after a long and dangerous journey brought it joyfully to Rome, treating it with the greatest care, in order that he might make it available to the world at large, to the use and profit of many. To provide convincing proof of this account, it is well to add the authentic testimony of a passage at the beginning of the Autograph:

'At the end of the year of grace 1615 I was in the city of Cairo, most famous of the cities of Egypt at that time, diligently investigating the neglected monuments of antiquity, and there I found this book, hidden away among men whose ignorant minds were incapable of appreciating it. After a long and difficult journey I finally brought it to Rome, in order that with its unique assistance the ancient language of Egypt, which had almost died out among the Egyptians themselves, might eventually live again and shed much light on sacred and secular literature. May posterity be pleased to accept my contribution to this enterprise, and the duty which I owe to the Eternal City and to my country, the fount of good learning. Farewell.'

Meanwhile D. Nicolaus Fabricius, royal senator at the court of Aix, that distinguished ornament of letters, had been fully informed of this treasure recently brought from Egypt, and left no stone unturned to publish it as soon as possible in a Latin translation. A suitable person to undertake this task was sought abroad, especially in France where the study of foreign languages and of letters in general flourished exceedingly. At length I, who had adopted France as my country when I left Germany on account of the Swedish disturbances there, was prevailed upon to undertake the work, though I was by no means equal to it, at the instigation of my friends and above all at the urgent request of my dear friend Fabricius. When word of these endeavours reached the ears of His Eminence Cardinal Barberini, he too devoted himself to the cause with no less enthusiasm. He wished me to come to Rome with all speed to carry out this work there and to revive the study of hieroglyphics. I reached Rome, not without some danger, began the work entrusted to me, and with God's help brought it to the desired conclusion within two years. The book was finished, then, and ready for the press, but it was held up by a journey to Sicily and Malta which I had undertaken, and by the lack of apparatus necessary to print the characters, and was delayed again and again. Because of these hindrances the work was at a standstill for several years, and the author's intention to publish it all but vanished. Indeed, it seemed not unlikely that the treasure rescued with such great effort from the moths and bookworms should return to its former chaos. While I was pondering these things, the Holy Roman Emperor, well knowing the reasons for this delay, of his great and natural munificence most generously provided funds sufficient to procure types of all the oriental languages and other things necessary to complete the work. I mention this in order that the reader may appreciate the incomparable virtues of this indomitable emperor, who was not so overwhelmed by the barbarity of war and wave after wave of invasion as to devote himself to Mars to the exclusion of Pallas Athene. More might be said here of this invincible emperor's great wisdom, of his enthusiasm for all the arts and his almost incredible kindness. However, I intend to consider these things elsewhere, and, since they could not be told here with sufficient brevity, I have contained myself for the present. Types were therefore acquired, thanks to the emperor's generosity, and the work so long awaited went to press and at last saw the light of day.

You will see that it is in three parts. The first section is concerned with grammar, the second with vocabulary, and the third contains a list of words arranged in alphabetical order. You will scarcely believe the pains we have taken to make an accurate translation of the names of things. Indeed we should have collapsed but for the assistance of two Copts and others, especially of Abraham Ecchell, a scholar in many branches of learning, including oriental languages, who helped us in all sorts of ways, notably by their careful collation of everything with the Autograph.

Moreover, we have taken care in our translation to render everything into Latin word for word. In the interests of integrity and also of clarity, we have shunned conjecture and marked with an asterisk those places where the translation is in doubt because damp has made the original illegible. To guard against serious error in the translation of other ambiguous and equivocal words, we have looked these up – and the extent of this task you may imagine – in the manuscripts of the Holy Scriptures at the Vatican. God willing, we have attained by our unremitting labours the degree of accuracy in translation necessary for the revival of the study of hieroglyphics and the restoration of this neglected discipline.

I trust that this will suffice to ward off the attacks of those who may gnaw at our work with envious teeth. This book has been promoted and eagerly awaited by the general public and by people of quality; indeed, the most eminent men of our time in the republic of letters, not only in Europe but also in Asia and Africa, have given it their approval and looked forward to its completion, as we could abundantly demonstrate from the letters which we have received from Jews, Greeks, Arabs, Armenians, Syrians, Ethiopians and Persians, from Constantinople, Aleppo, Damascus, Alexandria, Cairo, Ephesus, Tunis and other places. However, we leave it to Oedipus to bear out what we have said. For, if the goodness of God prolongs his life, Oedipus will declare how much we have achieved in reviving this language. Unless I am much mistaken, students of these abstruse subjects in future times will admit that the monumental labours of Oedipus could never have been brought to fruition without the help of this language, and we trust that we shall win some thanks from a grateful posterity when in due course it reaps the full harvest of our work. What we have done is to produce a Silenus, rough and uncultured at his first appearing, but who in his own time will, we have no doubt, shine forth and light up dark places. These are the facts of which, O Reader, we thought it would be well to inform you. And so Farewell, and be good enough to further my work by letting me know if you discover anything which may help Oedipus.

Lingua Aegyptiaica, 1643

Translated from the Latin by H. Powell

How the Rosetta Stone came to the British Museum

TOMKYNS HILGROVE TURNER

SIR TOMKYNS HILGROVE TURNER (1766?-1843) was a professional soldier all his life and achieved considerable distinction both in his military career and as an antiquarian. From 1793 onwards he was continuously engaged in campaigns in the Low Countries and France, and in 1801 he went with his regiment to Egypt, where he fought in the battles of Aboukir Bay and Alexandria. After the capitulation of this city, one of the articles of the surrender terms required the French to hand over many of the antiquities their scientific commission had collected, and it was Turner who negotiated the actual transfer of these objects, and insisted that the collection should include the most important find brought to light by the French – the Rosetta Stone. Turner wrote an account of these transactions for the Society of Antiquaries, on whose premises the stone was displayed before its removal to the British Museum, where it has subsequently remained.

Read 8 June, 1810

Argyle Street, 30 May, 1810

Sir,

The Rosetta Stone having excited much attention in the learned world, and in this Society in particular, I request to offer them, through you, some account of the manner it came into the possession of the British army, and by what means it was brought to this country, presuming it may not be unacceptable to them.

By the sixteenth article of the capitulation of Alexandria, the siege of which city terminated the labours of the British army in Egypt, all the curiosities, natural and artificial, collected by the French Institute and others, were to be delivered up to the captors. This was refused on the part of the French General to be fulfilled, by saying they were all private property. Many letters passed; at length, on consideration that the care in preserving the insects and animals had made the property in some degree private, it was relinquished by Lord Hutchinson; but the artificial, which consisted of antiquities and Arabian manuscripts, among the former of which was the Rosetta Stone, was insisted upon by the noble General with his usual zeal for science. Upon which I had several conferences with the French General Menou, who at length gave way, saying, that the Rosetta Stone was his private property; but, as he was forced, he must comply as well as the other proprietors. I accordingly received from the under secretary of the Institute, Le Pere, the secretary Fourier being ill, a paper, containing a list of the antiquities, with the names of the claimants of each piece of sculpture: the stone is there described of black granite, with three inscriptions, belonging to General Menou. From the French sçavans I learnt, that the Rosetta Stone was found among the ruins of Fort St Julien, when repaired by the French, and put in a state of defence: it stands near the mouth of the Nile, on the Rosetta branch, where are, in all probability, the pieces broken off. I was also informed, that there was a stone similar at Menouf, obliterated, or nearly so, by the earthen jugs being placed on it, as it stood near the water; and that there was a fragment of one, used and placed in the walls of the French fortifications of Alexandria. The Stone was carefully brought to General Menou's house in Alexandria, covered with soft cotton cloth, and a double matting, where I first saw it. The General had selected this precious relick of antiquity for himself. When it was understood by the French army that we were to possess the antiquities, the covering of the stone was torn off, and it was thrown upon its face, and the excellent wooden cases of the rest were broken off; for they had taken infinite pains, in the first instance, to secure and preserve from any injury all the antiquities. I made several remonstrances, but the chief difficulty I had was on account of this stone, and the great sarcophagus, which at one time was positively refused to be given up by the Capitan Pasha, who had obtained it by having possession of the ship it had been put on board of by the French. I procured, however, a centry on the beach from Mon. Le Roy, prefect maritime, who, as well as the General, behaved with great civility; the reverse I experienced from some others.

When I mentioned the manner the stone had been treated to Lord Hutchinson, he gave me a detachment of artillerymen, and an artillery-engine, called, from its powers, a devil cart, with which that evening I went to General Menou's house, and carried off the stone, without any injury, but with some difficulty, from the narrow streets, to my house, amid the sarcasms of numbers of French officers and men; being ably assisted by an intelligent serjeant of artillery, who commanded the party, all of whom enjoyed great satisfaction in their employment: they were the first British soldiers who entered Alexandria. During the time the Stone remained at my house, some gentlemen attached to the corps of sçavans requested to have a cast, which I readily granted, provided the Stone should receive no injury; which cast they took to Paris, leaving the Stone well cleared from the printing ink, which it had been covered with to take off several copies to send to France, when it was first discovered.

Having seen the other remains of ancient Egyptian sculpture sent on board the Admiral, Sir Richard Bickerton's ship, the *Madras*, who kindly gave every possible assistance, I embarked with the Rosetta Stone, determined to share its fate, on board the *Egyptienne* frigate, taken in the harbour of Alexandria, and arrived at Portsmouth in February 1802. When the ship came round to Deptford, it was put in a boat and landed at the Custom-House; and Lord Buckinghamshire, the then Secretary of State, acceded to my request, and permitted it to remain for some time at the apartments of the Society of Antiquaries, previous to its deposit in the British Museum, where I trust it will long remain, a most valuable relick of antiquity, the feeble but only yet discovered link of the Egyptian to the known languages, a proud trophy of the arms of Britain (I could almost say *spolia opima*), not plundered from defenceless inhabitants, but honourably acquired by the fortune of war.

I have the honour to be, Sir,
Your most obedient, and most humble servant,
H. Turner, Major General.
Nicholas Carlisle, esq.,
Secretary to the Society of Antiquaries, &c., &c.

Archaeologia, vol xvi, 1812

Champollion deciphers the hieroglyphs

JEAN FRANCOIS CHAMPOLLION (*1790-1832*) *was born at Figeac and early showed signs of an amazing aptitude for languages which was fostered and encouraged by his self-effacing elder brother. When he was sixteen years old he read a paper to the Academy at Grenoble which astonished the scholars who heard it and, at an age when most pupils were still seeking admission, he was made a teacher. His work was often interrupted by the political disturbances of the age, but in 1821 he was able to bring out the paper which proved to be the definitive solution to the Egyptian hieroglyphs. His ideas were in direct contradiction to those propounded by most scholars of his day, and met with bitter opposition, but his work successfully withstood all tests and acceptance could not long be denied. In 1831 a Chair was specially created for him at the Collège de France in recognition of his achievement.*

Letter to M. Dacier concerning the alphabet of the phonetic
hieroglyphs

Sir,

It is to your generous patronage that I owe the indulgent attention which the *Académie Royale des Inscriptions et Belles-Lettres* has been pleased to accord to my work on the Egyptian scripts, in allowing me to submit to it my two reports on the *hieratic*, or priestly, script and the *demotic*, or popular one; after this flattering trial, I may as last venture to hope that I have successfully shown that these two types of writing are neither of them composed of alphabetic letters, as had been so widely supposed, but consist of *ideograms*, like the hieroglyphs themselves, that is, expressing the *concepts* rather than the *sounds* of a language; and to believe that after ten years of dedicated study I have reached that point where I can put together an almost complete survey of the general structure of these two forms of writing, the origin, nature, form and number of their signs, the rules for their combination by means of those symbols which fulfil purely logical and grammatical functions, thus laying the first foundations for what might be termed the *grammar* and *dictionary* of these two scripts, which are found on the majority of monuments, and the interpretation of which will throw so much light on the general history of Egypt. With regard to the *demotic* script in particular, there is enough of the precious Rosetta inscription to identify the whole; scholastic criticism is indebted first to the talents of your illustrious colleague, M. Silvestre de Sacy, and successively to the late M. Akerblad and Dr Young, for the first accurate ideas drawn from this monument, and it is from this same inscription that I have deduced the series of demotic symbols which, taking on syllabic-alphabetic values, were used in *ideographic* texts to express the proper names of persons from outside Egypt. It is by this means also that the name of the Ptolemies was discovered, both in this same inscription and in a papyrus manuscript recently brought from Egypt.

Accordingly, it only remains, in completing my study of the three types of Egyptian writing, for me to produce my account of the pure *hieroglyphs*. I dare to hope that my latest efforts will also have a favourable reception from your famous society, whose goodwill has been so valuable an encouragement to me.

However, in the present condition of Egyptian studies, when relics abound on every side, collected by kings as much as by connoisseurs, and when, too, with regard to these relics, the world's scholars eagerly devote themselves to laborious researches and strive for an intimate understanding of those written memorials which must serve to explain the rest, I do not think I should delay in offering to these scholars, under your honoured auspices, a short but vital list of new discoveries, which belong properly to my account on the *hieroglyphic* script, and which will undoubtedly spare them the pains I took in establishing them, and perhaps also some grave misconceptions about the various periods of the history of Egyptian culture and government in general: for we are dealing with the series of *hieroglyphs* which, making an exception to the general nature of the signs of this script, were given the property of expressing word *sounds*, and served for the inscription on Egyptian national monuments of the *titles, names* and *surnames of the Greek or Roman rulers* who successively governed the country. Many truths concerning the history of this famous country must spring from this new result of my researches, to which I was led quite naturally.

The interpretation of the *demotic* text on the Rosetta inscription, by means of the accompanying Greek text, had made me realise that the Egyptians used a certain number of *demotic* characters, which assumed the property of expressing sounds, to introduce into their ideographic writings *proper names* and *words foreign to the Egyptian language*. We see at once the indispensable need for such a practice in an ideographic system of writing. The Chinese, who also use an ideographic script, have an exactly similar provision, created for the same reason.

The Rosetta monument shows us the application of this auxiliary method of writing, which I have termed *phonetic*, that is, expressing the sounds, in the proper names of the kings *Alexander* and *Ptolemy*, the queens *Arsinoe* and *Berenice*, in the proper names of six other persons, *Aetes, Pyrrha, Philinus, Areia, Diogenes* and *Irene*, and in the Greek words *ΞΥΝΤΑΞΙΣ* and *ΟΥΗΝΝ*. . . .

The hieroglyphic text of the Rosetta inscription, which would have lent itself so felicitously to this study, owing to its cracks, yielded only the name *Ptolemy*.

The obelisk found on the island of Philae and recently brought to London also contains the hieroglyphic name of a Ptolemy, written in the same symbols as on the Rosetta inscription and similarly enclosed in a cartouche, and this is followed by a second cartouche, which must contain the proper name of a woman, a Ptolemaic queen, since this cartouche ends with the feminine hieroglyphic signs which also follow the hieroglyphic proper names of every Egyptian goddess without exception. The obelisk was, as it were, *tied* to a pedestal bearing a Greek inscription which is a supplication from the priests of Isis at Philae to the king, Ptolemy, his sister Cleopatra and his wife Cleopatra. If this obelisk and its hieroglyphic inscription resulted from the plea of the priests, who actually mention the consecration of a similar monument, the cartouche with the female name could only be that of a Cleopatra. This name, and that of Ptolemy, which have certain like letters in Greek, had to serve for a comparative study of the hieroglyphic symbols which composed the two; and if identical signs in these two names stood for *the same sounds* in both cartouches, they would have to be *entirely phonetic* in character.

A preliminary comparison had also made me realise that these same two names, written phonetically in the demotic script, contained a number of identical characters. The resemblance between the three Egyptian scripts in their general principles caused me to look for the same phenomenon and the same correspondences when the same names were given *in hieroglyphs*: this was soon confirmed by simple comparison of the hieroglyphic cartouche containing the name Ptolemy and that on the Philae obelisk which I believed, according to the Greek text, must contain the name Cleopatra.

The first sign in the name *Cleopatra*, which resembles a kind of *quadrant*, and which would represent the *K*, should have been absent from the name Ptolemy. It was.

The second sign, a *lion couchant*, which would give the *Λ*, is exactly similar to the fourth sign in the name Ptolemy, also an Λ ($\Pi\tau o\lambda$).

The third sign in the name Cleopatra is a *feather* or *leaf*, standing for the short vowel E; we also see two similar *leaves* at the end of the name Ptolemy, which, from their position, can only have the value of the diphthong AI, in $AIO\Sigma$.

The fourth character in the cartouche for the hieroglyphic Cleopatra, the representation of a kind of *flower with a bent stem*, would stand for the O in the Greek name of this queen. It is in fact the third character in the name Ptolemy ($\Pi\tau o$).

The fifth sign in the name Cleopatra, which appears as a parallelogram and must represent the Π, is equally the first sign in the hieroglyphic name Ptolemy.

The sixth sign, standing for the vowel A of $K\Lambda EO\Pi ATPA$, is a *hawk*, and does not occur in the name Ptolemy, nor should it.

The seventh character is an *open hand*, representing the T; but this hand does not occur in the word Ptolemy, where the second letter, the T, is expressed by a *segment of a circle*, which, none the less, is also a T; for we shall see below why these two hieroglyphs have the same sound.

The eighth sign of $K\Lambda EO\Pi ATPA$, which is a frontal *mouth*, and which would be the P, does not occur in the cartouche of Ptolemy, nor should it.

Finally, the ninth and last sign in the queen's name, which must be the vowel A, is in fact the *hawk* which we have already seen representing this vowel in the third syllable of the same name. This proper name ends in the two hieroglyphic symbols for the feminine gender: that of Ptolemy ends in another sign, which consists of a bent shaft, equivalent to the Greek Σ, as we shall see below.

The combined signs from the two cartouches, analysed phonetically, thus already yielded us twelve signs, corresponding to eleven consonants, vowels or diphthongs in the Greek alphabet, A, AI, E, K, Λ, M, O, Π, P, Σ, T.

The phonetic value of these twelve signs, already very probable, becomes indisputable if, applying these values to other cartouches or small enclosed panels containing proper names and taken from Egyptian hieroglyphic monuments, we are enabled to read them effortlessly and systematically, producing the proper names of rulers foreign to the Egyptian language. . . .

You, sir, will doubtless share all my astonishment when the same alphabet of phonetic hieroglyphs, applied to a host of other cartouches carved on the same piece of work, will give you titles, names and even surnames of Roman emperors, spoken in *Greek* and written with these same phonetic hieroglyphs.

We read here, in fact:

The imperial title *Αυτοκρατωρ*, occupying a whole cartouche to itself, or else followed by other *still persisting* ideographic titles, transcribed *ΑΟΤΟΚΡΤΡ, ΑΟΤΚΡΤΟΡ, ΑΟΤΑΚΡΤΡ* and even *ΑΟΤΟΚΛΤΛ*, the *Λ* being used as a bastard substitute (pardon the expression) for the *P*.

The cartouches containing this title are almost always next to, or connected with, a second cartouche containing, as we shall shortly see, the *proper names* of emperors. But occasionally we also find this word in absolutely isolated cartouches. . . .

But it remains, sir, for us to survey briefly the nature of the phonetic system governing the writing of these names, to form an accurate estimate of the character of the signs used, and to investigate the reasons for adopting the image of one or another object to represent a particular consonant or vowel more than another. . . .

I am in no doubt, sir, that if we could definitely determine the object represented or expressed by all the other phonetic hieroglyphs comprised in our alphabet, it would be a relatively easy matter for me to show, in the Egyptian-Coptic lexicons, that the names of these same objects begin with the consonant or vowels which their image represents in the phonetic hieroglyph system.

This method, followed in the composition of the Egyptian phonetic alphabet, gives us an idea to what point we could, if we wished, continue multiplying the number of phonetic hieroglyphs without sacrificing the clarity of their expression. But everything seems to indicate that our alphabet, by and large, contains them. We are, in fact, justified in drawing this conclusion, since this alphabet is the result of a series of phonetic proper names carved on Egyptian monuments during a period of about *five centuries* in various parts of the country.

It is easy to see that the vowels of the hieroglyphic alphabet are used indiscriminately one for another. On this point we can do no more than establish the following general rules:

1. The hawk, the ibis and three other kinds of bird are consistently used for *A*;

2. The leaf or feather can stand for both the short vowels *Ă* and *Ĕ*, sometimes even *Ŏ*.

3. The twin leaves or feathers can equally well represent the vowels *I* and *H*, or the diphthongs *IA* and *AI*.

All I have just said on the origin, formation and anomalies of the *phonetic hieroglyph* alphabet applies almost entirely to the *demotic phonetic* alphabet. . . .

These two systems of phonetic writing were as intimately connected as the *hieratic ideographic* system was with the *popular ideographic*, which was no more than its descendant, and the *pure hieroglyphs*, which were its source. The demotic letters are generally, in fact, as I have said, the same as the *hieratic* signs for hieroglyphs which are themselves phonetic. You, sir, will have no difficulty in recognising the truth of this assertion, if you trouble to consult the comparative Table of hieratic signs classified beside the corresponding hieroglyph, the Table which I presented before the *Académie des Belles-Lettres* more than a year ago. So there is basically no other difference between the *hieroglyphic* and *demotic* alphabets but the actual form of the signs, their values and even the reasons for those values being identical. Finally I would add that since these popular phonetic symbols were merely unchanged hieratic characters, there cannot, of necessity, have been more than *two* phonetic writing systems in Egypt;

1. the *phonetic hieroglyph* script, used on public monuments;
2. the *hieratic-demotic* script, used for Greek proper names in the middle text of the Rosetta inscription and the demotic papyrus in the royal library . . . , and which we shall perhaps see one day used to transcribe the name of some Greek or Roman ruler in the rolls of papyrus written in the hieratic script.

Phonetic writing, then, was in use among every class of the Egyptian nation, and they employed it for a long time as a necessary adjunct to the three ideographic methods. When, as a result of their conversion to Christianity, the Egyptian people received the alphabetic Greek script from the apostles, and then had to write all the words of their maternal tongue with this new alphabet, adoption of which cut them off for ever from the religion, history and institutions of their ancestors, all monuments being, by this act, 'silenced' for these neophytes and their descendants, yet these Egyptians still retained some trace of their ancient phonetic method; and we see in fact that in the oldest Coptic texts, in the Theban dialect, most of the short vowels are completely omitted, and that often, like the hieroglyphic names of Roman emperors, they consist of no more than strings of consonants interspersed at long intervals by a few vowels, almost always long. This resemblance seemed to me worth noting. The Greek and Latin writers have left us no formal remarks on the Egyptian phonetic script; it is very difficult to deduce even the existence of this system, forcing the sense of certain passages where something of the kind would seem to be vaguely hinted at. So we must abandon the attempt to study through historical tradition the period when the phonetic scripts were introduced into the ancient Egyptian picture-writing.

But the facts speak well enough for themselves to enable us to say with fair certainty that the employment of an auxiliary script in Egypt to represent the sounds and articulations of certain words preceded Greek and Roman domination, although it seems most natural to attribute the introduction of the semi-alphabetic Egyptian script to the influence of these two European nations, which had long been using a true alphabet.

Here I base my opinion on the two following considerations, which, sir, may seem to you a solid enough weight to tip the scales.

1. If the Egyptians had invented their phonetic script in imitation of the Greek or Roman alphabets, they would naturally have established a number of phonetic signs equal to the known elements of the Greek or Latin alphabet. But there is nothing of the kind; and the incontestable proof that the Egyptian phonetic writing arose for a totally different purpose from that of expressing the sounds of proper names of Greek or Roman rulers is found in the Egyptian transcription of these very names, which are mostly corrupted to the point of being unrecognisable; firstly by the suppression or confusion of most of the vowels, secondly by the persistent use of the consonants T for Δ, K for Γ, Π for Φ; and lastly by the accidental use of Λ for P and P for Λ.

2. I am positive that the same signs in *phonetic hieroglyphs* used to represent the sounds of Greek and Roman proper names were also used in ideographic texts carved long before the Greeks reached Egypt, and that they already had, in certain contexts, the same value representing sounds or articulations as in the cartouches carved under the Greeks and Romans. The development of this valuable and decisive point is connected with my work on the pure hieroglyphs. I could not set out the proof in this letter without plunging into extraordinarily prolonged complications.

Thus, sir, I believe that *phonetic* writing existed in Egypt at a far distant time; that it was first a necessary part of the ideographic script; and that it was then used also, after Cambyses, as we have it, to transcribe (crudely, it is true) in ideographic texts the proper names of peoples, countries, cities, rulers and individual foreigners who had to be commemorated in historic texts or monumental inscriptions.

I dare say more: it would be possible to recover, in this ancient Egyptian phonetic script, imperfect though it may be in itself, if not the source, at least the model on which the alphabets of the western Asiatic nations were framed, above all those of Egypt's immediate neighbours. If you note in fact, sir:

1. that each letter of the alphabets which we term Hebrew, Chaldean and Syriac bears a distinguishing name, very ancient appellations, since they were almost all transmitted by the Phoenicians to the Greeks when the latter took over the alphabet;

2. that the *first consonant or vowel of these names* is also, in these alphabets, the *vowel or consonant to be read,*

you will see, with me, in the creation of these alphabets, a perfect analogy with the creation of the phonetic alphabet in Egypt: and if alphabets of this type are, as everything indicates, primitively formed from signs representing ideas or objects, it is evident that we must recognise the nation who invented this method of written expression in those who particularly used an ideographic script; I mean, in sum, that Europe, which received from ancient Egypt the elements of the arts and sciences, is yet further in her debt for the inestimable benefit of alphabetic writing.

However, I have only tried here to indicate briefly the many important consequences of this discovery, and it arose naturally from my main subject, the *alphabet of the phonetic hieroglyphs,* the general structure of which, together with some applications, I proposed to expound at the same time. The latter produced results which have already met with a favourable response from the illustrious members of the *Académie,* whose scholastic studies have given Europe the first principles of solid learning, and continue to offer her the most valuable of examples. My attempts may perhaps add something to the record of definite achievements by which they have enriched the history of ancient peoples; that of the Egyptians, whose just fame still echoes round the world; and it is certainly no little achievement today that we can take with assurance the first step in the study of their written memorials, and thence gather some precise notion of their leading institutions, to which antiquity itself gave a name for wisdom which nothing has yet overthrown. As for the remarkable monuments erected by the Egyptians, we can at last read, in the cartouches which adorn them, their fixed chronology from Cambyses and the times of their foundation or their successive accretions under the various dynasties which ruled Egypt; the majority of these monuments bear simultaneously the names of pharaohs and of Greeks and Romans, the former, characterised by their small number of signs, perpetually resisting every attempt to apply to them successfully the *alphabet* I have just discovered. Such, sir, I hope, will be the value of this work, which I am flattered to produce under your honoured auspices; the enlightened public will not refuse me its admiration or its support, since I have obtained those of the venerable Nestor of scholarship and French literature, whose devoted studies honour and adorn them, and who, with a hand at once protective and encouraging, is ever pleased to support and guide, in the hard course which he has so gloriously covered, so many young imitators who have later wholly justified his enthusiastic patronage. Happy to rejoice in my turn, I would not, however, venture to make a reply but for my deep gratitude, and my respectful affection; permit me, I beg you, sir, to repeat publicly all my assurances of that affection.

Paris, 22 September 1822   J. F. CHAMPOLLION the younger

Lettre à M. Dacier Relative à l'alphabet des Hiéroglyphes Phonétiques, 1822
Translated from the French by V. M. Conrad

A fantastic interpretation of the Great Pyramid

CHARLES PIAZZI SMYTH

CHARLES PIAZZI SMYTH (*1819-1900*) *was born in Naples, and his second name was chosen in honour of the famous Sicilian astronomer. He justified this choice by making astronomy his career, obtaining first a post as assistant in the Royal Observatory at the Cape of Good Hope, and then the appointment of Astronomer-Royal of Scotland. As long as he confined himself to astronomy and the related fields of meteorology and spectroscopy he produced results of great value and originality, but in middle life he developed an interest in pyramidology, and made a journey to Egypt to survey and measure the Great Pyramid, being firmly convinced that these measurements held invaluable revelations about the past and future of the human race. Among his curious delusions was the notion that the design of the pyramid had been divinely revealed to 'its creator Melchisedec', that it heralded the beginning of the millennium in 1882 – a prophesy he had the misfortune to live to see disproved – and that the measurements, properly interpreted, would produce a cryptographic solution to the problem of squaring the circle. His actual interpretations are too lengthy and too fantastic to come within the scope of this book, so a part of his explanatory introduction has been selected.*

The Pyramids of Egypt have very safely, because according to the collected opinions of the leading antiquaries of all nations, been allowed to be the most ancient existing remains of the most ancient form and fashion of the architecture of that most anciently inhabited land they are found in. They constitute, exhibit, and illustrate, therefore, the nearest approach amongst the intellectual works of man to his doing immediately after the days of the Biblical Dispersion of mankind; and are, in fact, the only *contemporary* proofs that can now be claimed or referred to, for what went on in those exceedingly early times before the birth of written history.

The number of these most remarkable monuments may amount to thirty-seven, or possibly thirty-eight; but that exact number is of little importance, for after the first seven or eight of the largest of them have been passed in review, built, too, as they are, with admirable skill in hewn stone, and appearing on that distant horizon like colossal crystals of mountain size, – the others fail so rapidly in height, breadth, quality of material and lasting power, as to have crumbled into rounded, ruinous masses, and in some of the later cases to be hardly distinguishable from moderate-sized hillocks.

They are, or were, all of them square-based Pyramids, with four triangular sloping flanks for sides, meeting towards the top in a point, over the centre of the base. They are, moreover, nearly solid constructions, whether built of stone or sun-dried brick; and are all situated on the Western, Lybian and more desert side of the Nile, occupying positions there, at intervals, along a line nearly seventy miles in length. This line begins near the Southern point of the Delta land of Lower, that is Northern Egypt, within view, but across the river, of the modern city of Cairo, and extending thence Southward or towards Upper Egypt. But never reaching it; for there all the architecture is of the adorned Temple kind, and is of a much later date in Egyptian history, though still of far greater antiquity than any of the Classic remains of Greece or Rome.

If, too, we should proceed, at this mere preliminary stage of our prospective and exclusive enquiry, to declare, that as to the Pyramids of Egypt in *general*, they were built to serve as lasting sepulchres for the great Egyptian dead, both Pharaohs and their relatives, we shall be supported by all the Egyptological science of modern times. And yet there is one amongst them which refuses to yield to this mode of explanation; and unfortunately it is the greatest, the best built, the best preserved of them all; one that for ages has acquired the name *par excellence* of the Great Pyramid, is spoken of more frequently than any other for and by itself alone, has attracted more frequent historic notice from travellers and writers of all times and all ages; has been considered also almost, if not absolutely quite, the earliest of this very early description of monument raised by man; and was held to be both the greatest and oldest of the seven wonders of the world in the days of the Greeks; while it is now the only one of them all which is still in existence on the surface of the earth.

Locally, this Pyramid is known as that of Jeezeh, Geezeh, or Ghizeh, because, standing on a low, flat-topped hill of that modern Arabic name, in the African desert position already described; where it has, however, several companions of later date and smaller size. Yet they are quite sufficient to discriminate all the travellers who visit them into two sharply divided classes; those who, with the world in general, are enthusiastic about 'the Pyramids' (*i.e.* in the plural) 'of Egypt', with anything else thoroughly Egyptian also; and, on the other side, those who confine their admiration and their interest to the one Great Pyramid, on account of what is there of anti-Egyptian character. For there have been, however it came about, such persons in all ages; though the idea has only begun to bear intellectual fruit in recent years, and has received at last a justification worthy of all Biblical scholars and Christian believers to occupy themselves with enquiring into.

This new idea which solves with a hitherto unknown certainty the chief standing mystery of the civilised world through all the ages, the said world owes to the late Mr John Taylor of London, in a book published in AD 1859, and entitled *The Great Pyramid; why was it built? and who built it?* He had not visited the Pyramid himself, but had been for thirty years previously collecting and comparing all the published accounts, and specially all the better-certified mensurations (for some were certainly poor indeed) of those who had been there; and while so engaged, and quite spontaneously (as he described to me by letter), the new theory opened out before him.

Though mainly a rigid induction from tangible facts of scientific bearing and character, Mr Taylor's result was undoubtedly assisted by means of the mental and spiritual point of view from whence he commenced his researches; and which is, in the main, simply this:

That whereas other writers have generally esteemed that a certain grand but unknown existency, whom they all allow, in their historical enquiries, did direct the building of the one Great Pyramid (and to whom the Egyptians in their early traditions and for ages afterwards gave an immortal and even abominable character) must, therefore, have been very bad indeed – so that the world at large, from that time to this, has ever been fond of treading on and insulting that dead lion whom they really knew nothing of – he, Mr John Taylor, seeing in every characteristic mention of them in the *Bible*, how religiously bad the idol-inventing Egyptians themselves were, was led to conclude that the unknown leader and Architect whom they hated, and could never sufficiently abuse, might perhaps have been pre-eminently *good*; or was, at all events, of a *purer religious faith* than that of the Mizraite sons of Ham.

Then, remembering, with *mutatis mutandis* what Christ himself says respecting the suspicion to be attached, when all the *world* speaks well of any one, Mr Taylor followed up this idea by what the Old Testament does record touching the most vital and distinguishing part of the Israelitish religion; and which is therein described, some centuries after the building of the Great Pyramid, as notoriously an 'abomination to the Egyptians'; and combining this with certain unmistakable and undisputed, by any one, historical facts, he successfully deduced sound and Christian reasons for believing that the director of the building, and perhaps his immediate assistants who controlled the myriads of *native* builders at the Great Pyramid, were by no means Egyptians, but strangers of the *chosen* race, sons of Shem, and in the line of, though preceding Abraham; so early, indeed, as to be closer to Noah than to Abraham. Men, at all events, who had been enabled by Divine favour to appreciate the appointed idea, as to the absolute necessity of a sacrifice and atonement for the sins of man by the blood and free-offering of a Divine Mediator, as in the most earnest and Evangelical form of Christianity.

This very crucial idea of our present faith was nevertheless of an antiquity coeval with the contest between Cain and Abel, and had descended through the Flood to certain predestined families of mankind; but yet was an idea which no one of Egyptian born would ever contemplate with a moment's patience. For every ancient Egyptian, from first to last, and every Pharaoh of them more especially, just as with the Ninevites and Babylonians generally, was an unmitigated Cainite in thought, act, and feeling to the very backbone; confident of, and professing nothing so much, or so constantly, as his own perfect righteousness and absolute freedom by his own innate purity, and by his own invariable, complete, and unswerving rectitude throughout his whole life from every kind of sin, large or small, against God or man.

On this general ground it was that Mr Taylor took his stand; and, after disobeying the world's long-formed public opinion of too passively obedient accord with profane Egyptian tradition, and after thereby also setting at naught some of the most time-honoured prejudices of modern Egyptological scholars, so far as to give a full, fair and impartial examination to the whole case from the beginning, announced that he had discovered in some of the arrangements and measures of the Great Pyramid – when duly corrected for injuries and dilapidations of intervening time – certain scientific results, which speak of neither Egyptian nor Babylonian, and much less of Greek or Roman learning, but of something much more than, as well as quite different from, any ordinary human ways of those several contemporary times.

For, besides coming forth *suddenly* in the primeval history of its own remote day, without any preliminary period of childhood, or known ages of evolution and preparation – the actual facts of the Great Pyramid, in the shape of builded proofs of an exact numerical knowledge of the grander cosmical phenomena of both earth and heavens – not only rise above, and far above, the extremely limited and almost infantine knowledge of science humanly attained to by any of the Gentile nations of 4,000, 3,000, 2,000, nay only 300 years ago; but they are also, in whatever of the great physical secrets of nature they chiefly apply to, essentially above the best knowledge of philosophers in our own time as well.

This is indeed a startling assertion to be put forth about an ancient stone monument. Never ventured, too, by any one, let it be duly borne in mind, for the 'Pyramids of Egypt' in the plural; but only for the one great and strange Pyramid *in* Egypt; and which, though standing *there*, is yet not at all *of*, or *according to*, native ideas, whether in science or religion, as they were graven in the hieroglyphics of Egypt, and as she herself has described them in her own history. Yet the assertion admits of the completest and most positive refutation, if at all as untrue for the Great Pyramid as it undoubtedly is for any other ancient building whatever. For the exact science of the present day, compared with that of only a hundred years ago, is a marvel of development; and is capable of giving out no uncertain sound, both in asserting itself, and stating not only the fact, but the order and time of the invention of all the practical means humanly necessary to the minutest steps of each separate discovery yet made.

Much more then can this modern science of the mathematical kind speak with positiveness, when comparing its own presently extended knowledge against the little that was known to man, by his own efforts and by his then school methods, in those early epochs before accurate and numerical physical science had begun, or could have been begun, to be seriously cultivated at all. That is, in the truly primeval day when men were few on the earth, and yet the Great Pyramid was built, finished, sealed up, and left as we see it now, modern dilapidations only excepted, in the midst of an unbelieving world, to guard its own secret through the ages, and serve at last its intended purpose, whatever that was to be, in the latter days of mankind.

Let us proceed, then, to examine all well known Great Pyramid facts by the light of modern science, so far as that can be brought to bear; keeping our eyes duly open all the time to the necessity of guarding, on one side against accidental coincidences in favour of this theory of the Great Pyramid; and on the other, to the possibility of any intentional features really detected there being common to any of the other Pyramids as well.

Before the many difficulties of such an enquiry, and the practical skill required, I should myself have been very loath to pronounce any positive conclusions on reading alone any number of so-called book authorities. But having actually visited the Pyramid field in Egypt; encamped there in 1864 and 1865 for several months, making daily use of a variety of scientific measuring apparatus; and since then having spent more than twenty years in working out, and fighting for, every step of the enquiry, I do humbly trust that, by the grace of God, I may not only have arrived at many true results, but may be able to show that the steps of the work and the progress of the proof are much easier than might have been anticipated to all who are in heart inclined to follow, and desire to make securely their own.

Our Inheritance in the Great Pyramid, 1890

The underwater tomb

WILLIAM FLINDERS PETRIE

SIR WILLIAM MATTHEW FLINDERS PETRIE (*1853-1942*) *was born at Charlton and took an early interest in antiquities. He began with a study of Stonehenge, and published a book on the subject in 1880, which was also the year of his first expedition to Egypt. He was largely responsible for the establishment of the Egyptian chronology in the form in which it is used today; and as founder of the British School of Archaeology in Egypt, under whose auspices the site of Memphis was discovered and excavated, he ensured the continuity of scientific study of Egyptian antiquities. The sites of his surveys and explorations included the temple of Tanis, the Greek city of Naucratis, the Delta towns, the Fayum, Meydum and the Pyramids of Giza.*

When considering the places favourable for future excavations I had named Hawara and Illahun, amongst other sites, to M. Grébaut; and he proposed to me that I should work in the Fayum province in general. The exploration of the pyramids of this district was my main object, as their arrangement, their date, and their builders were quite unknown. Hawara was not a convenient place to work at, as the village was two miles from the pyramid, and a canal lay between; I therefore determined to form a camp of workmen to live on the spot, as at Daphnae. For this purpose I needed to recruit a party from a little distance, and began my work therefore at the ancient Arsinoe or Crocodilopolis, close to Medinet el Fayum. Here I cleared the pylon of the temple, of which a few disturbed blocks remain, and found a second mention of Amenemhat II beside that already known; but his work had all been altered and rebuilt, probably by Ramessu II. Four or five different levels of buildings, and reconstruction could be traced, and the depth of rubbish over the approach to the temple in the shallowest part of the mounds was twenty-four feet. Within the great enclosure of mud-brick wall, the site of the temple could be traced by following the bed of sand, on which the foundations had been laid; but scarcely a single stone was left. One re-used block had a figure of a king of the nine-teenth dynasty, probably Ramessu II; and this leads us to date as late as

Ptolemy II the temple which we can trace here. He doubtless built a large temple, as the place received much attention in his time, and was dedicated to his sister-wife Arsinoe: she was specially worshipped along with the great gods, as we know from the stele of Pithom. The only early objects found here were flint knives in the soil of the temple; these belong to the twelfth dynasty, as we know from later discoveries.

A short work of a few days at Biahmu resolved the questions about the so-called pyramids there. So soon as we began to turn over the soil we found chips of sandstone colossi; the second day the gigantic nose of a colossus was found, as a broad as a man's body; then pieces of carved thrones, and a fragment of inscription of Amenemhat III. It was evident that the two great piles of stone had been the pedestals of colossal seated monolithic statues, carved in hard quartzite sandstone and brilliantly polished. These statues faced northward, and around each was a courtyard wall with sloping outer face, and red granite gateway in the north front. The total height of the colossi was about sixty feet from the ground. The limestone pedestal rose twenty-one feet, then the sandstone colossus had a base of four feet, on which the figure, seated on its throne, rose to a height of thirty-five feet more. Thus the whole statue and part of its pedestal would be visible above the enclosing courtyard wall, and it would appear from a distance as if it were placed on a truncated pyramid. The description of Herodotos, therefore, is fully accounted for; and it shows that he actually saw the figures, though from a distance, as any person who visited them closely would not have described them in such a manner.

Having by this time formed and organised a good body of workmen, I moved over to Hawara, with as many men as I wanted; and the only difficulty was to restrain the numbers who wished to work. The pyramid had never been entered in modern times, and its arrangement was wholly unknown; explorers had fruitlessly destroyed much of the brickwork on the north side, but yet the entrance was undiscovered. In Roman times the stone casing had been removed, and as the body of the structure was of mud bricks, it had crumbled away somewhat: each side was therefore encumbered with chips and mud. After vainly searching the ground on the north side for any entrance, I then cleared the middle of the east side, but yet no trace of any door could be found. As it was evident then that the plan was entirely different to that of any known pyramid, and it would be a hopeless task to clear all the ground around it, I therefore settled to tunnel to the midst. This work was very troublesome as the large bricks were laid in sand, and rather widely spaced; hence as soon as any were removed, the sand was liable to pour out of the joints, and to loosen all the surrounding parts. The removal of each brick was therefore done as quietly as possible, and I had to go in three times a day and insert more roofing boards, a matter which needed far more skill and care than a native workman would use. After many weeks' work (for there was only room for one man), I found that we were halfway through, but all in brick. On one side of the tunnel, however, I saw signs of a built wall, and guessing that it had stood around the pit made for the chamber during the building, I examined the rock-floor, and found that it sloped down slightly, away from the wall. We turned then to the west, and tunnelling onwards, we reached the great roofing beams of the chamber in a few days. No masons of the district, however, could cut through them, and I had to leave the work till the next season. Then, after a further search on all the four sides for the entrance, the masons attacked the sloping stone roof, and in two or three weeks' time a hole beneath them was reported; anxiously I watched them enlarge it until I could squeeze through, and then I entered the chamber above the sepulchre; at one side I saw a lower hole, and going down I found a broken way into the sandstone sepulchre, but too narrow for my shoulders. After sounding the water inside it, a boy was put down with a rope-ladder; and at last, on looking through the hole, I could see by the light of his candle the two sarcophagi, standing rifled and empty. In a day or two we cleared away the rubbish from the original entrance passage to the chamber, and so went out into the passages, which turned and wandered up and down. These were so nearly choked with mud, that in many parts the only way along them was by lying flat, and sliding along the mud, pushed by fingers and toes. In this way, sliding, crawling, and wading, I reached as near to the outer mouth of the passage as possible; and then by measuring back to the chamber, the position of the mouth on the outside of the pyramid was pretty nearly found. But so deep was it under the rubbish, and so much encumbered with large blocks of stone, that it took about a fortnight to reach it from the outside.

The pyramid had been elaborately arranged so as to deceive and weary the spoiler, and it had apparently occupied a great amount of labour to force an entrance. The mouth was on the ground level, on the south side, a quarter of the length from the south-west corner. The original explorers descended a passage with steps to a chamber, from which apparently there was no exit. The roof consisted of a sliding trap-door, however, and breaking through this another chamber was reached at a higher level. Then a passage opened to the east, closed with a wooden door, and leading to another chamber with a trap-door roof. But in front of the explorer was a passage carefully plugged up solid with stone; this they thought would lead to the prize, and so all the stones were mined through, only to lead to nothing. From the second trap-door chamber a passage led northward to the third chamber. From that a passage led west to a chamber with two wells, which seemed as if they led to the tomb, but both were false. This chamber also was almost filled with masonry, which all concealed nothing, but had given plenty of occupation to the spoilers who removed it in vain. A filled-up trench in the floor of the chamber really led to the sepulchre; but arriving there no door was to be found, as the entrance had been by the roof, an enormous block of which had been let down into place to close the chamber. So at last the way had been forced by breaking away a hole in the edge of the glassy-hard sandstone roofing block, and thus reaching the chamber and its sarcophagi. By a little widening of the spoilers' hole I succeeded in getting through it into the chamber. The water was up to the middle of my body, and so exploration was difficult; but the floor was covered with rubbish and chips which might contain parts of the funereal vessels, and therefore needed searching. The rubbish in the sarcophagi I cleared out myself; and then I set some lads to gather up the scraps from the floor on the flat blade of a hoe (as it was out of arms' reach under water), and after searching them they threw them into the sarcophagi. Thus we anxiously worked on for any inscribed fragments; my anxiety being for the cartouche of the king, the boys' anxiety for the big bakhshish promised, at *per* hieroglyph found, extra value given for cartouches. The system worked, for in the first day I got the coveted prize, a piece of an alabaster vessel with the name of Amenemhat III, proving finally to whom the pyramid belonged; and other parts of inscribed vessels were found. Still there was a puzzle as to the second sarcophagus, which had been built up between the great central one and the chamber side. On clearing in the chamber which led to the sepulchre, however, they found a beautiful altar of offerings in alabaster, covered with figures of the offerings all named, over a hundred in all, and dedicated for the king's daughter, Neferu-ptah; near it were parts of several bowls in the form of half a trussed duck, also bearing her name: so doubtless the second interment was hers; and she must have died during her father's life, and before the closing of the pyramid. Of the actual bodies I found a few scraps of charred bones, besides bits of charcoal and grains of burnt diorite in the sarcophagi; also a beard of lazuli for inlaying was found in the chamber. The wooden inner coffins, inlaid with hard stone carving, had therefore been burnt. The chamber itself is a marvellous work; nearly the whole height of it is carved out of a single block of hard quartzite sandstone, forming a huge tank, in which the sarcophagus was placed. In the inside it is twenty-two feet long and nearly eight feet wide, while the sides are about three feet thick. The surface is polished, and the corners so sharply cut that I mistook it for masonry, until I searched in vain for the joints. Of course it was above water level originally; but all this region had been saturated by a high level canal of Arab times. Afterwards I had all the earth removed from the pyramid passages as far as practicable, but nothing further was found there. No trace of inscription exists on either the walls or sarcophagi; and but for the funereal furniture, even the very name would not have been recovered.

Ten Years' Digging in Egypt, 1892

The discovery of the Amarna tablets

ERNEST BUDGE

Sir Ernest Alfred Wallis Budge (*1857-1934*) *was born in Cornwall and educated at Christ's College, Cambridge, where he became Assyrian and Hebrew Scholar. He entered the service of the British Museum in 1883 and ultimately became Keeper of Egyptian and Assyrian antiquities; in 1920 he was knighted for his services to archaeology. He made many expeditions to the eastern Mediterranean region, and besides conducting excavations he obtained for the British Museum a large number of antiquities, papyri and manuscripts, in the Greek, Coptic, Arabic, Syriac and Ethiopic languages. His most significant acquisition, however, was a collection of documents written at the end of the XVIII dynasty, known as the Amarna tablets.*

In the course of the day a man arrived from Hajjî Kandîl, bringing with him some half-dozen of the clay tablets which had been found accidentally by a woman at Tall al-'Amârnah, and he asked me to look at them, and to tell him if they were *kadim*, i.e. 'old' or *jadid*, i.e. 'new' – that is to say, whether they were genuine or forgeries. The woman who found them thought they were bits of 'old clay', and useless, and sold the whole 'find' of over 300 tablets to a neighbour for 10 piastres (2s.)! The purchaser took them into the village of Hajjî Kandîl, and they changed hands for £E10. But those who bought them knew nothing about what they were buying, and when they had bought them they sent a man to Cairo with a few of them to show the dealers, both native and European. Some of the European dealers thought they were 'old' and some thought they were 'new', and they agreed together to declare the tablets forgeries so that they might buy them at their own price as 'specimens of modern imitations'. The dealers in Upper Egypt believed them to be genuine, and refused to sell, and, having heard that I had some knowledge of cuneiform, they sent to me the man mentioned above, and asked me to say whether they were forgeries or not; and they offered to pay me for my information. When I examined the tablets I found that the matter was not as simple as it looked. In shape and form, and colour and material, the tablets were unlike any I had ever seen in London or Paris, and the writing on all of them was of a most unusual character and puzzled me for hours. By degrees I came to the conclusion that the tablets were certainly not forgeries, and that they were neither royal annals nor historical inscriptions in the ordinary sense of the word, nor business or commercial documents. Whilst I was examining the half-dozen tablets brought to me, a second man from Hajjî Kandîl arrived with seventy-six more of the tablets, some of them quite large. On the largest and best written of the second lot of tablets I was able to make out the words 'A-na Ni-ib-mu-a-ri-ya', i.e. 'To Nibmuariya', and on another the words '(A)-na Ni-im-mu-ri-ya shar mâtu Mi-is-ri', i.e. 'to Nim-muriya, king of the land of Egypt'. These two tablets were certainly letters addressed to a king of Egypt called 'Nib-muariya' or 'Nim-muriya'. On another tablet I made out clearly the opening words 'A-na Ni-ip-khu-ur-ri-ri-ya shar mâtu (Misri)', i.e. 'To Nibkhurririya, king of the land of (Egypt') and there was no doubt that this tablet was a letter addressed to another king of Egypt. The opening words of nearly all the tablets proved to be letters or despatches, and I felt certain that the tablets were both genuine and of very great historical import-ance.

Up to the moment when I arrived at that conclusion neither of the men from Hajjî Kandîl had offered the tablets to me for purchase, and I suspected that they were simply waiting for my decision as to their genuineness to take them away and ask a very high price for them, a price beyond anything I had the power to give. Therefore, before telling the dealers my opinion about the tablets, I arranged with them to make no charge for my examination of them, and to be allowed to take possession of the eighty-two tablets forthwith. They asked me to fix the price which I was prepared to pay for the tablets, and I did so, and though they had to wait a whole year for their money they made no attempt to demand more than the sum which they agreed with me to accept.

I then tried to make arrangements with the men from Hajjî Kandîl to get the remainder of the tablets from Tall al-'Amârnah into my possession, but they told me that they belonged to dealers who were in treaty with an agent of the Berlin Museum in Cairo. Among the tablets was a very large one, about 20 inches long and broad in proportion. We now know that it contained a list of the dowry of a Mesopotamian princess who was going to marry a king of Egypt. The man who was taking this to Cairo hid it between his inner garments, and covered himself with his great cloak. As he stepped up into the railway coach this tablet slipped from his clothes and fell on the bed of the railway, and broke in pieces. Many natives in the train and on the platform witnessed the accident and talked freely about it, and thus the news of the discovery of the tablets reached the ears of the Director of Antiquities. He at once telegraphed to the Mudir of Asyût, and ordered him to arrest and put in prison everyone who was found to be in possession of tablets, and, as we have seen, he himself set out for Upper Egypt to seize all the tablets he could find. Meanwhile, a gentleman in Cairo who had obtained four of the smaller tablets and paid £E100 for them, showed them to an English professor, who promptly wrote an article upon them, and published it in an English newspaper. He postdated the tablets by nearly 900 years, and entirely misunderstood the nature of their contents. The only effect of his article was to increase the importance of the tablets in the eyes of the dealers, and, in consequence, to raise their prices, and make the acquisition of the rest of the 'find' more difficult for everyone.

By Nile and Tigris, vol. I, 1920

12. The sarcophagus of Sekhem Khet, found inside the buried pyramid of Saqqara. It was empty!

28

13. Carter and his colleagues at the doorway of Tutankhamen's tomb.

Tutankhamen

HOWARD CARTER

HOWARD CARTER (1873-1939) *was born in Swaffham, Norfolk, and educated privately. At the age of seventeen he entered the service of the Egyptian Exploration Fund, and Flinders Petrie was among those who supervised his training in archaeological techniques. He took part in several excavations under the auspices of the Fund until 1899 when he was appointed Inspector General of the Antiquities department of the Egyptian government. From 1902 onwards he supervised Davis' excavations in the Valley of the Kings, which brought to light the tombs of Tuthmoses IV and Queen Hatshepsut. After this he was engaged to take charge of an excavation under the patronage of Lord Carnarvon, and in 1922 he discovered the tomb of the XVIII dynasty pharaoh Tutankhamen, which was the first and only intact royal burial to be discovered in the Valley of the Kings.*

It was on February 3 (1924) that we first had a clear view of this sepulchral masterpiece, ranking as it does among the finest specimens of its kind the world possesses. It has a rich entablature consisting of a cavetto-cornice, taurus moulding and frieze of inscription. But the outstanding features of the sarcophagus are the guardian goddesses Isis, Nephthys, Neith and Selkit, carved in high relief on each of the four corners, so placed that their full spread wings and outstretched arms encircle it with their protective embrace. Round the base is a dado or protective symbols *Ded* and *Thet*. The corners of the casket rested upon alabaster slabs. Between the last shrine and the sarcophagus there were no objects, save for a *Ded*-symbol placed on the south side for 'Strength' and possibly 'Protection' of the owner.

As our light fell on the noble quartzite monument, it illuminated, in repeated detail, that last solemn appeal to gods and men, and made us feel that, in the young king's case, a dignity had been added even to death. With the profound silence that reigned the emotion deepened, the past and present seemed to meet – time to stand and wait, and one asked oneself, was it not yesterday that, with pomp and ceremony, they had laid the young king in that casket? – so fresh, so seemingly recent, were those touching claims on our pity that, the more we gazed on them, the more the illusion gathered strength. It made one wish that his journey through those grim tunnels of the Underworld might be unperturbed until he attained complete felicity! – as those four goddesses, sculptured in high relief at the corners, seemed to plead as they shielded their charge. For in them had we not a perfect Egyptian elegy in stone?

The lid made of rose granite tinted to match the quartzite sarcophagus, was cracked in the middle and firmly embedded in the rebated top edges. The cracks had been carefully cemented and painted over to match the rest, in such a way as to leave no doubt that it had not been tampered with. Undoubtedly the original intention must have been to provide a quartzite lid in keeping with the sarcophagus itself; it would therefore appear that some accident had occurred. It may be that the intended lid was not ready in time for the burial of the king, and that this crudely made granite slab was substituted in its place.

The crack greatly complicated our final effort, the raising of this lid, for had it been intact the operation would have been far easier. The difficulty, however, was overcome by passing angle irons along and closely fitting the sides of the slab, which permitted it to be raised by differential pulleys as one piece. . . .

Many strange scenes must have happened in the Valley of the Tombs of the Kings since it became the royal burial ground of the Theban New Empire, but one may be pardoned for thinking that the present scene was not the least interesting or dramatic. For ourselves it was the one supreme and culminating moment – a moment looked forward to ever since it became evident that the chambers discovered, in November 1922, must be the tomb of Tut-ankh-Amen, and not a cache of his furniture as had been claimed. None of us but felt the solemnity of the occasion, none of us but was affected by the prospect of what we were about to see – the burial custom of a king of ancient Egypt of thirty-three centuries ago. How would the king be found? Such were the anticipatory speculations running in our minds during the silence maintained.

The tackle for raising the lid was in position. I gave the word. Amid intense silence the huge slab, broken in two, weighing over a ton and a quarter, rose from its bed. The light shone into the sarcophagus. A sight met our eyes that at first puzzled us. It was a little disappointing. The contents were completely covered by fine linen shrouds. The lid being suspended in mid-air, we rolled back those covering shrouds, one by one, and as the last was removed a gasp of wonderment escaped our lips, so gorgeous was the sight that met our eyes: a golden effigy of the young boy king, of most magnificent workmanship, filled the whole of the interior of the sarcophagus. This was the lid of a wonderful anthropoid coffin, some seven feet in length, resting upon a low bier in the form of a lion, and no doubt the outermost coffin of a series of coffins, nested one within the other, enclosing the mortal remains of the king. Enclasping the body of this magnificent monument are two winged goddesses: Isis and Neith, wrought in rich gold-work upon gesso, as brilliant as the day the coffin was made. To it an additional charm was added, by the fact that, while this decoration was rendered in fine low bas-relief, the head and hands of the king were in the round, in massive gold of the finest sculpture, surpassing anything we could have imagined. The hands, crossed over the breast, held the royal emblems – the Crook and the Flail – encrusted with deep blue faience. The face and features were wonderfully wrought in sheet-gold. The eyes were of aragonite and obsidian, the eyebrows and eyelids inlaid with lapis lazuli glass. There was a touch of realism, for while the rest of this anthropoid coffin, covered with feathered ornament, was of brilliant gold, that of the bare face and hands seemed different, the gold of the flesh being of different alloy, thus conveying an impression of the greyness of death. Upon the forehead of this recumbent figure of the young boy king were two emblems delicately worked in brilliant inlay – the Cobra and the Vulture – symbols of Upper and Lower Egypt, but perhaps the most touching by its human simplicity was the tiny wreath of flowers around these symbols, as it pleased us to think, the last farewell offering of the widowed girl queen to her husband, the youthful representative of the 'Two Kingdoms'.

Among all that real splendour, that royal magnificence – everywhere the glint of gold – there was nothing so beautiful as those few withered flowers still retaining their tinge of colour. They told us what a short period three thousand three hundred years really was – but Yesterday and the Morrow. In fact, that little touch of nature made that ancient and our modern civilisation kin.

Thus from stairway, steep descending passage, Antechamber and Burial Chamber, from those golden shrines and from that noble sarcophagus, our eyes were now turned to its contents – a gold-encased coffin, in form a recumbent figure of the young king, symbolising Osiris or, it would seem, by its fearless gaze, man's ancient trust in immortality. Many and disturbing were our emotions awakened by that Osiride form. Most of them were voiceless. But, in that silence, to listen – you could almost hear the ghostly footsteps of the departing mourners.

Our lights were lowered, once more we mounted those sixteen steps, once more we beheld the blue vault of the heavens, where the Sun is Lord, but our inner thoughts still lingered over the splendour of that vanished Pharaoh, with his last appeal upon his coffin written upon our minds: 'Oh Mother Nût! spread thy wings over me as the Imperishable Stars.'

The Tomb of Tut-ankh-Amen, vol. II, 1927

14. Opening the doors of the shrine which contained
the golden coffins of Tutankhamen.

The golden coffin

HOWARD CARTER

Thus our season had begun. The Valley, awakened from its summer sleep for the last two days by bawling workmen and screaming boys, was at peace again, and quiet will possess it until the winter migrants and their followers invade its golden silence.

The Antechamber freed of its beautiful furniture, the Burial Chamber denuded of its golden shrines, leaves the now open stone sarcophagus in the centre with its coffins within alone retaining their secret.

The task before us now was to raise the lid of the first outermost coffin, as it rested in the sarcophagus.

This great gilded wooden coffin, 7 feet 4 inches in length, anthropoid in shape, wearing the *Khat* head-dress, with face and hands in heavier sheet-gold, is of *Rishi* type – a term applied when the main decoration consists of a feather design, a fashion common to coffins of the preceding Intermediate and Seventeenth Dynasty Theban periods. During the New Empire, in the case of burials of high officials and commoners, the style of decoration of coffins completely changes at the beginning of the Eighteenth Dynasty; but in the case of the royal coffin, as we now see, the older fashion still survived, with only very slight modification, such as the addition of figures of certain tutelary goddesses. This is a complete inversion of the usual order of things – fashion generally changing more rapidly with the upper than with the lower stations in life. May not this connote some religious idea in connexion with a king? There may be tradition behind it. The goddess Isis once protected the dead body of Osiris by taking him within her wings, thus she protects this new Osiris as represented by the effigy.

After careful study of the coffin it was decided that the original silver handles – two on each side – manifestly made for the purpose, were sufficiently well preserved still to support the weight of the lid, and could be used without danger in raising it. The lid was fixed to the shell by means of ten solid silver tongues, fitted into corresponding sockets in the thickness of the shell (four on each side, one at the head-, and one at the foot-end) where they were held in place by substantial gold-headed silver pins. Could we remove the silver pins by which the lid was fixed to the shell of the coffin without disturbing the coffin in the sarcophagus? As the coffin filled up nearly the whole of the interior of the sarcophagus, leaving only the smallest space, especially at the head- and foot-ends, it was by no means easy to extract the pins. By careful manipulation, however, it was found possible to withdraw them, with the exception of the pin at the head-end where there was only space enough enough to pull it half out. It had therefore to be filed through before the inner half could be withdrawn.

The next step was to place in position the hoisting tackle necessary for lifting the lid. This tackle consisted of two sets of three sheaf pulley-blocks provided with automatic brakes, fixed to an overhead scaffold, the pulleys being slung so as to come immediately above the centre of the lid opposite each pair of handles. The tackle was attached to the handles of the lid of the coffin by means of slings, and thus a correct centralization of its weight was assured, otherwise there would have been a danger of the lid bumping against the sides of the sarcophagus the moment it became free and pendent.

It was a moment as anxious as exciting. The lid came up fairly readily, revealing a second magnificent anthropoid coffin, covered with a thin gossamer linen sheet, darkened and much decayed. Upon this linen shroud were lying floral garlands, composed of olive and willow leaves, petals of the blue lotus and cornflowers, whilst a small wreath of similar kind had been placed, also over the shroud, on the emblems of the forehead. Underneath this covering, in places, glimpses could be obtained of rich multi-coloured glass decoration encrusted upon the fine gold-work of the coffin.

Some time was spent in the previous summer working out the methods to be followed in this undertaking, and in providing the necessary appliances, thus it was completed in one morning when otherwise it would have occupied several days at least. The tomb was closed, everything being left undisturbed to await Mr Harry Burton's photographic records.

Thus far our progress had been fairly satisfactory, but we now became conscious of a rather ominous feature. The second coffin, which, so far as visible through the linen covering, had every appearance of being a wonderful piece of workmanship, showed distinct signs of the effect of some form of dampness and, here and there, tendency for its beautiful inlay to fall away. This was, I must admit, disconcerting, suggesting as it did the existence of former humidity of some kind within the nest of coffins. Should this prove the case, the preservation of the royal mummy would be less satisfactory than we had hoped.

On October 15 Mr Burton arrived, and on the 17th, early in the morning, he successfully completed the photographic records of the shroud and floral garlands that covered the second coffin, as it rested, within the shell of the first, in the sarcophagus.

These records complete, we had now to consider how best to deal with the second coffin, as well as the shell of the first. Manifestly, our difficulties were increased on account of the depth of the sarcophagus, and it was evident that the outer shell and the second coffin, neither of which was in a condition to bear much handling, must be raised together. This was eventually accomplished by means of pulleys as before, attachment being attained by means of steel pins passed through the tongue-sockets of the first outermost shell. In this way hoisting was possible with minimum of handling.

In spite of the great weight of the coffins – far heavier than at first seemed possible – they were successfully raised to just above the level of the top of the sarcophagus, when wooden planks were passed under them. In the confined space, and with the restricted head-room available, the task proved one of no little difficulty. It was much increased by the necessity of avoiding damage to the fragile gesso-gilt surfaces of the outermost coffin.

Further records having been taken, I was then able to remove the chaplet and garlands, and roll back the covering shroud. It was one more exciting moment. We could now gaze, with admiring eyes, upon the finest example of the ancient coffin-maker's art ever yet seen – Osiride, again in form, but most delicate in conception, and very beautiful in line. As it now lay in the outer shell which rested upon the modern improvised trestles, it presented a wonderful picture of Majesty lying in State.

The chaplet and garlands placed upon the shroud in memory of 'the wreaths given to Osiris on his triumphant exit from the Judgment-hall of Heliopolis', which, as Dr Gardiner remarks, reminds us of the 'crown of righteousness' (2 Tim. iv. 8), were but illustration of Pliny's description of ancient Egyptian wreaths. When the care and precision with which these are fashioned is recognised, there is strong reason for the belief that this particular occupation with the ancient Egyptians, as in later days, must have been a specialised trade.

This second coffin, 6 feet 8 inches in length, sumptuously inlaid on thick gold-foil with cut and engraved opaque glass, simulating red jasper, lapis lazuli and turquoise respectively, is similar in form and design to the first. It symbolises Osiris, it is *Rishi* in ornament, but it differs in certain detail. In this case the king wears the *Nemes* headdress, and in place of the protective figures of Isis and Nephthys, the body is embraced with the wings of the vulture Nekhebet and of the serpent Buto. The arresting feature is the delicacy and superiority of the conception, which confer upon it at once the position of a masterpiece.

We were now faced by a complicated problem, not unlike the one we had to solve two seasons before when the covering shrines were dismantled. It was again a case of the unexpected happening. Conclusions drawn from former evidence or example are not to be trusted. For some unknown reason the reverse too often proves to be the case. On seeing that there were handles on the outer coffin for lowering or raising it, we were led to expect similar metal handles on the second coffin. There was none, and their absence placed us in a dilemma. The second coffin proved exceedingly heavy; its decorated surface very fragile; it fitted the outer shell so closely that it was not possible to pass one's little finger between the two. Its lid was fixed, as in the case of the outer coffin, with gold-headed silver pins which, as the coffin lay in the outer shell, could not be extracted. It was evident that it would have to be lifted in its entirety from the outer shell before anything further could be done. Thus the problem which confronted us was to discover a method of doing this with the minimum risk of damage to its delicate inlay, that had already suffered from some kind of humidity, the origin of which was then unknown.

It may be, under the strain of such operations as these, that one is too conscious of the risk of irreparable damage to the rare and beautiful object one desires to preserve intact. Much in the early days of Egyptian archaeological research had undoubtedly been lost to us by too eager or careless handling, more still from want of necessary appliances at the right moment; but against ill-luck, even when every possible precaution has been taken, no man is secure. Everything may seem to be going well until suddenly, in the crisis of the process, you hear a crack – little pieces of surface ornament fall. Your nerves are at an almost painful tension. What is happening? All available room in the narrow space is crowded by your men. What action is needed to avert a catastrophe? There is, too, another danger. As the lid is being raised, the excitement of seeing some new and beautiful object may attract the workmen's attention; for a moment their duty is forgotten, and irreparable damage in consequence may be done.

Such are often the anxious impressions uppermost in the arch-aeologist's memory when his friends enquire what his emotions in these thrilling moments may have been. Only those who have had to handle heavy yet fragile antiquities in circumstances of similar difficulty, can realise how exacting and nerve-racking the strain and responsibility may become. Moreover, in the case before us, we could not be sure that the wood of the coffin was sufficiently well preserved to bear its own weight. However, after long consultations, and having studied the problem for nearly two days, we devised a plan. To remove the second coffin from the shell of the first, some points of attachment were necessary. There were, it will be remembered, no handles, so it was judged best to make use of the metal pins which fastened down the lid.

Inspection showed, however, that although the space between the shell of the outer coffin and the second coffin was insufficient to enable us to withdraw these pins entirely, they could still be pulled out about a quarter of an inch, so as to permit stout copper wire attachments to be fixed to them and to the overhead scaffold. This we did successfully. Strong metal eyelets were then screwed into the thickness of the top edge of the shell of the outer coffin so as to enable it to be lowered from the second coffin by means of ropes working on the pulleys.

On the following day, after these preparations, we were able to proceed with the next stage. It proved to be one of the most important moments in the dismantling of the tomb. The process adopted was the reverse of that which might at first appear to be the natural order of things. We lowered the outer shell from the second coffin, instead of lifting the second coffin out of the first. The reason for this was that the head-room was insufficient, and the weight being stationary, there would be less risk of undue stress upon those ancient silver pins. The operations proved successful. The shell of the outer coffin was lowered once more into the sarcophagus, leaving for a moment, the second coffin suspended in mid-air by means of the ten stout wire attachments A wooden tray sufficiently large to span the opening of the sarcophagus was then passed under it, and thus the second coffin strongly supported, stood before us free and accessible. The wire attachments having been severed, the overhead gear removed, Mr Burton made his records, and we were able to turn our energies to the raising of its lid.

The entire inlaid surface was indeed, as already mentioned, in a very fragile condition, and any handling, so far as possible, had to be avoided. In order therefore to lift the lid without causing injury, metal eyelets, to serve as handles, were screwed into it at four points where there would be no danger of permanent disfigurement. To these eye-lets our hoisting tackle was fixed, the gold-headed silver nails were extracted and the lid was slowly raised. There was at first some slight tendency for the lid to stick, but gradually it rose from its bed and, when high enough to clear the contents of the coffin, it was lowered on to a wooden tray placed at the side to receive it. This revealed a third coffin which, like its predecessors, was Osiride in form, but the main details of the workmanship were hidden by a close-fitting reddish-coloured linen shroud. The burnished gold face was bare; placed over the neck and breast was an elaborate bead and floral collarette, sewn upon a backing of papyrus, and tucked immediately above the *Nemes* headdress was a linen napkin.

Mr Burton at once made his photographic records. I then removed the floral collarette and linen coverings. An astounding fact was dis-closed. This third coffin, 6 feet $1\frac{3}{4}$ of an inch in length, was made of solid gold! The mystery of the enormous weight, which hitherto had puzzled us, was now clear. It explained also why the weight had dimin-ished so slightly after the first coffin, and the lid of the second coffin, had been removed. Its weight was still as much as eight strong men could lift.

The face of this gold coffin was again that of the king, but the features though conventional, by symbolising Osiris, were even more youthful than those on the other coffins. In actual design it reverted to that of the outermost coffin, inasmuch as it was *Rishi*, and had engraved upon it figures of Isis and Nephthys, but auxiliary to this design were winged figures of Nekhebet and Buto. These latter protective figures, emblematic of Upper and Lower Egypt, were the prominent feature, for they are superimposed in gorgeous and massive cloisonné work over the richly engraved ornament of the coffin – their inlay being natural semi-precious stones. In addition to this decoration, over the conventional collarette of 'the Hawk' – again in auxiliary cloisonné work – was a double detachable necklace of large disk-shaped beads of red and yellow gold and blue faience, which enhanced the richness of the whole effect. But the ultimate details of the ornamentation were hidden by a black lustrous coating due to liquid unguents that had evidently been profusely poured over the coffin. As a result this unparalleled monument was not only disfigured – as it afterwards proved, only temporarily – but was stuck fast to the interior of the second coffin, the consolidated liquid filling up the space between the second and third coffins almost to the level of the lid of the third.

These consecration unguents, which had obviously been used in great quantity, were doubtless the cause of the disintegration observed when dealing with the outer coffins which, as they were in a practically hermetically sealed quartzite sarcophagus, cannot have been affected by outside influences. As a further result it may be mentioned that the covering shroud and floral collarette mingled with blue faience beads had suffered, and although these at first appeared to be in good condition, they proved so brittle that the material broke the very instant it was touched.

We raised the third coffin contained in the shell of the second, which now rested on the top of the sarcophagus, and moved them into the Antechamber where they were more accessible, both for examination and manipulation. It was then that the wonder and magnitude of our last discovery more completely dawned upon us. This unique and wonderful monument – a coffin over 6 feet in length, of the finest art, wrought in solid gold of $2\frac{1}{2}$ to $3\frac{1}{2}$ millimetres in thickness – represented an enormous mass of pure bullion.

How great must have been the wealth buried with those ancient Pharaohs! What riches that valley must have once concealed! Of the twenty-seven monarchs buried there, Tut-ankh-Amen was probably of the least importance. How great must have been the temptation to the greed and rapacity of the audacious contemporary tomb robbers! What stronger incentive can be imagined than those vast treasures of gold! The plundering of royal tombs, recorded in the reign of Rameses IX, becomes easily intelligible when the incentive to these crimes is measured by this gold coffin of Tut-ankh-Amen. It must have represented fabulous wealth to the stone-cutters, artisans, water-carriers and peasants – to contemporary workers generally, such as the men implicated in the tomb robberies. These plunderings occurred in the reigns of the latter Ramessides (1200-1000 BC) and are recorded in legal documents now known as the Abbott, Amherst, Turin, and Mayer papyri, discovered in Thebes about the beginning of last century. Probably the thieves, who made their practically ineffectual raid on Tut-ankh-Amen's tomb, were aware of the mass of bullion covering the remains of the young Pharaoh under its protective shrines, sarcophagus and nested coffins. . . .

The external ornaments and inlaid gold trappings having been removed, the king's mummy lay bare with its simple outer coverings and gold mask. It occupied the whole of the interior of the gold coffin, measuring in total length 6 feet 1 inch.

The outer wrappings consisted of one large linen sheet, held in position by three longitudinal (one down the centre and one at each side) and four transverse bands of the same material, corresponding in position to the flexible inlaid gold trappings already mentioned. These linen bands had evidently been fastened to the linen covering by some such adhesive as Herodotus has described. They were doubled, and varied from 2¾ to 3½ inches in width. The central longitudinal band, beginning in the middle of the abdomen (in reality thorax), was passed under the lower layer of each of the three transverse bands, over the feet, under the soles, and doubled back below the second layer of transverse bands. At each side of the feet the linen wrappings had been rubbed, the result probably of friction against the sides of the metal coffin during transport to the tomb. The mummy lay at a slight angle, suggesting that it had been subjected to some shock when lowered into the sarcophagus. There was also similar evidence to imply that the unguents had been poured over the mummy and coffin before they were lowered into the sarcophagus – the liquid being at different levels on the two sides, suggesting the tilting of the coffin.

In consequence of the fragile and carbonised condition of the linen swathing, the whole of the exposed surface was painted over with melted paraffin wax of such a temperature that when congealed it formed a thin coating on the surface, with minimum penetration of the decayed wrappings beneath. When the wax had cooled, Dr Derry made a longitudinal incision down the centre of the outer binding to the depth penetrated by the wax, thus enabling the consolidated layer to be removed in large pieces. Nor did our troubles end here. The very voluminous under-wrappings were found to be in even worse condition of carbonisation and decay. We had hoped, by removing a thin outer layer of bandage from the mummy, to free it at the points of adhesion to the coffin so that it might be removed, but in this we were again disappointed. It was found that the linen beneath the mummy and the body itself had been so saturated by the unguents which formed a pitch-like mass at the bottom of the coffin and held it embedded so firmly, that it was impossible to raise it except at risk of great damage. Even after the greater part of the bandages had been carefully removed, the consolidated material had to be chiselled away from beneath the limbs and trunk before it was possible to raise the king's remains.

The bandages that actually enveloped the head were in a better state of preservation than those on the rest of the body, inasmuch as they had not been saturated by the unguents, and consequently had only suffered from indirect oxidation. This was also the case to a large extent with the wrappings on the feet.

The general system of bandaging so far as could be discovered was of normal character; it comprised a series of bandages, sheets and pads of linen, where the latter were required to complete the anthropoid form, the whole showing evidence of considerable care. The linen was evidently of a very fine cambric-like nature. The numerous objects found upon the mummy were enclosed in alternate layers of the voluminous wrappings, and literally covered the king from head to foot; some of the larger objects were caught up in many different layers of bindings which were wound crosswise and transversely.

Although the actual examination had necessarily to be carried out beginning from the feet upwards, for the sake of clarity, in the following description, I will describe it from the head downwards, enumerating each object and point of interest in proper sequence.

Upon the top of the head was a large pad of conic form, composed of wads of linen, wrapped in the manner of a modern surgical head-bandage, and in shape suggestive of the *Atef* crown of Osiris, without such accessories as the horns and feathers. The purpose of this pad is obscure; from its shape it might be thought to be a crown, but, on the other hand, it could well be merely a tall pad to support and fill the empty space within the hollow of the *Nemes* headdress of the gold mask, especially in view of the fact that the mask is an integral part of the external equipment of the mummy, making it coincide with the effigies upon the coffins.

Beneath this crown-like pad, lying on the back of the mask, was a small amuletic *Urs* pillow, or head-rest, made of iron, which, according to the 166th Chapter of the 'Book of the Dead', has the following significance: 'Rise up from non-existence, O prostrate one . . . over-throwest thou thy enemies, triumphest thou over what they do against thee.' Such amulets are usually made of haematite, but in this case pure iron has taken the place of that ore, a fact that gives us a very important milestone in the development and growth of the history of civilisation....

Next to the pad and encircling the top of the head, was a double tie (the Arabic *aqal*), not unlike that of the Bedouin headdress, made of fibre tightly bound with cord and having loops at the ends to which were doubtless attached tapes for tying at the back of the head. Its use is unknown, its like or parallel never before having been found. It suggests a relief to the head from the pressure of a crown.

The removal of a few layers of wrappings revealed a magnificent diadem completely encircling the king's head – an object of extreme beauty and of simple fillet type. In design it comprises a richly ornamented gold ribbon of contiguous circles of carnelian, having minute gold bosses affixed to their centres, with, at the back, a floral and disk-shaped bow, from which hang two ribbon-like gold appendages similarly decorated. On both sides of the fillet are appendages of a like but broader kind, and having a massive pendent uraeus attached to their front margins. The insignia of northern and southern sovereignty of this diadem, I should here mention, were found lower down, separate, and on the right and left thighs respectively and as the king lay within the sarcophagus, east and west – his head towards the west – the uraeus of Buto being on the left side, and the vulture of Nekhebet on the right, the insignia took their correct geographical position, as did also those emblems on the coffins. Both of these golden emblems of royalty have grooved fastenings on the back, into which fit corresponding T-shaped tongues upon the diadem. They are thus movable and could be fitted on to whatever crown the king might have worn.

The golden Nekhebet with obsidian eyes is a remarkable example of fine metal-work. The shape of the head, occiput covered with wrinkles, and at the back of the neck a partial collar of short stiff feathers, make it quite clear that the bird, representing the Upper Egyptian goddess, was *Vultur auricularis*, Daud. – the sociable vulture. This particular species is today plentiful in Nubia, but uncommon in the middle and southern provinces of Egypt, but seldom if ever seen in Lower Egypt.

This diadem must have had a very early origin, inasmuch as it seems to have derived its name *Seshnen* and form from the circlet-ribbon worn on the head by men and women of all classes, as far back as the Old Kingdom, some 1,500 years before the New Empire. . . .

More than often when this type of diadem is depicted upon the monuments, the king is represented wearing it around a wig in coniunction with, and surmounted by, the *Atef* crown of Osiris.

Around the forehead, underneath a few more layers of linen, was a broad temple-band of burnished gold terminating behind and above the ears. At its extremities are slots through which linen tapes were passed and tied in a bow at the back of the head. This band held in place over the brow and temples, a fine cambric-like linen *Khat* headdress, unfortunately reduced by decay to such an irreparable condition that it was only recognisable from a portion of the kind of pigtail at the back, common to this headdress. Sewn to this *Khat* headdress were the royal insignia, being a second set found upon the king. The uraeus, with body and tail in flexible sections of gold-work threaded together, and bordered with minute beads, was passed over the axis of the crown of the head as far back as the *lambda*, whilst the Nekhebet vulture (in this case with open wings, and with characteristics identical with those already described) covered the top of the head-dress, its body being parallel with the uraeus. In order that the soft linen of this head-dress should take its conventional shape, pads of linen had been placed under it and above the temples.

Beneath the *Khat* headdress were further layers of bandaging that covered a skull-cap of fine linen fabric, fitting tightly over the shaven head of the king, and embroidered with an elaborate device of uraei in minute gold and faience beads. The cap was kept in place by a gold temple-band similar to that just described. Each uraeus of the device bears in its centre the *Aten* cartouche of the Sun. The fabric of the cap was unfortunately much carbonised and decayed, but the bead-work had suffered far less, the device being practically perfect, since it adhered to the head of the king. To have attempted to remove this exquisite piece of work would have been disastrous, so it was treated with a thin coating of wax and left as it was found.

The removal of the final wrappings that protected the face of the king needed the utmost care, as owing to the carbonised state of the head there was always the risk of injury to the very fragile features. We realised the peculiar importance and responsibility attached to our task. At the touch of a sable brush the last few fragments of decayed fabric fell away, revealing a serene and placid countenance, that of a young man. The face was refined and cultured, the features well formed, especially the clearly marked lips, and I think I may here record, without wishing to encroach on the province of Drs Derry and Saleh Bey Hamdi, the first and most striking impression to all present – namely, the remarkable structural resemblance to his father-in-law, Akh-en-Aten – an affinity that has been visible on the monuments.

The Tomb of Tut-ankh-Amen, vol. II, 1927

The buried pyramid

ZAKARIA GONEIM

ZAKARIA GONEIM was born in Egypt. He took his diploma in Egyptology from the University of Giza in 1934 under the supervision of Newberry, Junker and Vikentiev. In 1937 he was appointed to the Antiquities Service, and began his career at Saqqara. In 1939 he was made Inspector of Antiquities at Aswan and Edfu, and in 1943, Conservator of the Theban necropolis. He carried out this work so successfully that in 1946 he was promoted to the post of Inspector-in-Chief of Upper Egypt, and in 1951 he was placed in sole charge of the antiquities of Saqqara. It was here that he made his remarkable discovery of a new pyramid enclosure. Unfortunately his work was interrupted by political and economic considerations in 1956, and he died in most unfortunate circumstances in 1959.

During the last few days of September 1951, Hofni and I went around the vast site looking for a suitable place to begin our work. Our attention was drawn to an outcropping of rubble masonry just appearing above the surface on the western border of the terrace. So we began to dig at this point. To our delight, on the first day a massive wall of rubble-coursed masonry appeared. We dug down to the bottom of the wall which was about 27 feet deep, and found that it was built on the rock strata and had a thickness of over 60 feet. It was built in three parts, like a sandwich. The middle of the sandwich was an upright course about 11 feet thick, faced on each side with another course about 41 feet thick, the outer sides of which sloped inward at an angle of 72 degrees. Architects call this type of construction a 'battered' wall.

This discovery reassured me that my original conception was correct, and during the following two months we continued to make further excavations at points along the length of this massive wall. I increased my gang of workmen to fifty. Under Hofni Ibrahim's direction, the 'Decauville' railway was laid down to carry the excavated sand and rock from the site to a suitable dumping-place. The terrace lies in the south-east corner of the great depression, which is situated to the south-west of Djoser's enclosure. I chose as my dumping-ground an area to the west of the west border of the terrace, having first examined the place by digging other trial pits to make sure that it was only rock strata and did not conceal tombs or monuments. The 'Decauville' is a light, narrow-gauge railway, which can be rapidly laid down and equally rapidly removed to a new site when required. Steel tip-trucks run along it, and the rumble of these, mingled with the songs and rhythmic chanting of the workmen, is a sound with which all Egyptian archaeologists are familiar. It is music to the excavator's heart!

The wall was built of large uniform blocks of local grey limestone, and the upper part appeared to have been quarried in antiquity. When I had defined this wall I searched for the corners, and eventually established the limits. I found that it was built around a rectangular enclosure, which had a north–south axis of about 1,700 feet and an east–west axis of about 600 feet.

The enormous thickness of this wall – 66 feet – and the fact that it was not faced with fine limestone, as was Djoser's circuit wall, puzzled me at first. Then I realised that it was really a foundation platform on which the upper wall had originally been built. The lie of the land showed why this was. Djoser's pyramid complex stands on a command-ing site on the very edge of the plateau, overlooking the valley; but the king for whom the newly discovered enclosure was built did not have this advantage. His monument had to be built in a depression, and in order to overcome this his architect had first built this massive stone platform of local limestone, which would not perhaps be visible to the eye, and on top of this he had built the *real* enclosure wall, of similar type to that of Djoser, projecting bastions and probably dummy gates, all of which would be visible from afar. Most of this 'curtain' wall had disappeared; the fine limestone of which it was built had been too great a temptation to subsequent builders. The kings of Ancient Egypt frequently plundered their ancestors' monuments, and this wall had fallen a victim like the rest. Nevertheless, I had no doubt that the uppermost wall had been completed, because we came across several fragments of it in the extreme northern limit of the enclosure, with panelled bastions and 'curtains' having the same measurements as those of Djoser's wall. This, incidentally, is one of the reasons why I believe that the king who built this enclosure was later than Djoser, since, if the latter king's monument had not already existed, the builders of this other structure would have raised it nearer to the edge of the plateau, not only because of the more advantageous position, but because they would have been nearer the western bank of the Nile, at which the facing stones would have to be unloaded. For although the cores of the pyramids were built of local limestone, the fine-grained stone needed for the facing-blocks was quarried from the hills on the eastern bank of the Nile.

Further excavations in the northern area of the rectangular terrace revealed several rubble walls, running parallel with one another in an east–west direction, and joined together with small cross-walls, also of rubble; the whole strikingly resembling some of the embankments and fillings in Djoser's step pyramid enclosure. It took us about two months to excavate and examine this bewildering complex of cross-walls, for it was difficult to know where to begin digging in this vast enclosure. I must emphasise at this point the immensity of the place. It was not like excavating a simple tomb in a small circumscribed spot, but comparable to digging out an area several times the size of Trafalgar Square in London. Dozens of times I went with Hofni Ibrahim to re-examine Djoser's enclosure, particularly at its northern end, in the hope of finding clues to the lay-out of the newly discovered enclosure. We found the same complex of walls in several places, but chiefly in the northern end.

The reason for the existence of these cross-walls was as follows. When the builders of that remote period wished to raise the level of an area, they first built cross-walls, dividing the area into compartments which they afterwards filled in with stone. Also it is very important to remember that the buildings in Djoser's enclosure were not real buildings intended for human habitation, but dummies. They were practically solid, and these walls were used in the construction of such dummy structures.

Let me put it this way. If one is excavating, say, a house or a temple, one can tell which were walls and which were spaces between the walls for chambers. But in this case the spaces left within the structures were so small that the whole construction looked as if it was one solid mass. Most of these buildings were, in fact, symbolic, and designed to represent certain elements in the king's palace at Memphis which were deemed necessary for his habitation in the after-life and to assert his rights of sovereignty.

The difficulty of establishing the lay-out of such buildings when they have been reduced to foundation-level can be imagined, and this was why I returned frequently to the enclosure of Djoser, which has been systematically excavated, to see if I could gain information which would enable me to interpret the lay-out of the new structure. The resemblances were striking, and I became increasingly convinced that this was indeed the enclosure of a step pyramid, though at the time few others believed me.

In work of this kind the archaeologist sometimes runs into blind-alleys – both literally and figuratively – and one such distraction occurred while we were digging in this area. We noticed that most of the fragments used in the fillings were chips of soft clay, called in Arabic *tafl*, which are usually found in the debris from subterranean galleries. This led us to suspect that there might be subterranean galleries underneath, perhaps leading to tombs, the more so since similar complexes of walls are found over such galleries in the northern part of Djoser's enclosure. So we searched for the entrance, and I remember my two chief workmen and I spent a long time conjecturing where it might be. The other workmen joined enthusiastically in the search, and, as usually happens on such occasions, each had his own special theory. Cries would go up 'The entrance is here! . . . No, it is here!' and so on, and every day brought new conjectures. It was very difficult to see one's way out of this maze, particularly as visitors and other archaeologists came to see us, and after viewing the site, expressed the opinion that the enclosure had never been completed and that we would find nothing.

The search for a tomb having proved vain, I decided at last to shift the whole work a few yards farther north. It was at Christmas 1951 that I told *Reis* Hofni to move the Decauville railway to the north. Imagine our joy when, on New Year's Day, 1952, we suddenly found a flight of steps leading to an enormous cross-wall, which ran from east to west across the enclosure. This wall was quite different from those I had discovered earlier. It was faced with fine white limestone and built with bastions and curtains, just like those of Djoser's enclosure wall. Also it was similarly panelled. For some reason it had never been completed and had been embedded in a mass of dry masonry composed of rubble cross-walls built at intervals over and against its bastions and curtains, the gaps being filled up with debris. Owing to this, the wall was found intact to the length of 138 feet at the very stage when its construction was broken off, probably because of an alteration in the architect's design. As it gradually revealed itself in all its beauty, exactly as the workmen had left it nearly five thousand years ago, I realised that here was a find of major importance. . . .

The New Year seemed full of hope for us all. Hofni, his brother, and the rest of the workmen were as delighted as I was. In the past they had worked on some great excavations, and it was a point of honour for them that at every site on which they worked something important should be found. Naturally, such expectations are not always realised, and when they are there is great rejoicing. Such experiences then become part of their life-history, which they tell to their children.

Perhaps some readers will wonder why such a fuss should be made of a mere stone wall. But this was no ordinary wall. It is very rare in Egypt to find such a structure untouched by time, and as we cleared more and more of its length, we found incontestable evidence that the White Wall, as we named it, must have been buried very shortly after its construction. We were looking at something which no human eye had seen for nearly fifty centuries.

This evidence consisted of marks and drawings in red paint left on the white limestone surface by the ancient builders. For instance, on some of the stone blocks were quarry marks, painted on the stones before they left the quarries on the opposite side of the Nile. Those on the White Wall were mere symbols of which the meaning is lost, but we know from other examples found in the later pyramids that some of these marks indicated the names of the gangs or crews who cut the stone. These crews are believed to have consisted of some eight hundred to a thousand men. For instance, here are the names of some of the crews who quarried stone for the Pyramids of Cheops and Mycerinus:

The Crew, Cheops excites love.

The crew, the White Crown of Khnmw-Khufu (Cheops) is powerful. Other marks have been translated as follows:

This side up

To be taken away

For the royal tomb (per nwb).

These roughly drawn signs and inscriptions bring one very near to the ancient builders. On the White Wall, for example, we found the actual levelling-lines, made by stretching a cord dipped in red paint across the surface and 'flipping' it, just as a modern mason does to this day. These were evidently made to ensure that workmen should lay the stones at the same level along the entire length of the wall. Even though this was perhaps only the second or third attempt at building monumental walls in stone masonry, the builders had evidently acquired great skill.

Then we found something which brought the remote past very near to us; a rare human touch on a royal Egyptian monument. Here and there the workmen had been beguiling a leisure moment by drawing on the wall, in red ochre or lamp-black, pictures of men, animals, and boats. There was a figure of a Lybian man in a long robe and tall head-dress, carrying a bow. The Lybians, nomads living in the West Desert, were of course foreigners to the Egyptians whose dress was quite dissimilar. Then there were unmistakable drawings of lions. At that time lions and other beasts of prey were still found in the deserts of Egypt, and the men must have seen them many times roaming the desert fringes. Other drawings showed boats, some with sails and some without, and barges similar to those which were used by the Ancient Egyptians to bring blocks of limestone from the east to the north-east bank of the Nile.

I must repeat at this point that no evidence had so far been uncovered to indicate that I had found a pyramid. I had found an enclosure which bore certain resemblances to that of King Djoser, and a magnificent cross-wall which was so like that of that king's enclosure wall as to leave no doubt that it must have been built at a period very close to that of Djoser. But that was all. Apart from the White Wall, visitors to the site in those early months of 1952 found little to impress them: only the bare plateau, of sand and rock, pitted with a few holes, from one of which the Decauville ran to the rubbish-dump. 'Where's the pyramid?' my professional colleagues would ask jocularly, and I had no answer; only an inner faith that somewhere beneath that vast expanse of sand I would eventually find what I was looking for. But when I thought of my modest and rapidly dwindling allowance I became anxious, for if the money was spent on fruitless digging, it might be difficult to obtain more. The site of each trial pit would have to be chosen with great care, and night after night, when I returned to my house after the day's work, I would study the plan of the area, consult the works of other archaeologists who had worked on pyramids, form and reject theories, and talk far into the night with my chief workmen, Hofni and Hussein.

At this stage I would like to refer my readers to the plan of the pyramid enclosure. . . . They will notice that north of the point where the White Wall joins the north–south walls of the enclosure there is a curious change of alignment. We discovered this shortly after the wall was revealed, and it puzzled me for some time. In fact, there were two features which gave me cause for thought. First, there was the fact that, from the White Wall onwards, in a northerly direction, the east–west walls of the enclosure did not follow the same line as before, but were inset to a depth of about 6 feet, forming an angle. This indicated either another monument attached to the first on the northern side, or else *an extension of the original monument*. Later I found that this latter supposition was correct.

The second strange feature was that this northern extension, beyond the White Wall, was raised above the level of the southern part of the enclosure, forming a kind of raised platform. Why was this done? Only further excavations will provide a final answer.

In the meantime, in an endeavour to find an answer to the puzzle, I began to excavate the whole breadth of the enclosure from west to east, following the line of the White Wall. We first encountered large blocks of fine limestone so arranged as to form a flight of steps built at the western end of the massive wall, and designed to facilitate its exploitation as a quarry.

The wall itself proved to be comprised of a thick, regularly built inner core of local limestone, faced outside with dressed white limestone. The whole outer face of the wall was panelled and constructed with bastions and curtains (panels). The whole magnificent structure presented exactly the same design as Djoser's enclosure wall. The panels had the same breadth and depth. The bastions and 'curtains' had the same measurements, with equal spaces in the larger bastions for carving imitation closed double gates, as in Djoser's wall. I was delighted, because it was now quite clear that I had found an enclosure built on lines similar to that of Djoser.

Throughout the rest of the 1952 season, from January to March, we continued to work on this wall, and excavated 150 feet of its length, only stopping when we found that at its eastern end, nearest to the necropolis, it had been damaged by quarrying.

However, we noticed two essential differences in the structural disposition of the stones. The dimensions of the stones here were much larger than those of Djoser's enclosure; in the new wall, the height of the course is 50–52 centimetres, while in the lower parts of Djoser's wall it is only 24–26 centimetres. On the other hand, the fine limestone was employed much more thriftily in the casing.

These two factors are extremely important in the dating of the monument. It is certain that already in Djoser's reign there had been a tendency to increase the size of the stone blocks, as the builders ultimately came to learn that an increase in size meant an economy in the work of cutting out the stones, and lent more strength and a greater degree of cohesion to walls. Therefore the size of the stones and the way in which they were used in this new wall suggest a date *later* than Djoser, although still Third Dynasty. The economy of the casing also suggests a more rational, hence more developed method of construction. But the wall had been abandoned during construction, and the northern limit of the enclosure had been moved 600 feet farther north. That it was abandoned during construction is proved by the fact that the sixth and uppermost course had not been faced and had been left rough. In addition, several partition walls of coarse limestone leaned directly against the panelled façade, and the surface of the wall had not been smoothed, but bore the numerous quarry marks and mason's lines which I have already described.

Throughout this time my workmen and I still kept a look-out for signs of subterranean galleries such as exist beneath the northern part of Djoser's enclosure, and one day we found something which raised our hopes. It was a hole made by one of the ancient tomb-robbers. . . . To the archaeologist such holes can be a cause of both hope and despair. Hope, because they indicate that, thousands of years ago, some enterprising rascal had known or suspected that there was a tomb near by; despair, lest he should have found and plundered it!

In this case hope triumphed. We went down the hole and followed the robber's tunnel for a distance of 62 feet. It plunged down into the rock and described a wide semicircle. We had to proceed carefully for fear of falling rock or a total collapse of the tunnel, but when Hofni and I reached the end and found only the rock, we were delighted and relieved. On this occasion the robber had drawn a blank and given up in disgust. But had he perhaps succeeded elsewhere? The answer to that question still lay in the future.

The period from January to the beginning of April 1952 was spent in clearing the White Wall down to its base, and along its length to the point where quarrying had damaged much of the structure. During this time the lay-out of the enclosure had become somewhat clearer to me. When I am excavating a site I always try to identify myself with the ancient builders, to get inside their minds in order to understand *why* their monument assumed its present shape. They often changed their plans during construction, and by observation and reflection, and by drawing on one's knowledge of other monuments, it is sometimes possible to estimate where and why such changes have occurred, and to make an intelligent guess at what may lie under the sand. . . .

For instance, I became fairly certain that the White Wall had originally formed the northern limit of the enclosure, but that for some reason not yet explained the builders decided to extend it to the north at a higher level. Also, that since this was clearly an enclosure, it must have had a central edifice, which should be near the geometrical centre of the *original* enclosure. It could be objected that the builders might have abandoned the enclosure before beginning the central edifice, whatever it was – pyramid or *mastaba*; but this was unlikely, since we know from other structures that the building of the various component parts went on at one and the same time. But there was no sign of any such central edifice, not even an outcropping of masonry such as had guided me to the enclosure wall.

Early in April I surveyed the original enclosure with a theodolite in order to determine its exact geometrical centre. I explained to Hofni my idea, and he showed an enthusiastic interest. He had not worked before on pyramids of this very early date, though he had played an important part in the excavation of the famous Pyramid of King Senusret II (Dyn. XII) at el-Lahun. In fact it was Hofni Ibrahim who found one of the most beautiful objects ever discovered in an Egyptian pyramid. Over thirty years ago he was working for Sir Flinders Petrie in the tomb of Princess Sit-Hathor-Iunet, daughter of Senusret II, when, during the clearing of a recess in the corner of the tomb, he found a rare specimen of the royal *uræus* or sacred snake, in gold, with a head of lapis-lazuli, eyes of garnet, and hood ornamented with carnelian, turquoise and lazuli. This royal symbol, signifying dominion over Lower Egypt, was worn by the Pharaohs in their crowns. Embedded in mud, it was overlooked by the tomb-robbers when they rifled the tomb, and had remained untouched for four thousand years until Hofni found it. He once told me that he often visits the Cairo Museum just to admire the *uræus* in it glass case, and to recall that day, thirty-six years ago, when he first held it in his hands. It is memories such as this which lend glory to the lives of these men, and inspire them with hope whenever they tackle a new site. So it was with considerable excitement that my workmen began the next phase of the excavation, which was to try to locate the central edifice, if it existed.

In all work of this kind luck and judgment both play their part, and on this occasion we were lucky. I had established the spot where the central building should lie, but when I gave instructions for the sinking of the first trial pit I had no idea whether we should strike the edge of the structure or some point within it. Judge my satisfaction when on January 29th, 1952, Hofni came to me excitedly and said that they had found masonry. By good fortune we had located the actual southern edge of the hidden structure, from which point it would not be difficult to follow it along to its corners, and define the limits of the whole edifice.

It proved to be composed of a series of independent walls leaning one on the other and inclining inwards at an angle of about 75 degrees, and *the stone courses were at right angles to the slope of the walls*. Readers who have carefully followed Chapter One, in which I described the construction of step pyramids, will realise that this was a valuable clue to the age of the structure. For in the few surviving examples of step pyramids we know, the accretion walls are built in this manner, whereas in later pyramids built subsequent to the time of Snofru the courses were laid horizontally. I immediately went to Monsieur Lauer, the architect of the Antiquities Department who has worked for many years on Djoser's step pyramid. (He is responsible for restoration and consolidation of monuments.) I found him as usual at work near this pyramid, and together we made our way to the terrace where Hofni, Hussein, and the other workmen were clearing the newly discovered walls. When he had seen and examined them he said to me: 'I have no doubt whatsoever that this forms part of a step pyramid.'

Even so, there were still many who doubted us, and unfortunately we had now come to the end of the 1952 season, and I knew it would be some time before these doubts could be finally resolved, as I was sure they would be. Excavations closed down in May 1952 and were not resumed until November 1953. Work had reached a critical point, and I felt I needed time to study the finds and decide carefully on my next course of action. It was also necessary to obtain an additional grant in order that the work could continue.

In November 1953 I reassembled my workmen, and once again the loaded trucks began to rumble along the Decauville as we laboured to uncover more of this mysterious building. I first concentrated my attention on finding its limits. First we extended the pit and assured ourselves that the structure continued on both the east and west sides. Then I gave orders to shift the work some distance to the west on the same line, at a point where I judged the corner of the building might be. We found that the southern side was covered up with soft clay resulting from the cutting of subterranean galleries, so this almost imperceptible evidence showed where the artificial fillings ended and the debris resulting from later quarrying of the pyramid began. When we dug below the desert surface, it was clear where this intentional covering material ended. Not long after this work was begun I was engaged at another point in the enclosure when Hussein Ibrahim, the brother of Hofni, came running towards me with outstretched arms and crying: 'Mabruk elnasia!' which means 'Congratulations! We have found the corner!'

I went back with him and found to my joy that they had struck the corner of a pyramid, for this I was now more convinced it was. It could hardly have been a mastaba, partly because of its size, but chiefly because no mastabas are known to exist with 'accretion walls' and inclined courses. These are typical of pyramid construction.

Every archaeological site has its own characteristics, and one has to work for a very long time to find them and to recognise what happened in ancient times. Because of the immense surface covered by the enclosure, I adopted the method of finding first the main points; otherwise I would have had to expend much time and money on fruitless labour before being able to understand the lay-out.

For example, having uncovered this first corner it was easy for us to find the other three. From the photographs it will be seen that this was a stepped structure, but that only one step remains. The masonry is of good quality, but the limestone blocks are relatively small, as in Djoser's pyramid. The builders had not yet reached the stage when they built with huge megalithic blocks. The whole structure is 400 feet square; the base thus presented is larger than that of Djoser's pyramid. In its unfinished state it has a maximum height of about 23 feet, but I believe that it might have been built originally to double this height and that it has been reduced by quarrying in later times. No traces of an outer casing were found, and it may be assumed that only the core of the pyramid was begun and that it was never finished.

This is a square layer-structure consisting of probably fourteen skins of masonry which diminished in height from the centre outwards and leaned on a central nucleus at an angle varying between 71 and 75 degrees, with the beds of the courses at right angles to the facing lines. The 'accretion faces' were left in the rough. Assuming that each pair of these skins of masonry was designed to form one step, as is the case in Djoser's pyramid, we may infer that the new pyramid was intended to have seven steps in place of Djoser's six.

Had this pyramid been finished, it would probably have stood to a height of about 230 feet, i.e. 30 feet higher than Djoser's. It stands directly on the rock, and was built of local, coarse grey limestone. The blocks are roughly squared and are set in a mortar composed of soft clay (*tafl*) obtained from the tunnelling of underground passages, mixed with limestone chips. The stones were generally laid in alternate courses of 'headers and stretchers' in imitation of mud-bricks. The courses are level and parallel, and the bedding joints are much wider than the rising joints. A fragment of a boundary *stela* bearing the name of Djoser was found re-used in the masonry, a further indication that the new pyramid must have been built at a later date than Djoser's.

The Buried Pyramid, 1956

Part Four

THE BOOK OF THE TOWERS

A second solution to the cuneiform script

HENRY RAWLINSON

Sir Henry Creswicke Rawlinson (1810–1895) was born at Chadlington in Oxfordshire. In 1827 he went to India as an officer cadet of the East India Company, and after six years he was transferred to Persia with several other officers to reorganise the troops of the Shah. At this time cuneiform writing was known in fairly substantial quantities but only the German Grotefend had found any clue to its decipherment and Rawlinson, who did not know of Grotefend's work, became deeply interested in the problem. With considerable danger and difficulty he scaled the rock of Behistun and transcribed part of the inscription, but international political friction made it necessary for him to leave the country before he finished the work. In 1840 he became political agent for Kandahar and requested to be sent to Turkish Arabia; he settled in Baghdad and continued his researches into the problem of the inscription. It was at this time that he transcribed, deciphered and interpreted the remainder of the Behistun inscription. During two years' leave in England he placed his valuable collection of antiquities in the charge of the British Museum, who gave him a grant to continue the excavations begun by Sir Austen Layard which he carried on until his retirement in 1855. He was awarded the K.C.B. for his work, and during the remainder of his life, which was largely spent in London, he continued to be active in cuneiform scholarship and in international affairs.

'On my arrival at Baghdad during the present year I deferred the completion of my translations, and of the Memoir by which I designed to establish and explain to them, until I obtained books from England which might enable me to study with more care the peculiarities of Sanskrit grammar; and in the mean time I busied myself with comparative geography. It was at this period that I received through the Vice-President of the Royal Asiatic Society, a letter from Professor Lassen, containing a précis of his last improved system of interpretation, and the Bonn alphabet I recognised at once to be infinitely superior to any other that had previously fallen under my observation. The Professor's views indeed coincided in all essential points with my own, and since I have been enabled, with the help of Sanskrit and Zend affinities, to analyse nearly every word of the Cuneiform inscriptions hitherto copied in Persia, and thus to verify the alphabetical power of almost every Cuneiform character, I have found the more reason to admire the skill of Professor Lassen, who with such very limited materials as were alone with his disposal in Europe, has still arrived at results so remarkably correct. The close approximation of my own alphabet to that adopted by Professor Lassen, will be apparent on a reference to the comparative table, and although in point of fact, the Professor's labours have been of no farther assistance to me than in adding one new character to my alphabet, and in confirming opinions which were sometimes conjectural, and which generally require verification, yet as the improvements which his system of interpretation makes upon the alphabet employed by M. Burnouf appear to have preceded not only the announcement, but the adoption of my own views, I cannot pretend to contest with him the priority of alphabetical discovery. Whilst employed in writing the present Memoir, I have had further opportunities of examining the Persepolitan inscriptions of Mr Rich, and the Persian inscription of Xerxes which is found at Ván; and I have also, in the pages of the *Journal Asiatique*, been introduced to a better knowledge of the Pehlevi, by Dr Müller, and I have obtained some acquaintance with Professor Lassen's translations, from the perusal of one of the critical notices of M. Jacquet.

'Having thus briefly described the progress of my Cuneiform studies during the last four years, and having explained the means by which I have been enabled to complete my alphabet, I have now to make a few particular remarks on the translations. This branch of the study although depending upon, and necessarily following the correct determination of the characters, is of course the only really valuable part of the enquiry. It is in fact the harvest springing from the previous cultivation of a rugged soil, and as far as I am aware, it has been hitherto but poorly reaped.

'The translations of Professor Grotefend and of Saint Martin are altogether erroneous and merit no attention whatever. The memoir of M. Burnouf on the inscriptions of Hamadán is confined to the illustration of twenty short lines of writing, containing an invocation to Ormand, a few proper names, and a bare enumeration of royal titles. Some of the grammatical peculiarities are, it is true, from their identity with similar formations in Zend, correctly developed; but the nature of the inscriptions has necessarily rendered the labours of the Paris secretary, ample and erudite as they are, deficient in historical interest; and the faulty condition of his alphabet has, moreover, led him into several important errors of translation. His incidental examination of the geographical names contained in one of Niebuhr's Persepolitan inscriptions constitutes by far the most interesting portion of his researches; yet in a list which exhibits the titles of twenty-four of the most celebrated nations of ancient Asia, he has correctly deciphered ten only of the names.

'Of Professor Lassen's translations I have no means of judging, except from the specimen which he has sent me of his system of interpretation applied to Niebuhr's Geographical inscription, and from M. Jacquet's critique on the same subject. The highly improved condition of the Bonn alphabet has rendered the Professor's identification of the geographical names at Persepolis far superior in correctness to that of M. Burnouf, but still he is not, I think, without error in his reading and appropriation of these names, and that he has also in many cases misunderstood both the etymology of the words and the grammatical structure of the language, will be apparent from the appendix to the present Memoir, where I have compared the Professor's translation of Niebuhr's inscription with my own.

'In the present case, then, I do put forth a claim to originality, as having been the first to present to the world a literal and, as I believe, a correct grammatical translation of nearly two hundred lines of Cuneiform writing, a memorial of the time of Darius Hystaspes, the greater part of which is in so perfect a state as to afford ample and certain grounds for a minute orthographical and etymological analysis, and the purport of which to the historian must, I think, be of fully equal interest with the peculiarities of its language to the philologist. I do not affect at the same time to consider my translations as unimpeachable; those who expect in the present paper to see the Cuneiform Inscriptions rendered and explained with as much certainty and clearness as the ancient tablets of Greece and Rome will be lamentably disappointed. It must be remembered that the Persian of the ante-Alexandrian ages has long ceased to be a living language; that its interpretation depends on the collateral aid of the Sanskrit, the Zend, and the corrupted dialects which in the forests and mountains of Persia have survived the wreck of the old tongue; and that in a few instances, where these cognate and derivative languages have failed to perpetuate the ancient roots, or where my limited acquaintance with the different dialects may have failed to discover the connexion, I have then been obliged to assign an arbitrary meaning, obtained by comparative propriety of application in a very limited field of research. I feel, therefore, that in a few cases my translations will be subject to doubt, and that as materials of analysis continue to be accumulated and more experienced Orientalists prosecute the study, it may be found necessary to alter or modify some of the significations that I have assigned; but at the same time I do not, and cannot, doubt, but that I have accurately determined the general application of every paragraph, and that I have been thus enabled to exhibit a correct historical outline, possessing the weight of royal and contemporaneous recital, of many great events which preceded the rise and marked the career of one of the most celebrated of the early sovereigns of Persia.'

When I wrote the foregoing introduction in the year 1839, it was my intention to have merely published the text of the Behistun Inscriptions, with a running commentary illustrative of such points of philology, history, and geography, as appeared particularly to deserve attention, and I confidently expected that the Memoir in this humble form would be ready for the press before the expiration of the year. As I proceeded however with my task the labour grew insensibly on my hands. The examination of a language, so venerable from its age, and so interesting from its close affinity to the Vedic Sanskrit, seemed to demand more care than could be bestowed on it in a mere series of critical notes; while the historical and geographical questions that started up in rapid succession at each progressive stage of the enquiry, threatened to bury the text under a load of commentary, and to obscure, or perhaps entirely efface, the force and perspicuity of the argument. I set to work, accordingly, in the autumn of 1839 to recast the Memoir, arranging the material under different heads, and devoting a separate chapter to the treatment of each particular subject. This distribution was of the greatest assistance to me. The progress of the work was necessarily slow, but it was constant and uniform; and I might have still hoped to publish the Memoir in its amended form in the spring of 1840, had not circumstances, over which I had no control, and which I could neither have desired nor foreseen, arrested my enquiries in mid-career and superseded for a long period the possibility of their resumption.

It is not my intention to dwell with any minuteness on the interruption which I thus sustained. Let it suffice to say that my services were called into activity by the Government, that I was suddenly transferred from the lettered seclusion of Baghdad to fill a responsible and laborious office in Afghanistan, and that I continued in that situation during the entire period of our eventful occupation of the country. Those who have experienced a difficulty of combining a sustained application to literary matters with the ordinary distractions of business, will I believe admit that in the emergent condition of the public service in Afghanistan, calling for undivided attention and untiring care, I had no alternative but the abandonment of antiquarian research. To have continued my labours on the inscriptions during the few hours of leisure that I could legitimately command would have produced no result; to have devoted any considerable portion of my time to the enquiry, would have been incompatible with my duty to the Government.

But years rolled on, and in December, 1843, I found myself again at Baghdad. The interest in the inscriptions with which my original researches had inspired me, had never flagged; it was sharpened perhaps by the accidents that had so long operated to delay its gratification; and I thus hastened with eager satisfaction to profit by the first interval of relaxation that I had enjoyed for many years to resume the thread of the enquiry. Mr Westergaard, well known for his contributions to Sanskrit literature, who had been travelling in Persia during the year 1843, for the express purpose of collecting Palaeographic and antiquarian materials, supplied me at this period in the most liberal manner with several new inscriptions which he had copied at Persepolis. The inscription on the portal close to the great staircase, which had escaped all former visitors, was of much value; equally so were the corrections of Niebuhr's inscriptions H and I, and the restoration of all the minor tablets upon the platform; but the gem of his collection, the most important record in fact of the class which exists in Persia, with the exception of the tablets of Behistun, I found to be the long inscription at Nakhsh-i-Rustam engraved on the rock-hewn sepulchre of Darius. This inscription was no less remarkable for its extent and interest than for the correctness of its delineation. I could not but observe indeed that Mr Westergaard's copy, defective as it necessarily was, both from the abrasion of the rock and from the difficulty of tracing letters through a telescope at so great an elevation, still indicated, in its superiority over all the specimens of Niebuhr, Le Brun, Porter, and Rich, the immense advantage which a transcriber acquainted with the character and language enjoys over one who can only depend for the fidelity of his copy on the imitative accuracy of an artist.

I have derived the greatest assistance in my recent labours from Mr Westergaard's inscriptions, as well as from the Median copy of the inscription at Nakhsh-i-Rustam, with which soon after my arrival at Baghdad I was most kindly furnished by M. Dittel, a Russian Orientalist, who was Mr Westergaard's coadjutor at Persepolis; and I trust that both these gentlemen will permit me to express in a public form, the obligations which I thus owe to them.

It is probable that with these extended materials at my command, and with the improved acquaintance with the language which such material supplied, I should have thought it advisable under any circumstances to undertake a third revision of the Memoir that I was writing; but such a course was rendered absolutely necessary by the fortunate result of a visit which I was enabled again to make to the rock of Behistun in the autumn of last year, and in which I succeeded in copying the whole of the Persian writing at that place, and a very considerable portion also of the Median and Babylonian transcripts. I will not speak of the difficulties or dangers of the enterprise. They are such as any person with ordinary nerves may successfully encounter; but they are such, at the same time, as have alone prevented the inscriptions from being long ago presented to the public by some of the numerous travellers who have wistfully contemplated them at a distance.

On returning to Baghdad from my tour in Southern Kurdistan, public avocations and indifferent health again prevented me for some time from continuing my labours. The same causes have operated, with more or less effect, in impeding their prosecution during the spring and summer, and if I had not been fortunately able to avail myself of the ready hand of Lieutenant Jones, an accomplished officer of the Indian Navy, who has delineated the sculptures of Behistun and contributed in a great measure to the execution of the text, I might have been altogether frustrated in my hope of early publication. I may observe, at the same time, that in February of the present year, I took the precaution of forwarding to the Royal Asiatic Society, a literal translation of every portion of the Persian writing at Behistun, and of thus placing beyond the power of dispute the claim of the Society at that date to the results which are published in the following Memoir.

I now proceed to notice the contemporaneous march of discovery upon the Continent during the interval which had elapsed since the publication of the Bonn and Paris Memoirs of 1836. Professor Lassen,

I believe, established a Journal at Bonn in the year 1838, devoted exclusively to the elaboration of Palaeography and Eastern literature, and in that journal, I have been given to understand several pages on the Cuneiform Inscriptions have from time to time appeared. One of these papers, containing a translation of the inscription of Artaxerxes Ochus, was explained to me (for unfortunately I am ignorant of German) by Dr Aloys Sprenger, at Calcutta, in 1843; but of the contents of the others I have no cognizance whatever. I am indebted to Mr Westergaard for the information that Professor Grotefend undertook in 1839 to call in question the discoveries of Professor Lassen, and to place in opposition to them the infallible claims of the antiquated alphabet of 1815, a proceeding which was justly regarded by the German literati as little better than fatuity.

Professor Grotefend may take up the high position of primitive, though imperfect discovery; but Professor Lassen may contest with him even in the numerical identification of alphabetical powers; while in all the essentials of interpretation the old has no pretention whatever to be brought into comparison with the modern system. I also learn from the same source that other Orientalists with whose labours I am very imperfectly acquainted have been engaged in the enquiry. To Dr Beer of Leipsic, it appears, is conceded in Germany the discovery of the two characters ⟨⟨ h, and ⟨⟨ y, and the lamented M. Jacquet is said to have appropriated to his own researches the determination of the letter ⟨⟨ ch and ⟨⟨ jh. The only identifications in the present Memoir that I presume to be essentially different from those which are universally received at present upon the Continent, are ⟨⟨ and ⟨⟨ m', but the attribution of the power sh, instead of s, to the character ⟨⟨, and of $t̆r$ (with a dormant rather than an articulated liquid) to the character ⟨⟨, are modifications of some consequence, and two new letters ⟨⟨ and ⟨⟨ will also be remarked, which I respectively represent by $ñ'$ and $ñ$. To those who are interested in tracing the exact progress of alphabetical announcement, the tabular statement which heads Chapter III, on the Persian Cuneiform alphabet, will afford full and satisfactory information. For the mere purpose of reading the inscriptions the phonetic powers which are given in the right-hand column of the Table will be an ample and sufficient guide.

It remains that I should pay another tribute to Professor Lassen's acumen and research. It appears that Mr Westergaard on his return to Europe at the commencement of 1844, placed his Persian inscriptions in the hands of Professor Lassen, and that these new materials were justly deemed of sufficient consequence to demand an elaborate and immediate analysis. Professor Lassen accordingly devoted an early number of his Journal to the subject, and he took occasion at the same time to collect all the other inscriptions of the class and to publish the whole series together, in an amended text, and with revised translations. This is I believe the last work that has appeared upon the subject, and as might have been expected, it anticipates in some degree the novelty of the present Memoir. I have received a copy of the pamphlet whilst I have been writing the following pages, and I have found it of the greatest convenience, as a manual of reference. The marginal notes, indeed, that I have added to the present text, will show the care with which I have consulted it; but at the same time, I am bound to say that my translations, already completed when the book arrived, were, if not independent of assistance, at any rate beyond the reach of alteration, and I have further to regret that an ignorance of German has deprived me of that aid on questionable points of grammar, which, if I had been able to follow the Professor's arguments, I could not have failed to derive from the matured opinions of so eminent and correct a scholar.

I have only further to observe, that although the present Memoir, in consequence of the great augmentation of material, has been re-written during the present year, it is, as far as the original materials extended, and in all essential points of grammatical and etymological construction, absolutely identical with that which I had brought into a forward state of preparation for the press in the year 1839. If the translations can be amended (and imperfectly acquainted as I am with the niceties of Zend and Sanskrit grammar, I submit them with diffidence and deference to the public,) they must be indebted for their improvement to a critical examination of the text; for the materials available for analysis or verification, are not, I believe, entirely exhausted; and unless excavations should be undertaken on a great scale either at Susa, Persepolis, or Pasargadae, we must rest content with the sorrowful convictions that we have here, comprised in a few pages, all that remains of the ancient Persian languages and all that contemporary native evidence records of the glories of the Achaemenides.

The Persian Cuneiform Inscriptions at Behistun, 1846

John R. Freeman

15. One of the oldest of "modern" maps: a sketch of the ruins of
Babylon, made in 1811 by the great explorer and linguistic
genius Claudius Rich.

Was Babylon here?

CLAUDIUS JAMES RICH

CLAUDIUS JAMES RICH (*1787-1820*) *was born at Dijon in Burgundy, but grew up in Bristol. He was always interested in languages and began to study Arabic at the age of nine. It was probably this skill which led the East India Company to post him to Egypt when he became a cadet in 1803, but on his way to his first appointment he was shipwrecked and after spending some time in Malta, then in Italy, he was directed to Constantinople and Smyrna. He travelled widely in Asia Minor and then moved on to Egypt. His knowledge of the Arab language and customs was so thorough that he was able to disguise himself as a Mameluke and journey undetected throughout Egypt, Syria and Palestine, even succeeding in entering the Great Mosque at Damascus. In 1807 he was appointed to Bombay but the Company shortly decided that his unique abilities could best be used in Asia Minor and posted him to Baghdad, where he proved a most able and respected administrator. His work did not occupy him so fully that he had no time for further studies; he made a journey to the ruins of Babylon in 1811, and in 1820 he planned a much more extensive expedition through Kurdistan, Nineveh, Shiraz, Persepolis and down the Tigris to Baghdad. There was, however, an outbreak of cholera at Shiraz and when Rich stopped to give what assistance he could he caught the disease himself and died. His books, manuscripts and many valuable antiquities were bought by the British Museum.*

Those who have investigated the antiquities of Babylon have laid much stress on the authority of Diodorus, probably adverting more to the quantity than the quality of the information he supplies. He never was on the spot: he lived in an age when, as he himself tells us, its area was ploughed over: he has therefore recourse to Ctesias; and it must be owned that the want of discrimination in the ancients, and the credulity of Diodorus himself, were never more strongly exemplified than in his choice of a writer who confounds the Euphrates with the Tigris, and tells us that Semiramis erected a monument to her husband, which from the dimensions he specifies must have been of superior elevation to Mount Vesuvius, and nearly equal to Mount Hecla. If these are not 'fairy tales', I certainly know not to what the term can be applied. When an author can in so many instances be closely convicted of ignorance and exaggeration, we are certainly not justified in altering what is already before our eyes, to suit it to his description. We have only the very questionable authority of Ctesias for the second palace, and the wonderful tunnel under the river; but even he does not say whether the Tower of Belus stood on the east or west side. Herodotus, who will ever appear to greater advantage the more he is examined and understood, is the only historian who visited Babylon in person; and he is in every respect the best authority for its state in his time. The circumference he assigns to it has been generally deemed exaggerated; but after all we cannot prove it to be so. He says nothing to determine the situation of the Palace (for he speaks but of one) and Temple; he has no mention of east or west, or of proximity to the river. It is true, it has been attempted to establish from him, that the Temple was exactly in the centre of one of the halves into which the city was divided by the river: which, by the way, if clearly made out, would not agree with Major Rennel's position of it on the river's banks: but the error appears to have arisen from translating μέσος, *centre*. . . . Strabo, as might be expected, contains much fewer particulars than Herodotus; and the other Grecian and Roman historians still less: they are consequently of little use in a topographical enquiry. It appears, therefore, that none of the ancients say whether the Tower of Belus was on the east or the west of the Euphrates; that its position in the centre of the city, or even of one of its divisions, is by no means clearly made out; and that while the description of the best ancient author involves no difficulties, the only particulars which embarrass us are supported by the sole testimony of the worst. . . .

I therefore repeat my belief, formed from the inspection of the ruins about Hilla, that they are of one character, and must be received altogether as a part of Babylon, or wholly rejected without reserve. And I must here state what seems to me to be the best evidence for their antiquity, independent of their appearance, dimensions, and correspondence with the descriptions of the ancients – The burnt bricks of which the ruins are principally composed, and which have inscriptions on them in the cuneiform character, only found in Babylon and Persepolis, are all invariably placed in a similar manner, viz. with their faces or written sides downwards. This argues some design in placing them, though what that might have been it is now impossible to say. It, however, proves sufficiently that the buildings must have been erected when the bricks were made, and the very ancient and peculiar form of characters on them in use. When these bricks are found in more modern constructions, as in Baghdad and Hilla, they are of course placed indifferently, without regard to the writing on them. In the greatest depth in the excavations at the Kassr, at the subterraneous passage or canal, I have myself found small pieces of baked clay covered with cuneiform writing, and sometimes with figures indisputably Babylonian: these shall be described when I come to speak of the Babylonian antiques. Had the ruins been more recent than is here presumed, these inscriptions would not have been found in this order and manner, and we should in all probability have found others in the character of language then in use. Thus, had the town been Mahometan or Christian, we might reasonably expect to meet with fragments of Coufic or Stranghelo. There is another equally remarkable circumstance in these ruins, and which is almost conclusive with respect to their antiquity. In the very heart of the mound called the Kassr, and also in the ruins on the bank of the river, which have been crumbled and shivered by the action of the water, I saw earthen urns filled with ashes, with some small fragments of bones in them; and in the northern face of the Mujelibè I discovered a gallery filled with skeletons inclosed in wooden coffins. Of the high antiquity of the sepulchral urns no one will for an instant doubt; and that of the skeletons is sufficiently ascertained, both from the mode of burial, which has never been practised in this country since the introduction of Islam, and still more by a curious brass ornament which I found in one of the coffins. These discoveries are of the most interesting nature; and though it is certainly difficult to reconcile them with any theory of these ruins, yet in themselves they sufficiently establish their antiquity. The two separate modes of burial too are highly worthy of attention. There is, I believe, no reason to suppose that the Babylonians buried their dead; the old Persians we know never did. It is not impossible that the difference may indicate the several usages of the Babylonians and Greeks, and that the urns may contain the ashes of the soldiers of Alexander and of his successors. . . .

It now remains for me to notice the most interesting and remarkable of all the Babylonian remains, viz. the Birs Nemroud. – If any building may be supposed to have left considerable traces, it is certainly the Pyramid or Tower of Belus; which by its form, dimensions, and the solidity of its construction, was well calculated to resist the ravages of time; and, if human force had not been employed, would in all probability have remained to the present day, in nearly as perfect a state as the pyramids of Egypt. Even under the dilapidation which we know it to have undergone at a very early period, we might reasonably look for traces of it after every other vestige of Babylon had vanished from the face of the earth. When, therefore, we see within a short distance from the spot fixed on, both by geographers and antiquarians, and the tradition of the country, to be the site of ancient Babylon, a stupendous pile, which appears to have been built in receding stages, which bears the most indisputable traces both of the violence of man and the lapse of ages, and yet continues to tower over the desert, the wonder of successive generations, – it is impossible that their perfect correspondence with all the accounts of the Tower of Belus should not strike the most careless observer, and induce him to attempt clearing away the difficulties which have been suggested by Major Rennel against its reception within the limits of Babylon. I am of opinion that this ruin is of a nature to fix of itself the locality of Babylon, even to the exclusion of those on the eastern side of the river: and if the ancients had actually assigned a position to the Tower irreconcileable with the Birs, it would be more reasonable to suppose that some error had crept into their accounts, than to reject this most remarkable of all the ruins. But there is no necessity for either supposition. From the view of the ancient historians, I have taken in the foregoing part of this Memoir, it will appear that none of them has positively fixed the spot where the Tower of Belus stood; and if we receive the dimensions of Babylon assigned by the best of the ancient historians – himself an eye-witness – both the Birs and the eastern ruins will fairly come within its limits. Against receiving his testimony we have only our own notions of probability. We have reduced the dimensions merely because they do not accord with our ideas of the size of a city: but we know Babylon to have been rather an inclosed district than a city; and there can of course be no hesitation in abandoning less accurate evidence, and receiving the statement of Herodotus, if there be any traces on the spot to justify it.

The whole height of the Birs Nemroud above the plain to the summit of the brick wall is two hundred and thirty-five feet (235). The brick wall itself which stands on the edge of the summit, and was undoubtedly the face of another stage, is thirty-seven (37) feet high. In the side of the pile a little below the summit is very clearly to be seen part of another brick wall, precisely resembling the fragment which crowns the summit, but which still encases and supports its part of the mound. This is clearly indicative of another stage of greater extent. The masonry is infinitely superior to any thing of the kind I have ever seen; and leaving out of the question any conjecture relative to the original destination of this ruin, the impression made by a sight of it is, that it was a solid pile, composed in the interior of unburnt brick, and perhaps earth or rubbish; that it was constructed in receding stages, and faced with fine burnt bricks, having inscriptions on them, laid in a very thin layer of lime cement; and that it was reduced by violence to its present ruinous condition. The upper stories have been forcibly broken down, and fire has been employed as an instrument of destruction, though it is not easy to say precisely how or why. The facing of fine bricks has partly been removed, and partly covered by the falling down of the mass which it supported and kept together. I speak with the greater confidence of the different stages of this pile, from my own observations having been recently confirmed and extended by an intelligent traveller, who is of opinion that the traces of *four* stages are clearly discernible. As I believe it is his intention to lay the account of his travels before the world, I am unwilling to forestall any of his observations; but I must not omit to notice a remarkable result arising out of them. The Tower of Belus was a stadium in height; therefore, if we suppose the eight towers or stages which composed the Pyramid of Belus to have been of equal height, according to Major Rennel's idea, which is preferable to that of the Count de Caylus (see *Mem. de l'Academie*, vol. xxxi), we ought to find traces of them in the fragment which remains, whose elevation is 235 feet; and this is precisely the number which Mr Buckingham believes he has discovered. This result is the more worthy of attention, as it did not occur to Mr B himself.

The Birs Nemroud is apparently the Tower of Belus of Benjamin of Tudela, who says it was destroyed by fire from heaven – a curious remark, as it proves he must have observed the vitrified masses on the summit. M. Beauchamp speaks of it under the appellation of Brouss: he never visited it himself; indeed the undertaking is not always practicable without a strong escort. The excellent Niebuhr, whose intelligence, industry, and accuracy cannot be too often praised, suspects the Birs to have been the Tower of Belus. He gives a very good account of it even from the hasty view which circumstance would allow of his taking. 'Au sud ouest de Hellè à 1¼ mille, et par conséquent à l'ouest de l'Euphrate, on trouve encore d'autres restes de l'ancienne Babylone: ici il y a toute une colline de ces belles pierres de murailles dont j'ai parlé; et au dessus il y a une tour qui à ce qui parait est intérieurement aussi toute remplie de ces pierres de murailles cuites; mais les pierres de dehors (qui sait combien de pieds d'épaisseur) sont perdues par le tems dans cette épaisse muraille, ou plutôt dans ces grands tas de pierres: il y a ici et là de petits trous qui percent d'un coté jusqu'à l'autre, sans doute pour y donner un libre passage à l'air, et pour empêcher au dedans l'humidité, qui auroit pu nuire au batiment.' (*Voyage*, vol. ii, p. 235.) In this description the Birs may be recognised, even through the obscurity of a job translation.

After this, I was certainly surprised to find that Major Rennel not only excludes it from the limits of Babylon, but even doubts the mound being artificial. So indisputably evident is the fact of the whole mass being from top to bottom artificial, that I should as soon have thought of writing a dissertation to prove that the Pyramids are the work of human hands, as of dwelling on this point. Indeed, were there anything equivocal in the appearance of the mound itself, the principles of physical geography utterly forbid the supposition of there being an isolated hill of natural formation in ground formed by the depositions of a river; and therefore, if any traveller fancied he saw a natural hill at Musseil, or any other place in that direction, he was most unquestionably mistaken.

The same reasons prove that there could never have been bitumen springs in Babylon. (See *Geog.* of Herod., p. 369.) Diodorus, indeed, does not say, as Major Rennel supposes, that bitumen was found in Babylon, – but in Babylonia, which is a very different thing.

The Birs Nemroud is in all likelihood at present pretty near in the state in which Alexander saw it; if we give any credit to the report that ten thousand men could only remove the rubbish, preparatory to repairing it, in two months. If, indeed, it required one half of that number to disencumber it, the state of dilapidation must have been complete. The immense masses of vitrified brick which are seen on the top of the mount appear to have marked its summit since the time of its destruction. The rubbish about its base was probably in much greater quantities, the weather having dissipated much of it in the course of so many revolving ages; and, possibly, portions of the exterior facing of fine brick may have disappeared at different periods.

In the foregoing observations I have endeavoured to show that the ruins of Babylon in their present state may be perfectly reconciled with the best descriptions of the Grecian writers, without doing violence to either. I feel persuaded that the more the subject is investigated the stronger will the conformity be found; but it is one in which the spirit of system would be peculiarly misplaced: and I am so far from being bigoted to my own opinions, that should I in the course of my researches happen to discover particulars which may reasonably appear to militate against them, I will be the first to lay them before the public.

Bagdad, July 1817.

P.S. Since writing the above I have received an extract from the Supplement to the fifth edition of the *Encyclopaedia Britannica*, containing a summary of my former accounts of Babylon, with the author's own ideas on the subject. It is peculiarly gratifying to me to find that my opinions have the confirmation of such a writer.

Second Memoir on Babylon, 1818

The walls of Babylon

ROBERT KOLDEWEY

ROBERT KOLDEWEY (1855-1925) studied architecture, archaeology and ancient history at Berlin, Munich and Vienna. His first archaeological investigation was on the Acropolis of Assos, after which he was commissioned by the German Archaeological Institute to excavate in Lesbos, and in 1887 the British Museum sent him to Iraq. For the next ten years he alternated between teaching at Gorlitz and excavating in the Mediterranean region. In 1897 the Deutsche Orient-Gesellschaft, wishing to acquire new finds of cuneiform tablets, commissioned him to survey for promising sites in Mesopotamia, and he reported favourably on Babylon. In 1899 he began to excavate, and remained there for the next eighteen years, only leaving during World War I when the British advance was on the point of cutting off his last retreat to safety. His expedition was perhaps the most scientific and certainly one of the best equipped of its time, being the first to instal a light railway for moving debris, and to employ over 200 men, and it is largely owing to his work that the legendary Babylon of the Bible became known and investigated as a historical and geographical fact.

In the time of Nebuchadnezzar the traveller who approached the capital of Babylonia from the north would find himself where the Nil Canal flows today, face to face with the colossal wall that surrounded mighty Babylon. Part of this wall still exists and is recognisable at the present time in the guise of a low earthen ridge about 4 to 5 kilometres in length. Up to the present we have only excavated a small part, so that it is only possible to give a detailed description of the most noteworthy features of these fortifications, that were rendered so famous by Greek authors.

There was a massive wall of crude brick 7 metres thick, in front of which, at an interval of about 12 metres, stood another wall of burnt brick 7·8 metres thick, with the strong wall of the fosse at its foot, also of burnt brick and 3·3 metres thick. The fosse must have been in front of this, but so far we have not searched closely for it, and therefore the counterscarp has not yet been found.

Astride on the mud wall were towers 8·37 metres (about 24 bricks) wide, that projected beyond the wall on both its faces. Measured from centre to centre these towers were 52·5 metres apart. Thus there was a tower at intervals of about 100 ells, for the Babylonian ell measured roughly half a metre.

Owing to the unfinished state of the excavations it is not yet possible to say how the towers on the outer wall were constructed. The space between the two walls was filled in with rubble, at least to the height at which the ruins are preserved and presumably to the crown of the outer wall. Thus on the top of the wall there was a road that afforded space for a team of four horses abreast, and even for two such teams to pass each other. Upon this crown of the wall the upper compartments of the towers faced each other like small houses.

This broad roadway on the summit of the wall, which was of world-renown owing to the descriptions of it given by classical writers, was of the greatest importance for the protection of the great city. It rendered possible the rapid shifting of defensive forces at any time to that part of the wall which was specially pressed by attack. The line of defence was very long; the north-east front, which can still be measured, is 4,400 metres long, and on the south-east the ruined wall can be traced without excavations for a length of 2 kilometres. These two flanks of the wall certainly extended as far as the Euphrates as it flowed from north to south. With the Euphrates they enclosed that part of Babylon of which the ruins exist at the present time, but according to Herodotus and others they were supplemented on the other side of the Euphrates by two other walls, so that the town site consisted of a quadrangle through which the Euphrates flowed diagonally. Of the western walls nothing is now to be seen. Whether the traces of a line of wall to the south near the village of Sindjar will prove to have formed part of them has yet to be ascertained.

The excavations carried on up to the present time have yielded no surrounding walls beyond this fortification. The circuit extended for about 18 kilometres. Instead of this, Herodotus gives about 86 kilometres and Ctesias about 65 kilometres. There must be some error underlying this discrepancy. The 65 kilometres of Ctesias approximate so closely to four times the correct measurement that it may well be suspected that he mistook the figures representing the whole circumference for the measure of one side of the square. We shall later turn more in detail from the testimony of the ancient writers to the evidence of the ruins themselves. Generally speaking, the measurements given are not in accordance with those actually preserved, while the general description, on the contrary, is usually accurate. Herodotus describes the wall of Babylon as built of burnt brick. To an observer from without it would no doubt appear as such, as only the top of the inner mud wall could be seen from outside. The escarp of the fosse was formed of the square bricks that are so extraordinarily numerous in Babylon, that measure 33 centimetres and bear the usual stamp of Nebuchadnezzar. Those of the brick wall are somewhat smaller (32 centimetres) and unstamped. These smaller unstamped bricks are common previous to the time of Nebuchadnezzar, but nevertheless they may very well date from the early years of his reign, as we shall see farther on. To what period the mud-brick wall may be assigned we do not yet know; it is certainly older. It apparently possessed an escarp, of which there are some scanty remains within the great brick wall. It appears to have been cut through on the outside by the latter.

Up to the present we have found about 15 of the towers on the mud wall only. They are the so-called Cavalier towers, and project both at the front and the back, thus placed astride on the wall. They were, of course, higher than the walls, but we can get no clue from the ruins as to the height of walls or towers, as only the lower parts remain. The towers are 3·36 metres wide and are placed 44 metres apart. Thus on the entire front there were about 90, and on the whole circumference – provided the town formed a square – there must have been 360 towers. How many there were on the outer wall we do not know. Ctesias gives the number as 250. No gateway has yet been found, which is not surprising, considering the limited extent of the excavations.

During the Parthian period these lines of fortification can have been no longer in a condition to afford protection. On the town side of the mud wall there are Parthian sarcophagi, inserted in holes dug in the wall itself.

While the foundations of the brick wall are below the present water-level, the mud wall stands on an artificial embankment. As a general rule mud walls were not provided with deep foundations. The mortar employed for the mud wall was clay, and for the brick wall bitumen was used. The same method of construction can be recognised in other parts of the city, where it is better preserved and can be more satis-factorily studied.

At the northern end of our line of wall, which enclosed the mound of ruins, called 'Babil', with a hook-like curve, the inner wall also was built of brick. This appears, at least, from the two deep trenches left by plunderers which occur here, but it must be inferred pending excavation. The digging for the valuable bricks which occurred in recent times has left deep traces in the otherwise smooth surface of the ground which we do not find in the attempted demolitions of more ancient times.

For this reason, with the exception of the portion near Babil there is nothing to be seen of the burnt-brick wall without excavating, while the mud wall, which has merely suffered from the ravages of time, has left behind a clearly marked line of ruins of some height. The town wall of Seleucia on the Tigris, likewise a mud wall, stands out similarly above its mounds of debris to a considerable height. It cannot therefore be said that a burnt-brick wall of 480 stadia, the gigantic dimensions recorded by Herodotus, must necessarily have left considerable and unmistakeable traces, and it is not this consideration that leads us to doubt the existence of an encircling wall of such dimensions, which has been accepted as an established fact since Oppert's excavations in Babylon. Neither does the immense size of itself demand dismissal as fantastic. The great wall of China, 11 metres high and 7·5 metres broad, with its length of 2,450 kilometres, is just 29 times as long as that of Herodotus. There are other overwhelming considerations which we shall investigate later. In any case the city, even in circumference, was the greatest of any in the ancient East, Nineveh itself not excepted, which in other respects rivalled Babylon. But the period in which the fame of Babylon's vast size spread over the world was the time of Herodotus, and then Nineveh had already ceased to exist.

A comparison with modern cities can scarcely be made without further consideration. It must always be remembered than an ancient city was primarily a fortress of which the inhabited part was surrounded and protected by the encircling girdle of the walls. Our great modern cities are of an entirely different character, they are inhabited spaces, open on all sides. A reasonable comparison can, therefore, only be made between Babylon and other walled cities, and when compared with them Babylon takes the first place, both for ancient and modern times, as regards the extent of its enclosed and inhabited area.

Nebuchadnezzar frequently mentions this great work in his inscriptions. The most important passage occurs in his great *Steinplatten* inscription, col. 7 1. 22-55: 'That no assault should reach Imgur-Bel, the wall of Babylon; I did, what no earlier king had done, for 4,000 ells of land on the side of Babylon, at a distance so that it (the assault) did not come nigh, I caused a mighty wall to be built on the east side of Babylon. I dug out its moat, and I built a scarp with bitumen and bricks. Its broad gateways I set within it and fixed in them double doors of cedar wood overlaid with copper. In order that the enemy who devised (?) evil should not press on the flanks of Babylon, I surrounded it with mighty floods, as is the land with the wave-tossed sea. Its coming was like the coming of the great sea, the salt water. In order that no breach should be made in it, I piled up an earthen embankment by it, and encompassed it with quay walls of burnt brick. The bulwark I fortified cunningly and made the city of Babylon into a fortress' (cf. H. Winckler, *Keilinschriftliche Bibliothek*, vol. iii, 2, p. 23). It can hardly be expected that we can yet reach absolute certainty as to the meaning of all the details here given. That can best be afforded by a complete excavation, which is urgently to be desired.

The Excavations at Babylon, 1914

A curious sculpture

ROBERT KOLDEWEY

At the north-east corner before our excavations began there was a great basalt figure of a lion trampling on a man who lay beneath him with his right hand on the flank of the animal, and the left on his muzzle. This latter has been chopped away by superstitious hands, and he is marked all over by the stones and flint balls that have been, and are still, flung at him; for he is regarded as the much-feared 'Djin'. On one side the Arabs have dug out a deep hole in his flanks, which is now filled in with cement. The reason of this is as follows. A European once came here, and enquired about the lion, which he had probably read of in the books of earlier travellers. The Arabs showed it to him, and after looking at it attentively, he chose from among the small holes in the basalt the right one, into which he thrust a key and turned it, whereupon his hand was immediately filled with gold pieces. Having accomplished his practical joke the traveller went his way, unable as he was to speak Arabic. The worthy Arabs, however, in order to render the treasure available, hammered this hole in the lion, which must have caused them immense labour, for the stone is extremely hard. The figure is not completely carved, and is still little more than blocked out. It therefore looks more ancient than it really is, for it can scarcely be earlier than the time of Nebuchadnezzar. People are divided as to its meaning. Some see in it Daniel in the lions' den, and others Babylonia above defeated Egypt. But a concrete past is throughout this period never represented otherwise than in reliefs, and, on the other hand, it is foreign to Babylonian art to take as a basis the representation of an abstract idea.

The Excavations at Babylon, 1914

Problems at the excavation of Nineveh

PAUL EMILE BOTTA

PAUL EMILE BOTTA (*1805-1870*) *was the son of a prominent Italian politician and historian. In 1826 he sailed on a voyage round the world which took him three years, and on his return he travelled extensively in the eastern Mediterranean region, including an expedition to Sennaar as physician to the Arab leader Mehemet Ali. He then entered the diplomatic service and in 1836 was posted to Tripoli where he remained for the next twenty years. It was during this stay that he made his expedition to the mounds of Kouyunjik and Khorsabad, the site of Nineveh, and began the excavations which were later continued by Layard. His work as both a diplomat and an antiquarian received recognition in 1845 when he was created a member of the Légion d'Honneur.*

I told you, Sir, that the wall turned northward at its extremity, and there formed a sort of recess; this measures about one metre and a half in depth, and is occupied by a symbolical half-length statue, representing the fore part of a bull, human headed, projecting from the wall. Although the legs are very natural and admirably sculptured, the upper portion is not only much decayed, but it appears entirely conventional. Scales, regularly striated, seem to indicate wings; the beard is formally plaited, and the fetlock is delineated by a broad band of horizontal furrows. The head is fallen and in bad condition, yet there can be no doubt that the face was human. This statue must have been about 5 metres high, and was carved out of one single block of gypsum.

Wall xxxiii, constituting the recess, displays another symbolical figure, viz. a winged personage with the head of a bird. The beak, though rather long, appertains to a bird of prey; the hair is stiffly plaited, and the head surmounted by a kind of tuft descending to the shoulders. The neck is encircled by a collar or carcanet, the arms and wrists are adorned with bracelets; the right hand is elevated, and the left certainly holds a basket similar to those carried by the winged figures of passage No. II. This personage is clad in a short tunic, and a fringed girdle of increased width at its extremity, hangs between his legs. In evidence of the profusion of sculptures decorating this monument, I must remark that the small surface of wall between the bull and this winged figure is likewise ornamented with bas-reliefs.

The construction of this edifice is invariably the same; always large and small gypsum slabs set upright against the earth of the mound. I cannot believe such walls have ever supported a stone roof, and this is one reason for my suspecting it was of wood. Nevertheless, I have acquired no certain knowledge on this subject; the charcoal, very abundant in some places, is not seen in others where, however, the walls offer an equally calcined appearance. I therefore remain undecided. I shall merely observe that the dimensions of the bull are so enormous, it is impossible to suppose it could have been conveyed to its place through narrow passages excavated in the mound. Perhaps it was stationed outside one of the portals. In this case, the wall must have formed the exterior part of this monument, and, consequently, the state of preservation in which both the sculptures and stone itself are found is fully explained. It would not have suffered by the falling in of the burning roof. But the time has not yet come for entering upon these discussions; when everything is disinterred we may probably understand all that at present seems doubtful. By making enquiries I have endeavoured, but in vain, to learn whether this village had not anciently some other name of more Chaldean sound than Khorsabad, or Khestéabad (for so it is still written); there is no local tradition on the subject, and even the inhabitants themselves were ignorant of the archaeological treasures lying buried under their feet, and which chance enable me to discover; my researches shall continue, notwithstanding. With regard to the future direction of the works, I have, Sir, the satisfaction of informing you that, in all probability, I shall encounter no further obstacles. His Excellency the Minister of the Interior having kindly assisted my labours, I am able to act more freely, and have succeeded in persuading the Chief of the village to vacate his house, which barred our passage; he will take up his abode in the plain, and the rest of the people will follow him; the entire mound will thus be left at my disposal, and nothing shall escape my scrutiny. I am, however, compelled to stop the excavations for some time; the air of Khorsabad is particularly unhealthy, as I not only myself experienced, but likewise all those who accompanied me. Already, I have frequently been obliged to change the workmen; and their head, who served me with intelligence, is now dangerously ill. For this reason I cannot return to Khorsabad before the heats are over, and were the works to proceed at this moment, such is the condition of the sculptures, they would be lost before I could go and draw them; I have therefore suspended my labours for a short period, and reinterred those parts which I had not time to copy. As for the others, I regret to say they will soon fall to atoms. Being no longer supported, the walls yield to the swelling of the ground, the action of the sun reduces the surface to powder, and even now a considerable portion has disappeared. This is truly grievous, but I can devise no remedy, unless the whole, as I draw it, should be again filled up, and thus preserved for future investigation; this is my present purpose, since, everything considered, it will always be possible to make a fresh clearing, whilst, by leaving the walls uncovered, in three months not a vestige of them would remain.

Letters on the Discoveries at Nineveh, 1850

Excavations at Nimrud

AUSTEN HENRY LAYARD

Sir Austen Henry Layard (*1817-1894*) *was born in Paris and was educated in Italy, France, Switzerland and England. His father was a Civil Servant and there is no doubt that his cosmopolitan upbringing contributed to his love of travel and the fine arts. He began his professional career in the office of a London solicitor, but after six years he left with the intention of travelling overland to Ceylon where he planned to follow his father into the Civil Service. When he reached the Near East, however, he gave up any idea of continuing his journey, and for some years engaged in unofficial diplomatic missions, during the course of which he became familiar with the ruins of Nimrud, Nineveh and Babylon. After securing official assistance and encouragement for his expedition he undertook the excavation of the mound of Nineveh, and shortly after this, of Babylon, acquiring the greater part of the magnificent collection of Assyrian sculptures now in the British Museum.*

I was again amongst the ruins by the end of October. The winter season was fast approaching, and it was necessary to build a proper house for the shelter of myself and servants. I marked out a plan on the ground, in the village of Nimroud, and in a few days our habitations were complete. My workmen formed the walls of mud bricks dried in the sun, and roofed the rooms with beams and branches of trees. A thick coat of mud was laid over the whole, to exclude rain. Two rooms for my own accommodation were divided by an Iwan, or open apartment, the whole being surrounded by a wall. In a second court-yard were huts for my Cawass, Arab guests, and servants, and stables for my horses. Ibrahim Agha displayed his ingenuity by making equidistant loopholes, of a most warlike appearance, in the outer walls; which I immediately ordered to be filled up, to avoid any suspicion of being the constructor of forts and castles, with the intention of making a permanent Frank settlement in the country. We did not neglect precautions, however, in case of an attack from the Bedouins, of whom Ibrahim Agha was in constant dread. Unfortunately, the only shower of rain, that I saw during the remainder of my residence in Assyria, fell before my walls were covered in, and so saturated the bricks that they did not dry again before the following spring. The consequence was, that the only verdure, on which my eyes were permitted to feast before my return to Europe, was furnished by my own property – the walls in the interior of the rooms being continually clothed with a crop of grass.

On the mound itself, and immediately above the great winged lions first discovered, were built a house for my Nestorian workmen and their families, and a hut, to which any small objects discovered among the ruins could at once be removed for safety. I divided my Arabs into three parties, according to the branches of the tribe to which they belonged. About forty tents were pitched on different parts of the mound, at the entrance to the principal trenches. Forty more were placed round my dwelling, and the rest on the bank of the river, where the sculptures were deposited previous to their embarkation on the rafts. The men were all armed. I thus provided for the defence of my establishment.

Mr Hormuzd Rassam lived with me; and to him I confided the payment of the wages, and the accounts. He soon obtained an extraordinary influence amongst the Arabs, and his fame spread through the desert.

The workmen were divided into bands. In each set were generally eight or ten Arabs, who carried away the earth in baskets; and two, or four, Nestorian diggers, according to the nature of the soil and rubbish which had to be excavated. They were overlooked by a superintendent, whose duty it was to keep them to their work, and to give me notice when the diggers approached any slab, or exposed any small object to view, that I might myself assist in its uncovering or removal. I scattered a few Arabs of a hostile tribe amongst the rest, and by that means I was always made acquainted with what was going on, could easily learn if there were plots brewing, and could detect those who might attempt to appropriate any relics discovered during the excavations. The smallness of the sum placed at my disposal, compelled me to follow the same plan in the excavations that I had hitherto adopted, – digging trenches along the walls of the chambers, and exposing the whole of the slabs, without removing the earth from the centre. Thus, few chambers were fully explored; and many small objects of great interest may have been left undiscovered. As I was directed to bury the buildings with earth after they had been examined, I filled up the trenches, to avoid unnecessary expense, with the rubbish taken from those subsequently opened, having first copied the inscriptions, and drawn the sculptures.

The excavations were recommenced, on a large scale by the 1st of November. My working parties were distributed over the mound – in the ruins of the N.W. and S.W. palaces; near the gigantic bulls in the centre; and in the south-east corner, where no traces of buildings had as yet been discovered.

It will be remembered that the greater number of slabs forming the southern side of the large hall in the N.W. palace had fallen with their faces to the ground. I was, in the first place, anxious to raise these bas-reliefs, and to pack them for transport to Busrah. To accomplish this, it was necessary to remove a large accumulation of earth and rubbish – to empty, indeed, nearly the whole chamber, for the fallen slabs extended almost half-way across it. The sculptures on nine slabs were found to be in admirable preservation, although broken by the fall. The slabs were divided, as those already described, into two compartments, by inscriptions which were precisely similar.

The sculptures were of the highest interest. They represented the wars of the king, and his victories over foreign nations. The upper bas-reliefs, on the first two slabs, formed one subject – the king, with his warriors, in battle under the walls of a hostile castle. He stood, gorgeously attired, in a chariot drawn by three horses richly caparisoned, and was discharging an arrow either against those who defended the walls; or against a warrior, who, already wounded, was falling from his chariot. An attendant protected the person of the king with a shield, and a charioteer held the reins, and urged on the horses. Above the king was the emblem of the supreme Deity, represented as at Persepolis by a winged figure within a circle, wearing a horned cap resembling that of the human-headed lions. Like the king, he was shooting an arrow, the head of which was in the form of a trident.

Behind the king were three chariots; the first drawn by three horses – one of which was rearing and another falling – and occupied by a wounded warrior demanding quarter of his pursuers. In the others were two warriors, one discharging an arrow, the other guiding the horses, which were at full speed. In each Assyrian chariot was a standard – the devices which were enclosed in a circle ornamented with tassels and streamers, being an archer, with the horned cap but without wings, standing on a bull; and the two bulls, back to back. At the bottom of the first bas-relief were wavy lines, to indicate water or a river, and trees were scattered over both. Assyrian footmen, fighting or slaying the enemy, were introduced in several places; and three headless bodies above the principal figures in the second bas-relief represented the dead in the background.

On the upper part of the two slabs following the battle-scene was the triumphal return after victory. In front of the procession were warriors throwing the heads of the slain at the feet of the conquerors. Two musicians, playing on stringed instruments, preceded the charioteers, who were represented unarmed, and bearing their standards; above them was an eagle with a human head in its talons. The king came next in his chariot, carrying in one hand his bow, and in the other two arrows – the attitude in which he is so frequently represented on Assyrian monuments, and probably denoting triumph over his enemies. Above the horses was the presiding divinity; also holding a bow. The attendant, who in war bore the shield, was now replaced by an eunuch, raising the open parasol – the Eastern emblem of royalty. The horses were led by grooms, although the charioteer still held the reins. Behind the king's chariot was a horseman leading a second horse, gaily caparisoned.

After the procession, was the castle and pavilion of the victorious king, – the former represented by a circle, divided into four equal compartments, and surrounded by towers and battlements. In each compartment were figures evidently engaged in preparing the feast: one was slaying a sheep; another appeared to be baking bread; and others stood before bowls and utensils placed on tables. The pavilion was supported by three columns; one surmounted by a fir-cone, – the emblem so frequently seen in the Assyrian sculptures; the others by figures of the ibex or mountain goat. It was probably of silk or woollen stuff, richly ornamented and edged with a fringe of fir-cones and tulip-shaped ornaments. Beneath the canopy was a groom cleaning one horse; whilst others, picketed by their halters, were feeding at a trough. An eunuch stood at the entrance of the tent, to receive four prisoners, who, with their hands bound behind, were brought to him by an Assyrian warrior. Above this group were two singular lion-headed figures, one holding a whip or thong in the right hand, and grasping his under jaw with the left, the other raising his hands. They were clothed in tunics, descending to the knees, and skins falling from the head, over the shoulders, to the ankles, and were accompanied by a man raising a stick.

The four following bas-reliefs recorded a battle, in which were represented the king, two warriors with their standards, and an eunuch in chariots, and four warriors, amongst whom was also an eunuch, on horses. The enemy were on foot, and discharged their arrows against the pursuers. Eagles hovered above the victors, and were feeding on the slain. The winged divinity in the circle was again seen above the king.

These bas-reliefs in many respects illustrate the manners and civilisation of the Assyrians. We here find the eunuch commanding in war and engaging with the enemy in combat, as we have before seen him ministering to the king during religious ceremonies, or waiting upon him as his arms-bearer during peace. That eunuchs rose to the highest rank among the Assyrians, and were even generals over their armies, we learn from Scripture, where the Rabaris, or chief of the eunuchs, is mentioned as one of the three principal officers of Sennacherib, and as one of the princes of Nebuchadnezzar. They appear, indeed, to have held the same important posts, and to have exercised the same influence in the Assyrian court, as they have enjoyed in Turkey and Persia, where they have frequently attained to the post of vizir or prime minister.

The horses of the archers were led by mounted warriors, wearing circular skull caps, probably of iron. Horsemen are frequently mentioned in the Bible as forming an important part of the Assyrian armies. Ezekiel (xxiii, 6.) describes 'the Assyrians clothed in blue, captains and rulers, all of them desirable young men, horsemen riding upon horses'; and Holofernes had no less than 12,000 archers on horseback. The rider is seated on the naked back of the horse, which is only adorned with a cloth when led behind the chariot of the king, probably for his use in case of accident to the chariot.

The horses represented in the sculptures appear to be of noble breed. Assyria, and particularly that part of the empire which was watered by the Tigris and Euphrates, was celebrated at the earliest period for its horses, as the same plains are to this day for the noblest races of Arabia. The Jews probably obtained horses for their cavalry from this country; and horses were offered to them by the general of the Assyrian king, as an acceptable present. On Egyptian monuments horses from Mesopotamia are continually mentioned amongst the spoil or tribute. The horse of the Assyrian bas-reliefs was evidently drawn from the finest model. The head is small and well shaped, the nostrils large and high, the neck arched, the body long, and the legs slender and sinewy. The prophet exclaims of the horses of the Chaldaeans, 'They are swifter than the leopards, and more fierce than the evening wolves'; and the magnificent description of the war-horse in the book of Job is familiar to every reader. At a later period the plains of Babylonia furnished horses to the Persians, both for the private use of the king and for his troops. The rich pasture-grounds of Mesopotamia must have always afforded them ample sustenance, whilst those vast plains, exposed to the heats of summer and cold of winter, inured them to hardship and fatigue.

Nineveh and its Remains, 1867

16. A winged bull with a human head comes to light during the Nimrud excavations, and with it the first news of the high culture of ancient Assyria.

17. A. H. Layard, the great excavator of Nineveh, at work; drawn in 1850 by a visitor to the site.

Discoveries and alarms

AUSTEN HENRY LAYARD

On the morning following these discoveries, I had ridden to the encampment of Sheikh Abd-ur rahman, and was returning to the mound, when I saw two Arabs of his tribe coming towards me and urging their mares to the top of their speed. On reaching me they stopped. 'Hasten, O Bey', exclaimed one of them – 'hasten to the diggers, for they have found Nimrod himself. Wallah! it is wonderful but it is true! we have seen him with our eyes. There is no God but God'; and both joining in this pious exclamation, they galloped off, without further words, in the direction of their tents.

On reaching the ruins I descended into the newly opened trench, and found the workmen, who had already seen me, as I approached, standing near a heap of baskets and cloaks. Whilst Awad advanced and asked for a present to celebrate the occasion, the Arabs withdrew the screen they had hastily constructed, and disclosed an enormous human head sculptured in full out of the alabaster of the country. They had un-covered the upper part of a figure, the remainder of which was still buried in the earth. I saw at once that the head must belong to a winged lion or bull, similar to those of Khorsabad and Persepolis. It was in admirable preservation. The expression was calm, yet majestic, and the outline of the features showed a freedom and knowledge of art, scarcely to be looked for in works of so remote a period. The cap had three horns, and, unlike that of the human-headed bulls hitherto found in Assyria, was rounded and without ornament at the top.

I was not surprised that the Arabs had been amazed and terrified at this apparition. It required no stretch of imagination to conjure up the most strange fancies. This gigantic head, blanched with age, thus rising from the bowels of the earth, might well have belonged to one of those fearful beings which are described in the traditions of the country as appearing to mortals, slowly ascending from the regions below. One of the workmen, on catching the first glimpse of the monster, had thrown down his basket and had run off towards Mosul as fast as his legs could carry him. I learnt this with regret, as I anticipated the consequences.

Whilst I was superintending the removal of the earth, which still clung to the sculpture, and giving directions for the continuation of the work, the noise of horsemen was heard, and presently Abd-ur rahman, followed by half his tribe, appeared on the edge of the trench. As soon as the two Arabs I had met had reached their tents, and published the wonders they had seen, every one mounted his mare and rode to the mound to satisfy himself of the truth of these inconceivable reports. When they beheld the head they all cried together, 'There is no God but God, and Mohammed is his Prophet!' It was some time before the Sheikh could be prevailed upon to descend into the pit, and convince himself that the image he saw was of stone. 'This is not the work of men's hands,' exclaimed he, 'but of those infidel giants of whom the Prophet, peace be with him! has said, that they were higher than the tallest date tree; this is one of the idols which Noah, peace be with him! cursed before the flood.' In this opinion, the result of a careful examination, all the bystanders concurred.

I now ordered a trench to be dug due south from the head, in the expectation of finding a corresponding figure, and before night-fall reached the object of my search about twelve feet distant. Engaging two or three men to sleep near the sculptures, I returned to the village, and celebrated the day's discovery by a slaughter of sheep, of which all the Arabs near partook. As some wandering musicians chanced to be at Selamiyah, I sent for them, and dances were kept up during the greater part of the night. On the following morning Arabs from the other side of the Tigris, and the inhabitants of the surrounding villages, congregated on the mound. Even the women could not repress their curiosity, and came in crowds, with their children, from afar. My Cawass was stationed during the day in the trench, into which I would not allow the multitude to descend.

As I had expected, the report of the discovery of the gigantic head, carried by the terrified Arab to Mosul, had thrown the town into commotion. He had scarcely checked his speed before reaching the bridge. Entering breathless into the bazaars, he announced to every one he met that Nimrod had appeared. The news soon got to the ears of the Cadi, who called the Mufti and the Ulema together, to consult upon this unexpected occurrence. Their deliberations, ended in a procession to the Governor, and a formal protest, on the part of the Mussulmans of the town, against proceedings so directly contrary to the laws of the Koran. The Cadi had no distinct idea whether the very bones of the mighty hunter had been uncovered, or only his image; nor did Ismail

Pasha very clearly remember whether Nimrod was a true-believing prophet, or an infidel. I consequently received a somewhat unintelligible message from his Excellency, to the effect that the remains should be treated with respect, and be by no means further disturbed; that he wished the excavations to be stopped at once, and desired to confer with me on the subject.

I rode to Mosul at once and called upon him accordingly. I had some difficulty in making him understand the nature of my discovery. At last he was persuaded that I had only discovered part of an ancient figure in stone, and that neither the remains of Nimrod nor of any other personage mentioned in the Koran had been disturbed. However, as he requested me to discontinue my operations until the excitement in the town had somewhat subsided, I returned to Nimroud and dismissed the workmen, retaining only two men to dig leisurely along the walls without giving cause for further interference. I ascertained by the end of March the existence of a second pair of winged-human-headed lions, differing from those previously discovered in form, the human shape being continued to the waist, and being furnished with human arms, as well as with the legs of the lion. In one hand each figure carried a goat or stag, and in the other, which hung down by the side, a branch with three flowers. They formed a northern entrance into the hall or chamber, of which the human-headed lions previously described formed the western portal. I completely uncovered the latter, and found them to be entire. They were about twelve feet high and twelve feet long. The body and limbs were admirably portrayed; the muscles and bones, although strongly developed, to denote power and strength, showed at the same time a correct knowledge of the anatomy and form of the animal. Expanded wings sprung from the shoulders and spread over the back; a knotted girdle, ending in tassels, encircled the loins. As these sculptures were placed against walls forming a doorway or entrance, and thus only one side of the body was to be seen, they were carved partly in full and partly in relief. The head and forepart, facing the chamber, were in full; the rest of the figure was sculptured in high relief; and that the spectator might have both a perfect front and side view, it was furnished with five legs; four on the side forming the entrance, and an additional leg in front. The slab was covered, in all parts not occupied by the image, with inscriptions in the cuneiform character. Remains of colour could still be traced in the eyes – the pupils being painted black, and the rest filled up with a white pigment; but no other parts of the sculpture. . . .

I used to contemplate for hours these mysterious emblems, and muse over their intent and history. What more noble forms could have ushered the people into the temple of their gods! What more sublime images could have been borrowed from nature, by men who sought, unaided by the light of revealed religion, to embody their conception of the wisdom and power of a Supreme Being! They could find no better type of intellect and knowledge than the head of the man; of strength, than the body of the lion; of ubiquity, than the wings of the bird. These winged human-headed lions were not idle creations, the offspring of mere fancy; their meaning was written upon them. They had awed and instructed races which flourished 3,000 years ago. Through the portals which they guarded, kings, priests, and warriors had borne sacrifices to their altars, long before the wisdom of the East had penetrated to Greece, and had furnished its mythology with symbols recognised of old by the Assyrian votaries. They may have been buried, and their existence may have been unknown, before the foundation of the eternal city. For twenty-five centuries they had been hidden from the eye of man, and they now stood forth once more in their ancient majesty. But how changed was the scene around them! The luxury and civilisation of a mighty nation had given place to the wretchedness and ignorance of a few half-barbarous tribes. The wealth of temples, and the riches of great cities, had been succeeded by ruins and shapeless heaps of earth. Above the spacious hall in which they stood, the plough had passed and the corn now waved. Egypt has monuments no less ancient and no less wonderful; but they have stood forth for ages to testify her early power and renown; whilst those before me had but appeared to bear witness, in the words of the prophet, that once 'the Assyrian was a cedar in Lebanon with fair branches and with a shadow-ing shroud of an high stature; and his top was among the thick boughs . . . his height was exalted above all the trees of the field, and his boughs were multiplied and his branches became long, because of the multitude of waters when he shot forth. All the fowls of heaven made their nests in his boughs, and under his branches did all the beasts of the fields bring forth their young, and under his shadow dwelt all great nations'; for now is 'Nineveh a desolation and dry like a wilderness, and flocks lie down in the midst of her: all the beasts of the nations, both the cormorant and bittern, lodge in the upper lintels of it; their voice sings in the windows; and desolation is in the thresholds'.

Nineveh and its Remains, 1867

The Gilgamesh Epic is found

GEORGE SMITH

GEORGE SMITH (1840-1876) was born in Chelsea, London. Lacking the advantage of extensive formal education, he began his professional career as a banknote engraver, but he spent so much of his spare time in the Assyrian Department of the British Museum that he attracted the attention of Sir Henry Rawlinson, who secured him a position in the Department. He shortly justified his appointment by the publication of an inscription fixing the date of the eclipse of the sun in 763 BC and of another which fixed the date of the Elamites' invasion of Babylon in 2280 BC. In 1872 he transcribed and translated the Gilgamesh epic, which was complete apart from seventeen lines. When this hiatus was discovered, the Daily Telegraph financed an expedition under Smith's leadership to find the missing lines, and almost unbelievably, these very lines were discovered on a tablet excavated early in the first season. The newspaper, considering that the purpose of the expedition was then fulfilled, declined further support and it was only by a fortunate chance that in its closing stages a group of tablets detailing the succession of the Babylonian dynasties was found. In 1874 and 1876 the British Museum financed two further expeditions under Smith's leadership, but he was not a man of strong constitution and the conditions of life and work in the desert proved too severe for his health. He contracted a fever and died at Aleppo in 1876.

Turning from this I rode through the low ground by the side of the Tigris, and then along the face of the cliffs overhanging the water, and soon arrived at Mosul, from which I crossed over to Kouyunjik to see the progress of the excavations. My trenches in the palace of Sennacherib proceeded slowly and produced little result, the ground being so cut up by former excavations that it was difficult to secure good results without more extensive operations than my time or means would allow; inscriptions, the great object of my work, were however found, and served as compensation for the labour.

In the north palace the results were more definite. Here was a large pit made by former excavators from which had come many tablets; this pit had been used since the close of the last excavations for a quarry, and stones for the building of the Mosul bridge had been regularly extracted from it. The bottom of the pit was now full of massive fragments of stone from the basement wall of the palace jammed in between heaps of small fragments of stone, cement, bricks, and clay, all in utter confusion. On removing some of these stones with a crowbar, and digging in the rubbish behind them, there appeared half of a curious tablet copied from a Babylonian original, giving warnings to kings and judges of the evils which would follow the neglect of justice in the country. On continuing the trench some distance farther, the other half of this tablet was discovered, it having evidently been broken before it came among the rubbish.

On the 14th of May my friend, Mr Charles Kerr, whom I had left at Aleppo, visited me at Mosul, and as I rode into the Khan where I was staying, I met him. After mutual congratulations I sat down to examine the store of fragments of cuneiform inscriptions from the day's digging, taking out and brushing off the earth from the fragments to read their contents. On cleaning one of them I found to my surprise and gratification that it contained the greater portion of seventeen lines of inscription belonging to the first column of the Chaldean account of the Deluge, and fitting into the only place where there was a serious blank in the story. When I had first published the account of this tablet I had conjectured that there were about fifteen lines wanting in this part of the story, and now with this portion I was enabled to make it nearly complete.

After communicating to my friend the contents of the fragment I copied it, and a few days later telegraphed the circumstance to the proprietors of the *Daily Telegraph*. Mr Kerr desired to see the mound at Nimroud, but, as the results from Kouyunjik were so important, I could not leave the site to go with him, so I sent my dragoman to show him the place, remaining myself to superintend the Kouyunjik excavations.

The palace of Sennacherib also steadily produced its tribute of objects, including a small tablet of Esarhaddon, king of Assyria, some new fragments of one of the historical cylinders of Assurbanipal, and a curious fragment of the history of Sargon, king of Assyria, relating to his expedition against Ashdod, which is mentioned in the twentieth chapter of the Book of Isaiah. On the same fragment was also part of the list of Median chiefs who paid tribute to Sargon. Part of an inscribed cylinder of Sennacherib, and half of an amulet in onyx with the name and titles of this monarch, subsequently turned up, and numerous impressions in clay of seals, with implements of bronze, iron, and glass. There was part of a crystal throne, a most magnificent article of furniture, in too mutilated condition to copy, but as far as it is preserved closely resembling in shape the bronze one discovered by Mr Layard at Nimroud.

On the evening of Saturday, the 17th of May, after paying the workmen, I started to examine the mounds of Khorsabad. I crossed the Tigris, and passed through the ruins of Nineveh, by the side of the Khosr river, and went over the country to the mound of Kalata. From the lateness of the hour, I was unable to inspect Kalata, and put up in a village near that mound. Rising early next morning, I went to the mound of Kalata, a large, conical artificial elevation, which had been tapped by former explorers. The only thing that could be seen of any account was a chamber in the side of the mound, which appeared to me like a tomb. The vault had been recently rifled of its contents, and I was told several antiquities had been found there. From Kalata I went to Barimeh, a well-built village near the foot of the mountains of Jebel Maklub, and, passing through a beautiful country, rode to Khorsabad. A fine stream, a tributary of the Khosr, flows from Barimeh to Khorsabad. In one place there is a pretty waterfall, and signs of cultivation and fertility are visible in every direction. The neighbouring mountains and streams, the fields and flowers combine to make this district a contrast to the vast brown plains of most of Assyria, and fully justify the choice of Sargon, who fixed on the site of Khorsabad to build his capital.

The ruins of Khorsabad represent the old Assyrian city of Dursargina, and consist of a town and palace mound. The wall of the town is nearly square, rather over a mile each way, the angles of the square facing the cardinal points. On the south-west face of the wall there is the fortified enclosure of a citadel, and on the north-west face, along which runs the stream from Barimeh, stands the palace platform, somewhat in form of the letter T, the base of the letter being turned to the northwest, nearest to the stream. This part of the mound near the water is the highest, and covers the remains of the palace and a temple. The excavations here by M. Botta have been made in a systematic manner, and have laid bare a considerable portion of the palace, some of which can still be seen; but most of it has been covered again, to preserve it.

I spent some time in inspecting these ruins, and then returned to Mosul.

I have said I telegraphed to the proprietors of the *Daily Telegraph* my success in finding the missing portion of the deluge tablet. This they published in the paper on the 21st of May 1873; but from some error unknown to me, the telegram as published differs materially from the one I sent. In particular, in the published copy occurs the words 'as the season is closing', which led to the inference that I considered that the proper season for excavating was coming to an end. My own feeling was the contrary of this, and I did not send this. I was at the time waiting instructions, and hoped that as good results were being obtained, the excavations would be continued. The proprietors of the *Daily Telegraph*, however, considered that the discovery of the missing fragment of the deluge text accomplished the object they had in view, and they declined to prosecute the excavations further, retaining, however, an interest in the work, and desiring to see it carried on by the nation. I was disappointed myself at this, as my excavations were so recently commenced; but I felt I could not object to this opinion, and therefore prepared to finish my excavations and return. I continued the Kouyunjik excavations until I had completed my preparations for returning to England, and in the north palace, near the place where I found the tablet with warnings to kings, I disinterred a fragment of a curious syllabary, divided into four perpendicular columns. In the first column was given the phonetic values of the cuneiform characters, and the characters themselves were written in the second column, the third column contained the names and meanings of the signs, while the fourth column gave the words and ideas which it represented.

I searched all round for other fragments of this remarkable tablet, pushing my trench farther through the mass of stones and rubbish, the remains of the fallen basement wall of the palace. Large blocks of stone, with carving and inscriptions, fragments of ornamental pavement, painted bricks, and decorations, were scattered in all directions, showing how complete was the ruin of this portion of the palace. Fixed between these fragments were found, from time to time, fragments of terra-cotta tablets; and one day a workman struck with his pick an overlying mass of mortar, revealing the edge of a tablet which was jammed between two blocks of stone. We at once cleared away the rubbish, and then, bringing a crowbar to bear, lifted the upper stone block, and extracted the fragment of tablet, which proved to be part of the syllabary, and joined the fragment already found. The greater part of the rest of this tablet was found at a considerable distance in a branch trench to the right. It was adhering to the roof of the trench, and easily detached, leaving the impression of all the characters in the roof.

Two other portions of the sixth tablet of the deluge series also came from this part. They relate to the conquest of the winged bull, and will be given with the other portions of the Isdubar series.

On my left in this excavation stood a mass of solid rubbish, which had been undermined during the former excavations; and a crack having started between this and the mound at the back of it, it stood as if ready to fall into the trench. For some time the workmen were afraid to touch it; but I expected some fragments there, so I directed them to attack it from the top, and was rewarded by several parts of tablets. A second trench on the right yielded a good text, being a variant account of the conquest of Babylonia by the Elamites, 2280 BC. Most of the fragments from this part were obtained with considerable difficulty, on account of the masses of stone which had to be removed to get at the inscriptions.

In the northern part of Sennacherib's palace I made some excavations, and discovered chambers similar to those in the south-east palace at Nimroud. Here no inscriptions rewarded me; but in the part of the temple area near this I discovered a new fragment of the cylinder of Bel-zakir-iskun, king of Assyria, 626 BC. Farther to the south-east in this part of the mound I discovered brick inscriptions of Shalmaneser, 1300 BC, and his son, Tugulti-ninip, 1271 BC, both of whom made restorations and additions to the temple of Ishtar. Here was a later wall, in constructing which some fine sculptures of the age of Assur nazir-pal, 885 BC, had been cut up and destroyed.

Such were my principal discoveries at Kouyunjik, and I closed the excavations there on the 9th of June. While I stayed at Mosul I made many friends among the Catholic missionaries and the merchants in the town, and in company with some of them, I paid a farewell visit to Nimroud on the 4th and 5th of June. On the 8th of June, as I was about to leave the country, I gave a farewell dinner to my friends, and next day we took leave of each other, I starting for Europe with my treasures.

Assyrian Discoveries, 1875

Early technical achievements

HERMAN HILPRECHT

HERMAN VOLRATH HILPRECHT (*1858-1925*) *was born in Hohenerxleben, Germany, and studied at the University of Leipzig. In 1886 he went to Philadelphia where he joined the staff of the University's department of Assyriology, and became curator of the Babylonian section of the University Museum. As a result of his excavations at Nippur he was invited to organize his finds, which were the statutory property of the Turkish government, in the Imperial Ottoman Museum at Istanbul, a job which occupied him from 1893 to 1909. His later years were clouded by his unjustifiable attempt to defend a mistake in his publication on the Nippur excavation, which ultimately led to his retirement, but the value of his work remains great.*

While examining the surroundings of this interesting edifice, Haynes came first upon the same gray or black ashes as are found everywhere in the court of the *ziggurrat* immediately below Naram-Sin's pavement, next upon 'lumps of kneaded clay', then upon several stray bits of lime mortar. All these traces of human activity were imbedded in the débris characteristic of the lower strata, which largely consist of earth, ashes, and innumerable potsherds. When he had reached a depth of nine feet from the top of the solid structure, – in other words, had descended about four feet below the bottom of the ancient curb on the south-east side of the stage-tower, – he found a large quantity of fragments of terra-cotta water pipes of the form here shown. Though the reports before me offer no satisfactory clue as to their precise use, there can be little doubt that they belong to the real pre-Sargonic period. I will try to explain their purpose later, Haynes' interpretation being better passed over in silence.

The explorer's curiosity was aroused at once, and having sunk his shaft a few feet deeper at the spot where the greatest number of these terra-cotta pipes were lying, he made one of the most far-reaching single discoveries in the lower strata of Nippur. After a brief search he came upon a very remarkable drain, reminding us of the advanced system of canalisation, as e.g. we find it in Paris at the present time.

It ran obliquely under the rectangular building described above, starting, as I believe, at a corner of the early sanctuary, but evidently having fallen into disuse long before the L-shaped building was erected. It could still be traced for about six feet into the interior of the ruins underlying the *ziggurrat*. But its principal remains were disclosed in the open court, into which it extended double that length, so that its tolerably preserved mouth lay directly below the ancient curb, – a fact of the utmost importance. For it constitutes a new argument in favour of the theory previously expressed that this curb marked the line of the earliest south-east enclosure of the *ziggurrat*, or whatever formerly may have taken the place of the latter. But it also follows that a gutter of some kind, which carried the water to a safe distance, must have existed in this neighbourhood outside the curb.

No sooner had Haynes commenced removing the débris from the ruined aqueduct, than he found, to his great astonishment, that it terminated in a vaulted section 3 feet long and was built in the form of a true elliptical arch, – the oldest one thus far discovered. The often ventilated question as to the place and time of origin of the arch was thereby decided in favour of ancient Babylonia. The bottom of this reliable witness of pre-Sargonic civilisation lies fifteen feet below Naram-Sin's pavement, or ten feet below the base of the curb, which it probably antedates by a century or two. We may safely assign it, therefore, to the end of the fifth pre-Christian millennium. It presented a number of interesting peculiarities. Being 2 feet 1 inch high (inside measurement), and having a span of 1 foot 3 inches and a rise of 1 foot 1 inch, it was constructed of well baked plano-convex bricks laid on the principle of radiating *voussoirs*. These bricks measured 12 by 6 by $2\frac{1}{2}$ inches, were light yellow in colour, and bore certain marks on their upper or convex surface, which had been made either by pressing the thumb and index finger deeply into the clay in the middle of the brick, or by drawing one or more fingers lengthwise over it. Primitive as they doubtless are, they do not (as Haynes inferred) 'represent the earliest type of bricks found at Nippur or elsewhere in Babylonia', – which are smaller and sometimes a little thicker, – though for a considerable while both kinds were used alongside each other and often in the same building. The curve of the arch was effected 'by wedge-shaped joints of the simple clay mortar used to cement the bricks'. 'On the top of its crown was a crushed terra-cotta pipe about 3 or $3\frac{1}{2}$ inches in diameter', the meaning of which Haynes declares unknown. I cannot help thinking that it served a purpose similar to the holes provided at regular intervals in our modern casing walls of terraces, etc.; in other words, that the pipe was intended to give exit to the rain water percolating the soil behind and above it, and in this way to prevent the softening of the clay cement between the bricks of the arch, and the caving-in of the whole vault which would result from it. This explanation being accepted, it necessarily follows that the floor of the court surrounding the earliest sanctuary was not paved with burned bricks, an inference entirely confirmed by the excavations.

There is much to be said in favour of the theory that this skilfully planned tunnel was arched over originally along its entire length. Like its vault, the lower part of the aqueduct presented several most surprising features. 'Just beneath the level of the pavement and in the middle of the water channel were two parallel terra-cotta tiles, 8 inches in diameter, with a 6-inch flanged mouth'. Haynes, regarding this tunnel as a drain rather than the protecting structure for a drain, was at a loss to explain their presence and significance. They were laid in clay mortar and consisted of single joints or sections, each 2 feet long, cemented together by the same material. We may raise the question: Why are there two small pipes instead of one large one? Evidently because they carried the water from two different directions to a point inside the sacred enclosure, where they met and passed through the arched tunnel together. They surely testify to a most highly developed system of drainage in the very earliest period of Babylonian history. I have, therefore, no doubt, that the so-called 'water-cocks' previously mentioned serve some purpose in connection with this complicated system of canalisation, and that in all probability they are to be regarded as specially prepared joints intended to unite terra-cotta pipes meeting each other at a right angle.

The mouth of the tunnel was provided with a T-shaped construction of plano-convex bricks, which Haynes is inclined to consider as 'the means employed for centring the arch', or as 'a device to exclude domestic animals, like sheep, from seeking shelter within it against the pitiless sun's rays in midsummer', while the present writer rather sees in it a strengthening pillar erected to protect the most exposed part of the tunnel at the point where the arching proper begins and the side walls are most liable to yield to the unequal pressure from the surrounding mass of earth. That the last-mentioned view is the more plausible and the explanation of the single pipe placed over the arch as given above is reasonable, follows from what happened in the course of the excavations. A few months after Haynes had removed the brick structure with its two arms, he reported suddenly that the arch had been 'forced out of its shape, probably from the unequal pressure of the settling mass above it, which had been drenched with rain water'. Truly the original purpose of these simple means, which had secured the preservation of the arch for six thousand years, could not have been demonstrated more forcibly. At the same time, Haynes, who never thought of this occurrence as having any bearing upon the whole question, could not have paid a higher compliment to the inventive genius and the extraordinary forethought of the ancient Babylonian architects.

Like all other parts, the long side walls of this unique tunnel were built with remarkable care. They consisted of eleven courses of bricks laid in clay mortar – a sure indication that the tunnel itself was not intended to carry water. The six lowest courses, the eighth, the tenth and eleventh, were placed flatwise with their long edge presented to view, while the seventh and ninth courses were arranged on their long edges like books on a shelf with their small edge visible. Considering all the details of this excellent system of canalisation in the fifth pre-Christian millennium, which not long ago was regarded as a prehistoric period, we may be pardoned for asking the question: Wherein lies the often proclaimed progress in draining the capitals of Europe and America in the twentieth century of our own era? It would rather seem as if the methods of today are little different from what they were in ancient Nippur or Calneh, one of the four cities of the kingdom of 'Nimrod, the mighty hunter before the Lord' (Gen. 10:9), at the so-called 'dawn of civilisation', – a somewhat humiliating discovery for the fast advancing spirit of the modern age! How many uncounted centuries of human development may lie beyond that marvellous age represented by the vaulted tunnel with the two terra-cotta pipes imbedded in cement at its bottom, four feet below the former plain level of 'the land of Shinar'!

Explorations in Bible Lands, 1903

The royal graves of Ur

CHARLES LEONARD WOOLLEY

Sir Charles Leonard Woolley (*1880-1960*) *was educated at St John's College, Leatherhead, and at New College, Oxford. Shortly after completing his studies at Oxford he was appointed an assistant curator at the Ashmolean Museum, and from this time the rest of his life was devoted to archaeology. He took part in many excavations; firstly he went to the Roman settlement at Corbridge, and then he joined the Oxford expedition to Nubia and then the British Museum excavation at Carcemish. The outbreak of war in 1914 found him in the Near East, where his local knowledge of Palestine and Egypt was invaluable when he joined Military Intelligence, but in 1916 he was taken prisoner by the Turks and held until the end of the war in 1918. The following year he returned to his excavations in Carcemish and in 1921 he spent a year at Tell el-Amarna. In 1922 he began the work which was to occupy him for the next twelve years and to produce the most spectacular and important discoveries since Schliemann's royal graves at Mycenae – the excavation of Ur of the Chaldees.*

Just outside the wall which enclosed the Temenos of Ur, the Sacred Area within which stood the terraced tower of the Moon God and the main temples of his cult, lay an open space which three thousand years before Christ was the burial-place of the citizens of Ur. Later on, in the days of Sargon of Akkad (about 2560 BC), the area was used again for the same purpose and the gravediggers disturbed hundreds of the earlier tombs; later still, after 2000 BC, houses were built over the ancient cemetery, and the discovery of old graves containing treasure induced men to tunnel deep into the soil in search of plunder. Thus, most of the royal tombs we found had been robbed long ago, and the repeated working of the soil had confused the stratification; but none the less it was clear that the original cemetery was a little earlier in date than the First Dynasty of Ur, a dynasty of kings whose historical existence had first been demonstrated by the excavation of the temple at al 'Ubaid set up by A-anni-pad-da, the second of the royal line.

Of more than a thousand graves of the early period only sixteen were royal tombs: the rest were the graves of private citizens dug as near as might be to the resting-place of the semi-divine ruler, just as today in a Moslem cemetery the humble headstones cluster round the domed *turbeh* of a religious sheikh . . .

A great square pit was dug deep into the soil, approached by a downward-sloping ramp. In the pit was built a tomb, of stone or brick, vaulted or domed: it might be a single chamber or it might be a miniature house with three or four rooms and a connecting passage; the inner face of the walls and the chamber floors were smoothly plastered with white cement. This was the tomb proper. Into it the body was brought and laid upon a bier, surrounded by offerings that testified to the wealth of the ruler in his lifetime and might serve his pleasure hereafter; two or three of his more intimate attendants were killed and their bodies set alongside the bier; then the tomb door was walled up. Next, there came down the ramp into the pit, whose earth sides were masked by reed matting, the whole company of those who were to accompany their royal master to the other world; ministers of the household, musicians, dancing women, male slaves and soldiers of the guard, even the chariot drawn by oxen or by asses, with the drivers, the grooms and the animals, assembled in ordered ranks at the bottom of the pit. Presumably some kind of service was held (in Queen Shub-ad's grave the fingers of the girl harpist were still touching the strings of the lyre), and at its end each took a little cup, filled it might be from a great bronze vessel set in the pit's centre, and drank a draught of a narcotic and lay down in his place and slept. And, from above, the mourners threw in the earth of the pit's making and buried the sleepers and the tomb chamber, and stamped the earth down and made of it a level floor for the next stage of the ceremony. For the filling of the pit was a slow process, done in stages. On the floor, still deep below the ground's surface, there was held a funeral feast and then two or three more human victims were sacrificed and laid out, and more earth was flung in and trodden down, for the same ritual to be repeated two or three times until the shaft was filled up level with the surrounding soil; probably, though for this we have no certain evidence, a funerary chapel was built above-ground to mark the spot, a chapel in which offerings would be made to the memory of the dead and services conducted in his honour.

This generalised description is no flight of fancy: it is based throughout on evidence afforded by the tombs themselves. In the case of PG 1054 we dug down methodically through floor after floor in the filling of the pit, each with its votive deposits and subsidiary burials, till we reached the little domed stone chamber with its blocked door, against which had been put the bones of sacrificed animals, and found inside it the gold-bedecked body with its dead attendants. In Queen Shub-ad's grave the musician with her harp and the singers formed a group apart; the grooms were there with the gaily-adorned and inlaid sledge-chariot drawn by two asses; the Keeper of the Wardrobe lay beside the flat chest which had held the royal dresses. Inside the tomb chamber the ladies-in-waiting were crouched beside the bier on which their mistress lay shrouded in beads of gold and lapis lazuli and carnelian, wearing over her elaborately adorned wig the massive gold hair-ribbon, the gold chaplets and the five-flowered hair-pin of a queen, while on a shelf at her side was put another court wig bound by a broad fillet of lapis lazuli against which were set marvellously-wrought little gold figures of animals and fruit and ears of corn.

The queen's grave had been dug in the shaft of a slightly older tomb, perhaps that of her husband whose last resting-place she wished to share. The grave-diggers had hit upon the vaulted roof of the old king's chamber and, tempted too far, had broken in and plundered it of all its wealth, and had placed the queen's wardrobe chest over the hole to hide the evidence of their misdoing. But they had not disturbed the 'death-pit'. There we found all in order. Eight soldiers with spears and helmets lay in double rank at the ramp's foot. Facing the ramp (evidently it had been backed down the slope) was the heavy chariot drawn by oxen wearing silver collars, the reins, decorated with huge lapis lazuli beads, attached to silver rings in their nostrils. The drivers and soldier attendants were with the car. Against the wall of the tomb-chamber were the harpist and the singers; soldiers guarded the walled-up door and stood against the matting-draped sides of the pit; there were 63 persons gathered there to die. In another case, PG 1237, the floor of the death-pit was covered with bodies all in ordered rows: 6 men on the entrance side and 68 women in court dress, red coats with beaded cuffs and shell-ring belts, head-dresses of gold or silver, great lunate ear-rings and multiple necklaces of blue and gold. Amongst them was one girl who was not wearing her silver hair-ribbon, – it was in her pocket, tightly coiled up like a rounded tape, as if she had been late for the funeral and had not had time to put it on. Here there were four harpists with their lyres, grouped together, and by them in an open space lay a copper cauldron; it was difficult not to connect this with the little drinking-bowl found by every one of the 74 bodies in the pit.

None of the private graves in the cemetery had anything corresponding to this wholesale slaughter. Even the richest of them, the grave of Meskalam-dug, which contained a princely wealth of arms and vessels in gold, silver, bronze and stone, had in it no bodies other than that of 'the lord of the good land' himself, solitary in a wooden coffin. The built grave-chamber and the human sacrifice were a privilege reserved for kings. It seems to imply a belief that those kings were at least semi-divine beings for whom death was but a transition; and if we may judge from the fact that so many people died with them without violence, to the accompaniment of music made by themselves and by means of a narcotic voluntarily drunk, surely these people were buoyed up by the confidence that going thus in their lord's company they assured themselves of a continuance of their service and of an honourable place in that other world.

In all the Sumerian literature that we possess there is no hint of any such ritual forming part of the funeral of a king; and since the discovery at Ur was unique of its kind some scholars were loth to accept any such interpretation of the evidence. They pointed out that the few names recovered from the 'Royal Tombs' did not figure in the lists of kings recorded by Sumerian annalists. The facts of the burials were beyond dispute, but they preferred to see in them a sacrifice offered to the acknowledged gods, a 'Fertility rite' in which a mystic marriage symbolising the earth's fruitfulness culminated with the killing of the bride and bridegroom. The first point is true enough. But the Sumerian annalists enumerate only the kings of those dynasties which claimed to rule the whole land of Sumer. The occupants of our Royal Tombs make no such claim, but they do call themselves 'kings'. Their names are not unlike those of the First Dynasty kings – they might well belong to the family – but judging by the archaeological evidence they are older in date, and, if so, were necessarily not dynastic kings but vassals, lords only of a single city. If they were the chosen victims of a 'Fertility rite' they would scarcely call themselves kings at all.

Further, Sumerian literature, which is rich in liturgical and religious texts, gives no hint whatsoever that there was any killing of the protagonists of a 'mystic marriage' rite; no human sacrifice is suggested anywhere as part of the orthodox religion. The assumption of the 'Fertility rite' therefore does just as much violence to the literary evidence as does the assumption that these are royal burials – more, in fact, for there is no description of any royal burial anywhere in Sumerian literature. Again, the 'mystic marriage' involves two people, bride and bridegroom, and if they had to be killed surely they would be buried together. But each of the Royal Tombs at Ur contains only one principal body. Yet a further argument is this: the need for the fruits of the earth is constant, and if a 'Fertility rite' is practised at all it should be a yearly ceremony, as indeed it was in Sumer in historic times. But in the graveyard at Ur, which must have been in use for many generations, there are only 16 'Royal Tombs'. Did men only 16 times in all those years take steps to secure a good harvest? And now the evidence of the Royal Tombs no longer stands alone. At Ur we have found that a thousand years later the great rulers of the Third Dynasty at Ur had vast tombs just outside the Temenos wall wherein numerous people were buried with them, tombs surmounted by a palace-temple in which the eldest son of the house maintained the worship of the king, who was deified in his lifetime and counted as a god after his death. It was an enduring tradition, though literature is silent regarding it, whereby God's 'tenant farmer' partakes of his divinity and does not die but is translated to the heavens.

Here then, in this prehistoric cemetery at Ur, we have the graves of kings and commoners to teach us something of the thoughts and beliefs of a people who have left us no real written testimony of themselves, and to tell us very much about their arts and crafts and the material setting of their lives. Only in one respect does the evidence here compare poorly with that from other sites – we have not found such portrait statues as were unearthed in great numbers at Tell Asmar in northern Iraq in the course of the American excavations there. The reason is that at Ur the site is a cemetery, whereas the building at Tell Asmar was a temple. To the ancient Sumerians, a statue was the last thing one would think of putting in a tomb. A statue represented either a god, in which case the shrine was the obvious place for it, or the human worshipper, and the proper place for the worshipper too was in the temple, where he might stand day and night before his god in perpetual adoration and prayer. For a complete picture of Sumer as it was five thousand years ago we must collect our evidence not from one only but from many sources which in recent years archaeology has opened up to us; but none the less the objects from the ceremony of Ur bear full witness to the quality of the civilisation which had been developed in the Euphrates valley throughout the periods of al'Ubaid, Uruk and Jemdet Nasr and was flourishing at the dawn of the historic age.

Ur; the First Phases, 1946

Part Five

THE BOOK OF THE ROCKS AND VALLEYS

Digging up Pergamon

CARL HUMANN

CARL HUMANN (*1839-1896*) *was a railway engineer who in 1861 concentrated his activities in southern regions for reasons of health. He immediately showed, firstly on Samos, an interest in archaeology. He became famous through his excavation of the Altar at Pergamon (reconstructed in Berlin) which he concluded in 1886.*

Pergamon, 19 December 1871

My dear Mr Curtius,

Five weeks have passed since I last wrote and had I not then promised you to write again in 8-14 days to give you the results of the excavations and to send you the plan of Pergamon, I should have written again long ago.

Well, up to today I had neither of these, or, at any rate, not in their completed forms. It has been raining solidly here for five weeks, and only since new moon has there been a north wind and, as a superfluous addition, bitter cold. There you have my complete excuse – I have not been wasting time. I profited from every half day, if it was not raining, by climbing up to the Acropolis with my people, and am at last happy to tell you that I have really managed to get things moving.

Remember the high, thick wall up there in which I showed you the two sculptures projecting from underneath? I have now got these out and at home, on *Prussian* ground. . . .

No. 1: This is the stone which lay on the left; the chest was visible. When I had blasted the wall down so far that we were close up to it I personally carefully removed stone after stone and found the neck and chin, then the left cheek and the eye. When I saw the eye I cried out: '*That's a dead man!*' For this statue, although completely and beautifully sincere, definitely had the emaciated and stark look of death. I am telling you this because it shows that one can set no great store by my *artistic* critical faculty. Eventually the statue was completely excavated and turned out to be a beautiful youth with curly hair, stretched out, the breast high and drumlike (25 centimetres) the right arm, unfortunately broken, raised, the left hanging down, the head slightly inclined to one side, the mouth half open, not distorted by pain, but rather by fatigue, as though asleep; only the wide-open, rolled back eyes showed that we were looking at a man killed in battle. Strength and beauty were here united in most marvellous harmony. To the left a leg belonging to another statue is visible.

No. 2 in the drawing shows an aged, bearded man who, defeated in battle, looks on grimly; this head, also, although the chin and nose are missing, is beautifully carved. At first I took it to be a lion's head, before the left shoulder and the beautifully modelled sleeper had been dug out. The eyebrows are like thick rolls, but not exaggerated. A hand, most probably not his, for it would have to be the right one, holds a shield over his head. This shield is carved very thin, hardly a fingerswidth thick; and for this reason, mostly broken. Behind stands a man of whom only the right arm, the right breast, and a part of the back of the head are preserved, who is in the act of hitting the old man with a club. Over the left shoulder he wore a lion skin, a paw of which is still preserved. Head, left arm and left breast are unfortunately no longer in existence, as they probably stood out too far from the wall.

No. 3, a horse's foot, belongs to this category too. I've never seen a foot like it before! All the bones in the joint show through the skin. I don't know which I prefer, No. 1 or 3.

The three listed pieces are all made of the same bluish-white marble. The first two are both 89 centimetres high. As various blocks have previously been found here and have unfortunately been destroyed, it is certain, also taking these two into account, that they were part of a continuous frieze which showed a battle between men.

Years ago I saw a block which showed a man with a lion (at that time this was sent to Constantinople to Mr Karatheodoris): as well as this there is No. 3, the horse's foot, and so we have a whole battle with men, horses, wild animals. The frieze could only have been part of a very important building, e.g. the Temple of Minerva of the Acropolis. Then, to my joy, it turned out that all the architectural fragments of the building, whose foundations and lower vaulting you admired, were also made of the same pure bluish-white marble, which is furthermore in agreement with the diameter of the columns of this temple, which I have not yet been able to measure accurately, and agrees with the frieze's height of 89 centimetres.

I hope it is not just the ecstacy of discovering something oneself which leads me to say that we have here a masterpiece of sculpture. My sketches drawn in the courtyard with frozen fingers, can only give you inaccurate impression of the beauty of these pieces. On top of this, the stonehard limestone of the wall still lies between all the most delicate parts, as I have left it there for safety's sake. No. 1 and 2 are broken in two places, but so conveniently that none of the finest parts are cut through. The great expanse and uneven load of the wall seems to have broken them. One can hardly still call them *Haut-reliefs* as the figures are completely rounded and look as though they have been stuck on to slabs of 15-20 centimetres thick and are therefore almost statues. The chest of the young man taken together with the slab is more than half a metre thick. All the drawings are drawn to a scale of 1.10 so that the sizes can in all cases be calculated. The hatching indicates what is broken off.

No. 4 is a bas-relief and shows armour. On the left shoulder are fringes such as those worn by our drum majors; both sides carry figures of warriors, very lovely, but too small to be drawn in here.

No. 5 is an inscription on a white slab of marble; I pulled 4 and 5 out of the wall.

6a and 6b were given me by a Turk. It is the same frieze which you saw on the gateway of a Han, but in a better state of preservation. Were I to draw the small winged lion for you with all its muscles, it would take half a day and also I was no longer able to go on using the page of the enclosed drawing. Therefore I have indicated only size and colour.

As well as this I have in the house a bas-relief from a grave showing a rider, in front of him, a tree with a serpent, but everything rather blurred; also a small Ionic capital and base of about 1½ feet in diameter, so pretty and delicate that it will please any architect and that Mr Surveyor (Adler) will immediately want to have it measured. Also a stele with an inscription which I have no more time to copy today; the upper half is broken off, though I have just been told that it is preserved in a house, here. I shall annex it tomorrow. *Ischallah!* (God be willing!) Then I shall have the fragments of the broken man we discovered and various architectural fragments.

Then I dug out a seated robed female figure, in brilliant white marble, of the best period! – Head, arms, one breast and the feet are missing; she sits on a pillow. Drawing to follow soon; I hope that she will be coming down from the hill tomorrow. The one naked foot which projected from the wall was knocked off two years ago and sent to Constantinople to the Turkish Museum. That one was magnificent. I hope that they will allow it to be retrieved later on. *Bakshish!* With that, everything's possible.

The probable throne and a statue will appear tomorrow or the day after, for I've almost reached them. I bought a storage vessel, of fired clay, higher than a man and too large to be encompassed by three, in a village five hours from here. According to the description, it must be this shape; but because of the boggy roads it is at present impossible to bring it back here.

I have not yet been able to copy half a dozen inscriptions in the Turkish churchyards; they are still unknown; three more are coming off the walls this week. I have sent someone off to Kilise-Keni; they are asking 10 lire for the stone. I have offered 2 and hope to get it.

The Greeks don't want to give up the stone from the church, they consider this a sin, and furthermore they are not allowed to send their native tradition abroad. Those stupid Bulgarians just want to haggle and hope to gain a giant sum for it.

In a mosque I found a large stone fruit-motif carving, almost one metre square, beautifully executed, grapes, plums, laurel, acorns, figs, palms. Our governor, as you know, my intimate friend, is taking great pains to acquire it for me; but the damned Imam thinks it would be sinful to give Unbelievers something from the mosque, in spite of the fact that I offered them 10 lire for it; I shall have to give the Imam a few pounds. For the rest I have succeeded in getting the Mufti and Kadi to their feet to prove from the Koran that the mosque should engage in a deal if a profit is to be had. *Baccalym!* I shall not tell you about my coins and clay vessels; this letter is too long as it is.

As soon as I have got all the statues which are still visible out of the walls, I shall begin excavations on the ruins of the Temple of Minerva and without doubt find still more reliefs. All the heads which are to be seen in the museum here were also found there. From there I shall get very valuable architectural fragments. I possess a column *con verde antico* of about 1½ metres long at Dikeli on the coast. I have since stopped the work at the burial mound of the Eye or of Attalos because I wanted to be present, and this was impossible. It won't run away.

My plan of Pergamon has, of course, got delayed on account of the weather and the excavations; 3 or 4 days' work, and then it's finished. For your use for the present I am sending you herewith a rough copy.

18. The Altar of Zeus at Pergamon, excavated by Carl Humann in 1884–6 and reconstructed in Berlin.

I have discovered a great deal. I shall stay here over Christmas because of the excavations and shall probably not go to Smyrna until next week. I am bringing the slabs of marble down from the Acropolis on a large sledge, but shall have to take it apart at the bottom and take it back up piece by piece. You know how high it is. I have had specially tough carts built in which to take the things to Dikeli on the coast, from where I shall send them to Smyrna either by boat, or, should there by then be a great deal of stuff, perhaps the imperial ambassador will be able to transport them.

I am sending this letter to Dr Luhrsen for his information, partly for his private interest and partly for official reasons, so that he can, in case of need, help me verbally and practically, although up to now I have not encountered any difficulties at all.

Should, at some point or other, the matter of costs arise, I confirm herewith that up to the present moment no costs at all have been incurred for the Government, and yet, everything that I have collected was on the Government's behalf, and is its own property.

Well, that's enough. I wish you, dear Mr Curtius, a very happy Christmas and New Year, and hope that you will soon give me the pleasure of a few lines. I shall write again.

With best wishes, Yours very sincerely,

Carl Humann

Der Pergamon-Altar, entdeckt, beschrieben und gezeichnet von Carl Humann,
1959
Translated from the German by C.M.Kaine

The discovery of the Hamah stones

WILLIAM WRIGHT

WILLIAM WRIGHT (*1837-1899*) *was the son of a farmer and grew up in County Down, Ireland, but his academic abilities gained him scholarships to study at Queen's College, Dublin. Here he decided to enter holy orders and become a missionary, and with this in view he studied at the theological seminaries of Dublin and Geneva. In 1865 he went to Damascus and remained in this region for the next ten years. In addition to his religious work he devoted much time to travel, and to the study of antiquities, making journeys in Palestine and Syria and northern Arabia, and writing accounts for the Pall Mall Gazette. It was during this time that he became interested in the newly discovered Hittite civilization, and, hearing of the inscribed stones which had been reported at Hamah, he determined to secure and study them.*

On the 10th of November, 1872, I set out from Damascus intent on securing the Hamah inscriptions.

Sixty years previously Burckhardt, in his exploration of Hamah, had discovered, in the corner of a house in one of the Bazaars, a stone covered with figures and signs, which he declared to be hieroglyphics, but different from the hieroglyphics of Egypt. Every one who cared to know anything of Syria, read Burckhardt's travels. All admitted his accuracy of observation and truthfulness of description, yet so little interest was taken in his discovery, even by professional explorers, that Porter, in Murray's *Handbook*, so late as 1868, declares 'there are no antiquities in Hamah'.

At length, in 1870, Mr J. Augustus Johnson, the American Consul-General, and the Rev. S. Jessup, an American missionary, stumbled on the Hamah inscriptions, and from that moment a period of zealous effort to secure them succeeded the long period of apathy and neglect. The newly kindled enthusiasm with reference to the curious hiero-glyphics, which had waited so long for an interpreter, seemed destined to endanger their existence, and from Damascus we watched, with almost breathless suspense, the various heroic but fruitless attempts to secure accurate copies.

The vague but much dreaded power of the American Consul, and the local knowledge and skill of an American missionary, availed not to enable them to make accurate transcripts of the re-discovered hieroglyphics.

In publishing a picture of one of the inscriptions, in the 'First Quarterly Statement of the American Palestine Exploration Society', in 1871, Mr Johnson says: 'We did not succeed in getting squeeze impressions, for fanatical Moslems crowded upon us when we began to work upon the stones, and we were obliged to be content with such copies of this and other inscriptions found on stones, *over* and *near* the city gate, and *in* the ancient bridge which spans the Orontes, as could be obtained by the aid of a native painter.' Mr Johnson must have been hard pressed, for he seems to have seen only one of the stones, as he describes the positions of the others incorrectly, doubtless having been led into error by the vague reports of the people; but his efforts were not in vain, and the imperfect facsimile of one of the inscriptions, published in the 'First Quarterly Statement of the American Palestine Exploration Society', did much to quicken interest in the new hiero-glyphics, and stimulated others to succeed where he had partially failed.

The imperfect tracings of the 'native painter' were seen by Messrs Drake and Palmer, on their way home through Beyrout, from their wanderings in the Desert; and the Palestine Exploration Fund sent Mr Drake back to Syria, to examine and copy the inscriptions. By his great skill in dealing with natives, Mr Drake partly succeeded in taking photographs and squeezes of the most important, but gathering angry mobs obliged him to hasten his operations before he had effected his purpose.

Captain Burton, then Her Majesty's Consul at Damascus, also visited Hamah. He gives a good description of the stones, and points out accurately the places where they were to be found, but he also had to be content with the decipherings of one Kostatin-el-Khuri. These he published in *Unexplored Syria* with the following explanation. 'The ten sheets accompanying this article had been applied to the blackened or reddened faces of the four stones, and the outlines were afterwards drawn with a reed pen. In a few cases the fancy of the copyist had been allowed to run wild', &c.

Captain Burton suggested that the stone should be secured 'by means of a Vizerial order, intended to be obeyed', and he adds: 'When at Hamah, I began to treat with the proprietor of No. 1, the Christian Jabbour, who, barbarously greedy like all his tribe, began by asking a hundred napoleons'.

The publication of the rude tracings in *Unexplored Syria* increased still more the general interest in the inscriptions, and a very large sum of money was offered for the smallest stone, but the people of Hamah would not part with it at any price. Then a new and altogether different set of men began to bully and barter for the coveted curiosities, and we saw with dismay a commencement of the fussy peddling which, a short time before, had led to the destruction of the Moabite stone. At this juncture my opportunity arrived, not only of securing but of saving the precious inscriptions.

The Sublime Porte, seized by a periodic fit of reforming zeal, had appointed an honest man, Subhi Pasha, to be Governor of Syria. Subhi Pasha brought a conscience to his work, and not content with redressing wrongs that succeeded in forcing their way into his presence, resolved to visit every district of his province, in order that he might check the spoiler and discover the wants of the people. He invited me to accompany him on a tour to Hamah, and I gladly accepted the invitation. Mr W. Kirby Green, our excellent Consul at Damascus, was also to be his guest. I thought it best to join the party in the neighbourhood of Hamah, lest familiarity should breed contempt before the critical moment had arrived for asking permission to copy the inscriptions. This I was able to do after lingering on my way among the village schools in Jebel Kalamoun.

Having spent a few days in Saidnâya, M'alûla, Yabrûd, Nebk, and Deir Atîyeb, among the handsomest peasantry of Syria, some of them speaking a *patois* of Syriac, and all of them speaking Arabic with a Syriac accent, I struck north by Hasya, and joined the Pasha's cavalcade at Hums.

The following day we started for Hamah with an enormous following. Chiefs from all parts flocked in with their retainers to do honour to the Waly. Princelings, whose possessions had been reduced to a horse, a few arms, and a richly braided jacket, galloped over the plain, wheeling and tossing their spears in the air, and showing wonderful feats of horsemanship. Bedawin hostages from the Desert, white-turbaned Ulema, sugar-loaf-topped Dervishes, priests and peasants made up a procession, ten deep, more than a mile long, and surrounded by a picturesque army of skirmishers, who kept up their antics for miles all round the main body during the whole journey.

On the 25th of November we arrived in Hamah, late in the afternoon. During the day,the Waly had consulted Mr Green and me as to his projects for ameliorating the condition of the people. We sat up late that night together, and I had an opportunity of asking his Excellency to aid me in getting perfect copies of the inscriptions. This he promised to do, and so gracious and kind was he, that he accompanied us to our beds to make sure that his guests were comfortable.

The next morning at an early hour Mr Green and I sallied forth in quest of the inscriptions. None of the books or articles referring to the inscriptions had reached us in Damascus before we set out, and we had to begin our operations without any advantage from the labours of our predecessors. Our first business was to find the inscribed stones, and this was not so easy as it might seem, for all whom we asked about them looked us steadily in the face, and swore vehemently that there were no stones such as we sought in Hamah.

In a large city of narrow crooked streets, it would have been a weary work to find the inscriptions for ourselves, and after so much disappointment we resolved to ask every person we met, in the hope that we might find some one not up to the plot of concealing the inscriptions from us. The first man we met after making this resolve proved to be Suliman-el-Kallas, in the wall of whose house was inscription H.1. The secret being out, we had no difficulty in finding all the stones, and they were also pointed out to the Waly.

Subhi Pasha, who was known in Europe as Subhi Bey before his appointment to Damascus, was descended from a noble Greek family. He was the most learned man among the Turks, and his private collection of coins and art treasures, the greater part of which has been since sold in London, brought him into scholarly relations with many of the savans of Europe. Subhi Pasha, who was the creator of the Constantinople Museum, recognised at a glance the great importance of the inscriptions, and sent a telegram to the Sultan asking him to accept the inscribed stones for the Museum.

I pointed out to His Excellency that such inscriptions ought to be the common property of all, that the scholars of Europe were waiting eagerly for accurate copies of them, and that they would doubtless open a new chapter in history which would show that a great people, called the Hittites in the Bible, but never referred to in classic history, had once formed a mighty empire in that region.

The Pasha not only consented to let me take copies of the inscriptions, but promised to bring the inscribed stones to the *Serai*, where I might copy them at leisure. Under other circumstances we should have experienced great difficulties in securing copies of the inscriptions, for the recent feeble attempts to get possession of the stones had brought the Hamathites to consider them of extraordinary value; and as we passed through the city to the baths with the Governor-General, we heard many expressions of muttered defiance, and threats of violence towards anybody that might venture to interfere with their sacred and venerable treasures.

Later in the day, when it became known that the Pasha would take the stones, we heard men vowing that they would destroy the inscriptions, as they have since done with that at Aleppo.

I saw now that a crisis was reached. For hundreds, perhaps thousands, of years these mute inscriptions had waited for some one to hear their story. Egyptian, Assyrian, Greek, Selucidae, Roman, Saracen, Crusader and Turk had passed them by as unworthy of even a passing notice; and now that travellers from the Isles of the Sea, eager to learn their secrets, had arrived, their voice was about to be hushed for ever. A greater calamity than that of the Moabite stone tragedy was imminent. A mighty Empire was about to claim its rightful position among the great nations of the ancient world, and a few fanatics were about to push it back into the outer darkness to which classic history had assigned it.

Mr Green and I saw that we must exert ourselves if we were to gain our purpose. We visited all the men in whose grounds or walls the stones were, and assured them, on the faith of a British Consul, that Subhi Pasha was altogether different from the other Pashas whom they had known; that he would pay full value, and more, for the stones; and now that the Sultan had replied by telegram accepting them, any one who interfered with the inscriptions would be most severely punished. We thus endeavoured to enlist the cupidity and fear of the Hamathites in favour of the stones.

We also laid the matter before the Waly, who placed the inscriptions under Ibrahim Pasha for the night, and he told off a number of soldiers for their protection. Hearing from some of our people that a formidable conspiracy was on foot for the destruction of the inscriptions, we told them candidly what we had heard, and assured them that dire punishment would fall on them if any mishap befell the stones. It was an anxious and sleepless night, and on the following morning the Waly, by our advice, paid sums varying from three to fifteen napoleons each for the stones, and the work of removing them to the *Serai* began.

The removal of the stones was effected by an army of shouting men, who kept the city in an uproar during the whole day. Two of them had to be taken out of the walls of inhabited houses, and one of them was so large that it took fifty men and four oxen a whole day to drag it a mile. The other stones were split in two, and the inscribed parts were carried on the backs of camels to the *Serai*. As the shrill-voiced Moslems were summoning from the minarets the faithful to prayer at set of sun, the last stone was to our great delight deposited in safety.

The removal of these mysterious relics produced a great commotion in Hamah. The fact of a British Consul and a Protestant missionary being the guests of the Waly of Syria, and accompanying him to mosques and baths, seemed strange and portentous in the eyes of fanatical Moslems, but was somewhat reassuring to the cringing native Christians. Celestial portents also combined to impress the Moslem mind; for on the night following the removal of the stones to the *Serai* a meteoric shower, in Eastern splendour, was seen by the Hamathites, who beheld in every brilliant sparkling train the wrath of Heaven fulminated against Hamah in the event of their sacred stones being taken away. The wrathful stars had appeared in accordance with an ancient prophecy.

There was much shouting and invoking the name of Mohammed and Allah during the night, and in the morning an influential deputation of green and white turbaned Moslems waited on the Waly to tell him of the evil omens, and to urge a restoration of the stones.

The Waly ordered coffee and cigarettes for all the members of the deputation, who squatted in solemn dignity around him. He listened patiently to all the speakers, several of whom spoke at great length and with much animation. When they had finished the Waly continued stroking his beard for some time. Then he asked, in a very grave manner if the stars had hurt any one. They replied they had not. 'Ah', said the Waly, brightening up and speaking with a cheery ringing voice that even the guards outside the door might hear, 'the omens were good. They indicated the shining approbation of Allah on your loyalty in sending these precious stones to your beloved Khalif, the Father of the Faithful'. The grave deputation rose up comforted. Each member kissed the Waly's hand and withdrew.

We had now got our hare, and we had to face the difficulty of cooking it. It was necessary to get transcriptions free from what Captain Burton called, in those which he reproduced, 'the vagaries of the native painter'. There was no photographer in Hamah, and we had no photographic apparatus with us, and we felt that it was of the greatest importance to secure exact facsimiles, as we knew not what might happen to the stones. I tried in vain to procure plaster of Paris in Hamah. I learned, however, that gypsum was found in the neighbourhood, and I sent two trusty men, well bribed, to search for it.

Then began the work of cleaning the inscriptions. The moss and dirt of ages had filled up the hollows between the raised characters. Lime mortar had been dashed into them, and during the lapse of ages it had grown almost as hard as the stone itself. It was a work that could be delegated to no one, and it required incessant scrubbing during the greater part of two days, with brush and water and pointed stick, to make the stones clean. Meantime the men had returned with a camel-load of gypsum in blocks. This had to be burnt, and pounded into powder.

Many attempts were made to decoy us from our labour to shoot woodcock, or to hunt wild boars, or to stalk gazelles and bustards; but we stuck to our task until we had two sets of perfect plaster casts of all the inscriptions. This work was fully shared in by Mr Green, who took my place at the inscriptions when I was obliged to be elsewhere, and who managed to make up for my absence from the Pasha's parties.

As soon as the casts were firm we despatched them by a safe man to Damascus, whence Mr Green sent one set to the Government for the British Museum, and at Mr Tyrwhitt Drake's request I sent the other set to the Palestine Exploration Fund. We had thus succeeded in placing within the reach of scholars exact facsimiles of the Hamah inscriptions, showing the actual lengths of lines and bars and characters and blanks, perfect even to the faults of the stone.

We now propose to investigate the records of Egypt and Assyria and the Hebrew Scriptures, with reference to the Hittites, before asking the question, Are these curious inscriptions Hittite remains?

The Empire of the Hittites, 1884

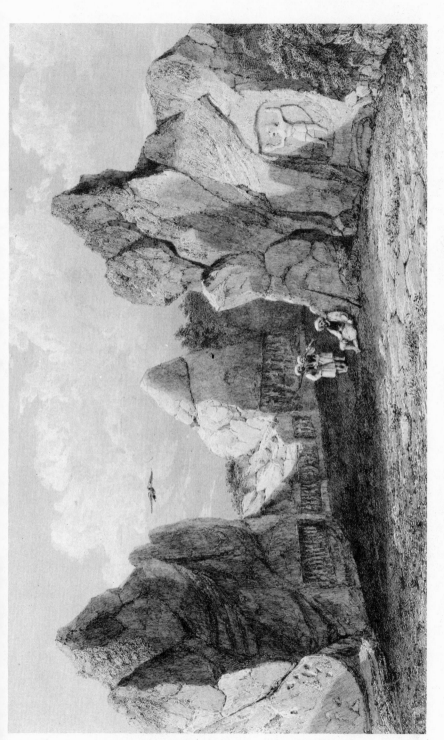

19. An early traveler's view of the Hittite rock sanctuary at Yazilikaya near Boghazköy, in what is today Turkey.

20. Sculpture and inscriptions of the Hittites from Karatepe. Three generations of scholars had tried in vain to decipher the writings of this people. Here at last the bi-lingual inscriptions were found that made decipherment possible.

To Boghazköy!

HUGO WINCKLER

HUGO WINCKLER (*1863-1914*) *was born in Saxony, and devoted all his academic career to the study of ancient texts. In 1904 he was appointed to the Chair of Oriental Languages at Berlin University, and contributed translations of the Amarna letters and the Code of Hammurabi, but he is better known for his findings at Boghazköy. Here his excavators discovered numbers of fine buildings and hoards of tablets, but unfortunately Winckler's interest was confined mainly to the subject-matter of the tablets and as a result much of the systematic recording of the excavation was neglected. Among the tablets he discovered and translated was a cuneiform version of the treaty between Ramesses II and the Hittites after the battle of Kadesh.*

The completion of this task was planned for the winter. An attempt was first made to obtain the relatively modest means needed for a preliminary expedition from influential sources who were actively concerned with the expedition. Meanwhile the scholars who had been consulted were of a different opinion on the subject of Boghazköy from my own, so I had to find another way of doing things. However, it turned out that the Near East Society and the Berlin Eastern Committee had limited funds obtainable. These could be made available for our purposes and the money, about the same amount again, which was missing was put at my disposal by my friends Dr Georg Hahn and the Military Chief Chaplain, Otto Strauss (Spendau). So by the summer we had the sum which we had estimated ready for our preliminary purpose and were in a position to prove who had been in the right about the potential prospects at Boghazköy.

On the seventeenth of July, early in the morning, we again rode into Zia-Bey's konak and were already greeted as old friends (with pleasant memories of Bakshish). As heir of an ancient race of princes, the Bey still enjoys a great deal of respect and one has to be sure of his influence if one wants to work in this district without difficulties. An expedition undertaken in the name of the Government would naturally not induce any obvious difficulties from anyone, but there are also others which are no smaller. And here the European is at a disadvantage because he has not the inexhaustible supply of time of the oriental. And the first requirement of this kind of warfare is time! We had stayed on very friendly terms with the Bey – he had made many requests, from a good bottle of cognac, to aid in a momentary difficulty – and for this in his own way he had also done us services. He supplied us, without any trouble at all, with a working party at his command – small services of friendship are well worth while in the Orient!

We were reckoning on about eight weeks' work and, as it was high summer, we wanted to spend them either in the tents or in huts made out of foliage. Memories of summer joys in the Lebanon were brought to my mind! Although here also in Asia Minor one goes higher up into the mountains in the summer to spend a summer holiday under canvas – which is what Zia-Bey did – I was bitterly disillusioned in my desire for warmth. We were able to camp at the foot of the actual peak of the Büyük Valley, at the source of an adequate spring. It is the place where, in the following year, our house was built. The modest tent which had to do for both of us offered us the kind of temperature, under the burning midday sun, which would have been not uncomfortable in a Turkish bath, but which was hardly refreshing for a midday nap. Soon after sunset the air cooled noticeably and with this drop in temperature a fierce evening wind blew down from the bare mountains, which led to a night in which there had to be good reason indeed to leave the warmth of the camp. So in the evening we sat in front of our tent in the howling wind to eat our evening meal, as our coats swelled with wind. Then, as a rule, one had cooled off enough to creep into one's tent, without all too many formalities, where there was just room enough for two men who were indefatigable at their work and between whom in this close contact there was never an irritated word or even an impatient thought, although at this time both had to suffer considerable physical hardship.

A bower of leaves accommodated the kitchen in which a cook of Bulgarian origin performed his duties in a pretty horrible fashion. He had recommended himself to my experienced friend on account of some knowledge of German, which should have made being here easier for me. The man had formerly been allowed to practise his art on the patients of a German hospital. I accepted his tricks with equanimity, for I set out on my travels with the idea that pleasure was not too eagerly to be sought. But my poor Macridi swallowed our anger twice and three times over for both of us and could not indemnify himself with clay tablets! A second arbour of leaves had to serve as shade for me in which to study the clay tablets and was soon ready to be put to extensive use. The whole camp was surrounded by a high fence woven of branches which at the same time acted as a badly needed windshield. Along a section of this, a bit lower down, a rather larger shelter made of branches had been erected which sheltered five beings who had never experienced better times in their whole lives – our horses! They earned their bread by doing almost nothing at all, whereas everyone else had more than enough to do. Their vicinity of course boasted a huge superfluity of flies, and for me this meant the pleasure of having to copy my clay tablets with covered head and neck and gloved hands, if I wanted to avoid stopping after each symbol to ward off the overpowering interest the friendly little animals took in my work. We are, of course, in our scholarship anxiously concerned to guard the spiritual right of the Firstborn.

From the camp sites (as now from the front of the house built in 1907) one looks out over the valley-bowl of Boghazköy and Jükbas to the chain of mountains which encloses it in the West. At the back lies the high Büyük Valley, which adjoins the eastern heights of the mountain basin.

So we had quickly settled ourselves in and my pencils were sharpened in readiness to record on paper the hoped-for treasured documents.

One should remind oneself of what had to be judged on the evidence of the facts known up to the present day with respect to what was expected to be discovered: the language of the lands which belonged to Arzawa, the land of the el-Amarna letters and the documents of the time of el-Amarna. The next step would therefore be to find information on Arzawa and to find its centre at Boghazköy. But already the size of the site of the town pointed to an especial significance of the place, and therefore of the country itself. We were not to be kept in suspense for too long. On 21st July the work on the Büyük Valley could be started and from the very first day onwards documents came to light. At first only small fragments. The ones which had been picked up earlier had been found on the slopes of the castle hill in the rubble which had rolled down, and inside a rather sharply defined strip. It therefore followed that the large expanse of mountainside had to be examined and in such a way that the rubble was cleared away from the bottom towards the top. It was work of not inconsiderable danger for the workmen, as an unwanted collapse of the overhanging earth and rock could at times be avoided only with the greatest precautions. The further into the mountain the work advanced, the larger became the fragments discovered. The productive strip narrowed a little towards the top, and our success showed that Macridi had from the start, with a lucky look, rightly gauged-round the actual site of the finds. Neither to the left or to the right of the strip was anything found and it was discovered in the following year that the actual source of the treasures had been at the edge of the mountain peak.

The majority of the pieces found this time showed the already familiar characters in the unknown language. The contents were varied, but at first too small to answer the problem which was primarily still unanswered: which part of the world we were in. That it had been a great centre was now quite clear and that it could not be the remains of the archives of an insignificant king, which came into our hands at the rate of 100-200 a day was also definite. The direction of Arzawa . . . also had to be discounted after the first few days.

Soon a few pieces in Babylonian yielded the information. At first they were small fragments of letters, completely in keeping with the expected el-Amarna type, the remains of the diplomatic correspondence between two kings. These were the King of Egypt and the King of (C)Hatti. Therefore after a few days no doubt remained that we found ourselves on the site of the capital of the Kingdom of the Hittites (?) and that we had found the royal archives of the rulers of the Hittites at the time when they had been in contact with Egypt. This was at the time of el-Amarna and the period immediately following, that is 15-13 centuries BC. The first pieces did not yet contain the names of the kings in question. Also a fairly well preserved tablet, which spoke of a treaty between Egypt and (C)Hatti, did not name, as was usual, the kings concerned in the treaty, so that at first closer determination was not possible; that one had hoped to find something of the negotiations and treaties between Ramesses II and (C)Hatti referring to the big treaty between Ramesses II and 'Chetafar,' as he was then called, was self-evident, but to find something directly relevant to this, I had not dared to hope – being impermeated with the pessimism of experience, which showed that the facts never actually took the expected course.

This time, however, that which we did dare not hope for became fact. On the 20th August, after about twenty days' work, the trench which had been laid in the rubble of the mountain side had reached the first dividing wall. Under this was found a beautifully preserved tablet the appearance of which already gave a promising impression. One look at it, and all the experiences of my life paled into insignificance. Here was written what one had perhaps jokingly referred to as an idle wish: Ramesses wrote to Chattusil – *ci devant* Chetafar – of the two-sided treaty. Although during the last days more and more fragments were found concerning the treaty between the two states, only here was it actually confirmed that the famous treaty which one knew from the hieroglyphic record on the temple wall at Karnak had also been elucidated by the other side concerned in the treaty. Ramesses with his titles and his descent described in exactly the same words as those of the text of the treaty, writes to (C)hattusil, who is similarly recorded, and the contents of the writing follows word for word the paragraphs of the treaty. It is therefore not the actual final text of the treaty, but a letter written on this subject, perhaps the final version sent by the Egyptian side, which was used as a basis by the Hattians for the final treaty. As well as this a small fragment (of the beginning of the tablet in question) of a second copy of this letter was found. Like other important legal records it was therefore kept in duplicate in the archives.

They were strange feelings, those which I of all people experienced when I looked at such a document. Eighteen years had passed since I had got to know the Arzawa Letter of el-Amarna in the former Bulaq Museum and the language of the Mitanni in Berlin. At that time in consequence of the facts revealed by the find at el-Amarna I had ventured to suggest that also the Ramesses Treaty could originally have been written in cuneiform, and now I held in my hand one of the very letters which had been exchanged on this very subject – in the most beautiful cuneiform script and good Babylonian! It was truly a rare coincidence in the life of a man, how the first venture into oriental territory planned by the Egyptians had now found its confirmation in the heart of Asia Minor. As wonderful as a fairy story from the *1001 Nights* seemed such a coincidence – and yet the next year was to bring things even more fairy-tale-like, when all the documents were found in which those figures again reappeared who had so often occupied my attention in those eighteen years. As the King of the Mitanni, Tusratta, appeared in a Hattian elucidation and as even the Prince of Amuri, Arizu, the enemy of Rib-Addi of Byblos and the pike in the Phoenician goldfish pond, appeared in the documents, which must have acted as a commentary to his letters from el-Amarna! It was indeed a rare combination of circumstances in the life of one man . . . !

Nach Boghazköy, Der Alte Orient, vol. 14, part 3, 1913
Translated from the German by C. M. Kaine

Hrozný deciphers the
Hittite cuneiform

L. MATOUŠ

FRIEDRICH (BEDRICH) HROZNÝ (*1879-1952*) *was born at Lysa nad Labem in Bohemia, and studied in Prague, Vienna, Berlin and London. In 1904 he took part in an expedition to northern Palestine, and in the following year he was appointed a professor of Prague University. He was attracted by the problem of the Hittite cuneiform and was immersed in his study of their decipherment when he was interrupted by the outbreak of the First World War, and conscripted into the army. Fortunately for oriental scholarship his commanding officer sympathized with his ambitions and understood the importance of his work, and he was excused from active duty in order to continue his researches. Basing his interpretation on his belief in the Indo-European origin of the Hittite language, he published his decipherment and translation of the cuneiform in 1915. Many and virulent attacks were made on his work by other scholars, but when his solution was applied to a large number of Hittite documents, including an extensive legal code, it was amply vindicated. During the remainder of his brilliant scholastic career he took part in several more expeditions and continued his work on decipherment problems, including an unsuccessful attempt on Cretan Linear B.*

The year 1913 marks the end of the first period in Hrozný's career. As has been stated before, the cultural history which he was planning, would – had he written it then – have left many aspects of the interrelations of the various Near Eastern cultures unexplained. The interruption in his plans which this year marks was only apparent, and actually to the advantage of his later work. He knew that more urgent tasks were calling him in other fields, that a whole complex of problems demanded elucidation, without the solution of which he would not be able to achieve the final synthesis he had in mind. It was characteristic of his mental quality never to lose sight of his appointed goal, never to be frightened from his path by even the most formidable obstacles he might encounter.

What were these pressing problems? Since the decipherment of cuneiform writing by Grotefend and Rawlinson, sufficient information had been gleaned from Sumero-Babylonian clay tablets to give a picture of the history and cultural life of the ancient Babylonians and Assyrians, but the history of Asia Minor remained a sealed book. The only sources of information available were indirect ones – Assyrian and Babylonian documents, Egyptian hieroglyphic texts, and the Bible, while the written documents of the nations of Asia Minor themselves remained incomprehensible. As early as 1906, the Berlin Assyriologist, Hugo Winckler (who had been Hrozný's teacher during the latter's stay in Berlin in the autumn of 1901), had succeeded in excavating near the Turkish village Boghazkeui in Asia Minor, some 145 km north of Ankara, the ruins of the ancient capital of the Hittite kingdom, Khattushash. These contained the archives of the Hittite kings on some 1,300 cuneiform tablets in the, as yet unknown, Hittite tongue. The archives of Boghazkeui, however, were not the first extant examples of the Hittite language. It was soon shewn that the language used in these inscriptions was identical with that of the country *Arzava* (i.e. western Cilicia), of which two examples had been found in letters discovered in 1888 in the archives of Tell el-Amarna, containing the correspondence of the Egyptian pharaohs, Amenophis III and IV, with contemporary kings and princes of Asia Minor. In view of the absence of contextual material, however, these letters continued to prove undecipherable. It was well known, from the cuneiform documents of Babylonia, that the Hittites had played an important part in the history of Mesopotamia. Hittite armies had been a source of constant anxiety to the mighty Babylonian empire from the first half of the second millennium BC onwards, and the fall of the great Khammu-Rabi dynasty is attributed to them by the Babylonian chronicles. According to the Bible, Heth was the son of Canaan, and the Old Testament always mentioned Syria as the home of the Hittites. These meagre biblical data had been somewhat improved upon by Egyptian sources, where the Hittites are mentioned in documents of the 18th to 20th dynasties, i.e. from 1500 to 1190 BC. It is quite clear, however, that on the strength of these indirect and fragmentary sources of information our ideas of the Hittites were incomplete and quite inadequate.

The task of elucidating the mysterious language of this unknown nation, which had lived in Asia Minor in the second millennium BC and which had left behind such vast numbers of cuneiform inscriptions in the Boghazkeui archives, can thus be seen as one of prime importance.

The work was facilitated somewhat by the fact that the cuneiform script could be read – though the language which it served to express had so far withstood all attempts at interpretation. Before Hrozný, the Berlin Assyriologist, Dr Weidner, Prof. Böhl of Gronhingen, and the discoverer of the archives, Hugo Winckler himself, had been working at this task. Hrozný offered to collaborate with the latter as early as 1910, but could not fully devote himself to this task, being engaged on his work on Babylonian wheat. It was only after this was completed and he had been officially commissioned (after Winckler's death in 1914) by the Berlin Oriental Society to publish the Hittite archives, that Hrozný really began his work of decipherment. Only the smaller portion of the inscriptions was in Berlin – the majority were kept at the Constantinople museum. In addition to the already mentioned Dr Weidner, Prof. Delitzsch had also been working on the Berlin inscriptions, as well as Dr O. Weber. Hrozný was not sent to Constantinople until April 1914, shortly before the outbreak of the Great War, in order to copy the inscriptions there together with the Berlin Assyriologist Dr Figulla, who had been working there since January 1, 1914. In order to make up for this delay, Hrozný did not lose a moment in copying inscriptions for the planned edition; at the same time he transcribed a number of tablets which he did not intend to publish, but which he required in connection with his work of decipherment. He spent his days copying tablets at the Ottoman Museum above the Golden Horn, and at night, often far into the early hours, he transcribed Hittite texts in his flat at Moda, on the Asiatic shore of the Marmorian Sea. The words thus transcribed he grouped into alphabetical dictionaries; not only by initials, but also by their endings, *a tergo* – this being an indispensable condition for the elucidation of unknown grammatical forms. The war caught him in the middle of this grinding labour, towards the end of August 1914, and necessitated his immediate return to Vienna. By then he had however already copied a sufficiently large number of inscriptions to continue his work, the fruits of which he presented to the public a year later.

The method which he adopted in deciphering this unknown tongue is not without interest. He chose for a starting point unilingual inscriptions which had to be elucidated on their own. There were, it is true, bilingual and even trilingual Hittite-Babylonian-Sumerian vocabularies, published in 1914 by Prof. Delitzsch, but their use offered too little opportunity of penetrating into the grammatical structure of the language. Hrozný found important aid, however, in proper names and

Sumero-Babylonian ideograms, i.e. cuneiform characters expressing complete words (word-pictures). It should be remembered that the Hittites, in taking over cuneiform spelling from the Babylonians, also adopted, not only ideograms, but entire words, which they spelt phonetically. Such word-pictures and loan-words often helped to elucidate the meaning of entire sentences. Adopting the method of combination, comparing phrases and meanings, progressing from the known to the unknown, Hrozný soon succeeded in understanding the structure of the tongue and in assigning it a place in the family of languages.

His starting point was the sentence: '*nu NINDA-an ezzateni vâdar-ma ekutteni*'. The only known factor here was the Sumero-Babylonian ideogram *NINDA*, meaning 'bread'. From examples in other places Hrozný established that the suffix *-an* was the termination of the Accusative Sing. Hrozný guessed correctly, as it turned out, that a sentence which gave emphasis to the word 'bread' might reasonably be expected to include the meaning 'to eat', which could be contained only in the word '*ezzateni*'. Since other passages had shown the suffix *-teni* to be the ending of the 2nd person pl. pres. or fut., he could venture a translation of the first half of the sentence: 'You (will) eat bread'. The structure of the second sentence was clearly parallel with the first, hence, if the noun corresponding the *NINDA* was *vâdar* – which might mean 'water', – then the verb on which the noun was dependent could only be '*ekutteni*' which in that case should mean 'drink'. Hrozný could now venture a reading of the entire sentence – '*Now you will eat bread, further you will drink water*'.

Hrozný at once identified the Hittite root '*ad-*', '*-ez*', contained in '*ezza-teni*', with the Latin '*edo*', the German '*essen*', the Old German '*ezzan*', i.e. with the roots of the Indo-European group, which included the family of Slav languages, the Germanic, Latin languages, etc. Similar affinities could be detected in the words of the second sentence also. The Hittite '*vâdar*' seemed related to the English 'water', the Czech '*voda*', and the root '*e(a)ku-*' contained in the word '*ekutteni*' – 'you (will) drink' revealed an affinity with the Latin '*aqua*'. The Indo-European character of the Hittite language was also shown clearly in its general structure, as in comparison of the personal pronouns – '*uga, ug*', 'I' and the Latin '*ego*', the Hittite '*kûish*', 'who', and the Latin '*quis*'. Another important characteristic was the declension of nouns and the conjugation of verbs, where especially the participles in '*-nt*' and the medio-passive forms in '*-ri*' point to the corresponding

Latin forms. Later detailed analysis showed that the general structure of the language placed it in the West Indo-European 'Kentum' group, i.e. in the same division as the Greek, Latin and Germanic languages.

Recognition that Hittite belonged to Indo-European stock was no mean surprise for Hrozný. That he had almost excluded this possibility is shown by the fact that among the books which he took to Constantinople, Indo-European philology was represented only by the small and quite inadequate manual by Meringer, from the Göschen collection. When Hrozný announced his conclusions for the first time at a meeting of the Near Eastern Society in Berlin, on November 24, 1915, they gave rise to a discussion lasting far into the night. In general, his conclusion that Hittite was an Indo-European language, was received with great scepticism. Attention was drawn in particular to the non-Indo-European physical character of the Hittite race, which, with its great curved nose and backwards sloping forehead seemed close to the 'Armenoid' type. The suggestion was made that Hittite was a Caucasian language, and Weidner even considered it closely related to Gruzinian. The most ferocious of Hrozný's opponents were Professors Bartholomae and Bork. On the other hand, Hrozný's lecture – repeated on November 16th at Vienna University under the aegis of the Eranos Vindobnensis Society, and published the same year under the title *'Die Lösung des hethitischen Problems'* (The solution of the Hittite problem) – was received by the press in Germany as well as in Austria with great respect, and commented upon as 'a milestone in the history of Indo-European philology and archaeology'. It must be admitted also that Hrozný's conclusions were often attacked on pettyfogging grounds. Thus, one comparative philologist refused even to consider his arguments, because Hrozný had claimed that the Hittite word *'vâdar'* was spelt with a long first syllable – which on the strength of the rules of comparative philology, he declared to be altogether inadmissible.

On December 1, 1915, Hrozný was called up for service with the Vienna Garrison Regiment, where, in view of his extreme shortsightedness, he served until the end of the war as a clerk. His superior officers showed unusual sympathy and understanding for his extra-military interests and made it possible for him to devote several hours daily to his Hittitological studies. Thus Hrozný was able to publish even before the end of the war at Leipzig the first grammar of the Hittite language, under the title *'Die Sprache der Hethiter, ihr Bau und ihre Zugehörigkeit zum indogermanischen Sprachstamm'* (The language of the Hittite, its structure and its membership of the Indo-Germanic stock). In this for the first time he published his conclusions as a systematic grammar and defined the position of Hittite within the Indo-European group – surely a remarkable achievement, if we remember that he had succeeded, within a mere three years, in doing what so many before him had tried to do in vain. He had solved the mystery of this strange tongue, the oldest Indo-European language so far known.

In order to prove the truth of his theories, Hrozný at once began a systematic translation of Hittite religious and historical inscriptions, which appeared at Leipzig in 1919 as '*Hethetische Keilschrifttexte aus Boghazköi in Umschrift und Übersetzung*' (Hittite cuneiform inscriptions from Boghazkeui in transcription and translation). The number of opponents and sceptics gradually grew smaller, and Indo-European philologists began to recognise the truth of his theories of Hittite as a Kentum language and of his readings and interpretations and of his view of Hittite grammar. The first to take Hrozný's side was the Norwegian philologist Marstrander in 1919. The following year, the German Indo-European philologist F. Sommer came to the conclusion, after many doubts, that Hittite was Indo-European in structure, but that its vocabulary was drawn mainly from indigenous Asia Minor sources. After this the number of Hrozný's followers grew steadily, and today there is not one among serious Indo-European scholars to doubt the truth of his interpretation. A just tribute was paid to Hrozný by the Professor of Hittitology at Leipzig University, Friedrich: '*Hrozný's name will always have an honourable place at the head of Hittit-ological studies. He saw and understood the basic characters of Hittite declension and inflexion so correctly that on the foundation laid by him others could build. It is not surprising in the work of a pioneer that he should occasionally make mistakes in the identification of forms. Hrozný, as the discovering genius, and Sommer as the careful methodician, are, as it were, the twin poles of Hittite philology*'. Thanks to Hrozný's brilliant pioneer labour, therefore, Hittitology quickly grew into an independent branch of philology and served to bring new light into the history of Asia Minor in the second millenium BC.

Bedrich Hrozný: The Life and Work of a Czech Oriental Scholar, 1949

Excavations at the Black Mountain

HELMUTH BOSSERT

HELMUTH BOSSERT (1889-1962) was born in Landau and educated at the Universities of Heidelberg, Strasbourg, Freiburg and Munich. For some years he remained a private scholar, concentrating his interest upon Near Eastern studies, but in 1934 he accepted the appointment of Professor of Near Eastern languages and culture at the University of Berlin, and at the same time became Director of the Institute for the exploration of Near Eastern languages and culture at the University of Istanbul. He led many expeditions in the field and made extensive studies of the Hittite hieroglyphs. Since 1947 he directed the excavation of the Hittite remains at Karatepe.

The exploration in Anatolia undertaken in summer 1945 by the Institute for Research in Ancient Oriental Civilisations of the University of Istanbul (the staff of the expedition, consisting of Prof. H. Th. Bossert, his assistants Dr Halet Çambel, Nihal Ongunsu and Muhibbe Darga, were accompanied by Bay Ali Riza Yalgin of the Direction of Antiquities from Ankara), led us along the road over the Taurus pass connecting Kayseri with south-eastern Anatolia and North Syria over Gezbel, Saimbeyll, Feke, Kozan and Ceyhan. Our aim was to determine as far as possible, the ancient Hittite road at the time of the New Hittite Empire. On our way we seized every opportunity of getting information from the inhabitants about possible Hittite monuments in the vicinity. In this way we collected a number of pieces of information which seemed worth while examining. Among others was a rumour about a supposedly Hittite lion-relief worked on the rock, somewhere in the mountainous region east of Kadirli. It being already very late in the season, we were unable to check this information right away and had to postpone the matter until the next year.

When, in February 1946, our group (composed of the same members) came into the same region – thanks to the helpfulness of Bay Hüsameddin Arkan, Director of Public Instruction in Adana – we felt it our duty to check the accuracy of this story; and in spite of the bad condition of the roads, impassable for motor-cars because of heavy rains during the past few days, we decided to set out for the mountainous region beyond Kadirli. Considering the difficulties of the trip under these conditions and the vagueness of our information, everybody tried to dissuade us from this undertaking and we ourselves were fully aware of the fact that though most rumours have some grain of truth in them, the whole matter could still prove to be a complete disappointment, for the relief in question might well be a Roman monument, especially since remains of this epoch are not at all rare in the region of Kadirli. After due deliberation we decided to continue our investigations in two different directions and to separate into two groups, of which one, consisting of Nihal Ongunsu and Muhibbe Darga, were to set out for Adana and thence to the Mersin region, while the other, consisting of myself and Dr Halet Çambel as well as Bay Naci Kum, Director of the Adana Museum, who had joined our group in the meantime and was kind enough to accompany us, were to set out for Kadirli.

On February 27 at 1 p.m. the three of us left Kozan in a horse-cart. At first the roads were fairly good and while we were crossing a not very high chain of hills no considerable difficulty was encountered. Having reached the village Koseli, in the plain east of this mountainous chain, however, we heard from the peasants that, owing to heavy rains, the road to Kadirli led through very swampy territory. We were therefore obliged to send back to Kazan our cart-driver who, besides not knowing the roads, had brought along horses in such poor condition that they could not be expected to overcome the difficulties of a march through swampy land; and we had to get a better one before it got too late in the day. With the kind assistance of the villagers this proved possible, and after a few minutes a new cart with strong horses was ready. A little beyond Koseli, after we had passed through the village Karaömerli and had inspected for pot-sherds the 'Mustafa Alinin Hüyügü' which lies close to the road, we found that the main road had completely disappeared in swampy territory, and we were very glad that we had got this new driver, who, through a labyrinth of cart-tracks, brought us safe and sound to Kadirli, in spite of darkness having set in in the meantime and in spite of an accidental fall into a ditch.

It was after 7.30 p.m. when we pulled up before the municipal office of Kadirli, where the local authorities, who in the meantime had been notified by telephone of our arrival, were already expecting us. They very kindly invited us to dine with them, and during the excellent dinner that was served right there in the town hall, we had the opportunity of talking to the *kaymakam* of Kadirli Bay Münir Alkan, Bay Ibrahim Savrun (the head of the municipality), Bay Tevfik Coşkun (a member of the municipal council) and Bay Hilmi Inan, the headmaster of the primary school of Kadirli. We explained our plans to them and asked them to give us more information about the lion-monument in question, Unfortunately none of these gentlemen had ever seen or heard about it, so that at first we felt quite depressed and disappointed. But, not losing hope altogether, we asked if there was not anybody in Kadirli who knew the region well, who had wandered around and might thus have come across our monument. Bay Ekrem Kuşçu, teacher at the primary school of Kadirli for the last 20 years, who was said to have wandered more than once all around the region, was described as being such a man. He was sent for immediately, arrived after a short while, and could, to our great joy, give us very exact information about the monument, which, he said, he had visited four times in the course of the years 1927-44.

According to what he told us, the lion-monument was not a rock-relief but a sculpture in the round, a lion-base. On it had stood, originally, the statue of a man; but the statue had fallen down and lost its head in the course of the years. The body was covered with a cuneiform inscription all over. The monument, he said, was about 5-5½ hours on horseback to the east of Kadirli, on top of a wooded elevation which was part of a long, wood-covered mountain called Karatepe. All around were lying fragments of stones with remnants of writing and reliefs. All these were worked in a kind of black stone which was not naturally to be found in the vicinity, and the stones must have been brought from a pretty great distance. Besides this, a very great number of similar black stones lay dispersed on the opposite side of the Ceyhan river, which flows past the Karatepe; and these, surely, could be nothing but the remains of an ancient city belonging to the castle. Bay Ekrem told us further that, according to the information he had obtained from the peasants, the statue, including the head, was still standing 60 years ago. We were, of course, curious to know if the teacher had found this remote monument by chance or if he had heard about it through the peasants. Thereupon he told us that his attention had been drawn to the monument in 1927 by the then 80-year-old Abdullah (who died in 1932), son of Vahab and father of the actual *muhtar* of Kizyusuflu (a village lying between the Karatepe and Kadirli). He went on to tell us the following story: in 1915 a wise *hodja* came to Kizyusuflu and stayed for two months as a guest at Abdullah's house. Unable to pay back his host for his hospitality, he proposed to give him the benefit of his wisdom by helping him in the discovery of a treasure. 'Show me a place', he said, 'and I will find a treasure for you'. Abdullah thereupon led him to the lion-monument, but the *hodja* explained that this was the funeral monument erected by his men to a king torn to pieces on a lion-hunt by the lion, and therefore, he declared, no treasure was to be found there, Abdullah must lead him to another place. Thereupon he led him to Bodrum, lower down on the Ceyhan river; but whether they found the treasure or not we do not know.

Bay Ekrem told us further that, except for the peasants and himself and one man from Mersin whom he knew, nobody, and in particular no expert, had yet visited this ancient site. He himself had in his time told Bay Ali Riza Yalgin, then Director of the Adana Museum, about it, but had not led him there. Bay Ali Riza, with whom we discussed the matter later, confirmed what the teacher had said – Ali Riza had been to Kadirli in the spring of 1939 to study the habits of the Turcomans of the region and had met the teacher on that occasion. Bay Ali Rizi drew our attention to an article entitled 'The Turcomans of Kadirli' published in the Türksözü appearing in Adana of April 19, 1939, where, basing himself on the oral information of the teacher, he writes: '. . . With all this, Kadirli is capable of giving us monuments of older epochs too. But these are up in the mountains and in an untransportable state. The ruins of Karatepeli on the Ceyhan river in particular may be considered among the more important ones worth while examining.'

On the strength of all this information we decided to ride out to the monument the next day, and we asked the teacher to be so kind as to guide us, which he readily agreed to do. Thanks to the hospitality of Bay Ibrahim Savrun and Tevfik Coşkun and their families, we spent a very restful night at Kadirli.

The next day at 8.30 a.m. the necessary number of horses stood ready in front of the town hall and we set out without delay. On the map, which we owe to the courtesy of the foresters at the District Forest Department of Kadirli, our marching-route is indicated by a line of dots and dashes. It led us at first in roughly eastern direction through a valley and up into the mountainous region, and then, always following the crest of the mountainous range, turned southeastwards at Döğüş-gedigi towards the Karatepe, a black mountain which could be seen in the distance. The way was quite practicable for the horses, though it consisted only of a narrow path. Favoured by the finest spring-weather we rode through budding shrubs, bushes, and low pines and after $3\frac{1}{2}$ hours reached Kizyusuflu, a village of widely scattered houses. There we obtained receptacles to contain the water for wetting the squeeze paper. One of the villagers, Haci Aga, accompanied us on foot. Always following the crest of the hills, we rode happily on and on, with a marvellous view of the snow-covered heights of the Anti-Taurus on the east and, to the south, the Amanus, which we had crossed only a few weeks ago. Our path now gradually descended into a valley and, after passing over another elevation, led us down to the Akyol (pronounced Agyol by the peasants). This is a very old caravan route still used by the inhabitants of the region when moving to and from their summer pastures. Before us now lay a densely wooded long mountain with a maximum height of approximately 500 m. This was the Karatepe, on the northern-most but lower spur of which the lion-monument was to be found.

The ascent to this place on a narrow shepherd's path did not offer any difficulty. In 15 minutes' time we had reached the summit and before us lay the ruins of the destroyed royal Hittite castle.

II

Not far from the place where the shepherd's path had led to the summit of the hill, the lion-monument we had been searching for was lying, overthrown. This base, which showed a relief of two lions held by a standing man, seemed not to be *in situ* and had probably originally been standing on a level place worked into the natural rock, not far away. The human statue belonging to it lay overthrown near by. Its head was missing and no fragments that might have belonged to it were visible, at least in the immediate vicinity. The statue was lying on its face; the rather smooth back was covered with a 20-line Old Aramaic inscription. Beginnings of lines on the front side, visible even without turning over the statue, showed that here another inscription had been engraved. Taking into consideration the great weight of the statue and the fact that the ground underneath was very rocky, we did not think it advisable to try and turn it over, for the probability of damaging the excellently preserved back would have been too great. The front part of the statue had been damaged already, probably at the moment of being violently thrown down from its base; and it is even possible that a fragment bearing an Old Aramaic inscription, lying near by, is a part of it. The first question that arose now, was whether we should try to copy the inscription on the back or whether we should do better, taking into consideration that we had only three hours at our disposal, to start with the squeezes immediately after taking the necessary photographs. As the inscription was partly covered with algae, which would not have everywhere permitted a sure reading without previous cleaning, it seemed preferable to start right away with the squeezes, even at the risk that, owing to the season, they might not get completely dry.

While one of us (H. Çambel) got busy with the photos and squeezes, the other (H. Th. Bossert) started to look for more remnants of inscribed or sculptured stones. Though it was rather hard to search, because of the thorny thickets abounding all around, the fact that the stones used for inscriptions and sculptures were blacker in colour and harder than the natural stone of the Karatepe mountain, was of great help. First, the movable stones in the immediate vicinity of the lion-base, which had partly sunk into the ground, were turned and a number of inscribed and sculptured fragments were thus exposed. Though the sculptures were, with one exception, very badly smashed, some, at least, could still be identified as 'Hittite' reliefs, which seemed to be in a style even more rustic than that of the reliefs of Zincirli and Islahite. Most of them had probably been part of such orthostats as are known from other Hittite buildings. Such a representation, as the three birds placed one above the other, in spite of all its naïvity, seems to suggest that new designs may be found on this site too. Some of the most important finds were, however, the fragments of Hittite hieroglyphic inscription, for nowhere hitherto have Old Aramaic and Hittite hieroglyphic stone inscriptions been found side by side. While the Old Aramaic inscriptions of Karatepe are, as far as we know today, all incised, there seems to be at least one among the hieroglyphic inscriptions which shows very careful relief-work. As far as the character of the hieroglyphic incised inscriptions can be judged, they seem to belong approximately to the same epoch as the Old Aramaic ones. Another great surprise was the discovery of a very small inscribed fragment, which, though bearing only a very few letters, could be identified as of the *boustrophedon* type. No such Aramaic inscriptions have been recognised up to now and there is no reason to believe that any such existed. It is therefore very probable that this inscription was not written in the Old Aramaic language, but rather in some non-semitic language, using Old Aramaic characters. Still further, we found the breast-fragment of another statue (?) bearing an Old Aramaic inscription, which we did not deem necessary to depict in this preliminary report, as only a very few letters were left visible on it.

Most of the finds made in this short time were clustered round the lion-base. On the remaining parts of the hill-top a great many stone fragments of the same type were noticed, but these seemed not to bear any kind of inscription or decoration, though this of course may have been merely accidental. Owing to the shortness of the time and the thickness of the bushes, which made it difficult to move about, the slopes and the foot of the hill could not be examined thoroughly, though in all probability numerous inscribed and sculptured fragments are still to be found there. Nevertheless, a column-base, evidently not *in situ*, of the same type as those of Zincirli, but without any plastic decoration, was noticed on the slope; and remains of a violently destroyed citadel wall were encountered at different spots. It should moreover be noted, that, approximately at the centre of the hill-top, a rocky formation could still be seen, from which the stone for the building of the citadel had evidently been taken. Two ditches, one in the vicinity of the lion-base, the other one nearer the border of the hill-top, bore witness to the fact that peasants or shepherds had now and then searched for treasure on the Karatepe . . . Pot-sherds were also looked for, but since the natural rock is very near the surface on the hill-top, rains have probably washed most of the sherds down the slopes and only a very few small, weathered pieces of a buffish earthenware could be found, which gave no clue whatsoever as to shape, type or epoch.

The woodiness of the territory prevented us from getting a view of the city ruins on the other side of the river. These ruins probably belonged to the Karatepe citadel. It was only from the top of a tree that a photograph could be taken of the area where the ruins are said to lie. Time being short and the Ceyhan river being very wide at this time of the year, it was not possible to get across to inspect the ruins.

It was now gradually getting dark and our guides were in a hurry to leave. The squeezes were far from being dry and the only thing we could do was to take them down carefully and dry them over a fire. We then packed them into a tin case, loaded the smaller fragments into our saddle-bags for subsequent deposition in the Adana Museum, and, having made a last photo of our group, set out for night quarters at Molla Mehmet's house in Kizyusuflu, 1½ hours' ride away.

The remains of inscriptions, reliefs, statues and the citadel wall which we left behind and which slowly disappeared from view, were solid witnesses that a new Hittite site had been won for science.

Karatepe, 1946

The Royal Residence on the 'River of Nymphs' (Nymphaios)

FRIEDRICH DÖRNER

FRIEDRICH KARL DÖRNER (*1911-*) *was born in Gelsenkirchen in Germany, and educated at the University of Greifswald, where he specialized in ancient history, classics and archaeology. He travelled extensively in the eastern Mediterranean region, and first came to Kommagene in Syria in 1938. He is a member of the German Archaeological Institute at Berlin and Istanbul, and of the Austrian Academy of Sciences, and has taught at the University of Tübingen. Since 1950 he has held the post of Professor of Ancient History at the University of Münster. It was in 1951 that he discovered the royal palace of Arsameia at Kommagene, and has been digging there ever since.*

The discovery of the Kommagenian royal residence of Arsameia on the River of the Nymphs was not a chance find but is the result of a systematic examination of the Kommagenian cultural region on the Upper Euphrates in the magnificent mountain world of the Antitauros. There are only a few references to this region in ancient literature. It makes its first appearance in the annals of the Assyrian kings, in which it is recorded that the rulers of Kummhi (Kommagene) were to deliver tribute to Assyria, and above all, the valuable cedar tree-trunks, then much in demand. Apparently Kummhi was then, in the reign of Sarrukin (Sargon) II, who reigned from 721 to 705, annexed to the Assyrian Empire.

Although the land, on account of its important crossing-points of the Euphrates, must have played a great role in respect of the connections between North Mesopotamia and the coast of the Mediterranean, and although its position was also very important for the traffic to the land route to Asia Minor, we hear nothing more of its history in the course of the following centuries. Kommagene is not mentioned again in the historical records until the first century BC, when the Romans tried to push their eastern boundary towards their Parthian enemies. It is understandable that these sources – written from a Roman point of view – do not contain much favourable comment on a country whose rulers tried to uphold their political and cultural independence in the fight between the Roman Empire and the Parthian kingdom.

To these ancient records was added an unhoped-for, lively increase of information, the results of a German expedition which went to Kommagene in 1883 under the leadership of Karl Humann and Otto Puchstein. The two scholars had been commissioned by the Academy of Sciences in Berlin to investigate the necropolis of the Kommagenian king, Antiochus I, which this ruler had erected for himself on one of the peaks of the Antitauros. It was proved that the fantastic-sounding accounts which the German engineer, Karl Sester, had sent to Berlin before anyone else, had not been exaggerations. A Town of the Dead did indeed exist on Nemrud Dagh, more than 2000 metres up, built by Antiochus 'as near as possible to the Heavenly Thrones'. One special find was the discovery there of a monumental inscription, a unique contemporary record, in which Antiochus had let his religious ideas be recorded for posterity. It was no less astonishing to see the king as the creator of a religion whose elements were those of the religions of the Greek and Persian worlds. In front of the more than 50 metres high burial mound the king had had himself represented in the circle of native gods – in monumental proportions, which the rulers of the east loved, stern and immovable, like the lifeless chunks of cliff on the mountain landscape.

In the publication of the results of their journey Humann and Puchstein expressed the wish that an intensive exploration should be instigated. But the sensational excavations on the west coast of Asia Minor came overpoweringly to the fore. They were, above all, much more easily accessible than the lonely, impassable mountain region. So it was more than half a century before scholarly interest in Kommagene was again aroused.

My first expedition to Kommagene, which I undertook in 1938 together with R. Naumann, unfortunately remained no more than a short prelude. But during all the war years I never forgot the promise which I had made to myself and to my local companions to return for new research work.

In 1951 I actually got there, and immediately, in the first days of the exploration, I was lucky enough to find the royal residence of Arsameia on the River of the Nymphs. We had already struck camp before sun-up and reached, after a long ride over a sun-scorched treeless high plateau, the little village of Alut. How good it was to stretch out on the colourful, hand-woven carpets which had been laid out in welcome for us by the villagers next to an ice-cold spring under shady trees. Quickly we unpacked our provisions; added to these by our hosts were fresh yoghurt and marvellous grapes. Then began the usual oriental word-play of From where and Where to. When the villagers heard from me that I was searching for the sites of ancient ruins, the Turkish name for the mountain which lay near by was mentioned for the first time: Eski Kale (i.e. Old Castle) where a 'Picture Stone' had been dug out. I was eager to examine this locality more closely; but, as is so often the case in the East, I had to fight my impatience; for Nuri, who seemed to know most about Eski Kale, had no desire at all to play the guide in the scorching heat and to show me the narrow track up to the steep heights. He suggested that we should wait for the cool of the evening here at the spring. So I saw the legend-surrounded castle hill for the first time in the light of the setting sun. Its slopes fell down steeply and precipitously on all sides; only from the south was an approach possible. But where was the castle which had given its name to this bleak, bare slope? I looked round in vain for traces of walls or for the remains of the fortifications. When I asked Nuri why this mountain had been named 'Old Castle', he just shrugged his shoulders and said in a circumspect manner, 'That's what my grand-father already called it.'

All the same I was eager to have a look at the 'Picture Stone'. It must have quite recently been excavated and left lying where it was found by peasants who were looking for stone for house-building, because it had been too heavy to get down into the valley. A prelimin-ary glance showed me that the piece in question was a fragment of a relief of Kommagene times showing the Persian god of light, Mithras, wearing a great crown of rays, the first important clue to the meaning of the 'Old Castle'!

With redoubled zest I searched further and soon discovered that the south flank had once been terraced and that when the walls had been destroyed they had buried all the buildings under them. An exposed, artificially flattened rock wall attracted my attention especially.

Could it be possible that the rock walls had not merely been worked but had also been covered with inscriptions? Momentarily it seemed as though this was so. In my excitement I came up closer to the rock and looked at it from the front, the light of the setting evening sun on my back; I could still see nothing more than a very cracked, shattered, grey wall of rock. Disillusioned, I turned away. It was obviously only my imagination which had been deceiving me. But then I suddenly saw something! In the slanting light, which came from the side, appeared the vertical and horizontal lines of letters, only very faintly recognisable, between the weatherbeaten marks of the stones. Excitedly I called for pick-axe and spade and there and then began to dust the lines of letters with my handkerchief and to clear away the earth from the wall of rock with my hands. Before the tools had been passed up to me I had already confirmed my guess: I stood before an inscription written in Greek letters.

The first blows of the pick-axe cleared away the rubble which had protected the letters on the lower level from destruction and weathering. More beautiful and undamaged than I had dared hope, the inscription emerged from the protecting soil. In the days which followed I tried to get rid of the rubble which had accumulated in front of the wall of rock. A first attempt at reading the letters showed that I had in front of me the end of an inscription arranged in several columns which, judging by the type of letters, belonged to the time of King Antiochus, i.e. the first half of the first century BC.

Of course I immediately tried to push forward to the beginning of the inscription. But this proved to be a difficult task because of the enormous amount of rubble. When eventually a third column followed the second, I was as happy about my discovery as I was despairing at the impossibility of penetrating any farther into the huge heaps of rubble of the terrace. But improvisation is the great art of every exploration! I therefore decided not to attempt a complete clearance but to grope my way along the rock wall along a tunnel. Luckily there was a bend in the wall after the fourth column, so that it now ran parallel with the slope. With the fifth column I had eventually found the beginning of the inscription.

Like the royal inscription on Nemrud Dagh, which it in many ways resembled, this inscription was also carved at the command of King Antiochus of Kommagene. In elevated language, beautifully written, the king here announced that his royal father, Mithradates Kallinikos, had chosen this place as his Hierothesion – i.e. as his sacred resting-place: he decreed that here a cult for both father and son should be practised, for which he was leaving exact instructions.

Luckily the king also makes reference to the site in the inscription. He praises the excellent location, for a fortification, which had led his ancestor Arsames to have a fortress built and a town founded, which in all times of need should be a reliable retreat for the royal house. Arsames had called the town Arsameia on the River of Nymphs in honour of himself and here 'in the suburbs of Arsameia' his father, in compliance with his own wishes, had been buried.

Had I not been firmly convinced that an excavation of the royal residence of Arsameia and the search for the royal tomb had great significance for our historical knowledge, and had I not had the confidence that we must succeed in the realisation of this plan, I would early have despaired of the immense difficulties. But where there is a will there is a way. It took two years until all the expert evidence had been given and the first excavation budget had been sanctioned by all the relevant parties. The Turkish Government had also given its permission for the excavations to be done at Arsameia on the River of the Nymphs, and so, in the autumn of 1953 and also 1954, I was able to carry out the excavation.

Of course our work was concentrated on the area of the Hierothesion of King Mithradates Kallinikos. The king's large inscription was completely uncovered; with this we found the magnificent relief with the scene of King Mithradates and the God Herakles greeting each other. Because of the quality of the work this find excels all other reliefs so far found in Kommagene and is of importance in the history of art as an excellent example of the reinterpretation which Hellenistic culture experienced in the oriental sphere.

But where was the king's tomb itself? Was it perhaps inside the castle hill? We had, in fact, beneath the third column, come up against a rounded arch hewn out of the rock which formed the entrance to a carefully worked rock passageway, within which a flight of rock steps led into the depths at an angle of inclination of 35-45 degrees.

The excavation of these presented us with a very difficult technical problem; for the entrance to the rock had been taken through serious fractures in the rock in a number of places, and the ancient builders had, unperturbed by the sequence of hard and soft parts of the rock, continued the stepped passage-way in the same direction as that taken at the start, even if in doing so, soft sections of varying depths had to be penetrated. Judging by the fragments we found, someone had, in ancient times, done exactly what we were doing and had propped up these very dangerous places with wooden supports. After each such disturbed section we always rediscovered the continuation of the rock passage and were eventually able to penetrate to a depth of 115 metres. But in the middle of a loamy layer we had to break work off, in autumn 1954, because of lack of the right technical equipment, so that the question of whether the passage really led to the tomb of King Mithradates or had served some other purpose within the sanctuary, still remained unanswered.

Simultaneously work on other parts of the southern slope was also in process, where we excavated a series of foundations of pedestals, some of which bore fragments of their reliefs. We also obtained important results from the excavation of the cultural levels on the heights of the mountain plateau. Here it was revealed that Eski Kale had also been inhabited in post-Kommagenian times until up to the middle ages, but, on the other hand, had also been inhabited, far before the Hellenistic foundation of Arsames, back in pre-historic times. So Eski Kale unexpectedly emerged from the darkness of history as a favoured settlement in Kommagene, and we can hope that by the exploration of the castle mound we may increase our knowledge about eastern Asia Minor in its role as a connecting link between the Mediterranean countries and the highly developed cultures of Asia.

Die Königsresidenz am Nymphenfluss, 1956

Translated from the German by C. M. Kaine

The discovery of Ugarit

CLAUDE SCHAEFFER

CLAUDE FREDERICK ARMAND SCHAEFFER (*1898-*) *was born in Alsace, studied archaeology at the Universities of Strasbourg and Paris, and married the daughter of an eminent archaeologist. He has not only worked in museums and on expeditions in the field, but has served as a consultant in the interests of antiquity to such government bodies as the* Commission des Fouilles et Missions Archéologiques *and the National Council of Scientific Research. He has made great contributions to Aegean archaeology in his work at Enkomi in Cyprus and his excavation of the site of ancient Ugarit, now called Ras Shamra, which he at first mistakenly identified as Sapuna.*

The excavations at Minet el Beida and Ras Shamra, begun in 1929 and continued in 1930, were undertaken at the suggestion of M. René Dussaud, Member of the Institute and Conservator at the Louvre. The natural harbour of Minet el Beida (the White Bay) lies facing Cyprus; and it was this fact which gave M. Dussaud the idea of a Mycenaean colony from Cyprus importing thither the copper which had to be disembarked for transport to the interior and to Mesopotamia. This theory was supported by the fact that 1000 metres from the bay is a huge *tell* (mound), called by the natives Ras Shamra (Cape Samphire), which might well hide the ruins of this assumed sea-port.

In 1928 there came the accidental discovery of a burial-vault at Minet el Beida, of corbelled construction and containing Mycenaean and Cypriote pottery dating from the 13th century BC. This was the first confirmation of the theories about the antiquity of Minet el Beida and Ras Shamra. The Académie des Inscriptions et Belles-Lettres, at M. Dussaud's suggestion, sent out an expedition to locate the ancient harbour, town and cemeteries of Minet el Beida. The direction was entrusted to the present writer, who chose as his assistant M Chenet, well known on account of his excavations of the Roman kilns and glass-factories of the Argonne.

Our excavations near the bay have revealed an important cemetery containing several large rectangular tombs with corbelled vaults, approached through a short vestibule or forecourt with stairway, the whole carefully built of well worked stone blocks. One of these tombs was hidden under a rather important building, to judge from the columns with attached walling which are all that remain of it today and which are not easy to explain. Directly communicating with the tombs were other still more important buildings, one of which was completely cleared this year; it contained thirteen halls, rooms and passages, without counting the upper story whose staircase with its landing are preserved. This building is generously provided with wells and water-channels, all of which have been rendered useless by artificial filling or concrete covers. Upon and beside these wells, along the passages, in the rooms and at the foot of nearly every column, were placed votive offerings of painted Mycenaean and Cypriote vessels, ordinary pots and objects of bronze, silver and gold, such as pins, lamps, knives and daggers. They prove that the building cannot have served a merely utilitarian purpose. Perhaps it may be regarded as one of those houses of the dead like those which some Egyptian pharaohs had built beside their funeral vaults. The comparison is strengthened by the fact that the civilisation of Ras Shamra, as we shall see presently, borrowed much from that of the Nile Valley.

A still more important series of discoveries awaited us to the north of the tombs, towards the sea. Here, at a depth of between o m. 50 and 1 m. 50, near a roughly built room, lay about 80 deposits consisting of Cypriote, Mycenaean and local pottery, bronze implements and weapons, stone weights conforming in part to the Egyptian mina of 437 grammes, shells or just plain pebbles from the shore close by. There were also curious stone tablets, pierced steles and stone phalli, large and very life-like. The richest deposit, near the centre of the group, contained two horus-hawks in the Egyptian style; one of them, of bronze, bore the double crown of Lower and Upper Egypt, the other, of bronze and gold, held the Uraeus between its feet. Not far off lay a statuette representing a seated deity with eyes of silver and enamel, giving a benediction with its outstretched hand, according to the manner of certain Syrian gods. The chief object of the group is the statuette (25 cm. high) of the Syrian god Reshef (sometimes identified with Baal); it is of silvered bronze, and the head and high coiffure are formed of a leaf of gold. The god is represented standing; formerly in his right hand he brandished a thunderbolt or battle-axe, while in his left he held a sceptre or spear, as he appears in other representations from Ras Shamra.

Not far from the majestic Reshef lay his colleague, the goddess Astarte with the Hathor coiffure, holding the lotus in her hands. Her fair, slender form is artistically wrought in gold leaf. A necklace of quartz and carnelian beads completed the hoard.

We must imagine that this hoard and those near it had been buried in honour of some great persons, probably the kings of the adjacent city of Ras Shamra, laid to rest in the vaults we found close by.

The first vault, whose covering-slabs were almost level with the surface, had been plundered by natives. In the debris from it was recovered Cypriote and Mycenaean pottery of the 13th century, an engraved spatula and a bronze bracelet.

Vault No. 2 had served as a quarry since ancient times. The three upper courses of the fine corbelled vault and that of the stairway had been carried away; the vault itself, the votive-niches in the walls, and the little recess alongside had all been robbed. Arrowheads, bronze spatulae and some pottery found on the floor of the tomb show that like the rest it belongs to the late Mycenaean period, and may be assigned to the 13th century BC.

The third vault, which is almost intact, was also visited by robbers in bygone times. They entered through a hole in the roof, carried off whatever valuable metal objects there may have been in the tomb, and blocked up the hole again after leaving. Happily their visit was clandestine, and in spite of the disorder they left behind them part of the grave-goods, which were very sumptuous, remained undisturbed and they did not even enter the passage. It was by this way through the entrance of the tomb we went in, collecting the native offerings of pottery which were placed in the corner of each step, leaving the middle of the staircase free. They consisted of Canaanite terra cotta lamps, small conical vases, a fine Mycenaean crater with overlapping ornament and a magnificent intact Egyptian two-handled vase of alabaster. On the threshold of the fine door of the vault lay a well preserved human skull; it is difficult to say whether it belonged to an attendant who was sacrificed and buried at the entrance of his master's tomb, or whether it had been thrown there by the robbers when they broke into the vault.

The skeletons – at least four in number – had suffered at the hands of the robbers, the bones were scattered and the skulls broken. But in their haste the robbers failed to search thoroughly the corners of the vault, where they missed finding rings and beads of gold or of silver and iron –

then regarded as a precious metal – haematite cylinder-seals, faience and alabaster vases and, above all, oval ivory boxes, one of which has a splendidly carved lid. It represents the Goddess of Fertility (the 'potnia theron'), seated on a throne flanked by two he-goats, and it is indisputably the finest Mycenaean ivory actually known. The pottery dates this vault too to the late Mycenaean (13th century BC).

Our excavations on the northern projection of the mound of Ras Shamra brought to light a large temple with two rectangular courts joined together and enclosed by thick walls. We found fragments of life-size granite statues of gods which had once stood on raised stone pedestals in the court; their style is that of the end of the 18th dynasty (1580-1350). From a stele dedicated by Mami, royal clerk of the Treasury, to Baal of Sapouna, we get the ancient name of the town. This large temple of Egyptian character reveals the strong influence exercised by the pharaohs or even their political control of the land of Sapouna in the 14th and 13th centuries BC. Beside it we found several shrines of lesser importance which appear to have been devoted to the cult of local divinities, two of whose images we found. One, female, was mutilated; the other, male, was fortunately intact. It represents a god in a standing posture, with an Egyptian coiffure of ostrich-plumes; on the forehead grows a spiral horn; in the left hand is a spear, and in the right the *hiq* – a kind of sceptre presented by the Egyptians to foreign rulers. The god is clothed simply in a loin-cloth kept in position by a belt with a big-pommelled dagger; he wears leather-thonged sandals with toes pointed after the Hittite style.

Beside the temple, as at Nippur, stood a school or seminary where the young priests must have learnt Sumerian – the Latin of those times – and the other languages used at Sapouna; where also they learnt the difficult profession of a scribe. We found their exercises in cuneiform writing, their lists of Sumerian and Babylonian (Accadian) words, as well as regular bilingual dictionaries intended to assist them in reading and composing religious and diplomatic documents. A letter quite in the style of the well-known Amarna correspondence refers to alterations of the frontier between three hitherto unknown Syrian towns – Halbini, Hazilu and Panashtai.

But what gives outstanding importance to the cuneiform tablets found at Ras Shamra is the fact that most of them contain a script that is wholly unknown and which had already become alphabetic. Professor Bauer of Halle and Father Dhorme of the Ecole Biblique at Jerusalem recognised a Semitic language in these documents; and they have put forward a preliminary explanation of it. The complete deciphering and first translation of the new writing are the work of M. Charles Virolleaud, the learned Assyriologist, to whom I entrusted the publication of the documents of Ras Shamra. He has just made a communication to the Académie des Inscriptions et Belles-Lettres concerning these texts, a portion of which is composed in almost pure Phoenician and whose contents are of capital importance for the religious history of the East. The principal document is a kind of epic poem in which the chief character is called Taphon, and which consists, in its present state, of nearly 800 lines. Chief among the divinities are the goddess Anat and the god Alein, son of Baal; but there are more than 20 others, among whom are Asharat, Astarte, Dagon, El-Hokmot the god of wisdom, and Din-el the Justice of God. The bilingual glossary contains a very complete list of words and some Sumerian phrases; but instead of the Babylonian which is usually employed in these glossaries to translate Sumerian, the glossary of Ras Shamra contains a language totally unknown up to the present. M. Thureau Dangin, the distinguished Assyriologist, will shortly make known its significance. The number of documents we found this year gives ground for supposing that the school of scribes possessed an important library, containing amongst other things large tablets of three or four columns each, which encourage us to expect a fine harvest of new historical knowledge.

Below the floor of the library and all around it we made numerous discoveries: – silver and bronze cups, copper ingots, a vase full of silver objects, and above all a splendid collection of 74 bronze implements and weapons in an exceptionally fine state of preservation. It consists of 4 swords, 2 daggers, 25 flat axes, 11 spearheads, 3 arrowheads, 6 chisels, 4 sickles, a fine tripod ornamented with pomegranate-flowers. The most valuable objects are 5 large implements of unknown use and 9 socketed adzes (herminettes), five of which have cuneiform inscriptions punched upon them, probably dedications. The presence of two cakes of metal and the fact that several of the weapons are unfinished show that the workshop where they were made cannot have been far distant.

At a lower level, clearly separated from the one above it, which belongs to the 14th and 13th centuries, we brought to light a cemetery of the 17th and 16th centuries completely free from Mycenaean influence. The pottery belongs to native Canaanite types, with blackish or reddish slip, unpainted.

Penetrating to a yet lower depth, at 7 metres down we found crude brick walls belonging to buildings that stood here long before the existence of the overlying cemetery; these must go back to the beginning of the 2nd or even to the 3rd millennium. The investigation of them must necessarily be postponed until the two upper levels have been cleared.

The French Excavations in Syria, Antiquity, vol iv, no 16, 1930

Solomon's foundries

NELSON GLUECK

NELSON GLUECK (*1900-*) *is a man whose life has always been directed by his undeviating devotion to scholarship. He took degrees in archaeological, oriental and Hebrew studies at the Universities of Cincinnati, Berlin, Heidelberg, Jena, and Hebrew Union College, and many other institutions have presented him with their highest academic honours. He first went to Jerusalem in 1928 as Fellow of the American School of Oriental Research, and from 1932 onwards he has pursued his explorations of Palestine with an enthusiasm which was undeterred by the harsh conditions of desert archaeology. For a long time he persistently ignored the dangerous political hostilities latent in the area, but by 1952 it was no longer possible for a leading Jewish scholar to live and work in the Arab states, so he turned his attention to the apparently empty and barren region of the Negev, where his explorations have made great contributions to Biblical and Oriental studies.*

We are of course speaking from hindsight about the copper and iron products of the Arabah and Ezion-geber. To our immense surprise, the excavations demonstrated that while Ezion-geber was undoubtedly a seaport, it was no less important as an industrial centre. There were nails and timbers and resin and ropes, which had undoubtedly been used to build and repair ships. There were fishhooks and net-weights and piles of sea shells related to the extensive fishing that had obviously been carried on in the rich waters of the eastern arm of the Red Sea, which is a fisherman's paradise even today. There were, to be sure, no traces of docks, but perhaps we should not have expected any. It is highly possible that the Tarshish ships were little more than small *dhows*, which were anchored offshore. And when, at times, a sudden storm blew up, and their mooring lines did not hold, they could be dashed to shore and broken to pieces on the rocks in the shallows. That is exactly what happened, as we have seen, to Jehoshaphat's fleet, about the middle of the ninth century BC.

What puzzled us greatly when we first commenced operations at Tell el-Kheleifeh was what seemed to us to be the particularly unfortunate location of the site. Situated in the centre of the Arabah rift, which is banked on either side by high hills leading, respectively, into Arabia and Sinai, it is open to the full fury of the almost constant winds that blow fiercely down the Wadi Arabah, as if forced through a wind tunnel. The result is an endless series of sandstorms, frequently so severe as to obscure vision. The architects of Ezion-geber could not possibly have chosen a more inclement site along the entire shoreline. It was understandable why they had not built farther to the west where the soil was poor and the water was worse, being completely undrinkable by either man or beast. But why, we asked ourselves at first in irritation at having to work eat and sleep in frequent sandstorms, had they not chosen a site farther to the east at Nabataean Aila or Arabic Aqabah, where the water is excellent, the soil is fertile and the winds are tempered by the hills? We began digging at the northwest end of Tell el-Kheleifeh, in order at least to have our backs and not our faces turned to the biting winds and blinding sandstorms. In the meantime, we fumed and fussed at what seemed to be the folly of Solomon's town planners. Their seeming madness, however, was soon explained.

The very first building brought to light at the northwest corner of the mound turned out to be the largest and most elaborate smelter ever discovered in antiquity. Each of the walls of its rooms was pierced by two rows of carefully constructed apertures, which could only be flues. The upper rows were intended to permit the gases formed in one chamber to penetrate into the second and so on and preheat its contents. It was easy to reconstruct the smelting process. The ores were given a preliminary 'roasting' at the individual mining sites in the Wadi Arabah, and then brought for further smelting and refining to Ezion-geber. Layers of ore were placed between layers of lime in large, thick-walled pottery crucibles.

Piles of charcoal from the wooded hills of Edom were packed all around them in the open furnace rooms of the smelter, with the fires being ignited in successive order at proper intervals of time. No hand-bellows system was necessary, because with brilliant calculation, Solomon's engineer had harnessed the winds to furnish a natural draft. The Bessemer principle of forced-air draft, discovered less than a century ago, was, in essence, already familiar some three millennia back. So well had the smelter been constructed that, when it had been completely exposed, we could place our hands on the flue holes in the wall at the south end of the structure and feel the air emerging, which had entered through the flue holes on the north side, a number of rooms away.

It became more apparent than ever, as a result of our excavations, why Edom and Judah had fought so long and so bitterly with each other over the Arabah and Ezion-geber although the Bible, however, as I have already pointed out, passes over in complete silence one of the main reasons for the prolonged warfare between them. The copper and iron mines of the Arabah and the control of access to the Red Sea were as much a cause of inextinguishable rivalry between them as oil in Arabia and along the Persian Gulf is a source of competition and conflict among many nations today. Both for Edom and Judah, the command of the resources of the Arabah and of the highway which led through it and the control of Ezion-geber:Elath, with its industries and access to the Red Sea, were indispensable to their safety, economic well being and potentialities of growth.

The turnabout ownership of Ezion-geber:Elath is illustrated by two names, one Edomite and the other Hebrew, which we came across in the excavations of the city of Elath. Built by the Judaeans on the ruins of Ezion-geber, it had been captured from them by the Edomites (II Kings 16:6), with whom it exited from history. The Edomite name occurred in seal impressions on the handles of a whole store-room full of fine pottery jars. On the handle of every one of them was stamped the following inscription: 'Belonging to Qausanal the Servant of the King.' We know that Qausanal is a typical Edomite name, the first part of which, Quas, is the designation of a familiar Edomite, Nabataean and Arabian deity. It seems likely that this Qausanal, who was undoubtedly an Edomite, was the governor of the district of Elath when it was under Edomite dominion. He acted as the personal representative, that is, the 'servant' of the Edomite king of the time.

The other inscription was found in an earlier level of Elath, when it was still in Judaean hands. It was part of what turned out to be the only seal signet-ring of a Judaean king ever discovered thus far. And thereby hangs a tale. At the last minute of the last day of the last of the three seasons of our excavations, I decided to make a final farewell tour of the site. Our Arabic foreman, Abbas, made the rounds with me. Yielding to a sudden impulse, I asked him to tear down with his pick-axe a bit of mud-brick wall that we had left standing until it was measured and photographed. As he pushed it over, he saw a tiny object that had lain underneath it, and quickly picked it up. 'What have you there, Abbas?' I asked him. Instead of replying, he asked me if the system of paying *baksheesh* for every object found still held good even though the expedition were formally over.

I must explain here that we paid our workmen a special reward for every object found, related to its market value, whether it was a broken bead or an ivory fragment or a piece of gold. This was necessary to ensure that every object got into our hands rather than into those of dealers, whose rates, incidentally, we were always prepared to match. Instead of keeping accounts, we would pay each workman immediately for the things he had found and had turned over to the staff member supervising the section he worked in as a pick-man, shovel-man or basket boy. By the time everyone concerned had looked carefully through the earth being dug up and removed, there was very little of value that escaped attention. In addition, we sometimes put the debris of entire rooms through sieves to make this assurance doubly sure.

I told Abbas that I would be delighted to pay him *baksheesh*, even at this stage of the game. He persisted and asked if I were willing to pay as much as a shilling or two for what he held in his closed fist. 'Hand it over, Abbas,' I said to him. He gave it to me. I took a hurried look, stuck it into an inner pocket, and told him to hold out his hands in cupped form. With that, I emptied into them all the silver and paper money in my pockets. It may have been the equivalent of fifty dollars. It was a lot of money for that part of the world. I could easily have engineered a minor revolution with it. He looked at the heap of shillings and pounds, which was indeed a veritable fortune to him, and, after a moment, said to me: 'Ya Mudir (O Master), but I can't possibly take all that money from you.' I assured him that I thought what he had found was worth a good reward, and that anyway I had intended giving him a parting gift. He had been most faithful and helpful during the years we had worked together, and we had become good friends. We embraced and took leave of each other, he back to Aqabah and the rest of us to our cars on the way to Amman and Jerusalem.

As soon as possible, I examined the find. It had been apparent immediately that it was some sort of a seal-signet ring, with an intact copper casing around a dirt-encrusted stone. It was the kind that was hung by a cord on the belt of a prominent person and served in effect as a badge of office (I Kings 21:8; Haggai 2-23). Cleaning it somewhat, I was able to make out what was engraved on the stone seal, which was stained green from the copper band around it. A horned ram, with a little man standing in front of it, was carved on it; and incised above it, in retrograde, in the clearest possible ancient Hebrew characters, was the inscription *LYTM*. The letter '*L*' means 'to' or 'belonging to'. And making allowance for the omission of vowels or vowel letters, which is characteristic of ancient Cannaanite writing, the three remaining consonants '*Y T M*' could signify nothing else than '*YOTAM*', which is the proper name of 'Jotham'. The translation of the entire inscription, therefore, is 'Belonging to Jotham'. This had to be a seal-signet ring of Jotham, King of Judah!

We know that a Jotham ruled Judah as regent during the last years of the reign of his father, Uzziah, who had been afflicted with leprosy, and that he succeeded him as king after his death. It was Uzziah who had built the new city of Elath on the sand-covered mound of the previously ruined and abandoned Ezion-geber. and it was during the reign of his grandson, Ahaz, the son of Jotham, that the Edomites drove out the Judaeans and established themselves firmly in Elath. It was, therefore, quite appropriate that the Qausanal impression should have been found in the Edomite stratum of Elath and the Jotham ring in the preceding Judaean one. There is little question but that this unique seal-signet ring lent royal authority to the governor, ruling the southernmost city of the kingdom of Judah, in the name of its king, Jotham.

Rivers in the Desert, 1959

The Dead Sea Scrolls

JOHN MARCO ALLEGRO

JOHN MARCO ALLEGRO (1923-) *was educated at Manchester University and after receiving an award for oriental research went to Magdalene College to study Hebrew dialects. He has conducted archaeological expeditions in Asia Minor, and published his results in lectures, broadcasts and television films as well as in print. In 1953 he was appointed British representative on the international team for editing the Dead Sea Scrolls, a task which called for the utmost skill and dexterity owing to the fragmentary condition of the material.*

The editing and publication of a complete scroll is a relatively simple task. The reading here and there may be difficult, but at least where the scroll is intact the position of the words and phrases is not in doubt. Very different is the preparation of hundreds of tiny fragments, many no bigger than a fingernail. All these must be laid out and minutely examined in the hope that they may connect with parent documents and be of use in reconstructing broken passages. The work of editing the fragments bought and excavated from the First Cave was entrusted to Fathers J. T. Milik and D. Barthélemy, both attached to the French School in Jerusalem. Starting work in 1952, the work appeared in 1955, having taken two full years to go through the Press. It is not surprising that the second-named collaborator was soon after flown home for extended medical treatment, although Milik has been able to continue on the work of preparing the Semitic texts of Murabba'at and, at the same time, by far the largest section of the fragments from the Fourth Cave. It is as well that the world should know the price in strained eyesight and mental fatigue which is being paid by scholars like these that it may have these priceless scroll fragments at the earliest possible moment.

As the Cave Four material flowed in, it became clear that its bulk was going to surpass by far anything found in the First Cave, and that it was beyond the capabilities of one or two scholars to edit in a reasonable time. De Vaux and Harding therefore decided that the work

21. Piecing together and deciphering the Dead Sea Scrolls.

should be shared by a team of scholars brought to Jerusalem and resident there for this purpose over several years, or at least for one year with return visits of several months each. Since the excavations have always been carried out by joint teams drawn from the French and American Schools, with the co-directorship of Lankester Harding, an Englishman, it was further decided that the Scrolls team should be of an international character. Thus there have been drawn to Jerusalem for this exciting work men from America, Britain, France, Germany, and Poland, eight of us in all. The whole project has been a happy example of close international collaboration, and a wonderful experience for all of us. The division of work has been roughly that the two American scholars, Dr Frank Cross and Father Patrick Skehan, have taken the biblical section, in all the remains of about a hundred different manuscripts, Father Jean Starcky the Aramaic works, Dr Claus Hunzinger the copies of the War Scroll and some papyrus manuscripts, Father Milik the apocryphal and pseudepigraphal works, the Manual and Damascus Documents manuscripts, and other sectarian works, Mr John Strugnell the hymn scrolls and other non-biblical works, and myself the Bible commentaries and some wisdom literature. The material from the other caves has been put in the care of Father Maurice Baillet of France. Even when we are not able to be in Jerusalem, much can be done on the photographs which we take to our home countries with us, but reference to the original pieces is absolutely essential to the work, and, all the time, examination of the unidentified fragments is continuing and pieces are being extracted for absent members of the team and put aside pending their return.

Naturally to bring out and keep a team of scholars for such work from the four corners of the globe is an expensive procedure. Some of the institutions to which the members are attached have financed their travel and residence, whilst for others it has been made possible by a generous grant from Mr John D. Rockefeller, under whose patronage the Museum in Jerusalem was first built and continues its work. The results of our labours will be published in a series of volumes, of which the first has been that of Barthélemy and Milik dealing with the Cave One fragments and excavations. Next will probably be the volume of the Murabba'at caves, then fragments from the minor caves, to be followed by the biblical volume of Cave Four, and the non-biblical volume(s). Again the cost of publication has been defrayed to a large extent by Mr Rockefeller's grant.

The fragments reach the Museum from Kando or the Bedouin in

cigarette cartons and the like, and are immediately stamped on the back with the code letters assigned to the various donors who have provided the money. Needless to say, that does not mean that those bodies will receive necessarily those pieces, for many will have been merged into their parent documents which may have been earmarked for elsewhere. In these cases as near an equivalent-sized fragment as possible will be allocated at the final distribution to replace the other. The fragments then have to be cleaned of the white dust with which most are covered. Sometimes this is so firmly engrained that no amount of brushing will remove it, and then we find that a very light brushing with a camel-hair brush touched with a non-acid oil, like castor oil, will make the marl translucent and bring up the writing very clearly. Very often it is not so much the dust that obliterates the writing as the colour of the leather itself, which has gone completely black from exposure to humidity and thus makes the writing indistinguishable from its surroundings. In these cases the process of infra-red photography has been particularly valuable in our work. We are very fortunate in having at the Museum a beautifully equipped photographic laboratory under the expert direction of Mr Nejid Anton Albina, who must by now be one of the world's foremost experts in this field. He used Kodak Infra-red plates and films, specially obtained from the United States, in conjunction with a red/violet, or a Red 3 filter fitted on to a Linhoff camera. Exposure at f.11 varies, of course, with the blackness of the subject and the distance from the lens, but to take our ordinary-sized glass plate of normally dark fragments (12 in. by 9½ in.) he sets his camera at about 32 in. from the subject, and gives exposures of six minutes between the hours of 8 and 10 a.m., and four between 10 a.m. and 2 p.m. A darker plate of fragments may need eight minutes, and exposures for particularly difficult pieces running over the hour are not uncommon. Such is the constancy of light in Jerusalem that he finds a light meter is unnecessary. Developing is done in ID 2 for five minutes and printed on soft or medium Bromide paper. The results on fragments where to the naked eye no writing at all was visible, are just amazing, and to this miracle we owe a very great deal of relief from serious eye-strain.

Very often the skin of the fragment is dry and brittle, sometimes tightly curled, and then it must undergo a process of hydration before it is safe to unroll it. The pieces requiring treatment are put into a glass vessel containing water at the bottom covered with a zinc perforated sheet and a sealed lid. After ten or fifteen minutes in hot weather the fragment is usually supple enough to allow gentle manipulation, but sometimes, with particularly coarse pieces, several hours of such treatment is necessary. If the piece is left too long, the result is a drop of liquid glue and one less epoch-making discovery. The clean fragments are laid out between the glass plates, several dozen or scores in each, and put out in the large room on trestle tables.

To the new collaborator entering the 'Scrollery' for the first time, the effect is rather shattering. He finds himself surrounded by about five hundred glass plates, packed with fragments of varying sizes, over which he will be the next year or two of his life crouching, trying to pick out pieces belonging to his documents, or seeking to identify new fragments. If he is a comparatively late-comer to the team, perhaps some of the results already obtained will strengthen his weakening resolve. In the corners of the room are the collected sections of other members of the team, and walking round he may see how pieces, no larger than the palm of the hand, have grown to cover complete volumes of text, and whose secrets will be proudly shown to him by the collaborator responsible. He may look wonderingly at a biblical text which is going to bring about a revolution in our ideas of text transmission, or on a commentary which throws new light on the messianic expectations of the time. He may find himself gazing at the Aramaic text of pseudepigraphal work never before seen in its original tongue, and all around him will be biblical texts older by a thousand years and more than Hebrew manuscripts of the Bible previously known. He will have walked into a new and exciting world, but the way to the revealing of its treasures is a hard one, and before he can be sitting down reading columns of text and preparing the transcriptions and translations for publication he has many months of extremely trying work ahead of him. Armed with one of his biggest fragments he will go slowly round those scores of unidentified plates seeking for the lost pieces. As he grows more proficient at the task he will be able to recognise a member of his flock from one letter or even part of a letter. One of the saving factors has been that of the four hundred or so manuscripts we have to deal with, surprisingly few have been written by the same scribe, so that by recognising the idiosyncrasies of one's own scribes you can be fairly sure that the piece belongs to his document. Of course, this is not always so, and often we may find, after some months of patient collecting, that we have more than one work on a plate, coming from the hand of the same scribe. However, besides the script there is the rather less dependable criterion for identification of the skin itself. Where this remains constant over the whole scroll, it can be a most useful means of quickly recognising parts from the same work. But, unfortunately, there are often extreme variations in colour and even texture where different skins have been sewn together to complete the work, or where disintegration of the scroll in antiquity has meant that different conditions have acted upon the pieces, so that one may be clean and supple, while its neighbour is darkened with moisture and warped completely out of shape. Warping is a major problem, for not only does it make pieces very difficult to join together even where the join is certain from the text, but it will distort the letters of the writing out of the true form, so that if there are only one or two letters on the piece, and the colour of the leather is changed from its parent document, it may be a long time before it is recognised as belonging to its own scroll.

Another cause of difficulty in joining is that worms or damp have often attacked the edges of fragments, so that real 'jig-saw puzzle' joins are no longer possible. This again is largely due to the scrolls having disintegrated in antiquity, and so frequently does this occur, and so often does one find tears which are certainly not new, that I am myself inclined to believe that the Fourth Cave was entered long ago and its contents maliciously damaged. Be that as it may, much of the relative positioning of the fragments in a document has to be done by 'dead reckoning' rather than edge-to-edge joins. This is not too difficult in the case of a biblical text where the order of the words is already known, although sources of trouble here are variant texts which we shall discuss in the next chapter. It is more difficult in the case of non-biblical works previously quite unknown or known only in translation.

An intriguing problem which has presented itself during the work has been the deciphering of a number of different secret codes in which several of the works were written. Happily they are nothing more complicated than new alphabets, which were composed by the Sectarians to keep certain works especially secret, and in one case they contrive to write most but not all of the words backwards, and use a mixture of four or five alphabets, including one or two of their own invention. Thus, for instance, one might come across a word written with a combination of alphabets in something after this fashion: Xϡy'b FƳ ᴋƴOβ ᴄϡX. The reader might like to work that one out for himself, with the clue that the alphabets represented in this imaginary example are Latin, Greek, Phoenician, and Aramaic, and the principle of using ancient letters for their modern equivalents is precisely that used by the author of this Qumran document. Having deciphered one column including a particularly puzzling phrase, it was encouraging to find another piece in a further purchase which contained the same phrase written, rather carelessly for the coder, in 'clear' Hebrew, confirming the decipherment.

Another code used entirely letters of their own invention, and begins in 'clear' Hebrew: 'the wisdom which he spoke to the Sons of the Dawn', and then goes on into this unknown script, beginning 'Listen ye'. One day, when the three of us, who then constituted the team, were tired of cleaning the thousands of fragments in the boxes before us, we decided to enliven the proceedings by having a competition to see who could crack the code first. The main difficulty was that being very fragmentary there were very few complete words, so that determining the relative frequency of occurrence of letters, which would normally have given the answer in a very short time, would not work so easily in this instance. Some of the letters looked something like the proto-Hebraic writing, a derivation from the ancient Phoenician script, but they made no sense when given these equivalents. Whilst Cross and I were tearing our hair over it after lunch that day, Milik strolled in and informed us that he had done it, or at least got enough of the letters to make a full decipherment eventually possible. He had guessed the meaning of one of the few complete words, which had the pattern *ABCBAD*. Since Hebrew is based on the triliteral root system there are not a large number of words possible with this combination, and a common group *LHTHLK*, the infinitive of the reflexive form of the verb *HLK* with the prefix *L*, meaning 'to walk about', gave him enough letters to break other smaller words, and thence to work through the whole fragment until he had the alphabet, or as much of it as could be obtained from the evidence available. There are, however, other cryptic scripts which have been impossible to decipher so far for want of sufficient material.

I have said that a factor which is apt to give trouble is the changing of skins part way through a scroll. Just as at times like this one wishes there had existed animals with skins large enough to suffice for a complete scroll, we often wish they had invented the fountain pen in the first century BC. Some of our scribes seem to have had 'quill trouble', in that the instrument kept wearing down and giving the writing a quite different appearance from that presented when the scribe had newly sharpened his pen. I have one manuscript in my section, a commentary on Isaiah, whose writing changes startlingly in the first two columns, and fragments coming from later columns look different again. Of course, close examination shows the same basic characteristics are still there, but when one is looking through fragments of only one or two letters for pieces to match, these variations can be most puzzling. It is by no means unknown, also, for the Qumran Scriptorium to play a very mean trick on the Jerusalem Scrollery by changing horses in midstream, or rather scribes in mid-scroll. This is quite unforgivable, and most trying.

The Dead Sea Scrolls, 1956

Part Six

—◆—

THE BOOK OF THE STEPS

The Pyramid of Cholula

ALEXANDER VON HUMBOLDT

ALEXANDER FRIEDRICH HEINRICH, BARON VON HUMBOLDT (*1769-
1859*) *was a great scholar, explorer and savant. He was born in Berlin and
after deep studies of many aspects of the natural sciences he was appointed
Assessor of Mines in the government service. He quickly rose to a high rank,
but, wishing to be free to travel, he then resigned. For the next five years after
his resignation he explored Central America and collected so vast an amount
of data on the geography, antiquities, meteorology and botany of the region
that it took him twenty-one years to arrange it for publication after his return
to Europe.*

The small city of Cholula, which Cortez, in his Letters to Charles V,
compares with the most populous cities of Spain, contains at present
scarcely sixteen thousand inhabitants. The pyramid is to the east of the
city, on the road which leads from Cholula to Puebla. It is well preserved on the western side, which is that represented in the engraving.
The plain of Cholula presents that aspect of barrenness, which is
peculiar to plains elevated two thousand two hundred metres above the
level of the ocean. A few plants of the agave and dracaena rise on the
foreground, and at a distance the summit of the volcano of Orizaba
is beheld covered with snow; a colossal mountain, five thousand two
hundred and ninety-five metres of absolute height, and of which I have
published a sketch in my Mexican Atlas, plate 17.

The teocalli of Cholula has four stories, all of equal height. It appears
to have been constructed exactly in the direction of the four cardinal
points; but as the edges of the stories are not very distinct, it is difficult
to ascertain their primitive direction. This pyramidical monument has a
broader basis than that of any other edifice of the same kind in the old
continent. I measured it carefully, and ascertained, that its perpendicular
height is only fifty metres, but that each side of its basis is four hundred
and thirty-nine metres in length. Torquèmada computes its height at
seventy-seven metres; Betancourt, at sixty-five; and Clavigero, at
sixty-one. Bernal Diaz del Castillo, a common soldier in the army of
Cortez, amused himself by counting the steps of the staircases, which

led to the platform of the teocallis: he found one hundred and fourteen in the great temple of Tenochtitlan, one hundred and seventeen in that of Tezcuco, and one hundred and twenty in that of Cholula. The basis of the pyramid of Cholula is twice as broad as that of Cheops; but its height is very little more than that of the pyramid of Mycerinus. On comparing the dimensions of the house of the Sun, at Teotihuacan, with those of the pyramid of Cholula, we see, that the people, who constructed these remarkable monuments, intended to give them the same height, but with bases, the length of which should be in the proportion of one to two. We find also a considerable difference in the proportions between the base and the height in these various monuments: in the three great pyramids of Geeza, the heights are to the bases as 1 to 1·7; in the pyramid of Papantla covered with hieroglyphics, this ratio is as 1 to 1·4; in the great pyramid of Teotihuacan, as 1 to 3·7; and in that of Cholula as 1 to 7·8. This last monument is built with unbaked bricks (*xamilli*), alternating with layers of clay. I have been assured by some Indians of Cholula, that the inside is hollow; and that, during the abode of Cortez in this city, their ancestors had concealed, in the body of the pyramid, a considerable number of warriors, who were to fall suddenly on the Spaniards: but the materials with which the teocalli is built, and the silence of the historians of those times, give but little probability to this assertion.

It is certain, however, that in the interior of this pyramid, as in other teocallis, there are considerable cavities, which were used as sepulchres for the natives. A particular circumstance led to this discovery. Seven or eight years ago the road from Puebla to Mexico, which before passed to the north of the pyramid, was changed. In tracing the road, the first story was cut through, so that an eighth part remained isolated like a heap of bricks. In making this opening a square house was discovered in the interior of the pyramid, built of stone, and supported by beams made of the wood of the deciduous cypress (*cupressus disticha*). The house contained two skeletons, idols in basalt, and a great number of vases, curiously varnished and painted. No pains were taken to preserve these objects, but it is said to have been carefully ascertained, that this house, covered with bricks and strata of clay, had no outlet. Supposing that the pyramid was built, not by the Toltecks, the first inhabitants of Cholula, but by prisoners made by the Cholulans from the neighbouring nations, it is possible, that they were the carcases of some unfortunate slaves, who had been shut up to perish in the interior of the teocalli. We examined the remains of this subterraneous house,

22. Baron Alexander von Humboldt (1769–1859) in his study. He was the greatest explorer and natural scientist of his era.

Drawing by Alexander von Humboldt

23. Humboldt's sketch of the pyramid of Cholula in Mexico.

and observed a particular arrangement of the bricks, tending to diminish the pressure made on the roof. The natives, being ignorant of the manner of making arches, placed very large bricks horizontally, so that the upper course should pass beyond the lower. The continuation of this kind of stepwork served in some measure as a substitute for the Gothic vault, and similar vestiges have been found in several Egyptian edifices. An adit dug through the teocalli of Cholula, to examine its internal structure, would be an interesting operation; and it is singular, that the desire of discovering hidden treasure has not prompted the undertaking. During my travels in Peru, in visiting the vast ruins of the city of Chimu, near Mansiche, I went into the interior of the famous Huaca de Toledo, the tomb of a Peruvian prince, in which Garei Gutierez de Toledo discovered, on digging a gallery, in 1576, gold amounting in value to more than five million of francs, as is proved by the book of accounts, preserved in the mayor's office at Truxillo.

The great teocalli of Cholula, called also the *Mountain of unbaked bricks* (tlalchihualtépec), had an altar on its top, dedicated to Quetzalcoatl, the god of the air. This Quetzalcoatl, whose name signifies serpent clothed with green feathers, from *coatl*, serpent, and *quetzalli*, green feathers, is the most mysterious being of the whole Mexican mythology. He was a white and bearded man, like the Bochica of the Muyscas, of whom we spoke in our descriptions of the Cataract of Tequendama. He was high priest of Tula (Tollan), legislator, chief of a religious sect, which, like the Sonyasis and the Bouddhists of Indostan, inflicted on themselves the most cruel penances. He introduced the custom of piercing the lips and the ears, and lacerating the rest of the body with the prickles of the agave leaves, or the thorns of the cactus; and of putting reeds into the wounds, in order that the blood might be seen to trickle more copiously. In a Mexican drawing in the Vatican library, I have seen a figure representing Quetzalcoatl appeasing by his penance the wrath of the gods, when, thirteen thousand and sixty years after the creation of the World (I follow the very vague chronology computed by Rios) a great famine prevailed in the province of Culan. The saint had chosen his place of retirement near Tlaxapuchicalco, on the volcano Catcitepetl (*Speaking Mountain*), where he walked barefooted on agave leaves armed with prickles. We seem to behold one of those *rishi*, hermits of the Ganges, whose pious austerity is celebrated in the Pouranas.

The reign of Quetzalcoatl was the golden age of the people of Anahuac. At that period, all animals, and even men, lived in peace; the earth brought forth, without culture, the most fruitful harvests; and the air was filled with a multitude of birds, which were admired for their song, and the beauty of their plumage. But this reign, like that of Saturn, and the happiness of the world, were not of long duration; the great spirit Tezcatlipoca, the Brahma of the nations of Anahuac, offered Quetzalcoatl a beverage, which, in rendering him immortal, inspired him with a taste for travelling; and particularly with an irresistible desire of visiting a distant country, called by tradition Tlapallan. The resemblance of this name to that of Huehuetlapallan, the country of the Toltecks, appears not to be accidental. But how can we conceive, that this white man, priest of Tula, should have taken his direction, as we shall presently find, to the south-east, towards the plains of Cholula, and thence to visit this northern country, whence his ancestors had issued in the five hundred and ninety-sixth year of our era?

Quetzalcoatl, in crossing the territory of Cholula, yielded to the intreaties of the inhabitants, who offered him the reins of government. He dwelt twenty years among them, taught them to cast metals, ordered fasts of eight days, and regulated the intercalations of the Tolteck Year. He preached peace to men, and would permit no other offerings to the Divinity, than the first fruits of the harvest. From Cholula Quetzalcoatl passed on to the mouth of the river Goasacoalco, where he disappeared, after having declared to the Cholulans (Cholotecatles) that he would return in a short time to govern them again, and renew their happiness.

It was the posterity of this saint, whom the unhappy Montezuma thought he recognised in the soldiers of Cortez. 'We know by our books,' said he, in his first interview with the Spanish General, 'that myself, and those who inhabit this country, are not natives, but strangers, who came from a great distance. We know also, that the chief, who led our ancestors hither, returned for a certain time to his primitive country, and thence came back to seek those, who were here established. He found them married to the women of this land, having a numerous posterity, and living in cities, which they had built. Our ancestors hearkened not to their ancient master, and he returned alone. We have always believed, that his descendants would one day come to take possession of this country. Since you arrive from that region, where the Sun rises, and, as you assure me, you have long known us, I cannot doubt, but that the king, who sends you, is our natural master.'

Another very remarkable tradition still exists among the Indians of Cholula, according to which the great pyramid was not originally destined to serve for the worship of Quetzalcoatl. After my return to Europe, on examining at Rome the Mexican manuscript in the Vatican library, I found, that this same tradition was already recorded in a manuscript of Pedro de Los Rios, a Dominican monk, who, in 1566, copied on the very spot all the hieroglyphical paintings he could procure. 'Before the great inundation, which took place four thousand eight hundred years after the creation of the World, the country of Anahuac was inhabited by giants (tzocuillixeque). All those who did not perish were transformed into fishes, save seven, who fled into caverns. When the waters subsided, one of these giants, Xelhua, surnamed the architect, went to Cholollan; where, as a memorial of the mountain Tlaloc, which had served for an asylum to himself and his six brethren, he built an artificial hill in form of a pyramid. He ordered bricks to be made in the province of Tlamanalco, at the foot of the Sierra of Cocotl, and to convey them to Cholula he placed a file of men, who passed them from hand to hand. The gods beheld with wrath this edifice, the top of which was to reach the clouds. Irritated at the daring attempt of Xelhua, they hurled fire on the pyramid. Numbers of the workmen perished; the work was discontinued, and the monument was afterwards dedicated to Quetzalcoatl.' . . .

This history reminds us of those ancient traditions of the East, which the Hebrews have recorded in their sacred books. The Cholulans preserved a stone, which, enveloped in a ball of fire, had fallen from the clouds on the top of the pyramid. This aerolite had the figure of a toad. Rios, to prove the high antiquity of this fable of Xelhua, observes, that it was contained in a hymn, which the Cholulans sung at their festivals, dancing round the teocalli; and that this hymn began with the words *Tulanian hulutaez*, which are words belonging to no dialect at present known in Mexico. In every part of the Globe, on the ridge of the Cordilleras, as well as in the isle of Samothrace in the Egean sea, fragments of primitive languages are preserved in religious rites.

The size of the platform of the pyramid of Cholula, on which I made a great number of astronomical observations, is four thousand two hundred square metres. From it the eye ranges over a magnificent prospect; Popocatepetl, Iztaccibuatl, the peak of Orizaba, and the Sierra de Tlascalla, famous for the tempests which gather around its summit. We view at the same time three mountains higher than Mount Blanc, two of which are still burning volcanoes. A small chapel, surrounded with cypress, and dedicated to the Virgin de los Remedios, has succeeded to the temple of the god of the air, or the Mexican Indra. An ecclesiastic of the Indian race celebrates mass every day on the top of this antique monument.

In the time of Cortez, Cholula was considered as a holy city. Nowhere existed a greater number of teocallis, of priests, and religious orders (*tlamacazque*); no spot displayed greater magnificence in the celebration of public worship, or more austerity in its penances and fasts. Since the introduction of christianity among the Indians, the symbols of a new worship have not entirely effaced the remembrance of the old. The people assemble in crowds from distant quarters at the summit of the pyramid, to celebrate the festival of the Virgin. A mysterious dread, a religious awe, fills the soul of the Indian at the sight of this immense pile of bricks, covered with shrubs and perpetual verdure.

We have above remarked the great similarity of construction between the Mexican teocallis and the temple of Bel, or Belus, at Babylon. The analogy had already struck Mr Zoega, though he had been able to procure but very incomplete descriptions of the group of the pyramids of Teotihuacan. According to Herodotus, who visited Babylon, and saw the temple of Belus, this pyramidical monument had eight stories. It was a stadium high, and the breadth of its basis was equal to its height. The outer wall which surrounded it, the περιβολος, was two stadia square. A common olympic stadium was one hundred and eighty-three metres: the Egyptian stadium was only ninety-eight. The pyramid was built of brick and asphaltum. A temple (ναος) was erected on its top, and another at its basis. The first, according to Herodotus, was without statues; it contained only a table of gold, and a bed on which reposed a female chosen by the god Belus. Diodorus Siculus, on the other hand, asserts, that the upper temple contained an altar, and three statues, to which, according to notions taken from the worship of the Greeks, he gave the names of Jupiter, Juno, and Rhea. But neither these statues nor any part of the monument existed in the time of Diodorus and Strabo. In the Mexican teocallis, as in the temple of Belus, the lower *naos* was distinguished from the temple on the platform of the pyramid. The same distinction is clearly pointed out in the letters of Cortez, and in the history of the conquest written by Bernal Diaz, who dwelt several months in the palace of the king Axajacatl, and consequently opposite the teocalli of Huitzilopochtli.

Researches Concerning the Institutions and Monuments of the Ancient Inhabitants of America, 1814

Travels in the Yucatan

JEAN DE WALDECK

JEAN FREDERIC MAXIMILIAN, COMTE DE WALDECK (1766-1875)
was the descendant of a noble German family who had settled in France.
Like Denon, he started his career as an art student under the tuition of the
painter David, and he too followed Napoleon's army to Egypt. When the
army withdrew, he remained in Egypt and travelled on his own initiative up
the Nile as far as Aswan. Encouraged by the success of this trip, he next
organized an expedition to cross the Sahara, but it ended in disaster with the
deaths of all the participators except himself. In 1821 he made his first journey
to Guatemala and in the next year he went to London to help with the
illustrations of a book on Palenque; there he met Lord Kingsborough, who
financed several of his expeditions to central America. After Kingsborough's
death, Waldeck found that he could not raise sufficient funds to publish the
results of his investigations, but an appeal to Prosper Mérimée and the French
Academy was finally successful and, at the age of one hundred, he was able to
publish his account of Palenque. His report on his earlier journeys in Yucatan
had been published in 1838 but, before the discoveries of John Lloyd Stephens
roused public interest in pre-Columbian archaeology, it attracted little
attention.

Prior to my expedition, the ruins of Uxmal had been visited only by
the owners of the neighbouring farm, worthy people for whom a
shattered city is no more than a quarry for building materials; but
these ruins, described with such poverty by Cogolludo and his successors, are the remains of a powerful city, comparable in size with our
greatest European capitals. What name can we give them? Could they
be part of Mani, even Itzalana perhaps? There are no historical records
to shed light on this important question; but I believe there are certain
reliable indications which can lead us to discover the truth.

In the first place, it is impossible that the dwellers in this city were of
a minor order; if it were so, what could we make of Mani, Mayapan,

Tichualajtun and other great cities whose ruins still stand? So there existed here a vast and powerful centre, a people great enough to give rise to an immense capital. We can dismiss the theory that these ruins belong to an outpost of another ancient city near by, for their position on a high mountain plateau is sufficient indication of an isolated city. On these two points, then, there can be no argument. If, further, we remember that Itzalana is known to have been near Mani, traces of which b strew the plain; that those latter ruins and the ones on the mountain summit are very close together; that there are no others in the vicinity; we can rest assured that the precincts I explored were indeed Itzalana. Finally, we know that the Itaexes were the cruellest of all the peoples in this region; the only teocalli in the whole of the Yucatan is in these ruins. This problem, which may not prove too weighty, has absorbed me for some time, and will no doubt be resolved when men skilled in deduction in this field follow my researches with their own, and dispel the gloom amidst which I hope to light a feeble candle.

The structures at Palenque are, with the exception of the palace, on a small scale; those at Uxmal are of colossal dimensions, and are all constructed of dressed stone. Four great principal buildings, separated by open spaces, enclose an area of 57,672 square feet. The longest side of this rectangle is 227 feet 8 inches long, the shortest 172 feet 9 inches, not counting the double gaps we see at each end of the structure, which are 20 feet long. The teocalli is built on a pyramid; its principal staircase has 100 steps, 1 foot high by 5 inches broad. This is the only known sacrificial temple in all Mexico. I should say that even this was not recognized, for the local people had nicknamed it the Tower of the Wizard, a name which bears no relation whatever to the function of a teocalli. As this monument is the highest and most singular of the five I saw, and the first I set eyes on, I followed my examination of it by naming it after my generous patron, Lord Kingsborough.

Asiatic influence can easily be discerned in the architecture of these monuments. The symbol of an elephant occurs on the rounded corners of the buildings, the trunk uplifted on the East side and lowered on the West. It is disappointing, however, that no whole figures remain; generally the legs are missing. These sculptures are life-size reliefs; their delineation is extraordinarily accurate in some places, yet poor in others. It is chiefly in the ornaments that we can admire the patience of the craftsmen employed on these buildings, and perceive the taste of these ancient peoples for monumental splendour.

The building which forms the North face of the structure and closes in the area I have described has a double gallery and measures 227 feet 8 inches long by 27 feet 8 inches wide; it contains 16 small rooms, 11 feet across and varying in depth from 22 feet to 26 feet 6 inches. I cannot tell whether this irregularity is significant, or merely the result of the builders' whim. Each room has an entrance, and we notice, on the inside, stone rings fixed at the height of the joist which forms the top of these doorways. These rings served doubtless to support the rod which held the tapestry or curtain which closed off each opening; we do not see here, as at Palenque, the stone hinges which are evidence of the firm seal which closed the doors of the edifices there. Above the doorways of these 16 rooms on the outside we see an enlarged version of the *calli* sign. There are 18 such signs, and we can guess that they were intended to mark a certain period of time which elapsed before the construction of the building. Equally, it might be that, as well as the katuns by which they marked the divisions of their era, the Mayas had another method of reckoning time, a symbolic system connected with their religious rites which is found in these calli. The age of the building is thus found to be 832 years; what is certain is that it existed a century before the conquest; since we can go back no farther, let us rest on this reliable evidence. Here, then, is an antiquity of 932 years up to the arrival of the Spaniards; moreover, since the invasion of the Yucatan took place in 1519, it follows that the Mayas were a nation, and had reached a high level of civilization, in A D 587. The plague which decimated the Toltecs did not, according to all the chronologies and dates we have collected, prolong its ravages beyond the year 1050. So we are left with a gap of 567 years between the period of Mayapan's magnificence and the plague which devastated Tula; it is therefore true to say, as I had always believed before this irrefutable proof, that it was the Mayas who passed on to the Toltecs and Aztecs their civilisation and part of their culture. Add the fact that we find not a single Aztec word in the Yucatec language – an impossibility if the Mayas were the last comers. The Mayas could be descended from the Palenqueans, and the lawgiver of Tula, Quetzalcoatl, could have been a grandson of Zamna, or descended from those who formed this leader's entourage when he came to civilize the Yucatan.

The ruins of Itzalana have one important difference from those of Palenque. Although the single or double galleries of Itzalana end pyramid fashion, we see no openings linking one gallery to another; nor are there any giving access from the interior to the outside. At

Palenque, by contrast, we find numerous high windows in the shape of the Greek *tau* (T) which served to admit air and light to the chambers. The only apertures in the rooms of the Uxmal buildings are a mere 6 inches deep, and are set opposite one another; from this arrangement it is clear that they were intended to support cross-beams from which hammocks were slung; so these rooms were bed-chambers. The absence of windows indicates, as I have said above, that the doorways were closed only by curtains; otherwise, in these completely sealed rooms, the heat would have been intolerable. The doors of the buildings at Palenque were wooden and turned on stone hinges, necessitating vents to the interior, and it was by means of the *tau* openings that light and air reached the galleries. These *tau* shapes were the symbol of the Lingam cult, in so far as it played a part in the religion of Palenque, where Buddhism seems, for the rest, to have been extremely pure.

The glyphs of Itzalana which are indisputably connected with those of the Toltecs and Aztecs are: *cohuatl, calli, miquiztli, atl* and *quiahuitl*, which can be identified with a *cipactli*. A representation of Tonatiuh in a mask is repeated seven times on the facade of one most remarkable edifice. These are the only signs in the ruins which show any kinship with those of Mexico; the rest are totally different; nor did I find there so much as one hieroglyph like those on the Toltec remains at Xochicalco.

The dress of the Itzalana statues is closer to the Palenquean style than to any other. The headdress worn by one sacrificer . . . occurs in a bas-relief at Ototiun; likewise with the same personage's cape. This correspondence points to a Palenquean tradition, an assumption which is supported by the close similarity of the Palenquean and Maya methods of building.

Between the construction of Maya buildings and Mexican – the sole example of which is Xochicalco – there is an important difference. The Toltecs first raised the main structure of their building, and carved the ornaments afterwards *in situ*. The Mayas followed the reverse procedure. If they wished to cover a façade with ornaments or symbolic figures, they began by painting the whole wall in the chosen colour; this background was almost always red, as with the structures at Palenque. This first task completed, they stuck on the painted wall the stone marquetry which would provide the decoration, colour-washing it with somewhat more care than the background. Blue was used here, for we can still see traces of this colour in the grooved lines of the squares which frame a type of small turned cross. Red and blue are the only colours I could distinguish on the sacrificial temple at Itzalana. However, yellow and white must also have been used, for these two tints are still visible on other buildings. . . . We notice that even tiny stones are shaped with enormous care, and the whole is an assemblage as perfectly fitted as a joiner's.

The boxes or coffers which adorn the façades of the buildings at Itzalana must draw the attention of artists and scholars. No one who makes a close examination of the cubes which compose this attractive decoration can doubt that the authors of this astonishing piece of cutting thoroughly understood the principles of geometry. I have measured every line, slid the lead over every join, and I have never found the slightest deviation beneath the cord. The native inhabitants of the country continually affirm that the Indians of old were barbarians. This ludicrous assertion, fostered by the Spaniards, who had a motive for spreading the belief that there had been nothing here before their arrival but misery and gloom, this assertion, I say, is proof that we need not hesitate to turn upon the modern people of the Yucatan their own reproach of barbarism. If they do not know how to appreciate the splendour and beauty of the ruins which bestrew their country's soil, it is because they themselves sleep in the profoundest ignorance. This truth needs no further demonstration.

Voyage Pittoresque et Archéologique dans la Province d'Yucatan et aux
Ruines d'Itzalane, 1838

Translated from the French by V. M. Conrad

The purchase of a city

JOHN LLOYD STEPHENS

JOHN LLOYD STEPHENS (*1805-1852*) *was born in Shrewsbury, New Jersey, and studied law, but his greatest interest was always the study of archaeology. He travelled extensively in the eastern Mediterranean area, and there he met Mr Frederick Catherwood, who had been attached to the unsuccessful Robert Hay expedition in Egypt. On his return to the United States he began to study the existing documents relating to the great Central American civilizations, which convinced him that surviving remains of extensive cities must await discovery in the jungles. His appointment to a diplomatic mission in the area gave him the opportunity he needed, and he secured the cooperation of Mr Catherwood to draw anything he might find and set off in search of ruins. His search was dramatically rewarded, and his account of his journey is lively and humorous as well as informative.*

All day I had been brooding over the title-deeds of Don Jose Maria, and, drawing my blanket around me, suggested to Mr Catherwood 'an operation'. (Hide your heads, ye speculators in up-town lots!) To buy Copan! remove the monuments of a by-gone people from the desolate region in which they were buried, set them up in the 'great commercial emporium', and found an institution to be the nucleus of a great national museum of American antiquities! But query, could the 'idols' be removed? They were on the banks of a river that emptied into the same ocean by which the docks of New-York are washed, but there were rapids below; and, in answer to my inquiry, Don Miguel said these were impassable. Nevertheless, I should have been unworthy of having passed through the times 'that tried men's souls' if I had not had an alternative; and this was to exhibit by sample: to cut one up and remove it in pieces, and make casts of the others. The casts of the Parthenon are regarded as precious memorials in the British Museum, and casts of Copan would be the same in New-York. Other ruins might be discovered even more interesting and more accessible. Very soon their existence would become known and their value appreciated, and the friends of science and the arts in Europe would get possession of them. They belonged of right to us, and, though we did not know how soon we might be kicked out ourselves, I resolved that ours they should be; with visions of glory and indistinct fancies of receiving the thanks of the corporation flitting before my eyes, I drew my blanket around me, and fell asleep.

At daylight the clouds still hung over the forest; as the sun rose they cleared away; our workmen made their appearance, and at nine o'clock we left the hut. The branches of the trees were dripping wet, and the ground very muddy. Trudging once more over the district which contained the principal monuments, we were startled by the immensity of the work before us, and very soon we concluded that to explore the whole extent would be impossible. Our guides knew only of this district; but having seen columns beyond the village, a league distant, we had reason to believe that others were strewed in different directions, completely buried in the woods, and entirely unknown. The woods were so dense that it was almost hopeless to think of penetrating them. The only way to make a thorough exploration would be to cut down the whole forest and burn the trees. This was incompatible with our immediate purposes, might be considered taking liberties, and could only be done in the dry season. After deliberation, we resolved first to obtain drawings of the sculptured columns. Even in this there was great difficulty. The designs were very complicated, and so different from anything Mr Catherwood had ever seen before as to be perfectly unintelligible. The cutting was in very high relief, and required a strong body of light to bring up the figures; and the foliage was so thick, and the shade so deep, that drawing was impossible.

After much consultation, we selected one of the 'idols' and determined to cut down the trees around it, and thus lay it open to the rays of the sun. Here again was difficulty. There was no axe; and the only instrument which the Indians possessed was the machete, or choppingknife, which varies in form in different sections of the country; wielded with one hand, it was useful in clearing away shrubs and branches, but almost harmless upon large trees; and the Indians, as in the days when the Spaniards discovered them, applied to work without ardour, carried it on with little activity, and, like children, were easily diverted from it. One hacked into a tree, and, when tired, which happened very soon, sat down to rest, and another relieved him. While one worked there were always several looking on. I remembered the ring of the woodman's axe in the forests at home, and wished for a few long-sided Green Mountain boys. But we had been buffeted into patience, and watched the Indians while they hacked with their machetes, and even wondered that they succeeded so well. At length the trees were felled and dragged aside, a space cleared around the base, Mr C.'s frame set up, and he set to work. I took two Mestitzoes, Bruno and Francisco, and, offering them a reward for every new discovery, with a compass in my hand set out on a tour of exploration. Neither had seen 'the idols' until the morning of our first visit, when they followed in our train to laugh at los Ingleses; but very soon they exhibited such an interest that I hired them. Bruno attracted my attention by his admiration, as I supposed, of my person; but I found it was of my coat, which was a long shooting-frock, with many pockets; and he said that he could make one just like it except the skirts. He was a tailor by profession, and in the intervals of a great job upon a round-about jacket, worked with his machete. But he had an inborn taste for the arts. As we passed through the woods, nothing escaped his eye, and he was professionally curious touching the costumes of the sculptured figures. I was struck with the first development of their antiquarian taste. Francisco found the feet and legs of a statue, and Bruno a part of the body to match, and the effect was electric upon both. They searched and raked up the ground with their machetes till they found the shoulders, and set it up entire except the head; and they were both eager for the possession of instruments with which to dig and find this remaining fragment.

It is impossible to describe the interest with which I explored these ruins. The ground was entirely new; there were no guide-books or guides; the whole was a virgin soil. We could not see ten yards before us, and never knew what we should stumble upon next. At one time we stopped to cut away branches and vines which concealed the face of a monument, and then to dig around to bring to light a fragment, a sculptured corner of which protruded from the earth. I leaned over with breathless anxiety while the Indian worked, and an eye, an ear, a foot, or a hand was disentombed; and when the machete rang against the chiselled stone, I pushed the Indians away, and cleared out the loose earth with my hands. The beauty of the sculpture, the solemn stillness of the woods, disturbed only by the scrambling of monkeys and the chattering of parrots, the desolation of the city, and the mystery that hung over it, all created an interest higher, if possible, than I had ever felt among the ruins of the Old World. After several hours' absence I returned to Mr Catherwood, and reported upward of fifty objects to be copied.

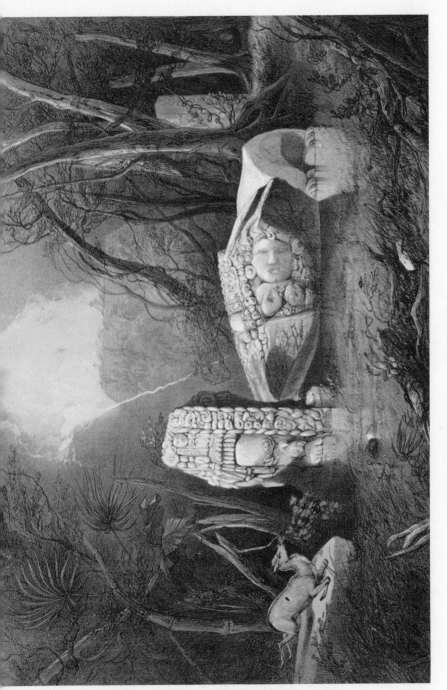

24. Frederick Catherwood's engraving of a fallen Maya stele at Copan in Honduras. Nothing was known to the civilized world of the vanished Maya culture. Catherwood's drawings in 1844 were the first pictures of its relics seen in the Western world.

25. Stucco head of a Mayan noble found in the crypt underneath the Temple of Inscriptions at Palenque, Mexico.

I found him not so well pleased as I expected with my report. He was standing with his feet in the mud, and was drawing with his gloves on, to protect his hands from the moschetoes. As we feared, the designs were so intricate and complicated, the subjects so entirely new and unintelligible, that he had great difficulty in drawing. He had made several attempts, both with the camera lucida and without, but failed to satisfy himself or even me, who was less severe in criticism. The 'idol' seemed to defy his art; two monkeys on a tree on one side appeared to be laughing at him, and I felt discouraged and despondent. In fact, I made up my mind, with a pang of regret, that we must abandon the idea of carrying away any materials for antiquarian speculation, and must be content with having seen them ourselves. Of that satisfaction nothing could deprive us. We returned to the hut with out interest undiminished, but sadly out of heart as to the result of our labours.

Our luggage had not been able to cross the river, but the blue bag which had caused me so many troubles was recovered. I had offered a dollar reward, and Bartolo, the heir-apparent of lesseeship of our hut, had passed the day in the river, and found it entangled in a bush upon the bank. His naked body seemed glad of its accidental washing, and the bag, which we supposed to contain some of Mr C.'s drawing materials, being shaken, gave out a pair of old boots, which, however, were at that time worth their weight in gold, being waterproof, and cheered Mr Catherwood's drooping spirits, who was ill with a pro-spective attack of fever and ague or rheumatism, from standing all day in the mud. Our men went home, and Frederico had orders, before coming to work in the morning, to go to Don Gregorio's and buy bread, milk, candles, lard, and a few yards of beef. The door of the hut looked toward the west, and the sun set over the dark forest in front with a gorgeousness I have never seen surpassed. Again, during the night, we had rain, with thunder and lightning, but not so violent as the night before, and in the morning it was again clear.

That day Mr Catherwood was much more successful in his drawings; indeed, at the beginning the light fell exactly as he wished, and he mastered the difficulty. His preparations, too, were much more com-fortable, as he had his water-proofs, and stood on a piece of oiled canvass, used for covering luggage on the road. I passed the morning in selecting another monument, clearing away the trees, and preparing it for him to copy. . . . Mr Catherwood went to the ruins to continue his drawings, and I to the village, taking Augustin with me to fire the

Balize guns, and buy up eatables for a little more than they were worth. My first visit was to Don Jose Maria. After clearing up our character, I broached the subject of a purchase of the ruins; told him that, on account of my public business, I could not remain as long as I desired, but wished to return with spades, pick-axes, ladders, crowbars, and men, build a hut to live in, and make a thorough exploration; that I could not incur the expense at the risk of being refused permission to do so; and, in short, in plain English, asked him: What will you take for the ruins? I think he was not more surprised than if I had asked to buy his poor old wife, our rheumatic patient, to practise medicine upon. He seemed to doubt which of us was out of his senses. The property was so utterly worthless that my wanting to buy it seemed very suspicious. On examining the paper, I found that he did not own the fee, but held it under a lease from Don Bernardo de Aguila, of which three years were unexpired. The tract consisted of about six thousand acres, for which he paid eighty dollars a year; he was at a loss what to do, but told me that he would reflect upon it, consult his wife, and give me an answer at the hut the next day. I then visited the alcalde, but he was too tipsy to be susceptible of any impression; prescribed for several patients; and instead of going to Don Gregorio's, sent him a polite request by Don Jose Maria to mind his own business and let us alone; returned, and passed the rest of the day among the ruins. It rained during the night, but again cleared off in the morning, and we were on the ground early. My business was to go around with workmen to clear away trees and bushes, dig, and excavate, and prepare monuments for Mr Catherwood to copy. While so engaged, I was called off by a visit from Don Jose Maria, who was still undecided what to do; and not wishing to appear too anxious, told him to take more time, and come again the next morning.

The next morning he came, and his condition was truly pitiable. He was anxious to convert unproductive property into money, but afraid, and said that I was a stranger, and it might bring him into difficulty with the government. I again went into proof of character, and engaged to save him harmless with the government or release him. Don Miguel read my letters of recommendation, and re-read the letter of General Cascara. He was convinced, but these papers did not give him a right to sell me his land; the shade of suspicion still lingered; for a finale, I opened my trunk, and put on a diplomatic coat, with a profusion of large eagle buttons. I had on a Panama hat, soaked with rain and spotted with mud, a check shirt, white pantaloons, yellow up to the knees with mud, and was about as outré as the negro king who received a company of British officers on the coast of Africa in a cocked hat and military coat, without any inexpressibles; but Don Jose Maria could not withstand the buttons on my coat; the cloth was the finest he had ever seen; and Don Miguel, and his wife, and Bartalo realised fully that they had in their hut an illustrious incognito. The only question was who should find paper on which to draw the contract. I did not stand upon trifles, and gave Don Miguel some paper, who took our mutual instructions, and appointed the next day for the execution of the deed.

The reader is perhaps curious to know how old cities sell in Central America. Like other articles of trade, they are regulated by the quantity in market, and the demand; but, not being staple articles, like cotton and indigo, they were held at fancy prices, and at that time were dull of sale. I paid fifty dollars for Copan. There was never any difficulty about price. I offered that sum, for which Don Jose Maria thought me only a fool; if I had offered more, he would probably have considered me something worse.

Incidents of Travel in Central America, 1842

The palace at Palenque

JOHN LLOYD STEPHENS

In the mean time work went on. As at Copan, it was my business to prepare the different objects for Mr Catherwood to draw. Many of the stones had to be scrubbed and cleaned; and as it was our object to have the utmost possible accuracy in the drawings, in many places scaffolds were to be erected on which to set up the camera lucida. Pawling relieved me from a great part of this labour. That the reader may know the character of the objects we had to interest us, I proceed to give a description of the building in which we lived, called the palace.

A front view of this building is given in the engraving. It does not, however, purport to be given with the same accuracy as the other drawings, the front being in a more ruined condition. It stands on an artificial elevation of an oblong form, forty feet high, three hundred and ten feet in front and rear, and two hundred and sixty feet on each side. This elevation was formerly faced with stone, which has been thrown down by the growth of trees, and its form is hardly distinguishable.

The building stands with its face to the east, and measures two hundred and twenty-eight feet front by one hundred and eighty feet deep. Its height is not more than twenty-five feet, and all around it had a broad projecting cornice of stone. The front contained fourteen doorways, about nine feet wide each, and the intervening piers are between six and seven feet wide. On the left (approaching the palace) eight of the piers have fallen down, as has also the corner on the right, and the terrace underneath is cumbered with the ruins. But six piers remain entire, and the rest of the front is open.

The building was constructed of stone, with a mortar of lime and sand, and the whole front was covered with stucco and painted. The piers were ornamented with spirited figures in bas-relief, one of which is represented in the engraving opposite. On the top are three hieroglyphics sunk in the stucco. It is enclosed by a richly-ornamented border, about ten feet high and six wide, of which only a part now remains. The principal personage stands in an upright position and in profile, exhibiting an extraordinary facial angle of about forty-five degrees. The upper part of the head seems to have been compressed and lengthened, perhaps by the same process employed upon the heads of the Choctaw and Flathead Indians of our own country. The head represents a different species from any now existing in that region of country; and supposing the statues to be images of living personages, or the creations of artists according to their ideas of perfect figures, they indicate a race of people now lost and unknown. The headdress is evidently a plume of feathers. Over the shoulders is a short covering decorated with studs, and a breastplate; part of the ornament of the girdle is broken; the tunic is probably a leopard's skin; and the whole dress no doubt exhibits the costume of this unknown people. He holds in his hand a staff or sceptre, and opposite his hands are the marks of three hieroglyphics, which have decayed or been broken off. At his feet are two naked figures seated cross-legged, and apparently suppliants. A fertile imagination might find many explanations for these strange figures, but no satisfactory interpretation presents itself to my mind. The hieroglyphics doubtless tell its history. The stucco is of admirable consistency, and hard as stone. It was painted, and in different places about it we discovered the remains of red, blue, yellow, black, and white.

The piers which are still standing contained other figures of the same general character, but which, unfortunately, are more mutilated, and from the declivity of the terrace it was difficult to set up the camera lucida in such a position as to draw them. The piers which are fallen were no doubt enriched with the same ornaments. Each one had some specific meaning, and the whole probably presented some allegory or history; and when entire and painted, the effect in ascending the terrace must have been imposing and beautiful.

The principal doorway is not distinguished by its size or by any superior ornament, but is only indicated by a range of broad stone steps leading up to it on the terrace. The doorways have no doors, nor are there the remains of any. Within, on each side, are three niches in the wall, about eight or ten inches square, with a cylindrical stone about two inches in diameter fixed upright, by which perhaps a door was secured. Along the cornice outside, projecting about a foot beyond the front, holes were drilled at intervals through the stone; and our impression was, that an immense cotton cloth, running the whole length of the building, perhaps painted in a style corresponding with the ornaments, was attached to this cornice, and raised and lowered like a curtain, according to the exigencies of sun and rain. Such a curtain is used now in front of the piazzas of some haciendas in Yucatan.

The tops of the doorways were all broken. They had evidently been square, and over every one were large niches in the wall on each side, in which the lintels had been laid. These lintels had all fallen, and the stones above formed broken natural arches. Underneath were heaps of rubbish, but there were no remains of lintels. If they had been single slabs of stone, some of them must have been visible and prominent; and we made up our minds that these lintels were of *wood*. We had no authority for this. It is not suggested either by Del Rio or Captain Dupaix, and perhaps we should not have ventured the conclusion but for the wooden lintel which we had seen over the doorway at Ocosingo; and by what we saw afterward in Yucatan, we were confirmed, beyond all doubt, in our opinion. I do not conceive, however, that this gives any conclusive data in regard to the age of the buildings. The wood, if such as we saw in the other places, would be very lasting; its decay must have been extremely slow, and centuries may have elapsed since it perished altogether.

The building has two parallel corridors running lengthwise on all four of its sides. In front these corridors are about nine feet wide, and extend the whole length of the building upward of two hundred feet. In the long wall that divides them there is but one door, which is opposite the principal door of entrance, and has a corresponding one on the other side, leading to a courtyard in the rear. The floors are of cement, as hard as the best seen in the remains of Roman baths and cisterns. The walls are about ten feet high, plastered, and on each side of the principal entrance ornamented with medallions, of which the borders only remain; these perhaps contained the busts of the royal family. The separating-wall had apertures of about a foot, probably intended for purposes of ventilation. Some were of this form ⊐⊏, and some of this ⊤⊤, which have been called the Greek Cross and the Egyptian Tau, and made the subject of much learned speculation.

The ceiling of each corridor was in this form ◻/. The builders were evidently ignorant of the principles of the arch, and the support was made by stones lapping over as they rose, as at Ocosingo, and among the Cyclopean remains in Greece and Italy. Along the top was a layer of flat stone, and the sides, being plastered, presented a flat surface.

The long, unbroken corridors in front of the palace were probably intended for lords and gentlemen in waiting; or perhaps, in that beautiful position, which, before the forest grew up, must have commanded an extended view of a cultivated and inhabited plain, the king himself sat in it to receive the reports of his officers and to administer justice. Under our dominion Juan occupied the front corridor as a kitchen, and the other was our sleeping apartment.

From the centre door of this corridor a range of stone steps thirty feet long leads to a rectangular courtyard, eighty feet long by seventy broad. On each side of the steps are grim and gigantic figures, carved on stone in basso-relievo, nine or ten feet high, and in a position slightly inclined backward from the end of the steps to the floor of the corridor. The engraving opposite represents this side of the courtyard, and the one next following shows the figures alone, on a larger scale. They are adorned with rich headdresses and necklaces, but their attitude is that of pain and trouble. The design and anatomical proportions of the figures are faulty, but there is a force of expression about them which shows the skill and conceptive power of the artist. When we first took possession of the palace this courtyard was encumbered with trees, so that we could hardly see across it, and it was so filled up with rubbish that we were obliged to make excavations of several feet before these figures could be drawn.

On each side of the courtyard the palace was divided into apartments, probably for sleeping. On the right the piers have all fallen down. On the left they are still standing, and ornamented with stucco figures. In the centre apartment, in one of the holes before referred to of the arch, are the remains of a wooden pole about a foot long, which once stretched across, but the rest had decayed. It was the only piece of wood we found at Palenque, and we did not discover this until some time after we had made up our minds in regard to the wooden lintels over the doors. It was much worm-eaten, and probably, in a few years, not a vestige of it will be left.

At the farther side of the courtyard was another flight of stone steps, corresponding with those in front, on each side of which are carved figures, and on the flat surface between are single cartouches of hieroglyphics. . . .

The whole courtyard was overgrown with trees, and it was encumbered with ruins several feet high, so that the exact architectural arrangements could not be seen. Having our beds in the corridor adjoining, when we woke in the morning, and when we had finished the work of the day, we had it under our eyes. Every time we descended the steps the grim and mysterious figures stared us in the face, and it became to us one of the most interesting parts of the ruins. We were exceedingly anxious to make excavations, clear out the mass of rubbish, and lay the whole platform bare; but this was impossible. It is probably paved with stone or cement; and from the profusion of ornament in other parts, there is reason to believe that many curious and interesting specimens may be brought to light. This agreeable work is left for the future traveller, who may go there better provided with men and materials, and with more knowledge of what he has to encounter; and, in my opinion, if he finds nothing new, the mere spectacle of the courtyard entire will repay him for the labour and expense of clearing it.

The part of the building which forms the rear of the courtyard, communicating with it by the steps, consists of two corridors, the same as the front, paved, plastered, and ornamented with stucco. The floor of the corridor fronting the courtyard sounded hollow, and a breach had been made in it which seemed to lead into a subterraneous chamber; but in descending, by means of a tree with notches cut in it, and with a candle, we found merely a hollow in the earth, not bounded by any wall.

In the farther corridor the wall was in some places broken, and had several separate coats of plaster and paint. In one place we counted six layers, each of which had the remains of colour. In another place there seemed a line of written characters in black ink. We made an effort to get at them; but, in endeavouring to remove a thin upper stratum, they came off with it, and we desisted.

This corridor opened upon a second courtyard, eighty feet long and but thirty across. The floor of the corridor was ten feet above that of the courtyard, and on the wall underneath were square stones with hieroglyphics sculptured upon them. On the piers were stuccoed figures, but in a ruined condition.

On the other side of the courtyard were two ranges of corridors, which terminated the building in this direction. The first of them is divided into three apartments, with doors opening from the extremities upon the western corridor. All the piers are standing except that on the northwest corner. All are covered with stucco ornaments, and one with hieroglyphics. The rest contain figures in bas-relief.

The first was enclosed by a border, very wide at the bottom, part of which is destroyed. The subject consists of two figures with facial angles similar to that in the plate before given, plumes of feathers and other decorations for headdresses, necklaces, girdles, and sandals; each has hold of the same curious baton, part of which is destroyed, and opposite their hands are hieroglyphics, which probably give the history of these incomprehensible personages. The others are more ruined, and no attempt has been made to restore them. One is kneeling as if to receive an honour, and the other a blow.

So far the arrangements of the palace are simple and easily understood; but on the left are several distinct and independent buildings, as will be seen by the plan, the particulars of which, however, I do not consider it necessary to describe. The principal of these is the tower, on the south side of the second court. This tower is conspicuous by its height and proportions, but on examination in detail it is found unsatisfactory and uninteresting. The base is thirty feet square, and it has three stories. Entering over a heap of rubbish at the base, we found within another tower, distinct from the outer one, and a stone staircase, so narrow that a large man could not ascend it. The staircase terminates against a dead stone ceiling, closing all farther passage, the last step being only six or eight inches from it. For what purpose a staircase was carried up to such a bootless termination we could not conjecture. The whole tower was a substantial stone structure, and in its arrangements and purposes about as incomprehensible as the sculptured tablets.

Left of the tower is another building with two corridors, one richly decorated with pictures in stucco, and having in the centre the elliptical tablet represented in the engraving opposite. It is four feet long and three wide, of hard stone set in the wall, and the sculpture is in bas-relief. Around it are the remains of a rich stucco border. The principal figure sits cross-legged on a couch ornamented with two leopards' heads; the attitude is easy, the physiognomy the same as that of the other personages, and the expression calm and benevolent. The figure wears around its neck a necklace of pearls, to which is suspended a small medallion containing a face; perhaps intended as an image of the sun. Like every other subject of sculpture we had seen in the country, the personage had earrings, bracelets on the wrists, and a girdle round the loins. The headdress differs from most of the others at Palenque in that it wants the plumes of feathers. Near the head are three hieroglyphics.

The other figure, which seems that of a woman, is sitting cross-legged on the ground, richly dressed, and apparently in the act of making an offering. In this supposed offering is seen a plume of feathers, in which the headdress of the principal person is deficient. Over the head of the sitting personage are four hieroglyphics. This is the only piece of sculptured stone about the palace except those in the courtyard. Under it formerly stood a table, of which the impression against the wall is still visible, and which is given in the engraving in faint lines, after the model of other tables still existing in other places.

At the extremity of this corridor there is an aperture in the pavement, leading by a flight of steps to a platform; from this a door, with an ornament in stucco over it, opens by another flight of steps upon a narrow, dark passage, terminating in other corridors, which run transversely. These are called subterraneous apartments; but there are windows opening from them above the ground, and, in fact, they are merely a ground-floor below the pavement of the corridors. In most parts, however, they are so dark that it is necessary to visit them with candles. There are no bas-reliefs or stucco ornaments; and the only objects which our guide pointed out or which attracted our attention, were several stone tables, one crossing and blocking up the corridor, about eight feet long, four wide and three high. One of these lower corridors had a door opening upon the back part of the terrace, and we generally passed through it with a candle to get to the other buildings. In two other places there were flights of steps leading to corridors above. Probably these were sleeping apartments.

In that part of the plan marked Room No. 1, the walls were more richly decorated with stucco ornaments than any other in the palace; but, unfortunately, they were much mutilated. On each side of the doorway was a stucco figure, one of which, being the most perfect, is given in the engraving opposite. Near it is an apartment in which is marked 'small altar'. It was richly ornamented, like those which will be hereafter referred to in other buildings; and from the appearance of the back wall we supposed there had been stone tablets. In our utter ignorance of the habits of the people who had formerly occupied this building, it was impossible to form any conjecture for what uses these different apartments were intended; but if we are right in calling it a palace, the name which the Indians give it, it seems probable that the part surrounding the courtyards was for public and state occasions, and that the rest was occupied as the place of residence of the royal family; this room with the small altar, we may suppose, was what would be called, in our own times, a royal chapel.

With these helps and the aid of the plan, the reader will be able to find his way through the ruined palace of Palenque; he will form some idea of the profusion of its ornaments, of their unique and striking character, and of their mournful effect, shrouded by trees; and perhaps with him, as with us, fancy will present it as it was before the hand of ruin had swept over it, perfect in its amplitude and rich decorations, and occupied by the strange people whose portraits and figures now adorn its walls.

Incidents of Travel in Central America, 1842

The elephant in America?

GRAFTON ELLIOT SMITH

SIR GRAFTON ELLIOT SMITH (*1871-1937*) *was born in Grafton, New South Wales, and studied medicine at the University of Sydney. In 1894 he began his research career in anatomy, specializing in the structure of the human brain, and in 1896 he came to England to continue his studies at Cambridge. In 1900 he accepted the post of Professor of Anatomy in the Government Medical School at Cairo, and during his stay in Egypt he developed an interest in the possibilities of applying his work to the study of archaeology and anthropology. He joined with a team of archaeologists in a survey of 20,000 Nubian burials and made extensive contributions to the science of palaeopathology. Throughout his further career as Professor of Anatomy at Manchester University and University College, London, he continued to preserve a lively interest in all aspects of magic and religion, early emigrations and diffusions of culture, and propounded a theory about the possible Egyptian origin of the Central American civilization which has many supporters today.*

The discussion of representations of the elephant has played an exceptionally prominent part in the interpretation of man's achievements in the past, so that the identification of conventionalised elephants has become one of the deciding issues in the great problem of the reconstruction of the early history of civilisation.

In his *History of New France*, published in 1744, Father Charlevoix gave an account of a tradition, that still survives among the North-American Indians, of a great elk, concerning which the late Sir Edward Tylor made the comment: 'It is hard to imagine that anything but the actual sight of a live elephant would have given rise to this tradition.' In 1813 Baron von Humboldt described the picture . . . of a creature with the head of an elephant, human hands, the feet of a bird, and, as Professor Seler pointed out some years ago, the wings of a bat, concerning which Humboldt made the following remarks: 'The disguise of the sacrificing priests presents some remarkable and apparently not accidental resemblances with the Hindoo Ganesa (the elephant-headed god of wisdom)'. One seems to recognise in the sacrificer's mask the trunk of an elephant. The snout of the tapir no doubt protrudes a little more than that of our pigs, but it is a long way from the tapir's snout to the trunk figured in the 'Codex Borgianus'.

During the intervening period there has been considerable controversy concerning these and many other pictures and sculptures. For instance, there is a picture in the 'Codex Cortes' . . . representing a human figure with an elephant's head. The identity of this elephant-headed god is obvious, because he carries thunderbolts, and is associated with a serpent coiled round so as to retain the water that should fall as rain. In other words, it is a child-like representation of an episode in the *Rig-veda*, in which the god Indra, who is associated with an elephant and with thunder, has a combat with the serpent Vritra, who is described in the Indian epic as holding up the water in precisely the same way as the Maya artist depicts the episode.

In another Maya Codex . . . the elephant-headed god is represented pouring out the rain from a vase, and putting his foot upon the head of the serpent so as to prevent the rain from reaching the earth. This again is another incident in the mythology of India, and one might collect scores of other pictures from these early American manuscripts which might serve as a child's guide to the *Rig-veda*. If it be objected that the *Rig-veda* was written perhaps twenty centuries before the American artist drew these pictures, it is important not to forget that the ancient Indian stories were still current in Java, Cambodia, and elsewhere in the neighbourhood of the south-east corner of Asia, at the time when the American artist on the opposite side of the Pacific was drawing his illustrations of the story.

During the last century there has been a great amount of controversy concerning certain architectural embellishments of the corners of Mayan buildings in Central America, which have been compared – and rightly compared – with similar adornments of Asiatic buildings, particularly those of Indo-China and Java, and have been claimed to represent the trunks of elephants. Anyone who studies the Asiatic evidence, however, will realise that these adornments do not usually represent elephants' trunks at all, but highly specialised and diverse forms of the makara, the Indian capricorn.

The upper end of a stela at Copan (eighth century AD) in Central American is shown in the photograph . . . of Dr Maudslay's drawing. The peculiar headdress of the central figure presents features distinctive of Java and Indo-China. Both in the ancient sculptures of Boro-budur, in Java, and in the Cambodian temples, a headdress such as is shown here is worn, as it still is by the Emperor of Annam. The most distinctive feature of this particular stela is the upper left-hand corner, which seems to be a conventionalised picture of an Indian elephant with a rider bending forwards on it, and also wearing an Indian turban. The mode of conventionalising the ear is found also in Asia, from India to Java; and the peculiar method of conventionalising the tusk and the under-surface of the trunk by two areas with cross-hatching, introduces exactly the methods employed by the Eastern Asiatic artists – in particular, those of China – at a time corresponding to that in which these American sculptures were made. These and many other representations of the elephant have been discussed for more than a century, but several new bits of information have come to light recently, which, as it seems to me, settle the question definitely once for all.

The elephant-like forms at the upper corners of Mayan buildings in Central America have been the subject of controversy for more than eighty years (see my book, *Elephants and Ethnologists*, 1924), but new evidence has just come to light to settle the matter once for all.

Mr J. Eric Thompson has just discovered in the Ayer Collection of the Newberry Library in Chicago the hitherto unpublished water-colour sketches (of which photographic copies are reproduced on page 85) made about ninety years ago by M. Frédéric de Waldeck, a French artist who has been described (by the historian Bancroft) as 'the most indefatigable and successful explorer of Palenque'. No one is likely to doubt the accuracy of the representation of the elephant's head, either in the profile views or in the front view with the mouth widely opened in the 'bun-catching' attitude. The lozenge-shaped form of the open mouth, the cut stumps of the tusks, and the markings of the under-surface of the trunk are all quite distinctive of the elephant.

Waldeck writes that the four strips (bas-reliefs in stucco) were found by himself on the floor of a subterranean room in the Palace at Palenque (of which Dr Alfred P. Maudslay, in *Biologica Centrali-Americana*, has given full information with exceptionally beautiful photographs and plans), and the photographs reproduced on page 85 were made from his water-colour sketches. The other photograph reproduces Waldeck's drawing (the shaded parts are restorations) of part of the wall in the same room.

My colleague, Professor Collie, has called my attention to the fact that the very un-Maya-like floral pattern intertwining both the elephants' heads (and their anthropomorphised derivatives on the second slab) suggest well-known Chinese motives of the T'ang period, which points to the eighth or ninth century AD – a date that seems to be appropriate for the Maya building in which the slabs were found. The third slab is of special interest because it represents a conventionalised tapir – the form of the ear, mouth, and snout being characteristic.

The design upon the wall is peculiarly interesting. The elephant's head is set upon the entwined snake, as so often happens in the Maya codices. But the Maya sculptor, unwittingly anticipating the controversies that were to develop ten centuries after him, has placed as heraldic supporters of the elephant two of the rival claimants put by modern ethnologists, the macaw on the right, and on the left a highly conventionalised tapir (compare the stucco slab) borne upon a bird's body. Here, then, is decisive evidence that ought to settle the elephant controversy once for all.

Other representations of elephants have been brought to light in San Salvador and Panama. In 1916 Dr Thomas Gann found in a mound at Yallock in Guatemala a cylindrical vase (now in the Bristol Museum) with polychrome paintings of two elephants, shown in the correct colour. . . . The form of the head, body, and legs does not admit of any doubt as to their identity as elephants; and the peculiarities of the lower jaw and teeth can be explained by studying the mode of conventionalising elephants in Java and elsewhere in the Eastern Asiatic area. During the centuries when the Indian Gupta phase dominated artistic expression in Indo-China and Indonesia, China also came under the sway of its influence. It is not a mere chance that Chinese art attained the zenith of its accomplishment during the T'ang period (AD 602-907). The influence of India left its mark upon Chinese Buddhistic art, and probably also upon that of the Nara period in Japan. But the great wave of culture that flowed over Eastern Asia and the Malay Archipelago in the eighth century swept out into Oceania also, and was carried to Central America. The Palenque bas-reliefs represent the elephant in association with floral designs suggestive of the T'ang period because they belong to that period and were expressions of the same inspiration.

The Elephant Controversy Settled by a Decisive Discovery
Illustrated London News, 15 January, 1927

The temple pyramid of Tepoxtlan

EDUARD SELER

EDUARD SELER (1859-1922) was born in Germany and planned to become a schoolmaster. A serious illness obliged him to seek a more sedentary occupation, so he turned to work as a translator. A book on pre-Columbian America aroused his interest in the subject, and he obtained an appointment in the Americanist department of the Berlin Ethnological Museum. By this time his health had substantially improved and in 1887 he left on an expedition to Central America. He made great contributions to the study of Maya and Aztec writings and expounded the complicated Aztec calendar system in addition to his field-work on the monuments of the area.

The causeway leading from the City of Mexico, which runs southward, formerly through the waters of the salt lake itself, now through meadow land, to Churubusco, the ancient Uitzilopochco, where the road branches off to Chalco, and to the margin of the great lava stream, which extends from a little volcano below the lofty Cerro de Ajusco to the plain lying 2,300 meters above the sea. A traveller leaving the city by this road sees before him a high mountain range, which connects the towering Ajusco with the snow-capped cone of Popocatepetl and in this direction forms the termination of the undrained basin of Mexico. This mountain range is crossed from Xochimilco by a long, gradually ascending path, which finally leads into extensive pine forests covering the whole breadth of the ridge. Another road, from Chalco, runs in the valley of Amecameca, immediately at the western base of Popocatepetl, to a less elevated path. In both places the mountain slopes on the south quite precipitously to the valleys below, the streams of which flow into the Rio de las Balsas. These are the valleys of Cuernavaca, situated about 1,600 meters above the sea, and of Yautepec, lying about 500 meters lower. They have been celebrated from ancient times for their mild climate. Here the Mexican kings had their pleasure gardens, in which they cultivated plants of the tierra caliente that did not thrive in Mexico itself. Cortes did not fail to include this district within the limits of his marquesado, and the viceroys, and also the unfortunate Maximilian, loved to sojourn in this favoured vale. Midway between Yautepec and Cuernavaca, directly at the foot of the lofty mountain range towering on the north, on a riblike spur at the upper end of a range of hills and ridges which divides the valleys of Yautepec and Cuernavaca, in the centre of a small plain forming the extreme northwestern extremity of the valley of Cuernavaca, lies the small town of Tepoxtlan. Although but three miles distant from each of the cities previously named, this place, because it is situated quite away from the great highroads radiating from the capital and at the foot of the mountain, has remained until very recently little known or investigated. The ancient inhabitants, who undoubtedly were of the same race as the Tlalhuies of Cuernavaca, have in the main shared the history of the latter. Cuernavaca, the ancient Quauhnauac, was the first territory which fell into the hands of the Mexicans when they began to spread beyond the limits of the valley. In the reign of the third Mexican king, Itzcouatl, who reigned in the second quarter of the fifteenth century, the siege and subjugation of Cuernavaca is reported, and under Motecuhzoma Ilhuicamina, the king succeeding Itzcouatl, Tepoxtlan is named in the Mendoza codex, together with Quauh-nauac, Uaxtepec, and Yautepec, among the conquered cities. The Historia Mexicana of the year 1576 (Aubin-Goupil codex) reports in connection with the accession to the throne in the year 1487 of King Ahuitzotl, which was celebrated with great sacrifices of captives, that new kings had been installed in Quauhnauac, Tepoxtlan, Uaxtepec, and Xiloxochitepec.

In the tribute list (Mendoza codex, page 26, no. 13) Tepoxtlan, the 'place of the axe', is again put with the same towns in the Uaxtepec group. Cortes came into contact with Tepoxtlan in the year 1521 on his march from Yautepec to Cuernavaca, when, because the inhabitants did not voluntarily surrender, he burned the town. Bernal Diaz extols the fine women (*muy buenas mugeres*) and the booty which the soldiers obtained here. After the establishment of Spanish rule Tepoxt-lan, with Cuernavaca, was included in the principality, which, with the title Marques del Valle de Oxaca, was awarded Cortes as recompense for his distinguished services. A manuscript Relacion of the year 1582, which is preserved with others of like character in the Archivo General de las Indias in Sevilla, refers to the place as Villa de Tepoxtlan, and mentions six estancias subordinate to it. In the same Relacion it is also stated that the Mexican language was spoken by the inhabitants, both by those who still lived in the place and those who, having become disgusted with the country, had emigrated to the neighbourhood of Vera Cruz. Through incorporation into the marquesado the town was doubtless saved from oppression and vexation by lesser encomenderos. In their isolated mountain home the people have been able to preserve their language and their old customs. The place has now a population numbering from 5,000 to 6,000 souls of fairly pure Indian descent, who speak pure, uncorrupted Mexican, are proud of their descent, and cling tenaciously to the ancient traditional customs. It is deserving of mention as an interesting fact that since last year a newspaper has been published here with the title El Grano de Arena, which, besides the Spanish text, always contains several columns of matter in the Mexican language.

As we passed through the town of Cuernavaca in December, 1887, on the return from our expedition to Xochicalco we were told that there was a pyramid in Tepoxtlan as interesting as that of Xochicalco. We wished to visit it, but the governor of the state of Morelos told us at that time – whether correctly I leave undecided – that he could not permit it, for 'these Indians are terrible'. As we had still so much else to see we did not insist upon it. Beyond this general report nothing has been known until very recently of the pyramid of Tepoxtlan, but two years ago, when the extraordinary session of the Americanist Congress was about to be held in Mexico and an effort was being made throughout the whole country to furnish something fresh in the nature of relics and finds for the scholars attending this meeting, the thought arose even in Tepoxtlan of freeing the pyramid of that locality from the rubbish hiding it from view and of opening up its interior chambers and outer walls. A young engineer, Francisco Rodriguez, a native of Tepoxtlan, followed out this idea with enthusiasm and strove to carry it into execution. He was able to induce the people of his district to furnish volunteer labour, and thus in the months of August and September, 1895, the pyramid was uncovered, a result of which the Tepoxtecs themselves are now quite proud. A description of the pyramid, including a plan of the structure, was submitted by Mr Rodriguez to the congress assembled in October of the year 1895. It has now been published in the proceedings of the congress. Later, accompanied by Mr Rodriguez, Mr Marshall II Saville visited the pyramid and took several photographs of it. In August, 1896, Mr Saville read a report on this pyramid before the American Association for the Advancement of Sciences, convened in Buffalo, which was published in volume 8 of the bulletins of the American Museum of Natural History, and again later in the journal Monumental Records. From this and from Mr Rodriguez's report I gathered the information which appears below:

The pyramid is situated about 2,000 feet above the town, on a cliff detached from the ridge of the mountain range, which north of the town rises rugged and precipitous above the level plain. The pyramid itself is not visible from the plain, but its approximate location is marked by huge crags which on the left project above the mountain ridge. From the foot of the precipice the road ascends through a small canyon. Several long flights of steps are encountered, some of them cut into the rock, others built of masonry. Carved inscriptions are to be seen here and there on the perpendicular walls of the ravine. About halfway to the top the road emerges from the canyon and winds aloft on the very face of the cliff. For nearly 100 steps, according to Saville's statement, the ascent is almost perpendicular. Steps are hewn into the rock or supported by masonry. When Rodriguez began his excavations here he was obliged to use ladders in two places, because the way was obstructed by fallen rock fragments. When the top of the cliff is finally reached it is seen to consist of two separate plateaux which are connected by a narrow neck. On the western one of these two plateaux is the temple pyramid; the eastern one is almost completely covered with foundation walls of buildings of different kinds and sizes, which probably were the dwellings of priests, and other buildings adjoining. Behind rises a rocky cliff covered with pine woods, which can only be reached from this spot, and here Mr Rodriguez found running water.

Viewed from the east side, the pyramid is seen to rise in three terraces over a rough substructure that forms a horizontal base on the uneven, rocky ground. . . . A flight of steps on this side leads up to the top of the first terrace, which, rising to a height of 9·5 meters above the rock foundation, forms the broad base of the building proper, formed by the two other terraces. A second stairway on the south side near the entrance of the temple leads to the top of the lower terrace. . . . On the west side, which is the front of the temple, this first terrace forms a small platform . . ., and in the centre of this there is a low rectangular bench, with serrated corners, up which flights of steps probably led on all four sides. The location of this little structure corresponds to the spot where, in the great temple of Mexico, stood the two round stones, the quauhxicalli and the temalacatl, and it was probably used for similar sacrificial purposes. I also found a very similar structure in Quiengola in the middle line of the platform of the east pyramid, whose front likewise faced the west. From this platform a stairway leads to the top of the second terrace and to the entrance of the temple itself, which the third terrace forms. This temple is formed of walls 1·9 meters thick, constructed of blocks of red and black tezontle (porous volcanic rock) with copious mortar of lime and sand, and reaching to a height of 2·5 meters. The roof has fallen in. From the ruins Mr Rodriguez was still able to determine that it had been a flat arch, with a maximum rise of 0·5 meter, a span of 5 meters, and a thickness of 0·7 meter, formed of pieces of tezontle and a great quantity of mortar, the use of which in thick layers made the construction possible. On the site of the front wall are to be seen the remains of two rectangular masonry columns, which left a wide central doorway with a narrow one on each side. The interior space is divided by a wall, 0·9 meter thick, pierced by a doorway, into two rooms, of which the front one runs back 3·73 and the inner one 5·2 meters, with a width of 6 meters. In the middle of the front room Rodriguez found a rectangular depression, and in it remains of charcoal and a couple of well-preserved pieces of copal. This was probably, therefore, the hearth where the sacred fire burned and whence, perhaps, glowing coals were obtained with which to burn incense to the god.

In the axis of the inner chamber against the rear wall stood the idol. The doorway connecting the two rooms has a width of 1·9 meters. It is flanked by two pillars, which are covered with stucco and richly ornamented. At the bottom there is a sort of fluting; above this a grecque in relief, like those in the palaces at Mitla, and at the top a picture of the sun, only the lower part of which is still preserved. All are painted in colour, and the colours are still tolerably fresh. In the place where the idol stood, in the rear room, Rodriguez found remains of a sub-structure among which were two sculptured fragments, one of them, according to his account, containing a bas-relief, of what character is not stated, painted in a deep red colour; the other, the relief picture of a Mexican royal crown (xiuh-uitzolli). Both pieces are now preserved in the cabildo of Tepoxtlan, in a room transformed into a museum. The most interesting feature of the inner apartment are the benches, ornamented on the front with carved stones. These run round a part of the front room and along the rear and both lateral walls of the back room. They display at the upper part a narrow, somewhat projecting frieze, on which, it seems, the twenty characters for the days are represented. Beneath this, on each lateral wall, there are placed four large slabs, with symbols in relief, apparently relating to the four cardinal points. On the south side we see what seem to be the four pre-historic ages; on the north side the gods corresponding to the four cardinal points are represented by their symbols. I must forgo attempting to explain these more exactly until casts or good photographs are submitted for study. The reliefs on the rear wall are, perhaps, of a still more interesting nature, but unfortunately here a portion of the bench is destroyed. It is to be hoped that Mr Saville, who has now started again for Tepoxtlan and Xochicalco, will bring home satisfactory casts and make known these representations.

Finally, in addition to the above, two stone tablets, which were found built into the south wall of the lower terrace of the pyramid, are of special importance. One contains the hieroglyph of King Ahuitzotl, who derived his name from a small ghostlike water animal, which, according to Mexican tales, played the rôle of a sort of nixy and was represented in this form. On the other slab a rabbit is depicted, and beside it are 10 circles, which would indicate the year 10 Tochtli, corresponding to the year 1502 of the Christian chronology, the last year of Ahuitzotl's reign, or the year of his death. Saville has interpreted these two tablets quite correctly, and he concludes that the year of the erection of the temple and its builder were thus immortalised. This is probably correct, in which case, in truth, 'the ancient temple of Tepoxtlan would be the only aboriginal structure still standing in Mexico to which we can with probability assign a certain date'.

It would next be desirable to know to which god sacrifices were offered in this place. Neither Rodriguez nor Saville have attempted to answer this question. I am fortunately in a position to be able to decide this matter beyond dispute. There was a class of deities among the Mexicans which excited the special wonderment and abhorrence of the monks and the Spaniards generally. These were the pulque gods, or the gods of drunkenness. As we say (in German) of a drunken man that 'he has got an ape', so the Mexicans, of course, with a doubtless wholly different train of thought, spoke of a rabbit (tochtli), under whose influence the intoxicated person acted. They said he had 'rabbited himself' (omotochtili), when anyone drank to insensibility and in this condition came to any harm. Hence the gods of drunkenness were also called Totochtin, 'rabbits'. The day ome Tochtli, '2 rabbits', was under their influence. Whoever was born on that day, if he did not take special precautions, seemed inevitably doomed to become a drunkard. Since there were different kinds of drunkenness, intoxication manifesting itself with different people in very different ways, the

'400 rabbits' (centzon totochtin) were spoken of 'as though one intended to say that pulque made innumerable kinds of drunkards'. Hence the pulque gods were also designated as centzon Totochtin, the '400 rabbits', and a large number of them were specified by particular names. Concerning the significance of these deities, this one fact is of primary importance, that they are all closely related to the earth goddess. Like her, they wear the golden Huaxtec nose ornament, shaped like a crescent, which was called yacametztli. This ornament is so characteristic of them that it is usually marked on all objects dedicated to the pulque gods. A second characteristic of these deities is the bi-coloured face, painted red and black. The two colours, in many parallel red and black longitudinal stripes, likewise served to denote an object as consecrated to the pulque gods. Thus, in the picture manuscript of the Biblioteca Nazionale in Florence, the *manta de dos conejos*, 'blanket of the 2 rabbits' (ome-tochtilmàtli), the shoulder covering of the pulque gods, and, in the same manuscript, the shield of Macuil-Xochitl, are marked in this way. These gods are characterised by a remark which occurs above them in the picture manuscript of the Biblioteca Nazionale in Florence still more exactly than by their relation to the earth goddess. The pulque gods in this manuscript are represented after or among the *fiestas móbiles*, immediately after the feast of flowers (chicome xochitl and ce xochitl), and it is stated in this place that 'when the Indians had harvested and gathered in their maize, then they drank to intoxication and danced while they invoked this demon and others of these four hundred'. It seems, therefore, that here we have to do with gods of husbandry, who were to impart virtue to the soil as the pulque – and this is always brought out – imparts courage and strength and was the drink of the fearless and strong, the eagles and jaguars (quauhtli and ocelotl), that is, the warriors.

Among the names by which these gods were known, in addition to ome Tochtli, '2 rabbits', which refers directly to their nature as pulque gods, we meet almost exclusively such as are derived from place names, or at least are formed in a similar manner to those derived from place names as Acolhua, Colhuatzincatl, Toltecatl, Totoltecatl, Izquitecatl, Chimalpanecatl, Yauhtecatl, Tezcatzoncatl, Tlaltecayoua, Pahtecatl, Papaztac, Tlilhua: and a pulque god Tepoxtecatl, a god of Tepoxtlan, is repeatedly and prominently mentioned.

If the fact is taken into consideration that the temple which I have described above is still called by the people 'casa del Tepoxteco', then the supposition is not far to seek that it is our Tepoxtlan from which the pulque god Tepoxtecatl derived his name, and this supposition is confirmed by two good witnesses. In the Relacion that I already mentioned at the beginning, which was the reply to an inquiry blank, dispatched under King Philip II with the same wording to all towns of the Spanish colonial territory, the question concerning the name of this place and the meaning of the name is answered thus: 'They say that the place is named Tepoxtlan because, when their ancestors settled this land, they found this name already in use, for those who settled there before (or first) said that the great devil, or idol, which they had, was called Ome tuchitl, that is, '2 rabbits', and that he bore the surname Tepoxtecatl'. The other testimony is furnished by the often-mentioned picture manuscript of the Biblioteca Nazionale in Florence, which, besides various other pulque gods, represents Tepoxtecatl in full figure and in hieroglyph and remarks concerning him: 'This is the representation of a great iniquity which was the custom in a village named Tepoxtlan; namely, when an Indian died in a state of intoxication the others of this village made a great feast to him, holding in their hands copper axes which were used to fell wood. This village is near Yautepeque. They are vassals of the Lord Marques del Valle'. . . .

It is to be hoped that the interest once aroused among the patriotic inhabitants of Tepoxtlan will continue, and that further investigation will produce other important material for the study of the ancient civilisation and history of these regions.

The Temple Pyramid of Tepoxtlan,

Bulletin of the Bureau of American Ethnology, No. 28, 1904

A royal tomb at Palenque

ALBERTO RUZ

ALBERTO RUZ (1906–) was educated at the Universidad Nacional in Cuba, then at the School of Anthropology and History in Mexico, and has devoted many years to his researches in archaeology and anthropology at the Universidad Autonoma of Mexico and in Paris. He has held progressively important posts in the National Institute of Anthropology and History of Mexico, and was finally appointed Director. In this capacity he has conducted many valuable investigations into the history of Central America, with particular emphasis on the civilization of the ancient Maya.

When in the spring of 1949 the National Institute of Anthropology and History of Mexico appointed me Director of Research at Palenque, I fully appreciated that this was the most important event in my professional life.

I knew that my predecessors had been explorers, artists, scientists, distinguished men, and that marvellous sculpture had been discovered there during the course of 150 years; but I was convinced that many other archaeological treasures still lay hidden in the rubble of the palaces, temples, and pyramids, and beneath the dense and mysterious Chiapas jungle which had been their jealous guardian.

A feature of my working plan was one which should always be present in the plans of archaeologists working in Mexico and Central America; to seek for architectural structures of an earlier date and lying beneath the actually visible building. It has, in fact, been proved that the ancient inhabitants of Central America were in the habit of building on top of older constructions, more with the object of increasing their height and bringing them closer to the heavens in which the gods lived than for any practical purpose.

For various reasons I decided to make such a search in the Temple of the Inscriptions. First, because it was the tallest building in Palenque and therefore the most likely to have been built on top of something older; secondly, because of its importance and its containing some fine, large, sculptured panels and one of the largest Mayan hieroglyphic inscriptions; and thirdly, because it had never been explored and its flooring was more or less intact – owing to its being made of great slabs instead of the more usual simple levelled plaster.

This temple is composed of a portico leading to a sanctuary and two lateral cells; and in the central room of the temple one of the slabs of the flooring caught my eye, as it had done with my predecessors on the site. This slab has round its edges two rows of holes provided with stone plugs. After thinking for some hours on its possible purpose, I came to the conclusion that the answer would be found underneath the stone; and accordingly I began to clear the floor beside it, in a place where the slabs had been already removed or broken by treasure-seekers, who had been discouraged from going on by meeting with a heavy filling of large stones.

Quite soon after beginning to remove the rubble I noticed that the temple's walls were prolonged under the floor instead of stopping at its level – a sure sign that there was 'something' to be found underneath. Elated by this prospect, I began excavating and on the next day – May 20, 1949 – there appeared that stone which in Mayan buildings is always used to close up a vault. The Mayans did not build a true arch, their vaulting being simply the result of bringing walls closer together by means of inclined facings which converge until there remains only a very small space to be closed with a single flat stone. A few days later I found a step, and then more and more steps. What had been found was an interior staircase descending into the pyramid and which for a reason which we then did not know, had been made impracticable by a filling of large stones and clay.

Four spells of work – each two-and-a-half months long – were needed before we were able to clear the filling from this mysterious staircase. After a flight of 45 steps, we reached a landing with a U-turn. There followed another flight, of 21 steps, leading to a corridor, whose level is more or less the same as that on which the pyramid was built – i.e., some 22 metres under the temple flooring. In the vaulting of the landing two narrow galleries open out and allow air and a little light to enter from a near-by courtyard.

Above one of the first steps we reached we found a box-shaped construction of masonry containing a modest offering: two ear-plugs of jade placed on a river stone painted red. On reaching the end of the flight we found another box of offerings, backing on to a wall which blocked the passage. This time it was a richer offering: three pottery dishes, two shells full of cinnabar, seven jade beads, a pair of circular ear-plugs also of jade, the plugs of which were shaped like a flower, and a beautiful tear-shaped pearl, with its *lustre* pretty well preserved. An offering of this kind, at such a depth, told us without any doubt that we were approaching the object of our search.

And, in fact, on July 13, 1952, after demolishing a solid obstruction some metres thick, made of stone and lime – this was very hard and the wet lime burnt the hands of the workmen – there appeared on one side of the corridor a triangular slab, 2 metres high, set vertically to block an entrance. At the foot of this slab, in a rudimentary stone cist, there lay, mixed together, the largely destroyed skeletons of six young persons, of whom one at least was a female.

At noon on the 15th of the same month we opened the entrance, displacing the stone enough for a man to pass through sideways. It was a moment of indescribable emotion for me when I slipped behind the stone and found myself in an enormous crypt which seemed to have been cut out of the rock – or rather, out of the ice, thanks to the curtain of stalactites and the chalcite veiling deposited on the walls by the infiltration of rain-water during the centuries. This increased the marvellous quality of the spectacle and gave it a fairy-tale aspect. Great figures of priests modelled in stucco a little larger than life-size formed an impressive procession round the walls. The high vaulting was reinforced by great stone transoms, of dark colour with yellowish veins, giving an impression of polished wood.

Almost the whole crypt was occupied by a colossal monument, which we then supposed to be a ceremonial altar, composed of a stone of more than 8 square metres, resting on an enormous monolith of 6 cubic metres, supported in its turn by six great blocks of chiselled stone. All these elements carried beautiful reliefs.

Finest of all for its unsurpassable execution and perfect state of preservation was the great stone covering the whole and bearing on its four sides some hieroglyphic inscriptions with thirteen abbreviated dates corresponding to the beginning of the seventh century AD, while its upper face shows a symbolic scene surrounded by astronomical signs.

I believed that I had found a ceremonial crypt, but I did not wish to make any definite assertions before I had finished exploring the chamber and, above all, before I had found out whether the base of the supposed altar was solid or not. On account of the rains and the exhausting of the funds available for this phase of the exploration, we had to wait until November before returning to Palenque. I then had the base bored horizontally at two of the corners; and it was not long before one of the drills reached a hollow space. I introduced a wire through the narrow aperture and, on withdrawing it, I saw that some particles of red paint were adhering to it.

The presence of this colouring matter inside the monolith was of supreme importance. The offerings found at the beginning and the end of the secret staircase had borne red paint; and the sides of the great stone showed traces of having been painted red all over. This colour was associated in the Mayan and Aztec cosmogony with the East, but also it is nearly always found in tombs, on the walls or on objects accompanying the dead person or on his bones. The presence of red in tombs came, therefore, to indicate resurrection and a hope of immortality. The particles of cinnabar adhering to the wire inserted into the centre of the enormous stone block was therefore unquestionable evidence of burial: and our supposed ceremonial altar must therefore be an extraordinary sepulchre.

To prove this it was necessary to lift the sculptured stone, which measured 3·80 metres by 2·20 metres (some 13 by 7 ft.), weighing about 5 tons and constituting one of the most valuable masterpieces of American pre-Hispanic sculpture. The preparations lasted two days in the midst of feverish tension. It was necessary to fell in the forest a hard-wood tree of the kind called in that region 'bari', and to cut it into sections of different lengths, lift these along a greasy path to the lorry, convey them by motor to the pyramid, move them by manpower to the temple, lower them by cables through the interior staircase and introduce them through the narrow aperture of the crypt.

The four major sections of the trunk were placed vertically under the corners of the stone and on top of each was placed a railway or motorcar jack. On November 27, at dusk, after a twelve-hour working day, the soul-shaking manœuvre took place. Every kind of precaution was taken to prevent the stone tipping up or slipping, and, above all, to prevent its suffering any damage. Handled simultaneously and without any jerking, the jacks lifted the stone millimetre by millimetre, and while this was happening slabs were placed underneath it to hold it up. When the jacks reached the limit of their extension, other sections of the tree were inserted and the operation was repeated. A little before midnight the stone was resting intact 0·60 metre above its original level on six robust logs of 'bari' and a few days later it was lifted to a height of 1·12 metres.

Once the stone left its seating and began to rise it could be seen that a cavity had been cut out of the enormous block which served it as a base. This cavity was of an unexpected shape, oblong and curvilinear, rather like the silhouette in schematised form of a fish or of the capital letter Omega (Ω), closed in its lower part. The cavity was sealed by a highly polished slab fitting exactly and provided with four perforations, each with a stone plug. On raising the slab which closed it we discovered the mortuary receptacle.

This was not the first time during my career as an archaeologist that a tomb had been discovered, but no occasion has been so impressive as this. In the vermilion-coloured walls and base of the cavity which served as a coffin, the sight of the human remains – complete, although the bones were damaged – covered with jade jewels for the most part, was most impressive. It was possible to judge the form of the body which had been laid in this 'tailored' sarcophagus; and the jewels added a certain amount of life, both from the sparkle of the jade and because they were so well 'placed' and because their form suggested the volume and contour of the flesh which originally covered the skeleton. It was easy also to imagine the high rank of the personage who could aspire to a mausoleum of such impressive richness.

We were struck by his stature, greater than that of the average Mayan of today; and by the fact that his teeth were not filed or provided with incrustations of pyrites or jade, since that practice (like that of artificially deforming the cranium) was usual in individuals of the higher social ranks. The state of destruction of the skull did not allow us to establish precisely whether or not it had been deformed. In the end, we decided that the personage might have been of non-Mayan origin, though it is clear that he ended in being one of the kings of Palenque. The reliefs, which we have still to uncover on the sides of the sarcophagus and which are now hidden under lateral buttresses, may tell us before long something of the personality and identity of their glorious dead.

Even if he had not been buried in the most extraordinary tomb so far discovered in this continent of America, it would still be perfectly possible to assess the importance of this personage from the jewels which he wore – many of them already familiar in Mayan bas-reliefs. As shown in some reliefs, he was wearing a diadem made from tiny disks of jade and his hair was divided into separate strands by means of small jade tubes of appropriate shape; and we discovered a small jade plate of extraordinary quality cut in the shape of the head of a Zotz, the vampire god of the underworld and this may have been a final part of the diadem. Around the neck were visible various threads of a collar composed of jade beads in many forms – spheres, cylinders, tri-lobed beads, floral buds, open flowers, pumpkins, melons, and a snake's head. The ear-plugs were composed of various elements, which together made up a curious flower. From a square jade plate with engraved petals, a tube, also of jade, projected and this ended in a flower-shaped bead; while on the back of the square plate (which carries a hieroglyphic inscription) a circular plug was fitted. All these elements would be united by a thread and it would seem that there hung as a counterpoise to them, behind the broad part of the ear, a marvellous artificial pearl, formed by uniting two perfectly cut pieces of mother-o'-pearl, polished and adjusted to give the impression of a pearl of fabulous size (36 mm). Over the breast lay a pectoral formed of nine concentric rings of twenty-one tubular beads in each. Round each wrist was a bracelet of 200 jade beads, and on each finger of both hands a great ring of jade. We found these still fixed on the phalanges, and one of the rings was carved in the form of a crouching man, with a delicate head of perfect Mayan profile. In the right hand he held a great jade bead of cubical form, and in the left, another, but this one spherical, the two being perhaps symbols of his rank or magical elements for his journey to another world. Near his feet we found another two great jade beads, one of them hollow and provided with two plugs in the shape of flowers. A jade idol of precious workmanship stood near the left foot and is probably a representation of the sun god. Another little figure of the same material must have been sewn above the breech-clout. From the mouth cavity we extracted a beautiful dark jade bead, which, according to the funeral rites of the Mayans, was placed there so that the dead person should have the means to obtain sustenance in the life beyond the tomb. At the moment of burial, the personage wore over his face a magnificent mask made of jade mosaic, the eyes being of shell, with each iris of obsidian, with the pupil marked in black behind. Of the hundreds of fragments, some remained on the face, adhering to the teeth and the forehead, but the greater part were lying on the left side of the head, clearly as the result of the mask's slipping off during the burial. The corpse must have been set in the sarcophagus entirely wrapped in a shroud painted red, and the same cinnabar colour adhered to the bones, the jewels and the bottom of the sarcophagus when the cloth and the flesh decomposed. The mask was fitted directly on the dead man's face, the fragments being stuck in a thin coating of stucco, the remains of which fitted to the human face. Nevertheless, the mask had to be prepared beforehand and may perhaps have been kept on a stucco head. It is perfectly possible that its main traits, realistic as they are, represent more or less those of the actual dead man. After the burial the sarcophagus was closed with its lid and covered with the enormous sculptured stone. Some jewels were thrown upon this – a collar with slate pendants and what was probably a ritual mask made of jade mosaic – and there were placed underneath the coffin various clay vessels, perhaps containing food and drink, and two wonderful human heads modelled in stucco, which had been broken from complete statues. At the closing of the crypt six young persons, perhaps sons and daughters of important persons at Court, were sacrificed to act as companions and servants of the dead man in the other world. In the best preserved of their skulls could be noted the cranial deformation and the mutilation of the teeth which were customary in the nobility alone. A serpent modelled in lime plaster seems to rise straight out of the sarcophagus and ascend the steps which lead to the threshold of the room. Here it is transformed into a tube, running as far as the flooring of the corridor and after this, it leads on to the temple, in the form of an echeloned moulding, hollow and superimposed on the steps. This amounts to a magical union, a conduit for the spirit of the dead man to ascend to the temple in order that the priests might continue to be in contact with his deified being and able to explain his mandates. Our search for an older building under the Temple of the Inscriptions could therefore not lead to the expected result, but in exchange, it revealed a tomb whose discovery leads to considerable modification of certain established concepts concerning the function of the American pyramid. It was formerly thought that this was solely a solid base for supporting a temple, unlike the Egyptian pyramids, which are vast mausoleums. Palenque's 'Royal Tomb', as it is now popularly called, with a certain intuitive propriety, perhaps – brings us a great deal closer to the Egyptian concept once we grant that the pyramid which hid it, although supporting a temple, was also constructed to serve as a grandiose funeral monument. The monumental quality of this crypt, built by thousands of hands to challenge the centuries and enriched with magnificent reliefs; the sumptuousness of the tomb itself, a colossal monument weighing 20 tons and covered all over with bas-reliefs of stupendous quality; the rich jade finery of the buried personage; all this expensive toil and this magnificence suggest to us the existence in Palenque of a theocratic system similar to that of Egypt, in which the all-powerful priest-king was considered during life or after death to be a real god. This Palencan Royal tomb also leads us to suppose that the attitude towards death of the Mayan *halach uinic* was very close to that of the pharaohs. The stone which covers the tomb appears to confirm this obsession and synthesises in its reliefs some essentials of the Mayan religion. The presence here, in a sepulchral slab, of motives which are repeated in other representations, gives perhaps the key to interpret the famous panels of the Cross and the foliated Cross (in Palenque) and also some of the paintings in the codices. On the stone in question we see a man surrounded by astronomical signs symbolising heaven – the spatial limit of man's earth, and the home of the gods, in which the unchanging course of the stars marks the implacable rhythm of time. Man rests on the earth, represented by a grotesque head with funereal traits, since the earth is a monster devouring all that lives; and if the reclining man seems to be falling backwards, it is because it is his inherent destiny to fall to the earth, the land of the dead. But above the man rises the well-known cruciform motif, which in some representations is a tree, in others the stylised maize plant, but is always the symbol of life resurgent from the earth, life triumphing over death.

Illustrated London News, 29 August 1953

Machu Picchu, the sacred city

HIRAM BINGHAM

HIRAM BINGHAM (1875–1956) *was born in Honolulu and educated at the Universities of Yale, California and Harvard. He also held the degree of Litt.D. from the University of Cuzco in Peru and had a distinguished political career in addition to his academic achievements. Shortly after graduating, he joined an expedition to South America, and since 1906 he made five trips devoted to exploration and research. His work brought to light much information about the splendid civilization of the Incas, and perhaps his most spectacular success was the discovery, during the campaign of 1911, of a magnificent stone-built Inca city in the mountain region of Machu Picchu.*

The ruins of what we now believe was the lost city of Vilcapampa the Old, perched on top of a narrow ridge lying below the peak of Machu Picchu, are called the ruins of Machu Picchu because when we found them no one knew what else to call them. And that name has been accepted and will continue to be used even though no one now disputes that this was the site of ancient Vilcapampa.

The sanctuary was lost for centuries because this ridge is in the most inaccessible corner of the most inaccessible section of the central Andes. No part of the highlands of Peru is better defended by natural bulwarks – a stupendous canyon whose rock is granite, and whose precipices are frequently 1,000 feet sheer, presenting difficulties which daunt the most ambitious modern mountain climbers. Yet, here, in a remote part of the canyon, on this narrow ridge flanked by tremendous precipices, a highly civilized people, artistic, inventive, well organized, and capable of sustained endeavour, at some time in the distant past built themselves a sanctuary for the worship of the sun.

Since they had no iron or steel tools – only stone hammers and little bronze crowbars – its construction must have cost generations, if not centuries, of effort. To prevent their enemies or undesirable visitors from reaching their shrines and temples, they relied, first, on the rapids of the Urubamba, which are dangerous even in the dry season and absolutely impassable during at least half of the year. On three sides this was their outer line of defence. On the fourth side the massif of Machu Picchu is accessible from the plateau only by a narrow razor-like ridge less than 40 feet across and flanked by precipices, where they constructed a strong little fort – a veritable Thermopylae. No one could reach the sacred precincts unless the Inca so decreed, as Friar Marcos and Friar Diego found to their cost.

While the lower slopes of Huayna Picchu are relatively easy of access in the dry season, the mass of Huayna Picchu is separated from the ruins by another razor-like ridge impassable on the east side and having only a footpath for sure-footed Indians on the west side. This trail passes for more than a hundred yards along a horizontal cleft in an overhanging precipice of sheer granite. Two men could defend it against an army and it is the only route by which Machu Picchu may be reached from Huayna Picchu.

So much for the northern approach. The east and west side of the ridge are sufficiently precipitous for fifteen hundred feet to be well-nigh unassailable. Rocks could easily have been rolled down upon invaders in the manner referred to by the conquistadors as a favourite method of Inca soldiers. If a path was maintained on each side, as is the case today, these paths, in turn, could easily have been defended by a handful of men. Wherever breaks in the precipices would give a foothold to intruders they were walled up and the natural defence strengthened.

On the southern side rise the precipitous cliffs of Machu Picchu Mountain. In ancient times they were flanked by two Inca roads. The road on the west side of the peak ran along another horizontal cleft or fault in the very face of a magnificent precipice. Traces can still be seen but rock slides have destroyed it. On the opposite side of the mountain the Inca road climbed the abrupt declivity by means of a stone stairway and circumvented the mountains by a trail which only goats could have followed with ease. Both of these roads led to the little ridge on which was the aforementioned Thermopylae, and which alone gave access to Machu Picchu Mountain from the plateau and the southern rim of the canyon. Both of them could have been readily defended in various places.

In accordance with their well-known practice, we found on top of both neighbouring peaks on Machu Picchu and Huayna Picchu the ruins of Inca signal stations, from which it was possible for messages to be sent and received across the mountains. The arrival of unwelcome visitors or even the distant approach of an enemy could have been seen and instantly communicated to the city. That on top of Machu Picchu was necessarily the more important. No pains were spared to make it safe and convenient. Its construction required great skill and extraordinary courage. It is located on top of one of the most stupendous precipices in the Andes. If any of the workmen who built the retaining wall on the very edge of the signal station slipped he must have fallen 3,000 feet before striking any portion of the cliff broad enough to stop his body. I do not mind admitting that when I took pictures from it I not only lay flat on my stomach, I had two trusty Indians hang on to my legs. It really was a dizzy height. But imagine building a wall on it!

The Sanctuary of Vilcapampa was regarded as so sacred that in addition to the outer defences and the reinforced precipices which protected the city against enemies, two walls were built to keep out visitors or workmen who had been allowed to pass the mountain Thermopylae. On the south side of the city are an outer wall and an inner wall. The outer runs along the ends of a magnificent tier of agricultural terraces. Near by are half a dozen buildings which may have been intended as barracks for the soldiers whose duty it was to protect the city on the only side where it could be reached by the ancient roads, and was comparatively vulnerable. There was still an inner line of defence. At the narrowest part of the ridge, just before one reaches the city from the south, a fosse, or dry moat, was dug, its sides faced with stone. Above it the wall of the city proper extends across the top of the ridge and down each side until it reaches precipitous cliffs which make the wall no longer necessary.

On the very top of the ridge the wall was pierced by a large gateway built of massive stone blocks. The gate itself, probably a screen of heavy logs lashed together, could be fastened at the top to a large ring-stone or eye-bonder firmly embedded above the lintel and underneath 6 or 8 feet of masonry. At the sides, the door could be fastened by a large cross-bar whose ends were tied to powerful stone barholds, stone cylinders, firmly anchored in holes left in the doorposts for that purpose. Such a door might, of course, have been smashed in by an attacking force using a large log as a battering ram. To avoid the likelihood of this the engineer who constructed the fortifications brought forward a salient from the wall at right angles to the doorway. By this means the defenders standing on top of the salient could have rained down a lateral fire of rocks and boulders on the force attempting to batter down the gate.

The walls of the city were too high to be scaled with ease. In fact, an attacking force which had been so fortunate as to overcome all the natural defences of this powerful stronghold and had circumvented the defenders of the several Thermopylae-like passes would have found themselves in a very bad situation when rushing along the terraces towards the inner fortifications. At the end of the terraces they would have found it necessary to jump down into the dry moat and scale its farther side as well as the city wall, all the time subjected to a shower of stones from the slings of the defenders. It is difficult to imagine that any attacking force could possibly have been large enough to overcome a vigorous defence even if the city were held by only a few score determined soldiers. Of course the walls served equally well in peace time to keep intruders from entering the sacred precincts of the sanctuary. In the *accla-huasi*, or houses of the Chosen Women of the Sun, no men were permitted to enter except the Emperor, his sons, the Inca nobles, and the priests.

The city gate shows evidences of being repaired. The top of the narrow ridge is at this point occupied by a large granite boulder which was worked into the fortifications, or, rather, the walls were strengthened by its being used as a member. As a result, the outer gatepost of the massive entrance rests on an artificial terrace. This terrace has settled a few inches, owing to erosion in the steep hillside. Consequently the wall has been thrown out of the perpendicular and has started to destroy the fine old gateway. It will not be long before the great lintel will fall and carry with it the repaired part of the wall which is superimposed above it. One clearly gets the feeling, in looking at the entrance to the citadel, that it was rather hastily repaired at a period long subsequent to its original construction, probably by Manco II.

Space was limited and the houses were crowded closely together, but an extensive system of narrow streets and rock-hewn stairways made inter-communication within the walls of the city comparatively easy. In fact, perhaps the most conspicuous feature of Machu Picchu is the quantity of the stairways, there being over one hundred, large and small, within its limits. Some of them, to be sure, have but three or four steps, while others have as many as a hundred and fifty. In several cases the entire flight of six, eight or even ten steps was cut out of a single boulder. The stairways which connect the various agricultural terraces follow the natural declivity of the hill even where it is so steep as to make them seem more like a ladder than a flight of stairs. In several places a little garden plot was tucked into a terrace less than eight feet square behind and above a dwelling house. In order to make little garden terraces like these accessible the Incas constructed fantastic stairways scarcely wide enough to permit the passage of a boy. Within the city, however, and particularly in the narrow streets or alleyways, the stairs were constructed on a comfortable grade.

The stairway or flight of steps as an ornamental or ceremonial motif in Inca architecture does not seem to occur here, although it might well have originated in this locality. In the ruins of a monolithic gateway at Tiahuanaco, Bolivia, in a curiously carved rock called Khenko, near Cuzco, are little flights of stairs which were carved for ceremonial or ornamental purposes and which serve no useful object as far as one can see. The stairways of Machu Picchu, on the other hand, with possibly one exception, all appear to be available for reaching locations otherwise difficult of access. While they are more numerous than was absolutely necessary, none of them appears useless, even today. The longest stairway, which may properly be described as the main thoroughfare of the city, commences at the top of the ridge at the terrace by which the highway enters the walls, and, roughly dividing the city into two parts, runs all the way down to the impassable cliffs on the north-eastern slope.

The central thoroughfare in the heart of the city consisted in part of this granite stairway of one hundred and fifty steps, and was the site of the principal waterworks. As usual, the Incas took great pains to do everything possible to provide adequate water.

There are several springs on the side of Machu Picchu Mountain, within a mile of the heart of the city. The little *azequia*, or conduit, which brought the water from the springs, may still be followed along the mountain side for a considerable distance. It has been partly destroyed by landslides but may be seen where it runs along one of the principal agricultural terraces, crosses the dry moat on a slender stone aqueduct, passes under the city wall in a groove less than 6 inches wide, and is carried along one of the terraces to the first of the series of fountains or little stone basins which are located near the principal stairway. The first four are south of the stairway. Near the fourth the stairway is divided into two flights. At this point there begins a series of twelve. The *azequia* runs south from the last fountain and empties into the moat.

The basins of the Stairway of the Fountains are usually cut out of a single block of granite placed on a level with the floor of the little enclosure into which the women came to fill their narrow-necked jars.

Frequently one or two little niches were constructed in the side walls of the enclosure as a shelf for a cup or possibly for the stoppers of the bottles, made of fibre or twisted bunches of grass. Sometimes a small lip was cut in the stone at the end of the conduit so as to form a little spout, thus enabling the water to fall clear of the back wall of the fountain. In other cases the water would usually pass through the narrow orifice with sufficient force to reach the opening of the jar without the necessity of the carrier dipping the water from the basin. In times of water scarcity, however, we may be sure that the latter method was followed, and that the reason for the sixteen basins was not only in order to permit many jars to be filled at once but to keep the all too precious fluid from escaping. The *azequia* is narrower than any I have seen elsewhere, being generally less than 4 inches in width.

The stone basins are about 30 inches long by 18 inches wide and from 5 to 6 inches in depth. In some places both the basin and the entire floor of the fountain enclosure are made of a single slab of granite. Sometimes holes were drilled in one corner of the basin to permit the water to flow through carefully cut underground conduits to the next basin below; in case of necessity these holes could easily have been plugged up to permit the basin to fill. The conduits run sometimes under the stairway and sometimes at its side. It is perhaps worth noting that the modern Peruvians call these fountains *baños*, baths, but it does not seem to me likely that they were used for this purpose. On account of the rarefied air, the cold, and the rapid radiation, even Anglo-Saxons do not bathe frequently in the Peruvian highlands, and the mountain Indians of today never bathe. It is hardly to be supposed, therefore, that the builders of Machu Picchu used these basins for such a purpose. On the other hand, the Incas were fond of making easy the work of the water carriers and providing them with nicely constructed fountains.

Possibly one reason for abandoning Machu Picchu as a place of residence was the difficulty of securing sufficient water. In the dry season the little springs barely furnished enough water for cooking and drinking purposes for the forty or fifty Indian workers and ourselves. In the earliest times, when the side of the mountain was forested, the springs undoubtedly did better; but with the deforestation which followed continued occupation and the resultant landslides and increased erosion of the surface soil, the springs must at times have given so little water as to force the city dwellers to bring the water in great jars on their backs for considerable distances.

It is significant that the sherds found near the city gate represent forty-one containers of liquid refreshment as compared with only four cooking pots, nine drinking ladles, and not a single food dish. Evidently the dispensers of *chicha* were stationed here. The results are the more striking when compared with the finds in the south-eastern quarter, where almost as many food dishes were found as jugs.

The largest flat space within the city limits lies in a swale at the widest part of the ridge. This was carefully graded and terraced, and at the time of our visit had recently been cultivated by Richarte and his friends. In fact, one would have to go a good many miles in the canyon of the Urubamba to find an equally large 'pampa' at an elevation of not less than 7,000 nor more than 10,000 feet. In other words, this little pampa offered an unusual opportunity to a people accustomed to raising such crops as flourished in Yucay and Ollantay-tambo. The fact that it was possible for them also to cover the adjacent hillside with artificial terraces which would increase the potentiality of the region as a food producer was doubtless as important a factor in the selection of this site as the ease with which it could be made into a powerful citadel or a very sacred sanctuary. One of the most carefully constructed stairways leads directly from the chief temples to the little pampa itself. It may have been the pampa where the *huilca* tree grew – the *huilca-pampa*.

There is only one city gate. The Northern, or Huayna Picchu side, was not defended by a transverse wall but by high, narrow terraces built on little ledges which would otherwise give a foothold on the precipices. Near these terraces there is a broad saddle connecting Machu Picchu with a conical hill that is part of a ridge leading to the precipi-tous heights of Huayna Picchu. South of the saddle, which was once covered with a dense forest, is a rude amphitheatre. It had been ter-raced and there are five or six different levels, recently used for the small plantations of the Indians. This might very well have been the special garden plot for raising food for the rulers. On the surface of the ground, among the cornstalks, pumpkin vines, and onion patches, we found occasional pieces of pottery.

Lost City of the Incas, 1951

Mann

26. The Inca's sacred city of Machu Picchu.

27. The centuries-old "Bridge of San Luis Rey," on the Apurímac River,
Peru. Though suspended by ropes "the thickness of a human body,"
it collapsed one day. Thornton Wilder made this catastrophe the
basis of his world-famous novel.

The bridge of San Luis Rey

VICTOR VON HAGEN

VICTOR WOLFGANG VON HAGEN (1909-) *was born in St Louis, Missouri, and the list of the explorations he has undertaken seems too many for one man's lifetime. In the Americas alone they include Mexico, Ecuador, the Upper Amazon, the Galapagos, the Honduras, Guatemala, North Panama, Columbia, the Amazon, Peru, the West Indies and Bolivia. He has not confined his journeys exclusively to the New World; in 1959 he undertook to trace the Imperial Roman road system from the Rhine to North Africa, and went on to visit Italy, Yugoslavia, Greece and Turkey. One of the most important assignments he has carried out was that of Director of the Inca Highway for the American Geographical Society when he traced the great post-road of the Incas from end to end.*

The walls of the tunnel, which was 250 yards long by actual measurement, were pierced with openings to allow in the light and air. Through these 'windows', into which I climbed, I could see the snow-topped peaks of Mt Marcani beyond us. The tunnel had been fashioned by the Incas much as the Romans mined rock. After a fierce fire had been built against it, water was thrown on the hot rock, splitting the friable lime and sandstone. The Incas, with their knowledge of working stone with stone, were presented with no problem. Their daring techniques in engineering were something else. At the end of the tunnel, which had once been connected with a stone stairway cut and built into the rock, we eased across that dangerous cleft and, gaining the circular stairway, went very slowly down the step-road. Cieza de Leon back in 1543 had had trouble with these same stairways, even when they were in good repair: 'Here the road is so rugged and dangerous, that some horses laden with gold and silver, had fallen in and been lost, without any chance of saving them.' Several hundred feet below, we came to what had been the platform, on which we found the remains of two enormous stone towers or pillars supporting the cables of the bridge. Two hundred feet directly in front of us, across the stygian gap of the river, we could clearly see the other side of this 'bridge of the . . . Apurimacchaca'. Cieza had written that it 'was the largest bridge encountered from Cajamarca . . . with the road well built along the sides of the mountains. . . . The Indians who built it must have performed herculean labour. . . .'

No precise data can be given for the bridge's construction. After the year 1300 the Incas expanded their realm, to the edge of the Apurimac and about this time, according to their chronicles, Inca Roca, then chieftain, finished the bridge. This would have been *circa* AD 1350. The detailed description of its structure is given by the Cuzco-born historian Garcilaso de la Vega, surnamed 'The Inca':

> The Apurimac bridge which lies on the royal road from Cuzco to Lima has its pillar support (he called it stirrup) made up of natural rock on the Cuzco side; on the other side (where we were now standing trying to figure it all out) was the stone tower, made of masonry. Under the platform that held this tower, five or six large wooden beams were inserted as thick as oxen – they stretched from one side to another. They were placed one higher than the other like steps. Around each of these beams, each of the suspension cables is twisted once so that the bridge will remain taut and not slacken with its own weight, which is very great.

Until nineteenth-century technology ushered in the use of iron chains for suspension cables, this Bridge of San Luis Rey, hanging by enormous rope-cables across the Apurimac, was one of the largest bridges of its type known. The Incas had no knowledge of the arch, nor, for that matter, did any other of the preliterate peoples in America. Depending as it does upon the principles of gravity, pressure and weight, the arch is yet earthbound and passive and therefore could not have been used here even had the Incas been familiar with it. Instead, they perfected the principles of the suspension bridge by reversing the arch-curve and giving it wings.

The Bridge of San Luis Rey, like all suspension bridges on the Royal Road, hung from rope cables hand-twisted from the fibres of the maguey plant. Those of this bridge, of 'the thickness of a man's body', were just laid over the high stone towers for their 'suspending' and then buried in the thick masonry on the platform of the towers. From the suspended cables, supports hung down, and to these the bridge platform made of wood planking was attached. Cables attached to the main bridge served as wind bracing.

Although the materials were primitive, the essential nature of the technology of the Inca suspension bridge is, in principle, the same as the best-constructed suspension bridges of today. Rope bridges have been built since immemorial times, but few other cultures before the advent of recent eras built so well as the Inca. This particular bridge indeed was so well made that it lasted for five hundred years, the cables, of course, being renewed every two years as a part of their work-service by Indians living at the *tampu* of Cura-hausi. This system of maintenance, so efficacious that the Spanish conquerors maintained it throughout the colonial period, disappeared only after the 'wheel' conquered the Andes, and the bridge which had served as a highway for foot and mule traffic for a period of five hundred years was allowed to fall into slow decay.

The Incas built for eternity; performance was to them, as it was with the Romans, the base of all their construction. If the Inca road system is here occasionally compared with the Roman road system, it is because, until very recent times, there have been no other communication systems that can be compared with either. Other civilizations had, of course, their highways, but until the advent of the Romans none maintained a road system.

However, structurally an Inca road differed greatly from a Roman road. The Romans employed heavy-wheeled carts with rigid front axles which necessitated a deep roadbed. The Incas, since their roads were travelled only by those on foot and by llama herds, had no need for the roadbed. But apart from this the two civilizations, Inca and Roman, were amazingly similar in their concept of road engineering. While there is no denying Rome's place in civilization's sun, the Incas, living on a neolithic cultural horizon tied to stone tools, still conceived a communication system that stands extremely high in comparison with the Roman.

The Romans had three thousand years of experience to draw on. The facets of Old World thought and techniques regarding the building of roads are a vast web stretching from the first wagon ruts of ancient India to the stoneways of the Persians. Remote as certain of these areas were, and removed from each other by time and space, the Romans had all these centuries of cultural heritage on which to draw. The Inca had none of these, yet an Inca road is in many aspects superior to a Roman road. Every feature of a Roman road is paralleled in an Inca road except that, for the most part, the Incas built – literally – in the clouds. The Apurimac Bridge, for example, was part of a highway which came from heights the like of which no Roman had ever seen. The passes the Romans conquered were as nothing compared to these in the Andes; Mont Blanc, the highest peak in Europe, is 15,800 feet high; yet here in Peru we have walked over Inca roads *built* at this height. The old Roman roads which crossed the spine of the Italian promontory of the Apennines were no higher than the city of Cuzco, which is 10,200 feet above the sea. Again we turn to our Cieza. As a boy in Spain, he knew the Roman Road. He had walked between Tarragone and Cadiz over the Via Augusta, built in the first century BC and rebuilt every quarter of the century by the Caesars. He drove his mules over the Via Argenta, which ran between Merida and Salamanca – a road which was started by Tiberius, continued by Nero and fully repaired by Caracalla in AD 214 – so he and others like him knew what they were saying when they wrote as a general rule that there is 'nothing in Christendom that equals the magnificence of the Inca roads.'

The remarkable thing is the similarity in approach to the 'idea' of roads between the Inca and the Roman. Both civilizations were of the land. Both had land armies, and land armies need roads; and since a road is only a road if one can go back over it, both believed that the road must be well built and well maintained. The Romans, it is true, ruled the straight line into civilization's thinking, whereas the Inca's road *surmounted* obstacles rather than avoided them, and as a general rule their engineers employed what I will call 'directional straightness' – that is, between two given points their road ran unerringly straight. Caius Caesar personally laid down vast stretches of road and the Claudian family, when public funds were not available, defrayed expenses for road-building out of its own privy purse. In Peru the road-building programme was also identified with the rulers and the roads were called after the Inca who built them. For example, one 2,500-mile-long road than ran to Chile was known as the Huayna Capac Nan, or the Road of Huayna Capac. Often an Inca would order a road to be built for himself grander than that of his predecessor. The Romans put up milestones as markers, while the Incas built their *topus* 'with the distance between them a Castilian league and a half'. Along their road, the Romans placed night quarters or *mansiones*; in Peru, the Incas erected and maintained *tampus* every four to eight or twelve miles (according to the difficulty and arduousness of the terrain) along the entire route of their roads. Roman couriers had a change of horse-mounts at *mutationes* to hurry up messages along the Imperial Way; the Incas, depending on foot, had their *chasqui* stations every two and a half miles as way stations for the trained runners who carried messages over the most terrifying terrain in the world.

The bridge, 'the little brother of the road', was ever an important link in the great Inca road system. How many of them there were along the length and breadth of the Andes we cannot be sure. But of them all, the Apurimac-chaca, the Bridge of San Luis Rey, was the greatest. Few who passed over it did so without pausing to wonder at this miracle of engineering. As to its length, the Inca historian, Garcilaso de la Vega, guessed it to be 200 paces long – 'although I have not measured it, I have asked many in Spain who did'. Cieza, that most accurate of observers, thought it was 'fifty estados' or about 85 metres (250 feet) in length. Sir Clements Markham, who crossed it in 1855, estimated the Apurimac-chaca at 90 feet and its elevation above the river's surface at 300 feet, while Lieutenant Lardner Gibbon, who made a survey of the Amazon for the United States Government in 1817, estimated its length at 324 feet.

When Squier came to the bridge in the summer of 1864, he and his companions lost no time extracting the measuring tapes and sounding lines. They found that the bridge was 148 feet long from end to end and that it was suspended 118 feet above the surging river. That was the first and last time this famous bridge was exactly measured, for although it was still hanging in 1890 it was no longer used and the cables, unreplaced, curved dangerously downward into the gorge and were slowly decaying with time. Squier also made several daguerreo-types of it, which he used in a somewhat dramatized and heightened version as a woodcut illustration in his book, *Peru, Land of the Incas.* Of the bridge, he wrote:

Between the precipices on either side, looking wonderfully frail and gossamer-like, was the famed bridge of the Apurimac. A steep, narrow path following for some distance a natural shelf, formed by the stratification of the rock, for the rest of the way hewn in its face, led up for a hundred feet to a little platform also cut in the rock where were fastened the cables supporting the bridge. On the oppo-site bank was another and rather larger platform roofed by rock where was the windlass (a feature added by the Spaniards) for making the cables taut and where, perched like goats on some mountain shelf, lived the custodians of the bridge. . . . It was a memorable incident in my travelling experiences – that crossing of the great swinging bridge of the Apurimac; I shall never forget it.

Later, in the beginning of the present century, Hiram Bingham, in speaking of the origins of his interest in Peru, said that this illustration of the bridge 'was one of the reasons why I decided to go to Peru'.

It is known that this dramatic picture of the bridge inspired Prosper Mérimée to use it as a literary device in a fictional piece on Peru, and that Thornton Wilder later, inspired both by the suggestions of the French writer and by the great span that crossed the Apurimac, and fascinated by its picturesque remoteness, wrote his literary masterpiece, *The Bridge of San Luis Rey*. With this book in hand I now stood looking down on the hiatus between the walls where the bridge once hung. Later I wrote Thornton Wilder from La Estrella hacienda. I knew that he regarded the bridge as a literary device, but so well had he described it that I felt that he must have seen, perhaps in some old issue of *Harper's Magazine*, a reproduction of Squier's stirring woodcut of this ancient bridge, which was in fact the actual hero of his novelette. 'It is best, von Hagen', he answered me, 'that I make no comment or point of it. . . . I wish I were with you and could see the great river and the gorge.'

The afternoon wind came up loud and shrill as we were standing on the platform that once held the great suspension cables of the bridge to set the foliage that clung to the rock walls rustling. We knew now that an old adage about the wind and the bridge was true, and that when the afternoon winds blew even the wind-braced cables could not hold the bridge steady and it would swing like a hammock.

It was late afternoon by the time we regained the boulder-strewn shores of the river. The sun was lighting the snow peaks while the shadows of the mountains fell across the canyon. A long shadow falling across the vertical cliffs gave a curious illusion of a hanging bridge. At that moment I must have been very close to the spot where Fra Juniper had stood looking upward at the bridge when a 'twanging noise filled the air . . . and he saw the bridge divide and fling the five people into the river below.'

' "Why did this happen to *those* five?" ' the Fra asked himself. 'If there were any plan in the universe at all, if there were any pattern in a human life, surely it could be discovered mysteriously latent in those lives so suddenly cut off. *Either we live by accident and die by accident* or we live by plan or die by plan.' With that soliloquy Wilder began his story. It is an ironic truth that if this tragic story had not been written, this wondrous bridge built in 1350 by the Inca Roca, which was to endure for five centuries as one of the greatest tributes to man's domination of wild nature, would have been lost to memory.

With the dying sun now playing fully on the glaciers, the river canyon became as bright as if it were full day. The shadows were gone and, with them, the illusion of the hanging bridge. When I next looked back, there was again only emptiness between the two vertical walls.

Highway of the Sun, 1956

A problem of Tihuanacu

ARTHUR POSNANSKY

ARTHUR POSNANSKY *was the Royal Bavarian Professor and Civil Geodetic Engineer, and for many years held the post of Professor of arch-aeology and physical anthropology at the University of La Paz. For more than fifty years he studied the antiquities of Tihuanacu in the High Andes of Bolivia, which many scholars claim to be the earliest civilization of the Western Hemisphere. The city reached its zenith long before the emergence of the empire of the Incas, and showed an astonishingly high standard of development at a time comparable to that of the earliest settlements of the Old World.*

For many, the group of ruins found 246 metres to the east of the Temple of the Sun, Kalasasaya, is a real mystery, and many investigators, including Squier, hold the opinion that it is a spot used for blood sacrifices. After long and conscientious studies we have come to the conclusion that what today is called 'Kantataita' is a model of a building of Tihuanacu, perhaps similar to the one which from the time of the French Mission (1903) has been called the 'Temple of the Sarcophagi', described in one of the previous chapters.

Now, of course, from the point of view of the modern engineer, to make a construction, no matter how large or small, the first thing that is done is to make a drawing, a plan, in which there are co-ordinated the ideas of form and appearance that will be given to the building, the accessories that it will have on the inside, and its exterior appearance and configuration. And since in our time one works on a dwelling or public building from say six months to a maximum of three years, and the one who plans it usually finishes it, a plan like the one described above is sometimes sufficient. But in the case of Tihuanacu, when the idea of 'time is money' did not exist, because there was more than enough time and the means, resources and systems of construction were still very rudimental – to such a degree that to move the surface of a stone a metre square they took months – a construction job might in spite of the many hands last a century or more, and even then not be finished. On this account, during the construction of a temple or palace of a public nature, it is unquestionable that the architects, and the directors of the work, were changed many times. Since there were no drawings or plans to which those who were continuing the work might refer, they would have needed something else to perpetuate the constructive idea, something which would incorporate the primitive concept and plan of the building on which they were working. This is why they adopted a system which is used in modern times to give a picture of the form and perspective of a building or monument which is to be constructed – in other words, a 'model'. In this era, the building is constructed on a small scale of stucco or some other material, in which one can see the perspective and main form of the building better than in a drawing. This is not only for the use of the architect of the project but especially for those untrained in this sort of material and unversed in the 'reading' of an architectonic plan with its different projections. It seems that this system of models is the one that was used in the Third Period of Tihuanacu to carry out a magnificent construction and, in our opinion, that which is today called Kantataita, is a horizontal model of a sumptuous construction. Also, a block near Puma-Punku, which the common people call 'the writing desk of the Inca', is nothing more than the vertical model of a façade, possibly of a building set to be constructed in the group now known as Puma-Punku and which actually is the Temple of the Moon of Tihuanacu.

With regard to Kantataita, this group of ruins is also completely destroyed. Everything that could be used in the way of slabs and finely carved stones, with and without figures, was carted off by both cultured and uncultured iconoclasts from Tihuanacu, the 'quarry of carved stones', long before the Conquest. Thus it is that considerable study, fancy and imagination are required to reconstruct in one's mind the form and appearance of this architectural group, which, like all in Tihuanacu, was not finished during its time. This group of buildings is apparently 40 m. long on the axis and perhaps 30 m. wide. But it is logical to suppose that a great number of the blocks found on the extreme western part belong rather to the sculptural atelier and would possibly have formed, when finished, a part of the great model or a part of another splendid building around this group. The principal part of the whole construction seems to be a slab of great dimensions which has caused some people to presume and still insist that this building was planned for 'blood sacrifices', the famous *Wilancha*, which the author has considered in other works. In the slab there is a square incision with a balcony on which it can be seen that there descend from the upper platform to the bottom, five little stairs composed of three steps. The idea of those who think that this was a sacrificial stone has its origin in the six holes carved on the upper platform of the block where, according to this opinion, there were six square columns which supported a flat stone to hold the sacrifice. The little steps served, according to those who hold the above opinion, to measure the amount of blood which ran from the chests or throats of the propitiatory victims.

Any person who studies Tihuanacu with care, rejects this idea at once. For example, in order to measure the blood, a single little step would have been sufficient, since the slab was level. What this slab actually represents is the model of a typical and genuine building of Tihuanacu. When the French Mission excavated the building called the 'Palace of the Sarcophagi', considered in a previous chapter, the section that was discovered then also had its balcony part, and showed exactly, even to the smallest details and with its little steps, the form seen in the slab that we are considering. Just as the last part of the balcony section of the model which is found to the east is broken, there is also broken the last but most marvellous stair which formed the entrance to the miniature building. This, without the least doubt, was in its turn also no more than a miniature of the three-coloured perron with three steps which gave access to the 'Palace of the Sarcophagi', of which, as well as of other details, we still have good photographs. Unfortunately, it was not possible to photograph the excavation of the French mission immediately, because of a lack of 24 × 30 plates and for other reasons. We say 'unfortunately' since on the following nights the oft-mentioned iconoclasts had already destroyed practically everything and carried off to the village tons of finely carved stones and beautiful slabs of all sizes. When we returned a few days later, there remained only the large blocks which could not be moved and transported. The two photographs (24 × 30) of this material, the only existing document-ation, show the remains of what was probably one of the most artistic buildings, of a rare and magnificent architectonic work of the pre-historic Americans. In the light of the foregoing discussion, we have no doubt that what is now popularly called 'Kantataita', is nothing more than a model of a building in construction in the Third Period. This structure was undoubtedly a semisubterranean building with an external platform at a greater height than the ordinary level of Tihuanacu. The slab which we have described and which is the principal part of the model, is 4·05 m. wide by 4 m. long, 30 cm. deep and the part to the west is somewhat sunken in. It is composed of hard andesitic material, which was employed in the most select constructions of the Third Period. On the west side of this group there is found in a great heap a quantity of blocks, some in the form of steps and others with typical staircase ornaments and we again emphasize that it is very difficult to decide whether they were all destined for the model or miniature building, or whether a portion of them was for other buildings and whether, finally, the model occupied a square of only thirty metres per side or whether it was larger. Future studies carried out on the basis of methodical excavations and reconstructions, will supply the last word on the subject of this mysterious construction, whose secret, as well as many others in Tihuanacu, may never be revealed to the man of today. The aforementioned topographical map which accompanies this volume will give the student a full idea of what still remains of this work on the surface of the ground.

Tihuanacu: Cradle of American Man, 1945

Part Seven

NEW METHODS IN ARCHAEOLOGY

Archaeology from the air

OSBERT CRAWFORD

OSBERT GUY STANHOPE CRAWFORD (1886-1957) was born in Bombay and came to England as a child. He was educated at Marlborough and Keble College, Oxford, where he read classics, but soon began to turn to the more technical aspects of archaeology. In 1914 he secured a place on an expedition to the Sudan, but this was cancelled on the outbreak of war. He joined the army and shortly transferred to the Royal Flying Corps, where he made many surveying flights. After the war he dug in Wales until 1920 when he was appointed Archaeological Officer to the Ordnance Survey. This work suited his tastes and talents to perfection, and he continued in this post until the first appearance of the periodical 'Antiquity', which he founded and continued to edit until his death.

We now come to the discovery of a technique which revolutionized field archaeology, that of air-photography. I have given elsewhere the main facts of its history and need not do so again. I would merely point out that the advantages of the vertical view of earthworks was fully realized by both Dr Williams-Freeman and myself long before we had either of us ever seen an air-photograph, and before our time by Colonel Sir Charles Arden-Close and by the late Sir Henry Welcome, who actually had vertical photographs taken from a box-kite of his excavations in the Sudan in 1913. What neither Dr Williams-Freeman nor I realized was the extraordinary clarity and sharp definition that would be given to earthworks by air-photographs. We were accustomed to look at them at close range; we used occasionally to see in the corn the track of a ploughed-up ditch showing as a broad greener band; but seen from near by from the opposite hill the outline was rather blurred. We longed to see it, not obliquely but in plan, as would be possible in an aeroplane, but we did not then realize that the greater distance given by the height would so greatly improve its appearance. It is exactly the same thing as the reduction by photography of a coarsely-drawn plan; the rough edges disappear, and what looked coarse becomes fine and pleasing.

I made several unsuccessful efforts after the 1914-18 war to get hold of some British air-photographs, and tried to interest the Earthworks Committee, also without success. Through the failure of their then honorary secretary to do anything the Committee lost the chance of its life-time. My expectations were at last satisfied when Dr Williams-Freeman asked me to come over to Weyhill and see some air-photographs with curious markings on them that had been shown to him by Air Commodore Clark Hall, then in command of the R.A.F. station there. What I saw far surpassed my wildest dreams, and I felt much the same excitement as, according to the poet, did stout Cortez on a memorable occasion. Here on these photographs was revealed the accurate plan of field-systems that must be at least 2,000 years old, covering hundreds of acres of Hampshire. There followed a period of intensive field-work over the area, supplemented by fresh air-photos taken in Hants and Wilts. The results were announced at a meeting of the Royal Geographical Society on 12th March 1923. The paper which I then delivered was published in the *Geographical Journal* for May of that year, and subsequently reissued with some alterations as an Ordnance Survey monograph (*Air Survey and Archaeology*, 1st edn. 1924, 2nd edn. 1928). In 1929, after we had had time to study air-photos more thoroughly, I wrote another monograph (*Air Photography for Archaeologists*) dealing not so much with the new discoveries themselves as with the ways in which they were revealed by photography. There was not, as some were almost inclined to think, any magic power in the camera; as a matter of fact it sees no more than does the naked eye. What it does is to make a document, the photographic print, which has all the properties of an original historical manuscript except its uniqueness – for it can be replaced if lost. This document can be studied at leisure in the home or office, and compared with others and with maps of the region – things that are impossible when observing from a fast-moving aeroplane. In this second monograph I classified the ancient sites revealed by air-photography into three groups: (1) shadow-sites; (2) soil-sites; (3) crop-sites; and that classification has been found adequate and still holds good, not only in this country, but all over the world.

During this same decade I took some air-photographs myself, working in collaboration with Mr Alexander Keiller in a specially chartered aeroplane from a base near Andover. The results were published in a joint book, *Wessex from the Air* (Oxford, 1928). Soon after this, I think about 1930, a private flier, Major George Allen, happened to pick up one of my Ordnance Survey monographs in a hotel at Southampton, and was immediately interested. He wrote to me about it, and began work on his own account. Having his own aeroplane he was a free agent and could go where he wished and take his own photographs. For a decade he continued to explore the country round Oxford and sometimes farther afield, and gradually accumulated a magnificent collection. The majority of his sites were crop-sites and new discoveries. He did more than anyone else to advance the new technique; and his untimely death by accident in 1940 was a very severe loss. He bequeathed his collection of photographs and records to the Ashmolean Museum at Oxford, where they are now available for the use of students. Comparable with Major Allen's work is that of Father Poidebard in Syria, where with the co-operation of the French Air Force he has surveyed the Roman frontier defences and discovered an enormous number of new Roman forts and roads. He has also succeeded in adding a fresh triumph, the photography of ancient remains beneath the sea (at Tyre) both from the air and below the water. (I tried out the possibilities of this myself in December 1928, when I flew over the harbour of Alexandria looking for the submerged quays there; but the sea was rough and muddy and I could see little or nothing.)

To return to the technique of air-photography, however. Shadow-sites are those whose surface is irregular, consisting of banks, mounds, ditches, and terraces whose presence is revealed by the shadows they cast when seen in the low light of the rising or setting sun. There is of course nothing at all mysterious about this process, which can be observed (though far less effectively) on the ground. Exactly the same principle is employed in photographing inscribed stones and carvings in low relief, where a side-light is necessary to bring out the detail. In explaining by examples how the shadow technique works I am neces-sarily anticipating somewhat, for I have to assume a familiarity with certain types of remains which I have not yet described; but it will be quite enough if for the moment they are regarded simply as banks (or whatever they may be) without worrying about their archaeological significance, which will appear later. The simplest and most familiar examples of banks are the ramparts of prehistoric hill-forts like Maiden Castle or Badbury Rings, or to take examples from Hampshire, St Catherine's Hill at Winchester, Tachbury Mount and Toothill near Romsey. These are all shadow sites of the most obvious kind. An observer visiting these hill-forts sees of course the shadows on the slopes away from the sun, but he gets no clear view of the hill-fort as a whole nor of its plan, for he is too near it. Returning to my analogy of the carved stone he is in the position of a fly on its surface. It is unnecessary to labour this point further; the basic principle is very easy to grasp.

Under the head of shadow-sites must also come, rather paradoxically, those where there are no shadows at all. When the land slopes towards the sun the banks on it reflect the light at a different angle and appear as brighter lines than the rest of the terrain. The light thus reflected is fore-shortened and condensed and therefore brighter. The banks of prehistoric fields show up in this way.

Shadow-sites can all be seen by an observer on the ground. Many of them were already known before they were photographed from the air; but even so air-photography has often revealed new features which had not been observed before. The classic example is the Trundle, a hill-fort near Worthing, where an air-photograph revealed within the ramparts a hitherto unnoticed circle which Dr Cecil Curwen subsequently excavated and proved to be the rampart of an earlier neolithic habitation-site. This led to a re-examination of other well-known hill-forts in some of which similar remains were found.

When taken in a good low light an air-photograph will reveal undulations in the surface so slight and broad that they might, and often did, escape the notice of a field archaeologist. When, however, with his attention thus drawn to them, he goes over the ground (as he always should) with the air-photograph in his hand, he can generally see something of them, however faintly. One of the chief services of air-photography has been to sharpen our eyes so that we can see these faint undulations. To the inexperienced eye they seem so slight as to be negligible; but no clue, however faint, should be neglected. Others brush them aside as products of the imagination, but air-photography has vindicated them, and their observers. It must be remembered, because it is a fundamental axiom of field archaeology, that in the chalk regions and in some (but not all) others, every irregularity of the surface is of human origin and demands an explanation. Broad low banks may seem trifles, but every gardener and every farmer knows that they are not. The cubic content of a bank that, though now only a few inches high, is several yards broad, represents long hours of human labour; and people do not undertake that for no purpose, or merely to mislead field archaeologists. The same remarks apply conversely to a silted-up ditch whose present depression may be a matter of a few inches only. Its original depth is probably not far short of its present width; the ditch of a levelled hill-fort may appear as a depression of a foot only with a width of fifteen feet representing perhaps a depth of ten feet. That is quite a formidable affair.

Soil sites are those which are revealed by disturbance and consequent discoloration of the surface. Except in deserts (where the few human sites are mostly shadow-sites) soil-sites usually occur on cultivated land when it is not bearing a crop. The marks are usually caused by the dispersal of the soil of banks and mounds and of the causeways of Roman or other made roads. In the chalk country such banks will have been made by digging a ditch and piling up the white chalk, which causes the resulting bank to remain visible even after many years of ploughing. Ditches and pits are sometimes revealed in bare soil even when they have become completely filled in and invisible as surface irregularities because their filling retains more moisture and thus has a darker appearance. For the same sort of reason a wet towel is darker than a dry one. Soil-sites are more common in winter and early spring, especially in a dry spring, than at other times of year. In the case of hill-forts it is usually the bank, or what remains of it, which shows up a soil-mark, and the ditch as a crop-mark. It is therefore a good thing to photograph such sites more than once at different times of the year and under the different conditions of moisture.

Crop-sites are perhaps the most important and the most numerous of all. Most of those known represent completely new discoveries. A crop-site is one that is revealed by the differential growth of a crop; the causes are excess and defect of moisture; ditches, pits, and post-holes, when they silt up, remain soft spots whose filling is of a different composition from that of the ground in which they are dug, whether that be chalk, sand, gravel, hard rock or even clay. When a crop of corn (and some other plants) is sown in a field containing such silted-up holes, the corn will grow better in the moister, more fertile soil of the silting, and will therefore be of a darker green colour. When seen from above those patches of darker green corn stand out in sharp contrast to the rest; and a vertical photograph of them gives an accurate plan of the bands or spots, which appear on it of course in black. No matter how long the holes have been filled up, the pattern is sharp and precise. The ditches of barrows that were ploughed flat in the Iron Age, some 2,000 years ago, have come to light again in this way as perfectly sharp, clear circles.

Even to give a list of the important discoveries of crop-sites made during the last quarter of a century would be impossible here, and I must confine myself to mentioning a few of them. The first and one of the most famous was the continuation of the avenue leading to Stonehenge. I saw it first in 1923, not on a print but on a negative that was taken in 1921 by the R.A.F. at Old Sarum, in the ordinary routine of practice. The existence of the ditches of the avenue was proved by excavation the same year. A little later, in 1926, Squadron Leader Insall, v.c., discovered not far away the timber circles which have been called Woodhenge, whose post-holes showed up as concentric ovals of dark spots enclosed within a dark ring marking the ditch. It was excavated later by the Cunningtons, who published their report in book form. One of the most striking crop-sites was that of Wood-bury. I found this myself in 1924, but was unable to photograph it, and it was rediscovered independently and a remarkably good photo-graph taken of it by a member of the R.A.F. photographic staff at Old Sarum in 1929. The site was selected for excavation by the Prehistoric Society, and two seasons' work were done there in 1938 and 1939, under the direction of Professor Bersu. It proved to be an Early Iron Age habitation-site. It was very well reconstructed by Jacquetta Hawkes in consultation with Professor Bersu, at Denham, and used in the film of prehistoric life. Major Allen discovered innumerable crop-sites in the Oxford district; and during the 1939-45 war Flight-Lieutenant D. N. Riley found more both in the same region and in the Fenland and other parts of East Anglia. Since the war Dr St Joseph has discovered many important crop-sites, including dozens of new Roman forts and marching camps.

In Iraq, Squadron Leader Insall discovered the site of Seleucia, the Hellenistic capital of Mesopotamia, by observing the rectangular lay-out, revealed partly by vegetation and partly by soil discoloration.

The remains of ancient irrigation-systems provide ideal subjects for both crop- and soil-sites. Those of Iraq can generally be seen as shadow-sites, for the ancient canals silted up their beds till they grew into great embankments. But there is a very good silted-up canal to be seen (as a soil- or crop-site) near Ur, complete with its distributary channels. The Romano-British drainage channels and associated field-systems and tracks are revealed in copious detail by air-photography, but remain for the most part unpublished. Extinct irrigation systems have been reported from Nubia, Turkmanistan and Soviet Azerbaijan, but neither Egyptologists nor apparently Soviet archaeologists have pub-lished any air-photographs of them.

28. An aerial view of an Etruscan necropolis. The hidden tombs show as patches of light. Both as an instrument of large-scale reconnaissance of extensive and difficult terrain and as a means of spotting buried ruins, graves, walls, streets, and canals, aerial photography has become a vital aid to archaeology.

29. Underwater exploration, one of archaeology's oldest dreams, began to come true
when Captain Jacques-Yves Cousteau developed the aqualung. It has now become
possible to locate by relatively simple means the innumerable shipwrecks of classical
antiquity along the Mediterranean seacoasts and to salvage their treasures.

One of the most important discoveries of crop-sites was made in Italy at the end of the last war by Mr John Bradford. Here turned up a wholly unsuspected group of Neolithic or Early Bronze Age hill-forts whose encircling ditches can be seen with astonishing sharpness and accuracy of outline on some air-photos taken partly during the war and partly on special archaeological reconnaissances undertaken by Mr Bradford immediately after it.

Crop-sites as yet unpublished have been recorded by photography in Siam and French Indo-China; and they have been seen also in North America by Dr St Joseph.

There are therefore crop-sites to be found in every continent (except, up to the present, Australia), and it is evident that we are merely at the beginning of discoveries. There is no reason to doubt that in favourable regions whole epochs of lost history may be recovered by air-photography followed up by scientific excavation. Obviously not all can be excavated; but when some have been and the plan-type thus securely established, air-photography will provide the data for distribution-maps of these types.

If one were to attempt to indicate where the most abundant harvest of crop-sites was likely to be gathered, one would find it difficult to exclude any country in the world outside the Polar Regions and the tropical forests and deserts. I did in fact intend at this point to make such an attempt, but on getting out my atlas and looking through it I gave it up. There are so few regions that are likely to be completely barren, and so many that will almost certainly be rich and productive. The harvest is indeed ready but the labourers are few, and often frustrated by official apathy or by their own lack of enterprise and initiative. I will confine myself to a bare list of some obviously promising regions: China, Indo-China and Siam, northern India, western Turkey, Thessaly and Thrace, central Europe from the Russian steppes (which must abound in crop-sites) to Hungary (where I have seen them myself), Nigeria, the corn-lands of North and South America. One would not look for crop-sites except where large level areas are under cultivation and where prehistoric man has been busy digging holes and ditches. The former considerations exclude many Mediterranean and most mountainous lands, and the latter such regions as Australia and parts of Central Asia where existence has been chiefly nomadic. But there is quite enough left to keep archaeologists busy for many centuries.

Archaeology in the Field, 1953

The blue museum

JACQUES-YVES COUSTEAU

JACQUES-YVES COUSTEAU (1910-) *was born in the Gironde and educated at naval college. During World War II, in which he served with such distinction as to be awarded the Croix de Guerre, he realized the need for a form of under-water movement more free than traditional helmet diving, and after much experimentation and some personal hazard he developed the aqualung. After the war he recognized the possibilities of his invention as an aid to oceanographic research, and since then his work in marine biology, exploration and archaeology has won for him many international honours.*

There are finer treasures in the Mediterranean, waiting within range of the lung. She is the mother of civilization, the sea girt with the oldest cultures, a museum in sun and spray. The grandest of undersea discoveries, to our taste, are the wrecks of pre-Christian ships on the floor. Twice we have visited classic wrecks and recovered riches beyond gold, the art and artifacts of ancient times. We have located three more such vessels which await salvage.

No cargo ship of antiquity is preserved on land. The Viking ships that have been found buried in the earth and the Emperor Trajan's pleasure barges which were recovered by draining Lake Nemi in Italy, are splendid examples of non-commercial vessels of ancient times, but little is known of the merchant ships that brought nations together.

My first clue to the classic ships appeared in the Bay of Sanary, where forty years ago a fisherman brought up a bronze figurehead. He died before I came to Sanary, and I have never been able to learn where he found it.

Years later Henri Broussard, leader of the Undersea Mountain-climbing Club of Cannes, came up from an aqualung dive with a Greek amphora. The graceful two-handled earthenware jar was the cargo cask of antiquity, used for wine, oil, water, and grain. The cargo ships of Phoenicia, Greece, Carthage, and Rome carried thousands of amphoras in racks in the hold. The bottom of the amphora is conical. On land it was punched into the earth. On shipboard it probably fitted into holes in the cargo racks. Broussard reported that he saw a pile of amphoras in sixty feet of water. He did not guess that it indicated a wreck, because the ship was completely buried.

We dived from the *Elie Monnier* and found the amphoras tumbled and sharded on a bed of compacted organic matter in a dusty grey landscape of weeds. With a powerful suction hose we tunnelled down to find the ship. A hundred amphoras came out of the shaft, most of them with corks still in place. A few had well-preserved waxen seals bearing the initials of ancient Greek wine merchants.

For several days we siphoned mud and amphoras. Fifteen feet down we struck wood, the deck planking of a freighter, one of two ancient cargo vessels that have been found. We were not equipped to carry out full-scale salvage and our time was limited. We went away with amphoras, specimens of wood, and the knowledge of a unique hydro-archaeological site which awaits relatively simple excavation. We believe the hull is preserved and could be raised in one piece. What things that wreck might tell of the shipbuilding and international commerce of the distant past!

Of ancient ships we know a smattering from murals and vase paintings, and can make fairly sound guesses at the science of their navigators. Their cargo ships were short and broad and probably could not work to windward. The few existing light-houses were fires kept burning on shore and there were no beacons or buoys on rocks and shoals. The skippers must have hated to lose sight of land and always tried to moor at night. The pilots must have inherited a knowledge of generations to risk voyaging a ship. Sentenced to skirt the shore, the ships were prey to sudden Mediterranean storms and treacherous rocks. Most of them that foundered, therefore, must have gone down in relatively shallow littoral waters, within diving range. Naval battles and piracy added to the toll of wrecks in shallow depths. I believe there are hundreds of ancient hulks preserved in accessible mud.

A ship that settled in less than sixty feet of water has probably vanished in the scattering action of tide and current, but if it landed deeper it lies in the calm museum of the floor. If the ship fell on rock bed and could not be wholly swallowed, it was overcome by the intense life of the sea. Algae, sponges, hydrozoa, and gorgoniae enveloped it. Hungry fauna sought food and shelter in the wreck. Generations of shellfish died and were crunched by other animals that rained excremental sand and mud which mounted as the wreck broke down. After centuries the simultaneous enveloping and consuming actions reached a common level and the sea bottom healed, leaving perhaps a scar.

A diver needs trained eyes to find the signs of such a wreck – a slight anomaly of the bottom contour, a odd-shaped rock, or the graceful curve of a weed-grown amphora. Broussard's amphoras must have been deck cargo. Amphoras in the hold would have been covered with the ship. Many ancient ships would have been lost beyond trace when coral or sponge divers ignorant of the probability that amphoras point to a ship beneath, removed the jars without noting their location.

Unmistakable were the signs of the only other classic cargo vessel ever found, the galley of Mahdia. The designation is, however, a misnomer; the ship had no tiers of oars; it was a pure sailing vessel which was specially designed to carry an incredible load for its day, at least four hundred tons. The argosy of Mahdia was built by the imperial Romans nearly two thousand years ago for the express task of looting the art treasures of Greece. Our finding of the argosy was the climax of an archaeological detective story.

In June 1907 one of the gnomelike Greek divers who roam far and deep in the Mediterranean was prospecting for sponges off Mahdia on the Tunisian east coast, when he found one hundred and twenty-seven feet down row after row of huge cylindrical objects, half-buried in the mud. He reported that the bottom was covered with cannon.

Admiral Jean Baehme, in command of the French Tunisian naval district, sent helmet divers to investigate. The objects consisted of sixty-three cannon lying in apparent order in a scattered oval on the sea plain, along with other large rectangular forms. All were heavily encrusted with marine life. The divers raised one of the cylinders. When the organisms were removed, marble fluting was revealed. The 'cannon' were Greek Ionic columns.

Alfred Merlin, the Government director of antiquities in Tunisia, sent the news to the famous archaeologist and art historian, Salomon Reinach. Reinach aroused art patrons to finance a salvage effort. Two Americans subscribed, an expatriate who styled himself the Duke of Lubar, after a Papal patent, and James Hazen Hyde, who gave $20,000. Reinach guaranteed no results, but Hyde was willing to back the effort. The expedition was in charge of a Lieutenant Tavera, who engaged experienced civilian divers from Italy and Greece, equipped with the latest helmet diving suits.

The depth was a serious problem at that stage of diving technique. That year the Royal Navy Deep Diving Committee was working out the first tables of stage decompression for operations to one hundred and fifty feet, of which Tavera did not yet have knowledge. Several divers were so heavily stricken with the bends that they could never work again. The difficult and dangerous operation was pursued for five years.

The argosy was a museum of classic sculpture. It held not only capitals, columns, plinths, and horizontal members of the Ionic order, but carved *kraters*, or garden vases, as tall as a man. The divers found marble statuary and bronze figures scattered across the floor as though they had been deck cargo, strewn as the ship side-slipped down like a falling leaf.

Merlin, Reinach, and other experts attributed these treasures to Athens of the first century BC. They believed that the argosy had foundered about 80 BC while carrying the loot systematically gathered by the Roman dictator Lucius Cornelius Sulla, who had sacked Athens in 86 BC. The evidence was that the architectural members constituted a complete temple or sumptuous villa which Sulla's art commissioners had taken apart in Athens for shipment to Rome. The ship was right off course for a journey from Greece to Rome, but that was a not uncommon dilemma for the clumsy sailing ships of that era. Enough *objets d'art* were brought up to fill five rooms of the Alaoui Museum in Tunis, where they may be seen today. In 1913 the salvage operation was broken off when financial aid ran out.

We first heard of the argosy in 1948, when we made an undersea archaeological investigation of the supposed sunken commercial harbour of ancient Carthage. The summer before, Air General Vernoux, commanding in Tunisia, had personally taken some curious aerial photos of the shallow water off Carthage. Through the clear sea were seen distinct geometrical forms that startlingly resembled the moles and basins of a commercial harbour. The photographs were examined by Father Poidebard, a Jesuit scholar, who was also an Air Force chaplain. He had found underwater remains of the ports of Tyre and Sidon in the early twenties and was eager to look into the Carthage discovery.

Father Poidebard came abroad the *Elie Monnier* and we took a ten-man diving team to examine the harbour. We found no trace of masonry or man-made construction, and to check our conclusions we had a powerful dredge cut trenches through the 'harbour' features. The dredgings held no traces of building material.

Then in the Tunisian archives and in the Alaoui Museum we came upon the story of the argosy of Mahdia. Merlin's monographs and Lieutenant Tavera's report led us to believe there were many treasures still left in the wreck. I had a thrill when I came across the name of Admiral Jean Baehme: he was my wife's grandfather. When we found Tavera's clear detailed sketches, showing the bearings of the wreck, we went after it.

We lay off shore in dazzling Sunday morning sunlight, studying the sketches. There were three drawings of landmarks which could be aligned to bring us over the argosy. The first alignment was a castle sighted past a stone butress in a ruined jetty. We saw the castle immediately, but there were four piers of the fallen jetty which could be lined up on it.

The second bearing was to bring a small bush on the dunes in line with the crest of a hill. In the thirty-five years since Tavera had drawn the lonely bush, a veritable forest had grown up around it. The last clue was a change in colour of a distant olive grove with a windmill in the foreground. We squinted through the glasses until our eyes wavered but saw no windmill. We made disparaging remarks about Lieutenant Tavera, now a deceased admiral, and wished he had studied treasure-map cartography from Robert Louis Stevenson.

We went ashore to look for the ruins of the mill. We loaded a truck with wooden beams and muslin to construct a signal beacon on the site. Up and down the dusty road we went, questioning the natives. No one remembered the mill, but someone suggested the old eunuch might know. We found him hobbling down the road, a withered octogenarian with a bald head and fluffy white side-whiskers. It was difficult to imagine him as he once must have been, the sleek and proud factotum of an Arabian Night's harem. His blank eyes lighted encouragingly. 'Windmill? Windmill?' he squeaked. 'I'll take you to it'. Carrying our gear we followed him several miles across country to a pile of rubble. We hurried to build the beacon. The ancient looked worried and mumbled to me 'I remember another mill further on'. He took us to a second heap of stones. As we regarded it with pain, he thought of still another ruined mill. The coast of Mahdia seemed to be a graveyard of windmills.

We returned to the *Elie Monnier* and held council. We decided to exert the maximum possibilities of aqualung search technique to rediscover the wreck as though we knew nothing of its location. That was not greatly exaggerating the situation. We had two facts – the, wreck was somewhere near and it was in one hundred and twenty-seven feet of water. Echo sound established that the floor was nearly level with slight variations in depth. We cruised until we found the depth area closest to Tavera's sounding.

On the sea floor we laid a steel wire grid covering one hundred thousand square feet, with fifty feet between each cross-line. The divers could then swim to and fro along the strips, surveying the terrain right and left for signs of wreck. It took us two days to canvass the grid. We would have found a watch dropped on the field. There was no Roman freighter in our web.

Lieutenant Jean Alinat proposed that he should go down on the undersea sledge. We towed him round the outskirts of the grid, but he found nothing. So passed the fifth fruitless day of our argosy hunt. That night we indicated our desperation by deciding to search closer to shore.

Next morning Commandant Tailliez waved the sledge aside and elected to be towed on a shotline by an auxiliary tender. In our campaigns against the unmanageable sea, I believe I felt the low point that morning, the sixth day of failure. I mentally composed a report to my superiors in Toulon explaining why I had had to work two naval vessels and thirty men for a week on a wreck that had been salved in 1913. Father Poidebard was beginning to remind me of an angry admiral.

A look-out shouted. Out on the sunny water bobbed a tiny dot of orange plastic, the personal signal buoy which Tailliez carried on his belt. When the little buoy comes up, the diver has marked something important. Tailliez broke water, tore out his mouth grip, and yelled. 'A column! – I've found a column'.

The old records indicated that one pillar had been dragged away from the wreck and abandoned when operations were terminated. The argosy was ours. We ran into Mahdia for the night and ordered champagne for all hands. What occurred in the bistros that night illustrates the problem of a crew that has found undersea treasure. The town buzzed with the news that we had found the galley's fabled golden statue, a mythological object locally venerated for a third of a century. Philippe's mollusc-eaten pillar became a fortune of gold. Admirers thronged abroad to congratulate us.

We began work at daybreak. Dumas and I went down and found the main wreck site. It looked nothing like a ship. The fifty-eight remaining columns were vague cylinders covered with thick blankets of vegetation and animals. They lay pounded, flattened into the muddy basement. We called on our imaginations to conjure up a picture of the ship. She must have been a whale of a vessel in her day. Tape measurements on the distribution of the columns outlined a ship perhaps one hundred and thirty feet long by forty feet wide, twice the displacement of the *Elie Monnier*, hanging in the sky above.

The argosy was lost in a bare prairie of mud and sand that spread beyond sight into the clear depths. It was an oasis for fish. Big rock bass swam in the drowned museum. We noticed there were no commercial varieties of sponges growing on the columns. The thoroughgoing Greek sponge divers of our day had apparently gleaned them all. Perhaps they had also removed some small *objets d'art* as a belated patriotic recovery of the Roman pillage.

We were confronted with a semi-industrial salvage operation. We were heirs of the great advances in diving science since Tavera's brave men had dared the wreck, and we had, in fact, a set of unique diving tables newly worked out under Lieutenant Jean Alinat's direction. They were designed for aqualung work, in which men could go down and come back quickly in a series of short dives, without building up the nitrogen saturation of prolonged single plunges. The latest helmet diving tables for a man who was to work forty-five minutes at a depth of the argosy required him to return by stages to decompress. He had to halt four minutes at a depth of thirty feet, proceed to twenty feet and spend twenty-six minutes, and halt for another twenty-six minutes at ten feet, before surfacing.

It cost him almost an hour to return from a three-quarter-hour dive. Alinat's schedule, in contrast, sent a man down for three fifteen-minute dives, alternated by three-hour rest periods. The independent diver needed only five minutes of stage decompression at ten feet after the third dive, one-twelfth of the helmet diver's decompression wait.

To make Alinat's theories work for an efficient attack on the Roman ship, the two-man team had to go down and come up on a rigid timetable. They could not be expected to consult their own wristwatches. We devised a 'shooting clock', a rifle-man on deck, who fired into the water five minutes after they gone down, again at ten minutes, and discharged three rounds at fifteen minutes as the imperative signal to surface. The shock impact of bullets could be heard distinctly in the wreck.

On the first day I saw a diver surface, holding up a small glittering object, and my heart leaped, for we had hoped to find Greek bronzes. It was merely a bullet from the shooting clock. The floor had become covered with them. It would have been fun to have been hiding behind a column when the next sponge diver sneaked down and saw the bottom gleaming with gold.

The timetable was also threatened by the fact that in wind and current the *Elie Monnier* swung wide off its anchor, so that the divers had long unpredictable diagonals to swim on their way to work, a drain of time and energy. Dumas hoisted out on deck a sling-load of miscellaneous dockyard scrap he had foraged, such as rusted girder bolts and hunks of plate. The divers laughed at the boyish simplicity of Didi's solution. Holding a fifteen-pound scrap iron against his belly, a diver could go sailing down, using his body as a hydrofoil to control his slanting glide. He could come on the wreck from any approach by adjusting his ballast. He could drag, side-slip, or plunge; arrive rested; and drop his iron season ticket.

Didi dutifully obeyed the shooting clock, until one day he spied something fascinating as he climbed from his third dive. The sun was still aglow on the floor. Dumas could not resist a lighting dive at it. He found nothing of interest and returned. At dinner he remarked on a twinge in his shoulder. We grabbed him instantly, locking him in the recompression chamber on deck, and dialled the inside pressure to four atmospheres. We could not take the chances on the bends, which can hit a diver some time after he surfaces. There was a phone from the recompression chamber to a loudspeaker in the divers' ready room. After we had eaten, Dumas took the microphone and broadcast a diatribe against the shipmates who starve a friend. We let him cool off for an hour. It was the only time we have used the recompression chamber on our dives.

The world of the argosy was twilight blue in which flesh became a greenish putty colour. The far-off sun gleamed on the chromed regulators, winked on the frames of the masks, and ensilvered our exhaust bubbles. The light-coloured sea-bed suffused a reflected light strong enough to make a colour movie of the divers at work. I believe it was the first colour film made at such a depth.

The Athenian marbles were dark bluish shapes, blurred with blankets of marine life. We dug under with our hands, dog-fashion, to pass cargo slings under them. As the stones were raised by a winch, colour grew on the crust and at the surface they swung into the air ablaze with life. As they lay draining on deck, the many-coloured coat of flora and fauna faded. We scraped, scrubbed, and hosed the snowy marble volutes and bared them to their first sun since ancient Athens.

Of the stones on the floor, we took four columns, two capitals, and two bases. We raised two mysterious leaden parts of ancient anchors, which were found near the supposed outlines of the ship in positions that indicated the anchors had been stowed when the vessel sank. She must have met her fate suddenly. The anchor parts, each weighing three-quarters of a ton, were oblongs with reinforced holes in the middle, obviously to take wooden posts that had rotted away. Such straight metal shapes could not have been the arms or hooks of the anchors. We dug around for the arms and found none. The finds could only have been the stocks, or top cross-bars. The rest of the anchors must have been made of wood. Here was a puzzle. Why did the ancients put the greatest weight at the top of the anchor?

We argued over evidence and supposition and formed a possible explanation. The ancient ships did not have anchor chain, but used rope. A modern anchored ship driven by wind or current keeps its hook fast by means of the horizontal stress on the lower end of the anchor chain. The Roman anchor rope drew taut in such conditions and would have lifted the wooden hooks if the top had not been weighted with a leaden stock, which provided the horizontal stress.

We worked six days in the Roman argosy, increasingly absorbed with its clues to original seamanship. We wanted to dig for the ship itself. Tavera's records indicated that the helmet divers had excavated extensively in the stern. I selected marbles from a compact area on the starboard ship amidships and sent them up to clear an area for excavation. We lowered a powerful water hose to blow away the earth. A slight current conveniently carried off the mud we raised. We supposed that the heavily laden vessel had burst her top framing outward in the crash and that the main deck had been hammered in by the deck cargo. The theory seemed to be borne out.

Two feet down we stubbed our fingers on a solid deck covered with leaden plates. The sea washed mud into the hole almost as soon as we clawed, but we felt enough of the sturdy deck to estimate that the Roman ship is two-thirds intact. We dug up an Ionic capital which was encased entirely in mud. No molluces or plants had reached it. It scrubbed down to the pristine beauty of the days when it was carved, before Christ was born.

I am confident that amidships there is unbreached cargo. I am certain that then as now the crew lived in the forecastle, the least desirable place of a ship, and that there are intimate possessions and tools buried there that could tell us about what kind of men sailed the Roman ship.

We were merely scratching at history's door in our few days in the huge argosy. We found iron nails corroded to needle thicknesses and bronze nails worn to bright threads. We turned up a millstone, with which the sea cooks had ground grains carried in amphoras. We brought up yard-long pieces of Lebanon cedar ribs covered with the original yellow varnish. (It would be useful to know how to make marine varnish that will survive twenty centuries of immersion.) I dug down five feet at the prow against the sliding sands and embraced the cedar stempost. I could barely touch fingertips round it.

Four years later in New York, I met the president of the French Alliances of the United States and Canada, a lively old gentleman named James Hazen Hyde, and linked his name with that of the patron who had helped salve the treasure of Mahdia. It was the same man. He invited me to dinner at the Plaza and I showed him the colour film of the divers in the wreck. 'Fascinating' he said 'You know I've never seen the things that were brought up. In those days one had a lot of money and a steam yacht. I was cruising in the Aegean while they were diving. I never got to the museum at Tunis. Salomon Reinach sent me photographs of the kraters and statues, I got a nice letter from Merlin, and the Bey of Tunis gave me a decoration. It is interesting indeed to see it after forty-five years'.

The Silent World, 1953

Atomic physics in archaeology

THOMAS GEOFFREY BIBBY

THOMAS GEOFFREY BIBBY (*1917-*) *was born in Westmorland and educated at Caius College, Cambridge. From 1947 to 1950 he was employed by the Iraq Petroleum Company, but since 1950 he has devoted himself exclusively to his work on archaeology. He now lives in Denmark, where he holds the post of Keeper and head of the Oriental Department of the Forhistorisk Museum.*

Once again the new method clears away a misconception. Just as De Geer showed that a year was a concept independent of man, so Professor Willard F. Libby of the University of Chicago, the inventor of the radio-active-carbon technique, has shown that time is a concept independent of years. The age of an object is not basically the number of years but rather the length of time which it has existed. Years, though not man-made, are man-employed as a unit for measuring time. But time goes on, regardless of whether man measures it in years or not.

Carbon is the basic ingredient for all organic matter, the major constituent of animal and vegetable life, and at the same time, in the form of carbon dioxide, one of the principal ingredients of the air. Carbon is absorbed from the carbon dioxide of the air by plants which release the surplus oxygen; and this assimilated carbon in the plants is in turn consumed by animals and by man. Both in plants and in animals the carbon is partly used to replace structural wastage and to build up new structure, the process we call growth. There is a constant influx of new carbon to any living growing organism, and a constant, though lesser, outflow of the old.

Now, carbon is not the simple element that it was believed in pre-atomic times to be. It consists of three isotopes, three distinct substances which are chemically indistinguishable but which have different physical characteristics, the most obvious being a different in atomic weight, 12, 13 and 14. Ordinary everyday carbon is of atomic weight

12. But C-12 is mixed with one part to several million of C-13 and C-14. These tiny proportions of the heavier carbon are manufactured in the upper levels of the atmosphere. There the carbon dioxide of the air is exposed to bombardment by cosmic rays, the unexplained streams of ionized particles which shower down upon the earth from outer space. When such a particle strikes an atom of carbon in the carbon-dioxide of the atmosphere, sufficient of the energy, or matter, of the particle is absorbed to convert the C-12 into C-13 or C-14.

This 'heavy carbon' is like the ordinary carbon, absorbed from the atmosphere, at first or second hand, by every living thing.

This process would be of only academic interest were it not for a very important fact. Carbon 14 is radio-active.

Now, radio-active materials do two things. They emit particles, the rate of emission of which can be measured on a Geiger counter, and in the process they break down into other normally non-radio-active substances. They break down at a fixed rate for each radio-active substance, so that it is possible to state that after a definite length of time the amount of radio-activity in a quantity of material will be reduced to half, and after the same period again to a quarter, and so on. This fixed period is known as the 'half-life' of the substance.

Libby, a gangling six-foot atomic chemist, first became interested in Carbon 14 in 1946, after an exciting four years on the Manhattan Project. And he reasoned out that, once the proportion of C-14 in the carbon of the atmosphere is kept constant by the continual streams of cosmic rays, and since every living creature keeps renewing its C-14 by absorption of the atmospheric carbon, then every living creature is radio-active, and to exactly the same degree.

This rather disturbing thought was still not of immediate concern to the prehistorian interested in determination of chronology. But in 1947 Libby took his reasoning a step further. When an organism dies, it ceases to absorb new carbon from the air. From that point the natural breakdown of its C-14 is not counter-balanced by new intake. There-fore its proportion of C-14 to C-12 will slowly drop – *and drop at a fixed rate*. The half-life of Carbon-14 was found to be 5,568 years, to an accuracy of 0·54 per cent. So that a tree cut down 5,568 years ago would produce only half as many clicks on a Geiger counter as a tree cut down yesterday.

Now the prehistorians woke up. For the reverse was also true. If a piece of wood gave only half the number of clicks given by a modern piece, then that piece of wood was 5,568 years old. And any other proportion of clicks could likewise be converted into a date, as far back as the limits of accuracy of the machine. A method of dating any prehistoric material containing carbon had suddenly appeared out of the blue.

And so it proved. A committee of four archaeologists was set up by the American Anthropological Association in February of 1948 and proceeded to submit samples of every conceivable type of prehistoric material containing carbon to Libby and his battery of Geigers. The first samples were objects of known date – wood from the graves of Egyptian Pharaohs and from Hittite palaces, ashes from Roman encampment and cloth from the Dead Sea scrolls. Libby was able to indicate a date conforming to within ten per cent with the date already known. This new method had proved itself.

Now the impossible could be attempted. The objects that were, by axiom, undatable could be tested. The embers of a fire from the cave at Lascaux dated the Stone Age habitation of the cave to 15,516 years ago; birchwood from the edge of the ice cap in northern Germany determined the retreat of the ice from that point as occurring 10,800 years ago; shells from one of the earliest agricultural settlements in the world, Jarmo in Iraq, gave a reading of 6,707 years.

We should not be misled by the apparent exactitude of the number of years resulting. In each case the number was accompanied by a statement of the permissible error, and which was usually up to, and sometimes over, ten per cent. But even a ten per cent inaccuracy is many times better than the highly subjective estimates previously possible. And better shielding of the Geigers from stray cosmic rays, better preparation of the samples, and greater care in their collection and transport have already resulted in a significant drop in the margin of error.

It is with the Geiger counter that the future of archaeological dating rests – until an even better method is found. Libby's machine has been duplicated at all the major centres of anthropological study in America, and a number have been erected in Europe, the first being at Cambridge and Copenhagen. And now, in the museum that Thomsen founded, only a short way from the rooms in which he first displayed his collection arranged by the system of three chronologically successive ages, a lead-shielded apparatus clicks busily, measuring out with increasing accuracy the age of the objects that he first dared to suggest were prehistoric.

The Testimony of the Spade, 1957

The Lerici Periscope

CARLO MAURILIO LERICI

CARLO MAURILIO LERICI (*1890- *) *was born in Verona and studied industrial and mechanical engineering at Turin Polytechnic. During the early part of his life he achieved considerable success as an industrial engineer, pioneering new geophysical methods of prospecting for oil and water, but his interest began to turn towards antiquity when his relatives asked him to design a suitable family mausoleum. With characteristic thoroughness he undertook a study of ancient models upon which to base his design, and his attention gradually became absorbed by the monuments of the fascinating and little-known civilization of the Etruscans. He is deeply concerned for the threatened safety of the Etruscan remains, and has devoted all the resources of his scientific training and archaeological knowledge to their discovery and preservation. His geophysical techniques, which he was the first to apply to archaeological problems, have achieved remarkable results; in the following passage (written in 1961) he quotes the discovery of 600 tombs at Cerveteri and 2,600 at Tarquinia, but by June 1964 these figures had risen to 950 at Cerveteri and 5,250 at Tarquinia.*

A few months ago the Lerici Foundation of the Milan Polytechnic was asked to organize an archaeological survey of the ancient city of Sibari and of other interesting remains in the area round the rivers Crati and Coscile in Calabria.

This is a large area, extending over several tens of square kilometres, so that emphasis was on the development of apparatus which would enable a small group of people to work very much faster than large teams using traditional methods.

That these new methods have proved themselves remarkably successful can be seen by the following list of discoveries made in five years by two people, with subsidiary labour recruited on the spot.

At Fabriano a necropolis.

At Cerveteri 600 tomb chambers containing 6,500 excavated objects.

At Vulci numerous structural remains of the ancient city, including the Tomb of the Inscriptions, with a large sculptured sarcophagus.

At Tarquinia, 2,600 tomb chambers, 20 of them painted.

At Sibari various remains of ancient buildings.

For comparison with previous work, it is sufficient to record that in the Tarquinia region it had previously taken the whole of the nineteenth century to record as many painted tombs as we have recorded in five years; that since 1892, i.e. during sixty-six years, not a single painted tomb had been discovered, and that during the last fifteen years an average of one tomb a year had been discovered in the Cerveteri region. A comparison with the records shows that our discoveries at Tarquinia which are still proceeding with success, will soon double the heritage of Etruscan pictures. The Polytechnic group has accomplished in five years what would previously have taken more than a century.

THE METHODS

The methods found to be most successful are: (1) measurement of the *electrical resistance* of the ground, by which changes under the surface are revealed, and (2) the use of *exploratory probes* at points indicated by resistance measurement. These probes can be used, either to bring up a complete sample of the soil strata as a core, or, if a tomb is pierced, to allow visual and photographic examination of the interior.

These methods have proved of outstanding value, and will be described in a section below. But other methods have also been used to gather useful information.

First among these is *aerial photography*. This is regularly used in our work. But two points should be noted. Firstly, the usual survey photographs are not the best for our purpose, since light and other factors should be so chosen as to emphasize archaeological detail. Also infrared photographs are of particular value. Secondly, we have shown in the sites so far surveyed that archaeological detail is not likely to appear if the remains are below 1·5–2 metres from the surface. In the Latium region, for instance, details of necropolises at Cerveteri and Tarquinia, and of inhabited settlements at Vulci, are only visible when closer to the surface. Thus about 50 per cent of the formations at Cerveteri and 75 to 80 per cent at Tarquinia are not visible in aerial photographs, while at Sibari aerial photographs are of very little value.

With these reservations, aerial survey offers an indispensable beginning to every large-scale archaeological project.

In cases where moisture in the soil renders resistance measurement less effective, this method may be supplemented by seismic recordings. Here, a small explosive charge is detonated at one point in the ground, and the multiple echoes at various receiving points are recorded.

ARCHAEOLOGICAL SURVEY BY MEASUREMENT OF THE ELECTRICAL RESISTANCE OF THE GROUND

If two metal rods (the electrodes) are pushed into the ground and a current passed between them, we can measure the electrical resistance between them in the normal way. The resistivity of a material is the resistance of a block of unit length and cross-section, in this case a cubic metre, and we can obtain the resistivity of the earth approximately from the resistance reading. As we move the electrodes farther apart, the resistance will increase, but if the earth is uniform the resistivity will remain constant. The farther apart the electrodes are placed, the more the current will travel to deeper layers as it passes from one electrode to the other. Thus if there is a lower layer of earth through which the current passes more easily (i.e. a lower resistivity), this will eventually start to contribute to the result, and the overall resistivity will fall. If the electrodes are over an empty tomb, the reverse may happen, since air has a very high resistivity, and the resistivity will rise, as the electrodes are moved apart. . . .

It can now be seen that any buried structures, such as tombs or buildings, can be detected and their depth estimated.

There are two methods of resistance survey: vertical and horizontal electrical soundings.

Vertical Electrical Soundings
The two middle electrodes are kept fixed, and the two outer electrodes are moved apart in stages. Thus we get a picture of the vertical structure of the soil below the apparatus.

Horizontal Electrical Soundings
To explore the nature of the ground at a fixed depth below the surface, we fix the distance between all four electrodes, and move the whole set together along the ground.

It is our common practice to determine first of all the layer structure of the ground with a few vertical soundings, and then to survey along a line with horizontal, and finally to confirm any discovery with a vertical sounding.

Equipment for Resistance Measurement

The portable apparatus for the surveys described above consists of two parts. The lower part is the power pack, which converts the current from a 12-volt battery to values suitable for the recording devices housed in the upper part. Readings can be taken in a few seconds. This apparatus has been developed by the Foundation. In use, it is mounted in the back of a jeep.

THE PROBES

The MacCullogh Motor-probe

This portable motor drill, weighing 40 kg., can be used in two ways. (A) With a twist-drill bit, holes may be bored up to 12 cm. in diameter. (B) With a core sampler in place of the twist-drill, a core of soil up to 40 cm. long may be withdrawn so that all the strata down to this depth are revealed.

Thus, when the resistance survey indicates a likely archaeological formation, the motor-probe may be used, either to bring up a sample of the soil, or to pierce a tomb-chamber.

The Periscope

When a tomb-chamber has been located and pierced by the motor-probe, the periscope can be lowered so that the interior of the chamber may be studied and photographed. This device was developed in the Polytechnic for our work. It consists of a compound tube from 3 to 5 metres long, with two windows at its lower end, the upper for viewing and photographing, and the bottom window for illumination of the chamber. A sequence of 12 photographs, with the periscope turned through 30 degrees after each exposure, will record the complete tomb.

In this way the periscope enables the tomb to be examined in all detail without entry. Thanks to this instrument the Milan Polytechnic now has archives of unprecedented scope covering the tombs of the seventh-third centuries BC. Some of these tombs must wait many months before they are opened.

A complete documentation in colour of all the new discoveries will be published in 1961 under the auspices of the Lerici Foundation of the Milan Polytechnic.

SOME PROBLEMS

The aim of the work described above is to defend and conserve our buried archaeological inheritance.

30. C. M. Lerici's periscope camera at work. The camera–eye explores the inside of an Etruscan grave: is it worth while to open it?

31. Objects inside an unopened Etruscan tomb, photo-graphed by the periscope camera.

It has been argued by our critics that these rapid methods do not allow the thorough and detailed examination that is required by archaeology today. This criticism can best be answered by stating the following facts.

1. Our survey leaves the tombs undamaged in every way, and located for subsequent detailed investigation, the probe hole being plugged.

2. Extensive cultivation in the last ten years is frequently preceded by deep-ploughing, using bulldozers. On several occasions these have irreparably damaged archaeological material near the surface. Furthermore, owing to the subsequent enrichment of the soil with fertilizers, salt-enriched water seeps into the buried remains and causes further damage. The Etruscan necropolis at Tarquinia offers an impressive example of this destruction. Deterioration is proceeding at such a rate that in a few years there will be very much less to recover.

3. Illegal research. Today illegal research in the archaeological zones of Italy forms the *larger part* of all excavations, because it is many times superior in efficiency of discovery to that carried out by the Administration of Antiquities and other authorized bodies. The damage caused by this robbery, either through the dispersal of unrecorded material or through negligent treatment, can be valued in billions of lire every year. The Milan Polytechnic has in its records examples of impressive gravity, such as the destruction of certain painted walls in the Tarquinia necropolis in order to penetrate the adjacent spaces and steal the antiquities. These facts must fully justify a rapid and careful survey of existing archaeological formations, with a view to their subsequent protection and conservation.

The speed of our discoveries has found the authorities unprepared; and in fact sufficient personnel and funds are simply not available in Italy to cover even the most important works of conservation.

As we work, we know very well that illegal excavators are carefully observing our survey. In many cases the Milan Polytechnic has had to provide day and night guards at its own expense. Notwithstanding, where the Polytechnic squad works, there the illegal excavators concentrate their work. There have even been attempts to export whole fragments of walls.

Conservation Required
After a tomb has been entered, it is most important to ensure that it remains so isolated that temperature and humidity remain as before,

and fairly constant. Measures may then be taken to remove incrustations of salts and to prevent further seepage. Some paintings, however, must be removed to stable environments. Here the methods of the Instituto Centrale at Rome have proved invaluable, and should be extended.

Methods used in the Archaeological Prospecting of Etruscan Tombs,
Studies in Conservation, vol. 6, no. 1, 1961

Photogrammetry

Archaeology, which has for so long depended upon the interpretive eye and mind of the scholar, is now beginning to take its place among the exact sciences, where the use of complex technical devices is gradually cutting down the possibility of error. As we have seen, machines can be used to locate the position of underground chambers, to ascertain the date of ancient artifacts, to trace the outline of earth-works invisible from ground level. They can also reproduce exact copies of carved or moulded surfaces, and may even one day help us to unravel forgotten languages.

The Documentation Centre was set up in May 1955 by the Antiquities Service of Egypt with the direct co-operation of Unesco. It is an Egyptian body, financed by the government of the United Arab Republic. Unesco has a representative on the Board of Directors of the Centre and provides technical aid in the form of international specialists.

From the days of Champollion – the founder of scientific Egyptology – the work of preserving monuments, organizing excavation work, research and documentation studies has been carried out by a great many foundations, museums and universities in Egypt, Europe and America. It has often been done most successfully, but almost inevitably in a piece-meal fashion. Never until now has so systematically organized a body as the Cairo Centre been at work in this field. Its operations have called for powerful resources and the services of large teams of full-time specialists working in a synchronized operation.

Originally, the Centre had chosen as its first task to make systematic surveys of the Necropolis of Thebes where the tombs, once well preserved, had shown signs of deterioration. The announcement of the High Dam project changed the order of priorities and began the race against time in Lower Nubia. In the next five years something like one hundred missions are planned with a clear-cut programme of work relating to the monuments threatened by the Aswan High Dam.

The archaeologists and philologists attached to the Centre co-ordinate all operations, taking into account existing documentation and data. They direct work in the field and then record the results of every mission on card indexes.

Facts needed to complement copies and descriptions are assembled by the technical section. Architects prepare plans, sections and elevations, complete to the most minute detail – every brick, every flagstone and even the smallest hole in a wall is marked in. Experts in architectural drawing trained at the Centre use photographs to prepare exact plans of groups of monuments. The old method of making tracings from actual monuments is no longer used except for small details, or in cases where monuments are too closely hemmed in or in too bad a state of preservation for satisfactory photographs to be taken. Copies of those reliefs which are renowned for their beauty or historical interest and of any hieroglyphic inscriptions likely to provoke controversy, are made by moulders, who also prepare architectural models.

Photographers find themselves working closely with many of the other specialists. Following details of the master plan, they develop their test film each day on the spot before sending the negatives to the developing laboratory in Cairo. At the same time they take identical photographs on colour film. Yet even all this work is not enough.

The photographic reproduction of works of art, and of sculpture in particular, is – as André Malraux has termed it – a phenomenon of recreation. Freed from the recesses where they were hidden away, sculptures seem to spring into life again when viewed in this new light, becoming familiar and acquiring fresh significance.

Photography, like drawing and even architectural plans, contains a certain element of subjectivity which can produce various degrees of distortion. To obtain the absolute accuracy demanded by scientific recording, use has been made of photogrammetry, a process that has been employed for the past forty years in the preparation of geographical maps.

This method was first used to survey a monument in 1850 and today provides invaluable documentary material for archaeologists. The stereoscopic photographs, taken with the aid of a phototheodolite, give precise information down to the smallest detail of a relief and thus make possible the creation of an absolutely faithful copy in reproductions, models and casts.

Photogrammetry opens up new horizons in the knowledge of forms and techniques. It may even make possible the discovery of architectural laws as yet undisclosed by Egyptologists, and may add to our knowledge of sculptural techniques. For instance, the contour lines taken on the face of the North-West Osirian colossus (23 feet) in the inner court of the Great Temple of Abu Simbel, and those taken on the face of the South colossus (65 feet) on the façade, show some striking resemblances between the two even down to the modelling of the cartilage of the nose.

When all the survey programmes are completed, the Documentation Centre of Cairo will be a rich, permanent source of information both for Egyptological studies and for works destined for the man in the street. As a safety measure, all the archives are to be microfilmed and one copy of every document will be given special security treatment to guard against any possible destruction or deterioration.

Thanks to the international action undertaken by Unesco there is now reason to hope that these majestic monuments will be saved from the encroaching waters and that present and future generations will still be able to visit the giant statues of Rameses II and the island temples of Philae. Furthermore, the extensive work undertaken by the Documentation Centre on Ancient Egypt will give the world's Egyptologists the possibility of adding to our knowledge of one of the areas of the Ancient World which has by no means finished yielding up its secrets.

Unesco Courier, February 1960

Computer decipherment?

In the latter half of 1960 a group of workers at the Institute of Mathematics of the Siberian Division of the USSR Academy of Sciences undertook an experiment in deciphering the Maya language with an electronic computer. The results of this work were reported at the Conference on Information Processing, Machine Translation and the Automatic Reading of Text, held at Moscow, January 21-30, 1961.

This was accompanied by publication of a reading (to be more precise – transliteration without translation) of fragments of Maya texts.

The value of the work of the Institute of Mathematics personnel lies in the fact that this was the first practical proof of the possibility of successful study by computer of ancient systems of writing. Theoretically this problem arose some years ago, after statistical methods had been successfully employed by 'manual' means for deciphering ancient systems of writing (by M. Ventris for the syllabic Cretan script, and by the present author with respect to the hieroglyphic Maya script). Thus, the use of computers for decipherment was a logical consequence and capping of a new stage in the development of the theory of decipherment characterized by large-scale employment of statistical methods.

In posing the general objective of investigating 'the possible applications of computers to solution of problems in ancient systems of writing and in developing a technique for effective employment of electronic computers towards this end' (Evreinov I, p. 3) the authors of these papers had the goal, with respect to Maya hieroglyphic texts, 'of establishing the relationship between the words of the lexicon and the manuscript texts, and of determining by this means the nature of the employment of the hieroglyphs and their meanings' (Evreinov I, p. 4). From the published materials it follows that, in fact, a somewhat narrower objective was posed – that of providing a transliteration of the hieroglyphic texts into Latin script (or, to be more exact, into the so-called 'traditional' Maya alphabet) with no effort at translation.

The authors were, of course, familiar with 'manual' decipherment of Maya writing and with the technique employed in it.

The Institute of Mathematics workers selected the Dresden and Madrid Maya codices for study. Palaeographic work (such as identification of symbols un-clearly written, discovery of errors in writing etc.) was not undertaken, as the workers used the present author's texts of all the manuscripts and certain Maya inscriptions in numeral coding (a three-digit number for each symbol), as well as a catalogue of the symbols with denotation of allographs. Omission of the Paris Codex from consideration was unfortunate inasmuch as the Madrid Codex is in considerably worse condition. Moreover, limitation of the raw material complicates the investigation. The major sources employed on the Maya language of the colonial period were the Motul Dictionary, the *Book of Chilam Balam of Chumavei* and the Codex Perez. . . .

The processing of the lexical data took place parallel to the processing of the hieroglyphic texts: the frequency of syllables and words was computed and, in addition, lists of words were compiled in accordance with their meanings (the animal and vegetable world, various trades, objects of daily life, gods, rituals, sacrifices, astronomical and calendrical terms, and the most commonly used words). In view of the substantial difference in the vocabulary of the Maya language during the colonial period and that of the hieroglyphic texts, these lists proved to be essentially useless.

In comparisons of the processed data, the symbols were compared with the syllables in frequency, the number of symbols in the hieroglyph was compared with the number of syllables in the word. ('The most efficient method was the so-called "rebus" method, based upon seeking points of correspondence between complexes containing specific numbers of symbols, and words containing the corresponding number of syllables' (Evreinov I, p. 10); in another paper we read that the 'rebus' method 'consists of the hieroglyphs being identified with words against the background of the subject of the section being dealt with, the meaning of symbols formerly defined, and the methods by which the symbols are employed in the given hieroglyph' (Ustinov, p. 15).) For hieroglyphs whose meaning was determined on the basis of the drawings, appropriate synonyms were chosen in accordance with lists by subject matter, and then one of them was chosen in accordance with conditions of the criteria of accuracy.

It must be noted that the authors developed no new methods whatever, but employed those long since utilized in the study of Maya codices, for the most part as far back as the last century. Uncoordinated employment of all these various methods is responsible for the confusion in the results and led to elementary errors and, in addition, changed the problem posed. In its final form the task undertaken proved to be the following: to provide a transliteration without translation of a text consisting of phrases accompanied by illustrations and written in unknown symbols in a known language. In this extremely simplified form, the problem has little in common with that of deciphering ancient systems of writing. Nevertheless the authors regard it as being 'similar in nature to the problems of machine translation and problems of study of signal systems', and compare the research process to translation of creative writings (Evreinov I, p. 11). The extensive employment of supplementary methods demonstrates that the authors were unable to employ statistical methods with satisfactory effect.

For the reasons detailed above, the results following twenty hours of computer processing of the data proved to be very modest. The authors themselves assert that they had read 'approximately forty per cent' of the Madrid and Dresden Maya codices (Ustinov, p. 25). What they probably meant is that they had succeeded in duplicating approximately forty per cent of the published 'manual' decipherment. This is approximately correct. The published 'Preliminary Results' (Predvaritel'nye rezul'taty) (Evreinov III) adduces transliterations of eight paragraphs (of 170) in the Dresden Codex and 27 (of 250) of the Madrid. A transliteration is provided of 367 hieroglyphs, including repetitions (all told, the codices contain about 5,300 differentiable hieroglyphs). If we eliminate repetitions, the authors provide a transliteration of sixty-seven hieroglyphs (representing words or combinations thereof). The so-called 'readings' (i.e. transliterations) of hieroglyphs – both by the Novosibirsk team, and in general in the literature of deciphering of the Maya script – are by no means of equal value throughout. . . .

For all practical purposes, this exhausts the results of decipherment in the true meaning of the term, i.e. determination of the phonetic reading of the symbols. The 'machine' decipherment yielded considerably fewer readings than the 'manual' and provided no correct new readings whatever (whereas in the incorrect readings it essentially repeated the early results of 'manual' decipherment). . . .

The authors assert that the results of their work confirm the assumption on which it was based. If, as the result of the 'machine' decipherment of the Maya script, confirmation was obtained of the author's 'hypothesis' of identity of the language of the hieroglyphic texts and the language of the 16th century Maya, this would mean that 'machine' decipherment is an absurdity. In reality this 'hypothesis' is wholly refuted by the results of the 'machine' decipherment (as otherwise it would not have been necessary to substitute the conventional names for the hieroglyphs in place of true readings). '

The authors' papers contain a number of erroneous propositions that tend to mislead the reader. It is impossible to examine them all in the present article, but it is necessary to pause to consider at least a few. The authors assert, for example, that 'investigation of the script of the ancient Maya was performed by mathematical methods and with an electronic computer. The processing of informational data of such great volume and diversity in any form of notation is virtually impossible without the employment of modern methods of research. So is disclosure of all the connections and laws of quantitative and qualitative aspects of the problem capable of shedding light on determination of the precise sense and phonetic significance of the symbol and hieroglyph' (Ustinov, pp. 12-13; compare also Evreinov II, p. 4). This assertion does not correspond to the facts. It is common knowledge that an increase in the amount of data does not complicate but facilitates decipherment, be it 'manual' or 'machine'. On the other hand, a reduction in the amount of material increases the volume of work required for decipherment to astronomical dimensions. It is when the volume of data is small (i.e. the inscription on a clay vessel from the Slavic burial ground in Alekonovo village, or the inscription on the Phaistos disk) that virtually insuperable difficulties for deciphering arise.

Further, the authors assert that 'in analysis of the archaic script of the Maya, in which heterogeneous material must be studied, it is impossible to limit oneself to some single method' (Evreinov I, p. 8). This assertion is not only untenable as theory, but has now since been refuted in practice by the fact of 'manual' deciphering which, as is well known, was accomplished exclusively by statistical means.

The problem before the writers was to employ modern computer equipment for an experimental decipherment of an ancient script. It was completely unimportant whether this script had already been deciphered or not, although for control purposes it made sense to start with an analysis of a script already deciphered. This was the reason for selection of the Maya script for the first effort (it would have been just as possible to employ Egyptian hieroglyphics, the cuneiform writing, etc.). The work carried out by the writers under review demonstrated in practice that modern computer technology can be employed in deciphering ancient systems of writing. The 'machine' deciphering confirmed the fact that when a script is studied objectively the results certainly agree. It must be observed that if the results of 'machine' decipherment had not coincided with those of the prior 'manual' work, it would have been necessary to review the 'machine' (and not the already proved 'manual') deciphering, as must actually be done with respect to that portion of the work in which obviously erroneous phonetic readings are adduced (although they, too, repeat previously published work). The 'machine' deciphering was successful only in part in duplicating the 'manual' work and added nothing to our knowledge of Maya script. In order to achieve results of practical significance for American studies, the authors will have to re-examine their theoretical postulates and considerably improve the methods of programming.

Soviet Anthropology and Archaeology, vol. 1, no. 3 Winter, 1962/3

SOURCES

J. M. Allegro: *The Dead Sea Scrolls*. London: Pelican Books; 1956. By permission of Penguin Books, Ltd.

G. B. Belzoni: *Narrative of Operations and Recent Researches in Egypt and Nubia*. London: John Murray; 1820.

Geoffrey Bibby: *The Testimony of the Spade*. New York: Alfred A. Knopf; 1956. By permission of the publishers.

Hiram Bingham: *Lost City of the Incas*. New York: Appleton-Century; 1951. By permission of J. M. Dent & Sons Ltd.

Helmuth Bossert: *Karatepe*. Istanbul: Istanbul University; 1946. By permission of Dr. E.-M. Fischer-Bossert.

P. E. Botta: *Letters on the Discoveries at Nineveh*. London: Longman, Brown, Green and Longmans; 1850.

R. L. S. Bruce-Mitford: *Recent Archaeological Excavations in Britain*. New York: Macmillan; 1957. By permission of Routledge & Kegan Paul, London.

E. A. W. Budge: *By Nile and Tigris*, Vol. I. London: John Murray; 1920. By permission of the publishers.

J. L. Burckhardt: *Travels in Nubia*. London: John Murray; 1819.

Howard Carter: *The Tomb of Tut-ankh-Amen*, Vol. II. London: Cassell and Company Ltd.; 1927. By permission of Curtis Brown Ltd.

J. F. Champollion: *Lettre à M. Dacier Relative à l'Alphabet des Hiéroglyphes Phonétiques*. Paris: Academie Royale; 1822.

Jacques-Yves Cousteau: *The Silent World*. New York: Harper and Row; 1953. By permission of Hamish Hamilton, London.

O. G. S. Crawford: *Archaeology in the Field*. New York: Frederick Praeger; 1953. By permission of J. M. Dent & Sons Ltd.

E. Curtius: *Archaeologische Zeitung*, Vol. XXXV, Part I. Berlin, 1877.

—— and F. Adler: *Olympia*, Vol. I. Berlin: A. Asher & Co.; 1870.

G. Dennis: *Cities and Cemeteries of Etruria*, 3rd edn., Vol. II. London: John Murray; 1883.

D. V. Denon: *Travels in Upper and Lower Egypt*. London: James Ridgway; 1802.

F. K. Dörner: "Die Königsresidenz am Nymphenfluss," *Kosmos*, Vol. LII. Stuttgart: Franck'sche Verlag; 1956. By permission of Professor Dr. F. K. Dörner and Franck'sche Verlag, Stuttgart.

Amelia Edwards: *A Thousand Miles Up the Nile*. London: George Routledge and Sons; 1889.

Earl of Elgin: *Memorandum on the Subject of the Earl of Elgin's Pursuits in Greece*. London: William Miller; 1811.

Arthur J. Evans: *The Palace of Minos*, Vol. III. London: Macmillan & Co. Ltd.; 1930. By permission of Agathon Press, Inc. *The Palace of Minos* was reprinted in 1964 by Biblo & Tannen, Inc., in co-operation with Agathon Press.

Fouilles de Delphes, Vol. 4, Part 5. Paris: École française d'Athènes; 1890.

Nelson Glueck: *Rivers in the Desert*. New York: Farrar, Straus & Giroux; 1959. By permission of Weidenfeld and Nicholson, London.

Augustus Goldsmidt: "The Plaster Corpses of Pompeii": see *Proceedings of the Society of Antiquaries of London*.

M. Zakaria Goneim: *The Lost Pyramid*. New York: Holt, Rinehart and Winston; 1956. By permission of Longmans, Green & Co., London.

Victor W. von Hagen: *Highway of the Sun*. New York: Duell, Sloan and Pearce; 1955. By permission of Mr. V. W. von Hagen.

H. V. Hilprecht: *Explorations in Bible Lands*. Edinburgh: T. and T. Clark; 1903.

C. Humann: *Der Pergamon-Altar*, ed. E. Schulte. Dortmund: Ardey Verlag; 1959.

Alexander von Humboldt: *Researches Concerning the Institutions and Monuments of the Ancient Inhabitants of America*. London: Longman, Hurst, Rees, Orme & Brown, J. Murray and H. Colburn; 1814.

Athanasius Kircher: *Lingua Aegyptiaica*. Rome: Hermann Scheus; 1643.

Robert Koldewey: *The Excavations at Babylon*. New York: Macmillan; 1915.

Henry A. Layard: *Nineveh and its Remains*. London: John Murray; 1867.

C. M. Lerici: Lecture to the Rotary Club of Rome. Milan Polytechnic, Lerici Foundation, 1958. By permission of Professor C. M. Lerici.

——: *Methods Used in the Archaeological Prospecting of Etruscan Tombs*. London: *Studies in Conservation*, Vol. 6, No. 1; 1961. By permission of Professor C. M. Lerici.

Paul MacKendrick: *The Mute Stones Speak*. New York: St. Martin's Press; 1962. By permission of Methuen & Co. Ltd., London.

A. E Mariette: *Monuments of Upper Egypt*. London, 1877.

Gaston Maspero: *Institut Egyptien Bulletin*, Series 2, No. 2. Marseilles, 1881.

L. Matous: *Bedrich Hrozny: The Life and Work of a Czech Oriental Scholar*. Prague: Orbis; 1949. By permission of Professor L. Matous.

Memorandum on the Subject of the Earl of Elgin's Pursuits in Greece: *see* Elgin.

Napoleon I: *Correspondance de Napoléon*, Vol. I. Paris: Imprimerie Impériale; 1858.

W. M. Flinders Petrie: *Ten Years' Digging in Egypt*. Edinburgh: Religious Tract Society; 1892. By permission of Miss A. Petrie.

Arthur Posnansky: *Tihuanacu: Cradle of American Man*. New York: J. Augustin; 1945.

Proceedings of the Society of Antiquaries of London, Series 2, Vol. II. London, 1863.

Henry Rawlinson: "The Persian Cuneiform Inscriptions at Behistun," *Journal of the Royal Asiatic Society*, Vol. 10. London, 1846.

Claudius Rich: *Second Memoir on Babylon*. London: Longman, Hurst, Rees, Orme and Brown, J. Murray; 1818.

Alberto Ruz: "An Astonishing Discovery," *Illustrated London News*, 29 August 1953, pp. 321–3. By permission of the publishers.

C. F. A. Schaeffer: "The French Excavations in Syria," *Antiquity*, Vol. IV, No. 16. London, 1930. By permission of Professor C. F. A. Schaeffer.

Heinrich Schliemann: *Ilios*. London: John Murray; 1880.

——: *Mycenae*. London: John Murray; 1878.

——: *Troy and its Remains*. London: John Murray; 1875.

Eduard Seler: "The Temple Pyramid of Tepoxtlan," *Bulletin of the Bureau of American Ethnology*, No. 28, pp. 341–52. Washington, 1904. By permission of the Smithsonian Institution, Washington.

George Smith: *Assyrian Discoveries*. London: Sampson Low, Marston, Low & Searle; 1875.

George Elliott Smith: "The Elephant Controversy Settled by a Decisive Discovery," *Illustrated London News*, 15 January 1927, pp. 86, 87, and 108. By permission of the publishers.

Charles Piazzi Smyth: *Our Inheritance in the Great Pyramid*. London: Charles Nisbet & Co.; 1890.

Sir Hans Sloane: *Printed Will and Codicils of Sir Hans Sloane, Bart*. London: John Virtuoso; 1753.

Soviet Anthropology and Archaeology, Vol. I, No. 3, Winter 1962/3, pp. 43–50. New York: International Arts and Sciences Press. By permission of the publishers.

John L. Stephens: *Incidents of Travel in Central America*. New York: Harper and Brothers; 1842.

Claude Tarral: "The Discovery of the 'Venus de Milo,'" *Revue Archéologique*, Series IV, Vol. VII, pp. 193–9. Paris, 1906.

Lord William Taylour: *The Mycenaeans*. New York: Praeger; 1964. By courtesy of Lord William Taylour.

General Sir Tomkyns H. Turner: "How the Rosetta Stone Came to the British Museum," *Archaeologia*, Vol. XVI, pp. 212–14. London, 1812.

Vittorino Veronese: "An Appeal" (by the Director-General of UNESCO), *UNESCO Courier*. Paris, February 1960.

Von Hagen, V. W.: *see* Hagen, V. W. von.

Von Humboldt, Alexander: *see* Humboldt, Alexander von.

J. F. M. Waldeck: *Voyage Pittoresque et Archaéologique dans la province d' Yucatan et aux ruines d'Itzalanes*. Paris: Dufour; 1838.

Horace Walpole: *The Letters of Horace Walpole*, Vol. III, ed. Mrs. Paget Toynbee. Oxford: Clarendon Press; 1903. By permission of the publishers.

Johann J. Winckelmann: *A Critical Account of the Situation and Destruction of Herculaneum and Pompeii*. London: T. Carnan and F. Newbery; 1771.

Hugo Winckler: "Nach Boghazköy," *Der Alte Orient*, Vol. 14, Part 3. Berlin: Vorder-asiatische Gesellschaft; 1913. By permission of J. C. Hinrichs Verlag, Leipzig.

William Wright: *The Empire of the Hittites*. London: James Nisbett; 1884.

C. Leonard Woolley: *As I Seem to Remember*. New York: Praeger; 1962. By permission of George Allen & Unwin, London.

——: *Digging Up the Past*. New York: Crowell; 1955. By permission of Ernest Benn Ltd., London.

——: *Excavations at Ur*. New York: Barnes and Noble; 1955. By permission of Penguin Books, London.

INDEX

A Note about the Editor

C. W. CERAM is a name known to everyone interested in archaeology. Born in 1915 in Berlin, he was known for many years under his real name, Kurt W. Marek, as a newspaperman, drama critic, and a leading figure in the publishing world. His first book, *Gods, Graves, and Scholars* (1951), brought worldwide fame to its author—it has now been a great popular and critical success in twenty-five languages—and immeasurably expanded popular interest and concern for the world's archaeological heritage. One might say that the saving of Abu Simbel, for example, as the result of a widespread popular outcry against its threatened disappearance at the bottom of the Nile, owes something to the world's having been for years alerted to the importance of such monuments by the books of C. W. Ceram and those who followed in his footsteps. He has since published *The Secret of the Hittites* (1956), the result of an invitation to participate in two digs in Turkey, uncovering the Hittite past; *The March of Archaeology* (1958); and in 1961, under his actual name, *Yestermorrow: Notes on Man's Progress*. Mr. Marek lives with his wife and son in Woodstock, New York.

A Note on the Type

THE TEXT of this book has been set on the Monotype in a type face named Bembo. The roman is a copy of a letter cut for the celebrated Venetian printer Aldus Manutius by Francesco Griffo, and first used in Cardinal Bembo's *De Aetna* of 1495—hence the name of the revival. Griffo's type is now generally recognized, thanks to the researches of Mr. Stanley Morison, to be the first of the old face group of types. The companion italic is an adaptation of a chancery script type designed by the Roman calligrapher and printer Lodovico degli Arrighi, called Vincentino, and used by him during the 1520's.

*Printed by Universal Lithographers, Inc.,
Lutherville, Timonium, Md.*

Bound by The Haddon Craftsmen, Inc., Scranton, Pa.